PRACTICALLY EVERYONE IS RAVING ABOUT THE PRACTICAL GUIDE TO PRACTICALLY EVERYTHING!

"If ever a book functioned as an instruction manual for almost every aspect of life, it's this ultimate consumer annual."

—Doug Hatt, *People*

"Open to any page and you're likely to find something you can use...this bulging paperback with all the right stuff is my pick for a stocking stuffer." —Gene Shalit, *Today*

One "of the most appealing gift books" of the year. "A most astonishing mix of the trivial and essential."

—Christopher Lehmann-Haupt, *The New York Times*

"Go ahead and buy a case of these and get the whole holiday shopping process over in a hurry. It's easily the most browseable book of the year." —*Book Page*

"It's a big fat book full of stuff you can really use...an endlessly interesting stack of facts that are absolutely not trivia." —*The Boston Globe*

"Like the classic early-American almanacs, [The Practical Guide] *is designed to tickle and intrigue readers as well as help them puzzle out the problems of daily life.* The Practical Guide *is alive with characters."* —Kevin McManus, *The Washington Post*

"Bernstein and Ma have taken a good idea (ask the experts what they do) and run with it." —*The Chicago Tribune*

"The best-looking new information book we've seen in a long time." —Judyth Rigler, *The San Antonio Express-News*

"In this chubby, comprehensive volume, Consumer Reports *meets* The World Almanac. *The diligent reporting and amusing titles make a fine mix, whether you are just browsing or bent on self-education."* —*Mademoiselle*

WITH HUNDREDS OF NEW EXPERTS TO
TIME AND MONE

"With the old Almanac and the old year, leave thy old Vices, tho' ever so dear."

Ben Franklin
Poor Richard's Almanac

THE PRACTICAL GUIDE TO PRACTICALLY EVERYTHING

1997 EDITION

PETER BERNSTEIN & CHRISTOPHER MA
EDITORS

RANDOM HOUSE NEW YORK

To our parents
Margaret and James Ma
Helen and Bob Bernstein, and
Sylvia Bernstein, a great grandmother

In the preparation of this book, every effort has been made to offer current, correct, and clearly expressed information. Nonetheless, inadvertent errors can occur and information can change. The information in the text is intended to afford general guidelines on matters of interest. Accordingly, the information in this book is not intended to serve as legal, accounting, tax, or medical advice. Readers are encouraged to consult with professional advisers concerning specific matters before making any decision, and the editors and publisher disclaim any responsibility for positions taken by readers in individual cases or for any misunderstanding on the part of readers.

 Published in the United States by Random House, Inc., New York, and simultaneously in Canada by Random House of Canada Limited, Toronto.

An earlier edition of this work was published in 1995 by Random House, Inc.

Library of Congress Cataloging-in-Publication Data is available.

ISBN 0-679-75492-X

Random House website address: http://www.randomhouse.com/

Printed in the United States of America on acid-free paper.

98765432

Second Edition

THE PRACTICAL GUIDE

CONTENTS

INTRODUCTION XI
CONTRIBUTORS XII

Chapter 1:
MONEY

INVESTING 2
THE LONG VIEW: Stocks for the 21st century .. 2
STRATEGIES: Why not to sell ... 4
STOCKS: Tips from the Motley Fool ... 7
EMERGING MARKETS: Around the world ... 11
DIVIDENDS: Companies that pay out ... 13
BONDS: The new inflation beaters ... 14
Where and how to buy ... 15
INVESTMENT CLUBS: Why women do better . 16
NEWSLETTERS: The top moneymakers ... 17
BROKERS: Tips for finding one ... 19
Cheap discount brokers ... 21
ONLINE: Money info on the Web ... 23
BOOKS: Ten moneymaking classics ... 24

MUTUAL FUNDS 25
BEST FUNDS: Morningstar's top picks ... 27
FUND FAMILIES: The worst and best ... 32
THE BASICS: Analyzing a fund ... 34
FEES: Loads vs. no-loads ... 36
FUND PICKING: Freshly minted funds ... 37
Big vs. small ... 37
INDEX FUNDS: Beating the market? ... 38
ASSET ALLOCATION: Ready-made portfolios . 39
MONEY MANAGEMENT: How the rich do it ... 42

RETIREMENT 44
HAVENS: Where the living is easy ... 44
ELDER COMMUNITIES: Beyond nursing homes ... 46
NEST EGGS: How much you need ... 49
Social Security ... 51
401(k)s ... 52
IRAs ... 54
Saving plans for the self-employed ... 55
Variable annuities ... 56
ESTATES: Avoiding taxes ... 57
WILLS: How to write one ... 59
PERSONAL FINANCE: Help for the elderly ... 60

REAL ESTATE 61
PRICES: Home values ... 61
The top housing markets ... 63
MORTGAGES: Buying vs. renting ... 65
Picking a mortgage ... 67
Mortgage tables ... 72
When to refinance ... 74
HOME INSURANCE: Hidden perils ... 75
VACATION HOMES: The top markets ... 76
FORECLOSURES: Houses on the cheap ... 78

COLLECTING 79
TRENDS: What's hot ... 79
ANTIQUES: Sizing up an heirloom ... 82
The allure of old silver ... 84
AUCTIONS: The Jackie O premium ... 86
COLLECTIBLES: Things worth saving ... 87
The Boomerabilia boom ... 88
FLEA MARKETS: Tips from a junkie ... 89
GEMSTONES: Buying the perfect ring ... 90
COINS & STAMPS: Minting a collection ... 92
FOSSILS: Dinosaur bones ... 95

THE PRACTICAL GUIDE

TAXES 96

CHANGES: Tips for tax day '97 96
DEDUCTIONS: 25 easily overlooked ones .. 101
COUPLES: Marriage can be taxing 103
CHARITY: Tax-free giving................ 104
TAX PREP: Picking an accountant........ 105
TAX FORMS: Filing electronically 107
HELP: The best software, etc............ 108
AUDITS: If the IRS drops by 109

DOLLARS & SENSE 110

KIDS: How much allowance............. 110
CREDIT CARDS: The best plastic.......... 114
GRATUITIES: Tipping tips................ 117
SHOPPING CLUBS: What's cheap.......... 118
BILLS: Online banking 119
CELLULAR PHONES: Picking a service 120
PHILANTHROPY: The best charities 121
INSURANCE: How to buy it.............. 124
DIVORCE: Lessons from Charles and Di .. 130
GETTING EVEN: Small claims court 132

Chapter 2:

HEALTH

GETTING FIT 134

WEIGHT GUIDE: New recommendations .. 135
EXERCISE: Benefits of different sports ... 137
TONE-UPS: Tips from Miss Galaxy 142
INJURIES: How to stay off the bench 146

HEALTHY EATING 148

FOOD VALUES: Daily nutritional needs... 149
VITAMINS: Food sources and benefits.... 151
CHOLESTEROL: What's healthy.......... 156
DIET: A look at the Asian pyramid 159
RED WINE: The health benefits 160
OLESTRA: Guilt-free potato chips 161
MILK: What low-fat means 161
FISH: A gourmet's taste guide 164
DESSERTS: Jacques Pépin's favorites ... 165
FRUIT: Picking what's ripe 169
COFFEE: Perfect espresso at home 172
TEA: A connoisseur's guide 173
BEERS: The best microbrews 175
DELI FOODS: What's safe 177
COOKBOOKS: Hall of Fame winners..... 178

LOOKING GREAT 179

SKIN CARE: How not to look your age 179
COSMETICS: A makeup artist's picks 183
HAIR CARE: Tips from "Friends" 184
COSMETIC SURGERY: A guide to common procedures 187
WRINKLES: Laser them away 189
IMPLANTS: Silicone's safety............ 193

HAVING CHILDREN 194

CHILDBEARING: The biological clock..... 195
DUE DATES: Figuring out yours 196
GENETIC TESTS: What you need to know .. 200
INFERTILITY: Help for couples 202
ADOPTION: Pitfalls to avoid 204
HYPERACTIVITY: Attention deficit disorder . 208

DOCTORS & MEDICINE 210

DOCTOR SELECTION: Tips from Dr. Koop .. 210
HMO'S: Does yours measure up? 215
HOSPITALS: The very best in America ... 217
MEDICAL BILLS: What procedures cost ... 226
ANTIBIOTICS: What's not working 228
GENERIC DRUGS: Paying less 230
PAIN RELIEVERS: Telling what's what 232
PSYCHOACTIVE DRUGS: Mending the mind 233
PHOBIC'S GUIDE: Foreign maladies....... 236
MELATONIN: What's behind the hype 237
BREAST CANCER: A woman's guide 238
MENOPAUSE: Hormone replacement therapy 241
BACK PAIN: Letting it go away 244
ALLERGIES: When to expect sneezes 250

TABLE OF CONTENTS

Chapter 3: SEXUALITY

WAYS & MORES 254

SEX DRIVE: Where it comes from 254
SEX ED: Explaining the stork to kids 259
SWEET TALK: The art of pillow talk 261
HARASSMENT: Over-the-line behavior 263
GAY RIGHTS: The new legal landscape ... 264
FOOT MASSAGE: Pleasuring the sole 266

RISKS & REMEDIES 269

CONTRACEPTION: The morning-after pill . 269
The pill, 25 years later............. 271
Choosing birth control protection... 272
ABORTION: Soon-to-be approved drugs ... 274
Reading the law's fine print 275
HIV: Testing and confidentiality 279
The risks from oral sex............. 280

Chapter 4: EDUCATION

K THROUGH 12 282

CHILD-REARING: Raising a moral child ... 285
SCHOOL REFORM: Where the action is 286
CHARTER SCHOOLS: Starting a school 288
STRESS: Dr. David Elkind advises 289
HOMEWORK: Appropriate help 292
FOREIGN LANGUAGES: When to start 295
SCIENCE: Bill Nye the Science Guy 296
MUSIC: Does it make you smarter? 298
SINGLE-SEX ED: Changing attitudes 300

COLLEGE & GRAD SCHOOL 302

EARLY ADMISSIONS: Why it's happening .. 302
TEST DATES: The SAT calendar 303
TOP COLLEGES: The *U.S. News* survey 306
FINANCIAL AID: Who qualifies and why ... 314
COMPUTERS: Campus cyberculture 317
GRAD SCHOOLS: America's best programs . 319

LIFELONG LEARNING 324

CONTINUING ED: Who needs what 325
LIBRARIES: A library lover's favorites ... 326
BOOKS: 20th century's most influential .. 327
ALUMNI PERKS: Ties that bind 330
RETIREMENT: Returning to the campus ... 331

Chapter 5: CAREERS

GETTING STARTED 334

JOBS: Where the work is 334
The fastest-growing professions 337
Top careers for women............. 338
Dream internships 340
GENERATION X: How to get ahead......... 342
PERSONALITY TESTS: For the clueless 344
CYBERSPACE: Online job-hunting 346
INTERVIEWS: What you can't be asked 348

PAY & PERKS 349

SALARIES: Getting a raise............... 349
How much you should be earning... 350
What 100 occupations pay 353
BENEFITS: What you should expect 356
VACATION: How to get more time off...... 357
FAMILY: What good companies offer 358
Baby leaves for moms—and pops.... 360

SMART MOVES 362

GETTING AHEAD: A coach's secrets........ 362
LEADERSHIP: Read your way to the top ... 365
HEADHUNTERS: How to get noticed 367
THE ZODIAC: Is success in your stars? 368
BOSSES: Dealing with a bully 370

THE PRACTICAL GUIDE

STRESS: Beating burnout 372
ENTREPRENEURS: Being your own boss . . . 374
The hottest franchises 376
HOME OFFICE: Best bets for big bucks 377
JURY DUTY: Tips from OJ's consultant 378
ERGONOMICS: Sitting pretty 379
OFFICE GIFTS: Beyond fruit baskets 380

Chapter 6:

HOUSE & GARDEN

AROUND THE HOUSE 382

DREAM HOUSE: What buyers want 383
RENOVATIONS: Costs and pay-offs 384
PAINT: A color expert's trade secrets 388
BEDS: How to buy the right one 391
LIGHTING: Smart ways to light a room . . . 392
PICTURE FRAMES: Do's and don'ts 393
WATER LEAKS: Plugging the problems 395
APPLIANCES: When to fix them 396
POLLUTANTS: If a home is a hot zone 398
Environmentally safe cleansers 400

HOME SAFETY 402

COP'S GUIDE: Keep your house safe 402
AUTO THEFT: How not to be a victim 404
ALARMS: Get your money's worth 405
SELF-DEFENSE: If you're attacked 406
GUN LAWS: A citizen's guide 409

GARDENING 411

CONTAINER GARDENING: Urban gardens . . . 411
GROWING ZONES: Where plants thrive 413
TOOLS: Where to buy the best 415
VEGETABLES: A planter's guide 417
FERTILIZERS: Organic alternatives 419
ROSES: No-fuss plants 423
LAWNS: Grasses for every occasion 427
HOUSEPLANTS: Indoor garden guide 429

PETS 431

EXOTICS: Hedgehogs to emus 431
DOG BREEDS: Canine personalities 433
INBREEDING: How to avoid a problem 435
DOG CARE: A holistic guide 436
CAT BREEDS: Meows for all seasons 437
CYBERPETS: Surrogates for busy people . 442

Chapter 7:

TRAVEL

HOT SPOTS 444

HAWAII: Hidden treasures 444
BEACHES: Dr Beach's secluded favorites . 451
PYRAMIDS: Mexico's Mayan ruins 452
THE CARIBBEAN: Island-by-island guide . . . 455
VIETNAM: Asia's newest jewel 464
COUNTRY HOUSES: England's finest 466
PARIS: New must-see sights 468
EUROPEAN INNS: Karen Brown's picks 469
VILLAS: A renter's guide 472
SHOPPING: Worldwide bargains 474
RESTAURANTS: Tastes of America 475
HONEYMOONS: Where Romeos go 478
RETREATS: Try a monastery 479

NATURAL TREASURES 480

NATIONAL PARKS: Crowdless parks 480
The top ten 484
The best guides 495
CONSERVATION: Imperiled wonders 496
LODGING: Cozy wilderness cabins 498
WILDLIFE: Eagles, manatees and more . . . 500
TRAILS: Paths across the U.S. 502
FALL FOLLIAGE: Best leaf drives 508

ADVENTURE 510

EXPLORING: The last great places 510
SAFARIS: Into Africa 515

TABLE OF CONTENTS

RAINFORESTS: Wet and wild 519
ECOTRAVEL: Green journeys. 522
HIKING: Ten great treks. 523
WALKS: The Swiss Alps. 526
BARGING: Slowly, thru Europe. 530
SIGHT-SEEING: Whale-watching 532
RAFTING: White-water runs 534
WILDERNESS SCHOOLS: Outdoor learning . 537

GETTING THERE 538

AIR TRAVEL: Safe planes, safest seats 538
Best airlines 541
If you're bumped; Frequent flyers . . 543
Cheap flights 545
TRAINS: Tips, trips and passes 549
CRUISES: Best new and old ships 552
Cabin picking tips 553
Traveling by trawler 555
LODGING: Motels matters 556
The best places to stay 557
ON THE ROAD: Weird attractions 558
U.S. mileage table. 560
BOOKS: Picking a guide 562

Chapter 8:

AUTOS

BUYING & LEASING 564

RESALE VALUES: After 5 years 565
BEST CARS: Picks from the 1996 models . . 567
BARGAINING: What dealers don't tell you . 571
LEASING: Should you buy or lease? 574
CRASH TESTS: How cars fare in a crunch . 576
INSURANCE: Costs for different models . . . 578
MOTORCYCLES: Tips for buying a bike . . . 582

DRIVING & MAINTENANCE 584

ROAD SAVVY: Lyn St. James on driving . . . 584
SAFETY: Equipment to keep you safe 588
TEEN DRIVERS: Smart driver's ed 589
CAR REPAIRS: Avoiding breakdowns 592

Chapter 9:

ENTERTAINMENT

MUSIC 596

ROCK & ROLL: Where history was made . . 596
INDIE LABELS: The next Pearl Jam 600
ROCK FESTS: Shows on the road 602
JUKEBOX: If you liked Janis Joplin 603
CLASSICAL MUSIC: Collector's musts 604
OPERA: Cecilia Bartoli's favorites 606

MOVIES 608

WEB SITES: Finding movie reviews 608
VIDEO GUIDE: Movies worth renting 611
STARSEARCH: Find your favorites 624
MAIL-ORDER VIDEOS: Beyond Blockbuster 625

GEAR & GADGETS 626

SHOPPER'S GUIDE: TVs, VCRs,
CD players, and more 626
HOME THEATERS: What to look for 629
SPEAKERS: Placement for the best sound 631
PHOTOS: Tips on picture-snapping 632

JUST FOR KIDS 633

KID MOVIES: The Movie Mom's latest 634
GOOSEBUMPS: R.L. Stine's picks 638
TOY RATINGS: The year's best toys 639
THRILLS: Best amusement parks 645
COOKING: Fun in the kitchen 648

Chapter 10:

COMPUTERS

HARDWARE 650

BUYING: What to look for 650
TECH GUIDE: Under the hood 652

THE PRACTICAL GUIDE

PLATFORMS: PC or Mac? 655
PERIPHERALS: Monitors and more 656
UPGRADES: Machine add-ons 659
NOTEBOOKS: A buyer's guide 660
HACKER'S GUIDE: Health hazards 662

SOFTWARE 664

CD-ROMS: From reference to weird 664
KIDS: Computer hints 670
Best bets for the under-10 set 672
DATABASES: For list lovers only 675
PERSONAL FINANCE: Best programs 677
TOOLS: Desktop publishing 679
Word processing 680

ONLINE 681

THE INTERNET: Signing up 681
Online services 683
E-MAIL: The cyber-postman 685
TECH TALK: Online lingo 686
BROWSERS: Tools you can use 688
HOT LIST: Web hangouts 689
THE WEB: Your very own home page 694
TROUBLE: How to avoid it 696

Chapter 11:

SPORTS & GAMES

A FAN'S GUIDE 698

BEING THERE: Hard-to-get tickets 698
Best sports values 699
Scalper's guide 700
BETTING: Winning the office pool 701
BASEBALL: Team guide 702
Cal Ripken's all-star advice 703
Spring training 704
FOOTBALL: Team guide 706
Should kids play tackle? 707
BASKETBALL: Team guide 708
Home hoops 709
HOCKEY: Team guide 710
HALLS OF FAME: Baseball to jousting 711

THE GREAT OUTDOORS 713

IN-LINE SKATING: A glider's guide 713
ROCK CLIMBING: Cliff walks 715
MARATHONS: Extreme races 717
BICYCLES: Pedaler's guide 718
GOLF: Best public courses 721
TENNIS: Tips from Zina 723
Picking a racquet 724
SOFTBALL: Hitting hints 725
FISHING: Angler's guide 726
Great streams 727
SNORKELING: Places to dive for 729
SWIMMING: Better strokes 731

WINTER FUN 733

SNOWBOARDING: Catching air 733
SKIING: Best resorts 735
Up-and-comers 738
New gear 739
ESCAPADES: Curling to ice climbing 741
HUNTING: Where, when and how 744
Falconry, sport of sultans 746

PARLOR GAMES 747

MONOPOLY: Tips from the champ 747
SCRABBLE: Words to master 749
BOARD GAMES: Checkers 750
Chess 750
Backgammon 752
CARD GAMES: Poker 753
Blackjack 755
Gin Rummy and Spades 756
Solitaire 758
POOL: Tips from a shark 759

INDEX 761
ACKNOWLEDGMENTS 786
READER'S QUESTIONNAIRE 787

INTRODUCTION

From the editors

DEAR READER,

When we published the first edition of *The Practical Guide to Practically Everything* last year, our goal was to provide up-to-date information and the very best advice from experts on all the subjects that can really make a difference in your daily life, from health and nutrition to money management and career planning, travel, home ownership, and consumer technology. Our inspiration was the traditional almanacs made famous by Benjamin Franklin and other early American publishers. This year we have redoubled our commitment to making this book practical, valuable, and time saving, and have added hundreds of new experts and many new features, including new sections on children, sports and retirement.

We've been enormously gratified by the feedback we've gotten from the hundreds of people we've met or received mail from over the last few months. From the reader in California who wrote to say that our auto chapter had saved him $600, to the Massachusetts woman who found our information on college financial aid of help to her daughter, to the correspondents who offered us suggestions from as far away as Belgium and Syria, we appreciate hearing from you.

A major occupational hazard of writing a book called *The Practical Guide to Practically Everything* is that it is sometimes assumed that we know practically everything, which of course is anything but the case. Among the queries that stumped us this year: how do you order guacamole dip in Swahili, and where can the actor who played Goober on *The Gomer Pyle Show* be found (see page 624 for the answer to the latter). One reader who called to question our recommendations on roses last year appears as our rose expert in this edition (page 423).

That's just the kind of collaboration we hope to have with you in the years to come. After all, a book like *The Practical Guide to Practically Everything* needs the help of practically everyone to stay current and compelling. So whether you're a new reader or an old friend, please pass the word that *The Practical Guide* is back and hopes to hear from you.

Christopher Ma and Peter Bernstein

CONTRIBUTORS

Editors: Peter Bernstein and Christopher Ma

Editorial Design: Janice Olson

Managing Editor: Mary Yee **Senior Editor:** Anna Mulrine

Senior Writers: Anna Isgro (Money), Michele Turk (Health, Sexuality)

Maps and Illustrations: Steve McCracken

Charts and Graphs: David Merrill

Reporters: Dan Avery (Entertainment), Patrick Brown (Autos), Sherrie Byrand (Sports & Games, Travel), Andrea Chipman (Money, Careers), Lavinia Edmunds (Education), Mary Kathleen Flynn (Computers), Shannon Henry (House & Garden, Entertainment), Jamie Krents (Entertainment), Doug Lederman (Sports & Games), Carol Levin (Computers), Christina Lowery (Education, Sexuality), Rita Pelczar (House & Garden), Mark Pener (House & Garden), Melissa Perenson (Computers), Jay Strell (Careers), Molly Tschida (Careers, Sexuality), Alex Ulam (Travel), Molly Ulam (Travel), Alex Wang (Entertainment), Leonard Wiener (Money), Saul Wisnia (Careers, Sports & Games), Drake Witham (Sports & Games)

Copy Editors: Eva Young, Michael Burke, Evan Stone

Production: Zachary W. Dorsey

Indexer: S. W. Cohen & Associates

Design Consultant: Rob Covey

CHAPTER ONE

MONEY

EXPERT QUOTES

"In the long run, I'm bullish. America has about 100 good years left."
—Phillip Carret, super-investor who turns 100 in 1996.
Page 2

"Baby boomers won't be choosing idle retirement. They are more adventurous."
—David Savageau, author of *Retirement Places Rated*
Page 44

"Most of the Kennedy items will probably not hold their value over the long haul."
—Bruce Wolmer, editor-in-chief, *Art & Auction*
Page 86

■ **THE YEAR AHEAD: CONTINUE** to bet on stocks, even if there is a bear market... **INVEST** in companies that put all their eggs in one basket... **WATCH** emerging stock markets in Poland, India, and Brazil... **TAP** the Web for valuable investing information... **BYPASS** your broker, buy stock directly from the company... **BEWARE** of freshly minted mutual funds... **PAY ATTENTION** to your 401(k)... **EXPECT** home prices to rise faster than inflation... **EYE** the art market as it stages a comeback... **START** paying your bills electronically...

INVESTING 2

MUTUAL FUNDS 25

RETIREMENT 44

REAL ESTATE 61

COLLECTING 79

TAXES 96

DOLLARS & SENSE 110

INVESTING

STRATEGIES: Why you shouldn't sell, PAGE 4 **EXPERT Q & A:** Smart tips from the Motley Fool, PAGE 7 **EMERGING MARKETS:** The best places to invest overseas, PAGE 11 **STOCKS:** Why dividends matter, PAGE 13 **BONDS:** One way to beat inflation, PAGE 14 **INVESTMENT CLUBS:** Why women do better than men, PAGE 16 **ADVICE:** How to find an honest broker, PAGE 19 **ONLINE:** A quick-click guide to cyber-investing, PAGE

THE LONG VIEW

INVESTING FOR THE NEXT 100 YEARS

A 100-year-old stock picker looks ahead

Philip Carret's name may not top everyone's list of legendary stock pickers, but it probably should. Even before superinvestor Warren Buffett was born, Carret (rhymes with beret) was practicing the precepts of value investing—that is, buying quality stocks and sticking with them for the long haul, a strategy that Carret outlined in 1930 in his first book, *The Art of Investing*. Buffett, who was a teenager when he first met Carret, has called him the man with the "best long-term record of anyone in America."

Carret, who turns 100 on November 28, 1996, has seen his share of market gyrations. He has lived through 31 bull markets, 30 bear markets, 20 recessions, and the Great Depression. In 1928, when the Dow Jones Industrial Average was at a mere 197, Carret started the Pioneer Fund, one of the first mutual funds. An original $1,000 investment in Pioneer would be worth more than $2 million today. Carret stepped down as chairman of Pioneer in 1983, although he still attends monthly board meetings.

Age has only slightly impinged on Carret's activities. He is writing his fourth book, *The Patient Investor*, works more than 40 hours a week, cooks his own meals, and regularly circles the world to view eclipses. Several years ago, Carret gave up management responsibilities at New York–based Carret & Company, the investment firm he founded that handles portfolios of at least $500,000. But he can still be found at his desk every weekday morning, promptly at 9:00 a.m, picking stocks. Here's some of his time-tested investing wisdom.

■ **What's your view of the current market?**

In the long run, I'm bullish. America has about 100 good years left.

■ **What stock picking lessons can you pass on to the average investor?**

Pick quality stocks with strong balance sheets, steady earnings, clever market strategies, and good management. Don't buy stock in companies that are highly leveraged or debt-heavy.

Be sure managers have a significant stake in their own companies—at least a year's salary. Be patient and don't try to time the market. Trading in and out of the market is the pinnacle of stupidity. Traders and timers always lose.

Don't become so emotionally attached to your investments that your judgment

EXPERT PICKS

A CENTENARIAN'S STOCKS FOR THE NEXT CENTURY

Philip Carret, 99 as this book went to press, and his disciples at Carret & Company, pick the following stocks for the long haul. They have the potential of greatly outperforming the market over a period of five years or so.

COMPANY / ☎	BUSINESS	COMMENTS
GREIF BROTHERS ☎614-363-1271	Fiberboard containers, packaging	*New management includes a long-experienced successor determined to enhance shareholder value.*
HIRSCH INTERNATIONAL CORP. ☎516-436-7100	Embroidery machinery for logos	*High quality, proprietary, state-of-the-art machinery; increasing demand for product.*
INACOM CORP. ☎402-392-3900	Computer networking systems and services	*Quality management; well qualified to ride wave of increased demand for networking services and hardware.*
ST JOE PAPER ☎904-396-6600	Paper manufacturer	*Well-positioned to capitalize on demand; good management; well-capitalized; secure; long-term quality holding.*
WALT DISNEY COMPANY ☎818-560-1000	Entertainment	*Good management; desirable franchises; strong balance sheet.*

becomes clouded. Take losses before they become drastic. On the other hand, don't be too anxious to take profits on gains made.

■ What's your best advice for personal money management?

Never borrow money to finance your investments. Avoid debt like the plague.

■ What's the most important characteristic an investor can have?

Patience.

■ Are stocks the best investment? What about bonds or hard assets?

Equities are where long-range growth and performance will be. I don't buy government bonds—I don't like to invest in the operations of insolvent organizations. Balance sheets are important and I wouldn't touch the government's balance sheet with a 10-foot pole.

As far as hard assets—only if you're very rich, and, even then, more than a 5 percent exposure is hard to justify.

■ What was your best investment?

Greif Brothers is one. Howard Buffett, Warren Buffett's father, recommended it almost 50 years ago. It grows steadily and is well-managed. Neutrogena is another one. I found Neutrogena soap in a hotel room and liked it. I bought the stock, making a nice profit. Then Johnson & Johnson took it over.

■ How do you know when to sell?

I don't like to sell and rarely sell unless a company's results are seriously disappointing or when whatever was attractive no longer holds true.

The hardest thing for amateur investors is to come to grips with the fact that everything isn't going to work every time. They have to learn to accept losses without becoming emotionally involved with the securities. When amateurs are emotionally involved, it becomes hard to admit they made a mistake and they ride a stock on down. Whereas when a professional senses a change in the fundamentals of an investment, he cuts bait and moves on to the next one.

STRATEGIES

WHY YOU SHOULD NEVER SELL

On Wall Street, patience is almost always rewarded

America has truly become a nation of investors. For the first time in more than two decades, Americans have more of their wealth invested in stocks, bonds, and mutual funds than in their homes, according to the Federal Reserve Board. Not since the go-go stock market of the late '60s have households had so much of their money tied up in financial assets.

With so much at stake, should the wise investor take some chips off the table? A widely held belief says, no. Over the long term, argues Jeremy J. Siegel, a finance professor at the University of Pennsylvania's Wharton School, stocks beat every other investment. Says Siegel, "Most people should buy a diversified list of stocks and use that as nearly 100 percent of their long-term holdings—and they should do that whether or not the valuations tend to be on the high side or on the low side when they buy." Siegel, whose strategy is detailed in his book, *Stocks for the Long Run* (Irwin, 1994), says it might be possible for some investors to time the market and buy and sell accordingly. But, he cautions, it's foolish to try. For truly long-term investing, says Siegel, there is never a bad time to buy stocks—or a good time to sell.

History is on his side. Measure stocks against bonds, cash, diamonds, you name it, and in the long run, stocks win. Stashing your cash in houses, gold, oil, or in collectibles is considered smart during times of high inflation, which can hurt stocks and bonds. But not over the long haul, according to R. S. Salomon, Jr., of STI Management, a Stamford, Conn. investment firm. After tracking the returns of different assets since the late 1970s, Salomon found that returns on tangible assets fluctuate wildly from year to year (see table, below). In the long run, though, financial assets beat out collectibles and hard assets.

■ STOCKS VS. BONDS VS. HARD ASSETS: AND THE WINNER IS...

Over the long haul, stocks and bonds beat tangible assets every time.

ASSET	20 YR.		10 YR.		5 YR.		1 YR.	
	Rank	Return[1]	Rank	Return[1]	Rank	Return[1]	Rank	Return[1]
STOCKS	**1**	13.8%	**1**	14.6%	**1**	11.4%	**1**	20.1%
BONDS	**2**	10.5	**2**	11.7	**1**	11.4	**3**	15.8
STAMPS	**3**	8.2	**8**	-0.5	**7**	1.3	**7**	0.8
3-MO. TREASURY BILLS	**4**	8.1	**4**	6.2	**4**	4.8	**4**	5.5
DIAMONDS	**5**	7.7	**5**	5.9	**10**	0.2	**8**	0.0
HOUSING	**6**	5.8	**6**	3.8	**5**	2.5	**11**	–1.4
GOLD	**7**	4.4	**7**	2.0	**8**	1.1	**6**	0.1
FOREIGN EXCHANGE[2]	**7**	4.4	**3**	9.1	**3**	6.4	**2**	19.8
OIL	**9**	2.7	**10**	–3.8	**6**	1.6	**5**	3.5
SILVER	**10**	0.9	**9**	–1.5	**8**	1.1	**10**	–0.1
SOTHEBY'S STOCK[3]		NA[4]		NA	**11**	–6.2	**8**	0.0
CONSUMER PRICE INDEX		**5.4**		**3.5**		**3.3**		**2.9**

1. Average annual returns as of the end of June 1995.
2. Combines money market returns with changes in exchange rates.
3. Proxy for art investment
4. Not applicable

SOURCE: R. S. Salomon, Jr., STI Management, Stamford, Conn.; Based on data from: Salomon Brothers Inc.; *The Diamond Registry*, Scott Publishing Co.; West Texas Intermediate; National Association of Realtors.

Pit stocks against cash and again stocks are tops. (By cash, we mean money invested in three-month Treasuries or a first-rate money market fund, not the reserve you stash for a rainy day.) Looking back 50 years, cash has beaten out stocks only 10 times, according to Ibbotson Associates, a Chicago research firm. One of those rare periods was between August 1993 and the end of 1994, when the returns of the 30-day Treasury bill outperformed the Standard & Poor's 500 stock index by 3 percentage points and the 20-year Treasury bond by 15 percentage points. Usually, though, periods when cash is king have not lasted longer than 24 months. After accounting for inflation, cash has returned an average 0.5 percent per year since 1926, compared with 6.9 percent for the S&P 500, according to Ibbotson.

What's an investor to do when market indicators, such as the Dow Jones Industrial Average and the S&P 500, hit rocky patches? Hold on tight, say buy-and-hold advocates, the road will eventually smooth out. What's more, market averages can sometimes be deceiving. Take, for example, the 16 years between the market peak in 1966 to the low in the summer of 1982—perhaps the most abysmal period for stock-market investors since the Great Depression of the 1930s. The Dow lost money at an average annual rate of 1.5 percent. The S&P gained a measly 0.9 percent annually. Treasury bills looked downright alluring with

EXPERT TIP

Which stocks do well in a bear market? Look at industries that led the way out of past recessions, advises Elaine M. Garzarelli, a respected Wall Street analyst. Here are her top five industry groups that have had big gains in the first 12 months after the market has bottomed out and their average percent gain.

Leisure time	**111.9%**
Retail drug stores	**97.1%**
Pollution control	**94.8%**
Newspaper publishing	**86.6%**
Homebuilding	**75.5%**

SOURCE: Garzarelli Capital Fund.

■ THE BULLS ARE BEATING THE BEARS

This century's bull markets have lasted longer and moved farther than the bear markets. On average, they've lasted about two years with a near 85 percent increase in the Dow Jones Industrial Average. The current bull started running on October 11, 1990, and was still going strong as of June 25, 1996. The average bear market during this century lasted 410 days, during which the Dow dropped some 30 percent.

■ BEAR MARKETS

Beginning date	Ending date	Number of days	Loss in Dow	Mos. to recover
2/9/66	10/7/66	240	–25.2%	6
12/3/68	5/26/70	539	–35.9%	22
4/28/71	11/23/71	209	–16.1%	64
1/11/73	12/6/74	694	–45.1%	4
9/21/76	2/28/78	525	–26.9%	6
9/8/78	4/21/80	591	–16.4%	10
4/27/81	8/12/82	472	–24.1%	4
11/29/83	7/24/84	238	–15.6%	3
8/25/87	10/19/87	55	–36.1%	23
7/16/90	10/11/90	87	–21.2%	5

SOURCE: Ned Davis Research, Inc.

■ BULL MARKETS

Beginning date	Ending date	Number of days	Gain in Dow
10/7/66	12/3/68	788	32.4%
5/26/70	4/28/71	337	50.6%
11/23/71	1/11/73	415	31.8%
12/6/74	9/21/76	655	75.7%
2/28/78	9/8/78	192	22.3%
4/21/80	4/27/81	371	34.9%
8/12/82	11/29/83	474	65.7%
7/24/82	8/25/87	1,127	150.6%
10/19/87	7/16/90	1,001	72.5%
10/11/90	——	2,084*	141.8%*

*As of June 25, 1996.

returns of 7 percent a year. But the picture wasn't as bleak as the market averages suggest. If you include stock dividend income, an important part of the market's total return, the S&P return jumps to 5.1 percent a year, according to Ibbotson. Also, not all stocks were losers: Returns for small-company stocks actually rose 12.7 percent a year, including reinvested dividends.

Furthermore, market averages become less significant for investors who regularly pump money into stocks, regardless of share prices. A strategy called dollar-cost averaging helps manage the risk of stock market ups and downs. By investing a set dollar amount regularly, say, $100 once a month, you get more shares when stock prices are low and fewer when prices are high. Over time, the practice reduces your average cost per share, improving your chances of becoming a slow but steady winner. Ibbotson figures that if you put $100 every month into S&P 500 stocks, you would have invested a total of $19,800 between 1966 and 1982. The total worth of your portfolio at the market low in August 1982: $32,600, or 64 percent more than your cost.

There are lessons to be learned from successful buy-and-hold investors. Take Anne Scheiber, the frugal spinster from New York City who died at age 101 in 1995. By reinvesting dividends, ignoring market fluctuations, and searching for solid stocks, she nurtured a nest egg of $20,000 or so into a $22 million fortune. No one can guarantee great stock market returns, but if you invest regularly, diversify your holdings, reinvest dividends, and have patience—you should be rewarded.

...AND WHEN YOU SHOULD SELL

Even buy-and-hold advocates would agree that there is a difference between trying to time the market and trying to reassess your holdings. Is it time to unload a few stocks? Ask yourself these questions before you dump them. Responses were culled from the best advice of financial planners:

■ Have a particular stock's underlying fundamentals changed?

Study the company's financials and management history. Are there signs of serious trouble? A few quarters of poor results doesn't necessarily signal a dog, but some pros say when a company reports earnings decreases of 5 percent or more over a 12-month period, it's probably time to unload. Others say a considerable slowdown in a company's sales growth can also be a sell signal.

■ How does the stock's performance compare with my goals for buying it?

If the stock price is dipping well below your goals for those shares, it may be time to cut your losses. Some investors say if a stock price falls 30 percent, it's time to unload it. On the other hand, a stock that rises 30 percent may also be a candidate for a sell.

■ How exposed to stocks is my portfolio?

A diversified portfolio that combines stocks, bonds, and cash—like money-markets and Treasury bills—is well buttressed against dips in the stock market. Even if stocks plunge 20 percent, say, you won't pulverize your holdings.

■ What are the costs of dumping?

You'll face hefty brokerage commissions when you sell. And, you may have to fork over plenty in taxes if you sell and show a profit on the investment.

■ Where would I invest the money?

Determine what your investment alternatives are. Nearly all other investment options—bonds, money-market funds, T-bills, hard assets—won't beat stocks over the long haul. For inflation-beating returns, there's just no match for the stock market.

EXPERT Q & A

SMART TIPS FROM A FOOL

Buying the dogs of the Dow can make you rich

The hottest, hippest investment gurus today are a pair of brothers, David and Tom Gardner, who go by the unlikely moniker, the Motley Fool. The brothers took the title from an obscure passage in Shakespeare's *As You Like It* and have turned it into an online household name. Their site on America Online (keyword: FOOL) has become a hotspring of investing tips and humor. The basis of their investment philosophy: Fools can almost always beat the so-called wise men of Wall Street.

Most investors would suffer the Motley Fool gladly: The Gardners' investing wisdom has resulted in an astounding 163 percent return on their online portfolio from its inception in August 1994 to the end of April 1996. By comparison, the stock market average came to 40 percent. Here, David Gardner, coauthor with his brother of *The Motley Fool Investment Guide* (Simon & Schuster, 1996), shares some of the Fool's wisdom.

■ What's your strategy for beating the Dow?

We use a systematic three-pronged approach to investing. We call it the three prongs of the foolish fork. First, we use the Dow dividend approach, popularized by one of our heroes, money manager Michael O'Higgins in his book *Beating the Dow*. The second prong is to pick good small-cap stocks, and the third prong is to sell stocks short.

■ Tell us about the Dow dividend approach.

We pick stocks from among those that make up the Dow Jones Industrials, which is an index of 30 of the largest American companies. We buy equal dollar amounts of some of these stocks and hold on to them. It's a simple approach that takes all the emotion out of investing. It can be used by any novice. All it takes is 30 minutes a year to run the numbers and make the buys and sells. You sit tight and one year later, you probably doubled the market returns.

■ Exactly how does your strategy work?

Here's how our Dow dividend approach works. First, get the names of the 30 companies on the Dow, which you can find in the stock pages of *The Wall Street Journal*. Then look at the share price relative to the company's dividend yield. Dividends are basically monetary rewards that the company

FACT FILE:

THE GREATEST INVESTOR OF ALL TIME

■ *In the pantheon of great investors, picking the best ever is a tough call. The roster includes* **John Maynard Keynes**, *the famous British economist and avid investor;* **Peter Lynch**, *who nurtured the Fidelity Magellan Fund into a giant; and* **George Soros**, *whose Quantum Fund made huge bets on foreign currencies and bonds, and mostly won. The winner, according to* The Wall Street Journal*:*

■ **Warren Buffett**, *chairman of Omaha-based Berkshire Hathaway, Inc. Buffett's 27 percent average annual return since 1957 actually trailed Soros's 34 percent since 1969, But the* Journal *gave him points for his style. Unlike Soros, Buffett rarely uses leverage, or debt, which can embellish investment results.*

takes from its profits and gives to shareholders. Generally, that amount is about 3 percent of a company's share price.

To find a company's dividend yield, you take the amount of the dividend paid per share and divide by the price of one share of stock. For example, say a company is paying $1 a share in dividends. If the stock is selling at $50 per share, divide $1 by $50 and you get a dividend yield of 2 percent, which represents a sort of interest payment you get for holding the stock over the next year.

■ How do you identify your targets?

You take the 30 companies and rank their dividend yields. Put the highest dividend yields at the top and the lowest at the bottom. A few, like Bethlehem Steel and Woolworth's, don't pay dividends so they go at the very bottom.

FACT FILE:

THE DOGS OF THE DOW

■ *These 10 bargain stocks, often called the "Dogs of the Dow," are the 1996 highest-yielding stocks of the Dow Jones 30. At the beginning of each year, buy the bargain 10 for that year, hold them for one year and then repeat the process. You'll almost always beat the market.*

COMPANY	YIELD*
PHILIP MORRIS	4.4
TEXACO	4.1
J.P. MORGAN	4.0
CHEVRON	3.8
EXXON	3.7
DU PONT	3.0
3M COMPANY	2.8
GENERAL ELECTRIC	2.6
INTERNATIONAL PAPER	2.6
EASTMAN KODAK	2.4

*As of Dec. 29, 1995. Yields are calculated by dividing the annual dividend by the stock price.

Source: John Downes, editor of *Beating the Dow*

Now, ignore the bottom 20 and focus on the top 10 yielding companies—sometimes called the Dogs of the Dow.

These are your targets. You buy equal dollar amounts of each of those 10 and hold them for one year. After one year, line them up again, according to their yields. Do this every year for two decades and you'd have returns of around 16 percent.

■ Can you do any better than 16 percent returns?

Yes. If you are selective, you can outperform the Dogs of the Dow by investing in fewer of them and saving on commission fees as well. You don't want to own just one stock, even if it's the best performer. You want to diversify. We took the top 10 yielders and lined them up by share prices. O'Higgins says that if you invest in the five with the lowest share price, you could wind up with average returns of 20 percent or so, which is great.

We took it one step further. We ranked the companies by share price from the highest to the lowest. We looked at the performance of each of those. O'Higgins says the one with the second lowest share price has been the best performer historically—somewhere around 29 percent. The worst performer of all, with returns of just 8 percent, was the one with the lowest price, which is the one at the top of the list. The third, fourth, and fifth outperformed the sixth through tenth.

We decided it would make sense to double up on the stock in the number two position and eliminate the one in the number one position. We call that group—numbers two, three, four, and five—the Foolish Four. Investing in them has returned more than 25 percent over the last two decades.

■ Why does the dividend approach work?

It works because you are buying the stocks when public sentiment is against the company and prices are at a real low. Remember that the companies that make up the Dow are not about to go out of business. Prices may be down temporarily, but they'll shoot back up. It's a safe strategy, too, because you're buying into huge companies and getting them at cheap prices. They won't go up every time, but for more than two decades, they have returned more than 22 percent a year, compared to 10.5 percent for the market average.

■ How does the second part of your investment strategy work?

The Dow dividend strategy is a starting point. If you're going to buy any other stocks, you're going to have to beat the performance of the Dow dividend stocks. The second prong of our investing strategy is to buy small-cap stocks. Stock prices track the performance of company earnings and the earnings of small companies multiply much faster than those of bigger companies. We use an extensive checklist of things to look at when picking small-cap growth stocks, including those with sales growth of more than 25 percent a year, and companies in which at least 15 percent of the stock is management-owned. Then we narrow down the list, read all their financial statements and annual reports, and hope we make the right choices. These small-cap companies have been the greatest performers in our portfolio with dramatic returns.

■ What about the third prong?

The third prong to our foolish fork is that we sell stock short. Selling short means you're making money when a given stock drops as opposed to rising. We believe that if you can find undervalued stock you can also find overvalued stock, so it's smart to have money down on both sides. You should never have more than 20 percent of your overall portfolio in selling short but we think it's good to have this hedge in down times.

■ Why are you bearish on mutual funds?

The rule of thumb is: 80 percent of all mutual funds have underperformed the market average. With a record like that, why bother?

■ Are stocks the only way to go?

For us, yes. We've never owned anything else. And that should be the case for mature investors. Even for complete novices, the Dow dividend approach is the way to go.

EXPERT LIST

20 UNDERACHIEVERS WORTH A BET

Each year, the Council of Institutional Investors, a Washington, D.C.–based group of huge pension funds, puts out a list of 20 companies that are underachievers—or that are poised for a turnaround. To make the list, a company must have total shareholder returns below its industry average for the year and for the five previous years. Once the companies beat the S&P 500 on their 5-year returns, they are thrown off the list.

The Council has found that investing in the 20 companies has paid off nicely. In the year after a company makes the list, its share price has risen an average 14 percent above the S&P. Earnings also improved as the companies refocused their operations and restructured their assets.

Here's the 1995 list:

ALZA CORP.
COOPER INDUSTRIES INC.
CRAY RESEARCH
EG&G INC.
GENUINE PARTS CO.
LONGS DRUG STORES INC.
MELVILLE CORP.
MORRISON KNUDSEN CORP.
NACCO INDUSTRIES
NORTHERN TELECOM LTD.
OGDEN CORP.
POTLATCH CORP.
SAFETY-KLEEN CORP.
SALOMON INC.
TENNECO INC.
TOYS "R" US INC.
TYCO INTERNATIONAL LTD.
UNITED STATES SURGICAL CORP.
UPJOHN CO.
YELLOW CORP.

SOURCE: Council of Institutional Investors, Washington, D.C.

EXPERT TIPS

WHY THE MARKET LOVES PURE PLAYS

Companies with all their eggs in one business stand out

What does the stock market prefer: Hotshot conglomerates or focused single-business companies? Despite all the hype about diversified conglomerates, it's the smaller, one-business companies—or pure plays—that the market values. According to a study by Stern Stewart, a New York–based financial management firm, investors know that being focused is better.

To determine how much wealth a company created from each dollar invested in it, Stern Stewart compared each company's market value with all the capital that was plowed into it over time. The results: Pure plays created an average $2.27 in market value for every dollar invested in them. Companies with five or more businesses trailed behind with an average $1.55.

■ PURITY OF PURPOSE PAYS OFF

Here's a list of all the companies that created at least $8 in market value for every dollar of debt and equity invested. (The study doesn't take into consideration dividends paid over the years.) No company with four or more businesses made the cut.

TYPE OF BUSINESS	MARKET VALUE PER $1 INVESTED
ONE BUSINESS	
ZEBRA TECHNOLOGIES	$17.52
INTUIT	$17.28
PARAMETRIC TECHNOLOGY	$16.53
CISCO SYSTEMS	$16.36
CHARTER MEDICAL	$16.32
LINEAR TECHNOLOGY	$15.06
CHEYENNE SOFTWARE	$14.91
AMERICAN POWER CONVERSION	$14.87
PAYCHEX	$13.29
CABLETRON SYSTEMS	$12.22
GENTEX	
BED, BATH & BEYOND	$11.14
FASTENAL	$11.12
FTP SOFTWARE	$10.32
AUTOZONE	$ 9.73
VENTRITEX	$ 9.57
WM. WRIGLEY JR.	$ 8.72
XILINX	$ 8.55
NEXTEL COMMUNICATIONS	$ 8.54
NEWMONT MINING	$ 8.36
ELECTRONIC ARTS	$ 8.35
GYMBOREE	$ 8.08
SUNSHINE MINING	$ 8.05
TWO BUSINESSES	
INTERNATIONAL GAME TECHNOLOGY	$8.02
THREE BUSINESS	
UST	$9.41

SOURCE: Stern Stewart.

■ What do you advise for investors who are reluctant to jump into the stock market?

A good starting point for leery investors is the Vanguard Index Trust 500 Portfolio. Index funds mimic the market and put you ahead of most other investors who own mutual funds run by managers. The Vanguard Index fund is run by computers, demands no research and mimics the Standard & Poor's 500. Managers of huge mutual funds are getting paid huge amounts but their funds are underperforming the index funds. We don't really think there's any other fund out there worth buying.

■ How do you weather bear markets?

We buy and hold and don't worry about it. The notions of bear and bull markets are short-term distinctions. I believe we live in an eternal bull market, when you look at it in the long term.

EMERGING MARKETS

TAKING YOUR MONEY ON TOUR

To make a packet abroad try investing in Poland, India, and Brazil

Putting money into foreign stocks is not for the faint-hearted. After spectacular gains in 1993—the average emerging-market stock fund gained 72 percent—the devaluation of the Mexican peso sent global markets crashing. The average emerging-market fund lost 10 percent in 1994 and 7 percent in 1995. What's more, the risks are high. Emerging stock markets lack the regulatory safeguards that protect U.S. shareholders. Many are dominated by just a few stocks or are rife with speculation.

With that kind of history, why bother venturing into emerging markets at all? Because that's where future growth is likely to be. While leading economies will only inch ahead in the next decade, the gross domestic product (GDP) in emerging markets will grow an average 4.9 percent a year, according to the World Bank. For intrepid investors who can tolerate the wild swings, fast-growing emerging markets may be the ticket for the coming decade.

The trick, of course, is to buy foreign stocks when they are down because they almost always go back up. Timing the market isn't easy, but analysts advise keeping a close eye on the movement of interest rates. Emerging markets seem to do best when U.S. bond yields are falling. Such was the case in 1993: U.S. interest rates were dropping and emerging markets were turning in booming results.

Where in the world to invest is another difficult dilemma. Leila Heckman, managing director of Global Asset Allocation at Smith Barney, has done an analysis of 39 countries around the globe, based on stock valuation, economic growth, risk, and interest rate environment. One of her favorite regions is Eastern Europe, especially the Czech Republic and Poland. "We are forecasting very attractive price/earnings (stock price divided by a company's earnings per share) ratios for these countries: 8.1 for the Czech Republic and 7.9 for Poland, compared to an average p/e ratio of 12 for the entire region," says Heckman. Russia is worth keeping an eye on, albeit a wary one, say some analysts. The market potential in the country is enormous but so are fears of political and exchange rate volatility.

Asia, with the exception of Japan, is another good bet. The Asian market as a whole is expected to see domestic growth rates of 5.4 percent by 2004. China, with its vast population and huge savings pool, is poised for the hottest growth: 8 percent to 10 percent a year over the next decade, according to the World Bank. Heckman also finds South Korea alluring, with its stable interest rates and a low projected p/e ratio. Hong Kong's string of disappointing years has made its stocks

■ BEST & WORST OF COUNTRY STOCKS

Emerging markets like India and the Czech Republic were among the worst performers of 1995. Analysts believe they'll rebound over the next few years.

BEST	Return rate*
Switzerland	45.0%
United States	38.2%
Sweden	34.1%
Spain	31.2%
Netherlands	28.9%
Belgium	27.3%
Jordan	24.8%
Hong Kong	22.6%
New Zealand	22.4%
Ireland	22.4%

WORST	Return rate*
India	–34.0%
Hungary	–33.6%
Pakistan	–32.3%
Taiwan	–30.7%
Venezuela	–30.2%
China	–25.5%
Czech Republic	–24.9%
Colombia	–24.5%
Mexico	–24.3%
Brazil	–18.5%

*One-year returns as of Dec. 31, 1995; denominated in U.S. dollars. SOURCE: Smith Barney.

especially cheap and China has promised to respect Hong Kong's bustling free-market economy when it takes over in 1997. But watch out: The market in Hong Kong has crashed four times in the past 30 years.

Many analysts are bearish on Japan. "Its banking system still has its share of problems, which are unlikely to be resolved anytime soon," says Heckman. On the positive side, Japan's GDP and exports are improving and low interest rates are helping to stimulate the economy. Some contrarians believe it may be time to get into Japan early, before the market makes a comeback.

In South Asia, India is expected to shine. Policy reforms over the past few years have slashed government controls on production, trade, and investment, although they've also caused some disarray. India's massive population and active stock market are attractive, as is a projected GDP growth rate of 8 percent by 2004, far outpacing the region. Indonesia is also enticing. Its companies are expected to show an earnings growth rate of 18 percent, on average, for several years to come.

Latin America has had a sizzling decade: Markets gained nearly 22 percent a year on average, according to Morgan Stanley Asset Management. Can the region keep it up for a few more years? Yes, says Morgan Stanley. Even though some Latin American countries, such as Mexico and Argentina, have taken a big hit in the recent past, at least three Latin economies are poised for big growth in the long term. Morgan Stanley projects a 16 percent annual rise in corporate profits for Chile and 18 percent for Peru over the next five years. But the hottest projections are reserved for Brazil, which is considered undervalued and has gone a long way toward curing economic ills such as inflation. Morgan Stanley expects corporate earnings in Brazil to shoot up at a 25 percent annual rate.

HOW TO GO ON A FOREIGN FLING

If you thrive on risk, try investing in companies overseas

Want a piece of the global action? The most common way to invest overseas is through mutual funds that specialize in foreign markets. One way to get a taste of global investing is through index funds, such as Country Baskets or World Equity Baskets (WEBs), which closely match a specific stock market index. The funds trade on the New York Stock Exchange and can be bought through brokers. But increasingly Americans are buying shares of individual foreign companies in the form of American depository receipts (ADRs).

ADRs are negotiable certificates issued by U.S. banks and represent a given number of shares in a foreign company. ADRs are registered with the SEC and traded like other securities on the over-the-counter or other U.S. exchanges. ADRs are sold in U.S. dollars through brokers, just like stocks. To buy one, just pick up the phone.

Getting timely information on the company whose stock you're buying isn't that easy, though. Pros generally advise that average investors stick with the 220 or so companies trading on the big exchanges that meet U.S. standards of accounting and disclosure. Voluminous data on ADRs are available in *Morningstar American Depository Receipts*, a biweekly report by Morningstar, the Chicago-based research company (☎ 800–876–5005). The report tracks 1,000 ADRs, with up to 10 years of data, business summaries, and market snapshots. The cost is steep: $335 per year, or $45 for a three-month trial subscription.

A caveat: Investing in ADRs is risky for several reasons. For one, the underlying stock is denominated in local currency, so that a strengthening dollar hurts an ADR's value. (The reverse is also true.) What's more, faraway economic and political developments can jolt an ADR's price.

STOCKS

A LITTLE EXTRA DIVIDEND

Why companies whose payout climbs regularly are a good bet

If the stock market has you jittery but you don't want to bail out altogether, look for stocks that have a habit of raising dividends year after year, no matter what. That's the strategy pushed by, among others, superinvestor Peter Lynch, now vice chairman of Fidelity Investments, who made a name for himself managing its Magellan fund for 13 years. As Lynch outlines it in the September 1995 issue of *Worth* magazine, investing in so-called dividend achievers is a way of getting the best of both worlds: Money to live on that normally comes from bonds, and growth that comes from stocks.

One reason that Lynch and others love dividend achievers is that these companies provide steadiness in rough times. Take, for example, American Home Products Corp., maker of Robitussin, Gulden's mustard, etc., which has had 43 years of dividend growth. If its stock were to skid 5 percent over the next year, an investor would still come out ahead, thanks to its 6 percent or so dividend. When directors raise dividends, they think future earnings will be good enough to allow the higher payouts, and they're usually right.

Lynch goes so far as to propose that investors sink 100 percent of their investment capital into a portfolio of companies that pay decent dividends. An easy way to invest in dividend achievers is to buy into an S&P 500 index fund, currently yielding about 3 percent. Or, you can be more selective and choose a few dividend achievers from the list in *Moody's Handbook of Dividend Achievers.* (Cost: $24.95. Call: ☎ 800–342–5647, ext. 0546.)

Of the 13,200 publicly traded stocks tracked by Moody's, about 10 percent increased their dividends in 1995. Of those, 342 companies have raised dividends for at least 10 years in a row. Winn-Dixie Stores holds the title for the longest stretch of annual dividend hikes: 52 years. Close behind is Ohio Casualty Corp., which has increased dividends for the past half century. Both companies ranked in the top third of Moody's list for total returns, that is, dividend income plus price appreciation.

The total returns of many of the dividend achievers compare favorably with other investments. And, when the bull market soars, the combination of price appreciation and reinvested dividends yielded some dazzling returns. Medtronic Inc., for example, which topped Moody's 1995 list of total return achievers, had a total return of 102.1 percent.

■ TOP DIVIDEND ACHIEVERS

The top 10, ranked by the average annual dividend growth rate, 1985 to 1995.

Company	Industry	Growth rate
Fed. National Mortgage Assoc. (Fannie Mae)	Financial	48.3%
Raymond James Financial	Brokerage	31.1%
Progressive Corp.	Insurance	29.2%
Allied Group	Insurance	29.1%
Wal-Mart Stores	Retail	27.5%
Arnold Industries	Trucking, warehousing	27.1%
Cintas Corp.	Manufacturing	25.9%
Circuit City Stores	Electronics retail	24.8%
Brady Co.	Manufacturing	24.7%
Sysco Corp.	Food service	24.3%

■ TOP IN TOTAL RETURNS

These companies earned investors the greatest total returns—stock-price appreciation plus dividends—in 1995.

Company	Industry	Return rate
Medtronic Inc.	Medical tech.	102.07%
American Business Prod.	Office products	97.40%
Wallace Computer Svs.	Computer svs.	91.73%
Loral Corp.	Def. electronics	88.95%
Monsanto Co.	Chemical	78.67%
Merck & Co.	Pharmaceutical	76.68%
Eli Lilly & Co.	Pharmaceutical	76.68%
Fannie Mae	Financial	75.05%

SOURCE: *Moody's 1996 Handbook of Dividend Achievers.*

BONDS

ONE WAY TO BEAT INFLATION

Uncle Sam's new bonds could boost your long-term savings

Economists have long clamored for bonds that eliminate inflation risks. Inflation can have an insidious effect on bonds, cutting the worth of a bond's coupon payments and its eventual redemption value. For example, if you bought a 30-year government bond in 1966 yielding 5 percent, the bond would now be worth only 85 percent of its original value, thanks to years of higher-than-expected inflation.

To remove some of that risk, the Treasury is issuing a new bond that offers returns that rise and fall in line with inflation. The new bonds are designed to help the average investor save for retirement, the kids' college tuition, and other long-term goals. All the details of the new bonds had yet to be worked out as this book went to press in mid-1996. But one thing was clear: The bonds will be denominated as low as $1,000, making them attractive for individual investors.

The big question: Are inflation-indexed bonds a better deal than regular fixed-income bonds? Yes and no, depending on the real interest rate an investor agrees to and the inflation rate over the life of the bond. In periods of high inflation, the new bonds will give you the necessary inflation protection and better returns. For example, assume that inflation starts at 3 percent a year, gradually rises to 5 percent over the first 10 years, and then to 9 percent over the next 20 years. If you invested in a conventional 30-year bond with a $1,000 face value paying 7 percent interest, your payout, in 1996 dollars, would be $1,297. The payout, in 1996 dollars, for an inflation-indexed bond would be $1,900.

But the bonds are no hedge for deflation, that is, when consumer prices are falling over a long period. Let's assume you bought that same bond when the inflation rate was 3 percent during the early years and then fell to 1 percent over the following years. The payout for the conventional bond: $2,320. For the inflation-indexed bond: $1,900. In this case, you would have fared better with a fixed-income bond. As it happens, deflationary times are less common than periods of inflation.

STAYING AHEAD OF THE CURVE

Want to know where bonds are headed? Consult the yield curve. The yield curve, which can be found in *The Wall Street Journal* or *Investor's Business Daily*, shows how interest rates and bonds of different maturities relate to each other.

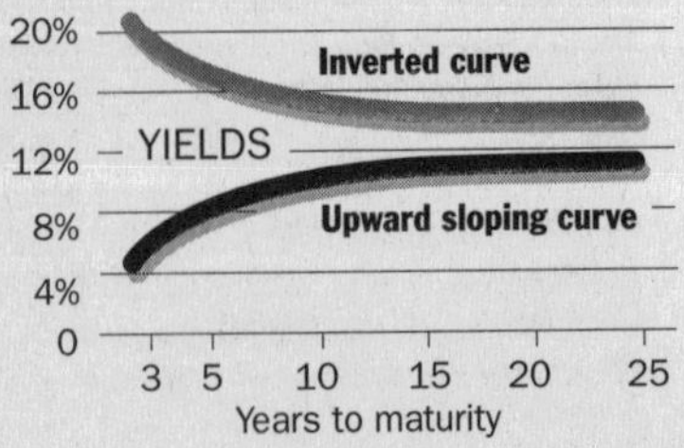

A normal curve moves upward, showing that interest rates rise as maturities increase. The curve turns downward, or inverts, when short-term rates are higher than long-term rates. When short- and long-term rates are about the same, the curve is flat—the market sees little difference between the short-term and long-term risks, so buying longer-term bonds gives you only a slight premium. When short-term yields exceed long-term yields, the curve inverts, a sign of a recession to come. In a recession, you want to be in long-term bonds; eventually the curve will normalize and the value of the bonds will rise.

BONDS

WHERE TO GET GOOD PAPER

Brokers, funds, and Uncle Sam all offer an on-ramp to investing

Once you've selected from the variety of available bonds—government bonds, U.S. Savings bonds, Treasury bills, Treasury notes, municipal bonds, and corporate bonds—how do you go about buying them? Depending on the type, you have a few choices.

Municipals and corporate bonds are bought through brokers. You can buy Treasuries through a bank, a broker, a mutual fund, or through a government program called Treasury Direct, ☎ 202-874-4000. The advantage of buying through the government is that there is no commission. For more information, write: Department of the Treasury, Bureau of the Public Debt, Washington, D.C. 20239.

You also can open an account and learn about scheduled bond auctions. Two- and three-year bonds are available for a minimum $5,000 investment. Five- and 10-year notes require a minimum $1,000 investment.

For greater diversification, you can turn to bond funds (see table below). You can invest in small amounts and a professional manager runs the show. A drawback: Bond funds constantly trade bonds and don't hold them to maturity, so you lose the guarantee that you'll get a bond's face value at a certain date.

When investing in bond funds, scrutinize fees and other expenses. After all, the return is so low, why dish out 4 or 5 percent? To find the true return, find out the yield and subtract the fund's annual expense ratio.

■ CHOOSING A BOND STRATEGY

The determining factor is when you expect to cash in

TIME FRAME	TYPE OF BOND	COMMENTS
Less than 1 year	**Any**	■ You may want to consider a money market fund for stability of principal.
1–2 years	**Short-term bond**	■ If interest rates are stable or fall, you could get higher than money market fund yields as well as potential capital appreciation. If interest rates rise, this fund could still be a good choice. Unless rates rise substantially, the income you get may make up some of the losses to principal and may still put you ahead of where you'd be in a money market fund.
2–4 years	**Federal or state tax-free bond, mortgage bond, government bond, investment grade bond**	■ If you're counting on the fund to supply you with a stream of income, keep in mind that higher yields can help compensate for some of the drop in the value of your account. If you invested to diversify a stock portfolio, keep in mind that the long-term price volatility of bonds is typically lower than that of stocks.
More than 4 years	**Aggressive bond**	■ Although interest rates can affect these funds, they tend to benefit from a healthy economy. Over the long term, income provides the bulk of total return in bond funds. If you are comfortable with the quality of risk, aggressive funds provide the highest income.

SOURCE: Fidelity Investments.

INVESTMENT CLUBS

WHY WOMEN DO BETTER THAN MEN

They're more analytical, pay attention to detail and have more patience

File this in the category of shattered myths: Men are not better investors than women. The proof: In 7 out of the past 10 years, women's investment clubs have outperformed men's clubs by an average of 12.8 percent compared to 12.5 percent for men—a slight edge, but still an edge.

In fact, the gap should be wider. "Women's clubs have become so popular that their ranks have swollen in recent years," explains Barry Murphy, marketing director for the National Association of Investors Corporation (NAIC), the parent organization of the nation's 21,000 investment clubs. "These new clubs are just learning the ropes and their early results have brought down the average."

Richard J. Maturi, author of *Main Street Beats Wall Street: How the Top Investment Clubs Are Outperforming the Pros* (Probus, 1995), offers some explanations about the hows and whys of investments clubs' performance.

■ Why do women's clubs do better?

Men are more apt to buy or sell impulsively. Women are more analytical, pay more attention to detail, and stick with their stock for the long run. Even though a stock isn't doing well one year, women have the patience to stick with it as long as the financials of the company look good.

■ Investment clubs are forming at the rate of 100 a week, double the 1980s' rate. Why the increased popularity?

Much of it has to do with the success of *The Beardstown Ladies' Common Sense Investment Guide* (Hyperion, 1994). The book tells about a dozen older women investing and beating many of the pros. People figure, if these ladies can do it, so can I.

■ Why do investment clubs as a whole often outperform the pros?

The biggest reason is that investment decisions are made collectively. Several people evaluating a stock purchase are less likely to make that big wrong decision that decimates the portfolio. Club investors who use the NAIC guidelines (☎ 810-583-6242) also run stock analysis programs, which an investor might not do alone.

■ What is the stock-picking credo of the NAIC members?

Look for companies with five-year growth rates in earnings and revenues of about 15 percent a year or more. Buy stocks when the price/earnings ratio (share price divided by the company's earnings per share) is at or below their average price/earnings ratio over the past five years. Then, unless the company's financials are unhealthy, stick with a stock, reinvesting dividends and earnings.

FACT FILE:

INVESTMENT CLUB HITS

■ *The 10 most popular stocks held by members of the nation's investment clubs, ranked by the dollar value of the holdings as of December 31, 1995. Most have made the list for years.*

	Value of Holdings
McDonald's	$299.7 million
AFLAC Inc.	$266.0 million
Merck & Co.	$185.9 million
PepsiCo	$156.2 million
Coca Cola Co.	$ 97.2 million
AT&T	$ 92.0 million
Intel	$ 64.4 million
Wal-Mart Stores	$ 52.9 million
Motorola	$ 51.3 milllion
RPM Inc.	$ 28.4 million

SOURCE: National Association of Investors Corp.

EXPERT LIST

THE BEST INVESTMENT NEWSLETTERS

Financial newsletters number in the hundreds—500 is a common estimate. So which tip sheets offer the most lucrative advice? For the rankings below, the Hulbert Financial Digest, *the bible of comparative newsletter performance, examined scores of newsletters over 5-year and 10-year periods ending December 31, 1995.* Hulbert *used two measures to rate the performance of the portfolios recommended by the newsletters: total-return and risk-adjusted. In cases where a newsletter recommended more than one portfolio, its ranking was based on an average of all its portfolios. As benchmarks,* Hulbert *used the total returns of the Wilshire 5000 and returns on a Treasury-bill portfolio. Risk-adjusted ratings are based on average monthly gains per unit of risk. The Wilshire 5000 is equal to 100, so the higher a newsletter's risk-adjusted rating, the better its performance. The best mutual fund newsletters are ranked similarly.*

TOTAL RETURN RATINGS

The total returns of the Wilshire 5000 and returns on a Treasury-bill portfolio were used for comparison.

■ TEN YEARS	Total ret.	Comp. annually
1. MPT Review	+791.8%	24.5%
2. California Technology Stock Ltr.	+532.8%	20.3%
3. Fundline	+328.7%	15.7%
4. Value Line Convertibles Survey	+322.5%	15.5%
5. The Chartist	+310.6%	15.2%
Wilshire 5000 total return	**+276.6%**	**14.2%**
T-bill portfolio	**+73.3%**	**5.7%**

■ FIVE YEARS		
1. OTC Insight	+390.0%	37.4%
2. The Prudent Speculator	+385.9%	37.2%
3. Turnaround Letter	+344.3%	34.8%
4. The Oberweis Report	+327.8%	33.7%
5. New Issues	+240.3%	27.8%
Wilshire 5000 total return	**+121.9%**	**17.3%**
T-bill portfolio	**+24.0%**	**4.4%**

■ MUTUAL FUNDS NEWSLETTERS, FIVE YEARS		
1. Timer Digest*	+194.5%	24.1%
2. Fundline	+175.8%	22.5%
3. Stockmarket Cycles*	+150.3%	20.1%
4. Equity Fund Outlook	+138.2%	19.0%
5. Fidelity Monitor	+131.6%	18.3%
Wilshire 5000 total return	**+121.9%**	**17.3%**
T-bill portfolio	**+24.0%**	**4.4%**

RISK-ADJUSTED RATINGS

Risk-adjusted ratings are assigned using the Wilshire 5000's rating of 100 as a benchmark.

■ TEN YEARS	Risk adjusted rating
1. Investech Mutual Fund Advisor	137.9
2. Zweig Performance Ratings Report	129.3
3. California Technology Stock Letter	123.0
4. MPT Review	122.4
5. Systems & Forecasts	116.7
Wilshire 5000	**100.0**

■ FIVE YEARS	
1. Value Line Convertibles Survey	131.4
2. Richard Band's Profitable Investing	128.0
3. Fidelity Insight	118.9
4. Fundline	113.6
5. NoLoad Fund Investor	112.7
Wilshire 5000	**100.0**

■ MUTUAL FUNDS NEWSLETTERS, FIVE YEARS	
1. Fidelity Insight	118.9
2. Fundline	113.6
3. NoLoad Fund Investor	112.7
4. Personal Finance*	108.5
5. Equity Fund Outlook	105.9
Wilshire 5000	**100.0**

*Fund Portfolio

SOURCE: *Hulbert Financial Digest*, 316 Commerce St., Alexandria, Va. 22314, ☎ 703–683–5905.

EXPERT SOURCES

WHERE TO GET THE TOP NEWSLETTERS

It pays to subscribe to one of the following publications

CALIFORNIA TECHNOLOGY STOCK LETTER
Mike Murphy, ed., $295
PO Box 308
Half Moon Bay, CA 94019
☎ 415-726-8495

THE CHARTIST
Dan Sullivan, ed., $150
PO Box 758
Seal Beach, CA 90740
☎ 310-596-2385

EQUITY FUND OUTLOOK
Thurman Smith, ed., $115
PO Box 76
Boston, MA 02117
☎ 617-397-6844

FIDELITY INSIGHT
Eric Kobren, ed., $99
PO Box 9135
Wellesley Hills, MA 02181
☎ 617-369-2100

FIDELITY MONITOR
Jack Bowers, ed., $96
PO Box 1294
Rocklin, CA 95677
☎ 800-397-3094

FUNDLINE
David Menashe, ed., $127
PO Box 663
Woodland Hills, CA 91365
☎ 818-346-5637

INVESTECH MUTUAL FUND ADVISOR
James B. Stack, ed., $175
2472 Birch Glen
Whitefish, MT 59937
☎ 406-862-7777

MPT REVIEW
Louis Navellier, ed., $245
PO Box 5695
Incline Village, NV 89450
☎ 702-831-1396

NEW ISSUES
Norman Fosback and Glen King Parker, eds., $95
3471 N. Federal Hwy.
Ft. Lauderdale, FL 33306
☎ 800-327-6720

NOLOAD FUND INVESTOR
Sheldon Jacobs, ed., $129
PO Box 318
Irvington, NY 10533
☎ 914-693-7420

OBERWEIS REPORT
James D. Oberweis, ed., $249
841 N. Lake
Aurora, IL 60506
☎ 708-801-4766

OTC INSIGHT
James Collins, ed., $195
PO Box 127
Moraga, CA 94556
☎ 800-955-9566

PERSONAL FINANCE
Stephen Leeb, ed., $39
1101 King St.
Alexandria, VA 22314
☎ 703-548-2400

THE PRUDENT SPECULATOR
Al Frank, ed., $175
PO Box 1438
Laguna Beach, CA 92652
☎ 310-587-2410

RICHARD BAND'S PROFITABLE INVESTING
Richard Band, ed., $99
7811 Montrose Rd.
Potomac, MD 20854
☎ 301-340-1520

STOCKMARKET CYCLES
Peter Eliades, ed., $198
PO Box 6873
Santa Rosa, CA 95406
☎ 707-579-8444

SYSTEMS & FORECASTS
Gerald Appel, ed., $195
150 Great Neck Rd.
Great Neck, NY 11021
☎ 516-829-6444

TIMER DIGEST
Jim Schmidt, ed., $225
PO Box 1688
Greenwich, CT 06836
☎ 800-356-2527

TURNAROUND LETTER
George Putnam III, ed., $195
225 Friend St., Suite 801
Boston, MA 02114
☎ 617-573-9550

VALUE LINE INVESTMENT SURVEY
Value Line, Inc., $525
711 Third Ave., NY, NY 10017
☎ 800-634-3583

ZWEIG PERFORMANCE RATINGS
Martin Zweig, publ., $205
PO Box 2900
Wantagh, NY 11793
☎ 516-785-1300

EXPERT Q & A

FINDING THE BEST BROKER

The nation's top stock cop on what to expect from your stockpicker

Few people can talk about the brokerage business with more authority than Arthur Levitt, Jr., the chairman of the Securities and Exchange Commission (SEC) and the nation's top market cop. A former broker, Levitt headed the American Stock Exchange for more than a decade. As SEC chief since 1993, he has made investor protection and education a top priority. We asked Levitt for tips on how to find a good broker and what to do about an unethical one.

■ How do you pick the best broker?

The best brokers ask you questions before you invest to understand fully your financial goals and your tolerance for risk. This is the only way that they can recommend a portfolio that matches your needs. Most serious problems arise when a broker recommends a stock or other financial product simply to earn a commission, rather than considering whether the product fits your needs.

The important thing in picking a broker is to look him or her in the eye and ask some tough questions. What is the broker's philosophy on how best to meet your goals? Has the broker ever been disciplined for wrongdoing? Does the broker seem more interested in selling you a stock than getting to know your financial situation and your future financial needs? Ask questions that will help you determine if the chemistry is right and whether the broker will always put your interests first.

■ What else should an investor ask a potential broker?

First, find out how your broker gets paid. Typically, brokers are paid by commissions that reward them for the quantity of business they do, not for the quality. Ask your broker a few questions, such as: Do you make more if I buy this mutual fund, for example, than if I buy this stock? Some brokerage firms allow you to pay a flat fee based on the amount of your assets under management. Ask the broker if you would be better off paying a flat fee or a commission.

■ How do I know if my broker is getting me the best price when I buy or sell stocks?

When your broker quotes you the price at which he'll sell you a stock or bond, ask how much he'd pay to buy it from you. The difference is the spread. You should ask your broker whether you could get a better price for a stock if you place a "limit" order, which specifies a price that falls in the middle of the spread. Also ask your broker if you could get a better price if he routed your order to a particular exchange or another market.

■ How do I know my municipal bond investments are in good hands?

For the first time, beginning in January 1996, your broker is able to obtain key data about the financial health of municipal bond issuers from national or state information centers. For example, your broker can find out if the bond issuer is delinquent on principal or interest payments, if its ratings have been downgraded, or if it has lost its tax-exempt status. Be sure to ask for this information.

■ In what other ways can investors better protect themselves?

Before you hire a broker, check out his record by calling the National Association of Securities Dealers' hot line (☎ 800–289–9999) or your state securities regulator. We hope to have those records on the Internet in 1997. Also, scrutinize your account statements for transactions that you didn't authorize, excessive commissions, and delays in executing orders. Complain if you suspect wrongdoing.

■ What should an investor do if he runs into a bad broker?

Most stockbrokers are honest professionals. But if you think you've encountered an uneth-

■ FEES: THE TALE OF THE TAPE

Brokerage firms are not created equal. In fact, the differences among them in commissions, fees, performance, and conduct are enormous, according to a study by the National Council of Individual Investors. The NCII studied the top 10 firms in the categories below. They found that the difference in commissions is up to 638 percent. From their survey, we picked the firms in each category with the highest and lowest brokerage commissions and annual IRA fees.

FULL SERVICE			
Commissions*	Average	$160	
	Highest	$177	Paine Webber
	Lowest	$130	Everen Securities
Annual IRA fees	Average	$34	
	Highest	$40	Smith Barney
	Lowest	$30	A.G. Edwards, Dean Witter Reynolds, Edward Jones & Co.
BANK-AFFILIATED			
Commissions*	Average	$101	
	Highest	$150	Nations Securities
	Lowest	$59	First Interstate Securities
Annual IRA fees	Average	$28	
	Highest	$40	First Interstate Securities
	Lowest	None	Citicorp Investment Services
DISCOUNTERS			
Commissions*	Average	$60	
	Highest	$89	Charles Schwab
	Lowest	$25	Pacific Brokerage**
Annual IRA fees	Average	$18	
	Highest	$40	Pacific Brokerage
	Lowest	None	Olde Discount, Waterhouse Securities, Kennedy Cabot & Co.
DEEP DISCOUNTERS			
Commissions*	Average	$32	
	Highest	$39	Investors National, Marsh Block & Co.
	Lowest	$24	Wall Street Equities
Annual IRA fees	Average	$27	
	Highest	$60	Brown & Co.
	Lowest	None	Kennedy Cabot & Co., Lombard Institutional

*Commissions based on 500 listed shares at $10. **Also a deep-discounter.

SOURCE: 1996 Annual Brokerage Firm Survey, National Council of Individual Investors. Survey copies are available for $5. Call ☎ 800-663-8516.

ical one, call our Office of Investor Assistance at ☎ 202-942-7040. We use "tips" from you to keep our securities markets free from fraud and bad brokers and bad financial planners. Report any problems promptly to the branch officer or the firm's compliance officer as well as to the NASD.

■ How do I settle a dispute with a broker?

Most investors agree to arbitrate disputes when they sign a customer agreement with a brokerage firm, so arbitration is the main route for settling disputes. You can file for arbitration with the NASD, or the New York Stock Exchange (☎ 212-656-3000), among other exchanges, or the American Arbitration Association (☎ 202-296-8510).

The SEC is working to improve the arbitration process to ensure that disputes are handled fairly. We're looking to expand the pool of arbitrators, give investors a greater say on who sits on their arbitration panel, and improve the training of arbitrators so that they better understand securities laws.

DISCOUNT BROKERS

TRADING ON THE CHEAP

Everything you need to know about discount brokers

Discount brokers account for about one-third of individual stock trades. Small wonder. While full-service brokerages provide customers with investment advice and other services, discount brokers stick to no-frills trading, passing the savings on to you. Cost-conscious investors can take a huge chunk out of commissions paid on trades by using discounters. But you have to know what you want and be comfortable making your own investment decisions.

When it comes to price breaks, discounters are great and getting better. While full-service brokerage firms increased their commissions by 3 percent on average in 1995, deep discounters cut rates by about 6 percent, according to Mercer Inc., a New York–based research firm. The average commission among the 10 cheapest discount brokers to trade 100 shares at $50 per share was $29.60, according to Mercer. The same trade would cost an average $52.70 at the Big Three regular discounters—Charles Schwab, Fidelity, and Quick & Reilly—and $103 at a full-service brokerage.

Which discount brokerage offers the best deal? That's tough to say because they set their prices differently. Rates are often based on the total dollar value of a transaction, the number of shares purchased, or simply a flat fee for each type of transaction. Sometimes, small commission and fees for non-routine trades are tacked on. Large dollar volume trades or those placed online often get further discounts at some firms.

As a result, some firms are cheaper for some trades and not for others. Before you pick a broker, advises the American Association of Individual Investors (☎ 312-280-0170), first compare the commissions the firm charges for the kinds of trades you're apt to make. Call the discounters directly, or use one of the surveys put out annually by Mercer (☎ 800-582-9854) or the AAII. After you've chosen a few candidates, ask for a commission schedule and description of services, fees, and bonus discounts. Keep in mind that some firms may charge a flat fee to open a new account, for example, and then high fees to wire funds or to get copies of reports.

■ THE TOP 10 DEEP DISCOUNTERS

Among these brokers with the cheapest commissions, Wall Street Equities charges the least to trade stocks. For bonds, Pacific is best at a low $25 commission.

Broker	☎	NUMBER OF offices / accounts	COMMISSION ON Min.	1 share @ $50	T-bill*	Load funds	No-fee no-load funds
Brown & Co.	800-822-2021	10/10,000	$29	$29	$38	No	No
Consolidated Financial	800-292-6637	1/3,000	$35	Neg.	$35	Yes	No
K. Aufhauser & Co.	800-368-3668	1/720,000	$25	$25	$39	Yes	No
Kennedy Cabot & Co.	800-252-0090	15/121,500	$20–$30	$20	$30	Yes	No
Lombard Institutional	800-566-2273	2/25,000	$34	$34	$34	Yes	No
National Discount Broker	800-888-3999	5/NA	$30	$30	$40	Yes	Yes
Pacific Brokerage Services	800-421-8395	4/120,000	$25	$25	$25	No	No
Recom Securities	800-328-8600	2/NA	$35	$35	$35	Yes	No
R.J. Forbes Group	800-488-0090	1/6,000	$35	$35	$50	Yes	No
Wall Street Equities	800-447-8625	1/5,000	$15	$15	N/A	No	No

*$10,000 Treasury bill at auction

SOURCES: Mercer Inc.; brokerage houses.

The Big Three discounters, and a few others, try to compete with full-service firms by offering research information, stock and bond picks, 24-hour phone service, asset management accounts with check-writing privileges and ATM cards, and margin accounts for trading instruments such as options, bonds, and certificates of deposit. Another plus is their extensive branch networks. The add-ons just keep coming. If you have an account with Schwab, for example, you now can also have dividends reinvested free, get a free retirement-planning software program, and a credit card that gives you points redeemable for free investment research.

Most discount brokerage customers use discounters for little more than trading stocks and bonds. But what if you wanted to get into zero coupon bonds, say, or futures? Which firm has the widest range of products? Two small outfits, Jack White and K. Aufhauser, were cited by *SmartMoney* magazine in July 1995 as tops in product offerings. Both carry futures trades, unit-investment trusts, and other esoteric investments. For investors who want to pick from a highly selective list of free no-load mutual fund offerings, Schwab is the place to go, according to *SmartMoney*. Of Schwab's 345 funds, 90 have performed in the top 25 percent of their peer groups over the past five years ending Jully 1995.

But don't expect a lot of handholding. You'll get little account maintenance and even less personal attention. If more attention and greater control over the price you pay is what you're after, you're better off with a full-service broker. Often, says Andre Scheluchin, managing editor of *Mercer's 1995 Discount Brokerage Survey*, it's not impossible to negotiate a cut in commission with a full-service broker. In fact, you may end up paying only slightly more than with a discounter.

It's a smart idea to check out a brokerage firm before doing business. Background information is available from the National Association of Securities Dealers (☎ 800–289–9999), or from the Central Registration Depository of your state securities agency, listed in the blue pages of the phone book.

EXPERT PICKS

BYPASSING YOUR BROKER

Want to cut your broker out altogether? More and more companies are letting investors buy stock directly—even if it's their initial purchase in the company. What's the appeal? First, says Charles Carlson, editor of *DRIP Investor* newsletter (☎ 219–852–3220) and author of *Buying Stocks Without a Broker* (McGraw-Hill, 1996), you can save a bundle by bypassing expensive brokers. Second, you're not sacrificing service. Many no-load stock programs, as they're known, are administered by large banks and offer services such as automatic withdrawals from your bank account to make electronic payments and redemption services that sell stock by phone. You can't lose, says Carlson. "You get a nice breadth of services and pay little, if any, fees." Here are Carlson's 10 favorite no-load stocks.

COMPANY	☎	MINIMUM INITIAL INVESTMENT
AFLAC	800–774–4117*	$750
Atmos Energy	800–774–4117	$200
Dial	800–453–2235	$100
Exxon	800–252–1800	$250
First USA	800–524–4458	$1,000
McDonald's	800–774–4117	$1,000
Morton International	800–774–4117	$1,000
Piedmont Natural Gas	800–774–4117	$250
Procter & Gamble	800–742–6253	$100
Wisconsin Energy	800–558–9663	$50

*This number for the NoLoad Stock Clearinghouse will provide information for these and many other stock-purchasing plans.

ONLINE

CYBER-INVESTING FOR NEWBIES

There's a ton of information on the Web if you can find it. Here's how.

Your computer can be a powerful at-your-fingertips investing tool. It can be a rich source of business news and details that can give you an edge over offline investors. But navigating the shifting seas of online investing can prove tough going even for non-novices. Newbies may find it positively intimidating.

Here's a four-step process to guide you through the cyber-maze—from researching your investment targets to executing your buy order.

1. LEARN THE LAY OF THE LAND. Start out by checking out the investment index pages on the World Wide Web. Among the best are Yahoo indexing service's financial listings *(http://www.yahoo.com)*. For an excellent primer on online investing, visit the American Association of Individual Investors' Web site *(http://www.aaii.org/)*, where you'll also find selected articles to sharpen your financial skills.

For the computer-challenged, the AAII offers a paper guide—a good, thorough and unbiased source on online investing—called *The Individual Investor's Guide to Computerized Investing* ($24.95, ☎ 800–428–2244).

2. CHAT WITH OTHER INVESTORS. The most reasonably priced access route to financial news and bulletin boards are the commercial online services: CompuServe (☎ 800–848–8199), Prodigy (☎ 800-PRODIGY), America Online (☎ 800–827–6364), and Microsoft Network (☎ 800–386–5550). Each offers free trial software, access to wire-service news and other financial publications, and to the Internet.

You should also visit the financial bulletin boards and investment forums, popular gathering places where users exchange advice. You can converse with a variety of Wall Street gurus, such as Peter Lynch on Prodigy and the Motley Fool on America Online, whose site is a popular place to go for investment advice with an attitude. Prodigy's Money Talk bulletin boards alone handle up to 40,000 messages a month.

A word of caution. Beware of quick-buck operators trying to pump up low-quality stocks in an attempt to stir up buys and boost the price. They'll dump the stocks after a few days and leave unsuspecting investors holding useless issues.

3. DO NITTY-GRITTY RESEARCH. Loads of raw data are available via the Internet. You can get full-text corporate filings on stocks and mutual funds from the Securities and Exchange Commission's Edgar database on the World Wide Web. Address: *http://www.sec.gov /edgarhrp.htm*. You'll find thousands of corporate and mutual fund filings, including prospectuses and corporate 10-Ks. For listings of stock quotes, try: *http://www.seccapl.com/cgi-bin/qs*. For a list of World Wide Web pages by public companies go to: *http://networth.galt.com/www/home/insider/publicco.html*.

4. PLACE YOUR ORDER. Once you've zeroed in on your target, you can use an online brokerage to place your order directly to the floor of the exchange. The larger online firms are the discount brokers: Charles Schwab (☎ 800–435–4000 *http://www.schwab.com*) available via proprietary software from Schwab; Fidelity On-Line Xpress (☎ 800–477–3902 *http://www.fid-inv.com*) available via proprietary Fidelity software; and PC Financial Network (☎ 800–825–5723), available through Prodigy and America Online. Executing trades online is catching on. The largest online broker, Schwab, has some 170,000 online accounts. According to a study by Forrester Research Inc., a Cambridge, Mass. Internet watcher, the number of online brokerage accounts is likely to more than double from 600,000 to 1.3 million by the end of the decade.

EXPERT SOURCES

TEN BOOKS WORTH THE INVESTMENT

Bookstores are bulging with tomes on how to invest your money. But separating treasures from trash can be an expensive and time-consuming process. With this in mind, we asked Yale Hirsch, editor of the 1996 Stock Trader's Almanac *(☎ 800–477–3400) and a publisher of investment newsletters for 35 years, for his favorite titles of recent years. Here are his picks, along with his comments. These volumes can't guarantee results but they will give you a head start.*

WHAT WORKS ON WALL STREET

James P. O'Shaughnessy (McGraw-Hill, 1996, $29.95)

■ This will be the stock market book of the 1990s. O'Shaughnessy has taken all the notable market strategies and tested them over the past 34 years of data to discover what really works on Wall Street.

STOCKS FOR THE LONG RUN

Jeremy J. Siegel (Irwin Professional Publishing, 1994, $27.50)

■ The more data Siegel analyzes, the more confident he is that stocks are superior long-term investments. His thorough analysis also explains why the market moves as it does and what to expect in the future.

MAIN STREET BEATS WALL STREET

Richard J. Maturi (Probus Publishing Co., 1995, $22.95)

■ Maturi explains why investment clubs outperform many of Wall Street's top money managers year after year. He covers key strategies and tactics, such as dollar-cost averaging and diversification.

MARKET MASTERS

Jake Bernstein (Dearborn Financial Publishing, 1994, $24.95)

■ An illuminating study of the minds of eight professional traders that helps identify their behavioral and psychological traits.

INVESTMENT BIKER: On the Road with Jim Rogers

Jim Rogers (Random House, 1994, $25)

■ Rogers gauges investment opportunities in six continents, which he toured by motorcycle in the early 1990s .

THE NEW SCIENCE OF TECHNICAL ANALYSIS

Thomas R. DeMark (John Wiley & Sons, 1994, $49.95)

■ Describes the sophisticated market timing models DeMark developed over the course of nearly 25 years. His empirical approach eliminates reliance on gut-feelings and guesswork.

THE WARREN BUFFETT WAY

Robert G. Hagstrom, Jr. (John Wiley & Sons, 1994, $24.95).

■ An in-depth look at the investment strategies of superinvestor Warren Buffett, who turned a $100 initial investment into a $19.4 billion business empire.

THE CRAFT OF INVESTING

John Train (HarperCollins, 1994, $22)

■ Train explains growth investing, value investing, emerging markets, when to buy and sell, losing strategies and how to avoid them—and much more.

BENJAMIN GRAHAM ON VALUE INVESTING

Janet Lowe. (Dearborn Financial Publishing, 1994, $22.95)

■ Celebrates the 100th anniversary of the birth of Graham, who literally created the framework for investment analysis, bringing the clarity of logic and reason to investing.

SOROS: The Life and Trading Secrets of the World's Greatest Investor

Robert Slater (Irwin Professional Publishing, 1996, $25)

■ Penetrates the myths swirling around this Hungarian-born investment titan, uncovering the brilliant techniques and insights that have led to his phenomenal success.

MUTUAL FUNDS

EXPERT LIST: The top 140 mutual funds, PAGE 27 **FUND FAMILIES:** The best and worst-performers, PAGE 32 **THE BASICS:** How to analyze a fund, PAGE 34 **FEES:** The surprising case for no-load funds, PAGE 36 **EXPERT Q&A:** Why you can't beat the market, PAGE 38 **ASSET ALLOCATION:** Are these funds for you? PAGE 39 **EXPERT PICKS:** How many funds should you own? PAGE 41 **MONEY MANAGEMENT:** Do the super-rich have an edge? PAGE 42

LONG-TERM INVESTING

PICKING THE BEST MUTUAL FUNDS

A new fund is born almost every day. Here are the top performers

Smart investors know that good mutual funds are those that show dynamite returns, have low expenses, and involve little risk. With more than 6,000 funds to choose from—and a new fund born every day or so—even savvy investors have a tough time finding the picks of the litter. With that in mind, Morningstar Inc., the Chicago-based investment information publisher, ranked the performance of the top mutual funds—according to data that really count.

The rankings that start on page 27 include the top 10 performing funds in each of 14 categories. The funds are ranked based on their annualized three-year return as of March 31, 1996, though returns for one year and five years are also provided. We settled on ranking funds by their three-year performance mainly because that seemed the most appropriate time horizon for the buy-and-hold investor.

The list of top performers also includes Morningstar's highly respected rating that takes into account a fund's fees and risk. Fees can pulverize a fund's returns and risk is perhaps an investor's biggest fear. Morningstar's ratings, which appear on the lists as stars, consider both factors. They are based on a fund's total return within its category after adjusting for sales loads, redemption fees, and other fund expenses. To account for risk, Morningstar compared the funds' performance with the risk-free returns that you'd get by buying three-month Treasury bills. After weighing those factors, Morningstar gave five stars to its top fund picks; four to above-average funds; three to average performers; and two stars or less to below-average funds.

A fund's category, or style, is worth some explanation. Different kinds of funds have different investment objectives; that's generally how funds are grouped so that investors can compare apples with apples. But, in truth, the dividing line between categories can be fuzzy. Typically, the funds themselves decide what category they belong in, not an independent authority or agency. And different publications often classify funds in different categories. What, for example, is the difference between a "growth" fund and an "aggressive growth" fund? How different will the investment strategy of one fund be from another? A careful investor will want to understand the fund classification categories. Following is a brief explanation of the categories Morningstar used to compile its rankings.

■ **AGGRESSIVE FUNDS:** They seek the rapid growth of capital, often through investment in smaller companies and with techniques involving greater-than-average risk, such as frequent trading, short-selling, and leveraging. This category includes small company funds, which seek capital appreciation by investing mainly in stocks of small companies, as determined by market capitalization.

■ **GROWTH FUNDS:** They invest primarily in equity securities. Current income, if it is considered at all, is a secondary objective.

■ **TOTAL RETURN FUNDS:** They include equity income funds that invest at least 65 percent of assets in equity securities with above-average yields, and growth and income funds that seek growth of capital and current income as near-equal objectives, primarily by investing in equity securities with above-average yield for appreciation.

■ **INTERNATIONAL FUNDS:** These include European stock funds, which generally invest at least 65 percent of assets in equity securities of European issuers; foreign stock funds, which invest primarily in equity securities of issuers located outside the United States; Pacific stock funds, which invest primarily in issuers located in countries in the Pacific Basin and Australia; and world stock funds, with holdings in equity securities of issuers located throughout the world, maintaining a percentage of assets (normally 25 to 50 percent) in the United States.

■ **SPECIALTY FUNDS:** They seek capital appreciation by investing in equity securities in a single industry or sector, like health, technology, utilities, or natural resources.

■ **HYBRID FUNDS:** These have substantial holdings in both stocks and bonds, or hold securities that have characteristics of both stocks and bonds.

■ **CONVERTIBLE BOND FUNDS:** They invest primarily in bonds and preferred stocks that can be converted into common stocks.

■ **CORPORATE BOND HIGH-YIELD FUNDS:** This type of fund will generally invest 65 percent or more of its assets in bonds rated below investment grade. The price of these issues generally is affected more by the condition of the issuing company (similar to a stock) than by the interest-rate fluctuation that usually causes bond prices to move up and down.

■ **CORPORATE BOND FUNDS:** These funds invest in fixed-income securities, primarily corporate bonds of various quality ratings. This category includes High-Quality Corporate Bonds funds that have at least 65 percent of their holdings in securities rated A or higher.

■ **GOVERNMENT BOND GENERAL FUNDS:** They invest in a blend of mortgage-backed securities, Treasuries, and agency securities.

■ **GOVERNMENT BOND TREASURY FUNDS:** These funds invest at least 80 percent of their assets in U.S. Treasury securities.

■ **GOVERNMENT BOND MORTGAGE FUNDS:** They generally invest 65 percent of their assets in securities that are backed by mortgages.

■ **INTERNATIONAL BOND FUNDS:** These funds seek current income with capital appreciation as a secondary objective by investing primarily in bonds denominated in currencies other than the U.S. dollar. These bonds are frequently issued by foreign governments. Also includes Short-Term World Income funds that seek income and a stable net asset value by investing mainly in various non-U.S.-currency-denominated bonds, usually with maturities of three years or less. Short-term world income funds seek higher yields than a money market fund and less fluctuation of their net asset value (NAV) than a world bond fund.

■ **MUNICIPAL BOND FUNDS:** These funds seek income that is exempt from federal income tax by investing primarily in bonds issued by any state or municipality.

EXPERT LIST

THE 140 TOP MUTUAL FUNDS

Here Morningstar, Inc., the Chicago-based investment information publisher, ranks the top 10 mutual funds in 15 different categories. The funds are ranked based on their three-year annualized return as of March 31, 1996. The rating column refers to Morningstar's exclusive five-star rating system. Notes explaining the rating system and various terms used throughout the tables can be found on pages 28 and 29.

FUND NAME	STYLE	TOTAL RETURN 1YR	3YR	5YR	M* RATING	EXPENSE RATIO	MAX SALES CHARGE	NET ASSETS $MM	PHONE
■ AGGRESSIVE GROWTH									
1. Putnam New Opportunities A	MG	44.28	**29.74**	29.42	★★★★★	1.13	5.75	295	800-225-1581
2. Stein Roe Capital Opportunities	MG	58.73	**29.40**	23.92	★★★★	1.05	0.00	681	800-338-2550
3. Putnam New Opportunities B	MG	43.27	**28.87**	NA	★★★★★	1.88	5.00D	247	800-225-1581
4. Overland Express Strategic Growth A	MG	39.30	**26.12**	NA	★★★★★	1.28	4.50	68	800-552-9612
5. Kaufmann	SG	40.17	**23.85**	24.22	★★★★★	2.29	0.00	358	800-237-0132
6. Alliance Quasar A	MG	64.64	**22.92**	16.19	★★★	1.83	4.25	203	800-227-4618
7. Alliance Quasar B	MG	63.65	**21.99**	15.28	★★★★	2.65	4.00D	29	800-227-4618
8. USAA Aggressive Growth	SG	53.09	**21.26**	16.33	★★★	0.86	0.00	486	800-382-8722
9. Putnam Voyager A	MG	37.57	**21.03**	19.13	★★★★★	1.07	5.75	658	800-225-1581
10. Keystone Small Company Growth (S-4)	MG	32.32	**20.85**	20.00	★★★★	1.78	4.00D	203	800-343-2898
■ GROWTH									
1. Franklin CA Growth	MB	40.37	**28.71**	NA	★★★★★	0.25	4.50	60	800-342-5236
2. Dominion Insight Growth	MG	66.05	**25.35**	NA	★★★★	2.38	3.50	149	800-880-1095
3. Excelsior Business & Industrial Restr	MB	36.49	**24.36**	NA	★★★★★	0.98	4.50	74	800-446-1012
4. Fidelity New Millennium	MG	54.10	**24.32**	NA	★★★★★	1.18	3.00	812	800-544-8888
5. Waddell & Reed Growth B	MG	26.65	**24.13**	NA	★★★★★	2.23	3.00D	202	913-236-2000
6. Robertson Stephens Value + Growth	LG	19.67	**23.81**	NA	★★★★★	1.68	0.00	973	800-766-3863
7. T. Rowe Price Mid-Cap Growth	MG	42.57	**23.20**	NA	★★★★★	1.25	0.00	419	800-638-5660
8. Mairs & Power Growth	LB	39.49	**22.03**	18.03	★★★★★	0.99	0.00	86	612-222-8478
9. Wasatch Growth	SB	39.05	**21.08**	15.42	★★★★	1.50	0.00	76	800-551-1700
10. MFS Value A	MB	41.11	**21.05**	19.28	★★★★★	1.35	5.75	288	800-637-2929
■ TOTAL RETURN									
1. Safeco Equity	LV	25.80	**20.08**	18.15	★★★★★	0.84	0.00	635	800-426-6730
2. Clover Capital Equity Value	MV	21.32	**19.98**	NA	★★★★★	1.10	0.00	65	800-932-7781
3. Oppenheimer Main St Income & Growth A	LB	27.99	**19.39**	27.53	★★★★★	1.07	5.75	284	800-525-7048
4. Babson Value	LV	29.01	**19.37**	17.76	★★★★★	0.98	0.00	414	800-422-2766
5. RIMCo Monument Stock	LB	33.57	**19.16**	NA	★★★★★	0.98	5.75	82	800-934-3883
6. Retirement System Core Equity	LB	36.53	**18.31**	NA	★★★★★	0.90	0.00	6	800-772-3615
7. Mutual Qualified	MV	27.28	**17.87**	18.67	★★★★★	0.72	0.00	356	800-553-3014
8. Dodge & Cox Stock	LV	29.26	**17.85**	16.00	★★★★	0.60	0.00	138	800-621-3979
9. Mutual Shares	LV	28.85	**17.62**	18.30	★★★★★	0.69	0.00	585	800-553-3014
10. First American Stock A	LV	29.10	**17.45**	14.57	★★★★	0.76	4.50	17	800-637-2548

■ EXPERT LIST

FUND NAME	STYLE	TOTAL RETURN 1YR	3YR	5YR	M* RATING	EXPENSE RATIO	MAX SALES CHARGE	NET ASSETS $MM	PHONE
■ INTERNATIONAL EQUITIES									
1. Seligman Henderson Global Smaller Co A	SG	32.63	**23.67**	NA	★★★★★	1.83	4.75	161	800-221-2450
2. Dean Witter European Growth	LG	27.76	**23.00**	15.49	★★★★	2.23	5.00D	990	800-869-3863
3. Wright EquiFund–Netherlands	MG	28.28	**20.17**	12.09	★★★★	2.00	0.00	9	800-888-9471
4. GAM Global A	LB	7.94	**19.93**	13.75	★★★	2.16	5.00	21	800-426-4685
5. Janus Worldwide	LG	36.93	**19.25**	NA	★★★★★	1.23	0.00	266	800-525-8983
6. Keystone Global Opportunities A	SG	26.66	**19.16**	19.51	★★★★	1.81	5.75	117	800-343-2898
7. Idex II Global A	LG	36.51	**18.64**	NA	★★★★	1.97	5.50	105	800-851-9777
8. Keystone Global Opportunities C	SG	25.62	**18.36**	NA	★★★★	2.56	1.00D	104	800-343-2898
9. Keystone Global Opportunities B	SG	25.74	**18.30**	NA	★★★★	2.56	5.00D	308	800-343-2898
10. Merrill Lynch Dragon D	LG	20.71	**18.28**	NA	★★	1.63	5.25	327	800-637-3863
■ SPECIALTIES									
1. Fidelity Select Electronics	MB	47.82	**37.18**	28.98	★★★★	1.71	3.00	100	800-544-8888
2. Franklin Global Health Care	SG	65.38	**35.70**	NA	★★★★★	0.25	4.50	60	800-342-5236
3. Midas	NA	74.58	**35.04**	23.93	★★★	2.15	0.00	94	800-400-6432
4. Seligman Communications & Information A	MB	18.96	**34.75**	27.24	★★★★★	1.61	4.75	217	800-221-2783
5. IDS Precious Metals A	NA	72.36	**32.29**	21.28	★★★	1.61	5.00	96	800-328-8300
6. T. Rowe Price Science & Technology	MG	45.27	**32.29**	24.81	★★★★★	1.01	0.00	260	800-638-5660
7. Lexington Strategic Investments	MG	13.87	**31.35**	9.89	★	1.70	5.75	75	800-526-0056
8. Fidelity Select Computers	MV	29.76	**31.16**	21.88	★★★	1.69	3.00	446	800-544-8888
9. Fidelity Select Medical Delivery	MB	27.41	**30.52**	14.63	★★★	1.45	3.00	288	800-544-8888
10. Alliance Technology A	MG	34.74	**30.49**	25.79	★★★★★	1.75	4.25	436	800-227-4618
■ HYBRID									
1. Oppenheimer Quest Opportunity Value A	LV/HI	35.34	**18.92**	20.33	★★★★★	1.69	5.75	559	800-525-7048
2. Westwood Balanced Ret	LB	30.32	**16.09**	NA	★★★★★	1.68	0.00	14	800-937-8966
3. Templeton Developing Markets I	MV	15.80	**16.06**	NA	★★★	2.10	5.75	261	800-292-9293
4. Founders Balanced	LB/HI	29.32	**15.57**	14.71	★★★★★	1.23	0.00	163	800-525-2440
5. Overland Express Asset Allocation A	LB	30.37	**14.22**	14.22	★★★★	1.30	4.50	53	800-552-9612
6. General Securities	LV	23.66	**13.87**	12.65	★★★★	1.50	0.00	36	800-577-9217
7. AIM Balanced A	LB/HI	31.89	**13.86**	15.44	★★★	1.25	4.75	125	800-347-4246
8. Vanguard/Wellington	LV/HL	26.66	**13.81**	13.59	★★★★	0.35	0.00	13	800-662-7447
9. Warburg Pincus Balanced	MV/HI	28.42	**13.69**	13.50	★★★★	1.53	0.00	21	800-927-2874
10. Flag Investors Value Builder A	LV/MI	28.88	**13.69**	NA	★★★★	1.35	4.50	198	800-767-3524

EXPLANATION OF TERMS

STYLE/SIZE
Growth-oriented funds (G) generally include companies with the potential to increase earnings faster than the rest of the market. Value-oriented funds (V) focus on stocks that are undervalued by the market. A blend of the two (B) may contain growth and value stocks, or stocks that exhibit both characteristics. Funds with median-market capitalizations of less than $1 billion are labeled small-company funds (S). Funds with median market capitalizations between $1 billion and $5 billion are labeled medium (M) offerings, and funds with median market capitalizations exceeding $5 billion qualify for the large (L) label. Fixed-income funds are split into three maturity groups—short (S), intermediate (I), and long (L)—and three credit quality groups—high (H), medium (M), and low (L). Funds with an average effective maturity of less than four years qualify as short-term bond funds; those with maturity longer than 10 years are long term.

TOTAL RETURN
Total return is calculated by taking the change in investment value, assuming the reinvestment of all income and capital-gains distributions during the period, and dividing by the initial investment value. Total returns for periods over

■ EXPERT LIST

FUND NAME	STYLE	TOTAL RETURN 1YR	3YR	5YR	M* RATING	EXPENSE RATIO	MAX SALES CHARGE	NET ASSETS $MM	PHONE
■ MULTISECTOR BOND									
1. Kemper Diversified Income A	ML	12.13	**9.08**	14.62	★★★	1.09	4.50	489	800-621-1048
2. Janus Flexible Income	ML	15.51	**8.61**	11.94	★★★★★	0.96	0.00	635	800-525-8983
3. Colonial Strategic Income A	SV/MI	14.47	**8.53**	11.60	★★★★	1.18	4.75	710	800-248-2828
4. John Hancock Strategic Income A	MI	15.41	**8.21**	10.66	★★★★★	1.09	4.50	360	800-225-5291
5. Oppenheimer Strat Income A	NA	15.88	**8.06**	10.24	★★★★★	0.99	4.75	334	800-525-7048
6. Colonial Strategic Income B	SV/MI	13.63	**7.71**	NA	★★★★★	1.97	5.00D	716	800-248-2828
7. MFS Strategic Income A	LG	15.76	**7.40**	9.36	★★★★	1.54	4.75	50	800-637-2929
8. Oppenheimer Strat Income B	NA	15.23	**7.27**	NA	★★★★	1.75	5.00D	225	800-525-7048
9. Putnam Diversified Income A	SG/MI	13.82	**7.26**	10.92	★★★★★	1.01	4.75	170	800-225-1581
10. Lazard Strategic Yield	MI	15.22	**7.25**	NA	★★★★★	1.08	0.00	97	800-823-6300
■ CONVERTIBLE BOND									
1. MainStay Convertible B	MV	17.40	**13.62**	17.97	★★★★★	1.90	5.00D	542	800-522-4202
2. Franklin Convertible Securities I	NA	24.38	**13.11**	15.85	★★★★★	1.03	4.50	99	800-342-5236
3. Oppenheimer Bond Fund for Growth M	MV	20.16	**13.03**	18.79	★★★★★	1.58	3.25	266	800-525-7048
4. Pacific Horizon Capital Income	LG	25.05	**12.48**	16.73	★★★★	0.97	4.50	246	800-332-3863
5. Calamos Growth & Income	LG	33.00	**12.29**	15.38	★★★★	2.00	4.75	5	800-823-7386
6. Calamos Convertible	LV	28.75	**12.13**	13.60	★★★	1.60	4.75	24	800-823-7386
7. Putnam Convertible Income-Growth A	LV	23.17	**12.12**	15.41	★★★	1.16	5.75	821	800-225-1581
8. SBSF Convertible Securities	LB	24.12	**11.27**	14.05	★★★★★	1.31	0.00	77	800-422-7273
9. Value Line Convertible	NA	26.33	**11.12**	14.21	★★★★	1.08	0.00	69	800-223-0818
10. Fidelity Convertible Securities	MB	20.21	**11.10**	16.35	★★★★★	0.70	0.00	109	800-544-8888
■ CORPORATE BOND - HIGH YIELD									
1. MainStay High-Yield Corporate Bond B	MV/LI	17.43	**12.85**	16.97	★★★★★	1.60	5.00D	178	800-522-4202
2. Northeast Investors	MV/LI	15.29	**12.76**	17.50	★★★★	1.02	0.00	891	800-225-6704
3. Fidelity Spartan High-Income	MV/LI	17.85	**12.66**	17.21	★★★★★	0.80	0.00	128	800-544-8888
4. Seligman High-Yield Bond A	LI	19.34	**12.12**	16.10	★★★★	1.13	4.75	215	800-221-2783
5. First Investors High-Yield A	LI	16.09	**10.77**	15.45	★★★★★	1.61	6.25	188	800-423-4026
6. First Investors Fund for Income A	SV/LI	16.22	**10.58**	15.83	★★★	1.18	6.25	423	800-423-4026
7. Kemper High-Yield A	LI	15.56	**10.57**	14.87	★★★★	0.90	4.50	244	800-621-1048
8. Fidelity Advisor High-Yield A	SV/LI	16.98	**10.54**	16.52	★★★★★	1.15	3.50	136	800-522-7297
9. Value Line Aggressive Income	LI	22.71	**10.47**	12.67	★★★★	1.27	0.00	48	800-223-0818
10. Colonial High-Yield Securities A	SV/LI	14.92	**10.35**	16.76	★★★★	1.23	4.75	454	800-248-2828

a year are expressed in terms of compounded average annual returns.

RATING
Morningstar rates a fund's return performance relative to its class based on total returns adjusted for maximum front-end and applicable deferred loads and redemption fees. It then calculates the fund risk, mindful that most investors' biggest fear is losing money (defined as underperforming the risk-free rate of return an investor can earn from the three-month Treasury bill). The fund's comparative Risk score is then subtracted from its Return score. The result is plotted along a bell curve to determine the fund's rating. The top 10 percent of the class receives five stars (Highest); the next 22.5 percent receives four stars (Above Average); the middle 35 percent earns three stars (Neutral or Average); those lower still in the next 22.5 percent receive two stars (Below Average); and the bottom 10 percent get one star (Lowest).

EXPENSE RATIO
The annual expense ratio expresses the percentage of assets deducted each fiscal year for fund operating expenses.

SALES CHARGE
Maximum level of various fees and sales charges imposed by a fund. A deferred sales charge (D) is paid when you sell a fund.

NET ASSETS
The mutual fund's year-end net assets, recorded in millions of dollars.

■ **EXPERT LIST**

FUND NAME	STYLE	TOTAL RETURN 1YR	3YR	5YR	M* RATING	EXPENSE RATIO	MAX SALES CHARGE	NET ASSETS $MM	PHONE
■ CORPORATE BOND									
1. Loomis Sayles Bond	ML	21.71	**12.49**	NA	★★★★★	0.84	0.00	311	800-633-3330
2. CGM Fixed-Income	LV	27.38	**11.47**	NA	★★★★★	0.85	0.00	33	800-345-4048
3. Strong Corporate Bond	ML	14.80	**10.14**	11.58	★★★★	1.10	0.00	273	800-368-1030
4. Alliance Bond Corporate Bond A	ML	27.52	**9.09**	13.44	★★★★	1.24	4.25	262	800-227-4618
5. Smith Barney Investment Grade Bond A	NA	15.84	**8.42**	NA	★	1.11	4.50	213	800-451-2010
6. Alliance Bond Corporate Bond B	ML	26.69	**8.37**	NA	★★	1.99	3.00D	315	800-227-4618
7. Managers Bond	ML	15.08	**8.27**	10.00	★★★★★	1.20	0.00	28	800-835-3879
8. Smith Barney Investment Grade Bond B	NA	15.27	**7.85**	11.10	★★★	1.57	4.50D	268	800-451-2010
9. IDS Bond A	ML	14.16	**7.77**	11.02	★★★★	0.78	5.00	254	800-328-8300
10. Invesco Select Income	ML	12.55	**7.48**	10.15	★★★★★	1.00	0.00	268	800-525-8085
■ GOVERNMENT BOND - GENERAL									
1. Strong Government Securities	HI	10.95	**6.51**	9.76	★★★★★	0.90	0.00	541	800-368-1030
2. Benham Long-Term Treasury & Agency	HL	13.46	**6.41**	NA	★★	0.67	0.00	109	800-331-8331
3. Loomis Sayles U.S. Govt Secs	HI	10.88	**6.36**	NA	★★★	1.00	0.00	23	800-633-3330
4. William Penn U.S. Govt Secs Income	HI	10.67	**6.25**	8.60	★★★	1.00	4.75	44	800-523-8440
5. Federated U.S. Govt Bond	HI	12.83	**6.14**	8.86	★★	0.85	0.00	86	800-245-5040
6. Sit U.S. Government Securities	HS	8.89	**5.99**	7.27	★★★★★	0.80	0.00	52	800-332-5580
7. Montgomery Short Govt Bond R	HS	8.18	**5.86**	NA	★★★★★	0.47	0.00	19	800-572-3863
8. State Street Research Govt Income A	HI	10.15	**5.83**	8.33	★★★	1.10	4.50	617	800-882-0052
9. California Investment U.S. Govt Secs	HL	10.55	**5.82**	9.23	★★★	0.64	0.00	29	800-225-8778
10. Nationwide U.S. Govt Income	HI	10.55	**5.72**	NA	★★★	1.08	5.00D	39	800-848-0920
■ GOVERNMENT BOND - TREASURY									
1. Benham Target Maturities 2020	HL	23.53	**9.82**	11.78	★	0.72	0.00	736	800-331-8331
2. Benham Target Maturities 2010	NA	19.11	**8.61**	12.49	★	0.71	0.00	114	800-331-8331
3. Benham Target Maturities 2015	HL	21.29	**7.65**	11.88	★	0.71	0.00	119	800-331-8331
4. Vanguard F/I Long-Term U.S. Treasury	HL	14.12	**7.35**	10.25	★★★	0.27	0.00	870	800-662-7447
5. Vanguard Admiral Long-Term U.S.	HL	14.22	**7.34**	NA	★★	0.15	0.00	176	800-662-7447
6. Benham Target Maturities 2005	HI	15.94	**6.51**	11.33	★★	0.71	0.00	233	800-331-8331
7. T. Rowe Price U.S. Treasury Long-Term	HL	12.97	**6.33**	8.98	★★★	0.80	0.00	71	800-638-5660
8. Wright U.S. Treasury	HL	13.84	**6.26**	9.58	★★	0.90	0.00	21	800-888-9471
9. ISI Total Return U.S. Treasury	HL	10.85	**6.25**	8.69	★★	0.80	4.45	196	800-955-7175
10. Flag Investors Total Ret U.S. Treas A	HL	10.85	**6.23**	8.69	★★	0.80	4.50	151	800-767-3524
■ GOVERNMENT BOND - MORTGAGE									
1. Fidelity Mortgage Securities	HI	11.65	**7.46**	8.12	★★★★★	0.77	0.00	490	800-544-8888
2. Smith Breeden Interm Duration US Govt	HI	9.69	**6.61**	NA	★★★★★	0.78	0.00	36	800-221-3138

■ **EXPERT LIST**

FUND NAME	STYLE	TOTAL RETURN 1YR	3YR	5YR	M* RATING	EXPENSE RATIO	MAX SALES CHARGE	NET ASSETS $MM	PHONE
3. Dreyfus Basic GNMA	NA	10.81	**6.25**	8.20	★★★★★	0.50	0.00	55	800-645-6561
4. Lexington GNMA Income	NA	10.37	**6.09**	7.89	★★★★	1.01	0.00	122	800-526-0056
5. Franklin Strategic Mortgage	NA	10.95	**5.91**	NA	★★★	0.00	4.25	6	800-342-5236
6. Vanguard F/I GNMA	NA	10.65	**5.87**	8.14	★★★★★	0.29	0.00	695	800-662-7447
7. Fidelity Spartan Ginnie Mae	HI	10.52	**5.76**	7.48	★★★★	0.65	0.00	442	800-544-8888
8. Kemper U.S. Govt Securities A	HL	10.95	**5.62**	7.60	★★★	0.72	4.50	437	800-621-1048
9. USAA GNMA	HI	9.41	**5.58**	7.90	★★★★	0.32	0.00	301	800-382-8722
10. Accessor Mortgage Securities	NA	9.44	**5.57**	NA	★★★★	1.31	0.00	60	800-759-3504

■ **INTERNATIONAL BOND**

FUND NAME	STYLE	1YR	3YR	5YR	M* RATING	EXPENSE RATIO	MAX SALES CHARGE	NET ASSETS $MM	PHONE
1. Fontaine Global Income	MG/HS	23.84	**14.79**	NA	★★★★★	1.21	0.00	1	800-247-1550
2. Federated International Income A	MI	7.71	**11.56**	NA	★★★★★	1.30	4.50	173	800-245-5051
3. G.T. Global High-Income A	LL	39.15	**11.50**	NA	★	1.75	4.75	151	800-824-1580
4. Federated International Income C	MI	7.02	**10.81**	NA	★★★★★	2.06	1.00D	12	800-245-5051
5. G.T. Global High-Income B	NA	38.10	**10.77**	NA	★	2.40	5.00D	231	800-824-1580
6. Benham European Govt Bond	HI	7.23	**10.67**	NA	★★★★★	0.82	0.00	256	800-331-8331
7. Lazard International Fixed-Income	HI	3.77	**10.02**	NA	★★★★★	1.05	0.00	51	800-823-6300
8. Capital World Bond	HI	11.63	**9.41**	9.61	★★★★	1.12	4.75	713	800-421-4120
9. T. Rowe Price International Bond	HI	5.38	**9.36**	11.53	★★★★★	0.98	0.00	102	800-638-5660
10. Franklin Templeton German Govt Bond	NA	1.93	**9.31**	NA	★★★	1.25	3.00	24	800-342-5236

■ **MUNICIPAL BOND**

FUND NAME	STYLE	1YR	3YR	5YR	M* RATING	EXPENSE RATIO	MAX SALES CHARGE	NET ASSETS $MM	PHONE
1. Smith Barney Managed Municipals A	HL	9.54	**7.82**	10.27	★★★★★	0.71	4.00	187	800-451-2010
2. Executive Investors Insured Tax-Exmpt	HL	9.34	**7.62**	8.62	★★	0.50	4.75	14	800-423-4026
3. STI Classic Invmt Grade T/E Bond Inv	HL	8.35	**7.50**	NA	★★★★	1.15	3.75	40	800-428-6970
4. Excelsior Long-Term Tax-Exempt	HL	9.32	**7.50**	9.57	★★★★	0.80	4.50	91	800-446-1012
5. Smith Barney Managed Municipals B	HL	8.70	**7.20**	NA	★★★★★	1.23	4.50D	733	800-451-2010
6. United Municipal High-Income A	LL	9.01	**7.19**	9.04	★★★★★	0.76	4.25	390	800-366-5465
7. Franklin High Yield Tax-Free Inc I	ML	8.80	**7.10**	8.91	★★★★★	0.60	4.25	378	800-342-5236
8. Van Kampen Amer Cap Tax-Fr High-Inc A	ML	6.76	**6.72**	6.00	★★★★	0.87	4.75	650	800-421-5666
9. Prairie Municipal Bond A	HI	8.06	**6.63**	8.40	★★★	0.07	4.50	7	800-370-9446
10. Calvert National Municipal Interm A	MI	7.44	**6.45**	NA	★★★★★	0.69	2.75	39	800-368-2748

All data are through March 31, 1996. Institutional, Restricted Access, and Closed funds were not included in the table.
SOURCE: Morningstar, Inc., Chicago, IL. ☎ 800–735–0700.

FUND FAMILIES

THE WORST-PERFORMING FUNDS

Some household names chalked up some pretty mediocre results

Sizing up individual mutual funds is fairly straightforward, but how do you compare performance among fund families? Morningstar Inc., the mutual fund research firm, tackled that problem for *SmartMoney* magazine (August 1995 issue) by examining a company's fund-by-fund performance over the six-year period ending March 31, 1995. Morningstar then arrived at an average for each family's basket of funds and assigned each company a score—from 5 (worst) to 1 (best).

The results: The best-known mutual fund families aren't necessarily the leaders of the pack. In fact, 31 multibillion-dollar companies, including Merrill Lynch and John Hancock, had a score above 3.0, meaning that on average their funds underperformed their peers. The seven worst performing families, which hold a grand total of 110 funds and $80 billion in mutual fund assets, have only five funds that rank in the top 20 percent of their peer groups.

Which of the biggest families were the biggest laggards? Prudential, with a 3.7 score, was near the bottom of the heap. The problem at Prudential, according to *SmartMoney*, is a carry-over of conservative insurance practices to the investment side of the company. Keystone, with 70 funds and $9 billion in assets, also rated a 3.7. Dragging down Keystone's performance were high annual expense charges, which cut into investor gains. Dean Witter scored 3.6, thanks to mediocre performances turned in by its 41 funds. Paine Webber, also with a 3.6 score, earned a dubious distinction—not one of its 51 funds showed positive returns during 1994.

IN THE DOG HOUSE

A year or two of poor results by a mutual fund can be forgiven. After all, this year's dog often turns into next year's darling, and vice versa. But a fund with a five-year stretch of bad returns deserves an investor's skepticism. Among the biggest funds, these showed below-average returns in their categories in each year of the five years ending December 31, 1995, according to Morningstar Inc. The poor performance is stated as the percentage points short of the average of its peers.

FUND	TYPE	ASSETS (millions)	% BELOW AVERAGE
CENTURY SHARES TRUST	Specialty financial	$267	–11.28
MATHERS	Asset allocation	$232	–9.34
ARIEL GROWTH	Small company	$121	–7.61
MFS-INTERMEDIATE INCOME B	Multisector bond	$233	–5.75
GT GLOBAL THEME HEALTH CARE A	Specialty health	$523	–4.65
DREYFUS GLOBAL GROWTH	World equity	$109	–4.62
MERRILL LYNCH TOMORROW B	Growth	$113	–4.38
BURNHAM A	Growth and income	$110	–3.69
ONE GROUP FIDUCIARY	Small company	$470	–3.67
DREYFUS	Growth and income	$2,810	–3.64

SOURCE: Morningstar Inc.

EXPERT LIST

HOW THE TOP MUTUAL FUND FAMILIES STACK UP

Dreyfus, Fidelity, Vanguard—they are household names. But how do they differ from each other and from other big fund families? The table below compares the biggest families[1], including both no-load funds, which charge no fees or commissions when you buy or sell fund shares, and load funds, which do levy them. Front-end loads are sales charges paid before an investor's money goes into the mutual fund. With back-end loads, sales charges are paid when an investor redeems or sells shares. The average expense ratio is the annual expenses shareholders can expect shown as a percentage of the funds' assets. For example, Vanguard's 0.40 percent average expense ratio means that the group's average stock fund costs 40 cents per $100 in assets to run. The industry average is 1.34 percent.

Fund Family ☎ Business hours[2]	Assets in $billions / TYPE[3]	Number of funds	Best fund *Worst fund*[4]	Exp. ratio front (F) back (B)	Initial minimum investment	Min. check-writing
CAPITAL RESEARCH & MGT. ☎ 800–421–9900 8 am–8 pm M–F	$155 LOAD	14 stk 11 bnd 3 mm[5]	**Fundamental Investors** *Tax–Ex Money Fnd. of America*	0.78% F	$250– $2,500	$250
DEAN WITTER INTERCAPITAL ☎ 800–869–3863 8 am–8 pm, M–F	$69 LOAD	19 stk 27 bnd 9 mm	**Dean Witter High Yield** *Dean Witter NY Muni MM*	1.75% B	$1,000– $10,000	$500
DREYFUS CORP. ☎ 800–782–6620 24 hours, 7 days	$76 NO LOAD	36 stk 70 bnd 33 mm	**Dreyfus New Leaders** *Dreyfus Cap Value; A*	0.92%	$2,500– $25,000	$500
FIDELITY MGT. & RESEARCH ☎ 800–544–8888 24 hours, 7 days	$384	83 stk 43 bnd 23 mm	**Fidelity Select Home Fin** *Fidelity Select Environment*	0.91%	$2,500– $10,000	$500
FRANKLIN ADVISORS, INC. ☎ 800–632–2180 9 am-11 pm, M-F; 11 am-8pm Sa	$105 LOAD	29 stk 55 bnd 6 mm	**Franklin Balance Sheet** *Franklin NY TF;Mf.*	0.65% F	$100	$100– $500
IDS MUTUAL FUND GRP. ☎ 800–328–8300 8 am– 8 pm, M–F	$63 LOAD	17 stk 16 bnd 3 mm	**IDS Precious Metals** *IDS Tax–Free Money; A*	0.90% F 1.64% B	$2,000	$500
MERRILL LYNCH ASSET MGT. ☎ 800–637–3863 9 am–5 pm, M–F	$155 LOAD	22 stk 27 bnd 28 mm	**Merrill Lynch Basic Value; A** *Merrill Sh–Tm Global; B*	1.07% F 2.09% B	$250– $5,000	$500
PUTNAM INVESTMENT MGT. CO. ☎ 800–225–8806 8:30 am–8pm, M–F	$91 LOAD	28 stk 21 bnd 5 mm	**Putnam New Oppty; A** *Putnam CA Tax–ex MM*	1.16% F	$500	$500
SMITH BARNEY INC. ☎ 800–221–8806 8 am–8 pm, M–F	$71 LOAD	28 stk 21 bnd 12 mm	**Smith Barney Spec Eqty; B** *Smith Barney Muni: CA MM; A*	0.86% F	$1,000– $10,000	NONE
VANGUARD GROUP ☎ 800–635–1511 8 am–9 pm, M–F; 9–4 Sa	$193 NO LOAD	33 stk 24 bnd 9 mm	**Vanguard Spl: Health** Vanguard NJ TX–Fr: MM	0.40%	$500– $50,000	$250

NOTES: **1.** Federated Investors is omitted from this list because it sells largely through bank trust departments. **2.** Eastern Standard Time. **3.** Assets as of Jan. 31, 1996. **4.** Based on growth rates from March 31, 1991 to March 31, 1996. **5.** mm means "money market."

SOURCES: Lipper Analytical Services, Inc.; Investment Company Institute; company reports.

THE BASICS

HOW TO ANALYZE A MUTUAL FUND

There's no lack of information out there. Here's what to focus on

Mutual fund investors can't make perfect choices every time—too many variables are stacked against them. They need to compile the ideal portfolio, buy into a fund at precisely the right time, and bail out just before the precisely wrong time. But investors can stay a step ahead and avoid serious blunders by knowing the basics of analyzing a mutual fund's performance. Here are a few simple lessons in evaluating a fund:

■ **RETURN**. Many investors obsess over a fund's yield, which tells you the current income distributed annually. But the true test of any fund, even one bought for income, is total return. Total return measures the increases and decreases of your investment over time, assuming the reinvestment of dividends and subtracting the fund's costs. If you'd rather skip the mathematics involved in calculating a fund's total return, just call the fund company's toll-free number and ask for it.

When comparing the total returns of several funds, be sure you're comparing only figures calculated over the same time period, say January 1 to December 31. Determine if sales charges have been deducted from total returns before you compare fund results. Some funds and most financial publications report total returns before sales fees and other costs have been deducted. Then run year-by-year and cumulative comparisons, say, over five years or since the fund's inception. If most of the cumulative gains have been earned over the past year or two, you're looking at a fund that could burn out.

■ **RISK**. It isn't easy to calculate or compare how much risk a mutual fund assumes but getting an idea of risk is important. A few statistical measures that give an idea of a fund's risk include a fund's beta, alpha, and standard deviation. Beta measures the volatility of a fund's return against an index, such as the Standard & Poor's 500. Aggressive investors prefer funds with a beta above 1.0, which means the fund's returns have moved up and down more than the S&P as a whole. A more conservative choice would be a fund with a .75 beta, for example, meaning it was 75 percent less volatile than the market.

Alpha reports how much the fund's performance deviated from its expected return. A fund with a positive alpha did better than expected. A negative alpha means the fund underperformed.

Academics especially like a risk measure called standard deviation. It gauges how widely a fund's return swings from one time period to another. A fund with volatile returns is supposedly more likely to show a big loss in the future.

■ **INVESTMENT STYLE AND MIX.** Two funds can fall under the same general investment category but have very different styles that affect their performance. The reason: interpretations of terms such as "aggressive growth" may vary from fund to fund. The prospectus will give you a precise explanation of a fund's strategy and investment objective. (Funds often change their investment style or management team, making past performance a nearly useless measure.) Check out a fund's mix of investments, too. Exposure to a vulnerable industry or to volatile foreign stocks can go a long way toward explaining a fund's performance.

■ **LEVERAGE**. Many funds hedge against possible changes in interest rates or currency values with strategies that may be risky. Be sure you're comfortable with a fund's hedging strategy. Can the fund invest in risky derivatives, fill up on Latin American stocks, sell short? Often, the techniques help returns, but just as often they can cause deep losses. Scrutinize the prospectus.

■ **TAXES**. Don't ignore the tax implications of

EXPERT Q & A

HOW GOOD ARE FUND RANKINGS?

A study finds that past performance isn't the key to the future

It's hard to find a business magazine that doesn't carry some ranking of mutual funds. The lists have become the standard for investors to gauge a mutual fund and to assess the performance of the manager who steers the fund. But critics say the swelling number of mutual fund rankings reinforce short-term thinking by moving the year's top performers into an elite class. Sure, those comprehensive lists sell magazines, but are they as valuable as investors may think? Bob Fischer, associate vice president of Legg Mason, an investment firm in Richmond, Va., asked himself that question and in 1995 set out to study the mutual fund rankings offered by major financial magazines. Fischer's conclusion: Investors beware. Here's why.

■ **Why did you decide to study mutual fund rankings?**

I've always been suspicious of the ratings that magazines give mutual funds. Do the *Money* "A" funds do better than its "C" funds, for example? Should you change from a fund with an "up" arrow in *Business Week* for one with three "up" arrows? I decided to see if the rankings were any use in predicting the future performance of the funds.

I studied the mutual fund rankings of four leading financial magazines: *Money*, *Forbes*, *Kiplinger's*, and *Business Week*. If the grades these magazines give mutual funds are useful in predicting the funds' future performance, then a fund that's rated "A" one year would do better than a "B" fund the following year, and so on.

■ **Did you find a link between a fund's ranking and its future performance?**

No. We found that there is absolutely no relationship between mutual fund ratings and future performance. One fund rated an "F" in *Forbes* in 1992, for example, and the following year outperformed those that had received a "B." Conversely, several funds that were ranked highly by *Business Week* trailed behind lower-ranked funds the following year.

■ **How many funds did you study?**

We studied the 1992 performance of 25 mutual funds from each magazine compared to their 1993 performance. We chose only growth and income funds as categorized by Morningstar.

■ **Wasn't that a rather limited study?**

That's a valid criticism, but we wanted a small enough number of funds in our sample so that it would be practical for an individual to own that number. I doubt that a more exhaustive study would have shown anything different.

buying a particular fund, but don't get carried away by potential tax bills either. There's no doubt that taxes can take the fun out of a mutual fund gain. If you're shopping for a tax-free fund, avoid those that post most of their income in gains. If you're buying stock funds, find out when the fund posts its annual gains, usually at year-end, and wait until after that move to buy in.

But don't pick a fund just for its tax advantages. A study by the *No-Load Fund Analyst,* a newsletter based in Orinda, Calif., found that there's not much change in equity-fund rankings on an after-tax basis. So, the report suggests, investors should focus first on performance, not taxes. Use the tax analysis only when you're deciding between two similar funds with comparable gross returns.

FUND FEES

WHERE LESS EQUALS MORE

No-load funds not only have fewer up-front charges but better returns

These days, investors bristle at paying commissions and sales charges when similar versions of a product are available without a fee. Hence, the attraction of no-loads, or mutual funds that don't charge a fee or commission to buy or sell its shares. No-loads grabbed 45 percent of sales in 1995, up from 31 percent in 1988. Small wonder that the big brokerage firms, long leaders of mutual funds with loads, or costly sales charges, are plunging into no-load waters.

■ WHAT TO AIM FOR

Your odds of getting better returns rise when you invest in lower-cost funds. Here are the average annual expenses you can expect for various stock and bond funds. A .77% expense ratio for municipal bond funds, for example, means the average such fund costs 77 cents per $100 in assets to run.

DIVERSIFIED U.S. STOCK FUNDS	1.29%
Aggressive growth	1.72%
Equity income	1.25%
Growth	1.28%
Growth and income	1.18%
Small company	1.37%
INTERNATIONAL STOCK FUNDS	1.77%
Diversified foreign	1.62%
Europe	1.90%
Pacific	1.84%
BOND FUNDS	
Corporate bonds	0.84%
Government bonds	0.91%
Municipal bonds	0.77%

SOURCE: Morningstar Inc.

Full-service broker Smith Barney recently introduced a deluxe service that includes no-fee transactions on mutual funds, stocks, and bonds. Investors get access to mutual fund and other investment research, and personal investment advice. The program isn't completely fee-free. Loads are waived, but there is a small yearly charge for the research and advice services based on the value of an investor's funds. Prudential Securities unveiled a no-load plan in late 1995 and other giant load firms are sure to jump in with no-load offerings.

The newcomers are pining after the business being snatched away by wildly successful programs like OneSource, offered by discount broker Charles Schwab. The plan offers one-stop shopping, making hundreds of no-load funds accessible with one phone call. All reporting is conveniently consolidated in one statement. For the services, investors pay only a small transaction fee, if any.

The lines between no-load and load funds were starting to blur even before the big boys got into the act. Sales charges on many traditional load funds have been shrinking. Up-front loads—which are paid at the time a mutual fund is purchased—have dropped from 8.5 percent in the early 1980s to about 4.5 percent and are expected to fall further.

As the question of fees begins to recede, other differences between no-loads and loads loom larger. Which are riskier, for example, and which are better performers? Conventional wisdom holds that no-loads take more risks because they want to make a bigger splash and attract aggressive investors. Not so, says a study by Morningstar Inc., the mutual fund research company. Based on standard measures, no-loads actually proved less risky on average than loads. Even on performance, Morningstar found that no-loads came out slightly ahead over the long haul. Over a five-year period, returns for no-load diversified equity funds came to 10.78 percent, compared to 9.83 percent for funds with loads.

Investors should focus less on the distinctions between load and no-loads, Morningstar concluded, and more on the services provided by load funds—and whether that advice is worth the added expense.

FUND PICKING

THE SHOCK OF THE NEW

Freshly minted funds often soar, but they can also fizzle fast

New mutual funds are cropping up faster than newly discovered planets these days. About 500 new funds were added to Morningstar Inc.'s database of funds in 1995. In fact, funds with a track record of less than five years attracted nearly one-third of all assets that flowed into equity mutual funds in 1995.

What's the appeal? For one thing, their small size gives fledgling funds the flexibility to move quickly as they discover promising new stocks or sectors. As a result, new funds usually turn in sizzling first-year returns. Take Dean Witter Capital Growth fund, which was born in 1991. One year later, its returns were an astounding 48 percent. The Pasadena Nifty Fifty, also born in 1991, posted a stratospheric 67.5 percent return one year later. Out of 368 diversified domestic stock funds launched in 1994, in fact, more than two-thirds returned at least 10 percent during the first five months of 1995, which comes to nearly 25 percent on an annualized basis, according to Morningstar Inc. And, on the downside, only a handful had negative returns.

But, as quickly as new funds soar, they can also fizzle and burn out. Three years after its inception Dean Witter Capital Growth fund posted an average 4.2 percent annual loss. The Pasadena Nifty Fifty managed a return of only 1.4 percent a year between 1992 and 1994. One reason for new-fund burnout is that as startups the funds often get special treatment from their fund families, skewing first-year results. Big fund families often give their startup funds more exposure to hot new stocks on the market. Although figures are hard to come by, experts say the new funds quickly turn around and sell the stock, resulting in a rapid spike in performance.

Still, if getting into a new fund seems irresistible, money managers say you should first consider putting your money into new small-cap funds (small-cap refers to market capitalization or the total value of a company's stock), which generally get better results than other types of new funds. Secondly, bone up on the fund's manager. What's his or her experience? Go with a manager who's a proven quantity and who sticks to a specialty area.

WHY BIGGER IS BETTER

Over the long haul, the lumbering giants outperform the smaller fry

Small funds are the darlings of gunslingers. They can quickly gain investing advantages, often producing hot-shot results. Big stock funds like Fidelity Magellan and Vanguard's Windsor, however, are seen as lumbering giants run by celebrity managers too busy to do the legwork. Can huge funds turn in respectable results? Morningstar Inc., the mutual fund research company, says, yes, bigger is often better.

Morningstar studied the performance of the 15 largest diversified stock funds, including heavyweights like Magellan and Windsor, from 1985 to 1995. The funds' returns were compared with those of all other diversified stock funds and the Standard & Poor's 500 index. The results: Every year, the 15 big boys outperformed the average for diversified equity funds. Among the 11 funds with 10-year records, almost all beat the S & P 500 in 5 years.

In addition to more consistent performance, another big fund advantage is deep research capabilities. In other words, there's no reason to ignore a fund just because it grows.

EXPERT Q & A

WHY YOU CAN'T BEAT THE MARKET

A stock market guru makes the case for index funds

Why search for just the right stock fund or manager when you can do better by investing in an unmanaged index fund? That's the question posed by proponents of index funds, which buy the stocks in the Standard & Poor's 500 to get the same performance as the index. Critics of index funds ask, why settle for mediocrity when you could hit on a fund that soars? As the debate rages on, investors have poured nearly $38 billion into index funds.

To get an expert's perspective, we consulted Princeton University economist Burton Malkiel, author of the classic investment book, *A Random Walk Down Wall Street* (W. W. Norton, 6th ed., 1996). Malkiel has long argued that investing in the stock market is like taking a random walk. Or, as he often stated, "A blindfolded chimpanzee throwing darts at the stock pages could select a portfolio that would do as well as the experts." Here are Malkiel's views on index funds.

■ Are index funds all they're cracked up to be?

I have argued for over 20 years that an indexing strategy—simply buying and holding the hundreds of stocks making up the broad stock market averages—is probably the most sensible one for individuals and institutional investors. With index funds, investors can buy different types of stocks and get the benefits of stock and bond investing with no effort, minimal expense, and big tax savings.

■ How have index funds performed?

Over the past 25 years, the Standard & Poor 500 Stock Index has outperformed about 70 percent of active investment managers. In 1995, more than 80 percent of the pros were trounced by the index. Statistics show similar results for professional investors like pension fund managers. And they've done well compared with other indexes, too, like the Wilshire 5000 Stock Index.

■ What's the biggest advantage of index funds?

The biggest benefit is the tax advantage of deferring capital gains taxes, or avoiding them altogether if the shares are left to an heir. Switching from stock to stock involves realizing capital gains that are subject to taxes, which cut net returns substantially. Index funds don't trade from security to security and therefore avoid capital gains taxes.

■ How do index-fund fees compare with those of traditional funds?

Very favorably. Fund expenses for actively managed funds average more than 1 percent a year, compared to less than .2 of a point for the largest public index funds.

■ What about the criticism that index funds simply guarantee mediocrity?

Well, you can't boast about the fantastic gains you've made by picking stock-market winners. But index fund investors are likely to get better results than those of the typical fund manager, whose huge fees and large portfolio turnover reduce returns. To many, the guarantee of playing at par with the stock market nearly every time is very attractive.

■ Which index funds do you like?

The popularity of Standard & Poor's 500 funds may have inflated their value. But indexing isn't simply buying the S&P 500. I also like funds that match other indexes such as the broader Wilshire 5000. Some good values may exist in small-cap stocks, in real estate investment trusts, and in foreign equities. There are funds that match those indexes, such as Morgan Stanley Capital International Index of European and Asian Stocks, as well as emerging-markets indexes. These index funds have also generally outperformed actively managed funds that invest in similar securities.

ASSET ALLOCATION

READY-MADE PORTFOLIOS

These funds decide for you how to balance your investments

Jittery about jumping into the stock market? Would you rather have someone else do the investment work for you? Many reluctant investors are calming their nerves these days by tossing out piles of prospectuses and investing in asset allocation funds. These funds serve as sort of mini portfolios that aim to give you the kind of balance you want.

Asset allocation funds invest broadly in stocks, bonds, and money market instruments. Their promise is to move your money among the various choices in order to seize maximum advantage of changing markets. Members of the extended family of asset allocation funds include balanced funds and the latest addition to the clan, lifestyle or life-cycle funds.

There are only a few hundred asset allocation funds around, a trickle in the large pool of 6,000 mutual funds. And they are fairly new—of the 235 funds tracked by Morningstar Inc., 165 are less than two years old. Even so, asset allocation funds managed to attract some $1.7 billion in assets in 1995, up from a mere $377 million in 1994.

Not everyone is enamored of the funds. Some financial experts say investors may be paying plenty just to calm their jitters. Others wonder about the funds' usefulness. The question in their minds: Are they really the first brick in an investment portfolio—or are they just a mediocre investment choice for lazy investors? Here are some pros and cons of asset allocation funds.

■ Who would gain from investing in asset allocation funds?

New or tentative investors stand to gain because the funds' managers tackle the big decisions: how much to invest and where. They are good choices for investors who want to diversify beyond stock funds but who may not have a large enough portfolio to do so on their own. Each fund serves as a stand-alone portfolio, buying stocks, bonds and cash in varying proportions. They are also appealing for those who have the money to diversify but don't have an interest in devising their own asset allocation plan.

■ Who doesn't need them?

Anyone who is investing for the long haul and has the stomach for stocks probably doesn't need asset allocation funds. If your portfolio already includes several different kinds of funds, you may be in good shape on your own. Fund managers will jiggle those assets

■ ASSETS AND LIABILITIES

Returns and expense ratios among asset allocation funds vary widely. Here's a snapshot of some of the more popular funds.

FUND	OBJECTIVE	TOTAL RETURN*	EXPENSE RATIO
BLANCHARD GLOBAL GROWTH	Long-term capital appreciation	12.71%	2.51%
FIDELITY ASSET MANAGER	Long-term reduced risk	18.16%	0.97%
STRONG ASSET ALLOCATION	High total return	21.95%	1.26%
VANGUARD ASSET ALLOCATION	High total return	35.46%	0.49%

*One year total return as of December 31, 1995.

SOURCE: Morningstar Inc.

around more than you will, but you'll be paying for all the fine-tuning.

■ Are the fees higher?

Asset allocation funds trade a lot, making their brokerage costs somewhat higher than other mutual funds. The costs aren't always reflected in a fund's expense ratio but they cut into returns. You should aim for an expense ratio that is no higher than 1 percent. You may be willing to go higher if you know the fund has a superior portfolio manager. You can find out the manager's experience by calling the fund company directly.

■ Finding the right mix.

Some asset allocation funds are geared for a certain stage of life, age, risk tolerance, investment goal, or some combination of these factors. The right mix depends mainly on how much time you have before you'll need the money. You can choose a portfolio geared to short, intermediate, or longer term needs. It's rare for an investor to have to cash in an entire portfolio, so some money should almost always be left in equities, which have the best performance record over the long haul.

A first fund might be one that buys blue-chip companies or that mimics a market index. When choosing a first stock fund, you're better off passing by the hotshots, advises A. Michael Lipper, president of Lipper Analytical Services, a research and consulting firm in Summit, N.J. "Funds that are hot are the most likely to disappoint."

■ What's their record?

Not all assets take their lumps at the same time, which can work to the advantage of asset allocation funds. When the stock market plunged in 1987, for example, many asset allocation fund managers switched to bonds. The bond market rallied, limiting the funds' losses to about 11 percent, compared to about 30 percent for stocks as a whole.

As a group, asset allocation funds have turned in a fair, if not stellar performance. Over the five-year period ending December 31, 1995, they returned 11.75 percent, compared with 16.64 percent for diversified equity funds and 8.36 percent for taxable fixed-income funds, according to Morningstar. But looked at individually, returns for asset allocation funds can swing wildly. For example, take the Quest for Value Opportunity A fund, which invests heavily in stocks. Its total three-year return rate of 17.20 percent handily beat the S&P 500's 14.69 percent return. At the other extreme, the Mathers Fund, which pumps its assets largely into bonds, showed a three-year total return rate of a measly 0.88 percent.

■ Beware of market timers.

Diversifying and trying to time the stock market are two entirely different things and asset allocation funds shouldn't be in the forecasting business, say experts. "Most asset allocation funds move money around based on their forecast of how one asset class is going to do and that's awfully hard to predict," says John Markese, president of the American Association of Individual Investors.

If an asset allocation fund is making dramatic swings among various asset groups, it may be trying to time the market. Aggressive market timers—those that have more than 150 percent turnover rate—are best avoided. How can you find out that information? One way is to check with one of the independent mutual fund rating services such as Chicago-based Morningstar Inc.

■ Know what you're buying.

It's often hard to know what you're buying with mutual funds—and this can be especially true of asset allocation funds. Some fund managers have great flexibility in shifting into more appealing assets at any given time. Others operate under a ceiling of how much can go into a given asset group. You can get information on how much leeway a manager has by calling the fund. Ask what, if any, investing parameters are placed on a fund's manager.

If it's safety you're after, be leery of some asset allocation funds that invest in more volatile areas like emerging markets, gold, or commodity-based stock. The peso's devaluation in 1994, for example, really whacked some of the funds.

EXPERT PICKS

HOW MANY FUNDS SHOULD YOU OWN?

There's a danger in owning too many. Simplify your portfolio

You've heard the message by now: investing in mutual funds gives you the immediate benefit of diversification, which lowers risk without hurting returns. But investors fond of fund collecting could be heading for mediocre results or, even worse, diminishing returns.

The problem with piling on funds is that you may be duplicating what's already in your portfolio. "With two to four funds you can own 1,000 stocks of many kinds from all over the world. How many stocks do you need?" asks Eric Kobren, president of Insight Management, Inc., a Wellesley, Mass., investment firm that publishes *Fidelity Insight*, an independent newsletter.

Indeed, a study by Professors Walt Taylor of the University of Southern Mississippi and Jim Yoder of West Georgia College found that a handful of stock funds are all you need to reduce risk. The study, which tracked 168 domestic stock funds from 1978 through 1989, found that most risk reduction, about 75 percent, occurred with just four funds. Beyond 15 funds, there was almost no lessening of risk.

Before you can consolidate wisely, says Kobren, look at the kinds of securities each fund owns. A good mix would include large- and small-company stocks and foreign stocks and bonds. Kobren believes just three well-chosen funds will do the job.

We asked Kobren to devise a diversified three-fund portfolio for a moderately aggressive investor and one for an investor with moderately conservative tastes. His choices for the more aggressive investor are Fidelity Value and Fidelity Growth Company, funds that invest in large company stocks, and Mutual Discovery, which emphasizes small-company and international stocks. Kobren says this diversity gives the portfolio less volatility than the Standard & Poor's 500.

For the moderately conservative investor, Kobren suggests a mix of less risky large-company stock funds through Mutual Beacon and Fidelity Equity Income II funds, augmented with exposure to bonds through Vanguard's Intermediate Corporate Bond fund. This mix, says Kobren, is about 75 percent less volatile than the S&P.

Here are Kobren's model portfolios, along with what percent of your assets to allocate to each fund and the funds' three-year return rates.

■ MODEL PORTFOLIOS: WHEN THREE FUNDS ARE ENOUGH

Eric Kobren, president of Insight Management, argues that most investors own too many funds. In most cases, no matter what type of investor you are, three will do.

FUND	TYPE	% ALLOCATION	3-YEAR RETURN*	PHONE
■ MODERATELY AGGRESSIVE				
FIDELITY VALUE	Growth	30%	18.84%	800–544–8888
FIDELITY GROWTH CO.	Growth	40%	18.63%	800–544–8888
MUTUAL DISCOVERY	Growth & income	30%	21.73%	800–448–3863
■ MODERATELY CONSERVATIVE				
FIDELITY EQUITY INC–II	Growth & income	50%	15.55%	800–544–8888
MUTUAL BEACON	Growth & income	35%	18.17%	800–448–3863
VANGUARD INTERMD CORP	Bond	15%	6.40%**	800–662–7447

*As of Feb. 29, 1996. **Since December 1993.

MONEY MANAGEMENT

DO THE SUPER-RICH HAVE AN EDGE?

Not really. These days, mutual funds often outperform private managers

When it comes to solid investment advice and stellar performance, the well-heeled with their private money managers have an advantage. Right? Wrong, say investment experts. By just about every measure, the differences between investing with large mutual fund managers and private money managers—who usually only take accounts of $1 million or so—are negligible. In many ways, mutual fund investors win out.

"The separate account environment is a vanity business, which has very little to do with cost, services, or performance," says Michael Stolper, head of Stolper & Co., a San Diego firm that tracks investment managers. "It's like driving a Honda versus a Mercedes. Everyone leaves and arrives at the same time. It's just a matter of preference."

Take investment performance. For the three years and five years that ended in December 1994, the latest available figures, there was no significant difference in the performance of stock investments held in private money managers' accounts and in mutual funds, according to data prepared by Chicago-based Stratford Advisory Group.

Are the wealthy getting better service? After all, private managers can find stocks that reflect the investor's risk tolerance, monitor the portfolio, and adjust it accordingly. "Those are false virtues," counters Stolper, "I'll go to a mutual fund anytime because I like the simplicity. I don't care whether I own Exxon or Mobil, I just want them to make money." Furthermore, he says, there's a wealth of public information available about funds in newspapers, magazines, and other sources. Private managers only periodically allow investors a peek at their data.

The rich, it turns out, are pretty much getting what they pay for. In other words, they aren't paying a premium for their privately managed accounts. In fact, costs associated with using a private money manager compared with mutual fund accounts are pretty much a wash. Most investment managers charge a flat fee of 1 percent of assets and scale back fees for larger accounts. Even after taking into consideration the added paperwork involved in recording transactions with private managers, costs usually come to 1.25 to 1.5 percent a year—about the same charged by most funds, says Michael Flynn, a consultant with the Stratford Advisory Group.

When it comes to a diversified portfolio, mutual fund investors have the upper hand. Private managers usually focus on a specialty, like small-company stocks for example, so in order for investors to diversify they may need more than one manager. Mutual fund investors get built-in diversity. In fact, says Stolper, the risk with mutual funds is that the investor may be overly diversified rather than overly concentrated. "If you're investing in more than 30 securities, you lose diversification and pick up redundancy," says Stolper.

The wealthy come out slightly ahead when taxes come into the picture. With private account managers, investors have a bit more room to maneuver: They can time sales of stock, using losses to offset gains and minimize tax bills. Mutual fund companies usually make distributions to investors in late December and even if the money is reinvested in fund shares, the distributions trigger tax liabilities.

All this blurring of lines between private money managers and mutual fund managers hasn't escaped the wealthy. A 1994 survey by Graystone Partners, a Chicago firm that tracks money managers and advises the very rich, showed that clients who had $100 million in assets were looking to put more of their assets into mutual funds within five years. Big institutional investors, meanwhile, have been pumping money into mutual funds for some time: Their share comes to $898 billion, rising from 32 percent of the total assets in 1988 to nearly 42 percent in 1994, according to the Investment Company Institute.

EXPERT PICKS

FUNDS THAT SERVE WITH A SMILE

Some treat your money with the respect it deserves

Service is the name of the game in the crowded field of mutual funds. Many fund companies are looking to grab market share by bending over backward to cater to investors. Which companies provide the best service? DALBAR, Inc., a Boston-based mutual fund research firm, tests about two dozen mutual fund groups each year before selecting a handful that provide kid-glove service to investors.

For the 1995 awards, DALBAR looked at more than 10,000 transactions designed to test 55 different aspects of service. The areas of service rated ranged from routine matters, such as opening an account and checking fund share prices, to whether dividends, annual reports, and tax statements were received on time. Aside from knowledge of actual data, the funds' representatives were also graded on their demeanor. For instance, did the rep have a pleasant, upbeat attitude, or was he or she abrupt, rude, or casual with the caller? Did the rep display confidence when giving responses? DALBAR invested about $180,000 of its own money in the funds and conducted more than 146,000 evaluations throughout the year before selecting the funds that would be awarded its excellence-in-service seal.

What should you do to get the best service from your funds? After many years of conducting its surveys, DALBAR has gleaned the following advice for investors:

■ **Ask how you can get your money out efficiently.** Ask the mutual fund company if you can get a checkbook and check-writing privileges so that if you want cash from your account, you can simply write yourself a check.

■ **Know how your money flows.** Find out beforehand what you must do to transfer money between funds or switch from reinvesting dividends to taking them in cash, or vice versa.

■ **Ask who to call for advice or help.** For example, funds should be able to tell you how to use your investment as collateral for a loan. Some funds will issue a certificate acceptable to the lender; a stockbroker, if you use one, should be able to put your account on margin.

■ AND THE WINNERS ARE:

DALBAR doesn't reveal the losers, but here's the list of winners of the 1995 DALBAR Quality Tested Service Seal.

FUND	ASSETS	☎ PHONE
THE BERGER FUNDS	$3 billion	800–551–5849
INVESCO FUNDS GROUP	$12.5 billion	800–525–8085
NEW ENGLAND FUNDS	$7 billion	800–283–1155
PUTNAM INVESTMENTS	$74.5 billion	800–225–2465
SELIGMAN FUNDS	$11 billion	800–221–2450
STATE STREET RESEARCH	$35 billion	800–882–0052
VAN KAMPEN AMERICAN CAPITAL	$25 billion	800–225–2222

RETIREMENT

ELDER COMMUNITIES: A nursing home isn't your only option, PAGE 46 **NEST EGGS:** Are you saving enough? PAGE 49 **SOCIAL SECURITY:** What to expect from Uncle Sam, PAGE 51 **EXPERT Q & A:** How to nurture your 401(k), PAGE 52 **SELF-EMPLOYED:** Best places to stash your cash, PAGE 55 **ESTATES:** Why the rich die richer, PAGE 57 **WILLS:** The way to write one, PAGE 59 **MONEY MANAGEMENT:** Financial housekeepers for the elderly, PAGE 60

EXPERT Q & A

WHERE THE LIVING IS EASY

Baby boomers are forsaking the Sun Belt and finding new territory

Each year about two million folks take their gold watches and head for the easy life. Not all join the exodus to the Sun Belt, though. In fact, the vast majority of retirees remain in their own hometowns. A tiny number—1 of every 70—make less-than-dramatic moves within their own state. Only about 5 percent actually pack up and move out of state, say retirement experts.

While that percentage sounds low, the ranks of retirement migrants add up to nearly half a million, a figure that's expected to rise significantly as baby boomers start hitting retirement age. By the year 2000, the number of Americans over 65 is expected to exceed 29 million.

Retirement experts say we'll see plenty of changes in retirement patterns in years to come. Some trends are already emerging. For one, more new retirees continue to work to some degree: 25 percent now hold seasonal or part-time jobs. For another, many relocating retirees are looking beyond Florida to more unusual locales. Increasing numbers are picking college towns, for example.

What factors should a new retiree consider before choosing a place to live out the golden years? We posed that question and others to David Savageau, author of *Retirement Places Rated* (Macmillan, 1995).

■ **Which states are retirees choosing?**

The Sun Belt states—Florida, Arizona, Texas, New Mexico, Nevada—have always attracted retirees and continue to do so. But the new trend is to look outside the Sun Belt. Many are turning to Washington state, Oregon, Colorado, Montana, and, in New England, Vermont and Maine. Though still minor players compared to Florida, the appeal of these states is increasing and will rise as baby boomers retire.

■ **Why are some states more appealing than others?**

Taxes play a big role. States with no taxes on personal income—Florida, Nevada, Texas, and Washington state—have historically lured retirees. South Dakota, Wyoming, and Alaska also have no taxes on personal income, although most people don't think of them as good places to retire.

Many states allow you to avoid taxes on retirement income. Mississippi, for example, has no tax on social security or pension benefits. Georgia has generous exemptions on retirement income, as does Colorado.

EXPERT PICKS

THE VERY BEST PLACES TO RETIRE

In his book Retirement Places Rated, *David Savageau graded 183 potential retirement spots across the country. He took into account seven factors: housing, climate, personal safety, availability of services and leisure activities, and the availability of part-time work. No spot rated a perfect 100. Here are Savageau's picks for the top 20 retirement places, the area's score, and its most attractive features.*

PLACE	SCORE	SELLING POINTS
1. Las Vegas, Nev.	84.47	Potential for part-time work
2. St. Petersburg–Clearwater, Fla.	83.88	Leisure activities and affordable housing
3. Bellingham, Wash.	83.25	Leisure activities
4. Fort Collins–Loveland, Colo.	83.09	Leisure activities and personal safety
5. Medford-Ashland, Ore.	82.37	Low cost of living
6. Tucson, Ariz.	82.26	Availability of services
7. Coeur d'Alene, Idaho	82.12	Leisure activities and low cost of living
8. Traverse City, Mo.	81.77	Affordable housing and personal safety
9. Phoenix-Mesa-Scottsdale, Ariz.	81.66	Potential for part-time work
10. Melbourne, Fla.	81.38	Affordable housing and leisure activities
11. Savannah, Ga.	80.95	Affordable housing and availability of services
12. Daytona Beach, Fla.	80.73	Low cost of living
13. Fort Myers–Cape Coral, Fla.	80.54	Potential for part-time work and leisure activities
14. Fayetteville, Ark.	80.18	Affordable housing and low cost of living
15. Gainesville, Fla.	80.08	Services and affordable housing
16. San Diego, Calif.	79.96	Potential for part-time work and services
17. San Antonio, Texas	79.78	Affordable housing and services
18. Camden, Me.	79.33	Personal safety, services and leisure activities
19. Austin, Texas	79.26	Services and affordable housing
20. Port Angeles–Sequim, Wash.	79.09	Personal safety and services

■ Will baby boomers differ in their retirement patterns?

Yes, they don't want to go to Florida. They say, "My parents went there, *ipso facto*, I'll stay out of that state." They won't be choosing idle retirement, that is, you won't find them lying on beaches and sitting around playing bridge. They are more adventurous and will look at nontraditional places like the Northwest, Colorado, the Carolinas, and New England states. They'll be willing to discover new places—college towns, mountain resorts, small towns—that are nice places to live.

In compiling my book, I've starting seeing boomers who are retiring. Many of them are former federal, state, or municipal employees taking early retirement. I see them setting up bed-and-breakfast inns and seeking out places like Durango and Grand Junction, Colo., and Sandpoint, Idaho.

■ What should you look for in a retirement place?

Most important is the cost of living. Your retirement location should cut your cost of living by at least 20 to 33 percent, money that you'll need later in life. It's just about impossible to cut your costs in half, however. Primary targets for cuts should be taxes and housing costs.

Look at the local quality of life: access to health care, the climate, and personal safety.

I would advise looking for nontraditional places that have four seasons—not spots that are uniformly paradise. Ideally, the place should be situated in the midst of protected land—a national forest, wildlife refuge or national park—that will provide an outlet for a desire to get outdoors and also a draw for tourism. Twenty years later when it comes time to dispose of the home, the place will be well-positioned for a sale.

Another bit of advice: Stay within a major media market. That's important not only for entertainment and information, but also because the trend is away from center cities to outlying areas. Try to avoid the sticks, though. Find a place where you can still catch PBS or buy a major newspaper at a corner convenience store. You don't have to play Columbus and discover some remote place.

■ Why the trend toward retiring in college towns?

College towns are great. They offer a good time. They are attracting lots of graduates from the '40s. In fact, college towns are over-represented in two age groups: 18 to 22 and over 65. They have rich, year-round calendars—academic, athletic, arts, and culture. For their scale, college towns provide a higher level of human services than other towns. Public transportation, health care, education, voluntary organizations—it's all in college towns.

College towns are good rental markets, with professors and students coming and going. If you're retiring and you don't know if you should buy, I say, "Rent, rent, rent," until you're sure. You can become a landlord and rent out to graduate students, for example, or become a tenant. By renting you avoid most of the cost of living differences involved in buying or living in an overpriced house.

Some good college towns are Bloomington, Ind., Princeton, N.J., Boulder, Colo., and Charlottesville, Va., among others. Some aren't great. College Park, Md., for example, is within the commuting range of big city problems, making it a less desirable place to retire.

ELDER COMMUNITIES

SURE BEATS A NURSING HOME

These days, you have a plethora of choices. Here's how to sort them out

The graying of America is in full swing: the over-85 group grew 275 percent between 1960 and 1994, according to the Census Bureau. Combined with longer life spans, Americans can expect to spend a fourth of their lives retired.

Not long ago, nursing homes were about the only option. Today, elders can pick from a variety of retirement communities, many in resort-like settings. There are nearly 700 retirement communities in the country, a figure that's expected to double in the next decade. Finding the right place requires a lot of legwork. And most have waiting lists ranging from 6 months to 10 years.

Before starting the search, advises Robert Greenwood of the American Association of Homes and Services for the Aging, ask yourself just what services you'll need. Do you need help with personal care? Do you need special meals? Will you need transportation? Do you intend this to be your last move?

We've tapped the experts and scoured the resources on retirement communities. Here's the lowdown, along with some pros and cons of each option.

CONGREGATE HOUSING OR INDEPENDENT LIVING

These communities are the ticket for active seniors who want to live independently but don't want to do chores like mowing the lawn and shoveling drives. Residents live in apartments, condos or single-family homes. The community provides the groundskeepers, social activities, and recreational facilities, which often include a golf course, swimming pools, and health clubs. The communities offer security and a range of amenities designed with the elderly in mind. Housing generally sells at market rates for comparable properties in the area. The communities charge monthly fees, which vary widely and which can be hefty.

For those still able to care for themselves, these communities are a good choice. But residents must provide their own health care, so that a move to an independent-living community probably won't be the last move the elder makes.

ASSISTED LIVING

This type of housing is for seniors who need help with personal care, such as dressing and grooming, but don't require 24-hour attention. Services vary widely from place to place. Some won't accept seniors who need wheelchairs, for example, or who have continence problems. Some offer housekeeping, others don't. Some can't handle special diets.

To determine if a community is right for you, inspect the place. Residents don't own their own rooms or units. Ask which room you would be given. Would you get the same room after a hospital stay? Can you come and go at will? Is transportation available? When are health-care providers on duty? Does the place seems safe and secure?

Assisted-living communities cost a bundle. Monthly fees can run from $1,000 to more than $3,000. There may also be entry deposits and processing fees, among other charges. Medicare and Medicaid usually won't help foot the bills, as they do for nursing homes.

When a resident's health declines, many places allow nurses to come in and help with the care. Fees for the services are tacked onto monthly charges. Many communities are not equipped to care for the incapacitated, who may have to move to nursing homes.

NURSING HOMES

Nursing homes, which provide round-the-clock care, have been tarnished with a bad reputation. Many deserve it, according to *Consumer Reports* magazine, which concluded in its August 1995 issue after a year-

EXPERT SOURCES

WHERE TO START YOUR SEARCH

Retirees contemplating a move to a retirement community face the daunting task of finding one that's right for them. Here are some helpful resources for the bewildered.

AMERICAN ASSOCIATION OF HOMES AND SERVICES FOR THE AGING

■ Offers publications such as *Continuing Care Retirement Community: A Guidebook for Consumers* ($6.95) and *Consumer's Directory of Continuing Care Retirement Communities* ($24.95).
☎ 800–508–9442

AMERICAN ASSOCIATION OF RETIRED PERSONS

■ This group can provide a bibliography of publications on retirement facilities, as well as the publication *Selecting Retirement Housing*.
☎ 800–424–3410

HEALTH CARE INFORMATION ANALYSTS, INC.

■ *The Directory of Retirement Facilities* is nearly 1,400 pages long and lists 22,000 facilities nationwide. It costs $249 but can be found in most libraries.
☎ 800–568–3282

NATIONAL ELDERCARE LOCATOR SERVICE

■ Funded by the U.S. Administration on Aging, this service gives out phone numbers of local private and public agencies that provide care for seniors.
☎ 800-677-1116

NEW LIFESTYLES

■ Free guides to retirement communities in 23 regions of the country.
☎ 800–869–9549

SENIOR SIGNPOSTS

It's never too soon to start planning retirement, nor is it ever too late. Here are the financial and legal mileposts you'll encounter as you look down the road and at what age you should expect them:

- **AGE 55:** Minimum age for many senior communities. If you retire or lose your job, you can withdraw from your Keogh, 401(k), and profit sharing without tax penalty or having to annuitize. You can sell your house tax-free on a capital gain of up to $125,000.

- **AGE 59-AND-A-HALF:** You can withdraw a lump sum from certain pension plans—IRA, Keogh, 401(k), without a tax penalty.

- **AGE 60:** You qualify for senior discounts from retail stores, hotels, movies, etc.

- **AGE 62:** You qualify for Social Security, but you'll get more if you wait until age 65.

- **AGE 65:** If you're getting Social Security benefits, you are automatically enrolled in the Medicare hospital insurance program. If you're not on Social Security, you must apply for Medicare coverage.

- **AGE 70:** Social Security benefits rise, if you're just starting; personal income—regardless of how much—doesn't reduce Social Security benefits.

- **AGE 70-AND-A-HALF:** You must start withdrawing from private plans, like IRA and Keogh, by April 1 or face tax penalties.

long investigation: "Many facilities range from inadequate to scandalous and the good ones are hard to find."

To find a good one, visit as many facilities as possible. By law, nursing homes must make government inspection reports available to the public. Look for any deficiencies and violations of health and safety laws.

The best places to get the lowdown on specific nursing homes, according to *Consumer Reports*, are the offices of the state ombudsmen, who serve as advocates for nursing home residents. To contact your ombudsman, call the state office on aging and ask for his or her name and number.

Nursing homes cost about $40,000 to $70,000 a year. Who pays? Residents, long-term health care insurance, and Medicaid. To qualify for Medicaid, however, a senior must impoverish himself to about $3,000 and enough to cover his burial. Nearly half of nursing home residents spend $40,000 or so before they qualify. Before signing a nursing home contract, ask if the place will guarantee a Medicaid bed as soon as the patient is eligible and if they'll guarantee a return bed after a hospital stay. Find out if costs for things like laundry and TV are covered by the daily rate and if they are covered by Medicaid.

LIFE-CARE COMMUNITIES

Also called continuing-care retirement communities, these are good places for seniors who don't want to move more than once. They offer a lifetime guarantee of room, board, and access to health care. Such communities include independent-living and assisted-living facilities, and nursing homes—on the same site or nearby.

You usually sign a contract that guarantees residence for life and pay a lump-sum entrance fee that can range from $40,000 to $400,000. There are also substantial monthly fees to cover utilities, property taxes, maintenance services, and such. Some communities are resident-owned: Members buy stock in proportion to the square footage of their apartments and put up money to buy the community's services and amenities. If the resident leaves, a portion or all of the fee is refunded.

NEST EGGS

HOW MUCH DO YOU NEED TO RETIRE?

More than you think. And, the onus is on you to find the funds

A good rule of thumb is that you'll need at least 70 percent of your annual preretirement income to maintain your standard of living during retirement. That may sound high, but isn't in reality. True, those who retire at 65 can expect to spend less on housing, food, entertainment, and transportation. But beyond that age, health care costs go way up. As a result, reports a study by Georgia State University's Center for Risk Management and Insurance Research, 60-something retirees will need 70 to 85 percent of what they earned before retiring.

Where does the average retiree's income come from? For those pulling in more than $20,000 a year in retirement income, the largest chunk, 39 percent, comes from personal savings and investments. Employer pensions contribute 15 percent and continued employment by one or both spouses provides 26 percent. Only 20 percent comes from Social Security benefits, according to the Treasury Department. But both Social Security and traditional pension plans are undergoing changes. Increasingly, the onus is on workers to fund their own retirement.

Two-thirds of Americans have never tried to figure out how much money they'll need when they retire. To get an idea of whether you'll have enough money for a comfortable retirement, first calculate the amount equal to at least 70 percent of your income. Then figure out if your retirement nest egg—including savings, 401(k)s, other pension plans, and Social Security benefits (see chart on page 51)—will generate enough income. The table below, developed by Westbrook Financial Advisers, Inc., a New Jersey retirement planning firm, will help you determine if you're putting enough aside. Remember that people are living longer these days; to ensure that you don't outlive your savings, you'll have to plan as if you and your spouse will live to 92.

If you find you're not saving enough, how

■ ARE YOU SAVING ENOUGH?

This table, developed by Westbrook Financial Advisers, will tell you if you have enough put aside to live well during your golden years. Find your approximate savings figure, then look at the number below the age when you want to call it quits. That's the amount you would receive in 1996 dollars for the rest of your life, including Social Security benefits, assuming a 3 percent annual inflation rate, a life expectancy of 92, and that the money is invested at 6.5 percent.

SAVINGS	AGE 50	AGE 55	AGE 62	AGE 65
$50,000	$8,875	$10,701	$14,428	$17,332
$100,000	$11,195	$13,168	$17,192	$20,276
$200,000	$15,836	$18,100	$22,721	$26,165
$300,000	$20,476	$23,033	$28,250	$32,054
$400,000	$25,116	$27,965	$33,779	$37,943
$500,000	$29,757	$32,898	$39,308	$43,832
$600,000	$34,397	$37,830	$44,837	$49,721
$700,000	$39,037	$42,763	$50,366	$55,610
$800,000	$43,678	$47,696	$55,895	$61,499
$900,000	$48,318	$52,628	$61,424	$67,388
$1,000,000	$52,958	$57,561	$66,953	$73,277

SOURCE: Westbrook Financial Advisers, Ridgewood, N.J., and New Canaan, Conn.

you face up to that shortfall depends on many factors including your age, of course, and how you are allocating your assets. No one type of investment always comes out on top and no one can predict which investment will do best at any time, so diversifying among stocks, bonds and money market securities makes sense. The level of risk you're willing to take is also important.

T. Rowe Price, the mutual fund family, has devised three possible retirement-investment strategies. The risk-averse, or those near retirement, should consider putting 40 percent of their assets into growth-oriented investments such as stocks or stock funds, 40 percent in bonds, and 20 percent in ultra-safe vehicles like Treasury bills, money market funds, and CDs.

If you have some time before you retire and can tolerate a moderate degree of risk, or if you are near retirement and want to assume risk because you have other assets or sources of income, you should emphasize growth stocks, in a mix that includes 60 percent stocks, 30 percent bonds, and 10 percent Treasury bills or money market funds.

If you have a long way to go before you retire and can stomach greater risk for potentially greater returns, consider a portfolio of 80 percent stocks and 20 percent bonds. Over the period 1950–1994, this strategy would have shown the greatest rewards, according to T. Rowe Price. An investor would have seen inflation-adjusted returns of 6.9 percent, compared to 4.4 percent from the risk-averse mix and 5.7 percent for the moderate-risk mix. But, of course, it was also the most volatile—swinging from gains of 42.6 percent in the best year to a 20 percent loss in its worst year.

Inflation can flatten your savings. To keep your money growing at an inflation-beating rate, be sure you are getting at least 2 to 4 percent returns after inflation. What's the best inflation-beating investment? Historically, stocks that return an average 10 percent are the best way to outpace inflation.

Sixty-six percent of Americans approaching retirement age regret that they didn't start saving sooner. Saving for retirement isn't easy, especially if you're already 40-something. According to Merrill Lynch, the investment firm, the average baby-boomer household saves at only one-third the rate needed to finance a comfortable retirement. The moral of this story: It's never too soon to start planning your retirement.

HOW TO BAIL OUT EARLY

You don't have to wait until you're 65 to enjoy the good life.

Jim Rogers was a high-charged Wall St. investor when at the ripe old age of 37, he dropped out to pursue his fantasy: retire early and motorbike around the world. Starting in 1990, Rogers lived out his adventure, logging 65,065 miles in 22 months. He recounts the tale in his book, *Investment Biker* (Random House, 1994). Not everyone who checks out early is as financially well-cushioned as Rogers was. But, even for him, early retirement held a few surprises, as he explains:

■ **Focus.** *"People who retire early, especially if they're young, need to have a focus. I knew I wanted adventure but because I didn't have a clear idea, I was exploding in all directions, wasting a lot of time."*

■ **You'll need plenty of money.** *"Don't forget, Social Security won't kick in at 42 and it costs more to retire at 40 or 50 than after 65, when you may have less energy."*

■ **No regrets.** *"I exult in what I've done. By retiring early, you get to do things you've only dreamed of and still be young enough to enjoy them. I can't imagine going around the world on a motorcycle at age 75."*

■ **Just do it.** *"Someday it will be too late. Why would anyone want to say: 'I'm glad I kept working and got to be a senior vp, but I never got to visit the Nile.' Everybody has dreams. Never living those dreams is a terrible tragedy."*

SOCIAL SECURITY

WHAT TO EXPECT FROM UNCLE SAM

It's not a golden handshake, but, at least, it's something

A retiree would have a tough time surviving on Social Security benefits alone. The average Social Security benefit paid to a 65-year-old retiree in 1995 was a meager $10,322. You can start taking Social Security benefits at age 62 but you'll suffer a permanent 20 percent cut in benefits. If you wait until 65 or beyond, you could get up to several thousand dollars more a year.

Keep in mind that legal changes have extended the age at which people will start getting Social Security payments in the future. The full retirement age will be increased in gradual steps. For example, benefits start at age 65 and 2 months for those born in 1938, at 65 and 4 months for those born in 1939, 65-and-a-half for those born in 1940, 65 and 8 months for those born in 1941, and 65 and 10 months for those born in 1942. Those born between 1943 and 1954 will have to wait until they reach 66. The steps increase until those born in 1960 reach full retirement age at age 67.

Working beyond your full retirement age can help you get higher Social Security payments because higher lifetime earnings mean higher benefits. But working while you're getting Social Security could lower your benefits. If you are 62 to 64 and earn more than $8,040, you could reduce your payments by $1 for every $2 you earn over the limit. If you are 65 to 69 and earn more than $11,160, your Social Security benefits are cut by $1 for every $3 you earn over your limit. Once you've hit 70, your benefits can't be cut, though, no matter how much you earn.

The table on this page estimates your annual benefits if you retire at 65. But benefits depend on your earnings history and that of your spouse, so you may want to contact the Social Security Administration, ☎800-772-1213, for a more accurate estimate.

With Congress tampering with Social Security, the future of benefits is unclear. Under current law, if you receive income in addition to Social Security benefits, and your adjusted income is more than $34,000 ($44,000 for couples), up to 85 percent of your benefits could be included in your taxable income. Congress has been tinkering with the amount subject to tax and inevitably will do so again.

At greatest risk are future Social Security benefits for those with higher incomes. Congress will most likely pass legislation restricting or eliminating their benefits. Within the next decade, predicts Ted Benna, author of *Escaping the Coming Retirement Crisis* (Pinon Press, 1995), it's possible that a person whose annual retirement income falls in the $40,000 to $50,000 range will see shrinking benefits. And those in the higher income ranges—say, $80,000 or above—probably won't get any benefits.

On another front, Social Security taxes have been climbing for two decades—from 5.85 percent of wages in 1977 to 7.65 percent in 1990. During that time, the maximum tax payable jumped from $965 to $4,682. The so-called FICA taxes are expected to shoot up further, predicts Benna, carving out 20 percent of your wages within the next 15 years.

■ WHAT SOCIAL SECURITY OWES YOU

The estimated benefits shown below assume that you work steadily over the years and retire when you turn 65. They do not reflect automatic cost-of-living adjustments.

ANNUAL WORKING INCOME	ANNUAL BENEFITS: Worker only	ANNUAL BENEFITS: Worker and spouse
$20,000	$9,420	$14,124
$30,000	$13,564	$18,840
$40,000	$13,812	$19,992
$50,000	$14,532	$21,792
$61,200 or more	$14,976	$22,464

SOURCE: Social Security Administration, 1995.

EXPERT Q & A

HOW TO NURTURE YOUR 401(K)

The man with a plan tells you how to maximize your savings

More and more workers are pumping money into their retirement piggy banks through 401(k) plans. The plans get their awkward name from a 1978 tax code provision that created them and are available through employers. A 401(k) lets participants invest pretax earnings in a personal account where money grows tax-free until retirement. There's an extra bonanza: Some employers will match employees' contributions.

The amount a participant can contribute in any one year is limited by the IRS and the employer. The 1996 maximum set by the IRS is $9,500. Most employers are expanding the number of investment choices they offer, which typically include a combination of company stock, money-market funds, and stock and bond mutual funds. Despite their appeal, experts say 25 percent of those eligible for 401(k)s don't participate, and an overwhelming number contribute less than they are allowed by law.

For help on how to nurture your 401(k), we turned to benefits consultant Ted Benna, the father of 401(k)s. In 1980, Benna created the first 401(k) plan for his own consulting firm. Today, he runs the 401(k) Association, a Langhorne, Pa., advocacy firm. Benna predicts that assets in all 401(k)s will bulge to more than $1 trillion within five years.

■ What's the big appeal of 401(k)s?

Normally, experts cite benefits like tax savings, or a company's matching contribution, or the ability to borrow or withdraw money when you need it. But I say the most important benefit is that they help participants become successful savers. They force you to save every pay period. They reverse the normal spend-save cycle, that is, I spend and intend to save but never have anything to save. A 401 (k) makes saving the first priority.

■ Are they superior to traditional pension plans?

One is not clearly superior. Traditional pension plans are wonderful if you manage to spend virtually all your career in one place and stay until retirement. But they are pretty rotten for employees who move from job to job, or who willingly or unwillingly retire in their mid-to-late 50s. That's because most of a pension plan's value builds from 55 to 65. The high cost of pension buildup is

■ SIZING UP THE BIG BOYS' PLANS

Not all 401(k) plans are created equal, even among the nation's largest companies. The maximum percentage of salary that an employee can contribute and the amount that an employer will match vary from company to company. So do the number and type of investments. Here's a scorecard comparing the plans of some of the largest companies.

Company	Max. employee pretax contribution	Employer match	INVESTMENT OPTIONS: Money market	Stocks	Bonds
AT&T (management)	16%	67%	1 fund	5 funds	2 funds
EXXON	14%	100%	0	2 funds	1 fund
GENERAL ELECTRIC	17%	50%	1 fund	1 fund	3 funds
GENERAL MOTORS (salaried employees)	15%	25%	1 fund	35 funds	4 funds
IBM	12%	50%	1 fund	4 funds	2 funds

SOURCE: Company reports.

one reason that downsizing companies target older employees.

For employees who are mobile, 401ks are definitely more beneficial. The ideal would be to work for a company that gives you both and most big companies still do.

■ What would a smart 401(k) plan look like in terms of asset mix?

That depends on how old you are and your investment goals. An aggressive strategy for a working 40-year-old would be to put 100 percent into stocks for an annual return of about 10.3 percent. For a person near retirement age, an aggressive plan would call for a mix of 60 percent stocks and 40 percent bonds. A conservative mix for a 40-year-old would be: 20 percent in stocks, 60 percent in bonds, and 20 percent in other fixed-income instruments.

For higher, most-aggressive rates of return, active workers need to invest in more volatile investments, like growth stocks. Retirees can probably get good rates by sticking to a mixture of more stable blue chip stocks, high-quality bonds, and other fixed-income vehicles.

■ Is a buy-and-hold strategy a good one for 401(k)s?

Yes, I normally recommend that people planning their retirement establish a strategy in terms of their investment objectives and stick to it and not get blown in the wind by what the stock market does every day.

■ There have been reports of possible misuse of 401(k) plan contributions. Should participants in 401(k)s be worried about fraud?

Yes and no. There have been cases where small companies started a 401(k) and a few months later went out of business and there was no money in the plan. But there are 250,000 plans out there and the number of cases where this happens is very small.

Where there's more need for concern is in a company of fewer than 25 employees that may be in serious financial difficulty. But larger employers have never been cited for improperly funding their plans.

One-half of the workforce has no form of private retirement coverage. For small companies, 401(k)s can cost about $3,000 and be complex to administer. We've come up with a 401(k) starter plan for very small employers that only costs between $500 to $700 to administer. Interested employers can call ☎800–320–401K.

■ What happens when a 401(k) participant switches companies?

You can transfer your fund directly into another company-sponsored plan or into an individual retirement account (IRA). You can also get a cash payment to roll the money over into an IRA. But getting the cash requires tax-withholding, so it's more advantageous to do a direct rollover.

One option that people are not commonly familiar with is that if their benefit payment is more than $3,500, they are allowed to leave it in their company plan.

■ Is taking a loan from your 401(k) wise?

No, it should be a last resort. For most people it's tough to repay the loan and continue to contribute to the plan. If you have an employer who's matching your contribution, you're missing out because you may not be able to put in the maximum amount allowed and repay the loan at the same time.

■ Will a good 401(k) alone provide adequate retirement income?

It certainly will. But you have to start early—at least at age 30. Also, between your contributions and your employer's matching, you have to save at least 10 percent of your income. And you have to invest it aggressively. You can't afford to have it sit in money-market investments, for example.

■ What happens when participants retire? Do they just sit back and enjoy their 401(k) windfall?

People are living 20 to 25 years in retirement these days and they have to continue to be active in managing their retirement money. The old idea of converting it to fixed income was okay when people lived 10 years during retirement. Today you must reinvest more aggressively during your retirement.

NEST EGGS

DON'T GIVE UP ON YOUR IRA

It may not be deductible but earnings compound tax-free

The thrill is long gone from Individual Retirement Accounts. They lost a lot of their appeal almost a decade ago when the law allowing tax-deductible contributions for most employed individuals was changed. But IRAs may still be a worthwhile tax saver for some workers, and as this book was going to press, Washington was abuzz with proposals to resuscitate them as a wealth-building tool. Ideas included extending the accounts beyond just employees so that even nonemployed spouses staying at home could open their own IRAs; easing restrictions on withdrawals before age 59½; and offering new choices in how the accounts can be set up to save taxes.

Deposits to IRAs—generally up to $2,000 a year—tumbled after a change in the law in 1987 narrowed the number of employees eligible to take a tax deduction for deposits.

EXPERT TIP

Though withdrawals from an IRA are generally not allowed without a tax penalty until you reach age 59½, you can begin pulling money out sooner if the withdrawals are in a series of substantially equal annual payments linked to your life expectancy. There are several approaches and formulas are tricky, so you may want some professional guidance.

The revised rules barred employees who were eligible for a retirement plan at work from fully deducting deposits to an IRA unless their adjusted gross income was below $40,000 on a joint return or $25,000 on a single return. (A partial deduction was left in place for incomes less than $10,000 above those amounts.) The change kept IRAs a potent tool for employees not covered by a plan at work by allowing them to continue to make fully deductible deposits regardless of their income. But a trap was set: If one spouse is in a retirement plan at work, a deduction could be barred for either spouse.

The change cooled the primary sizzle of an IRA—the tax deduction for deposits—but left another benefit untouched: Investment earnings in the account could compound each year without a yearly tax bite. That translates into bigger returns from mutual funds, stocks, certificates of deposit, or other assets into which an IRA's balance is put. But few people have been lured into making nondeductible deposits just to get the tax-deferred compounding. There's more paperwork and recordkeeping required in such nondeductible IRAs and the benefits of tax-deferred compounding become significant only after many years of reinvestment.

Taking money out of an IRA can be tricky. Withdrawals are fully taxed if you got deductions for your deposits and partly taxed if you didn't. Currently, moreover, withdrawals before age 59½ are generally subject to a penalty of 10 percent off the top, plus regular tax. And after age 70½, you must begin taking out money at a pace designed to deplete the account over your life expectancy.

These rules do not apply when you remove money to switch investments—from an IRA at one mutual fund to another fund, for example. You can make an unlimited number of direct transfers when the firm holding your IRA sends the withdrawal directly to a new account. But if you make a rollover yourself, you can do that only once every 12 months for each IRA you have (you can have as many accounts as you wish). The funds being rolled over can remain in your hands for no more than 60 days or they'll be taxed and subject to the 10 percent withdrawal penalty.

SELF-EMPLOYED

WHERE TO STASH YOUR CASH

If you want to retire in style, consider one of these savings plans

The self-employed are different from the run-of-the mill working stiff: They can salt away a sizable portion of their income each year and shelter it from taxation. A tax deduction for deposits to a retirement plan provides an immediate reward, while investment earnings in the account compound without a tax bite. The money isn't taxed until withdrawn.

In the easiest maneuver, under the current law, you can divert up to 13.0435 percent of your self-employment income to an IRA-like simplied employee pension (SEP) plan, up to a maximum annual contribution of $22,500. The paperwork is minimal and mutual funds and others offer readymade plans.

More complex are Keogh retirement plans. They can shelter more income than a SEP and withdrawals may qualify for more favorable tax treatment. But, as with SEPs, withdrawals before age 59½ are generally subject to a 10 percent early withdrawal penalty.

The most popular type of Keogh is a so-called profit-sharing plan. It's flexible since you can vary the share of income that you save each year. As with a SEP, a maximum of 13.0435 percent of self-employment income—up to $22,500 a year—can be set aside. (Self-employment income in these cases is what is left after subtracting business expenses and the deduction you get for half of your self-employment Social Security tax.)

An antidote for people who feel constrained by the $22,500 limit is to fund a money purchase Keogh plan. You'll be locked into saving a fixed percentage of income, but that can be up to 20 percent—to a maximum annual contribution of $30,000. Want greater flexibility on making deposits? Many advisers suggest that you can open both a profit sharing and a money purchase plan. You get a combined contribution limit of 20 percent and a top deposit of $30,000, yet can set the fixed money purchase deposit low enough to be manageable.

Don't be misled by rules that say you can put 15 percent of your income in a SEP or profit-sharing Keogh, or up to 25 percent into a money purchase Keogh or a paired profit-sharing and money purchase plan. Those percentages apply to self-employment income after you have subtracted the deposit itself. That's tricky math. It's easier to use the equivalent limits of 13.0435 and 20 percent of income before subtracting the deposit.

The most aggressive savings tactic is to open what's known as a defined benefit Keogh plan. Someone who is, say, 10 or 15 years from retirement can shelter a very large portion of income since these plans generally allow whatever is needed to be set aside to fund a predetermined retirement benefit. These plans, however, are the most complex of all and you'll need professional help setting one up.

People who hire employees may face an extra burden. They may have to provide retirement benefits for workers if they fund a SEP or Keogh for themselves. But look on the bright side, you'll not only be funding your own retirement but helping others look forward to life on Easy Street, as well.

EXPERT TIP

The deadline to open a new Keogh plan for 1996 is generally December 31, but deposits for 1996 can be made until the filing deadline in 1997 for your '96 return, including any extension you get. For a SEP, you have until the filing deadline for your 1996 tax return, including any extension, to both set one up and make a contribution.

NEST EGGS

A NO-BRAINER INVESTMENT?

Variable annuities are popular but may not be your best bet

They have so much going for them that variable annuities seem like a no-brainer investment. For starters, variable annuities, which are essentially mutual funds in an insurance wrapper, are tax-friendly. Earnings are tax-deferred until you start withdrawing the money. They are also versatile, allowing you to invest in a menu of mutual funds, stocks, bonds, and money markets. No wonder, investors poured in more than $50 billion in 1995.

But they carry huge downsides and many investors should put their money elsewhere. Many variable annuities carry penalties for withdrawing funds before the end of the term, often starting as high as 9 percent. And, as with other retirement accounts, the IRS hits you with a 10 percent tax penalty on earnings if you withdraw your money before you turn 59½. Ongoing expenses can be hefty, too. The average expense ratio of variable annuities can average up to a full percentage point more each year than fees on comparable mutual funds. Because expenses are paid directly out of earnings, your yield and total return can take a big hit.

Before deciding, says Steven B. Weinstein, editor of the *Arthur Andersen Personal Financial Planning Newsletter*, ask yourself the following:

Have you already made the maximum contributions available to other tax-advantaged investment plans? Do you plan to hold your investment at least until you are 59½? If you are in the 28 or 31 percent federal tax bracket, do you intend to hold the annuity for at least 10 years? If you are in the 36 percent or higher tax bracket, do you expect to hold the investment for at least 15 years for bonds and at least 20 years for stocks? And, do you expect to be in a lower tax bracket when you retire and annuity withdrawals begin?

Variable annuities are for you if you answer yes to Weinstein's questions. A bit of advice: Pick solid, aggressive funds with low fees and stick with them for the long haul.

■ BEST AND WORST OF THE BUNCH

Morningstar Inc. rates variable annuities based on performance and risk in one comprehensive evaluation. Morningstar gives five stars to annuities, or subaccounts, as they are called, with the most attractive risk/reward profile. The least attractive get one star.

Subaccount	Objective	Five-year ann. return*	Rating
BEST PERFORMERS			
1. UNUM VA I Dreyfus Small Cap	Aggressive	55.62%	★★★★★
2. Manulife Account 2 Lifestyle Emerging Growth Equity	Aggressive	22.08%	★★★★
3. Anchor National ICAP II Capital Appreciation	Aggressive	21.20%	★★★★
4. MONYMaster Enterprise Managed	Balanced	19.90%	★★★★★
5. Life of Virginia Commonwealth	Aggressive	19.47%	★★★★
WORST PERFORMERS			
1. Guardian Investor/Guardian Real Estate Account	Specialty	–6.08%	★
2. Anchor National ICAP II Foreign Securities	International stock	1.26%	★
3. PaineWebber Advantage Annuity Global Growth	International stock	1.35%	★
4. Bankers Security USA Plan Alliance S/T Multi-Mkt	International bond	1.75%	★
5. Prudential VIP-86 Real	Specialty	2.91%	★★

*As of February 29, 1996

SOURCE: Morningstar Inc.

EXPERT Q & A

THE RICH DIE RICHER

And so can you. A noted trust and estates lawyer tells you how

The very rich are different from you and me, as F. Scott Fitzgerald once noted. One big difference is that even after they leave their worldly fortune, the rich manage to shield it from the tax man. What lessons can a person of average means learn from how the wealthy plan their estates? William D. Zabel, a senior partner with Schulte Roth & Zabel, a New York and Palm Beach law firm, has given legal advice to very rich clients for more than 30 years. "With some sophistication and planning," says Zabel, author of *The Rich Die Richer and You Can Too* (William Morrow and Co., Inc. 1995), "everyone can make estate and gift taxes essentially voluntary rather than mandatory." Here are some pointers:

■ How do the rich die richer?

Most Americans pay little, if any, attention to estate planning. The rich, however, are accustomed to trying to preserve and protect their money and they focus heavily on estate plans.

■ How hefty are estate taxes and what are some tax-saving techniques?

Every American citizen has a one-time $600,000 exemption from federal, estate, and gift taxes ($1.2 million for a couple). A transfer of these amounts can be made during your lifetime as a gift or at death through a will or a trust. Beyond that exemption, estate taxes kick in, with rates between 37 and 55 percent, and an extra 5 percent surcharge for estates of $10 million to $21 million.

Some tax-saving techniques include setting up a charitable trust to defer or eliminate taxes, setting up a family foundation that will get the money that would have gone to taxes, and freezing the value of a closely held business. Another strategy is to make low-interest loans to children to avoid gift taxes.

■ How much of an estate that's left to a spouse can be given free of estate and gift taxes?

Under federal tax laws, no matter how rich you are, you can leave 100 percent of your estate to your spouse free of estate and gift taxes. Still, you can restrict what happens to your estate after your spouse dies—an important factor to consider if there are children from a former marriage. The most common device used is a so-called QTIP trust (qualified terminable interest property). Simply put, you would say: "I give all the income for life to my wife but at the death of my wife the property will pass to my children."

■ How can gifts to children and grandchildren escape gift taxes?

Each year, you can give $10,000 ($20,000 per couple) to as many recipients as you wish free of gift taxes. The best time to make these gifts is early in January of each year so death during the year won't preclude the gifts.

During your lifetime you can also pay college or medical costs tax-free for children,

■ THE ESTATE TAX BITE

Your heirs only pay the top rate on the top end of your estate.*

If estate is above this base	Your tax is this...	Plus this % over base
$600,000	$0	37%
$750,000	$55,500	39%
$1,000,000	$153,000	41%
$1,250,000	$255,500	43%
$1,500,000	$363,000	45%
$2,000,000	$588,000	49%
$2,500,000	$833,000	53%
$3,000,000	$1,098,000	55%
$10,000,000	$4,948,000	60%
$21,040,000	$11,572,000	55%

* Table does not account for taxable gifts.
SOURCE: Internal Revenue Service.

grandchildren, or others. But payment must be made directly to the school or the provider of the medical services.

■ What's a good way to restrict the use of money left to kids?

Setting up a trust is the traditional way. You can include conditions that require children not to smoke or drink, for example. You can indicate that if they don't complete their education, they won't get the money. One way to provide incentive for children to earn money is to set up a trust that will match income produced. You can't include conditions that are against public policy, such as requiring that a son divorce his wife.

■ What about giving to charity?

The most common tax technique is the charitable remainder trust, of which there are several varieties. Such a trust allows you to sell an asset without incurring a capital gains tax; increase your life income and your spouse's income; and get an immediate charitable income-tax deduction. At the death of both spouses, the income goes to the charity of their choice. This sort of trust lets you have your charitable cake and still eat a good part of it.

FACT FILE:

WHY THE KENNEDYS AREN'T ROCKEFELLERS

■ *Joe Kennedy, father of JFK, paid $100,000 for a mansion in Palm Beach, Florida, in 1933. His heirs sold it for $4.9 million in 1995. Here's what some equivalent commitment to some other investments would be worth over the same time period.*

S&P 500	**$5.5 million***
Coca-Cola stock	**$71.9 million***
Renoir painting	**$88.8 million**
Exxon stock	**$250 million****

*Dividends spent **Dividends reinvested
SOURCE: *Forbes Magazine*, June 19, 1995.

■ How useful are life insurance trusts as tax shelters?

A so-called irrevocable life insurance trust is the safest and most effective means of leaving substantial funds to children free of all death taxes. You can leave an unlimited amount of insurance proceeds to your spouse tax-free, but that doesn't avoid death taxes, it only defers them. The primary purpose of a life insurance trust is to avoid an estate tax in both spouses' estates and leave the insurance proceeds to younger generations tax-free. There's an added benefit: You can pass millions of dollars to grandchildren and escape estate taxes and the fairly new tax called the generation-skipping tax. In very high brackets, this tax can almost double the death taxes for assets left to grandchildren.

■ What's the difference between an executor, a trustee, and a guardian? How should they be chosen?

An executor carries out the terms of the will. He or she collects the assets, has them appraised, invests or sells them, pays the death taxes, if any, and distributes the assets according to the will. A trustee oversees property that's held in trust and administers it for the benefit of the trust's beneficiaries.

Choose them *very* carefully: If they turn out to be the wrong person for the job, they can destroy the value of a will or estate plan. Family members, friends, lawyers, accountants, or bank and trust company officials can be chosen as trustees and executors. Integrity and good judgment are the most important factors to look for.

Guardians are surrogate parents for children whose parents die unexpectedly. It's vital for parents, regardless of their assets, to appoint guardians for their children. Otherwise, a court will do it for them. Blood relatives are usually chosen, but the best guardians are those who share the same traditions and values as the parents, and, of course, who have a willingness to love and care for the minor children.

EXPERT Q & A

DO YOU NEED A WILL?

The answer is probably yes. Here's why and what it should include

More than half of American adults do not have wills, according to the American Association of Retired Persons. True, if your estate is under $600,000—and that's the case for most Americans—your heirs may be exempt from paying estate taxes, but that doesn't mean that you don't need a will. What are the potential consequences of not planning for the disposition of your estate? For some expert answers, we spoke with Boston attorney Alexander Bove, the author of *The Complete Book of Wills & Estates* (Henry Holt, 1989).

■ What happens if I don't have a will?

If you have no will, your estate will end up in probate court and many important decisions will be out of your hands. Normally, you name an executor, a trusted friend or family member who is responsible for determining taxes, assets, bills, and debts to be paid on your estate. Without a will, the court becomes the executor and your estate is divided under state laws.

■ What are the most important components of a will?

As a rule, wills are broken up into two parts. Bequests include specified property, such as amounts of money, real estate, and stocks that are left to a designated beneficiary. The residue is everything else, or everything not specifically defined, and will normally go to the primary beneficiary of the estate, usually a spouse, children, or both. Only property in your name at the time of your death can be passed on to your heirs.

■ What are living wills, health care proxies, and durable powers of attorney, and why are they important?

A living will is a declaration that indicates whether you would want to be kept alive by artificial means in the event that you are diagnosed with a terminal illness.

A health care proxy allows you to appoint someone to make medical decisions for you.

A durable power of attorney names someone to make financial transactions for you. If you don't have a durable power of attorney, and if your assets or property need to be transferred, your beneficiaries would have to go to probate court in order to appoint a conservator or guardian.

■ How often should I update my will?

Whenever there is a major change in the tax laws, or if there is a change in your family or your family's finances.

■ How can I provide for minor children?

If you have minor children, you should be sure to name a trusted relative or friend as the guardian who will be responsible for the "person and property" of the minors.

■ What is the difference between a will and a living trust?

A living trust is a legal document that you create while you are alive; you can transfer assets to the trust while you are alive, and the trust governs the assets. You may be your own trustee. Whatever is in the trust does not have to pass through probate. Whatever you do not put into the trust goes into a will.

A living trust—including a will, a durable power of attorney, and health care proxy—and a living will are the typical documents in a modern estate plan.

■ How much should I pay to have a will drawn?

That depends on the complexity of the estate. The process of drawing up a will can range between $50 and $5,000, depending on how complicated it is. Often the amount of property is not as important a factor as the family circumstances.

FINANCIAL HOUSEKEEPERS

$$$ MANAGEMENT MADE EASY

A new breed of helpers can help you with your bills

"*What do you mean I'm out of money, I still have some checks left.*" That refrain can, of course, apply to a person of any age. But nearly one-quarter of people over 85 need help managing their money, according to the National Institutes of Health. Traditionally, relatives step in to help seniors whose eyesight is failing, for example, or who can no longer cope with the complexities of insurance policies. But now there are daily money-management services. Unlike financial planners who focus on long-term financial goals, these services balance check books, file insurance claims, prepare taxes, and handle other mundane money matters.

Some are nonprofit services funded by charities. Fees are sometimes determined based on the elder's income. Some are profit-making firms that charge between $45 and $60 per hour. Typically, managers spend one to six hours a month per client.

To find a service, call the Eldercare Locator Service (☎800–677–1116) or the American Association of Retired Persons' Legal Counsel for the Elderly (☎202–434–2120). Or, call your state agency on aging or county department of human services. Be sure to check referrals out with the Better Business Bureau or the Chamber of Commerce, for example, and look for managers or volunteers with some professional financial experience.

EXPERT SOURCES

NOT SHY ABOUT HELPING YOU RETIRE

Even though some of these organizations are after your business, their pamphlets, books, and retirement kits can be helpful as you devise a retirement strategy. Many are free.

■ **THE DREYFUS PERSONAL RETIREMENT PLANNER**
Dreyfus Investments
☎800–443–9794

■ **RETIREMENT PLANNING GUIDE**
Fidelity Investments
☎800–544–4774

■ **RETIREMENT PLANNING GUIDE KIT**
T. Rowe Price. (A software version costs $15.)
☎800–541–6066

■ **ANNUITIES: BUILDING YOUR RETIREMENT NEST EGG**
National Association of Life Underwriters
☎202–331–6000

■ **PLANNING YOUR RETIREMENT: A SINGLE PERSON'S GUIDE TO RETIREMENT PLANNING**
American Association of Retired Persons
✉AARP Fulfillment–EE0996
601 E St., N.W.
Washington, D.C. 20049

■ **VANGUARD RETIREMENT PLANNER**
Vanguard Group. (A hardcover book or software kit. Each costs $15 plus $2.50 shipping.)
☎800–933–1970

■ **THE CONSUMER'S GUIDE TO MEDICARE AND SUPPLEMENT INSURANCE** *and*
■ **CONSUMER'S GUIDE TO LONG-TERM CARE INSURANCE**
The Health Insurance Association of America
☎202–824–1600

■ **UNDERSTANDING SOCIAL SECURITY**
Social Security Administration
☎800–772–1213

REAL ESTATE

HOMEBUYER'S MARKET: The top 134 markets, PAGE 63 **MORTGAGES:** Should you buy or rent? PAGE 65 **EXPERT LIST:** Which mortgage is for you? PAGE 67 **EXPERT TIPS:** What lenders want to know, PAGE 71 **REFINANCING:** When to trade in a mortgage, PAGE 74 **HOME INSURANCE:** Covering the cost of your prized possessions, PAGE 75 **VACATION HOMES:** The hot markets, PAGE 77 **FORECLOSURES:** Houses for bargain-basement prices, PAGE 78

PRICES

HOW MUCH IS YOUR HOME WORTH?

Our expert says the value of your humble abode should appreciate

The good old days of solid housing profits are long gone. In fact, the heady '80s may have been an aberration. For some time now, home prices have done little more than march to the tune of the inflation rate. Over the past five years, inflation has averaged 3.1 percent a year, while the median increase in home sale prices during that time was 3.2 percent annually, according to Regional Financial Associates, a West Chester, Pa., economic consulting firm.

Fortunately, the picture for the rest of the century is slightly rosier, says David Lereah, chief economist for the Mortgage Bankers Association. Lereah expects home price increases to edge out the inflation rate by nearly a percentage point. Of course, housing demand and prices vary from region to region, but the combination of low interest rates and modest inflation that Lereah foresees should gladden the hearts of nearly all. Sellers can expect some gains, however humble. Low rates will spur buyers and those sitting on the sidelines to make purchases. And homeowners will take advantage of low rates to refinance or borrow to fund home renovations.

Here's what Lereah sees in his crystal ball for the near future:

■ What's the outlook for home sales and prices?

Pretty favorable. Beyond 1996, we'll continue to have numbers due to baby boomers, immigration patterns, and minority growth. Sales of new and existing homes will be healthy and home price increases should outpace the projected inflation rate for the foreseeable future. The most important factor is the economy. I believe we'll see low interest rates and low inflation for the rest of the decade, creating a favorable backdrop for housing.

■ Do you see any downturn looming?

There will be a slight downturn when we have a recession, which could come in 1997 or 1998, although that's anybody's guess. A recession will bring down consumer confidence and slow home buying, but even then, I foresee only a temporary adjustment, thanks to all the other favorable factors.

■ How low will mortgage rates go and which types of mortgages will be most popular?

I believe we'll see a 6.25 percent rate on a 30-year fixed mortgage sometime into 1997. As long as interest rates are low, the 30-year fixed mortgage will always be the popular choice.

HOW MUCH A MONTH?

Homebuying costs in major markets

The average monthly payment (including taxes and insurance)

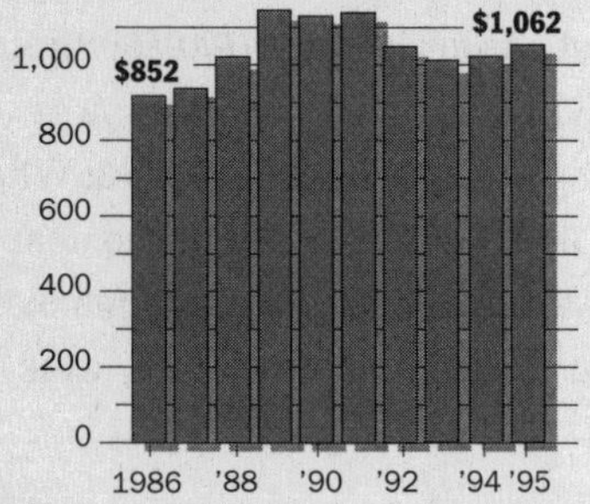

HOW MUCH DOWN?

Initial outlay for a house in major market

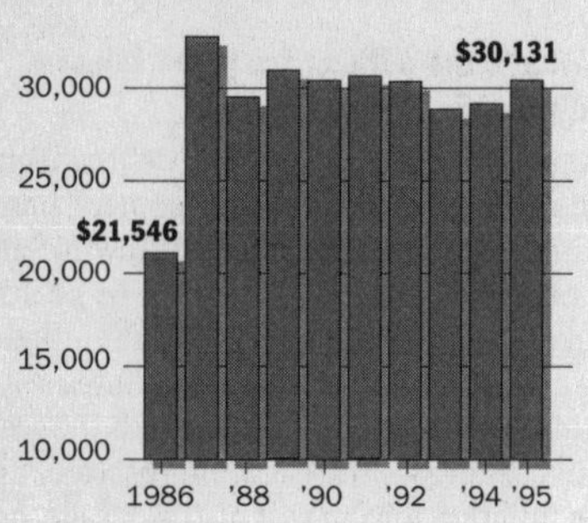

ROLLER-COASTER RATES

Average mortgage interest rates

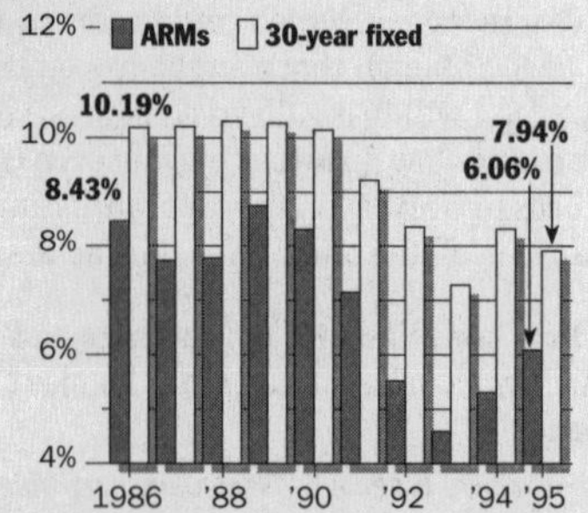

SOURCES: Monthly payment and initial outlay from Chicago Title and Trust Co.; mortgage rates from Mortgage Bankers Association of America.

The 15-year fixed mortgage also gains in popularity as rates fall. Adjustable rate mortgages (ARMS) will lose their popularity; interest rates are just too low.

When is it a good time to refinance?

When it comes to refinancing, the rule of thumb is: If you're paying more than one point over the current mortgage interest rate, start calling lenders.

Will the future be kind to first-time buyers?

Yes. Low interest rates bring in first-time buyers and all the new types of people, immigrants and minorities, coming into the home market. Asians and Hispanics will help lift prices because they are the populations growing at rapid paces. Lenders are reaching out to minorities and low-income groups, and that means we'll have greater demand for starter homes. This will be a major force for the remainder of the decade.

What's in the cards for trade-up homes?

If the economy continues to expand, the trade-up market will be healthy. I believe the market will stay healthy for the rest of the decade except for a short recessionary period. Higher-priced homes may see some depression in prices further down the line because baby boomers may find it hard to sell their four-bedroom, three-bath suburban houses.

How are baby boomers affecting the real estate market?

Baby boomers are aging, and we're finding that when they age they increase their housing consumption. They will continue to buy homes at a more rapid pace until age 72.

The good news is they'll continue to buy homes in places like Florida or Arizona. People also start to save, invest, and bring down their debt at age 45, which is the age that baby boomers are entering. We'll see an increase in home-buying during the next decade but a decrease in mortgage volume because they won't have to take out a mortgage to buy smaller homes at lower prices. Growth of mortgage debt will come down, and the rate of home sales will go up.

HOMEBUYER'S GUIDE

THE TOP 134 HOUSING MARKETS

Ever-lower mortgage rates are expected to boost the median price of existing homes nationwide to $117,300 in 1996, up from $112,900 in 1995. Home prices rose everywhere except in the Northeast in 1995, where they fell 1.6 percent to a median price of $136,900. Homeowners in the Midwest saw the value of their homestead rise the most: 6.5 percent to $93,600. The market rankings cover median prices for single-family detached and attached existing homes.

Metropolitan area	1995	% change from '94
1. Salt Lake City–Ogden, Utah	$113,700	16.0
2. Detroit, Mich.	$98,200	12.9
3. Nashville, Tenn.	$107,300	11.2
4. Amarillo, Texas	$71,000	10.1
5. Colorado Springs, Colo.	$114,700	10.1
6. Kalamazoo, Mich.	$82,200	9.9
7. Portland, Ore.	$128,400	9.8
8. Omaha, Neb.	$83,000	9.8
9. Baton Rouge, La.	$84,600	9.3
10. Raleigh–Durham, N.C.	$125,900	9.3
11. Eugene–Springfield, Ore.	$104,900	9.0
12. Denver, Colo.	$127,300	9.0
13. Akron, Ohio	$92,100	8.5
14. Canton, Ohio	$84,000	8.4
15. Richmond–Petersburg, Va.	$103,100	8.1
16. Topeka, Kan.	$68,200	7.7
17. Sarasota, Fla.	$104,500	7.7
18. Lincoln, Neb.	$82,500	7.7
19. Mobile, Ala.	$75,100	7.4
20. Louisville, Ky.	$86,400	7.3
21. Springfield, Mo.	$78,300	7.3
22. Champaign, Ill.	$79,400	7.2
23. Davenport, Iowa	$66,200	7.1
24. South Bend/Mishawaka, Ind.	$69,300	7.1
25. Chattanooga, Tenn.	$82,800	6.8
26. Fargo, N.D.	$82,900	6.8
27. Des Moines, Iowa	$87,000	6.5
28. Waterloo/Cedar Falls, Iowa	$56,500	6.4
29. Albuquerque, N.M.	$117,000	6.4
30. Cleveland, Ohio	$104,700	6.3
31. Gainesville, Fla.	$89,900	6.3
32. Greensboro/Winst. Salem, N.C.	$102,500	6.1
33. Tulsa, Okla.	$78,500	5.9
34. Phoenix, Ariz.	$96,800	5.9
35. Aurora–Elgin, Ill.	$131,600	5.8
36. Greenville–Spartanburg, S.C.	$92,400	5.7
37. Lansing.–E. Lansing, Mich.	$79,800	5.7
38. Appleton, Wis.	$85,100	5.6
39. Oklahoma City, Okla.	$70,400	5.5
40. Austin/San Marcos, Texas	$101,400	5.4

A DECADE-LONG LOOK AT HOUSING PRICES

In 1995, the average price gain was a flimsy 1.7 percent—due in part to buyers settling for less-expensive homes. Here's a look at average home prices in major markets:

SOURCE: Chicago Title and Trust Co.

■ HOMEBUYER'S GUIDE

Metropolitan area	1995	% change from '94
41. Tucson, Ariz.	$100,500	5.3
42. Little Rock–N. Little Rock, Ark.	$79,000	5.3
43. Kansas City, Mo.	$91,700	5.3
44. Saginaw–Bay City–Midland, Mich.	$62,000	5.3
45. Milwaukee, Wis.	$114,700	5.2
46. Minneapolis–St. Paul, Minn.	$106,800	5.2
47. Toledo, Ohio	$77,600	5.1
48. Sioux Falls, S.D.	$84,200	5.1
49. Columbia, S.C.	$91,800	5.1
50. Gary–Hammond, Ind.	$91,600	5.0
51. Knoxville, Tenn.	$93,600	4.9
52. Dayton–Springfield, Ohio	$88,300	4.9
53. Grand Rapids, Mich.	$80,600	4.8
54. Corpus Christi, Texas	$77,600	4.7
55. Columbus, Ohio	$99,100	4.5
56. Montgomery, Ala.	$85,800	4.4
57. Springfield, Ill.	$79,100	4.4
58. Indianapolis, Ind.	$94,600	4.3
59. Lake County, Ill.	$136,200	4.1
60. Cedar Rapids, Iowa	$86,200	4.1
61. Atlanta, Ga.	$97,400	4.1
62. Pensacola, Fla.	$79,500	4.1
63. Cincinnati, Ohio	$100,400	4.0
64. Spokane, Wash.	$98,400	4.0
65. Charleston, W.V.	$81,700	3.9
66. Wichita, Kan.	$76,500	3.8
67. Miami, Fla.	$107,100	3.8
68. Lexington–Fayette, Ky.	$90,880	3.8
69. Madison, Wis.	$120,000	3.4
70. Birmingham, Ala.	$103,600	3.4
71. Green Bay, Wis.	$89,500	3.3
72. San Antonio, Texas	$80,800	3.3
73. Shreveport, La.	$72,500	3.3
74. Peoria, Ill.	$70,100	3.2
75. Ocala, Fla.	$61,400	3.2
76. St. Louis, Mo.	$87,700	3.2
77. W. Palm Bch.–Boca Raton, Fla.	$121,300	3.1
78. Biloxi–Gulfport, Miss.	$73,100	3.1
79. Rockford, Ill.	$87,500	3.1
80. Bradenton, Fla.	$91,000	3.1
81. Youngstown–Warren, Ohio	$65,000	3.0
82. Charleston, S.C.	$94,300	2.9
83. Tampa–St. Pete–Clearwater, Fla.	$78,300	2.8
84. Ft. Lauderdale–Hollywood, Fla.	$105,900	2.7
85. Las Vegas, Nev.	$113,500	2.7
86. Reno, Nev.	$137,100	2.6
87. Chicago, Ill.	$147,800	2.6
88. Tacoma, Wash.	$121,400	2.1
89. Tallahassee, Fla.	$99,000	2.0
90. Seattle, Wash.	$159,000	2.0
91. Mel.–Titusville–Palm Bay, Fla.	$78,200	2.0
92. Pittsburgh, Pa.	$82,100	1.7
93. Dallas, Texas	$96,400	1.5
94. Jacksonville, Fla.	$83,100	1.5
95. Ft. Worth–Arlington, Texas	$83,700	1.5
96. New Orleans, La.	$78,000	1.4
97. Daytona Beach, Fla.	$69,600	.9
98. Charlotte–Gast.–Rock Hill, N.C.	$107,200	.7
99. Middlesex–Hunterdon, N.J.	$171,400	.4
100. Memphis, Tenn.	$86,500	.2
101. Monmouth–Ocean, N.J.	$137,200	.1
102. Boise, Idaho	$98,900	–.1
103. Ft. Myers–Cape Coral, Fla.	$77,700	–.1
104. Boston, Mass.	$179,000	–.2
105. Worcester, Mass.	$130,100	–.4
106. San Francisco, Calif.	$254,400	–.5
107. Atlantic City, N.J.	$107,000	–.6
108. Philadelphia, Pa.	$118,700	–.7
109. Providence, R.I.	$115,800	–.7
110. Rochester, N.Y.	$85,000	–.7
111. Washington, D.C.–Md.–Va.	$156,600	–.8
112. Springfield, Mass.	$106,700	–.9
113. Anaheim–Santa Ana, Calif.	$208,800	–1.0
114. Newark, N.J.	$185,100	–1.2
115. Buffalo–Niagara Fallls, N.Y.	$81,300	–1.2
116. Bergen–Passaic, N.J.	$189,700	–1.6
117. Houston, Texas	$79,200	–1.6
118. Orlando, Fla.	$89,200	–1.7
119. Trenton, N.J.	$129,000	–1.8
120. New York City–North N.J.–Long Is., N.Y.	$169,700	–2.0
121. Syracuse, N.Y.	$81,200	–2.3
122. San Diego, Calif.	$171,600	–2.5
123. Nassau–Suffolk, N.Y.	$155,300	–2.5
124. Hartford, Conn.	$129,400	–3.0
125. Honolulu, Hawaii	$349,000	–3.1
126. El Paso, Texas	$72,900	–3.2
127. New Haven–Meriden, Conn.	$135,100	–3.2
128. Beaumont, Texas	$62,800	–3.4
129. Sacramento, Calif.	$120,200	–3.5
130. Baltimore, Md.	$111,300	–3.6
131. Los Angeles–Long Beach, Calif.	$179,900	–4.9
132. Albany–Schenectady–Troy, N.Y.	$105,900	–5.4
133. Riverside–S. Bernardino, Calif.	$120,900	–6.4
134. Richland/Kenn./Pasco, Wash.	$100,900	–9.3

SOURCE: National Association of Realtors®.

MORTGAGES

SHOULD YOU RENT OR BUY A HOME?

A formula for the biggest investment decision you're likely to make

It's often difficult to remember that buying a home is an investment fraught with some of the risks of Wall Street. And much as you might wish to own a place of your own, you might feel somewhat better about parting with your hard-earned down payment if you were convinced that you were making a savvy investment. A quick rule of thumb: You can assume you're probably better off renting if you do not itemize deductions on your tax returns or if you plan to move in a few years.

Gaylon Greer, professor of real estate at the University of Memphis, has devised a more sophisticated formula by adapting for potential homeowners a calculation used to decide whether to rent or buy. Keep in mind that Greer's calculation only considers the financial aspects of the decision. Here's how it works:

Consider the hypothetical predicament of Tracy and Jeff Summers, who are renting an apartment in Chicago for $1,200 a month. They are considering buying a similar-sized home for $200,000 and plan to live in the house for seven years.

■ **STEP 1:** Figure out the yearly financial cost for each scenario. For renting, that would be the Summers's annual rent of $14,400. For buying, it would be the after-tax costs of mortgage payments, property taxes, and maintenance.

Greer suggests estimating the annual maintenance costs at about 1 percent of the

■ WHERE BUYING BEATS RENTING

A deep dip in mortgage rates, along with higher rents, has made owning a house cheaper than renting for the first time in recent years.

In 38 of the 74 most populous metro areas, it is now less expensive to own a four-bedroom house than to rent a two-bedroom luxury apartment, according to a study by the E & Y Kenneth Leventhal Real Estate Group in 1995. When the firm measured housing affordability in early 1994, renting was cheaper in most of the markets. Another finding: The most affordable housing can be found in Tornado Alley, or the area running from north of Texas to Missouri. In most of the West Coast, however, housing costs remain sky-high.

This table shows the percentage of median household income that goes toward paying housing costs—mortgage and rent—in the most affordable and least affordable areas across the country.

Metropolitan area	Single-family home costs*	Rental costs*
THE TEN MOST AFFORDABLE HOUSING MARKETS		
1. Dallas–Ft. Worth, Texas	16.5%	19.1%
2. Houston, Texas	18.6	18.2
3. Indianapolis, Ind.	19.0	20.1
4. Kansas City, Mo.	18.4	20.9
5. Oklahoma City, Okla.	19.2	20.0
6. Richmond, Va.	19.7	20.2
7. Louisville, Ky.	19.8	20.0
8. Jacksonville, Fla.	18.3	22.3
9. Central N.J.	23.0	17.8
10. St. Louis, Mo.	19.4	22.6
THE TEN LEAST AFFORDABLE HOUSING MARKETS		
1. San Francisco, Calif.	63.0	35.5
2. Honolulu, Hawaii	60.6	37.1
3. New York, N.Y.	49.3	33.3
4. Los Angeles, Calif.	51.8	29.6
5. Oakland–East Bay, Calif.	40.8	28.7
6. San Diego, Calif.	36.0	30.8
7. Boston, Mass.	39.7	26.8
8. Tucson, Ariz.	28.7	33.4
9. Sarasota-Bradenton, Fla.	33.3	28.8
10. San Jose, Calif.	34.1	27.3

*As a percentage of disposable median household income.

SOURCE: E&Y Kenneth Leventhal Real Estate Group

house's value for a new home. For an older house, he suggests up to 3 or 4 percent. The local tax assessor can give you property tax rates.

The Summerses estimated spending about $2,000 a year on maintenance and paying $8,000 in property taxes. Their yearly mortgage payments come to approximately $16,000, assuming a $180,000 mortgage at 8.1 percent. However, the total yearly cost of buying is brought down substantially once you factor in the fact that property tax and mortgage payments are mostly tax-deductible. Since the Chicago couple falls into the 39.6 percent income tax bracket, they can roughly estimate that the government pays that percentage of their costs. Therefore their total yearly costs for buying would be $16,000.

■ **STEP 2:** Figure how much you stand to recoup when you sell your house. You should expect anywhere from 8 to 10 percent of the final value to be consumed by transaction costs, such as brokerage and legal fees. After subtracting their transaction costs, the Summers estimate getting $290,000 for their house after living there for seven years. And they will still owe about $165,000 on their mortgage, so after taxes their net gain will be approximately $90,000.

■ **STEP 3:** Estimate how much you might make if you had invested your money in something other than a home—such as corporate or municipal bonds, or shares of corporate stock. You can use the table on this page to give you the value today of a dollar available at various points in the future. The table is based on an 8 percent rate of return on high-grade corporate bonds. This number can change—if it does you can use a present value table found in any finance book.

Each number corresponds to a year, so for year one, the factor will be .9259. Multiply that number by the annual cost of $16,000 to get a "present value equivalent" for the first year cost of ownership. Continue with similar calculations for each year you plan to live in the house. At the end you will add what you can expect to recoup from selling the house and the down payment. You should end up with something like this. Parentheses indicate negative numbers, or costs.

Year	(Cost) or benefit	Factor	Present value equivalent
1	($16,000)	.9259	($14,814.40)
2	($16,000)	.8573	($13,716.80)
3	($16,000)	.7983	($12,772.80)
4	($16,000)	.7350	($11,760.00)
5	($16,000)	.6806	($10,889.60)
6	($16,000)	.6502	($10,403.20)
7	($16,000)	.5835	($9,336.00)
7*	$90,000	.5835	$52,515.00
Present value equivalent (Total)			**($31,177.80)**
Include:			
Down payment to buy			**($20,000.00)**
Net present value equivalent			**($51,177.80)**

* Sold in seventh year.

■ **STEP 4:** Go through the same calculation for renting—minus the down payment and net gain from selling. The lower cost is the best financial option.

Year	(Cost) or benefit	Factor	Present value equivalent
1	($16,000)	.9259	($14,814.40)
1	($14,400)	.9259	($13,332.96)
2	($14,400)	.8573	($12,345.12)
3	($14,400)	.7983	($11,495.52)
4	($14,400)	.7350	($10,584.00)
5	($14,400)	.6806	($9,800.64)
6	($14,400)	.6502	($9,362.88)
7	($14,400)	.5835	($8,402.40)
Present value equivalent (Total)			**($75,323.52)**

The bottom line for the Summerses: They should buy the house. Figuring the present value of their money, they will come out ahead by over $20,000 if they go ahead and purchase the home.

Of course, even if the result favors renting, you might still decide to buy the house you saw because it has such a lovely view from the kitchen window. That's simply a different definition of present value.

EXPERT LIST

WHICH MORTGAGE IS FOR YOU?

It's hard to keep track of all the different kinds of mortgages currently being offered, much less choose the one that's the best deal for you. Here's an explanation of some of the most popular varieties, adapted from The Mortgage Money Guide, *published by the Federal Trade Commission, along with the pros and cons of each and some expert tips.*

FIXED-RATE MORTGAGE

Fixed interest rate, usually long term; equal monthly payments of principal and interest until debt is paid.

■ **PROS:** Offers some stability and long-term tax advantages.

■ **CONS:** Interest rates may be higher than other types of financing. New fixed rates are rarely assumable.

■ **EXPERT TIP:** Can be a good financing method, if you are in a high tax bracket and need the interest deductions.

FIFTEEN-YEAR MORTGAGE

Fixed interest rate. Requires down payment or monthly payments higher than 30-year loan. Loan is fully repaid over 15-year term.

■ **PROS:** Frequently offered at slightly reduced interest rate. Offers faster accumulation of equity than traditional fixed-rate mortgage.

■ **CONS:** Has higher monthly payments. Involves paying less interest but this may result in fewer tax deductions.

■ **EXPERT TIP:** If you can afford the higher payments, this plan will save you interest and help you build equity and own your home faster.

■ IT'S HARDER THE FIRST TIME

With lower mortgage rates, first-time homebuyers can afford more expensive houses. The National Association of Realtors' first-time home buyer index shows the ablity of renters who are prime potential first-time buyers to qualify for a mortgage on a starter home. When the index equals 100, the typical first-time buyer can afford the typical starter home under existing financial conditions with a 10 percent down payment. The first-time buyer median income represents the typical income of a renter family with wage earners between the ages of 25 and 44 years. The 1995 first-time buyer index shows that the qualifying income needed for conventional financing on a $96,000 starter home was $30,720. Yet the median income of prime first-time buyers was $24,637, leaving an average shortfall of $6,083. As a result, a typical first-time buyer could only afford a home costing $80,000 or so, some $16,000 less than the cost of the average starter home.

FIRST-TIME BUYERS AFFORDABILITY INDEX

YEAR	Starter home price	Loan	Mortgage rate	Monthly payment	Payment as % of income	Prime first-time median income	Qualifying income	Index
1991	$85,300	$76,770	9.30%	$648	33.3%	$23,345	$31,120	75.0
1992	$88,100	$79,290	8.11%	$602	30.6%	$23,625	$28,887	81.8
1993	$90,800	$81,720	7.16%	$566	28.9%	$23,475	$27,186	86.4
1994	$93,300	$83,970	7.47%	$600	29.8%	$24,154	$28,792	83.9
1995	$96,000	$86,400	7.85%	$640	31.1%	$24,637	$30,720	80.2

Source: National Association of Realtors.

■ EXPERT LIST

ADJUSTABLE RATE MORTGAGE

Interest rate changes over the life of the loan, resulting in possible changes in your monthly payments, loan term, and/or principal. Some plans have rate or payment caps.

■ **PROS:** Starting interest rate is slightly below market. Payment caps prevent wide fluctuations in payments. Rate caps limit amount total debt can expand.

■ **CONS:** Payments can increase sharply and frequently if index increases. Payment caps can result in negative amortization.

■ **EXPERT TIP:** Remember that if your payment-capped loan results in monthly payments that are lower than your interest rate would require, you still owe the difference.

RENEGOTIABLE RATE MORTGAGE

Interest rate and monthly payments are constant for several years; changes possible thereafter. Long-term mortgage.

■ **PROS:** Less frequent changes in interest rates offer some stability.

■ **CONS:** May have to renegotiate when rates are higher.

BALLOON MORTGAGE

Monthly payments based on fixed interest rate; usually short term; payments may cover interest only with principal due in full at end of term.

■ **PROS:** Offers low monthly payments.

■ **CONS:** Possibly no equity until loan is fully paid. When due, loan must be paid off or refinanced. Refinancing poses high risk if rates climb.

■ **EXPERT TIP:** Some lenders guarantee refinancing when the balloon payment is due, although they do not guarantee a certain interest rate.

GRADUATED PAYMENT MORTGAGE

Lower monthly payments rise gradually (usually over 5 or 10 years), then level off for duration of term. With adjustable interest rate, additional payment changes possible if index changes.

■ **PROS:** Easier to qualify for.

■ HOW MUCH INCOME YOU NEED TO GET A MORTGAGE

Figures are based on a 30-year loan and assume a down payment of 20 percent of purchase price.

Interest rate	$50,000 loan	$75,000 loan	$100,000 loan	$150,000 loan	$200,000 loan	$250,000 loan
6%	$16,754	$25,131	$33,508	$50,261	$67,015	$83,769
6.5%	$17,451	$26,176	$34,901	$52,352	$69,802	$87,253
7%	$18,163	$27,244	$36,325	$54,488	$72,651	$90,814
7.5%	$18,889	$28,334	$37,779	$56,668	$75,558	$94,447
8%	$19,630	$29,445	$39,260	$58,889	$78,519	$98,149
8.5%	$20,383	$30,574	$40,766	$61,149	$81,532	$101,915
9%	$21,148	$31,722	$42,296	$63,444	$84,593	$105,741
9.5%	$21,925	$32,887	$43,849	$65,774	$87,698	$109,623
10%	$22,711	$34,067	$45,423	$68,134	$90,845	$113,557
10.5%	$23,508	$35,262	$47,016	$70,523	$94,031	$117,539
11%	$24,313	$36,470	$48,626	$72,940	$97,253	$121,566
11.5%	$25,127	$37,690	$50,254	$75,380	$100,507	$125,634

NOTE: Calculations assume property taxes equal 1.5 percent of purchase price and hazard insurance costs 0.25 percent of purchase price.

SOURCE: Fannie Mae.

■ EXPERT LIST

■ **CONS:** Buyer's income must be able to keep pace with scheduled payment increases. With an adjustable rate, payment increases beyond the graduated payments can result in additional negative amortization.

SHARED APPRECIATION MORTGAGE

Below-market interest rate and lower monthly payments, in exchange for a share of profits when property is sold or on a specified date. Many variations.

■ **PROS:** Low interest rate and low payments.

■ **CONS:** If home appreciates greatly, total cost of loan jumps. If home fails to appreciate, projected increase in value may still be due, requiring refinancing at possibly higher rates.

■ **EXPERT TIP:** You may be liable for the dollar amount of the property's appreciation even if you do not wish to sell at the agreed-upon date. Unless you have the cash available, this could force an early sale of the property.

ASSUMABLE MORTGAGE

Buyer takes over seller's original, below-market rate mortgage.

■ **PROS:** Lower monthly payments.

■ **CONS:** May be prohibited if "due on sale" clause is in original mortgage. Not permitted on most new fixed-rate mortgages.

■ **EXPERT TIP:** Many mortgages are no longer legally assumable. Be especially careful if you are considering a mortgage represented as "assumable."

SELLER TAKE-BACK

Seller provides all or part of financing with a first or second mortgage.

■ **PROS:** May offer a below-market interest rate.

■ **CONS:** May have a balloon payment requiring full payment in a few years or refinancing at market rates, which could sharply increase debt.

■ **EXPERT TIP:** If an institutional lender arranges the loan, uses standardized forms, and meets certain other requirements, the owner take-back can be sold immediately to Fannie Mae. This enables seller to obtain equity promptly.

■ PAYMENTS MONTH-BY-MONTH

The following chart shows the maximum monthly amount you could spend for home payments and total monthly credit obligations at a variety of income levels and meet the guidelines required by most lenders. As a rule of thumb, no more than 28 percent of your gross monthly income should be used for your mortgage payment (principal, interest, taxes, insurance, condo fees, owners association fee, mortgage insurance premium) and no more than 36 percent of your gross monthly income should be going toward your mortgage payment plus all other monthly credit obligations (car loans, credit cards, utility payments).

Your gross annual income	Monthly mortgage payments	Maximum monthly credit obligations
$20,000	$467	$600
$30,000	$700	$900
$40,000	$933	$1,200
$50,000	$1,167	$1,500
$60,000	$1,400	$1,800
$70,000	$1,633	$2,100
$80,000	$1,867	$2,400
$90,000	$2,100	$2,700
$100,000	$2,333	$3,000
$130,000	$3,033	$3,900
$150,000	$3,500	$4,500
$200,000	$4,667	$6,000

SOURCE: *Unraveling the Mortgage Loan Mystery,* Federal National Mortgage Association.

■ EXPERT LIST

WRAPAROUND

Seller keeps original low-rate mortgage. Buyer makes payments to seller, who forwards a portion to the lender holding original mortgage.

■ **PROS:** Offers lower effective interest rate on total transaction.

■ **CONS:** Lender may call in old mortgage and require higher rate. If buyer defaults, seller must take legal action to collect debt.

■ **EXPERT TIP:** Wraparounds may cause problems if the original lender or the holder of the original mortgage is not aware of the new mortgage. Some lenders or holders may have the right to insist that the old mortgage be paid off immediately.

GROWING EQUITY MORTGAGE

Rapid payoff mortgage. Fixed interest rate but monthly payments may vary according to agreed-upon schedule or index.

■ **PROS:** Permits rapid payoff of debt because payment increases reduce principal.

■ **CONS:** Buyer's income must be able to keep up with payment increases. Does not offer long-term tax deductions.

LAND CONTRACT

Seller retains original mortgage. No transfer of title until loan is fully paid. Equal monthly payments based on below-market interest rate with unpaid principal due at loan end.

■ **PROS:** Payments figured on below-market interest rate.

■ **CONS:** May offer no equity until loan is fully paid. Buyer has little protection if conflict arises during loan.

■ **EXPERT TIP:** Land contracts are being used to avoid the "due on sale" clause. The buyer and seller may assert to the lender who provided the original mortgage that the clause does not apply because the property will not be sold to the end of the contract. Therefore, the low interest rate continues.

BUY-DOWN

Developer (or other party) provides an interest subsidy that lowers monthly payments during the first few years of the loan. Can have fixed or adjustable interest rate.

■ **PROS:** Offers a break from higher payments during early years. Enables buyer with lower income to qualify.

■ **CONS:** With adjustable rate mortgage, payments may jump substantially at end of subsidy. Developer may increase selling price.

■ **EXPERT TIP:** Consider what your payments will be after the first few years. They could jump considerably. Also check to see whether the subsidy is part of your contract with the lender or with the builder. If it's provided separately with the builder, the lender can still hold you liable for the full interest rate.

RENT WITH OPTION

Renter pays "option fee" for right to purchase property at specified time and agreed-upon price. Rent may or may not be applied to sales price.

■ **PROS:** Enables renter to buy time to obtain down payment and decide whether to purchase. Locks in price during inflationary times.

■ **CONS:** Payment of option fee. Failure to take option means loss of option fee and rental payments.

REVERSE ANNUITY MORTGAGE

Equity conversion. Borrower owns mortgage-free property and needs income. Lender makes monthly payments to borrower, using property as collateral.

■ **PROS:** Can provide homeowners with needed cash.

■ **CONS:** At end of term, borrower must have money available to avoid selling property or refinancing.

■ **EXPERT TIP:** You can't obtain a RAM until you have paid off your original mortgage.

SOURCE: *The Mortgage Money Guide*, Federal Trade Commission.

EXPERT TIPS

WHAT LENDERS WANT TO KNOW

You can speed up the loan application process by having the right information with you when you meet with your mortgage lender. Here—from the Federal National Mortgage Association, the government-chartered company otherwise known as Fannie Mae that buys mortgages from 3,000 lenders nationwide—are some of the things lenders look for:

■ **PURCHASE AGREEMENT/SALES CONTRACT:** Outlines the terms and conditions of the sale.

■ **YOUR ADDRESSES:** All from last seven years.

■ **EMPLOYMENT INFORMATION:** Name, address, and phone number of all employers for the past seven years.

■ **SOURCES OF INCOME:** Two recent pay stubs and your W-2 forms for the previous two years. Verification of income from social security, pension, interest or dividends, rental income, child support, and alimony may also be needed.

■ **CURRENT ASSETS:** The balance, account number, name and address of financial institutions for your savings, checking, and investment accounts. Recent statements should suffice. Real estate and personal property can also be listed on your application as assets. Bring an estimate of market value.

■ **CURRENT DEBTS:** Names and addresses of all creditors plus account numbers, current balances, and monthly payments. Recent bank statements may be required.

■ **SOURCE OF DOWN PAYMENT**. May be savings, stocks, investments, sale of other property, or life insurance policies. May also be from relatives if money doesn't have to be repaid.

■ DOES YOUR MORTGAGE LENDER MAKE THE GRADE?

The best lenders help you refinance when rates fall. The following mortgage originators came out on top in a consumer survey done in 1995 by DALBAR Inc., a Boston research firm. Customers chose them as providers of the best service after the mortgage was granted. What makes the lenders stand out? Their willingness to provide refinancing when interest rates fall and help in special situations such as a sudden job loss or the death of a spouse, say satisfied customers.

Customers rated lenders on a scale of 4, very satisfied, 3, satisfied, 2, dissatisfied and 1, very dissatisfied.

RANK	COMPANY	RATING
1.	Source One Mortgage	3.64
2.	Chase Manhattan	3.63
3.	Weyerhauser Mortgage	3.50
4.	Glendale Federal Bank	3.43
5.	BancBoston	3.40
	Marine Midland Bank	3.40
6.	Director's Mortgage	3.38
	Keycorp	3.38
	BancOne	3.38
7.	American Savings Bank	3.33
	Barclays American	3.33
	Great Western Bank	3.33
8.	Countrywide Mortgage	3.31
9.	Home Savings	3.29
	Security Pacific Housing	3.29
10.	G.E. Capital	3.25

HOMEBUYER'S GUIDE

MAKING SENSE OF YOUR MORTGAGE PAYMENTS

These tables show what your monthly payments (principal and interest) will be assuming different interest rates and loan terms. For example, monthly payments for a $90,000, 30-year fixed mortgage at 8 percent would be $660.39. For amounts over $100,000, add the numbers for the amount equal to the amount of mortgage.

AMOUNT	MONTHLY PAYMENTS (principal and interest)					
FINANCED	5 years	10 years	15 years	20 years	25 years	30 years
6% ANNUAL PERCENTAGE RATE						
$25,000	$483.33	$277.56	$210.97	$179.11	$161.08	$149.89
$30,000	$579.99	$333.07	$253.16	$214.93	$193.30	$179.87
$35,000	$676.65	$388.58	$295.35	$250.76	$225.51	$209.85
$40,000	$773.32	$444.09	$337.55	$286.58	$257.73	$239.83
$45,000	$869.98	$499.60	$379.74	$322.40	$289.94	$269.80
$50,000	$966.65	$555.11	$421.93	$358.22	$322.16	$299.78
$60,000	$1,159.97	$666.13	$506.32	$429.86	$386.59	$359.74
$70,000	$1,353.30	$777.15	$590.70	$501.51	$451.02	$419.69
$80,000	$1,546.63	$888.17	$675.09	$573.15	$515.45	$479.65
$90,000	$1,739.96	$999.19	$759.48	$644.79	$579.88	$539.60
$100,000	$1,933.29	$1,110.21	$843.86	$716.44	$644.31	$599.56
7% ANNUAL PERCENTAGE RATE						
$25,000	$493.03	$290.28	$224.71	$193.83	$176.70	$166.33
$30,000	$594.04	$348.33	$269.65	$232.59	$212.04	$199.60
$35,000	$693.05	$406.38	$314.59	$271.36	$247.38	$232.86
$40,000	$792.05	$464.44	$359.54	$310.12	$282.72	$266.13
$45,000	$891.06	$522.49	$404.48	$348.89	$318.06	$299.39
$50,000	$990.06	$580.55	$449.42	$387.65	$353.39	$332.66
$60,000	$1,188.08	$696.66	$539.30	$465.18	$424.07	$399.19
$70,000	$1,386.09	$812.76	$629.18	$542.71	$494.75	$465.72
$80,000	$1,584.10	$928.87	$719.07	$620.24	$565.43	$532.25
$90,000	$1,782.11	$1,044.98	$808.95	$697.77	$636.11	$598.78
$100,000	$1,980.12	$1,161.09	$898.83	$775.30	$706.78	$665.31
8% ANNUAL PERCENTAGE RATE						
$25,000	$506.91	$303.32	$238.91	$209.11	$192.95	$183.44
$30,000	$608.29	$363.98	$286.70	$250.93	$231.54	$220.13
$35,000	$709.67	$424.65	$334.48	$292.75	$270.14	$256.82
$40,000	$811.06	$485.31	$382.26	$334.58	$308.73	$293.51
$45,000	$912.44	$545.97	$430.04	$376.40	$347.32	$330.19
$50,000	$1,013.82	$606.64	$477.83	$418.22	$385.91	$366.88
$60,000	$1,216.58	$727.97	$573.39	$501.86	$463.09	$440.26
$70,000	$1,419.35	$849.29	$668.96	$585.51	$540.27	$513.64

■ HOMEBUYER'S GUIDE

AMOUNT FINANCED	MONTHLY PAYMENTS (principal and interest) 5 years	10 years	15 years	20 years	25 years	30 years
$80,000	$1,622.11	$970.62	$764.52	$669.15	$617.45	$587.01
$90,000	$1,824.88	$1,091.95	$860.09	$752.80	$694.63	$660.39
$100,000	$2,027.64	$1,213.28	$955.65	$836.44	$771.82	$733.76
9% ANNUAL PERCENTAGE RATE						
$25,000	$518.96	$316.69	$253.57	$224.93	$209.80	$201.16
$30,000	$622.75	$380.03	$304.28	$269.92	$251.76	$241.39
$35,000	$726.54	$443.36	$354.99	$314.90	$293.72	$281.62
$40,000	$830.33	$506.70	$405.71	$359.89	$335.68	$321.85
$45,000	$934.13	$570.04	$456.42	$404.88	$377.64	$362.08
$50,000	$1,037.92	$633.38	$507.13	$449.86	$419.60	$402.31
$60,000	$1,245.50	$760.05	$608.56	$539.84	$503.52	$482.77
$70,000	$1,453.08	$886.73	$709.99	$629.81	$587.44	$563.24
$80,000	$1,660.67	$1,013.41	$811.41	$719.78	$671.36	$643.70
$90,000	$1,868.25	$1,140.08	$912.84	$803.75	$755.28	$724.16
$100,000	$2,075.84	$1,266.76	$1,014.27	$899.73	$839.20	$804.62
10% ANNUAL PERCENTAGE RATE						
$25,000	$531.18	$330.38	$268.65	$241.26	$227.18	$219.39
$30,000	$637.41	$396.45	$322.38	$289.51	$272.61	$263.27
$35,000	$743.65	$462.53	$376.11	$337.76	$318.05	$307.15
$40,000	$849.88	$528.60	$429.84	$386.01	$363.48	$351.03
$45,000	$956.12	$594.68	$483.57	$434.26	$408.92	$394.91
$50,000	$1,062.35	$660.75	$537.30	$482.51	$454.35	$438.79
$60,000	$1,274.82	$792.90	$644.76	$579.01	$545.22	$526.54
$70,000	$1,487.29	$925.06	$752.22	$675.52	$636.09	$614.30
$80,000	$1,699.76	$1,057.20	$859.68	$772.02	$726.96	$702.06
$90,000	$1,912.23	$1,189.36	$967.14	$868.52	$817.83	$789.81
$100,000	$2,124.70	$1,321.51	$1,074.61	$965.02	$908.70	$877.57
11% ANNUAL PERCENTAGE RATE						
$25,000	$543.56	$344.38	$284.15	$258.05	$245.03	$238.08
$30,000	$652.27	$413.25	$340.98	$309.66	$294.03	$285.70
$35,000	$760.98	$482.13	$397.81	$361.27	$343.04	$333.31
$40,000	$869.70	$551.00	$454.64	$412.88	$392.05	$380.93
$45,000	$978.41	$619.88	$511.47	$464.48	$441.05	$428.55
$50,000	$1,087.12	$688.75	$568.30	$516.09	$490.06	$476.16
$60,000	$1,304.54	$826.50	$681.96	$619.31	$588.07	$571.39
$70,000	$1,521.97	$964.25	$795.62	$722.53	$686.08	$666.63
$80,000	$1,739.39	$1,102.00	$909.28	$825.75	$784.09	$761.86
$90,000	$1,956.81	$1,239.75	$1,022.94	$928.97	$882.10	$857.09
$100,000	$2,174.24	$1,377.50	$1,136.60	$1,032.19	$980.11	$952.32

SOURCE: *The Mortgage Money Guide,* Federal Trade Commission.

REFINANCING

WHEN TO TRADE IN A MORTGAGE

The right answer may be a lot sooner than you think. Here's why

The conventional wisdom is that interest rates have to drop 2 percent to make refinancing attractive. The conventional wisdom may be wrong. In fact, if you're planning to live in your house for many years, refinancing to a lower rate by as little as 1 percent can be profitable.

For a typical mortgage that involves refinancing costs of 1 percent of the total loan, the accounting firm of Ernst & Young figures that, if you can lower your interest rate by a single percentage point, the new loan will put you ahead after just 18 months.

FACT FILE:

MONEY IN THE BANK?

■ *Payments and savings on a $100,000 mortgage refinanced to 7 percent.*

Current rate	Current monthly payment	Monthly savings at 7%	Annual savings at 7%
8.0%	$734	$69	$828
8.5%	$769	$104	$1,248
9.0%	$805	$140	$1,680
9.5%	$841	$176	$2,112
10.0%	$878	$213	$2,556
10.5%	$915	$250	$3,000
11.0%	$952	$287	$3,444
11.5%	$990	$325	$3,900
12.0%	$1,029	$364	$4,368
12.5%	$1,067	$402	$4,824
13.0%	$1,106	$441	$5,292

SOURCE: Mortgage Bankers Association of America.

Refinancing can give you other opportunities—like switching from a 30-year fixed mortgage to 15 years. The switch usually bumps up your monthly payments, but it will also reduce the overall cost of your loan, and the interest rate you pay will generally be about a half percentage point lower than a 30-year mortgage. Another benefit: You build up more equity in your home that you can tap into later. Recent data show that a third of the holders of 30-year mortgages choose 15-year loans when they refinance.

That may not be a good decision, though. For example: If you get a $150,000, 30-year mortgage at 7.3 percent, you will pay $229,208 in interest over the life of the loan. A 15-year mortgage at 6.8 percent would cost less than half that—$89,612. The difference in monthly payments is $304—$1,028 for the 30-year mortgage versus $1,332 for the 15-year mortgage.

But suppose you opt for the 30-year loan and invest the $304 difference in the stock market, where it earns 7 percent after tax. (The historic return on stocks is about 10 percent before taxes.) And suppose you also invest the extra tax savings generated by the longer-term loan. Since the loan amortizes more slowly than a 15-year mortgage, more of your monthly payment is tax-deductible interest. After 10 years, the 30-year loan looks like a much better deal. By the end of 15 years, the holder of the 30-year loan would have earned enough on his investment to pay off the remaining debt on the house and still have some $10,000 left.

After choosing a mortgage, you'll have to decide about refinancing costs: covering them at the outset by paying points or spreading them over the life of the loan by accepting a slightly higher interest rate. In most cases, you should opt for not paying points. By investing the money you would have paid in points, you can build up a tidy nest egg over the life of your mortgage, which should amount to more than you'd save if you paid the points and invested the amount you saved in lower interest costs. The bottom line: the best mortgage for you will be the one whose term most closely matches the time you expect to keep your house.

INSURANCE

THE PERILS OF OWNING A HOME

Standard policies often don't cover the possessions you prize the most

If you're a proud homeowner, of course you need home insurance (see "How to Buy What You Really Need," page 124). And you may be able to cut your premium significantly by taking advantage of the discounts insurers offer (see the table below).

But that doesn't mean that you're sufficiently covered. For example, your policy may cover jewelry up to a specified amount against certain named "perils," but if your necklace is stolen and "theft" is not one of the named perils, you're out of luck—unless you have a rider, an extra piece of insurance that covers special property in special circumstances. If you own any of the following items, you might consider adding a rider to your policy:

■ **JEWELRY**. Many basic insurance policies exclude theft from named perils when it comes to jewelry and limit coverage to a maximum payout of $1,500. A jewelry rider—also known as a "personal articles policy"—should itemize each piece of jewelry insured, including its appraised value.

■ **SILVERWARE.** Silverware is generally covered for everything but theft and is usually limited to $2,500 worth of coverage.

■ **ORIENTAL RUGS.** Standard homeowner policies limit the reimbursement for damage to $5,000 on any one rug and $10,000 total.

■ **ART OR ANTIQUES.** Basic policies usually limit contents coverage to 50 percent to 75 percent of the face value of your homeowner's policy.

■ **COMPUTER GEAR.** Your homeowner's policy may not cover the full cost of tech stuff, particularly if you have a home office. It should cost $50 to $100 to increase coverage to $10,000 from the standard $2,500 for office equipment.

■ DISCOUNTS FOR HOME INSURANCE

Some 20 million homeowners can cut their home insurance bills by up to 50 percent or more, say experts, yet many are unaware they may qualify for discounts. Most insurers, for example, will shave your premium if you let them know you've installed or upgraded a home security system. To find out what you qualify for, call your insurance carrier and ask.

TYPE OF DISCOUNT[1]	STATE FARM	ALLSTATE	AMEX	AMICA	AETNA	USAA[3]
New Home	20%	25%	15%	20%	20%	20%
Less than 7 years old	3%	6%	2%	10%	12%	8%–18%
Less than 10 years old	NONE	NONE	NONE	4%	9%	2%–6%
Less than 12 years old	NONE	NONE	NONE	NONE	3%	NONE
Central alarm	15%	10%	15%	5%	20%	15%
Fire/smoke alarm	4%	3%	15%	2%	7%	2%
Sprinklers	10%	10%	NONE	13%	7%	8%
Home/auto combination	NONE	5%	15%	NONE	5%	NONE
Renovations	NONE	25%	15%	NONE	NONE	NONE
Retirees	NONE	10%	NONE	NONE	NONE	NONE
Customer for 3+ years	5%	NONE	NONE	NONE	5%	NONE
Customer for 6+ years	10%	NONE	NONE	NONE	NONE	NONE
$1,000 deductible[2]	24%–33%	21%	25%	19%	22%	30%–32%

NOTES: **1.** Type and amount of discount may vary from state to state. **2.** Standard deductible ranges from $100 to $250. **3.** Eligibility restricted to present and former U.S. military officers and their families. SOURCE: Company reports.

VACATION HOMES

HEADING FOR THE HILLS

Forget bigger digs, boomers are nudging prices up on second homes

Baby boomers have pretty much settled into their primary homes, but they won't sit still for long. A study by the American Resort Development Association in 1995 found that 35 percent of those polled believed there was a good chance that they'd buy vacation property within the next decade. Only 16 percent had a similar response in 1990. The group most likely to buy a second home—35- to 54-year-olds with no kids at home—could double by the year 2000, according to *American Demographics* magazine.

With boomers set to charge into the vacation home market, prices of second homes could nudge upward, says Karl Case, a principal in the Cambridge, Mass., real estate research firm Case Shiller Weiss. That bodes well for early birds who get into the market now. We asked Case to give us the lowdown on the second-home market:

■ What should a buyer consider when looking for a vacation home?

A buyer should look at a vacation home as an investment and a consumer durable good. Often buyers focus on the investment part and forget that the most important part is the actual benefits you get from living in or using the home. Of course, the home should be located at a spot where the buyer wants to spend a lot of time. The buyer should also be sure that he or she has the time to use it.

■ Is a second home a good investment?

Remember that the return on your investment includes your use of the home or renting it out. The biggest mistake people make is buying property that sits vacant 10 months of the year. Letting a vacation home sit idle is like running a factory at less than capacity. Of course, a buyer wants to buy a home in an improving market. But picking markets is like picking stocks: The ones we know are good are already expensive and the ones that aren't so strong are less expensive. Occasionally, you can find an underpriced market because of regional economic conditions. Property in Crested Butte, Colo., for example, was inexpensive after the oil debacle in Texas in the 80's, when many owners were forced to sell. Opportunities like that are rare, though. Often, property a little off the beaten track in an area is usually significantly less expensive. If it's in a growing area, off the beaten track can become the beaten track.

■ What areas of the country are appealing in terms of affordable vacation homes?

Look at the regional economic trends. Vacationers in the Northeast tend to favor spots like Cape Cod, Maine, or Vermont. When the Northeast economy is performing poorly, those areas tend to depreciate. As the economy bounces back, the areas recover, as they are now doing. Right now, southern California is doing poorly and the Midwest and Mountain States are doing well. There are probably good opportunities in the spots where southern Californians normally vacation. Investing in property in the upper Midwest a few years ago would have produced a good return.

■ What's the future for vacation-home prices?

Vacation-home prices will move upward as baby boomers enter their prime earning years. They are facing low interest rates and a peaking stock market. Boomers are also about to receive a substantial transfer of wealth from their parents. Many of the boomers have equity built up in their first homes. Diversifying into real estate is likely to be an attractive alternative for them. That combination of factors bodes well for the second home market generally.

■ What's the most valuable tip you would give someone looking for a second home?

Love it before you buy it. Use it and take care of it.

HOMEBUYER'S GUIDE

THE HOT VACATION HOME MARKETS

The following vacation spots won out in a survey of more than 170 second-home markets around the country. Conducted by the CENTURY 21® real estate system, the survey studied factors such as home price appreciation between 1994 and 1995, the availability of the widest range of recreational opportunities (beach access, fishing, golfing, camping, etc.), and proximity to urban areas. Some spots fared better than others in individual factors. Brainerd, Minn., for example, was tops in the lifestyle category, while Houghton, Minn., stood out for its affordability. More vacation home shoppers are buying with the intention of using the retreat as a retirement home (see "Plan to retire" in the table below). Indeed, in some areas such as Durango, Colo., and Cape May, N.J., 50 percent of buyers had retirement in mind.

Location	Avg. price[1]	1994–1995 increase	Plan to retire	Nearest city	Dist. from nearest city (miles)
WEST					
Madras, Ore.	$85,000	9%	NA[2]	Bend, Ore.	45
McCall, Idaho	130,000	8%	30%	Boise, Idaho.	90
Durango, Colo.	150,000	3%	50%	Farmington, N.M.	45
Lake Tahoe, Calif.	200,000	0%	10%	Reno, Nev.	60
Twain Harte, Calif.	129,500	0%	50%	Modesto, Calif.	64
MIDWEST					
Sturgeon Bay, Wisc.	90,000	13%	10%	Green Bay, Wisc.	45
Brainerd, Minn.	127,000	NA	20%	St. Cloud, Minn.	65
Nashville, Ind.	89,000	5%	30%	Bloomington, Ind.	15
Detroit Lakes, Minn.	60,000	5%	20%	Fargo, N.D.	45
Houghton, Mich.	45,000	0%	25%	Marquette, Mich.	100
Lake James, Ind.	275,000	20%	20%	Ft. Wayne, Ind.	45
SOUTH					
South Hill, Va.	125,000	2%	30%	Richmond, Va.	90
Ocean City, Md.	150,000	0%	15%	Salisbury, Md.	30
Lake Marion, S.C.	150,000	0%	50%	Columbia, S.C.	60
Clayton, Ga.	90,000	0%	50%	Gainesville, Ga.	50
Emerald Isle, N.C.	150,000	11%	25%	Jacksonville, N.C.	30
NORTHEAST					
Lower Cape May, N.J.	92,500	0%	50%	Atlantic City, N.J.	35
Bridgewater, N.H.	100,000	2%	10%	Concord, N.H.	30
Monticello, N.Y.	85,000	0%	10%	Middletown, N.Y.	20
Sandwich, Mass.	135,000	0%	35%	Boston, Mass.	65
Lake of the Pines, Pa.	110,000	-6%	20%	Stroudsburg, Pa.	12

NOTES: **1** Average price for a 1,500 sq. foot home **2** NA (not available) SOURCE: Century 21 Real Estate Corp.

FORECLOSURES

HOUSES ON THE CHEAP

Well, somebody has to buy these thousands of troubled properties

To many people, buyers of foreclosed properties are like vultures descending on luckless prey. But somebody has to buy the thousands of troubled properties on the market each year, and the plucky, patient buyers who survive the process are often rewarded.

The best time to close in on a troubled property is after the foreclosure process has been completed and the house is in the hands of the lender, says Ted Dallow, author of *How to Buy Foreclosed Real Estate for a Fraction of Its Value* (Adams Publishing, 1991). Such properties are called OREs, or owned real estate. By taking this route, rather than buying directly from the owner of a property in the foreclosure process, you'll eliminate surprises—such as tax liens on a house whose owner hasn't paid property taxes. Lenders are also usually anxious to unload the properties—on which they have to pay taxes and other expenses—and will chip away at prices.

Government agencies, such as the Veterans Administration and the Federal Housing Administration, and mortgage providers like Fannie Mae and Freddie Mac, have loads of foreclosed properties on their hands. The FHA alone forecloses on nearly 30,000 properties a year. The agencies advertise in the real estate section of local newspapers, running long lists of available properties. Fannie Mae (☎ 800–732–6643) will send you a list of its foreclosed properties. You can also locate foreclosed properties from real estate agencies, which often represent FHA and VA properties. Or, advises Dallow, go to local banks and talk with the officer in charge of foreclosure.

Once you spot a good prospect, try to find out how long the lender has held it, which will give you an idea of how eager he is to unload it. Then bargain hard to bring down the price, interest rate financing, and closing costs.

A PIECE OF THE DESERT AND A BURRO TO BOOT

Those newspaper ads touting sales of cheap public land are come-ons. Homesteading laws were repealed in 1976. Occasionally, though, the Interior Department's Bureau of Land Management (☎202–452–7780) sells off parcels of land considered to be "excess" public acreage.

■ Most of the land is in 11 western states, although there are some scattered parcels in the East. You can buy a few acres or several thousand.

■ Don't expect dirt cheap prices; the government can't accept offers below fair market value.

■ Dreaming of digs in the desert? You can buy up to 320 acres of arid or semiarid land—but you'll have to install an irrigation system, which could run $250,000 or more.

■ Sales are usually held at a site near the property, but you don't have to be present to make an offer. You can send a sealed bid. After the bid is accepted, it will probably take a year or two before you get title to your property.

■ Want your own wild horse or burro? Some 7,000 wild horses and 750 burros are put up for sale each year by the BLM. A horse goes for $125; burros are a steal at $75. A bonus: If the mare or jenny you buy has an unweaned foal, you get the offspring for free.

COLLECTING

ANTIQUES: How to tell if furniture is authentic, PAGE 82 **SILVER:** The allure of the old, PAGE 84 **AUCTIONS:** The Jackie O premium, PAGE 86 **EXPERT PICKS:** Collectibles that won't break the bank, PAGE 87 **FLEA MARKETS:** An expert's tips on how to shop for bargains, PAGE 89 **GEMS:** Everything you'll need to know to pick the best ring, PAGE 90 **COINS:** Why you shouldn't collect money to make money, PAGE 92

TRENDS

THE FINE ART OF ART COLLECTING

After the '80s boom and '90s bust, old and new masters are affordable

The art market boom of the '80s turned into a bust in the early '90s, but signs abound that the market has bounced back. At Christie's, for example, art sales rose more than 20 percent in 1995. And galleries are opening, not shuttering doors. "It's not yet a boom," says James Goodman, owner of New York's Goodman Gallery and president of the American Art Dealers Association, "but the market is healthy again."

What has emerged, however, is a different landscape, and to get a handle on the changes we canvassed some movers and shakers in the art world. Here's the scene they sketched.

PAINTINGS BY THE NUMBERS

When it comes to art sales, it's the megamillion-dollar paintings that grab the headlines, such as a Vincent Van Gogh that sold for $82.5 million a few years back.

But art is not just for the super rich. Even those with modest purses can be collectors. The average price for all art sold at auction in 1994 was $8,200, according to *Art & Auction* magazine. Considering that many pieces sold for multimillions, that means many works are going for way under $8,200.

In fact, quality art from rising stars, or prints by established favorites like Roy Lichtenstein or Jasper Johns, can be had for a few thousand dollars or under. Even lesser-known masters are within reach: A painting by Domenico Maria Fratta, an 18th-century artist, for example, recently sold at Christie's for $1,560.

Whatever you buy, cautions Christie's managing director Patricia Hambrecht, who collects 19th- and 20th-century drawings, "Buy the best quality you can afford. Ideally, you'll want to own something fresh to the market. But you should also love it."

EXPERT QUOTE

"Art is something to collect because it adds to your enjoyment of life and it adds to your aesthetic and spiritual life. But it won't line your pocketbook."

—*Bonnie Stretch, managing editor of* ARTnewsletter

WHY ANDY WARHOL'S NOT HOT

Impressionist art and some contemporary works have survived the recent shakeout, although they are generally commanding lower prices than during the go-go '80s. On the other hand, prices of more recent modern pieces, such as Andy Warhol's, are lagging behind the market's recovery. In the heady '80s, frenzied buyers gobbled up abstract art that made social statements and stretched the limits of abstraction. Many collectors today don't want to be challenged by the art on their walls, says Edward Boyer, a New York art dealer: "What sells mostly is a comforting realism—works that are pretty, realistic, and more decorative than complex."

A tepid market is a bargain market, of course, and contrarian investors may see this as a good time to buy quality abstract art. "It may be undervalued now," says Boyer, "but it will eventually bounce back when people rediscover art-for-art's sake."

ART VS. STOCKS

Most art forms defy financial analysis because each work is highly individual. However, in his book, *Art Auction Trends* (Connemara-Coleman, 1992), James Coleman suggests that a wily art investor can beat the market. Coleman compared the investment value of selected artists' works to the consumer price index and the Standard & Poor's 500. Between 1971 and 1991, 68 percent of the artists studied by Coleman kept pace with inflation and 54 percent outperformed the S&P 500.

EXPERT SOURCES

There are dozens of publications available that track trends and gossip. Among them:

ARTnewsletter ☎ **212-398-1690**
Eye on Art ☎ **212-877-5117**
Print Collector's Newsletter ☎ **212-988-5959**
Baer Faxt ☎ **212-260-1372**

When it comes to liquidity, art is not the best asset to own, unless you want to take an immediate loss. With stocks and bonds, for example, you pay a 1 or 2 percent commission when you buy or sell. With a work of art you have to pay 20 percent or more on each end, so the art has to increase in value at least 40 percent before you begin to realize a penny of profit.

THE FINE PRINT ON PRINTS

The uniformity of prints, which are generally created in batches of 50 or 100, allows some financial comparison. A 1993 study by James Pesando, a University of Toronto economist, analyzed the sales between 1977 and 1992 of 27,961 prints by 28 modern artists, including Picasso and Matisse. The results: Those who invest in prints are in for a wild ride. Annual returns swung from a disastrous -35.34 percent a year to a robust 47.18 percent. In fact, similar prints that sold within a few weeks of each other varied in price by as much as 30 percent. The overall picture was discouraging. The mean return for the prints was 1.51 percent a year, whereas a low-risk government bond would have gotten you a 2.54 percent return.

Print collectors face another obstacle. Art dealers sometimes use terms loosely, so clarifying terms can help prevent ripoffs. An "original," for example, can refer not only to the artist's actual original piece but also to any lithograph or serigraph that is part of a limited edition signed and numbered by the artist. (A lithograph is a print made through a process in which ink is applied on a smooth stone or plate. A serigraph is a print made by pressing pigments through a silk screen with a stencil design.) "Limited edition" simply means that the number of pieces issued has been limited. The question, of course, is limited to what? Fifty, 500, or 5,000? The fewer the number, the more valuable the piece. Only a handful of states, among them New York and California, require dealers to indicate the size and year of their limited-edition prints.

ART FOR ART'S SAKE

The consensus: Don't buy art solely as an

EXPERT SOURCES

HOW MUCH IS THAT MASTERPIECE IN THE WINDOW?

Collectors can save a bundle if they know the financials on a piece of fine art, say, or the going rate for antiques and collectibles. Surfing the Web, collectors can find everything from price guides for paintings to who craves your old cookie jar. There are dozens of online art and antique trading networks and bulletin boards. We've sifted through scores of services online—they seem to come and go daily. The following have shown some staying power.

ANTIQUE & COLLECTIBLE EXCHANGE
http://www.worldint.com/ace
■ The original online marketplace for antiques and collectibles
■ **Cost to sellers:** $195 per year for unlimited advertising, including color photos.
☎800-643-2204

ANTIQUE NETWORKING
http://www.smartpages.com/antique
■ Online database
■ **Cost:** $4.95 per search; 50 searches for $25
☎800-400-8674

ARTNET AUCTIONS PRICES ON-LINE
http://www.artnet.com
■ Everything there is to know about the fine arts market
■ **Cost:** Free software. Searches cost $1.75 per minute, reduced rates after the first hour.
☎800-4-ARTNET

CHRISTIE'S
http://www.christies.com
■ Online auction catalogs, schedules and highlights of sales
■ **Cost:** Free
☎212-546-1000

COLLECTOR'S ATLAS
http://www.worldint.com/atlas
■ Guide to art, antiques and collectibles worldwide, or in your own hometown
■ **Cost to sellers:** $45 to $300 to advertise
☎800-643-2204

COLLECTOR ONLINE
http://www.collectoronline.com/collect
■ Want ads, an auction calendar, and an antiques mall that shows inventory for sale
■ **Cost for buy/sell ads:** $10 per two weeks with photo
☎800-546-2941

COLLECTOR'S SUPERMALL
http://www.csmonline.com
■ *Antique Trader* magazine's Web site for antiques and collectibles
■ **Cost for ads:** $5 and up
☎800-364-5593

INTELLASEARCH
http://www.intellasearch.com
■ Online marketplace for antiques and other collectibles
■ **Cost:** $13 per month plus $25 to $45 for software
☎800-947-5390

SOTHEBY'S
http://www.sothebys.com
■ Auction calendar, tips on collecting items the house sells, and information about artists
■ **Cost:** Free
☎212-606-7000

investment. Burton Fredericksen, senior research curator of the J. Paul Getty Museum, who is writing a history of art collecting, believes that the works of perhaps only two artists, Leonardo da Vinci and Raphael, have held consistent price values over the past 500 years. Even an artist with the stature of Rembrandt has seen ups and downs. Moreover, the art that's esteemed and coveted today may end up in tomorrow's trash heap. Two highly sought artists of the 19th century, for example, were David Teniers and George Morland, now virtually unknown. Whether Picasso or Andy Warhol, say, will follow them into oblivion is anyone's guess.

ANTIQUES

SIZING UP AN HEIRLOOM

Examine the finish, hardware, feet, and even the smell, says our expert

How can a casual buyer tell if that attractive antique chest is genuine, a reproduction, a mongrel, or a fake? Sam Pennington, editor of *Maine Antique Digest* (☎800–752–8521), says when you're trying to determine whether an antique is authentic, you should examine several things: finish, backboard, drawers, hardware, and feet. "Sometimes, even smell will help," says Pennington. "You shouldn't detect any oil or paint-type odor, which suggests the piece has been recently worked on. Good, early, untouched furniture gives off a wonderful nutty smell from inside the drawers. Once you smell it, you never forget it." Here are Pennington's tips on sizing up an antique chest, bed, mirror, and chair from the 18th to early 19th century.

CHEST OF DRAWERS

■ In American chests, backboards generally tell you a lot. Look at the back carefully. It's usually made of pine and should be well darkened with age and exposure to air and dirt.

■ The older or earlier the finish, the better. A piece should not be refinished or painted. It should have a uniform patina and age to it.

■ Pull out the drawers. Dovetails—a special type of tongue-in-groove joint—on drawers are important. They should be hand done. Often cabinet makers would number the drawers in pencil and the numbers are sometimes still visible. There should be no shellac or finish on the inside of the drawers. Glue or black gunk is a sign of repair. The color of the wood inside the drawers should vary. The bottom drawer should be darker in the front and lighter to the rear. The bottom of the bottom drawer should be darkest of all—it gets more exposure. The middle drawers, which get less exposure to light, shouldn't show as much darkness as the bottom drawer.

■ Look at the hardware. Is there an extra set of holes? Then the original hardware has probably been replaced.

■ Check out the feet. Do they look as old as the chest? If the feet have been replaced, the price of the piece goes way down.

ANTIQUE BED

■ Tastes in beds have changed over the years and many antique beds have been altered to changing tastes. As a result, beds don't bring a lot of money.

■ There were no king-size beds 100 years ago, of course, so if the bed's been used, the rails will probably have been lengthened. Another compromise you may have to accept is the addition of box spring holders.

■ Look at the legs. Most early beds were too high for modern tastes and people have cut off the legs.

■ Beds should be made of all hard woods, such as mahogany, maple, cherry, walnut, or birch. The main things to look for in the wood are signs of smeared stain or wood that doesn't match.

■ Antique beds should have hand-fashioned bedbolts holding them together.

■ If it's a tall poster bed, look for the original tester (pronounced "teester"), the framework that holds the cloth canopy over the bed.

■ If there is carving on the bed, be sure it's consistent with the bed's style and period.

ANTIQUE MIRROR

■ The nicest thing to find in a mirror is a label. Labeled furniture is rare but you find more labels on mirrors than on any other

HOW TO RECOGNIZE FAMOUS NAME ANTIQUES

English designers Thomas Chippendale, George Hepplewhite, and Thomas Sheraton helped make the 18th century the golden age of furniture.

CHIPPENDALE 1750–1785

■ **CHAIR.** S-shaped curved legs and ball-and-claw feet. Back is fiddle-shaped with decorative carvings.

■ **CHEST.** Rococo carving often used. Big brass pulls on drawers. Legs curved, ball-and-claw feet common.

■ **MIRROR.** Frames made of thinly cut mahogany and often feature elaborate, pierced-scroll fretwork.

HEPPLEWHITE 1785–1810

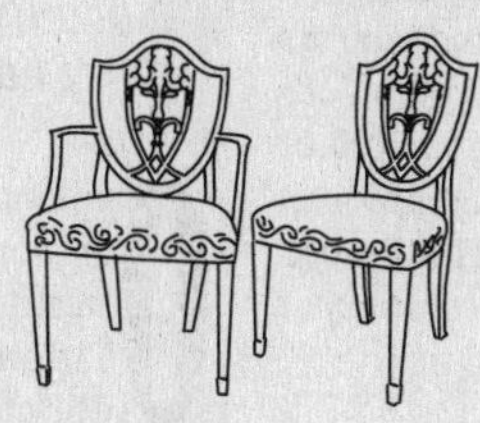

■ **CHAIR.** Distinctive shield-shaped chair backs. Legs usually tapered, with spade feet.

■ **CHEST.** Usually made of fancy woods, often with inlays. Feet curve outward. Oval brass drawer pulls.

■ **MIRROR.** Frames are elaborate and heavily gilt. Typical design features a floral urn atop an oval inlay.

SHERATON 1790–1830

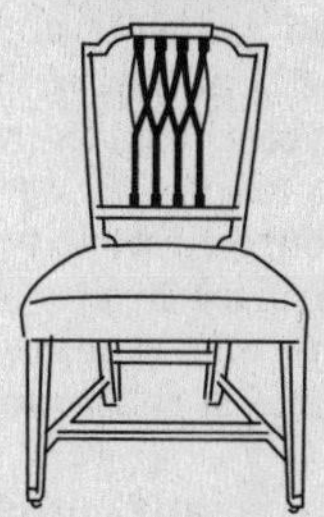

■ **CHAIR.** Thin, tapered legs. Brass castors under feet. Chair backs usually square or rectangular.

■ **TABLE.** Typically drum-shaped. Curved and fluted legs. Top often covered with leather.

■ **TESTER CANOPY BED.** Foot and head posts usually lightly tapered. Edge of headboard arched or flat.

antique. It's nice to know who made the piece and it helps date it.

■ If the mirror was made before 1830, the back shouldn't have circular saw marks on it. It should have plane marks instead.

■ Look for major replacements. Curlicues, or ears, on a mirror often break and get replaced. A number of those round mirrors have eagles or gilded work on them—it's hard to tell if they were made in 1820 or 1920—but you want to look for obvious changes in the finish or breaks in the design. The early ones were made of gesso, plaster with gold leaf rubbed on to it.

■ If it's an early mirror, the glass will be wavy. You'll see some breaks in the reflectivity. More likely, though, the glass has been replaced. I'd rather have the original glass, if possible.

ANTIQUE CHAIR

■ A really early chair may have sat in a cellar or on a dirt floor and part of its feet may have rotted away. Look for replacement of the bottom three or four inches of the legs, which seriously lessens the value.

■ If the chair is upholstered, try to see the frame under the upholstery. See if it's the original frame and that no one has put in a bigger wing than was there, for example. Be very careful if it's the original upholstery; that makes the chair worth a lot more. You don't see much original upholstery anymore.

■ Beware of a chair that has screws in it. The chair will be unstable because screws don't hold well in wood under the stress of a chair.

■ A Windsor chair with its original paint is more valuable than if it's been stripped down. In a Windsor chair, the legs are generally made of maple or birch, the seat is usually pine, the spindles and back are hickory or ash, and the arms might be oak. So, to get a uniform color, Windsor chairs were painted. Collectors are really after a Windsor with the original paint.

HEIRLOOMS

THE ALLURE OF OLD SILVER

Not only is used stuff better, you don't have to fork over a fortune

Opulence doesn't come cheap. Setting a dinner table for four with sparkling sterling silverware by top names like Tiffany, Georg Jensen, Gorham, or Christofle can set newlyweds or anyone else back about $3,000. One five-piece place setting of Jensen's popular Pyramid pattern, for example, goes for about $750.

There is a way to slice the price of silver: Buy it secondhand. Even aside from cheaper prices, says Connie McNally, managing editor of *Silver* magazine, "It's always best to buy silver on the secondary market because older silver is heavier and much better crafted than today's silver."

Auction houses are a good source for used silver. Big New York auction houses like Christie's and Sotheby's put silver on the block a few times each year, and many smaller houses across the country also hold silver auctions occasionally. All kinds of patterns go up for auction, says McNally. You can get a few pieces, or complete sets of silverware for 12, 18, or 24.

Buyers at auction pay a buyer's premium, usually an additional 15 percent above the purchase price. Even with the premium, though, the final cost is generally below retail. Tiffany's popular Take The Wave Edge pattern, for example, sells at retail for about $485 a place setting, or $97 a piece. At a recent Christie's auction a service of 110 pieces sold for $5,520—or $51 a piece—including the premium. Sotheby's silver auctions often include Georg Jensen's Acorn pattern, a current favorite, for about $50 a piece. One piece of Acorn sells for $200 or so at retail.

Many novices shy away from auctions but they shouldn't. Nearly half the participants at silver auctions are amateurs. Dealers tend to keep their distance because the going auction prices may be a steal for consumers but they don't give dealers much room to turn around and sell the silver at a profit.

Another source for discount silver: dealers who specialize in secondhand and antique silver. You can find them at antique malls, flea markets, and in shops devoted solely to buying and selling silver at off-prices. Silver dealers are particularly good if you want to locate an odd piece or two to fill out your set, although chances of finding an entire set of the pattern you want are somewhat slim. If you're buying a complete set of silverware from a dealer, he may hesitate to reveal if it was assembled from a variety of sources. Be sure to inspect the pieces carefully to see if they are true matches and in comparable condition.

Specialized publications are another way to shop for silver for less. Magazines like *Silver* (☎ 619–756–1054), *Maine Antique Digest* (☎ 800–752–8521), and *Antiques and the Arts Weekly* (☎ 203–426–3141) run ads regularly from silver dealers, listing available patterns and prices. Or you can contact the dealers and request a search for pieces in your pattern.

A cautionary note from McNally: Buy from a reputable source and check silver carefully. Sometimes monograms, or initials of former owners, are removed from old silver, a process that can alter part of the pattern and remove some silver as well. One tell-tale sign is a dip or hollow area where the monogram used to be.

SILVER MARKS: LOOK FOR A LION OR A KING

Silver can be easily altered or imprinted with a phoney hallmark, so it pays to know your silver. Sterling silverware is made by mixing pure silver with copper or some other alloy to make it harder and more durable. Three grades of silver are commonly used: Sterling, which is 925 parts per 1,000 pure silver; English, at 975; and European Continental, at 800. To identify silver flatware, turn the piece over. You may need a magnifying glass to decipher the markings on the back.

Before 1860, American silversmiths marked their wares on the back with their initials or full name. Silver made in America after 1860 is marked with the word "sterling." Sometimes there may also be initials or a silver maker's identification. For example, the markings for American Gorham are a lion, an anchor, a "G" and the word "sterling."

British silver has a complete set of hallmarks, including when and where it was made. Look for a king's or queen's head, a lion, or a leopard, among assorted other markings. A lion signifies that the piece is sterling silver. A leopard's head means it was made in London. A king's or queen's head indicates that the piece was made during the reign of the monarch depicted. There are often other marks as well, which can be identified by referring to one of the many tomes on silver markings, such as *The Book of Old Silver* (Crown Publishers, 1937; available in libraries) by Seymour B. Wyler, the definitive source for silver marks.

The marking on European Continental silver is "800," the designation for Continental-grade silver. Russian pieces are engraved with an "840." Pieces with no markings are either silver plate or some other alloy. Silver plating, which began on a large scale in the 19th century, consists of a metal base with a thin silver coating, usually applied by electroplating. Silver plated ware sells for about one-third the price of sterling.

AUCTIONS

THE JACKIE O PREMIUM

Her knickknacks fetched a First Lady's ransom. Will the values last?

An old French schoolbook fetches $37,000. Four worthless cookie jars go for $12,000. What's going on? These are not your garden variety garage sale knickknacks. The textbook is signed by Jacqueline Bouvier (later Kennedy Onassis); the jars held sweets for pop artist Andy Warhol. And, as auction connoisseurs know, when the rich and famous clean house, even the trash is valuable.

Celebrity and historic significance can drive prices through the roof. Sotheby's 1987 auction of a cache of jewels owned by the Duchess of Windsor was valued at $5 to $7 million. The actual take: More than $50 million. The price of fame was even more astounding at the 1996 Sotheby auction of Jackie Kennedy Onassis memorabilia. Nearly 6,000 items, valued at about $4 million, went on the block. The final take: $34.5 million.

The sales prices estimated by the auction houses are an assessment of fair market value. But those prices don't consider what an object would bring without the cachet of having belonged to someone famous. The Jackie premium, for example, amounted to more than $29 million. In the Kennedy sale, the "multiples," or how many times higher the sales prices were than the estimates, outstripped any known auction, according to Sotheby chairman Diana Brooks.

Objects worn or used often by the famous can fetch the highest premiums. A torn, faded stool with a stained satin cover used in the Kennedy household was valued at $100 or so. Sale price: $33,350. A very used set of John F. Kennedy's MacGregor woods with a scuffed black-and-red golf bag was valued at $700 to $900. Actor Arnold Schwarzenegger, spouse of J.F.K.'s niece, Maria Shriver, grabbed them for $772,500. Art and antique furnishings can incite less fervor: Jackie's signed 1797 painting of a Polish aristocrat by Martin Drolling carried a presale estimate of $80,000 to $120,000. It went for $167,500, not far from its intrinsic value.

Can the other new owners expect to turn a profit on their acquisitions? It's unlikely. The Duchess of Windsor's gold, turquoise, diamond, and amethyst necklace, for instance, sold at auction in 1987 for $605,000. Two years later, it only fetched $154,000. As for the collectors of Kennedy memorabilia, they may have been better off buying on the open market, where prices for Kennedy collectibles have been flat for years. Says Bruce Wolmer, editor-in-chief of *Art & Auction* magazine, "Most of the Kennedy items will probably not hold their value over the long haul. They won't lose it completely; they won't go back to being $150, say. But it will be very hard for people to get back all of what they've spent."

FACT FILE:

THE PRICE OF CELEBRITY

■ *Is charisma contagious? A double dose of famous owners can fetch the highest premiums:*

OBJECT(S) *Why*	VALUE	SOLD FOR
4 Cookie jars *Owned by Andy Warhol*	$20	$12,000
Plastic eye glasses *Belonged to Buddy Holly*	$100	$45,100
Fake pearl necklace *Worn by Jackie Kennedy*	$75	$211,500
20th-century sword *Gift to the Prince of Wales from George V*	$10,000	$1.47 mill.
40-carat Lesotho III diamond ring *Engagement ring Onassis gave to Jackie*	$600,000	$2.58 mill.

SOURCES: Sotheby's, Christie's, Impostor's jewelers, LensCrafters.

EXPERT LIST

COLLECTIBLES THAT WON'T BREAK THE BANK

The law of supply and demand is what drives prices. An exquisite, rare piece is worthless if no one wants it. We asked Donald R. McLaughlin, an antique dealer and president of the World Antique Dealers Association, to pick items worth collecting that cost $500 or less. Before you buy, advises McLaughlin, pick an area and bone up on it by reading and visiting antique shops, auctions, and museums.

1. Glass pieces from the American brilliant period (1880–1905) retain their popularity. Typically the pieces are made of thick, heavy, clear glass and are elaborately worked.

2. American pottery from the Arts and Crafts period (early 1900s) has skyrocketed in value but you can still buy much for under $500. Some of the pottery was made in Ohio by the Rookwood, Weller, and Roseville companies.

3. Heisey glass, made in clear crystal and in a variety of colors, has retained its value. The pieces are signed with a diamond "H" and were made in Newark, Ohio, in the early 1900s to the late 1950s.

4. Victorian jewelry has been popular for some time. Art Deco pieces, including jewelry that uses Bakelite, a heavy and durable plastic, are currently sought after.

5. Shelley bone china from England is a current craze. There are several hundred patterns of the fine bone china. Shelley dates from 1929 and is still made today.

6. Antique dolls—even those from the 40s, 50s, and 60s—have appreciated in value. Black dolls of all periods are also in demand, part of the larger market for black memorabilia.

7. Quality furniture from the 1940s through 1960s. Pieces made especially for Williamsburg, for example, and any good Baker or other high-quality furniture made in Michigan and South Carolina. These will become the Americana of the future.

8. Political memorabilia will always be popular. There's a big market for Civil War flags and Vietnam military items. Royalty memorabilia and coronation items from England, Germany, and Sweden are also sought after.

9. Marbles from the turn of the century through the 1920s and 1940s were made of quality glass. They are hard to find but worth it. Some of the marbles, called sulfides, came with animal figures inside.

10. Toys from the early 1900s. The better condition they're in, the more they'll increase in value. Newer toys should be bought in the original boxes. Banks disguised as ships, cars, horses, and other animals are especially in demand. Mechanical banks usually cost more than $500.

11. Premiums that were given away by companies and radio stations are hot, especially gas station collectibles, such as little Sohio gas company tin banks, and advertising calendars and glasses. Radio premiums offered during old programs like *Orphan Annie* and *Dick Tracy* include badges, belt buckles, and secret decoders. You can sell a good radio premium ring for more than a gold or precious-stone ring.

12. Small silver items, like early silver boxes, and silver made in the South are good choices, as well as ornate silver made by Tiffany, Gorham, and some Chicago silversmiths. Also anything made by the Danish silversmith Georg Jensen, but especially the Acorn pattern, is sought after.

TRENDS

THE BOOM IN BOOMERABILIA

Trolls, smiley faces, and Barbie dolls are in demand

Aging baby boomers are rushing to collect memorabilia that hark back to their salad days. Sociologists say boomers are turning to childhood souvenirs to take the edge off their fast-paced, anxiety-ridden lives. Then again, the trend may be no more than a nod to nostalgia, made affordable by adult salaries. Auction houses like Sotheby's have pushed boomerabilia aggressively. And a magazine has cropped up to cover the market: *Baby Boomer Collectibles* (☎ 800–334–7165; $18.95 for 12 issues). Original 1960s trolls, those cheap, weird plastic figures, are trading for $400 or so. And Pez candy dispensers, first produced in 1952, can fetch up to $2,000.

A few caveats about collecting mass-produced boomerabilia: For one, experts say the market is ripe for a shakeout that will set more realistic values to the goods. In fact, fickle collectors are already shunning old lunch boxes, which were the prized collectibles of the '80s. What's more, prices would dive if, say, caches of original trolls were discovered in a warehouse somewhere. Also, not all original goods are necessarily valuable—any defects slash the object's value significantly. Here's a sampling of hot boomerabilia:

■ **WOODSTOCKIANA.** Vintage mementos from the three-day love fest in August 1969, on a dairy farm in Bethel, New York, is a growing part of the $10 million or so rock-and-roll collecting binge. Fifteen years ago, the original Woodstock posters by Arnold Skolnick went for about $20; today they fetch up to $1,000. In 1993, Sotheby's sold a lot including two Woodstock posters, tickets, and a program for $2,700—more than triple their estimated take.

■ **AQUARIANA.** Dealers say there's a surge of interest in other 1960s souvenirs—mostly plastic knickknacks and doo-dads painted in neon colors. Products emblazoned with the era's ubiquitous, yellow smiley face are hot, as are tie-dyed shirts, crocheted vests, and Vietnam-era peace-sign items. A plastic peace-sign mobile can fetch $50; a cookie jar bidding you to "Have a Nice Day" can go for $100.

■ **HOT WHEELS.** The tiny metal cars sold for a mere 75¢ in the 1970s and now carry suggested prices of up to $2,000 each. The prices of Hot Wheels, put out by Mattel in 1968, are going up faster than older toys, like Lionel trains, says Terry Kovel, co-author of *Kovel's Antiques and Collectibles Price List.* But note that only Hot Wheels in mint condition—no scrapes or wear on the wheels—will bring in top dollar.

■ **BARBIE BONANZA.** Rare, vintage Barbie dolls that kids played with in the 1960s fetch up to $4,000 apiece. Even the more recent models are appreciating fast. We're not talking about the ordinary Barbies that line the aisles of toy stores, but the special collector dolls that Mattel has been making in limited quantities. The first Holiday Barbie doll, for example, introduced in 1988 for about $30, now goes for up to $800. Several publications keep the pulse on the Barbie market: *Miller's Market Report* (☎ 800–874–5201), a monthly newsletter for $24.95; and *Barbie Bazaar* (☎ 414–658–1004) at $26.95 for six issues a year.

■ **PASSION FOR PEZ.** What some people won't do for a Pez—those cheap plastic gizmos that dispense tiny candy bricks from the heads of Bugs Bunny, Minnie Mouse, Fred Flintstone, and others. A few years back, an ad ran in a New Haven, Conn., newspaper offering big money for old Pez dispensers. That night, dozens of rare models disappeared from Pez headquarters near New Haven. The going rate these days for a green-haired Wonder Woman, for example, is $242. Older models go for far more. Several newsletters keep track of Pez happenings. Among them: *Pez Collectors News*, c/o Richard Belyski, PO Box 124, Sea Cliff, N.Y. 11579.

EXPERT TIPS

CONFESSIONS OF A FLEABITTEN JUNKIE

Make a list, pack a lunch, avoid hot collectibles, and always haggle

Flea markets carry something for everyone: affordable antiques, kitschy velvet paintings, new and old clothes, gems and costume jewelry, often plants and produce, and just plain junk. Every size pocketbook is represented—from 25¢ postcards to $2,000 restored Coke machines. The markets attract collectors and treasure hunters of all kinds, including the likes of Barbra Streisand and Michael Jackson, who have been spotted in flea markets from London to Pasadena.

The rules of flea-marketdom are easy. "What's your best price?" is a choice phrase that sellers expect to hear. Regulars don't expect miracle finds every time. They say that most dealers know the value of their goods and how much profit they are willing to forsake. Expert foragers say the best times to pick up bargains are on rainy mornings and late in the day, when dealers may be feeling desperate. Then again, latecomers miss the first pickings.

Mary Randolph Carter is an advertising executive for a tony New York designer during the week. But when the weekend comes she engages in her favorite sport, "junking," scouring flea markets, garage sales, auctions, and junk shops in search of hidden treasures. We asked Carter, author of *American Junk* (Viking Studio Books, 1994), for some tips on how to be a successful flea market forager.

✔ Junking really starts on Friday, when the local newspapers list tag sales, flea markets, and auctions coming up that weekend. I mark the ones that look interesting, cut them out and tape them in my notebooks.

✔ It helps to bring a small magnifying glass to look for chips, cracks, dates, marks, names of artists, and manufacturing trademarks. You should probably bring along a measuring tape, although I don't use one. I use my eye.

✔ For a long day of junking, you don't want to waste time stopping for food. Take along a cooler in the car filled with bottled water, juices, carrot sticks, fruit, and yogurt. You don't have to add junk food to junk hunting.

✔ Making a list of the things you're looking for helps keep you focused, especially if you're going to a huge market or auction.

✔ I prefer junking alone. Going with a friend can be fun, except when you fixate on the same things. Then we have a "who grabs it first gets it" code.

✔ There's a lot of stuff out there for a dollar or two. Take along 20 singles and a few fives or tens. Sometimes you can make a deal by saying, "Gee, I only have five dollars."

✔ Always haggle, unless the item is really cheap. Before I bargain, I accumulate a pile of things I'd like. A dealer is more apt to make a deal on a bunch of things rather than one item.

✔ Paintings are great—they're inexpensive and come in all sizes. It's nice to collect different themes, like dogs or landscapes.

✔ Junk shops are great places. It's more difficult to find great treasures at tag sales, garage sales, and yard sales. They sell mostly utilitarian junk. If you've had a bad day finding what you want at those kinds of sales, hit a good junk shop and get a good fix.

GEMSTONES

BEYOND THE GLITTER

Everything you need to know about choosing the perfect ring

To the Greeks, diamonds were tears of the gods. To the Romans, they were splinters from falling stars. Today, the sparkling chunks of crystallized carbon are not only a girl's best friend but also a $2.6 billion business. More than three-quarters of all first-time brides get diamond engagement rings, according to industry figures. Unfortunately for grooms, tastes in engagement rings change with the wind. The wise groom would do well to keep up if he wants to get off on the right foot.

In the 1980s, the object of many a new bride's desire was a sapphire and diamond ring. The model: a large oval sapphire surrounded by 14 diamonds and set in 18-carat gold that Prince Charles presented to Lady Di when he popped the question. But, like their marriage, that style has hit on hard times. "She's no longer the model brides seek when they go into the state of matrimony," says Eileen Farrell, communications director of the Jewelers of America.

Prospective brides now want rings that bring to mind homier models: their grandmothers. Industry officials say the current rage is antique rings, "retro" styles, and new diamond rings set in platinum—in short, the kind of ring that Grandma wore. Platinum, a highly durable metal that looks like silver but is pricier than both silver and gold, is back with a vengeance. It went out of fashion during World War II, but retailers now say it's the setting of choice for engagement rings and wedding bands.

Shopping for an engagement ring poses a dilemma: Does the groom scour the shops alone and surprise his intended with his choice? Or does he shop with the bride so that she gets what her heart desires? There are no hard answers, but retailers report that more couples comb the stores together, with the groom returning alone to make the purchase.

The average engagement ring costs about $1,600. Getting a good value requires knowing the four C's: cut, clarity, color, and carat weight. The size of the diamond shouldn't be the prime consideration. Size increases the cost of the diamond, but size alone is almost meaningless if the stone is poorly cut, is flawed, or has poor color. Cut is actually most important because it sets apart the dull diamond from a dazzler.

Diamonds come in a variety of cuts, with the round or brilliant cut being the most popular—65 percent of diamonds sold in 1994 were round. Marquise, or a sort of diamond shape, followed at 24 percent and the rest were pear-shaped and assorted other cuts. More than half of engagement rings bought in 1994 were diamond solitaires, that is, unembellished with other gems.

Tiffany's and Cartier's may have a certain cachet, but they don't have a monopoly on fine diamonds. Just shop at a trustworthy jeweler who will be around if there's a problem or if you later decide to restyle the ring. But if it's an investment-quality ring you're after, the ones from the big name stores hold their value best. "Winston, Van Cleef & Arpels and Tiffany signify a certain quality of stones and a certain quality of classic design. People are willing to pay a premium for that," says John Block, jewelry director of Sotheby's New York. Small wonder that flashy real estate magnate Donald Trump presented his betrothed, Marla, with a 7.45-carat flawless, emerald-cut diamond from New York's Harry Winston, Inc.

■ SOME POPULAR CUTS

Brilliant Marquise Pear

Emerald Oval Square

PUTTING A LITTLE SPARKLE IN YOUR LIFE

The value of most gemstones is pretty steady compared to commodities like coffee and gold, changing no more than 10 or 15 percent in a year. But like any commodity, their value is tied to the vagaries of the global marketplace—a mine strike can send prices up just as a glut can send prices down. With that in mind, these numbers were compiled by Richard Drucker, who publishes a guide to per-carat wholesale gem values, to give a feel for how gems are priced across a wide spectrum of quality. They are accurate as of January 1, 1996, and have been modified to reflect retail prices.

GEMSTONE	WEIGHT	GRADE			
		Commercial	Good	Fine	Extra Fine
RUBY	1/2 carat	$55	$550	$1,500	$3,000–$5,000
	1 carat	$150	$2,200	$4,900	$7,800–$14,400
SAPPHIRE	1/2 carat	$30	$125	$250	$600–$1,400
	1 carat	$100	$600	$1,600	$3,600–$6,500
EMERALD	1/2 carat	$35	$350	$1,300	$2,700–$5,000
	1 carat	$80	$1,500	$3,500	$6,400–$15,000
AMETHYST	1 carat	$2	$6	$16	$36–$50
	3 carats	$6	$24	$60	$120–$210
PINK	1 carat	$30	$40	$100	$200–$300
TOURMALINE	3 carats	$120	$210	$420	$810–$1,080
GREEN	1 carat	$20	$40	$80	$150–$200
TOURMALINE	3 carats	$90	$150	$360	$600–$900
PERIDOT	1 carat	$8	$24	$50	$80–$120
	3 carats	$24	$72	$150	$240–$360
AQUAMARINE	1 carat	$20	$50	$150	$380–$600
	3 carats	$90	$300	$900	$1,650–$2,550
RHODOLITE	1 carat	$4	$20	$40	$60–$120
GARNET	3 carats	$24	$120	$180	$270–$540
TANZANITE	1 carat	$90	$130	$250	$440–$630
	3 carats	$450	$900	$1,500	$2,100–$2,700

■ **DIAMONDS.** *The Gemological Institute of America has developed a grading system for diamonds measuring "the four C's": carat weight, color, clarity, and cut. The best diamond would be an "ideally cut DIF"*

COLOR is graded from D (the best) to Z. (D to M is the general range, though.)
CLARITY ranges from best to worst as follows: "internally flawless" (IF), "Very, very slightly included" (VVS1), VVS2, "Very slightly included" (VS1), VS2, "Slightly included" (SI1), SI2, "Imperfect" (I), I2, and I3.
CUT can range from ideal cut to poorly cut. (Well-cut is a good standard.)

GIA Standard	WEIGHT	COLOR / CLARITY			
		G / VS1	H / VS2	I / SI1	J / SI2
DIAMOND	1/2 carat	$3,200	$2,500	$2,100	$1,500
(well-cut)	1 carat	$9,800	$8,800	$7,600	$6,000

SOURCE: (For gemstone table) Richard Drucker, Publisher, *The Guide*.

EXPERT Q & A

MINTING A COIN COLLECTION

If you think collecting money will make you money, think again.

One attraction of coin collecting is the beauty and historic value of what are essentially high-grade government documents. But no doubt the possibility of striking gold by discovering a rare and expensive coin buried in an old penny jar, say, is also a lure for America's two million numismatists. The chances of that happening are practically nil, according to veteran collectors. Coin collecting probably won't turn you into Midas, but if you're willing to bone up on the hobby, buy wisely, and wait patiently, you might even show a modest return for your efforts.

Meager monetary rewards haven't stopped coin collectors over the years. The hobby probably dates back to the Renaissance when royal families collected large copper coins struck during the days of the Roman Empire. As a result, coin collecting has become known as "the hobby of kings, the king of hobbies." We asked George Cuhaj, managing editor of the *Standard Catalogue of World Coins* (Krause Publications, $49.95) about the current trends in coin collecting:

■ Which coins make good collectibles right now?

U.S. coins in demand right now are large cents from 1793 to 1814, which were thicker and larger than today's quarter. Silver coins with the bust-image of Liberty (1796–1838) and those struck with the image of Liberty seated (1839–91) are also in demand.

You'll pay a premium for them, though. A Seated Liberty half dollar from 1856 to 1866, for example, goes for $400 to $2,500. A Bust Design silver dollar dated in the 1820s retails for $700 to $1,200. The higher end of those price ranges is for coins in so-called brilliant, uncirculated condition—a top grade. You can find these coins in lesser condition for as little as $50 or so, but those aren't usually in demand and won't appreciate. Buy coins of the best quality you can afford. That way you

FACT FILE:

LOOSE CHANGE: WHO'S WHO ON COINS

■ *Pennies can be a nuisance but the coins are actually helping to cut the federal deficit. The federal government makes money on every cent it mints, thanks to an arcane tradition that gives the Treasury three-tenths of a cent for every penny it produces. In 1995, it raked in nearly $400 million on the 13 billion pennies it minted. The Susan B. Anthony dollar, which was minted from 1979 to 1980, was a flop—consumers confused the coin with a quarter—and the Treasury stopped making it. Some 497 million Susan B. Anthonys are in circulation but another 260 million are stashed away in government vaults.*

AMOUNT	FRONT	BACK	CIRCULATION*
Penny	Abraham Lincoln	Lincoln Memorial	170 billion
Nickel	Thomas Jefferson	Monticello	20 billion
Dime	Franklin Delano Roosevelt	Torch,olive and oak branches	25 billion
Quarter	George Washington	Heraldic eagle	23 billion
Half-dollar	John F. Kennedy	Presidential coat of arms	N/A
Dollar piece	Susan B. Anthony	Flying eagle	497 million

*Estimates as of the end of 1995

SOURCE: U.S. Mint.

stand the best chance of realizing a profit after a reasonable time.

■ Which foreign coins are appealing?

The better grade coins of Germany have always had good collector appeal. A Hesse-Darmstadt, for example, a five-mark coin from the 1890s that sells for $1,700 to $2,500, is highly sought after. Commemoratives issued by the Federal Republic of Germany in the 1950s have also appreciated. The Nuremberg Museum's five-mark commemorative goes for $1,200 to $1,600. Ancient coins in superior quality are also in demand.

■ Are ancient coins readily available?

Yes, you can get them at coin shows and through dealers of ancient coins. Coins are made of durable metals and age doesn't always play a part in a coin's price. You can collect coins from ancient Greece and Rome and pay just a few dollars. You can get a bronze lepon (a coin of the Palestinian state, which is now Israel) with the name Pontius Pilate on it for $45 to $65. Others from the same era can be had for $20.

■ How do you know they're not fakes?

Every ancient coin has its own personality. Coins today are very uniform. Old coins were struck by hand and are irregular in shape. They usually don't have complete dates or designs; those that do command higher prices.

The potential of buying a fake is there. Familiarize yourself with the coins , and go to a reputable dealer.

■ Can a collector make money from coins in circulation?

Finding rare or expensive coins in circulation has always been hard. Coins in circulation are usually too worn to be valuable. A novice collector simply trying to assemble a set of recent circulating coins will even have a hard time. For example, there are few so-called wheat ear pennies, those made before 1959, and few silver coins made before 1964 in circulation. If you find one somewhere, it's likely to be worn and have little resale value. You can buy one of these coins in uncirculated condition from a dealer, of course. You'll pay from about $50 to more than $200, depending on its quality, date and mark. But you'll do well when you resell it later, providing you've taken care of it.

I'm not sure if any modern coin now circulating will appreciate in value. Modern coins are utilitarian—they're meant to be

FACT FILE: FACE VALUE: WHO'S WHO ON BILLS

■ *Ben Franklin still graces the $100 bill, but close observers of the bills issued since early 1996 will notice Ben's portrait is larger and slightly off-center. The redesign makes it tougher to counterfeit and reduces wear on the bill's portrait. Older versions are still in circulation and will gradually be replaced. Other denominations will be redesigned at the rate of one denomination every 6 to 12 months.*

AMOUNT	FRONT	BACK	CIRCULATION*
$1	George Washington	U.S. Seal	$5,970,314,609
$2	Thomas Jefferson	Signers of Declaration	$1,024,970,270
$5	Abraham Lincoln	Lincoln Memorial	$7,030,455,545
$10	Alexander Hamilton	U.S. Treasury	$13,212,968,860
$20	Andrew Jackson	White House	$78,339,902,280
$50	Ulysses Grant	U.S. Capitol	$43,449,352,950
$100	Benjamin Franklin	Independence Hall	$237,450,441,500
$500	William McKinley	Ornate Denomination	$145,159,500
$1,000	Grover Cleveland	Ornate Denomination	$168,451,000
$5,000	James Madison	Ornate Denomination	$1,770,000
$10,000	Salmon Chase**	Ornate Denomination	$3,450,000

*As of September 1995 **U.S. Supreme Court Justice 1864–73 SOURCE: U.S. Treasury.

IF STAMPS ARE YOUR PASSION

You wouldn't want to put these stamps on your mail

Printing stamps is so simple a process these days that botched-up stamps are a rarity. But on those rare occasions, collectors stand to win big. Take a recent snafu, involving a 1995 stamp honoring Richard Nixon. Out of some 80 million stamps that were printed, 160 contained major mistakes. Nixon's portrait is off center, for one, and his name is printed upside-down. The lucky recipients of these stamps struck gold: One misprinted Nixon stamp sold for $14,500 at a Christie's auction in early 1996.

Inverts, as the upside-down stamps are called in the philatelic world, have occurred before. In 1918, a biplane was printed upside down, for example, and in 1986 collectors discovered some upside-down candlestick stamps. According to *Linn's Stamp News*, which reported the Nixon error, the value of inverts depends on the stamp's age—and how many misprints are around. Inverts can fetch from 15¢ for a 1962 botched-up stamp that was reproduced aplenty to $225,000 for a rare 100-year-old stamp commemorating Christopher Columbus.

EXPERT SOURCES

Essential for stamp collectors and aspiring philatelists.

AMERICAN PHILATELIC SOCIETY
Annual membership dues, $25
■ Oldest and largest, services include insurance and certification.
☎ **814–237–3803**

LINN'S STAMP NEWS
$2 per issue, $39 per year (52 issues)
■ All the stamp news that's fit to print.
☎ **800–448–7293**

THE SCOTT CATALOG
Scott Publishing Co., Annual, $34 per vol.
■ Definitive numbers and prices.
☎ **800–572–6885**

spent. My advice is: Spend those Susan B. Anthony's. They haven't increased in value and aren't apt to.

■ What factors affect coin prices?

Demand and popularity. Take sea salvage coins: When a shipwreck is found, usually tens of thousands of coins are found. The rarer gold coins are taken by serious collectors and dealers, but the more common silver coins aren't absorbed and the market becomes flooded. A common shipwreck coin is a Spanish piece of eight real struck between 1714 to 1740. You can pick one up for $30 to $75.

Sea salvage coins are often not in the best condition. Many come with a certificate indicating that it came from a shipwreck, which is nice historically but doesn't do much for its value. One thing is certain about Spanish shipwrecks—there will always be more discovered.

■ Is this a good time to start a collection?

Historically speaking, it's always a good time. Right now there are lots of new issues being minted for circulation in the recently independent nations of the former Soviet Union. It's popular for collectors to fill out whole sets of coins from new countries.

An aspiring collector should visit coin shops, shows, and auctions, read trade publications, auction catalogs, and dealer fixed-price lists to get a feel for what's being offered. You can get a free sample of the major coin weeklies, *Numismatic News* (☎800–258–0929) and *Coin World* (☎800–253–4555).

If you want your collection to appreciate, buy the best quality, or grade of preservation, that you can afford. But first enjoy the history of the coin, learn about its designers and heraldry, and about the times it was minted. Then, if it happens to increase in value, all the better.

ARCHEOLOGY

THE FOSSIL FRENZY

Collectors are coveting T-rex bones, shark teeth, and meteorites

A Romanian cave bear from the Ice Age for $29,000. A skeleton of a pachycephalosaurus dino for $24,000. A 512-pound meteorite for $32,500. These items were among the 385 lots of rare objects at the standing-room-only sale by Phillips Fine Art Auctioneers in New York in late 1995.

Fossils are the collecting craze of the '90s, a trend spurred on partly by the hit movie, *Jurassic Park*. The MidAmerica Paleontology Society (4800 Sunset Dr., S.W., Cedar Rapids, IA 52404), which puts out a newsletter and a directory of fossil clubs around the country, has grown from 450 members a few years ago to 750. The group's annual fossil show, held in Macomb, Ill., each spring attracts hundred of dealers.

Is there big money to be made in the fossils trade? Not for the most part. The market can be volatile. "Fossils are just like coins, stamps, and other collectibles. What's rare today becomes common tomorrow if someone discovers more," says Glenn Rockers, a fossil dealer in Kansas.

A prickly problem for collectors is: Who owns a fossil unearthed on public lands? The government or the finder? As Congress thrashes out this thorny problem, a collector who digs up a vertebrate fossil from federal lands could end up in a courtroom.

If hunting fossils is more appealing to you than owning them, you can join up with organized fossil expeditions, such as those run by paleontologist Robert Bakker (☎ 800–DIG–DINO), who was a consultant for *Jurassic Park*. These treks can last from one day to several and take you to Wyoming, Colorado, Mexico—even Argentina and Mongolia.

EXPERT PICKS

THE BEST DINOS—IN CAPTIVITY

Robert Bakker, a paleontologist and consultant for the blockbuster movie Jurassic Park, *lists these among his favorite museums for viewing dinos:*

ROYAL TYRRELL MUSEUM OF PALEONTOLOGY

■ The best in the world—biggest display, greatest variety, best lighting.
Drumheller, Alberta, Canada 20J OYO
☎403–823–7707

MUSEUM OF THE ROCKIES

■ This outstanding collection is strong on the end of the dinosaur age. Includes duckbills and a four-foot-long cast of a *Tyrannosaurus rex* skull.
Bozeman, Mont. 59715
☎406–994–2251

DINOSAUR NATIONAL MONUMENT

■ The park covers more than 200,000 acres and has an excavation quarry rich in fossils.
Dinosaur, Colo./Utah 81610 ☎970–374–3000

TATE MUSEUM

■ A new hands-on museum at Casper College in Wyoming. You can clean dinosaur bones, make plaster replicas, etc.
Casper, Wyo. 82601
☎307–268–2447

CARNEGIE MUSEUM

■ Great variety. Up-to-date displays. Three specimens of *T. rex* bones and a juvenile *Camarasaurus lentus*, a four-legged browser, that's nearly intact.
Pittsburgh, Pa. 15213
☎412–622–3270

YOUR TAXES

TAXPAYER ALERT: Who must file a tax return, PAGE 99 **DEDUCTIONS:** Twenty-five that are often overlooked, PAGE 101 **COUPLES:** The penalties of getting married, PAGE 103 **CHARITY:** Getting a tax break for giving, PAGE 104 **TAX PREP:** How to pick an accountant, PAGE 105 **FILING:** Some common tax errors to avoid, PAGE 106 **TAX FORMS:** Should you file electronically? PAGE 107 **AUDITS:** If the IRS comes knocking at your door, PAGE 109

CHANGES

GETTING READY FOR TAX DAY '97

Knowing the new wrinkles in the rules could save you big money

Fiddling with the tax code has become the number one sport in Washington. Revising the rules—as well as endlessly chewing over proposals for change—seems the order of the day. And after more than a decade of almost nonstop refurbishing there's no end in sight. As this book was going to press in early summer, Republicans and Democrats were noodling a new set of major revisions (though nobody expects any major tax changes until after the '96 election, if then). Also getting a lot of ink these days is the idea of a flat tax that applies to almost all income with minimal deductions. (Don't count on that happening any time soon, though). Here, however, are 16 recent changes in the law, rules that are worth knowing about, and some tips that could save you money.

■ **TAX RATES:** Roller coaster fans should love the ups and downs of tax rates. Back in 1981 the top rate was 70 percent; then it was cut to 50 percent in 1982 and to 28 percent in 1988; now it's back to 39.6 percent, but flat-tax proposals would chop it again. Even without legislated changes, rates effectively drop each year because of automatic adjustments for inflation. A couple filing jointly moves to a tax rate of 28 percent from 15 percent in 1996 when their taxable income after deductions tops $40,100. The 28 percent rate began to bite faster in 1995—at $39,000 of income.

Adding insult to high-income people is a rule that lets taxpayers whose income tops a certain level—$117,950 for 1996—to claim only part of their itemized deductions. The only good news is that the trigger is boosted yearly for inflation, so 1996's trigger is $3,250 higher than in 1995.

Another hit: High-income families—over $176,950 for couples, over $147,450 for people filing as a head of household—can't deduct the entire amount normally allowed for personal and dependent exemptions. But thanks to inflation adjustments the triggers are almost 3 percent higher than for 1995.

■ **STANDARD DEDUCTION:** That pile of receipts for tax-deductible expenses may not be necessary any longer. You need them to claim itemized deductions, but if your outlays for mortgage interest, local tax, and charitable donations are modest, you may do better taking a standard deduction, a fixed amount you can subtract from your income without showing how much you actually spent. What's nice is that the amount is adjusted yearly for inflation.

Couples filing a joint return get $6,700 for 1996, up from $6,550 in 1995; singles get $4,000, up from $3,900; heads of household get $5,900, up from $5,750. People 65 or older get bigger amounts than younger filers. A single older filer gets a $5,000 standard deduction; a couple in which both spouses are at least 65 gets $8,300.

■ **SOCIAL SECURITY BENEFITS:** There was a time when Social Security benefits were tax-free. But starting in 1984, up to half became subject to tax. Beginning in 1994, up to 85 percent of benefits became taxable. A retiree's vulnerability to tax varies with income. The first step: Add to adjusted gross income (generally, income before personal deductions and exemptions) the amount of any tax-free interest and one-half of your Social Security benefits. When the total is less than $25,000 for a single person or $32,000 for a couple, there's no tax on the benefits.

Up to half the benefits are taxable above those limits until a second threshold is passed—$34,000 for a single person and $44,000 for a couple. After that point, up to 85 percent of benefits get taxed.

■ **NANNY TAX:** Obeying the requirement to pay Social Security and federal unemployment tax on household workers has gotten a bit easier. After public attention focused on the so-called nanny tax following the troubles that some early Clinton appointees faced because they hadn't paid the amounts due, Congress revamped the levy. People who employ domestic workers won't owe Social Security tax for 1996 unless the worker's wages hit $1,000—up from $50 before the law was changed in 1994. Unemployment tax generally applies when you pay $1,000 or more in any quarter. No Social Security tax is due at all now on household workers under 18 who don't do the work as a principal occupation—a student, say, who babysits or tends your lawn. But unemployment tax could be due if you pay quarterly earnings over $1,000.

Those who do owe the tax may find compliance easier. Instead of quarterly filings, you now include the tax and paperwork with your income tax returns using a new Schedule H. You may, however, want to increase withholding from your paychecks or make quarterly estimated tax payments to avoid owing a bundle at tax filing time.

■ **MORTGAGE POINTS:** Here's an example of a recent shift in IRS policy that can save tax for people who are primed to take advantage of it. The IRS now says that people who buy homes can deduct not only the points they pay to obtain a mortgage but can also deduct any points paid on their behalf by the seller. Points are a lump-sum interest charge often required up front by mortgage lenders. People who missed the break when they bought a home on which the seller paid points can file an amended return to claim a deduction for those points. You have three years from the due date of a return in which to amend it.

■ **CHARITABLE DONATIONS:** Your word may be as good as gold, but the IRS is demanding more hard proof these days when sizable charita-

■ HOW TAX RATES BITE HARDER AS INCOME RISES

A look at 1996 taxable income by filing status

Tax rate	Married filing jointly	Head of household	Single	Married fiing separately
15%	$0–$40,100	$0–$32,150	$0–$24,000	$0–$20,050
28%	$40,100–$96,900	$32,150–$83,050	$24,000–$58,150	$20,050–$48,450
31%	$96,900–$147,700	$83,050–$134,500	$58,150–$121,300	$48,450–$73,850
36%	$147,700–$263,750	$134,500–$263,750	$121,300–$263,750	$73,850–$131,875
39.6%	$263,750+	$263,750+	$263,750+	$131,875+

NOTE: Taxable income is gross income after subtracting exemptions, deductions, and other allowances. A tax rate applies only to the portion of overall income that falls within that specific bracket.

SOURCE: Internal Revenue Service.

ble deductions are claimed. When a charitable donation totals $250 or more, a canceled check is no longer sufficient to back up a deduction. You need written acknowledgement of the gift from the charity, and the receipt must be in your hands before you file your tax return. The IRS is also ordering charities to give more information about how much of a donation is deductible when a gift or premium is given to donors as an incentive. That's to enforce a rule that you can't deduct the part of a donation that covers the cost of a treat—say, a meal or performance at a charitable benefit—that's more than nominal.

■ **HOME OFFICE:** More people than ever are working out of their homes, but Uncle Sam is not very avuncular about tax breaks for doing so. You generally can't depreciate the part of a home used as an office, claim a share of rent, or deduct a portion of utility bills, taxes, and upkeep unless you spend most of your business hours at home engaging in the activity that generates income. Performing vital administrative chores isn't enough. A handyman using the office to set up jobs and send out bills probably does not qualify for a deduction; a sales representative doing business by phone probably does. Someone who regularly meets with clients at home may qualify for an exception that allows a deduction in such cases.

Don't assume a deduction will be worth the effort. Depreciation must be stretched out over up to 39 years and the share of a home's expenses you can deduct may be modest. Deducting an office can also trigger a tax bite on the profit you make when you sell the home. However, phone calls and equipment are deductible even if the office itself isn't.

■ **BUSINESS MEALS:** No one can argue that eating while on a business trip isn't a necessity, but how well you eat is a matter of debate. Before 1987, you could deduct 100 percent of business meals—when traveling or entertaining clients locally. To raise revenue and cut down on dining at taxpayers' expense, the law was changed to allow a deduction for only 80 percent of a meal. The latest change, begun in 1994, cuts the deduction to 50 percent.

But here's a new IRS rule that could make record keeping less cumbersome. Spend under $75 on a meal and you no longer need to document the deduction with a receipt. Previously the IRS required a receipt at $25. But remember, you still must be ready to establish when, where, and why a meal or other expense was incurred—with, say, a business diary. (The new rule on receipts also applies to most business-related entertainment and travel, but you still need a receipt for a hotel room, no matter how inexpensive.)

■ **BUSINESS EQUIPMENT:** Small entrepreneurs who buy new equipment in 1996 can sidestep depreciation deductions that are spread over several years and deduct all at once up to $17,500 in such spending. This break—known as "first-year expensing" or a "Section 179 deduction"—has been a favored tax incentive. Congress doubled it from $5,000 to $10,000 in 1987 and then raised it to $17,500 starting in 1993.

There are tricky rules to watch out for, however. You can claim first-year expensing for only part of the cost of equipment used less than 100 percent for business, for

FACT FILE:

MARK YOUR CALENDAR

■ *An extension is granted for filing your return, not for paying any tax due. Interest and a possible penalty will be charged on tax not paid by the April deadline. An extension at least precludes a penalty for filing the return late.*

TAX FILING DEADLINES

For filing 1996 income tax returns:	April 15, 1997
With extension, using Form 4868:	August 15, 1997
With second extension, using Form 2688:	October 15, 1997

example, but the equipment must be used for business more than half the time during its normal depreciation lifetime.

■ **SELF-EMPLOYED HEALTH INSURANCE:** A special tax provision allows self-employed people to deduct 30 percent of their health insurance premiums as an adjustment to income, bypassing the income barriers for qualifying to deduct medical expenses as an itemized deduction. The adjustment—which had been 25 percent—expired at the end of 1993, but has since been reenacted retroactive to the start of 1994 and increased to 30 percent for 1995 and later. People who filed returns for 1994 before the reinstatement can still file an amended return to claim the deduction.

An IRS ruling opens a bigger break for some. The IRS says it is permissible for a self-employed person to hire a spouse and deduct 100 percent of the cost of the spouse-employee's health coverage as a business expense. Since it's OK to provide family coverage to a spouse-employee, this tactic can provide a self-employed person with fully deductible medical protection.

■ **EMPLOYEE COMMUTING:** Free parking at work is an untaxed fringe benefit for most workers, but employees in areas where the value of parking is high may have to treat part of the perk as taxable income. When the monthly value of employer-paid parking tops $165 in 1996, the excess is counted as taxable income. Employers who encourage mass transit for commuting can provide up to $65 of transit passes or reimbursement a month before any of the benefit is taxable.

■ **EDUCATIONAL ASSISTANCE:** Payments by an employer for tuition, fees, and books so that an employee can earn a degree, say, at night school, are no longer considered a tax-free fringe benefit. Those payments must be considered taxable income unless Congress reenacts the exemption for such educational aid. But payments by an employer to help you improve or maintain the skills you use in your current job—not to prepare for a new one—may still be tax-free.

■ WHO MUST FILE

Your tax rate depends on your personal or family status as of the last day of 1996.

Filing status	Age	Gross income at least
SINGLE (including legally separated)		
	Under 65	$6,550
	65 or older	$7,550
MARRIED filing joint return (living together)		
	Both spouses under 65	$11,800
	One spouse 65 or older	$12,600
	Both spouses 65 or older	$13,400
MARRIED filing joint return (not living together)		
	Any age	$2,550
MARRIED filing separate return		
	Any age	$2,550
HEAD OF HOUSEHOLD		
	Under 65	$8,450
	65 or older	$9,450
QUALIFYING WIDOW or widower with dep. child		
	Under 65	$9,250
	65 or older	$10,050
DEPENDENT CHILD (any investment income)		
	Any age	$651
DEPENDENT CHILD (job income only)		
	Any age	$4,001

NOTE: Figures are for 1996 returns to be filed in 1997. The income levels are the thresholds for having to file a return, not necessarily for having to pay tax. Head of household status applies to single people and separated married people who care for a child or relative. A qualifying widow or widower is one whose spouse died in one of the three most recent tax years. People with income from self-employment must file a return if their net income from self-employment (after business deductions) totals $433.13 or more.

SOURCE: Based on IRS rules and inflation-adjusted allowances for 1996.

■ **MEDICARE TAX:** After wages and self-employment income top a certain amount—$62,700 in 1996—the Social Security tax ends. (Employees and employers each pay 6.2 percent on a worker's wages.) But Medicare tax now continues without limit—at 1.45 percent for both employee and employer. Self-employed people pay both the employee and employer shares of Social Security and Medicare tax, but the double bite is eased by special deductions that a self-employed person can claim when completing his or her tax return.

■ RETIREMENT DISTRIBUTIONS: The Treasury has set a trap for people who receive a lump-sum payout from a retirement plan after they quit a firm to change jobs or to retire. You could end up paying tax when none will be owed, and then have to wait for a refund. There's generally no tax on a retirement plan payout if it is rolled over within 60 days into another retirement plan—such as another employer's plan or an individual retirement account. The catch: 20 percent of a lump-sum payout will be withheld for possible tax when an employee takes the cash rather than telling his or her ex-employer where to directly reinvest it. So if you complete a rollover on your own after taking the cash—and want to avoid any tax—you'll have to tap other savings to make up for the portion of the distribution withheld. You won't get back the withheld amount until you file your tax return.

■ ESTIMATED TAX: The IRS expects you to pay tax on your income throughout the year, not wait until tax filing time to settle up. The basic rule: You're subject to a penalty if more than 10 percent of your 1996 tax liability is outstanding at the filing deadline in April 1997. (Owing less than $500 usually is OK.) But there is a simplified way to escape punishment. As long as the total of 1996's withholding and required quarterly estimated tax payments at least equals your total tax for 1995, you can generally avoid a penalty next April no matter what you owe. One exception: Someone whose adjusted gross income for 1995 was more than $150,000 won't escape a penalty unless the tax collected during 1996 adds up to at least 110 percent of 1995's liability.

■ EARNED-INCOME CREDIT: A special tax break for lower-income people who hold jobs and have children has been expanded—and can mean a bigger tax refund or a boost in weekly take-home pay. For 1996, single or married people get a tax credit of up to $2,152 when they care for one child and $3,556 when they care for more. The credit is subtracted from tax owed; if the tax falls to zero with credit left over, the taxpayer collects the difference from the government. The credit, designed to reward working, generally rises at first as job income grows then gradually phases out. For 1996, the credit doesn't end until total income is $25,078 when there's one child and $28,495 when there are more. People eligible for the credit can claim part of it in advance—lifting take-home pay up to $108 a month—by giving their employers a Form W-5. An additional twist: Workers without children can get a credit of up to $323 for 1996 when their income is below $9,500.

New legislation bars people with more than a small amount of investment income from claiming the credit. For 1996, that applies to those who get more than $2,350 of interest, dividends, or other proceeds from investments.

■ HOW YOUR ITEMIZED DEDUCTIONS STACK UP

The amounts shown are calculated from official early estimates for 1994 returns filed in 1995 and are the averages claimed by taxpayers who deducted those specific expenses. People with incomes over a certain ceiling ($117,950 for couples and single people for 1996) may be prohibited from deducting 100 percent of what they claim. The medical deduction is the amount claimed that exceeds 7.5 percent of adjusted gross income; the miscellaneous total is the amount exceeding 2 percent of adjusted gross income.

Adjusted gross income	Interest on home mortgage	Taxes	Medical expenses	Contributions	Misc.
$20,000–$30,000	$4,764	$2,229	$2,898	$1,217	$3,185
$30,000–$50,000	$5,095	$3,109	$4,266	$1,453	$3,007
$50,000–$75,000	$5,950	$4,415	$5,583	$1,616	$3,259
$75,000–$100,000	$7,196	$6,208	$7,788	$2,380	$3,942
$100,000–$200,000	$9,103	$10,031	$8,061	$4,071	$6,131

DATA: Statistics of Income Bulletin, Internal Revenue Service.

EXPERT LIST

TWENTY-FIVE EASILY OVERLOOKED DEDUCTIONS

Expenses for everything from contact lenses to dry cleaning could help you lower your tax bill. IRS regulations allow many personal and business expenses to be deducted from your gross income before you figure your tax liability. The more you can subtract, the more you reduce the amount of your taxable income. Here's a list from Ernst & Young, one of the nation's largest accounting firms, of 25 deductions that are easily overlooked:

1. APPRAISAL FEES: When paid to determine value of a charitable gift or extent of a casualty loss.

2. BUSINESS GIFTS: No more than $25 to any one person per year.

3. CELLULAR TELEPHONE: When used in your business, or required by your employer, the cost of the phone may be deductible, plus phone calls made.

4. CHARITABLE EXPENSES FOR VOLUNTEER WORK: Twelve cents a mile for use of your car, plus out-of-pocket spending for such items as uniforms and supplies.

5. COMMISSIONS ON SALE OF ASSETS: Brokerage or other fees to complete a sale are taken into account when you figure your profit or loss (generally added to your cost for the asset).

6. CONTACT LENSES: Also include the cost of eyeglasses or cleaning solution.

7. CONTRACEPTIVES: Legitimate medical items include birth control pills. Also abortions.

8. DRUG AND ALCOHOL ABUSE TREATMENT: Includes meals and lodging when staying at a treatment center, but not programs to quit smoking.

9. EDUCATIONAL EXPENSES: To improve or keep up your skills at your current job.

10. EMPLOYMENT AGENCY FEES: Whether you get a new job or not; but not if you're looking for your first job or switching occupations. Résumé and travel costs also are deductible.

11. FOREIGN TAX: If you pay tax to another country on income from foreign investments, you can get a deduction or credit for those payments when figuring your U.S. tax.

12. GAMBLING LOSSES: Only up to the amount of reported winnings.

13. LAUNDRY SERVICE ON A BUSINESS TRIP: You needn't pack for an entire trip.

14. MOVING EXPENSES: When changing jobs or starting work for the first time, and only if new job must mean a 50-mile or longer extra commute if you don't move.

15. PREMIUM ON TAXABLE BONDS: Investors who buy taxable bonds for more than face value can gradually deduct the excess each year they own the bond.

16. MEDICAL TRANSPORTATION: If driving, you can claim ten cents per mile plus tolls and parking.

17. ORTHOPEDIC SHOES: The extra amount over the cost of normal shoes.

18. PENALTY FOR EARLY WITHDRAWAL OF SAVINGS: When a certificate of deposit is cashed in before maturity, a penalty is deductible as an adjustment to income.

19. POINTS ON A HOME MORTGAGE: Deductible as a lump sum when paid on a loan to buy or remodel a main residence; deductible gradually over the life of the loan when paid to refinance a mortgage.

20. SELF-EMPLOYMENT TAX: Adjustment allows the self-employed to reduce taxable income by half their self-employment Social

■ **EXPERT LIST**

Security and Medicare tax.

21. SPECIAL SCHOOLING: For the mentally or physically impaired when the school is primarily to help them deal with their disability.

22. SUPPORT FOR A VISITING STUDENT: Up to $50 per month in housing, food, and support for live-in exchange student is deductible—only if you're not reimbursed.

23. TAX PREPARATION: Accountant's fees, legal expenses, tax guides, and computer programs.

24. WORK CLOTHES: When required for work, but not suitable for ordinary wear.

25. WORTHLESS STOCK: Claimed as a capital loss in the year it first has no value. (Less than one cent per share generally is considered worthless.)

NOTE: Some deductions are limited. For example, only the portion of total medical expenses exceeding 7.5 percent of your adjusted gross income is deductible. "Miscellaneous" deductions, including most employment-related and investment expenses, are deductible only to the extent they exceed 2 percent of adjusted gross income.

SOURCE: Adapted from *The Ernst & Young Tax Guide 1996*, Peter W. Bernstein, ed., John Wiley & Sons, 1995.

TEN SOURCES OF TAX-FREE INCOME

The biggest stream of tax-free income for many people comes from Social Security benefits. It's wholly untaxed unless your income exceeds a certain level—roughly $25,000 for single people and $32,000 for couples. Here are other types of income that can elude income tax.

■ **CHILD SUPPORT:** Unlike alimony—which is taxable—parents who collect child support from an ex-spouse do not report it as income.

■ **DISABILITY INCOME:** Worker's compensation benefits because of a job injury are generally not taxed.

■ **GIFTS:** Bequests and gifts are tax free; any gift or estate tax that may be due is paid by the giver.

■ **LIFE INSURANCE:** Beneficiaries don't pay tax on insurance proceeds, but an owner of a policy who cashes it in faces tax on proceeds that exceed the total amount of premiums paid.

■ **RENTAL OF A HOME:** Income from renting a vacation or other home for 14 or fewer days a year isn't taxable.

■ **SALE OF A RESIDENCE:** People who are 55 or older when they sell their principal residence can—once in a lifetime—permanently escape tax on up to $125,000 of any profit.

■ **U.S. SAVINGS BONDS:** Interest on bonds bought since 1990 can be wholly or partly tax free for parents who redeem the bonds to pay college tuition—but income and other limits apply.

■ **SCHOLARSHIPS:** Untaxed when the recipient is a candidate for a degree and the money is for tuition, fees, and supplies and isn't payment for work.

■ **MUNICIPAL BONDS:** Federal income tax doesn't apply to interest from state and local government obligations—but the interest could lift the amount of Social Security benefits subject to tax.

■ **WELFARE PAYMENTS:** Aid to families with dependent children, emergency disaster relief, compensation to crime victims—all can qualify as tax-free assistance.

COUPLES

WHY NOT TO GET MARRIED

Love doesn't conquer all. Your taxes could go up when you tie the knot

Should you get married? For most people that's not a decision dictated by tax considerations, but many newlyweds find that tying the knot means a present to Uncle Sam. If both spouses work, higher taxes often come with the wedding.

The National Bureau of Economic Research estimated that 52 percent of married taxpayers filing jointly in 1994 paid a so-called marriage penalty averaging $1,244. That's the additional tax two singles end up paying jointly after getting married.

At its simplest, the marriage penalty results from the higher effective rate that two singles can face when their incomes are combined. Two unmarried people in 1996, for example, each pay a tax rate of just 15 percent on the first $24,000 of their taxable income. A couple filing jointly pays that bottom rate on a combined $40,100 of income—not the $48,000 that applies in total to two singles.

To be sure, a single person pays more tax than a couple with the same amount of income. The marriage penalty arises when two singles marry and their income is combined—pushing them into a higher economic stratum for the levying of tax.

The penalty can vary widely depending upon the amount of income and specific deductions. A single person who doesn't itemize deductions, for example, gets a 1996 standard deduction of $4,000. A couple gets $6,700—not twice as much. Two single taxpayers can each claim rental property losses of up to $25,000 a year; if they marry they're subject to a combined $25,000 limit. Similarly, a single investor can write off $3,000 of capital losses against other income; a couple gets the same amount in total.

The other side of the coin: Some couples get a marriage bonus—the couple pays less tax than the partners would have paid in total as singles. That's typically the case when one spouse was working before marriage and the other wasn't, or when one spouse earns a lot more than the other. In those cases, some of the earnings of the higher-income spouse are subject to a lower effective tax rate when the income is melded with the little or no earnings of the other partner. The NBR study for 1994 estimated that 38 percent of couples got an average bonus of $1,399.

■ PAYING A PENALTY

The penalty can vary widely depending on deductions. A single person who doesn't itemize deductions, for example, gets a 1996 standard deduction of $4,000. A couple gets $6,700.

	Jane (single)	John (single)	Jane & John (married)
Gross income	$40,000	$35,000	$75,000
Personal exemption	–$ 2,550	–$ 2,550	–$ 5,100
Standard deduction	–$ 4,000	–$ 4,000	–$ 6,700
Taxable income	$33,450	$28,450	$63,200
Tax	$ 6,246	$ 4,846	$12,483
Combined tax as singles: $11,092			**PENALTY: $ 1,391**

■ GETTING A BONUS

When one spouse earns a lot more than the other, some of the earnings of the higher-income spouse are subject to a lower effective tax rate when the incomes are melded.

	Mary (single)	Bill (single)	Mary & Bill (married)
Gross income	$10,000	$60,000	$70,000
Personal exemption	–$ 2,550	–$ 2,550	–$ 5,100
Standard deduction	–$ 4,000	–$ 4,000	–$ 6,700
Taxable income	$ 3,450	$53,450	$58,200
Tax	$ 518	$11,846	$11,083
Combined tax: $12,364			**BONUS: $ 1,281**

Note: Tax based on 1996 tax rate schedules.

CHARITY

WHEN GIVING IS ALSO GETTING

Donate more to your favorite causes and get a deduction, to boot

Sometimes you can do good for others while also helping yourself at tax time. Older taxpayers, for example, can assure themselves of lifetime income—in some case boosting their current return from investments—by arranging now to commit some of their assets to a favorite charity after they die. That also nets them a current income tax deduction for the gift.

Many charities, as well as attorneys and financial advisers, can help you set up a trust—known as a charitable remainder trust—to bequeath assets to a charity, but draw investment income from them while alive. Charities also offer simpler pooled income funds, which operate somewhat like mutual funds. They accept deposits of cash and securities earmarked for the charity's use, but pay income to you during your life.

The deduction you earn for a gift in such circumstances will be for only a portion of its value since the charity cannot touch the assets until you die—or, depending upon your wishes—until, say, both you and your spouse die. The younger you are the longer the charity will probably have to wait and thus the smaller the deduction.

Advance giving plans can be fine-tuned. It's possible, for example, to target assets for a charity now to get a current tax deduction, but delay receiving income from the assets until you retire. That can mean bigger tax savings now when you may be in a high tax bracket and more payments later on because you delayed the start of payouts. Older donors can turn in stocks that have greatly appreciated in value but pay puny dividends, then get higher incomes when a trust reinvests them in higher-paying securities. You can also fashion a plan that assures you a fixed income or one whose payments will vary with the performance of stock and bond markets. The point to remember: The more you give, the more tax benefits you can get.

EXPERT TIPS

FIVE SMART PLANNING MOVES

Planning ideas that make a difference, from the experts at Ernst & Young

1. Consider giving gifts to your children. You may be able to shift income to them since children are usually in lower tax brackets and so pay less in taxes. However, if your children are under age 14, their income above certain levels will be subject to the special "kiddie tax" rates.

2. Charitable contributions are subject to certain tax limitations. Some of your contributions to charities may not be deductible if you exceed the prescribed limits or do not meet the substantiation requirements.

3. Focus on the after-tax yield when comparing the return on different investments.

4. Make your contributions to an IRA or Keogh plan early in the year. The combination of making contributions early in the year and compounding will make your money grow faster.

5. Contribute the maximum to your 401(k) plan early in the year. If you wait too long, you may not be able to contribute the full amount because of limitations.

SOURCE: Adapted from *The Ernst & Young Tax Saver's Guide 1996*, Peter W. Bernstein, ed., John Wiley & Sons, 1995.

TAX PREPARATION

HOW TO PICK AN ACCOUNTANT

Half of Americans get help. Here's some help about finding help

Here's how the instructions on an IRS tax form no bigger than a postcard might read if we had a really simple flat tax: Write down your total income for 1996. Now, send it in.

Of course, that's not the type of flat tax most citizens have in mind. And it's unlikely that in our lifetime any tax form put out by the IRS will be that short and simple. But, there's no doubt that an awful lot of Americans find the current tax system too complicated—so complicated, in fact, that they shy away from doing their own taxes. Currently, about half of taxpayers pay for help to complete their returns.

If your affairs are plain vanilla—your income coming from wages and simple investments, for example, and your deductions are the typical ones of, say, mortgage interest, donations, and local tax—you shouldn't fear doing your own return. But some people prefer not to devote the time, no matter how straightforward their return. And professional help may be in order if you're grappling with complex areas—running a business or rental property, say, or you've been through a financial whirl because of a divorce or complex investment.

Picking the right help, however, requires a bit of effort. Anyone can hang out a shingle as a tax preparer, whether qualified or not. And someone skilled in dashing off simple returns could miss tax-saving breaks or run afoul of the rules when wading into a more complicated return. Remember, you are ultimately responsible for any extra tax, interest or penalties that are assessed because of goofs—not your accountant.

Recommendations from friends or relatives are a good way to narrow the field when choosing a tax preparer. When a return involves special circumstances ask a preparer if he or she is familiar with what has to be done. Don't neglect local taxes—if you've moved from one state to another and owe tax in both, that can be daunting to some preparers. A preparer should match your tax style. If you're willing to take aggressive positions in gray areas, you won't be happy with a preparer who is very conservative, or vice versa.

Discuss fees up front. In many cases it's a flat amount. When charges are by the hour, ask for an estimate of the time needed. The cost can run from $50 or so on common returns to several hundred dollars for modestly involved ones—and up to several thousand dollars for elaborate ones. A lot depends on the type of preparer—listed below in order of generally rising expertise and cost.

■ **SEASONAL PREPARERS:** Operate only during the tax season; vary widely in knowledge; may be OK for common returns, but can fall behind on changes in the law and rules; check credentials and recommendations carefully.

■ **CHAINS:** Trained preparers, but many may be part-timers with limited knowledge beyond routine matters; a personalized, extra-cost service may be offered for complex or high-income returns; may be too conservative in trying to whittle tax for some tastes

■ **PUBLIC ACCOUNTANTS:** Full-time professionals, generally meet some state regulatory rules but with much fewer educational requirements than certified public accountants (CPAs); often specialize in small businesses.

■ **ENROLLED AGENTS:** Accredited by the IRS; must have worked as an IRS examiner or passed a stringent test; must take part in continuing education; good for all-year guidance. National Association of Enrolled Agents (☎800-424-4339) provides names of members.

■ **CERTIFIED PUBLIC ACCOUNTANTS (CPAS):** Highly trained and regulated; range from small operations to national firms with many partners; big firms are often not geared to handle individual returns except for the wealthy; may be overkill; good for strategic planning.

■ **TAX ATTORNEYS:** Not for completing returns; useful for guidance on major estate or other tax planning; needed for tax litigation; may work with your accountant.

It's in your interest to help a preparer by supplying organized, complete, and pertinent records. You should have documentation to support your income and deductions, including tabulations of the amounts. Bring along your W-2 forms for wages. You may also need 1099 forms for interest and dividends, statements for the purchase and sale price of securities you've traded, and receipts for business expenses. Ask what you should bring, and the degree of detail. You might save on the fee by tallying some totals yourself.

You can't expect a course in taxation, but when a return is complete it's reasonable to look it over and ask for explanations of items or calculations you don't understand.

A tax deduction for the cost of doing your return? Probably not. The fees are generally considered a miscellaneous deduction and nothing is deductible until the total of miscellaneous items tops 2 percent of your adjusted gross income. But fees related to a business tax schedule on your return may be deductible separately.

COMMON TAX ERRORS TO AVOID

Some things to remember before you sign the check

■ Include your Social Security number on each page of your tax return.

■ Make sure you have claimed all of your dependents, such as elderly parents who may not live with you.

■ Recheck your cost basis in the shares you sold this year, particularly shares of a mutual fund. Income and capital gains dividends that were automatically reinvested in the fund over the years increase your basis in the mutual fund and thus reduce a gain or increase a loss that you must report.

■ Fill out Form 8606, Nondeductible IRA Contributions, for your contributions to an IRA account, even if you don't claim any deductions for the contributions.

■ Are your W-2s and 1099s correct? If they're not, have them corrected so IRS records agree with the amount shown on your return.

■ If you are married, see if filing separate returns rather than a joint return is more beneficial.

■ If you are single and live with a dependent, see if you qualify for the lower tax rates available to a head of household or surviving spouse with a dependent child.

■ If you worked for more than one employer, be sure to claim the credit for any overpaid Social Security taxes withheld.

■ Check last year's return to see if there are any items that carry over to this year, such as charitable contributions or capital losses that exceeded the amount you were previously able to deduct.

■ If you did not pay enough taxes during the year, fill out form 2210, Underpayment of Estimated Tax, to figure the underpayment penalty

■ Don't report a state tax refund as income if you didn't claim an itemized deduction for the tax when it was originally paid.

TAX FORMS

SHOULD YOU FILE ELECTRONICALLY?

It may cost a bit more and, believe it or not, there are extra forms to fill

Yes, you can still file your return by mail, on paper—but new electronic means of filing promise faster refunds, fewer errors in processing and cost savings for the government.

Already, millions of taxpayers file returns via computer—shaving the normal wait for refunds to about half the typical six-week wait. And during the 1996 filing season the IRS expanded a program that allows filing by phone—opening it nationwide to single taxpayers who had under $50,000 of income and didn't itemize deductions. Those taxpayers could punch in data about their income and withheld tax and immediately be informed of how much tax they owed or the size of a refund. Nothing had to be mailed in—except a check if tax was due.

The IRS wants to get away from paper returns to curtail the math and other errors it must fix—some the fault of taxpayers and others caused by IRS personnel as they copy data from paper returns. One problem: Organized fraudulent claims for refunds that rely on the speed of electronic processing to bypass normal policing. However, the IRS has been instituting safeguards to counter potential fraud.

The main drawback to taxpayers of filing by computer is the extra charge that computer filers typically incur. The IRS has been considering allowing people to file from their home computers directly to the IRS, but so far you've had to go through an intermediary. That can be a preparer who's done your return or, in the case of people using tax software, a transmitting service that is offered as an option with the program. Fees have ranged from about $10 to $40. And there's still been paperwork—you've had to complete Form 8453 to authorize electronic filing and attach your W-2. But the IRS has been considering doing away even with that leftover paperwork.

Really impatient types can get a refund loan—made by banks through preparers such as H&R Block. You get your money in a day or two and the refund pays off the loan. But lenders have turned cautious and first-time refund borrowers may be limited in the amount they can get. The charge for a loan varies—ranging perhaps from $30 to $90 for loans of up to $3,500. Though these short-term loans have never been much of a bargain, many people find the cost minor when it facilitates a rapid flow of money back from the government.

A note to people who get refunds by mail: It's smart to keep the IRS apprised of your whereabouts. You can send in an address change using Form 8822. The post office returned 98,000 refunds to the IRS in 1995 because of outdated or incorrect addresses. The average orphan refund: $834.

EXPERT TIP

One way to speed a refund, and also preclude theft, is to have the IRS deposit the money directly to your bank account. That option was made available this past filing season to almost all filers. Direct deposit had previously been open only to people filing their returns electronically or using tax software to prepare a special 1040PC return.

To set up direct deposit and trim perhaps a week off the normal wait for a check, you supply information about your bank account on Form 8888 and attach it to your return.

TAX INFO

FOR THE DAZED AND CONFUSED

Low-cost aid from tax guides, tax software, and the IRS

Every tax filer can sometimes use a helping hand. But you don't have to spend a wad of money getting advice from professional tax preparers. Low-cost expert aid for many filers can come from tax guide manuals and computer tax preparation software.

BOOKS

Among the most reliable and comprehensive companions when doing your return are three top-selling manuals (about $15) that annually help decipher the latest IRS instructions, pass on useful tips, and explain updates in the rules that result from revisions in the law, court decisions, and changes of heart by the IRS.

The *Ernst & Young Tax Guide* reprints the IRS's free general purpose tax guide—known as Publication 17—and extensively annotates it with tips, clarifications, and planning hints from the accounting firm's experts. (Full disclosure: This guide is also edited by one of the editors of *The Practical Guide to Practically Everything*.) J. K. Lasser's *Your Income Tax* provides a wealth of well-organized nuts and bolts assistance with lots of examples. *Consumer Reports Books Guide to Income Tax* spices its many practical examples of how the rules work with lots of tips and cautionary notes. All three are likely to answer virtually any question you might typically face.

SOFTWARE

Computer owners are turning in greater numbers to software for hands-on help in filling out their returns and calculating tax. You can use the programs—about $25 to $50—to directly enter data onto an electronic tax form, getting on-screen help as you go along, or choose an interview format: The program asks about your finances and family and puts the material you supply where it belongs, deciding what forms and schedules you need. Later, you can print a completed return for mailing or utilize an option to file the return electronically. Companion software is available for doing state returns and costs $25 to $30. They can transfer needed information from the federal return.

The best-selling program is TurboTax, which consistently wins top reviews. Its Macintosh version is MacInTax. A close runner-up in ease of use is Kiplinger TaxCut, which features well-informed advice from *Kiplinger's Personal Finance* magazine.

But these programs may not provide all the light that's needed when taxpayers wrestle with knotty issues for the first time—claiming depreciation, for example, or reporting on investments. The printed tax guides are better at helping out in unfamiliar territory. The software often works well when you already have an idea of what must be done. Bugs also crop up: putting data in the wrong place, misfiguring deductions, and not taking account of dollar limits that apply to certain breaks. So carefully review your return before sending it off and register your program—that lets the software firm notify you of problems. You can also check with a firm's online support service for reports of problems.

THE IRS

You can whiz through cyberspace to the IRS. People missing a form can download what they need by dialing into the agency on the Internet's World Wide Web. Point a Web browser to http://www.irs.ustreas.gov to connect. You can also view and download IRS tax guidance publications. Online instructions explain the process and point you to free software you may have to download in order to view and print forms and publications.

To reach the IRS the old-fashioned way, call ☎ 800–829–3676 for mail delivery of forms and publications, including publication 910, *Guide to Free Tax Services*.

TAX AUDITS

IF THE IRS COMES KNOCKING

Chances are, you'll end up paying after an audit by the IRS

The IRS leaves a lot of returns unaudited, but its examiners are getting nosier about the ones they do examine. While in the past, IRS personnel may have left it at checking the validity of your tax deductions, these days they're on order to do more snooping for income you may have neglected to report.

The IRS's lethal weapon of choice is what's popularly called a lifestyle audit. Examiners take a global view of your financial and family affairs to see if your reported income is sufficient to support the lifestyle you're enjoying. Besides asking you for receipts for charitable donations, proof of business expenses, and details of investment transactions, auditors today may ask how you can afford that car and a second home on your income. Questions about the amount of your mortgage payment, whether your children work, what appliances you've recently bought, where you went to college, and whether you've been divorced are also fair game.

The IRS's top audit targets are generally upper-income professionals, self-employed people, investors claiming big losses, and people with considerable income from tips—but no group is immune. About 80 percent of audits end up pulling in extra tax, so emerging unscathed is a long shot.

Audits come in three flavors. Least intimidating is a correspondence audit—usually a letter asking for documentation to back up a single item. More fearsome are office audits in which you go to an IRS office for a face-to-face probe that may cover more topics in greater detail. At the top tier are field audits, which most often involve business-related returns and are conducted by top-trained agents at a taxpayer's home or office.

When the IRS contacts you, it has usually found something suspicious. Virginia accountant Richard Greene, who specializes in helping taxpayers under attack, warns that the IRS has the presumption of correctness, so you have to show why any proposed changes are wrong. Mail audits can often be handled on your own, but you may want guidance from an accountant on deeper probes.

You'd be wise not to insist on total victory. Give the auditor a few small wins so the IRS can close your case and move on. But also be wary. The examiner you meet is likely to be friendly and even sympathetic, cautions Greene, yet his or her job is to extract more tax from you. And like elephants, the IRS never forgets: If you have been audited before, the IRS will remember. Don't repeat past mistakes.

■ WHO GETS CHECKED THE MOST BY THE IRS

A look at individual tax returns audited in 1994 shows that estates are the most likely to attract Uncle Sam's attention:

TYPE OF RETURN	PERCENTAGE AUDITED
PERSONAL	
Income under $100,000	0.83%
Income over $100,000	2.94%
SELF-EMPLOYED	
Gross revenue under $100,000	3.64%
Gross revenue over $100,000	3.57%
FARMERS	
Gross revenue under $100,000	1.16%
Gross revenue over $100,000	1.74%
ESTATES	
Assets under $1 million	8.20%
Assets $1 million to $5 million	22.78%
Assets over $5 million	48.00%

NOTE: Personal income is the total before subtracting investment or tax shelter losses.
SOURCE: Internal Revenue Service.

DOLLARS & SENSE

CREDIT CARDS: The most popular and the best, PAGE 114 **SHOPPING CLUBS:** Where the bargains are, PAGE 118 **BILLS:** Online banking has arrived, PAGE 119 **PERSONAL TECH:** Straight talk about phones, PAGE 120 **CHARITIES:** What you should know before you give, PAGE 121 **INSURANCE:** How to buy what you really need, PAGE 124 **DIVORCE:** Lessons from the War of the Waleses, PAGE 130 **SMALL CLAIMS:** A consumer's guide to getting even, PAGE 132

EXPERT Q & A

CAN I HAVE MY ALLOWANCE?

Free advice from Dr. Tightwad on teaching your kids about money

If your spendthrift preteen regularly asks you for more pocket change and your college student treats her credit card like cash, you're not alone. There are ways, however, to teach your children how to manage their funds. We asked Janet Bodnar, a senior editor at *Kiplinger's Personal Finance* magazine who also writes a *New York Times* syndicated column under the alias "Dr. Tightwad," for her best advice on all the most vexing money questions you and your kids will confront from 6 to 60—give or take a few years!

■ When should you start giving allowances, and how much money should you give kids at different ages?

It is appropriate to start the allowance around the age of six or so, when the child is in the first grade. Three or four is a little too early, since most kids at that age have a really abstract idea of money. If you're going to start at first grade you should start with at least $1 a week, since if they play two video games at the movies, that eats up their whole allowance. It's also easy for you to manage and for them to manage, because $1 is a nice round sum (if they want to save a portion of it, they can). First grade is also a good time because that's when they're starting to learn about money in school.

The average allowance for six- to eight-year-olds is $2 a week, but it also depends on whether a child is an older child or younger sibling. You can get away with less for an oldest child because he or she has nothing to look up to. If the child is a younger sibling, and older siblings are getting $3, you might find yourself giving them allowances at an earlier age and giving more than you would otherwise. For 9- to 11-year-olds, $4 a week is the average; for 12- to 13-year-olds, $6; for 14- and 15-year-olds, $10; and it kind of tops out there.

■ At what point during the week should you give your kids their allowance?

On your payday you have money on your mind and cash in your pocket, so it's a good time to pay the kids. Sunday, at the beginning of the week, is also good. Parents tend to give allowances at the end of the week, and the kids spend it over the weekend—although a lot of kids are pretty sensible with money.

■ What should kids be required to pay for with their allowance?

It will vary. If you talk to 10 parents, they'll

WORK NOW, EARN MORE LATER

If you think that your teenager's after-school job is harming his or her future prospects, you may be mistaken. A study by Christopher Ruhm, an economics professor at the University of North Carolina at Greensboro, suggests that, on the contrary, such work can have a positive effect on long-term employment, fringe benefits, and occupational status. The study found the correlation is particularly strong for high school seniors. But, working can exact a short-term cost. A 1991 study by professors of psychology Laurence Steinberg of Temple University and Sanford Dornbush of Stanford University found that teens who worked 20 hours or more a week after school got grades half a letter lower than youngsters who worked fewer than 10 hours a week. Kids who spent more than 20 hours at work compensated for shorter hours spent on school work by cheating, copying assignments, and cutting classes more frequently. More alarming are the results of another Steinberg study: Teens who worked more than 20 hours a week used drugs and alcohol 33 percent more often than those who didn't work at all. Kids who work between 1 and 10 hours a week, however, tend to have slightly higher grade point averages and spend more time doing their homework than kids who are not employed.

■ THE REWARDS OF WORKING IN HIGH SCHOOL

Professor Ruhm's study examined the number of hours worked per week as a junior or senior in high school and annual earnings 6 to 9 years after high school graduation.

High school employment hours	Number of respondents	Annual earnings
JUNIOR WORK HOURS		
0	370	$13,856
1–20	553	$17,592
>20	139	$19,241
SENIOR WORK HOURS		
0	282	$12,765
1–20	494	$16,703
>20	289	$19,789

From "Is High School Employment Consumption or Investment?" Christopher J. Ruhm, University of North Carolina Greensboro and National Bureau of Economic Research. Revised: December 1994.

require kids to pay for different things. It doesn't matter how much or how little you require kids to pay for out of their allowance—as long as you require them to pay for something. Young children should start out by paying for the one thing that they most like to spend your money on—something within the dollar-a-week budget. Make that their responsibility. As they get older, you can expand that. If they are getting $5 a week, it is reasonable to expect them to pay for movie admission, snacks, or rent video games with their money.

■ Should you give your kids a clothing allowance, and if so, when?

I think that clothing allowances are probably a good thing. This topic comes up around the age of 15. At the age of 18, especially if they go off to college, they are going to have access to credit cards, and they don't even need your permission. You really want them to be able to spend money wisely. Kids have a skewed notion of buying clothes. They think of fancy jackets and cool shoes, but clothes also include underwear and socks. You want them to go through their clothes and take an inventory of what they need. I recommend starting with catalogs. Say, for example, "I would typically spend $200 for you per season. Here is the J. Crew or L.L. Bean catalog; if you had $200, how would you spend it? Some of those things you might be able to order from catalogs but other things you could get less expensively." They learn if they want a $40 shirt, they'll have to get regular jeans, not designer jeans, etc. Take them with you on a practice shopping excursion, and choose the

EXPERT SOURCES

MAKING KIDS MONEY-SMART

Several studies show that today's kids know less about financial matters than did children 30 years ago. What's the best way for parents to teach their kids money skills? By being good role models and discussing family finances on a regular basis, say experts. Some teaching aids:

PUBLICATIONS

Much of the information provided by the groups below is available free.

NATIONAL CENTER FOR FINANCIAL EDUCATION
☎619-232-8811
■ Kids' books about money. A catalog listing 150 publications costs $2.

CONSUMER FEDERATION OF AMERICA
1424 16th St. N.W., Suite 604, Washington, D.C. 20036
■ Send self-addressed, stamped envelope for brochures about saving and spending.

FEDERAL RESERVE BANK OF NEW YORK
Publications Department
☎212-720-6130
■ Comic books about inflation, trade, etc.

SECURITIES INDUSTRY ASSOCIATION
☎212-608-1500
■ Offers a game for kids called the Stock Electronic Market game.

NATIONAL ASSOCIATION OF INVESTORS CORPORATIONS
☎810-583-6242
■ Information about forming or joining a stock investment club.

LIBERTY FINANCIAL COMPANIES, INC./STEINROE
☎800-403-5437
■ *The Young Investor Parents' Guide* helps parents introduce their kids to the basics of investing.

BOOKS

A PENNY SAVED...Teaching Your Children the Values and Life-Skills They Will Need to Live in the Real World
Neale Godfrey and Tad Richards, Simon & Schuster, $18.95
■ A guide for teaching preschool-to-teenage kids the value of money. Covers spending, saving, lending, borrowing, taxes, and interest.

MONEY SMART KIDS (AND PARENTS, TOO!)
Janet Bodnar Kiplinger, Kiplinger Washington Editors, Inc., $12.95.
■ An all-in-one guide covering topics ranging from allowances and baseball card collections to gift-giving and college funds.

OTHER

STEINROE'S YOUNG INVESTOR FUND
☎800-338-2550
Min. investment: $1,000
■ For parents who want to teach their young kids about equities, this fund invests largely in stocks with kid-appeal, including Coca-Cola, Hershey's, and McDonald's. Includes newsletters, parents' guide, coloring book for children under seven, and IBM-compatible computer game for older kids. The fund has had a mediocre average annual return of 6.3 percent since its creation.

stores ahead of time. From a kid's standpoint, things generally just get handed to them. You want to teach them what is flattering and what isn't; what is well made and what isn't. You don't want to just peel off the bills and send them to the mall. Give them a grasp of how much things really cost.

■ Should you pay kids for chores?
I really think you should separate chores and allowances, or you end up paying kids for things they should be doing for free—cleaning up their rooms, for example. I think definitely kids should do additional chores, and they should be paid on a chore-by-chore

basis. Parents pay kids for chores because they want to teach them about working for pay, which is certainly a fine value. Baby-sitting for younger kids, washing the car, cleaning the garage—if you can agree on a price, inspect the job, and pay for it, it saves time. Washing dishes, cleaning up your room, taking out the trash, setting the table—they should be doing those kinds of chores without pay. I don't think you should get into the habit of paying for basic things because you just set yourself up for problems you might not anticipate.

■ What about baby-sitting for siblings or family members?

It depends on the circumstance. If you have to run to the grocery store after school, no, but if it is something you would pay for—say, it's Saturday night and your child could go out and get another baby-sitting job—you should pay your kids just as you would anyone else. It is okay to pay less than the going rate as long as you don't take advantage of them.

■ How should parents advise children who make money from part-time jobs?

You don't want to give kids the wrong idea that all money is discretionary. If they make $80 a week, they think that's great, but you have to teach them that in the real world, $80 a week is not enough to live on. Nowadays kids can't graduate from high school and go off and get a job that will pay a living wage, so it is appropriate to make kids put some money away for college, whether it's 25 percent, or whatever. It isn't really their money. You as a parent are legally within your rights to take that money and use it for family expenses—although few parents would exercise this right. You should say, if you want to take a part-time job, this is how much time you should work because your studies come first.

You should also give them more financial responsibility, including spending their own money for school field trips, etc. So you can expand the number of things they are paying for. Kids seem to be able to handle around 10 to 15 hours of work a week without too much suffering. But once it gets past that, there seem to be problems—especially after 20 hours a week. Family members don't see each other as often, and the parents don't seem to have as much control. But for some kids work is good, because if they are really unsuccessful in school, they can get job skills.

THOUGHTS FOR YOUR PENNIES

Some 170 billion pennies are in circulation, whether jammed into jars or coffee cans, lodged in car seats, or actually doing business. Is your private stash dragging you down? Here are ways to lighten the load:

■ GIVE THEM TO CHARITY. Many charities run penny drives and will happily take your load—and you'll also get a tax deduction. Salvation Army stores accept caches of pennies and will give you a receipt for tax purposes. Or, you can organize your own penny drive. A nonprofit group called Common Cents New York (☎ 212–736–6437) will help you set up a drive for a good cause.

■ TRADE THEM FOR STAMPS. Chances are your local post office has a vending machine that takes pennies along with other coins. Some 4,500 of the machines have been installed since 1994. Aside from using up your pennies, you can also usually avoid the long lines at the stamp counter.

■ TURN THEM INTO DOLLARS. Most banks will give you 50-penny wrappers to neatly contain your pennies and will then change them into dollars. But policies regarding pennies vary from bank to bank, so check with your branch before you show up with your penny jar.

CREDIT CARDS

A PRO' S PLASTIC PICKING POINTERS

Avoid the hype, be wary of rebates, and closely eye interest rate charges

If your mailbox regularly fills up with pre-approved credit card offers, you're not alone. But accepting every invitation is generally not a good idea—two cards are more than enough for most consumer needs. The most important thing for credit card shoppers to keep in mind when selecting a card is their own spending habits. We asked Ruth Susswein, executive director of Bankcard Holders of America (BHA), a consumer advocacy group, for tips on how to select and use credit cards wisely.

■ What is the most important thing to keep in mind when choosing a credit card?

Most people should base their decision on rate, because most people—about 70 percent—carry a balance and pay interest. The average balance is $1,800 and the average interest rate is 18 percent, so you want to do better than that.

If you are someone who doesn't pay interest and puts a lot of money on your card, then you are an ideal candidate for a rebate/frequent flyer card. Consumers who don't pay interest but spend less can still benefit from these cards, but it will take more time to earn a free trip or a rebate of real value. For example, if a person spends less than $3,000 a year with Discover's rebate card, he or she is taking in $13 at the end of the year (See "The Five Largest Rebate Cards," page 116). The same person will spend over $300 in interest if he or she carries a balance. If you are going to use a rebate or airline mileage card, you should be using that card for all your expenses.

■ Should I take advantage of temporary low-rate, pre-approved offers? Are there disadvantages to changing cards regularly?

We haven't seen anyone hurt by rate-hopping. A lot of the plans are for six months, but we recommend that you go for a teaser rate that lasts a year. You may or may not be able to get an extension, because the bank is not looking to maintain that low rate. If things are competitive, the policy that month might be to extend the rate for six months.

■ Is it worth bargaining with my current issuer if I am offered a better rate?

Certainly. We recommend negotiating the rate. Before you even start looking for another card, it's worth a phone call.

■ My card no longer requires a minimum payment. Should I pay it anyway?

Many issuers have now dropped their minimum payment entirely or lowered it. But even if you are paying $2 a month on every $100 of your balance, $1.50 of that will be interest. We recommend you always pay more than the minimum. You can also pay the balance off in full, and that is the best way to deal with a credit card, because then you're getting a free loan every month.

■ Any other pointers?

Make every effort to pay your bills on time, because many card issuers are beginning to penalize consumers for paying their bills late, skipping payments, or going over their credit limit. We've seen issuers as much as double their rates for these consumers.

EXPERT SOURCES

If you've been denied credit within the past 60 days, you can check on your report at no cost. One of the four big credit-rating agencies can tell you how:

CSC Credit Serv.	**☎ 800-392-7816**
Equifax	**☎ 800-685-1111**
Trans Union	**☎ 800-851-2674**
TRW	**☎ 800-392-1122**

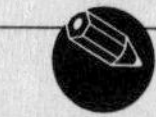

CONSUMER'S GUIDE

THE MOST POPULAR AND BEST CREDIT CARDS

We've listed the largest credit card issuers as well as the top low-interest, rebate, airline mileage, and secured credit cards in the following guide. The interest rates shown are as of February 1996, and can, of course, vary. Do check before signing up. We've listed the rates for standard cards in all cases; fees and perks for gold cards tend to be higher. Diner's Club and American Express cards are excluded here since they are charge cards and must be paid in full each month

■ THE TEN BIGGEST CREDIT CARD ISSUERS

The 10 biggest credit card companies are ranked by numbers of card holders. While both Visa and MasterCard are widely accepted in the United States, cardholders who travel abroad should be aware that Visa is more frequently recognized overseas.

Issuer ☎	No. of accounts	Interest (standard card APR)[1]	Annual fee	Grace period (days)	Annual cost on $1,800 balance[2]	Card choices
1. DISCOVER ☎800-955-7010	36,100,000	19.8% VARIABLE	Classic: None Gold: $40	25	$356.40-$396.40	Discover
2. CITICORP ☎800-462-4642	25,400,000	17.9% VARIABLE	Classic: None Gold: $50	30	$322.20-$372.20	Visa, MasterCard
3. AT&T UNIVERSAL ☎800-662-7759	17,600,000	18.4% VARIABLE	Classic: $20 Gold: $40	25	$351.20-$371.20	Visa, MasterCard
4. MBNA AMERICA ☎800-421-2110	17,000,000	18.4% VARIABLE	Classic: $20 Gold: $40	25	$351.20- $371.20	Visa,
5. FIRST CHICAGO CORP. ☎800-368-4535	15,700,000	18.4% VARIABLE	None	25	$331.20	Visa, MasterCard
6. HOUSEHOLD ☎800-477-6000	13,100,000	18.9% VARIABLE	Classic: None Gold: $39	25	$340.20- $379.20	Visa, MasterCard
7. CHASE MANHATTAN ☎800-282-4273	10,300,000	18.9% VARIABLE	Classic: $20 Gold: $50	30	$360.20- $390.20	Visa, MasterCard
8. FIRST USA ☎800-537-6954	9,800,000	13.99%	None	25	$251.82	Visa, MasterCard
9. CHEMICAL BANK ☎800-356-5555	6,800,000	17.8% FIXED	Classic: $20, Gold: $40	25	$340.40- $360.40	Visa, MasterCard
10. CAPITAL ONE ☎800-952-3388	6,100,000	15.9% VARIABLE	None	25	$286.20	Visa, MasterCard

■ THE FIVE BEST LOW-RATE CARDS*

Banks usually offer a range of interest rates that depend on the cardholder's perceived credit risk. Arkansas rates are also among the most attractive because of the state's strict usury laws. All these cards use the average daily balance method of calculating the balance; the difference is that some include new purchases, while others don't.

Issuer ☎	Interest (standard card APR)	Annual fee	Grace period (days)	Annual cost on $1,800 balance	Card choices	New purchases included or excluded
1. CITIZEN'S BANK (RI) ☎800-438-9222	5.9% FIXED	None	25	$106.20	Visa	Excluded
2. BANK OF BOSTON (MA) ☎800-252-2273	6.65% FIXED	$18	25	$137.70	Visa, MasterCard	Included
3. AMERICAN EXPRESS/CENTURION (True Grace) (DE) ☎800-467-8462	7.9% FIXED	None	25	$142.20	Optima	Excluded
4. AFBA INDUSTRIAL BANK (CO) ☎800-776-2265	8.5% FIXED	None	25	$153	Visa, MasterCard	Included

■ **EXPERT LIST**

Issuer ☎	Interest (standard card APR)	Annual fee	Grace period (days)	Annual cost on $1,800 balance	Card choices	New purchases included or excluded
5. RUKEYSER'S WALL ST. CLUB/ UNION PLANTERS BANK (TN) ☎800-971-4653	8.4% VARIABLE	None	25	$151.20	MasterCard	Included

* National Issuers.

■ THE FIVE LARGEST REBATE CARDS

Consumers can now charge their way to rebates on everything from Rolling Stones merchandise to investments in Fidelity money markets. To get the greatest benefit, however, cardholders should plan to make use of the rebates and charge all of their purchases to their cards.

Issuer ☎	Interest (standard card APR)	Annual see	Annual cost on $1,800 balance	REBATE
1. AT&T SOMETHING EXTRA ☎800-662-7759	17.15% VARIABLE	$20	$310.70–$328.70	One pt. for every dollar on monthly statements. Rewards incl. discounts on rental cars; free CDs, phone service, airline tickets, or reduced credit card interest rate.
2. GM/HOUSEHOLD BANK ☎800-947-1000	17.25% VARIABLE	Classic: 0 Gold: $39	$310.50–$349.50	5% rebate on every dollar (up to $500/year or $3500/7 years for Classic, more for Gold. Redeemable on GM vehicles. Switch to MCI earn $30 GM rebate; save 10% on calls.
3. SMARTRATE/DISCOVER ☎800-347-2683	19.8% VARIABLE	None	$356.40	Cash bonus up to 1% paid yearly, based on annual purchases, calculated monthly.
4. APPLE COMPUTER/CITIBANK ☎800-374-9999	16.65% VARIABLE	$20/ exc. year	$299.70–$319.70	2 1/2% annually for first $3,000, 5% on purchase over $3,000. (up to $500 a year). Can be donated to educational institution.
5. GE REWARDS/CAPITAL CONSUMER CARD CO. ☎800-677-1050	18.15% VARIABLE	None	$326.70	Tiered rebate structure; up to 2% cash back on annual purchases up to $10,000 ($140 annually). Discount coupons worth more than $2,500 annually.

■ THE FIVE LARGEST AIRLINE MILEAGE CARDS

All major U.S. airlines now offer a credit card, and the programs listed here all have generous tie-in programs. In addition, both American Express and Diner's Club offer mileage plans that can be applied to a number of airlines, although it takes longer to qualify for rewards.

Issuer ☎	Interest (standard card APR)	Annual fee	Annual cost on $1,800 balance	REBATE
1. AMERICAN AIRLINES AADVANTAGE/CITIBANK ☎800-843-0777	$16.65 VARIABLE	$50	$349.70	1 mile for each dollar charged; 2,500 bonus miles for new cardholders, 20,000 miles required for free ticket.
2. UNITED AIRLINES MILEAGE PLUS/FIRST CARD ☎800-537-7783	17.15% VARIABLE	Classic:$60 Gold:$100	$368.70–$408.70	1 mile for each dollar charged, 20,000 miles required for free trip in continental U.S., 50,000 mile limit per year.
3. CONTINENTAL ONE PASS/ MARINE MIDLAND BANK 800-850-3144	19.95% (GC) 18.95% (G) VARIABLE	Classic: $45 Gold: $65	$404.10–$406.10	1 mile for each dollar charged, 5,000 bonus miles for new cardholders, 20,000 miles to obtain free ticket
4. USAIR/NATIONS BANK ☎800-732-9194	17.15% VARIABLE	Classic: $35 Gold: $55	$343.70–$363.70	1 mile for each dollar charged, 2,500 mile bonus for new cardholders.
5. NORTHWEST WORLDPERKS/ FIRST BANK SYSTEM ☎800-225-2525	17% VARIABLE	Classic: $55 Gold: $85	$361–$391	1 mile for each dollar charged, 20,000 miles needed for free ticket.

■ EXPERT LIST

■ FIVE GOOD SECURED CREDIT CARDS

For many, including students and those with bad or nonexistent credit histories, getting a credit card is a hurdle. "Secured" cards require cardholders to make a deposit to be held as collateral on which interest is paid. Interests tend to be high and credit limits low, but there are deals.

Issuer ☎	Interest (standard card APR)	Annual fee	Grace period (days)	Card choices	Minimum deposit/ interest
1. FEDERAL SAVINGS BANK (AR) ☎800-285-9090	10.2% VARIABLE	$39	25	Visa, MasterCard	$250/2.5%
2. CALIFORNIA COMMERCE BANK (CA) ☎800-222-1234	12% FIXED	$80	25	Visa, MasterCard	$300/2.25%
3. PEOPLE'S BANK (CT) ☎800-262-4442	16.9% FIXED	$25	25	MasterCard	$500/2%
4. BANCO POPULAR (NY) ☎800-232-6255	18% FIXED	$25	25	MasterCard	$500/3%
5. AMERICAN PACIFIC BANK (OR) ☎800-879-8745	18.9% VARIABLE	$30	30	Visa, MasterCard	$400/4.5%

NOTES: **1.** Fixed rates can be changed within 15 days' notice. **2.** Annual cost on $1,800 balance includes annual fee, where applicable. SOURCES: Top Ten Card Issuers, RAM Research. All other tables: Bankcard Holders of America (BHA).

Complete updated listings of these and other cards are available for $4 to $5 from Bankcard Holders of America, 524 Branch Drive, Salem, VA, 24153, ☎ 703-389-5445. Top Ten Issuers Scoreboard available from RAM Research, PO Box 1700, Frederick, MD 21702, ☎ 800-344-7714.

TIPS ON TIPPING

The following table reflects the current conventional tipping wisdom. The amounts reflect standard gratuity rates in the United States. Overseas, traditions can differ from country to country; it is best to consult a guidebook for the country you will be visiting to learn the local customs.

■ AIRPORT

Car-rental shuttle driver	$1 per use
Hotel courtesy van	$1
if driver helps with luggage	$2
Taxi dispatcher	None
Taxi driver	10–15%
Car service	Gratuity included, or 15% of bill
Curbside baggage handler	$1–$1.50 per bag

■ HOTEL

Doorman for special service	$1–$2
baggage depending on number of bags	$1–$2
Bellhop for taking luggage to room	$1–$2 /bag
for delivering messages or packages	$1–$2 /del.
Message service	None
Housekeeper	$1–$2 per day
for special service	$1–$2 per day
Room-service waiter	15–20%
(if service is included in the bill)	5% or $1 min.
Concierge for tickets, etc.	$5–$10

■ RESTAURANT

Coffee-shop waiter	13–17% of bill
Maitre d' to get a good table	$5 for two $10 for four or more
(double amounts for five-star restaurants)	
Waiter	15–20% of bill
(if gratuities are included, an additional tip is warranted for special service)	
Wine steward	10% of wine bill
Bartender	15% of liquor bill
Hat/coat check	$1 per coat (or per person)
Door attendant	$1–$2 for cabs

■ OTHER

Parking valet	$1–$2 per use
Rail porter	$1 per bag

SHOPPING CLUBS

WHERE THE BARGAINS ARE

Grab your shopping carts, get set, and head for the nearest warehouse

Industrial-sized cans of fruit cocktail. Monster jars of mayo. Jumbo packages of toilet paper rolls. Bulk buyers stocking up for a nuclear winter can still make out like bandits at the warehouse stores and price clubs that dot the American landscape. But these outlets have been busy broadening their appeal. While bulk sales make up most of their business, increasingly these stores are appealing to family consumers with more practical "multi-pack" packaging and an expanding range of products, including clothing, office supplies, and electronics.

The cheapness comes at a price. Clubs are able to offer good deals to customers because they cut their operating costs and profit margins dramatically. In return, customers should not expect frills. Most clubs offer only a few brands in a category, and merchandise can change from week to week, so shoppers loyal to a brand may be disappointed. Also, clubs rarely provide shopping bags, although some offer used boxes for stacking food items.

Most clubs still require shoppers to become "members." At the top three chains—Price-Costco/Price Club, Sam's Club, and BJ's Wholesale Club—membership fees range from $25 to $35 for individuals, which usually include cards for the primary member and his or her spouse. Business memberships—a minority of club members but a majority of sales—usually cost the same as the individual membership, plus an average of $15 for additional company members. Other membership qualifications have mostly been dropped.

Everything isn't a bargain. As the table below shows, some prices are no cheaper than you'd find at your local pharmacy, supermarket, or even the electronics store.

■ ONE SMART SHOPPER'S SHOPPING LIST

We priced a dozen items at two Washington, D.C.-area shopping clubs and compared them with the price of identical items at nearby stores. Here are the results:

PRODUCT	PRICE CLUB (unit price)	BJ'S	SAFEWAY	CVS PHARMACY	CIRCUIT CITY
MAGNAVOX 19" Color TV with Smart Sound (Model 19PR14C)	$189.99	$188.99	—	—	$189.00
SONY 5-Disc Carousel CD Player (Model CDPC-365)	$179.99	$179.99	—	—	$179.98
FUJI 35 mm. color Film Pack: 4 24-exp.s, 2 36-exp. rolls	$13.99	$14.49	$16.38	—	—
CREST Tartar Control Toothpaste 3-tube pack (1 8.2 oz. tube)	$6.49 ($2.16)	$6.49 ($2.16)	$7.77 ($2.59)	$9.69 ($3.23)	—
PAMPERS Stretch Medium Diapers Size 3 (1 diaper)	128/box $23.49 ($.18)	128/box $24.99 ($.20)	32/box $7.29 ($.23)	24/box $6.99 ($.29)	—
TIDE Ultra Laundry Detergent (1 lb.)	280-oz. box $17.49 ($1.00)	280-oz. box $16.99 ($.97)	198-oz. box $17.49 ($1.41)	98-oz. box $9.39 ($1.53)	—
9-LIVES Plus Cat Food (can)	36 5.5-oz cans $8.99 ($.25)	24 5.5-oz. $5.69 ($.24)	2 5.5-oz. $.76 ($.38)	1 5.5-oz. $.39/can	—
PREGO spaghetti sauce w/mushrooms (1 lb.)	67-oz. jar $3.15 ($.75)	67-oz. jar $2.99 ($.72)	28-oz. jar $2.55 ($1.07)	—	—
JIF Creamy Peanut Butter (1 lb.)	2 40-oz. jars $6.79 ($1.36)	2 40-oz. jars $6.49 ($1.30)	28-oz. jar $4.39 ($2.51)	—	—
Boneless, skinless **chicken breasts** (1 lb.)	4-lb. pkg. $2.50/lb.	4-lb. pkg. $2.50/lb.	1.5- to 2-lb.pkg. $4.99/lb.	—	—

BILLS

THE NEXT BEST THING TO NOT PAYING

Forget about writing checks—online banking has arrived

Pretty soon old-fashioned checkbooks may be going the way of the abacus—quaint curiosities that you're more likely to find in a museum than a desk drawer. Electronic bill-paying services are rapidly proliferating. The cost of paying with pen and checkbook is roughly comparable to paying electronically, but the amount of time you spend at least triples—and you have to find a mailbox.

What features should you be looking for in an online banking program? The most basic services limit themselves to paying your bills each month, while others act as virtual electronic bankers, providing users with access to everything from balance statements to transfer of funds. The most elaborate programs enable consumers to initiate loans and purchase stocks or foreign currency. At the moment, however, the more comprehensive programs are generally limited to the largest national banks.

We compared the features of four of the most popular programs (see box below). The cost of accessing each of the programs varies.

Citibank Bank/Direct Access offers electronic bill-paying services only to Citibank customers. They are free to customers with average accounts of $500 or more; those with less pay $5 a month. Users receive $50 for signing up.

Quicken and Microsoft Money are software programs that are available wherever software is sold. Quicken retails for $49.99–$59.99; Microsoft Money retails for $24.88. With both programs, additional fees vary with the bank. (Besides paying bills, Quicken also has additional money management features, such as tax planning, insurance inventory, and payroll/cash flow tracking for small businesses.)

To use Prodigy Bill Payer you have to sign up for Prodigy's online service. Basic Prodigy service is $9.95/month for 5 hours online, including banking services, with fees varying according to bank. Users whose banks are not on the system can have simple bill-paying services for an additional $9.95 a month for the first 30 payments, and additional payments for $3.50 each.

BILL-PAYING OPTIONS

We compared four of the most popular programs with a range of features:

FUNCTIONS	CITIBANK DIRECT ACCESS	INTUIT QUICKEN	MICROSOFT MONEY	PRODIGY BILL PAYER
Printout of ATM record	Yes	Yes	Yes	Yes
Transfer $ bet. accounts	Yes	Yes	Yes	Yes
Pay bills electronically	Yes	Yes	Yes	Yes
Loan information/ application option	Yes	Varies by bank	No	Only available at two banks
Stock information	Research, prices, purch. online	Research, prices available	No	Payment by all, price quotes by 2 banks only
Buy travelers checks	Yes	No	No	No
View credit card account and pay credit card bills	Yes	Yes	No	Yes
Order foreign currency	Yes	No	No	Only at 2 banks

PERSONAL TECH

STRAIGHT TALK ABOUT PHONES

Having trouble sorting through the static? Check here for assistance

It wasn't long ago when the biggest decision a phone user had to make was which long distance company to choose. (AT&T, MCI, and Sprint, which control over 90 percent of the market, now offer almost identical discount plans.) But these days the choices have multiplied. Which kind of mobile phone should I buy? Can I get a free phone? What kind of hidden charges can I expect? And that's just the beginning. AT&T and MCI recently offered their customers the opportunity to sign up for access to the Internet; other phone companies are sure to follow. Here, we've tried to sort through the static.

■ Should I get a cellular or PCS phone?

Chances are you won't have this choice yet. Personal communications systems (PCS) use an entirely digital system; cellular phones, by contrast, run on both analog and digital systems. PCS phones have less static interference and greater security because of an improved encoding system.

As this book was going to press, PCS was only available in the Washington, D.C./Baltimore metropolitan area through Sprint. If you live there and only make mobile calls within that area, PCS is a preferable choice. You won't, however, be able, at least for now, to make calls outside the calling area.

■ Which carrier should you choose?

Where you live determines your access to providers. Currently, Cellular One is the only nationwide carrier. But in most major markets, you have a choice. In the Northeast, for instance, Bell Atlantic/Nynex offers its own service. AT&T is expanding beyond its current markets in the West and South.

Your choice should be partly influenced by the calling area offered (the "coverage"). Even in the same metropolitan region, different carriers offer different coverages. In Washington, for example, Cellular One's coverage includes D.C. and its suburbs, rural Virginia, and the Eastern Shore. Sprint's coverage, on the other hand, is restricted to a narrow band around Washington and Baltimore.

All carriers offer various calling plans with dramatically different monthly charges. Examine your calling habits before making a choice (i.e., what time of the day you most often use the phone and for how long). Depending on the plan you choose, expect to pay a fixed fee that includes a certain number of calling "minutes." Once you use up the free time, expect a flat fee per minute, with different rates for day and evening calls.

■ Can you get a free cellular phone, just for signing up?

Most cellular plans come with a free, basic analog phone. Or you can buy fancier models for $20 to $1,000. Digital phones start higher, at around $200, and go up to $1,500.

■ What about hidden charges?

You can expect to pay a one-time installation fee. Some carriers also charge an activation fee of $35 to $50, although it's often waived. It doesn't hurt to ask to have this fee waived, even if a special isn't being offered.

You'll pay more for additional features—such as call forwarding, call waiting, detailed billing, and conference calling.

■ How long a commitment do you need to make when you sign up?

The minimum commitment is usually a year. If you commit for two years, most companies will offer additional discounts.

■ For car use, should I get a portable phone or one that's mounted in my car?

Mounted car phones have in the past been more powerful than battery-charged mobile phones, which lacked mobility. Now, however, you can buy a booster kit that gives a mobile phone the same power as a mounted car phone when it's used in the car.

EXPERT Q & A

CHARITY BEGINS WITH YOU

Good causes abound. Here's what you should know before you give

Americans gave nearly $130 billion to charity in 1994, and as federal budget cutbacks begin to be felt, demand for donations and competition among charities is expected to increase. Donors who want to make sure their hard-earned cash is put to the best use will have to choose between competing causes. We spoke with Stacy Palmer, managing editor of *The Chronicle of Philanthropy*, to get expert advice.

■ What are the important things for people to keep in mind when choosing a charity?

They really have to think hard about what causes they care about—not just the ones that solicit through the mail. It's only certain kinds of charity that raise money through the mail. It's the smaller, local social service charities that are going to be most affected by the federal cuts and are going to be really dependent on private donations. Arts groups are also going to be particularly hard hit.

■ How much of your income should you give to charities?

Charities recommend giving 5 percent of your income or your time, or some combination of the two. But most people don't give that much. For some charities, volunteer help is just as important as cash.

■ What should potential donors beware of?

Giving by telephone. That is where the most abuses occur. People should be extremely

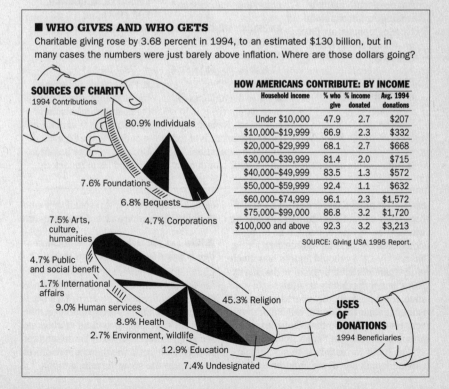

■ WHO GIVES AND WHO GETS

Charitable giving rose by 3.68 percent in 1994, to an estimated $130 billion, but in many cases the numbers were just barely above inflation. Where are those dollars going?

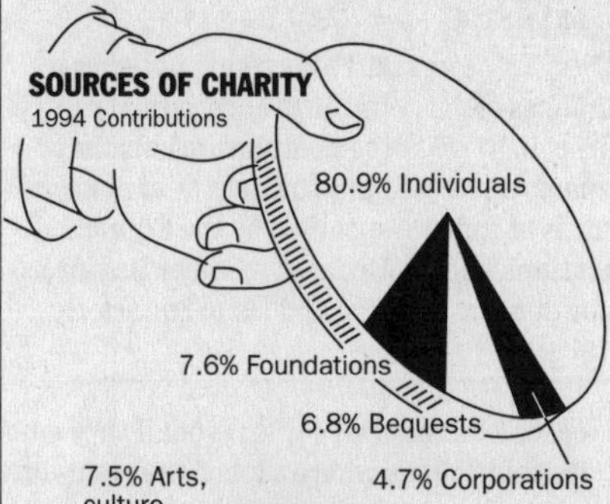

SOURCES OF CHARITY
1994 Contributions

80.9% Individuals
7.6% Foundations
6.8% Bequests
4.7% Corporations

HOW AMERICANS CONTRIBUTE: BY INCOME

Household income	% who give	% income donated	Avg. 1994 donations
Under $10,000	47.9	2.7	$207
$10,000–$19,999	66.9	2.3	$332
$20,000–$29,999	68.1	2.7	$668
$30,000–$39,999	81.4	2.0	$715
$40,000–$49,999	83.5	1.3	$572
$50,000–$59,999	92.4	1.1	$632
$60,000–$74,999	96.1	2.3	$1,572
$75,000–$99,000	86.8	3.2	$1,720
$100,000 and above	92.3	3.2	$3,213

SOURCE: Giving USA 1995 Report.

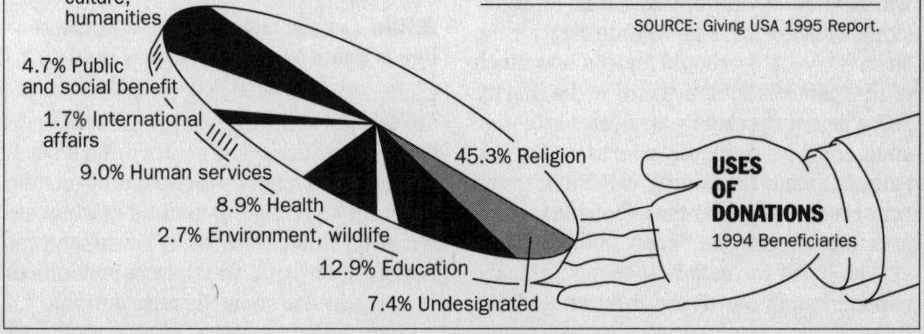

USES OF DONATIONS
1994 Beneficiaries

7.5% Arts, culture, humanities
4.7% Public and social benefit
1.7% International affairs
9.0% Human services
8.9% Health
2.7% Environment, wildlife
12.9% Education
7.4% Undesignated
45.3% Religion

EXPERT SOURCES

WHO'S WATCHING OUT FOR YOUR MONEY?

Americans have been bombarded in recent years with media reports of unsavory fraud rings posing as charities and philanthropic organizations. How can you make sure your money is going to truly worthy causes? The following watchdog groups monitor charities around the country and issue regular reports that are available to the public:

NATIONAL CHARITIES INFORMATION BUREAU
Dept. 6005,
19 Union Square West,
New York, NY 10003
☎212-929-6300

■ Provides brief surveys of nearly 400 charities in its *Wise Giving Guide,* published quarterly. Charities evaluated as to their management of finances, truth in fund-raising, and accountability. Single copies are free; an annual subscription costs $35.

PHILANTHROPIC ADVISORY SERVICE
(Council of Better Business Bureaus) 4200 Wilson Blvd., Arlington, VA 22203
☎703-276-0100

■ Information about 250 of the most visible national charities, including programs, finances, fund-raising practices, and governance. For information on local charities contact the Philanthropic Advisory Service or its local Better Business Bureau. PAS has a number of publications and a Web site: *http://www.bbb.org/bbb/*

AMERICAN INSTITUTE OF PHILANTHROPY
4579 Laclede Ave., Suite 136, St. Louis, MO 63108
☎314-454-3040

■ Rates the finances of over 300 charities in 37 categories. Reports on executive salaries at individual organizations and offers advice for donors. Charities with substantial endowments are given lower ratings since they are seen as requiring less in the way of donations. The quarterly *Charity Rating Guide and Watchdog Report* is available for $3 a copy; a one-year subscription costs $35.

EVANGELICAL COUNCIL FOR FINANCIAL ACCOUNTABILITY
PO Box 17456,
Washington, D.C. 20041
☎703-713-1414

■ This group publishes a list of 817 accredited religious organizations that abide by a set of criteria specified by the Council. Updated member lists are free and issued quarterly.

careful and always ask for something in writing. They should ask the person calling whether he is paid to call—is he a professional solicitor, or is he volunteering for the charity? And they should find out how much of the money is actually going to the charity. Ask whether the charity is registered in your state. Some states require charities to be registered to make that kind of call. But it's very, very risky to give over the telephone to some organization you don't know well.

Watch out for callers who say they are raising money for dying children and diseases like cancer. People respond very emotionally. That's where a lot of the scams are.

■ How can you make sure your organization is going to use your money well?

Charities—especially legitimate charities—are usually willing to send an annual report or their provisional tax return. That's how you can see what they are spending on their program expenses, their fund-raising, etc. A charity is not required by law to send you its tax return, but if you show up at its offices, it is required to show the return to you.

PHILANTHROPIST'S GUIDE

CHARITIES THAT MAKE A DIFFERENCE

Each year, The Chronicle of Philanthropy *ranks charities according to their private income and the percentage of donations that are used for program support. Here are the largest foundations by category:*

CHARITY	LOCATION	PRIVATE INCOME ($millions)	SHARE FOR PROGRAMS (%)	TELEPHONE
■ HUMAN SERVICES				
Salvation Army	Alexandria, Va.	$726.00	86.23	703-684-5500
American Red Cross	Washington, D.C.	$497.32	91.87	202-639-3286
Second Harvest	Chicago, Ill.	$425.07	99.75	302-263-2303
YMCA of the USA	Chicago, Ill.	$375.14	N/A	312-977-0031
Catholic Charities	Alexandria, Va.	$336.17	75.39	703-549-1390
■ RELIEF AND DEVELOPMENT				
World Vision	Monrovia, Calif.	$220.25	76.80	818-303-8811
AmeriCares Foundation	New Canaan, Conn.	$204.57	98.85	203-972-5500
MAP International	Brunswick, Ga.	$125.38	95.20	912-265-6010
Catholic Relief Services	Baltimore, Md.	$97.84	91.88	410-625-2220
■ CONSERVATION				
Nature Conservancy	Arlington, Va.	$172.14	60.50	703-841-5300
Ducks Unlimited	Memphis, Tenn.	$40.63	77.18	901-758-3825
World Wildlife Fund	Washington, D.C.	$39.12	88.12	202-778-9753
North Shore Animal League	Port Washington, N.Y.	$29.27	69.55	516-883-7575
Natural Resources Defense Council	New York, N.Y.	$23.11	62.85	212-727-4400
■ HEALTH				
American Cancer Society	Atlanta, Ga.	$373.07	72.31	404-841-0700
American Heart Association	Dallas, Texas	$249.06	77.43	214-373-6300
March of Dimes Birth Defects Found.	White Plains, N.Y.	$119.18	75.91	914-428-7100
National Easter Seal Society	Chicago, Ill.	$117.49	79.21	312-726-6200
Planned Parenthood Fed. of America	New York, N.Y.	$116.00	76.76	212-261-4300
■ RELIGION				
Campus Crusade for Christ Int.	Orlando, Fla.	$168.65	84.87	407-826-2200
Christian Broadcasting Network	Virginia Beach, Va.	$108.95	87.21	804-579-7000
Focus on the Family	Colorado Springs, Colo.	$89.41	75.70	719-531-3400
Billy Graham Evangelistic Assoc.*	Minneapolis, Minn.	$77.79	77.06	612-338-0500

Source: *The Chronicle of Philanthropy*, November 2, 1995.
*Figures are for Billy Graham Evangelistic Association and six affiliated organizations.

The thing to keep in mind with small charities is that they tend to spend a lot on fund-raising and administration, because they're getting started and trying to make their appeal. So it doesn't necessarily mean they're a fraud just because they're spending 30 to 40 percent on fund-raising. Small charities are sometimes shunned because of that and they shouldn't be.

■ What can you do if you think you have been taken advantage of by a fraudulent organization?

You should report that right away. Go to your state attorney general. Most states have a person or an office that specifically works on consumer protection. The other thing to do is to call an organization like the Better Business Bureau.

INSURANCE

HOW TO BUY WHAT YOU REALLY NEED

If you read nothing else before you buy insurance, read this

Buying insurance is right up there with going to the dentist on most folks' list of things they hate to do. And worse, unlike going to the dentist, buying insurance requires some know-how. Studies by the nonprofit National Insurance Consumer Organization show that more than 9 out of 10 Americans buy and carry the wrong types and amounts of insurance coverage.

The insurance industry doesn't make it any easier. Sorting through all the policies offered requires the patience of a crossword puzzle addict and the mathematical skills of an astrophysicist.

FACT FILE:

HOW LONG WE LIVE

■ *The average American born in 1990 can expect to live more than 26 years longer than his ancestor born in 1900.*

LIFE EXPECTANCY IN YEARS

Year born	Male	Female
1900	46.6	48.7
1910	48.6	52
1920	54.4	55.6
1930	59.7	63.5
1940	62.1	66.6
1950	66.5	72.2
1960	67.4	74.1
1970	68	75.6
1980	70.7	78.1
1990	72.7	76.1

SOURCE: 1995 *Life Insurance Fact Book Update*, American Council of Life Insurance.

Some simple guidelines can help, though. Find a strong, healthy company that tailors policies to the coverage you need, and then focus on getting the best value for your dollar. Here's how to figure out what kind and just how much coverage you really need for the most common varieties of insurance.

LIFE INSURANCE:

Your life insurance needs will vary over the course of your life, peaking as you cope with hefty mortgage payments and big tuition bills for your kids, and falling after you've retired.

■ **How much you need:** Whatever policy you buy, the most important thing is that you end up with enough coverage.

The amount of life insurance you need roughly correlates with your family's annual living expenses for the number of years you'll need the insurance. Add together all of your family's expenses for the years you'll need insurance. You should include future college costs, mortgage payments, costs to settle your estate and an emergency fund (typically, three months' salary). Then subtract all family income other than your salary. Be sure to include Social Security and pension payments as well as any income you may receive from your investments. Adjust both your future expenses and income to take account of inflation. The result of this calculation is how much life insurance you need. Some experts suggest an even simpler formula: multiply your annual take-home pay by five.

■ **What your options are:** Term insurance will pay your survivors a death benefit if you die while the contract is in force. It is often called "pure" insurance because it offers a death benefit without a savings component. A term life insurance policy can be locked in for 1 to 20 years. It is often the best—and cheapest—bet for families who want to provide for the future in the event of the loss of a breadwinner and who want to target the years when their insurance needs will be greatest.

A term insurance policy can often be rolled into a whole life policy later. "Whole life" (also called guaranteed-permanent) insurance provides a death benefit until you reach the age of 90 or 100, as long as you pay fixed premiums—premiums that cannot have unscheduled increases. Whole life insurance premiums are substantially higher at first than the same amount of term insurance, but term insurance premiums skyrocket as you get older. With whole life, you are betting that you will be around awhile, paying the higher premium at first and then averaging the cost out over a lifetime.

If you are older, the kids have graduated from college, and the mortgage is paid off, the fixed premiums of a whole life policy might be more attractive. These policies also offer an investment opportunity. Here, part of your premium payment is invested into a plan where earnings are tax deferred, so that the policy builds "cash value" over the years. At some point, the cash value of the policy should be enough to pay your premiums. "Cash-value" policies can help build wealth for you, and possibly your heirs—life insurance proceeds are not subject to income tax, or, for the most part, estate tax. However, they still need to be carefully evaluated. You should weigh each policy's returns against those you're getting from your other investments.

■ **What to watch out for:** Remember, the agent's computer models showing the projected returns are estimates, and are by no means guaranteed.

Not all policies that appear to provide fixed premiums and cash values are guaranteed-permanent insurance. Universal life, for example, is a form of cash-value insurance that combines term insurance with a "side fund" that is credited with earnings. Instead of making fixed premium payments, you have the flexibility to decide the size and frequency of your payments to the side fund, which accumulates interest on a tax-deferred basis. You get death-benefit protection as long as the amount in the side fund can cover the cost of the insurance.

If you make low payments to the side fund early on, you will have to make sharply higher payments later to maintain death-benefit protection. This flexibility means that universal life can function more like term or guaranteed-permanent insurance, depending on how you fund it.

Variable life insurance products can be even riskier. You choose among the investment options offered by the insurance company—stocks, bonds, fixed-rate funds, etc. Depending upon how the investments perform, you either build up cash value in the policy or not.

DISABILITY:

Disability insurance may be the most important kind of insurance to have. Indeed, during the peak-earning years of your career, the possibility of suffering a long-term disability is considerably greater than the possibility of death. The Society of Actuaries says that a 35-year-old is three times likelier to become

FACT FILE:

HOW WE DIE

■ *More than half the deaths in the United States stem from heart disease or cancer.*

CAUSES OF DEATH IN THE U.S.

Heart disease	32.4%
Cancer	23.6%
Cerebrovascular disease	6.7%
Influenza and pneumonia	3.6%
Diabetes	2.4%
Diseases of arteries, arteriole	1.9%
Chronic liver disease/cirrhosis	1.1%
Other diseases	21.9%
TOTAL NATURAL CAUSES	93.7%
Motor vehicle accidents	1.8%
Suicide	1.3%
Homicide	1.0%
Other accidents	2.1%
TOTAL EXTERNAL CAUSES	6.3%

SOURCE: *1995 Life Insurance Fact Book Update*, American Council of Life Insurance.

EXPERT LIST

INSURANCE COVERAGE NOT TO BUY

The CFA Insurance Group is a nonprofit organization that promotes the interests of insurance buyers. Here is its list of coverage not worth buying.

■ **Air travel insurance:** It costs too much and pays back only about 10 cents for each dollar of premiums. It is not comprehensive. You're more likely to die from a heart attack.

■ **Rain insurance:** It pays if it rains a lot on your vacations.

■ **Life insurance if you're single:** If you have no dependents, there is no economic reason to buy life insurance since there is no economic catastrophe associated with your death.

■ **Life insurance if you're married with children and your spouse has a good job:** If one of you dies, can the other get along on one income? If so, perhaps no life insurance is necessary beyond that which you have at work.

■ **Mail order life insurance:** Stay away unless you compare its price to annual renewable term insurance and find it cheaper.

■ **Insurance that pays only if you're hurt or killed in a mugging:** A classic example of "junk" insurance. This risk is covered by good life and health policies.

■ **Contact lens insurance:** The cost of a premium is about equal to the cost of a lens at a discount eyeglass store.

■ **Cancer insurance:** What good is a cancer insurance policy if you have a heart attack? To buy specific illness coverage is like buying toothpaste one squeeze at a time.

■ **Rental car insurance:** Your own auto insurance policy probably covers you if you do damage to a rental car. Also, many credit cards cover this.

■ **Life or health insurance sold to cover a car or other loan.**

■ **Health insurance that pays $100 a day while you are in the hospital in lieu of comprehensive coverage.**

■ **Health insurance on your pet.**

SOURCE: The CFA Insurance Group, Washington, D.C.

disabled for three months before reaching 65 than he is to die younger than 65.

■ **How much you need:** You can figure out how much disability insurance you need in the same way that you calculated your life insurance needs. Take your annual expenses and subtract your family's annual income without your salary. Buy as much disability insurance up to that level as you can. Generally, insurers will sell you only enough insurance to replace 60 percent of your income, so that, they say, you will have an incentive to return to work.

■ **What your options are:** The cost of disability income insurance depends on factors like your age, your profession, the amount of time you've worked or owned your business, whether you smoke and, more recently, whether you're a man or a woman. Since women file for disability benefits more often than men, many insurance companies have recently begun to raise women's rates, while at the same time lowering the rates for men.

■ **What to watch out for:** Look for a policy that can't be canceled and has no increase in premium until you are 65. Get a cost-of-living adjustment provision, so that your benefits increase once a year for as long as you are disabled. You should also insist on a provision allowing you to boost your coverage as your income increases.

Pay particular attention to the definition of disability. Some insurers say you qualify for benefits if you are unable to do your job, others only if you are unable to do any job. Residual or partial disability benefits can be tacked on to provide a percentage of lost income if you take a lower-paying job because of your disability. Set as long a waiting period as you can afford before the benefits kick in—delaying payments for three months to a year can substantially reduce premiums. A final tip: You can usually earn substantial premium discounts from insurers simply by doing things such as supplying a copy of your tax return at application time or prepaying a few years' premium up front.

HEALTH:

You're probably covered by group health insurance by your employer, but if you're not, you can buy individual coverage that will meet your needs—at a higher cost.

■ **How much you need:** At a minimum, you should buy a catastrophic policy that protects you from serious and financially disastrous losses that can result from an illness or injury. You need to factor in how much you must absorb in deductibles and copayments.

■ **What your options are:** Even if you buy a comprehensive policy that covers most medical, hospital, surgical, and pharmaceutical bills, it won't cover everything. You may need additional single-purpose coverage. You may want a Medicare supplement policy to fill in the gaps in your Medicare coverage if you are over 65. Private insurers offer "MedSup" specifically to cover Medicare copayments and deductibles. Some also cover outpatient prescription drugs. Hospital indemnity insurance pays you cash benefits for each day you are hospitalized, up to a designated number of days. The money can be used to meet out-of-pocket medical copayments or any other need. Specified disease policies—usually for cancer—are not available in every state. Even so, benefits are limited.

Depending on your age and circumstances, a long-term care policy might be a good idea. This type of policy covers the cost of custodial care either in a nursing home or in your own home. The Health Insurance Association of America estimates that nursing home care costs $30,000 to $50,000 per year or more, depending on where you live. Having someone in your home three days a week to care for you can cost almost $7,500 a year. If those kinds of expenses make you shudder, a long-term care policy can offer some relief. But remember this: If you are 65, there's slightly more than a 60 percent chance you'll never collect anything from a long-term care policy.

■ **What to watch out for:** You can reduce your premiums by opting for a large deductible—you will pay the entire amount due up to a certain limit. You may be able to save more by enrolling in a managed care plan, such as a health maintenance organization (HMO). If you have a problem getting insurance because of a pre-existing condition, find out if your state is one of the growing number that have risk pools, which provide insurance for people who can't get it elsewhere.

HOMEOWNER'S:

It doesn't matter what you paid for your house. What you need to insure is the cost to rebuild it. The two figures can be wildly different.

■ **How much you need:** The conventional formula for gauging how much insurance you need on your home is to figure out how much it would actually cost to rebuild it, then tack on the extras, such as the cost of central air conditioning or a new furnace. If you can't afford insurance for 100 percent of the house's value, make sure you're covered for at least 80 percent. That way, if you suffer a partial loss—say, a fire destroys your bedroom—an insurer will likely cover the entire cost. If you're less than 80 percent insured, your insurer will only pay that percentage of partial damages.

■ **What your options are:** There are three types of homeowner's policies: cash-value, replacement cost and guaranteed replacement cost. Cash-value insurance is the least expensive. It will pay you whatever your valuables would sell for today, which is unlikely to buy you a similar new item. Replacement cost insurance will replace the item that was lost or damaged with something new, but not necessarily the same as the one you lost, because this type of insurance usually comes with a price cap. You'll be able to replace, say, your furnace, but not necessarily with the best model. Guaranteed replacement cost insurance has no cap and offers the best coverage. The only thing it generally will not cover is the cost of upgrading your house to meet building codes that may have changed since the policy was issued.

Homeowner's insurance also includes liability coverage. Most policies come with up to $300,000 worth of coverage. Unless your total assets are less than that, you should probably pay a little more and get more coverage. For example, experts counsel that if you have $200,000 to $500,000 in assets, you need about $1 million in liability coverage. The best way to do this is to buy an "umbrella policy" that covers both your home and car. Liability coverage comes fairly cheap. It's unlikely that a claim against you will exceed $300,000, so underwriters can afford to give you a price break. A $300,000 to $1 million umbrella liability policy will cost anywhere from $80 to $300 annually, the average being about $150. For another $1 million in coverage, double the price.

■ **What to watch out for:** Cash-value coverage may be a little risky, since an investment you made years ago that is still holding up—such as a good furnace—may now be worth just a fraction of its cost. Replacement-cost coverage, which usually costs 10 percent to 20 percent more, is preferable—and worth it. You should be sure to find out if there are any caps on what will be reimbursed for individual items, such as jewelry. For example, the amount you can recover if all of your jewelry is stolen may be, say, $1,000, if that is the amount of the cap for jewelry. If you have valuables that are worth more, you may want to buy more insurance by adding riders to your policy. This generally costs about $1.50 per $100 of insurance.

AUTO:

In most states, drivers are required to have liability insurance for each driver, for accidents, and for the other person's car in case of an accident.

■ **How much you need:** Generally, insurance experts counsel that you buy as much liability coverage as you're worth. You should also consider an "umbrella policy," described above, that covers both your home and car.

■ **What your options are:** Collision and comprehensive coverage accounts for 30 percent to 45 percent of your premium. If the cost of your collision and comprehensive insurance is more than 10 percent of your car's Blue Book value, it probably makes sense to drop it. Remember, though, that if you get into an accident, you'll have to decide if it's worth getting your car fixed.

Uninsured or underinsured motorist coverage also is sometimes desirable, but it is probably cheaper to purchase it in your home or life policy. You may be able to slash the price of your car insurance by adding safety or antitheft features to your car, maintaining a safe driving record, or simply by driving a low number of miles each year.

■ **What to watch out for:** For an old jalopy, the insurance cost may not be worth the amount you'd receive in the event of an accident. The most you'll get if your car is damaged is the Blue Book value of the vehicle—not that much if your car is more than five years old.

A last tip: Medical payment, income replacement, and rental car insurance can add substantially to your premiums and may be covered elsewhere. Some credit card companies, for example, offer rental car insurance.

EXPERT SOURCES

HELP IS JUST A PHONE CALL AWAY

Some sources for insurance advice, discounts, and information

BASIC INFORMATION

General information and advice by phone:

NATIONAL INSURANCE CONSUMER HELPLINE
■ Sponsored by the insurance industry. Offers general information and advice about choosing the right policy, though it will not offer advice on specific products. It can help with life, health, home, and auto insurance.
☎ 800–942–4242

THE INSURANCE INFORMATION INSTITUTE
■ A nonprofit trade group for property and casualty insurers, answers questions on homeowners and car insurance.
☎ 212–669–9200
For information about fee-only insurance alliances in your area:
☎ 800–874–5662

THE HEALTH INSURANCE ASSOCIATION OF AMERICA
■ Provides information on health insurance.
☎ 202–824–1600

THE AMERICAN COUNCIL OF LIFE INSURANCE
■ The industry's trade organization.
☎ 202–624–2000

YOUR STATE INSURANCE DEPARTMENT
■ Can tell you what products and companies are available in your area. Usually able to assist consumers with complaints. Check directory assistance for toll-free number.

INDEPENDENT APPRAISERS

Unlike insurance agents, who get a commission, independent appraisers do not have a vested interest in the kind of insurance you buy.

THE CFA INSURANCE GROUP
■ A nonprofit public interest group. Provides general tips on buying any kind of insurance. An actuary will evaluate computer illustrations of cash-value policies you're thinking of buying or currently own for a flat $40 fee for the first one, $30 for each additional assessment, and $75 for second-to-die policies.
☎ 202–547–6426

THE LIFE INSURANCE ADVISERS ASSOCIATION
■ Charges $150 to $200 an hour to analyze a policy and help you identify exactly what you need.
☎ 800–521–4578

PRICE QUOTES

To shop insurance rates by phone without dealing with an agent:

INSURANCE QUOTE
■ Provides quotes free of charge over the phone for term insurance and whole life insurance.
☎ 800–972–1104

SELECTQUOTE
■ Identifies companies that give you the best rates for term insurance and sells policies by mail.
☎ 800–343–1985

QUOTESMITH
■ Will search pool of policies sold by independent agents and provide quotes free of charge.
☎ 800–556–9393

INSURANCE INFORMATION
■ Will find cheapest policies for $50 fee. Full refund if it doesn't save you $50 over your current policy.
☎ 800–472–5800

WHOLESALE INSURANCE NETWORK
■ Will give you prices for low-load policies.
☎ 800–808–5810

DIVORCE

LESSONS FROM CHUCK AND DI

Ask for the crown jewels, get everything on paper, avoid confrontations

In their four years of living apart, Prince Charles and Princess Diana helped to keep an army of tabloid journalists employed; now that the couple has announced they are formally calling it quits after 14 years of marriage, the royal lawyers have joined the fray. Luckily for Diana, modern princesses rejected by their spouses no longer face death by drowning or beheading, as was the case in earlier times. Indeed, Diana will receive a financial settlement of a reported $23 million.

"It's not like a normal case where she gets the money and runs like hell," said Ray Tooth, a British divorce lawyer, shortly after the royal divorce was announced. But mere commoners can learn some lessons from the War of the Waleses. To find out what they are, we spoke to Donald Schiller, a partner with the Chicago law firm Schiller, DuCanto & Fleck, the largest divorce law firm in the country.

■ **HIRE AN EXPERIENCED LAWYER.** After hashing out their lives in public, Charles and Diana, of course, depended on high-priced solicitors to reach a civil settlement. But even if your divorce is amicable, Schiller recommends getting professional counsel. His only possible exception: a short, uncomplicated marriage with no children, no real estate, and opposing parties certain that they know each other's assets and income.

Make sure that your attorney is highly experienced in divorce law. Don't assume a friend's lawyer is right for you; if you need one, call your local bar association for a directory of lawyers. Above all, says Schiller, "a lawyer who promises too much and agrees with everything you say is not someone to hire. You don't want to make fantastic claims."

■ **BE CLEAR ABOUT WHAT'S IMPORTANT TO YOU.** After her private meeting with Charles and other royal negotiators, Diana made sure a spokesperson publicly conveyed her terms: She would continue to live in Kensington Palace and participate in all decisions involving Princes William and Harry. Common folk are less likely to benefit from a public airing, but they do need to make their goals clear to their lawyer. Divorcing spouses should realize that the divorce document is an important one, Schiller emphasizes. Everything important to you should be in it.

■ **AVOID BEING CONFRONTATIONAL.** Once both prince and princess had admitted to adultery and Diana had questioned Charles's fitness for the throne, it was too late for the Waleses to take the high road. But that doesn't mean all couples have to start off from a confrontational position. A low-key approach to negotiation is not a sign of weakness, Schiller insists. If you want to get nasty, you can always do so later if your spouse refuses to cooperate. It's best to keep your bargaining chips in hand; otherwise, you will have nothing to hit the other side with later on.

■ **GO FOR THE CROWN JEWELS.** In addition to free rent at Kensington Palace, Diana's estimated annual expenses include, among other things, $450,000 for household expenses, $153,000 for clothing, and $6,400 for hair coloring and beauty treatments. But financially dependent women of more modest means also need to make sure they are provided for adequately with temporary support until a final agreement is worked out. If you are a woman whose husband won't support you adequately, Schiller recommends that you attempt to get copies of your past three to five years of IRS returns, including family business returns if any, and make an inventory of all your assets and liabilities before you meet with your lawyer. If your spouse has threatened to hide all the assets, leave town, or clean out the house, Schiller advises, you should seek an injunction or restraining order.

■ **DON'T TREAT THE KIDS AS A PRIZE:** As the second and third in line for the British throne,

Princes William and Harry are literally royal treasures; consequently, matters surrounding their custody arrangements were resolved with the utmost care. The boys will continue to split their time between their parents. Schiller suggests that most children would be better off if all custody cases were handled this gingerly. Unfortunately, he says, parents who think about winning custody as if it is a prize can create serious psychological problems for their kids. Parents should isolate the children from the process as much as possible.

Divorcing parents should also beware of joint custody, which only works with couples who cooperate. Even then, Schiller notes, the respective rights of the parties, including parenting time, should be well defined in a joint parenting agreement.

As a rule, Schiller says, the more you have in a divorce settlement that's specific, the less likely it is to lead to more fighting. Both spouses should plan arrangements as if they are not going to get on after the divorce: "It's much easier to give up rights through custom and practice than to get them later on."

EXPERT TIPS

BROTHER, CAN YOU SPARE A LOAN?

Borrow from a family member, but don't expect a sweetheart deal

Many of the wealthiest philanthropists in recent history have been stingy about parting with their hard-earned dough, especially when the recipients were family members. The late Jean Paul Getty, an eccentric billionaire who made his fortune in oil, only reluctantly agreed to lend his son $1 million to pay ransom to Italian kidnappers who were holding Getty's grandson captive. But even for willing relatives and the not-so-wealthy, family loans entail risks. We spoke with D. J. Shah, a Weston, Mass., financial planner and consultant, for some tips.

■ **MAKE THE TERMS OF THE LOAN CLEAR.** If the amount of the loan is not substantial, consider making it a gift. You can give any number of individuals up to $10,000 annually, without incurring gift tax.

If the loan is for a significant amount and you expect to be paid back, treat it as a business transaction: Define the expectations, when the loan will be paid back, what the interest will be, etc. Whenever a note is written between family members, it is useful to add a paragraph saying that the lender can sell the note to a third party for collection purposes.

■ **WATCH OUT FOR UNCLE SAM.** Lenders should always charge interest, particularly on loans of $1,000 and up. If you don't, the IRS assumes that you earned interest on the loan amount and will treat it as a gift. This could result in a double tax bill—income and gift—for the lender.

Avoid offering your borrower a below-market interest rate. Again, the IRS could cite unusually favorable terms as evidence that the loan was, in fact, a gift. How much interest should you charge? The U.S. Treasury publishes three separate rates—for short-, medium-, and long-term loans—based on the average rate of U.S. obligations. The rates are updated quarterly.

■ **GO AFTER DEADBEATS.** The IRS doesn't want people transferring wealth without paying taxes. If you have tried unsuccessfully to collect a loan, and have documented your efforts, you can write it off as a bad debt—lenders usually need only to show the effort. With family members, however, if you've made an effort to collect and it did not affect the borrower's credit rating, the IRS may argue that you did not try hard enough. If a payment is late, however, the borrower can make up for it later.

CONSUMER'S GUIDE

HAVING YOUR DAY IN SMALL CLAIMS COURT

Mad as hell at your neighbor who mistakenly cut down one of the trees on your property? Furious at the dry cleaner who ruined your new suit? Peeved at the mechanic who did everything but fix your car? Disputes like these, where the anger quotient is high and the dollar value relatively small, usually end up in small claims court. The filing fee is nominal, often $25 or less, and most cases are settled within two months. Although you can hire a lawyer to present your case, in most states, representation isn't necessary. Many states now send cases to mediators, who help the parties reach a compromise, and arbitrators, whose decisions are binding. The following are state-by-state guidelines from the National Center for State Courts in Williamsburg, Va.

State	Maximum dollar amount	Jury trials	Lawyers permitted
Alabama	$1,500	No	Optional
Alaska	$5,000	No	Yes
Arizona	$1,500	No	No
Arkansas	$3,000 [1]	No	No
California	$5,000	No	No
Colorado	$3,500	No	No
Connecticut	$2,000	No	Yes
Delaware	$2,000	No	Yes
District of Columbia	$5,000	Yes	Yes
Florida	$2,500	Yes	Yes
Georgia	$25,000 [2]	Yes [3]	Yes
Hawaii	$2,500 [4]	No	Yes
Idaho	$3,000	No	No
Illinois	$2,500	Yes	Yes
Indiana	$3,000	No	Yes
Iowa	$3,000	No	Yes
Kansas	$1,000	No	No
Kentucky	$1,500	No	Yes
Louisiana	$2,000	No	Yes
Maine	$3,000	No	Yes
Maryland	$2,500	No	Yes
Massachusetts	$1,500 [5]	Yes	Yes
Michigan	$1,750	No	Yes
Minnesota	$5,000	No	Yes
Mississippi	$1,000 [6]	N/A	N/A
Missouri	$3,000	No	Yes
Montana	$3,000	No	No
Nebraska	$1,800	No	No
Nevada	$7,500 [7]	No	Yes
New Hampshire	$2,500	No	Yes
New Jersey	$1,500	No	Yes
New Mexico	N/A	N/A	N/A
New York	$3,000	N	Yes
North Carolina	$3,000	No	Yes
North Dakota	$3,000	No	Varies
Ohio	$2,000	No	Yes
Oklahoma	$3,000	Yes	Yes
Oregon	$2,500	No	No
Pennsylvania	$5,000	No	Yes
Rhode Island	$1,500	No	Yes
South Carolina	$2,500	Yes	Yes
South Dakota	$4,000	No	Yes
Tennessee	$10,000–$15,000	No	Yes
Texas	$5,000	Yes	Yes
Utah	$5,000	No	Yes
Vermont	$3,500	Yes	Yes
Virginia	N/A	N/A	N/A
Washington	$2,500	No	No
West Virginia	N/A	N/A	N/A
Wisconsin	$4,000	Yes	Yes
Wyoming	$2,000	No	Yes

NOTES:

N/A=Information not available

Maximum Dollar amount=maximum amount of suit

1. (Municipal Court); $300 (Justice of the Peace)
2. (Civil Court); $5,000 (Magistrate Court); $7,500 (Municipal Court)
3. Except Magistrate Court
4. Except in residential security deposit cases
5. $2,000 for District Court Department
6. (Justice Court); $50,000 (County Court)
7. (Justice Court); $2,500 (Municipal Court)

SOURCE: From *State Court Caseload Statistics*, 1994.

CHAPTER TWO

HEALTH

EXPERT QUOTES

"It's not about how much weight you lift, but about how hard you squeeze."
—Ursula Sarcev, Miss Galaxy 1994
Page 142

"Go with what's happening (to your hair). It's not going to look exactly the same every day."
—John Barrett, hairstylist for the TV show "Friends"
Page 184

"Patients should write down their symptoms and complaints before visiting a doctor."
—Dr. C. Everett Koop, the former Surgeon General
Page 210

■ **THE YEAR AHEAD:** **LOOK FOR** weight-training to gain in popularity among health-minded Baby Boomers... **EXPECT** women taking folic acid supplements to have fewer babies with birth defects... **BEWARE** the hype over soy protein's ability to lower cholesterol levels dramatically... **TUNE IN** to the value of some alternative medicine treatments... **RAISE** a fuss if your HMO isn't serving your needs... **ENJOY** what Retin A can do for your wrinkles and age spots...

GETTING FIT 134

HEALTHY EATING 148

LOOKING GREAT 179

HAVING CHILDREN 194

DOCTORS & MEDICINE 210

GETTING FIT

BODY SHAPE: Weight around the belly is riskier than weight around the hips, PAGE 136 **EXPERT LIST:** The health benefits of 30 physical activities, PAGE 137 **EXERCISE GUIDE:** The calories burned in 30 minutes, PAGE 138 **WORKOUTS:** Exercises to increase strength and endurance, PAGE 140 **BODY TONING:** Expert tips from Miss Galaxy, PAGE 142 **FOOTWEAR:** Fitting a running shoe properly, PAGE 144 **INJURIES:** How to stay off the bench, PAGE 146

LIFELONG HEALTH

EXERCISING IS THE BEST DEFENSE

The new weight guidelines are must reading for those who like living

When it comes to health, not only are you what you eat, but what you weigh also tends to affect your health in later life. Bad eating and exercise habits developed during youth have produced a population in which one in three Americans is overweight. The sedentary lifestyle, and the extra pounds that lie around the midriffs of Americans at middle age, is a lethal combination. Lack of regular physical activity causes about 12 percent of all U.S. deaths each year.

The latest effort to blunt this trend is the federal government's new weight tables, revised by the U.S. Department of Agriculture and the Department of Health and Human Services for the first time in five years. Their message: Weight gain should not be synonymous with aging. That's a point that bears attention because in recent years the weight tables had become gradually more lenient about sanctioning middle-aged spread. For example, the 1990 version of the guidelines envisioned a man (or woman) five feet, eight inches tall, age 19 to 34 weighing between 125 and 164. The same man at age 35 was allowed to weigh between 138 and 178. But the new chart (see accompanying graphic) establishes strict er weight ranges—similar, ironically, to those proposed in the ideal weight chart issued by the Metropolitan Life Insurance Company in 1959, which was based on actuarial data showing the heights and weights at which customers lived the longest. Under the newest guidelines, the healthy weight range for the same five-feet, eight-inch man is now between 125 and 165 pounds—even if he's five years older.

The new guidelines don't differentiate between appropriate weights for men and women, but they do specify that the higher end of the range only applies to people with more muscle and bone. In other words, a person shouldn't necessarily allow himself to reach the upper limit.

The new chart should serve as a deterrent to weight gain, says Dr. Walter Willett, chairman of the nutrition department at the Harvard School of Public Health, because it's difficult to lose weight once it's been put on. "When you see your weight creeping up after age 21," says Willett, "take action in the first few pounds of weight gained, and make permanent, not modest adjustments in lifestyle. Don't wait until you get high blood pressure, diabetes, or a heart attack." That statement is supported by a 1995 study by Harvard researchers that found that thin women live

■ YOUR IDEAL WEIGHT, THE LATEST EDITION

The new guidelines, which apply to both men and women regardless of age, prescribe acceptable ranges rather than specific weights because people the same height may have different amounts of muscle and bone. The farther you are above the healthy weight range for your height, the higher are your risks of developing weight-related health problems.

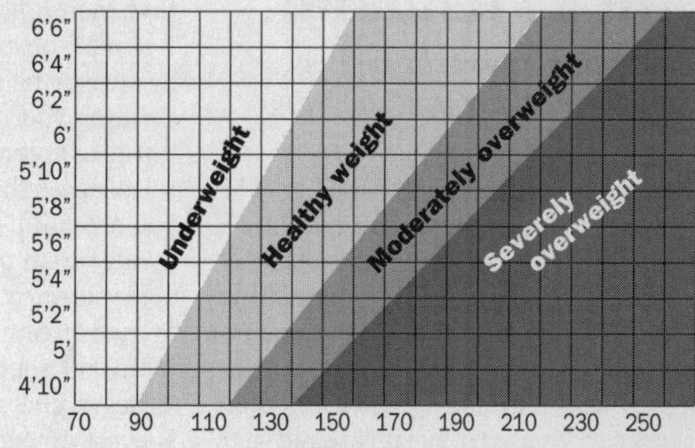

longer and suggested that even a modest weight gain of 10 to 15 pounds may be unsafe. The 14-year study of nearly 116,000 female nurses found that women who gained as little as 11 to 18 pounds in adult life faced a 25 percent greater chance of suffering a heart attack than women who gained fewer than 11 pounds after they reached age 18. The authors of the study criticized the 1990 weight tables, saying that they "provide false reassurance" to people who weren't defined as "overweight."

As the government guidelines make clear, staying trim and healthy not only requires watching your weight and eating a balanced diet, but regular exercise also: "30 minutes or more of moderate physical activity on most—preferably all—days of the week." Even activities like taking the stairs instead of the elevator can make a difference.

Other health authorities concur. In 1995, the federal Centers for Disease Control (CDC) and the American College of Sports Medicine also challenged the conventional wisdom that only an intense workout can reduce your risk of heart disease, hypertension, diabetes, osteoporosis, anxiety, depression, and some cancers. Everyday activities like gardening, housework, and mowing the lawn were all promoted in the joint recommendation.

However, to increase longevity, more intense exercise may be needed, according to a study that monitored the exercise habits and longevity of 17,000 Harvard alumni for 26 years. But the optimal amount of exercise is yet unproved, says Dr. Steven Blair, director of research at the Cooper Institute for Aerobics Research in Dallas, Texas.

Experts do agree that exercise will yield health dividends no matter how inactive a person may have been in earlier life. For instance, a study published recently in the *Journal of the American Medical Association* (JAMA) found that men who had maintained or improved their physical fitness over time were less likely to die than men who had not. Even men deemed highly unfit to begin with cut their risk of dying in half after becoming moderately fit. The more their fitness improved, the more they reduced their risk.

Even if you're overweight, exercising can reduce your risk of disease, according to a study conducted at the Cooper Institute for Aerobics Research, which found that obese men who exercise fare better than sedentary obese men. "Leading an active life will reduce the risk of becoming obese," says lead author Dr. Steven Blair. "And if you are obese and are fit, you're better off."

BODY SHAPE

THE TALE OF THE TAPE MEASURE

Weight around the belly is riskier than around the hips

How your weight is distributed may be even more important than how much weight you have in the first place, at least when it comes to determining risks to your health. If you are carrying around too much weight in your upper body, your health is at far greater risk than if you are carrying extra weight around your hips, buttocks, and thighs.

All of that excessive fat above the hips, around the belly, and in the upper torso has been found by researchers to be associated with an increased risk of breast and uterine cancer, heart disease, and diabetes, as well as a host of other ailments.

To assess whether your weight distribution puts you at higher risk, ask yourself whether your body more closely resembles the shape of an apple or the shape of a pear. "Apples" carry extra weight in the upper body and are often bigger at the waist than in the hips—traits found more often in men than in women. "Pears," on the other hand, carry their weight low. Their waists are smaller than their hips and they are usually women.

A more precise assessment can be obtained by measuring your hips and waist, and then dividing your waist measurement by your hip measurement. If the result is 0.75 or less, you are pear-shaped. If the result is 0.75 to 0.80, you are mildly apple-shaped. And a result greater than 0.80 puts you squarely in the apple category. If that's the case, you'd benefit from directing some of your energy toward taking off some pounds in the right places.

Researchers at the University of Glasgow suggest an even easier way to gauge your health risks from carrying too much weight in the wrong places. Their recent study found significantly higher health risks among women whose waists measure more than 34.5 inches and for men whose waists exceed 40 inches. Their advice: To ward off health problems, keep your waist size to 31.5 inches if you are a woman, and to 37 inches if your chromosomes make you a "he."

EXERCISING TO YOUR HEART'S CONTENT

Checking your pulse rate is one of the best ways to gauge whether you're exercising hard enough to improve your heart and lungs. The American Heart Association advises that you push your heart beat during exercise to between 50 percent and 70 percent of your maximum heart rate (calculated by subtracting your age from 220). Anything lower than 50 percent does little for your heart's conditioning; anything higher than 75 percent can cause problems unless you're in superb shape. When you're just starting an exercise program, cardiologists recommend aiming for the lower part of the target heart zone and gradually stepping up your pace.

AGE	Target heart rate beats per minute	Maximum heart rate
20	100–150	200
25	98–146	195
30	95–142	190
35	93–138	185
40	90–135	180
45	88–131	175
50	85–127	170
55	83–123	165
60	80–120	160
65	78–116	155
70	75–113	150

IMPORTANT NOTE: A few high blood pressure medicines lower the maximum heart rate and thus the target zone rate. If you are taking high blood pressure medications, call your physician to find out if your exercise program needs to be adjusted.

EXPERT LIST

PLAYING THE FIELD

Find a hill and climb it, pick a path and jog it. It doesn't take a big budget to get in shape, as the following analysis from Dr. David R. Stutz, author of 40+ Guide to Fitness *(Consumer Reports Books, 1994) illustrates.*

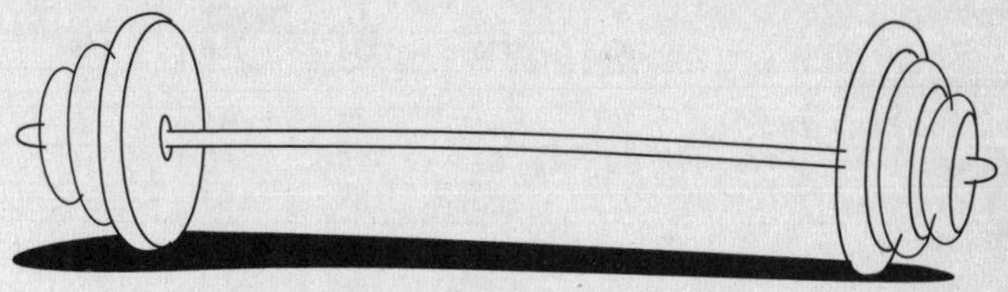

ACTIVITY	IMPROVES HEART AND LUNG FITNESS[1,2]	BURNS CALORIES[1,2]	TONES AND BUILDS MUSCLES[2]	LOWERS STRESS[1]
AEROBIC DANCE	Very good	Very good	Poor	Very good
ALPINE SKIING	Fair	Fair	Good	Good
BASEBALL	Fair	Fair	Fair	Good
BASKETBALL	Very good	Very good	Fair	Good
BICYCLING	**Excellent**	**Excellent**	Good	**Excellent**
BOWLING	Poor	Poor	Fair	Good
CROSS-COUNTRY SKIING	**Excellent**	**Excellent**	Fair	**Excellent**
FISHING (SITTING)	Poor	Poor	Fair	**Excellent**
FOOTBALL	Good	Good	Fair	Good
GARDENING	Poor	Fair	Fair	**Excellent**
GOLF	Poor	Poor	Poor	Good
HIKING AND CLIMBING	Very good	Very good	Fair	**Excellent**
HOCKEY	Very good	Very good	Fair	Good
HORSEBACK RIDING	Fair	Fair	Fair	**Excellent**
JOGGING AND RUNNING	**Excellent**	**Excellent**	Fair	**Excellent**
MARTIAL ARTS	Very good	Very good	Very good	Good
RACQUETBALL AND SQUASH	Very good	Very good	Fair	Good
ROPE JUMPING	**Excellent**	**Excellent**	Fair	Very good
ROWING AND CANOEING	**Excellent**	**Excellent**	Very good	**Excellent**
SAILING	Poor	Poor	Fair	**Excellent**
SKATING OR ROLLERBLADING	Good	Very good	Fair	Good
SOCCER	Very good	Very good	Fair	Good
STAIR CLIMBING	Good	Good	Very good	Very good
SWIMMING LAPS	**Excellent**	**Excellent**	Good	**Excellent**
TENNIS	Good	Good	Fair	Good
VOLLEYBALL	Good	Good	Fair	Good
WALKING (NORMAL)	Fair	Good	Poor	**Excellent**
WALKING (SPEED)	Very good	Very good	Fair	**Excellent**
WEIGHT TRAINING	Fair	Good	**Excellent**	Good
WOODWORKING	Poor	Poor	Fair	Very good

NOTES: **1.** Largely dependent upon duration of activity. **2.** Largely dependent upon intensity of effort.
SOURCE: Dr. David R. Stutz.

EXERCISER'S GUIDE

A SPORTING MENU

From puttering around to Olympic skiing, the estimated calories burned during 30 minutes of activity depends on body weight and intensity of effort.

ACTIVITY	WEIGHT						
	105	120	135	150	165	180	195
DAILY ACTIVITIES							
Work, sedentary office	36	41	46	51	56	61	66
Cooking	60	68	77	85	94	102	111
Cleaning (heavy)	107	123	138	153	169	184	199
AEROBICS							
Low-impact dance	119	136	153	170	188	205	222
High-impact dance	167	191	215	239	263	286	310
Water	95	109	122	136	150	163	177
ALPINE SKIING							
Moderate (recreational)	119	136	153	170	188	205	222
Vigorous (steep slope)	167	191	215	239	263	286	310
BASEBALL	119	136	153	170	188	205	222
BASKETBALL							
Half-court	143	164	184	205	225	245	266
Full-court (slow)	191	218	245	273	300	327	355
Full-court (fast break)	315	360	405	450	495	540	585
BICYCLING							
10–12 mph	143	164	184	205	225	245	266
12–14 mph	191	218	245	273	300	327	355
14–16 mph	239	273	307	341	375	409	443
BOWLING	72	82	92	102	113	123	133
CALISTHENICS							
Light	107	123	138	153	169	184	199
Heavy	191	218	245	273	300	327	355
CROSS-COUNTRY SKIING							
2.5 mph	167	191	215	239	263	286	310
4–5 mph	191	218	245	273	300	327	355
FISHING							
Sitting	60	68	77	85	94	102	111
Standing	84	95	107	119	131	143	155
FOOTBALL							
Playing catch	60	68	77	85	94	102	111
Touch or flag	191	218	245	273	300	327	355
GARDENING	95	109	123	136	150	164	177
GOLF							
Pulling cart	119	136	153	170	188	205	222
Carrying clubs	131	150	169	187	206	225	244
HIKING AND CLIMBING							
Cross-country hiking	143	164	184	205	225	245	266
Rock climb (mountain trek)	191	218	245	273	300	327	355
Rock climb (vigorous)	253	289	325	361	398	434	470
HORSEBACK RIDING							
Leisure riding	95	109	123	136	150	164	177
Posting to trot	143	164	184	205	225	245	266
Galloping	188	215	242	269	296	323	350

■ **EXPERT LIST**

ACTIVITY	WEIGHT						
	105	120	135	150	165	180	195
ICE OR ROLLER SKATING/BLADING							
Sustained moderate	167	191	215	239	263	286	310
Vigorous (9+ mph)	215	245	276	307	338	368	399
JOGGING AND RUNNING							
12 min./mile pace	191	218	245	273	300	327	355
10 min./mile pace	239	273	307	341	375	409	443
8 min./mile pace	298	341	384	426	469	511	554
6 min./mile pace	382	436	491	545	600	655	709
MARTIAL ARTS							
Tae kwon do, karate, judo	239	273	307	341	375	409	443
Tai chi	95	109	123	136	150	164	177
RACQUET AND COURT GAMES							
Racquetball (social)	167	191	215	239	263	286	310
Racquetball (competitive)	239	273	307	341	375	409	443
Handball and squash	286	327	368	409	450	491	532
ROPE JUMPING							
Slow	191	218	245	273	300	327	355
Moderate	239	273	307	341	375	409	443
Fast	286	327	368	409	450	491	532
ROWING AND CANOEING							
Leisurely	84	95	107	119	131	143	155
Vigorous sustained	167	191	215	239	263	286	310
Very vigorous	286	327	368	409	450	491	532
SAILING							
Leisurely	72	82	92	102	113	123	133
Racing	109	136	153	170	188	205	222
SOCCER							
Casual	167	191	215	239	263	286	310
Competitive	239	273	307	341	375	409	443
SWIMMING							
Laps freestyle (moderate)	191	218	245	273	300	327	355
Laps freestyle (fast)	239	273	307	341	375	409	443
TENNIS							
Social doubles	119	136	153	170	188	205	222
Social singles	157	180	202	225	248	270	293
Competitive doubles	172	196	221	245	270	295	319
Competitive singles	227	259	291	324	356	389	421
VOLLEYBALL							
Leisurely	74	85	96	106	117	128	138
Competitve	167	191	215	239	263	286	310
WALKING							
24 min./mile pace	72	82	92	102	113	123	133
20 min./mile pace	84	95	107	119	131	143	155
17min./mile pace	95	109	123	136	150	164	177
15 min./mile pace	107	123	138	153	169	184	194
12 min./mile pace	119	136	153	170	188	205	222
WEIGHT TRAINING							
Free weights or machines	143	164	184	205	225	245	266
Circuit weight training	191	218	245	273	300	327	355

SOURCE: Dr. David R. Stutz.

BUILDING STRENGTH AND ENDURANCE

The American College of Sports Medicine recommends these exercises to build strength. Be sure to exhale on exertion and to inhale when returning to start.

■ ARMS, SHOULDERS, AND CHEST

SINGLE-ARM ROW: Pull weight to shoulders, then ease to floor. Don't lift with your back.

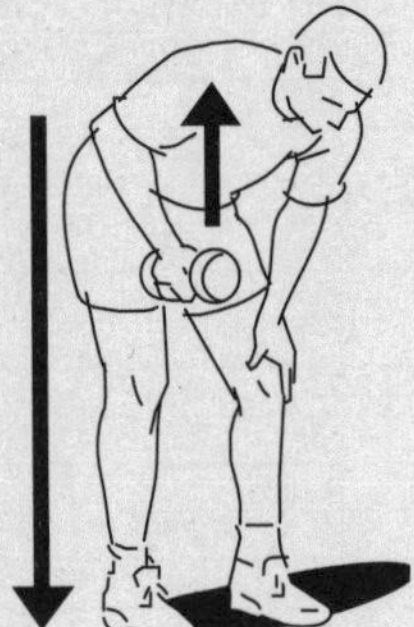

CHAIR PUSH-UP: Keep your hands below your shoulders, and position the chair so that it doesn't slide.

■ ABDOMINALS

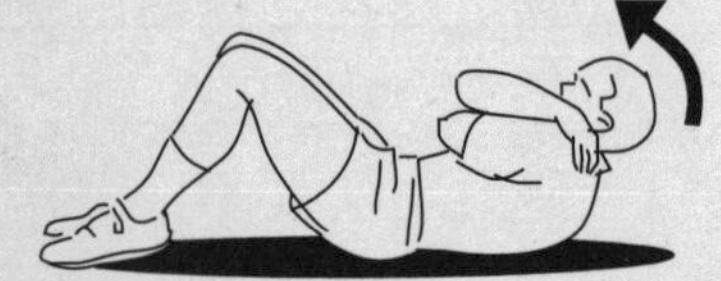

SHOULDER CURL-UP: Lift your back off the floor. But don't sit all the way up; it may strain your back. Use a pad if possible.

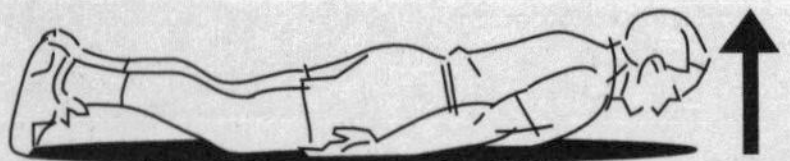

PRONE NECK LIFT: Keep hands up and lift neck. But avoid arching it backward.

■ LOWER BODY

SEATED STRAIGHT-LEG LIFT: Raise your entire leg off the chair by keeping the knee locked. Good for the quadriceps, the muscle that extends the leg.

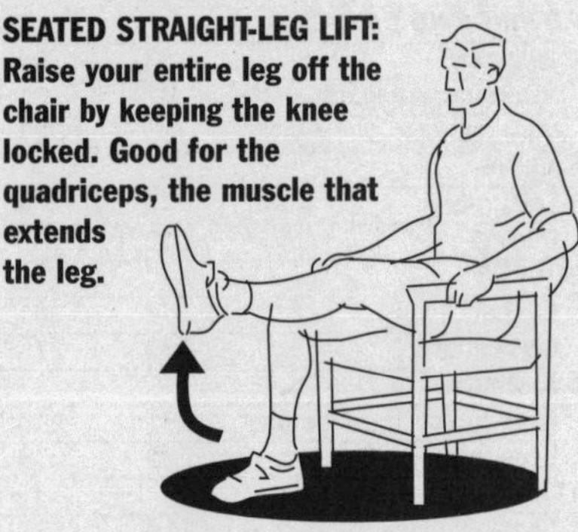

SOURCE: *American College of Sports Medicine Fitness Book,* Human Kinetics, 1992.

■ LESS EFFECTIVE TRADITIONAL EXERCISES

BICYCLES

DONKEY KICKS

KNEE BENDS

JUMPING JACKS

STAY FLEXIBLE IN WHAT YOU DO

Stretching is important before and after workouts. Limber up with this routine from the American College of Sports Medicine.

■ NECK

■ SHOULDER, CHEST, AND BACK

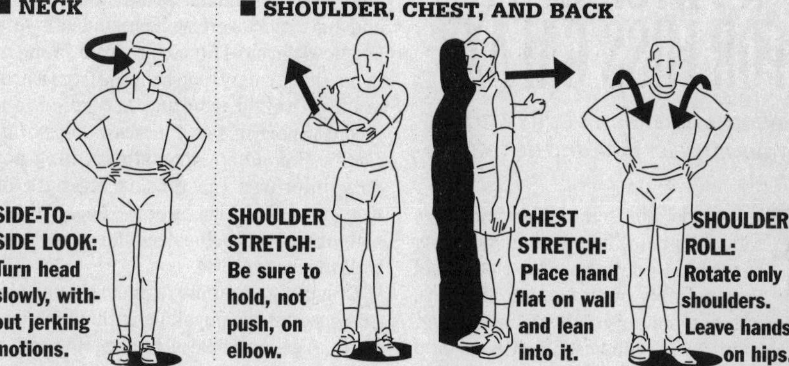

SIDE-TO-SIDE LOOK: Turn head slowly, without jerking motions.

SHOULDER STRETCH: Be sure to hold, not push, on elbow.

CHEST STRETCH: Place hand flat on wall and lean into it.

SHOULDER ROLL: Rotate only shoulders. Leave hands on hips.

■ ABDOMINALS AND LOWER BACK

STANDING CAT-STRETCH: Don't arch your back.

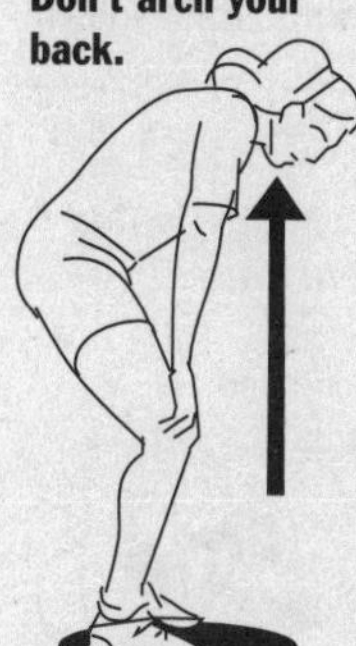

KNEE TO CHEST: One knee at a time, then both. Keep hands under thighs.

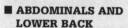

SEATED TOE-TOUCH: Keep legs straight, toes pointed. Don't bounce.

■ LOWER BODY

WALL LEAN: Keep your back heel on the ground and feet turned inward.

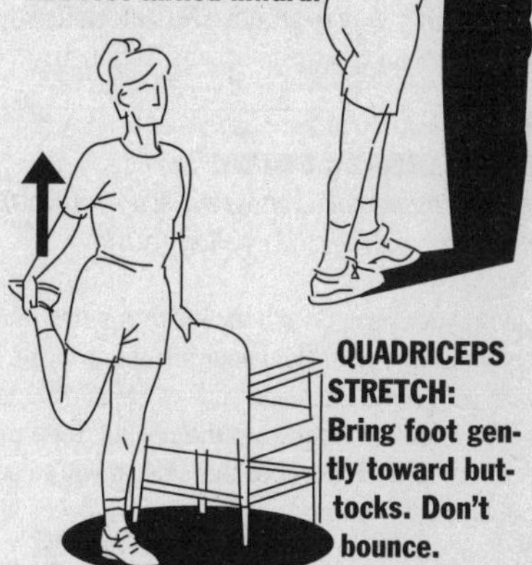

QUADRICEPS STRETCH: Bring foot gently toward buttocks. Don't bounce.

■ LESS EFFECTIVE TRADITIONAL EXERCISES

HURDLER STRETCH

BACK BENDS

THE PLOW

STANDING TOE-TOUCH

EXPERT TIPS

A PHYSIQUE FIT FOR MISS GALAXY

Follow this champ's advice to give your muscles tone and definition

Ever wonder how some amateur athletes can run a marathon even though they appear to be out of shape? How could they possibly be fit enough to run 26 miles, yet appear so flabby? Aerobic exercises improve cardiovascular fitness and endurance and can help you lose weight, but they don't necessarily tone or sculpt your muscles. Even if you're an avid jogger, swimmer, or cyclist, you can run, paddle, or pedal forever, but your muscles still may not be as toned as you'd like them to be.

The only way to achieve muscle definition is to lift weights or do strength training, or anaerobic, exercises that use the body's weight as resistance, says Ursula Sarcev, winner of the 1994 Miss Galaxy fitness competition. Miss Galaxy's advice is borne out by the American College of Sports Medicine, which recommends that both aerobic and anaerobic exercise be included in any balanced physical fitness program. Women, in particular, may reap benefits from a program of weight training. According to a recent report in the *American Journal of Health Promotion*, strength training not only improves the muscle strength of women in their 40s but also boosts their body image and self-esteem far more than walking for exercise.

Designing a training regimen should take into account the physique with which you begin. A general rule of thumb: How much weight you lift depends on whether you want to build muscle mass or merely tone and shape your muscles. If you carry more weight and body fat than you are happy with in a certain area, you'll want to go with lighter weights and higher repetitions, say, 25 to 30, to help burn fat. "Don't use too much weight in areas you want to slim down

■ DUMBBELL FLIES:

Tones the pectoral chest muscles without making you look like a bodybuilder.

Lie on your back on a bench with a small dumbbell in each hand. Hold your arms out to the side with your arms bent and your wrists turned toward each other. Lift up toward the ceiling, then bring both arms back down to the side. If you raise the bench so it's on an incline, you'll work muscles higher in your chest. If you lower the bench so your head is below your torso, you'll work the lower chest muscles.

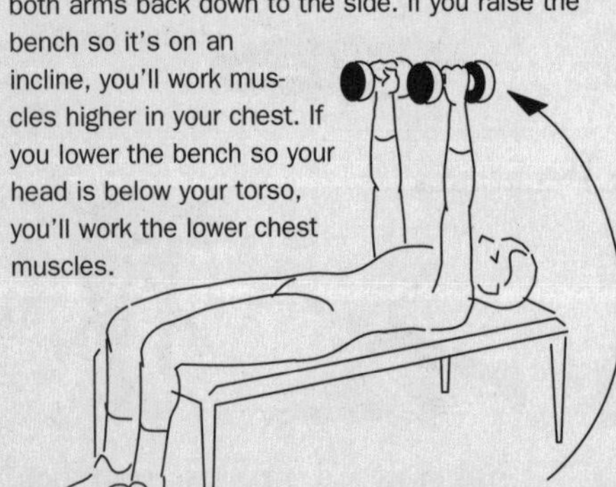

■ BICEP CURLS:

Tones and shapes the biceps; builds muscles if more weight is used.

Hold a dumbbell in each hand and stand with your arms at your side and your palms facing forward. Curl the dumbbell up toward your chest and turn your wrist out when you are at the end of the curl. Lower the weight slowly because you're resisting weight and strengthening your muscles as you go down, too. Do 15 to 20 repetitions, alternating arms or lifting both at the same time.

because you'll end up building up that area," advises Sarcev. If you're trying to put on weight in specific areas, go with heavier weights and do fewer reps, about 8 to10.

A professional body builder, Sarcev says that the key to achieving maximum results is proper form. For starters, always contract your muscles from the moment that you start an exercise until you're finished. "You're not doing anything if you just lift up and down," she explains. "It's not about how much weight you lift, but about how hard you squeeze." Also, you want to make sure that you extend your muscle entirely with each repetition. "The biggest mistake I see is when people don't have full range of motion, which is like working half the muscle," says Sarcev. "You'll make much more progress if you use less weight, but use the full range of motion."

Even if you don't have access to a gym, you can invest in inexpensive equipment, such as small free weights, that will help you slim down or build up specific muscle groups. Miss Galaxy recommends these exercises to tone you up and shape common trouble spots.

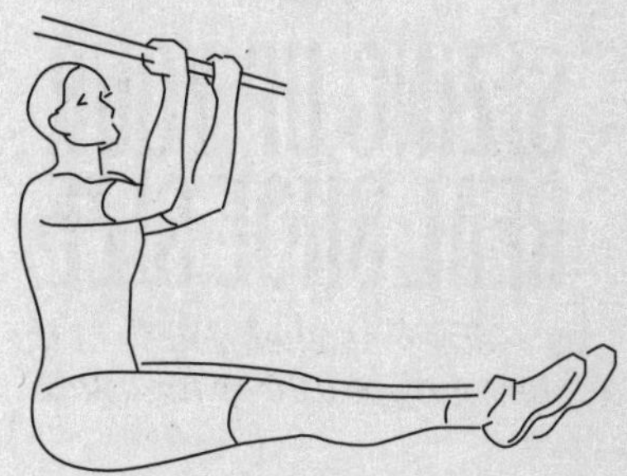

■ LEG RAISES:
The best way to tone the lower abdomen.

To begin, hang from a bar and lift your legs straight in front of you as high as possible, at least at a 90-degree angle. Eventually try to work up to 15 to 20 leg raises, but try not to swing. It's a difficult maneuver, so beginners should start by lifting their knees up while someone helps balance them.

■ LUNGES:
Trims and tones the quadriceps in the legs and gluteal muscles in the buttocks. Using dumbbells adds resistance and helps build muscle rather than slimyou down.

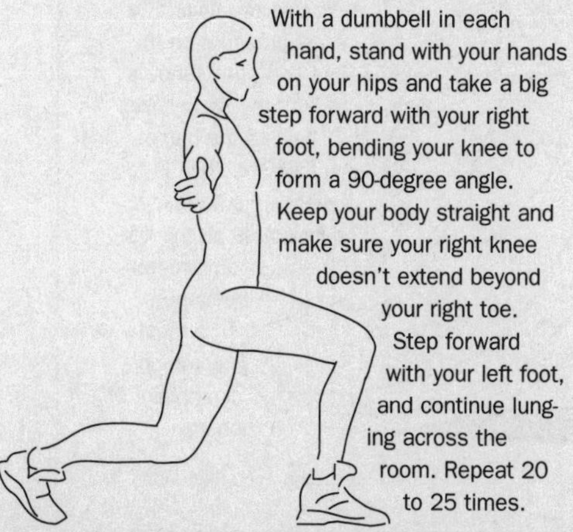

With a dumbbell in each hand, stand with your hands on your hips and take a big step forward with your right foot, bending your knee to form a 90-degree angle. Keep your body straight and make sure your right knee doesn't extend beyond your right toe. Step forward with your left foot, and continue lunging across the room. Repeat 20 to 25 times.

■ STEP-UPS:
A simple exercise, yet far more effective at trimming and toning the buttocks than the step machine.

Step up onto a bench or high step, then step down, squeezing your muscles with each step. Do 15 to 20 repetitions on each leg. The higher the bench, the harder the workout.

FOOTWEAR

SIZING UP YOUR REAL SHOE SIZE

A 9 1/2-size foot when you're at the store may be a 10 by nightfall

The adage, "If the shoe fits, wear it," may be good advice in most situations, but it's no guarantee that your next pair of exercise shoes will fit you properly when you get them home from the store and lace them up. That's because foot sizes vary depending on the time of day, the temperature of your feet, and what you've been doing with them. A long jog in warm weather, for example, can expand a runner's feet as much as a half size.

If it's been a while since you bought your last pair of exercise shoes, weight changes, aging, or injuries can also affect your shoe size. Foot specialists advise that the best time of day to shop for shoes is at the end of the day when your feet are at their largest. Good shoes should feel comfortable right away, not just when they've been "broken in." Make sure there's a space the width of your thumbnail between the top of the shoe and the tip of your longest toe on your longer foot.

Running shoes should be replaced after logging 250 to 450 miles, and walking shoes after 400 hours of use. And when choosing a workout course, don't run on sand and sidewalks. "When your foot hits sand, it keeps going because the sand gives," warns sports podiatrist Dr. Stephen Pribut, and your Achilles tendon can be severely strained. Concrete, unfortunately, doesn't give at all, sending shock waves up the legs, knees, and back.

■ FITTING A RUNNING SHOE PROPERLY

Forget fancy designs and high-tech gizmos; here's what you really need for comfortable running:

■ **SQUEEZE THE BACK TO FIND A SOLID COUNTER.** This is the stiff cup that keeps your ankle steady to help avoid sprains.

■ **CHECK FOR A HEEL LIFT.** Although flat shoes offer the agility necessary for lateral motion, shoes with a 1/2- to 3/4-inch lift in the heel provide the shock absorption needed to prevent shin-splints and other pavement-pounding-induced ailments. Look for a flared outsole. It promotes stability and makes the shoe more durable.

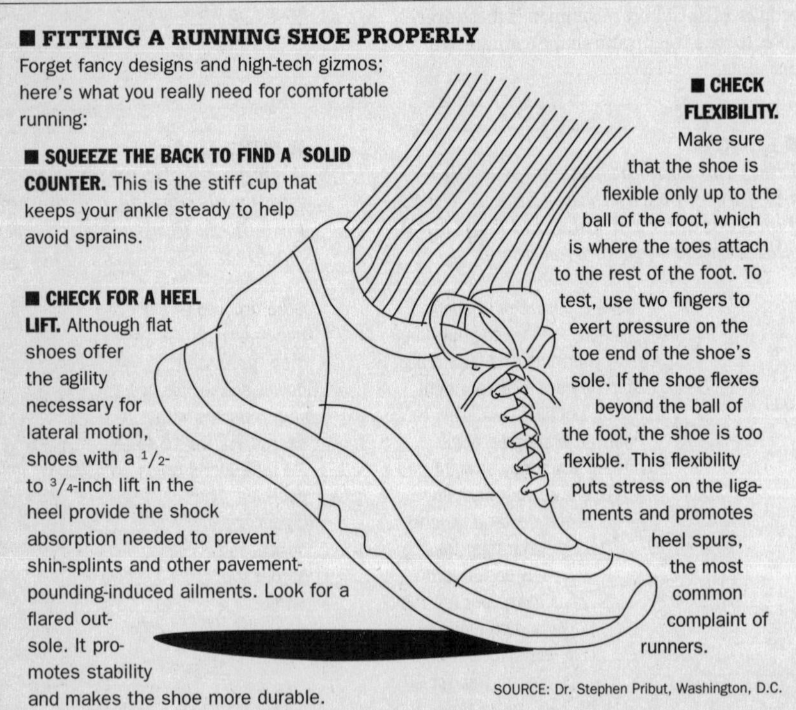

■ **CHECK FLEXIBILITY.** Make sure that the shoe is flexible only up to the ball of the foot, which is where the toes attach to the rest of the foot. To test, use two fingers to exert pressure on the toe end of the shoe's sole. If the shoe flexes beyond the ball of the foot, the shoe is too flexible. This flexibility puts stress on the ligaments and promotes heel spurs, the most common complaint of runners.

SOURCE: Dr. Stephen Pribut, Washington, D.C.

PARENT'S GUIDE

FIT ENOUGH TO BE PRESIDENT

During the Kennedy administration, the man in the Oval Office exhorted his fellow Americans to test their fitness in a 50-mile walk. Now, the President's Council on Physical Fitness and Sports has issued a new challenge to children ages 6 to 17. Children who score at or above the following levels for their age and sex on all five of the suggested events qualify for the President's Physical Fitness Award and are eligible for both a presidential commendation and a badge.

AGE	Curl-ups (per minute)	Shuttle run (seconds)	V-sit reach (inches)	Sit and reach (centimeters)	1-mile run (minutes)	Pull-ups
BOYS						
6	33	12.1	3.5	31	10:15	2
7	36	11.5	3.5	30	9:22	4
8	40	11.1	3.0	31	8:48	5
9	41	10.9	3.0	31	8:31	5
10	45	10.3	4.0	30	7:57	6
11	47	10.0	4.0	31	7:32	6
12	50	9.8	4.0	31	7:11	7
13	53	9.5	3.5	33	6:50	7
14	56	9.1	4.5	36	6:26	10
15	57	9.0	5.0	37	6:20	11
16	56	8.7	6.0	38	6:08	11
17	55	8.7	7.0	41	6:06	13
GIRLS						
6	32	12.4	5.5	32	11:20	2
7	34	12.1	5.0	32	10:36	2
8	38	11.8	4.5	33	10:02	2
9	39	11.1	5.5	33	9:30	2
10	40	10.8	6.0	33	9:19	3
11	42	10.5	6.5	34	9:02	3
12	45	10.4	7.0	36	8:23	2
13	46	10.2	7.0	38	8:13	2
14	47	10.1	8.0	40	7:59	2
15	48	10.0	8.0	43	8:08	2
16	45	10.1	9.0	42	8:23	1
17	44	10.0	8.0	42	8:15	1

SOURCE: President's Council on Physical Fitness and Sports.

EXPERT Q & A

HOW TO STAY OFF THE BENCH

The N. Y. Knicks' doc on avoiding injuries and healing quickly

Professional athletes "play hurt," it is often said, and no wonder, for getting hurt is as much a part of most pro athletes' careers as collecting paychecks. Football great Joe Montana suffered serious injuries to his throwing arm, basketball legend Larry Bird was plagued by back pain and tennis star Martina Navratilova is known for her weak knees.

But sports injuries aren't limited to the pros. Weekend athletes are also prone to injury because they tend to overdo exertion even though they're out of shape. Usually it's minor damage, resulting in annoying aches and pains, but as you get older, you get more susceptible to serious injuries because your muscles aren't as strong as they once were. Scientists have found that many people, even those who get regular aerobic exercise, suffer rapid erosion of muscle mass after age 45 or so.

Weight training can help ward off injury by counteracting the subtle muscle atrophy that accompanies aging, and it can also play a role in recuperation. In general, it's safe to resume activity and do strengthening exercises a couple of days after the swelling and pain subside, says Dr. Norman Scott, chief of orthopedics at Beth Israel Medical Center North in New York City. Scott, also the team physician for the New York Knicks basketball team and the 1992 Olympic basketball team (known as "The Dream Team"), says there's little difference between the injuries sustained by recreational and professional athletes, except the pros are more likely to suffer serious injuries because they play with more force. Below, Scott helps explain what causes some common athletic injuries, how to avoid them, and what to do if you get laid up:

NECK: *Serious neck injuries are rare among athletes other than those who participate in contact sports like football and rugby. However, weightlifting, wrestling, even racquet sports like tennis can cause chronic aches and pains, especially flare-ups along the nerve route.*

■ **CAUSES:** Neck injuries in older amateur athletes are usually a sign of arthritic changes (joint inflammation), which are often totally asymptomatic. Strenuous neck movements often result in an inflammation that is associated with pain running down the arm into the fingers.

■ **PREVENTION:** Better overall conditioning is the best way to prevent neck injuries.

■ **TREATMENT:** If discomfort is acute, avoid exercise and don't stretch the muscle. Apply ice immediately and don't apply heat until 48 to 72 hours after the injury occurs. If necessary, take non-steroidal anti-inflammatory medications like Motrin, Advil, or Aleve (the same is true of all minor injuries).

BACK: *Almost any sport that requires trunk rotations, as in golf or racquet sports like tennis and racquetball.*

■ **CAUSES:** Most back injuries are muscular in origin, but, depending on your age, back pain can also be due to arthritic changes like osteoarthritis or degenerative arthritis.

■ **PREVENTION:** The best way to prevent back pain is through good overall conditioning and following a good stretching program to increase flexibility.

■ **TREATMENT:** Apply ice early on, then apply heat after 72 hours. Water therapy like swimming helps decrease spasms. Try gentle stretching exercises, including an abdominal strengthening workout.

SHOULDER: *Pitching, racket sports, golf, lifting weights, and other activities where you put your arm in an overhead position.*

■ **CAUSES:** The most common cause is bursitis, an inflammation of a normal structure called the bursa. Shoulder injuries are much more common as a person gets older due to muscle atrophy. Damage to the rotator cuff, a group of tendons that allows you to raise your arm up and down, is usually caused by repetitive motions like pitching a baseball.

■ **PREVENTION:** A program for stretching and strengthening muscles can reduce your chances of getting a shoulder injury.

■ **TREATMENT:** Continue to move the shoulder; if you don't, it can freeze up very quickly. Rotate your arms and shoulder, moving your hand in front of your body, then backwards, and up and down; also try to stretch from side to side, bringing your right hand over to touch your left shoulder.

KNEE: *Any sport that requires a pivoting motion, like tennis and basketball; runners are also prone to knee injuries.*

■ **CAUSES:** The knee is a joint that's especially susceptible to injuries, usually caused by sudden rotational movements.

■ **PREVENTION:** Develop very strong leg muscles by biking, lifting weights, and using step machines.

■ **TREATMENT:** Follow the RICE principle: Rest (but don't completely immobilize it), Ice, Compression (wrap the knee to reduce swelling), and Elevation. Apply ice for 48 hours, then progress to strengthening exercises. Sprained ligaments will need 3 to 12 weeks of rehabilitative exercise, but a torn ligament or cartilage may need surgery.

ANKLE: *Ankle injuries are common in any sport that requires a lot of running, such as jogging, racquet sports, baseball, and football.*

■ **CAUSES:** Sprains and strains are common injuries that occur when the joint or ligaments connecting bones are overstretched or twisted.

■ **PREVENTION:** Make sure you warm up—and your sneakers aren't untied.

■ **TREATMENT:** Again, follow the RICE principle, applying ice immediately. If the swelling is slight, you can exercise the following day, but keep your ankle wrapped or wear high-top sneakers. Try strengthening exercises a couple of days after swelling and pain subside.

ELBOW: *Besides tennis, you can develop tennis elbow from any sport that requires that you rotate your hand up and down repeatedly, as when you swing a golf club incorrectly.*

■ **CAUSES:** Tennis elbow (pain in the forearm and wrist) is a very common injury caused by too much tension on the tendons around the bony prominence of the elbow.

■ **PREVENTION:** Strengthening exercises, like squeezing a rubber ball, build muscles in your forearm.

■ **TREATMENT:** Apply ice. If necessary, take anti-inflammatory medications.

■ WHERE BRUISES COME FROM

Below are the estimates of the number of product-related injuries that occurred while playing various sports in 1994, derived from data collected in hospital emergency rooms. The sports that result in the greatest number of injuries aren't inherently more dangerous than other sports, however, since far more people play a sport like basketball than golf.

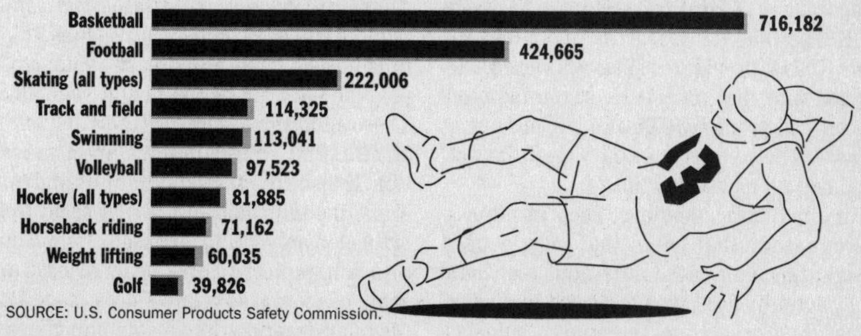

SOURCE: U.S. Consumer Products Safety Commission.

HEALTHY EATING

VITAMINS: Folic acid is crucial for women, PAGE 152 **CHOLESTEROL:** Does soy lower cholesterol? PAGE 158 **WINE:** Red wine may help you live longer, PAGE 160 **FISH:** Health benefits depend on the type you eat, PAGE 162 **DESSERTS:** Guilt-free recipes from chef Jacques Pépin, PAGE 165 **FRUIT:** A buyer's guide to ripeness, PAGE 169 **TEA:** How to make the best cup, PAGE 173 **BARBECUING:** Tips for reducing carcinogens when you grill, PAGE 174

EXPERT Q & A

YOU ARE WHAT YOU MUNCH

For those whose appetite is being ruined by all those diet studies

Eat this. Avoid that. Take dietary supplements. Forget it, on second thought. Every week, it seems, there's another medical study that either touts the benefits of a diet rich in one or another vitamin, or dashes the hopes that some previously favored nutrient can help ward off disease and keep you in the pink of health.

For those who want a bottom line, however, the newest dietary guidelines from the U.S. Department of Health and Human Services (HHS) and the U.S. Department of Agriculture (USDA) provide one: Eating a varied, balanced diet that meets the recommended dietary allowances (RDAs) for various nutrients will help you reduce the risk of disease and live a long healthy life.

If that sounds obvious, keep in mind a recent study that found that most people think they eat a more nutritious diet than they actually do. Asked to record in diaries what they in fact ate, the study's subjects discovered that they consumed far more fat-filled junk food than they thought they did, and that their intake of fruits, vegetables, and whole grains didn't begin to satisfy the guidelines urged by the USDA's food pyramid.

Here, Dr. Walter Willett, chairman of the nutrition department at the Harvard School of Public Health, puts the latest nutrition research in perspective:

■ What is the relationship between diet and disease?

We thought for a long time that diet influenced heart disease and cancer, but now it also seems important for preventing diseases like cataracts. We've also learned that while some aspects of diet are probably undesirable and to be avoided, eating foods that are protective, such as fruits and vegetables, seems to be more important.

■ What benefits are there from eating lots of fruits and vegetables?

There are dozens of studies that show reduced risk of various cancers—lung, colon, prostate, stomach, and breast—among people who eat a lot of fruits and vegetables. There's additional evidence that high intake of vitamin C can help in cataract prevention. It also appears that vitamins and minerals like folic acid in the diet seem to be critical in preventing birth defects, and may also help protect against heart disease and some cancers (see related story, page 152). Macular degeneration, a common cause of blindness, is also related to low intake of fruit and vegetables, particularly dark green leafy vegetables.

Diets rich in vegetables and fruits probably contain other nutrients that are not well-recognized. For example, phytochemicals, chemicals found in plant foods that prevent cancer in people, are probably important. And there's evidence that people who eat a lot of foods containing fiber have a considerably lower risk of heart disease.

■ What are antioxidants and what role do they play in protecting against disease?

We are constantly being bombarded with oxidative stresses—molecules that can damage DNA and other cell structures. Some of these stresses come from cigarette smoke and sunlight, but many are produced by the normal working of the cells' machinery. Antioxidants are compounds that prevent damage due to oxidative stress. Some antioxidant vitamins derived from the diet, such as vitamin C, E and carotenoid compounds such as lycopene also protect us from these stresses. We can get most antioxidants adequately from our diet if enough fruits and vegetables are eaten.

■ What's the optimum amount of fat intake?

Fat has been labeled the worst aspect of the diet. We've known for a long time, however, that it's the type of fat that's important. There's little evidence that body fat is related to the amount of fat in the diet. We've seen a steady decline of total fat in recent years, yet obesity has been on the increase. Efforts should be aimed at getting a healthier type of fat and limiting calories modestly overall.

■ Is there really a healthy fat?

Minimizing fat from animal sources, particularly red meat and dairy fat, which are high in saturated fat, and from partially hydrogenated vegetable oil like vegetable shortening and margarine, is what's important. Almost anything commercially fried should be avoided. Liquid vegetable oils are a better choice. We're not sure which are the healthiest, but there are many studies show-

■ VITAL INGREDIENTS

How much is too much? How little is too little? The FDA recommends the following for a healthy diet, assuming a daily intake of 2,000 calories—about the amount required by a young woman.

FOOD COMPONENT	MAXIMUM DAILY VALUE
Fat	65 g
Saturated fatty acids	20 g
Cholesterol	300 mg
Total carbohydrate	300 g
Fiber	25 g
Sodium	2,400 mg
Potassium	3,500 mg
Protein*	50 g

*The DV for protein does not apply to certain populations; for these groups, FDA nutrition experts recommend the following:

Children 1 to 4 years:	16 g
Infants less than 1 year:	14 g
Pregnant women:	60 g
Nursing mothers:	65 g

NUTRIENT	MINIMUM DAILY VALUE
Vitamin A	5,000 International Units (IU)
Vitamin C	60 mg
Thiamin	1.5 mg
Riboflavin	1.7 mg
Niacin	20 mg
Calcium	1.0 g
Iron	18 mg
Vitamin D	400 IU
Vitamin E	30 IU
Vitamin B 6	2 mg
Folic acid	0.4 mg
Vitamin B 12	6 micrograms (mcg)
Phosphorus	1 g
Iodine	150 mcg
Magnesium	400 mg
Zinc	15 mg
Copper	2 mg
Biotin	0.3 mg
Pantothenic acid	10 mg

SOURCE: U.S. Food and Drug Administration.

ing that olive oil confers beneficial effects on cholesterol levels.

■ Are fat-free prepared foods and baked goods healthy alternatives?

Most fat-free sweets and baked goods are loaded up with sugar instead of fat; they may actually be worse than some products with fat. There's evidence that eating refined carbohydrates like white bread or white rice has a worse effect on blood cholesterol than a diet with a lot of monounsaturated fat: Low-fat, high-carbohydrate diets tend to lower HDL cholesterol (the good cholesterol) as well as LDL cholesterol (bad cholesterol). Eating lots of sugar also displaces other nutrient-rich sources of calcium from the diet. In many cases, it's better to substitute a good fat for a bad fat than to replace it with a sugar or refined carbohydrate, which still has lots of calories.

■ Is it necessary to limit salt in the diet?

Extra salt in the diet will tend to increase blood pressure slightly, but still importantly. The best thing to do is cut down slowly and then it won't be missed. Most salt in our diet comes from commercially prepared foods, so beware. Although one study found that low-salt intake might be associated with heart disease, there's not much evidence that low salt intake is a problem in this country.

WHY A PILL A DAY WON'T KEEP DOCTORS AWAY

New research suggests that it's really not beneficial to take vitamin supplements

There's bad news for those who thought that popping an antioxidant vitamin pill every day might help them live longer. Just a few years ago, vitamins E, C, and A (beta carotene) seemed to offer real hope in preventing the nation's two biggest killers, heart disease and cancer, especially in people who don't get optimal amounts of these vitamins from their diet.

The evidence that consuming foods rich in antioxidant vitamins is beneficial remains overwhelming. But the latest research casts doubt on the value of dietary supplements in protecting against disease. One trial, known as the Physician's Health Study of 22,000 male doctors, concluded that the health benefits of taking beta carotene pills was nonexistent. Another study, known as CARET (Beta Carotene and Retinol Efficacy Trial) found that taking beta carotene supplements may actually increase the risk of lung cancer and heart disease. The study of 18,300 men and women at high risk of lung cancer because of histories as smokers, former smokers, and asbestos workers, was stopped prematurely when researchers discovered that those taking the supplements faced a 28 percent increased risk of lung cancer and a 17 percent increase in the number of deaths, compared to those taking a placebo. The results echo those from a 1994 study of heavy smokers in Finland that also found that beta carotene supplements increased the risk of lung cancer. It remains to be seen whether beta carotene supplements can confer health benefits in otherwise healthy nonsmokers.

"The finding should make us particularly cautious," says Dr. Walter Willett, chairman of the nutrition department at the Harvard School of Public Health. "It's possible that high doses of these supplements were interfering with other compounds that are beneficial." There is some evidence, however, that taking vitamin E supplements may protect against heart disease, he says, although few foods are a natural source of vitamin E.

What conclusion is to be drawn for now? You're probably better off skipping your daily vitamin and reaching for a piece of fruit instead.

EXPERT LIST

THE HOME VITAMIN SHELF

Your body needs vitamins to form blood cells, build strong bones, and regulate the nervous system, but it can't generate them on its own. Here are the FDA's daily values for essential vitamins and the foods that contain them.

VITAMIN A

DAILY VALUE:	5,000 international units
1 scrambled egg:	420 IU
1 cup nonfat milk:	500 IU
1 nectarine:	1,000 IU
1 piece watermelon:	1,760 IU

■ **WHAT IT DOES:** Aids in good vision; helps build and maintain skin, teeth, bones, and mucous membranes. Deficiency can increase susceptibility to infectious disease.

■ **WHAT IT MAY DO:** May inhibit the development of breast cancer; may increase resistance to infection in children.

■ **FOOD SOURCES:** Milk, eggs, liver, cheese, fish oil. Plus fruits and vegetables that contain beta carotene. You need not consume preformed vitamin A if you eat foods rich in beta carotene.

■ **SUPPLEMENTATION:** Not recommended, since toxic in high doses.

VITAMIN B1 (THIAMIN)

DAILY VALUE:	1.5 milligrams
1 slice enriched white bread:	0.12 mg
3 oz. fried liver:	0.18 mg
1 cup black beans:	0.43 mg
1 packet instant oatmeal:	0.53 mg
1 oz. dry-hull sunflower seeds:	0.65 mg

■ **WHAT IT DOES:** Helps convert carbohydrates into energy. Necessary for healthy brain, nerve cells, and heart function.

■ **FOOD SOURCES:** Whole grains, enriched grain products, beans, meats, liver, wheat germ, nuts, fish, brewer's yeast.

■ **SUPPLEMENTATION:** Not necessary, not recommended.

VITAMIN B2 (RIBOFLAVIN)

DAILY VALUE:	1.7 milligrams
1 oz. chicken:	0.2 mg
1 bagel:	0.2 mg
1 cup milk:	0.4 mg
1 cup cooked spinach:	0.42 mg

■ **WHAT IT DOES:** Helps cells convert carbohydrates into energy. Essential for growth, production of red blood cells, and health of skin and eyes.

■ **FOOD SOURCES:** Dairy products, liver, meat, chicken, fish, enriched grain products, leafy greens, beans, nuts, eggs, almonds.

■ **SUPPLEMENTATION:** Not necessary and not recommended.

VITAMIN B3 (NIACIN)

DAILY VALUE:	20 milligrams
1 slice enriched bread:	1.0 mg
3 oz. baked flounder or sole:	1.7 mg
1 oz. roasted peanuts:	4.2 mg
1/2 chicken breast:	14.7 mg

■ **WHAT IT DOES:** Aids in release of energy from foods. Helps maintain healthy skin, nerves, and digestive system.

■ **WHAT IT MAY DO:** Megadoses lower high blood cholesterol.

■ **FOOD SOURCES:** Nuts, meat, fish, chicken, liver, enriched grain products, dairy products, peanut butter, brewer's yeast.

■ **SUPPLEMENTATION:** Large doses may be prescribed by doctor to lower blood cholesterol. May cause flushing, liver damage, and irregular heart beat.

VITAMIN B5 (PANTOTHENIC ACID)

DAILY VALUE:	7 milligrams
8 oz. nonfat milk:	0.81 mg
1 large egg:	0.86 mg
8 oz. low-fat fruit-flavored yogurt:	1.0 mg
3 1/2 oz. liver:	4.57 mg

■ **WHAT IT DOES:** Vital for metabolism, pro-

A VITAMIN TODAY NOT TO TURN AWAY

The need for folic acid is particularly crucial for women of childbearing age

Folic acid deserves more respect. Not only does the little-known B vitamin found in leafy green vegetables like spinach and brussels sprouts prevent birth defects in newborns, but it may also protect against heart disease. Yet a recent survey of women aged 18 to 45 found that only half of those surveyed had ever heard of folic acid, and only 15 percent knew that the government recommends that women of childbearing age take the vitamin daily.

Folic acid is also the only known method of preventing neural tube defects such as spina bifida and anencephaly (the absence of a brain) in babies, although a new study suggests that vitamin B12 may also play a role. To help protect against such defects, the Food and Drug Administration (FDA) recently announced that all enriched foods like flour, pasta, and rice will be fortified with folic acid beginning in 1998. (The last time a food was fortified was in 1943, when flour was supplemented with vitamins and iron.)

While researchers have long suspected that folic acid wards off heart disease, a new study by researchers at the University of Washington has established the mechanism likely involved. Taking folic acid supplements could prevent up to 50,000 strokes and heart attacks a year, the researchers estimate.

Folic acid is needed most during the first three to six weeks of pregnancy, and since most women don't realize they're pregnant until after the first month or so, they should begin taking folic acid before they get pregnant, says Dr. Richard Johnston, a Yale pediatrics professor and medical director of the March of Dimes Birth Defects Foundation. To be effective, folic acid must be taken every day, he adds, because the body doesn't store this vitamin. Says Johnston: "The only sure way a woman has of getting enough folic acid is to take a vitamin every day."

duction of essential body chemicals.

■ **FOOD SOURCES:** Whole grains, beans, milk, eggs, liver.

■ **SUPPLEMENTATION:** Not necessary, not recommended. May cause diarrhea.

VITAMIN B6 (PYROXIDINE)

DAILY VALUE:	2.0 milligrams
1 bran muffin:	0.11 mg
1 cup lima beans:	0.3 mg
3 oz. cooked bluefin tuna:	0.45 mg
1 banana:	0.7 mg

■ **WHAT IT DOES:** Vital in chemical reactions of proteins and amino acids. Helps maintain brain function and form red blood cells.

■ **WHAT IT MAY DO:** May help to boost immunity in the elderly.

■ **FOOD SOURCES:** Whole grains, bananas, meat, beans, nuts, wheat germ, brewer's yeast, chicken, fish, liver.

■ **SUPPLEMENTATION:** Large doses can cause numbness and other neurological disorders.

VITAMIN B12

DAILY VALUE:	6.0 micrograms
1/2 chicken breast:	0.29 mcg
1 large egg:	0.77 mcg
1 cup nonfat milk:	0.93 mcg
3 1/2 oz. lean beef flank:	3.05 mcg

■ **WHAT IT DOES:** Necessary for development of red blood cells. Maintains normal functioning of nervous system.

■ **FOOD SOURCES:** Liver, beef, pork, poultry, eggs, milk, cheese, yogurt, shellfish, fortified cereals, and fortified soy products.

■ **SUPPLEMENTATION:** Not usually necessary, but people who are on strict vegetarian diets may need supplementation.

■ EXPERT LIST

VITAMIN C (ASCORBIC ACID)

DAILY VALUE:	60 micrograms
1 orange:	70 mcg
1 green pepper:	95 mcg
1 cup cooked broccoli:	97 mcg
1 cup fresh orange juice:	124 mcg

■ **WHAT IT DOES:** Helps promote healthy gums and teeth; aids in iron absorption; maintains normal connective tissue; helps in the healing of wounds. As an antioxidant, it combats the adverse effects of free radicals.

■ **WHAT IT MAY DO:** May reduce the risk of lung, esophagus, stomach, and bladder cancers, as well as coronary artery disease; may prevent or delay cataracts and slow the aging process.

■ **FOOD SOURCES:** Citrus fruits and juices, strawberries, tomatoes, peppers, broccoli, potatoes, kale, cauliflower, cantaloupe, brussels sprouts.

■ **SUPPLEMENTATION:** 250–500 mgs a day for smokers and anyone not consuming several fruits or vegetables rich in C daily. Larger doses may cause diarrhea.

VITAMIN D

DAILY VALUE:	400 international units
1 oz. cheddar cheese:	3 IU
1 large egg:	27 IU
1 cup nonfat milk:	100 IU

■ **WHAT IT DOES:** Strengthens bones and teeth by aiding the absorption of calcium. Helps maintain phosphorus in the blood.

■ **WHAT IT MAY DO:** May reduce risk of osteoporosis, forestall breast and colon cancers.

■ **FOOD SOURCES:** Milk, fish oil, fortified margarine; also produced by the body in response to sunlight.

■ **SUPPLEMENTATION:** 400 IU for vegetarians, the elderly, those who don't drink milk or get sun exposure. Toxic in high doses.

VITAMIN E

DAILY VALUE:	30 international units
1/2 cup boiled brussels sprouts:	1.02 IU
1/2 cup boiled spinach:	2.7 IU
1 oz. almonds:	8.5 IU

■ **WHAT IT DOES:** Helps form red blood cells. Combats adverse effects of free radicals.

■ **WHAT IT MAY DO:** May reduce the risk of esophageal or stomach cancers and coronary artery disease; may prevent or delay cataracts; may boost immunity in the elderly.

■ **FOOD SOURCES:** Vegetable oil, nuts, margarine, wheat germ, leafy greens, seeds, almonds, olives, asparagus.

■ **SUPPLEMENTATION:** 200–800 IU advised for everybody; you can't get that much from food, especially on a low-fat diet.

BIOTIN (VITAMIN B)

DAILY VALUE:	300 micrograms
1 cup cooked enriched noodles:	4 mcg
1 large egg:	11 mcg
1 oz. almonds:	23 mcg

■ **WHAT IT DOES:** Important in metabolism of protein, carbohydrates, and fats.

■ **FOOD SOURCES:** Eggs, milk, liver, mushrooms, bananas, tomatoes, whole grains.

■ **SUPPLEMENTATION:** Not recommended.

FOLATE (VITAMIN B)

(Also called Folacin or folic acid)

DAILY VALUE:	400 micrograms
1 orange:	47 mcg
1 cup raw spinach:	108 mcg
1 cup baked beans:	122 mcg
1 cup asparagus:	176 mcg

■ **WHAT IT DOES:** Important in synthesis of DNA, in normal growth, protein metabolism. Reduces risk of certain birth defects, notably spina bifida and encephaly.

■ **WHAT IT MAY DO:** May reduce the risk of cervical cancer.

■ **FOOD SOURCES:** Leafy greens, wheat germ, liver, beans, whole grains, broccoli, asparagus, citrus fruit, and juices.

■ **SUPPLEMENTATION:** 400 mcg, from food or pills, for all women who may become pregnant, to help prevent birth defects.

SOURCE: U.S. Food and Drug Administration; *Food Values of Portions Commonly Used*, Jean A. P. Pennington, Harper & Row, 1980.

EXPERT LIST

THE MINERAL MINDER

Minerals help your body form bones, regulate the heart, and synthesize enzymes, but experts say too many, or too few, can lead to heart disease, diabetes, or even cancer. Here are the FDA's daily values and where to get them.

CALCIUM

DAILY VALUE:	1 gram
1 cup hard ice cream:	0.18 g
1 cup nonfat milk:	0.3 g
2 oz. cheddar cheese:	0.41 g
8 oz. nonfat yogurt:	0.45 g

■ **WHAT IT DOES:** Helps form strong bones and teeth. Helps regulate heartbeat, muscle contractions, nerve function, and blood clotting.

■ **WHAT IT MAY DO:** May reduce the risk of high blood pressure, high cholesterol, and colon cancer.

■ **FOOD SOURCES:** Milk, cheese, butter and margarine, green vegetables, legumes, nuts, soybean products, hard water.

■ **SUPPLEMENTATION:** Most Americans don't consume enough calcium, but megadoses are not recommended. High intakes may cause constipation and increase some men's risk of urinary stones.

IRON

DAILY VALUE:	18 milligrams
1 slice whole wheat bread:	1 mg
3 scrambled eggs:	2.1 mg
3 oz. lean sirloin steak, broiled:	2.6 mg
3 oz. fried liver:	5.3 mg
1 packet instant oatmeal:	6.7 mg

■ **WHAT IT DOES:** Vital in forming hemoglobin (which carries oxygen in blood) and myoglobin (in muscle).

■ **FOOD SOURCES:** Red meat, poultry, liver, eggs, fish, whole-grain cereals, and breads.

■ **SUPPLEMENTATION:** Often (but not always) advised for dieters, strict vegetarians, menstruating women, pregnant women, infants, and children. Large doses may damage the heart, liver, and pancreas.

PHOSPHORUS

DAILY VALUE:	1 gram
6 scallops:	0.2 g
1 cup nonfat milk:	0.25 g
3 oz. broiled trout:	0.26 g
1 cup tuna salad:	0.28 g
1 cup low-fat cottage cheese:	0.34 g

■ **WHAT IT DOES:** Helps form bones, teeth, cell membranes, and genetic material. Essential for energy production.

■ **FOOD SOURCES:** Nearly all foods, including red meat, poultry, liver, milk, cheese, butter and margarine, eggs, fish, whole-grain cereals and breads, green and root vegetables, legumes, nuts, and fruit.

■ **SUPPLEMENTATION:** Not recommended. Deficiencies in Americans are virtually unknown. Excessive intake may lower blood calcium level.

POTASSIUM

DAILY VALUE:	3,500 milligrams
1 cup nonfat milk:	406 mg
1 banana:	451 mg
1 baked potato, with skin:	844 mg
1 cup cooked spinach:	839 mg

■ **WHAT IT DOES:** Needed for muscle contraction, nerve impulses, and function of heart and kidneys. Aids in regulation of water balance in cells and blood.

■ **WHAT IT MAY DO:** May fight osteoporosis and help lower blood pressure.

■ **FOOD SOURCES:** Unprocessed foods such as fruits, vegetables, and fresh meats.

■ **EXPERT LIST**

■ **SUPPLEMENTATION:** Not usually recommended. Take only under a doctor's advice and supervision.

IODINE

DAILY VALUE:	150 micrograms
1 oz. cheddar cheese:	12 mcg
1 tsp. iodized salt:	400 mcg

■ **WHAT IT DOES:** Necessary for proper thyroid gland function and thus normal cell metabolism. Prevents goiter (enlargement of thyroid).

■ **FOOD SOURCES:** Milk, cheese, butter and margarine, fish, whole-grain cereals and breads, iodized table salt.

■ **SUPPLEMENTATION:** Not recommended. Widely dispersed in the food supply, so even if you eat little iodized salt, you probably get enough iodine.

MAGNESIUM

DAILY VALUE:	400 milligrams
1 slice pumpernickel bread:	22 mg
1 tbsp. peanut butter:	28 mg
1/2 cup peas:	31 mg
1 baked potato:	55 mg
1/2 cup cooked spinach:	79 mg

■ **WHAT IT DOES:** Aids in bone growth, basic metabolic functions and the functioning of nerves and muscles, including the regulation of normal heart rhythm.

■ **FOOD SOURCES:** Milk, fish, whole-grain cereals and breads, green vegetables, legumes, nuts, and hard water.

■ **SUPPLEMENTATION:** Not usually recommended. Deficiency is rare.

ZINC

DAILY VALUE:	15 miligrams
8 oz. lowfat fruit yogurt:	1.52 mg
1 cup boiled lentils:	2.5 mg
3.5 oz. roast turkey, dark:	4.4 mg

■ **WHAT IT DOES:** Stimulates enzymes needed for cell division, growth, and repair (wound healing). Helps immune system function properly. Also plays a role in acuity of taste and smell.

■ **FOOD SOURCES:** Red meat, fish, seafood, eggs, milk, whole-grain cereals and breads, legumes.

■ **SUPPLEMENTATION:** Not recommended, except by a doctor for the few Americans who have low zinc levels.

COPPER

DAILY VALUE:	2 milligrams
2/3 cup seedless raisins:	0.31 mg
1 oz. dry roasted pistachios:	0.34 mg
1/2 cup boiled mushrooms:	0.39 mg

■ **WHAT IT DOES:** Helps in formation of red blood cells. Helps keep the bones, blood vessels, nerves, and immune system healthy.

■ **FOOD SOURCES:** Red meat, poultry, liver, fish, seafood, whole-grain cereals and breads, green vegetables, legumes, nuts, raisins, mushrooms.

■ **SUPPLEMENTATION:** Not recommended. A balanced diet includes enough copper.

SOURCE: U.S. Food and Drug Administration; *Food Values of Portions Commonly Used*, Jean A. P. Pennington, Harper & Row, 1980.

FACT FILE:

ZINC AWAY A COLD?

■ *We've all heard that vitamin C may help stave off the common cold, or at least lessen its symptoms. But there's also mounting evidence that the mineral zinc may reduce the length of time people suffer symptoms of a cold. A 1992 study of students at Dartmouth College found that 42 percent of those with colds who ate zinc lozenges reported milder symptoms than those who took a placebo.*

EXPERT Q & A

A SHORT COURSE ON CHOLESTEROL

Cut saturated fat intake and exercise to lower your "bad" cholesterol

Cholesterol is "bad" except when it's "good." Having high cholesterol is unhealthy except when it's the type that's desirable. If you're confused about the role of cholesterol in the body, here is Dr. James Cleeman, coordinator of the National Cholesterol Education Program (NCEP) at the National Heart, Lung, and Blood Institute of the National Institutes of Health, to explain:

■ What is cholesterol?

Cholesterol is a fatty, waxy substance that's an important component of cell membranes and is important in making hormones. When too much cholesterol circulates in the blood, however, it leaves deposits on the walls of the arteries, especially the coronary arteries that supply the heart. Over time, the buildup of cholesterol and fatty substances, called plaque, gets larger and thicker and starts to impede the flow of blood. In some cases, a clot may also form. When that happens, the flow of blood to that vessel may completely stop, robbing the heart muscles of oxygen and causing a heart attack. Clotting can also cause angina—pain caused by too little blood flow to a portion of the heart muscle.

■ How much cholesterol is unhealthy?

In people age 20 and over, a total cholesterol count of less than 200 mg/dl is considered desirable. A cholesterol count between 200 and 239 mg/dl is considered borderline high, and 240 or greater is definitely too high. In children 2 to 19, acceptable total levels are less than 170 mg/dl, 170 to 199 mg/dl is borderline, and 200 mg/dl and above is high.

■ What's the difference between "good" cholesterol and "bad" cholesterol?

Cholesterol is carried along in the blood by attaching itself to proteins, forming a package called a lipoprotein, which is essentially a transport mechanism. Low-density lipoprotein (LDL) is the substance by which cholesterol is transported to the cell; high-density lipoprotein (HDL) is thought to be the vehicle by which cholesterol is transported away from the cells to the liver for excretion. LDL is known as "bad" cholesterol because it's the major culprit in atherosclerosis, which develops when plaque is deposited in the arteries. HDL, on the other hand, is "good" cholesterol because it prevents cholesterol from building up in artery walls.

■ What gives a person high cholesterol?

Most people eat their way into having high cholesterol. There aren't many whose genetic makeup is so bad that they're going to have high cholesterol no matter what they do.

■ How often should cholesterol tests be taken?

Adults 20 years of age and older should have both a total cholesterol and HDL-cholesterol test, without fasting, at least once every five years. If those are fine, you don't have to do anything else. But if there's a problem, then you should have a total lipoprotein profile to determine your LDL-cholesterol level.

Most children don't have to be tested for cholesterol levels unless there is a family history of high cholesterol or heart disease striking before age 55.

■ What are the best ways to lower cholesterol?

First, watch the composition of your diet. For the roughly 40 million people who need cholesterol lowering but don't have coronary heart disease already, a Step One diet is the place to begin. A Step One diet takes 8 to 10 percent of its calories from saturated fat, about 30 percent from total fat, and allows less than 300 milligrams a day of dietary cholesterol. Try that for a period of time, rechecking your cholesterol at four to six weeks, and then again at three months.

■ FAT ATTACK

Saturated fat slows down the elimination of cholesterol in your bloodstream, and that can lead to heart disease. Here are some household oils listed by saturated fat content per single tablespoon serving.

Saturated fat | Polyunsaturated fat | Monounsaturated fat | Other fat

Product	Calories	Total fat
Canola oil	120	14 g.
Safflower oil	125	14
Sunflower oil	125	14
Corn oil	125	14
Olive oil	125	14
Regular soft margarine	100	11
Peanut oil	125	14
Veg. shortening	115	13
Lard	115	13
Butter	100	11

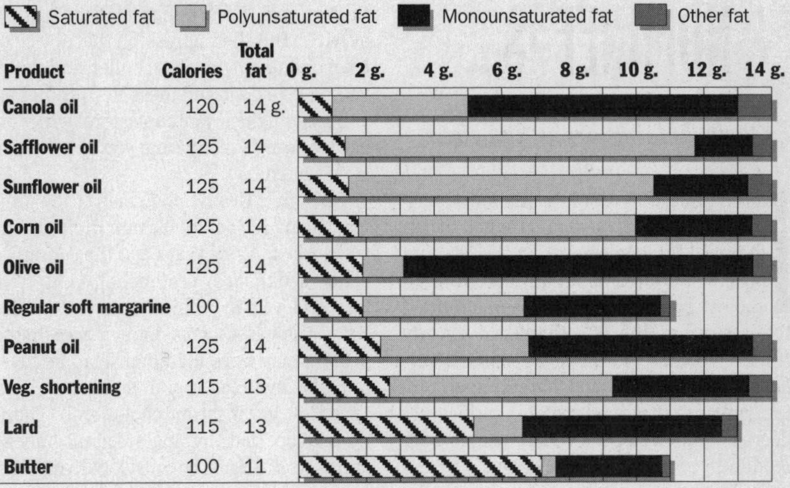

0 g. 2 g. 4 g. 6 g. 8 g. 10 g. 12 g. 14 g.

SOURCE: U.S. Department of Agriculture.

If that's not lowering your cholesterol enough, you need to move to the Step Two diet, which reduces the saturated fats to less than 7 percent of calories and the cholesterol to less than 200 milligrams a day. Saturated fat is the key culprit. For a patient who has coronary disease and has already had a heart attack or angina, the Step Two diet would be the first step because you want as much LDL-cholesterol lowering as possible.

■ Which foods should be eaten or avoided?

To reduce saturated fat and cholesterol, substitute lower-fat items for higher fat ones: Drink skim or 1% milk instead of whole milk, limit yourself to no more than six ounces a day of chicken, fish and lean cuts of meat, and concentrate on fruits, vegetables, and grains. Organ meats are very high in dietary cholesterol and probably should be restricted. Eggs are also very high in dietary cholesterol—three to four egg yolks a week are probably okay, but not more.

If you are overweight, you will lower your LDL-cholesterol and raise your HDL-cholesterol if you lose weight. By reducing your weight, you also lower your risk of coronary disease. Physical activity can also help lower LDL-cholesterol and raise HDL-cholesterol, even if you don't need to lose weight.

■ Who should take drugs to reduce cholesterol?

Drugs would be considered if dietary therapy doesn't get you far enough after six months, but they would be added to the dietary therapy, not substituted for it. Maintaining the diet will help keep the dose of drugs as low as possible. The only exception is a patient with coronary disease and a very high cholesterol level; some physicians might move fairly quickly to drug therapy in such cases.

We estimate that 85 percent of coronary patients could benefit from cholesterol lowering and only about 27 percent of these patients are actually doing diet therapy. It's particularly important that coronary patients have their cholesterol lowered. They account for about half the heart attacks that occur each year, which is 12 or 13 million.

NUTRITION

AND THIS YEAR'S NOMINEE IS...

Soy may help cut cholesterol. Garlic's claims are still unclear

In the 1970s, nutritionally minded Americans cut back on meat and turned to fish to fight high cholesterol. In the '80s, oat bran was touted as an antidote to high cholesterol. Now, soy has been anointed the cure-all of the '90s, thanks to a study reported recently in the *New England Journal of Medicine* that found that eating soy protein rather than animal protein significantly decreases cholesterol levels in people with moderate to high cholesterol levels. Ironically, the study is by Dr. James Anderson, the same doctor who discovered that oat bran can lower cholesterol in some circumstances.

Anderson, an endocrinologist at the University of Kentucky College of Medicine, and his colleagues analyzed 38 studies involving 730 men and women to determine if there's any correlation between eating soy protein and cholesterol levels. The researchers concluded that a diet consisting of 31 to 47 grams of soy protein a day—that's at least three glasses of soy milk a day or two or three cups of tofu—can reduce total cholesterol levels by an average of 9 percent, and cut LDL-cholesterol (the bad kind) by nearly 13 percent. Eating soy protein was most beneficial for those with extremely high cholesterol levels—counts of 335 milligrams per deciliter or above. They experienced a 20 percent reduction in their cholesterol level.

Perhaps the most astonishing finding is that soy protein cuts cholesterol levels no matter what else a person eats. "It's better to eat a healthy diet, but soy works even if you don't," says Anderson. Heart disease is much less common in Asian countries like Taiwan and Japan, notes Anderson, where soy is incorporated into many meals.

The benefits of adding soy to the diet shouldn't be oversold, however. "It probably does help to lower cholesterol somewhat," says Dr. James Cleeman, coordinator of the National Cholesterol Education Program at the National Heart, Lung and Blood Institute at NIH. "But the impression that soy or oat bran or fish oil is a magic bullet, and that all you have to do is add these to your diet and you're going to lower cholesterol while otherwise doing exactly what you're doing now is mistaken."

Dr. Ronald Krauss, chairman of the American Heart Association's nutrition committee, agrees. A few years ago the committee concluded that soy protein helps lower cholesterol levels in rabbits but not in humans. Krauss now sees increasing evidence that soy protein may work in humans, but he says it must be included in a diet that's well balanced and low in fat and cholesterol. "There's no evidence that any single food substance in and of itself should be considered a medicine or an antidote to prevent disease."

For those intrigued enough with the soy studies to try incorporating the protein in their diet, soy researcher Anderson suggests adding soy flour and soy milk to homemade muffins, or substituting tofu for cottage or ricotta cheese in lasagna. But, he cautions, to confer health benefits, soy must contain isoflavones, a natural chemical found in some plant foods. Isoflavones are found in most soy products except those made of soy protein concentrates like soy-vegetable burgers.

If soy products leave you cold, there's also the "garlic effect" to consider. In recent years, several studies have shown that eating garlic can lower cholesterol levels. According to an analysis of four studies at New York Medical College, one-half to one clove of garlic a day can reduce total cholesterol by nine percent. The "garlic effect" worked even when garlic tablets, powder, or extract was substituted for garlic in a person's food.

The studies have been criticized, however, as too small and poorly designed to establish clearly whether garlic lowers cholesterol. If you want to try eating a daily clove, however, there's no evidence that it's dangerous—except perhaps in social situations.

EXPERT TIPS

VEGETARIAN WAYS THAT MAKE SENSE

There's a right and wrong approach to skipping meat

If "Eat your veggies!" was a refrain you often heard from your mother as a child, give dear old Ma some credit. It's now widely recognized that eating too much meat can lead to chronic diseases while a diet rich in vegetables, fruits, and grains is more nutritious than even your mother may have suspected.

Indeed, several recent studies have shown that a vegetarian-based diet contributes to lower mortality rates from some cancers, and less obesity, coronary heart disease, high blood pressure, and diabetes. Even the U.S. government has given the seal of approval to vegetarianism. Last year, the U.S. Department of Health and Human Services (HHS) and the U.S. Department of Agriculture (USDA) acknowledged for the first time that you can get most necessary nutrients from a vegetarian diet as long as you eat adequate amounts of a variety of foods. Although fewer than seven percent of Americans consider themselves full-fledged vegetarians, many others are cutting back on the amount of meat, fish, and poultry in their diets.

Suzanne Havala, nutritional adviser to the Vegetarian Resource Group, and author of *Shopping for Health: A Nutritionist's Aisle-by-Aisle Guide to Smart Low-Fat Choices at the Supermarket* (HarperCollins, 1995), offers these suggestions on how to follow a nutritious vegetarian diet:

■ **Eat a variety of foods.** Fruits, fresh vegetables, whole grain breads, cereal, and legumes (dried beans and peas) are the foods basic to good health. Although supplementing a vegetarian diet with extra protein was once thought necessary, you should get all the pro-

■ **THE ASIAN PYRAMID**

People in Asian countries tend to live longer than Americans. Scientists think this may be attributed in part to a diet that features very little meat.

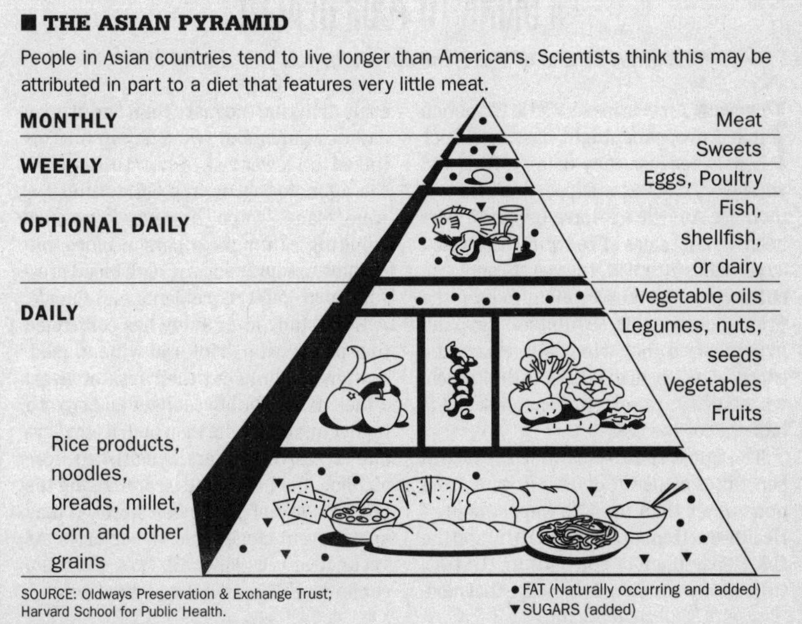

SOURCE: Oldways Preservation & Exchange Trust; Harvard School for Public Health.

tein you need from a varied diet. Vegetarians and non-vegetarians alike have a difficult time meeting the RDA (recommended dietary allowance) for iron and zinc, but that's only if you fail to eat a balanced diet. Vegans (vegetarians who eat no foods derived from animals or dairy products) need an alternate source of vitamin B12, which occurs in animal products; they can get it from supplements, B12-fortified cereal, or soy milk.

■ **Limit egg yolks and high-fat dairy products like cheese.** Egg yolks should be limited to three a week and milk to three servings a day. When people include too many animal products in their diet, they displace plant foods that contain antioxidant vitamins, fiber, and other health-supporting vitamins and minerals. Just because a product is made with soy doesn't mean it's low in fat, either. Soy dairy products, like soy yogurt, cheese, and some soy milk can also be high in fat.

■ **Beware of high-fat vegetarian foods.** Peanut butter, tahini, nuts, seeds, butter, margarine, cream cheese, mayonnaise, and oil are vegetarian foods that are high in fat.

■ **Learn low-fat cooking techniques.** Fried foods are high in fat. Instead, learn to stir-steam in nonstick pans, using water in the bottom of the pan instead of oil or butter. You can also steam vegetables in the microwave, a technique that preserves nutrients more than other methods because it cooks so quickly.

■ **Add flavor to food without adding fat.** You can make salad dressing with flavored vinegars and pureed fruit, use mustard or chutney on sandwiches, or experiment with herbs, spices, and salsa.

■ **If you do eat meat, make it a minor part of your meal rather than the focal point of your plate.** Try to break out of the mindset that meat is the main part of the meal. Many people slowly convert to a vegetarian diet by eating more meatless meals. But have realistic expectations; it takes time to develop new habits and replace old traditions with new ones.

A DRINK TO YOUR HEALTH

A glass or two of red wine may help you live a long time

For years, Americans scoffed at the notion that Europeans might have healthier hearts because they drink a little red wine every day. But as supporting evidence mounts, Americans have begun to take heed. In fact, sales of red wine have risen 80 percent since 1991, the year French scientist Serge Renaud brought to light the French paradox on *60 Minutes*. Reynaud hypothesized that wine counteracts the effects of a rich, high-fat diet in the French, whose death rate from heart disease is half that of the U.S.

The latest endorsement of the health benefits of moderate drinking comes from none other than the U.S. Department of Health and Human Services (HHS) and the U.S. Department of Agriculture (USDA). Officials there now acknowledge that moderate drinking (no more than one drink a day in women and two a day in men) is linked to a lower risk of heart disease. As the agencies' "Dietary Guidelines for Americans" warn, however, excessive drinking can make a person more vulnerable to some cancers, high blood pressure, birth defects, accidents, and suicide.

Still, study after study has confirmed that people who drink red wine in moderation not only cut their risk of heart attack in half, but live longer and enjoy a higher quality of life than both teetotalers and excessive drinkers. Scientists believe alcohol cuts heart disease by raising the body's levels of good cholesterol. It may also prevent clogging of the arteries. As yet unclear is whether all types of alcohol confer health benefits or just red wine.

OLESTRA

GUILT-FREE CHIPS YOU CAN TASTE

Snack foods made with fake fat are here but not all effects may be good

As a scientific achievement, Procter & Gamble's development of the fat substitute olestra may not rank with the landing of a man on the moon, but the hype surrounding its approval by the Food & Drug Administration is impressive even by NASA's standards. Manufacturers have already begun selling snack foods like potato chips made with olestra, sold under the brand name Olean. Potato chips made with olestra should have less than half the calories and none of the fat of other brands.

Using olestra in other foods like ice cream, salad dressing, or oil will require another FDA review. Unlike other fake fats, olestra can be used to cook foods and may eventually be available as an oil or shortening.

Olestra is made by combining sugar with fatty acids, which produces a substance that tastes like fat, looks and feels like vegetable shortening, yet doesn't add fat to food because it isn't digested or absorbed by the body.

FDA approval aside, however, olestra's metabolic effects aren't fully understood. Products with olestra will be required to warn of potential side effects, including "abdominal cramping and loose stools," and P&G will have to monitor olestra's long-term effects closely over the next two years. The FDA is also requiring that vitamins A, D, E and K be added to products made with olestra because it inhibits the absorption of these essential vitamins. Says Dr. Ronald Krauss, chairman of the American Heart Association's nutrition committee: "This is a whole new concept—taking a chemical and calling it a food—and we still have a lot of questions about that."

THE BEVERAGE OF CHAMPIONS

Milk is a great source of dietary calcium and need not be fattening

Christie Brinkley and Lauren Bacall drink milk. So do the female cast members of TV's *Friends*. And why shouldn't they? Milk is one of the best sources of dietary calcium, which protects against osteoporosis in women.

Yet despite the Milk Industry Foundation's ads featuring milk-moustachioed celebrities touting milk's benefits, many people—especially women—don't touch the stuff because they think it's fattening. In fact, skim and 1% milk are low in fat and calories. The misperception that milk products are high-fat stems in part from the way milk is labeled. For example, 2% milk is labeled low-fat even though it has five grams of fat per 8-ounce serving—10 times as much fat as a glass of skim milk. (The relative calcium content is the same.)

That labeling will soon change. Under legislation proposed by the Food and Drug Administration, dairy products can't be labeled low-fat if they have more than three grams of fat per serving. Instead, 2% milk will be labeled reduced fat; 1% milk will continue to be labeled low-fat; and skim milk will be called fat-free or nonfat.

■ IS IT REALLY LOW-FAT?

New labeling proposed by the FDA should clarify what it means to be low-fat:

Type	Fat content (grams) per 8 ounce serving	Calories
Whole milk	8	150
2% milk	5	120
1% milk	2–3	110
Skim milk	0.5 or less	80

SEAFOOD

A FISH TALE THAT NEEDS FOLLOWING

The benefits of eating fish may depend on what kind you choose

Here's a fishy debate: Does eating fish help ward off heart disease? The most recent study suggests that eating certain types of fish like tuna and salmon can reduce the risk of sudden death from heart disease. But a larger, earlier study found no such effect.

In the latest study, researchers at the University of Washington in Seattle, where moderate seafood consumption is a way of life, compared the diets of a group of Seattle-area residents who suffered cardiac arrest with a second group of randomly chosen people in the same 24- to 74-year-old age group. Researchers looked not only at how much fish was eaten by the subjects, but at the level of fatty acids in the participants' blood cell membranes.

Cardiac arrest, which occurs when the heart suddenly stops beating, appears in about two people per 10,000, and is responsible for about one-quarter of deaths from heart disease, says lead researcher David Siscovick, co-director of the Cardiovascular Health Research Unit at the University of Seattle.

The Seattle study suggests that even modest consumption of fish rich in omega-3 fatty acids (a type of oil unique to fish) reduced the risk of cardiac arrest. Researchers found that eating the equivalent of one to two servings of fish a week, depending on the type of fish, cuts in half the risk of cardiac arrest. When at least five percent of the fatty acids in a person's cell membranes were composed of omega-3 fatty acids, that person lowered his risk of cardiac arrest by

HEART-HEALTHY WITH FISH OIL

While the effectiveness of omega-3 fish oil has not been conclusively shown to prevent heart disease, here's a lineup of the fish and shellfish with the highest concentrations of the oil. Fish caught in the wild generally contain more omega-3 than farm-raised fish.

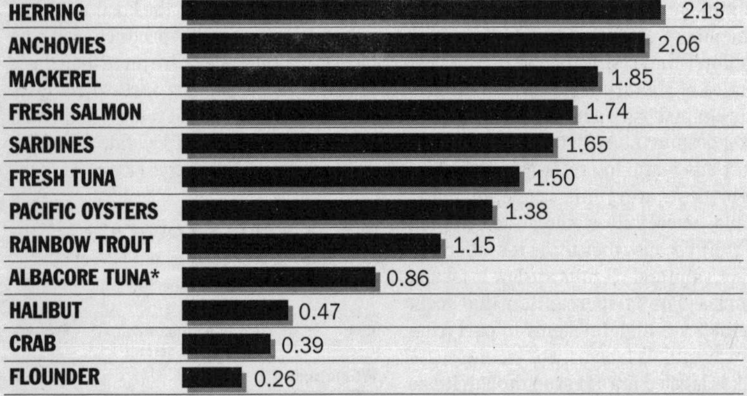

* Canned in water. Tuna packed in water has more omega-3 than tuna packed in oil.

SOURCE: University of Washington Cardiovascular Health Research Unit, *Washington Post* staff reports.

70 percent. Although studies in animals have found similar results, it's not clear why omega-3 fatty acids reduce the risk of heart attack.

What is evident, says Siscovick, is that "when it comes to these types of fatty acids, you are to a large extent what you eat." Increasing your dietary intake of these fatty acids by eating fish like salmon, albacore tuna, herring, and mackerel once or twice a week "results in changes that may influence short- and long-term health in a matter of days or weeks," says Siscovick. The research suggests, however, that frying fish reduces some of the benefits so it's best to grill, poach, or broil fish, which also leaves out saturated fat.

While the University of Seattle study found that eating certain oily fish regularly helps protect against cardiac arrest, a much larger study by researchers at Harvard last year found that eating fish doesn't appear to prevent heart disease. The Harvard investigators questioned more than 44,000 apparently healthy men (all health professionals) about their eating habits, then monitored their health for six years. The study, which focused on overall risk of heart disease, not just cardiac arrest, found that men who ate fish frequently—up to seven times a week—were just as likely to be stricken with and die from heart disease as those who ate it once a month. Even taking fish oil supplements conferred no additional benefits.

Previous reports linking fish consumption to reduced rates of heart disease prompted many Americans to add fish to their diet, and some even took fish oil capsules, which have not been proven effective at preventing heart disease. Over a decade ago, researchers recognized that in Greenland, where fish oils are a staple in the diet, heart disease is rare. The Japanese, who also eat a lot of fish, also tend to be heart-healthy. But until the health benefit of eating fish is more clearly established, don't feel you have to turn your table into the equivalent of Seattle's fish market.

■ HOW TO CLEAN A FISH

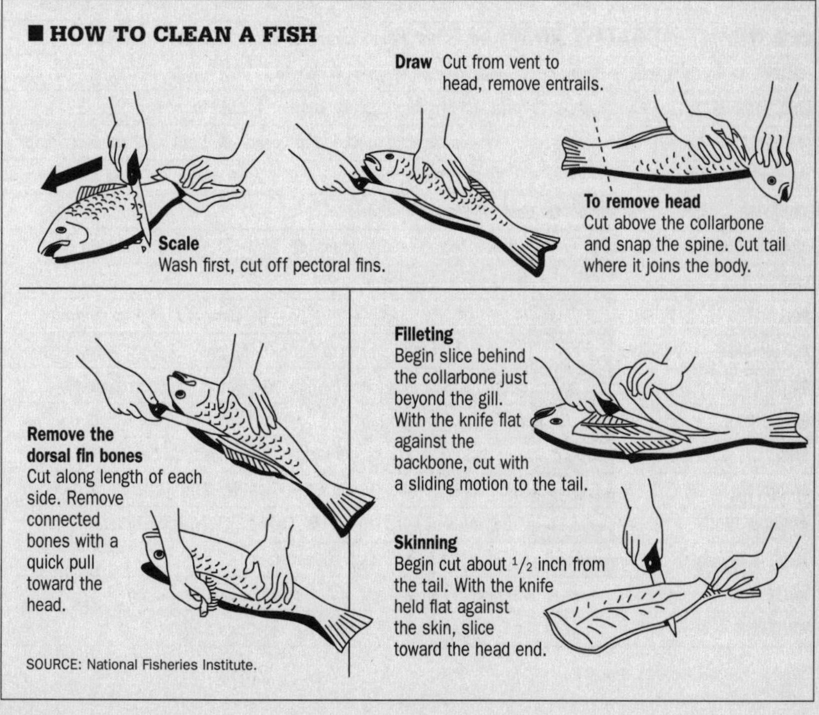

Scale
Wash first, cut off pectoral fins.
Draw Cut from vent to head, remove entrails.
To remove head
Cut above the collarbone and snap the spine. Cut tail where it joins the body.
Remove the dorsal fin bones
Cut along length of each side. Remove connected bones with a quick pull toward the head.
Filleting
Begin slice behind the collarbone just beyond the gill. With the knife flat against the backbone, cut with a sliding motion to the tail.
Skinning
Begin cut about 1/2 inch from the tail. With the knife held flat against the skin, slice toward the head end.

SOURCE: National Fisheries Institute.

GOURMET'S GUIDE

TREASURES FROM THE DEEP BLUE

These days Americans can get fish caught in waters the world over in supermarkets and restaurants. But according to the National Fisheries Institute's study of data collected by the National Marine Fisheries Service, most Americans' idea of fish is still the old standby: canned tuna. If you're one of these folks and you want to expand your taste horizons, the guide below will help you decide between bluefish and mahi mahi the next time you're in the grocery store or scanning the restaurant menu.

FISH	SOURCE	TYPE OF MEAT	*FLAVOR*
SEA BASS	Northeast Atlantic coast	**Dark**	*Light to moderate*
STRIPED BASS	Atlantic and Pacific coastal waters; also farm-raised	**Light**	*Light to moderate*
BLUEFISH	Atlantic coastal waters	**Dark**	*Light to moderate*
CARP	Freshwater lakes, ponds worldwide	**Light**	*Wild carp may taste muddy*
FARMED CARP	Farms worldwide	**Light**	*Farmed carp is light to moderate*
CATFISH	Lakes, ponds, and rivers; also farmed	**White**	*Wild catfish may taste muddy*
FARMED CATFISH	Farms worldwide	**White**	*Farmed catfish light to moderate*
COBIA	Mid-Atlantic from U.S. to Argentina	**White**	*Light to moderate*
COD	North to mid-Atlantic or North to mid-Pacific, depending on species	**White**	*Very light, delicate*
FLOUNDER	Atlantic, Pacific coasts, Asian Pacific coast, and Bering Sea	**White**	*Very light, delicate*
GROUPER	Tropical and subtropical coastal waters and Atlantic coast	**Light**	*Very light, delicate*
HALIBUT	North Atlantic or Pacific coast, depending on species	**White**	*Very light, delicate*
LAKE HERRING	Lakes and rivers in Canada and northern U.S.	**Light**	*Light to moderate*
MACKEREL	Atlantic or Gulf coast, Pacific, European Atlantic coast, Indian Ocean	**Light**	*Pronounced flavor*
MAHI MAHI	Off Hawai'i and Florida, Gulf Stream, Pacific Calif. to S. America	**White**	*Light to moderate*
MONKFISH	North to mid-Atlantic	**Light**	*Light to moderate*
ORANGE ROUGHY	Deep ocean waters off New Zealand and Australia	**White**	*Very light, delicate*
PIKE	Rivers and streams worldwide	**Light**	*Light to moderate*
POLLOCK	North Pacific or both sides of North Atlantic and the North Sea	**Light**	*Light to moderate*
RED SNAPPER	Gulf coast and Atlantic coast from North Carolina to Florida	**Light**	*Light to moderate*
SALMON	Northern Atlantic or Pacific, rivers when spawning; also farmed	**Light**	*Light to moderate*
SAND SHARK	Western Atlantic	**Light**	*Light to moderate*
SMELT	Lakes, rivers, and northern Atlantic and Pacific coasts	**Light**	*Very light, delicate*
SWORDFISH	Off Calif., New England, Hawai'i, Spain, Japan, Greece, S. America	**Light**	*Light to moderate*
RAINBOW TROUT	North American rivers and streams; also farmed	**Light**	*Very light, delicate*
TUNA	Tropical to temperate waters worldwide	**Dark**	*Light to moderate*
WALLEYE	Northern North American lakes and rivers	**Light**	*Very light, delicate*
WHITEFISH	Northern United States and Canadian lakes	**White**	*Light to moderate*

SOURCE: National Fisheries Institute.

TREATS

THE JACQUES PEPIN WAY

Tips from a master chef on creating delicious–but not sinful–desserts

When it comes to cooking, low-fat need not mean bland taste, insists Jacques Pépin, the celebrated French chef whose low-fat recipes prove his point. "French cooking is associated in this country with the three-star chefs who present a very expensive, esoteric, rich cuisine. People believe that's what most French food is like, which is a misunderstanding," says Pépin.

Pépin started his formal apprenticeship at age 13 and became the personal chef to French President Charles de Gaulle before leaving France for the U.S. in 1959. Since then, he cofounded the American Institute of Wine and Food, became dean of programs at the French Culinary Institute in New York City and is featured on the PBS series *Today's Gourmet*. Here are Pépin's tips for making delicious low-fat desserts without sacrificing flavor:

■ **USE RIPE FRUIT.** There's an enormous variety of taste you can bring out of fresh, ripe fruit. When fruit is ripe, it can have a very sweet, intense flavor. Fruits naturally high in sugar like pineapples and strawberries can be used to make desserts like sorbet without adding much sugar, but tart and acidic fruits usually need sugar.

■ **USE FRUIT THAT'S IN SEASON.** It's important to buy fruit in season—like bananas in the winter and berries and melon in the spring and summer. Seasonal fruits are less expensive and taste better.

■ **RELY ON NATURAL INGREDIENTS.** It's best to be true to Mother Nature unless you have a health problem like diabetes. Sugar substitutes cut calories, but they also sacrifice taste. Try using jam instead: It's sweet like sugar and also adds flavor because it's made with concentrated fruit.

■ **USE PASTRY DOUGH INSTEAD OF COOKIE DOUGH.** Cookie dough can't roll very thin and it's high in fat. Pastry dough has a lot of water so it can be expanded to create a rich dessert like crêpes or wafers with a minimal amount of fat.

■ **DON'T SKIMP ON PORTIONS.** Many diet cookbooks reduce calories and fat by diminishing portion sizes. But it's important to have volume so you're satisfied. For example, a soufflé with berries and egg whites is enormous, yet has a minimum amount of calories and fat.

■ **SUBSTITUTE EGG WHITES FOR WHOLE EGGS.** Egg whites are a coagulant that holds things together and add volume but have no fat. You might use one egg and three egg whites in a recipe to compromise.

■ **CONSIDER ADDING A LITTLE ALCOHOL.** Cooking alcohol will eliminate most of its calories because alcohol rises in the form of vapor, but the flavor remains.

■ **USE NONSTICK COOKWARE.** Nonstick skillets and cookie sheets will prevent food from sticking without adding any fat.

■ **USE UNSWEETENED COCOA POWDER.** Bittersweet or semisweet chocolate is made with unsweetened cocoa powder plus vegetable shortening, which means that 50 percent of its calories can be from fat. Unsweetened cocoa powder has very little fat—but don't confuse it with ground chocolate used to make instant cocoa drinks.

■ **CREATE THE LOOK AND TEXTURE OF RICH DESSERTS.** If a dessert is supposed to look creamy like custard, you can make a low-fat version that appears authentic by using canned fruit and adding yogurt to emulsify it. It won't have the taste of butter or cream, but it will feel like it does.

RECIPES

SIMPLE AND SIMPLY DELICIOUS

Jacques Pépin classics to fill out your sweet tooth, not your waist

The key to making low-fat food taste good, explains chef Jacques Pépin, is relatively simple, straightforward cooking—a style he learned in his parents' restaurant in the French countryside. But anyone who has tried to transform mouth-watering desserts into healthy eats just by cutting out the butter, cream or sugar knows that something's missing—usually the flavor. Pépin's approach emphasizes moderation rather than deprivation. "People get terrified about a piece of butter," he says. "You can't have that type of food every day, but you're not going to die if you eat it once in a while."

The following dessert classics taken from *Jacques Pépin's Simple and Healthy Cooking* (Rodale Press, 1994) are among the celebrated chef's favorites:

FRUIT SORBETS

6 SERVINGS

Sorbets are excellent do-ahead desserts. This assortment features fresh fruit. The fruit is pureed, then combined with a sugar syrup before being frozen in a commercial ice cream maker. Strawberries, watermelon, pineapple, kiwi and grapefruit—the fruits used here—all make delicious sorbets.

Sugar Syrup:
- **1 cup water**
- **1 cup sugar**

■ **TO MAKE THE SUGAR SYRUP:** Place the water and sugar in a small saucepan and warm the mixture over low heat, stirring, until the sugar is dissolved. Cool the syrup to room temperature and store it in a jar, covered, in the refrigerator. This makes about 1 1/2 cups of syrup.

Since the addition of too much sugar will prevent a sorbet from freezing properly, most professional kitchens use a Baumé hydrometer, which measures the density of sugar syrup. Syrup is added to a fruit puree until the hydrometer registers the proper level. I have tried to approximate this technique by suggesting the amount of syrup that should be added to each of the fruit purees.

Strawberry Sorbet:
- **2 1/2 cups pureed strawberries**
- **3/4 cup sugar syrup**
- **2 tablespoons lemon juice**

Watermelon Sorbet:
- **3 cups pureed watermelon**
- **1/4 cup sugar syrup**
- **1 tablespoon lemon juice**

Pineapple Sorbet:
- **2 cups pureed pineapple**
- **1/4 cup sugar syrup**
- **1 tablespoon lemon juice**

Kiwi Sorbet:
- **2 cups pureed kiwi**
- **1 cup sugar syrup**
- **1 tablespoon lemon juice**

Grapefruit Sorbet:
- **2 cups grapefruit juice**
- **1 cup sugar syrup**

■ **TO MAKE THE SORBET:** In a bowl, combine the amount of puree, syrup and lemon juice (if called for) specified for the type of sorbet you're preparing. Transfer the mixture to an ice cream maker and freeze according to the manufacturer's instructions.

Per serving:

Strawberry Sorbet:	120 calories
0.3 g. fat (2% of calories)	0 g. saturated fat
0 mg. cholesterol	1 mg. sodium
Watermelon Sorbet:	127 calories
0.5 g. fat (2% of calories)	0 g. saturated fat
0 mg. cholesterol	3 mg. sodium
Pineapple Sorbet:	128 calories
0.3 g. fat (2% of calories)	0. gr. saturated fat
0 mg. cholesterol	1 mg. sodium
Kiwi Sorbet:	167 calories
0.3 g. fat (1% of calories)	0 g. saturated fat
0 mg. cholesterol	4 mg. sodium
Grapefruit Sorbet:	151 calories
0 g. fat (0% of calories)	0 g. saturated fat
0 mg. cholesterol	0 mg. sodium

CRÊPES

12 CRÊPES

For me, crêpes are best when eaten as suggested here—hot from the pan with a light coating of homemade jam. Make them ahead and refrigerate or freeze them. Notice that these crêpes, made in an 8-inch nonstick skillet, are larger than conventional crêpes.

½ cup all-purpose flour
2 egg whites
¼ cup skim milk
1 tablespoon canola or peanut oil
1½ teaspoons sugar
½ teaspoon vanilla extract or 1 tablespoon dark rum
Assorted jams, such as raspberry, plum, apricot, or quince (optional)

■ PLACE the flour in a medium mixing bowl. Whisk in the egg whites and ¼ cup milk, beating the mixture with a whisk until it is smooth. Then whisk in the oil, sugar, vanilla or rum and the remaining ½ cup milk.

■ LIGHTLY coat an 8-inch nonstick skillet with vegetable cooking spray and set it over high heat until hot. Place 2 tablespoons of the crêpe batter in the bottom of the skillet and immediately tilt and shake the skillet until its entire bottom is covered lightly with the batter. (The faster the batter is spread, the thinner the crêpe will be.)

■ ALLOW the crêpe to cook over medium to high heat for 35 to 45 seconds, until it is browned on the bottom. Then, using a fork, loosen it around the edges. Grab hold of the crêpe along one side with both hands, carefully turning it over in the skillet, and cook it for 30 seconds on the other side. Transfer the crêpe to a platter and continue making crêpes in the skillet (no additional spray is needed) until the batter is gone. (You should have about 12 crêpes.)

If desired, spread each crêpe with about 1 teaspoon of jam and serve immediately, 2 per person. Or securely wrap and refrigerate or freeze the crêpes.

Per plain crêpe:	47 calories
1.8 g.fat (3.5% of calories)	0.1 g. saturated fat
0 mg. cholesterol	17 mg. sodium

BARBARA WALTERS' BAKED APPLE DELIGHT

The TV personality gets top ratings for her desserts, too.

Ousted Senator Robert Packwood is a man of dubious judgment when it comes to sexual propriety. But he apparently knows a good dessert when he tastes one. In his now-infamous diaries, the former Oregon senator pronounced the baked apple dish that he was served by television star Barbara Walters at a brunch at her apartment "wonderful." Walters later provided the recipe to the *Washington Post*. Here's what the *Post* reported:

- **Wash the apple and take the core out with a grapefruit knife. With the same knife, take out the remaining seeds.**
- **Rub just a little butter onto the outside of the apple to make the skin soft.**
- **Grease the pan. Pour apple juice into the middle of the apple where you took the core out. Then pour enough apple juice into the pan to cover the bottom of the apple.**
- **Sprinkle cinnamon onto the apple. Bake at 350°F for 45 minutes.**

ANGEL CAKE

12 SLICES

This light, airy cake is an American classic that's best made in an angel food cake pan.

¾ cup sifted confectioners' sugar
1 cup sifted cake flour
10 egg whites (1½ cups)
1 teaspoon almond extract
1 ¼ cups granulated sugar

■ PREHEAT the oven to 350 degrees F.

■ COMBINE the confectioners' sugar and flour in a small mixing bowl.

■ PLACE the egg whites in a large copper or

stainless steel mixing bowl and add the almond extract. Beat the mixture by hand with a large balloon whisk or with an electric mixer (fitted with a whisk attachment) at medium to high speed. When the whites hold a firm peak, gradually beat in the granulated sugar, then continue beating the mixture for 10 seconds, until the whites are stiff and shiny.

■ SIFT the flour mixture on top of the egg whites and fold it in with a rubber spatula just until it is incorporated. Do not overmix! Pour the batter into a 10-inch tube pan.

Bake in the center of the oven for 35 minutes, or until the cake springs back when lightly touched. Immediately invert the pan onto an overturned metal funnel or a cake rack and cool it completely.

To remove the cake from the pan, run a thin-bladed knife around the edges of the cake. Invert the cake onto a serving plate, cut (or pull apart with forks) and serve.

Per slice:	147 calories
0 g. fat (0% of calories)	0 g. saturated fat
0 mg. cholesterol	46 mg. sodium.

CHOCOLATE SAUCE

6 SERVINGS

Because this concentrated chocolate sauce is made with unsweetened cocoa powder instead of chocolate, which is high in fat, it is suitable for people on low-fat diets. The sauce goes well with Angel Cake.

½ cup water
½ cup sugar
½ cup unsweetened cocoa powder

■ COMBINE the water and sugar in a medium saucepan and bring the mixture to a boil. Boil for 1 minute, then add the cocoa and whisk the mixture until it is well blended.

■ STRAIN the sauce into a jar and set it aside; it will thicken as it cools. When it is cool, cover the jar with a tight-fitting lid and store in the refrigerator. Rewarm the sauce or serve it cold over cake or frozen yogurt.

Per serving:	74 calories
0.7 g. fat (7% of calories)	0 g. saturated fat
0 mg. cholesterol	5 mg. sodium.

RASPBERRY SOUFFLÉS IN RASPBERRY SAUCE

6 SERVINGS

This showy dessert contains egg whites with a little sugar and a puree of fresh berries; it has a wonderful color and concentrated berry taste. I make individual soufflés here, but you can also make one large dessert in a 1-quart mold (bake for 25 to 30 minutes).

10 ounces fresh raspberries or 1 package (10–12 ounces) frozen unsweetened berries, thawed
⅓ cup seedless raspberry jam
1 teaspoon peanut or corn oil
4 large egg whites
⅓ cup sugar
½ cup fresh raspberries

■ TO make the sauce, place the 10 to 12 ounces of raspberries in a food processor or blender. Add the jam and process until the mixture is pureed. Strain the puree.

■ PREHEAT the oven to 400 degrees F. Brush 6 molds (½- to 1-cup capacity) with the oil.

■ PLACE the egg whites in a large copper or stainless steel mixing bowl. Beat with a large balloon whisk or with an electric mixer with a whisk attachment at medium to high speed. When the whites hold a firm peak, gradually beat in the sugar. Continue beating for 10 seconds, until the whites are stiff and shiny.

■ CRUSH the ½ cup of raspberries coarsely and fold them into the egg white. Divide the mixture among the molds so that it extends in soft peaks above the tops of the molds.

■ PUT the molds on a baking tray and bake 12 to 15 minutes, until the tops are browned and the soufflés are well-inflated and firm.

To serve, put 2 tablespoons of sauce on each of 6 dessert plates. Run a knife around the edge of the soufflés, unmold them and place a soufflé, brown side up, in the center of each plate. Drizzle the top of each soufflé with a tablespoon of sauce. Serve immediately.

Per serving:	135 calories
1.1 g. fat (7% of calories)	0.1 g. saturated fat
0 mg. cholesterol	39 mg. sodium

FRUIT

RIPE FOR THE PICKING

A grocery shopper's guide to choosing fresh fruits

For many consumers, buying fresh produce is like a game of roulette. There's no telling whether their fruits and vegetables will be fresh and ripe at home because they don't know how to choose produce at the grocery store.

Even some shoppers who consider themselves knowledgeable produce pickers are merely misinformed victims of old wives' tales. Contrary to popular belief, watermelon thumping, cantaloupe shaking, and pineapple plucking are not valid tests for determining ripeness, according to the Produce Marketing Association.

Experts there offer these tips for choosing the ripest of the most popular fresh fruits:

■ APPLES
Fruit should be firm, well-colored, and mature. Should have no soft spots or broken or shriveled skin.

■ APRICOTS
Plump fruit with golden-orange color. When ripe, flesh will yield to gentle pressure when touched. Avoid hard and overly firm fruit.

■ AVOCADOS
When ripe, fruit yields to gentle pressure when touched. Firm avocados will ripen at room temperature. Should have no bruises or hard and soft spots.

■ BANANAS
Look for firm, bright-colored fruit without bruises. Fully ripe when skin turns yellow with brown and black flecks. Can be purchased green and stored at room temperature to ripen.

Only refrigerate ripe bananas. Refrigeration will turn skins black, but will not affect fruit quality.

■ CANTALOUPES
Will have a cantaloupe smell, yield to pressure on the blossom end, and have a yellowish cast under the netting when ready.

Leave cantaloupes at room temperature to soften and become juicier.

■ CHERRIES
Should be plump with firm, smooth, and brightly colored skins and intact stems. Avoid cherries with blemished, rotted, or mushy skins or those that appear either hard and light-colored or soft, shriveled, and dull.

■ GRAPEFRUIT
Should be firm, springy to the touch, heavy for size, well shaped, and thin-skinned.

Grapefruit may show russeting (browning of the peel) or regreening, which do not affect fruit quality.

■ GRAPES
Bunches should be well colored with plump fruits firmly attached to green, pliable stems. Grapes should not leak moisture.

■ HONEYDEWS
Will have a creamy yellow skin and a slightly soft blossom end. An unripe honeydew has

EXPERT TIP

To speed the ripening of soft fruits such as avocados, bananas, kiwis, nectarines, peaches, pears, plums, and tomatoes, store them in a paper bag with an apple. The apple will boost the partly ripe fruit's exposure to ethylene, a gas required for ripening.

—The Produce Marketing Association

white skin with a green tint and a hard blossom end, and will ripen at room temperature.

Choose melons that are heavy for their size and are well shaped. Unlike cantaloupe, honeydew does not have a distinctive aroma.

■ KIWIFRUIT
Choose firm, plump, light brown kiwi that gives slightly to the touch. Harder fruit can be purchased and ripened at room temperature at home.

■ LEMONS
Should have a pleasant citrus fragrance. Should be firm, heavy for size, and have thin smooth skins.

■ LIMES
Should be plump and heavy for their size, with glossy skin.

■ NECTARINES
Look for a creamy yellow background color without any green at the stem end. Firm fruits can be ripened at home. When they yield slightly to pressure, they're ready to eat.

■ ORANGES
May regreen after harvest, but this is natural and does not indicate unripeness. To get the juiciest fruit, choose oranges that feel heavy for their size.

■ PEACHES
Fruits should smell peachy and have no tinge of green in the background color of the skin. The amount of red blush does not indicate ripeness. Buy peaches that are fairly firm and a little soft. They should give a bit when squeezed in the palm of the hand. Stored in a paper bag, they will soften and get juicier, but not sweeter.

FACT FILE:

FRUITS THAT DO NOT RIPEN AFTER HARVEST:

- *Apples*
- *Grapefruit*
- *Lemons*
- *Oranges*
- *Strawberries*
- *Tangelos*
- *Cherries*
- *Grapes*
- *Limes*
- *Pineapples*
- *Tangerines*
- *Watermelons*

■ PEARS
Will yield to gentle pressure near the stem end and side when they are ready to eat. Ripen at home at room temperature.

■ PINEAPPLES
Will have a strong pineapple aroma. Should be heavy for their size, well shaped and fresh-looking with dark green crown leaves and a dry, crisp shell. Ripeness is not indicated by shell color or pulling crown leaves.

■ PLUMS
Choose plump fruit with good color for the variety. Skin should be smooth, without breaks or discolorations. Flesh should be fairly firm to slightly but not excessively soft. To ripen at home, store in a paper bag.

■ STRAWBERRIES
Should be plump, firm, well rounded, and have an even bright red color with natural shine. Caps should be fresh-looking, green, and in place. When possible, avoid fruit that is white near the caps. This is called white shoulders, and it can mean two things: either the fruit was picked too soon, or the berries are fully ripe but missing some color due to a lack of sunshine.

■ TANGERINES
Look for fruit with deep, rich color and "puffy" appearance. Good-quality fruit should be heavy for its size. Avoid fruit with soft or water-soaked spots or mold.

■ WATERMELONS
Should have a dull (as opposed to shiny) rind, a dried stem, and a yellowish underside where the watermelon has touched the ground. Immature watermelons have a shiny rind and a white, pale green, or light yellow underside. Thumping does not indicate ripeness.

COFFEE

A COFFEE LOVER'S WORLD TOUR

From the mountains of Colombia to Java, beans to suit every palate

Coffee beans are like wine grapes. Where they are grown and how they are raised shapes their taste profoundly. Even the most casual of coffee drinkers will taste the difference, for instance, between the light-bodied coffee produced from beans cultivated in the high Sierras in southern Mexico and the "buttery" full body and spicy aroma of Indonesian-grown coffees. For a taster's tour of coffees around the world, sip on:

■ **CENTRAL AND SOUTH AMERICA.** Coffees from south of the U.S. border are usually light-to-medium bodied with clean lively flavors. Colombian coffees have a brisk snappy quality—called "acidity" by coffee connoisseurs although it has nothing to do with pH factor. Their aroma is heady and distinctive. Costa Rican beans, particularly those from the mountainous Pacific region known as Tres Rios, are medium-bodied when brewed, with a tangy aroma. Guatemalan beans, particularly those from the Antigua region, produce a richer and more complex flavored coffee than any other Central American variety. Kona coffee is smooth and even. Although it is raised in Hawaii, not Latin America, it is a close cousin to that region's products in taste and aroma.

■ **EAST AFRICA.** Medium to full-bodied generally, the coffees of East Africa combine the brisk, refreshing quality found in Central American coffees with flavors that seem floral or resemble fine red wine at times. Kenyan coffee is especially known for its combination of heartiness and winelike flavor. The Arabica beans native to Ethiopia produce a brew that is medium-bodied with a deep, near-floral aroma and taste. Arabian Mocha is smooth, delicate, winy, and aromatic all at once. It comes from Yemen, where coffee was first grown. It is sometimes blended with Java beans from Indonesia to produce Arabian Mocha Java.

■ **INDONESIA.** Full-bodied and smooth, Indonesian coffees are quite different in taste and aroma from those of Latin America. Indonesian coffees often have exotic floral or spice-like aspects to their aroma and flavor. The best-known coffee from the region is Estate Java, which is rich and full-bodied with a deep spicy aroma.

SOURCE: Adapted from "The World of Coffee," Starbucks Coffee Company, 1995.

EXPERT SOURCES

GETTING YOUR JAVA THROUGH THE MAIL

True coffee aficionados relish coffee from microroasters who import coffee beans from all over the world and roast them in small batches. Below are some roasters that offer great mail-order coffee:

ROASTERS SELECT COFFEE OF THE MONTH CLUB

■ This Seattle company features one coffee per month from 26 American microroasters. For $9.95 a month, you get a one- or two-pound selection, a newsletter, and a sweet. ☎ 800–JAVAS–2–U

UNCHARTED GROUNDS

■ After sampling 100 gourmet coffees each month, the staff chooses one coffee to send members at $8.95 for 3/4 pound. ☎ 800–242–2226

NORTHWESTERN COFFEE MILLS

■ This Wisconsin coffee roaster has been in business for over 100 years. Discounts for bulk orders. ☎ 800–243–5283

MONTANA COFFEE TRADERS

■ For some local flavor, try the Buffalo or Grizzly blends. This microroaster also has a coffee-of-the-month club. ☎ 800–345–JAVA

PEET'S COFFEE & TEA

■ A Berkeley, California company that offers coffees from around the world and exotic house blends. It has a coffee-of-the-month club and gift items by mail. ☎ 800–999–2132

THE PERFECT ESPRESSO IN YOUR OWN HOME

Coffee-drinkers may be calling the '90s the Coffee Bar Decade. All across America, coffee bars have replaced the other kind of bar as destination hangouts for those seeking gourmet caffeine and social company. But you don't have to head down the street for a good cup of espresso. Jerry Baldwin, chairman of Peet's Coffee & Tea, the Berkeley, Calif., institution where the coffee revolution began over 30 years ago, offers these tips on making espresso fit for a Medici in your own home.

"To enjoy good espresso at home," says Baldwin, "you need a machine that uses steam." Stovetop "moka pots" or electric models selling for under $100 do not generate enough pressure to produce the intense flavor of espresso.

"Home grinding is essential because finely ground coffee goes stale in just a few hours. Precise grinding is crucial in the formation of golden-brown *crema*, the true sign of a well-made espresso. Crema will not form if the coffee is improperly ground: if it is too coarse, the espresso will come through in less than 15 seconds and there will be too much fluid; if it is too fine, longer than 20 seconds will be required and there will be only a small amount of bitter fluid." (White crema is another indication that the infusion was too slow.)

"If the coffee is fresh, making the appropriate adjustments to the grind should produce the result you're aiming for—1 1/2 to 2 oz. of rich, brown ambrosia with the desired crema—though you might also try tamping the coffee into the portafilter more or less firmly to slow down or speed up the process."

TEA

TASTES WORTH A TRIP TO CHINA

The world's greatest tea masters on the perfect cup of tea

For over two millennia tea has been extensively cultivated in the East, especially in China. Yet most consumers are unfamiliar with the growing and production processes required to develop fine teas. That is not the case for Donald R. Wallis and Roy Fong, founders of the American Tea Masters Association based in San Francisco. An organization for tea cognoscenti, the Tea Masters Association imports connoisseur-grade tea from Chinese tea farmers who raise their crops according to the Association's demanding standards. The group then sells these stocks to its members, at $150 to $2,500 a pound. Some 421 varieties of the finest teas are available, and nonmembers can order through a catalog as well.

Not everyone can match Wallis and Fong's tea connoisseurship. (Wallis drinks 20 to 30 cups a day.) But even an introduction by them to the world of tea will delight you. Their report:

The tea plant, *Camellia sinensis*, is a member of the large family of flowering camellias that often decorate parks and gardens. The world's most popular beverage today, tea is produced everywhere from China to South America. The best known is black tea, although technically it is actually reddish in color. The mislabeling is thought to date to the 1600s, when a dark oolong tea from the Wu Yi mountains in China may have been exported via Dutch traders to Europe, and thanks to its dark color, incorrectly named black tea. Today, other types of tea, such as green, oolong, yellow, white, and puerh, are also popular.

In Western countries, tea is usually sold in teabags that infuse within a matter of seconds and produce a drink, referred to in its liquid form as liquor, which is somewhat more astringent than loose whole-leaf teas.

Every tea has an optimum technique for preparation, but the consumer can rely on a few basic tips.To avoid a bitter liquor, many commercial teabags may often be improved by steeping for 30 seconds or less in an open cup with very hot but not boiling water—temperatures generally not exceeding 185 degrees F. The resulting liquor will exhibit a lighter, sweeter flavor, and the bag may be infused a second or third time. Properly prepared tea should not taste bitter.

Loose whole-leaf tea is usually best prepared fresh by the cup. Loose green teas also enjoy lower temperature water and may be improved by steeping them for only a minute or two. The liquor is then drained from the leaves using a small utility strainer or the lid of a Chinese covered teacup (gaiwan) to retain the leaves in the cup. The leaves may be used again for additional infusions with slightly increased water temperature and steeping time, as desired. All subsequent infusions should be completed within an hour or so of the first immersion.

White and yellow teas are prepared in a similar manner. Loose red (black), oolong, and puerh teas may be prepared at higher water temperatures, but for the gourmet palate never at the boiling point. To the gourmet, tea is not a strong, coarse beverage that overwhelms the senses with bitter vengeance, but a smooth, sweet, and subtle taste sensation.

EXPERT SOURCE

For more information on tea connoisseurship or a catalog of special teas for mail order, contact:

The American Tea Masters Association
41 Sutter Street #1191
San Francisco, CA 94104
☎ 415-775-4227

EXPERT TIPS

CHARCOAL TASTE WITHOUT HARM

Outdoor grilling is healthy if you keep the fat down and don't char

Barbecuing is by nature a healthy cooking technique—never mind that using charcoal to grill your food can produce carcinogens if the flame comes in direct contact with your dinner, or if there's a lot of smoke produced by grease dripping on the hot coals or coils in your grill. You'd have to grill every day for years to be threatened by these effects, says Melanie Polk, a registered dietitian and director of nutrition education for the American Institute for Cancer Research. Far more unhealthy is the propensity of many backyard enthusiasts for turning the barbecuing rite into a fat-filled, high-calorie fête. Here, Melanie Barnard, the author of *Low-Fat Grilling*, (HarperPerennial, 1995, $10) and a regular columnist for *Bon Appetit*, offers lowfat tips:

■ **Use nonstick vegetable spray.** Before you put the grill rack over the fire, spray it with a nonstick cooking spray, then let the rack heat up for at least five minutes before adding food.

■ **Prepare low-fat marinades.** The basic ingredients are vinegar or lemon juice, molasses, sugar or honey, seasonings, and just a few drops of oil to preserve the food's moisture.

■ **Grill vegetables.** Fresh vegetables need just a little fat to keep them from sticking to the grill. Sprinkle them with lemon juice and herbs, then brush them with a light coat of olive or canola oil.

■ **Remove the skin from chicken.** The skin adds a lot of fat to a chicken breast. And you can grill chicken without any additional fat.

■ **Try grilling seafood.** Fish needs just a smidgen of oil or mayonnaise to seal in the flavor. Grill clams in the shell for a five-minute meal that has practically no fat.

■ **Use small portions of meat and add vegetables.** Try recipes like lamb kebobs with vegetables or a grilled steak salad.

GRILLING WITHOUT CARCINOGENS

The technique you use can cut the health risks of barbecuing substantially. To control carcinogens when barbecuing, dietitian Pamela Savage-Marr of the American Dietetic Association has these tips:

■ Choose low-fat meats so there's not as much fat to drip and cause smoking.

■ Cover the grill with foil and punch holes in it, so fat can drip away but smoke can't get back in contact with the food.

■ Avoid flare-ups by keeping food as far from coals as possible. Keep a water bottle close by so you can squirt water on the grill if flames get too high.

■ Precook poultry or meat if you wish to be extra-cautious, then throw it on the grill for just a few minutes to get the charcoal flavor. If you're cooking vegetables or fish, wrap it in foil, which protects it from smoke but preserves the flavor and juices.

■ If you do char food, scrape off the blackened bits to eliminate excessive exposure to carcinogens, and remove charred food from the grill to avoid burning food again.

EXPERT PICKS

THE BEST BREWS ANYWHERE

Picking the top 10 American beers is almost an impossibility, or so says Christopher Finch, author of A Connoisseur's Guide to the World's Best Beers *(Abbeville, 1996) and co-author of* America's Best Beers *(Little, Brown, 1994) with W. Scott Griffiths. But the beermeister who's tried everything offers this list of his favorite craft brewers from coast to coast.*

ANCHOR BREWING COMPANY
San Francisco, California

■ Fritz Maytag's company, which he took over in 1965, sets the standards by which American craft brewing should be judged. Anchor Steam Beer is a world classic and Liberty Ale is one of my top choices among widely distributed ales.

CELIS BREWERY
Austin, Texas

■ Pierre Celis is one of the world's master brewers and a legend in his native Belgium. Celis White, his Texas interpretation of a classic Belgian wheat beer style, is a brew that no beer lover should miss. The brewery's other beers are almost as good.

GREAT LAKES BREWING CO.
Cleveland, Ohio

■ Operating one of the nation's great brewpubs, Patrick and Daniel Conway serve consistently excellent beers, notably The Commodore Perry's IPA and Moon Dog Ale.

MENDOCINO BREWING COMPANY
Hopland, California

■ Founded in 1983, by Michael Leybourn, Mendocino Brewing provided California with its first modern brewpub. Its beers, now thankfully well-distributed, include the creamy, British-accented Red Tail Ale. I hesitate to call any single beer my favorite, but I can't think of an American brew I like better.

NEW BELGIUM
Fort Collins, Colorado

■ A great Belgian-style ale brewery in the shadow of the Rockies? It's almost unthinkable, but New Belgium's beers are superb. Try Fat Tire Ale or the delectably meaty Tripple.

PIKE PLACE BREWER
Seattle, Washington

■ Founded by America's premier quality beer importer, Charles Finkel (Merchant du Vin), this tiny microbrewery produces some of the fullest bodied beers in America. The XXXXX Stout is outstanding, as is the chewy basic Pale Ale and the ambrosial Old Bawdy Barley Wine.

ST. STAN'S BREWERY
Modesto, California

■ This brewery makes some of the most distinctive beers in America, very smooth and satisfying in the German tradition—top fermented like ales, yet different. Its Red Sky Ale is worth trying.

SIERRA NEVADA BREWING CO.
Chico, California

■ Founded in 1981 by Ken Grossman and Paul Camusi, this company produces a range of exceptional beers. The Pale Ale, the Porter, and the Stout are all first rate examples of their styles, as is the formidable Bigfoot Barleywine.

TABERNASH (COLORADO BREWING COMPANY)
Denver, Colorado

■ Tabernash Weiss is the best German-style wheat beer brewed in America, bar none. Tabernash also brews some of the most authentic German-style lagers to be found on this side of the Atlantic.

ZIP CITY BREWING CO.
New York, New York

■ American craft brewing generally does much better with ales than with lagers. Like Tabernash, Zip City provides a welcome exception to this rule. Try Marzen or the meaty Dunkel.

REMEDIES

SOUP ISN'T JUST FOR THE SOUL

If you've got a cold, grandmother's recipe is a good place to start

Jewish grandmothers have known for generations that chicken soup can fight congestion caused by the common cold. But most scientists have long dismissed chicken soup as an old-fashioned remedy that didn't hurt—but it probably didn't help, either.

The first real evidence that chicken soup might have curative powers came in a study in 1978. Researchers compared whether eating chicken soup could increase the rate mucus and air flowed through nasal passages better than drinking hot or cold water. It did.

A more recent study conducted by Dr. Stephen Rennard, chief of pulmonary and critical care medicine at the University of Nebraska Medical Center, confirmed chicken soup's ability to unclog nasal passages. Rennard suspected the soup slows the movement of white blood cells called neutrophils that can cause inflammation. He tested his theory in a laboratory by releasing neutrophils in the top half of a container divided by a strainer that contained bacteria that attracts neutrophils in the bottom half. Then he added the soup and measured how quickly the neutrophils moved toward the bottom. Both canned and homemade soup inhibited neutrophil movement, but plain water did not.

Rennard, however, won't say that chicken soup actually cures the common cold and hasn't performed the experiment in humans. "There's no doubt that chicken soup can contain lots of medicinal compounds, but whether they're good or bad for you remains undetermined," he says. "But if your grandmother always told you to take chicken soup when you have a cold, I wouldn't dispute that."

HOW TO CARVE A TURKEY

Show off at the table next Thanksgiving dinner. Here's what to do:

1. Remove drumstick and thigh by pulling leg away from body. Joint connecting leg to backbone will often snap free or may be severed easily with knife point. Cut dark meat from body by following body contour carefully with a knife.

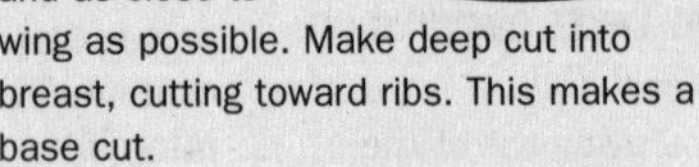

2. Place drumstick and thigh on cutting surface and cut through connecting joint.

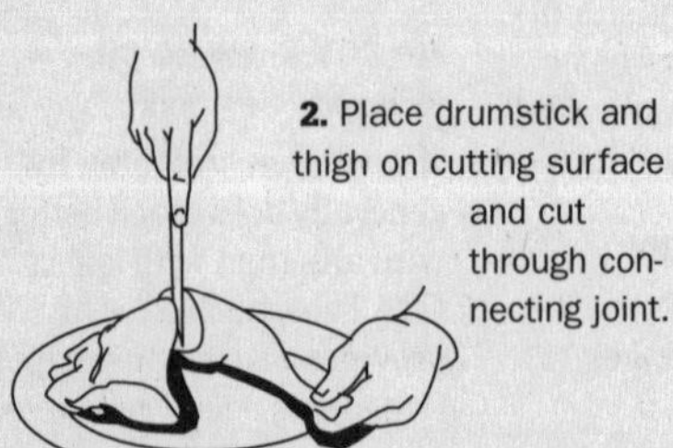

3. Hold turkey breast firmly on carving surface with fork. Place knife parallel and as close to wing as possible. Make deep cut into breast, cutting toward ribs. This makes a base cut.

4. Slice breast by carving downward, ending at base cut. Keep slices thin and even.

SOURCE: National Turkey Federation.

DELI FOODS

WHEN YOUR ORDER IS HOT PASTRAMI

Hold the mayo, hold the meat and you'll be just fine

Americans love to nosh on ham and cheese with mustard, and submarine sandwiches from their local deli. But is this lunchtime ritual healthy? Unfortunately, bacon, ham, pastrami, and corned beef are dietary no-no's. Add mayo and you're really in trouble: one tablespoon has 100 calories and 11 grams of fat. Beware, too, of cheese, which adds another 100 calories and 10 grams of fat. If you're tired of turkey and grilled chicken breast, try a roast beef sandwich with mustard.

Besides unhealthy amounts of fat, the other deli food concern is bacterial contamination, but this problem is rare. Refrigerating food at 40 degrees F or below prevents most food-borne bacteria from multiplying, says the U.S. Department of Agriculture (USDA). But a bacterium named listeria—and listeriosis, the life-threatening illness it can cause—is hardy enough to survive refrigeration.

Cases of listeriosis have been linked to soft cheese, hot dogs, milk, and processed meat. Healthy people rarely contract listeriosis, but pregnant women, newborns, people over age 60, and those with compromised immune systems are more susceptible.

To reduce your risk of common foodborne illnesses, Bessie Berry, acting director of the USDA Meat and Poultry Hotline, advises that you check the temperature in the deli refrigerator to ensure that it is 40 degrees or lower. Most delis have a thermometer that is visible to customers. Also avoid meat that is touched excessively. Food handlers' gloves should be changed each time meat or other food is touched. Finally, ask the butcher to slice meat rather than buy pre-packaged or pre-sliced meat. The product will be fresher.

GERM WARFARE

Use temperature to kill bacteria before they make you sick.

240°	Canning temperatures for low-acid vegetables, meat, and poultry in pressure canner.
212°	Canning temperature for fruits, tomatoes, and pickles in water bath canner. Cooking temperatures destroy most bacteria. Time required to kill bacteria is decreased as temperature is increased.
165°	Warming temperatures prevent growth but allow survival of some bacteria.
140°	Some bacterial growth may occur. Many bacteria survive. **DANGER ZONE. Temperatures in this zone allow rapid growth of bacteria and production of toxins by some bacteria.**
60°	Some growth of food-poisoning bacteria may occur. (Do not store meats, poultry, or seafoods for more than one week in the refrigerator.)
40°	Cold temperatures permit slow growth of some bacteria that cause spoilage.
32°	Freezing temperatures stop growth of bacteria, but may allow bacteria to survive. (Do not store food above 10° F for more than a few weeks.)

SOURCE: U.S. Department of Agriculture.

EXPERT PICKS

THE JAMES BEARD COOKBOOK HALL OF FAME

The Cookbook Hall of Fame recognizes books that have significantly influenced the way we think about food and honored authors who possess an exceptional ability to communicate their gastronomic vision via the printed page. The first cookbook was inducted into the Hall of Fame in 1977.

1995 LE TECHNIQUE *and* **LA METHODE,** *Jacques Pépin, Times Books;* Le Technique, *1976, $25;* La Methode, *1979, out of print*

1994 GREENE ON GREENS, *Bert Greene, Workman Press, 1989, $15.95*

1993 ALICE LET'S EAT, AMERICAN FRIED AND THIRD HELPINGS (THE TUMMY TRILOGY), *Calvin Trillin, FS&G, 1994, $16*

1992 SIMPLE FRENCH FOOD, *Richard Olney, Macmillan, 1992, $13*

1991 THE SILVER PALATE COOKBOOK, *Julee Rosso and Sheila Lukins with Michael McLaughlin, Workman Press, 1982, $12*

1990 THE FOOD OF FRANCE and **THE FOOD OF ITALY,** *Waverley Root, Random House, 1992, $13*

1989 THE ART OF EATING, *M. F .K. Fisher, Macmillan, 1990, $16*

1988 No award given

1987 FOODS OF THE WORLD *(18 volumes, 1969–1972), Time-Life Books, $19.95–$25*

1986 MASTERING THE ART OF FRENCH COOKING, VOLUMES ONE AND TWO, *Volume One by Julia Child with Simone Beck and Louisette Bertholle; Volume Two by Julia Child with Simone Beck, Knopf, 1970, $25 each*

1985 THE AMERICAN WOMAN'S COOKBOOK, *edited by Ruth Berolzheimer, Culinary Arts Institute, 1948, out of print*

1984 GEORGE AUGUSTE ESCOFFIER COOKBOOK COLLECTION, *George Auguste Escoffier, Van Nostrand Reinhold, 1979, $64.95*

1983 THE JAMES BEARD COOKBOOK, *James Beard, Dutton, 1970, out of print*

1982 THE BETTY CROCKER COOKBOOK, *edited by Marjorie Child Hustad, Bentham, 1987, $7.99*

1981 THE NEW YORK TIMES COOKBOOK, *Craig Claiborne, HarperCollins, 1990, $30*

1980 THE CORDON BLEU COOKBOOK, *Dione Lucas, Little , Brown, 1947, $25*

1979 THE FANNIE FARMER COOKBOOK, *Fannie Merritt Farmer, 1983, $6.95*

1978 THE JOY OF COOKING, *Irma Rombauer, Dutton, 1991, $9.98*

1977 THE SETTLEMENT COOKBOOK, *Mrs. Simon (Lillian) Kander, Simon & Schuster, 1976, $25*

■ SELECTED JAMES BEARD FOUNDATION 1996 COOKBOOK AWARD WINNERS

GENERAL

JIM FOBEL'S BIG FLAVORS, *Jim Fobel, Clarkson Potter, 1995, $19.95*

INTERNATIONAL

SUSANNA FOO CHINESE CUISINE: THE FABULOUS FLAVORS & INNOVATIVE RECIPES OF NORTH AMERICA'S FINEST CHINESE COOK, *Susanna Foo, Chapters, 1995, $35*

HEALTHY-FOCUS

LIGHTER, QUICKER, BETTER: COOKING FOR THE WAY WE EAT TODAY, *Richard Sax and Marie Simmons, William Morrow, 1995, $25*

VEGETARIAN

HIGH-FLAVOR, LOW-FAT VEGETARIAN COOKING, *Steven Raichlen, Viking, 1995, $24.95*

LOOKING GREAT

CONTACTS: Lenses with built-in UV-filters can protect your eyes from the sun, PAGE 180 **MAKEUP:** Choosing the right look for your age, PAGE 182 **HAIR:** Every day can be a good hair day, PAGE 184 **BALDNESS:** New techniques offer hope for thinning hair, PAGE 185 **COSMETIC SURGERY:** A guide to common procedures, PAGE 187 **SKIN:** Laser technology can help erase wrinkles, PAGE 189 **BREASTS:** The latest on silicone implants, PAGE 193

SKIN CARE

HOW NOT TO SHOW YOUR SKIN'S AGE

You can't erase genetic makeup; you can avoid damage from the sun

At first, it's merely a few laugh lines around your eyes, then tiny wrinkles appear around the mouth. Gradually, eyelids begin to droop and a double chin shows up uninvited. As inevitable as the aging process may be, however, there is great variability in how youthful different people appear at the same age. Everyone wants to look like Grace Kelly at age 50, Audrey Hepburn at age 60, or Claudette Colbert at 70, but few people take the preventive measures necessary to maintain youthful-looking skin.

Two factors are critical in determining how your skin ages: genetics and sun exposure. To some extent your skin's appearance is predetermined by genetic traits inherited from your parents. In addition, fair-skinned people are more likely than the more dark-complexioned to age prematurely or to develop skin cancer from sun exposure. That's because the fairer-skinned have less pigment to protect them from the sun's rays and are more susceptible to the process known as photoaging, which comes from the cumulative exposure a person receives to the sun.

Photoaging actually plays a bigger role in your skin's appearance than your chronological age. Skin can age as a result of getting too much sun over a short period of time, as well as from the gradual damage of long-term exposure. But most damage occurs by the time you reach age 18. "If you were dealt a bad hand genetically, and you want to make sure you don't get advanced signs of aging, the best thing you can do is avoid the sun," explains Dr. Cherie Ditre, a prominent Philadelphia dermatologist and researcher. Below is a guide to what you can expect of your skin from your 20s through your 50s, and what you can do to combat the toll of time:

■ **THE TWENTIES.** "No one is as gorgeous as a woman in her early 20s. This is the best you're ever going to look," says Dr. Wilma Bergfeld, head of clinical research for the department of dermatology at the Cleveland Clinic Foundation and past president of the American Academy of Dermatology. By the time you reach the late 20s, fine lines will probably develop around the mouth and eyes and be noticeable when you wear makeup. If you become pregnant, you may develop brown spots on your face, either now or later; sun exposure exacerbates the problem.

But how fast your skin ages depends on whether you stay out of the sun and use sunscreen religiously (see box). Other skin-saving strategies include not smoking, controlling your weight, and maintaining good health. "It's like anything else—if you wait until the damage is done, it's pretty hard to turn it around," says Bergfeld.

■ THE THIRTIES. The first real signs of aging usually become apparent after age 30. That's when you'll start to notice more fine wrinkles, see the skin on your eyelids begin to droop, and find the circles under your eyes becoming darker and maybe even puffy. Smokers will develop even more lines around their eyes and mouth.

For many women, the discovery of those first few wrinkles are enough to send them directly to the cosmetics counter. Happily, some products show promise in counteracting the damaging effects of the sun. There's no doubt, says Bergfeld, that simply moisturizing can reduce fine wrinkling up to about 16 percent.

If you're looking for something more potent, moisturizers containing alpha hydroxy acids (AHAs) derived from fruit, sugar cane, or lactic acid exfoliate, or shed the upper layer of skin, exposing newer skin. Recent research by Dr. Ditre, a clinical assistant professor of dermatology at Hahnemann University Hospital and Abington Memorial Hospital near Philadelphia, suggests that using AHAs can even reverse some of the signs of photoaging. In a study of 17 adults with severely sun-damaged skin, a lotion with a 25 percent concentration of AHA thickened the outer layers of the skin, increased its elasticity, and lightened age spots. (Over-the-counter formulations contain anywhere from a 2 percent to 10 percent concentration of AHA and prescription formulas have about 15 percent.) There is no evidence, however, that you can prevent wrinkles or turn back the aging clock with AHAs, even in the higher concentrations found in prescription-only formulas. AHAs, says, Ditre, are "not a facelift in a jar."

FACT FILE:

CONTACTS CAN PROTECT AGAINST THE SUN

■ *Most people know that their skin needs sun protection. But too much sun can also increase the risk of developing premature cataracts or degeneration of the retina. Now there are contact lenses that can absorb the sun's harmful rays. A study by Dr. Nadia-Marie Quesnel of the University of Montreal College of Optometry found that contact lenses with a built-in UV filter provide better protection against UV rays than regular contacts. However, warns Quesnel, UV-blocking lenses don't eliminate the need for sunglasses.*

■ THE FORTIES. Between ages 40 and 50, your skin loses its collagen and elastin (tissues that keep skin firm and plump), which means wrinkles get bigger and deeper and your skin begins to sag. In addition, your skin gets drier and appears more sallow, pores get larger, eyelids droop more, frown lines show themselves, and flat brown spots called liver or age spots appear.

At this stage, says Bergfeld, you should routinely inspect your face and body for potentially cancerous lesions and investigate any suspicious moles or growths, because you're more susceptible to developing skin cancer. (By the year 2000, skin cancer is expected to be the most widely diagnosed cancer in the United States.)

If you already have extensive wrinkling, you may be a candidate for Retin A at this age. Recently reformulated and renamed Renova, the acne cream derived from Vitamin A has long been prescribed to fight wrinkles, even though it was only recently approved by the Food and Drug Administration (FDA) to treat sun-damaged skin. As the first wrinkle cream to be approved by the FDA, Renova diminishes fine wrinkles and lightens and smoothes skin that has turned brown or rough. Renova cannot increase elasticity, eliminate deep

A GUARDIAN ANGEL WHEN YOU'RE IN THE SUN

Sun smarts begin with a cream or lotion with a rating of at least SPF 15

It's hard to pinpoint when Americans went around the bend in worshiping the bronzed god, but Hollywood no doubt bears a large measure of blame. Even before the movies went Technicolor and George Hamilton and Annette Funicello could prove by their antics that the suntanned really had more fun, moviegoers had already been subjected to years of glamorous Hollywood palm-tree and fun-in-the-sun imagery.

That cinematic fantasy, happily perpetrated by suntan lotion advertising, remains alive today. According to a recent survey for the American Academy of Dermatology, 59 percent of Americans view a tan as a sign of health and find that it enhances appearance.

The key to being "sun smart" is to use a sunscreen on exposed skin whenever you're outside. To help you choose the appropriate level of protection, the U.S. Food and Drug Administration now requires all sunscreen makers to rate the protective power of each of their products. A sunscreen with a sun protection factor (SPF) of 2, for example, allows you to stay in the sun without getting burned for twice as long as would otherwise be possible without a screen; an SPF of 8 gives you eight times the protection, and so on.

Words of wisdom to keep in mind:

- **Choose a sunscreen with at least SPF 15.** Dermatologists say this is necessary to ensure the filtering out of most UV-B rays, the part of the ultraviolet light spectrum most responsible for sunburn and skin cancer.

- **Make sure the sunscreen also guards against UV-A rays.** SPF only address a sunscreen's ability to guard against UV-B radiation. Researchers have recently discovered that another kind of ultraviolet radiation, known as UV-A radiation, harms the skin's connective tissue, resulting in visible aging and contributing to skin cancer in some cases.

- **Reapply sunscreen after exercise or swimming.** Water magnifies the power of ultraviolet rays, ensuring that you will burn even more quickly in the water than on the beach unless the sunscreen you use is water-resistant. Even if it is, it's a good idea to reapply it after leaving the water to ensure full protection.

wrinkles, or rejuvenate dull or sallow skin, however. "It can't turn an old bag who's never taken care of her skin into a youthful 20-year-old," says Bergfeld, "but it can bring about an impressive skin change that people notice."

Drawbacks shouldn't be ignored, however. Most people who use it experience temporary redness, dryness, itching, peeling, and a slight burning sensation. For pregnant women and nursing mothers, the medication is entirely off-limits. Moreover, the cream has no lasting benefits if you stop using it.

- **THE FIFTIES.** The changes that began two decades ago evolve still more—deeper wrinkles, especially around the eyes and lips; sagging, dry skin; and age spots. By now, your wrinkles are clearly noticeable if you've spent a lot of time tanning yourself over the years, or if you smoke. (Smokers are especially prone to develop lines around the mouth.) You're also more likely to see wrinkles if your weight has fluctuated significantly. "It's like stretching a balloon," says Bergfeld. "If it collapses after a while, the skin is real wrinkled and the wrinkles are exaggerated." Aesthetically at least, it's better to keep on a few extra pounds because it acts as a filler, says Bergfeld. "Aging women may have to put up with a fatter body for a better-looking face."

MAKEUP

FLATTERING LOOKS FOR TODAY'S FACES

What worked when Sophia Loren held sway may be out of vogue today

Still wearing the same bright red lipstick, jet black liquid eyeliner, and turquoise eyeshadow you wore when you were in your 20s? Then you're probably in a makeup rut, says cover girl makeup artist Liz Michael, who has worked her wonders for magazines like *Vanity Fair*, *Mademoiselle*, and the international editions of *Vogue* and *Elle*. "Women tend to get stuck in a look they think suits them and then wear it for life," says Michael. "The problem is our faces change and styles of makeup change, and we invariably look older and dated if we don't update."

In fact, wearing the same makeup that made you look attractive and young in years past can add 10 years to your face now, says Michael. "You can either add or take years off your face simply by deciding how to apply makeup." Here is what Michael advises:

■ **Build up a makeup "wardrobe."** Among the basic things every woman should have: a foundation (or sheer coverage like a face tint, tinted moisturizer, concealer, or loose powder); two shades of blush (one neutral, warm, and sandy and one a bit more rosy); three shades of lip color; an eye pencil (dark brown suits almost everyone); two basic eyeshadows; and a couple of lip pencils.

■ **Opt for light, sheer coverage.** As you get older, it's important to wear less makeup. Heavy, cakey foundations and blood-red lips look aging. Older women tend to wear all-in-one makeup in a compact, but they look heavy on an older woman. Instead, try a light reflective foundation that makes skin look luminous and dewy, but doesn't emphasize lines.

■ **Learn to apply blush skillfully.** Applying a subtle stroke of blush to the right area is the key to updating your look. A hint of rosy blush on the apples of the cheeks —where you naturally blush—will give you a more natural, youthful look. It looks softer, modern, and more flattering than vivid, dark blush; most women tend to apply blush in the same way, almost like a contour, and it looks very dated and unrealistic.

■ **Use face powder.** A lot of women feel that powder makes them look older, but the new formulations are very sophisticated and lighter than ever. Before, you could get light, medium, and dark, but now there are so many colors—and you can also buy custom blends. A light dusting is all you need, just enough to set makeup. A lot of women don't use it, but it makes skin look clean and finished. Without it, the face looks messy.

■ **Avoid the matte look.** Today, everything is about shine—how to look luminous and glowy. Makeup with shine looks more youthful and natural, whereas matte makeup looks pasty. However, if your skin tends to be shiny and oily, it's the last thing you want to use.

■ **Apply eyeliner with a light touch.** Instead of using a liquid eyeliner, a dark, neutral pencil smudged around the eyes will give eyes subtle definition and a much softer look. Many women tend to put black eyeliner on in a line, like the Sophia Loren look—which was great on Sophia Loren in the '50s. But using a grayish black or brownish black will look a lot less harsh.

■ **Choose subtle, sheer lip color.** Instead of vivid red lips, opt for a sheer, creamy texture in a more subtle color. If you love reds, go with a soft, muted plum or brown-red, but avoid orange-red (the kind that was big in the '50s). And throw away dry, matte lipsticks—they look horribly aging.

■ **Change your makeup seasonally.** The easiest way to update makeup seasonally is with new lipstick—at least three times a year. Lip color dramatically changes your look. This

EXPERT PICKS

COSMETICS THAT WILL MAKE YOUR DAY

Among Liz Michael's favorite beauty aids:

FOUNDATION

EXACT MAKEUP 2 MAKEUP+
by Prescriptives
■ There are 100 shades for every skin tone. Formula #2 is a good, natural foundation for normal skin.

ENLIGHTEN SKIN-ENHANCING MAKEUP
by Estée Lauder
■ An oil-free liquid with a natural finish. Makes skin look silky.

CELLULAR TREATMENT FOUNDATION/SATIN
by La Prairie
■ A good quality foundation that doubles as a treatment. It provides great coverage and makes skin look incredible.

SATIN FINISH FOUNDATION
by M.A.C
■ An emollient formula that makes skin look dewy and young. It's incredible on older skin.

POWDER & BLUSH

CUSTOM BLEND POWDER
by Prescriptives
■ It's the best on the market. Comes in many shades and is talc-free so it won't clog pores and make skin look pasty.

CHEEK COLOR
by Prescriptives
■ It's very sheer, very silk, and comes in tons of colors for all skin types.

TRANSPARENT FACECOLOR ALLOVER TINT
by Prescriptives
■ An oil-free cream that you can use to create a little glow and color instead of blush—or wear it all over. Gives skin a satin-like finish.

EYE SHADOW

COMPACT DISC EYE SHADOW IN BROWN #7
by Estée Lauder
■ A basic brown that looks good on anyone.

SATIN TAUPE
by M.A.C
■ A grayish brown frost with a hint of silver. It's glamorous yet natural and it looks good on everyone.

LIP COLOR

PLUM STAIN
by Prescriptives
■ Sheer, with a little more color than your lips. Looks good on almost anyone.

DIFFERENT LIPSTICK IN TENDER HEART
by Clinique
■ A light, slightly glossy brown with hint of pink. Great on blondes and women with fair skin.

RAISIN by Face Stockholm
■ A deep, red brown—a great red.

MASCARA

FRINGE BENEFITS MASCARA
by Origins
■ Silky and glossy, with an exceptional brush.

doesn't mean jumping on the latest color trend, but maybe just changing the texture to something creamier or glossy. Sometimes it's fun to have something a little offbeat.

■ **Don't try to match your makeup with your clothes.** That's a very outdated practice. Makeup selection depends on taste and style, skin tone, hair color, and the amount you want to wear. Sometimes you can play up colors you're wearing, but you should avoid clashing—if you're wearing a pink outfit, you don't want to wear brown lipstick.

■ **Be wary of trends.** You have to be young and hip to wear trendy makeup. Even though there's a return to orange, for example, it's for younger people. If you're much older, trendy makeup colors and styles usually look dated. Remember, you don't have to wear what's in fashion: It's about adapting and updating to what's going to work for you now.

EXPERT TIPS

A LITTLE HELP FROM FRIENDS

The hair stylist for the hit TV show on why Jennifer Aniston's do works

When you're an actress on one of television's top-rated shows, looking your best is an occupational imperative. Even Courteney Cox and Jennifer Aniston, stars of the TV series *Friends*, need help to pull this off. Week after week, one of the people they turn to is John Barrett, cast hair stylist for the show.

The key to making every day a good hair day is a good haircut, says Barrett, who recently opened his own salon, the John Barrett Salon at Bergdorf Goodman in New York City. Unless you have wavy hair, which is somewhat more forgiving, Barrett recommends getting a haircut every four to six weeks to keep it manageable. His advice on how to get a result you'll enjoy:

■ **If you don't have a stylist you're comfortable with, stop people whose style and cut you admire and ask them who cut their hair.** If you like, says Barrett, bring pictures to show the stylist the look you want, but be open to the stylist's suggestions. Your face shape should play a role in determining the cut and style, says Barrett. "One reason the Jennifer Aniston hairdo is so popular is that it's a long, layered shag, and you can easily adjust it to the shape of your face." For instance, if you have a round face, cut the layers shorter so they stay below the cheekbone. If you have a longer face, you'll want longer layers so they bulb out around the face.

■ **When picking a hair stylist, don't repeat your mistakes.** "If you do get a bad cut, it's almost always a bad idea to go back to the same person to fix it," says Barrett. "You'll dig your grave even more."

■ **Don't have any expectations about what your hair will look like.** It's best not to start out with a set idea of what your hair is going to do on a given day. Go with what's happening that day; it's not going to look exactly the same every day.

■ **Don't fight your hair's natural tendencies.** If you've got very curly hair that's difficult to style, there's no point in going for a look that's silky smooth. Take what you've got and work with it rather than setting yourself up for failure.

■ **Experiment with new products.** Styling products can make a big difference, especially for people with thick, curly hair. For example, if you towel dry your hair, then apply a little Kiehl's Creme with Silk Groom; it should stay put most of the day. For someone with long, shoulder-length, straight hair, try Big Curls by Conair, fat hot rollers that won't give you a "roller set" look, just a bit of a lift. And two products used often on the set of *Friends*: Sebastian Thick Ends gel, which doesn't get dry and flaky like many other styling gels, and Sebastian Shapier hairspray, which is very light.

■ **Don't wash your hair too much.** Washing hair takes all of the oil out of it. If you wash it every other day and just rinse it with water on the off-day, it will look more full of life than if you wash it every day. Also, use an intensive conditioner once a week.

■ **Blow-dry the roots first.** The secret of controlling hair and giving it volume is adequately drying the roots. Whatever you do at the roots determines how the style comes out. Many people blow-dry the ends, then wonder why nothing happens. Even if you don't want to get volume, it's hard to get control unless you lift the hair up at the roots somewhat, then dry them, pulling the hair out toward the end. If you want extra volume, get a light hair spray and while the brush is still in your hair, lift the hair up and spray the roots. This technique will give your hair a definite lift. After the hair is dry, put a tiny bit of styling lotion on your fingertips and apply it to the ends, which will give hair a very finished look.

HAIR LOSS

IF YOU HAVE A SAMSON PROBLEM

From minoxidil to hair transplants, what you can do to treat balding

Women have been ridiculed throughout the ages for resorting to extreme measures for the sake of beauty. But when it comes to hair loss, men are equally vain. Lured by ads promising a "miracle cure" that will restore hair to its youthful fullness, balding men spend thousands of dollars on desperate measures to salvage their locks and their looks. "It's so traumatic, they'll go to any lengths to get their hair back," says Dr. Deirdre Marshall, associate clinical professor of plastic surgery at the University of Miami Medical School and chief of plastic surgery at the Miami Veterans Hospital. One example: a balding Buffalo surgeon bolted his toupee to his head with metal pegs and now sells the device to anyone who will pay his $3,000 to $5,000 fee.

But there are less drastic, medically sound ways that can help achieve a fuller head of hair. The least invasive option is using minoxidil (brand name, Rogaine), the only proven medical method to thwart hair loss and grow new hair. However, spraying Rogaine on thinning hair daily doesn't have a dramatic effect on its growth, and the new hair is baby fine.

Rogaine has been prescribed by doctors since 1988, but it recently became available over-the-counter (a month's supply costs about $30). Rogaine works best in men with typical male pattern baldness (known as androgenetic alopecia), in which the hair line is receding at the corners of the forehead and crown. It is also effective in women with thinning hair. According to its manufacturer, Pharmacia & Upjohn, Inc., however, it's not suitable for those whose hair loss is patchy or sudden, involves someone with no family history of hair loss, or is accompanied by other symptoms. People with high blood pressure also should not use Rogaine, because it may induce hypertension.

The only tried-and-true hair replacement method is a hair transplant, a surgical technique that involves moving tiny pieces of the scalp from the back of the head, where hair is plentiful, to the area on top or in front of the head, where balding is occurring.

Transplant technology has advanced significantly since hair transplants were first performed nearly 40 years ago. Under the early approach, 25 to 50 hairs were replanted in one place in the balding scalp, creating a patch of conspicuous "plugs." More sophisticated techniques made it possible to perform "minigrafts," in which two to six follicles are transplanted in tiny clusters or circles.

Today, smaller groups of just one to four hairs called "micrografts" are transplanted in a staggered pattern, creating a more natural hair line. Marshall notes, however, that this procedure is more difficult and takes more time. Sometimes, micrografts and minigrafts are used together.

The best candidates for transplants are those with typical male pattern baldness. The procedure also works well on many women, who tend to lose hair all over, which makes the transplant less noticeable. Men and women should consider undergoing transplant surgery as soon as they start to lose hair, says Dr. Barry Resnik, a clinical instructor of dermatology at the University of Miami Medical School: "When you have enough hair, it looks imperceptible."

There are other less common hair transplant procedures. If you have a receding hairline across the front of your head, there is the scalp flap, for instance. A chunk of scalp (and the hair attached to it) is removed from the back of the head and rotated toward the front of the head, which produces a thick, but artificial-looking mane, because hair is growing in the wrong direction. To avoid that problem, the flap and the connected arteries can be severed from the back of the head, then reattached to the front. This surgery is much more costly and risky than transplanting hair grafts, but it does allow hundreds of hairs to be replanted in one session.

EXPERT TIPS

WHEN A WIG LOOKS ABOUT RIGHT

A man who buys a hairpiece wants it to look as natural as the hair he once had. But many end up disappointed, even after spending an average of $1,300 on a hairpiece. Here, Anthony Santangelo, president of the American Hair Loss Council, offers some tips on how to get your money's worth:

DO'S:

- Do visit at least two establishments and communicate your expectations clearly. The stylist you choose should know exactly what you want your new hair to look like and be able to tell you what a hairpiece can and can't do for you.

- Do make sure the style of hairpiece fits your lifestyle. If you plan to wear the hairpiece once in a while and take it off daily, you'll probably opt for one that's taped to the skin for a day or two, or one that clips to existing hair for three to four days. If you'd like to swim and sleep in it, you'll need a hairpiece that's glued or weaved into existing hair, which will last four to six weeks.

- Do consider how versatile you want your hair to be. A hairpiece made of human hair will offer the most flexibility and will allow you to use styling gels and mousse and comb and blow-dry it into different styles. Synthetic hair isn't as easy to style and offers just one look.

- Do match the hairpiece to your existing hair style and color.

- Do keep regular appointments for maintenance. As your natural hair grows and loses its style, the hairpiece will also begin to look shabby. When you get your hair trimmed, have the hairpiece checked too.

DON'T'S:

- Don't choose a hairpiece with too much hair. If the hair you have left is thin, the hairpiece shouldn't be thick and dense.

- Don't select an unrealistic hairline. A 40-year-old shouldn't have a 20-year-old hairline with bangs covering his forehead and eyebrows.

- Don't try to cover up gray hair with the hairpiece. If you have some gray, work with it and match the hairpiece with your natural color as it looks now.

For men with a U-shaped bald spot on top of their head, a scalp reduction is another option. In this procedure, the bald spot is cut out of the top of the head, then the skin with hair is pulled higher on the head and the edges are sewn together.

The average cost of a transplant is $2,100, but more than one surgery is often necessary. Nor do these surgeries prevent further balding behind newly transplanted hair. "If patients keep going bald, and they want to have a normal-looking hair pattern, they'll have to come back and have more transplants," says Dr. Marshall.

While there's no board certification required of doctors who treat hair loss, most are dermatologists or plastic surgeons. Be sure to select a well-trained doctor who's performed the surgery often.

Beware of glorified beauty salons where surgery is supervised by a doctor, but performed by a nonmedical technician. "The biggest mistake an amateur surgeon will make is plant the plugs in a way that can only be combed in the wrong direction," cautions Resnik. And there's no more expensive way to get a hair transplant than to have it botched so badly that you need to have it repaired.

EXPERT LIST

TINKERING WITH MOTHER NATURE

Facial implants and chemical peels have joined tummy tucks and nose jobs in the panoply of cosmetic procedures that appearance-conscious Americans are resorting to in increasing numbers. The American Society of Plastic and Reconstructive Surgeons provides this guide to today's most-elected interventions with nature.

BREAST ENLARGEMENT

Augmentation Mammoplasty. *Enhances the size and shape of breasts using artificial implants.*

■ **PROCEDURE:** Lasts 1 to 2 hours. Local anesthesia with sedation, or general. Usually outpatient.

■ **SIDE EFFECTS:** Temporary pain. Swelling, soreness, numbness of abdominal skin, bruising, tiredness for several weeks or months.

■ **RECOVERY:** Back to work in 2 to 4 weeks. More strenuous activity after 4 to 6 weeks or more. Fading and flattening of scars: 3 months to 2 years.

■ **RISKS:** Blood clots. Infection. Bleeding under the skin flap. Poor healing resulting in conspicuous scarring or skin loss. Need for a second operation.

■ **DURATION:** Permanent.

BREAST LIFT

Mastopexy. *Raises and reshapes sagging breasts by removing excess skin and repositioning remaining tissue and nipples.*

■ **PROCEDURE:** Lasts 1 1/2 to 3 1/2 hours. Local anesthesia with sedation, or general. Usually outpatient. Sometimes inpatient 1 to 2 days.

■ **SIDE EFFECTS:** Temporary bruising, swelling, discomfort, numbness, dry breast skin. Permanent scars.

■ **RECOVERY:** Feeling better, back to work in a week.

■ **RISKS:** Thick, wide scars; skin loss; infection. Unevenly positioned nipples. Permanent loss of feeling in nipples or breast.

■ **DURATION:** Variable; gravity, pregnancy, aging, and weight changes may cause new sagging. May last longer when combined with implants.

CHEMICAL PEEL

Phenol, trichloracetic acid (TCA). *Restores wrinkled, blemished, unevenly pigmented or sun-damaged facial skin, using a chemical solution to peel away skin's top layers. Works best on fair, thin skin with superficial wrinkles.*

■ **PROCEDURE:** Takes 1 to 2 hours for full face. No anesthesia—sedation and EKG monitoring may be used. Usually outpatient. Full-face phenol peel may require admission for 1 to 2 days.

■ **SIDE EFFECTS:** Both: Temporary throbbing, tingling, swelling redness; acute sensitivity to sun. Phenol: Permanent lightening of treated skin; permanent loss of ability to tan.

■ **RECOVERY:** Phenol: Formation of new skin in 7 to 21 days. Normal activities in 2 to 4 weeks. Full healing and fading of redness in 3 to 6

■ **SEX DISTRIBUTION**

Eyelid surgery is most popular among women, but men prefer to have their noses altered.

Sex distribution of aesthetic procedures, 1994

Procedure	Women	Men
Eyelid surgery	83%	17%
Nose reshaping	71%	29%
Liposuction	87%	13%
Collagen injections	96%	4%
Facelift	92%	8%

SOURCE: American Society of Plastic and Reconstructive Surgeons, Inc.

■ EXPERT LIST

months. TCA: New skin within 5 to 10 days.

■ **RISKS:** Both: Tiny whiteheads (temporary); infection; scarring; flare-up of skin allergies, fever blisters, cold sores. Phenol: Abnormal color changes (permanent); heart irregularities (rare).

■ **DURATION:** Phenol is permanent, although new wrinkles may form as skin ages. TCA is variable (temporary).

COLLAGEN/FAT INJECTIONS

Plumps up creased, furrowed, or sunken facial skin; adds fullness to lips and backs of hands. Works best on thin, dry, light-colored skin.

■ **PROCEDURE:** Lasts 15 minutes to 1 hour per session. Collagen: usually no anesthesia; local may be included with the injection. Fat requires local anesthesia. Outpatient.

■ **SIDE EFFECTS:** Temporary stinging, throbbing, or burning sensation. Faint redness, swelling, excess fullness.

■ **RISKS:** Collagen: allergic reactions including rash, hives, swelling, or flulike symptoms; possible triggering of connective-tissue or autoimmune diseases. Both: contour irregularities; infection.

■ **DURATION:** Variable, from a few months to as long as a year.

DERMABRASION

Mechanical scraping of the top layers of skin using a high-speed rotary wheel. Softens sharp edges of surface irregularities, including acne and other scars and fine wrinkles, especially around mouth.

■ **PROCEDURE:** Lasts a few minutes to 1½ hours. May require more sessions. Anesthesia: Local, numbing spray, or general. Usually outpatient.

■ **SIDE EFFECTS:** Temporary tingling, burning, itching, swelling, redness. Lightening of treated skin, acute sensitivity to sun; loss of ability to tan.

■ **RECOVERY:** Back to work in 2 weeks. More strenuous activities in 4 to 6 weeks. Fading of redness in about 3 months. Return of pigmentation/sun exposure in 6 to 12 months.

■ **RISKS:** Abnormal color changes (permanent). Tiny whiteheads (temporary). Infection. Scarring. Flare-up of skin allergies, fever blisters, cold sores.

■ **DURATION:** Permanent, but new wrinkles may form as skin ages.

EYELID SURGERY

***Blepharoplasty**. Corrects drooping upper eyelids and puffy bags below the eyes by removing excess fat, skin, and muscle. (May be covered by insurance if used to improve vision.)*

■ **PROCEDURE:** Lasts 1 to 3 hours. Usually, local anesthesia with sedation, occasionally general. Usually outpatient.

■ **SIDE EFFECTS:** Temporary discomfort, tightness of lids, swelling, bruising. Temporary dryness, burning, itching of eyes. Excessive tearing, sensitivity to light for first few weeks.

■ **RISKS:** Temporary blurred or double vision; blindness (extremely rare). Infection. Swelling at corners of eyelids; tiny whiteheads. Slight asymmetry in healing or scarring. Difficulty in clos-

■ **AGE DISTRIBUTION**

People want nose work first, but face lifts become increasingly popular as the years go by.

Number of aesthetic procedures by age group, 1994.

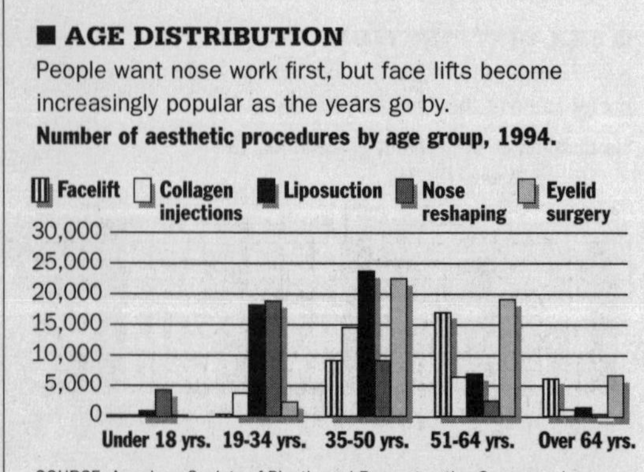

SOURCE: American Society of Plastic and Reconstructive Surgeons, Inc.

■ **EXPERT LIST**

ing eyes completely (rarely permanent). Pulling down of the lower lids (may require further surgery).

■ **RECOVERY:** Reading in 2 or 3 days. Back to work in 7 to 10 days. Contact lenses in 2 weeks or more. Strenuous activities, alcohol in about 3 weeks. Bruising and swelling gone in several weeks.

■ **DURATION:** Several years to permanent.

FACE-LIFT

***Rhytidectomy**. Improves sagging facial skin, jowls, and loose neck skin by removing excess, tightening muscles, redraping skin. Most often done on men and women over 40.*

■ **PROCEDURE:** Lasts several hours. Anesthesia: Local with sedation, or general. Usually outpatient. Some patients may require short inpatient stay.

■ **SIDE EFFECTS:** Temporary bruising, swelling, numbness, and tenderness of skin; tight feeling, dry skin. For men, permanent need to shave behind ears, where beard-growing skin is repositioned.

■ **RECOVERY:** Back to work in 10 to 14 days. More strenuous activity in 2 weeks or more. Bruising gone in 2 to 3 weeks. Limit exposure to sun for several months.

■ **RISKS:** Injury to the nerves that control facial muscles, loss of feeling (usually temporary but may be permanent). Infec-

WIPING AWAY THE SIGNS OF AGING

High-tech lasers do a great job with facial creases, but it's a pricey new technique

A new technique known as laser resurfacing that literally zaps wrinkles off your face is the latest high-tech innovation to stave off the signs of aging.

The CO2 laser, the type used for aesthetic treatments such as removing visible blood vessels, port wine stains, birthmarks, and tattoos, produces intense, short bursts of light that vaporize skin tissue. The laser removes thin layers of damaged skin, smoothes the skin's surface, and allows new collagen to form, giving skin a tighter appearance. Laser resurfacing (also known as laserbrasion or laser peeling) can remove age spots, soften fine wrinkles, lift droopy eyelids, and heal acne scars.

Sound too good to be true? Well, consider the cost: about $3,000 to $5,000 to "resurface" the entire face and roughly $2,000 for specific areas like crow's feet—fees that are rarely covered by health insurance.

Despite its high price tag, laser resurfacing is quickly becoming one of the most popular cosmetic procedures because it's safer and more precise than another popular nonsurgical method of smoothing aging skin—chemical peels that use various types of acid to exfoliate and remove the superficial layers of skin. Unlike moderate or deep-depth chemical peels that can scar the skin or cause an infection, laser resurfacing doesn't cause significant scarring and is bloodless and relatively painless. While skin will appear red for a couple of weeks, and a flushed look may persist for more than a month, "The laser is probably a safer way to do skin resurfacing because you can see how deep into the skin you're going," says New York City plastic surgeon Dr. Paul Weiss. With chemical peels, he explains, you only know how deep you go by the type of chemical used.

A caveat: Laser resurfacing has only been performed for a few years and there are no studies yet proving its long-term safety and effectiveness. "Because the procedure doesn't have a long track record, we have to be cautious in whom we recommend it to," says Dr. Weiss. A further caution: Patients considering laser resurfacing should make sure the dermatologist or plastic surgeon has ample experience in this procedure because in the wrong hands, the laser could burn facial skin.

■ EXPERT LIST

tion. Poor healing, excessive scarring. Change in hairline.

■ **DURATION:** Usually about 5 to 10 years.

FACIAL IMPLANTS

Change the basic shape and balance of the face using carefully styled implants to build up a receding chin, add prominence to cheekbones, or reshape the jawline. Implants may be natural or artificial.

■ **PROCEDURE:** Lasts 30 minutes to 2 hours. Anesthesia: Local with sedation, or general. Usually outpatient. Occasionally requires overnight stay.

■ **SIDE EFFECTS:** Temporary discomfort, swelling, bruising, numbness and/or stiffness. In jaw surgery, inability to open mouth fully for several weeks.

■ **RECOVERY:** Back to work in about a week. Normal appearance in 2 to 4 weeks. Activity that could jar face after 6 weeks or more.

■ **RISKS:** Shifting or imprecise positioning of implant, or infection around it, requiring a second operation or removal. Excess tightening and hardening of scar tissue around an artificial implant ("capsular contracture"), causing an unnatural shape.

■ **DURATION:** Permanent.

FOREHEAD-LIFT

Brow-lift. *Minimize forehead creases, drooping eyebrows, hooding over eyes, furrowed forehead, and frown lines by removing excess tissue and redraping skin. Most often done on people over 40.*

■ **PROCEDURE:** Length: 1 to 2 hours. Anesthesia: Local with sedation, or general. Usually outpatient.

■ **SIDE EFFECTS:** Temporary swelling, numbness, headaches, bruising. Possible itching and hair loss for several months. Change in hairline.

■ **RECOVERY:** Back to work in 7 to 10 days. More strenuous activity after several weeks. Bruising gone after 2 to 3 weeks. Limited exposure to sun for several months.

■ **RISKS:** Injury to facial nerve, causing loss of motion, muscle weakness, or asymmetrical look. Infection. Broad or excessive scarring.

■ **DURATION:** Usually about 5 to 10 years.

HAIR REPLACEMENT SURGERY

Fill in balding areas with the patient's own hair using a variety of techniques including scalp reduction, tissue expansion, strip grafts, scalp flaps, or clusters of punch grafts.

■ **PROCEDURE:** Lasts 1 to 3 hours. Some techniques may require multiple procedures over 18 months or more. Anesthesia: Usually local with sedation. Flaps and tissue expansion may may be done under general anesthesia. Usually outpatient.

■ **SIDE EFFECTS:** Temporary aching, tight scalp. An unnatural look in early stages.

■ **RECOVERY:** Back to work: usually in 2 to 5 days. More strenuous activities after 10 days

FACT FILE:

ORDERING BODY PARTS A LA CARTE

■ *"Celebrities set the tone for what we think of as beauty," says Dr. Alan Matarasso, associate clinical professor of plastic surgery at Albert Einstein College of Medicine in New York City. Some people—especially women—request the facial features of a star. Some of the more common requests: Claudia Schiffer's lips, Sharon Stone's nose, and 15 years after her death, Grace Kelly's facial shape. Most surgeons warn patients, however, that changing a feature won't make them look exactly like the celebrity.*

■ EXPERT LIST

to 3 weeks. Final look: may be 18 months or more, depending on procedure.

■ **RISKS:** Unnatural look. Infection. Excessive scarring. Failure to "take." Loss of scalp tissue and/or transplanted hair.

■ **DURATION:** Permanent.

LIPOSUCTION

Suction-assisted lipectomy. *Improve body shape using tube and vacuum device to remove unwanted fat deposits that don't respond to dieting and exercise. Locations include chin, cheeks, neck, upper arms, above breasts, abdomen, buttocks, hips, thighs, knees, calves, ankles.*

■ **PROCEDURE:** Lasts 1 to 2 hours or more, depending on extent of surgery. Anesthesia: Local, epidural, or general. Usually outpatient. Extensive procedures may require short inpatient stay.

■ **SIDE EFFECTS:** Temporary bruising, swelling, numbness, burning sensation.

■ **RECOVERY:** Back to work in 1 to 2 weeks. More strenuous activity after 2 to 4 weeks. Swelling and bruising may last 1 to 6 months or more.

■ **RISKS:** Infection. Excessive fluid loss leading to shock. Fluid accumulation. Injury to the skin. Bagginess of skin. Pigmentation changes (may become permanent if exposed to sun).

■ **DURATION:** Permanent, with sensible diet and exercise.

MALE BREAST REDUCTION

Gynecomastia. *Reduce enlarged breasts in men using liposuction and/or cutting out excess glandular tissue. (Sometimes covered by medical insurance.)*

■ **PROCEDURE:** Lasts 1½ hours or more. Anesthesia: general or local. Usually outpatient.

■ **SIDE EFFECTS:** Temporary bruising, swelling, numbness, soreness, burning sensation.

■ **RECOVERY:** Back to work in 3 to 7 days. More strenuous activity after 2 to 3 weeks. Swelling and bruising subsides in 3 to 6 months.

■ **RISKS:** Infection. Excessive fluid loss leading to shock. Fluid accumulation. Injury to the skin. Bagginess of skin. Pigmentation changes (may become permanent if exposed to sun). Excessive scarring if tissue was cut away. Need for second procedure to remove additional tissue.

■ **DURATION:** Permanent.

NOSE SURGERY

Rhinoplasty. *Reshape nose by altering size, removing hump, changing shape of tip or bridge, narrowing span of nostrils, or changing angle between nose and upper lip. May relieve some breathing problems.*

■ **PROCEDURE:** Length: 1 to 2 hours or more. Local anesthesia with sedation, or general. Usually outpatient.

■ **SIDE EFFECTS:** Temporary swelling, bruising around eyes and nose, and headaches. Some bleeding and stuffiness.

■ **RECOVERY:** Back to work or school in 1 to 2 weeks. More strenuous activities after 2 to 3 weeks. Avoid hitting nose or sunburn for 8 weeks. Final appearance after a year or more.

■ **RISKS:** Infection. Small burst blood vessels resulting in tiny, permanent red spots. Incomplete improvement, requiring additional surgery.

■ **DURATION:** Permanent.

TUMMY TUCK

Abdominoplasty. *Flatten abdomen by removing excess fat and skin and tightening muscles of abdominal wall.*

■ **PROCEDURE:** Lasts 2 to 5 hours. Anesthesia: General, or local with sedation. In- or outpatient.

■ **SIDE EFFECTS:** Temporary pain. Swelling, soreness, numbness of abdominal skin, bruising, tiredness for weeks or months.

■ **RECOVERY:** Back to work in 2 to 4 weeks. More strenuous activity after 4 to 6 weeks or more. Fading and flattening of scars in 3 months to 2 years.

■ **RISKS:** Blood clots. Infection. Bleeding under the skin flap. Poor healing resulting in conspicuous scarring or skin loss. Need for a second operation.

■ **DURATION:** Permanent.

Source: American Society of Plastic and Reconstructive Surgeons, Inc.

THE OTHER SIDE OF THE COIN

From Manhattan to Hollywood, what plastic surgery costs

Procedure	Nat'l Average	CALIFORNIA	NEW YORK	FLORIDA	TEXAS
BREAST AUGMENTATION	$2,754	$3,141	$3,522	$2,756	$2,718
BREAST LIFT	$3,063	$3,385	$4,010	$3,113	$2,970
BREAST RECONSTRUCTION					
Implant alone	$2,340	$2,719	$2,885	$2,468	$2,444
Tissue expander	$2,846	$2,881	$3,561	$3,204	$2,999
Latissimus dorsi	$4,509	$4,536	$5,395	$5,147	$5,031
TRAM (pedicle) flap	$6,143	$5,187	$7,483	$6,489	$6,209
Microsurgical free flap	$6,758	$5,685	$6,692	$7,262	$6,711
BREAST REDUCTION	$4,525	$4,929	$5,432	$5,293	$4,515
BREAST REDUCTION IN MEN	$2,325	$2,687	$3,061	$2,470	$2,026
BUTTOCK LIFT	$3,084	$2,798	$5,120	$3,175	$3,566
CHEEK IMPLANTS	$1,895	$1,870	$2,654	$1,701	$1,530
CHEMICAL PEEL					
Full face	$1,634	$1,849	$2,217	$1,668	$1,454
Regional	$682	$762	$869	$711	$626
CHIN AUGMENTATION					
Implant	$1,221	$1,380	$1,907	$1,153	$901
Osteotomy	$2,077	$2,342	$2,990	$2,133	$1,413
COLLAGEN INJECTIONS PER 1 CC	$266	$296	$328	$278	$259
DERMABRASION	$1,551	$1,840	$2,267	$1,486	$1,344
EYELID SURGERY					
Both uppers	$1,514	$1,601	$1,939	$1,469	$1,524
Both lowers	$1,519	$1,633	$2,151	$1,447	$1,478
Combination of both	$2,625	$2,784	$3,594	$2,564	$2,593
FACE-LIFT	$4,156	$4,448	$5,410	$4,026	$4,148
FAT INJECTION					
Head/neck	$636	$702	$695	$717	$695
Trunk	$622	$571	$794	$645	$300
Extremities	$663	$572	$794	$644	$689
FOREHEAD-LIFT	$2,164	$2,484	$3,207	$2,002	$1,852
LIPOSUCTION—any single site	$1,622	$2,028	$2,346	$1,603	$1,563
MALE-PATTERN BALDNESS					
Plug grafts–per plug	$101	$162	$152	$297	$23
Strip grafts–per strip	$1,096	$869	$1,500	$1,150	$1,200
Scalp reduction–all stages	$1,720	$2,549	$2,357	$2,084	$1,350
Pedicle flap–all stages	$2,699	$5,308	$2,525	$3,067	$1,600
Tissue expansion–all stages	$3,081	$3,609	$4,175	$3,244	$2,000
NOSE RESHAPING (primary)					
Fee for open rhinoplasty	$2,997	$3,390	$4,371	$2,947	$3,019
Fee for closed rhinoplasty	$2,825	$3,131	$4,160	$2,705	$2,689
NOSE RESHAPING (secondary)					
Fee for open rhinoplasty	$2,615	$3,130	$3,426	$2,806	$2,662
Fee for closed rhinoplasty	$2,649	$2,958	$3,841	$2,819	$2,525
RETIN-A TREATMENT per visit	$92	$56	$83	$58	$39
THIGH LIFT	$3,090	$3,093	$4,723	$3,115	$3,098
TUMMY TUCK	$3,618	$4,085	$4,774	$3,754	$3,581

SOURCE: American Society of Plastic and Reconstructive Surgeons, Inc., 1994.

BREASTS

IF A WONDER-BRA WON'T SUFFICE

Silicone implants aren't as risky as it was thought, says new research

What you see is not always what it seems, and nowhere is this truer than in the continuing controversy over the safety of cosmetic breast implants. In 1992, the Food and Drug Administration (FDA) banned the use of silicone gel–filled breast implants, though not saline-filled implants, after receiving nearly 100,000 reports of adverse reactions. In 1995, silicone implant manufacturers were also ordered to set aside $4 billion to cover potential damages to 400,000 women who are part of a class-action lawsuit against them in the courts.

Behind the crackdown was a fear that silicone-enhanced chests pose a significant risk of connective-tissue diseases that affect the immune system. Several recent studies, however, suggest that implants probably pose a minimal risk to women's health. In the largest of the studies, Dr. Charles Hennekens, a well-respected researcher at Brigham and Women's Hospital in Boston, found that women with implants face a small increased risk of suffering potentially fatal connective-tissue diseases such as rheumatoid arthritis, Sjogren's syndrome, polymyositis, dermatomyositis, and scleroderma.

Hennekens' survey of 400,000 women revealed that women with implants (the researchers didn't note whether respondents had silicone- or saline-filled implants) were 24 percent more likely to have connective tissue diseases than women without implants. However, the study also indicated that only about 1 percent of women with implants will be afflicted with a connective tissue disease, which is statistically significant enough to suggest a small causal relationship between connective tissue disease and implants. There are several methodological reasons why the researchers suspect that the risk might be overstated, however, including the possibility that a disproportionate number of women who developed problems may have responded to the questionnaire.

Nevertheless, both sides in the breast implant debate claim the latest study boosts their position. Manufacturers say that the study exonerates them, while women who filed lawsuits against the manufacturers claim the new study demonstrates that implants are unsafe.

Meanwhile, the FDA ban on silicone breast implants remains in place, while its policy on allowing saline implants continues. Even saline implants, the agency cautions, carry risks. According to the FDA, between 5 percent and 50 percent of implants leak or rupture, and scar tissue can cause the breast to harden and require follow-up surgery. The conclusion: There's always a cost to trying to improve nature.

FACT FILE:

THE BARBIE TRAP

■ *Anyone who has ever laid eyes on a Barbie doll knows that her curvy figure would be difficult to replicate in nature, but just how unreal the Mattel doll is as a physical ideal for women can only be appreciated if you put Barbie's dimensions into human context. Blown up to life-size, the doll would measure 40–18–32 inches around the chest, waist, and hips, a tale of the tape that has earned Barbie many critics. Yet the doll's popularity shows no sign of abating: according to Mattel, there are two Barbies sold every second.*

HAVING CHILDREN

PREGNANCY: Figuring out your due date, PAGE 196 **PRENATAL TESTING:** What tests are available and when women should have them, PAGE 200 **INFERTILITY:** Options for couples having trouble conceiving, PAGE 202 **ADOPTION:** Avoiding the pitfalls, PAGE 204 **EARLY DISCHARGE:** Are hospitals jeopardizing the health of new mothers and their babies? PAGE 206 **ATTENTION DEFICIT DISORDER:** Help for the hyperactive child, PAGE 208

CHILDBEARING

A LATE DATE WITH MOTHERHOOD

Having a child when you're 40 is no longer rare—or even that risky

Late motherhood, like late marriage, has been a hallmark of the Baby Boom. Just one generation ago, most women finished childbearing by the time they reached age 30. Today, delaying childbirth has become a common practice for career women. In 1993, 29 percent of all births were to women aged 30 to 39, compared to 19 percent in 1980, according to the National Center for Health Statistics. And between 1980 and 1993, the number of American women who postponed childbearing until their early 40s more than doubled, from 24,000 to 59,000.

But how long can motherhood be postponed without jeopardizing the health of a mother or her child? Until recently, labor and delivery were deemed more complicated for older women, but there's little evidence that women in their 30s and 40s face extra risks in either the maternity or delivery process compared with younger moms. Studies have shown that the risks associated with delaying pregnancy are minimal if a woman is healthy.

In fact, one of the biggest factors in gauging the health of a pregnancy—at any age—is the health of the mother before she conceives. "The barometer for the outcome of a pregnancy is the health of the mother going into the pregnancy," says Dr. Yvonne Thornton, director of the perinatal diagnostic testing center at Morristown Memorial Hospital in New Jersey. "If you're a healthy woman, you're going to have a healthy pregnancy." The misconception that it's unsafe to delay childbearing past age 35 stems from the difficulties women had long ago when large families were the norm, because multiple births can take a toll on the body, says Thornton.

To be sure, women over 35 are more likely to have preexisting medical conditions—such as hypertension and diabetes—that can cause complications in pregnancy. They also are more likely to develop these problems while they're pregnant. But women today are much more likely to be in better health than their ancestors were at the same age.

"If you're pregnant and healthy at 35, you shouldn't think of yourself as any different than anyone else," says Dr. Alan Kessler, associate professor of clinical obstetrics and gynecology and chief of the division of gynecology at New York Hospital–Cornell University Medical Center. By eating right, not smoking, and limiting weight gain to only what's necessary to nourish the fetus, a pregnant woman will greatly enhance her chances of a successful pregnancy, regardless of her age.

The bigger problem for many women who postpone childbearing is declining fertility. While a British woman made headlines several years ago when she gave birth at age 59 using donor eggs, by the time a woman reaches age 40, her chances of conceiving decrease significantly—even with fertility techniques such as IVF or using donated eggs (see related story, page 202).

Having a child with a genetic defect is another risk that's clearly age-related: The chances of having a child with a chromosomal abnormality increases as a woman ages. For example, the probability of giving birth to an infant with Down's syndrome is 1 in 885 at age 30, 1 in 365 at 35, 1 in 109 at 40, and 1 in 32 by age 45. Advances in genetic testing now enable doctors to screen for many genetic abnormalities (see related story, page 200). The tests are recommended for all women aged 35 and older. Ironically, says Dr. Kessler, "Most babies born with Down's syndrome today are to women under 35 because they don't take advantage of the testing."

Because older women are more likely to have a baby with a chromosomal abnormality, they're also more likely to suffer a miscarriage. Nearly one-third of all fetuses fail to survive past 12 weeks, and in women over age 35, that probability rises to 40 percent.

But the notion that labor and delivery are substantially more difficult for older women is a myth, doctors say. While some women who give birth to their first child in their 20s report having more difficulties in the delivery of later children, this is probably related to their declining health over the years, not just age. There are physiological changes that occur in pregnancy that are easier to handle at a younger age because your body is healthier, says Dr. Kessler: "The cardiovascular system of a 40-year-old isn't the same as that of a 20-year-old, and the amount of stress your body can take is different."

Studies indicate that older mothers are more likely to undergo cesarean sections, although there is no compelling medical explanation why the surgery is needed. The increased rate of C-sections may not be due to age, but due to physician bias. For example, in so-called premium pregnancies—when it may be a couple's only chance of having a baby because they've had fertility problems—doctors may be more likely to perform a C-section to ensure a safe delivery.

So how late is too late? It's possible and safe to become pregnant until a women reaches menopause, which typically occurs around the age of 51. That's when a woman's body becomes incapable of having children because she can no longer ovulate. (No doctor, of course, recommends waiting until the eve of menopause to test one's fertility.)

Instead, women should worry less about whether they can conceive and have a healthy baby and give more consideration to whether they can care for a child for the next 18 years, says Dr. Thornton. "The problem isn't delayed childbearing—it's delayed childrearing," she says. "You don't want your child to be running around outside while you're at the old folks' home sipping your dinner out of a straw."

■ THE BIOLOGICAL CLOCK

Recent data show that there were 4,240,000 babies born in the United States in 1993. Three-fourths were to women in their 20s and early 30s, but the biggest increases were for older women.

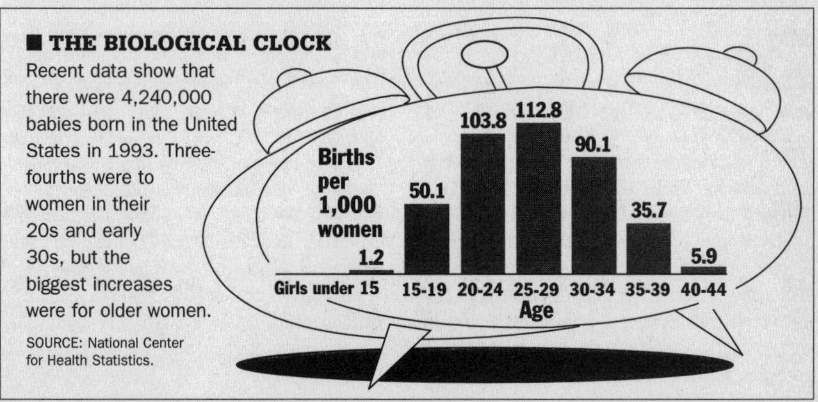

SOURCE: National Center for Health Statistics.

THE STORK'S GUIDE

FIGURING YOUR DUE DATE

While the average pregnancy is 280 days from the last menstrual period, it is normal to give birth anywhere from 37 to 42 weeks after your last period. To use this chart to determine your estimated delivery date, locate the bold-faced number that represents the first day of your last menstrual period. The light-faced number below it represents the expected delivery date.

JAN	**1**	**2**	**3**	**4**	**5**	**6**	**7**	**8**	**9**	**10**	**11**	**12**	**13**	**14**	**15**		**JAN**
OCT	8	9	10	11	12	13	14	15	16	17	18	19	20	21	22		OCT
JAN	**16**	**17**	**18**	**19**	**20**	**21**	**22**	**23**	**24**	**25**	**26**	**27**	**28**	**29**	**30**	**31**	**JAN**
OCT	23	24	25	26	27	28	29	30	31	1	2	3	4	5	6	7	NOV
FEB	**1**	**2**	**3**	**4**	**5**	**6**	**7**	**8**	**9**	**10**	**11**	**12**	**13**	**14**	**15**		**FEB**
NOV	8	9	10	11	12	13	14	15	16	17	18	19	20	21	22		NOV
FEB	**16**	**17**	**18**	**19**	**20**	**21**	**22**	**23**	**24**	**25**	**26**	**27**	**28**				**FEB**
NOV	23	24	25	26	27	28	29	30	1	2	3	4	5				DEC
MAR	**1**	**2**	**3**	**4**	**5**	**6**	**7**	**8**	**9**	**10**	**11**	**12**	**13**	**14**	**15**		**MAR**
DEC	6	7	8	9	10	11	12	13	14	15	16	17	18	19	20		DEC
MAR	**16**	**17**	**18**	**19**	**20**	**21**	**22**	**23**	**24**	**25**	**26**	**27**	**28**	**29**	**30**	**31**	**MAR**
DEC	21	22	23	24	25	26	27	28	29	30	31	1	2	3	4	5	JAN
APR	**1**	**2**	**3**	**4**	**5**	**6**	**7**	**8**	**9**	**10**	**11**	**12**	**13**	**14**	**15**		**APR**
JAN	6	7	8	9	10	11	12	13	14	15	16	17	18	19	20		JAN
APR	**16**	**17**	**18**	**19**	**20**	**21**	**22**	**23**	**24**	**25**	**26**	**27**	**28**	**29**	**30**		**APR**
JAN	21	22	23	24	25	26	27	28	29	30	31	1	2	3	4		FEB
MAY	**1**	**2**	**3**	**4**	**5**	**6**	**7**	**8**	**9**	**10**	**11**	**12**	**13**	**14**	**15**		**MAY**
FEB	5	6	7	8	9	10	11	12	13	14	15	16	17	18	19		FEB
MAY	**16**	**17**	**18**	**19**	**20**	**21**	**22**	**23**	**24**	**25**	**26**	**27**	**28**	**29**	**30**	**31**	**MAY**
FEB	20	21	22	23	24	25	26	27	28	1	2	3	4	5	6	7	MAR
JUN	**1**	**2**	**3**	**4**	**5**	**6**	**7**	**8**	**9**	**10**	**11**	**12**	**13**	**14**	**15**		**JUN**
MAR	8	9	10	11	12	13	14	15	16	17	18	19	20	21	22		MAR
JUN	**16**	**17**	**18**	**19**	**20**	**21**	**22**	**23**	**24**	**25**	**26**	**27**	**28**	**29**	**30**		**JUN**
MAR	23	24	25	26	27	28	29	30	31	1	2	3	4	5	6		APR

SOURCE: *Planning for Pregnancy, Birth, and Beyond*, American College of Obstetricians and Gynecologists, 1993.

■ THE STORK'S GUIDE

JUL	**1**	**2**	**3**	**4**	**5**	**6**	**7**	**8**	**9**	**10**	**11**	**12**	**13**	**14**	**15**		**JUL**
APR	7	8	9	10	11	12	13	14	15	16	17	18	19	20	21		APR
JUL	**16**	**17**	**18**	**19**	**20**	**21**	**22**	**23**	**24**	**25**	**26**	**27**	**28**	**29**	**30**	**31**	**JUL**
APR	22	23	24	25	26	27	28	29	30	1	2	3	4	5	6	7	MAY
AUG	**1**	**2**	**3**	**4**	**5**	**6**	**7**	**8**	**9**	**10**	**11**	**12**	**13**	**14**	**15**		**AUG**
MAY	8	9	10	11	12	13	14	15	16	17	18	19	20	21	22		MAY
AUG	**16**	**17**	**18**	**19**	**20**	**21**	**22**	**23**	**24**	**25**	**26**	**27**	**28**	**29**	**30**	**31**	**AUG**
MAY	23	24	25	26	27	28	29	30	31	1	2	3	4	5	6	7	JUN
SEP	**1**	**2**	**3**	**4**	**5**	**6**	**7**	**8**	**9**	**10**	**11**	**12**	**13**	**14**	**15**		**SEP**
JUN	8	9	10	11	12	13	14	15	16	17	18	19	20	21	22		JUN
SEP	**16**	**17**	**18**	**19**	**20**	**21**	**22**	**23**	**24**	**25**	**26**	**27**	**28**	**29**	**30**		**SEP**
JUN	23	24	25	26	27	28	29	30	1	2	3	4	5	6	7		JUL
OCT	**1**	**2**	**3**	**4**	**5**	**6**	**7**	**8**	**9**	**10**	**11**	**12**	**13**	**14**	**15**		**OCT**
JUL	8	9	10	11	12	13	14	15	16	17	18	19	20	21	22		JUL
OCT	**16**	**17**	**18**	**19**	**20**	**21**	**22**	**23**	**24**	**25**	**26**	**27**	**28**	**29**	**30**	**31**	**OCT**
JUL	23	24	25	26	27	28	29	30	31	1	2	3	4	5	6	7	AUG
NOV	**1**	**2**	**3**	**4**	**5**	**6**	**7**	**8**	**9**	**10**	**11**	**12**	**13**	**14**	**15**		**NOV**
AUG	8	9	10	11	12	13	14	15	16	17	18	19	20	21	22		AUG
NOV	**16**	**17**	**18**	**19**	**20**	**21**	**22**	**23**	**24**	**25**	**26**	**27**	**28**	**29**	**30**		**NOV**
AUG	23	24	25	26	27	28	29	30	31	1	2	3	4	5	6		SEP
DEC	**1**	**2**	**3**	**4**	**5**	**6**	**7**	**8**	**9**	**10**	**11**	**12**	**13**	**14**	**15**		**DEC**
SEP	7	8	9	10	11	12	13	14	15	16	17	18	19	20	21		SEP
DEC	**16**	**17**	**18**	**19**	**20**	**21**	**22**	**23**	**24**	**25**	**26**	**27**	**28**	**29**	**30**	**31**	**DEC**
SEP	22	23	24	25	26	27	28	29	30	1	2	3	4	5	6	7	OCT

■ GROWTH OF THE FETUS FROM 8 TO 40 WEEKS

Week	**8**	**12**	**16**	**20**	**24**	**28**	**32**	**36**	**40**
Length	1 in.	3 in.	6.5 in.	10 in.	13 in.	14.5 in.	16 in.	18 in.	20 in.
Weight	0.07 oz.	0.6 oz.	5 oz.	12 oz.	1.3 lb.	2 lb.	3.5 lb.	5.5 lb.	7.5 lb.

SOURCE: *American Medical Association Encyclopedia of Medicine*, Random House, 1989.

PREGNANCY

WHAT TO EXPECT WHILE EXPECTING

It may sound simple, but just wait until motherhood confronts you

Most women know that the satisfactions of motherhood come accompanied by certain side effects of pregnancy such as morning sickness, cravings, and fatigue. Yet first-time mothers are usually unprepared for many aspects of pregnancy, labor, delivery, and ultimately, parenthood. Here's a guide to what most often surprises new parents:

EXPECT that something can go wrong. Most women assume everything is going to go along smoothly, but that's not always true, says Dr. Ioannis Zervoudakis, associate professor of clinical obstetrics and gynecology at New York Hospital–Cornell University Medical College. For example, preterm labor, the need for bed rest, and loss of time from work are not that rare. Between 7 and 10 percent of babies are born prematurely; roughly 3 to 4 percent of babies are born with some type of birth defect, out of which 1 to 2 percent are minor, such as a red spot on the skin, or one blue and one brown eye; others are intermediate birth defects that can be repaired. The rest are serious chromosomal abnormalities like Down's syndrome. "Most women don't think about the possibility that their baby might be born with birth defects," says Dr. Zervoudakis. "Then if a bad outcome happens, they are very surprised and unprepared."

EXPECT to be a parent. Most women focus on the birth itself rather than what will happen after they deliver the baby, says Marion McCartney, a certified nurse-midwife and past president of the National Association of Childbearing Centers. "It's as if you only envision up to the wedding and not the rest of the marriage," she says. "Whether you go home after eight hours or eight days, you still hit the same wall of responsibility. Most people leave the hospital or birthing center and think, 'They're letting me leave with this baby? I don't know what I'm doing.' "

EXPECT that you'll need help after the baby is born. Women should realize that they'll need people to help care for them when they leave the hospital, says McCartney. Parents need to look for providers who can also teach the new mother. Even before the baby is born, all new mothers should take breast-feeding and parenting classes, McCartney urges.

EXPECT to tend to the baby around the clock. "The thing women are most unaware of is the tremendous time a newborn baby requires during the first months and years of life," says ob/gyn Zervoudakis. "A baby really does demand 24-hour attention, and many times it's a big surprise to women what a big change in lifestyle it is."

EXPECT to look pregnant after the baby is born. "Women envision their stomachs flat again right after they first have a baby, and they think they're going to leap back into their prepregnancy clothes," says nurse-midwife McCartney. "But when they stand up they still look five months pregnant." At the end of two weeks, most women will have lost 20 pounds, but it's still "loose like dough" after two weeks. "You have to do abdominal exercises to tighten the muscles," she advises.

EXPECT to be unprepared. Most women who become pregnant have no idea what they're getting themselves into, says Dr. Yvonne Thornton, director of the perinatal diagnostic testing center at Morristown Memorial Hospital in New Jersey. Women need to realize that nothing they do (or read) can really prepare them for the experience of childbirth and parenthood. "The women who have had children will never tell the ones who haven't the real story," contends Thornton, "from the morning sickness to the labor to the breast-feeding to the diapers to the potty training to, 'Mom, can I have the keys to the car?' "

KEEPING YOUR BABY FROM HARM'S WAY

Beware of what these agents could do to the fetus

AGENT	REASONS USED	EFFECTS
ALCOHOL	Part of regular diet, social reasons, dependency.	Growth and mental retardation.
ANDROGENS	To treat endometriosis.	Genital abnormalities.
ANTICOAGULANTS Warfarin (Coumadin, Panwarfin) and dicumatrol	To prevent blood clotting; used to prevent or treat thromboembolisms (clots blocking blood vessels).	Abnormalities in bones, cartilage, and eyes; central nervous system defects.
ANTITHYROID DRUGS Propylthiouracil, iodide, and methimazole (Tapazole)	To treat an overactive thyroid gland.	Underactive or enlarged thyroid.
ANTICONVULSANTS Phentoin (Dilantin), trimethadione (Tridione), paramethadione (Paradione), valproic acid (Depakene)	To treat epilepsy and irregular heartbeat.	Growth and mental retardation, developmental abnormalities, neural tube defects.
CHEMOTHERAPEUTIC DRUGS Methotrexate (Mexate) and aminopterin	To treat cancer and psoriasis.	Increased rate of miscarriage, various abnormalities.
DIETHYLSIBESTROL (DES)	To treat problems with menstruation, symptoms of menopause and breast cancer, and to stop milk production; previously used to prevent preterm labor and miscarriage.	Abnormalities of cervix and uterus in females, possible infertility in males and females.
LEAD	Industries involving lead smelting, paint manufacture and use, printing, ceramics, glass manufacturing, and pottery glazing.	Increased rate of miscarriage and stillbirths.
LITHIUM	To treat the manic part of manic-depressive disorders.	Congenital heart disease.
ORGANIC MERCURY	Exposure through eating contaminated food.	Brain disorders.
ISOTRETINOIN (Accutane)	Treatment for cystic acne.	Increased rate of miscarriage, developmental abnormalities.
STREPTOMYCIN	An antibiotic used to treat tuberculosis.	Hearing loss.
TETRACYCLINE	An antibiotic used to treat a wide variety of infections.	Underdevelopment of tooth enamel, incorporation of tetracycline into bone.
THALIDOMIDE	Previously used as a sedative and a sleep aid.	Growth deficiencies, other abnormalities.
X-RAY THERAPY	Medical treatment of disorders such as cancer.	Growth and mental retardation.

SOURCE: *Planning for Pregnancy, Birth, and Beyond*, American College of Obstetricians and Gynecologists, 1993.

EXPERT Q & A

MEDICAL CHECK-UPS IN UTERO

Today's tests for genetic defects make far more information available

Ten tiny toes, 10 tiny fingers: The emotional climax of any pregnancy comes when the doctor places the newborn baby on the mother's belly and assures the parents that he or she is healthy. But many mothers no longer have to wait until the child is born to learn whether their baby is likely to be healthy. As more women postpone having children until their mid- to late 30s, genetic tests that offer women a chance to learn the likelihood that the baby will have a serious birth defect are being administered far more frequently.

Below, Lee Fallon, a certified genetic counselor and supervisor of genetic counseling at the Genetics and IVF Institute in Fairfax, Va., answers some of the most common questions asked about genetic testing by prospective parents:

■ Which birth defects are most common?

The two most common birth defects are congenital heart defects and cleft lip and palate. One in 500 to 1,000 babies is born with either cleft lip or cleft palate and one in 100 to 200 is born with heart defects. Two other common birth defects are neural tube defects such as spina bifida and anencephaly (the absence of a part of the brain or a damaged spinal cord) and chromosomal abnormalities such as Down's syndrome, the most common type of serious chromosomal disorder.

■ At what age are women at risk of having a baby with chromosomal abnormalities?

A woman in her 20s has about a 1 in 500 chance of having a baby with a chromosomal abnormality. It's about 1 in 380 by age 30, 1 in 180 at age 35, 1 in 100 by age 38, and 1 in 50 by age 41; then it doubles almost every year after that. However, 80 percent of children with Down's syndrome are born to women in their 20s, many of whom, because they face less risk, don't choose to undergo more advanced diagnostic tests.

■ What is the AFP test?

The AFP test is a blood test that measures a chemical called alpha-fetoprotein (AFP), which is produced inside the liver of the fetus. If the spinal fluid were leaking into amniotic fluid, there would be a higher concentration of AFP in the amniotic fluid, and therefore a higher level would usually get into the blood of the mother.

The test, which is normally offered to all pregnant women, is most accurate at detecting spina bifida and anencephaly, which are suspected when there's an elevated AFP level, but it can also help detect Down's syndrome.

■ What is ultrasound screening and who should have it done?

An ultrasound test is usually offered only when there's another risk factor for a genetic disorder or birth defect like a family history or an abnormal AFP test. Ultrasound uses sound waves that emit from a transducer (a reverse microphone) and bounce off structures. It allows us to look at the physical development of the baby and get a general picture of the legs, arms and body. The denser the structure, such as bone, the brighter the image. For example, a birth defect like anencephaly is very accurately picked up on ultrasound because you can see the part of the skull that's not formed.

■ How likely are these basic screening tests to detect problems?

The AFP Plus test detects 80 to 85 percent of cases of spina bifida and about 65 percent of Down's syndrome, which means that almost one in three cases would not show up. When ultrasound is done after 18 weeks, it will detect most serious heart defects and more than 50 percent of neural tube defects, and it's even more likely to detect major physical problems.

■ WHEN THERE'S A FAMILY HISTORY

Some defects are more likely to recur if parents already have one child with the defect.

DISORDER	RISK OF HAVING A FETUS WITH THE DISORDER		
	Overall		With one affected child
DOMINANT GENE			
Polydactyly	1 in 300 to 1 in 100		50%
Achondroplasia	1 in 23,000		50%
Huntington's disease	1 in 15,000 to 1 in 5,000		50%
RECESSIVE GENE			
Cystic fibrosis	1 in 2,500	White persons	25%
Sickle-cell anemia	1 in 625	Black persons	25%
Tay-Sachs disease	1 in 3,600	Ashkenazi Jews	25%
Beta-thalassemia	1 in 2,500- 1 in 800	Persons of Mediterranean descent	25%
X-LINKED			
Hemophilia	1 in 2,500	Men	50% for boy, 0% for girl
CHROMOSOMAL			
Down's syndrome	1 in 800	Average risk increases with mother's age	1%–2%
Klinefelter syndrome	1 in 800	Men	No significant increase
Turner syndrome	1 in 3,000	Women	No significant increase
MULTIFACTORAL			
Congenital heart disease	1 in 125		2%–4%
Neural tube defects	1 in 1,000 to 1 in 500		2%–5%
Cleft lip/cleft palate	1 in 1,000 to 1 in 500		2%–4%

SOURCE: *Planning for Pregnancy, Birth, and Beyond,* American College of Obstetricians and Gynecologists, 1993.

■ Are further tests necessary if the results of AFP and ultrasound are normal?

It's important to understand the difference between screening tests like AFP and ultrasound and diagnostic tests like amniocentesis or chorionic villus sampling (CVS). A screening test doesn't give you a yes or no answer; it just tells you if your risk is average or above or below average, whereas diagnostic tests almost always give you a yes or no answer. If you have an abnormal result from a screening test, you most likely have a healthy pregnancy, but you may want to have a diagnostic test. A normal result on a screening test doesn't mean you have a healthy pregnancy, but your chances of developing certain problems are lower than most.

■ What's the difference between amniocentesis and the diagnostic test CVS?

Amniocentesis involves withdrawing about a tablespoon of amniotic fluid surrounding the fetus with a thin needle from the mother's abdomen. Cells in the fluid shed from the baby can be used to determine if the baby has a chromosomal or genetic abnormality. CVS involves removing a small amount of cells called the chorionic villi that form the placenta by inserting either a catheter into the cervix or a needle into the mother's abdomen, then genetic tests are performed on the cells.

■ Who should undergo diagnostic tests?

These tests are usually offered only to women who will be age 35 or older at the time their baby is due, unless there's another indication, such as if a woman has already had a baby with a chromosomal abnormality or there's another hereditary risk. Amniocentesis may also be offered to women at least 14 weeks pregnant because of an AFP or ultrasound finding, but the window of opportunity has closed by that time to perform CVS, which is done between 10 and 13 weeks of pregnancy. Most facilities will provide these tests to younger women if requested, but most insurers consider it optional and would not cover the cost. (Amniocentesis costs about $1,500; CVS costs $1,500 to $1,800).

■ How does a woman decide which diagnostic tests to undergo?

Whether to undergo any of these tests is the decision of the woman or the couple. Amniocentesis is the more commonly available test. CVS is usually performed if a woman desires results early in her pregnancy, if a woman has had a previous pregnancy with chromosomal abnormalities, or if the couple is at risk of having a child with a genetic disease. However, CVS isn't available everywhere.

■ How effective are amniocentesis and CVS at detecting abnormalities?

Both amniocentesis and CVS have greater than 99 percent accuracy in detecting chromosomal abnormalities.

■ What are the risks associated with the various screening and diagnostic tests?

The AFP and ultrasound screening tests pose no risk to the baby; both amniocentesis and CVS carry a risk of causing miscarriage. On average in the U.S., the risk of miscarriage associated with CVS is one in 100 to 200, and it's one in 200 to 400 for amniocentesis.

■ What factors should a couple consider in deciding whether a woman should be tested?

Couples should think about whether the information the test provides has a real benefit such as peace of mind or being able to make a decision about the pregnancy. Some decide to have the test because they feel that any risk of an abnormality would justify finding out. Others decide to have the test not based on the statistics, but on fear of the unknown.

■ Do some women over age 35 choose not to undergo any screening tests?

People who decide not to have testing done feel they would not do anything different in the pregnancy and taking a risk—however small—of losing that pregnancy is too great of a tradeoff. If there is a problem, the choices available are limited. Because we can't cure these conditions, the options are continuing the pregnancy knowing the diagnosis or terminating the pregnancy.

INFERTILITY

HIGH-TECH WAYS TO HAVE A BABY

Options for couples having trouble conceiving are greatly expanded

Late marriages and biological clocks are frequent factors. Environmental toxins, previous surgery, and declining sperm counts may also play a role. And sometimes there's no explanation why about 1 out of every 12 couples in the U.S. has been reported unable to conceive in a year of trying. This is despite the fact that more than half of women trying to conceive already had at least one child. The experience can be emotionally and financially draining, not to mention disappointing, since many couples don't get to bring home a baby even after trying for years.

In some cases the causes of infertility seem clear cut. The age of the mother is one of the biggest factors that influence the ability to conceive because as women age, they are less likely to ovulate. Certain women who don't release enough eggs can be treated with a fertility drug such as Clomid. (There's evidence that women who take some of these fertility drugs face a greater risk of ovarian cancer, although that's still unclear.) Other factors that can prevent successful conception include tubal scarring and blockage, poor sperm quality, or a low sperm count.

The procedures used to correct these problems vary. Sometimes couples just need to adjust their schedules (see box), undergo minor surgery to correct problems in their reproductive organs, or take prescription medications to conceive. But others must subject themselves to demanding and costly tests and treatments like hormone injections, egg retrieval, and embryo transfers.

So-called assisted reproductive technologies have become incredibly advanced since the birth of Louise Brown through in vitro fertilization (IVF) in 1978. Newer technologies such as gamete intrafallopian transfer (GIFT) and zygote intrafallopian transfer (ZIFT) have also become more widespread. With GIFT, the sperm and egg are inserted into the fallopian tubes, where fertilization occurs naturally. For IVF and ZIFT, fertilization of the eggs by the sperm takes place in the laboratory and the fertilized egg is placed directly into the woman's uterus for IVF, or her fallopian tubes for ZIFT.

One area that has progressed tremendously is in treating male infertility, which accounts for as much as 40 percent of all cases. For example, intracytoplasmic sperm injection (ICSI), which involves injecting a single sperm into an egg, then returning the egg to the uterus, is a technique designed to overcome infertility caused by weak or abnormal sperm. A recent report suggests that whether the procedure is successful depends at least in part on the age of the mother: Researchers found that the older the woman, the less likely that the fertilized egg would implant in her uterus.

But these high-tech treatments have their limits. A good rule of thumb in judging a treatment's efficacy, says Joyce Zeitz of the Fertility Institute in Birmingham, Ala., is after following a procedure for six full cycles without success, try something else. One of the most difficult decisions is when to quit. When a couple thinks they've done everything they can, the decision is sometimes complicated by a doctor's optimism that he or she can find a treatment that will work.

Some fertility clinics publish exaggerated success rates, which can also inflate couples' confidence that eventually they will conceive. In fact, the Federal Trade Commission has won cease and desist agreements against five clinics that ran misleading ads. The success rate for assisted reproductive technologies averages about 20 percent, ranging from 18 percent for IVF to 30 percent for GIFT. One researcher reported a success rate of nearly 40 percent using ICSI. Although only one in seven couples conceive on the first try using more established assisted reproductive technologies like IVF, the success rate increases after several tries.

Only 10 states require insurance companies to cover such procedures, which can cost anywhere from $6,000 to $10,000 a try. One study estimated that the cost of IVF can range from $66,000 for a couple that conceives after the first try to up to $800,000 for couples that try repeatedly to conceive.

WHEN BIRDS LIKE BEES THE BEST

Time your love-making to the day of ovulation if you're hoping to conceive

New research may make it easier for couples to conceive simply by clarifying exactly when a couple is most likely to conceive. The study, conducted by researchers at the National Institute of Environmental Health Sciences and published in the *New England Journal of Medicine*, concluded that a woman's chances of becoming pregnant are greatest if she has sexual intercourse on the day of ovulation (when the egg is released from the ovary), or in the five days before she ovulates.

The finding challenges the conventional wisdom that a woman is fertile from about three days prior to ovulation to about three days afterward. Most surprising was the finding that a woman's chances of conceiving after ovulation are virtually nil. Not one of the study's 221 women who were trying to become pregnant conceived as a result of having intercourse after they ovulated, while 10 percent of those who had intercourse five days before ovulating and 33 percent of those who had intercourse on the day of ovulation became pregnant. To take advantage of this timing information, women must first predict when they will ovulate, which they can do by either using over-the-counter ovulation tests or by charting basal body temperature.

EXPERT TIPS

MAKING AN ADOPTION WORK

To avoid pitfalls, examine your motivation before you begin

Parental rights battles like the "Baby Jessica" and "Baby Richard" cases have made Americans more aware of the anguish associated with adoption. While most adoptive parents don't experience that degree of trauma, they routinely have to contend with endless waits, exorbitant costs, and bureaucratic runarounds. Deb Harder, program director of Adoptive Families of America, a nationwide nonprofit agency that provides information and assistance to adoptive parents, has this advice on how to avoid being victimized or caught up in "the system":

■ **Examine what's motivating you to adopt.** The first step for anyone considering adoption is to make sure you're firmly committed to rearing and nurturing a child. Look very carefully at your skills and strengths as a person and how they translate to being an effective parent. If you're dealing with infertility, it's important to have gone through a grieving process and acknowledge that you're unlikely to bear children. You should look at adoption not as a second best option, but as an alternative to bearing a child.

■ **Decide what kind of child you will be an effective parent for.** Many families only consider adopting a healthy, same-race infant, and don't think of a child born in another country or one with special needs. Some folks are prepared to parent a child with special needs, but others might not be equipped to. Likewise with kids from other cultural backgrounds. You have to consider how you are going to incorporate that heritage into day-to-day life.

■ **Learn state laws.** Among the first things a family should do is contact their state department of social services and talk to an adoption supervisor to find out what they are legally required to do to complete an adoption in their state.

■ **Choose the type of adoption you're interested in.** One of the first decisions is whether you'd like to adopt through a public agency, which primarily works with kids in foster care and group home settings, and rarely handles healthy, same-race infants; or a private agency, which specializes in healthy, same-race infants and children with special needs, and in some cases arranges international adoptions. You can also opt for an independent, or private adoption, in which adoptive parents work with a lawyer or other non-agency adoption provider to find a birth parent or child. There are certain risks with private adoptions and more of a safety net with an agency.

■ **Assess the costs.** The cost of adopting a child ranges from $8,000 to $20,000, depending on the type of adoption. International adoptions tend to be more expensive, because there are hidden costs such as long-distance calls and travel expenses. Private adoption has the reputation of being more expensive, because the costs usually aren't set up front, while some agencies may charge on a sliding scale basis.

Different agencies have different fee structures, services, and missions. Try to get details about the services they provide and insist that they assign a service to each fee.

■ **Expect to be scrutinized during the selection process.** Many private agencies allow birth mothers a say in choosing which couple they want to adopt their child. Agencies can and do compile a book of dossiers with biographical information about prospective families for birth mothers to review. Your age may also be a factor. One reason many adoptive parents look at international programs is that some agencies have a 35- to 40-year-old age cap for adoptive parents, but many international programs have wider age ranges.

■ **Be honest during the "home study."** All prospective adoptive parents must undergo a home study, a means by which agency personnel can assess the qualities needed to be an effective parent with what your qualities are. It's not unlike applying for a mortgage. For example, they assess what's motivating you to adopt, how you were parented, and how you plan to discipline the child. They'll also ask for references and look at your finances and psychological stability. If you have a criminal history or a history of psychiatric illnesses, you don't want to lie about the situation—it will cause greater problems than if you're up front and explain what's what.

■ **Decide whether you want an open or confidential adoption.** In years past, you could be pretty sure an adoption would be confidential and records would be sealed. But open adoption, in which the birth and adoptive families establish communication, is becoming more common. If the agency allows open adoption, consider what degree of openness you're interested in. It's a highly emotional time for adoptive and birth parents, so it's hard to assess what you're going to be comfortable with long-term.

■ **Find out how quickly adopted children go home with adoptive families.** The number of families seeking to adopt is greater than the number of healthy, same-race infants available, which means the wait can take anywhere from 9 to 24 months. It varies more than it used to because of the degree of openness, which also means you have greater opportunity to be selected ahead of time. The agency should be able to give you a time line as to what to expect, but bear in mind that nothing is written in granite. Be flexible, but assertive. Remember, the agency will control if and when your child comes home to you.

■ **Make sure the people you're working with are reputable.** The people you're working with must be competent, qualified, and ethical or the whole thing is jeopardized. If you opt for a private adoption, don't go to a family lawyer unless he or she has experience in adoption. And bear in mind that just because a lawyer knows how to complete an adoption according to the letter of the law doesn't mean he or she has a background in the sociological and psychological aspects of adoption. If you are trying to arrange an international adoption, be aware that what is culturally acceptable in other countries may be way outside of our experience or what we deem acceptable. For example, many international programs will request "gifts" that may look like bribes in the U.S.

■ **Weigh the risks and benefits of "legal risk."** In an agency adoption, the baby usually stays with a foster family during a waiting period mandated by the state (from 48 hours to three months), until the adoption becomes final. But if you arrange what's called legal risk, you take custody of the adopted child immediately after birth, but the birth parents can come forward and reclaim the child during that period. You can arrange this through both agency and private adoptions, but most agencies don't tell you it's an option unless you ask. Chances are you'll immediately bond with the child, so it's an extremely painful experience for adoptive families to go through to have the birth mother renege, and if they do, there's not a lot of recourse.

EXPERT SOURCES

If you want more information about adoption, contact one of the following organizations:

Adoptive Families of America
☎ **800-372-3300**

National Adoption Information Clearinghouse
☎ **301-231-6512**

The National Adoption Center
☎ **800-TO-ADOPT**

EARLY DISCHARGE

"DRIVE-THROUGH" CHILDBIRTH

Some experts think hospitals are discharging new mothers too early

Shorter hospital stays for new mothers and their infants have become standard practice in hospitals across the country. The average length of stay has decreased from four days in 1970 to 48 hours in 1992, according to the Centers for Disease Control and Prevention, and nowadays, most women and their babies leave the hospital within 12 to 24 hours if they've experienced an uncomplicated vaginal birth, and between 48 and 72 hours after cesarean births. Although shorter hospital stays were initiated by women who wanted to "demedicalize" childbirth and go home sooner to be with their families, the latest trend has been driven by insurance companies attempting to curb health care costs.

While early discharge seems to work for healthy patients, critics charge that "drive-through deliveries" jeopardize the health of the newborn. For example, there's evidence that early discharge places infants at increased risk of undetected jaundice (yellowing of the skin that occurs when a pigment called bilirubin builds up in the blood), because the condition often doesn't manifest itself until two or three days after birth.

The American Academy of Pediatricians (AAP) and the American College of Obstetricians and Gynecologists (ACOG) have called for 48-hour stays for vaginal births and 96-hour stays for cesarean births. At least 16 states have passed laws mandating minimum stays, in fact, and a similar bill has been introduced in Congress. President Clinton has also backed proposals to lengthen maternal stays in hospitals.

Most new mothers discharged early will fare better if they learn to identify the symptoms of potential problems like jaundice *before* they go into labor, says Dr. Ioannis Zervoudakis of New York Hospital–Cornell University Medical College. Prenatal education can also help teach new mothers how to breast-feed properly and often enough to prevent dehydration.

RATING A NEWBORN'S HEALTH

Within a minute of delivering a baby, the obstetrics team will check the newborn's heart rate, respiration, muscle tone, reflexes, and coloration and record a score designed to reflect how that baby came through the delivery process. That rating, known as an Apgar score, is compiled by issuing a ranking between zero and two for each of the vital signs and indicators listed above, and then adding each of the numbers together to arrive at a single score. The process is then repeated five minutes after birth and the two sets of observations are compared to gauge the baby's progress in adjusting to his or her new environment. But Apgar scores are not intended as a reliable predictor of a baby's long-term health prospects, only of how the newborn is adapting to life outside a mother's womb.

COMPONENT	APGAR SCORE		
	0	1	2
HEART RATE	Absent	Slow (< 100 beats/min.)	>100 beats/min.
RESPIRATIONS	Absent	Weak; hypoventilation	Good, strong cry
MUSCLE TONE	Limp	Some flexion	Active motion
REFLEX IRRITABILITY	No response	Grimace	Cough or sneeze
COLOR	Blue or pale	Body pink; extremities blue	Complete pink

SOURCE: *Planning for Pregnancy, Birth, and Beyond,* American College of Obstetricians and Gynecologists, 1993.

VISION

FOUR EYES MAY BE TWO TOO MANY

New research: It may be wrong to put glasses on kids too early

Many children begin wearing eyeglasses when they first develop vision problems—sometimes before they can even read. But a new study suggests that wearing glasses early in life may actually exacerbate rather than correct vision problems.

Researchers at the University of Houston studied 11 infant Rhesus monkeys to determine whether lenses could correct nearsightedness or farsightedness. Each monkey wore headgear with lenses that simulated either nearsightedness or farsightedness, and researchers then measured the effects of the lenses on the eye's growth. In almost all of the monkeys who wore lenses to correct nearsightedness, the eye being tested grew longer than normal and became more myopic. Where lenses to correct farsightedness were used, the eye became more flat and farsighted.

Researchers suspect that the monkeys were somehow able to detect visual errors and grow in such a way as to correct the problem. Their conclusion: The results "show that changing the focus of the eye of infant primates with a simple spectacle lens can change the way the eye grows."

The researchers point out that since primates' eyes closely resemble human eyes in the first few years of life, results from visual tests on monkeys can usually be extrapolated to humans because their visual systems are so similar. With further research, the scientists believe, it may turn out that poor vision in children may gradually improve over time without glasses. However, researchers caution that because humans and monkeys develop at different rates, the results may be applicable only to infants and not older children, who typically don't start wearing glasses until they reach school-age.

RECOMMENDED CHILDHOOD IMMUNIZATION SCHEDULE

The Centers for Disease Control, the American Academy of Pediatrics, and the American Academy of Family Physicians are America's leading authorities on childhood immunization. Below is their unified immunization schedule, released in January 1996.

Vaccine	First dose	Second dose	Third dose	Fourth dose	Fifth dose	Sixth dose
Hepatitis B[1]	Before 2 mos.	1–4 mos.[2]	6–18 mos.			
Diphtheria, Tetanus, Pertussis (DTP)	2 mos.	4 mos.	6 mos.	12–18 mos.[2]	4–6 yrs. (booster)[3]	11–16 yrs.
H. influenza type B	2 mos.	4 mos.	6 mos.	12–15 mos. (booster)[4]		
Polio	2 mos.	4 mos.	6–18 mos.	4–6 yrs.		
MMR	12–15 mos.	4–6 yrs. or 11–12 yrs.[2]				
Chicken Pox[1]	12–18 mos.					

NOTES: 1. Unvaccinated children should be vaccinated between ages 11 and 12. 2. Allow at least one month after previous dose before administering next. 3. Allow at least five years after previous dose before administering next. 4. Children who get an H. influenza vaccine known as PRP–OMP do not require a dose at 6 months, but still require the booster.
SOURCE: Centers for Disease Control, the American Academy of Pediatrics, and the American Academy of Family Physicians, 1996.

EXPERT Q & A

THE HYPERACTIVE CHILD

Diagnosing ADHD early can make all the difference to childhood

To skeptics, ADHD is a much overstated explanation for behavior that is only to be expected in children. But to families with children who seem constantly driven to distraction, learning to recognize and get help for Attention Deficit Hyperactivity Disorder is crucial. Here, Dr. Russell A. Barkley, professor of psychiatry and neurology and director of psychology at the University of Massachusetts, and author of *Taking Charge of ADHD* (Guilford Publications, 1995), explains the disorder and its treatments:

■ What are ADHD's characteristics?

The three primary problems are hyperactivity, inattentiveness, and impulsiveness. The most obvious characteristics include being very active, being impatient, and doing very uninhibited things like cutting people off in conversations. Then there are the problems for which the disorder is named, problems with concentration and attention that mainly involve not being able to persist in things that are tedious or boring.

Rather than being just an attention deficit, the disorder is really a fundamental problem with how children develop the ability to control their behavior. It tends to come on early, usually in preschool years, and it's relatively chronic. For most kids who have it, problems will persist for at least 10 years, and in some cases, well into adulthood.

■ How is ADHD diagnosed?

Since there are no objective tests available to diagnose mental disorders, including ADHD, a diagnosis is based upon interviewing the individual and finding out the nature of his complaints, then looking at the history of the individual and comparing this information to what we know about children's mental disorders.

To help in this process, the American Psychiatric Association has developed a set of guidelines that clinicians should follow. It includes a list of 18 possible behaviors of kids with ADHD. In addition, the symptoms have to appear before a child is seven and have to cause problems, such as impairment in school, social life, and community or family function. For example, failing in school, getting thrown out of preschool or being forbidden to return to the houses of relatives because the child's behavior was so obnoxious. Finally, it has to be established that the child doesn't have another disorder like retardation or autism that looks like ADHD.

■ What causes ADHD?

There are many causes of ADHD, but chief among them is heredity, which probably accounts for 70 percent or more of the cases. When there's a clear family history, we often find that about 35 percent of the siblings have the disorder and there's a 40 to 50 percent chance that one of the two parents is an adult with ADHD. In the 30 percent of kids who didn't inherit the behavior pattern, anything that could injure or cause a development problem in the front part of the brain during pregnancy, such as exposure to alcohol and nicotine, or after the child is born, could give rise to this problem.

■ Why have so many kids been diagnosed with ADHD?

Even though there has been no rise in the prevalence of ADHD, the public has become increasingly aware of this disorder, which means more kids are getting referred for it. In public health, that's exactly what you want to see—people who previously were undiagnosed and untreated are now getting help.

■ When should parents seek help?

All children show a few symptoms of ADHD, but what really distinguishes people with ADHD from the rest of us is how extreme it is, how often it occurs, and how much trouble it gets them into. A parent should ask, for instance, if a child requires much more supervision than others his age, or is being refused permission to go to neighbors' homes because he's been so unruly, aggressive and disruptive.

■ When are medications required?

Medications are probably going to be needed for 60 to 80 percent of all kids who are diagnosed with ADHD. That's why we've seen a rise in drugs like Ritalin in the past 10 to 20 years. That simply reflects the fact that over the past 5 years or so, we have come to the realization that medications, rather than being something we turn to after we've tried everything else and failed, are the most effective treatments.

■ How does Ritalin actually work?

It energizes or stimulates the brain's ability to inhibit behavior and allow time for thinking and reflection. In other words, it's stimulating the self-control mechanisms of the brain. The kids are less active, but they're also better able to concentrate and follow through on work and instructions, less impulsive, less restless, and as a result they're better controlled.

For about 70 percent of kids, stimulant medications like Ritalin will make them indistinguishable from other children. About 30 percent will either have no response to medications or a modest response—enough that we might keep them on it.

■ What drawbacks do these medications have?

Stimulants like Ritalin are pretty safe medications with few side effects. One is the loss of appetite usually right around lunch time, so the children don't eat quite as much as they normally would. A few children lose a couple of pounds the first year or so, though many will regain the weight later. In a few rare cases, children lose much more weight and have to be put on "drug holidays" and taken off medications for weekends in summers, so that they can regain the lost weight. It used to be we took everyone off on weekends in summers because of the fear of growth problems, but studies have shown us that these drugs don't affect bone growth or height in most children.

A few children do have serious growth problems, however, that need to be monitored by physicians. In addition, about 2 to 3 percent of children may develop nervous tics, and about 5 to 10 percent of kids have a bad reaction to the medication. Not only does it not help them, it actually makes them worse, so they need to try another type of medication. For example, antidepressant medications are now believed to benefit some ADHD children.

■ Are drugs the only effective treatment?

It's often said that medications should never be used alone, and that's probably true. You also have to counsel people about their disability in order to help them live with it, cope with it, and deal with it more effectively. Short-term counseling that educates individuals and their families about the nature of the disorder can be very useful. In addition, about 60 to 70 percent of the kids we see are going to need extra help in school, not only with managing their behavior but also with managing their assignments and workload. About 40 percent of kids will need formal special education. In addition, there are some parents who need help in learning more effective strategies for how to raise a child with a behavioral disability.

The thing to realize is the best treatment is diagnosis. Once people know what the child has, they can approach that child from a very different frame of reference and understand that this child isn't acting naughty, this child doesn't have a moral failing, this child doesn't have bad parents, this child has a developmental disability.

■ Can ADHD be outgrown?

Yes, though we're realizing that far more people continue to have the problem than we once thought. I would estimate that 20 to 30 percent of children with ADHD do fully outgrow the condition by the time they reach adulthood. The rest continue to manifest some or all of these symptoms.

DOCTORS & MEDICINE

HMOS: Making them work for you, PAGE 213 **EXPERT LIST:** The best hospitals in America, PAGE 217 **GENERIC DRUGS:** When paying less is hip, PAGE 230 **BREAST CANCER:** Knowing the risk factors, PAGE 238 **PROSTATE CANCER:** Diagnosis is easier than ever, PAGE 242 **BACK PAIN:** A new study says it may be overtreated, PAGE 244 **CHIROPRACTIC:** Should you trust a chiropractor? PAGE 246 **ALTERNATIVE MEDICINE:** Yoga may be of help, PAGE 247

EXPERT Q & A

WHAT TO LOOK FOR IN A DOCTOR

Dr. C. Everett Koop on finding the right doctor in today's environment

Like it or not, managed care is rapidly replacing fee-for-service medical treatment in the lives of most Americans. Understandably, the change has provoked great confusion and concern about the quality of medical care today. One common complaint is that doctor-patient trust has been destroyed by the dollars-and-cents mentality that now pervades the profession.

Former United States Surgeon General C. Everett Koop, a longtime consumer health advocate, recently published a self-help guide, *Dr. Koop's Self-Care Advisor: The Essential Home Health Guide* (Time Life Medical, 1996), to help educate health care consumers and encourage them to take a more active role in the health care decisions affecting them. Here, Dr. Koop discusses how consumers can get the most out of a visit to the doctor:

■ How should patients choose a doctor?

The answer to this question is different than it was a few years ago because of managed care. With 66 percent of the country now in managed care, most people don't have much choice. The patients with the greatest leeway are those on Medicare. But if you do have a choice of doctors, one of the things I think people find most helpful is referrals from patients who are satisfied with their doctor. If a doctor doesn't listen to you or doesn't communicate, that's not a doctor to seek out unless there's something very special about him and his knowledge.

■ Is choosing a doctor different for women than for men?

Some women feel that there are sexual overtones with a male physician and don't feel comfortable—it's just chemistry. But a lot of people, even women, still prefer a male physician. That's going to change in another five years or so because in many of our medical schools, more than half of the class are women. I think it will be for the better. Studies have shown that when a physician asks a patient a question, he tends to interrupt long before the patient finishes. But men physicians interrupt in 15 seconds and women in 45 seconds.

■ How can patients determine whether their doctor is qualified to treat their condition, or whether they need to see a specialist?

That's a real tough one. It's almost a moot question in some HMO's. I recently saw an internal document of a managed care company that said that the only three diagnoses that can be referred out to a dermatologist are squamous cell carcinoma, basal cell carcinoma, and melanoma. There are a lot of things in dermatology that are tougher to handle. If you have an honest primary care physician and you ask, "Do you know as much about what you want me to do as a specialist would," a good answer would be, "No, I don't, but I know enough so that I'm doing the right thing for you." Depending on your confidence in your doctor, you would accept that. You don't have to know everything to be able to do the right thing. It's the tricky situations where a difference of opinion can make a real difference in the patient's quality of life, or even life itself. And sometimes people understand by attitude, innuendo, and body language what their doctor's comfort level is with what he's telling them.

■ What if you do need a specialist?

Many people know a doctor, he may even be a friend they don't use professionally, who can recommend a specialist. Patients can also ask what a doctor's background is. If your primary care physician says, "I think you should see a gastroenterologist," then the patient has the right to ask whether this man is truly a specialist and has board certification—which means he has passed an exam recognizing his expertise in a particular field of medicine. He may be great, but if you're looking for concrete ways to track down a person's credentials, that is one. If you visit the doctor you've been referred to, and he says, "You ought to have X, Y, and Z done," you say, "Are there other options?" When he answers, ask, "How often have you done X, Y, and Z, and what are the results?" The more that patients ask that, the more honesty they're going to get from physicians.

■ Is there any statistically reliable way to gauge a physician's skill?

In many places now, the batting average of doctors and hospitals in the management of certain problems is being made available. In Pennsylvania, for instance, every doctor who does open heart surgery is not only listed with his mortality rate overall, but also his mortality rate in different hospitals where he works because sometimes it's quite different. You have pretty good objective evidence, all based on the same kind of statistics. Say your cardiologist says that there are three surgeons to consider in your town, and you can see that one has a 95 percent success rate, one a 92 percent rate, and one an 89 percent. That gives you a place to go. You then can talk to the doctor with the lowest rating and he may say, "I'm different than the other two because I take every patient that comes my way, and sometimes I take very high-risk patients, and of course they tend to have more problems than the others, while my competitor only takes patients that he knows he's going to succeed with." There are ways you can ferret out the answers you want, but it takes digging.

■ How can patients get their doctor to listen to their questions and help ensure successful treatment?

Most people know in general what their problem is before they go see a doctor; at least their symptoms point to something they fear. Patients should have their symptoms and

EXPERT SOURCE

A new video series, "At Time of Diagnosis," developed and hosted by America's best-known doctor, the former surgeon general, C. Everett Koop, takes the mystery out of being sick. Each of the 30 half-hour videos includes four sections: understanding the diagnosis, what happens next, treatment and management and issues and answers. The videos by Patient Education Media, Inc., a subsidiary of Time–Life, are sold in pharmacies nationwide and cost $19.95 each.

complaints written down so that they don't forget any of them. More important still, they should have the questions they want to ask their doctors written down. Experience shows that when their own health is concerned, a lot of things fly out of patients' heads in their doctor's office.

■ What if seeing a doctor is intimidating?

Patients always hold doctors in great awe and are embarrassed to ask questions. As a pediatric surgeon, I found that parents asked questions without embarrassment because the child meant so much to them. But when it's about themselves, they don't want to appear foolish. One of the things patients must realize is, there's no foolish question and there's no question that they can ask that the doctor hasn't heard before. If they realize that, it takes away some of the fear. If you don't understand a doctor, ask to have it put in plain language. Your doctor may get annoyed with you, but you're paying for his service and you're entitled to be satisfied when you leave his office.

■ When do you recommend getting a second opinion?

Second opinions are very important for surgical procedures, especially those that even the laity knows are not always successful, like operations for lower back pain. Then there are the situations where one doctor says you need your gallbladder out and "I can do that through three little incisions with a laparoscope and you'll be out the next day," and another doctor says, "You need an old-fashioned surgical procedure"—then a second opinion is necessary. Insurance companies are willing to pay for second opinions because if the second opinion is not to have surgery and the patient believes it, they save money.

■ Is it harder to get a second opinion when you're in a managed care situation?

With any HMO you have a built-in constraint on referrals because they're trying to save money. So you probably don't have as many referrals outside the HMO. Many times in fee-for-service medicine, a doctor will refer a patient to a surgeon he trusts and accept his judgment about whether that surgery is necessary. In the managed care situation, you might be able to choose from more than one specialist within the plan, but patients may be suspicious that all the specialists work for the same boss and are giving them the party line. Second opinions also benefit managed care companies, and managed care companies are as liberal with second opinions as they are with any referrals outside of their own group.

■ What questions should patients ask before undergoing surgery?

Ask about your particular situation and why it's absolutely necessary to have surgery. Then ask about the risk versus the benefit and whether you have something that is premalignant or just a nuisance that is bothering you. If you ask questions like this, you can weigh whether the surgery's risk is relatively small and is worth the benefit. I don't think patients should think about the economics of it if it's at all possible to do so.

■ Should patients in an HMO question a decision not to treat their condition?

They have every right to. The fee-for-service doctor can be accused of doing too many things in order to make money, but the managed care doctor can be accused of doing too few things in order to save money for his company. One of the sad things about managed care is that in some systems the physician gets docked for doing too much—if he has too many referrals, if his prescriptions are too expensive, if he is seeing too many patients for 20 minutes instead of 15. That all comes out in the computer and he could get less income at the end of the month. No matter how bad fee-for-service is, with ethical physicians you always knew the doctor had the ability to be the patient's advocate, whereas in an HMO system the doctor is primarily an advocate for the company and himself. It's the same thing for a test. If a doctor says, "You ought to have a stress test," some people won't think the system should be charged for that. They should say, "Doctor, talk to me about why you think it's important that I should have the test." But that demands a frankness with doctors that patients are frequently loath to show.

EXPERT TIPS

MAKING HMOs WORK FOR YOU

It takes skill and assertiveness to get the most out of the new plans

Members of managed care health plans take heart: Recent research has shown that the quality of care in managed care health plans is generally as good as in fee-for-service situations. A 1996 study by KPMG Peat Marwick, a financial services and consulting firm, of 11 million patients treated in cities with a high level of managed care found that the 3,700 hospitals surveyed reported significantly lower costs, shorter lengths of stay, and lower mortality rates than the national average. Another study of 8,000 heart attack survivors found that those enrolled in health maintenance organizations (HMOs) were less likely to undergo angioplasty (surgery to enlarge blood vessels) than those patients insured by other health care plans, yet short-term survival rates were about the same. To ensure top treatment, you have to be your own health care watchdog, however. Geraldine Dallek, director of health policy for Families USA, a national, non-profit health consumer group, offers this advice on how to be a savvy medical consumer in the changing world of health care:

■ **Analyze each health care plan according to your special needs.** Look at a plan in terms of what medical conditions you or your family members will need to be treated for. If you have a special problem or concern, make sure the plan will provide you access to the drugs, specialists, or hospitals you need. And don't make a decision solely on cost, unless you

■ **THE NEW HEALTH CARE LANDSCAPE**

Fewer than half of all Americans still see doctors on a fee-for-service basis.

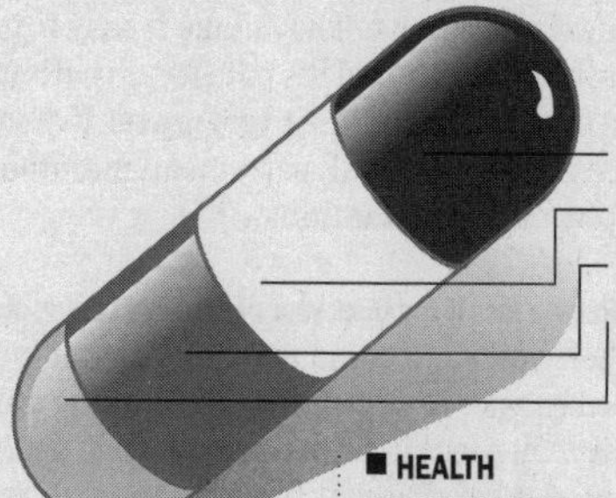

TYPE OF HEALTH CARE	ENROLLMENT
FEE-FOR-SERVICE	30%
HEALTH MAINTENANCE ORGANIZATION	27%
PREFERRED PROVIDER ORGANIZATION	24%
POINT-OF-SERVICE	19%

■ **FEE-FOR-SERVICE** Private care where the patient chooses any doctor he or she wants to see. The patient pays according to the service rendered.

■ **HEALTH MAINTENANCE ORGANIZATION (HMO)** Managed care where the patient is limited to seeing doctors employed by the HMO, and there is a set fee for the visit, no matter what service is performed.

■ **PREFERRED PROVIDER ORGANIZATION (PPO)** Managed care where the patient chooses from a list of specific doctors in his or her area and pays a set fee for the consultation, no matter what service is performed.

■ **POINT-OF-SERVICE** Managed care where the patient chooses from a list of doctors a primary care physician who coordinates all of his or her care. Patients who want to see a specialist must obtain the primary care physician's approval first.

SOURCE: KPMG Peat Marwick LLP, survey of employer-sponsored health benefits, 1995.

can't afford anything but the cheapest plan.

■ **Find out what's covered, and what's not, before you sign up with a health plan.** If you're concerned about special medical needs or problems, ask which services are covered in the benefits package offered and which have to be paid for out-of-pocket. Be sure to ask your doctor if the plan imposes any limits on his ability to talk to you about your medical needs.

■ **Ask your primary care doctor which, if any, plans he or she participates in.** You may not want to join an HMO if you've already established a relationship with a physician not on the list. However, you can opt for a point-of-service plan that allows you to go outside the HMO's network of providers for an additional fee.

■ **Learn when referrals are allowed, and when they're not.** Most HMOs require that patients first see a primary care doctor, who determines whether you need to see a specialist. Sometimes decisions are not in the primary care doctor's hands. Ask him under what circumstances he would give a referral, and whether somebody else approves referrals, which is likely the case if you're in an HMO. If you have a particular illness like Multiple Sclerosis (MS), make sure your plan allows you access to a specialist in MS.

■ **Compare the out-of-pocket costs of the health plans you're considering.** In many fee-for-service plans you pay an annual deductible and a percentage of each medical bill. Look at how much your monthly premium and deductibles will be as well as your maximum out-of-pocket costs—it could be $2,500 or $12,000. If you're in an HMO, you may have to pay a fixed amount, and in PPOs, a percentage of the cost of each visit. Managed care plans are generally cheaper than fee-for-service plans, but be sure to compare co-payment requirements for prescription drugs and office visits for HMOs.

■ **Know which hospitals and network of providers you'll be limited to if you sign up.** Many people are reluctant to enroll in managed care plans because they're concerned that if they get sick the plan won't allow them to get the best possible treatment at so-called centers of excellence. If you're not satisfied with the choice of hospitals, try a preferred provider organization (PPO), which usually offers a range of hospitals in the plan, or an HMO with a point-of-service option.

Make sure you look at the whole range of providers. With some HMOs you don't actually receive medical care from the HMO's total network, or main group of doctors, but from a contracting medical group or independent practice association (IPA), a network of providers that contracts with the HMO. So the HMO may have a wonderful list of doctors, but that isn't going to help you at all. For example, your care could be very limited if your IPA only has two heart specialists they've contracted with.

■ **Use the coordinated care and preventive services provided by managed care.** There are benefits to joining a managed care plan aside from reduced cost. In the best plans, somebody really is coordinating your care and making sure you get the referrals you need, and that's a huge plus. HMOs do a very good job of providing preventive care because it's very cost-effective. They make it easy to get preventive care, and it's paid for, so patients are much more willing to get preventive services like a physical, pap smear, mammography or immunizations.

■ **Raise a fuss if you think your needs aren't being met.** When you're in a managed care plan, you need to take responsibility for making sure that what needs to get done gets done. If you're denied a service you think is critical, you should first talk to your primary care doctor. You can also file a grievance with the HMO challenging a health care provider's judgment and requesting that a decision not to provide or pay for care be reconsidered. All HMOs have grievance procedures, although they do vary. If need be, investigate whether there's an outside group available to help you. Some communities have nonprofit advocacy groups and at least half of all states have hot lines that you can call to complain and ask for an investigation if you have a grievance.

HEALTH PLANS

DOES YOUR HMO MEASURE UP?

Report cards can shed light on whether your plan is a good one

Membership in health maintenance organizations (HMOs) has doubled in the last decade, from roughly 21 million Americans enrolled in 1985 to 42 million today. But when it comes to selecting an HMO or other managed care plan, most people usually end up judging by word of mouth, or simply base the decision on cost, because there's scant information available comparing the quality of care offered by the nation's 574 HMOs.

Managed care report cards that evaluate health plans using standardized criteria are one tool that can educate consumers and make it easier for them to reliably compare the performance of HMOs nationwide. Several business coalitions, large employers, and nonprofit organizations have completed report cards on managed care plans, and some health care plans publish their own report cards or surveys of members. The National Commission for Quality Assurance (NCQA), a nonprofit organization that recently tested a system of standardized performance measures, highlights key measures to consider when reading report cards:

■ **MEMBER SATISFACTION:** Most report cards include a survey of member satisfaction. Two of the most telling measures are the percentage of enrollees who would recommend the plan to others and how many intend to switch plans.

■ **ACCESS TO CARE:** Common complaints about HMOs include longer waits for visits and a limiting choice of doctors. You can learn how difficult it is to see a specific doctor, how long it takes to get an appointment, and whether members think exams are sufficiently thorough.

■ **DELIVERY OF SERVICES:** One key indicator of HMO quality is how well a plan delivers preventive services like childhood immunizations, cholesterol screenings, and pap smears. Report cards also evaluate a plan's ability to treat serious conditions. For example, you can compare the percentage of members in different plans who undergo operations like coronary bypass, angioplasty, and cesarean sections. A study at a New Orleans hospital found that merely using report cards lowered the cesarean section rate by 30 percent. However, it's difficult to gauge how well an HMO provides care because there's no consensus on the appropriate level of care needed for individual patients.

If you rely on a report card to evaluate a health plan, be sure that the data are audited by an outside company and are based on standard performance measures like HEDIS (the Health Plan Employer Data and Information Set), which apply uniform criteria when analyzing a plan. Report cards should also compare a plan's performance against widely accepted benchmarks such as those defined by the federal government's Healthy People 2000, the nation's health goals for the year 2000.

EXPERT SOURCE

The National Commission for Quality Assurance (NCQA) began a voluntary accreditation process for HMOs in 1991. Consumers can find out how a plan fared on a range of criteria, including whether it checks its doctors' histories for malpractice and encourages members to take preventive tests. For a free copy of the NCQA accreditation status list, call ☎ 202-955-3515.

THE PATIENT'S BILL OF RIGHTS

Patients should be considered partners in their hospital care. The American Hospital Association has proposed a patient's bill of rights to help make your care as effective as possible.

WHILE YOU ARE A PATIENT IN THE HOSPITAL, YOU HAVE THE RIGHT:

■ TO CONSIDERATE and respectful care.

■ TO BE WELL INFORMED about your illness, possible treatments, and likely outcome and to discuss this information with your doctor. You have the right to know the names and roles of people treating you.

■ TO CONSENT TO OR REFUSE a treatment, as permitted by law, throughout your hospital stay. If you refuse a recommended treatment, you will receive other needed and available care.

■ TO HAVE an advance directive, such as a living will or health-care proxy. These documents express your choices about your future care or name someone to decide if you cannot speak for yourself. If you have a written advance directive, you should provide a copy to the hospital, your family, and your doctor.

■ TO PRIVACY. The hospital, your doctor, and others caring for you will protect your privacy as much as possible.

■ TO EXPECT that treatment records are confidential unless you have given permission to release information or reporting is required or permitted by law. When the hospital releases records to others, such as insurers, it emphasizes that the records are confidential.

■ TO REVIEW your medical records and to have the information explained, except when restricted by law.

■ TO EXPECT that the hospital will give you necessary health services to the best of its ability. Treatment, referral, or transfer may be recommended. If a transfer is recommended or requested, you will be informed of risks, benefits, and alternatives. You will not be transferred until the other institution agrees to accept you.

■ TO KNOW if this hospital has relationships with outside parties that may influence your treatment and care. These relationships may be with educational institutions, other health-care providers, or insurers.

■ TO CONSENT OR DECLINE to take part in research affecting your care. If you choose not to take part, you will receive the most effective care the hospital otherwise provides.

■ TO BE TOLD of realistic care alternatives when hospital care is no longer appropriate.

■ TO KNOW about hospital rules that affect you and your treatment and about charges and payment methods. You have the right to know about hospital resources, such as patient representatives or ethics committees that can help you resolve problems and questions about your hospital stay and care.

YOU HAVE RESPONSIBILITIES AS A PATIENT. You are responsible for providing information about your health, including past illness, hospital stays, use of medicine. You are responsible for asking questions when you do not understand information or instructions. If you believe you can't follow through with your treatment, you are responsible for telling your doctor.

The hospital works to provide care efficiently and fairly to all patients and the community. You and your visitors are responsible for being considerate of the needs of other patients, staff and the hospital. You are responsible for providing information for insurance and for working with the hospital to arrange payment, when needed.

Your health depends not just on your hospital care but, in the longterm, on the decisions you make in your daily life. You are responsible for recognizing the effect of lifestyle on your personal health.

A hospital serves many purposes. Hospitals work to improve people's health; treat people with injury and disease; educate doctors, health professionals, patients, and community members; and improve understanding of health and disease. In carrying out these activities, their institution works to respect your value and dignity.

EXPERT LIST

THE BEST HOSPITALS IN AMERICA

Each year, the magazine U.S. News & World Report *publishes a special report ranking America's best hospitals in 16 categories. The magazine's rating system was designed by the National Opinion Research Center, a social-science research group at the University of Chicago. The model combines three years' worth of reputational surveys conducted by the magazine. Board-certified specialists from across the country in each of the highlighted categories were asked to nominate the five best hospitals in their specialties, without regard to cost or location. Only major academic hospitals providing comprehensive, state-of-the-art care were eligible for consideration. Among the objective measures also factored in were everything from the ratio of nurses and board-certified specialists to hospital beds and the availability of advanced technology in various specialties, to death rates in fields where that is relevant.*

■ AIDS: Hospitals specializing in AIDS patients focus on the prevention and treatment of infections and related complications that develop as the body's immune system deteriorates. Outpatient care has become standard in many of the hospitals; inpatient wards include pediatric intensive care units.

	Hospital	Overall score	Reputational score	Ratio of staff to beds: Residents	R.N.s	Brd.-cert. M.D.s	Mortality rate	Tech. score	Dischg. plan
1	**San Francisco General Hospital Medical Center**	100.0	59.1%	1.19	1.52	0.011	0.95	8	2
2	**Johns Hopkins Hospital, Baltimore***	66.1	31.2%	0.73	1.43	0.084	0.97	11	2
3	**Massachusetts General Hospital, Boston***	62.3	26.8%	1.00	1.14	0.085	0.88	11	2
4	**U. of California, San Francisco Medical Center***	55.0	19.4%	1.03	1.82	0.435	0.89	10	2
5	**UCLA Medical Center, Los Angeles***	54.2	19.7%	1.52	1.20	0.023	0.66	11	2
6	**U. of Miami, Jackson Memorial Hospital***	42.8	15.4%	0.85	1.39	0.046	1.12	8	2
7	**Memorial Sloan-Kettering Cancer Center, N.Y.***	41.4	12.6%	0.38	1.37	0.074	0.91	7	2
8	**New York U. Medical Center, New York***	39.5	9.7%	1.30	1.15	0.360	0.98	8	2
9	**New York Hospital–Cornell Medical Center***	37.9	10.9%	0.79	1.00	0.113	1.07	10	2
10	**U. of Washington Medical Center, Seattle***	35.6	4.3%	1.05	2.06	0.440	0.84	8	2
11	**Stanford U. Medical Center, Stanford, Calif.***	35.4	6.1%	1.34	0.86	0.147	0.90	9	2
12	**Beth Israel Hospital, Boston***	35.2	4.4%	0.57	1.93	0.590	0.85	8	2
13	**New England Deaconess Hospital, Boston***	35.2	7.2%	1.08	1.33	0.089	0.99	9	2
14	**Duke U. Medical Center, Durham, N.C.***	34.5	5.0%	0.91	1.61	0.081	0.90	10	2
15	**UCSD Medical Center, San Diego***	33.6	2.8%	1.65	2.17	0.049	0.75	8	2
16	**Columbia-Presbyterian Medical Center, N.Y.***	33.0	8.3%	0.85	1.05	0.111	1.25	11	2
17	**Northwestern Memorial Hospital, Chicago***	32.7	6.4%	0.43	1.03	0.134	0.99	9	2
18	**Rush-Presbyterian–St. Luke's Med. Ctr., Chicago***	32.3	2.9%	1.05	1.24	0.224	0.81	10	2
19	**Mount Sinai Medical Center, New York***	31.6	4.9%	0.99	1.50	0.253	1.09	9	2

TERMS:

REPUTATIONAL SCORE: Percentage of doctors surveyed who named the hospital.

RESIDENTS TO BEDS: Ratio of interns and residents to beds.

R.N.s TO BEDS: Ratio of full-time registered nurses to beds.

BOARD-CERTIFIED M.D.s TO BEDS: Ratio of doctors certified in a specialty to the number of beds.

MORTALITY RATE: Ratio of actual to expected deaths (lower is better). Rate is specialty-specific except for AIDS and gynecology.

TECHNOLOGY SCORE: Specialty-specific index from 0 to 11 (AIDS).

DISCHARGE PLANNING: Number of post-discharge services available, from 0 to 2.

* Indicates member of Council of Teaching Hospitals.

■ **EXPERT LIST**

	Hospital	Overall score	Reputational score	Ratio of staff to beds: Residents	R.N.s	Brd.-cert. M.D.s	Mortality rate	Tech. score	Dischg. plan
20	**University Hospital, Portland, Ore.***	31.1	0.3%	1.54	2.31	0.164	0.80	9	2
21	**Boston City Hospital**	31.0	1.8%	1.64	1.37	0.545	0.75	7	2
22	**Barnes Hospital, St. Louis***	30.8	4.0%	0.89	0.82	0.273	0.98	9	2
23	**Montefiore Medical Center, Bronx, N.Y.***	30.3	6.2%	0.53	1.28	0.095	1.19	10	2
24	**Henry Ford Hospital, Detroit***	30.2	1.3%	1.34	1.50	0.301	0.96	10	2
25	**Cleveland Clinic***	30.1	1.2%	1.22	1.47	0.015	0.87	10	2

■ **CANCER:** Cancer is a group of diseases in which cells grow uncontrollably and spread throughout the body. Treatment for most cancers includes a combination of surgery, chemotherapy, and radiation. The top hospitals are on the cutting edge of experimental treatments.

	Hospital	Overall score	Reputational score	Ratio of staff to beds: Residents	R.N.s	Brd.-cert. M.D.s	Mortality rate	Tech. score	Inpatient op. to beds
1.	**Memorial Sloan–Kettering Cancer Center, New York***	100.0	70.8%	0.38	1.37	0.083	0.97	9	7.93
2.	**U. of Texas M.D. Anderson Cancer Center, Houston***	93.2	63.1%	0.70	1.88	0.010	0.27	11	7.18
3.	**Dana–Farber Cancer Institute, Boston**	74.1	46.7%	0.49	1.58	0.964	0.01	4	12.91
4.	**Johns Hopkins Hospital, Baltimore***	47.7	28.7%	0.73	1.43	0.011	0.53	11	1.57
5.	**Mayo Clinic, Rochester, Minn.***	42.3	27.5%	0.24	0.77	0.026	0.57	8	3.03
6.	**Stanford U. Hospital, Stanford, Calif.***	30.9	15.3%	1.34	0.86	0.028	0.80	10	1.64
7.	**U. of Washington Medical Center, Seattle***	30.7	13.1%	1.05	2.06	0.039	0.58	9	2.11
8.	**Duke U. Medical Center, Durham, N.C.***	28.7	12.3%	0.91	1.61	0.028	0.71	12	2.76
9.	**University of Chicago Hospitals***	25.1	8.1%	1.64	1.38	0.034	0.59	11	2.76
10.	**Roswell Park Cancer Institute, Buffalo**	24.7	8.5%	0.68	2.58	0.000	0.52	9	14.09
11.	**U. of Calif. San Francisco Medical Center***	21.2	6.0%	1.03	1.82	0.021	0.59	11	0.92
12.	**Massachusetts General Hospital, Boston***	21.1	7.3%	1.00	1.14	0.011	0.80	12	2.41
13.	**UCLA Medical Center, Los Angeles***	19.4	4.4%	1.52	1.20	0.031	0.42	11	2.03
14.	**Hospital of the U. of Pennsylvania, Philadelphia***	19.2	4.0%	1.72	1.33	0.033	0.86	10	1.87
15.	**U. of Calif. Davis Medical Center***	19.2	0.8%	1.54	2.81	0.017	0.61	11	1.29
16.	**Indiana U. Medical Center, Indianapolis***	18.4	3.4%	1.10	1.86	0.022	0.57	11	1.31
17.	**UCSD Medical Center, San Diego***	16.8	0.4%	1.65	2.17	0.058	0.54	8	1.66
18.	**University Hospital, Portland, Ore.***	16.2	0.0%	1.54	2.31	0.017	0.40	9	1.45
19.	**Fox Chase Cancer Center, Philadelphia**	16.1	3.7%	0.36	1.42	0.290	0.14	7	15.49
20.	**University Medical Center, Tucson, Ariz.***	15.9	3.0%	0.74	1.73	0.053	0.71	9	1.51
21.	**U. of Nebraska Medical Center, Omaha***	15.9	2.8%	1.37	1.23	0.000	0.89	10	0.99
22.	**U. of Wisconsin Hospital and Clinics, Madison***	15.8	2.0%	1.30	1.24	0.039	0.62	11	2.14
23.	**Cleveland Clinic***	15.8	1.9%	1.22	1.47	0.009	0.64	11	1.80
24.	**Vanderbilt University Hospital and Clinic, Nashville***	15.6	1.9%	1.21	1.29	0.011	0.64	12	1.82
25.	**University Hospitals of Cleveland***	15.5	0.0%	1.60	1.73	0.032	0.79	12	1.54

TERMS:

REPUTATIONAL SCORE: Percentage of doctors surveyed who named the hospital.

RESIDENTS TO BEDS: Ratio of interns and residents to beds.

R.N.s TO BEDS: Ratio of full-time registered nurses to beds.

BOARD-CERTIFIED M.D.sTO BEDS: Ratio of doctors certified in a specialty to the number of beds.

MORTALITY RATE: Ratio of actual to expected deaths (lower is better). Rate is specialty-specific except for AIDS and gynecology.

TECHNOLOGY SCORE: Specialty-specific index from 0 to 12 (cancer), 0 to 10 (cardiology), 0 to 11 (endocrinology).

INPATIENT OPERATIONS TO BEDS: Ratio of annual inpatient specialty-related procedures to beds.

* Indicates member of Council of Teaching Hospitals.

SOURCE: Reprinted from *U.S. News & World Report*, July 24, 1995. ©1995.

■ **EXPERT LIST**

■ **CARDIOLOGY:** At cardiology departments, doctors treat a variety of heart and circulatory disorders from abnormal rhythm of the heart to congestive heart failure. Most hospital cardiac units can perform routine procedures such as coronary bypass surgery, but complex cases that may involve valve problems or congenital heart disease are best treated at a large medical center.

Hospital	Overall score	Reputational score	Ratio of staff to beds: Residents	R.N.s	Brd.-cert. M.D.s	Mortality rate	Tech. score	Inpatient op. to beds
1. Cleveland Clinic*	100.00	49.9%	1.22	1.47	0.035	0.90	10	9.03
2. Mayo Clinic, Rochester, Minn.*	93.4	49.0%	0.24	0.77	0.053	0.82	8	6.57
3. Texas Heart Institute–St. Luke's Episcopal, Houston*	81.4	24.6%	0.26	1.36	0.064	1.52	9	10.00
4. Massachusetts General Hospital, Boston*	73.3	32.5%	1.00	1.14	0.034	0.71	10	7.24
5. Duke University Medical Center, Durham, N.C.*	63.7	25.1%	0.91	1.61	0.054	0.85	10	6.30
6. Brigham and Women's Hospital, Boston*	56.3	23.2%	1.49	0.79	0.071	1.03	9	5.70
7. Stanford University Hospital, Stanford, Calif.*	54.1	20.3%	1.34	0.86	0.102	0.93	9	5.19
8. Emory University Hospital, Atlanta*	48.3	17.6%	0.71	1.28	0.037	0.95	8	9.57
9. Johns Hopkins Hospital, Baltimore*	40.5	15.6%	0.73	1.43	0.033	1.21	10	4.66
10. U. of Calif. San Francisco Medical Center*	37.0	8.4%	1.03	1.82	0.043	0.96	9	2.51
11. Columbia-Presbyterian Medical Center, New York*	33.7	10.8%	0.85	1.05	0.044	1.16	10	3.76
12. UCLA Medical Center, Los Angeles*	33.4	4.2%	1.52	1.20	0.034	0.68	10	3.68
13. U. of Alabama Hospital, Birmingham*	31.9	10.2%	0.82	0.92	0.040	1.17	9	6.48
14. Beth Israel Hospital, Boston*	31.7	3.4%	0.57	1.93	0.087	0.87	9	10.50
15. UCSD Medical Center, San Diego*	30.9	0.6%	1.65	2.17	0.100	0.80	7	3.04
16. University of Chicago Hospitals*	29.7	1.0%	1.64	1.38	0.033	0.79	10	4.24
17. Methodist Hospital, Houston*	29.6	8.6%	0.19	1.33	0.058	1.13	9	5.03
18. Cedars-Sinai Medical Center, Los Angeles*	29.4	7.5%	0.51	0.83	0.113	1.06	9	6.95
19. Mount Sinai Medical Center, New York*	29.1	2.0%	0.99	1.50	0.068	0.84	8	3.94
20. Barnes Hospital, St. Louis*	28.8	6.9%	0.89	0.82	0.000	1.06	10	5.45
21. University Hospital, Portland, Ore.*	28.6	0.0%	1.54	2.31	0.043	0.93	9	2.76
22. Hospital of the U. of Pennsylvania, Philadelphia*	28.4	0.8%	1.72	1.33	0.035	0.91	9	4.88
23. New York Hospital–Cornell Medical Center*	28.3	4.7%	0.79	1.00	0.034	0.96	9	3.80
24. U. of Washington Medical Center, Seattle*	28.0	0.0%	1.05	2.06	0.132	0.75	8	4.35
25. U. of California Davis Medical Center*	27.9	0.3%	1.54	2.81	0.017	1.02	9	3.22

■ **ENDOCRINOLOGY:** Clinical endrocrinologists diagnose and treat patients with problems involving the hormone-secreting endocrine glands, which affect a person's rate of growth, metabolism, and sexual development. These specialized internists consult with other physicians on a wide range of disorders such as diabetes, osteoporosis, thyroid disorders, infertility, high cholesterol, and hormone-producing tumors.

Hospital	Overall score	Reputational score	Ratio of staff to beds: Residents	R.N.s	Brd.-cert. M.D.s	Mortality rate	Tech. score
1. Mayo Clinic, Rochester, Minn.*	100.0	65.1%	0.24	0.77	0.060	0.48	8
2. Massachusetts General Hospital, Boston*	92.0	58.2%	1.00	1.14	0.085	0.93	11
3. U. of California San Francisco Medical Center*	52.2	24.0%	1.03	1.82	0.435	0.78	10
4. Johns Hopkins Hospital, Baltimore*	41.8	18.4%	0.73	1.43	0.084	0.68	11
5. Barnes Hospital, St. Louis*	39.1	17.8%	0.89	0.82	0.273	0.86	11
6. UCLA Medical Center, Los Angeles*	37.9	14.1%	1.52	1.20	0.023	0.34	11

■ **EXPERT LIST**

Hospital	Overall score	Reputational score	Ratio of staff to beds: Residents	R.N.s	Brd.-cert. M.D.s	Mortality rate	Tech. score
7. University of Chicago Hospitals*	35.5	12.5%	1.64	1.38	0.074	0.78	11
8. U. of Michigan Medical Center, Ann Arbor*	34.9	12.8%	1.00	1.29	0.086	0.62	10
9. New England Deaconess Hospital, Boston*	34.7	13.0%	1.08	1.33	0.089	0.72	10
10. U. of Washington Medical Center, Seattle*	34.2	11.3%	1.05	2.06	0.440	1.00	10
11. Brigham and Women's Hospital, Boston*	33.5	13.1%	1.49	0.79	0.179	0.89	10
12. Parkland Memorial Hospital, Dallas*	28.1	10.4%	1.35	0.93	0.039	1.00	10
13. Duke U. Medical Center, Durham, N.C.*	27.1	6.7%	0.91	1.61	0.081	0.69	11
14. Vanderbilt U. Hospital and Clinic, Nashville*	26.8	7.9%	1.21	1.29	0.171	0.93	11
15. U. of Va. Health Sciences Center, Charlottesville*	26.3	6.0%	1.41	1.92	0.101	0.90	10
16. Beth Israel Hospital, Boston*	25.9	5.0%	0.57	1.93	0.590	0.86	9
17. Stanford U. Hospital, Stanford, Calif.*	25.4	5.2%	1.34	0.86	0.147	0.38	11
18. University Hospital, Portland, Ore.*	24.9	2.3%	1.54	2.31	0.164	0.73	9
19. U. of Pittsburgh–Presbyterian University Hospital*	24.3	3.1%	1.48	2.10	0.291	0.91	9
20. UCSD Medical Center, San Diego*	22.9	0.8%	1.65	2.17	0.049	0.55	8
21. Columbia-Presbyterian Medical Center, New York*	22.6	8.2%	0.85	1.05	0.111	1.35	10
22. Cleveland Clinic*	22.5	5.5%	1.22	1.47	0.015	1.02	11
23. Hospital of the U. of Pennsylvania, Philadelphia*	22.5	2.4%	1.72	1.33	0.007	0.71	11
24. U. of Texas M.D. Anderson Cancer Center, Houston*	21.7	2.2%	0.70	1.88	0.083	0.48	11
25. U. of Calif. Davis Medical Center*	20.7	0.0%	1.54	2.81	0.032	0.90	10

■ **GYNECOLOGY:** Usually linked with obstetrics and the care of routine and high-risk pregnancies, gynecology departments also run the gamut of medical specialties. For example, cancers of the reproductive tract demand doctors trained in oncology as well as gynecology.

Hospital	Overall score	Reputational score	Ratio of staff to beds: Residents	R.N.s	Brd.-cert. M.D.s	Mortality rate	Tech. score	Inpatient op. to beds
1. Johns Hopkins Hospital, Baltimore	100.0	29.5%	0.73	1.43	0.046	0.97	10	0.46
2. Mayo Clinic, Rochester, Minn.	95.4	30.0%	0.24	0.77	0.014	0.72	6	0.35
3. U. of Texas M.D. Anderson Cancer Center, Houston	85.9	22.5%	0.70	1.88	0.040	0.38	9	0.75
4. Brigham and Women's Hospital, Boston	80.9	20.9%	1.49	0.79	0.127	0.91	9	0.66
5. Massachusetts General Hospital, Boston	57.7	12.0%	1.00	1.14	0.046	0.88	10	0.53
6. Los Angeles County–USC Medical Center	55.9	11.7%	1.21	1.30	0.021	0.88	7	0.03
7. Duke U. Medical Center, Durham, N.C.	53.9	10.2%	0.91	1.61	0.028	0.90	10	0.45
8. Cleveland Clinic	50.3	8.8%	1.22	1.47	0.009	0.87	9	0.48
9. University of Chicago Hospitals	49.2	7.2%	1.64	1.38	0.036	0.80	10	0.37

TERMS:

REPUTATIONAL SCORE: Percentage of doctors surveyed who named the hospital.

RESIDENTS TO BEDS: Ratio of interns and residents to beds.

R.N.s TO BEDS: Ratio of full-time registered nurses to beds.

BOARD-CERTIFIED M.D.s TO BEDS: Ratio of doctors certified in a specialty to the number of beds.

MORTALITY RATE: Ratio of actual to expected deaths (lower is better). Rate is specialty-specific except for AIDS and gynecology.

TECHNOLOGY SCORE: Specialty-specific index from 0 to 11 (endocrinology and gynecology), 0 to 9 (neurology).

INPATIENT OPERATIONS TO BEDS: Ratio of annual inpatient specialty-related procedures to beds.

* Indicates member of Council of Teaching Hospitals.

SOURCE: Reprinted from *U.S. News & World Report*, July 24, 1995. ©1995.

■ **EXPERT LIST**

Hospital	Overall score	Reputational score	Ratio of staff to beds: Residents	R.N.s	Brd.-cert. M.D.s	Mortality rate	Tech. score	Inpatient op. to beds
10. UCLA Medical Center, Los Angeles	49.1	7.8%	1.52	1.20	0.028	0.66	10	0.49
11. Memorial Sloan-Kettering Cancer Center, New York	45.6	9.4%	0.38	1.37	0.007	0.91	7	0.50
12. Parkland Memorial Hospital, Dallas	43.9	10.2%	1.35	0.93	0.024	1.22	9	0.11
13. Stanford U. Hospital, Stanford, Calif.	43.0	6.1%	1.34	0.86	0.107	0.90	9	0.39
14. U. of Calif. San Francisco Medical Center	42.6	5.3%	1.03	1.82	0.043	0.89	9	0.21
15. Hospital of the U. of Pennsylvania, Philadelphia	39.7	4.5%	1.72	1.33	0.036	0.97	10	0.35
16. Yale–New Haven Hospital, New Haven, Conn.	38.4	5.9%	1.12	1.23	0.103	1.06	9	0.60
17. U. of Washington Medical Center, Seattle	37.1	2.2%	1.05	2.06	0.093	0.84	9	0.59
18. Roswell Park Cancer Institute, Buffalo	36.1	2.5%	0.68	2.58	0.023	0.56	8	0.91
19. Beth Israel Hospital, Boston	35.3	3.0%	0.57	1.93	0.132	0.85	7	0.55
20. UCSD Medical Center, San Diego	35.0	0.8%	1.65	2.17	0.078	0.75	7	0.33
21. U. of North Carolina Hospitals, Chapel Hill	33.8	4.5%	1.41	1.71	0.064	1.23	9	0.50
22. Thomas Jefferson University Hospital, Philadelphia	33.4	1.9%	0.96	1.44	0.102	0.85	9	0.41
23. University Hospital, Portland, Ore.	33.1	0.0%	1.54	2.31	0.055	0.80	8	0.38
24. U. of Calif. Davis Medical Center	32.8	0.5%	1.54	2.81	0.025	1.01	9	0.36
25. Northwestern Memorial Hospital, Chicago	32.8	4.6%	0.43	1.03	0.088	0.99	9	0.44

■ **NEUROLOGY:** Neurology delves into disorders of the central nervous systems and muscles and has recently been marked by promising experimental therapies, such as the drug Betaseron for mulltiple sclerosis and Tacrine for Alzheimer's disease. Hospitals with outstanding neurology departments often have centers dedicated to epilepsy or other specific diseases.

Hospital	Overall score	Reputational score	Ratio of staff to beds: Residents	R.N.s	Brd.-cert. M.D.s	Mortality rate	Tech. score
1. Mayo Clinic, Rochester, Minn.*	100.0	51.5%	0.24	0.77	0.035	0.72	6
2. Johns Hopkins Hospital, Baltimore*	80.7	38.7%	0.73	1.43	0.014	0.84	9
3. U. of Calif. San Francisco Medical Center*	63.9	27.3%	1.03	1.82	0.029	0.91	8
4. Massachusetts General Hospital, Boston*	61.8	28.6%	1.00	1.14	0.014	1.00	9
5. Columbia-Presbyterian Medical Center, New York*	54.8	23.7%	0.85	1.05	0.040	1.02	9
6. UCLA Medical Center, Los Angeles*	41.4	9,6%	1.52	1.20	0.056	0.69	9
7. Cleveland Clinic*	40.6	10.6%	1.22	1.47	0.023	0.62	9
8. New York Hospital–Cornell Medical Center*	40.2	12.8%	0.79	1.00	0.024	0.78	7
9. Barnes Hospital, St. Louis*	39.6	12.5%	0.89	0.82	0.042	0.87	9
10. Hospital of the U. of Pennsylvania, Philadelphia*	36.1	9.2%	1.72	1.33	0.051	1.02	9
11. Duke U. Medical Center, Durham, N.C.*	33.2	8.6%	0.91	1.61	0.017	0.89	9
12. Brigham and Women's Hospital, Boston*	31.1	5.3%	1.49	0.79	0.036	0.79	8
13. New York University Medical Center*	28.6	3.7%	1.30	1.15	0.024	0.73	7
14. University of Illinois Hospital and Clinics, Chicago*	27.7	2.4%	1.29	1.95	0.017	0.50	6
15. Stanford University Hospital, Stanford, Calif.*	27.5	3.2%	1.34	0.86	0.031	0.79	9
16. University of Chicago Hospitals*	27.3	1.5%	1.64	1.38	0.023	0.67	9
17. University of Washington Medical Center, Seattle*	27.0	2.6%	1.05	2.06	0.047	0.89	8
18. Beth Israel Hospital, Boston*	26.8	1.1%	0.57	1.93	0.087	0.82	7

SOURCE: Reprinted from *U.S. News & World Report*, July 24, 1995. ©1995.

■ **EXPERT LIST**

Hospital	Overall score	Reputational score	Ratio of staff to beds: Residents	R.N.s	Brd.-cert. M.D.s	Mortality rate	Tech. score
19. Rush-Presbyterian–St. Luke's Medical Center, Chicago*	26.7	2.4%	1.05	1.24	0.031	0.53	8
22. U. of Pittsburgh–Presbyterian U. Hospital*	26.0	2.1%	1.48	2.10	0.066	1.05	7
21. University Hospital, Portland, Ore.*	25.8	0.6%	1.54	2.31	0.063	0.95	7
22. Mount Sinai Medical Center, New York*	25.4	1.9%	0.99	1.50	0.026	0.78	7
23. U. of Iowa Hospital and Clinics, Iowa City*	24.9	4.6%	0.96	1.34	0.015	0.97	9
24. U. of Michigan Medical Center, Ann Arbor*	24.9	5.3%	1.00	1.29	0.014	1.02	8
25. Georgetown University Hospital, Washington, D.C.*	24.7	1.1%	0.92	1.59	0.028	0.77	8

■ **ORTHOPEDICS:** The branch of surgery dealing with problems of bones, joints, and muscles covers patients from children born with skeletal defects such as spina bifida to seniors crippled by diseases such as osteoporosis. Athletes of all ages with knee or elbow injuries also receive care from professionals in this specialty, a major player in the field of sports medicine. A top hospital can benefit those requiring complicated bone surgery like total hip replacement and delicate hand or facial surgery. Once an orthopedic problem is corrected, intensive rehabilitation is often needed for a full recovery of function, so physical therapists play a key role in the department.

Hospital	Overall score	Reputational score	Ratio of staff to beds: Residents	R.N.s	Brd.-cert. M.D.s	Mortality rate	Tech. score	Inpatient op. to beds
1. Mayo Clinic, Rochester, Minn.*	100.0	41.7%	0.24	0.77	0.023	0.55	4	1.89
2. Hospital for Special Surgery, New York*	95.9	36.6%	0.68	0.78	0.271	0.24	4	17.09
3. Massachusetts General Hospital, Boston*	76.5	28.7%	1.00	1.14	0.026	0.72	5	2.29
4. Johns Hopkins Hospital, Baltimore*	45.3	14.4%	0.73	1.43	0.026	0.80	5	1.11
5. Duke U. Medical Center, Durham, N.C .*	41.0	11.4%	0.91	1.61	0.016	0.75	5	1.54
6. UCLA Medical Center, Los Angeles*	38.2	10.5%	1.52	1.20	0.015	0.93	5	1.72
7. Cleveland Clinic*	37.7	8.8%	1.22	1.47	0.020	0.65	5	2.33
8. Hospital for Joint Diseases–Orthopedic Inst., New York*	33.9	7.6%	0.27	1.26	0.277	0.11	4	9.68
9. U. of Washington Medical Center, Seattle*	31.3	5.9%	1.05	2.06	0.070	0.72	4	1.54
10. U. of Iowa Hospitals and Clinics, Iowa City*	31.2	7.9%	0.96	1.34	0.020	0.92	5	1.08
11. Hospital for the U. of Pennsylvania, Philadelphia*	28.7	3.9%	1.72	1.33	0.036	0.61	5	1.65
12. Stanford U. Hospital, Stanford, Calif.*	26.9	4.0%	1.34	0.86	0.068	0.63	5	2.34
13. U. of Michigan Medical Center, Ann Arbor*	25.0	5.7%	1.00	1.29	0.025	1.16	5	1.21
14. U. of Texas M.D. Anderson Cancer Center, Houston*	24.4	2.9%	0.70	1.88	0.022	0.20	5	0.69
15. Brigham and Women's Hospital, Boston*	23.7	3.6%	1.49	0.79	0.034	0.79	4	2.37
16. UCSD Medical Center, San Diego*	23.1	1.0%	1.65	2.17	0.097	0.66	2	0.96
17. Thomas Jefferson University Hospital, Philadelphia*	22.9	2.5%	0.96	1.44	0.034	0.61	4	1.73
18. Vanderbilt University Hospital and Clinic, Nashville*	21.6	2.3%	1.21	1.29	0.018	0.80	5	1.62
19. University of Chicago Hospitals*	21.4	0.5%	1.64	1.38	0.011	0.55	5	1.38
20. U. of Wisconsin Hospital and Clinics, Madison*	21.1	1.0%	1.30	1.24	0.014	0.57	5	1.66
21. Harborview Medical Center, Seattle*	21.1	5.3%	0.37	1.73	0.049	1.24	2	1.21
22. U. of Calif. Davis Medical Center*	20.8	0.9%	1.54	2.81	0.021	1.10	4	1.42
23. U. of North Carolina Hospitals, Chapel Hill*	20.8	0.6%	1.41	1.71	0.018	0.68	4	1.21
24. Rush-Presbyterian–St. Luke's Medical Center, Chicago*	20.4	2.0%	1.05	1.24	0.039	0.76	4	1.83
25. University Hospitals, Oklahoma City*	20.1	0.0%	1.60	1.56	0.023	0.53	4	0.90

■ **EXPERT LIST**

■ **UROLOGY:** Urology departments treat problems of the female urinary tract and the male urinary and reproductive systems. Much of the focus of urologists is on the prostate, and these specialists help men sort out difficult options when faced with cancer. Prostate surgery and radiation can induce incontinence or impotence.

Hospital	Overall score	Reputational score	Ratio of staff to beds			Mortality rate	Tech. score	Inpatient op. to beds
			Residents	R.N.s	Brd.-cert. M.D.s			
1. Johns Hopkins Hospital, Baltimore*	100.0	63.5%	0.73	1.43	0.084	0.94	11	1.346
2. Mayo Clinic, Rochester, Minn.*	89.7	56.6%	0.24	0.77	0.060	0.74	8	2.840
3. Cleveland Clinic*	65.0	34.2%	1.22	1.47	0.015	0.62	10	1.593
4. UCLA Medical Center, Los Angeles*	59.8	29.6%	1.52	1.20	0.023	0.46	11	2.364
5. Stanford U. Hospital, Stanford, Calif.*	46.6	22.5%	1.34	0.86	0.147	0.96	11	1.692
6. Duke U. Medical Center, Durham, N.C.*	44.1	19.8%	0.91	1.61	0.081	0.86	11	1.680
7. Massachusetts General Hospital, Boston*	43.2	20.2%	1.00	1.14	0.085	0.92	11	2.018
8. Barnes Hospital, St. Louis*	42.3	21.3%	0.89	0.82	0.273	1.08	11	1.520
9. U. of Texas M.D. Anderson Cancer Center, Houston*	37.7	13.7%	0.70	1.88	0.083	0.51	10	1.763
10. Memorial Sloan-Kettering Cancer Center, New York*	34.8	16.0%	0.38	1.37	0.074	0.98	8	2.255
11. Baylor U. Medical Center, Dallas*	28.8	9.4%	0.29	1.38	0.093	0.72	8	1.439
12. New York Hospital–Cornell Medical Center*	28.6	10.3%	0.79	1.00	0.113	0.90	9	1.430
13. U. of Calif. San Francisco Medical Center*	28.1	8.2%	1.03	1.82	0.435	1.02	10	1.404
14. Indiana U. Medical Center, Indianapolis*	27.5	8.4%	1.10	1.86	0.107	1.13	10	1.401
15. U. of Washington Medical Center, Seattle*	26.9	4.9%	1.05	2.06	0.440	0.80	10	1.601
16. U. of Pittsburgh–Presbyterian U. Hospital*	26.8	2.9%	1.48	2.10	0.291	0.73	8	2.864
17. Hospital of the U. of Pennsylvania, Philadelphia*	25.6	4.6%	1.72	1.33	0.007	0.87	11	2.560
18. University Hospital, Portland, Ore.*	25.0	1.0%	1.54	2.31	0.164	0.53	9	2.083
19. U. of California Davis Medical Center*	24.8	0.5%	1.54	2.81	0.032	0.47	10	1.244
20. Columbia-Presbyterian Medical Center, New York*	23.9	7.4%	0.85	1.05	0.111	1.07	10	1.454
21. Emory University Hospital, Atlanta	23.8	4.8%	0.71	1.28	0.039	0.70	8	2.553
22. Brigham and Women's Hospital, Boston*	23.4	6.3%	1.49	0.79	0.179	1.16	10	1.350
23. UCSD Medical Center, San Diego*	23.0	0.5%	1.65	2.17	0.049	0.47	7	1.403
24. U. of Michigan Medical Center, Ann Arbor*	22.2	3.0%	1.00	1.29	0.086	0.77	10	1.301
25. U. of Iowa Hospitals and Clinics, Iowa City*	21.6	4.0%	0.96	1.34	0.053	0.92	11	1.301

TERMS:

REPUTATIONAL SCORE: Percentage of doctors surveyed who named the hospital.

RESIDENTS TO BEDS: Ratio of interns and residents to beds.

R.N.s TO BEDS: Ratio of full-time registered nurses to beds.

BOARD-CERTIFIED M.D.s TO BEDS: Ratio of doctors certified in a specialty to the number of beds.

MORTALITY RATE: Ratio of actual to expected deaths (lower is better). Rate is specialty-specific except for AIDS and gynecology.

TECHNOLOGY SCORE: Specialty-specific index from 0 to 5 (orthopedics), 0 to 6 (pediatrics), 0 to 8 (psychiatry), 0 to 9 (neurology), 0 to 10 (cardiology, gynecology, rehabilitation), 0 to 11 (endocrinology, urology), 0 to 26 (ophthalmology).

INPATIENT OPERATIONS TO BEDS: Ratio of annual inpatient specialty-related procedures to beds.

DISCHARGE PLANNING: Number of post-discharge services available, from 0 to 2.

GERIATRIC SERVICES; Include comprehensive geriatric assessment, Alzheimer's diagnostic assessment services, geriatric acute care, geriatric clinics, adult day care, respite care, emergency response for the elderly, senior membership services, and patient-representative services.

* Indicates member of Council of Teaching Hospitals.

SOURCE: Reprinted from *U.S. News & World Report*, July 24, 1995. ©1995.

■ **EXPERT LIST**

THE FOLLOWING FOUR FIELDS WERE BASED ON REPUTATIONAL SCORES ONLY BECAUSE DEATH RATES HAVE LITTLE OR NO RELATION TO TREATMENT IN THESE AREAS.

■ **OPHTHALMOLOGY:** Ophthalmology procedures, including surgery for cataracts, glaucoma, and detached retina, are generally done on an outpatient basis.

	Hospital	Reputational score	Board-cert. M.D.s to bed	Technology score	Inpatient ops. to bed
1.	Wilmer Eye Institute, Johns Hopkins Hospital, Baltimore*	57.4%	0.027	25	15.5
2.	Bascom Palmer Eye Institute, U. of Miami	53.7%	1.894	4	37.8
3.	Wills Eye Hospital, Philadelphia	44.8%	1.100	3	44.5
4.	Massachusetts Eye and Ear Infirmary, Boston	41.8%	0.024	4	78.4
5.	Jules Stein Eye Institute, UCLA Medical Center, Los Angeles*	33.1%	0.048	25	14.6
6.	U. of Iowa Hospitals and Clinics, Iowa City*	18.8%	0.023	24	25.5
7.	Barnes Hospital, St. Louis*	10.3%	0.057	23	11.1
8.	U. of Calif. San Francisco Medical Center*	9.7%	0.090	25	18.3
9.	Mayo Clinic, Rochester, Minn.*	8.3%	0.015	18	21.5
10.	Duke U. Medical Center, Durham, N.C.*	8.0%	0.018	25	15.3
11.	Manhattan Eye, Ear and Throat Hospital, New York	6.8%	2.330	1	95.9
12.	Doheny Eye Institute, Los Angeles	6.8%	0.762	0	31.3
13.	New York Eye and Ear Infirmary	6.6%	2.631	3	52.2
14.	U. of Michigan Medical Center, Ann Arbor*	5.4%	0.028	23	16.8
15.	Baylor U. Medical Center, Dallas*	4.7%	0.019	20	19.3
16.	Emory University Hospital, Atlanta*	4.2%	0.030	16	17.2
17.	U. of Illinois Hospital and Clinics, Chicago*	3.7%	0.022	19	13.7

■ **PEDIATRICS:** Desperately or chronically ill children can benefit from the range of specialists and level of counseling at a children's hospital or at the pediatric ward of a teaching hospital.

	Hospital	Reputational score	Board-cert. M.D.s to bed	Technology score	Inpatient ops. to bed
1.	Children's Hospital, Boston*	44.0%	0.307	5	1.60
2.	Children's Hospital of Philadelphia*	32.2%	0.133	4	1.89
3.	Johns Hopkins Hospital, Baltimore*	30.2%	0.069	6	1.43
4.	Children's Hospital Los Angeles	12.3%	0.051	0	1.45
5.	Children's Hospital of Pittsburgh*	9.1%	0.656	3	2.06
6.	Children's National Medical Center, Washington, D.C.*	8.6%	0.233	4	1.82
7.	Univ. Hospitals of Cleveland (Rainbow Babies and Children's Hospital)*	8.0%	0.279	6	1.73
8.	Children's Hospital, Denver	7.9%	0.468	5	1.74
9.	Children's Hospital Medical Center, Cincinnati*	7.7%	0.418	5	2.18
10.	Children's Memorial Hospital, Chicago*	6.3%	0.208	5	1.99
11.	Children's Hospital and Medical Center, Seattle*	6.2%	0.717	5	2.23
12.	Mayo Clinic, Rochester, Minn.*	6.1%	0.021	5	0.77
13.	Columbia-Presbyterian Medical Center, New York*	5.7%	0.179	6	1.05
14.	Texas Children's Hospital, Houston*	5.6%	0.411	4	1.97
15.	UCLA Medical Center, Los Angeles*	5.5%	0.128	5	1.20
16.	U. of Calif. San Francisco Medical Center*	5.3%	0.233	5	1.82
17.	Massachusetts General Hospital, Boston*	5.2%	0.069	5	1.14
18.	Stanford University Hospital, Stanford, Calif.*	5.2%	0.145	3	0.86
19.	Children's Medical Center of Dallas	4.7%	0.712	4	1.77

SOURCE: Reprinted from *U.S. News & World Report*, July 24, 1995. ©1995.

■ **EXPERT LIST**

■ PSYCHIATRY: Despite the increasing numbers of drugs for treating mental illness—Prozac, for example—psychotherapy still goes hand in hand with psychopharmacology. A good hospital employs drugs and talk therapy—as well as follow-up care after a patient is discharged.

	Hospital	Reputational score	Board-cert. M.D.s to beds	R.N.s to beds	Discharge planning	Technology score
1.	C.F. Menninger Memorial Hospital, Topeka, Kan.	14.4%	0.172	0.48	2	6
2.	Massachusetts General Hospital, Boston*	14.1%	0.032	1.14	2	7
3.	McLean Hospital, Belmont, Mass.	12.9%	0.370	0.66	2	8
4.	Johns Hopkins Hospital, Baltimore*	12.9%	0.032	1.43	2	8
5.	New York Hospital–Cornell Medical Center*	12.1%	0.227	1.00	2	8
6.	Mayo Clinic, Rochester, Minn.*	10.8%	0.024	0.77	2	8
7.	Columbia-Presbyterian Medical Center, New York*	9.2%	0.147	1.05	2	7
8	Sheppard and Enoch Pratt Hospital, Baltimore	8.6%	0.079	0.28	2	7
9	New York University Medical Center*	7.9%	0.120	1.15	2	2
10.	UCLA Neuropsychiatric Hospital, Los Angeles	6.7%	0.009	0.52	2	5
11.	Duke University Medical Center, Durham, N.C.*	6.4%	0.047	1.61	2	6
12.	Yale–New Haven Hospital, New Haven, Conn.*	5.8%	0.083	1.23	2	8
13.	Institute of Living, Hartford, Conn.	5.0%	0.158	0.45	2	8
14.	Hospital of the University of Pennsylvania, Philadelphia*	5.0%	0.074	1.33	2	6
15.	Mount Sinai Medical Center, New York*	4.0%	0.136	1.50	2	7

■ REHABILITATION: Rehabilitation units help patients return to lives as normal as possible following strokes, head and spinal injuries, falls, and sports injuries. The team includes physical, speech, and occupational therapists; psychologists; social workers; doctors and nurses.

	Hospital	Reputational score	Board-cert. M.D.s to beds	R.N.s to beds	Discharge planning	Geriatric services	Technology score
1.	Rehabilitation Institute of Chicago	38.7%	0.094	0.52	1	1	7
2.	U. of Washington Medical Center, Seattle	30.4%	0.044	2.06	2	4	9
3.	Mayo Clinic, Rochester, Minn.	27.0%	0.013	0.77	2	5	7
4.	Rusk Institute for Rehabilitation Medicine (New York U. Medical Center)	21.9%	0.023	1.15	2	1	8
5.	Craig Hospital, Engelwood, Colo.	17.7%	0.114	0.41	2	1	5
6.	The Institute for Rehabilitation and Research, Houston	16.6%	0.011	0.35	1	0	6
7.	Los Angeles Co.–Rancho Los Amigos Medical Center, Downey	13.0%	0.004	1.01	2	6	9
8	Baylor University Medical Center, Dallas	12.7%	0.004	1.38	2	4	8
9	Ohio State U. Medical Center, Columbus	11.1%	0.012	1.11	2	5	9
10.	Thomas Jefferson U. Hospital, Philadelphia	8.9%	0.033	1.44	2	3	9
11.	U. of Michigan Medical Center, Ann Arbor	8.6%	0.005	1.29	2	8	10
12.	Kessler Institute for Rehabilitation, West Orange, N.J.	8.1%	0.102	0.50	2	1	6
13.	Moss Rehabilitation Hospital, Philadelphia	6.8%	0.123	0.28	2	1	6
14.	Spaulding Rehabilitation Institute, Boston	5.7%	0.004	1.14	2	4	9
15.	Columbia-Presbyterian Medical Center, New York	5.0%	0.012	1.05	2	4	10

TERMS:

REPUTATIONAL SCORE: Percentage of doctors surveyed who named the hospital.

R.N.s TO BEDS: Ratio of full-time registered nurses to beds.

BOARD-CERTIFIED M.D.s TO BEDS: Ratio of doctors certified in a specialty to the number of beds.

TECHNOLOGY SCORE: Specialty-specific index from 0 to 6 (pediatrics), 0 to 8 (psychiatry), 0 to 10 (rehabilitation), 0 to 26 (ophthalmology).

INPATIENT OPERATIONS TO BEDS: Ratio of annual inpatient specialty-related procedures to beds.

DISCHARGE PLANNING: Postdischarge services available, from 0 to 2.

GERIATRIC SERVICES: Include comprehensive geriatric assessment, Alzheimer's diagnostic assessment services, geriatric acute care, geriatric clinics, adult day care, respite care, emergency response for the elderly, senior membership and patient-representative services.

* Indicates member of Council of Teaching Hospitals.

EXPERT LIST

THE DOCTOR'S BILL TODAY WILL BE...

Each year, the publication Medical Economics *compiles data on medical charges by physicians in private, office-based practices across the country. The figures below represent median fees for a variety of medical procedures in 1995. The survey sample was designed to be representative by type of practice, age, geographic region, and gender. Overall, the survey found that fees for medical services and procedures increased less than 4 percent over the previous year.*

PEDIATRICIANS

History, examination of normal newborn	$120
Immunization, DPT	$25
MMR virus vaccine	$44
Circumcision, clamp procedure, newborn	$113

OBG SPECIALISTS

Circumcision, clamp procedure, newborn	$135
Total hysterectomy, abdominal	$2,295
Complete OB care, routine delivery	$2,020
Routine delivery by family physicians	$1,544
Complete OB care, cesarean section	$2,479
Dilation and curettage (for abortion)	$712
Dilation and curettage (diagnostic)	$600
Laparascopy with fulguration of oviducts	$1,150

GENERAL SURGEONS

Total hysterectomy, abdominal	$1,894
Appendectomy	$1,090
Laparoscopy, surgical; appendectomy	$1,293
Cholesystectomy	$1,747
Laparoscopy, surgical; cholecystectomy	$2,133
Inguinal hernia repair, age five and over	$1,043
Gastrectomy with gastroduodenostomy (partial stomach removal for ulcers)	$2,429

■ OFFICE VISIT FEES FOR A NEW PATIENT

Consider the AMA's evaluation of a new patient in which the physician must: 1. compile a comprehensive history; 2. undertake a comprehensive exam; 3. perform medical decision making of moderate complexity. In a case whose description is adapted here from the journal *Medical Economics*, the problems are of moderate to high severity, typically requiring 45 minutes of physician time. Examples might include a patient in his mid-60s experiencing chest pains possibly related to cardiologic difficulty, or a woman in her mid-30s with an infertility problem.

	East	South	Midwest	West	Urban	Suburban	Rural
Cardiologists	$125	$117	$120	$142	$125	$125	N/A
Family physicians	$94	$92	$90	$107	$100	$95	$90
Gastroenterologists	$134	$119	$114	$146	$130	$129	$121
General practitioners	$99	$88	$87	$110	$100	$95	$80
General surgeons	$100	$100	$100	$125	$103	$105	$100
Internists	$100	$110	$95	$126	$116	$100	$95
OBG specialists	$105	$100	$90	$105	$100	$100	$90
Orthopedic surgeons	$115	$110	$100	$125	$125	$115	$99
Pediatricians	$69	$80	$85	$100	$75	$80	$80
All surgical specialists	$100	$102	$100	$123	$110	$102	$100
All non-surgeons*	$100	$100	$90	$117	$105	$100	$90
All doctors	$100	$100	$95	$120	$105	$100	$90

*Includes family physicians and general practitioners. SOURCE: *Medical Economics*, continuing survey, 1995.

■ **EXPERT LIST**

Modified radical mastectomy	$1,999
Excision of cyst fibroadenoma from breast tissue, one or more lesions	$585

ORTHOPEDIC SURGEONS

Colles fracture, closed manipulation (wrist injury common in those over 40)	$588
Open treatment of hip fracture	$2,459
Knee arthroscopy with meniscectomy (Removal of cartilage in knee)	$2,071
Total hip arthroplasty	$4,217
Diagnostic knee arthroscopy (Fiber-optic examination of knee interior)	$933
Total knee arthroplasty	$4,242

CARDIO SURGEONS

Replacement of aortic valve with cardiopulmonary bypass	$5,000
Insertion of permanent pacemaker with transvenous electrodes, ventricular	$1,500
Coronary artery bypass, with three coronary grafts	$5,299

CARDIOLOGISTS

Cardiac catheterization	$700
Echocardiography	$350

NEUROSURGEONS

Cranioplasty	$3,500
Craniotomy for evacuation of hematoma (Removal of part of skull to remove potentially fatal blood clot)	$4,286
Neuroplasty (median nerve)	$1,077
Diskectomy, anterior and osteophytectomy, cervical, single interspace	$3,677

GASTROENTEROLOGISTS

Upper gastrointestinal endoscopy, including esophagus, stomach, and either duodenum and/or jejunum, diagnostic	$475
Liver biopsy, percutaneous needle	$250
Dilation of esophagus by unguided sound or bougie	$150

SOURCE: *Medical Economics*, continuing survey. 1995. Reprinted by permission.

■ OFFICE VISIT FEES FOR AN ESTABLISHED PATIENT

Doctors' fees tend to be higher in the East and West than in the Midwest and South. In one situation whose AMA description is adapted from the publication *Medical Economics*, the doctor seeing an established patient for an office or other outpatient visit must deal with at least two of three components: 1. an expanded problem-focused history; 2. an expanded problem-focused examination; 3. medical decision making of low complexity. Usually, the problems presented are of low to moderate severity (e.g., an office visit for a patient in his mid-50s, for managing hypertension).

	East	South	Midwest	West	Urban	Suburban	Rural
Cardiologists	$55	$50	$50	$49	$50	$50	N/A
Family physicians	$45	$44	$42	$50	$47	$45	$40
General practitioners	$50	$40	$42	$48	$50	$45	$37
Gastroenterologists	$50	$50	$45	$50	$50	$50	$45
General surgeons	$50	$47	$45	$54	$50	$50	$45
Internists	$50	$45	$40	$50	$50	$50	$43
OBG specialists	$66	$50	$50	$55	$50	$55	$45
Orthopedic surgeons	$60	$50	$50	$52	$55	$55	$45
Pediatricians	$44	$43	$40	$50	$43	$46	$37
All surgical specialists	$60	$50	$50	$55	$51	$53	$45
All non-surgeons*	$50	$45	$42	$50	$48	$46	$40
All doctors	$50	$45	$45	$50	$50	$50	$42

*Includes family physicians and general practitioners. SOURCE: *Medical Economics*, continuing survey, 1995.

EXPERT Q & A

MIRACLE DRUGS THAT FAIL

Years of misuse have left antibiotics less effective than before

When antibiotics were first prescribed in the 1940s, they were universally hailed as miracle drugs. They lived up to their reputation until recently: They controlled bacterial-based threats like pneumonia and were on their way to conquering deadly diseases like tuberculosis. But antibiotics have lost their edge in the last few years because disease-causing bacteria have become resistant to many antibiotic drugs.

In 1995, researchers at the Centers for Disease Control and Prevention (CDC) found a dramatic increase in reported cases of antibiotic-resistant strains of the bacteria that cause pneumonia, meningitis, and other diseases. Roughly 25 percent of patients who were studied had developed infections resistant to penicillin, the most commonly prescribed antibiotic. Virulent strains causing once-conquered diseases like tuberculosis have also returned—but they're deadlier now because they can survive drug treatment.

Antibiotics are losing their effectiveness, according to the experts, primarily because patients have used them inappropriately. Dr. Stuart Levy, director of the Center for Adaptation Genetics and Drug Resistance at Tufts University School of Medicine, and author of *The Antibiotic Paradox: How Miracle Drugs Are Destroying the Miracle* (Plenum Publishing, 1992) explains how consumers can learn to use antibiotics responsibly:

■ When should antibiotics be used?

Antibiotics are designed to treat bacterial infections, not viral infections such as the common cold. They are prescription drugs for a very good purpose, and they should only be used when prescribed by a physician because they can have severe side effects—gastrointestinal problems, cramps, diarrhea, rash, dizziness, and nausea.

■ Why are antibiotics less effective than they were when they were discovered 50 years ago?

Because consumers are overusing and misusing antibiotics and taking their medical care into their own hands. At least 50 percent of antibiotics are clearly used inappropriately—maybe more. For instance, instead of taking the complete 3- to 10-day course of treatment of drugs, patients stop taking the prescription prematurely. They have leftover antibiotics and they use them the next time they don't feel well, and they keep using them until the bottle runs out.

■ Why is it dangerous not to take the complete antibiotic prescription even when you feel better?

The five- or seven-day course of treatment is prescribed to get rid of every living infectious bacterium. If you stop midway, you don't get rid of all the bacteria, and this allows more resistant strains to take over. Clinical studies show that to ensure that the bacterial infection is eradicated, you should take the full course of treatment. If you don't, you run the risk of the infection coming back because you have allowed less susceptible strains to grow up and cause a new infection that can't be cured with the antibiotic. The main reason tuberculosis has made a comeback is because patients didn't complete the full six-month course of treatment.

■ Why shouldn't you take antibiotics occasionally when you don't feel well?

Resistant strains have also developed because many people casually reach for antibiotics when they have viral infections like a cold. If you take an antibiotic every once in a while like you take an aspirin, you're not going to treat any infection, even if you had one. Instead, you propagate resistant strains of bacteria, which may cause another infection in you or in another member of your family. You carry and pass on resistant strains of a bacterium like pneumococcus, which can lead to pneumonia and meningitis in children, without actually succumbing to it yourself.

■ What does casual use of antibiotics do to your body's ability to fight bacterial infections?

If you take an antibiotic when you don't need one, then when you really need an antibiotic to treat a serious illness, it may not work. If you don't have a bacterial infection, you're treating the body's environment. Most bacteria are friendly, but if we eliminate them with antibiotics, we set up an environment where resistant, harmful strains can grow.

■ Are antibiotics overprescribed?

Yes. Physicians overprescribe for one main reason: consumer expectation. Physicians often tell me that they prescribe antibiotics even when they're pretty sure it's not a bacterial infection because if patients come in for a visit, they expect a prescription. And if they don't get it, they demand it or they go to another doctor. Unfortunately, some physicians practice defensive medicine and prescribe antibiotics to make sure a patient doesn't sue if they've been misdiagnosed.

■ Which conditions are overtreated?

Many symptoms like a sore throat or a runny nose are treated with antibiotics but the cause may not be a bacterial infection like strep throat. And ear infections, which could be viral in nature, shouldn't always be treated with antibiotics.

■ What should consumers ask if their doctor prescribes an antibiotic?

Ask why you need an antibiotic. If the answer is a virus, then you can ask why he's treating a virus with an antibiotic. Also, make sure you understand how long and when you should take the drug.

■ What can people do who have developed drug-resistant strains of bacterial infections?

Fortunately, patients aren't resistant to the drugs, but their infections are. We can reverse the situation if we begin to use drugs in a rational way. The body's environment may be polluted with resistant organisms, but there are still susceptible strains out there. If we stop polluting the environment with antibiotics, the susceptible strains will come back, and if infectious, that can be treated effectively.

■ Are there some infections for which antibiotics just don't work anymore?

Yes. Now we're confronting the legacy we started in the 1960s. And the whole reason this subject has reached the level of consciousness it has today is because we're running out of antibiotics to treat common infections like pneumonia, urinary tract infections, ear infections, and less common ones like meningitis and tuberculosis. Patients are dying of tuberculosis and enterococcus, a bacterium that can lead to life-threatening blood infections, because we don't have drugs to treat some of the resistant infections. People are dying because the bacteria are resistant not to just one drug but to many, and sometimes there's just one drug left that might work. For these patients, it's like a return to the pre-antibiotic era, because antibiotics can't help them.

FACT FILE:

DOSING UP

A 1995 Gallup poll released by the American Lung Association found that Americans are ill informed about antibiotics:

- *Sixty percent of those surveyed believe that antibiotics are effective at treating viral infections.*
- *More than half who have taken antibiotics stop taking them when they feel better rather than complete the full course of treatment.*

EXPERT Q & A

WHEN PAYING LESS IS HIP

The do's and don'ts of using generic drugs to cut your bills

Cost-conscious consumers have long known that they can save 30 percent to 50 percent of their prescription drug bills by using generic rather than brand-name drugs. As the average price of prescription drugs climbs year after year, more and more people are growing wise to the ways of generic drugs, whose prices have remained steady. In 1985, 14 percent of prescriptions were filled with generic drugs compared with approximately 45 percent in 1994.

In fact, one way managed care plans keep costs down is by urging their members to use generic rather than brand-name prescription drugs. But many consumers aren't sure whether it's safe to substitute their prescriptions with generic drugs, or if they're as reliable as brand-name drugs. Dr. Brian Strom, a professor of biostatistics and epidemiology and director of the Center for Clinical Epidemiology and Biostatistics at the University of Pennsylvania, helps explain the similarities and differences between brand-name and generic drugs:

■ What are generic drugs and how do they differ from brand-name drugs?

All drugs have generic or scientific names that identify their active ingredients. The active ingredient in generic drugs—what makes a drug work—is the same as in brand-name drugs, and it's in the same amount. In some cases, it's exactly the same drug, but it has a different name. The only question is whether the manufacturing process may have changed things. The process of manufacturing the drugs may vary and the fillers—the inactive ingredient in drugs—may be different.

■ Are generic drugs as reliable as brand-name drugs?

In the 1980s, there was a scandal involving brand-name drugs marketed in generic form that had not undergone the proper testing. But consumers no longer have to worry whether generic drugs are safe. People can have allergic reactions to a generic drug's inactive ingredients, but the same problem can occur with the inactive ingredients in a brand-name drug. Brand-name companies give the impression that generic drugs aren't as reliable, but if you looked at the drug recalls by the Food and Drug Administration (FDA), that's not at all clear. In drugs that have been approved in a generic equivalent, there are extremely few, if any examples that have been shown to be unsafe or unequal.

■ How does the FDA evaluate drugs?

The FDA process is pretty rigorous. Before a brand-name drug can be marketed, its manufacturer has to go through extensive testing in people to make sure that it's safe and effective. If a generic drug manufacturer changes the manufacturing process when it markets a generic drug, it has to measure the rate of drug absorption and demonstrate that roughly the same amount of the drug appears in the blood in roughly the same time as the brand-name drug. There's no test of the generic drug's effectiveness, however—only whether it absorbs in the body at roughly the same rate as its brand-name counterpart.

■ Why are generic drugs less expensive than brand-name drugs?

Generic drug manufacturers charge just what it costs to manufacture the drug, whereas brand-name drug manufacturers base their prices on the market rate, and are hugely profitable ventures. In addition, brand-name manufacturers make a huge investment in testing many, many drugs that don't work and are never marketed. Generic drug manufacturers don't incur the initial, expensive costs of developing and testing drugs. And generic drugs—which are sometimes made by the same companies that manufacture brand-name drugs—aren't advertised.

■ Are generic drugs always less expensive?

A generic drug will almost always be cheaper than the brand-name drug. But it's important to check the prices from one pharmacy to the next, because prices can vary for the same drugs.

■ Why are some drugs not available in generic form?

When a new drug is marketed and sold in the United States, patent laws prevent any drug manufacturer from producing the same drug until the patent expires. Until recently, patents on new drugs barred a drug from being sold in generic form for 17 years. Last year's world trade agreement extended patent protection three years so the United States complies with the rest of the world's patent rules, which allow 20-year patent protection on new drugs. That means that some drugs, like the world's largest-selling drug, Zantac, won't be available in generic form until a few years later than expected. (A generic version of Zantac, used to treat ulcers, will be available in July 1997, unless legislation is passed shortening the protection on pharmaceuticals.)

■ Can generic and brand-name drugs be used interchangeably?

It's fine to take a generic drug instead of a brand-name drug, but switching back and forth may be ill advised. If you're taking a certain class of drugs, the so-called critical dose drugs, you shouldn't change back and forth because the rate of absorption could be slightly different. Since most drugs are given in larger doses than necessary, if you take a little more of these drugs, you could have a problem. For example, people who take blood thinners, anti-seizure medications, and some diabetes drugs should check with their pharmacist or doctor to find out whether the drug is a critical dose drug.

■ A DRUG BY ANY OTHER NAME...

Here's a sample of cost differences between brand-name drugs and their generic equivalents. By using generics, your savings can sometimes be substantial.

DRUG BRAND NAME *Generic name*	*Dosage/Quantity* *Uses*	Average price Brand *Generic*
ATIVAN *Lorazepam*	***1 mg. tablet/60*** *To treat anxiety disorders.*	$46.10 *$5.49*
CARDIZEM *Diltiazem HCl*	***60 mg. tablet/90*** *To treat high blood pressure and reduce chest pain.*	$62.94 *$37.17*
DIABINESE *Chlorpropamide*	***250 mg. tablet/60*** *To treat diabetes.*	$47.24 *$5.76*
ELAVIL *Amitriptyline*	***25 mg. tablet/90*** *To treat diabetes.* *To treat diabetes.*	$36.48 *$5.49*
HYTONE *Hydrocortisone*	***2.5%. cream/30 g.*** *To reduce itching and redness of skin caused by irritants like poison ivy.*	$21.14 *$8.65*
KEFLEX *Cephalexin*	***500 mg. capsule/20*** *To prevent and treat bacterial infection.*	$57.20 *$8.49*
LOPRESSOR *Metroprolol*	***50 mg. tablet/60*** *To treat cardiovascular problems like high blood pressure.*	$83.74 *$30.10*
PERCOCET *Oxycododone/APAP*	***5 mg./325 tablet/90*** *To relieve pain.*	$60.86 *$12.91*
VENTOLIN/PROVENTIL *Albuterol Sulfate*	***4 mg. tablet/90*** *To treat asthma and other lung problems.*	$47.63 *$12.44*

SOURCE: Health Care Financing Administration, 1994.

HOW DO YOU SPELL RELIEF?

Do you always reach for the same over-the-counter pain reliever whether you have a throbbing headache, a swollen ankle or premenstrual cramps? Certain painkillers work wonders with some conditions, but should be avoided in other situations. Here's a guide to help you choose the appropriate over-the-counter pain reliever:

ASPIRIN

■ **USES:** The granddaddy of painkillers, this anti-inflammatory drug reduces fever, relieves muscle stiffness and joint pain caused by some forms of arthritis, and may help migraine headache sufferers. Aspirin is the only pain reliever also shown to reduce the risk of heart attack or stroke.

■ **WARNINGS:** Like all anti-inflammatory drugs (including ibuprofen, naproxen sodium, and ketoprofen), aspirin can upset the stomach, and should be avoided by those who experience stomach problems like ulcers or heartburn. It can also raise blood pressure and cause bleeding. If you take a blood thinner, don't use aspirin or other anti-inflammatory drugs.

ACETAMINOPHEN

Tylenol

■ **USES:** Acetaminophen provides immediate relief for pain and fever without causing stomach irritation, bleeding, or nausea that can occur with anti-inflammatory drugs. It's also a more effective fever-fighter for children, and is the best choice for post-operative pain and for people taking blood thinners, because anti-inflammatory drugs can cause bleeding. However, because it's not anti-inflammatory, acetaminophen won't reduce swelling or stiffness.

■ **WARNINGS:** Acetominophen should not be mixed with alcohol. Heavy drinkers and people with liver, renal, or kidney disease should avoid using the drug.

IBUPROFEN

Advil, Motrin, Nuprin

■ **USES:** Ibuprofen provides immediate relief for headaches, fever, and inflammation and is especially effective for menstrual cramps. Like all anti-inflammatory pain relievers, ibuprofen can also relieve minor aches and pains.

■ **WARNINGS:** Like aspirin, ketoprofen, and naproxen sodium, ibuprofen can upset the stomach and may cause other gastrointestinal problems. It should be avoided by people with asthma, high blood pressure, kidney disease, and cirrhosis, and those taking lithium or diuretics.

KETOPROFEN

Orudis KT, Actron

■ **USES:** Orudis KT and Actron were approved as over-the-counter drugs in 1995 to reduce fever and relieve the discomforts of arthritis, menstrual cramps, and other pains. Ketoprofen provides fast relief yet seems to cause fewer stomach problems than other anti-inflammatory drugs.

■ **WARNINGS:** Precautions are the same as for aspirin and ibuprofen.

NAPROXEN SODIUM

Aleve

■ **USES:** Naproxen sodium is effective at reducing pain and fever for 8 to 12 hours, a longer period of time than acetaminophen, ibuprofen, or ketoprofen. It's an anti-inflammatory, but it's gentler on the stomach than aspirin.

■ **WARNINGS:** Precautions are the same as for aspirin and ibuprofen.

PSYCHOACTIVE DRUGS

MEDICINES TO MEND YOUR MIND

Substantial relief for sufferers of depression and anxiety

Depression and anxiety are closely related mental illnesses that are among the most common psychiatric problems suffered by Americans. In recent years there have been a number of advances in treating mental disorders with psychoactive drugs, but each medication has its drawbacks. Following is a guide to help understand depression and anxiety and the medications available to treat the disorders:

DEPRESSION

Ten million American adults will suffer a bout of depression this year alone, according to the National Institute of Mental Health. Women are twice as likely to experience depression as men, yet even so the condition will afflict 1 in 10 men over their lifetime. The telltale symptoms include persistent feelings of sadness or irritability, changes in weight or appetite, impaired sleep or concentration, fatigue, restlessness, thoughts of death or suicide, and loss of interest in ordinary activities or sex.

Even though the disorder is very common, nearly two-thirds of depressed people don't get appropriate treatment because they don't seek it or their symptoms aren't recognized, according to the National Institute of Mental Health. Primary care physicians are the health care providers most likely to see depressed patients, but they're also most apt to underdiagnose and undertreat it, says Dr. John Whipple, staff psychiatrist for the adult outpatient unit at the Menninger Clinic in Topeka, Kansas.

The consequences are enormous. Prolonged untreated depression is associated with higher rates of heart attack and stroke, especially in older people, and it's estimated that at least half of all people who commit suicide are severely depressed.

Yet depression is a very treatable illness. According to the National Institute of Mental Health, 80 to 90 percent of those with serious depression can improve significantly, reducing and eliminating symptoms and restoring normal function. The most common treatments for depression are psychotherapy and antidepressant medications, which are often

THE "DOCTOR" WILL SEE YOU NOW

When seeking help from a mental health professional, knowing who you're dealing with is not always clear. Here's who does what:

■ **PSYCHIATRISTS** are medical doctors licensed by the state where they practice. They must complete four years of medical school and a four-year residency training, and are the only mental health professionals authorized to prescribe medications.

■ **CLINICAL PSYCHOLOGISTS** have completed a doctoral program in psychology, including at least two years of supervised clinical work. They are licensed by the state where they work to diagnose and treat mental health problems.

■ **THERAPISTS** can be psychiatrists, psychologists, licensed social workers—or anyone who hangs up a shingle and says he or she is a therapist. It's a generic term used to describe anyone who provides any type of counseling, but it doesn't mean the provider is necessarily trained or licensed to do so.

used in combination and may be more effective than either treatment alone.

Whipple says the decision depends on which treatment the patient prefers, the severity of symptoms, and whether there is a medical risk if the patient is left untreated. How long the depression has existed is also a factor. "If someone has struggled with depression for many months without resolution and it's clearly getting worse," says Whipple, "or if it was triggered by stress, but the stress is gone and the depression is still there, these are reasons to start medications."

According to guidelines released by a panel convened by the Agency for Health Care Policy and Research (AHCPR), antidepressants are an appropriate medication for patients with moderate to severe depression. They are also used to treat dysthymia, a more mild, chronic form of depression.

ANXIETY

Experiencing anxiety at some point in life is normal, but for people who suffer anxiety disorders, it becomes overwhelming and completely disrupts one's life. Anxiety disorders encompass several distinct disorders:

- **PANIC DISORDERS** occur when a person experiences recurrent panic attacks, which are overwhelming, immobilizing fears with no apparent cause.

- **GENERALIZED ANXIETY DISORDERS** are characterized by unrealistic, persistent fears or concerns that something bad is going to happen.

- **PHOBIAS** occur when people dread a situation or object and go to great lengths to avoid it. Examples include fear of heights (acrophobia), agoraphobia (fear of being trapped), and numerous social phobias.

- **OBSESSIVE-COMPULSIVE DISORDERS** result in persistent irrational thoughts such as contamination that are relieved by repeating routine acts like washing your hands.

- **POST-TRAUMATIC STRESS DISORDER** afflicts survivors of extraordinary trauma, such as war or violent crime.

Although anxiety disorders are more common than depression, people who suffer depression are more likely to seek treatment than those with anxiety disorders. According to the Anxiety Disorders Association of America, just 23 percent of those who suffer an anxiety disorder will undergo treatment.

Both antianxiety medications and cognitive behavioral therapy, which teaches patients how to allay their fears and modify anxiety-producing behaviors, can relieve the symptoms of all types of anxiety disorders. Receiving both treatments simultaneously appears more effective than either one alone, says Dr. Jack Gorman, professor of clinical psychiatry at the Columbia University College of Physicians and Surgeons, and author of *The Essential Guide to Psychiatric Drugs* (St. Martin's Press, 1995).

About 70 percent of patients with panic disorders respond to behavioral therapy and medications both, says Gorman, but it's unclear which works best for individuals. "We don't yet have a good feeling as to which patients do better with which treatment, so it's often up to the patient," says Gorman.

Untreated, anxiety disorders can lead to depression, substance abuse, suicide, and possibly increased risk of heart attack.

Because patients respond differently to therapy, doctors treating depression and/or anxiety must determine which medication to prescribe on an individual basis, based upon the nature of the illness, previous reactions to particular drugs, other medical problems or medications that a patient may be using, and side effects associated with the drug.

It's also common to be afflicted with two distinct anxiety disorders or to experience symptoms of both depression and anxiety at the same time. This can complicate treatment, because physicians must determine which is the predominant disorder. For example, depression over the loss of a job can trigger anxiety about finding employment, or vice-versa. Gorman estimates that 50 percent of people with anxiety disorders will ultimately develop depression: "All of the anxiety disorders are frequently complicated by depression, and when they are, it's a good idea to use medications."

EXPERT LIST

MORE THAN JUST PROZAC

Below is an outline of the major classes of psychoactive medications used to treat anxiety disorders and depression. All are antidepressants except the benzodiazepines, which are used to depress or slow the central nervous system.

SELECTIVE SEROTONIN REUPTAKE INHIBITORS (SSRIS)

Prozac (fluoxetine), Paxil (paroxetine), Zoloft (sertraline)

■ **USES:** Often the first course of treatment for depression, this new category of antidepressants has received considerable attention because of Prozac's popularity. It's the most widely used psychoactive drug in the country and one of the top 10 medications prescribed overall. While SSRIs may be no more effective than other types of antidepressants, they have fewer and less severe side effects than most antidepressants. SSRIs are also used to treat patients with panic disorder, social phobias, and obsessive-compulsive disorder.

■ **PRECAUTIONS:** SSRIs may cause insomnia, drowsiness, anxiety, agitation, diarrhea, headache, and nausea, and can disrupt sexual function.

TRICYCLICS (TCAS)

Elavil (amitriptyline), Norpramin (desipramine), Tofranil (imipramine), Anafranil (clomipramine), Pamelor (nortriptyline), Sineqan (doxepin)

■ **USES:** For many years, TCAs were the most widely prescribed antidepressants, but they aren't prescribed as frequently nowadays because they're associated with several short-term and long-term side effects. However, they are still used to treat generalized anxiety disorder and obsessive-compulsive disorder.

■ **PRECAUTIONS:** Side effects include weight gain, dry mouth, blurred vision, drowsiness, heart rhythm disturbances, insomnia, constipation, decreased sexual ability, dizziness, headache, nausea, difficulty urinating and sleeping.

MONOAMINE OXIDASE INHIBITORS (MAOIS)

Marplan (isocarboxazid), Nardil (phenelzine), Parnate (tranylcypromine)

■ **USES:** Usually not the first treatment selected, MAOIs are prescribed more often for depressed patients who have failed to respond to other treatments, can't tolerate the side effects, or have an atypical form of depression. They're also used to treat social phobias.

■ **PRECAUTIONS:** MAOIs can produce toxic food-drug interactions known as the "cheese reaction" that can cause severe hypertension, headaches, and heart palpitations. Those taking MAOIs must be extremely cautious about their diet and avoid food containing a substance called tyramine, found in most types of cheese, beer, yeast, wine, chicken liver, lox, soy sauce, and licorice.

BENZODIAZEPINES

Valium (diazepam), Ativan (lorazepam), Xanax (alprazolam)

■ **USES:** Traditionally, benzodiazepines were the most commonly prescribed medications to treat anxiety disorders, but they're less popular now because new drugs have replaced them that cause fewer side effects. They're still used to treat generalized anxiety disorder, however.

■ **PRECAUTIONS:** Technically they are not addictive, but people can develop a physical dependency to benzodiazepines and experience withdrawal symptoms like anxiety, insomnia, and agitation when they stop treatment. These drugs, which are also prescribed as sedatives, cause drowsiness and cannot be taken together with alcohol.

PHOBIC'S GUIDE

YOU THINK YOU FEEL STRANGE?

Mental disorders can sometimes be triggered by cultural assumptions

Feeling shaky? Wondering if your head is about to explode or if you'll ever be able to sleep again? The doctor's diagnosis of what ails you could depend on how exotic your cultural background is. Increasingly, mental health professionals are taking note of the cultural differences in patients complaining of unexplained disorders, and finding that what may seem like hypochondria to some makes perfect sense to those of other cultures, from Hopi Indians to Japanese workers. Here's how the American Psychiatric Association's diagnostic manual describes a few of these remarkable syndromes:

■ **AMOK**: Brooding, followed by a violent outburst or homicidal behavior, mostly by men. The apparent trigger—a perceived slight or insult. Found primarily in Malaysia; with similar patterns in other parts of southeast Asia and the Pacific, Puerto Rico, and among the Navajo.

■ **ATAQUE DE NERVIOS:** A spate of uncontrollable shouting, weeping, trembling, sometimes accompanied by seizurelike or fainting episodes and suicidal gestures. Triggered by a stressful family event such as a relative's death, divorce, or other trauma. Found in Latin America and Mediterranean countries.

■ **BRAIN FAG:** A condition afflicting high school or college students stressed out by too much schooling. Difficulties involve concentrating, remembering, and thinking. Also include blurring of vision and burning sensation around head and neck. Students commonly complain of "brain tiredness" or fatigue. Found in West Africa.

■ **GHOST SICKNESS:** A preoccupation with death and the departed, characterized by bad dreams, loss of appetite, fainting, dizziness, loss of consciousness, and feelings of suffocation and danger. Has witchcraft associations for some. Found among American Indian tribes.

■ **KORO:** Sudden intense anxiety that the penis (and in women the vulva and nipples) will recede into the body, possibly causing death. Also known as shuk yang, shook yong, and suo yong (Chinese); jinjinia bemar (Assam); or rok-joo (Thailand). Found in Malaysia and other areas of south and east Asia.

■ **LOCURA:** A severe psychosis tied to feelings of inherited vulnerability and/or reaction to life difficulties. Among the symptoms are incoherence, hallucinations, and possible violent behavior. Found in United States and Latin America.

■ **MAL DE OJO:** Mal de ojo is Spanish for "evil eye." The condition is most widespread in children, and is marked by fitful sleep, unexplained weeping, diarrhea, vomiting, and fever. May be found in women, too. Found in Mediterranean countries and elsewhere.

■ **PIBLOKTOQ:** Up to 30 minutes of extreme excitement, followed by seizures and coma lasting as long as 12 hours. The afflicted person may tear off clothing, break furniture, shout obscenities, eat feces, and perform other irrational acts while stricken. Found among Eskimos.

■ **SHENKUI OR SHEN-K'UEI:** Panic symptoms attributed to excessive loss of semen from too much sexual intercourse, masturbation, or nocturnal emissions. Symptoms include dizziness, backache, insomnia, frequent dreams, sexual dysfunction. Found in China.

■ **TAIJIN KYOFUSHO:** Intense fear that one's body, physical appearance, or bodily functions will displease, embarrass, or offend others. Found in Japan.

SOURCE: Adapted from *Diagnostic and Statistical Manual of Disorders*, 4th ed., American Psychiatric Association, 1994.

ELIXIRS

MELATONIN MANIA

Hype and hope over a hormone's powers confuse the public

If Ponce de Leon had known about melatonin, he might never have gone looking for the fountain of youth and discovered Florida. But the Spanish explorer didn't have the benefit of today's best-seller lists, which have included books like *Stay Young the Melatonin Way* and *The Melatonin Miracle* for months. Although there is little evidence of the hormone's impact as a dietary supplement on humans, some researchers suspect that it may prevent everything from cancer to Alzheimer's disease.

When taken in pill form, melatonin is widely accepted as an antidote for jet lag, because it helps the body's internal rhythms adjust faster to new time zones. Research also shows that taking less than one milligram of melatonin an hour or two before bedtime can enhance a person's ability to doze off and stay asleep throughout the night, a finding that's made it a popular remedy among shift workers like nurses.

The hormone is secreted by the brain's pineal gland, a pea-sized organ that helps regulate sleep by adjusting the body's clock to daylight and darkness. Although the hormone is plentiful in youth, it wanes as people age, which may explain why older people sometimes have trouble sleeping. So far, melatonin appears to be nontoxic, even in huge doses. Subjects have been given up to 2,000 times the dose available in the capsules sold in most health food stores—with few ill effects. But there's concern that melatonin may turn out to be a disaster like the sleep aid L-tryptophan, which poisoned 1,200 people and killed 35 in the 1980s, because its long-term effects on humans are unknown.

While melatonin appears to be safe, its ability to prevent disease is far from clear. Laboratory tests have shown that the hormone strengthens the immune system and acts as an antioxidant that protects the body against toxic compounds called free radicals that damage cells and can lead to cancer and other diseases. In one experiment, researchers swapped the pineal glands of 10 old mice with those of 10 young ones. The young mice died prematurely while the older ones exceeded their life expectancies.

"Disease after disease is free radical–based, and if you can delay that part of the disease by taking melatonin or any antioxidant, you're a step ahead," argues Dr. Russel Reiter, author of *Melatonin: Your Body's Natural Wonder Drug* (Bantam, 1995). While melatonin does not reverse the aging process, it may delay the onset of some diseases like Alzheimer's and Parkinson's, he says.

But that kind of endorsement is rare among physicians. "The claims that melatonin should be applied to humans based upon the data out there are premature," warns Dr. Andrew Monjan, chief of the neurobiology of aging branch at the National Institute on Aging. Further study is needed, he contends, to set appropriate dosage levels and to see if there are any adverse effects to chronic use. Monjan recommends taking melatonin, even as a sleep aid, only under a doctor's supervision because there's no data on whether long-term use is safe or effective. (Even Reiter, who takes one milligram a day to counteract the effects of a hypertension drug, doesn't advise taking melatonin unless there's a medical condition you're being treated for by a doctor).

Monjan also questions whether melatonin works the same way in humans as in rats, because unlike humans, rats sleep in the daytime. But Reiter argues, "An antioxidant is an antioxidant." What's involved, he says, is "a chemical reaction that requires nothing of the body and is not unique to a species. It will prevent free radical damage in a test tube, in a rat, a frog or a human." Ponce de Leon, where are you?

EXPERT Q & A

SAYING NO TO BREAST CANCER

Knowing the risk factors will cut your risk of being a victim

Breast cancer is the most common form of cancer among American women. According to the American Cancer Society, 184,000 American women develop breast cancer and 44,000 die of the disease annually. Although more women now die of lung cancer and heart disease, breast cancer is the leading cause of death in women aged 40 to 55. Dr. A. Marilyn Leitch, chair of the American Cancer Society's Breast Cancer Subcommittee and an associate professor in surgical oncology at the University of Texas/Southwestern Medical Center, explains the risks, the precautions that should be followed, and the treatment options that are available:

■ Do one in eight women really develop breast cancer?

The numbers sound so much more horrifying if you don't look at the risk in relation to a woman's age. One in 8 women will get breast cancer assuming a lifespan of 85 to 90 years. If you live to age 60, your risk decreases to about 1 in 29, if your lifespan is 50, it's about 1 in 40, and at age 40, 1 in 65.

■ What are the symptoms of the disease?

The most common symptom is a painless mass found during a breast self-exam. Less common signs are nipple discharge, a change in the appearance of the skin on the breast such as redness or nipple dimpling, or a lump or swelling under the arm.

■ Who is most at risk of breast cancer?

All women—and men to a minor degree—are at risk of breast cancer. Advancing age is the most important risk factor—the older a woman gets, the more likely she is to get breast cancer. Roughly 77 percent of women diagnosed with breast cancer in a given year are over age 50.

■ Are there other factors that predispose a woman to developing breast cancer?

Yes, but these aren't as important as a woman's age. They include a prior diagnosis of breast cancer or a family history of breast cancer (the closer the relative is, the greater the risk). Having a breast biopsy in the past which shows abnormal changes in the breast's fibrocystic tissue, menstruating at an early age or having a late menopause, never having a baby, or getting pregnant for the first time after age 30 are also risk factors.

■ What can women do to protect themselves from the disease?

Self-exam is the most common way to detect breast cancer. All women—with or without risk factors—should be doing breast self-exams every month by the time they are age 20. It's ideal to do the exam about five to seven days after a woman's period starts, when breasts are the least tender or full. Post-menopausal women should perform self-exams at the same time each month. Statistically, most women aren't going to detect any abnormalities, but if something seems out of the ordinary, you'll be able to detect it because you'll be familiar with how the breast tissue feels. Examination by a health care professional can also help detect breast cancer. Between the ages of 20 and 40, women should be examined by their doctor every two to three years, and every year after age 40.

■ What is a mammogram and is the procedure safe?

A mammogram is an X ray of the breast that can detect smaller tumors before they can be felt in physical exams. Mammograms are the second most common method of detecting breast cancer. The theoretic risk of radiation is extremely low compared to the risk of getting breast cancer. Today, the technical aspects of doing mammographies have become very rigorous, and women are only exposed to very low doses of radiation. In addition, the Mammography Quality Standards Act, which requires mammography facilities to be certified by the Food and Drug Administration, ensures that high-quality equipment and technicians are used.

■ Who should get mammograms?

The American Cancer Society recommends that a woman should have her first mammogram by age 40, then every one to two years between ages 40 and 49. After a woman reaches age 50, she should have a mammogram every year.

■ Are mammograms effective in younger women?

One of the arguments for not doing mammograms in women aged 40 to 49 is that their breasts are more dense, so it's hard for the X ray to see through them. But that's become less of an issue in the past decade as mammography technique has improved. There's no question that there's a benefit to a woman who has her cancer diagnosed early—she has more treatment options and she's going to live longer. A review published last year that analyzed various studies showed that mammography screening can reduce mortality in women under age 50 by 24 percent.

■ How much do mammograms cost?

A diagnostic mammogram costs more than a screening mammogram because it requires more work on the part of the technician and the radiologist. A screening mammogram costs between $65 and $100, and a diagnostic mammogram usually costs anywhere from $100 to $150, although the price varies depending on where you are in the country. Most insurance carriers cover routine mammographies, although some have stopped paying for mammograms for women under age 50 because of the revised guidelines.

■ What does it mean if a woman finds a lump during a self-exam?

Sometimes a lump is just a thickening in the breast tissue that does not need further treatment, but all women who find a lump should have it checked by their primary care doctor to determine whether it's what's called a dominant mass. If it is, women over 30 should have a mammogram to evaluate the lump and a biopsy in which a needle is inserted into the lump to determine whether it's a solid tumor or a fluid-filled cyst. If it's

■ PERFORMING A BREAST SELF-EXAMINATION

1. Once a month, after your period, examine your breasts. Get to know their shape and texture, and be alert to changes. Raise each arm above your head and turn from side to side, looking for changes in appearance.

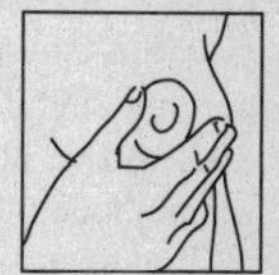

2. Squeeze the nipple to check for discharge. Check surface for peculiarities. Orange-peel texture could indicate a lump.

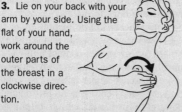

3. Lie on your back with your arm by your side. Using the flat of your hand, work around the outer parts of the breast in a clockwise direction.

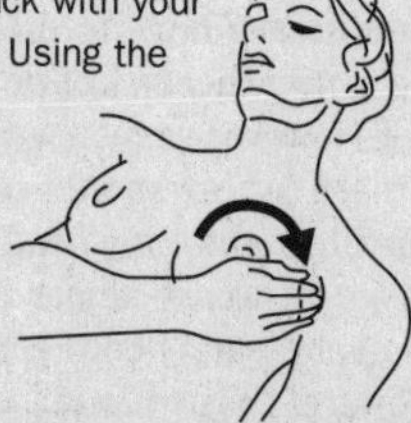

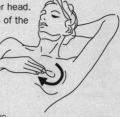

4. Raise arm over head. Check inner parts of the breast, along collarbone and into armpit. Stretching the skin makes detection easier.

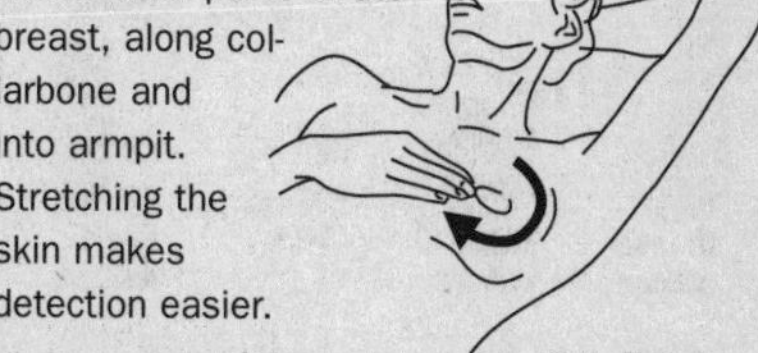

SOURCE: *American Medical Association Encyclopedia of Medicine*, Random House, 1989.

solid, the cells will be examined under a microscope to determine if the lump is benign or malignant.

■ What are the treatment options once you're diagnosed with breast cancer?

Most women with breast cancer are candidates for a breast-saving surgery called lumpectomy, which involves removing the cancerous tumor in the breast and lymph nodes under the arm, then getting radiation treatment to the entire breast. Women can also choose a mastectomy, which involves removing the breast, then they can have the breast reconstructed afterward if they want.

■ What are the chances of beating the disease through various treatments?

It depends on the stage of disease when patients are treated. The majority of women diagnosed with breast cancer can certainly expect to be alive in five years, but the earlier you detect it, the better your odds of surviving the disease. In five years, roughly 95 percent of white women whose tumor is confined to the breast and 75 percent of women whose tumors have spread to the lymph nodes will be alive. However, the survival rates are consistently lower for black women; we don't know whether it's because they don't have access to care or because of biologic differences. In 1995, the National Cancer Institute (NCI) announced the first decrease in the incidence of breast cancer mortality in decades, but it was primarily for white women. The mortality rate actually increased for black women.

■ FEAR OF DYING

Breast cancer is one of the most haunting problems facing women, yet there's evidence that *fear* of cancer is disproportionate to its actual incidence. A 1992 Gallup poll of more than 1,000 women found that breast cancer is by far the disease women are most concerned about, even though they are more likely to die of other causes:

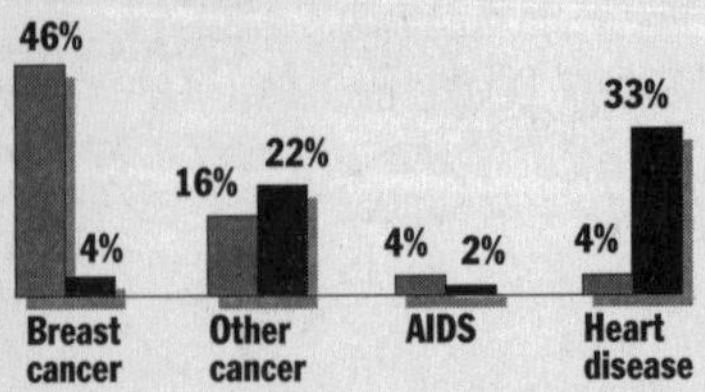

SOURCE: National Center for Health Statistics.

■ Can a low-fat diet or exercise reduce your risk of breast cancer?

It seems there is some relationship between obesity, a high-fat diet, and the development of breast cancer. Breast cancer is more common in countries where there's a high fat content in the diet, like the U.S., and is quite low in countries that have a lower fat content, like Japan. The decreased risk may be related to reducing the level of estrogen in the body. Younger women who are very athletic and women who have multiple pregnancies have fewer menstrual periods, which may have a protective effect because fewer hormones are produced, and women who are overweight tend to produce more estrogen. A 1994 study suggests that women who exercise when they're first menstruating through their reproductive years can greatly reduce their risk of premenopausal cancer, possibly because it can reduce the number of menstrual cycles. A couple of studies have suggested that reduction of weight and fat in the diet improves outcome even after a woman develops breast cancer.

■ Now that a gene that is thought to be associated with breast cancer has been identified, should women undergo genetic testing for breast cancer?

At the present time, there is not a single test readily available to the average woman to determine her risk of developing breast cancer. However, women with a family history of breast cancer should contact a university medical center involved in studying genetic risks of breast cancer in high-risk populations to learn about genetic testing and to donate their blood, which might help researchers learn more about the disease.

MENOPAUSE

BETTER LIVING WITH CHEMISTRY

Hormone replacement therapy can help, but don't expect a panacea

Baby boomers, who have always shown a talent for reinventing themselves and the society in which they live, now must redefine themselves as the menopausal generation. By the year 2000, about 60 million boomer women will reach age 45 and be faced with the dilemma of whether to take hormone replacement therapy, or HRT, to compensate for the loss of estrogen that accompanies menopause and the aging process.

Menopause occurs when the ovaries stop producing the hormone estrogen, which begins on average around the age of 51. Estrogen is an important factor in keeping the heart, bones, and skin healthy. As its production declines, women often complain of a loss of vaginal elasticity and lubrication, which can ruin a woman's libido.

Hormone replacement therapy not only relieves the "hot flashes" and vaginal dryness associated with menopause, but it also helps ease other menopausal symptoms such as mood swings, headaches, and thinning facial skin. There's also solid evidence that it can prevent osteoporosis, or bone loss, and that it significantly reduces a woman's risk of heart disease. Studies of women who took supplemental estrogen have repeatedly shown a 50 percent reduction in the incidence of heart disease.

HRT is not without its potential side effects, however. The American College of Obstetricians and Gynecologists has reported, for instance, that about 10 percent of women receiving HRT complain of breast tenderness, fluid retention, swelling, mood changes, and pelvic cramping. Another large recent study, which tracked the medical condition of 121,000 nurses over nearly two decades, found that women who use HRT face a 32 percent higher risk of breast cancer than those who did not take extra hormones. For women who elect HRT, that means the chances of getting breast cancer by age 60 are about one in 300 to 350, versus about one in 400 to 450 among those who eschew HRT.

Research has also suggested that estrogen supplements can increase a woman's risk of uterine cancer. To combat that risk, doctors now prescribe estrogen in combination with another substance called progestin, which mimics a hormone similar to estrogen. Taken together, the two substances have been shown to raise the level of "good cholesterol" in the blood, which helps cut the risk of heart disease, though not breast cancer.

Whether you're a good candidate for HRT depends on your individual circumstances, says Dr. Wulf Utian, director of obstetrics and gynecology at University Hospitals of Cleveland and executive director of the North American Menopause Society. Different dosages, hormone combinations, and ways of administering the hormones can—and should be—tailored to individual needs. For example, women in a high-risk group for heart disease or osteoporosis may be prime candidates for HRT. But if a woman has a high risk of breast cancer, her doctor may recommend a low-fat diet and regular exercise instead. In some circumstances, doctors may also recommend tamoxifen, an estrogen-like drug. Although it's still under investigation, it seems to have favorable effects on cholesterol levels and prevents bone loss and breast cancer but may increase the risk of uterine cancer.

This underscores that HRT is not a panacea for growing old, and "simply writing a prescription is not going to be the answer," says gynecologist Wulf Utian. Many women obviously concur with Utian. Surveys show that the average amount of time women stay on hormone therapy is just nine months, which confers health benefits during that period but not afterward. Yet women in the United States on average can expect to live one-third of their lives after menopause, even without a silver bullet.

PROSTATE CANCER

THIS SLEEPER NEEDS WATCHING

Diagnosis is easier than ever, but there's a debate about treatment

Bob Dole is among the afflicted. So is retired general Norman Schwarzkopf and junk bond developer Michael Milken. Nearly a quarter-million American men develop prostate cancer each year, making it the most common cancer in men, and after lung cancer, the second leading cancer killer among men.

Detecting prostate cancer is easier than ever, thanks to a blood test called the PSA (see box, facing page), which enables doctors to detect small tumors confined to the prostate. Most doctors agree that not all prostate cancers need to be treated, but it remains unclear which patients with localized prostate cancer will benefit from treatment, and no method exists to measure how effective those treatments are. "If we knew that finding cancer early would improve the chances of survival, we would have no problem treating everyone with prostate cancer," says Dr. Mark Austenfeld, a urologist at the University of Kansas Medical Center and a member of a special American Urological Association (AUA) study panel on the subject.

Prostate cancer is typically diagnosed late in life and grows slowly. In fact, only one in ten cancers ever becomes aggressive, or life-threatening, and many men with prostate cancer will die with the disease, not of it. Studies of autopsy results suggest that almost half of all men aged 70 to 80 have prostate cancer at the time of death, and the majority of men over age 90 have the disease—often without knowing it—yet they die of other illnesses. Unfortunately, it's difficult to determine accurately which cancers will advance quickly and spread, and which might remain harmless for as long as a decade without progressing.

Some doctors adopt a "surveillance" approach, examining the patient periodically to determine if the disease is spreading rather than rushing to treatment. Other doctors err on the side of caution, treating most cases by either removing the prostate with an increasingly common surgical procedure called radical prostatectomy, or administering radiation therapy that kills the cancer cells.

To help clarify the treatment options, the American Urological Association recently released guidelines for both doctors and patients that spell out factors to consider when choosing a treatment:

■ **Consider the stage and grade of a tumor.** A patient's prognosis depends on the grade and stage of his tumor. That means estimating the size of the tumor and the extent to which it has spread to other parts of the body. A grade is assigned to a tumor based on the results of an ultrasound test and biopsy, procedures that help determine how aggressive the tumor is, or how quickly it's expected to grow. Patients with small, low-grade tumors fare better than patients with high-grade tumors, regardless of the type of treatment. Some patients with low-grade tumors diagnosed

FACT FILE:

A TOMATO A DAY

■ *A study by Harvard University researchers suggests that tomatoes in the diet can help ward off prostate cancer. Men who ate at least 10 servings a week of tomato-based products had a 45 percent less chance of getting prostate cancer; men who ate at least 4 servings lowered their risk by 20 percent. The reduced risk may be derived from the antioxidant lycopene, abundant in tomatoes.*

WHEN A TEST OF ONE'S MANHOOD MAKES SENSE

As all men of a certain age know, a digital rectal exam in the doctor's office was for years the only screening test available to detect prostate cancer. But a more accurate test has now been developed that measures the amount of a protein in the blood called prostate specific antigen, which is produced exclusively by the prostate gland. The higher a man's PSA count, the greater the possibility that he has some prostatic disease.

The PSA test does have limitations: It will yield positive results in two-thirds of the men who take it, but only 30 to 40 percent of those with high PSA levels will actually have prostate cancer. PSA levels are also elevated in men with an enlarged prostate, a noncancerous condition known as benign prostatic hyperplasia, or BPH. An even more precise test may soon become available. Known as the "free PSA" test, it isolates free-floating PSA, which is common in men with prostate cancer, rather than measuring total PSA levels like the current test. The new test will reduce the high-false-positive rate and differentiate BPH from cancerous tumors. It may also help detect which tumors are slow-growing and which are aggressive.

Here's what men should keep in mind:

- All men, especially African American men and men with a family history of prostate cancer, are at risk.
- There are no symptoms in the disease's early stages, but there will be urinary difficulties and some pain as it progresses.
- The American Cancer Society and the American Urological Association recommend that all men age 40 and older have an annual digital rectal exam (DRE). African American men and those with a family history should also have an annual PSA test beginning at age 40. All men 50 and older are advised to undergo a DRE and a PSA test annually. However, a task force convened by the U.S. Public Health Service advises against routine prostate cancer screening because there's not enough evidence that early detection saves lives.

Despite its shortcomings, the PSA test detects prostate cancer better than a mammogram detects breast cancer.

at an early stage may choose surveillance as a treatment option.

■ **Take into account a patient's age, health, and life expectancy.** Because it's difficult to accurately determine the grade and stage of the cancer, doctors also rely on a patient's age, health, and life expectancy at the time of diagnosis to determine whether he's a good candidate for treatment. According to the guidelines, a man's life expectancy should be at least 10 years to be considered a candidate for treatment because that's how long it usually takes prostate cancer to spread and become fatal.

The younger a man is the more likely he will benefit from treatment because the disease will probably progress during his lifetime if left untreated. Regardless of the size and grade of the tumor, prostate cancer needs to be treated in someone age 50 or younger, says Austenfeld.

■ **Understand the side effects of treatment.** Some patients are reluctant to undergo prostate surgery because it may result in impotence and pain. But removal of the entire prostate greatly reduces the likelihood that the cancer will recur. With radiation therapy, the risk of impotence and incontinence is somewhat less, but the cancer may recur because the prostate remains in place.

Because the best treatment for prostate cancer remains unclear, patients need to be involved in making decisions, particularly if their case is borderline. Says Austenfeld: "We can't definitely say which treatments are preferable so we have to rely to some extent on patient preferences."

EXPERT TIPS

LETTING BACK PAIN GO AWAY

A new study suggests that back problems are greatly overtreated

In both his life and death, America's 35th president, John F. Kennedy, had little in common with most of his countrymen. But the chronic back problems that sometimes landed him in a rocking chair are a familiar plight for all-too-many Americans. One-third of all adults will experience back pain by age 30, three-fourths by age 40, and everybody experiences some back pain by age 50. In fact, it is the number one cause of disability in Americans under age 45, and more people seek medical care because of back pain than any other complaint except colds and upper respiratory illnesses, according to the American Academy of Orthopedic Surgeons.

Whether most back problems require medical treatment is debatable, however. A blue ribbon panel convened by the Agency for Health Care Policy and Research (AHCPR) recently found that nearly 90 percent of patients suffering from low back pain will get better within a few weeks without any medical treatment. The panel's chairman, Dr. Stanley Bigos, professor of orthopedic surgery and environmental health at the University of Washington in Seattle, discusses the new guidelines for treating acute low back problems and offers tips to help understand and manage back pain:

■ **Physical activity is the best way to relieve back pain.** Our panel looked at over 11,000 abstracts and 4,600 articles to help us understand what interventions medical science can or can't support. We asked, if one group gets treatment and the other doesn't, is there a difference that's beneficial? In going through that process, we realized that the real key to treatment is trying to avoid resting too much or too long—and for those whose symptoms last for a while, trying to build their tolerance for activity through exercise. Nine out of 10 people get over their problem during the first month. A study on nurses in Sweden shows that training specific back muscles can actually reduce the number of days people complain about their backs tenfold and the number of days missed at work fivefold. That's among people who have to lift patients all day, which is rather rigorous work.

■ **Gradually build endurance and stamina to increase your ability to tolerate activity.** Nobody's been able to show exactly what exercises people should do to minimize back pain, but there are some things that can be done safely that don't stress the back any more than sitting on the side of the bed before you get up in the morning. People can begin rather early walking, stationary biking, even jogging.

■ **If necessary, use over-the-counter pain relievers or spinal manipulation to temporarily ease the pain.** Part of treating back pain is keeping the patient reasonably comfortable early on when the symptoms first hit, when they're usually at their worst. But in almost 80 percent of patients the severe pain usually passes in three to four days. Spinal manipulation (see "Cracking the Armor of MDs," page 246) and acetaminophen (Tylenol), along with nonsteroidal anti-inflammatory medications like Aleve and ibuprofen (Advil) taken in the proper doses in combination, are usually as beneficial, or more beneficial than stronger, prescription medications.

Spinal manipulation offers relief for about the same amount of time as over-the-counter medications, but you can't repeat it as often. Although it's not as effective as these medications, it seems to be safer and doesn't cause ulcers. However, nothing totally wipes out the pain, it just takes the edge off it. And neither is a treatment—it's a means of controlling symptoms so people can stay active.

■ **Prevent back pain by keeping active.** There's nothing you can do to guard against back

■ **THE RIGHT MOVES...**

Once you have back symptoms, you can try to decrease how much they impact you. If you lift something, keep it close to your belly button, because it puts less stress on your back.

DON'T...

TO LIFT IT SAFE:

DO...

- Plan ahead and don't be in a hurry.
- Be careful not to lift something too heavy or awkward by yourself. Get help.
- Keep your feet a shoulder-width apart. Bend at the knees.
- Tighten your stomach muscles.
- Position a person or object close to your body before lifting.
- Lift with your legs.
- Avoid twisting your body; instead point your toes and pivot.
- Maintain the natural curve of your spine, and don't bend at the waist.

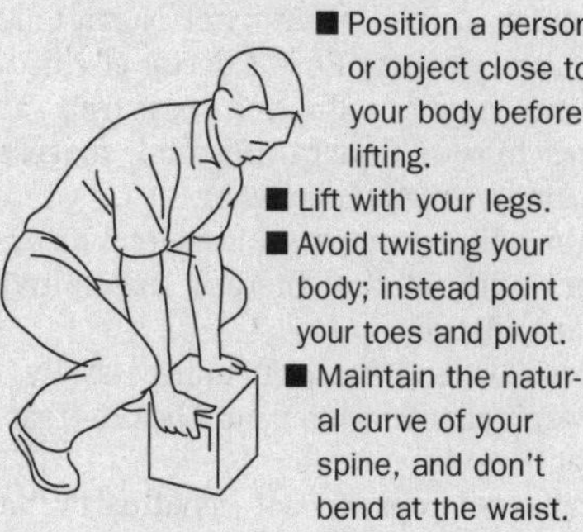

pain except try not to become debilitated by inactivity. It's especially important to exercise as we get older, because over our life we lose a great deal of muscular protection.

■ **Seek medical attention if your pain persists.** For the most part, acute back problems last less than three months. Chronic back problems are the ones that limit someone more than three months, and once someone has back symptoms, they may recur quite frequently. Whether you should seek medical attention depends on what you're kept from doing by your symptoms and how severe the pain is initially. If your symptoms last more than a month, your activity is really limited, and you don't seem to be headed in the right direction, you should try to figure out why you're so slow to recover. We usually start out by reviewing information from the physical exam, or ordering lab tests like a bone scan or an X ray, depending upon the patient's original complaint. We try to gather other information before doing imaging studies like MRIs or CAT scans, because those tests can be confusing and, if used alone, can give a false-positive rate of as high as 30 percent in people age 30.

■ **Choose a physician who really understands back problems.** The type of provider you choose isn't as important as the individual and the understanding he or she may have about back problems. They have to be trained well enough to look for the red flags and make sure they aren't missing something serious. Try to find clinicians that are going to keep you active. If somebody says, "I want you to go home and lie down for a few weeks," run the other way.

■ **Keep in mind that surgery is rarely necessary.** Whether or not surgery is required depends on how strong the findings are from different tests. Only one to two percent of patients who suffer from back pain will have findings compatible with a good surgical outcome—but half of them get over their symptoms within a month. That's why the new AHCPR guidelines advise physicians to wait a month before intervening unless certain red flags indicate that some sort of dangerous condition is present like cancer, an infection, or significant trauma like a fracture.

Relying too much on the wrong information—like imaging studies which have high false-positive rates—has led to a fair number of unsuccessful surgeries. If you're even a millimeter off whatever is causing the back symptoms, you might as well operate on the hand or the foot—the results will be the same. You won't take care of the problem and the place you operated on will be worse off. Americans seem to get operated on for back pain more than people in other Western cultures.

CHIROPRACTICS

CRACKING THE ARMOR OF MDs

Established medicine may not like it, but chiropractors do help some

Should you trust a chiropractor? The very notion makes many medical doctors, disturbed by what they see as a growing trend by chiropractors to tout themselves as primary care providers capable of treating the entire family, cringe.

But spinal manipulation—the mainstay of the nation's 50,000 licensed chiropractors—is increasingly being accepted by medical authorities as a means of controlling low back pain. Spinal manipulation involves adjusting by hand the 24 vertebrae stacked on top of each other, to restore normal movement in joints that aren't functioning properly.

Last year, a panel assembled by the Agency for Health Care Policy and Research (AHCPR), a branch of the U.S. Department of Health and Human Services, found that spinal manipulation is safe during the first month a patient experiences low back symptoms, as long as there has been no nerve damage. The scant research available on spinal manipulation indicates that it's probably safe if pain continues more than one month, but its effectiveness is unproved, according to the panel. Medical doctors maintain that people with chronic low back pain require a multidisciplinary effort because the short-term benefits conferred by spinal manipulation will disappear quickly.

"Manipulation is a very reasonable option for people who don't want to take medication," says Dr. Paul Shekelle, an internist at the West Los Angeles Veterans Administration Medical Center. Shekelle led a 1990 study by the RAND Corporation that also found that spinal manipulation can provide short-term relief from acute low back pain. There's only a one in a million occurrence, says Shekelle, that a serious complication will result from spinal manipulation—provided it's limited to the lower, or lumbar spine.

Spinal manipulation is covered by most insurance plans, but chiropractors maintain that it's less likely to be paid for in managed care health plans because primary care doctors are reluctant to refer patients to chiropractors. Spinal manipulation is also performed by doctors of osteopathy (physicians who emphasize the unity of the body, and believe that changes in one system such as the musculoskeletal system can affect how other systems and organs function), and some orthopedists and physical therapists as well. In choosing a provider, "the difference between clinicians is greater than between professions," says Shekelle, and getting a proper diagnosis is crucial.

In a 1992 article published in the *Journal of Family Practice*, Peter Curtis, a family physician at the University of North Carolina, and Geoffrey Bove, a doctor of chiropractic now conducting research at Massachusetts General Hospital, suggest choosing a chiropractor who:

- primarily treats musculoskeletal disorders with manual therapy like spinal manipulation
- doesn't extend treatment unnecessarily
- doesn't charge a lump sum before treatment begins
- graduated from a school accredited by the Council on Chiropractic Education, 4401 Westown Parkway, Suite 120, W. Des Moines, IA 50265, ☎ 515-226-9001.

If you don't see any results after three or four weeks of treatment, warns Bove, you should question whether your chiropractor's approach is likely to work—just as you would a medical doctor. The idea that once you start seeing a chiropractor, you must keep going, is a myth, says Bove. Yet many musculoskeletal problems are related to lifestyle issues, such as a poor diet, inactivity, obesity and stress. Unless those behaviors change, chiropractics will not rid a patient of his symptoms, Bove explains. "But some people say they'd rather come see me once a week than change their lifestyle."

EXPERT Q & A

WHAT DOCTORS DON'T LEARN

Biofeedback, visual imagery, and yoga may have uses

Homeopathy? Acupuncture? Massage therapy? Ten or 20 years ago these practices were dismissed as black magic by medical doctors and regarded with suspicion by most Americans. But alternative therapies are entering mainstream medicine. In 1993 the National Institutes of Health opened an Office of Alternative Medicine to oversee scientific research on alternative therapies. The federally funded agency recently awarded grants to eight specialty centers charged with evaluating various alternative therapies. A landmark study on alternative medicine published in the *New England Journal of Medicine* found that in a single year alternative approaches were used by more than one-third of Americans to treat a serious illness—with an out-of-pocket cost of $10 billion. Dr. James Gordon, the founder and director of the Washington, D.C.–based Center for Mind-Body Medicine and author of *Manifesto for a New Medicine: Your Guide to Healing Partnerships and the Wise Use of Alternative Therapies* (Addison-Wesley, 1996), discusses the changing status of alternative therapies:

■ What is alternative medicine and how does it differ from holistic or mind-body medicine?

Alternative medicine is basically everything your physician didn't learn in medical school. It uses the techniques of other healing systems, cultures, and approaches as an integral part of medical care. Holistic medicine, which comes from the Greek word *holos*, meaning whole, was developed in the 1970s to describe medicine that understood the whole person in his or her total environment and appreciated that a human being was different from and greater than the sum of his or her parts. Mind-body medicine refers to the effects of the mind on the body and the reciprocal effects of the body on the mind. It emphasizes the largely untapped power we all have to affect our health simply by using our minds through biofeedback, visual imagery, meditation, and relaxation. Some physical exercises, like yoga and tai chi, can also profoundly affect mental and emotional function.

■ How does alternative medicine differ from conventional medicine in its approach to treating illness?

The understanding that dominates our health care is that if somebody has a disease, we have to go in and find out what the biological basis is and develop something to solve the biological problem. When you focus on a specific biological reaction and develop a drug for that, like antibiotics, you destroy the bacteria you want to destroy. But in the process you may wipe out all the other bacteria and affect the immune system negatively. A more holistic approach might be to ask, "What can people do for themselves to strengthen their immune system so they don't get infections?" Instead of attacking the disease process as if it were the offender, you strengthen the whole human being so the disease process no longer has a place.

Most of the people I've seen come because conventional medicine has not done what they hoped it would do. Some of the studies coming out are having some effect, too. When a perfectly good study comes out that shows that garlic can lower cholesterol, people have to say, "Well, maybe there's something to it." Where we have made significant gains—for example, in cardiovascular disease—those gains have mostly come about because of patterns in diet and exercise rather than anything we've developed as far as drugs or surgery.

LITTLE NEEDLES THAT CAN

Western medicine is finally waking up to acupuncture's potential

"I have seen the past and it works." Those words were spoken in 1971 by the late *New York Times* columnist James Reston after he received acupuncture treatments in China following an appendectomy. Despite acupuncture's 5,000-year history in the East, it was Reston's endorsement that introduced Americans to the practice of inserting extremely fine needles into the skin to help balance the body's energy flow. The Chinese claim is that imbalances in energy lead to a host of ailments, and that inserting needles into specific "points" all over the body can rectify these problems by either enhancing or reducing energy.

In fact, acupuncture can relieve pain caused by arthritis, bursitis, headaches, muscle aches, and menstrual cramps by releasing chemical substances called endorphins, which increase the threshold of pain in the brain. Acupuncture has also been found to control drug and alcohol addictions. Studies also show that it may speed recovery of some stroke victims.

Acupuncture is not a cure-all, however, and shouldn't be used for conditions like cancer that may require surgery or drug treatment. "If an acupuncturist tells you he'll cure you, beware," says Dr. Xiao Ming Tian (who prefers to be called Dr. Ming), an orthopedic surgeon and pathologist who specializes in acupuncture and is a consultant to the National Institutes of Health.

Today's acupuncturists are better trained than in the 1970s, when a three-week course was the only training some acupuncturists in the United States underwent. Today, 24 states require acupuncturists to be licensed or certified. As acupuncture's credibility grows, many physicians are beginning to blend Chinese medicine with Western medicine.

Acupuncture is considered painless and safe, provided the practitioner is qualified, uses disposable needles, and employs precautions like wearing gloves at all times. Ming reports that in the past 23 years there have been only six cases of malpractice in the United States.

Acupuncture was considered an experimental treatment by the Food and Drug Administration until recently, when the agency classified the needles as medical devices. Although the FDA didn't declare the needles useful in treating specific conditions, the new classification is expected to make insurance coverage for acupuncture more likely.

■ Which alternative treatments are the best-established?

The best evidence shows that we can use our minds to change in a positive direction many physiological functions that were believed to be beyond our voluntary control 30 years ago. For example, you can lower blood pressure, relieve pain, and improve functioning in asthma patients. There's a good deal of evidence that relaxation therapies like biofeedback, hypnosis, and visual imagery are effective for treating insomnia and pain. There are also very good studies on acupuncture and herbal therapies; they're just not known in this country because most of them have been done in Asia and Europe.

Other research focuses on the use of chiropractic to treat lower back pain and on the effectiveness of homeopathic remedies for a variety of conditions including hay fever in children and arthritis. Studies of therapeutic touch show that when people bring their hands close to other people trained as healers, it relaxes them and improves their physiological functioning.

■ How do nutrition and exercise fit in?

They are also considered alternative therapies, because they're not ordinarily a part of physicians' practices. There's no real understanding of the use of nutritional supplementation or of diets like the Mediterranean diet, which can help prevent cardiovascular disease. The same with exercise. Most doctors know a bit about aerobic exercise, but they don't know anything about yoga or tai chi, which are enormously helpful in treating many chronic conditions. For example, there are many studies done in India where people have used yoga as part of the treatment for asthma, arthritis, hypertension, anxiety, and depression—with good results.

■ What should patients look for in a physician who practices alternative medicine?

At a minimum, every physician using alternative approaches should know about relaxation therapies, self-awareness, meditation, nutrition, and exercise. Beyond that, it's hard to know which system will be most effective. Sometimes you'll have a sense of which techniques are most important to you. For example, if you have a bad back or musculoskeletal problems, it's best to go to someone who knows manipulation in addition to conventional medicine. If you have food allergies, clearly you want somebody who knows about nutrition. If you have chronic pain, acupuncture is a good bet. It's important to work with someone who knows at least one approach well but won't beat you over the head with it whether it works or not.

■ How does the relationship between alternative practitioners and their patients differ from the typical doctor-patient relationship?

It involves a teaching relationship—which is not primarily the kind of relationship doctors have with patients. What you want are people who are going to help you learn how to take care of yourself, not people who are going to make you dependent on them. Alternative medicine practitioners often use groups as a way of maximizing therapeutic work, because we've found that people can help each other make real changes not only in psychology, but in basic biological processes, simply by sharing their experiences.

The most striking study was done at Stanford University, where one group of women with breast cancer received the conventional medical treatment—surgery, chemotherapy, and sometimes radiation—and another group, in addition, met together with a psychiatrist once a week for an hour and a half for a year. Women in the support group lived on average 18 months longer than women not in the support group.

■ Does insurance cover alternative therapies?

A lot of things are considered part of general medical treatment—so if I'm a doctor and I do homeopathy or nutritional counseling, that's covered. Most plans also cover chiropractic, and in some states acupuncture. But that's not the case for many of the services by practitioners who are not medical doctors.

■ What should a patient do if his doctor is reluctant to discuss alternative therapies?

Roughly 70 percent of patients receiving alternative therapies don't discuss it with their doctor because they fear their doctors will not only not be sympathetic, but will be angry with them. That has to change. Part of being a scientist is keeping an open mind and waiting until all the evidence is in. If patients find doctors irritated with them, or condescending, for being interested in alternative therapies, it's time to say, "That's unacceptable; take a look at the evidence. I need you to help me and not make uninformed judgments."

■ Are there any dangers to using alternative medicine?

Any health care practitioner should be optimistic and inspire hope, but I would be wary of anyone who promises miracles. One of the shortcomings of alternative medicine is that some practitioners think their method is going to cure everything. And some alternative practitioners have an antagonism toward traditional medicine. You need someone who can see the strengths and weaknesses of all the approaches. Alternative therapies can be used just as stupidly as conventional therapies.

STEELING YOURSELF FOR THE SNEEZE SEASON

Spring marks the start of the dreaded hay fever season for as many as 1 in 10 Americans who are allergic to airborne pollen. Allergy sufferers spend over $650 million each year on doctor's fees, allergy shots, and prescription drugs to combat their sneezing and sniffling. Unfortunately, no area is completely pollen-free. Depending on where you live, the pollen season runs from February or March until October. The farther north you live, the later the season's start. Trees pollinate first, then grasses and weeds.

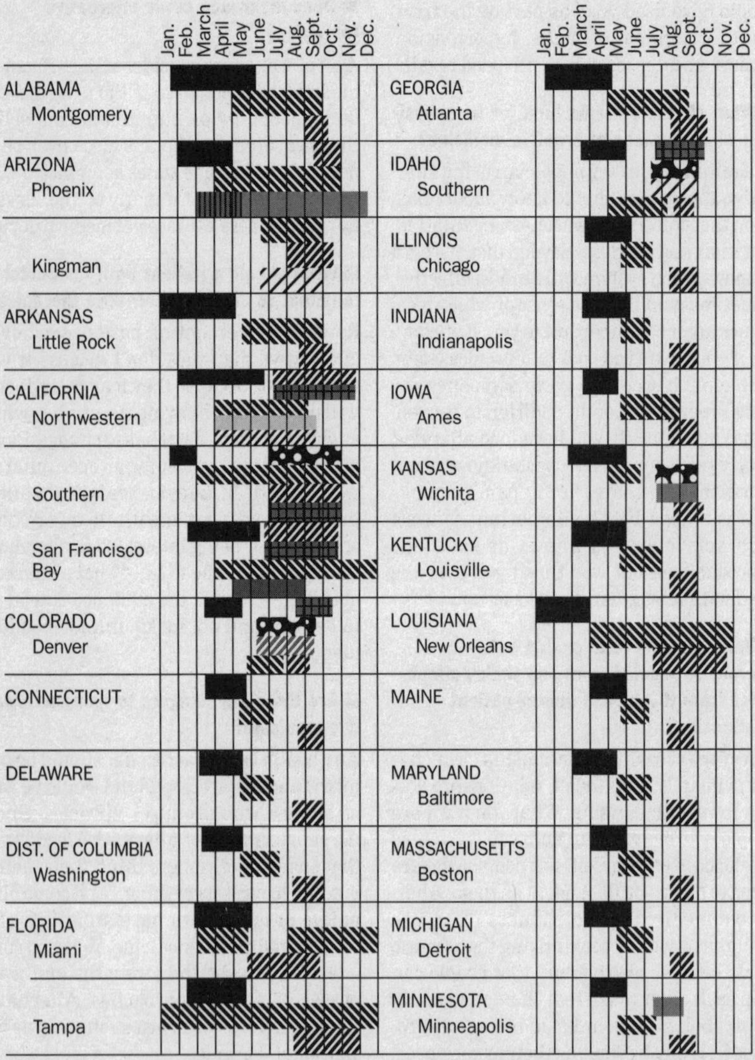

Jan. Feb. March April May June July Aug. Sept. Oct. Nov. Dec.

ALABAMA
Montgomery

ARIZONA
Phoenix

Kingman

ARKANSAS
Little Rock

CALIFORNIA
Northwestern

Southern

San Francisco Bay

COLORADO
Denver

CONNECTICUT

DELAWARE

DIST. OF COLUMBIA
Washington

FLORIDA
Miami

Tampa

Jan. Feb. March April May June July Aug. Sept. Oct. Nov. Dec.

GEORGIA
Atlanta

IDAHO
Southern

ILLINOIS
Chicago

INDIANA
Indianapolis

IOWA
Ames

KANSAS
Wichita

KENTUCKY
Louisville

LOUISIANA
New Orleans

MAINE

MARYLAND
Baltimore

MASSACHUSETTS
Boston

MICHIGAN
Detroit

MINNESOTA
Minneapolis

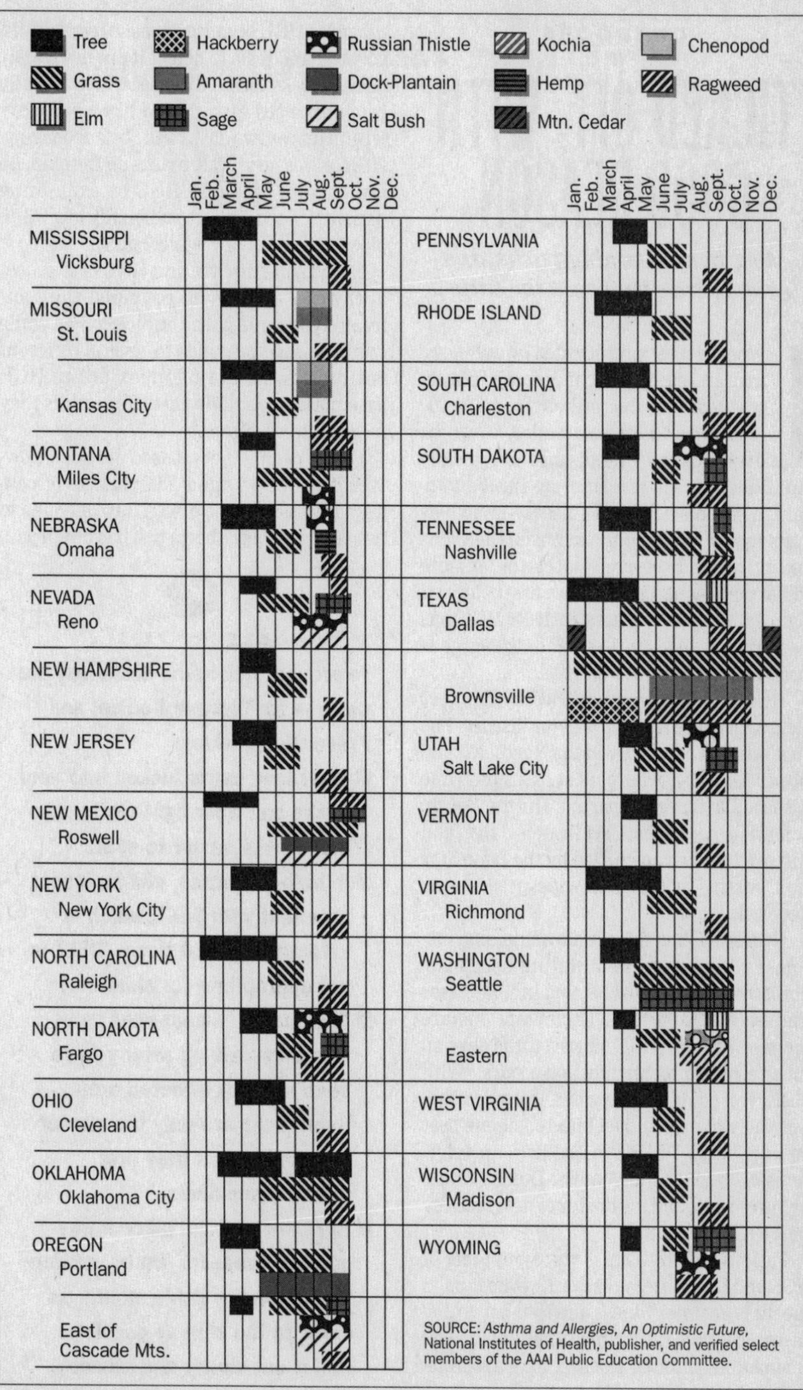

SOURCE: *Asthma and Allergies, An Optimistic Future*, National Institutes of Health, publisher, and verified select members of the AAAI Public Education Committee.

OUTDOORS

TICKED-OFF, WITH GOOD REASON

More bad news about ticks, and Lyme disease isn't even the culprit

Lyme disease, long dreaded by outdoorsmen and parents of children who play in wooded areas, has afflicted some 70,000 Americans. Left unattended, it can be disabling, but the disease is typically mild and not life-threatening. But be vigilant: a second tick-borne disease known as human granulocytic ehrlichiosis (HGE) has recently been discovered that can be far more lethal than Lyme disease. Since first being recognized as a new illness in 1994, HGE has been diagnosed 150 times and already has been blamed for four fatalities.

HGE is a bacterium carried by the deer tick, which also transmits Lyme disease. The tick is found primarily in the Northeast and upper Midwest, where most cases of Lyme disease have been reported. (In the South, scientists have identified a potentially fatal disease that is transmitted by the Lone Star tick, but this tick is not as widespread as the deer tick.)

HGE and Lyme disease have similar symptoms: a high fever, debilitating headache, chills, tired, achy muscles, and in some cases nausea and vomiting. The symptoms are more severe with HGE, however, and develop much sooner after an infection occurs. "With HGE, you could be fine when you go to bed, but you wake up and feel like someone beat you up," says Dr. Johan Bakken, an infectious disease specialist at the Duluth Clinic in Minnesota, and the doctor to first identify the HGE bacterium.

Patients often dismiss the symptoms of HGE and Lyme disease as the flu, even though the flu is a winter illness and tick-borne diseases are typically transmitted during the spring and summer. Doctors may also misdiagnose HGE because it was so recently discovered and tests to detect it are not widely used. Unlike Lyme disease, which usually produces a red rash shaped like a bull's-eye within one or two days of the bite occurring, HGE leaves no telltale marks on the skin. So far, doctors diagnose HGE by examining patients' blood for an abnormally low white blood cell count or platelet count.

Both Lyme disease and HGE can almost always be contained, provided they are treated promptly with antibiotics. But while Lyme disease responds to several different antibiotics, including amoxicillin, HGE patients may actually get worse unless they receive doxycycline.

Before ceding the woods to the ticks, however, keep this in mind: The chances of contracting a tick-borne disease are only one to two percent, even when a tick has bitten you.

EXPERT TIPS

To prevent tick-borne diseases, the Centers for Disease Control and Prevention advises:

- **Wear long pants tucked into your socks and wear light clothing to make ticks easier to spot.**
- **In high-risk areas, use an insect repellent with DEET, which is effective against ticks. (DEET is not appropriate for children.)**
- **Thoroughly inspect your body, hair, and clothing after you've been in a tick-infected area. Some ticks are only the size of a pinhead when they first attach themselves.**
- **To remove a tick, place a fine-pointed tweezers firmly, but gently behind the tick's mouth, as close to the skin as possible. Pull it out slowly and steadily.**

CHAPTER THREE

SEXUALITY

EXPERT QUOTES

"Estrogen is the Marilyn Monroe in us. It gives a woman curves and makes her receptive."
—Dr. Theresa Crenshaw, author of *The Alchemy of Love and Lust*
Page 255

"Honesty is definitely not called for" when talking to a partner about something that turns you off.
—Isadora Alman, syndicated sex columnist
Page 261

"One-half of unintended pregnancies could be prevented if women knew about emergency contraception."
—Dr. James Trussell, Princeton University
Page 270

■ **THE YEAR AHEAD: LOOK FOR** increased interest in testosterone replacement therapy by both men and women... **PREPARE** to discuss sexuality issues with children at an earlier age... **EXPECT** more debate about the practice of circumcision in the United States... **GET READY** for major new legal rulings that better define the rights of gay couples... **WATCH FOR** further medical breakthroughs in treating impotence... **FORGET** unprotected oral sex with a stranger...

WAYS & MORES 254

RISKS & REMEDIES 269

WAYS & MORES

PUBERTY: The body's wonder years, PAGE 256 **STATISTICS:** The numbers on things sexual, PAGE 258 **PARENTING:** What to tell your kids about sex, PAGE 259 **COMMUNICATION:** How to talk your way to satisfaction, PAGE 261 **WORKPLACE:** Effective ways to handle sexual harassment, PAGE 263 **FOOT MASSAGE:** Stimulating the senses, from the ground up, PAGE 267 **AGING:** Passion doesn't have to end in the golden years, PAGE 268

EXPERT Q & A

CHECKING UP ON YOUR SEX DRIVE

For men, it's testosterone, for women, estrogen that make whoopee

When Masters and Johnson conducted their groundbreaking research on the sex lives of Americans in the 1960s, they were among the first to treat sexuality as a medical topic. In recent years, sexual therapists and their patients have focused more intently on what influences the body's sex drive and, in turn, human relationships. Dr. Theresa Crenshaw, a sexual medicine specialist and author of *The Alchemy of Love and Lust* (G.P. Putnam's Sons, 1996), explains how hormones govern our sex lives and what we can do to handle them:

■ **Which hormones most strongly regulate sexuality?**

They all do at different times. That's why I refer to it as "sex soup." And as the ingredients change, so does the predominant sexual pattern and many other attitude-related behaviors. The relationship between hormones and sex drive is incestuous, intimate, and strong.

■ **What are the main differences in male and female sex hormones?**

Men have much more testosterone, but women have other hormones such as estrogen and progesterone. In men, the levels of these hormones and their pattern or rhythm changes during the day. About every 15 to 20 minutes testosterone oscillates in men, which influences a man's behavior—chief among these is the desire for orgasm. Women have more hormones, which makes their sex drive more complex. It means there are more sexual gears for women that generally follow the monthly cycle. For example, when estrogen predominates, a woman may be receptive and passive, but as she passes ovulation she enters the proceptive or seductive nature of her sex drive.

■ **How do differing sex drives of men and women affect their behavior and relationships?**

It's normal for people to have different sex drives and different rhythms. One partner could be a morning person and the other could be an afternoon person, or if they both have the desire three times a week it could be three different days. Unless a couple learns to handle, negotiate, and make the best of different sex drives early on in their relationship, they're destined for problems.

■ What role does estrogen play in a woman's sexual behavior?

It's the Marilyn Monroe in us. It gives a woman her curves, it's the gentle, nondemanding, nondomineering side, and it makes her willful, ready, and receptive for a man. It may also impair a woman's judgment slightly and reduce her selectiveness.

■ How does testosterone affect sex drive?

Testosterone makes us irritable, aggressive, belligerent, and testy—that's where the word comes from. Both men and women have testosterone, but it's in much lower doses in women. We know from studies in animals that testosterone makes a male want to be separate and alone. In addition, sexual fantasies are testosterone-dependent, and the hormone provokes an interest in genital sex and orgasm in both sexes. Curiously enough, it encourages masturbation rather than intercourse.

■ What happens to sex drive as we age?

In men, testosterone begins decreasing ever so slowly in their 30s and continues to decrease throughout a man's life. As a result, sex drive diminishes and all the hormones and mechanisms that make erection predictably available become unpredictably available. The frequency of sex goes down and for some men they aren't able to have sex at all.

In women who aren't given hormone replacement therapy (see related story, page 241) during menopause, testosterone becomes more powerful in their systems than it was before. Since estrogen disappears, the remaining testosterone has more power, relative to the ratio of other hormones that previously overwhelmed the testosterone. That's why some elderly women get mustaches and their voices get lower.

■ Do males experience menopause?

Male menopause, or viropause, is similar to menopause in women, with two distinctions. First, the predominant hormones lost in men are testosterone and DHEA, as opposed to estrogen and progesterone in the female. The second major difference is that women sometimes go through 10 to 15 years of unpleasant symptoms that are quite acute and distinct compared to the man's transition. A woman begins menopause when she's 40 to 45 and finishes in her late 50s. But the man begins to creep unknowingly into it in his 30s. It's gradual and indistinct and the changes don't knock him across the head. Most men don't suddenly wake up with hot flashes the way women do, which is one of the reasons so few physicians and therapists believe it occurs at all. It's less obvious clinically until it reaches the endpoint in the 60s and 70s, but if you don't recognize it or give a man treatment until then, he's gone through all the hard parts alone.

■ Can testosterone supplements boost a man's sex drive?

Testosterone replacement therapy (TRT) is usually excellent if it's properly delivered. But testosterone is overprescribed to the younger man who comes in complaining that his erections aren't strong enough and to younger men who have normal or abundant levels of testosterone. Then as a man ages and actually needs testosterone, physicians become stingy.

■ What are the potential side effects of testosterone replacement therapy?

While it will not cause prostate cancer, it may fertilize one that's already there. In addition, testosterone causes salt retention and in this way can raise blood pressure. But as long as you're aware of these risks and proceed with caution, testosterone can be prescribed safely for the majority who need it.

■ Can women also benefit from testosterone replacement?

Testosterone has the potential to improve sex drive tremendously in women and to improve mood and spirits. Women might consider testosterone replacement if their testosterone levels are not what they should be. Symptoms of low testosterone levels include low sex drive, quietude, passivity, and depression. It's all part of menopause.

THE BODY'S WONDER YEARS

Most teens will probably tell you that "normal adolescent development" is an oxymoron. But despite the awkwardness that goes with the change from child to adult, the transition is usually a predictable one.

■ PHYSICAL DEVELOPMENT IN ADOLESCENT GIRLS

	AGE CHANGE USUALLY BEGINS	AGE CHANGE USUALLY STOPS	REMARKS
INCREASE IN RATE OF GROWTH	10 to 11	15 to 16	If noticeable growth fails to begin by 15, see your doctor.
BREAST DEVELOPMENT	10 to 11	13 to 14	Noticeable development of breasts (one of which may begin to grow before the other) is usually the first sign of puberty. If change doesn't begin by 16, see a doctor.
EMERGENCE OF BODY HAIR	**Pubic:** 10 to 11 **Underarm:** 12 to 13	13 to 14 15 to 16	Development of body hair is extremely variable and largely dependent on heredity. Pubic hair usually darkens and thickens as puberty progresses.
DEVELOPMENT OF SWEAT GLANDS UNDER ARMS AND IN GROIN	12 to 13	15 to 16	Sweat glands are responsible for increased sweating, which causes underarm odor, a type of body odor not present in younger children.
MENSTRUATION	11 to 14	15 to 17	Menstruation often begins with extremely irregular periods but by age 17, a regular cycle (3 to 7 days every 28 days) usually becomes evident. If menstruation begins before 10 or has not begun by 17, talk to your physician.

■ PHYSICAL DEVELOPMENT IN ADOLESCENT BOYS

	AGE CHANGE USUALLY BEGINS	AGE CHANGE USUALLY STOPS	REMARKS
INCREASE IN RATE OF GROWTH	12 to 13	17 to 18	If noticeable growth fails to begin by 15, see your doctor.
ENLARGEMENT OF GENITALS	**Testicles and scrotum:** 11 to 12 **Penis:** 12 to 13	 16 to 17 15 to 16	As testicles grow, the skin of the scrotum darkens. The penis usually lengthens before it broadens. Ability to ejaculate seminal fluid usually begins about a year after the penis starts to lengthen.
EMERGENCE OF BODY HAIR	**Pubic:** 11 to 12 **Underarm:** 13 to 15	15 to 16 16 to 18	Development of body hair is extremely variable and largely dependent on heredity. Development of hair on abdomen and chest usually continues into adulthood.
DEVELOPMENT OF SWEAT GLANDS UNDER ARMS AND IN GROIN	13 to 15	17 to 18	Sweat glands are responsible for increased sweating, which causes underarm odor, a type of body odor not present in younger children.
VOICE CHANGE	13 to 14	16 to 17	Enlargement of the larynx, or voice box, may make the "Adam's apple" more prominent. The voice deepens at 14 to 15, and may change rapidly or gradually. If childlike voice persists after 16, see your doctor.

SOURCE: *American Medical Association Family Medical Guide*, 3rd edition (Random House, 1993).

INTIMATE EXPERIENCES

Most Americans—over 80 percent of all adults under age 60—have one or no sex partners in any given year. Over a lifetime, men tend to have more sex partners than women.

MEASURES OF SATISFACTION WITH PRIMARY PARTNER

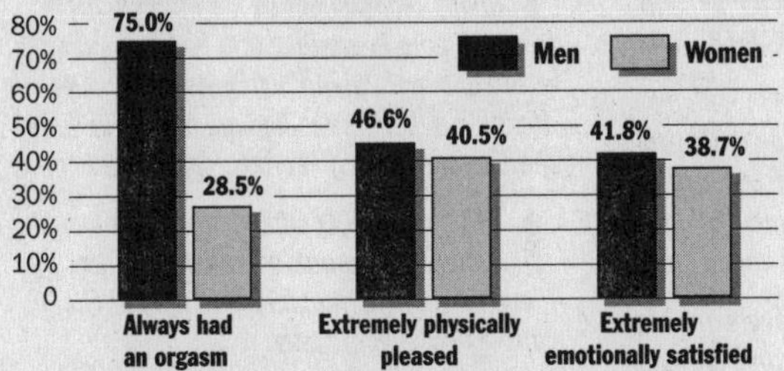

NUMBER OF SEX PARTNERS IN THE PAST 12 MONTHS

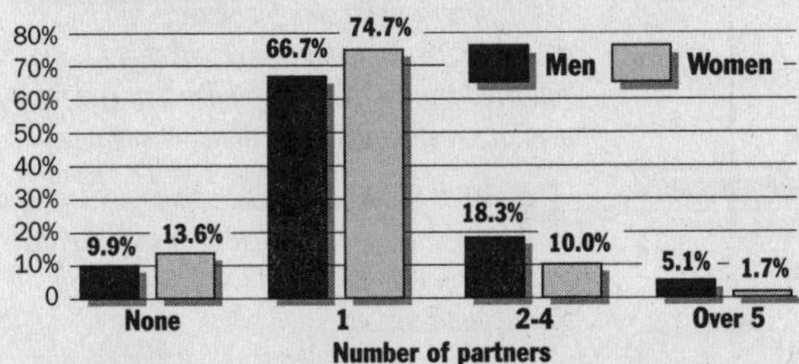

NUMBER OF SEX PARTNERS SINCE AGE 18

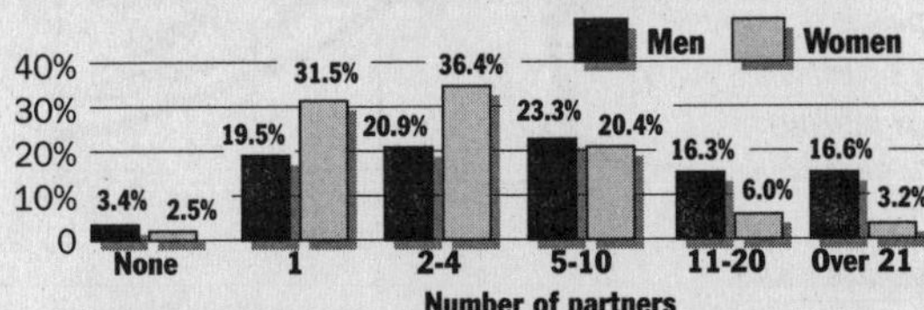

RELATIONSHIP OF WOMEN RESPONDENTS TO MAN WHO FORCED THEM TO DO SOMETHING SEXUAL

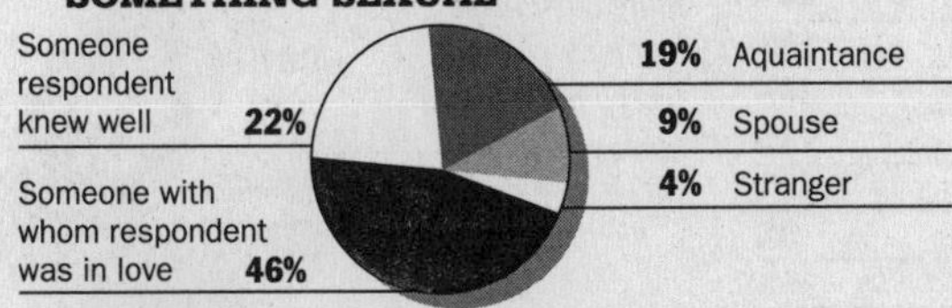

SOURCE: *The Social Organization of Sexuality: Sexual Practices in the United States* (University of Chicago Press, 1994).

- **For those who reached sexual maturity in the 1970s and 1980s, 48 percent of men and 37 percent of women lost their virginity by age 16.**
- **Some 92 percent of men report that having intercourse for the first time was something they welcomed; only 71 percent of women were ready for the experience.**
- **When asked which from a list of sexual practices was very appealing, watching a partner undress was second only to vaginal intercourse for men. For women, receiving oral sex finished a distant second to intercourse, but was slightly preferred to watching a partner undress.**
- **Only one in 50 men and just under one in 100 women identify themselves as homosexual.**
- **Although cause-and-effect cannot be proved, those with a single partner generally report themselves happier than those with more than one or no sexual partners.**

SEX BY THE NUMBERS

Ever since researcher Alfred C. Kinsey published his famous statistical portrait of male sexual behavior in 1948, Americans have sought to quantify what their fellow citizens were doing in the bedroom. A few reference points:

PENIS ENVY: *The circumcision rate in the United States is about 60 percent. In Europe, Russia, China, and Japan it's near zero.*

SPERM STORY: *The average male produces sperm at the rate of 500 million per day. Between 120 million and 600 million sperm are released during one ejaculation.*

HIGH-TEST: *Testosterone levels are highest in the early morning, and lowest in the late afternoon and evening. October is the high point of the year for testosterone levels, February is the nadir.*

NIGHT MOVES: *Average erections per night by age*

Adolescence:	4
Age 30-39:	3
Age 40-69:	2+
Age 70+:	1.7

FOLLOW YOUR NOSE: *When Dr. Alan Hirsch, neurological director of the Smell & Taste Treatment and Research Foundation, set out to find which scents men found most sexually arousing, as measured by penile blood flow, here's what he discovered turned men on the most:*

SCENT	INCREASE IN PENILE BLOOD FLOW (AVG.)
Lavender and pumpkin pie	40%
Doughnut and black licorice	32%
Pumpkin pie and doughnut	20%
Orange	20%
Lavender and doughnut	18%
Black licorice	13%
Black licorice and cola	13%
Doughnut and cola	13%
Buttered popcorn	9%
Vanilla	9%

SET FOR LIFE: *A woman is born with about 400,000 eggs in her ovaries, all that will ever be available to her. But she will only experience about 500 menstrual cycles during her lifetime so her egg supply is more than ample for any reproductive needs.*

SEXY IS AS SEXY DOES: *During intercourse, a woman's breast size may increase as much as 25 percent, and the nipples by 1 centimeter.*

MISSIONARY ZEAL: *The Indian sex manual, the* Kama Sutra, *documents 529 different positions for sexual intercourse. Kinsey and other researchers have reported that man-on-top positions are far and away the most common.*

SLOW BURN: *Men reach their sexual peak at age 17 or 18 and slowly decline from there. Women are at their most receptive around age 40.*

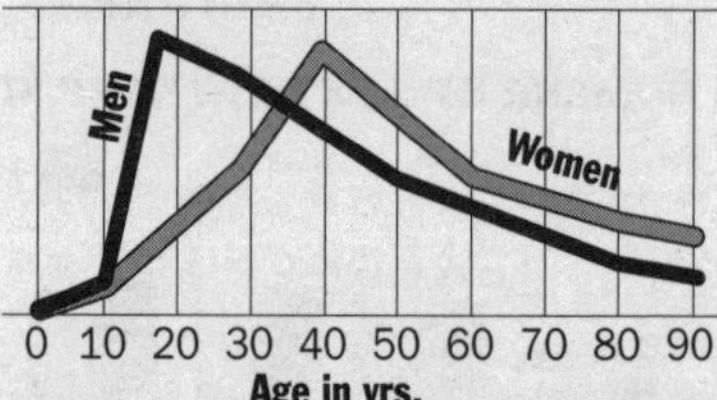

FOR LOVE OR MONEY: *A recent poll by Roper/Starch Worldwide for* Worth *magazine found that more than three times as many people worry more about money than they think about sex.*

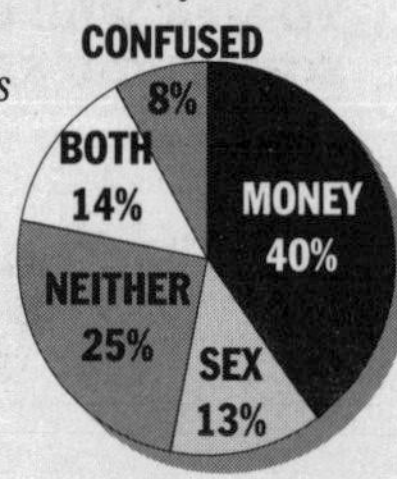

SOURCES: *Esquire* magazine; the Massachusetts Male Aging Study, John McKinley, dir.; *Redbook* magazine; additional reporting.

EXPERT Q & A

WHEN THE STORK WON'T DO

Don't be surprised by children's questions, prepare for them

What should they know? When should they know it? Sooner rather than later these days, every parent must deal with the question of when and how to discuss sexual issues with children. Here, Anne C. Bernstein, a professor of psychology at the Wright Institute in Berkeley, Calif., and author of *Flight of the Stork: What Children Think (and When) About Sex and Family Building* (Perspectives Press, revised 1994), has the following advice:

■ What is a parent's role as a sex educator?

A parent's first task is to create an atmosphere of trust so the child will see him or her as a reliable source of information and someone he or she can come to with questions. Another part of the parent's role is to convey values so the child is clear about the parent's feelings about what sexual relationships should be. Schools should make sure children are exposed to certain basics—factual information about what they need to do to keep themselves safe and to prevent untoward health consequences like unplanned pregnancies and sexually transmitted diseases (STDs). But I don't think parents should ever hold back on educating their children because they're expecting a school to do it.

■ What do children want to know first?

The first question is, "Where do babies come from?" The youngest child assumes that every baby that exists has always existed and the only problem is figuring out where they were before. They wonder about the place it came from—the doctor's, a store, or God's place (they imagine infants in the clouds waiting to be delivered). Then as they begin to understand that things have causes, their questions become more complex. They wonder, how did it happen? And why now? It's important for kids to have a clear sense of cause and effect, not just in sexuality but in every aspect of their lives. They need to understand that consequences are to a large extent based on their actions and aren't arbitrary or capricious.

■ How should parents respond?

Start by making it a dialogue, not a lecture. Find out what they want to know and answer it truthfully and simply. Sometimes it's helpful to ask them what they think, to find out exactly what the question is and what the gap is in their knowledge. You can say, "A lot of kids your age are interested in how babies are made. Do you have any questions about that? I want to make sure you're getting information from somebody who knows what they're talking about." The idea is to convey information that is accurate and will minimize anxiety and misunderstanding. Parents should also tailor the information they convey to the child's level of understanding.

■ How much should you really tell really young children?

Before they reach kindergarten, children should recognize anatomical differences between boys and girls, the names of the body's sexual parts and socially shared words for elimination. They should understand that babies grow within their mother's body and if they ask how, they should be told that babies are made by mothers and fathers together. They might not understand how it happens, but the idea that it takes two people to make a baby is important information, because you want children to know they are biologically related to both parents (if it's true). I don't expect every child will or has to understand things the way an adult would. I do think misunderstandings that cause distress or could lead to harm need to be addressed, which is why I advocate talking about the womb or uterus as opposed to the belly—so we don't confuse kids about how the digestive and reproductive systems are different.

■ What should be said to children who are a little older?

As they get older (about seven or eight), they become more interested in the social relations involved in reproduction—how does love go into making a baby and what does marriage have to do with making a baby? As they enter puberty, they've begun to think about their own sexuality and values, which become more central in their thinking about sexuality. That's why parents need to be clear about their own values. I think it's important to tell children about your values without telling them they need to have the same ones.

EXPERT QUOTE

Being honest is not the same as telling all about your own sex life. Do as I say, not as I did, can be an awkward tack to take when it comes to talking to your child about sexual experimentation. But if your child asks about your sexual coming-of-age, total candor may be ill-advised, says psychologist Anne C. Bernstein of the Wright Institute in Berkeley, Calif. "Don't lie, because that makes you a less truthful source," says Bernstein. "Tell them within limits—but you don't need to go into detail about your sex life." That's especially true if you're not proud of some of the choices you made when you were younger. "You can say, 'When I was younger, I did some things that hurt me and I would prefer that you not make the same mistakes, and let me tell you why,'" suggests Bernstein.

■ At what age should contraception be discussed?

Contraception comes into it fairly early on because kids may ask why certain people have been married so long, but don't have kids. You need to explain that every time you have intercourse, you don't have a baby. Explain that people use birth control if they have sexual intercourse, but don't want to have a baby.

■ What should parents tell their kids about AIDS and other STDs?

AIDS education is more and more something that has to happen early, primarily because with the increased prevalence of AIDS in many communities, children need to understand it's not easily communicable and they won't catch it from someone who's infected unless they engage in high-risk behavior. Kids should know that some infections you can catch sexually are very serious, and that's another reason why it's essential to be responsible in expressing their sexuality.

■ How should parents discuss homosexuality with their kids?

When to talk about homosexuality depends on a child's exposure to it. In a community with many openly gay families, where it's part of the social landscape, bring it up early on. Parents need to let kids know that there are people who fall in love with people of the same sex as well as with people of the opposite sex. If there are family members or people in your community who are homosexual, treat it as matter-of-factly as you can. It's impossible not to convey your values, but I recommend that people express their values as values and not facts when discussing homosexuality—and everything, really. Say, "This how I feel about it and why," but don't convey it as an immutable truth. Kids will be exposed to other values and they will question something if they've heard it as a truth.

EXPERT TIPS

PILLOW TALK THAT KEEPS YOU COZY

Satisfaction requires self-knowledge and a willingness to communicate

No matter how savvy, how sexy, how self-assured, and how liberated you may be, you wouldn't be human if you haven't had your share of embarrassing sexual situations. If people can get embarrassed at the dinner table for spilling a drink or failing to suppress a belch, just think of the possibilities for embarrassment when the atmosphere is charged and you're using your body for far more than eating a lobster. Isadora Alman, syndicated sex and relationship columnist, board-certified sexologist, and author of *Let's Talk: A Guide to Improving Communication, Sex Information: May I Help You* (Down There Press, 1992), and other publications, has this advice on communicating with a lover:

■ The first thing you have to examine in any dilemma, sexual or otherwise, is yourself.

Figure out who you are and take an honest look at your wants and needs. "I want to be cuddled" is very different from "I want to have sex." If you know what your feelings, wants, and needs are, it's much easier to understand your reactions to specific situations and much easier to communicate with your partner. This also means knowing what it is you feel about your partner—you might be so head-over-heels for one person that you'd dress up in a Barney the Dinosaur costume to fulfill a fantasy, but for another you'd only be willing to go from a buzz cut to a bob.

Self-knowledge is extremely important in examining why something embarrasses you or makes you uncomfortable. Do you find a certain sexual position embarrassing because you don't like the view it gives your lover of that extra roll of fat, or because it doesn't stimulate you in any erotic way, or because it makes you feel as if your partner is trying to dominate you? Maybe you should suggest to your partner that you save that position for a "lights off" encounter, or maybe you need to say that you need some kind of extra stimulation, or that you simply don't like it because it makes you feel as if you should be on a Nova special about animal mating rituals.

■ Communicating what's going on in your own brain and body takes tact.

You have to know yourself well enough to know how honest you want to be with your partner. If you don't like the way you look in one position, you need to know what options you would feel comfortable with, but you don't have to say why necessarily.

In telling your partner something about him or her that you don't like, honesty is definitely not called for. If you are becoming a bit repulsed by the extra love handles your partner is collecting, a blunt "Your body is beginning to disgust me," is definitely not the best tactic. Maybe, "I'm thinking about joining a gym and starting some weight training...maybe we could do it together," would be better. And if what is bothering you about the person is something he or she cannot change, like height, a hairy back, or lip shape, don't bring it up. Why make someone feel awkward or bad about something he or she has no control over?

■ Communications need not be verbal.

Some therapists say we should all be perfectly honest in bed all the time, but to bring everything to a screeching halt because your partner needs a map to your body can not only do damage to the evening, but to your relationship. Instead, try something nonverbal. Take his or her hand and guide it, or flop over and present the part of your body you want lavished with attention. You might also decide that you are willing to go without reaching the ultimate in physical ecstasy

KEEPING YOUR WITS WHEN THINGS GET STEAMY

Wondering what the etiquette is for handling a sexual embarrassment? Being able to laugh will help you deal with even the most absurd sexual situations. Here's how Isadora Alman would handle some touchy situations:

■ **At the office, a coworker of the opposite/same sex has clearly expressed a romantic interest in you. How do you tell that person you are gay or straight?**

Let me illustrate with a story. Years ago, I suggested to a man I knew that we get to know each other a little better. He responded with lavish compliments—he thought I was funny and smart, he enjoyed spending time with me, etc. He acknowledged who I was and made it clear that it wasn't any fault of mine, but that his tastes ran to tall, big-boned blondes, which I am not. Afterward, I felt really good about myself, never mind that I had been rejected.

The same tactic can be used to tell someone you are gay or straight. Tell your coworker you like this and that about him or her, but that your taste happens to run to girls—or boys, whichever it is. This is a situation where total honesty is certainly NOT called for. If, for example, you aren't attracted to a person because he or she is too fat, too old, or too hairy, there is no reason to bring it up.

■ **After dating someone for some time, you finally lean over to kiss him—and dislodge his previously undisclosed toupee.**

Try to ignore it. Maybe you can subtly put it back in place with the next kiss or head caress. If it's already on the floor or otherwise past the point of playing dumb, you'd better acknowledge it, hopefully with a tension-breaking joke.

■ **As the passions rise in your first sexual encounter with someone, your partner begins to "talk dirty." You want to burst out laughing.**

It may not be the words your partner uses, but just the fact that there are words at all that bothers you, so first figure out what you don't like about it. Try a nonverbal tactic. Stick your fingers in his or her mouth. If this doesn't work, you may need to bring it up outside of bed. You could say, "I love that you are so excited, but I find it distracting to have so much talking…maybe you could nibble on my ear."

■ **You and your partner agree to play out each other's fantasies. After hearing what is wanted of you, it holds no appeal.**

Ask yourself whether or not you are willing to do this for your partner. If you are willing, then do it wholeheartedly. Anything that you don't know how to do is awkward the first time, so find out exactly what he or she wants and figure out how do it. There are books, videos, and advisers on everything from sex toys to bondage to how to give a massage. Get into the fun of it, practice on your own, and then DO IT.

that particular time and bring it up in conversation outside of the already charged sexual situation.

■ **If you are finding it difficult to bring something up, admitting your embarrassment often makes it easier.**

Try saying, for instance: "You don't know how embarrassed I am to have this conversation, but..." If you absolutely cannot bring it up, write a note, being sure to put it in a place where your partner will find it privately. I feel very strongly that when telling your partner that you don't like one thing, you have the responsibility to suggest an alternative. Instead of saying, "I hate it when you suck on my toes," say, "I'm afraid the toes don't do it for me…but what does is the back of my knees, or the nape of my neck, or my armpit."

EXPERT TIPS

WHEN NO MEANS NO HARASSMENT

To ward off workplace trouble, women have to speak up early

Since Anita Hill leveled her claims against Clarence Thomas, sexual harassment has been a highly charged issue in nearly every institution and industry in the country. Yet the rules on relating to colleagues in the workplace remain murky. Between 40 and 60 percent of working women have experienced some form of sexual harassment, according to the American Psychological Association. Below, Ellen Bravo, executive director of the 9 to 5 National Association of Working Women and co-author of *The 9 to 5 Guide to Combating Sexual Harassment* (John Wiley and Sons, 1992), offers some tips for both women and men on navigating today's tension-filled work environment:

■ **NIP IT IN THE BUD.** Sexual harassment often starts out with an unexpected comment. If an issue about appearance or behavior throws you off guard at a business meeting, that's the intention. It's often dismissed as frivolous, but if it persists, you wonder if you misled him. There are many ways to stop it—by not laughing and changing the subject, or by saying, "I'm not comfortable with this." Typically, a harasser will dismiss these attempts by denial, accusing you of exaggerating, or by threatening you. But unless you stop it right away, he can say he thought the behavior was welcome.

■ **SAY NO CLEARLY, BUT DIPLOMATICALLY.** Start by saying, "Please don't take this wrong," or "I don't want to make a big deal about this. I know you're saying it in fun, but would you mind not saying it?" Chances are, if you preface it that way you'll get them to see the need to change their language and you'll get the behavior that's bothering you to stop.

■ **SAY IT IN WRITING, IF NECESSARY.** If it doesn't stop right away, saying it in writing is often effective. There should be three parts to a memo: describe in detail what the behavior was ("Yesterday when you told me about your sexual exploits over the weekend..."), how it made you feel ("I was embarrassed and thrown off guard..."), and what you want done ("As I said yesterday, I don't want you to do this again to me or to anyone else."). You don't have to send it to anyone else or threaten him, but it's your way of saying, "I know my rights." Keep a copy for yourself, and document your experiences in a notebook in which you can't add or remove paper.

■ **THINK HOW TO HAVE THE MAXIMUM IMPACT.** Realize this is a lack of power on your part, not a lack of intelligence. If the behavior is repeated and it's a pattern, and you realize it's being done to others too, you should pursue the formal complaint process. Saying to your company, there's a need for training in my department, is another way to get the message out that there will be consequences for this kind of behavior without naming names.

■ **SEEK A LAWYER'S ADVICE.** Consider seeking a onetime appointment with a lawyer to help appraise your case and learn what your rights are and other steps you should take. Or call the 9 to 5 National Association of Working Women at ☎ 800-522-0925.

■ **HELP CHANGE YOUR WORK ENVIRONMENT.** Volunteer to be on a task force or request a meeting to develop a policy—it's not a quick fix, not just a lecture and a list of do's and don'ts on the wall. A strong statement from top officials clearly defines channels familiar to everyone and includes more than one person you can report to. It should also include a complaint process, due process for the accused, prompt and effective investigation, discipline appropriate to the offense, protection against retaliation, counseling if appropriate, and a follow-up mechanism to ensure good training for everyone in the workplace.

GAY RIGHTS

THE SAME-SEX FRONTIER

For gays and lesbians, the legal landscape is changing rapidly

Nature or nurture? In the never-ending quest to understand human behavior, this question has been posed on seemingly countless fronts: Why is a person obese, a repeat sex offender, an alcoholic, gay or straight? In the realm of sexual preference, the issue has been particularly incendiary, with some people claiming that choosing a same-sex partner is merely a "social deviancy" dictated by life circumstance and others arguing that just as a person cannot help that he or she has red and not brown hair, an individual has no control over sexual preference.

Several recent research reports have fueled this debate. In 1993, Dr. Dean Hamer of the National Cancer Institute published a study in the journal *Science* suggesting that a gene located on the X chromosome somehow influences a man's choice of sexual partners—at least some of the time. Meanwhile, researchers in the Netherlands have reported finding a small structure in the brain that differs substantially between ordinary men and transsexuals who have been surgically transformed from men into women. The Dutch discovery is the first indication that there might be a difference in transsexual brains, and could partly explain why such individuals describe themselves as "women trapped in men's bodies."

Such findings may eventually reduce the social—and legal—stigma that many gays and lesbians must contend with today. The legal landscape that permits such discrimination is changing, however. In the last several years, courts have handed down crucial decisions and companies have enacted groundbreaking policies that directly affect gay and lesbian civil rights. Here are five major areas in which the law is in a state of flux:

DISCRIMINATION IN EMPLOYMENT, HOUSING, AND MILITARY SERVICE

The United States military is one of the last government employers that treats lesbians and gay men differently on the basis of sexual preference. In July 1993, President Clinton issued a new version of the military's policy, referred to as "Don't Ask, Don't Tell." This policy supposedly banned discrimination by barring recruiting officers from making sexual preference a criterion for employment and officers from factoring sexual preference into promotion or even daily treatment of those under their command. But many gay rights advocates argue that the current policy continues to impose discriminatory rules on gay service members in every aspect of their public and private lives, making it impossible for them to be open and honest about their sexual preference. A federal district court found the policy unconstitutional in March of 1995, but the government is appealing the decision, which is expected to be ruled on very soon.

Several housing discrimination suits may also break new legal ground soon. In one closely watched case that could have great impact nationally, a California landlord has been sued for rejecting an unmarried couple as tenants on the ground that it was her religious right not to rent an apartment to an unmarried couple. The case parallels other situations in which religion has been invoked as a shield against a range of antidiscrimination laws nationwide.

MARRIAGE AND PARENTING RIGHTS

Under current law, no state will grant a civil marriage license to same-sex couples. But a case that would allow single-sex marriages in Hawaii could have vast repercussions for gay and lesbian civil rights nationwide. Today, for example, companies can deny health care benefits to a gay employee's domestic partner because that couple is not legally married. Since marriage licenses granted in one state have always been honored by other states, a decision by Hawaii to recognize same-sex marriages could well result in same-gender couples traveling to our 50th state to "tie the knot," with the expectation that their marriage will be fully recognized in their home state.

To avoid this possibility, 32 states had introduced some type of legislation by May of 1996 that would allow them to ignore the marital status of same-sex couples married in Hawaii. Five states have passed such legislation, 15 have been unable to do so, and 12 are pending, even though such laws are sure to be challenged as unconstitutional. The Hawaii trial is to begin in August of 1996 and a decision is expected by the end of 1997.

Meanwhile, New York State's highest court has recently ruled that the children of lesbian and gay parents may establish legal ties with both of their parents, meaning that gay and lesbians have the legal right to adopt children. New York joins Massachusetts and Vermont as the only states with statewide high court rulings allowing second-parent adoptions. Lower- level appellate courts in Illinois, New Jersey, and the District of Columbia have also granted second-parent adoptions, and several other states are expected to follow.

ANTIGAY INITIATIVES

Ten years after the Supreme Court heard its last gay rights case and delivered a major blow to the gay rights movement, the Court issued a ruling that gave gays and lesbians reason to cheer. In May 1996, the Supreme Court struck down what was known as Colorado's Amendment 2, a constitutional amendment approved by Colorado voters that denied civil rights protections to homosexuals. Amendment 2 prohibited all branches of state government in Colorado from passing antidiscrimination legislation for gays and lesbians.

That meant that to seek antidiscrimination protections, gay Coloradans would first have had to amend the state's constitution, a process to which no other group would have been subjected. While the decision will bar other states from adopting similar provisions, it remains unclear what broader political and legal effects the decision is likely to have on homosexuals.

AIDS/HIV-RELATED POLICY

A key legal question is whether asymptomatic HIV infection, in which a person is HIV-positive but is not showing any symptoms, is a protected disability under the Americans With Disabilities Act. The legislative history of the ADA as well as subsequent cases identify HIV infection as a disability under the Act. But in May 1995, the first federal appeals court to rule on the issue held that asymptomatic HIV is not automatically a covered disability under the law. According to the court, judges must make a factual determination in each case as to whether a person is disabled by his or her infection. If that ruling holds up, it could make it difficult for people living with HIV to deal with insurance caps on their health care plans. In the scenario that worries gay rights activists, an employer provides a group health insurance plan with a limitation on HIV-related expenses that is substantially lower than benefits for all other medical expenses. For many people with HIV—asymptomatic or symptomatic—such a cap makes it impossible for them to obtain recommended treatments.

Other AIDS-related cases currently in the court system include ones involving employment discrimination, discrimination against HIV-positive health care workers, limited or denied access to health care, and the right to privacy.

IMMIGRATION

In June 1994, U.S. Attorney General Janet Reno issued an order that upheld a 1990 Board of Immigration Appeals ruling that allowed lesbians and gay men to be considered a social group for the purposes of determining political asylum eligibility. Since then, over a dozen people have been granted political asylum because of their sexual orientation. In all immigration cases, each person's situation is required to be considered individually.

■ **FOR MORE INFORMATION:** On these and other gay-rights cases, write to Lambda Legal Defense and Education Fund at 666 Broadway, New York, NY 10012–9849, or call ☎ 212–995–8585.

MASSAGE

AT THE FOOT OF THE BED

The pleasures of foot massage have been treasured for centuries

In the opening of the film *Pulp Fiction*, Vincent and Jules, hitmen with a knack for scintillating dialogue, can be found debating the meaning of a foot massage after their boss orders that his wife's chaperon be thrown from a window. His transgression? He gave the boss's spouse a foot massage.

The lure of the foot massage isn't difficult to understand. It's indulgent, seductive, sensual—and clearly off-limits unless it's done by an intimate partner. What else confers so much pleasure?

Exactly.

In fact, the feet were considered a private part long before Hollywood declared them decadent. In ancient China, society girls willingly subjected themselves to having their feet bound to become more desirable to men. The crippling procedure involved folding the toes underneath the foot and compressing the arch by wrapping tight bandaging around the heelbone and forefoot. Women with Golden Lotuses—perfectly shaped tiny feet—set the standard for beauty and were highly alluring to male suitors. But Golden Lotuses weren't just a status symbol; they

■ ON WINGED FEET

The quickest way to a person's soul may be through his soles.

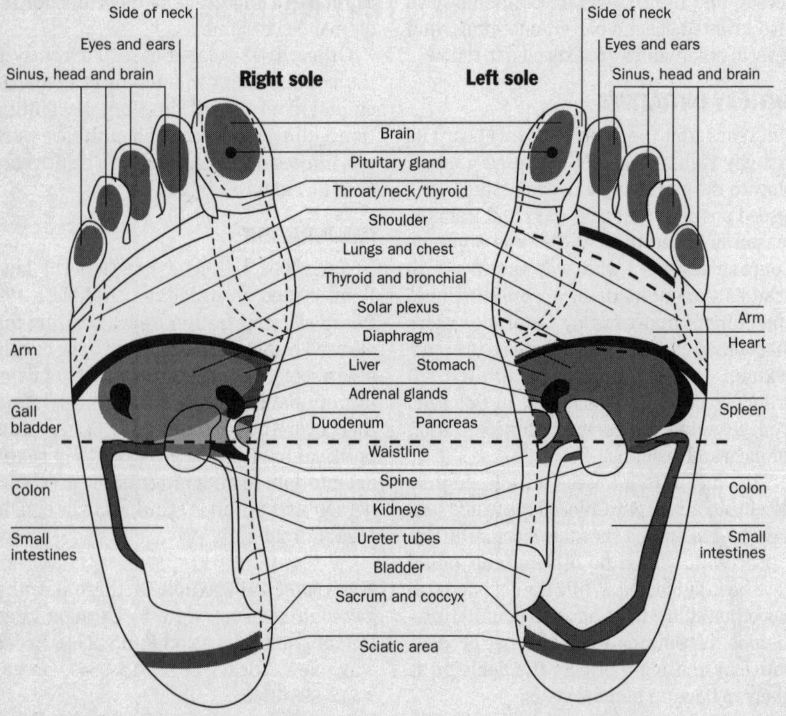

were also considered an erotic body part—regarded as a woman's most desirable physical asset.

Today, instead of subjecting themselves to the pain of foot-binding, women are more likely to pamper their feet with pedicures and foot massages that make their feet look and feel more attractive. Properly done, a foot massage can be refreshing, making tension disappear from the entire body. What's more, there's evidence that a therapeutic foot massage technique known as reflexology not only relieves stress and tension, but improves circulation, alleviates minor aches and pains brought on by stress, and promotes healing.

How does it work? There are thousands of nerve endings in the feet connected to nerves throughout the human body and when muscles tighten, it restricts blood flow to the area of the body under stress. Every body part and organ is connected to a reflex point on a person's foot and by massaging the foot in specific points on this map, it soothes the corresponding body parts.

By applying pressure to an area just below the ball of the foot, for example, you can help relieve a stomachache. Pushing about an inch higher will comfort and refresh the lungs (you can only work the heart by applying pressure to the left foot). "All of this is based on the belief that the body has the power to heal itself," explains Lucy Ostergren, a reflexologist at the New Age Health Spa in Nerversink, N.Y. "When the nerves relax, then the muscles relax, when the muscles relax, then the blood flows more freely."

EXPERT TIPS

HOW TO GIVE A FOOT MASSAGE

A little technique goes a long way in reflexology

Imagine that a Lilliputian-size person is contained inside your foot, and his body parts correspond with various reflex points on the soles of your feet. For instance, the big toe is connected with the head, the spine runs vertically along the inside of the feet, and the intestines, colon, liver, and pancreas are in the arch of the foot. Of course, it takes practice to find the reflex points and some are more difficult to find than others, but there's no harm in trying. Here Susan Ciminelli, owner of the Susan Ciminelli Day Spa in New York City, explains how to give a reflexology foot massage in three easy steps:

Step 1: Warm the foot and knead it a little to get the circulation going. Rub a little lotion or aromatic oil on your hands to make it easier to massage.

Step 2: Start at the top of the foot with the big toe and work down to the heel, using your thumb or knuckle to gently push each point. If you push gently and hold a reflex point, it will send a message to sedate the corresponding body part, but if you "pulse" the point by pushing in and out, it will stimulate the connecting part. Never pump or pulse the adrenal points or the intestine (see graphic), just push in and hold them.

Step 3: Gently rub the sensitive areas and hard spots to help break up calcium deposits. If you hit a point that hurts, you've found a trouble spot. For example, if someone has a stomachache, when you massage the corresponding reflex point, it's going to hurt. When that happens, push gently and hold the points, but don't pump them.

EXPERT Q & A

LETTING PLEASURE GROW ON YOU

Sexual activity in later life can rival finding the fountain of youth

Growing older doesn't mean giving up a sex life, according to the first national survey to examine the sex lives of older Americans. The survey, commissioned by *Parade* magazine, found that fully 40 percent of older Americans, with an average age of 74, remain sexually active—and happy with their lives. Sex isn't their first priority, however: Nearly 9 in 10 surveyed said companionship is what mattered most in an intimate relationship.

Dr. Robert N. Butler, professor of geriatrics and adult development at Mt. Sinai Medical Center in New York, and co-author of *Love and Sex after 60* (with Myrna I. Lewis, Ballantine, revised 1993), puts the issue in perspective:

■ What physical changes can people expect as they grow older?

If they don't have any diseases, the main change is in time. It takes longer for sexual arousal, and the sexual act may take longer. Also, there's also a longer period from one sexual encounter to another.

■ Which medical problems are most likely to interfere with sexual activity later in life?

Atherosclerosis (hardening of the arteries) is one of the main causes of sexual problems because it reduces blood supply to the sexual organs. Circulatory supply can also be influenced by diabetes. And drugs like antihypertensives and antidepressants can impair sexuality. Sometimes you can lower the dose, other times the drug isn't necessary at all, or you might be able to switch the drug and find that the person recovers his or her sexuality.

■ What impact does menopause have on a woman's sexuality?

In 99 percent of cases, it doesn't affect desire. However, a small percentage think of the end of fertility as the end of sexuality. Deciding whether to use hormone replacement therapy (see related story, page 241), is important. If you don't, vaginal dryness and discomfort can occur because of the absence of estrogen, but you can apply over-the-counter estrogen creams or lubricants that are safe.

■ Which seniors are most likely to be sexually active?

Those that are physically in good shape, emotionally involved, and intellectually curious are generally sexually active. If you're healthy, your partner is healthy, and you love each other, then sex will be very frequent. If you or your partner is ill, or you haven't been affectionate for 20 years, it's not age as much as the state of the relationship.

■ If you are sexually active and older, are there any other health precautions you need to worry about?

If you can walk up two flights of stairs or two city blocks, you use up the same oxygen and energy as the sexual act. You can handle sexuality even after bypass surgery if you can handle the most basic physical activity. By not having sex because you fear something's going to happen, you can work up more sexual tension than by going through the sexual act.

■ What are the benefits of maintaining an active sex life?

For one, it's a natural and appropriate expression of a relationship. As people get older, and hopefully if they love one another and are concerned about each others' pleasures, a degree of intimacy emerges. Some young people understand that and are terrific in their sensitivity to each other, and some people never are. By and large, older people become masterful because they really do become more sensitive to their partners and more concerned with his or her needs.

RISKS & REMEDIES

THE PILL: Despite common perception, experts say it's safe, PAGE 271 **LOVER'S GUIDE:** Protection for every occasion, PAGE 272 **VASECTOMIES:** The pros and cons of a man's option, PAGE 273 **ABORTION:** RU-486 is just one of several drugs to induce abortion, PAGE 274 **ABORTION LAW:** The legal parameters, PAGE 275 **STD'S:** Common diseases and treatments, PAGE 277 **AIDS:** Home-testing is now available for HIV, PAGE 279

CONTRACEPTION

THE MORNING AFTER A MISTAKE

Pills that cut the risks of pregnancy after sex are poorly understood

It's a simple, harmless, inexpensive, and effective method of preventing unintended pregnancies, yet until recently it was one of the best-kept secrets in modern medicine. The so-called "morning after pill" is actually a combination of high-dose birth control pills that alter the lining of the uterus, preventing the fertilized egg from implanting in the uterus. The pills, which contain the hormones estrogen and progestin, are administered in two doses: the first must be taken within 72 hours after intercourse, a second dose 12 hours later.

The use of emergency contraceptives was recently endorsed by the Food and Drug Administration (FDA) as an effective method of preventing an unplanned pregnancy. However, emergency contraceptives weren't prescribed by most doctors until recently because the FDA hasn't specifically approved birth control pills or the IUDs as emergency contraceptives, in part because no manufacturer has submitted a new drug application for the pills. Physicians can legally prescribe them, however, in a practice known as "off-label" drug use.

Nearly 6 in 10 pregnancies in the United States are unintended, according to a 1995 report by the Institute of Medicine, the research branch of the National Academy of Sciences. Among teenagers, more than 4 in 5 pregnancies are unplanned or unwanted, and it is common for many sexually active women who have engaged in unprotected sex to feel powerless about their situations.

Emergency contraceptive pills are by far the most common-

FACT FILE:

BIRTH CONTROL BY THE NUMBERS

■ *Sterilization is the most used contraceptive method in the U.S.*

■ FOR WOMEN	Percent who use it
Pill	25%
Spermicides (foams, creams, gels)	6%
Diaphragm/cervical cap	5.7%
Sponge	1.1%
Implants (Norplant)	1%
IUD	1%
■ FOR MEN AND WOMEN	
Sterilization/tubal ligation	27%
Condoms	19%
Withdrawal/rhythm	7%

SOURCE: Ortho Annual Birth Control Study, 1993.

ly used method of emergency contraception, although fertilization can also often be stymied by taking two doses of minipills (birth control pills that contain only progestin) or by inserting a copper-T intrauterine device (IUD) within seven days of unprotected sex. The pills are deemed safe for nearly all women, although many women who take them experience nausea.

Using emergency contraceptive pills reduces the risk of pregnancy by 75 percent, according to Dr. James Trussell, director of the office of population research at Princeton University. For instance, if 100 women have unprotected sex once in the middle of their menstrual cycle—when they're most fertile—about 8 will become pregnant. But if the same women had used emergency contraceptive pills after having intercourse mid-cycle, only 2 would become pregnant. Emergency use of the IUD is even more effective and can be left in place for 10 years afterward.

"A maximum of one-half of unintended pregnancies could be prevented if women knew about emergency contraception," says Dr. Trussell. "That doesn't mean they would use it, but they could use it."

A 1995 survey by the Henry J. Kaiser Family Foundation, a nonprofit health research organization, found that while most obstetricians were very familiar with emergency contraceptives, nearly 80 percent of respondents had prescribed them five times or less in the previous year. Likewise, most women have heard of emergency contraceptives but they don't know how or when to use them. Another survey conducted in 1994 by the Kaiser Family Foundation found that only 1 percent of American women have used the morning after pill.

Although emergency contraceptives still aren't widely used, they're gradually gaining recognition among women. In the first two months after a nationwide emergency contraception hotline was launched (see panel, this page), more than 20,000 calls were received. Dr. Trussell urges doctors to educate patients about the availability of emergency contraceptives, and even advocates prescribing them to sexually active patients before they become pregnant so that they'll have the pills on hand if the need arises. "Anyone can have it sitting around in the medicine cabinet if the condom breaks," he says.

But emergency contraceptives remain controversial because of misperceptions. A survey of 550 Princeton University students found that 95 percent of respondents knew about emergency contraceptives, yet over 50 percent confused the morning after pill with RU-486, the abortion pill. Unlike RU-486, emergency contraception is used much sooner, preventing rather than aborting a pregnancy.

Critics of emergency contraception also maintain that because emergency contraceptives are becoming more readily available, women might stop using other forms of birth control. But Trussell predicts the opposite might occur if doctors who prescribe emergency contraceptives use the opportunity to educate and counsel women about birth control options. "What emergency contraceptives can do," he says, "is provide a bridge to talk to a clinician about an ongoing method of contraception."

While there's no evidence linking an increased use in emergency contraceptives to reduced rates of abortion, Dr. Trussell predicts it could happen. Says Trussell: "I believe we would see a drop in abortion if doctors routinely prescribed emergency contraceptives and if more women knew about it."

EXPERT SOURCE

A nationwide telephone hotline is now available at ☎ 800-584-9911, to help women learn how to obtain and use emergency contraceptives. The automated hotline, which operates 24 hours a day in English and Spanish, also offers referrals to doctors who prescribe emergency contraceptives, including the name, telephone number, and location of three doctors in their geographic area.

EXPERT Q & A

IS THE PILL FOR YOU?

Many Americans suspect "The Pill" of being unsafe. They're wrong

Since it was introduced more than 35 years ago, oral contraceptives have become a widely used and accepted form of birth control—so common that taking "The Pill" has become for many a rite of passage. Yet there remains much public confusion about the safety of birth control pills. A recent survey by the Henry J. Kaiser Family Foundation, a nonprofit health research organization, found that only one-quarter of reproductive-age women considered the pill to be very safe while nearly 30 percent regarded the pills as either very unsafe or somewhat unsafe.

Here, Jacqueline Darroch Forrest, vice president for research at the Alan Guttmacher Institute, a nonprofit research, policy, and educational organization, addresses the most commonly asked questions about the pill's potential risks and benefits:

■ Has the pill changed much since it was first introduced 35 years ago?

The pill women are taking today typically has much lower doses of progestin and estrogen, and in recent years new progestins have also been introduced. The decrease, especially in the estrogen dose, was done because high doses of estrogen were shown to be linked to cardiovascular problems. As far as we can tell, there remain protective benefits against ovarian and endometrial cancer (cancer of the lining of the uterus) in the lower dose.

■ Do birth control pills increase the risk of blood clotting?

Questions have been raised by a recent British study of pills with a certain type of progestin, but even if they are true, the risk is extremely low. In addition, only one of the compounds in that research is available in the U. S. Women need to understand we're not talking about "the pill," but about a variety of formulations, most of which contain a synthetic progestin and a synthetic estrogen. They're not all the same progestins and they're not all the same dosage even within the same family of oral contraceptives. If a woman is concerned about what she's using, she should talk to her clinician and possibly choose another oral contraceptive.

■ Is it safe to use the pill long-term?

Yes. However, the image of women using pills for 10 to 20 years isn't typical. In fact, the average length of pill use is about 5 years. That's because the majority of couples, once they've had as many kids as they want, undergo sterilization. Early on there was this idea that after a couple of years you need to give your body a rest, but that was debunked years ago. In fact, the Food and Drug Administration has no age limit on pill use if you're not a heavy smoker and you have no contraindications to using the pill.

■ Does the pill affect a woman's chances of getting cancer?

We have very clear evidence of the reduction in risk of endometrial and ovarian cancers. And with ovarian cancer that's quite important because it's the only thing we know that women can do to decrease that risk, and up until now it's been very difficult to diagnose and has usually been diagnosed very late. Breast cancer is in some ways scarier in women, but ovarian cancer is deadlier.

With breast cancer, the information on balance is that women who use the pill really don't face much difference in terms of their overall risk of breast cancer compared to women who haven't used the pill. However, there's some indication that there might be an increase in breast cancer diagnosed at early ages among women who have used the pill, especially if they've used it for a long time. On the other hand, studies have shown there may be a lower risk of breast cancer diagnosed at older ages.

LOVER'S GUIDE

PROTECTION FOR EVERY OCCASION

Birth control techniques don't work unless they're used regularly. The following efficacy rates, provided by the U.S. Public Health Service, are yearly estimates based on several studies. Methods that are dependent on conscientious use are subject to a greater chance of human error and reduced effectiveness. Without contraception, some 60 to 85 percent of sexually active women would likely become pregnant within a year.

MALE CONDOM

About 85 percent effective

■ **USE:** Applied immediately before intercourse; used only once and discarded. Nonprescription.

■ **RISKS:** Rare irritation and allergic reactions.

■ **STD PROTECTION:** Latex condoms help protect against sexually transmitted diseases, including herpes and HIV.

FEMALE CONDOM

74 to 79 percent effective

■ **USE:** Applied immediately before intercourse; used only once and discarded. Nonprescription.

■ **RISKS:** Rare irritation and allergic reactions.

■ **STD PROTECTION:** May give some protection against sexually transmitted disease, including herpes and HIV; but not as effective as male latex condom.

SPERMICIDES USED ALONE

70 to 80 percent effective

■ **USE:** Applied no more than an hour before intercourse. Nonprescription.

■ **RISKS:** Rare irritation and allergic reactions.

■ **STD PROTECTION:** Unknown.

DIAPHRAGM WITH SPERMICIDE

82 to 94 percent effective

■ **USE:** Inserted before intercourse; can be left in place 24 hours, but additional spermicide must be inserted if intercourse is repeated. Prescription.

■ **RISKS:** Rare irritation and allergic reactions; bladder infection; very rarely, toxic shock syndrome.

■ **STD PROTECTION:** None.

CERVICAL CAP WITH SPERMICIDE

At least 82 percent effective

■ **USE:** Can remain in place for 48 hours, not necessary to reapply spermicide upon repeated intercourse; may be difficult to insert. Prescription.

■ **RISKS:** Abnormal Pap test; vaginal or cervical infections; very rarely, toxic shock syndrome.

■ **STD PROTECTION:** None.

PILLS

97 to 99 percent effective

■ **USE:** Pill must be taken on daily schedule, regardless of the frequency of intercourse. Prescription.

■ **RISKS:** Water retention, hypertension, mood change, and nausea. In rare cases, blood clots, heart attacks, strokes, gallbladder disease, and liver tumors. Not usually recommended for women who smoke, especially over age 35.

■ **STD PROTECTION:** Confers some protection against pelvic inflammatory disease.

IMPLANT (NORPLANT)

99 percent effective

■ **USE:** Effective 24 hours after implantation for approximately five years; can be removed by physician at any time. Requires prescription, minor outpatient surgical procedure.

■ **RISKS:** Menstrual cycle irregularity; headaches, nervousness, depression, nausea, and dizziness, change of appetite, breast tenderness, weight gain, enlargement of ovaries and/or fallopian tubes, excessive growth of body hair; may subside after first year.

■ **STD PROTECTION:** None.

INJECTION (Depo-Provera)

99 percent effective

■ **USE:** One injection every three months. Prescription.

■ LOVER'S GUIDE

■ **RISKS:** Amenorrhea, weight gain, other side effects similar to Norplant.
■ **STD PROTECTION:** None.

IUD

95 to 96 percent effective

■ **USE:** After insertion, stays in until physician removes it. Prescription.
■ **RISKS:** Cramps, bleeding, pelvic inflammatory disease, infertility; rarely, perforation of the uterus.
■ **STD PROTECTION:** None.

PERIODIC ABSTINENCE

53 to 86 percent effective

■ **USE:** Requires frequent monitoring of the body's functions and periods of abstinence; can be used in conjunction with barrier methods to increase effectiveness. Instruction provided by a physician or a family-planning clinic.
■ **RISKS:** None.
■ **STD PROTECTION:** None.

SURGICAL STERILIZATION

Over 99 percent effective

■ **USE:** Vasectomy (for men) is a onetime procedure usually performed in a doctor's office under local anesthesia; tubal ligation (for women) is a onetime procedure performed in an operating room and requires the use of general anesthesia.
■ **RISKS:** Pain, infection, and, for tubal ligation, possible surgical complications and bleeding.
■ **STD PROTECTION:** None.

THE VASECTOMY OPTION

Reversing the process is sometimes possible, but you better not count on it

When it comes to birth control techniques, most of the options belong to women. But when it comes to sterilization, the man takes center stage. That's because vasectomy has long been regarded as both a simpler and safer procedure than its female equivalent, tubal ligation. For couples who are ready to conclude their childbearing, vasectomy is the better course, say doctors. More than half a million men elect this option each year.

Not that vasectomy carries no worries. Two recent studies have raised the possibility that men with vasectomies may have some higher risk of developing prostate cancer. While the research is considered too preliminary to require revising current medical practice, further investigation of the question is warranted.

In a vasectomy, the tube that carries sperm to the penis is cut. The procedure can be done on an outpatient basis for about $450 and requires only 15 to 20 minutes. The doctor injects a local anesthetic in the scrotum and around each of the two vas deferens, the tubes that carry sperm from the testicles to the penis. After making a small incision in the scrotum, the doctor cuts and closes the tube with ties. After the operation, a man will still produce sperm, but the sperm can't enter the penis. Seminal fluid continues to be produced, nevertheless, and erection and ejaculation still take place.

Postoperative complications are relatively rare, and minor in most cases. They can include bleeding, infection, and the development of painful lumps in the scrotum. Risks can be greatly minimized by having the operation done by a doctor who performs it frequently.

Reversal of a vasectomy is often possible, but success is by no means a certainty. Advances in microsurgery techniques make the chances of successfully reconnecting the vas deferens 98 percent, but even if the vas is reconnected, there is only a 50 to 70 percent chance that the man will be able to fertilize an egg. That's because men who have had vasectomies often form antibodies against their own sperm. The antibodies don't appear to harm the man's health, but they can destroy fertility.

ABORTION DRUGS

REVOLUTIONIZING A GREAT DEBATE

Two drug regimens that can end pregnancies easily may win favor

Two new prescription drug regimens that are considered safe and effective alternatives to surgical abortion may soon be available for use by women in the privacy of their doctor's office. RU-486, the French "abortion pill," is expected to be approved by the Food and Drug Administration for use in the United States very shortly. The drug has been widely used in other countries, but efforts to introduce it to women in the U.S. have met with ongoing opposition from abortion foes.

Another, less publicized drug combination involves taking two medications, methotrexate and misoprostol, that are already available for other medical purposes. One large study found that the two drugs, when used in succession, effectively terminated pregnancy in 96 percent of the cases studied.

To induce an abortion using these drugs, a woman is first injected with methotrexate, which interrupts the growth of the embryo, in effect stopping the pregnancy. Three to seven days later, the woman receives a suppository of misoprostol, which causes uterine contractions, cramping, and bleeding to occur. Typically, it takes a few days for the abortion to occur, although it can take up to one month. In addition, approximately one-quarter to one-half of women who take the drugs need a second suppository to induce the abortion.

While both drugs have already been cleared by the FDA for unrelated purposes—methotrexate for cancer and arthritis, and misoprostol for ulcers—neither drug is approved for abortions. But the combination is occasionally used to treat abortion "off-label," which is the term that describes the widespread practice of prescribing drugs for unapproved purposes, provided clinical studies have proved that they're safe and effective.

RU-486, or mifepristone, as it will be known in the U.S., will be administered in the same manner. First, a woman receives mifepristone tablets during a visit to her doctor. Thirty-six to 48 hours later, misoprostol—the same drug that is sometimes used in combination with methotrexate—is also administered. Most women will have the abortion in the next four hours; if the drug fails to work, a surgical abortion is performed. Total cost for a medical abortion using mifepristone is expected to be about $325, which is slightly less than for surgical abortions.

Since 1989, mifepristone has been widely available in France, where 70 percent of eligible women have opted for a medical abortion over a surgical one. About 30 percent of all abortions in France are performed using mifepristone in combination with a drug like misoprostol, and more than 50,000 European women have used the drugs to induce abortion. Studies have shown that mifepristone alone is effective at inducing abortion between 65 and 80 percent of the time, and is 95 percent effective when used in combination with a drug that induces abortion.

RU-486 is only available to French women during the first 49 days of pregnancy. How effective it is if administered later in pregnancy is unclear, but the longer a woman waits, the less effective the method appears, according to officials who have been tracking research on American women at the Population Council.

While a medical abortion takes longer than a surgical abortion and is slightly less effective, it can be done much earlier in the pregnancy than surgical abortions, which usually aren't performed until the sixth week of pregnancy. "As soon as tests show you're pregnant, you can take this," says Sandra Waldman, a spokesperson for the Population Council. In addition, no anesthesia is required and the drugs cause few side effects. Both modes of medical abortion typically cause heavy bleeding, abdominal cramps and pain, however, and mifepristone can cause nausea, headache, and fatigue, and methotrexate typically causes nausea, vomiting, and diarrhea.

ABORTION LAWS

SPEAKING OF ABORTION

Defining limits to a woman's right to terminate pregnancy

A woman's right to elect an abortion remains the law of the land under Roe v. Wade and subsequent Supreme Court decisions. But that web of judicial rulings has left the states free to legislate numerous restrictions on the exercise of that right. A glossary of the different types of restrictions is adapted below from information supplied by the National Abortion Rights Action League. Not all of the 50 states have enacted all of these laws.

ABORTION BAN—The state prohibits virtually all abortions, but the ban is unconstitutional and therefore unenforceable. In "Pre-Roe" states, the ban in question predates Roe v. Wade. In "Post-Roe" states, the state has amended and reenacted its pre-Roe ban. Either way, the ban has no legal force.

INFORMED CONSENT—No abortion is allowed unless a woman receives state-prepared materials and counseling on adoptions and abortion alternatives, is told the doctor's qualifications, and has the risks of the procedure explained to her.

MINOR'S ACCESS—Requires one parent's written consent for a minor under 18. Permits abortion without parental consent if court order indicates woman is well informed and sufficiently mature.

PHYSICIAN-ONLY REQUIREMENT—Only a state-licensed physician may perform abortion procedures.

PUBLIC FUNDING—Regulation that a woman eligible for state medical care can't use such funds for abortion unless her life is at risk.

VIABILITY TESTING—Bars physician from performing abortion from 18th week on.

CONSCIENCE-BASED EXEMPTION—Spares any person or hospital from performing a role in an abortion.

POST-VIABILITY RESTRICTIONS—No abortion is allowed after viability unless necessary to preserve woman's health. In event of such, a second physician is required to provide medical attention to the fetus.

CLINIC VIOLENCE AND HARASSMENT—Provides criminal penalties for anyone physically preventing an individual from entering or exiting a health care facility.

HUSBAND CONSENT/HUSBAND NOTICE—No abortion for a married woman living with her husband without his consent.

INSURANCE—No abortion coverage under group health insurance for state workers.

WAITING PERIOD—No abortion unless a woman has waited 24 hours after hearing a state-mandated lecture about fetal development, abortion alternatives, and possible effects on future pregnancies.

LEGISLATIVE DECLARATION (PRO-CHOICE)—A law indicating legislative intent to protect a woman's right to choose abortion.

LEGISLATIVE DECLARATION (ANTI-CHOICE)—A law indicating intent to ban abortion.

MEDICAL ABORTION—State resolutions in favor of research and trials of RU-486 and other nonsurgical abortion.

PUBLIC FACILITIES—No use of public facilities to perform abortion services.

COUNSELING BAN—A state "gag rule" that bars state-funded abortion counseling or referrals.

SOURCE: National Abortion Rights Action League.

IMPOTENCE

PRIMING THE PUMP WITH SCIENCE

Some preventive maintenance will spare many men difficulties in bed

Just mentioning the word "impotence" is enough to make many men cringe. The condition afflicts 10 to 20 million American men, yet few of them feel comfortable even discussing their sex lives with their doctors.

The embarrassment need not be chronic. While impotence was long regarded as a psychological problem for which few medical treatments were available, doctors have come to realize recently that its causes are usually physiological in nature. The chances that a man will experience impotence increase with age, although it isn't clear whether advancing age itself is a risk factor for impotence or medical conditions that accompany aging lead to impotence. Regardless, studies show that 40 percent of men at age 40 suffer from impotence, 50 percent at age 50, 60 percent at 60, and so on.

Two of the most common medical conditions associated with impotence are diabetes and heart disease. Both illnesses can cause nerve damage, blood vessel damage, or tissue damage, thus leading to a complete breakdown of the hydraulic system's ability to initiate an erection.

In fact, just possessing risk factors for heart disease can be enough to cause impotence. For example, high blood pressure can injure the lining of the blood vessels, which leads to blocked arteries and impotence. Smoking is likely to aggravate the situation, since it contributes to hypertension. A high-cholesterol diet is also bad because it clogs the circulation to the heart, legs, and penis, making an erection difficult or impossible to maintain. Ironically, impotence can also be a side effect of many medications used for treating hypertension, diabetes, and heart disease, as well as certain antidepressant drugs.

If preventive measures to stop smoking and to watch one's weight, cholesterol, and blood pressure fail to work, drugs to treat impotence can help many men. The Food and Drug Administration (FDA) recently approved Caverject, an injectable drug to treat what is known technically as erectile dysfunction. Although a generic version of the drug, alprostadil, has been used to treat impotence for over a decade, the new formula has fewer side effects.

Studies have shown that more than 80 percent of patients who took Caverject, which must be injected into the penis, were able to maintain an erection sufficient to experience sexual intercourse. At $20 to $25 for a single injection, Caverject is very expensive, unfortunately, and some patients recoil at the notion of giving themselves an injection every time they want to have sex. The alternatives, such as penile implants and a vacuum device that draws blood into the penis, are equally unappealing to many men.

To overcome this reluctance to existing forms of impotence treatment, researchers are also at work on developing an anti-impotence drug that might someday be available in pill form. In three recent clinical trials, for instance, Viagra (generic name: sildenafil) improved men's ability to get erections significantly. In one trial of 351 men, between 65 and 88 percent reported improved erections (the success varied depending on the dose), compared to just 39 percent of those who took a placebo.

Although the drug seems promising, Dr. Perry Nadig, clinical professor of urological surgery for the University of Texas Health Science Center in San Antonio, cautions that the studies were only performed on limited numbers of patients, none of whom appeared to have any physical cause for their impotence. That could mean that it will be far less effective for the majority of those afflicted. In any case, further studies are necessary before it's approved for widespread use—and that probably will take several more years.

STDS

LOVERS AND OTHER STRANGERS

Sexually transmitted diseases can't just be kissed off

According to a recent study, men with two to four sex partners over a lifetime have a 1 in 29 chance of contracting a bacterial sexually transmitted disease such as syphilis or gonorrhea. For women with an equivalent number of partners, the risk is about twice as high. The patterns are similar for viral STDs such as genital herpes and hepatitis B. But men tend to have more partners than women. When that is taken into account, the chance of getting an STD is ultimately about the same for both sexes. Following are descriptions of the most common STDs from the Centers for Disease Control and Prevention:

BACTERIAL VAGINOSIS

Also called Gardnerella or Hemophilus.

■ **HOW SPREAD:** Through sexual intercourse and possibly through towels and wet clothing. A common cause of vaginitis.

■ **SYMPTOMS:** Grayish vaginal discharge is common. Untreated, it can cause reproductive problems, abnormal Pap smears, and urinary tract infections.

■ **TREATMENT:** Metronidazole.

CHLAMYDIA

Caused by the bacterium Chlamydia trachomatis.

■ **HOW SPREAD:** Vaginal or anal intercourse, mother to child during birth, hand-to-eye contact if hands have infected discharge.

■ **SYMPTOMS:** Appear 7 to 14 days after exposure. In women, it can cause infertility or pregnancy complications, vaginal discharge, painful urination, vaginal bleeding, bleeding after sex, and lower abdominal pain. In men, chlamydia causes burning during urination, urethral discharge, and inflammation of the urethra. Four-fifths of women have no symptoms.

■ **TREATMENT:** Tetracycline. The Centers for Disease Control and Prevention now recommend Doxycycline as the treatment of choice because it only has to be taken twice a day. Erythromycin for pregnant women. Chlortetracycline for eye infections.

CRABS/PEDICULOSIS PEDIS

Caused by crablike lice that live in eyebrows, pubic, armpit, and chest hair.

■ **HOW SPREAD:** Physical contact with someone who is infected, or using towels, clothes, or bedding of a person who has crabs.

■ **SYMPTOMS:** Intolerable itching in the genital or other areas.

■ **TREATMENT:** A lotion called Kwell can be prescribed. After treatment, clean clothes, towels, and bed linen. The crab will die in 24 hours.

GENITAL WARTS

Caused by human papilloma virus, a virus similar to the one that causes skin warts.

■ **HOW SPREAD:** Sexual intercourse.

■ **SYMPTOMS:** Appears three weeks to eight months after exposure. Small, painless warts can appear on the labia, vulva, cervix, or anus in women. In men, warts appear on the penis or scrotum. Using a condom can help prevent infection.

■ **TREATMENT:** Laser beam can burn off warts, or Podophyllin or trichloracetic acid can be applied.

GONORRHEA

Caused by gonococcus, a bacterium.

■ **HOW SPREAD:** Sexual intercourse, oral sex, from mother to child during birth, from hand-to-eye contact. For women, from being inseminated by infected semen.

■ **SYMPTOMS:** Appear two days to three weeks after infection. In women, thick discharge, burning or painful urination, pain in lower abdomen, vomiting, fever, irregular periods, a rash, chills, fever, pain in the wrists and fingers, hands, feet, and toes. Some 80 percent of women have no symptoms. In men, thick milky discharge, pain during urination. Almost all men show symptoms.

■ **TREATMENT:** The CDC recommends ceftriaxone. Since people are often infected with gonorrhea and chlamydia at the same time, the CDC also recommends seven days of taking Doxycycline to treat chlamydia. Pregnant women should take Erythromycin.

HERPES

Two types of herpes are caused by the herpes simplex virus. Type I is characterized by cold sores and fever blisters on the mouth; Type II by sores and blisters on the genitals.

■ **HOW SPREAD:** Sexual intercourse or oral sex with someone who has an active infection. The disease is most contagious when sores exist, but infection can occur even when there are no symptoms.

■ **SYMPTOMS:** Appear 2 to 20 days after infection, but most people don't have symptoms until much later. Tingling, itching in the genital area, burning sensations, pain or feeling of pressure in the legs, buttocks, or genitals, sores starting with one or more bumps that turn to blisters. Women can have sores on cervix with no noticeable symptoms. Blisters rupture in a few days and heal without treatment. Active sores may make urination painful. Also may be a dull ache or sharp pain in the genitals.

■ **TREATMENT:** No cure at present. CDC recommends keeping sores dry and clean. If very painful, xylocaine cream or ethyl chloride may be helpful. The antiviral drug acyclovir may reduce outbreak recurrence.

HIV INFECTION/AIDS

Caused by the HIV virus.

■ **HOW SPREAD:** Sexual intercourse, anal sex, blood transfusions, sharing of needles with an infected person. The virus is found in blood, semen, and vaginal secretions, so any contact with these bodily fluids with someone who is infected, such as in unprotected sexual intercourse, could lead to infection.

■ **SYMPTOMS:** Fatigue, weight loss, swollen glands, and skin problems such as seborrheic dermatitis. Bronchial infections, sores in the mouth, fever, night sweats, loss of appetite, headache, trouble swallowing. In women, also recurrent yeast infections, chronic pelvic inflammatory disease, and severe genital herpes.

■ **TREATMENT:** Several medications in a new class of drugs called protease inhibitors, which reduce the amount of HIV in the blood, are now being used. Used in combination with standard AIDS drugs such as AZT, protease inhibitors have prolonged some patients' lives.

NONGONOCOCCAL URETHRITIS (NGU)

Caused by Ureaplasma Urealyticum bacterium.

■ **HOW SPREAD:** Contracted through sexual intercourse. It can be found in apparently healthy people with no signs of infection.

■ **SYMPTOMS:** In men, symptoms include discharge from the penis and inflammation of the urethra. Some researchers think NGU causes pregnancy problems in women, but more research needs to be done.

■ **TREATMENT:** Tetracycline is the standard treatment. Doxycycline or Erythromycin may also be prescribed.

SCABIES

Caused by tiny parasitic mites.

■ **HOW SPREAD:** Sexual contact, towels, clothes, and even furniture.

■ **SYMPTOMS:** Intense itching, red bumps on breasts, waist, genitals, buttocks, or hands.

■ **TREATMENT:** Kwell, which is also used to cure crabs. For pregnant women, Eurax.

SYPHILIS

Caused by a bacterium called spirochete.

■ **HOW SPREAD:** Sexual or skin contact with infected person, or from mother to unborn child. Spreads from open sores or rashes and can penetrate mucous membranes and broken skin anywhere on the body.

■ **SYMPTOMS:** Appear 9 to 90 days after infection with a painless sore resembling a pimple. In men, pimple could appear on penis or scrotum. Left untreated, could lead to rash, sore throat, swollen painful joints, aching bones, hair loss, or raised area around the genitals. After 10 to 20 years, bacteria can invade the heart and brain, causing heart disease, blindness, mental incapacity, crippling.

■ **TREATMENT:** Penicillin by injection, Doxycline, or tetracycline pills.

AIDS

HIV TESTS: THE NEXT GENERATION

Do-it-yourself kits have arrived, and so have other effective methods

No disease probably has ever received as much public attention in as short a time as AIDS, yet health officials estimate that two-thirds of Americans at risk for contracting HIV still have not undergone testing and don't know if they are infected with the virus that causes AIDS and might be infecting others.

Now the Food and Drug Administration has authorized a do-it-yourself test kit that it hopes will encourage more people to learn their HIV status and to seek treatment if needed. Called Confide, the new testing system was developed by Direct Access Diagnostics, a subsidiary of Johnson & Johnson. It is the first HIV test kit ever to be approved by the FDA for home use.

Previously, HIV testing was only available at medical facilities like community health clinics, doctors' offices, publicly funded testing centers, and blood collection organizations. But according to a poll by the National Center for Health Statistics, 22 percent of those surveyed said they would opt for a home test over going to a testing facility. Among those at high risk of contracting AIDS, 31 percent said they would choose a home test over other testing methods.

Many people have resisted being tested until now because of a lack of privacy at testing centers and a fear that test results would not be kept confidential. Some worry, for instance, that their HIV status will be released to insurance companies and employers who will deny them health insurance coverage or discriminate against them in some way if their test result is positive.

The Confide home test involves pricking your finger with a lancet to draw a small blood sample, then smearing it on a test card precoded with an identification number. Unlike home pregnancy or cholesterol testing kits, however, the HIV home-testing system can't deliver instant results. Instead, the card must be mailed in an enclosed prepaid, preaddressed envelope to a medical laboratory for analysis.

Results can be obtained within a week by calling a toll-free number and punching in your confidential identification number. Negative test results are provided through an automated message system, though a counselor is also on hand to answer questions. If a test result is positive or incon-

TEST RESULTS THAT AREN'T KEPT SECRET

Confidentiality isn't always the policy of some AIDS testing centers

If you decide to undergo testing for HIV at a testing center, it's important to understand the difference between the confidentiality policies of different types of facilities. Confidential AIDS testing centers keep a medical record of your name and test result, which may be submitted to the state health department or your doctor, if you wish.

At some facilities, your HIV status may be included in your medical records as a matter of course and may affect your ability to obtain or keep health insurance. In anonymous testing, which isn't available in all states, you are provided an identification number to prevent unauthorized release of your HIV status.

To find testing facilities near you, or for more information about AIDS and AIDS testing, contact the Centers for Disease Control and Prevention's National AIDS Hotline at ☎ 800-342-AIDS.

ORAL SEX IS DEADLY SERIOUS IN AN AGE OF AIDS

New research suggests that unprotected oral intercourse is very risky

One more sexual activity has just been added to the category of high-risk behaviors known as "unsafe sex." New research offers the first strong evidence that the AIDS virus can be contracted through oral sex, refuting the widely held belief that AIDS is not easily transmitted through the mouth.

While many people are aware that unprotected sexual intercourse and IV drug use constitute high-risk behavior that could put them in danger of contracting the AIDS virus, few are aware that unprotected oral sex also poses a significant threat. This is despite the fact that the Centers for Disease Control and Prevention has long considered oral sex a potential mode of transmission and has consistently urged that condoms should be worn during oral sex.

Now, researchers at the Dana-Farber Cancer Institute in Boston have found that rhesus monkeys orally exposed to SIV (simian immunodeficiency virus) become infected with the virus. SIV is an AIDS-like virus in monkeys that closely resembles the AIDS virus in humans. Researchers placed a solution containing SIV on the tongues of seven adult monkeys; six of the animals became infected with the virus and two of them have died of SIV.

The monkeys had no sores or cuts in their mouths that might help explain why so many developed the virus. What's more, researchers discovered that the dose required to infect the monkeys with SIV was 6,000 times lower than that required if the virus were transmitted through the rectum. At this stage, though, researchers do not consider oral intercourse more dangerous than anal intercourse.

Further research is necessary to determine exactly how the virus is transmitted orally and how much of a risk this type of exposure poses. One message is welcome, however: It's still highly unlikely, say the researchers, that the virus can be transmitted by casual contact like kissing or sharing utensils—the virus is not found in high enough concentrations in saliva.

clusive, the call is answered by a trained bilingual counselor, who notifies the caller of the test results and provides local medical and social service referrals and emotional support and advice.

The kit, which costs about $40, is already available in Texas and Florida and will soon be sold at pharmacies, college health centers, and clinics nationwide. Eventually, it is also expected to be available through a national toll-free telephone number.

For those who hate needles or go faint at the sight of blood, the Food and Drug Administration has also recently approved a painless new HIV test called the OraSure HIV-1 Oral Specimen Collection device. For about the same cost as a blood test, OraSure allows a person to undergo testing without giving a blood sample. It is not a home test, however, and can only be offered in medical facilities where blood tests for HIV are already being conducted.

OraSure tests for HIV antibodies by drawing from the mouth a sample of fluid called oral mucosal transudate (OMT). Unlike saliva, OMT contains a high concentration of AIDS antibodies in infected individuals. To obtain the sample, a small, specially treated pad is held by a handle against a patient's lower cheek and gum for two minutes. Then the pad is placed in a vial and sent to a lab, where it is analyzed in much the same way as blood samples are. In a study of more than 3,500 individuals at 11 sites across the country, OraSure samples proved accurate more than 99 percent of the time, making it as reliable as traditional blood tests in detecting HIV.

CHAPTER FOUR

EDUCATION

EXPERT QUOTES

"Children are going to learn morality from how you treat them."
—Dr. Stanley Greenspan, child psychiatrist
Page 285

"Bad experiences [do not] prepare children for other bad experiences."
—Dr. David Elkind, author of *The Hurried Child*
Page 289

"For students interested in improving their writing, computers have made it easier."
—Professor Sherry Turkle, author of *Life on the Screen*
Page 317

■ **THE YEAR AHEAD: PAY ATTENTION** to state efforts to develop content standards for their school systems... **PARE DOWN** the organized extracurricular activities that your child takes on... **SEEK** a professional diagnosis if you think your child has a learning disability... **CONSIDER** the advantages of applying for "early admission" to college... **KNOW** what college loan options are available to your family... **CARRY ON** your lifelong learning through special alumni programs...

K THROUGH 12 282

COLLEGE & GRAD SCHOOL 302

LIFELONG LEARNING 324

K THROUGH 12

MORALITY: How to raise a moral child, PAGE 285 **CHARTER SCHOOLS:** Experiments in alternative education, PAGE 288 **HOMEWORK:** Making sure you're really helping, PAGE 292 **READING:** The harmful effects of pushing too early, PAGE 293 **FOREIGN LANGUAGE:** Learning a second tongue is easier if you start young, PAGE 295 **SCIENCE:** TV's Science Guy shows why science is cool, PAGE 296 **SCHOOLS:** Is single-sex or coed better? PAGE 300

EXPERT Q & A

TEACHING A CHILD TO BE A THINKER

To turn a kid into a problem-solver, practice active role-playing early on

Why are some children voracious learners throughout childhood while others lose their natural curiosity at an early age? The key to developing intellectually active children, says leading child psychiatrist Dr. Stanley Greenspan is to exercise their natural abilities through strong parental involvement in the kind of "emotional play" that children most value. Greenspan, who is the author of such landmark books as *Playground Politics: The Emotional Life of the School-Age Child,* with J. Salmon (Addison-Wesley, 1993) and *The Challenging Child,* with J. Salmon (Addison-Wesley, 1995) explains:

■ How should parents encourage the learning process in the very young?

The key for babies—and for children of all ages—is to have the child emotionally involved and to use his feelings as a critical part of the learning process. With a 12-month-old baby, for example, you're often confronted with two very diametrically opposed approaches to learning. You can show the baby pictures and match those pictures to words in a very didactic, drill-oriented approach to learning. Or you can do what I've called "floor time" with the child, which is when you're on the floor with the child, playing together and following the child's natural lead. For instance, you're playing with a ball or truck, and the child takes the object and you grab it back and hold it up and the child tries to get it back, and there is a rapid back-and-forth interaction where there's a strong sense of play.

In the situation with more dynamic interaction, without being aware of it you're exercising all that child's emerging abilities. Compare that to the looking at pictures, where you're only exercising a very narrow area of cognition in a somewhat sterile and rote manner. If you want to produce a person who loves learning, and as an adult is going to be a problem-solver who can think on his feet, the more interaction there is between adult and child at this age, the better.

■ Why does an emotionally involved approach to learning work best for infants?

When we follow the child's natural interests—by taking his ball and hiding it, for instance, so that the child is figuring out where the ball went and how he is going to get it—the child is doing a lot of cause-and-effect thinking. In order to get the ball, he's got to be motivated, he's got to have desire. This emotionally fueled thinking, in which the child is getting his motor system acting in a purposeful way, is helping him become a patterned thinker. That's exactly the kind of ability we want in an adult—a person who can figure things out.

■ How should a young child's love of learning be nurtured as she or he grows?

Neurophysiologically, a child has the capacity to create mental images or symbols around 18 months to 2 years of age. A couple of things happen as a result of this ability to create multisensory images of sound, sight, smell, and texture. We see a child's language come in, and we see the child's ability for more complex imitations and for the beginning of what we call pretending.

If you don't involve your child in much interaction, the child will use lots of words in a rote way. His nervous system is programmed to have that ability, just the same as it is for walking. To derail that ability, you really have to severely deprive a child. But if you want a child to use his words and symbols in a thinking way, the child has to associate the images his mind is able to create with something meaningful.

There is a difference between just labeling something "juice," for example, and attaching to it some inner desire or wish. Is "juice" simply something orange that you eat, or does it have a variety of subtle textures, tastes, and satisfactions that are different when you're hungry or thirsty? Juice is a complicated thing to get to know—you know it more and more as your experience with it grows. The same is true of love, or justice, you acquire those concepts as a result of experience.

■ Are there any particularly effective techniques for enhancing a young child's intellectual development?

Again, the way to develop a child's thinking ability is to tune in to the child at his developmental level. For the 30-month-old, that's the world of ideas. Try using dolls and action

FROM NEWBORN TO PRESCHOOLER

"The child is father of the man," wrote Wordsworth. The following developmental timeline shows the progression that takes place in the early years:

- **DURING FIRST MONTH:** The average daily weight gain: two-thirds of an ounce; the average daily height gain: one to one-and-a-half inches
- **BY END OF FIRST MONTH:** Hears well generally. May turn head toward family and voices that sound interesting
- **BY END OF THIRD MONTH:** Begins to babble and imitate some sounds and develop a social smile
- **BY END OF SEVEN MONTHS:** Responds to own name and uses voice to express joy and displeasure
- **BY FIRST BIRTHDAY:** May walk two or three unassisted steps and can say "Dada" and "Momma" and respond to "no"
- **BY 15 TO 18 MONTHS:** Says several simple words, including own name
- **BY 18 TO 24 MONTHS:** Follows simple instructions and begins make-believe play
- **BY THIRD BIRTHDAY:** Understands most sentences and uses pronouns and some plurals. Can also express a wide range of emotions and separates from parents easily
- **SOMETIME DURING FOURTH YEAR:** Has active vocabulary of 300 to 1000 words. Understands the concepts of "same" and "different" and tells stories

SOURCE: Adapted from *Caring for Your Baby and Young Child,* American Academy of Pediatrics, Bantam Books, 1993.

figures to create a drama, for instance. Talk to the doll and get the child to imitate something you do. Then act out another situation, and challenge the child to respond spontaneously. You might pretend the doll is feeding, for instance, and say, "I want more of that," and see what the child says. What you're doing is expanding the child's use of symbols in a highly spontaneous way that is driven by the child's natural interests. Not only is he very involved, but he's learning causal thinking at a symbolic level.

A parent only has a limited amount of time and can choose between rote learning or the "floor time" approach. In floor time, you might start off by pointing at a book and saying to your child, "You want to read?" Then when you read a sentence, you might get the child to do some pretend play that relates to what you read. You read, interact, read, interact, as opposed to just reading a whole story to him.

■ What concepts should a parent help introduce to a preschool child?

Concepts of causality, concepts of time, concepts related to space and quantity, and the meaning of words—all things that are part of any preschool agenda. To the extent that they're introduced through dynamic interaction, all the better. Do this through problem-solving discussions in which you try to be logical and reality-based. You might talk about what your child did at school, whom he played with, what he did, what he liked and didn't like, why he doesn't want to go to sleep on time. You're much more intrigued by a child who gives you a good lawyer's argument for staying up an extra 15 minutes than by just saying that the child has to go to sleep, no more arguments, because he's three-and-a-half years old. If you spend 10 minutes on a good debate, you've exercised that logical side in a way in which the kid really cares.

■ How can you help a child make the transition from preschool to a more formal school setting?

For most kids in most communities, the transition from preschool to a more formal structured school experience is a gradual process. It usually starts between ages two and three with a play group, and a new person called a teacher, about two mornings a week. By ages three to four it's probably two to three hours daily. By kindergarten, or what's sometimes called the transition year, what happens is still play-oriented but will be every weekday until two or three in the afternoon with the same teacher. The teacher's object is to move the child gradually into more problem-solving exercises that are still dynamic. From day one the child is learning that there are authority-based expectations in life as well as interactions that encourage a child to march to his own drummer.

At home as well, with children ages three to five, you should be having reality-based problem-solving discussions, and working with him on reality-based chores, whether it's helping you to do the dishes or setting the table or helping you make something or doing something on his own. As a child gets older, you expect more. Cleaning up his own toys, putting clothes away, figuring out what he wants to have for dinner and telling you in advance.

■ What makes children resist a structured school environment?

The education system we now have is really set up for about 10 percent of the kids who are self-learners. The pencil-and-paper work you find in many places requires a child who is already very motivated. But these expectations are very unrealistic.

Children do easily what's easy for them and will go against what's hard for them. Children will also rebel if they're angry with you. For example, children who sit and read are usually natural readers. Children who want to go out on the playground and shoot baskets are natural basketball players. You take a kid who can't throw the ball, and he's not going to want to play basketball. Similarly, the kid who has fine motor problems will not want to draw or write letters. You make a mistake to assume that the five- or six-year-old kid who sits and reads or writes is more motivated than the one who doesn't. At that level a child does what comes naturally. Motivation is not a big factor until the age of 10 or more.

HOW TO RAISE A MORAL CHILD

Empathy is the key to developing morality, says Dr. Stanley Greenspan

"Children are going to learn morality not from what you tell them, but from how you treat them," says child psychiatrist Stanley Greenspan, whose latest book, *The Growth of the Mind and Its Endangered Future* (Addison-Wesley, 1996), discusses how children develop their sense of morality. The way a child is treated is crucial, says Greenspan, whose research has shown that morality depends on a person's ability to feel empathy for someone else, and to have empathy a child must first develop what Greenspan calls "a sense of shared humanity." That sense of shared humanity, or "buying into the human race," comes from a child experiencing intimacy and warmth in a relationship with another person, whether that figure is the child's parents, relative, or other close contact. It's impossible to develop a concern for others, Greenspan argues, unless someone in your life has shown concern for you.

That sense of shared humanity is only the starting point, however, for encouraging morality in children. "You can't empathize with someone else unless you can picture what the other person wants and desires and are able to put yourself in the other's shoes," says Greenspan. "If you can't put yourself in another's shoes, you can't really contemplate how your actions are going to affect them."

Empathy is essential, Greenspan says, because it helps guide children's judgments in cases where there may not be a clear-cut rule to follow, and a child may have to decide how to handle a moral dilemma on his own. If you simply tell a child, "You don't do this, you don't do that," says Greenspan, some children will obey out of a fear of being "a bad person," without really understanding what that means. Such children have what Greenspan calls "a concrete sense of morality, and can just as soon be immoral as moral" if a new authority figure with less savory rules appears. To make moral judgments, stresses Greenspan, "the kind we want in our Supreme Court justices, comes from a sense of empathy."

■ **What if a child just can't handle the academic demands of early schooling?**

When a child rebels, you have to figure out what's hard for him and what's easy. Let him spend at least half his time on things that he's relatively competent at, and use those activities to develop his thinking skills. If a child has good gross motor skills and is a good athlete, for example, you can teach him about thinking and lots of things through sports. You can teach about math, for instance, by asking how many people are on both the child's and other guy's team, or how many seconds it will take to get from here to there.

Spend the other half of your time on the remedial areas. There, the key is to break the task down into smaller steps. It's like hitting a new golf or tennis stroke—break it down into simple enough steps, so that there's mastery associated with each step. Teachers often aren't given enough training in the steps involved in motor control. The person who says, "You can't coddle kids," doesn't realize that the nervous system has to be trained through a gradual procss. You can't skip over six steps—it just doesn't work. If you say, "Just tough it out," you'll get 70 percent of the kids dropping out of school in the sixth grade. There's no way that any child, short of having a very severe problem with nervous system development, shouldn't be able to read, write, and do arithmetic. That's a complete failure on our part. Parents need to work with their boards of education to made the educational system more dynamic and interactive.

SCHOOL REFORM

STATES ARE WHERE THE ACTION IS

The drive toward national education standards is being tested

It's been well over a decade since a blue-ribbon commission probing the health of the nation's schools declared that if a foreign enemy had tried "to impose on America the mediocre educational performance that exists today, we might well have viewed it as an act of war." The publication of that report, "A Nation at Risk," in 1983, left many families assuming that the war on educational mediocrity would have to be led by Washington. In fact, school reform has always been more the province of state and local authorities and the teachers whose paychecks they fund.

Nowhere has this been more evident than in policy-makers' recent support for outcomes-based education, an approach that turns on the notion that education should be judged by results, or outcomes, rather than inputs such as money or "seat-time," which is how teachers sometimes refer to the time their students spend in the classroom.

Federally sponsored efforts to identify what every student should know by grades 4, 8, and 12 have been a cornerstone of the Clinton administration's educational program, Goals 2000, which was approved by Congress in 1994. In the legislation, Congress set up a National Educational Standards and Improvement Council to "certify" the standards being developed by leading professional associations in every major academic field with funding from the Department of Education. But the Clinton administration's effort has come under attack by those who fear too much federal meddling in the classroom. And the details have been attacked by critics as being sometimes unrealistically comprehensive, not stringent enough, and overly political correct.

While the federal initiative founders politically, standards-setting is taking firm root at the state level. As of January 1, 1996, 27 states had adopted some sort of standards, and 23 (including the District of Columbia) were developing them. The National Governors Association hopes to promote this trend with major new initiatives. At a recent education summit at Palisades, NY, IBM Chairman Louis Gerstner urged corporate America to support the standards movement, even suggesting that companies consider how tough a state's education standards are, and how well it trains its students to meet those standards, in determining where to locate new plant facilities.

Of the states that already have standards, seven have changed theirs to match federal benchmarks, which now exist for the arts, business, civics, English, foreign language, geography, mathematics, and science. Other states are using the federal guidelines together with a wide variety of other sources to revamp their stated standards. Some states differ on the length of time a student should spend on a given subject, others on the content of the curriculum, still others on what every child must prove he or she knows.

Another prominent effort to develop a comprehensive set of standards for all major academic disciplines is being spearheaded by the Washington, D.C.–based National Center for Education in the Economy in collaboration with the Learning Research and Development Center of the University of Pittsburgh. Entitled New Standards, this effort is notable because in addition to describing what students should know by a given age (which NS has taken from the standards developed by each discipline), NS specifies the ways students should demonstrate their knowledge and skills, and provides teachers and schools with the tests to measure students' performances.

New Standards has come up with a two-part assessment system that may allay the fear of those that balk at the thought of national standardized tests. In addition to examinations at grades 4, 8, and 10, NS uses a portfolio system that shows a variety of a

EXPERT SOURCES

GETTING A FIX ON THE NEW STANDARDS

Booklets containing the curricular standards being developed by educators for the nation's schools come in a variety of core subjects. They attempt to describe all a student should know by a certain year—both the content and how a student should be able to demonstrate such knowledge. Prices for the booklets range from $9 to $25. To obtain copies of the standards for different disciplines, contact:

ARTS

MUSIC EDUCATORS NATIONAL COUNCIL
1806 Robert Fulton Dr.
Reston, VA 22091
■ Ask for *National Standards for Art Education.*
☎800–828–0229

CIVICS

CENTER FOR CIVIC EDUCATION
5146 Douglas Fir Rd.
Calabasas, CA 91302
■ Ask for *National Standards for Civics and Government.*
☎800–350–4223

ENGLISH

NATIONAL COUNCIL OF TEACHERS OF ENGLISH
1111 W. Kenyon Rd.
Urbana, IL 61801
■ Ask for *Standards for English and Language Arts.*
☎800–369–6283

FOREIGN LANGUAGE

AMERICAN COUNCIL ON THE TEACHING OF FOREIGN LANGUAGES
6 Executive Blvd.
Yonkers, NY 10701–6801
■ *National Standards in Foreign Language Education.*
☎914–963–8830

GEOGRAPHY

THE NATIONAL GEOGRAPHIC SOCIETY
PO Box 1640
Washington, D.C. 20013
■ Ask for *Geography for Life: National Standards.*
☎800–368–2728

HISTORY

UCLA NATIONAL CENTER FOR HISTORY IN THE SCHOOLS
10880 Wilshire Blvd.
Ste. 761, Los Angeles, CA 90021–4108
■ Ask for *National Standards for United States History* for kindergarten through 4th grade or 5th through 9th grade. Standards for world history are also available.
☎310–824–4702

MATH

NATIONAL COUNCIL OF MATHEMATICS
1906 Association Dr.
Reston, VA 22091
■ Ask for *Curriculum and Evaluation Standards for School Mathematics.*
☎703–620–9840

SCIENCE

NATIONAL RESEARCH COUNCIL
2101 Constitution Ave., N.W.
Washington, D.C. 20418
■ Ask for *National Science Education Standards.*
☎202–334–1399

student's work over time. Included are writing samples, as well as math and science assignments. Putting a portfolio together is itself intended to be a part of the learning experience because the child has to recognize what makes one analytic piece better than another. Evaluation takes place at several points in the year when the teacher, or possibly an outside consultant (depending on the state requirements), reviews the materials and assesses a student's progress.

To find out more about where the standards-setting movement stands in your state, contact your state's board of education. To receive copies of the federally developed benchmarks or more information on New Standards, see the addresses and phone numbers in the box above.

CHARTER SCHOOLS

DO-IT-YOURSELF CLASSROOMS

Experimental schools give critics a chance to do it their own way

Talk to parents and teachers enmeshed in the public school system and you'll often hear a common refrain: "My kids hate school. I want education to be inspiring for them." "I can't be expected to teach a class of 40 students." "Too little money, that's why our school doesn't have enough computers." "Students in this country aren't equipped for college or the working world when they graduate." As part of the effort to combat these frustrations, 22 states[1] have enacted laws in recent years that allow parents and teachers to establish experimental, or charter schools, that function outside the normal public school system. The following information, from Jeanne Allen, president of The Center for Education Reform, a Washington, D.C.-based nonprofit organization, explains what this movement is all about:

■ What are charter schools?

Charter schools are individual public schools that are autonomous from the public school system. While they are technically still public schools, they do not have to adhere to many of the rules and regulations governing public schools—for instance, they have complete control over their budgets, curriculum, scheduling, personnel, and the standards to which they hold their students. Typically, charter schools organize around a central idea—the ideas ranging from providing bilingual education to improving the attendance rate of an inner city school, to learning auto mechanics or hotel management, to only serving homeless children. As of January 1996, approximately 260 charter schools exist. This number is expected to have dramatically increased during the year.

■ Who may start a charter school?

Each state has a different set of criteria for who is allowed to start a charter school. In all cases, teachers and administrators of existing schools can apply to state or local authorities (which one depends on the state) for charter status. In certain states, parents, businesses, and other community organizations, such as museums and youth service organizations, are allowed to as well.

■ What is the appeal of such schools?

Charter schools offer teachers and parents control in areas where their hands were previously tied—how to allocate resources, how much time to spend on a given subject, and how to teach. Freed from the budgetary constraints imposed by the school district, charter schools have implemented innovative cost-cutting measures that allow them to have more money for such things as teachers and computers.

Some, for example, opt to forgo janitorial and maintenance costs by requiring parents to volunteer one hour a week. Others, such as the Vaughn Next Century Learning Center in California, have increased their daily student attendance rate by calling parents whenever a child is absent—and brought in more funds as a result, since some districts allocate funds based on attendance. In the case of Vaughn, the school immediately used its budget flexibility to hire four new teachers,

EXPERT SOURCES

For more on charter schools: Contact U.S. Department of Education ☎ 202-401-2000, or the Center for Education Reform, 1001 Connecticut Avenue, Suite 204, Washington, D.C. 20036. ☎ 800-521-2118.

reduce class size from 32 to 26 and add a 27-computer lab and a teachers resource center.

■ Is a charter school subject to the same academic standards as public schools?

While charter schools allow educators and parents the freedom to choose how to teach, students not only must meet state academic standards, but must also meet any goals delineated in the charter proposal. Failure to do so means the school is closed down. Proponents argue that such a clear-cut "succeed and live, or fail and die" approach provides a tremendous incentive for the school's administration and teachers to make sure their students meet their standards.

■ How detailed a plan must you have to start a charter school?

In each state, the law differs on who may apply for charter school status and who has the decision-making power to grant this status. The "powers that be" can range from a local school district to the state board of education, and from a community college to the state superintendent. Charter organizers must submit a proposal with a clearly defined mission and goals, a solid administrative and financial structure, a comprehensive curricular plan, and an assessment plan to measure results.

At the core of every charter proposal is the premise that, in exchange for a waiver of most of the education regulations of the state, the school will show satisfactory achievement by its students. A charter's achievement standards are generally expected to be equal to, or, more often, higher than the state's average student achievement. Schools must sign a performance contract with the state that requires them to meet the standards they have proposed; if they don't meet these achievement levels, their charter is simply revoked. They will also be shut down if they are not fiscally sound, or if they violate any civil, safety, or health codes.

1. Alaska, Arkansas, Arizona, California, Colorado, Connecticut, Delaware, Florida, Hawaii, Idaho, Illinois, Louisiana, Massachussetts, Mississippi, Minnesota, New Hampshire, New Jersey, North Carolina, Ohio, Pennsylvania, Texas, Wyoming.

EXPERT Q & A

THE CHILD WHO DOES TOO MUCH

The more activities kids take on, the less enriched their educations are

Every parent knows the exasperation that comes from having a child who "acts up"—whether it be the 5-year-old who is terrorizing other children at nursery school, the 7-year-old who throws a fit every morning before leaving the house, or the 10-year-old who refuses to do her homework. What can a parent do in such cases? Dr. David Elkind, a leading child development expert, shares his views about how to evaluate and cope with your child's behavior. Elkind is professor of child study at Tufts University and author of *The Hurried Child* (Addison-Wesley, 1988) and *Ties That Stress* (Harvard University Press, 1994):

■ How can you tell the difference between a child who is acting up because of stress, and one who is precocious and simply wants more stimulation?

Parents experience very different demands from children depending on what that child is experiencing. For example, a gifted child might demand constant stimulation to try to satisfy his or her voracious appetite for information—a chorus of whys ringing in your ears all day. That's very different from a child who battles for attention and presents parents with strain and power struggles.

You need to look at how many demands there are on a child. Is the child being shuttled from activity to activity? Is he having to adapt to too many places and people each day (e.g., school, daycare, baby-sitters)? The more changes a child experiences in a day, the more stress he feels. Also, if you are troubled or there is some type of distress in the family, your child will often mirror it.

■ What can be done to relieve stress at school?

Increasingly, schools make inappropriate demands on a child. With so many early education programs, educators are assuming that children know their numbers and letters at a younger and younger age. This might not be the case, and it is no reflection on the child's intelligence. Different children have different rates of development, and the education system is often too inflexible to deal with that fact.

One suggestion for avoiding stress is to keep your child out of the system a bit longer. If your child has a September or October birthday, especially for boys, you may want to wait an extra year before enrolling him. This is certainly much preferred to starting your child and then having him repeat a year, something I am opposed to for the most part. There is such a stigma for kids who are held back that if you are in the situation of deciding between holding your child back a year, I recommend allowing him to continue to the next grade, and providing additional tutoring. That way, the child is not "penalized."

■ How many activities can a child manage adequately?

I tell parents that there is no need for a child to have any organized activity like sports or music before the age of five or six. For school-age children, a sport, a musical instrument, and maybe a "peer activity" like scouts, is plenty. These should not take more than a few hours a week. It is very important for a child not to have all his time programmed. Children must learn to manage their own time. I see a lot of new college students who simply do not know how to manage their time because they had such "planned" lives. This causes a great deal of difficulty when they reach college, where it is left up to each individual to allocate time properly and handle a range of tasks all at once.

■ How do you allow a child to manage his or her own time, yet limit television or video watching?

You can certainly lay down some ground rules. For instance, you allow your child a certain number of hours of Nintendo per week, and the rest must be spent doing other things. You are not saying that he or she can't do something, but you are setting limits on it.

■ What's the best way to help a child deal with a stress that won't go away, like a death, divorce, or a move?

The most important thing is to talk to your child and help him or her deal with his or her feelings. If someone has died, it's very important for the child to talk about that person and to articulate how he or she feels. Similarly, if a child sees something frightening on TV, the child needs to talk about it and be allowed to work through his or her emotions.

■ When is professional help or therapy advisable?

While there are cases where a child needs therapy, a parent must be very careful. Being sent to see someone can label the child as abnormal and become yet another form of stress. When there is a problem for which a parent wants to seek professional counseling, this should be done as a family, as opposed to sending only the child. A child never experiences spontaneous combustion; he or she does not become emotionally distressed overnight, but over a period of years as a result of family behavior patterns. That's the reason I will not see individual children in therapy anymore. I will see and work with families, but not individuals. Even when a child is experiencing a physiological problem, such as Attention Deficit Disorder, the parents need counseling as well.

■ What is the biggest mistake parents make in helping children deal with life's stresses?

One of the biggest mistakes is to think that bad experiences prepare children for other bad experiences. I believe that the more good experiences parents can give their children—doing things with their children, giving them loving and successful experiences—the better they feel about themselves, the better the relationships they have with their parents, the better they are able to cope when something difficult does happen.

EXPERT TIPS

THE RIGHT WAY TO TALK THE TALK

Parents and teachers need each other, but often don't communicate

Every parent knows the frustration of a child not wanting to go to school, a teacher calling to say that your pride-and-joy has been disruptive, or a disappointing report card arriving in the mail. When your child is at school during the day, the teacher is his or her link to the world. But communicating well with your child's teacher can be difficult. What seems green to you may seem blue to your child's teacher. Dr. Lilian Katz, professor of early childhood development at the University of Illinois and the director of the Educational Resources Information Center, a federally funded clearing house of information regarding early childhood education, offers these tips on how to talk to your child's teacher better:

■ **The best way to communicate with a teacher is to speak very directly and honestly about your concerns.** It is very important to get the teacher's view as well as your child's view when a question or problem arises. If you want a third party's opinion, you can also ask the principal to bring in a specialist or another outside person to assess the situation. Trying to do that assessment yourself is not something you should do, however. Your child will act completely differently with you present, and you simply can't be objective about your own child.

The younger the child, the more important it is to be in regular communication with the child's teacher, as young kids are not very reliable reporters. Obviously, as children get older, they have private lives into which they will not want their parents intruding.

■ **Don't expect every school or every teacher to fit every child.** Children need to know that they are not going to like every teacher they have. It is a parent's responsibility to help them cope with that. Similarly, a child does not need to be overly coddled because he or she has an unpleasant situation. While it is important for parents to be empathetic, try to help a child understand that not everything in life is fun, and that he or she may have to do things even when they are not fun.

■ **Try to understand the teacher's perspective.** Parents should remember that teachers are under a lot of pressure. Not only is he or she trying to cope with, sometimes, up to 35 children in one room, which could mean over 150 in any given day, but they are under tremendous legal pressure. I've seen teachers very fearful to so much as touch a child, afraid that somewhere down the line, they will be accused of some type of misconduct. Also, parents should understand that teachers themselves go through different phases in their teaching careers. I tell disgruntled parents the same thing I tell teachers who are frustrated with overly anxious parents: they are just people, try to understand their point of view.

■ **Don't give your child a reason to dismiss his or her teacher.** It is very important that parents not criticize the teacher or the school in front of the child. This gives the child permission to be defiant, which solves nothing. For example, my son came home one day in a fit because his teacher wouldn't let him go to the library during his English class. I explained that if she knew him as well as I did, she probably would have let him go on his own. But the fact is, she has 130 to 140 kids to be responsible for every day and she has to have certain rules to maintain control over each class. In this case, he needed help understanding why a certain rule existed. He certainly didn't need to hear, "Oh, that stupid woman. I can't believe she wouldn't let you..."

As a parent, you should do what you can to ensure the child's life is fulfilling outside of school, through relationships, activities, and the like. But do not overindulge simply because the situation is not perfect.

HOMEWORK

A HELPING HAND AT DAY'S END

Some sound advice on how a parent can aid in after-school work

For parents anxious to help their children' s learning, getting involved with homework is one of the best methods. Yet all too often, homework becomes a battle ground for wars of words between parent and child.

"The relationship [of parent helping the child] is supposed to go on for years," says Joyce Epstein, who has studied homework issues extensively as director at the Johns Hopkins Center on Families, Communities, Schools and Children' s Learning. "You have to be careful that one night of confrontation doesn't ruin you for 12 years of school."

To develop good family communications, says Epstein, it's important how a parent talks to a child about school. "Many parents are told or advised to ask their child, 'How was school today?' as a way of interacting," says Epstein. "Better to ask: 'Show me something you learned in math today,' because that makes the youngster demonstrate and re-create, rather then comment on nothing." From there, she says, parents can build the kind of interaction that will not only help the child's work but will improve the way the parent and child communicate. Other pitfalls that parents must avoid include:

■ A confrontational attitude in which the parent challenges the child, rather than allowing the child to demonstrate what he or she has learned.

■ Giving up the guidance role too early, particularly with adolescents. Studies have found, says Epstein, that parents tend to talk less to their children as they reach high school, even though these students continue to need positive interaction on their work.

■ Taking on the teacher role, which sets up resistance in the child.

Epstein's research has shown a strong connection between parents' involvement in learning activities at home and gains in skills in reading and other subject areas. Concerned about lost learning opportunities at home, Epstein and a team of Hopkins educators designed TIPS (Teachers Involve Parents in Schoolwork)—homework assignments in which students discuss something interesting about their schoolwork with someone at home. Instead of dittoed exercises to be done in one night, homework becomes a source of games, interviews, and experiments conducted by the child with the help of a parent over a period of two to three days.

Epstein's research reveals that middle-school teachers who systematically involve families are more likely to see parents as allies, and to foster good communication between parent and child about school and homework. In the TIPS model, parents take on a variety of roles. For a lesson on the use of proper nouns, students play a game with the parent naming proper nouns from a list of common nouns such as *cereal* and *tennis shoe*. For a lesson called "Test Your Nerves," the parent is the test subject in an experiment in which a child observes and charts nervous reactions, such as blinking. All of the activities conclude with discussion on whatever phenomenon is studied.

"Schools are calling for more homework," says Epstein. "But what is really needed is better homework. Instead of assigning another page of math problems, teachers need to step back and see how to engage children in extra minutes of thought."

■ **For more information:** TIPS manuals and activities booklets are available for elementary and middle grades. Write the Dissemination Office, Center on Families, Communities, Schools and Children's Learning, The Johns Hopkins University, 3505 N. Charles Street, Baltimore, MD 21218, or call ☎ 410-516-8808.

EXPERT Q & A

READ THIS FOR YOUR CHILD'S SAKE

Lighten up, parents. Pushing reading too early is a big mistake

To be a good reader in school is to be considered smart. To be a bad reader, far too often, is to be labeled stupid. Research over the past few decades shows that difficulty in reading is due not to inferior intelligence but to specific learning disabilities that are neurological disorders, which can be helped and sometimes corrected through proper training. Still, parents go to extraordinary lengths to ensure that their child master the art of reading—from reading to the child while still *in utero* to buying a Speak & Spell when the child is a mere two years old. Harvard School of Education professor Jean Chall, author of *Learning to Read, the Great Reading Debate* (McGraw Hill, 1970) and other seminal books in the education field, shares her perspective on teaching reading:

■ At what age should a child learn to read?

That is difficult to answer as every child varies greatly. Traditionally, American schools teach children at age six, but many schools begin teaching informally in kindergarten and pre-kindergarten. I am wary of telling parents to start too early, because if a child does not immediately succeed, the parent has a hard time relaxing and letting the child go at his or her own pace.

■ What teaching methods are used today?

For the past century, there has been debate over two major methods of teaching reading. The first is known now as the "whole language" approach and is what American schools have been moving toward over a number of years. This approach focuses on content, meaning, and ideas—rather than teaching the "code" that is language, which is done in the more formal "phonic method." "Whole language" is taught by reading to the child and stressing the meaning of what the child is reading. "Whole language" teachers assume that a child who understands what is being read will eventually figure out from the context how to identify, or read, the words on a page.

■ Which teaching method works best?

Over the years, research has proved that the use of both methods—the "whole language" and the "phonic"—is the best way for a child to master reading. While the "whole language" approach, which includes reading to children and getting them interested in both the activity of reading and the story they are reading, is helpful, phonics must be taught. Children must be taught that one of the squiggles they see on a page is a "p" and another a "b" and that those two letters sound different and are written differently. Getting the print off the page requires a different ability than being able to understand the meaning of what is written. It is very important for normal progress, and especially for children at risk, that both methods be taught.

■ How do you lay the groundwork for reading in a young chiild?

You can start developing the skills needed in reading at a very young age. I, again, caution parents to not push their children too fast. Besides reading to children, parents can start "ear training" their child by playing rhyme games. This develops the child's ability to discern different sounds and to realize that certain words begin, look, and sound the same. In reading to children, parents also can point to words as they go, teaching the child that the funny lines on the page are the words you are saying. All of this "early teaching" should not be a serious thing. It should be a fun activity. There is plenty of time for serious learning later.

■ When should you "get serious"?

Once a child is in school, the learning of reading is inevitably more serious. If children do not already know how to identify and write letters, and to recognize words, they start to learn it in a systematic way. I am reluctant to tell parents when to teach reading to their children, as they often embark on too serious a task too early for the child.

■ How many children suffer from learning disabilities?

Most schools cite a 10 to 15 percent learning disability rate among their student body; some as high as 20 percent. Many children have some kind of reading difficulty.

■ What if your child is having difficulty with reading?

You must get a professional diagnosis. While the teacher might say the child is merely disinterested but will get over it, disinterest or poor performance in reading can stem from a number of things, some being very specific learning disabilities that can be identified and worked on. Correcting these early can circumvent a lot of potential problems later in school. Learning disabilities have now been shown to be neurological problems that can be corrected with the proper training.

■ What kind of specialist is it best to see?

Every school should have a reading specialist that can assess your child and explain to you why the child might be experiencing difficulty. If the school has no specialist, ask about private tutors, talk to other parents, consult a local university, but find an outside specialist. It is very tricky for parents to deal with their own child's learning disabilities and I most certainly do not recommend it.

GLASSES FOR THE EARS

Surprising insights into what causes some language learning disorders

For many children with serious language learning disorders, which often develop into dyslexia, even tutoring seems to come up short. Researchers Paula Tallal of Rutgers University and Michael Merzenich of the University of California School of Medicine in San Francisco have developed radical new treatments with intriguing preliminary results.

The treatments use a computer to enhance sounds that are difficult for some children to hear. The technique is designed for children who cannot distinguish between certain sounds, or phonemes, such as "ka" and "ta." By using a computer to make sounds longer and at times louder, some children have been able to advance a full two years in their verbal comprehension skills over the course of a month.

Why some children cannot hear such sounds is unclear. Explanations range from genetic flaws to trauma suffered as a result of chronic ear infections. But whatever the cause, Dr. Tallal suspects that by turning the computer into a therapeutic device, the brain cells in a child's auditory cortex can be trained to better recognize fast-changing acoustic cues, which is critical in the ongoing processing of speech.

To boost results still further, a third researcher, Dr. William Jenkins of the University of California School of Medicine in San Francisco, and Dr. Steven Meller of Rutgers have even employed video game techniques. They developed computer games and listening exercises using the processed speech. As his subjects watch animals fly across the screen and are rewarded by bells and flashing lights when they score well, they are being drilled in hearing pairs of tones and phonemes at ever faster speeds. The researchers stress that such techniques need more study and may not help with all reading problems, but they are a promising beginning.

To find out more: Scientific Learning Principles, 1 Kearny St., Ste. 501, San Francisco, CA 94108; e-mail *Miller@.scilearn.com* or online at *http://www.ld.ucsf.edu*

EXPERT TIPS

ACQUIRING A SECOND TONGUE

Children develop foreign language skills by starting young

America has always been a culture of many immigrants and many languages, but the "American language," it was always understood, was English. Yet you can go for hours today without hearing English spoken in many American cities, and because of the global economy, foreign language ability is increasingly important even for Americans. But U.S. schools lag far behind their international counterparts in requiring foreign language training. Starting when a child is young is critical, argues foreign language expert Nancy Rhodes, who is Associate Director for English Language and Multi-Cultural Education at the Center for Applied Linguistics in Washington, D.C. Rhodes offers this advice on training children to speak foreign tongues:

■ **Start foreign language training early.** After 12 or 13, it is very difficult to learn a language and be able to speak it like a native speaker and develop a high level of fluency. Some studies comparing second-grade learners with eighth-grade learners have found that eighth-graders learn more quickly and can do more grammar than the second-graders can. The older students are more thorough learners, as is the case with any subject area. But young kids like playing with language, they like making new sounds. They're not inhibited or embarrassed by making strange sounds, so it's ideal for them to learn a foreign language. If you wait until kids are in adolescence, they are very inhibited and very worried about how they appear to their peers.

■ **Don't worry that studying a foreign language will harm a child's native language ability.** Studying another language helps you learn more about your native language. All of the research results show that it actually enhances your native language abilities. By the time children in foreign language immersion programs get to fifth or sixth grade, they score as well or better in English than their peers who have been studying only in English.

■ **If you have a choice, elect a program that integrates foreign language instruction into the rest of the curriculum.** Typically, schools don't start foreign language teaching until about middle school or high school, but about a fifth of the elementary schools in the U.S. teach some type of foreign language, either before or after school, or during the school day. It could be just an introduction, or it could be an immersion-type experience in which the foreign language is the medium of instruction, so that the students are not just learning language, but they're learning all their content areas through the foreign language.

The successful programs are integrated into the school day so that everybody sees foreign language as part of the curriculum, not as some add-on that you only do if you have some extra time.

■ **When a family is multilingual, be as consistent as possible about who speaks what.** Children can learn five or six different languages. Children in many other countries do learn five or six languages at once. The important thing is to separate the language for the kids. If the mother speaks English, for example, and the father speaks Spanish, they should try to keep those roles the same so that the child will see that there are two separate languages. Do not be surprised or alarmed, however, if a child exposed to more than one language when young mixes the languages he or she hears. This is normal and is a phase. Be careful not to react with impatience, nor to curtail speaking additional languages. Remember that by teaching a foreign language early, you are imparting a great gift.

EXPERT TIPS

THE SCIENCE GUY'S MAGIC FORMULAE

The TV science maven's tips for tuning kids onto the natural world

Ask kids today what they think is "cool," and the answer might be Power Rangers, Bart Simpson, or baggy pants. The word "science" would be far down the list. But Bill Nye the Science Guy makes science jump to life six days a week on national television. The Seattle resident contends that figuring out the way things work really is enough to blow one's mind, young and old, if you just remember where and how to look. Here, television's Science Guy explains how to help your child understand the natural world's amazing ways:

■ **IT'S ALL SCIENCE.** Take virtually anything—the food you eat, the seasons of the year, the blood that comes out of a cut, something rancid in the refrigerator—we understand it all with science.

Consider our sun. This is something I encourage everyone to truly ponder, because it's amazing. Take a globe and a light and try to understand why there are seasons, days, and years. Many people don't really understand the intimate connection between one year and the earth's trip around the sun, nor do they seem to remember the relative size and distance that the two are from each other. If the earth were one centimeter, the sun would be 109 centimeters, and they would be 100 meters apart. This is a vast distance and yet, somehow, just the right amount of sunlight reaches earth to allow life as we know it.

■ **TAKE TIME TO STOP AND SMELL THE ROSES.** An age-old adage, but a good one.The world around you—whether you live in New York City or the mountains of Colorado—is rife with things to look at and figure out. Flowers? Bees? They are so cool. Look at them closely, figure out how they work. Pick up a leaf and look at the intricate system of veins. That leaf contains an amazing circulation system. Talk about it; get excited about it.

To see circulation "in action," put one end of a celery stick in water and food coloring and watch the coloring appear in the leaves. As far as I'm concerned, flowers, bees, spiders, and trees could pretty much take up a whole summer, not to mention frogs and fish, but I guess you need some free time.

■ **DON'T CONDESCEND.** Don't turn the activity into "I, Adult, will now impart to you, Child, my knowledge." That is the quickest way to throw a wet blanket on anyone. Make it an adventure—find things out together.

■ **DON'T KNOW EVERYTHING.** Don't be afraid to admit that you may not fully understand how a fish breathes in water, for example. "I don't know" is a great answer, as long as "let's find out" is next.

■ **LET THEM MAKE A MESS.** They, of course, will have to clean it up. But as long as your kids are being safe, don't be too concerned with neatness. Kids are often less squeamish than adults and often "the gross stuff" is considered most cool, so steel your nerves and pick up the worm, look at it, see how it moves, find out what it does.

EXPERT SOURCES

For more experiments guaranteed to work, consult either *Bill Nye the Science Guy's Big Blast of Science* (Addison-Wesley, 1993, $12.95), *Bill Nye the Science Guy's Consider the Following* (Disney Press, 1995, $9.95), or log onto his Web site at *http://nyelabs.kcts.org.*

DO TRY THESE YOURSELF AT HOME

Experiments that never cease to amaze the Science Guy

▼ Baking soda and vinegar together make carbon dioxide: a solid plus a liquid and voilà, a gas. My variation on this classic experiment is to put the vinegar in a bottle (a soda bottle works well) and the baking soda in a balloon.

Fit the balloon on the mouth of the bottle. When you're ready, shake the baking soda into the vinegar. Carbon dioxide is created and the balloon blows up. That in itself is good, but you can keep going. Take the balloon off and insert a lit match into the neck of the bottle. It goes right out because of the CO_2.

▼ To take it even further: In an aquarium or even a mayonnaise jar, place candles of various heights and light them. Then, pour the carbon dioxide, just as you would a liquid, from the bottle into the jar or aquarium. Because CO_2 is heavier than air, you can watch the candles go out in sequence, from shortest to tallest.

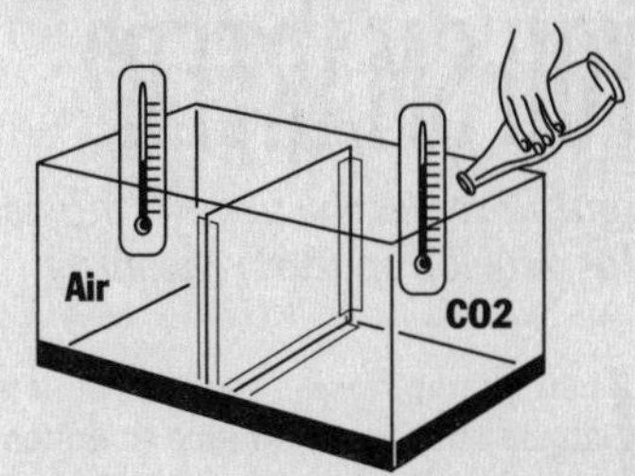

▲ Another fascinating CO_2 experiment demonstrates the "greenhouse effect." Partition an aquarium with cardboard, taping it well so air can't leak from one side to the other. Pour CO_2 in one side, and let the other side remain regular air. Place a thermometer in each side and flood lights above each. You will see that the side with CO_2 goes up a few degrees more than the other. A certain amount of carbon dioxide makes the earth's atmosphere warm enough to support life. Excess CO_2, however, is producing climatic changes.

▼ Try this and see if you can figure out what's happening. Cut the top end off of a 2-liter soda bottle. Fill the bottom with about an inch of water with blue food coloring in it and set the top section on the bottom section, cap down. Fill the top with ice. The result will be droplets forming on the inverted top section. The question: Why isn't there any blue food coloring in the droplets? The answer: When water evaporates, it leaves its impurities behind.

THE ARTS

DOES MUSIC MAKE YOU SMARTER?

Intriguing research suggests music helps develop spatial reasoning

When champions of the liberal arts argue that there's more to education than just reading, writing, and arithmetic, music and arts are often cited for their value in stimulating students' creativity and expanding their cultural horizons. Now there is evidence that students who receive formal musical training may enjoy higher standardized test scores and demonstrate greater powers of spatial reasoning than students who do not get this experience.

According to data released by the College Entrance Examination Board, for instance, students who reported coursework or experience in music performance scored 23 points higher on the verbal portion of their Scholastic Assessment Test (SAT) in 1995, and 19 points higher on the math component of the exam than the entire pool of test-takers. Students who reported taking music appreciation classes at school scored 33 points higher on their verbal SAT and 26 points higher on the math portion of the test than the test-taking universe as a whole.

While it is impossible to establish any cause-and-effect relationship between musical training and academic performance based on the SAT data, two recent studies by researchers at the Center for the Neurobiology of Learning and Memory at the University of California at Irvine suggest that there may indeed be a causal link between music and spatial intelligence. Spatial intelligence is the ability to perceive the visual world accurately, to form mental pictures of physical objects, and to recognize when objects differ physically. Having well-developed powers of spatial reasoning is considered crucial for excelling at complex mathematics and playing chess, among other things.

In one of the two studies, the UC Irvine team led by psychologist Frances Rauscher and neuroscientist Gordon Shaw compared the spatial reasoning abilities of 19 preschool children who took music lessons for eight months to the performance of a demographically comparable group of 15 preschool children who received no music training. The researchers found the first group's spatial reasoning dramatically better. The team also reported that the ability of the music students to do a puzzle designed to measure their spatial reasoning powers rose significantly during the experiment.

A second study, which replicated and expanded on results of an earlier study in the journal *Nature* in 1993, found that when college students listened to 10 minutes of Mozart's piano sonata K.448, their spatial IQ scores rose more than when these students spent the same amount of time sitting in silence or performing relaxation exercises. Curiously, the researchers observed no improvement in the students' spatial skills after 10 minutes of listening to the avant-garde composer Philip Glass or to a highly rhythmic dance piece, suggesting that hypnotic musical structures do nothing to improve spatial skills.

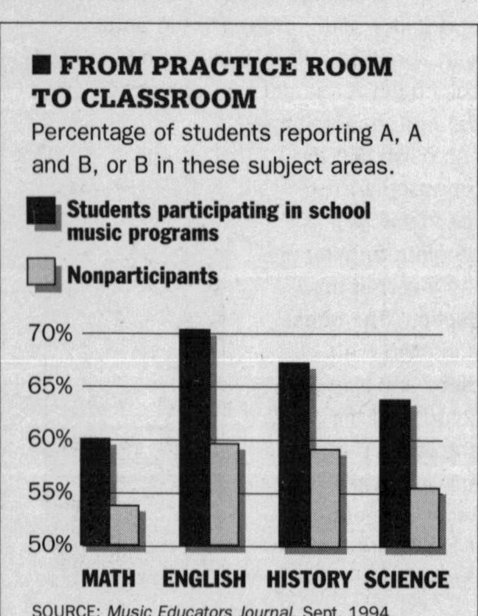

SOURCE: *Music Educators Journal*, Sept. 1994.

■ STARTING YOUNG

The median age musicians start lessons is 9.4 years. Age when all current or former players first learned to play:

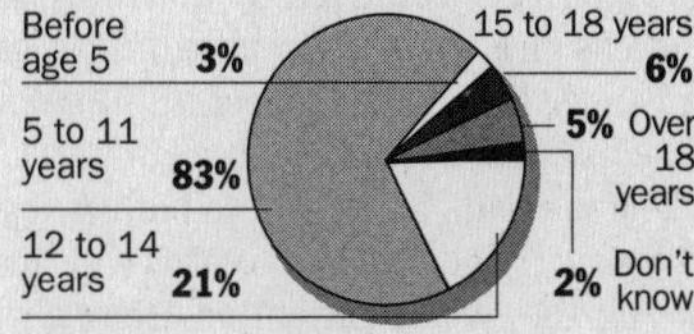

■ FIRST TEACHERS

Where current or former players learn to play. Total exceeds 100 percent due to multiple response.

Took private lessons	**40%**
Took lessons at school	**26%**
Taught self	**17%**
Took band or orchestra at school	**16%**
Parent or family member taught	**5%**
Friend taught	**4%**

■ TUNE-IN TIME

What makes players start an instrument:

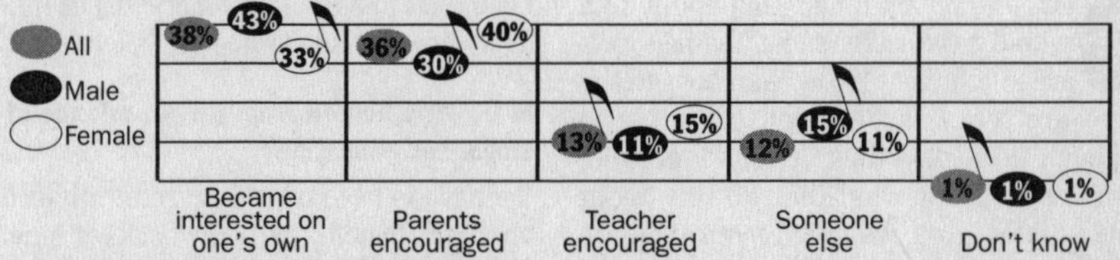

■ CHOOSE YOUR INSTRUMENT

The 10 most popular musical instruments, and what beginners will pay for them:

INSTRUMENT	ALL PLAYERS	MALE	FEMALE	BEGINNER PRICE RANGE
PIANO	34%	17%	50%	$1,200–$3,200
GUITAR	22%	36%	8%	$160–$200 (acoustic) $179–$300 (electric)
DRUMS	6%	11%	1%	$600–$800; individual drum $150
FLUTE	5%	2%	8%	$235–$400
ORGAN	4%	1%	7%	$250–$550
SAXOPHONE (ALTO)	4%	5%	3%	$475–$800
KEYBOARD	4%	4%	4%	$250–$550
CLARINET	4%	1%	6%	$250–$400
TRUMPET	3%	6%	1%	$343–$500
VIOLIN	3%	2%	4%	$285

■ THE TEEN BEAT

What teenagers say about the benefits of music:

It is an activity a child can enjoy all his or her life	**91%**
It helps instill appreciation of arts and culture in general	**90%**
It helps children make friends	**72%**
It teaches children self-discipline	**62%**
It provides a sense of accomplishment	**57%**
Performing in front of others helps develop poise and confidence	**51%**
It helps develop child's creativity	**49%**
It provides a child with another means of self-expression	**48%**
Teens who play an instrument are less likely to get in trouble with the law	**47%**

SOURCE: Reprinted with permission from the National Association of Music Merchants.

EXPERT Q & A

KEEPING GIRLS ON THE FAST TRACK

Single-sex education is only one way to help young women's self-esteem

Sixty percent of elementary school girls say they are "always happy the way I am." Fewer than half that many high school girls feel the same. Teenage girls are much more likely than boys to say they are "not smart enough" or "not good enough" to achieve their dreams. Moreover, when specifying what they do like about themselves, girls are much more likely to name a physical trait, while boys target a talent or ability.

These disturbing findings were published in "Shortchanging Girls, Shortchanging America," the result of an extensive survey of 3,000 girls and boys by the American Association of University Women in 1991. The blow to girls' confidence documented in the report may manifest itself in a host of disturbing behavior, from performing poorly in school to suffering depression to severe eating disorders. According to the National Institute of Mental Health, an estimated 5 percent of high-school and college-age girls suffer from some type of severe eating disorder and 15 percent have "substantially disordered" eating attitudes and behaviors.

Among some educators it has been popular to argue recently that the way to stem the precipitous drop in girls' self-esteem is to encourage single-sex education for young women. Here, Susan McGee Bailey, Executive Director of the Center for Research on Women at Wellesley College and principal author of the report, "How Schools Shortchange Girls," discusses the research and argues that it is important that we change how and what we teach boys and girls, rather than simply divide the sexes:

■ Are girls really at a disadvantage in mixed-sex classrooms?

Studies show that boys receive more of a teacher's attention than do girls. They tend to be more assertive than girls and to have that quality encouraged by their teachers, whereas girls are not. Because of this, girls and shyer boys begin to feel inhibited and self-conscious about speaking out.

The message being sent to both sexes is: "It's okay for boys to behave this way and if they do, they will get attention. However, it's not okay for girls to behave this way." This message that good girls are those that listen well and remain quieter is all wrong. We need boys to be good listeners just as much as we need girls to be good speakers.

■ Do girls benefit from the experience of single-sex education?

We have to be extremely careful in talking about the benefits and drawbacks of single-sex education because the research that looks at it in any comprehensive way is very limited. Although many girls and women who have been to all-girls' schools seem to have benefited from the experience, you have to take into account that all of these schools are private. I believe we must look at what is possible in the public school system and assess what is causing an unequal educational experience for boys and girls.

■ What is it about an all-girls school that seems to benefit students?

Many girls say they feel less inhibited and a more integral part of the class in such schools. They say it is easier to pursue and excel at typical "boy things," such as math and science, with no stigma attached. This, of course, parlays into girls' feeling more confident, more independent, and more assured about themselves.

In addition, many who have attended all-girls schools claim that because of the absence of boys in the school day, there was less of an emphasis on physical appearance than in a coeducational school. Women who are products of single-sex education often cite this absence of scrutiny from boys in the classroom as a relief.

■ What would explain why girls feel less inhibited in all-girls schools?

Girls' schools will often use more women as examples in teaching—more women's experiences and women as role models. The message is, "Look, women do excel and can be leaders in any field—so, of course, can you." In addition, pursuits that are typically "for boys" are necessarily "for girls" when there are no boys around—this includes both academic pursuits such as math and science and extracurricular activities, such as leadership roles and sports. But all-girls schools can reinforce stereotypical gender roles just as easily as mixed-sex schools. I believe mixed-sex schools can provide positive rather than negative experiences to girls as well as boys if we change the way we teach.

■ What can teachers in a mixed-sex school do to combat sexism in the classroom?

The most important thing is to talk about it head-on. Students need to talk about what their perceptions of the issue are. Some boys might argue that the girls in the class are favored while girls will contend that boys blurt out the answers all the time and don't give them a chance. Once the issue is on the table and is recognized, then the entire class—teachers and students—can deal with how to change.

We also need to prepare our teachers for the classroom and provide professional development once they are there. Teachers need to understand how their techniques and expectations of students can either reinforce traditional gender roles, or challenge them.

■ How can a parent whose daughter may be suffering in school because of gender help?

Parents need to be supportive and reinforce that support when their daughters do speak out and take a chance. Girls need to feel that their parents are proud of them when they do step outside the "traditional girl model," rather than to feel that they've done something inappropriate.

Parents should also encourage their daughters to be involved in some type of single-sex activity, although it certainly does not have to be in school. The benefits of participating in Girl Scouts or an all-girls team are also tremendous. Girls learn to appreciate other girls and therefore to think more highly of themselves.

This is certainly not limited to girls. Parents of both sexes should encourage their children to be involved in certain same-sex activities, as well as mixed-sex activities.

■ When do girls most need to spend time with other girls?

I think the middle-school years are particularly important. That's when girls are beginning to question themselves and are trying to figure out how they can be popular with boys, etc. This is the time that girls are shown to have a tremendous drop in their self-esteem. It's at this time that they need confidence and need to feel good about being strong and outspoken, smart, and good about their bodies.

Many parents and teachers of young children say that they try to be equitable and give boys dolls and engage girls in a rousing game of catch, but that the kids are simply not interested. One reason is that in early elementary years, play groups often become defined along stereotypical gender lines. Parents and teachers need to be very inventive in the games that kids play in order that both sexes do all kinds of things, not merely what is considered gender appropriate.

EXPERT SOURCES

For more on single-sex ed:

■ Center for Research on Women
Wellesley College, 106 Central,
Wellesley, MA 02181-8259
☎ 617-283-2500 or

■ American Association of University Women
1111 16th Street, N.W.,
Washington, D.C. 20036
☎ 202-785-7700.

COLLEGE & GRAD SCHOOL

GETTING IN: New ways to get and submit applications, PAGE 304 **SATS:** The scale has changed, PAGE 305 **RANKINGS:** The best colleges in America, PAGE 306 **BEST VALUES:** Good deals for the money, PAGE 312 **FINANCIAL AID:** Options for helping to pay the high cost of tuition, PAGE 314 **COMPUTERS:** E-mail, the Internet, and cyberculture on campus, PAGE 317 **EXPERT LIST:** The best graduate schools, PAGE 319

ADMISSIONS

APPLYING EARLY TO CLAIM A SEAT

If you need financial aid, you may need to try to be admitted early

Few rites of passage can compare to the excitement a student feels at heading off to college for the first time. Even fewer experiences are likely to produce as much anxiety as the college admissions. Now that experience is coming earlier for thousands of high school students. More and more students elect to apply to the school that is their first choice by November 1 of their senior year, giving their word that if accepted, they will agree to attend. In exchange, colleges are notifying applicants of "early decision" acceptances by mid-December. Students who fail to win early acceptance may still be admitted as part of the regular admissions process, but they must wait until April to learn whether they have been accepted.

Some educators argue that by forcing seniors to choose in the first few weeks of the year where it is they want to spend the next four years of life, colleges are making it impossible for students to truly investigate their choices and make informed decisions. Students should not apply for early admissions, warn these critics, simply from fear of competition.

It is difficult not to feel the pressure to apply early, however. In a survey of six highly selective colleges, 9,874 students applied early and one-third were accepted, according to Wintergreen/Orchard House, a New Orleans publisher of college data. For some schools that meant one-third of their freshman class was full before regular pool admissions began.

Most schools with early admissions programs have a "binding decision" policy, meaning that if a student is accepted early, he or she agrees to attend, regardless of where else he or she may have applied. The binding policy is often referred to as "early admission," while a nonbinding policy is termed "early action." From the colleges' standpoint, early admissions allow them to better manage their admissions and financial aid process, ensure that they achieve full enrollment, and that the freshman class is full of students they truly want.

There is some evidence to suggest, however, that students prefer not to be bound by admissions decisions too early. In 1995, for instance, the only two nonbinding Ivy schools, Harvard and Brown, received an increase in early applicants of 31 percent and 10 percent, respectively. At Harvard 33 percent of the freshman class last year was admitted early; at Brown the early acceptance success rate was 20 percent. Unless early admissions decisions are

■ DATES TO REMEMBER IN APPLYING FOR COLLEGE

If you need to take the SATs during the 1996–97 school year, here's when to do it. SAT I stands for the Scholastic Assessment Test, a three-hour test of verbal and math ability that is meant to determine how well a student may succeed academically during the first year of college. SAT II refers to subject tests formerly known as Achievement Tests.

■ TEST DATES FOR SAT I AND SAT II:

1996-1997 National test dates	TEST	U.S. registration deadlines	U.S. late registration deadlines	International special requests deadlines	International registration deadlines
Oct. 12, 1996	**SAT I and SAT II**	Sep. 13, 1996	Sep. 20, 1996	N/A*	N/A*
Nov. 2, 1996	**SAT I and SAT II**	Sep. 27, 1996	Oct. 9, 1996	Sep. 4, 1996	Sep. 27, 1996
Dec. 7, 1996	**SAT I and SAT II**	Nov. 1, 1996	Nov. 13, 1996	Oct. 9, 1996	Nov. 1, 1996
Jan. 25, 1997	**SAT I and SAT II**	Dec. 20, 1996	Jan. 2, 1997	Nov. 27, 1996	Dec. 20, 1996
Mar. 15, 1997	**SAT I only**	Feb. 7, 1997	Feb. 19, 1997	N/A	N/A
May 3, 1997	**SAT I and SAT II**	Mar. 28, 1997	Apr. 9, 1997	Mar. 5, 1997	Mar. 28, 1997
June 7, 1997	**SAT I and SAT II**	May 2, 1997	May 14, 1997	Apr. 9, 1997	May 2, 1997

*The October 1996 administration may be offered at international centers; refer to the 1996–97 International Bulletin for more information.

■ PRELIMINARY SAT (PSAT) AND NATIONAL MERIT SCHOLARSHIP QUALIFYING TEST (NMSQT)

Test dates	October 15, 1996	Tuesday
for 1996–97:	October 19, 1996	Saturday

■ ADVANCED PLACEMENT (AP)

Exam dates	May 5–9, 1997	Monday through Friday
for 1996–97:	May 12–16, 1997	Monday through Friday

■ SAT II SUBJECT TEST DATES FOR 1996–97

School-based test dates		SAT II: Subject test offered*	Registration deadlines
November 7, 1996	Thursday	**French with listening**	October 4, 1996
November 8, 1996	Friday	**Japanese with listening**	October 4, 1996
November 12, 1996	Tuesday	**Spanish with listening**	October 4, 1996
November 13, 1996	Wednesday	**German with listening**	October 4, 1996
November 14, 1996	Thursday	**English Language Proficiency Test**	October 4, 1996
November 15, 1996	Friday	**Chinese with listening**	October 4, 1996
April 29, 1997	Tuesday	**English Language Proficiency Test**	March 28, 1997

*Only at participating schools; test center availability pending.

SOURCE: College Board.

binding, however, many schools contend that it is nearly impossible to estimate how many early acceptances will result in enrollment. In 1994, for instance, Princeton had to move prefabricated housing on campus to accommodate unexpected students.

Whether the growth in early decisions has made admission more difficult for those who wait until the regular admissions deadline is a matter of debate. As Hank Ewert, a college counselor in Austin, Texas, says: "Most likely, the student who did not get in the regular pool would not have gotten in early."

While applying early may not make admission easier, there may be a sound financial reason to do so. With tuition costs rising and limited amounts of financial aid to award, colleges may exhaust much of their financial aid pool on their early acceptance cases, leaving little for students who are accepted later. If you are applying to a school that lacks the financial wherewithal to guarantee that if it accepts you, it will find the financial aid needed for you to attend, you may find yourself on the short end of the financial stick if you pass up the chance to apply early.

GETTING IN

STREAMLINING THE PROCESS

It's getting easier for applicants to get and submit key information

As labyrinths go, the college admissions process can't match the challenges posed by many federal agencies, but the number of hurdles that a college applicant and his or her family must clear in order to land a spot in the groves of academe has never been anything to underestimate. But with 1.5 million students applying for college annually, admissions, testing, and financial aid officials have been making a concerted effort to reduce the paperwork and simplify the application process for prospective college students.

For those savvy with their computers, a Web site administered by the College Board could drastically reduce the application headaches. Several parts of the admissions process can now be completed online via the Web site at *http://www.collegeboard.org,* and Nika Ganley, director of online services for the College Board, expects more services to be added rapidly. Already, it is possible to:

EXPERT SOURCE

One application fits all:
To obtain a copy of the Common Application and a list of colleges and universities that accept it, write:

National Association of Secondary School Principals
1904 Association Drive
Reston, VA 22091

- REGISTER for the Scholastic Assessment Test (SAT).

- OBTAIN information on Advance Placement exams.

- GET INFORMATION on specific colleges and universities nationwide, including applications for many. A student can download the application, work on it, and in some cases, upload the application and send it in to the admissions office. Others make the application available online, but still want it mailed in.

- OBTAIN detailed information on financial aid, from how to calculate the Estimated Family Contribution (see related story, page 314) to what the various options are for students in different situations.

- TAP INTO discussion groups for parents, students, and professionals.

What's more, over 164 colleges and universities now accept a standard application form called the Common Application. Students can submit copies of the same form, with the same essay question, to any of the participating schools, which include many prestigious institutions, from Harvard to Johns Hopkins and Pomona.

Just because a college accepts the Common Application, however, doesn't mean that it may not require supplemental information from applicants. Harvard, for example, requires candidates to identify more completely specific academic, extracurricular, and vocational interests, and to list nonacademic honors and to provide advanced placement test scores. The university also allows the candidate to send music tapes, slides of artwork, or samples of academic work, and gives applicants a chance to answer a second essay question if the topic required by the Common Application seems too restrictive.

Still, the rise of the Common Application, along with the College Board's streamlining, can greatly reduce the amount of paperwork, and stress, that students with college in their eyes must face.

SAT TESTS

WHEN "AVERAGE" LOOKS HIGHER

The scale's changed, but test averages haven't really jumped

Walk into a group of students immediately after they took the Scholastic Assessment Test (SAT) and you would hear, "What does 'ineluctable' mean?" "Do you think you did better on math or verbal?" "I didn't have enough time!!!" While not all colleges place the weight they once did on this three-hour test of verbal and mathematical ability, a student's score is still widely used as an important criterion for college admissions. The rise of SAT preparation classes over the past five years indicates the ever-increasing worry of performing well on this test.

But what is "performing well"? This question has just become more difficult to answer, following a "recentering" of SAT scores. The change, announced by the College Board in June, 1994, and put into effect in April, 1995, is supposed to reestablish today's average score near that of a previous recentering in 1941, when the average was established as 500 for both the verbal and math components of the SATs. Since then, national averages have fallen to 423 on verbal and 479 on math. The 1995 recentering moved the national averages up about 75 points on the verbal section and 20 points on the math.

The College Board maintains that the recentering does not change the relative standing of test takers to each other. "By placing the performance average at the intuitive average, halfway between 200 and 800," says Bradley J. Quin, associate director of the SAT program, "recentering will clarify the score's relationship to actual performance and reduce confusion among students competing for admission to college in the same year. With both averages near 500, students will immediately know where they stand in the test-taking population, and make better comparisons of their verbal and mathematical abilities." A score that is above or below the average before the recentering will still be so after the recentering; the average is just different.

According to test officials, the change is not supposed to affect the test's level of difficulty, the students' test performance, the ability of schools, colleges, and others to track score trends, or standards used in admissions and scholarship decisions. For uncentered SAT scores over the last 27 years, and estimates of what those scores would have been had the new recentering been in effect, see the table below.

To better assess a student's potential academic success, the College Board has also added an essay segment to the reading comprehension section of the SAT. In the past, both the verbal and math sections of the test were strictly multiple choice.

■ WHAT'S THE SCORE?

If you took the SAT before 1995, your test scores were based on a slightly different scale for comparing the score to actual academic performance. The table below helps you translate your score in today's world.

YEAR	UNRECENTERED		RECENTERED (est.)	
	VERBAL	MATH	VERBAL	MATH
1969	463	493	540	517
1974	444	480	521	505
1979	427	467	505	493
1984	426	471	504	497
1989	427	476	505	501
1994	423	479	500	504

NOTE: All scores in the table represent the 50th percentile, and all figures for 1969 are based on estimates. In the recentered columns, figures for 1974 through 1989 were obtained by applying a prediction equation to college-bound senior means and standard deviations on the original scale. Figures for 1994 are based on individual students' scores that have been recentered. SOURCE: College Board.

EXPERT LIST

THE BEST COLLEGES IN AMERICA

Every year U.S. News & World Report *publishes a widely followed special report that ranks America's best colleges and universities by several objective measures such as test scores and student/faculty ratios, as well as by academic reputation. Highlights from the 1995–96 survey appear below.*

■ BEST NATIONAL UNIVERSITIES

The 229 national universities from which these top-ranked institutions were selected have comprehensive program offerings, place great emphasis on faculty research, and award many Ph.D's. For the fifth year in a row, Harvard finished first in this category in 1995.

Rank / School	Overall score	Academic reputation	SAT / ACT 25th–75th percentile	Freshmen in top 10% of HS class	Acceptance rate	Student / faculty ratio	Education expenditures per student
1. Harvard University (Mass.)	100.0	1	1320–1480	91%	14%	11/1	$39,525
2. Princeton University (N.J.)	98.8	4	1280–1470	91%	14%	8/1	$30,220
2. Yale University (Conn.)	98.8	4	1290–1460	95%	19%	11/1	$43,514
4. Stanford University (Calif.)	98.1	1	1270–1450	90%	20%	12/1	$36,450
5. Massachusetts Inst. of Technology	98.0	1	1290–1470	94%	30%	10/1	$34,870
6. Duke University (N.C.)	96.8	8	1220–1410	90%	30%	12/1	$31,585
7. California Institute of Technology	95.5	8	1350–1480	100%	25%	6/1	$63,575
7. Dartmouth College (N.H.)	95.5	17	1250–1430	89%	23%	10/1	$32,162
9. Brown University (R.I.)	95.3	14	1210–1410	89%	22%	13/1	$22,704
10. Johns Hopkins University (Md.)	94.6	4	1210–1400	75%	44%	7/1	$58,691
11. University of Chicago	94.4	8	1180–1400	75%	50%	13/1	$38,380
11. University of Pennsylvania	94.4	14	1190–1380	80%	36%	11/1	$27,553
13. Cornell University (N.Y.)	94.0	8	1180–1380	83%	33%	13/1	$21,864
13. Northwestern University (Ill.)	94.0	14	1160–1360	85%	39%	11/1	$28,052
15. Columbia University (N.Y.)	93.8	8	1210–1410	76%	24%	12/1	$31,510
16. Rice University (Texas)	93.6	20	1270–1470	88%	22%	8/1	$24,167
17. Emory University (Ga.)	90.5	32	1140–1325	80%	49%	12/1	$31,054
18. University of Notre Dame (Ind.)	90.1	36	1150–1360	81%	42%	13/1	$15,122
19. University of Virginia	89.6	17	1110–1340	77%	44%	14/1	$13,349
20. Washington University (Mo.)	89.2	26	1130–1330	63%	65%	10/1	$48,309
21. Georgetown University (D.C.)	88.9	27	1150–1360	74%	24%	12/1	$20,126
22. Vanderbilt University (Tenn.)	88.8	27	1120–1310	78%	58%	11/1	$24,794
23. Carnegie Mellon University (Pa.)	87.2	20	1150–1370	62%	59%	9/1	$25,026
24. U. of Michigan at Ann Arbor	86.9	8	1060–1300	65%	68%	16/1	$15,470
25. Tufts University (Mass.)	86.6	49	1160–1330	62%	45%	13/1	$19,466
SCHOOLS RANKED 26TH TO 50TH							
26. U. of California at Berkeley	86.4	4	1110–1370	95%	40%	17/1	$15,140
27. U. of North Carolina at Chapel Hill	86.1	20	1010–1250	72%	39%	15/1	$17,284
28. U. of California at Los Angeles	84.6	20	1000–1270	93%	50%	20/1	$20,241
29. University of Rochester (N.Y.)	84.0	49	1020–1250	49%	63%	13/1	$28,299
30. Brandeis University (Mass.)	82.4	43	1130–1340	43%[2]	68%	10/1	$17,371
31. Wake Forest University (N.C.)	81.9	73	1150–1350	68%	44%	9/1	$46,622
32. University of Wisconsin at Madison	81.2	17	940–1230	40%	69%	15/1	$11,857

■ **EXPERT LIST**

Rank / School	Overall score	Academic reputation	SAT / ACT 25th–75th percentile	Freshmen in top 10% of HS class	Acceptance rate	Student / faculty ratio	Education expenditures per student
33. Lehigh University (Pa.)	80.3	73	1025–1240	42%	64%	13/1	$15,226
34. College of William and Mary (Va.)	79.9	36	1120–1340	70%	40%	12/1	$10,172
35. Case Western Reserve University (Ohio)	79.6	49	1110–1380[2]	69%	81%	13/1	$20,672
36. New York University	78.6	43	1055–1255	60%	52%	14/1	$23,242
37. Boston College	78.1	64	1120–1300	66%	41%	17/1	$11,628
38. Tulane University (La.)	77.9	49	1070–1290	42%	73%	14/1	$17,835
39. Rensselaer Polytechnic Institute (N.Y.)	77.5	49	1070–1300	56%	88%	17/1	$15,536
40. University of California at Davis	77.1	36	930–1200	95%	70%	24/1	$15,905
41. Penn State U. at Main Campus	77.0	27	960–1201	38%	54%	18/1	$10,185
42. Georgia Institute of Technology	76.9	27	1170–1330	90%	59%	19/1	$12,128
43. University of California at San Diego	76.2	43	980–1240	95%	64%	23/1	$18,668
44. University of Southern California	75.7	36	1000–1230	40%	72%	15/1	$17,822
45. Rutgers U. at New Brunswick (N.J.)	74.4	49	960–1220	35%	55%	19/1	$11,027
45. U. of Illinois at Urbana-Champaign	74.4	20	23–28	50%	76%	18/1	$8,515
47. University of Florida	73.4	43	980–1220	60%	64%	19/1	$16,638
48. University of California at Irvine	72.4	49	890–1140	85%	73%	21/1	$16,191
49. Syracuse University (N.Y.)	72.0	64	990–1220	33%	67%	11/1	$14,813
50. University of Washington	71.6	27	920–1190	40%[2]	61%	14/1	$15,632

NOTE: Schools with the same numbered rank are tied. Key to numbered notes is on page 308. Reputational surveys conducted by Market Facts, Inc.

■ BEST NATIONAL LIBERAL ARTS COLLEGES

The 161 liberal arts colleges from which these outstanding schools were picked are highly selective in their admissions and award more than 40 percent of their degrees in the liberal arts each year. Amherst College, which ranked number one in 1994, did it again in 1995.

Rank / School	Overall score	Academic reputation	SAT / ACT 25th–75th percentile	Freshmen in top 10% of HS class	Acceptance rate	Student / faculty ratio	Education expenditures per student
1. Amherst College (Mass.)	100.0	1	1210–1420	72%	20%	8/1	$22,227
2. Swarthmore College (Pa.)	99.4	3	1250–1440	87%	30%	9/1	$23,715
2. Williams College (Mass.)	99.4	1	1240–1450	82%	27%	9/1	$22,929
4. Bowdoin College (Maine)	96.6	5	1180–1350[1]	80%	30%	11/1	$19,612
5. Haverford College (Pa.)	96.2	8	1200–1390	75%	39%	11/1	$18,826
5. Wellesley College (Mass.)	96.2	3	1170–1360	83%	39%	10/1	$23,067
7. Middlebury College (Vt.)	94.7	16	1140–1340	62%	32%	10/1	$21,265
8. Pomona College (Calif.)	94.6	8	1270–1420	74%	34%	10/1	$21,147
9. Bryn Mawr College (Pa.)	92.9	8	1150–1350	71%	56%	9/1	$21,139
10. Smith College (Mass.)	92.2	8	1090–1290	59%	53%	11/1	$21,935
11. Carleton College (Minn.)	91.0	5	1160–1390	70%	57%	11/1	$18,700
12. Wesleyan University (Conn.)	90.7	5	1140–1360	67%	36%	12/1	$16,831
13. Vassar College (N.Y.)	90.4	14	1140–1320	58%	50%	10/1	$17,687
14. Grinnell College (Iowa)	89.9	8	1160–1370	64%	64%	9/1	$19,256
15. Washington and Lee University (Va.)	89.7	25	1200–1340	77%	29%	10/1	$17,196
16. Claremont McKenna College (Calif.)	89.6	16	1190–1370	71%	42%	9/1	$18,380

■ EXPERT LIST

Rank / School	Overall score	Academic reputation	SAT/ACT 25th–75th percentile	Freshmen in top 10% of HS class	Acceptance rate	Student / faculty ratio	Education expenditures per student
17. Colgate University (N.Y.)	89.4	18	1110–1280	53%	51%	11/1	$16,033
18. Bates College (Maine)	88.9	18	1170–1330[1]	54%	34%	10/1	$17,165
19. Colby College (Maine)	88.2	18	1105–1295	62%	40%	12/1	$16,845
19. Mount Holyoke College (Mass.)	88.2	18	1020–1250	53%	65%	10/1	$19,425
21. Davidson College (N.C.)	87.9	14	1160–1350	79%	37%	11/1	$18,386
22. Oberlin College (Ohio)	85.4	8	1110–1340	51%	66%	11/1	$18,289
23. Hamiton College (N.Y.)	85.1	25	1030–1250	46%	51%	10/1	$18,289
23. Trinity College (Conn.)	85.1	25	1080–1260	45%	59%	10/1	$19,360
25. Connecticut College	83.8	30	1064–1282	48%	49%	12/1	$15,620
SCHOOLS RANKED 26TH TO 40TH							
26. College of the Holy Cross (Mass.)	81.4	34	1110–1310	61%	46%	12/1	$13,011
27. University of the South (Tenn.)	81.0	39	1060–1260	54%	68%	11/1	$19,705
28. Colorado College	80.4	25	1090–1290	48%	55%	11/1	$15,350
29. Franklin and Marshall College (Pa.)	80.3	30	1070–1290	50%	66%	11/1	$15,878
30. Bucknell University (Pa.)	80.2	25	1110–1260	49%	59%	14/1	$14,146
31. Union College (N.Y.)	78.3	43	25–31	46%	53%	12/1	$15,866
32. Barnard College (N.Y.)	78.2	18	1120–1310	51%	49%	11/1	$13,408
33. Lafayette College (Pa.)	77.3	39	1010–1220[1]	37%	59%	11/1	$16,840
34. Macalester College (Minn.)	76.3	18	1130–1350[2]	53%	58%	11/1	$15,869
35. Sarah Lawrence College (N.Y.)	75.8	43	1070–1300	58%[3]	56%	6/1	$15,548
36. Kenyon College (Ohio)	75.5	30	1070–1290	43%	79%	11/1	$14,570
37. Scripps College (Calif.)	73.8	34	1020–1250	45%	78%	9/1	$19,179
38. Wabash College (Ind.)	71.2	56	1010–1270	44%	78%	11/1	$16,229
39. Occidental College (Calif.)	70.3	34	960–1210	52%	54%	9/1	$16,066
40. Dickinson College (Pa.)	70.1	43	960–1180[1]	37%	83%	11/1	$14,767

NOTES: **1.** Standardized aptitude tests (SAT I/ACT) not required. **2.** Data not submitted in the form requested by *U.S. News*. **3.** High school class standing data were based on fewer than 40 percent of enrolled freshmen.

■ BEST REGIONAL UNIVERSITIES

These institutions award a full range of bachelor's degrees and at least 20 master's degrees each year. Schools in this category have been subdivided into four regions: North, South, Midwest, and West.

Rank / School	Overall score	Academic reputation	Student selectivity	Faculty resources	Financial resources	Retention rank	Alumni satisfaction
NORTH							
1. Villanova University (Pa.)	100.0	1	4	6	23	2	58
2. Fairfield University (Conn.)	98.6	4	12	14	15	3	36
3. Providence College (R.I.)	97.1	3	10	23	39	1	11
4. University of Scranton (Pa.)	95.7	17	11	15	27	4	18
5. Simmons College (Mass.)	94.4	10	29	9	4	21	19
6. Ithaca College (N.Y.)	93.3	4	24	10	22	22	46
7. Loyola College (Md.)	92.1	4	5	55	26	6	28
8. Manhattan College (N.Y.)	91.8	10	14	31	17	17	37
8. Rochester Inst. of Tech. (N.Y.)	91.8	2	15	15	6	35	72

■ **EXPERT LIST**

Rank / School	Overall score	Academic reputation	Student selectivity	Faculty resources	Financial resources	Retention rank	Alumni satisfaction
8. Trenton State College (N.J.)	91.8	4	1	13	55	16	108
11. St. Michael's College (Vt.)	90.3	10	26	47	21	8	15
12. Alfred University (N.Y.)	88.5	10	18	27	7	43	21
13. St. Joseph's University (Pa.)	88.1	10	7	44	62	12	41
14. Hood College (Md.)	88.0	9	30	36	16	31	8
15. La Salle University (Pa.)	82.4	17	32	45	45	19	77
SOUTH							
1. University of Richmond (Va.)	100.0	1	5	2	6	1	6
2. Rollins College (Fla.)	98.0	3	8	4	3	3	22
3. Stetson University (Fla.)	95.9	3	15	1	3	11	21
4. Loyola University (La.)	92.9	8	18	3	11	7	51
5. Berea College (Ky.)	92.3	5	7	7	2	27	14
6. James Madison U. (Va.)	90.7	2	2	13	83	2	20
7. Samford University (Ala.)	89.8	5	9	5	22	23	55
8. Appalachian State U. (N.C.)	87.1	10	11	12	70	6	47
9. Converse College (S.C.)	86.3	24	23	23	5	12	15
10. Centenary Col. of Louisiana	85.0	14	31	11	12	28	24
11. The Citadel (S.C.)	83.2	5	54	24	34	8	45
12. Mercer University (Ga.)	83.0	8	12	8	7	56	38
13. Mary Washington Col. (Va.)	81.8	10	4	55	77	4	12
13. Spring Hill College (Ala.)	81.8	17	34	40	15	15	17
15. U. of N.C. at Charlotte	81.0	10	30	9	60	21	86
MIDWEST							
1. Valparaiso University (Ind.)	100.0	2	8	14	5	3	14
2. Creighton University (Neb.)	98.1	2	24	9	1	7	15
3. Drake University (Iowa)	97.9	2	14	1	2	17	28
4. John Carroll University (Ohio)	95.4	5	28	11	23	1	24
5. University of Dayton (Ohio)	95.3	11	34	4	5	2	36
6. Butler University (Ind.)	94.6	5	18	14	20	9	42
7. Bradley University (Ill.)	93.8	5	18	14	20	9	42
8. Baldwin-Wallace Col. (Ohio)	91.8	11	15	22	20	5	50
9. Xavier University (Ohio)	91.5	5	36	25	7	10	13
10. Calvin College (Mich.)	89.5	5	17	37	31	13	1
11. University of Northern Iowa	87.5	1	23	18	57	21	30
12. North Central College (Ill.)	87.3	17	10	35	19	24	4
13. University of Evansville (Ind.)	87.2	16	30	10	24	23	29
14. Drury College (Mo.)	84.9	23	11	26	17	32	5
15. U. of St. Thomas (Minn.)	81.8	11	43	53	14	6	64
WEST							
1. Trinity University (Texas)	100.0	1	3	1	1	2	19
2. Santa Clara University (Calif.)	96.6	2	2	16	5	1	21
3. Gonzaga University (Wash.)	93.3	3	13	9	21	8	11
4. St. Mary's College of Calif.	91.6	9	8	14	23	4	26
5. U. of Portland (Ore.)	90.9	9	14	8	17	11	22

■ EXPERT LIST

Rank / School	Overall score	Academic reputation	Student selectivity	Faculty resources	Financial resources	Retention rank	Alumni satisfaction
6. University of Redlands (Calif.)	90.6	13	21	4	2	15	13
7. Linfield College (Ore.)	88.2	13	5	32	22	6	2
8. Loyola Marymount U. (Calif.)	87.7	5	51	17	7	3	20
9. Seattle University	87.3	9	27	2	8	24	32
10. Cal Poly at San Luis Obispo	85.9	3	6	12	53	21	38
11. Western Washington U.	82.5	9	12	13	72	15	46
12. Whitworth College (Wash.)	82.2	6	11	53	31	10	18
13. Seattle Pacific University	81.7	16	28	18	13	26	23
14. St. Mary's U. of San Antonio	81.5	16	29	15	33	13	61
15. Pacific Lutheran U. (Wash.)	78.4	6	20	80	15	5	15

■ BEST REGIONAL LIBERAL ARTS COLLEGES

The 423 schools from which these colleges have been identified are generally less selective than the national liberal arts colleges. Some 60 percent of the bachelor's degrees they award are in occupational, technical, and professional fields.

Rank / School	Overall score	Academic reputation	Student selectivity	Faculty resources	Financial resources	Retention rank	Alumni satisfaction
NORTH							
1. Susquehanna University (Pa.)	100.0	1	8	8	10	6	4
2. Le Moyne College (N.Y.)	95.5	3	12	6	36	3	26
3. Elizabethtown College (Pa.)	93.5	6	5	7	15	17	32
4. Stonehill College (Mass.)	93.4	3	4	21	43	2	15
5. St. Anselm College (N.H.)	92.5	2	17	9	50	4	19
6. Regis College (Mass.)	89.2	10	35	5	14	16	6
7. Messiah College (Pa.)	89.0	10	3	27	32	8	22
8. King's College (Pa.)	88.0	6	28	17	45	6	7
9. St. Vincent College (Pa.)	87.9	20	10	19	21	11	8
10. Rosemont College (Pa.)	86.8	23	14	24	4	13	2
SOUTH							
1. Mary Baldwin College (Va.)	100.0	1	29	12	2	3	6
2. Berry College (Ga.)	99.5	1	14	15	4	6	30
3. Roanoke College (Va.)	98.8	3	34	4	8	4	23
4. Emory and Henry College (Va.)	98.4	3	22	11	34	1	2
5. Columbia College (S.C.)	95.3	9	31	7	18	11	12
6. Lyon College (Ark.)	94.4	5	1	1	1	47	20
7. John Brown University (Ark.)	92.7	27	2	20	26	8	14
8. Ouachita Baptist U. (Ark.)	92.0	19	5	9	67	4	43
9. Maryville College (Tenn.)	91.7	5	7	5	7	53	3
10. David Lipscomb U. (Tenn.)	90.3	9	32	14	30	11	67
MIDWEST							
1. St. Mary's College (Ind.)	100.0	4	25	2	5	1	24
2. St. Norbert College (Wis.)	98.7	2	14	7	24	6	15
3. Marietta College (Ohio)	97.0	15	15	10	6	5	17

■ **EXPERT LIST**

Rank / School	Overall score	Academic reputation	Student selectivity	Faculty resources	Financial resources	Retention rank	Alumni satisfaction
4. Ohio Northern University	96.0	10	11	13	11	9	34
5. Millikin University (Ill.)	94.8	2	22	7	25	12	52
6. Taylor University (Ind.)	94.0	10	1	23	43	3	38
7. Otterbein College (Ohio)	93.6	4	12	34	28	3	30
8. Mount Union College (Ohio)	92.1	15	15	5	54	14	12
9. Simpson College (Iowa)	91.8	10	13	6	56	18	22
10. Augustana College (S.D.)	91.5	4	10	21	36	22	27
WEST							
1. Albertson College (Idaho)	100.0	15	5	1	2	4	13
2. Texas A&M U. at Galveston	98.0	3	3	6	12	12	19
3. LeTourneau University (Texas)	94.9	6	6	11	23	8	4
4. Northwest Nazarene Col. (Idaho)	94.7	15	9	2	15	7	9
5. Evergreen State Col. (Wash.)	94.1	1	11	18	20	5	15
6. George Fox College (Ore.)	93.9	2	7	16	17	11	8
7. Texas Lutheran College	92.7	3	16	12	19	10	5
8. Pacific Union College (Calif.)	88.5	15	1	34	5	3	7
9. Oklahoma Baptist University	87.2	3	4	24	30	13	12
10. College of Santa Fe (N.M.)	87.1	6	22	14	14	9	36

SOURCE: *U.S.News & World Report, America's Best Colleges 1996 College Guide*, ©U.S.News & World Report.

■ A WORD ON METHODOLOGY

The *U.S. News* methodology for ranking America's colleges and universities has two components: a reputational survey taken among college administrators, together with a collection of more objective statistical measures of an institution's educational quality.

■ **Reputation:** According to *U.S. News*, over 2,700 college presidents, deans, and admissions directors participated in the 1995 survey of academic reputations. Participants were only asked to score institutions in the category to which their own schools belonged. The respondents were expected to assign each school to one of four quartiles based upon their assessment of a school's academic quality, and an average score was computed for each school.

■ **Student selectivity:** In measuring selectivity, the survey took into account the acceptance rate and actual enrollment of students offered places in the admissions process, the enrollees' high-school class rankings, and the average or midpoint combined scores on the SATs or ACTs.

■ **Faculty resources:** Faculty resources were judged by the ratio of full-time students to full-time faculty, excluding professional schools (such as law, dental, and medical), as well as the percentage of full-time faculty with Ph.D's or other top terminal degrees, the percentage of part-time faculty, the average salary and benefits for tenured full professors, and the size of the undergraduate classes.

■ **Financial strength:** This was calculated by dividing the institution's total expenditures for its education program during the previous year, including such things as instruction, student services, libraries and computers, and administration, by its total full-time enrollment.

■ **Alumni satisfaction:** This was a measure only weighed in the national universities and national liberal arts categories. It was derived from the average percentage of alumni giving during the two previous years. While alumni satisfaction does not appear in all the tables for space reasons, it was a factor in compiling the overall rankings.

PARENT'S GUIDE

THE BEST VALUES ON CAMPUS

The best faculty and educational program in the world won't matter to you if you can't afford them. To enable families to relate the cost of attending to the quality of education involved, U.S. News & World Report *developed a "best value" rating system that identifies colleges and universities that score high on overall quality as well as reasonableness of cost. The "best values" are based on an institution's "sticker price," the published price for tuition, room, board, and fees. For many students the actual price of attending that college will be less because of merit awards and need-based grants.*

■ NATIONAL UNIVERSITIES

Rank/ BEST VALUES	Total Cost
1. Brigham Young U. at Provo (Utah)	$7,415
2. University of Florida	$11,410
3. U. of North Carolina at Chapel Hill	$14,152
4. University of Texas at Austin	$11,651
5. Texas A&M at College Station	$11,651
6. Georgia Institute of Technology	$13,338
7. University of Wisconsin at Madison	$14,155
8. University of Tennessee at Knoxville	$9,718
9. University of Georgia	$10,649
10. Rice University (Texas)	$17,013
11. Rutgers at New Brunswick (N.J.)	$13,685
12. U. of Illinois at Urbana-Champaign	$13,866
13. SUNY at Binghamton	$13,333
14. University of Washington	$13,641
15. SUNY at Buffalo	$12,324
16. Iowa State University	$11,574
17. University of Hawai'i at Manoa	$9,762
17. University of Virginia	$17,852
19. University of Minnesota at Twin Cities	$13,560
20. Pennsylvania State U. at Main Campus	$15,610
21. Baylor University (Texas)	$12,533
22. University of California at Los Angeles	$17,452
23. University of Iowa	$12,588
24. University of Kentucky	$11,564
25. Auburn U. at Main Campus (Ala.)	$10,848
26. University of California at Berkeley	$18,512
27. University of Kansas	$11,444
28. University of California at Davis	$17,156
29. Florida State University	$12,835
30. Ohio University	$12,295
31. University of Missouri at Columbia	$13,532
32. Purdue U. at West Lafayette (Ind.)	$14,438
33. SUNY at Albany	$13,692
34. College of William and Mary (Va.)	$18,800
35. Miami University at Oxford (Ohio)	$14,450
36. California Institute of Technology	$22,781
37. North Carolina State U. at Raleigh	$13,730
38. Wake Forest University (N.C.)	$19,700
39. Virginia Tech	$13,859
40. Northwestern University (Ill.)	$22,965
41. University of California at Irvine	$17,713
42. University of California at San Diego	$18,904
43. University of Arizona	$12,168
44. Indiana University at Bloomington	$14,918
45. University of Notre Dame (Ind.)	$22,627
46. University of Delaware	$15,576
47. University of Michigan at Ann Arbor	$21,968
48. Michigan Technological University	$12,869
49. Michigan State University	$15,424
50. Ohio State University at Columbus	$14,607

■ NATIONAL LIBERAL ARTS COLLEGES

Rank/ BEST VALUES	Total Cost
1. Washington and Lee University (Va.)	$19,615
2. Grinnell College (Iowa)	$21,410
3. University of the South (Tenn.)	$20,595
4. Wabash College (Ind.)	$18,355
5. Amherst College (Mass.)	$26,625
6. Williams College (Mass.)	$26,510
7. Wellesley College (Mass.)	$25,810
8. Carleton College (Minn.)	$24,425
9. Claremont McKenna College (Calif.)	$24,100
10. Davidson College (N.C.)	$23,990
11. Swarthmore College (Pa.)	$27,165
12. Bowdoin College (Maine)	$26,500
13. Centre College (Ky.)	$17,450
14. Haverford College (Pa.)	$26,625
15. Pomona College (Calif.)	$26,300
16. Colorado College	$22,646
17. Macalester College (Minn.)	$21,661
18. Middlebury College (Vt.)	$27,190
19. Smith College (Mass.)	$26,484
20. Bryn Mawr College (Pa.)	$26,715
21. Wheaton College (Ill.)	$16,670
22. Furman University (S.C.)	$18,744

■ PARENT'S GUIDE

23.	Wesleyan University (Conn.)	$26,630
24.	Vassar College (N.Y.)	$26,570
25.	Colgate University (N.Y.)	$26,415
26.	Bates College (Maine)	$26,300
27.	Colby College (Maine)	$26,650
28.	Bucknell University (Pa.)	$24,395
29.	Mount Holyoke College (Mass.)	$26,865
30.	Hamilton College (N.Y)	$25,950
31.	Trinity College (Conn.)	$26,370
32.	Oberlin College (Ohio)	$26,716
33.	Rhodes College (Tenn.)	$20,832
34.	Connecticut College	$26,325
35.	College of the Holy Cross (Mass.)	$25,765
36.	Franklin and Marshall College (Pa.)	$25,630
37.	DePauw University (Ind.)	$20,720
38.	Lawrence University (Wis.)	$22,095
39.	Kenyon College (Ohio)	$24,660
40.	Illinois Wesleyan University	$19,810

■ REGIONAL UNIVERSITIES

SOUTH

1.	Berea College (Ky.)	FREE
2.	Winthrop University (S.C.)	$9,792
3.	Appalachian State University (N.C.)	$11,317
4.	The Citadel (S.C.)	$10,854
5.	Harding University (Ark.)	$10,483
6.	Meredith College (N.C.)	$10,500
7.	Samford University (Ala.)	$12,548
8.	James Madison University (Va.)	$12,974
9.	University of North Carolina at Charlotte	$11,798
10.	University of North Florida	$10,990

NORTH

1.	Trenton State College (N.J.)	$12,759
2.	Shippensburg U. of Pennsylvania	$12,498
3.	Bloomsburg University of Pennsylvania	$11,870
4.	Millersville University of Pennsylvania	$13,112
5.	Rutgers at Camden (N.J.)	$13,538
6.	SUNY Coll. of Arts & Scis. at Geneseo	$13,250
7.	SUNY College at Fredonia	$13,389
8.	University of Scranton (Pa.)	$19,634
9.	St. Michael's College (Vt.)	$19,960
10.	Loyola College (Md.)	$20,870

WEST

1.	Cal. Polytech. St. U. at San Luis Obispo	$12,824
2.	Western Washington University	$12,909
3.	Calif. Polytechnic State U. at Pomona	$12,448
4.	California State University at Fresno	$12,206
5.	St. Mary's University of San Antonio	$13,968
6.	University of St. Thomas (Texas)	$13,350
7.	Trinity University (Texas)	$18,584
8.	University of Portland (Ore.)	$17,540
9.	Gonzaga University (Wash.)	$18,540
10.	Humboldt State University (Calif.)	$14,328

MIDWEST

1.	University of Northern Iowa	$9,746
2.	Northeast Missouri State University	$8,894
3.	U. of Wisconsin at Stevens Point	$10,843
4.	University of Wisconsin at Eau Claire	$11,452
5.	Drury College (Mo.)	$13,087
6.	Valparaiso University (Ind.)	$16,310
7.	Creighton University (Neb.)	$16,110
8.	Calvin College (Mich.)	$14,890
9.	Bradley University (Ind.)	$16,110
10.	University of Dayton (Ohio)	$17,170

■ REGIONAL LIBERAL ARTS COLLEGES

SOUTH

1.	Mississippi University for Women	$6,753
2.	Louisiana College	$8,931
3.	Ouachita Baptist University (Ark.)	$9,970
4.	Flagler College (Fla.)	$8,670
5.	David Lipscomb University	$10,765

NORTH

1.	York College of Pennsylvania	$9,300
2.	Grove City College (Pa.)	$9,648
3.	Le Moyne College (N.Y.)	$17,100
4.	St. Vincent College (Pa.)	$15,885
5.	Messiah College (Pa.)	$16,234

WEST

1.	Texas A&M at Galveston	$9,460
2.	Oklahoma Baptist University	$9,734
3.	LeTourneau University (Texas)	$11,350
4.	Okla. Christian U. of Science and Arts	$10,760
5.	Texas Lutheran College	$12,232

MIDWEST

1.	College of the Ozarks (Mo.)	FREE
2.	Dordt College (Iowa)	$13,130
3.	Cedarville College (Ohio)	$12,576
4.	Augustana College (S.D.)	$15,152
5.	Taylor University (Ind.)	$16,064

METHODOLOGY NOTE: These ratings were based solely on the quality rankings for *U.S. News & World Report*'s 1995 edition of *America's Best Colleges*, divided by the total of tuition, required fees and room and board for the 1995–96 academic year. The higher the ratio of quality (a school's overall score) to price, the better the value. Because the best values are by definition at the better schools, only a proportion of all schools were considered.

FINANCIAL AID

LOOKING TUITION BILLS IN THE EYE

Know your options for meeting the staggering cost of college today

The average cost for a year at a private four-year college was $19,763 in the 1994–95 school year. Without some financial assistance from the government, educational institutions, or other private sources, more than half of college students would come up short at tuition time. Jack Joyce, Associate Director for Information and Training Services at the College Board, sponsors of the SATs and an organization dedicated to broadening access to higher education, has this advice for students and families on applying for financial aid.

■ Who is eligible for financial aid?

Well over half the students that are in college, and in some institutions, probably three-quarters of the students enrolled. But there is no one income number or other characteristic that determines a student's eligibility for aid.

■ How is a student's eligibility for financial aid determined?

At least two application forms and two formulas are used to determine a student's eligibility for financial aid. The most commonly used process starts with an application form that's called the Free Application for Federal Student Aid, or FAFSA. It collects a fairly limited amount of information on a family's income and assets. That information is used in the "federal methodology," which is a formula approved by Congress to determine a student's eligibility for federal financial aid programs.

Many colleges that have their own nonfederal financial aid collect some additional information on what is called the CSS/Financial Aid PROFILE.™ That form requests more details about a family's assets situation, including such things as home equity, and a little more information on other expenses the family has, such as medical and dental expenses. It is used to support a more traditional and sensitive need-analysis. This formula, known informally as the Institutional Methodology, was developed with the intent of providing a reasonable guideline as to a family's ability to contribute toward college costs.

■ Does it matter if the student is applying to a private or a state school?

In general, students applying to a state institution or public university where federal financial aid is all that is available would probably have to complete only the FAFSA. If they are applying to private colleges or universities, they would also be asked to complete the PROFILE. Students should understand that forms and procedures do change from year to year. It's important for a student to ascertain what application forms are required for financial aid and what kind of deadlines the colleges, universities, and scholarship programs have.

■ Do both the federal and institutional methodologies look at stocks and other investments to see if a student qualifies?

There is no consideration of assets in the federal formula for a family whose taxable income is less than $50,000 and who files one of the simplified versions of the federal tax return, the 1040A or 1040EZ. For others, both methodologies collect and consider information on assets, including the value of stocks and bonds and anything else that would generate interest or dividend income.

■ How does family size affect a family's eligibility for financial aid?

The number of siblings and the size of the household is an important consideration. The other important factor is the number of family members enrolled in college at the same time. A family might not be eligible for much financial aid this year, but next year, when the family's twins are enrolled, the family would suddenly be eligible for considerably more aid.

■ What are the major loan options and what are their differences?

The Stafford loan is the most widely available option. Right now it comes in two flavors. The first is available to families as part of the Federal Family Education Loan Programs (FFELP). The eligibility is determined by the school, which helps the family apply for the loan through a private lender, but the government pays the interest on the loan while the student is enrolled in school. For the past couple of years there's been a parallel program called the Federal Direct Student Loan Program. That program eliminates the private lender as the middle man and has the school not only determine eligibility for the loan but actually deliver the loan proceeds to the student. But from the student's perspective the differences are transparent. In both cases the terms are the same, the repayment obligation is the same, and the amount they can borrow is the same.

There is also the Perkins Loan Program, which is available to the neediest of students. The amount of money a college has for this program varies from school to school and depends on how many students an institution has applying for financial aid. Because it is intended for students with the highest need, it is a little more competitive than the Stafford program.

■ Are there any other loans?

Thanks to a major change in the FFELP and Direct Loan programs, a student who is not eligible for a loan based on need would still be eligible for an unsubsidized Stafford loan, in which the student would be responsible for the interest that accrues while she or he was in school. The student can either arrange to pay the interest while enrolled or opt to have the interest capitalized while he or she attends school and then repay both principal and interest later. Compared to a commercial loan, it would still be an attractive option.

In addition, there is the Federal PLUS loan, which is available to parents as opposed to the students themselves. Right now a parent would be able to borrow as much as the full cost of education for a son or daughter, minus any financial aid, including subsidized or unsubsidized Stafford loans, regardless of income level. Repayment would generally begin within 60 days of the receipt of the loan. The interest rate is similar to the Stafford loan, but it's determined a little differently each year. Some families advocate home equity loans or home equity lines of credit as a more attractive option. There are others that have investments they may draw upon. But PLUS is a source for a number of parents.

■ WHAT A YEAR OF COLLEGE COSTS

Tuition and fees at four-year colleges and universities rose 6 percent during the school year 1995–96. At two-year institutions the increase was 4 to 6 percent.

SECTOR		TUITION AND FEES	BOOKS AND SUPPLIES	ROOM AND BOARD	TRANS-PORTATION	OTHER EXPENSES	ESTIMATED TOTAL EXP.
TWO-YEAR PUBLIC	Resident	$1,387	$577	NA[1]	NA[1]	NA[1]	NA[1]
	Commuter			$1,752[2]	$894	$1,142	$5,752
TWO-YEAR PRIVATE	Resident	$6,350	$567	$4,243	$578	$972	$12,710
	Commuter			$1,796[2]	$902	$1,220	$10,835
FOUR-YEAR PUBLIC	Resident	$2,860	$591	$3,963	$565	$1,306	$9,285
	Commuter			$1,721[2]	$929	$1,348	$7,449
FOUR-YEAR PRIVATE	Resident	$12,432	$585	$5,199	$521	$1,010	$19,763
	Commuter			$1,845[2]	$863	$1,169	$16,910

1. Sample too small to provide meaningful information. 2. Board only.

SOURCE: College Entrance Examination Board, 1995.

EXPERT TIPS

MASTERING THE COLLEGE AID GAME

An insider's guide to maxing out financial aid

Most people who apply for financial aid for school have only a hazy idea of how colleges make their decisions. But there are some important facts everyone should know before they even sit down to fill out the forms. Kalman Chany, president of Campus Consultants Inc., a firm that guides parents through the financial aid process, and author of *The Princeton Review Guide to Paying for College 1997 Edition* (Random House, 1997), has the following tips on how to qualify for the most financial aid possible.

■ **UNDERSTAND THE ANGLES.** The theory is, the money goes where it's most needed. But in reality, people who better understand the system and how it works are going to get the most money. Few families understand how the aid process works. Most people are just gambling. Anyone can benefit, you just have to understand it.

■ **DON'T RULE OUT ANY SCHOOL AS BEING TOO EXPENSIVE.** Private schools are more flexible, and may be able to offer more financial aid since they are not as regulated as state schools. If a family can afford $10,000 and it's looking at a $30,000 school, it might be eligible for $20,000 in financial aid.

■ **THINK LOCAL.** If you really need the money, the worst thing you can do is go to a state school outside of the state in which you live. It's not popular and it's not good politically to give lots of aid to a student who is from out of state. The student isn't able to qualify for state aid. Instead, look at the state school in your state, or a private college in your state or out of state.

■ **KNOW THE TIMELINE.** The family income that the institutions will look at starts in January of the child's junior year in high school and ends in December of the child's senior year in high school. During that time, parents should be wary of selling stock, withdrawing from pensions prematurely, or withdrawing from IRAs prematurely.

■ **PUT ASSETS IN THE PARENT'S NAME.** In aid formulas, the student's solvency is weighed more heavily than the parents'. If you want to hope for financial aid, put the money in the parent's name, not in the child's name.

■ **IN DIVORCE SITUATIONS, ASSUME THE CUSTODIAL PARENT HAS THE ONUS.** The parent who had custody of the child for the previous 12 months—that is, the parent that the child lived with when the child was a senior in high school—is the parent whose income will be scrutinized. The custodial parent should fill out the financial aid forms. Some schools will look at both parents, but the majority don't.

■ **POSTPONE THE WEDDING BELLS.** If a parent is planning on remarrying, he or she should wait until the child is out of college before heading to the altar. If a parent remarries, the stepparent's income will be analyzed as if it is that of a natural parent. This could cause financial aid to be lost.

■ **DON'T RELY ON THE SCHOOL'S FINANCIAL AID ADMINISTRATOR.** Financial aid administrators work for the school. They are going to put the school ahead of the family. Ask them what to do, how to save money, and they won't answer. They'll tell you the rules but they put the needs of the school first.

■ **SAVE REGULARLY.** Above all, parents should set aside as much money as they can on a regular basis. They should get into the habit of saving regularly. Parents shouldn't be intimidated by statistics quoting the astronomical cost of tuition. They should just save as much as they can, as regularly as they can.

CYBERCULTURE

THE COMPUTER AS A CLASSMATE

Today's college experience is being deeply altered by online computing

College has long been a time of exploration and new experiences—students are challenged by new ideas and confronted with classmates of vastly different backgrounds. In the past, many of these experiences were at least sparked by encounters with new people, from professors and classmates to roommates and dining hall companions. Now, computers and technology are changing the way many college students are studying and socializing.

As Professor of the Sociology of Science at the Massachusetts Institute of Technology and author of *Life on the Screen: Identity in the Age of the Internet* (Simon & Schuster, 1995), Sherry Turkle has been chronicling this transformation. Turkle's groundbreaking studies have led some to call her the "Margaret Mead of cyberspace." Says Turkle:

■ Computers are changing the way students are communicating on campus and creating new communities of interest as well.

E-mail has added a whole new dimension to the way people interact. People now have both virtual relationships and face-to-face relationships, even with people that live down the hall or in the same fraternity. Some conversations and relationships may seem easier to have on e-mail, while others seem easier face-to-face. Rather than limiting conversation, and encouraging people to stay in their "own little world," as some argue, for many students computers have opened up a parallel track of communication.

■ Computer technology is opening up new ways for students and teachers to exchange information and gain access to research materials.

Technology has allowed people to conduct all kinds of business and socializing from their computer. Most of the work-day for many professionals, or study-day for many students, occurs in front of a terminal in one locale. Not only can information be obtained about what books and articles are available, but in some cases whole databases of articles can be "tapped into."

While not all professors do, I link all my readings for my classes to my Web page. Not only can my students download readings, but they can ask questions of both me and other students electronically. It is very important for students and professors to meet face-to-face, but for many "houskeeping" chores or questions that need rapid answers, it can be very convenient to communicate via computer.

■ Communications online provide students with new ways to explore their identities.

One pastime that is very popular amongst "the wired" population is to play in different Multi-User Domains (MUDs). MUDs are virtual spaces in which players can move around and interact with other players, each identifying themselves however they choose. They provide worlds for anonymous social interaction; one can play a role as far away from one's "real self" as one chooses. Because one's body is represented by one's own textual description, the obese can be slender, the beautiful plain, and the "nerdy" sophisticated. In this way, individuals can explore different aspects of themselves free from labels of gender, sexuality, race, etc.

College itself used to be thought of as a space in which psychological, intellectual, and sexual exploration were all permitted. In this day and age, however, that is not the case. Students are concerned with the ramifications of every move—will it affect their job eligibility, will they contract some type of disease, will they somehow limit themselves? I see the computer and cyberspace becoming a much-needed space of consequenceless exploration—a place to play. This is true for college students, as well as the rest of us.

Some people argue that by playing such games individuals—especially those who do so fanatically—are merely escaping their reality. And of course things can be taken to an extreme. But I believe that many individuals are using cyberspace for exploring various parts of themselves and for working out significant problems.

■ The computers that we use today teach us new ways to think about knowing.

Traditionally, most of us have operated under the assumption that to know something was to open the hood and see inside. This model remained in place when computers came along—that to understand a computer was to learn a computer language and know how to program. Now, however, we are very comfortable navigating around a computer and identifying things graphically by pointing and clicking without understanding how it works. In other words, we've become accustomed to not peering beneath the surface—which I think is a danger. In some ways this new view of what it is to know is very positive—you see this when you watch young people learn how to play a videogame—they learn by playing. They don't check the manual. Learning is involved with an activity and discovery. But there are some aspects of this way of knowing that we need to look at critically.

Just as we have habits of reading—asking questions of every text, such as who wrote it, why, under what circumstance, what was the point of view, we need to become schooled and disciplined in the new "reading" habits for reading software, the reading habits for a culture of simulation. In a simulation game of a presidential election, for example, players need to realize that while a decision to run a negative advertising campaign against an opponent may increase their popularity votes, setting up the game in that way betrays the decision of the game's programmer. It does not necessarily correspond to a reality. Young people are learning about how things work by playing simulations and we need to teach them how to be more critical about them.

Learning how to be a critical and responsible citizen in a culture so dependent on simulation must start very early. Just as parents discuss with their children the books they read and the television programs they watch, they should do the same for computer programs and games. Part of the difficulty in this is that parents and many teachers are not themselves comfortable or familiar with computer use.

■ Computers can increase students' degree of participation in their own learning.

Instead of reading a book and then heading to the library for further information about a given subject, one can read a text on screen and click on a specific word that will bring up an entirely different screen of information. The ease with which one can do this makes it more likely that students will explore the areas they are interested in.

■ Computers change the writing process.

Computer technology has reinforced the principle that writing is a process of revision and editing. For some, it has been negative. Students who are not interested in writing sometimes feel that because they can cut and paste things together and print out a text so that it "looks" beautiful, anything goes. But for students interested in improving their writing, computers have made it easier to treat a text as a "work in progress." This is one example of how computer technology can be used in positive and negative ways. What we make of it depends on us. In education it is not a panacea but an opportunity.

EXPERT LIST

THE BEST GRADUATE SCHOOLS IN AMERICA

If attending graduate school figures into your plans, a recent study by the National Research Council (NRC), a highly respected research organization, is must-reading. For the first time since 1982, the NRC has released comprehensive ratings of the best graduate schools in the United States. The evaluation of 3,634 doctoral programs in 274 universities nationwide took more than four years to complete and involved over 8,000 faculty members. Ratings were based on a combination of factors, including scholarly quality, educational effectiveness, and change in program quality over the last five years. (Duplicate rankings are ties.)

Rank	Quality	Effectiveness
ART HISTORY		
1. Columbia University	4.79	4.29
1. New York University	4.79	4.32
3. University of California Berkeley	4.67	4.18
4. Harvard University	4.49	4.11
5. Yale University	4.44	4.36
6. Princeton University	4.04	3.78
7. Johns Hopkins University	3.93	3.46
8. Northwestern University	3.83	3.57
9. University of Pennsylvania	3.80	3.51
10. University of Chicago	3.74	3.49
COMPARATIVE LITERATURE		
1. Yale University	4.70	4.30
2. Duke University	4.51	3.80
3. Columbia University	4.44	3.82
4. Harvard University	4.37	3.81
5. Princeton University	4.32	3.96
6. Cornell University	4.31	3.78
7. Johns Hopkins University	4.18	4.12
8. University of California Irvine	4.06	3.63
9. Stanford University	4.05	3.75
10. University of California Berkeley	4.00	3.83
ENGLISH LANGUAGE & LITERATURE		
1. Yale University	4.77	4.43
1. University of California Berkeley	4.77	4.53
1. Harvard University	4.77	4.14
4. University of Virginia	4.58	4.27
5. Duke University	4.55	3.98
5. Stanford University	4.55	4.30
7. Cornell University	4.49	4.43
8. University of Pennsylvania	4.47	4.24
8. Columbia University	4.47	3.91
10. University of Chicago	4.41	4.20
LINGUISTICS		
1. Massachusetts Institute of Technology	4.79	4.39
2. Stanford University	4.59	4.01
3. University of California Los Angeles	4.56	4.17
4. University of Massachusetts Amherst	4.44	4.44
5. University of Pennsylvania	4.16	3.68
6. University of Chicago	3.97	3.64
6. University of California Berkeley	3.97	3.40
8. Ohio State University	3.80	3.46
9. Cornell University	3.78	3.89
10. University of California Santa Cruz	3.66	3.80
MUSIC		
1. Harvard University	4.59	4.26
2. University of Chicago	4.53	4.32
3. University of California Berkeley	4.51	4.11
4. City University of New York Graduate School and University Center	4.41	3.79
5. Yale University	4.40	4.11
6. Princeton University	4.39	4.18
7. University of Pennsylvania	4.35	3.79
8. University of Rochester	4.24	4.03
9. University of Michigan	4.16	4.03
10. U. of Illinois Urbana-Champaign	4.11	3.60
PHILOSOPHY		
1. Princeton University	4.93	4.56
2. University of Pittsburgh	4.73	4.43
3. Harvard University	4.69	3.77
4. University of California Berkeley	4.66	3.66
5. University of Pittsburgh Program in History and Philosophy of Science	4.47	4.26
6. University of California Los Angeles	4.42	4.01
7. Stanford University	4.20	4.02
8. University of Michigan	4.15	3.88
9. Cornell University	4.11	4.14
10. Massachusetts Institute of Technology	4.01	3.91
RELIGION		
1. University of Chicago	4.76	4.01
2. Harvard University	4.73	4.10
3. Princeton University	4.33	3.89

■ EXPERT LIST

Rank	Quality	Effectiveness
4. Duke University	4.25	3.90
5. Emory University	4.05	3.59
6. University of Virginia	3.96	3.46
7. Vanderbilt University	3.85	3.50
8. Princeton Theological Seminary	3.84	3.61
9. University of California Santa Barbara	3.82	3.33
10. Jewish Theological Seminary	3.74	3.26
10. University of Pennsylvania	3.74	3.22

BIOCHEMISTRY & MOLECULAR BIOLOGY

Rank	Quality	Effectiveness
1. University of California San Francisco	4.84	4.73
2. Massachusetts Institute of Technology	4.83	4.68
2. Stanford University	4.83	4.59
4. University of California Berkeley	4.81	4.66
5. Harvard University	4.80	4.44
6. Yale University	4.59	4.32
7. California Institute of Technology	4.57	4.41
8. University of Wisconsin Madison	4.55	4.30
9. University of California San Diego	4.53	4.37
10. Johns Hopkins University	4.38	4.26
10. Columbia University	4.38	4.25

CELL & DEVELOPMENTAL BIOLOGY

Rank	Quality	Effectiveness
1. Massachusetts Institute of Technology	4.86	4.66
2. Rockefeller University	4.77	4.54
3. University of California San Francisco	4.76	4.57
4. California Institute of Technology	4.73	4.68
5. Harvard University	4.70	4.33
6. Stanford University Sch. of Medicine	4.55	4.39
7. University of California San Diego	4.50	4.15
8. University of Washington	4.48	4.23
9. Washington University	4.39	4.24
10. Yale University	4.37	4.22

ECOLOGY, EVOLUTION, & BEHAVIOR

Rank	Quality	Effectiveness
1. Stanford University	4.51	4.23
1. University of Chicago	4.51	4.31
3. Duke University	4.49	4.33
4. Cornell University	4.44	4.24
5. University of California Davis	4.42	4.12
6. Princeton University	4.34	3.96
7. University of Washington	4.30	4.20
8. University of California Berkeley	4.29	4.15
9. University of Wisconsin Madison	4.18	4.13
10. State U. of New York Stony Brook	4.12	3.86
10. University of Texas Austin	4.12	3.77

MOLECULAR & GENERAL GENETICS

Rank	Quality	Effectiveness
1. Massachusetts Institute of Technology	4.88	4.75
2. University of California San Francisco	4.87	4.80
3. Harvard University	4.77	4.55
4. California Institute of Technology	4.51	4.47
5. Stanford University	4.48	4.44
6. University of California San Diego	4.44	4.17
7. University of Wisconsin Madison	4.33	4.40
8. Yale University	4.32	4.29
9. Johns Hopkins University	4.26	4.01
10. University of California Berkeley	4.21	4.18

NEUROSCIENCES

Rank	Quality	Effectiveness
1. University of California San Diego	4.82	4.48
2. Yale University	4.76	4.44
3. Harvard University	4.73	4.33
4. University of California San Francisco	4.66	4.45
5. Stanford University	4.64	4.56
6. Columbia University	4.58	4.29
7. Johns Hopkins University	4.47	4.33
8. Washington University	4.43	4.42
9. University of California Berkeley	4.32	4.12
10. California Institute of Technology	4.30	4.22
10. University of Pennsylvania	4.30	4.17

PHARMACOLOGY

Rank	Quality	Effectiveness
1. Yale University	4.45	4.32
2. U. of Texas Southwestern Medical Center	4.39	4.04
3. University of California San Diego	4.36	3.87
4. Johns Hopkins University	4.21	4.22
5. Duke University	4.18	4.03
6. Vanderbilt University	4.17	4.15
7. Harvard University	4.14	4.00
8. University of North Carolina Chapel Hill School of Arts and Sciences	4.03	3.99
9. University of Washington	4.02	4.01
9. University of Pennsylvania	4.02	4.02

PHYSIOLOGY

Rank	Quality	Effectiveness
1. Yale University	4.48	4.38
2. University of California San Diego	4.47	4.25
3. University of Pennsylvania	4.27	3.95
4. University of California Los Angeles	4.23	4.02
5. University of California San Francisco	4.21	4.00
5. Baylor College of Medicine	4.21	3.84
7. University of Washington	4.20	4.10
7. Stanford University	4.20	4.17
9. University of Virginia	4.19	3.83
9. Columbia University	4.19	3.83

AEROSPACE ENGINEERING

Rank	Quality	Effectiveness
1. California Institute of Technology	4.61	4.43
2. Massachusetts Institute of Technology	4.54	4.31
3. Stanford University	4.50	4.26

■ **EXPERT LIST**

Rank	Quality	Effectiveness
4. Princeton University	4.30	4.03
5. University of Michigan	4.05	3.80
6. Cornell University	3.93	3.75
7. Purdue University	3.71	3.46
8. University of Texas Austin	3.67	3.64
9. Georgia Institute of Technology	3.66	3.49
10. University of California San Diego	3.62	3.27
10. University of California Los Angeles	3.62	3.44

BIOMEDICAL ENGINEERING

Rank	Quality	Effectiveness
1. Massachusetts Institute of Technology	4.62	4.17
2. University of California San Diego	4.45	4.43
3. University of Washington	4.35	3.85
4. Duke University	4.33	3.63
5. University of Pennsylvania	4.28	3.82
6. Johns Hopkins University	4.25	4.09
7. University of California San Francisco	4.19	3.89
8. University of California Berkeley	4.08	3.84
9. University of Utah	3.97	3.69
10. Rice University	3.94	3.95

CHEMICAL ENGINEERING

Rank	Quality	Effectiveness
1. University of Minnesota	4.86	4.57
2. Massachusetts Institute of Technology	4.73	4.43
3. University of California Berkeley	4.63	4.43
4. University of Wisconsin Madison	4.62	4.37
5. University of Illinois Urbana-Champaign	4.42	4.28
6. California Institute of Technology	4.41	4.24
7. Stanford University	4.35	4.31
8. University of Delaware	4.34	4.21
9. Princeton University	4.14	4.02
10. University of Texas Austin	4.08	3.73

CIVIL ENGINEERING

Rank	Quality	Effectiveness
1. Massachusetts Institute of Technology	4.61	4.47
2. University of California Berkeley	4.56	4.22
3. Stanford University	4.44	4.29
4. University of Texas Austin	4.42	4.27
5. University of Illinois Urbana-Champaign	4.41	4.23
6. Cornell University	4.30	4.08
7. California Institute of Technology	4.27	4.42
8. Princeton University	3.99	3.89
9. Northwestern University	3.96	3.73
10. University of Michigan	3.90	3.82

ELECTRICAL ENGINEERING

Rank	Quality	Effectiveness
1. Stanford University	4.83	4.68
2. Massachusetts Institute of Technology	4.79	4.61
3. University of Illinois Urbana-Champaign	4.70	4.57
4. University of California Berkeley	4.69	4.46
5. California Institute of Technology	4.46	4.34
6. University of Michigan	4.38	4.17

PAYING FOR YOUR GRAD SCHOOL MEAL TICKET

Plan on working at least part-time and borrowing a bunch to pay the tab

Federal financial aid for graduate students is similar to aid for undergraduates, according to Bart Astor, editor of *College Planning Quarterly*, with a few key differences: Graduate students are not eligible for such major federal scholarship programs as the Pell Grant, but the federal Stafford and Direct Loan programs have higher maximum amounts students can borrow; and all grad students are considered independent of their parents (i.e., only the student's income—and spouse, if appropriate—is used to determine the expected contribution for federal aid).

Another big difference is in how grad students pay for their education. Most graduate school aid comes from sources other than the federal government, and is not based on need. Also, a majority of grad students attend school part-time and maintain full-time jobs elsewhere; many receive tuition assistance from their employers. Of full-time students, many are awarded teaching and research assistantships or work for professors and are funded by research grants. Students attending the professional schools (medicine, law, etc.) usually do not work and have to borrow large amounts to pay for their schooling. There are private loan programs available to these students; the schools themselves can lead students in the right direction.

■ **EXPERT LIST**

Rank	Quality	Effectiveness
7. Cornell University	4.35	4.08
8. Purdue University	4.02	3.94
9. Princeton University	4.01	4.00
10. University of Southern California	4.00	3.71
10. University of California Los Angeles	4.00	3.79

MATERIALS SCIENCE

Rank	Quality	Effectiveness
1. Massachusetts Institute of Technology	4.61	4.22
2. Northwestern University	4.47	4.08
3. Cornell University	4.35	4.10
4. University of California Berkeley	4.33	4.08
5. University of Illinois Urbana-Champaign	4.29	3.93
6. Stanford University	4.24	4.00
7. University of Massachusetts Amherst	4.20	4.21
8. University of California Santa Barbara	4.18	3.65
9. Pennsylvania State University	3.97	3.83
10. University of Pennsylvania	3.79	3.62

MECHANICAL ENGINEERING

Rank	Quality	Effectiveness
1. Stanford University	4.77	4.50
2. Massachusetts Institute of Technology	4.65	4.45
3. University of California Berkeley	4.54	4.50
4. California Institute of Technology	4.35	4.30
5. University of Michigan	4.22	4.00
6. Princeton University	4.19	4.09
7. Cornell University	4.15	3.99
8. University of Minnesota	4.09	3.85
9. University of Illinois Urbana-Champaign	4.07	4.02
10. University of California San Diego	4.04	3.59
10. Purdue University	4.04	4.01

ASTROPHYSICS & ASTRONOMY

Rank	Quality	Effectiveness
1. California Institute of Technology	4.91	4.75
2. Princeton University	4.79	4.38
3. University of California Berkeley	4.65	4.53
4. Harvard University	4.49	3.92
5. University of Chicago	4.36	3.85
6. University of California Santa Cruz	4.31	4.14
7. University of Arizona	4.10	3.69
8. Massachusetts Institute of Technology	4.00	3.68
9. Cornell University	3.98	3.97
10. University of Texas Austin	3.65	3.39

CHEMISTRY

Rank	Quality	Effectiveness
1. University of California Berkeley	4.96	4.72
2. California Institute of Technology	4.94	4.75
3. Harvard University	4.87	4.57
3. Stanford University	4.87	4.57
5. Massachusetts Institute of Technology	4.86	4.70
6. Cornell University	4.55	4.40
7. Columbia University	4.54	4.37

Rank	Quality	Effectiveness
8. University of Illinois Urbana-Champaign	4.48	4.38
9. University of Wisconsin Madison	4.46	4.26
9. University of Chicago	4.46	4.20
9. University of California Los Angeles	4.46	4.00

COMPUTER SCIENCES

Rank	Quality	Effectiveness
1. Stanford University	4.97	4.60
2. Massachusetts Institute of Technology	4.91	4.62
3. University of California Berkeley	4.88	4.58
4. Carnegie Mellon University	4.76	4.38
5. Cornell University	4.64	4.47
6. Princeton University	4.31	3.84
7. University of Texas Austin	4.18	3.81
8. University of Illinois Urbana-Champaign	4.09	3.93
9. University of Washington	4.04	4.05
10. University of Wisconsin Madison	4.00	3.87

GEOSCIENCES

Rank	Quality	Effectiveness
1. California Institute of Technology	4.87	4.63
2. Massachusetts Institute of Technology	4.67	4.52
3. University of California Berkeley	4.45	4.09
4. Columbia University	4.38	4.14
5. Stanford University Program in Geophysics	4.33	3.96
6. University of California San Diego	4.23	4.06
7. University of Chicago	4.22	4.03
8. Harvard University	4.20	3.80
9. Stanford University	4.15	4.06
9. Cornell University	4.15	3.71

MATHEMATICS

Rank	Quality	Effectiveness
1. University of California Berkeley	4.94	4.37
1. Princeton University	4.94	4.69
3. Massachusetts Institute of Technology	4.92	4.57
4. Harvard University	4.90	4.58
5. University of Chicago	4.69	4.64
6. Stanford University	4.68	4.41
7. Yale University	4.55	4.11
8. New York University	4.49	4.26
9. University of Michigan	4.23	3.84
9. Columbia University	4.23	3.94

OCEANOGRAPHY

Rank	Quality	Effectiveness
1. University of California San Diego	4.69	4.21
2. Massachusetts Institute of Technology	4.62	4.31
3. University of Washington	4.31	4.07
4. Columbia University	4.30	4.00
5. Oregon State University	3.88	3.46
6. University of Rhode Island	3.68	3.53
7. University of Hawaii Manoa	3.50	3.11
8. State U. of New York Stony Brook	3.49	3.28

■ EXPERT LIST

Rank	Quality	Effectiveness
9. Florida State University	3.48	3.28
10. University of Maryland College Park	3.42	3.17

PHYSICS

Rank	Quality	Effectiveness
1. Harvard University	4.91	4.71
2. Princeton University	4.89	4.69
3. Massachusetts Institute of technology	4.87	4.64
3. University of California Berkeley	4.87	4.49
5. California Institute of Technology	4.81	4.61
6. Cornell University	4.75	4.54
7. University of Chicago	4.69	4.55
8. U. of Illinois Urbana-Champaign	4.66	4.39
9. Stanford University	4.53	4.35
10. University of California Santa Barbara	4.43	3.91

STATISTICS & BIOSTATISTICS

Rank	Quality	Effectiveness
1. Stanford University	4.76	4.44
1. University of California Berkeley Program in Statistics	4.76	4.33
3. University of California Berkeley Program in Biostatistics	4.43	4.01
4. Cornell University	4.37	4.06
5. University of Chicago	4.34	4.09
6. University of Washington Program in Biostatistics	4.21	4.08
7. Harvard University	4.17	3.80
8. University of Wisconsin Madison	4.06	4.07
9. U. of Washington Program in Statistics	4.01	3.85
10. Purdue University	4.00	3.61

ANTHROPOLOGY

Rank	Quality	Effectiveness
1. University of Michigan	4.77	4.40
1. University of Chicago	4.77	4.19
3. University of California Berkeley	4.51	3.93
4. Harvard University	4.43	3.67
5. University of Arizona	4.11	3.60
6. University of Pennsylvania	3.94	3.68
7. Stanford University	3.71	3.63
8. Yale University	3.67	3.43
8. University of California Los Angeles	3.67	3.50
8. University of California San Diego	3.67	3.44

ECONOMICS

Rank	Quality	Effectiveness
1. University of Chicago	4.95	4.63
1. Harvard University	4.95	4.33
3. Massachusetts Institute of Technology	4.93	4.71
4. Stanford University	4.92	4.58
5. Princeton University	4.84	4.69
6. Yale University	4.70	4.01
7. University of California Berkeley	4.55	4.05
8. University of Pennsylvania	4.43	3.91
9. Northwestern University	4.39	4.04
10. University of Minnesota	4.22	4.08

HISTORY

Rank	Quality	Effectiveness
1. Yale University	4.89	4.55
2. University of California Berkeley	4.79	4.50
3. Princeton University	4.75	4.48
4. Harvard University	4.71	4.02
5. Columbia University	4.63	4.29
6. University of California Los Angeles	4.59	4.07
7. Stanford University	4.56	4.44
8. University of Chicago	4.49	4.20
9. Johns Hopkins University	4.42	4.37
10. University of Wisconsin Madison	4.37	4.33

POLITICAL SCIENCE

Rank	Quality	Effectiveness
1. Harvard University	4.88	4.17
2. University of California Berkeley	4.66	4.13
3. Yale University	4.60	4.24
3. University of Michigan	4.60	4.31
5. Stanford University	4.50	4.02
6. University of Chicago	4.41	3.83
7. Princeton University	4.39	3.91
8. University of California Los Angeles	4.25	3.62
9. University of California San Diego	4.13	3.70
10. University of Wisconsin Madison	4.09	3.86

PSYCHOLOGY

Rank	Quality	Effectiveness
1. Stanford University	4.82	4.64
2. University of Michigan	4.63	4.40
3. Yale University	4.62	4.31
4. University of California Los Angeles	4.61	4.05
5. University of Illinois Urbana-Champaign	4.58	4.36
6. Harvard University	4.48	4.09
7. University of Minnesota	4.46	4.33
8. University of Pennsylvania	4.35	4.18
9. University of California Berkeley	4.33	4.03
10. University of California San Diego	4.32	4.12

SOCIOLOGY

Rank	Quality	Effectiveness
1. University of Chicago	4.77	4.26
2. University of Wisconsin Madison	4.74	4.61
3. University of California Berkeley	4.56	3.60
4. University of Michigan	4.39	4.08
5. University of California Los Angeles	4.36	3.79
6. University of North Carolina Chapel Hill	4.31	4.00
7. Harvard University	4.18	3.58
8. Stanford University	4.08	3.77
9. Northwestern University	4.07	3.61
10. University of Washington	4.03	3.73

SOURCE: National Research Council.

LIFELONG LEARNING

LIBRARIES: Brown University president Vartan Gregorian shares his choices for top libraries around the world, PAGE 326 **BOOKS:** The New York Public Libary picks the books that have most influenced life in the 20th century, PAGE 327 **ALUM PERKS:** Your alma mater may offer many exciting opportunities, PAGE 330 **RETIREMENT:** Why college towns are becoming popular places for spending the golden years, PAGE 331

CONTINUING EDUCATION

HOW NOT TO BE OBSOLESCENT

For many, keeping a job will be hard without ongoing training

If "downsizing" is not a concept that figures in your career plans, the idea of continuing education is a notion to bone up on. Whether you're an architect or a teacher, a doctor or a police officer, it's increasingly evident that to keep your job and be able to perform in a changing work world, additional training and credentials will frequently be necessary.

The traditional assumption that a few years' training at the start of a person's career prepares an individual for a lifetime is no longer viable, says Kay Kohl, Executive Director of the National University of Continuing Education Association (NUCEA), a nonprofit organization devoted to advancing continuing education in colleges and universities. "The flow of new knowledge in the workplace is so great and so rapid that one needs new skills and knowledge to stay occupationally competent." In today's world, for example, the half-life of a computer engineer is 2½ years, explains Kohl. "Technology is changing so fast, 50 percent of that person's knowledge will be obsolete in a mere 2½ years." In fields such as engineering, architecture, medicine, and even accounting, where there are both new materials and new methods of handling old problems, a life of continuing education will be essential.

Nor will those in "nontechnical" fields be able to rest on their laurels. Jobs are more multidisciplinary than ever before, requiring people to handle a multitude of new tasks. State requirements in different professions are also being raised. To respond to these trends in the workplace, colleges and universities are developing programs that integrate two or more fields. Johns Hopkins, for example, has a degree program designed for managers within the criminal justice system, recognizing that it will take training that goes well beyond criminology and basic management to be a police chief of a large city like Los Angeles. Another popular master's program, Environmental Policy and Management, provides far better training for a person who envisions working for an organization like The Nature Conservancy than an individual would find in either an environmental policy or a management program.

While many individuals seek additional training as a way of keeping up or staying a step ahead of their colleagues, many also do so to avoid breaking state law. Increasingly, states are mandating continuing education for a variety of professions. For

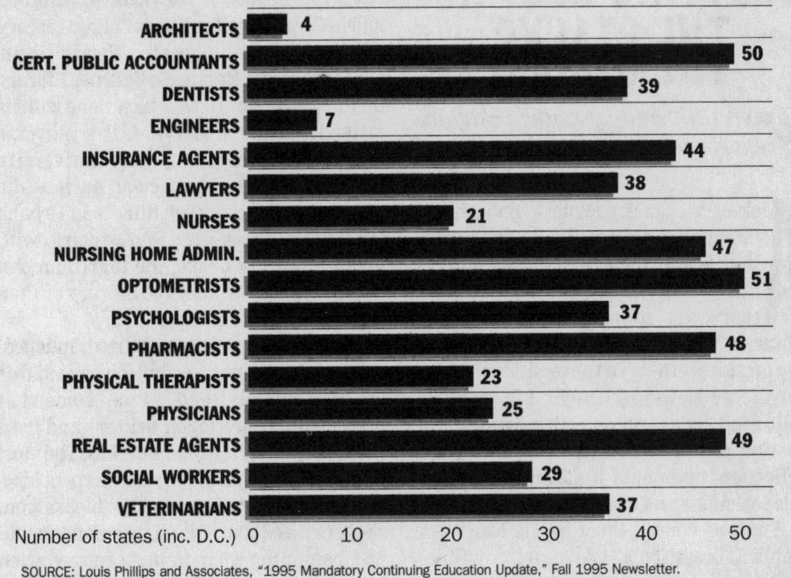

instance, between 1981 and 1993, 28 states approved mandatory continuing education for lawyers, joining 9 other states that already had such requirements. Meanwhile, 27 states raised their training requirements for real estate brokers.

Mandatory professional training usually means that individuals must complete a certain number of hours of study provided by an approved institution or attend a certain number of hours of conferences and workshops. (See the chart above for the number of states requiring continuing education, by profession.)

Those who expand their training are likely to reap rewards. The NUCEA estimates that three out of four jobs in today's marketplace require some type of postsecondary education. Of the new jobs that will be created by the year 2005, the bulk will be in managerial, professional, and technical occupations. Since these three areas already have the highest proportion of workers with college degrees and are the most sought after, it will take higher levels of education and training to compete for these jobs.

It's no surprise then that American workers are returning to school in record numbers. Part-time students are now the fastest-growing population in higher education,comprising over one-half of all enrolled students. Close to 4 million of them are older women, in many cases trying to juggle job, family, and schooling.

While there is some federal aid available to part-time students to finance continuing education, support from your employer may be your best bet. Over 90 percent of major companies offer continuing education benefits today. For some, this means financing classes, while others offer stock options for those who successfully complete classes. While it might seem like a hassle, additional training may well help you hold on to your job, qualify for a raise, or increase your stock portfolio. The alternatives may not be nearly as appealing.

LIBRARIES

GETTING LOST IN THE STACKS

Brown University president Vartan Gregorian on his favorite libraries

Asking Vartan Gregorian to name his 10 favorite libraries is like asking him to list his favorite 10 colors. "The world is full of a myriad of beautiful hues, and there are hundreds of wonderful libraries," says Gregorian, who before becoming president of Brown University was Director of the New York Public Library. The following "is not an objective list of great institutions," he says. "It is more a personal reflection" on some of his favorite libraries. His selections and commentary:

First, of course, must be the New York Public Library (*http://www.nypl.org*), where I spent eight rich years. The NYPL is in a class by itself in the sheer size and diversity of its holdings, and because of its writers' room where so many major works of both fiction and nonfiction were done, from Robert Caro's multivolume biography of Lyndon Johnson to Rachel Carson's *Silent Spring*.

Next I think of the Library of Congress (*http://lcweb.loc.gov*), our nation's premier library. No country in the world boasts a greater national library, and what a glory it is for a nation barely 200 years old that did not have the patronage of an aristocracy to shape its beginnings.

Another favorite is the British Library (*http://portico.bl.uk*), which was, is, and I hope will remain one of the great libraries of the world. On a similar scale is the Bibliothèque Nationale (*http://www.bnt.fr*) in Paris, of which I have personal memories from having spent many happy days there. Unlike our Library of Congress, the Bibliothèque Nationale began as a royal collection as early as the 15th century, and one can hardly imagine the depth and variety of its holdings.

Also in Europe is the Vatican Library, with its universal holdings on every possible topic and its current accessibility, which ranks it as one of the great libraries in the world. At Oxford is the Bodleian Library, and in Cambridge, the King's College Library.

The greatest university library in the United States is Harvard's Widener Library (*http://www.harvard.edu*), which along with its sister libraries at Harvard, is a universe apart. Some of the public university libraries are also spectacular, such as the one at the University of Illinois in Urbana (*http://www.grainger.uiuc.edu*), which is, with about 8 million books, the fourth largest library in the U.S. after the Library of Congress, the NYPL, and Harvard.

There are also the specialized, independent research libraries that we have in this country, which tend to be somewhat unknown but are much beloved and have absolutely irreplaceable materials. The most famous of these perhaps is the Pierpont Morgan Library, which is only a few blocks from the NYPL and contains all that money could buy, beginning early in this century when Morgan began his collecting.

Others of this type of library, founded by wealthy and enlightened individual collectors, are the Huntington Library, near Los Angeles, and the Folger Library in Washington, D.C. The Folger began as a library for the study of Shakespeare and has since branched out productively to a library for the study of Renaissance England.

Only after I came to Brown University did I realize that on our campus is the very prototype and model of all such libraries in the United States, the John Carter Brown Library (*http://www.brown.edu/Facilities/University Libr*). It is the greatest in the world for the study of the history of the expansion of Europe to America between 1492 and 1825.

Finally, there are our town and small city libraries. Surely it was one of the greatest philanthropic acts of all time that Andrew Carnegie built some 1,600 public libraries in the U.S. The tradition of making reading material available easily and freely continues. One can hardly overestimate their value in the success of this country.

EXPERT LIST

BOOKS THAT SHAPED THE 20TH CENTURY

To celebrate its centennial, the New York Public Library recently mounted an exhibit of books that its staff considered among the most influential of the 20th century. For more discussion of what makes these books great, see The New York Public Library's Books of the Century *(Oxford University Press, 1996).*

LANDMARKS OF MODERN LITERATURE

Anton Chekhov. **Tri sestry [The Three Sisters],** 1901

Marcel Proust. **A la recherche du temps perdu [Remembrance of Things Past],** *1913–27*

Gertrude Stein. **Tender Buttons,** *1914*

Franz Kafka. **Die Verwandlung [The Metamorphosis],** *1915*

Edna St. Vincent Millay. **Renascence and Other Poems,** *1917*

William Butler Yeats. **The Wild Swans at Coole,** *1917*

Luigi Pirandello. **Sei personaggi in cerca d'autore [Six Characters in Search of an Author],** *1921*

T. S. Eliot. **The Waste Land,** *1922*

James Joyce. **Ulysses,** *1924*

Thomas Mann. **Der Zauberberg [The Magic Mountain],** *1924*

F. Scott Fitzgerald. **The Great Gatsby,** *1925*

Virginia Woolf. **To the Lighthouse,** *1927*

Federico García Lorca. **Primer Romancero gitano [Gypsy Ballads],** *1928*

Richard Wright. **Native Son,** *1940*

W. H. Auden. **The Age of Anxiety: A Baroque Eclogue,** *1947*

Ralph Ellison. **Invisible Man,** *1952*

Vladimir Nabokov. **Lolita,** *1955*

Jorge Luis Borges. **Ficciones [Fictions],** *1944: 2nd augmented edition, 1956*

Gabriel García Márquez. **Cien años de soledad [One Hundred Years of Solitude],** *1967*

Toni Morrison. **Song of Solomon,** *1977*

NATURE'S REALM

Maurice Maeterlinck. **La vie des abeilles [The Life of the Bee],** *1901*

Marie Sklodowska Curie. **Traité de radioactivité [Treatise on Radioactivity],** *1910*

Albert Einstein. **The Meaning of Relativity,** *1922*

Roger Tory Peterson. **A Field Guide to the Birds,** *1934*

Aldo Leopold. **A Sand County Almanac,** *1949*

Konrad Z. Lorenz. **Er redete mit dem Vieh, den Vögeln und den Fischen: King Solomon's Ring [King Solomon's Ring: New Light on Animal Ways],** *1949*

Rachel Carson. **Silent Spring,** *1962*

Smoking and Health, *Known as The Surgeon General's Report, 1964*

James Watson. **The Double Helix: A Personal Account of the Discovery of the Structure of DNA,** *1968*

Edward O. Wilson. **The Diversity of Life,** *1992*

PROTEST & PROGRESS

Jacob Riis. **The Battle with the Slum,** *1902*

W. E. B. DuBois. **The Souls of Black Folk,** *1903*

Upton Sinclair. **The Jungle,** *1906*

Jane Addams. **Twenty Years at Hull-House,** *1910*

Lillian Wald. **The House on Henry Street,** *1915*

Lincoln Steffens. **The Autobiography of Lincoln Steffens,** *1931*

John Dos Passos. **U.S.A.,** *1937*

John Steinbeck. **The Grapes of Wrath,** *1939*

James Agee and Walker Evans. **Let Us Now Praise Famous Men,** *1941*

Lillian Smith. **Strange Fruit,** *1944*

Paul Goodman. **Growing Up Absurd,** *1960*

James Baldwin. **The Fire Next Time,** *1963*

Malcolm X. **The Autobiography of Malcolm X,** *1965*

Randy Shilts. **And the Band Played On,** *1987*

Alex Kotlowitz. **There Are No Children Here,** *1991*

COLONIALISM & ITS AFTERMATH

Joseph Conrad. **Lord Jim,** *1900*

Rudyard Kipling. **Kim,** *1901*

■ EXPERT LIST

Mohandas K. Gandhi. **Satyagraha [Non-Violent Resistance],** *1921–40*
E. M. Forster. **A Passage to India,** *1924*
Albert Camus. **L'étranger [The Stranger],** *1942*
United Nations Charter, *1945*
Edward Steichen. **The Family of Man: The Photographic Exhibition Created by Edward Steichen for the Museum of Modern Art,** *1955*
Chinua Achebe. **Things Fall Apart,** *1958*
Frantz Fanon. **Les damnés de la terre [The Wretched of the Earth],** *1961*
Jean Rhys. **Wide Sargasso Sea,** *1966*
Tayeb el-Salih. **Mawsim al-Hijra ila al-Shamal [Season of Migration to the North],** *1969*
V. S. Naipaul. **Guerrillas,** *1975*
Buchi Emecheta. **The Bride Price,** *1976*
Ryszard Kapuscińiski. **Cesarz [The Emperor],** *1978*
Rigoberta Menchú. **Me llamo Rigoberta Menchú y ási me nacio conciencia [I, Rigoberta Menchú],** *1983*
Marguerite Duras. **L'amant [The Lover],** *1984*

MIND & SPIRIT

Emile Durkheim. **Le suicide: étude de sociologie [Suicide: A Study in Sociology],** *1897*
Sigmund Freud. **Die Traumdeutung [The Interpretation of Dreams],** *1900*
Havelock Ellis. **Studies in the Psychology of Sex,** *1901–28*
William James. **The Varieties of Religious Experience: A Study in Human Nature,** *1902*
Kahlil Gibran. **The Prophet,** *1923*
Bertrand Russell. **Why I Am Not a Christian,** *1927*
Margaret Mead. **Coming of Age in Samoa,** *1928*
Jean-Paul Sartre. **L'étre et le néant [Being and Nothingness],** *1943*
Dr. Benjamin Spock. **The Common Sense Book of Baby and Child Care,** *1946*
The Holy Bible. Revised Standard Version, *1952*
Paul Tillich. **The Courage to Be,** *1952*
Ken Kesey. **One Flew Over the Cuckoo's Nest,** *1962*
Timothy Leary. **The Politics of Ecstasy,** *1968*
Elisabeth Kübler-Ross. **Death and Dying,** *1969*
Bruno Bettelheim. **The Uses of Enchantment,** *1976*

POPULAR CULTURE & MASS ENTERTAINMENT

Bram Stoker. **Dracula,** *1897*
Henry James. **The Turn of the Screw,** *1898*
Arthur Conan Doyle. **The Hound of the Baskervilles,** *1902*
Edgar Rice Burroughs. **Tarzan of the Apes,** *1912*
Zane Grey. **Riders of the Purple Sage,** *1912*
Agatha Christie. **The Mysterious Affair at Styles,** *1920*
Dale Carnegie. **How to Win Friends and Influence People,** *1936*
Margaret Mitchell. **Gone with the Wind,** *1936*
Raymond Chandler. **The Big Sleep,** *1939*
Nathanael West. **The Day of the Locust,** *1939*
Grace Metalious. **Peyton Place,** *1956*
Dr. Seuss. **The Cat in the Hat,** *1957*
Robert A. Heinlein. **Stranger in a Strange Land,** *1961*
Joseph Heller. **Catch-22,** *1961*
Truman Capote. **In Cold Blood: A True Account of a Multiple Murder and Its Consequences,** *1965*
Jim Bouton. **Ball Four: My Life and Hard Times Throwing the Knuckleball in the Big Leagues,** *1970*
Stephen King. **Carrie,** *1974*
Tom Wolfe. **The Bonfire of the Vanities,** *1987*

WOMEN RISE

Edith Wharton. **The Age of Innocence,** *1920*
Carrie Chapman Catt. **Woman Suffrage and Politics: The Inner Story of the Suffrage Movement,** *1923*
Margaret Sanger. **My Fight for Birth Control,** *1931*
Zora Neale Hurston. **Dust Tracks on a Road,** *1942*
Simone de Beauvoir. **Le deuxième sexe [The Second Sex],** *1949*
Doris Lessing. **The Golden Notebook,** *1962*
Betty Friedan. **The Feminine Mystique,** *1963*
Maya Angelou. **I Know Why the Caged Bird Sings,** *1969*
Robin Morgan, editor **Sisterhood is Powerful: An Anthology of Writings from the Women's Liberation Movement,** *1970*
Susan Brownmiller. **Against Our Will: Men, Women, and Rape,** *1975*

■ EXPERT LIST

Alice Walker. **The Color Purple,** *1982*

ECONOMICS & TECHNOLOGY

Thorstein Veblen. **The Theory of the Leisure Class: An Economic Study of Institutions,** *1899*

Max Weber. **Die protestantische Ethik und der Geist des Kapitalismus [The Protestant Ethic and the Spirit of Capitalism],** *1904*

Henry Adams. **The Education of Henry Adams,** *1907*

John Maynard Keynes. **The General Theory of Employment, Interest and Money,** *1936*

Milton Friedman. **A Theory of the Consumption Function,** *1957*

John Kenneth Galbraith. **The Affluent Society,** *1958*

Jane Jacobs. **The Death and Life of Great American Cities,** *1961*

Helen Leavitt. **Superhighway—Super Hoax,** *1970*

E. F. Schumacher. **Small Is Beautiful: A Study of Economics as if People Mattered,** *1973*

Ed Krel. **The Whole Internet: User's Guide & Catalog,** *1992*

UTOPIA & DYSTOPIAS

H.G. Wells. **The Time Machine,** *1895*

Theodor Herzl. **Der Judenstaat [The Jewish State],** *1896*

L. Frank Baum. **The Wonderful Wizard of Oz,** *1900*

J. M. Barrie. **Peter Pan in Kensington Gardens,** *1906*

Charlotte Perkins Gilman. **Herland,** *1915*

Aldous Huxley. **Brave New World,** *1932*

James Hilton. **Lost Horizon,** *1933*

B. F. Skinner. **Walden Two,** *1948*

George Orwell. **Nineteen Eighty-four,** *1949*

Ray Bradbury. **Fahrenheit 451,** *1953*

Anthony Burgess. **A Clockwork Orange,** *1962*

Margaret Atwood. **The Handmaid's Tale,** *1985*

WAR, HOLOCAUST, TOTALITARIANISM

Arnold Toynbee. **Armenian Atrocities: The Murder of a Nation,** *1915*

John Reed. **Ten Days That Shook the World,** *1919*

Siegfried Sassoon. **The War Poems,** *1919*

Jaroslav Hašek. **Osudy dobrého vojáka Svejkā za svêtové války [The Good Soldier Schweik],** *1920–23*

Adolf Hitler. **Mein Kampf,** *1925*

Erich Maria Remarque. **Im Westen nichts Neues [All Quiet on the Western Front],** *1928*

Anna Akhmatova. **Rekviem [Requiem],** *1935–40*

Ernest Hemingway. **For Whom the Bell Tolls,** *1940*

Arthur Koestler. **Darkness at Noon,** *1941*

John Hersey. **Hiroshima,** *1946*

Anne Frank. **Het Achterhuis [The Diary of a Young Girl],** *1947*

Winston Churchill. **The Gathering Storm,** *1948*

Mao Zedong. **Quotations from Chairman Mao,** *1966*

Dee Alexander Brown. **Bury My Heart at Wounded Knee: An Indian History of the American West,** *1970*

Aleksandr I. Solzhenitsyn. **The Gulag Archipelago, 1918–1956: An Experiment in Literary Investigation,** *1973*

Michael Herr. **Dispatches,** *1977*

Art Spiegelman. **Maus: A Survivor's Tale, 2 vols.,** *1986–91*

OPTIMISM, JOY, GENTILITY

Sarah Orne Jewett. **The Country of the Pointed Firs,** *1896*

Helen Keller. **The Story of My Life,** *1903*

G. K. Chesterton. **The Innocence of Father Brown,** *1911*

Juan Ramón Jiménez. **Platero y Yo [Platero and I: An Andalusian Elegy],** *1914*

George Bernard Shaw. **Pygmalion,** *1914*

Emily Post. **Etiquette in Society, in Business, in Politics, and at Home,** *1922*

P. G. Wodehouse. **The Inimitable Jeeves,** *1923*

A. A. Milne. **Winnie-the-Pooh,** *1926*

Willa Cather. **Shadows on the Rock,** *1931*

Irma S. Rombauer. **The Joy of Cooking: A Compilation of Reliable Recipes with a Casual Culinary Chat,** *1931*

J. R. R. Tolkien. **The Hobbit,** *1937*

Margaret Wise Brown. **Goodnight Moon,** *1947*

Harper Lee. **To Kill a Mockingbird,** *1960*

Langston Hughes. **The Best of Simple,** *1961*

Elizabeth Bishop. **The Complete Poems, 1927-1979,** *1983*

Source: Reprinted with permission of The New York Public Library.

ALUMNI PERKS

KEEP LEARNING TO STAY YOUNG

Your alma mater may offer nifty opportunities, so take advantage

Whether you donned cap and gown decades ago or received your hard-earned diploma only a few years back, your alma mater may very well have a host of services—both educational and practical—that would interest you. While certain benefits are limited to alumni, many programs are open to alumni and friends, so pester those you know about what their alma mater can offer you, as well as ringing up your own.

Across the country, colleges and universities are offering a wide variety of "lifelong learning" opportunities that range from weekend seminars to evening lectures given by a current professor, to correspondence courses via the Internet or with mailed materials, to trips around the world, accompanied by a professor. The number and variety of offerings, of course, depend on the size of the school. Oberlin College, for example, offers only four trips per year, with a professor in tow to give lectures. In 1996 destinations included South Africa, accompanied by a political science professor, and Greece.

Larger schools, however, are able to offer a much wider variety of programs. Stanford and Yale both operate over 50 travel programs per year and the University of Texas, over 90. One of Stanford's most popular offerings is the Stanford Summer Sierra Camp, a week-long camp for alums and their families in the Sierra Nevada. The camp is run by current Stanford students and offers a wide range of recreational activities for parents and children alike. While the camp has a more recreational bent, most travel programs offered through alumni associations have an educational draw—a professor who accompanies travelers and gives lectures throughout. Judy Coles, Director of University Relations for Yale University, cites three of Yale's most popular trips as: the Memphis-to-New Orleans cruise on the famed *Delta Queen*, with noted scholar of the American West Howard Lamar; Waterways of Russia; and a week-long London Theater Seminar, in which participants attend the theater in the evenings and devote the mornings to attending lectures and engaging in discussions of what they have seen.

While such treks may be a preferred and luxurious way to learn, many alumni associations offer educational opportunities to those who cannot fit such a trip into their schedules or budgets. These range from one-day seminars in cities across the country, to taped lectures by distinguished professors, to week-long "summer colleges." Many schools will package a series of lectures—either video, audio, or written—by a given professor with suggested reading material and discussion questions. They encourage their alumni to organize a group of people to meet once a month, work through the syllabus, and discuss the lectures and readings. Often, the association will then send the professor to the last meeting of the said "class" to conduct the discussion. For universities, this is an important way to keep alumni connected with the school and with its professors.

Distance education via the Internet is another area in which alumni associations are experimenting. Andy Shaindlin, Associate Director/Director of Alumni Education Programs for Brown University, created the first alumni online course offering. He explains that it is similar to a local chapter's miniclass—a series of lectures, readings, and discussions—except that everything takes place online. Many associations are in a development phase in this area, but it's worth looking into as you can be in Manhattan or Madagascar and still enroll in the course.

On the more practical side of things, your alumni association may offer useful benefits, such as life or temporary medical insurance, home loans, discounts on long distance service, and a credit card. All of these should be carefully looked into before signing up. Not that your alma mater is purely mercenary, but alumni associations do have to generate a certain amount of money to operate. The degree to which this is true varies from school to school, as certain associations are completely financially independent and others receive some school funding. At Stanford University, for example, members must pay a membership fee to be part of the Alumni Association, and thus eligible for programs and benefits. This fee ranges from $50 annually to $450 for life membership (for individuals who graduated over five years ago). Other colleges and universities automatically enroll their graduates in the alumni association, thus enabling them to be eligible for certain benefits. Free enrollment does not mean one should not read the fine print when it comes to offerings such as credit cards and loans. The credit card, for example, may not be such a great deal for you, but as you spend dollars, a certain percentage goes to the alumni association.

While some of the programs and benefits offered by schools and their alumni offices are limited to alums of that school, many are not. Beyond looking to a friend or spouse's alma mater for exciting lectures and trips, you should be aware of what universities in your area with which you may have no affiliation have to offer you. Stanford's association, for example, administers programs targeted to individuals outside the Stanford family. These include professional education classes in middle and high level management, marketing, and publishing, as well as the Stanford Instructional Television Network, a closed circuit television lecture system targeted to engineering professionals in the Silicon Valley.

LATER LIFE

SEE YOU AROUND THE CAMPUS

Retiring alums and faculty are choosing their old college towns

Many Americans now consider moving into a retirement community as part of their life plan, just as much as getting married, buying a house, and having children. Increasingly, the destination retirees are choosing is the place they spent their "wild days"—college.

In the last 10 years, more than 50 retirement communities from Charlottesville, Va., to Minneapolis, Minn., have opened in college towns, and experts expect that number to increase four-fold in the next decade. While some of these communities are affiliated with a particular school and open only to that school's alumni and former faculty, others are open to anyone interested in the lifestyle of a campus town. Such an arrangement has tremendous draws for both the potential residents and the college, says Patti O'Neil of the Marriott Corporation, whose retirement communities throughout the nation include the Colonnades, which is affiliated with the University of Virginia.

To explain the appeal of a college-based retirement center, one need only consider why people fear getting old and why certain communities have negative associations, says O'Neil. As one 92-year-old Houston woman who is not in a retirement home explains, "I don't want to be surrounded by a bunch of boring, lackluster old people!" Knowing they will be surrounded by others who have a similar educational background, are likely to have led interesting lives, and still maintain their interest in intellectual and social pursuits makes the choice to live in a college-based retirement community desirable to many.

The best of the university-centered retirement centers provide not only a pretty place to live and excellent health care facilities, but a stimulating environment. The calendar can include everything from basketball games to French farces to lectures by leading intellectuals. There is usually access to other school facilities, such as libraries, and, in the case of the Colonnades at the University of Virginia, a golf course, too.

In addition, residents are able to take or audit university classes, as well as organize classes among themselves by arranging for a professor from the school to teach. Close proximity and discounted rates give you another chance to learn Chinese or take that Latin American history course that you always regretted skipping when you were young. And if your group is embarking on a trip to Greece, you can bring in a professor to teach conversational Greek and a course on Socrates if you wish.

Colleges also view the close existence of a group of former students a plus. Catering to the needs of their students throughout a lifetime engenders a loyalty that serves a college well—both financially and otherwise. Active and satisfied alumni are ones who will not only help their alma mater and its students while they are active, but may even remember their schools in their wills.

The cost of such stimulating living communities varies greatly. You may be asked to pay a membership fee that can range from $50,000 to over $250,000. Monthly fees for services such as food, transportation, and cleaning can range from $1,000 to over $3,000. Sometimes the monthly fees are a fixed rate for all services, but charging residents for only what they use is increasingly common. In still other cases, residents are charged a straight rental fee plus a flat monthly charge for services used.

EXPERT PICKS

THE BEST CAMPUS RETIREMENT COMMUNITIES

Dr. Leon Pastalan, Professor of Architecture and Urban Planning at the University of Michigan and co-editor of University Linked Retirement Communities *(Haworth Press, 1994), recommends the following university- and college-affiliated retirement communities. Communities associated with universities are likely to offer many more services. Many universities, for instance, have medical schools and hospitals close at hand.*

UNIVERSITY-AFFILIATED RETIREMENT COMMUNITIES

■ **Meadowwood at the University of Indiana**
Bloomington, IN
☎812-336-7060

■ **The Colonnades at the University of Virginia**
Charlottesville, VA
☎703-448-8983

■ **University of Minnesota Retirees Association**
Minneapolis, MN
☎ 612-625-4700

COLLEGE-AFFILIATED RETIREMENT COMMUNITIES

■ **Henton at Elon**
Elon College, NC
☎910-584-4410

■ **Kendel at Oberlin College**
Oberlin, OH
☎216-775-0094

■ **College Harbor at Eckerd College**
St. Petersburg, FL
☎813-866-3124

POPULAR COLLEGE RETIREMENT TOWNS

■ **Burlington, Vermont**
(University of Vermont)

■ **Ft. Collins, Colorado**
(Colorado State University)

■ **Oxford, Mississippi**
(University of Mississippi)

■ **State College, Pennsylvania**
(Penn. State University)

■ **Corvallis, Oregon**
(Oregon State University)

CHAPTER FIVE

CAREERS

EXPERT QUOTES

"If your industry is hell-bent on downsizing into a broom closet, you need to ask yourself, 'What is my future?'"

—Nuala Beck, head of an employment consulting firm
Page 334

"When you're in a position of leadership, those under your supervision should always be working with you, not for you."

—John Wooden, UCLA's legendary basketball coach
Page 362

"If you're looking for a job, one thing to keep in mind is to never take a headhunter's call raw."

—Gerard Roche, one of corporate America's leading headhunters
Page 367

■ **THE YEAR AHEAD: SEEK OUT** jobs that take advantage of new technologies... **EXPECT** downsizing to continue... **DON'T COUNT** on a big raise, unless you're a CEO... **WATCH OUT** as companies squeeze employee benefits... **SEARCH** for the internships of your dreams... **LEARN** the new rules of success from Generation X... **SEARCH** cyberspace to find a new job... **DON'T ANSWER** every question in a job interview... **BEWARE** of brutal bosses... **DO** your homework before starting your own business... **THINK TWICE** before giving your boss a Christmas gift...

GETTING STARTED 334

PAY & PERKS 349

SMART MOVES 362

GETTING STARTED

EXPERT LIST: The 30 fastest-growing professions, PAGE 337 **THE GLASS CEILING:** The top career tracks for women, PAGE 338 **INTERNSHIPS:** From the set of *Baywatch* to the Coors Brewery, PAGE 340 **STRATEGIES:** A Generation Xer's guide to success, PAGE 342 **TESTS:** Psychological profiles can help the clueless find a job, PAGE 344 **JOB HUNTING:** Forget the classifieds, try cyberspace, PAGE 346 **INTERVIEWS:** What you can and can't be asked, PAGE 348

OUTLOOK

WHERE THE BEST JOBS WILL BE

The so-called "knowledge" professions will be hot in the 21st century

Ring out the old economy and welcome the new one. That's the message economists, management consultants, and career counselors are espousing these days. In their view, the economy is going through some fundamental changes. Indeed, many argue that the changes will be as fundamental as those brought on by the Industrial Revolution. And workers will have to adapt or suffer the consequences. The best jobs for the future, says Nuala Beck, who heads her own employment consulting firm in Toronto and is the author of *Shifting Gears* (HarperCollins, 1992), which identifies the changes in the modern economic environment, will be in the "knowledge" professions: computers, biotechnology, and health care. Companies in these areas are most likely to offer the most competitive salaries and the best possibilities for advancement. Here's Beck's analysis of the developments that will shape the workplace of the future.

■ What are the job trends for the 21st century?

When you look at industries that have a future in the new economy, there are signposts that people looking for a job should read. The clear engines of growth in this new economy are smart industries, which depend on highly skilled workers. Smart industries outperform those in the traditional manufacturing sector. As a result, the nature of work, where we work, how we work, the tools of our trade, if you will, are also changing as we move from an old economy into a new economy.

■ Are the current economic changes substantially different from those that occurred earlier in this century?

It is important to recognize that there is nothing new about the fact that new economies replace old economies. If you go back to the era of the Industrial Revolution, it was driven by important engines of growth: railroads, coal, steel, and textiles. That era has evolved into a mass-manufacturing era, which began in 1918 and was driven by whole new engines of growth—autos, housing, retailing, and mighty machine tool industries. But the mass-manufacturing era ended in 1981, after one oil shock too many.

The new economy is not based on mass manufacturing; it's based on information technology. And in this new economy, there are four major engines of growth. Engine one is computers and semiconductors; engine two is health and medical technology; engine three is communications and telecommunications; and engine four is instrumentation, which also includes robotics. These are the industry sectors of the economy that are leading the way forward, so it should come as no surprise that the new jobs are in these areas and in the industries that serve as suppliers to the new engines.

■ What are the signs that a particular industry is not going to adjust well to the new economy?

Although you should not focus so much on whether a company is downsizing, it is a telling sign. A lot of companies think that it is a lot easier to go backward than forward. What they're basically telling you is, we have no way to grow in the present time. We don't have the slightest notion of how we're going to grow. If they looked at the amount they spent on buyouts, think of how much they could have spent on growth.

If your industry is hell-bent on downsizing into a broom closet, you need to ask yourself, "What is my future?" There are scores

EXPERT PICKS

Here are the job creators with the highest percentage of knowledge workers (professionals, engineers, scientists, technicians, etc.), the industries where the best jobs will be in the future.

- **Home health care**
- **Motion picture production**
- **Offices of optometrists, etc.**
- **Community-based care services**
- **Child day care**
- **Computer software**
- **Veterinary services**
- **Management, public relations**
- **Cable and pay TV**
- **Elementary, secondary schools**

SOURCE: Nuala Beck & Associates.

■ SIGNS OF THE TIMES

Are you in a growing or declining occupation? The following numbers cover the number of jobs created or lost in various fields from January 1990 through June 1995.

Industry	Jobs Created or lost (1,000s)
■ THE TOP 20 INDUSTRIES FOR JOBS	
Temp and full-time employment agencies	899
Restaurants and bars	738
Local government administration	359
Hospitals	345
Recreation (health clubs, casinos, etc.)	344
Home health care	339
Nursing and personal care	310
Medical doctors' offices	290
Computer software	255
State government administration	228
Trucking and parcel delivery	222
Business services (security, drafting, etc.)	204
Residential care (rehab centers, etc.)	195
Management consulting, public relations	179
Social services	166
Offices of optometrists, podiatrists, etc.	144
Child day care	136
Grocery stores	133
Motion picture production	127
Elementary and secondary schools	106
■ THE 20 WORST INDUSTRIES FOR JOBS	
Aircraft and parts	–251
Savings institutions	–184
Search and navigation equipment	–128
Computer hardware	–116
Missiles, space vehicles, and parts	–90
Women's clothing stores	–83
Variety stores	–66
Commercial banks	–63
Residential construction	–60
Women's clothing manufacturing	–58
Railroads	–51
Machinery wholesalers	–48
Electronic components	–47
Masonry, stonework, and plastering	–47
Federal government manufacturing	–44
Instrumentation	–44
Subdividers and developers	–42
State hospitals	–42
Petroleum wholesalers	–41
Steel mills	–39

SOURCE: Nuala Beck & Associates.

of industries where it doesn't matter how good you are at what you do. It doesn't matter how great your skills are, or whether you graduated at the top of your class, how long you've been on the job, or how loyal you've been. When the ship starts to sink, it doesn't do any good to sit by the railing.

■ Are there ways to avoid becoming a victim of downsizing?

If you are in an industry that's downsizing like mad, you have two options: You can stay right where you are and play the odds that the person sitting beside you will get axed but you won't. Or you can take your skills and transport yourself into an industry that is growing.

If you pick an industry with a future, the job can change, the nature of the work and the company can change, but if you pick a field that has a future, you will have a future too.

■ What is the job outlook for new college graduates?

When young people of today think about their future in this age of change, they need to think about the opportunities that await them in the new economy, and I tell people, never mind the old economy. It was a world that was never your world anyway. There's something different and something better that is emerging for them.

The reason that I say something better is emerging is because of a key factor: It's a knowledge economy. In the new economy, you'll get paid to think, not just to do.

Getting a college education is not necessary. Not every young person is going to be able to or have an interest in going on to higher education. Such a person should think about becoming a driver for a medical lab. Think about becoming a bookkeeper for a software firm. There are lots of jobs for people who work on the loading dock, in distribution, in accounts receivable.

But there is no mistaking the fact that we have upped the education ante. The best advice is to train for jobs that exist.

■ How should graduates in the humanities and social sciences market themselves in the workplace?

If I had a daughter who said, "I'd love to go to college and get a B.A. in English," I'd say, "That's a wonderful idea, and you should think of becoming an editor for software manuals." It isn't what young people study. It's where they apply what they've learned. If someone would love to get a B.A. in English, he or she should do it, but then when the time comes, he or she should apply it to an industry that has a real future.

FACT FILE:

YOU'RE IN THE WRONG JOB IF...

Economist Nuala Beck says these are some of the telltale signs that a company won't make it in the "new" economy:

- *If the decor is some variation of avocado green and orange, the last time the company could afford to paint the place was 20 years ago.*
- *When you ask what systems are in place to protect against viruses and you're sent to the company nurse.*
- *If the hallways feature plaques commemorating the history of the company. The employer is dedicated to the past, not the future.*
- *If you hear lots of R words—like restructuring, refinancing, retirement, and reorganization.*
- *When there are more vice presidents than there are lead hands on the factory floor.*

EXPERT LIST

THE 30 FASTEST-GROWING PROFESSIONS

The best job opportunities often are not where the most jobs are, but instead where the most growth is. Explosive growth in a relatively small pool indicates an industry in need of a rapid infusion of labor. Overall, the projected rate of growth will be much slower than it has been in years past. From 1983 to 1994, total employment grew 24 percent, but projected growth for 1994–2005 is only 13.9 percent.

The service-producing industries will be unaffected by this sluggish growth. The aging U.S. population and medical advances will create a boom for health-care services, which will account for almost one-fifth of all job growth from 1994 to 2005. Also, there will be growth in the computer science and systems analysis fields. The following numbers from the U.S. Bureau of Labor Statistics show the 30 professions expected to experience the fastest growth between 1994 and 2005.

CHANGE IN EMPLOYMENT 1994–2005

Occupation	Jobs in 1994	Anticipated % change	Anticipated no. of new jobs
Homemaker–home health aides	598,000	107	640,000
Computer scientists and systems analysts	828,000	91	755,000
Physical therapy assistants and aides	78,000	83	64,000
Occupational therapy assistants and aides	16,000	82	13,000
Physical therapists	102,000	80	81,000
Human services workers	168,000	75	125,000
Services sales representatives	612,000	72	441,000
Occupational therapists	54,000	72	39,000
Medical assistants	206,000	59	121,000
Paralegals	111,000	58	64,000
Medical record technicians	81,000	56	45,000
Special education teachers	388,000	53	206,000
Correctional officers	310,000	51	158,000
Operations research analysts	44,000	50	22,000
Guards	867,000	48	415,000
Speech-language pathologists and audiologists	85,000	46	39,000
Private detectives and investigators	55,000	44	24,000
Surgical technologists	46,000	43	19,000
Dental assistants	190,000	42	79,000
Dental hygienists	127,000	42	53,000
General office clerks	2,946,000	NA	26,000
Teacher aides	932,000	39	364,000
Securities and financial services sales representatives	246,000	37	90,000
Emergency medical technicians	138,000	36	49,000
Respiratory therapists	73,000	36	26,000
Management analysts and consultants	231,000	35	82,000
Radiologic technologists	167,000	35	59,000
Employment interviewers	77,000	35	27,000
Social workers	557,000	34	187,000
Preschool teachers and child-care workers	1 million+	33	358,000
Restaurant and food service managers	526,500	33	192,000

SOURCE: U.S. Bureau of Labor Statistics.

EXPERT PICKS

THROUGH THE GLASS CEILING

Our expert picks the top career tracks for women

Women make up 46 percent of the workforce, but they still are largely absent from the top executive ranks of most major corporations. In fact, there's only one woman CEO in the Fortune 500 companies—Marion Sandler at Golden West Financial. That doesn't mean there haven't been breakthroughs. In some fields the gains have been remarkable either because women are attracted to those fields or there are fewer barriers to advancement or a combination of both. For the last five years until she resigned as editor of *Working Woman* magazine in mid-1996, Lynn Povich has been surveying the landscape. Each year, the magazine publishes listings of the hottest careers for women. Here's Povich's assessment of fields where women have made the most progress and other potential targets for success.

■ **BATTLE OF THE SEXES**

The average weekly salaries of men and women in different fields:

OCCUPATION	MALE	FEMALE
College and university teachers	$894	$689
Computer scientists	$879	$724
Elementary school teachers	$666	$586
Farm workers	$248	$232
General office supervisors	$730	$504
Insurance adjusters	$672	$414
Physicians	$1,186	$885
Police and detectives	$645	$576
Secretaries and typists	$399	$385
Truck drivers	$449	$331

SOURCE: *The American Workforce: 1992–2005*, U.S. Bureau of Labor Statistics, 1994.

■ **WOMEN-OWNED BUSINESS.** A lot of women are leaving larger companies to either start their own businesses or work for smaller companies. Many women are finding the corporate culture at larger companies so hostile that, after working for 15 years or so, they leave to start up their own companies. Women-run businesses are starting up twice as fast as men-run businesses, and the revenue growth of women-owned firms is much faster.

■ **FRANCHISES.** One of the big booms for women in franchises is business financial services, as well as franchises that cater to women with children—everything from maternity clothes and play centers to taxi shuttle services for kids. Health care and nondurable manufacturing (plastic, rubber, and leather products; printing and publishing) are also strong choices.

■ **SPECIALTY MEDICINE.** In medicine, the big specialties right now are obstetrician-gynecologists and fertility doctors (who study the causes of infertility). More women are expressing a preference for going to female doctors (especially OB-GYNs), and at the same time more women are choosing to go into that specialty. Women make up nearly 20 percent of all fertility doctors. Another hot area: genetic counseling.

■ **LAW.** Women are making headway as specialized attorneys—especially in elder law (lawyers who work specifically with older clients) and the broader field of health law. These fields are tied strongly into the baby boomers, who are thinking earlier about the well-being of their parents, their own retirement, and health issues that may arise down the road.

What we know about women is that they don't like those sort of corporate-hostile takeover lawyer jobs, and so there are a lot more women in intellectual property law—which has to do with protecting your name online or protecting your name if you're creating new products, like those in biotechnology. Biotechnology patent attorneys, for example, do research into the creation of new drugs—sometimes from natural sources

NINE CUTTING-EDGE JOBS FOR WOMEN

Each year, Working Woman *magazine compiles a report on the hottest careers for women. Here's the 1995 list of jobs on the cutting edge.*

JOB	$ Salary	✔ Women's Appeal
BIOETHICIST	Entry for philosophy prof, $35K; medical and law faculty, $60K–$100K.	*Universities and hospitals offer good perks and benefits.*
BIOLOGIST	With bachelor's, median $22K; with master's, median $28K; with PhD., median $55K.	*Better record for women in top management than many sciences.*
COMPUTER-SOFTWARE ENGINEER	Entry, $31K–$50K; supervisory engineer, $55K–75K; top, $61K–$91K.	*Huge growth but still male-dominated.*
ENVIRONMENTAL MANAGER	Entry, $28K–$35K; midlevel, $40K–$70K; top, $60K–$130K.	*AT&T, Du Pont, Exxon, and IBM are among the companies with environmental engineers and good hiring and promoting records for women.*
FERTILITY SPECIALIST	Average, $80K for academics; $181K for practicing doctors.	*Opportunities for job sharing and flexible hours in private practice.*
INFORMATION-SYSTEMS MANAGER	Average: manager, $44K; director of IS operations, $66K; VP, $93K.	*Room for working off-hours or off-site. Women increasingly being recruited.*
MULTIMEDIA MANAGER	Average, $50K+.	*Done on a project-by-project basis, allowing some flexible scheduling.*
PHARMACOECONOMIST	$60K–$200K.	*No discernible wage gap. Few women in academic and administrative posts.*
UTILITIES-MARKETING MANAGER	Entry, $25K; supervisor, $37K–$56K; marketing manager, $52K–$80K.	*Women should gain foothold with shift from tech to business.*

SOURCE: *Working Woman* magazine.

like the rain forests, sometimes chemically—then help with the related patenting issues.

■ **PHYSICAL THERAPY AND REHABILITATION.** Women have always been drawn to this field, but now more and more are getting involved with the rehabilitation of both older folks and aging baby boomers who are having knee or back problems and related ailments.

■ **FINANCIAL SERVICES.** More financial service companies want women to sell to women to bring in women. If you're a brokerage firm or a bank and you want to reach out to women, it's better to have your salesperson or your broker be a woman.

■ **TELECOMMUNICATIONS MARKETING.** The telecommunications business is expanding, and the computer and the TV businesses are also going into telecommunications. They're all going to need marketing, an area women happen to be very skilled in. Marketing is a field where there has been less discrimination in the past, and women have been let into the pipeline. The strongest marketing companies have been home products companies like Procter & Gamble and food companies like General Foods and Kraft. Since the buyers of those products are women, those companies have always trained a lot of women.

■ **SOFTWARE DEVELOPMENT.** It has traditionally been difficult for women to get into the harder sciences, but as computer software goes mainstream, there are a lot more women involved in content development as technical writers and online content writers. Companies are realizing they need people who can communicate clearly, not just "techies."

■ **EXECUTIVE RECRUITING.** Companies looking for women to fill positions need to have recruiters who know where the qualified women are, so a lot more women are filling these recruiting slots.

EXPERT LIST

THE INTERNSHIPS OF YOUR DREAMS

Sure, you can work as an intern at a place where you might dream of having a career, and that's not such a bad idea. A recent survey by Northwestern University found that 26 percent of those hired by a variety of corporations had been interns—up from 17 percent in 1993. But an internship can also be an excuse to try something just for fun, or to work in an environment that seems glamorous or otherwise unreachable. Mark Oldman and Samer Hamadeh, co-authors of America's Top Internships *(Villard Books, 1995) and* The Internship Bible *(Random House, 1995) have compiled a list of "dream" internships. Here are 10 of their top picks, along with contact addresses. Usually it's better to write or fax first, and follow up with a call.*

BAYWATCH

■ **THE JOB:** The TV show offers a 16- to 22-week internship to three or four interns a year to work in production, casting, and editing.

■ **THE REWARDS:** There's no stipend, although for many, soaking in the atmosphere of the set will be compensation enough. Perks include invitations to company parties and the chance to attend production meetings.

✏Internship Coordinator
The Baywatch Production Co.
Berk, Schwartz, Bonann Productions
5433 Beethoven Street
Los Angeles, CA 90066
☎310–302–9199 (Fax)

BUCKINGHAM PALACE

■ **THE JOB:** Built in 1703, the Palace is an internship site for 140 young people each summer, including three to five U.S. citizens, to work for eight weeks as "wardens" in security, ticket office, state rooms, and gift shops when the rooms are open to the public.

■ **THE REWARDS:** Interns are paid 200 pounds a week (about $350) plus free lunch daily. They also receive a 20 percent discount on souvenirs in the gift shop.

✏Visitor Office
Buckingham Palace
London, England SW1A 1AA
☎44–171–930–4832

COORS BREWING COMPANY

■ **THE JOB:** The brewery accepts 20–40 interns a year for a 9- to 12-week program. In the past, interns have worked in purchasing, engineering, project management, accounting, biology/microbiology, telecommunications, recreation, and journalism/public relations.

■ **THE REWARDS:** Undergraduate interns earn $390–$430 per week. Graduates earn $390–$580 a week. There's a company store where interns can receive discounts on beer (if they are of legal drinking age) and discounted logo items.

✏Coors Brewing Company
311 Tenth Street
Mail No. NH210
c/o College Recruiting Representative
Golden, CO 80401

DALLAS COWBOYS

■ **THE JOB:** The football organization accepts 16 interns each year. Internships last 10–14 weeks and run summer, fall, and spring. Interns work in public relations, marketing, television, sales and promotion, and the ticket office.

■ **THE REWARDS:** Interns get a paltry $300–$500 stipend but also free Cowboys paraphernalia and invitations to social events.

✏Internship Coordinator
Dallas Cowboys
1 Cowboys Parkway
Irving, TX 75063
☎214–556–9900
☎214–556–9970 (Fax)

FORTY ACRES AND A MULE

■ **THE JOB:** Director Spike Lee named his film company after the promise made to freed black slaves by Union General William T. Sherman at the conclusion of the Civil War. He

■ **EXPERT LIST**

hires 15 interns each year; interns work 8–11 weeks each—but only when the company is shooting a film.

■ **THE REWARDS:** No pay, but interns receive a discount on film merchandise, attend a number of parties, occasionally work as extras, and have the chance to mingle with the stars.

✏Forty Acres and a Mule Filmworks, Inc.
Internship Program
124 De Kalb Avenue
Brooklyn, NY 11217
☎718–624–3703

JIM HENSON PRODUCTIONS

■ **THE JOB:** The place Miss Piggy calls home selects 25 interns each year to work 12–16 weeks during the summer, fall, and spring. Interns work in the studio, consumer products, design services, production accounting, and public relations.

■ **THE REWARDS:** No pay, but interns attend studio tapings, enjoy a friendly workplace, and schmooze with the Muppets.

✏Internship Coordinator
Jim Henson Productions
117 East 69th Street
New York, NY 10021
☎ 212–794–2400
☎ 212–988–3112 (Fax)

THE LATE SHOW WITH DAVID LETTERMAN

■ **THE JOB:** The Late Show selects 30 interns yearly to fill 14- to 16-week internships during the fall, spring, and summer. Interns might work in talent, research, production, writing, music, or assist the Pet and Human Trick Coordinator. Be forewarned: the busywork quotient here is high.

■ **THE REWARDS:** No pay, but perks include free Late Show paraphernalia, occasional opportunities to perform in one of the show's skits, and the chance to chat up celebrities and, occasionally, Dave himself.

✏Internship Coordinator
Late Show with David Letterman
1697 Broadway
New York, NY 10019
☎ 212–975–5300

NIKE

■ **THE JOB:** The athletic shoe empire hires 15 applicants each year to fill 10-week summer internships. Interns work in a variety of divisions, including marketing, finance/accounting, and customer service.

■ **THE REWARDS:** Pay is $320 per week. Interns also get to enjoy the benefits associated with Nike's 75-acre Nike World Campus. Every Thursday there is an afternoon party for employees.

✏Internship Program
Nike
One Bowerman Drive
Beaverton, OR 97005
☎ 503–671–6453

PEGGY GUGGENHEIM COLLECTION

■ **THE JOB:** The art museum accepts 90 interns each year to fill 4- to 12-week internships. Interns open and close the galleries, sell catalogs and tickets, check bags, staff the checkroom, help administrative staff, and assist with special events.

■ **THE REWARDS:** Interns get the equivalent of $650–$800 a month, participate in discussions, lectures, and field trips and are invited to attend the Venice Biennale, the world's oldest art event.

✏Studentship Coordinator
Peggy Guggenheim Collection
Dursoduro 701
30123 Venezia, Italy
☎ 39–41–520–6288

POLO RALPH LAUREN

■ **THE JOB:** The fashion and home furnishings company selects 12 interns each year to fill 8- to 12-week internships in the summer, fall, winter, and spring. Interns are placed in New York in the public relations, advertising, and design departments, or in New Jersey in the production or finance departments.

■ **THE REWARDS:** Interns are not paid, but each is assigned a mentor and gets to have two luncheons with company executives, including the chairman.

✏Internship Coordinator
Polo Ralph Lauren
650 Madison Avenue
New York, NY 10022
☎ 212–318–7000

SOURCE: *The Princeton Review Student Access Guide: The Internship Bible,* 1996 Edition and *The Princeton Review Student Access Guide: America's Top Internships,* 1996 Edition.

STRATEGIES

A SLACKER'S GUIDE TO GETTING AHEAD

A Generation Xer tells you how to succeed in the Nasty Nineties

Slackers, for those of you who don't know, is the pejorative sobriquet for the twentysomethings that have been pouring into the workplace. According to the stereotype, these Gen Xers lack the drive and ambition that it takes to succeed. They're strictly 9-to-5ers who split right from the office to the brew pub or the couch in front of the TV set.

But, it turns out that so-called slackers may be misdiagnosed. According to a recent Roper Starch Worldwide survey on retirement attitudes, it seems that slackers may be more mindful about saving than the Baby Boomers, who are pointing the finger at them. And in other ways, slackers may be more suited for today's career realities than others.

> **FACT FILE:**
>
> **RÉSUMÉ ROULETTE**
>
> ■ *Number of résumés received by AT&T each year:* **1 million.** *Number of résumés received by Apple Computer each week:* **3,000.** *Number of résumés received each week by large companies:* **1,000.**
>
> ■ *Amount of time human resource managers say they spend reading most résumés:* **30 seconds to 4 minutes.**
>
> Source: *The Washington Post.*

"We've seen our parents put in 80-hour weeks, hit middle age, get laid off and divorced," Bradley G. Richardson, the twentysomething author of *Jobsmarts for Twentysomethings* (Vintage Books, 1995), told *The Wall Street Journal* recently. "We've seen what blind loyalty can do."

Richardson himself was just a college kid with no drive and mediocre grades when his father's company went bankrupt. Those unfortunate circumstances forced him into debt and a reality check. He got a good job in the high-tech industry upon graduation, but after writing his book quit in 1995 to form his own consulting firm in Plano, Texas. That's one of the new maxims of success in the '90s: You can't be afraid to quit and try something totally new. Here, Richardson describes some other slacker success strategies.

STRATEGY #1: JUST DO IT. The workplace has changed a great deal, and companies are no longer going to come to you. Campus recruiting is way down, and you have to be a lot more creative about finding a job. One of my favorite quotes is: "Whatever you want to do, or dream you can, begin it." Just shut up and do it. That's great initial advice for anyone.

STRATEGY #2: GET A LIFE. I grew up in west Texas, where we had these really corny high school coaches who were always saying, "You've got to set some goals, son." But it's really true. When you tell someone what you want to do, you can be held accountable. You're either going to do it or you're going to look stupid. Writing things out is also great. One day when I was working in high-tech, I was thinking about where I wanted to be and how I wasn't there yet. I pulled out a piece of paper and started brainstorming on everything I wanted to do—no matter how unrealistic. Now I look at that list about once a year—with things on it like, "I want to own a beach house" and "I want to own a company someday"—and about half of them have already happened.

STRATEGY #3: NETWORK, NETWORK, NETWORK. Almost 80 percent of all jobs are found through some kind of connection or relationship. A lot of young people think networking means being some cheesy insurance or car salesman, or using your friends to be political. That's not it. People hire people they know and trust, pure and simple A lot of it is simply making your goals, needs, wants, and options available to people. I've read about someone in a newspaper, then called and done business with him just by saying I saw the story. Never underestimate who your friends, your parents, or your parents' friends may know, and always treat secretaries and assistants like gold. They're often your best way into a company.

STRATEGY #4: TREAT FINDING A JOB LIKE A FULL-TIME JOB. Sending out 500 résumés and waiting for the phone to ring is not a job search. Employers don't know you; it's up to you to make yourself known. Set up your house as an office, setting specific times to write letters, make follow-up calls, and be available. It sounds corny, but it creates a mind-set. Don't sit around in your boxers and baseball cap making business calls. Treat it like a job.

STRATEGY #5: READ THE TRADES, SURF THE NET. If you want to be a professional, start thinking, acting, and reading like a professional right now—before you get there. If you're trying to get a job with Reebok, don't wait until you get the job before you start checking out the footwear industry, learning which athletes are endorsing which shoes, and reading the trade journals. Most articles and stories quote executives. Learn who they are, then contact them. Surf the Net. There is so much information available on the Internet about companies now, there is no excuse why you can't do your homework before an interview.

STRATEGY #6: FIND SOME SOUL MATES. It's healthy to have some people who know what you're going through and can identify with and support you. When you come back from a great interview, they can be happy for you, and when you're dejected and have had some doors slammed in your face, they can pick you up.

STRATEGY #7: TANGIBLE RESULTS ARE WHAT COUNTS. What speaks to employers in virtually any business are tangible results in numbers and figures. If you waited tables to work your way through school, did you train new staff members? That's a leadership skill you can take to employers. If you've worked in retail before, don't just put "Sales Associate—Gap," say "Sales Associate—increased sales X percent; in charge of $X worth of stock." Employers are not just interested in what you've done, but how you've done it.

STRATEGY #8: ASK QUESTIONS DURING INTERVIEWS. The worst thing you can do when an interviewer ask if you have any questions is say, "No, I think you covered everything." Always have questions, and ask them even if you know the answers. Sometimes you'll have to interview with several people at the same company, but if you ask every person the same questions, you'll get different responses—and a better idea about the job. You'll also be showing your interest.

STRATEGY #9: KEEP LEARNING. The best thing you should have learned from college is how to learn. For instance, someone 55 years old who runs a company probably started when there were no computers in the workplace, but he's survived by adapting. That's the modern work environment. It's not just your formal education; it's on-the-job training and life training. Learn a new language, learn a new skill—that's how you grow and make yourself marketable.

STRATEGY #10: TRY ANYTHING. Recent grads always worry and say, "Oh no, I don't know what I want to do!," but that's OK. Not everyone does right away. But while you're figuring it out, you can find out what you don't want. It's a process of elimination.

STRATEGY #11: INFORMATIONAL INTERVIEWS CAN BE GREAT. Find out what a person likes most about his or her job, what he or she likes least, and how he or she got started. Keep a file, and anytime you read about someone and think, "That sounds like a neat job," make a note of it and give that person a call. The more you know about everything out there, the easier it will eventually be to make your choice.

PERSONALITY TESTS

WHAT SHOULD I DO WHEN I GROW UP?

The clueless might get some clues from a psychological profile

The title of a recently published book captures the thought: *I Can Do Anything, If I Only Knew What It Was* (by Barbara Sher and Barbara Smith, Delacorte, 1994). But what is it? One way to find out is to take a personality test. The tests are becoming increasingly popular among individuals to help determine what career may best suit them. You can take them on the cheap by buying modified versions in a book. But the full-dress tests, administered by career counselors, psychologists, or psychiatrists, can cost hundreds of dollars—and produce uncertain results.

The Rorschach test, invented in the 1920s, was the first and is still widely used by psychiatrists. It is supposed to reveal an individual's underlying personality through his or her reaction to a series of inkblot designs. More popular these days are the Myers-Briggs Type Indicator and the Strong Interest Inventory. Unlike the Rorschach, both involve completing a lengthy questionnaire and attempt to gauge an individual's interests and temperament through the answers.

Until recently, personality tests were thought to be best only for individuals looking to change careers in midstream, but increasingly, the tests are being administered to people of all ages and at various stages of their lives. Some colleges are administering the tests to freshmen to help students plan their short-term and long-term goals. College career centers give the tests to graduating seniors before heading into the "real" world. In the business world, many corporations are using the tests to determine hirings (and promotions), saving the company the expense of hiring an individual whose personality does not complement the job or work environment. "These tests help people to understand what motivates them," says Irene Mendelson, a professional career counselor and president of BEMW Inc., in Bethesda, Md. "It also gets

EXPERT SOURCES

OTHER PLACES TO FIND THE REAL YOU

The perfect job probably doesn't exist but these tomes can help you find one that works for you:

WHAT COLOR IS YOUR PARACHUTE? (1996 ED.)
by Richard Bolles (Ten Speed Press).
■ This book has been a best-seller since it was first published 25 years ago. It is considered the bible for job hunters and career changers alike.

WISHCRAFT: HOW TO GET WHAT YOU REALLY WANT
by Barbara Sher (Ballantine Books, 1983).
■ The first—and some say better—book by the author of *I Can Do Anything*, it helps readers find the special interests and passions that move and motivate them.

COMPLETE JOB SEARCH HANDBOOK
by Howard Figler (Henry Holt, 1988).
■ Figler identifies 20 different skills that are crucial to successful job hunting. The author especially recommends the chapter "Zen of the Career Search," which discusses how intuition and gut-instinct play a vital role in helping individuals choose and find appropriate careers.

at the underlying issues in their lives and allows them to work and understand themselves better."

Most professionals agree that taking the test under the supervision of an accredited career counselor or psychiatrist is the best option—and the most expensive. Most of the tests cost between $200 and $300, which includes follow-up counseling sessions.

Here's a brief assessment of the two most popular tests:

■ **MYERS-BRIGGS TYPE INDICATOR (MBTI).** The most popular of the personality tests, the MBTI categorizes people based on four scales of personal preferences: extroversion-introversion, sensing-intuition, thinking-feeling, and judging-perceiving. The answers place individuals in one of 16 personality groups. Once MBTI identifies your type, a counselor will provide you a list of job fields best suited for you. The drawback of MBTI is that it's a personality, not a skills, test.

If you decide to take the test yourself, take a look at *Do What You Are*, by Paul Tieger and Barbara Barron-Tieger (Little Brown and Co., 1995). The book includes a list of careers that appeal to the different MBTI personality types.

■ **STRONG INTEREST INVENTORY.** Many counselors recommend taking this test in conjunction with Myers-Briggs. The interest inventory collects information about an individual's interests and recommends potential occupations based on work activities involved, the traits of the working environment, and personality characteristics that can affect work. Individuals are categorized by one of the six occupational types (realistic, investigative, artistic, social, enterprising, and conventional) that correspond with a list of career options. This test works best for college students or individuals with a college degree.

Before taking either test, you should contact a professional career counselor (or call the National Board for Certified Counselors ☎ 910-547-0607). Or check with the career office at a local university. Many allow students or alumni to take these tests free.

THE POWER LUNCH

A few years ago, Jonathan Karp was a twentysomething kid fresh out of Brown University working as a lowly editorial assistant at Random House and struggling to make it big in the world of publishing. Then he had a bright idea: invite Michael Korda, editor-in-chief of Simon & Schuster and author of *Power!* and *Success!* out to lunch, quiz him about how to get ahead, and then write a gushy article about the encounter for the company magazine. The gambit worked. Today, Karp, now 32, has a window office, rides in limos with the top brass, and gets to edit books, like this one. (He's also handling authors like Mario Puzo, who penned *The Godfather* and *The Last Don*.) Here are some of Korda's rules of power lunching, as recorded by Karp at the Grill Room of the Four Seasons in New York City:

■ **Tip like crazy.** Whenever you're eating, ultimately, it is the captain and the waiters who will decide whether you have a satisfactory meal, and your author or agent will go back saying, "What a suave, intelligent, capable person he or she is," or whether they will leave saying, "What a putz!"

■ **Always eat at the same restaurant.** If you eat at the same restaurant, you tip every day, and eventually your investment will pay off, because as you come in, people will say, "How nice to see you! The usual table?" It will all be smooth and seamless and perfect.

■ **If you're hosting, take guests where people will recognize you and make a fuss over you.** Because, ultimately, you're having lunch with people to run up a flag that says, "Hi. I'm attractive, ambitious, a terrific editor."

GETTING HIRED

JOB HUNTING IN CYBERSPACE

Forget the classifieds? More and more jobs are being posted online

Looking for a job is stressful enough these days, so it is nice to know that you can initiate your search from the comfort of your own home if you have a computer and modem. While most of the online services, including America Online and CompuServe, offer their own job sites and résumé posting services, the real action these days is on the World Wide Web.

The good news is that job bank sites and those offering employment advice continue to spring up with endless variety. Everyone from unemployed graduate students to large employers seem to have their own Web sites. A quick search turned up hundreds of specialized job banks targeted to academics, journalists, unemployed DJs, and agricultural laborers from British Columbia, among others. The number of jobs available can range from dozens to thousands.

Still, it's useful to remember the simple caveat that holds true for all Internet users: beware of junk. As employment sites go, anything that seems fairly selective—whether it is Crews for Cruise (for aspiring Love Boat staff) or Truck Driver's Job Directory—is probably too narrow and skimpy to be of much help to the average hunter, and unless you have unlimited free time, you should steer clear. Major sites, such as Com-

EXPERT SOURCES

WANTED: HELP FOR THE JOBLESS

New job-related Web sites appear on the Internet every day, but like everything else in cyberspace, finding the most valuable sites can be a time-consuming process. First-time surfers might want to browse a bit, but there are some good general sites that will point you toward specialized jobs and give you a broader idea of what is out there. We listed some of our favorite picks. Aim your browser at one of these sites:

AMERICA'S JOB BANK

http://www.ajb.dni.us/

■ One of the most clearly designed sites, it enables users to search job banks nationwide by category and employer. Employer listings range from Alaska's Denali National Park Resorts to the National Institutes of Health. Visitors can also access 10 state employment service Web sites and look at federal job opportunities, including the military.

CAREERPATH

http://www.careerpath.com/

■ This site connects users to the classified pages of the *Boston Globe*, *Chicago Tribune*, *Los Angeles Times*, *New York Times*, *Washington Post*, and *San Jose Mercury News*.

E-SPAN EMPLOYMENT DATABASE SEARCH

http://www.espan.com/

■ CompuServe's own personalized employment site, E-Span offers a variety of services. After registering, users have access to the site's Interactive Employment Network, with its links to job banks across the country. The Network will store information on the user's education, experience, desired salary, and geographic location. Users can post their résumés on E-Span and access other information, such as tips for interviewing.

puServe's E-Span and America's Job Bank (see the Expert Sources box on facing page) are likely to have a greater range and number of possibilities.

Before you start posting your qualifications, have a good idea of what's available in your prospective field. One good place to start: the employment site offered by the Yahoo browser *(http://www. yahoo. com/Business_and_Economy/Employment/Jobs/)*, which gives visitors a comprehensive list of more than 170 linked sites. The Companies link, for instance, sends Net cruisers to a list of 186 firms offering jobs, with descriptions of the companies; similarly, the government site lists federal departments and agencies with their openings.

Figures on the success rate of job hunts through résumé bulletin boards are hard to come by, but some experts say companies, especially those devoted to cutting-edge technology, are impressed by the initiative of job seekers who are Internet-savvy. Many services will store your résumé or help you set one up, and E-Span allows you to store a "user profile" of desired job specifications, by category, so that you can run a tailored search of its job bank every time you log on. E-Span will even e-mail you job listings matching your profile. As computer job banks develop, it will become even easier for services to forward your résumé to other job sites in your specialty.

As a rule of thumb, résumés should be short and pithy, to make them easier to skim and cheaper for prospective employers to download. Always include your e-mail address, if you have one.

In addition to offering job bank and résumé posting services, a number of the larger sites provide a range of career services, including chat areas where you can get feedback on your résumé from other job hunters, tips on writing cover letters, and updated listings of headhunters and job fairs from around the country. E-Span, CareerMosaic *(http://www. careermosaic.com/cm/)* and CWeb *(http://cww. cweb. com)* are some of the best to try. A number of sites will also refer visitors to career advisory services and books on finding employment through the Internet.

BETWEEN THE LINES

These days, with such intense competition for jobs, many classified ads may not actually be as great as they look. Of course, you can't really know what the job entails until you investigate, but it's useful to be able to translate the euphemisms. Kathryn Carmony, a writer for *Lumpen* magazine, devised a useful guide to deciphering what employers *really* mean in the classifieds. Here are excerpts:

Progressive company— *Employees get to wear jeans every other Friday*

Team player— *Must deal with dangerously territorial co-workers with rabid personalities*

Word processing skills essential— *There's a crippling case of carpal tunnel syndrome in your future*

Public Relations Receptionist Professional appearance important— *$20K/year job that requires $100K/year wardrobe*

Salary range $24,000 to $32,000— *The salary is $24,000*

Will train— *Prior conviction of a felony or two no problem*

B.A. required, master's preferred— *Must be an M.A. willing to work on a B.A.'s salary*

Civil service— *This job was filled from the inside six months ago*

Outstanding benefits package— *Health insurance*

Tons of variety!— *We took all the heinous tasks no other employee would do and rolled them into one job*

Dedicated— *You're looking at a minimum of 80 hours a week from now until we force you into early retirement*

Salary negotiable— *We'll take the lowest bidder*

Gal Friday— *Anyone who actually applies for this job deserves it*

SOURCE: Kathryn Carmony, from *Lumpen* (April 1995), 2558 W. Armitage Ave., Chicago, IL 60647.

JOB INTERVIEWS

WHAT YOU CAN'T BE ASKED

Sure, you want the job but you don't have to answer every question

Are you frequently sick? Have you ever been arrested? Do you have any addictions? Does stress sometimes affect your ability to be productive? If a job interviewer asks you any of these questions, he or she may have broken the law.

Increasingly, the job interview is becoming a legal minefield. In 1994 the Equal Employment Opportunity Commission issued 49 pages of new guidelines on how to conduct job interviews without running afoul of federal disability discrimination laws. The guidelines stemmed from the passage of the 1990 Americans with Disabilities Act (ADA), a landmark civil rights law for the country's disabled population. Employers are critical of the new guidelines, which they believe further muddy an already murky situation. The guidelines do contain some subtle distinctions. "Do you drink alcohol?" for example, is permissible. "How much alcohol do you drink per week?" is not.

An interviewer trying to put an applicant at ease by asking a few personal questions can quickly cross into forbidden territory. How a question is asked can determine whether it is permissable or not. But, in general, any question may be considered illegal if it is used to judge a candidate in a manner that is not job-related. Following is a guide to some of the questions you can and can't be asked. If you feel you've been discriminated against, you can call the Equal Employment Opportunity Commission, ☎ 800–669–4000.

CAN: Employers can ask you questions that relate specifically to your ability to perform the job with or without "reasonable accommodations." For example, if a job involves lifting weights, you may be asked whether or not you can lift those weights.

CAN'T: You can't be asked to take any medical or psychological test before being offered a job.

CAN: It is permissible to ask how many days you took off work the previous year, since the answer will not necessarily lead you to reveal any hidden disabilities.

CAN'T: You can't be asked any follow-up questions about a particular disability, even if you volunteer that you took time off from a previous job because of that disability.

CAN: You can be asked general questions about minor impairments, such as, "Do you have 20/20 vision?" If you admit your eyesight is not perfect, however, you do not have to say how bad your eyesight actually is.

CAN'T: You can't be asked about any addictions you may have.

CAN: You can be asked about illegal drug use and required to submit to drug tests. But you can only be asked about legal drug use (alcohol intake, supervised medications, etc.) if the prospective employer believes a positive drug test may have been the result of your taking prescribed medicines.

CAN'T: The results of tests you've taken to explore your honesty, taste, and habits can't be submitted to psychological analysis.

CAN: You can be asked to take a fitness test.

CAN'T: Your blood pressure or other medical tests (except tests for illegal drugs) can't be taken after a fitness test.

CAN: If a conditional offer of a job has been made, you may be required to undergo medical and psychological tests at the employer's expense. But the offer can only be withdrawn if as a result of the tests it can be proved that any disability you may have would make you incapable of carrying out the job even after "reasonable accommodations" were made.

PAY & PERKS

REALITY CHECK: Why you must earn four times your age, PAGE 350 **EXPERT TIPS:** How to ask for a raise, PAGE 351 **JOBS:** What 100 occupations pay, PAGE 353 **BENEFITS:** More options and more costs, PAGE 356 **VACATION:** Are you getting enough? PAGE 357 **EXPERT Q & A:** How to make sure your company is family-friendly, PAGE 358 **FAMILY LEAVE:** Will I get my job back? PAGE 360 **EXPERT PICKS:** The top companies for working moms, PAGE 361

SALARIES

IF YOU THINK YOU DESERVE A RAISE

Bosses are hogging the big dollars. Here's what to do to buck the trend

There are some eye-popping numbers at the top of the scorecard of what the top corporate chieftains took home in 1995 in total compensation, which includes salary, bonus, the value of restricted stock grants, gains from exercising stock options, and other long-term incentive payouts. CEO John F. Welch, Jr., of General Electric had total compensation of nearly $22 million. CEO Stanley Gault of Goodyear Tire & Rubber Co. earned $16.5 million. CEO Eckhard Pfeiffer of Compaq Computer Corp. made $16.1 million. CEO Reuben Mark of Colgate-Palmolive Co., $15.1 million. And the list, based on a compensation survey by William M. Mercer, Inc. for *The Wall Street Journal*, goes on and on. Overall, CEOs' salaries and bonuses soared 10.4 percent in 1995, reflecting a 14.2 percent gain in corporate profits.

That didn't leave much for the rest of us. Overall, U.S. wages and benefits climbed just 2.9 percent, the smallest advance in 14 years. The pay of white-collar subordinates down the hall from the CEO's corner office grew a moderate 4.2 percent. Furthermore, a Mercer survey predicts that average pay increases for 1996 will remain about level with those for 1995, No wonder millions of middle-class Americans are feeling squeezed. For most, salaries are barely keeping pace with inflation. And the outlook is for more of the same over the next few years.

The explanations for stagnating wage and benefit packages are depressingly familiar: increased domestic and foreign competition

FACT FILE:

IT PAYS TO ASK

■ *Percentage of those who have asked for a raise in their current job, and percentage of those who asked and got one:*

■ **Asked for raise**
■ **Asked and got the raise**

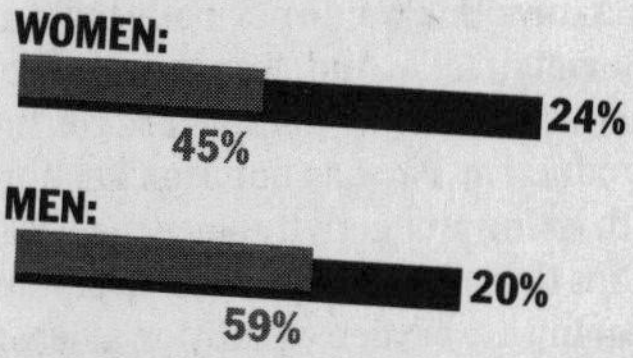

WOMEN: 24% (asked for raise); 45% (asked and got the raise)

MEN: 20% (asked for raise); 59% (asked and got the raise)

SOURCE: Lutheran Brotherhood and Louis Harris & Associates.

WHY YOU MUST EARN FOUR TIMES YOUR AGE

Maintaining a middle-class lifestyle is going to cost you

Twenty years ago, according to a popular equation, earning a thousand dollars annually for every year of your life would provide you with a comfortable middle-class lifestyle. Unfortunately, those days are long gone. Thanks to inflation and other economic changes over the past two decades, the average American now needs to earn four times his or her age to live the good life, according to *Fortune* magazine.

Fortune made its calculation by looking at two 45-year-old middle managers, Harry and Sally, as its representatives for 1975 and 1995 respectively. Each has two kids and lives in New Jersey. Harry's 1975 salary equals his age: $45,000, while Sally made the same salary adjusted for inflation up to 1995, or $127,000. While payroll taxes were higher in Harry's day, *Fortune* notes, the overall costs of maintaining a middle-class suburban existence have sped ahead of inflation in the intervening years.

Housing and education are the main culprits. Sally must spend $24,000 a year for mortgage and taxes on her $250,000 house, while Harry paid only $6,000 in 1975 on the $65,000 the house cost back then—a difference of 42 percent after inflation. Both Harry and Sally were planning to send their children to Princeton University, an investment for which Harry had to put away $8,000 annually. By contrast, Sally had to save $38,000 to meet future tuition payments. Finally, Sally is spending an additional $9,000 a year to add to her 401(k) retirement plan, plus $2,000 in annual medical premiums. Back in the 1970s, *Fortune* notes, Harry's employer picked up the entire tab for both benefits. The result of the extra cost for benefits, college, and housing? An additional $53,000 for Sally, requiring her to make close to $180,000, or four times her age, just to stay even.

■ HOW SALLY FELL BEHIND HARRY

Not only has the cost of living risen, companies aren't picking up the tab for employees' health and retirement.

	HARRY (1975)	SALLY (1995)
SALARY	$45,000	$127,000
HOUSE	$6,000	$24,000
KIDS IN COLLEGE	$8,000	$38,000
MEDICAL INSURANCE	0	$2,000
RETIREMENT	0	$9,000
DISPOSABLE	$31,000	$54,000

Sally would have to be earning almost $180,000 in 1995 dollars to have kept up with Harry.

in a fast-developing global economy; companies shifting more of the burden for rising health costs to their employees; and downsizing-induced anxiety, which tempers the wage pressures that would normally build as unemployment falls. And, ironically, wages have been stagnating as workers are getting more productive. Pay has not been keeping pace with rising productivity since the 1980s.

Perhaps it wouldn't be so bad if everyone were bearing the burden equally or, at least, if bosses weren't gobbling up so much of the pie. A recent study by Graef Crystal, a compensation expert, found the pay gap between chief executives and workers has grown from 41:1 in 1975 to 225:1 in 1994.

One way to beat the trend is to become a boss. Another option is to switch industries. Not surprisingly, industries that are booming pay better than those that aren't. High-tech fields such as computer services and telecommunications posted the highest average pay increases for 1995—5.2 percent and 4.8 percent respectively; they are expected to be the leaders once again for 1996, according to the Mercer study.

Some employers are trying to compensate for stagnant salaries by improving working

EXPERT TIPS

BEST WAYS NOT TO GET A RAISE

In this era of downsizing, the last thing most people want to do is risk their job by asking for a raise. While it is never possible to predict exactly how your boss will react, there are a few mistakes you want to make sure to avoid. Alisa Mosley, director of Career Connections at the University of South Carolina, offers some tips for employees looking to increase their take-home pay.

■ TIMING IS EVERYTHING

Don't ask for more money when your firm has just lost a major contract. Similarly, if your company has gone through difficult times, downsizing, or just released earnings that are down, you're better holding off. If you have recently done something that wasn't particularly positive, you wouldn't want to call attention to yourself, either.

If you work for a large organization that has a formal human resources policy, probably the best time to ask for a raise is at your performance review. If you're working for a small company without a structured policy, the best time to approach your boss is when you've done something that's really had a positive impact on the organization (e.g., you've made a big sale, brought in a new client, implemented a new computer system, etc.).

■ DO YOUR HOMEWORK

If you really feel like you're being underpaid compared to other people doing the same work, get some general salary information for that position that you could quote—professional associations publish salary surveys and state employment services also publish statistics. But keep in mind that salaries for the same position can vary from place to place. So the more localized the information, the better. Don't try to find out how much your co-workers are being paid if your company prohibits this practice.

■ DON'T TAKE A NEGATIVE APPROACH

When enumerating the reasons why you deserve a raise, note accomplishments, not sacrifices made. Don't assume that you deserve a raise just because you've been there a long time or because someone else got a raise. You need to be able to demonstrate your contribution and worth to an organization.

■ AVOID BLACKMAIL

Be assertive, but not aggressive. Clearly state what you want and why you deserve it. If you use an ultimatum as part of your raise negotiation, you need to be prepared to follow through. Don't threaten to quit unless you are willing to walk out the door.

conditions. Many, for example, are offering more flexible schedules. The Mercer study found that almost half of the companies surveyed are considering offering flex time, up from the 45 percent that currently do so. One of every five employers is considering offering workers the opportunity to telecommute, up from 15 percent in an earlier survey.

Still hankering for bigger bucks? More companies these days are offering onetime bonuses keyed to meeting specific goals. That keeps base pay low, but allows recognition of achievements that improve the bottom line. More companies are also experimenting with "skill-based pay," evaluation systems that determine raises by skills, not job title, reasoning that this way workers will take more responsibility for their own career development. The approach has worked with factory workers, but is spreading to white-collar jobs.

WHO'S GETTING AHEAD AND WHO'S FALLING BEHIND

Every American worker has a feeling about what's happening in his or her occupational field, but what's the big picture? Here are some numbers that point to current trends in the workplace. Among other things, they confirm everyone's sneaking suspicion that the wealthy are only getting wealthier, while the poor aren't much better off than they were 20 years ago.

■ TOP OF THE HEAP

Ratio of average CEO's salary to that of average American workers:

1973–1975	41:1
1987–1989	141:1
1992–1994	225:1

■ PREMIER JOBS

Professions from which the top 1 percent derive their income:

Management/executive	41%
Medical	22%
Sales	19%
Law	12%
Other	6%

SOURCE: Graef Crystal, The Crystal Report.

■ UPS AND DOWNS

Share of net worth held by top 1 percent of households

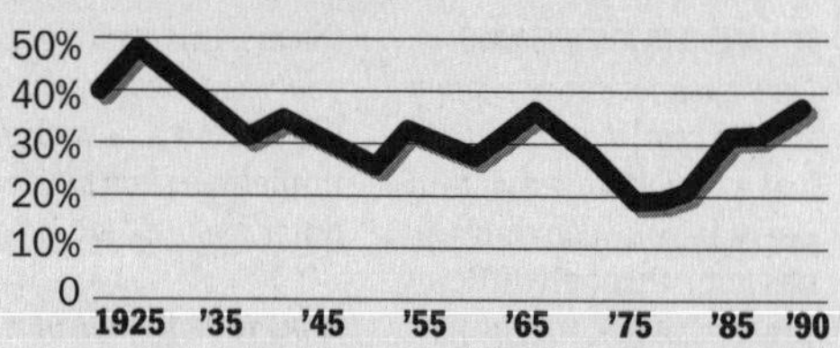

SOURCE: U.S. Bureau of Census.

■ LESS AND MORE

Changes in average household incomes (1994)

	1973	**1994**
Poorest fifth	$7,981	$7,762
Next poorest fifth	$19,988	$19,224
Middle fifth	$32,661	$32,385
Next richest fifth	$46,953	$50,395
Richest fifth	$83,271	$105,945

■ MORE IN THE MIDDLE

Percentage of families at various incomes

1969 **1994**

0 10% 20%

Less than $10,000

$10,000-$14,999

$15,000-$24,999

$25,000-$34,999

$35,000-$49,999

$50,000-$74,999

$75,000-$99,999

$100,000 and over

SOURCE: U.S. Bureau of the Census.

■ THE RICH GET RICHER

Changes in average family income (1977–1992)

Poorest fifth	–17%
Next poorest fifth	–7%
Middle fifth	+1%
Next richest fifth	+6%
Richest fifth	+28%
Top 1%	+91%

SOURCES: Center on Budget and Policy Priorities, Congressional Budget Office, U.S. Department of Commerce, Prof. Edward N. Wolff, NYU.

■ THE MORE YOU KNOW

Changes in average earnings by education level (1979–1992)

	Men	**Women**
Didn't finish high school	–23%	–7%
High school graduate	–17%	1%
Some college	–7%	8%
College graduate	5%	19%

SOURCES: Morgan Stanley & Co.; U.S. Department of Labor; Merrill Lynch.

EXPERT LIST

WHAT 100 OCCUPATIONS PAY

Updated every two years by the Bureau of Labor Statistics, the Occupational Outlook Handbook *is a treasure trove of useful information. The book covers the training and education needed, earnings, working conditions, and employment prospects for jobs from accountant to zoologist. Below are the salaries of 100 occupations from that book. In real life, of course, salaries can vary considerably by region, level of experience, and other factors, but the list does give a good comparison of average incomes.*

TITLE	NO. OF JOBS	STARTING SALARY	MEDIAN SALARY[1]	TOP SALARY
■ EXECUTIVE, ADMINISTRATIVE, AND MANAGERIAL OCCUPATIONS				
ACCOUNTANT	962,000	$27,900 yr.	$25,400–$77,200 yr.	$84,500 yr.
FUNERAL DIRECTORS	26,000	N/A	$44,062–$62,506 yr.	N/A
HOTEL MANAGERS	105,000[2]	N/A	$57,000 yr.	$81,000 yr.
INSPECTORS	157,000	$18,700–$41,000 yr.	$26,630–$62,970 yr.	N/A
ADVERTISING AND MARKETING MANAGERS	461,000	$22,000 yr.	$44,000 yr.	$98,000+ yr.
PERSONNEL MANAGERS	513,000[3]	$25,800–$38,700 yr.	$25,000–$52,800	N/A
RESTAURANT MANAGERS[2]	526,500	N/A	$28,600 yr.	$45,000+ yr.
EXECUTIVE CHEFS	526,500	N/A	$37,000 yr.	$43,000+ yr.
■ PROFESSIONAL SPECIALTY OCCUPATIONS				
ENGINEERS	1,327,000	$34,100–$55,300 yr.	$46,600 yr.	$105,700 yr.
ARCHITECTS	91,000	$24,700 yr.	$38,900–$50,000 yr.	$110,000+ yr.
ACTUARY	17,000	$36,000 yr.	$46,600–$72,700 yr.	$96,000 yr.
SYSTEMS ANALYSTS[3]	828,000	$35,000–$54,000 yr.	$44,000 yr.	$69,400+ yr.
MATHEMATICIANS	14,000	$30,300–$35,600 yr.	$35,000–$52,500 yr.	N/A
STATISTICIANS	14,000	N/A	$56,890–$60,510 YR.	N/A
BIOLOGICAL SCIENTISTS	118,000	$22,900–$48,000 yr.	$37,500 yr.	$73,900+ yr.
CHEMISTS	97,000	$29,300–$52,900 yr.	$45,400–$66,000 yr.	N/A
METEOROLOGISTS	6,600	$22,000–$37,000 yr.	$50,540 yr.	N/A
ASTRONOMERS AND PHYSICISTS	20,000	N/A	$64,000	$77,000
LAWYERS	656,000	$37,000–$80,000+ yr.	$115,000 yr.	$1 million+ yr.
ECONOMISTS	48,000	$27,600 yr.	$70,000 yr.	$95,000 yr
PSYCHOLOGISTS	144,000	N/A[4]	$26,000–$58,000 yr.	N/A
URBAN PLANNERS	29,000	$28,300 yr.	$30,000–$42,000	$63,000 yr.
HUMAN SERVICES WORKERS	168,000	$13,000–$20,000 yr.	$18,000–$27,000 yr.	N/A
SOCIAL WORKERS	557,000	N/A	$17,500–$30,000 yr.	$44,000 yr.
PROTESTANT MINISTERS	300,000	N/A	$40,000 yr.	N/A
RABBIS	4,225	N/A	$38,000–$62,000 yr.	N/A
ROMAN CATHOLIC PRIESTS	51,000	N/A	$29,000	N/A
ARCHIVISTS	19,000	$18,700–$41,100 yr.	$50,000	$100,000
LIBRARIANS	148,000	$28,300 yr.	$35,000–$58,200 yr.	N/A
ELEMENTARY SCHOOL TEACHERS	1.6 million	$20,000–$25,000 yr.	$36,400[4]	N/A

■ **EXPERT LIST**

TITLE	NO. OF JOBS	STARTING SALARY	MEDIAN SALARY[1]	TOP SALARY
DENTISTS	164,000	N/A	$97,450–$132,500 yr.	N/A
PHYSICIANS	539,000	N/A	$156,000	N/A
VETERINARIANS	56,000	$30,694	$59,188 yr.	N/A
DIETITIANS	53,000	N/A	$29,600–$41,600 yr.	N/A
OCCUPATIONAL THERAPISTS	54,000	N/A	$39,634 yr.	$49,392 yr.
PHYSICAL THERAPISTS	102,000	N/A	$37,596 yr.	$61,776+ yr.
PHYSICIAN ASSISTANTS	56,000	$44,176	$53,284 yr.	N/A
REGISTERED NURSES	1,906,000	N/A	$682 wk.	$1,005 wk.
SPEECH-LANGUAGE PATHOLOGISTS	85,000	N/A	$693 wk.	N/A
WRITERS and EDITORS	272,000	$18,000	$30,000–$60,000 yr.	N/A
PHOTOGRAPHERS	139,000	N/A	$25,100 yr.	$46,300+ yr
DANCERS	24,000	$475 wk.	$610 wk.	N/A
■ TECHNICIAN AND RELATED SUPPORT OCCUPATIONS				
EKG TECHNICIANS	15,000	N/A	$18,396 yr.	$22,985 yr.
EMERGENCY MEDICAL TECHNICIANS	138,000	$19,919–$23,861 yr.	$23,330–$33,962	N/A
NUCLEAR MEDICINE TECHNICIANS	13,000	N/A	$35,027	$41,598
AIRCRAFT PILOTS	90,000	$13,000–$27,900 yr.	$37,500–$81,000 yr.	$200,000
AIR TRAFFIC CONTROLLERS	23,000	$22,700	$59,800	N/A
COMPUTER PROGRAMMERS	537,000	$25,000–$54,000	$38,400 yr.	$60,600+ yr.
ENGINEERING TECHNICIANS	685,000	$16,590 yr.	$34,530–$51,060 yr.	N/A
PARALEGALS	110,000	$14,000–$32,000 yr.	$31,700	N/A
■ MARKETING AND SALES OCCUPATIONS				
CASHIERS	3,005,000	$4.25 hr.	$228 wk.	$421+ wk.
COUNTER AND RENTAL CLERKS	341,000	$4.25 hr.	$266 wk.	$586+ wk.
INSURANCE AGENTS and BROKERS	418,000	N/A	$31,620 yr.	$69,900+ yr.
REAL ESTATE AGENTS	374,000	N/A	$593 wk.	$1,447+ wk.
SERVICE SALES REPRESENTATIVES[4]	612,000	$24,600–$31,600 yr.	$28,800–$32,900 yr.	N/A
TRAVEL AGENTS	122,000	N/A	$21,300 yr.	$38,400+ yr.
■ ADMINISTRATIVE SUPPORT OCCUPATIONS				
BANK TELLERS	559,000	N/A	$15,300 yr.	$24,200 yr.
COMPUTER OPERATORS	259,000	$20,000–$31,500 yr.	$21,300 yr.	$39,500+ yr.
GENERAL OFFICE CLERKS	2,946,000	$13,000 yr.	$19,300 yr.	$32,200+ yr.
MAIL CLERKS	127,000	N/A	$322 wk.	$437 wk.
MAIL CARRIERS	320,000	$25,240 yr.	$34,566 yr.	N/A
SECRETARIES	3.3 million+	N/A	$26,700 yr.	$38,400 yr.
STENOGRAPHERS, COURT REPORTERS, MEDICAL TRANSCRIPTIONISTS[5]	105,000	N/A	$399 wk.	$790+ wk.
TEACHER AIDES	932,000	N/A	$8.29–$8.77 hr.	N/A
TELEPHONE OPERATORS	310,000	N/A	$398 wk.	$604+ wk.
DATA ENTRY KEYERS	1.1 million	N/A	$17,600 yr.	N/A

■ **EXPERT LIST**

TITLE	NO. OF JOBS	STARTING SALARY	MEDIAN SALARY[1]	TOP SALARY
■ SERVICE OCCUPATIONS				
CORRECTIONAL OFFICERS	310,000	$19,100 yr.	$22,900 yr.	$57,100 yr.
FIREFIGHTERS	284,000	N/A	$630 wk.	$975+ wk.
POLICE OFFICERS	682,000	N/A	$34,000–$42,800 yr.	$62,100 yr.
SHORT-ORDER COOKS	760,000	N/A	$6.50 hr.	N/A
WAITERS	1.8 million+	N/A	$256 wk.	$430+ wk.
BARTENDERS	373,000	N/A	$299 wk.	$514+ wk.
DENTAL ASSISTANTS	190,000	N/A	$329 wk.	N/A
MEDICAL ASSISTANTS	206,000	N/A	$7.51–$13.12 hr.	N/A
OCCUPATIONAL THERAPY ASSISTANTS	16,000	N/A	$25,300	N/A
PHYSICAL THERAPY ASSISTANTS and AIDES	78,000	$22,500 yr.	$24,000	N/A
COSMETOLOGISTS	709,000	N/A	$14,800	N/A
PRESCHOOL TEACHERS	1 million+	N/A	$260 wk.	$430+ wk.
FLIGHT ATTENDANTS	105,000	$12,700 yr.	N/A	$40,000 yr.
HOMEMAKER-HOME HEALTH AIDES	598,000	$4.90–$6.86 hr.	$5.69–$8.11	N/A
JANITORS	3,168,000	N/A	$293 wk.	$407+ wk.
■ MECHANICS, INSTALLERS, AND REPAIRERS				
ELEVATOR INSTALLERS	24,000	$410–$574 wk	$820 wk.	$923 wk.
AUTOMOTIVE BODY REPAIRERS	209,000	N/A	$456 wk.	$790+ wk.
AIRCRAFT MECHANICS	119,000	$8.70–$13.56 hr.	$36,858 yr.	$53,872 + yr.
VENDING MACHINE REPAIRERS	19,000	N/A	$8.30 hr.	$22 hr.
■ CONSTRUCTION TRADES OCCUPATIONS				
CARPENTERS[6]	992,000	N/A	$424 wk.	$785+ wk
CARPET INSTALLERS	66,000	N/A	$412 wk.	$751+ wk.
ELECTRICIANS	528,000	N/A	$574 wk.	$971+ wk.
PAINTERS[6]	439,000	N/A	$381 wk.	$721+ wk.
PLUMBERS[6]	375,000	N/A	$530 wk.	$970+ wk.
■ PRODUCTION OCCUPATIONS				
BUTCHERS	351,043	N/A	$329 wk.	$702+ wk.
JEWELERS	30,000	N/A	$400 wk.	N/A
MACHINISTS	376,000	N/A	$520 wk.	$880+ wk.
TOOL AND DIE MAKERS	142,000	N/A	$660 wk.	$1,130+ wk.
POWER PLANT OPERATORS	43,000	N/A	$857 wk.	N/A
TREATMENT PLANT OPERATORS	95,000	N/A	$27,100 yr.	$42,100 yr.
PRINTING PRESS OPERATORS	244,000	N/A	$432 wk.	$787+ wk.
BUS DRIVERS	568,000	N/A	$401 wk.	$758+ wk.
TRUCK DRIVERS	2,900,000	N/A	$8.06–$14.87 hr.	N/A

NOTES: **1.** In general, employees of the federal government earn less than those in the private sector. **2.** Includes assistant managers; represents all restaurant and food service managers. **3.** Includes computer scientists. **4.** Earnings depend on performance. Some sales reps are paid a straight salary, while others work solely on commission. Incentive pay can add up to 75 percent to base salary. **5.** Court reporters generally earn higher salaries. **6.** Excluding the self-employed, who sometimes earn more.

SOURCE: *Occupational Outlook Handbook*, Bureau of Labor Statistics, Spring 1996.

EMPLOYEE BENEFITS

MORE CHOICES, LESS COVERAGE

Here's the deal: You get lots of options but lots more of the cost

The news about employee benefits will hardly seem like news to the average American worker: benefits have been getting skimpier over the past few years. A 1995 survey of 929 firms by the U.S. Chamber of Commerce found that employee benefits decreased by 0.8 percent in 1994 measured by dollars spent per employee per year. That is in contrast to an 8.6 percent increase posted in 1994.

The most striking trend concerns medical benefits: Most employers decreased their share of medical costs per employee in 1994 after a significant increase in 1993. This was largely due to employers passing more of the cost on to workers, and more employees entering managed care programs. To slash medical costs, smaller firms, in particular, are increasingly joining co-ops for health insurance. Overall, all medically related benefits, including health insurance, disability, dental insurance, and wellness programs, decreased $241 per employee in 1994, after increasing $491 the previous year. Meanwhile, corporate payments to pension accounts have grown.

The extent to which employees have been losing benefits, of course, depends on where they work. Generally, large firms provide more benefits than small firms. Also, benefits vary from industry to industry. In 1994, manufacturing firms paid, on average, $16,253 per employee in benefits; nonmanufacturing firms just $14,333.

The best advice for benefit-hungry employees: Go west. Employers in the western states are more generous than those in the Rust Belt. Companies in the western United States had 43.4 percent of payroll going to benefits in 1994. Companies in the East North-Central United States (Illinois, Indiana, Michigan, Ohio, and Wisconsin) spend just 38.5 percent of payroll costs on benefits. What accounted for the difference? Many workers in the West are younger and more mobile, the Chamber of Commerce survey found, and better benefits attract better workers.

Chances are your company—whether it's large or small—now offers you as many benefit choices as there are items at the salad bar in the company cafeteria. Here are some of the current benefit choices.

■ **PENSION AND INVESTMENT PLANS.** The trend is toward defined contribution plans, in which employer contributions are matched by the employee, and away from traditional defined benefit plans, which put a greater emphasis on the employer's guarantee of a retirement income. Defined contribution plans—of which 401(k)s are the most common—can be taken with you if you change jobs or start your own business. New federal legislation is designed to make retirement benefits more portable. Also, many companies, concerned about their future liability for retired employees who are financially unstable, are offering investment education seminars and a greater choice of investment plans.

■ **HEALTH CARE.** More companies are moving away from traditional fee-for-service plans and toward managed care. Nearly two-thirds of companies were following this trend in 1995, according to *Money* magazine. But many firms are also offering a wider selection of managed care options and helping their workers to choose the plans that are best for them. As more fee-for-service doctors join managed care plans, employees in traditional health programs might find they can save money by changing to an HMO—without necessarily losing the physicians they are familiar with.

■ **LIFE INSURANCE.** The main differences are between plans that are fully employer-paid, and those that depend on employee contributions. Some companies offer a combination of both. Most core plans provide a cash payout equal to one times the employee's most recent annual salary, sometimes with a cash maximum.

■ **DISABILITY INSURANCE.** Employers differ in their formulas for calculating short-term disability payments. Some companies use the "salary continuation method" in which employees receive their entire salary (or a percentage of their salary depending on the years they have worked) for a defined period of time before long-term disability benefits kick in. Other employers use the "accrual" method. Your benefits are based on the amount of time you've worked for the company. Unlike other benefits, however, this one is crucial for all jobholders. Workers should consider buying supplemental coverage if their disability benefit will not replace at least 60 percent of their current compensation to age 65.

■ **FLEXIBLE BENEFITS.** Increasingly, you can order your benefits *à la carte*. Each employee receives a certain number of credits to use as he or she sees fit. For instance, you may be able to "buy" additional vacation days with part of your salary, "sell" credits for cash, or use them to purchase extra life insurance or health insurance. Employees covered under their spouse's health plan might want to cash in their own health benefits and invest the money in a company stock purchase plan or some other savings options. An increasing number of companies also let you put a percentage of your pretax salary in "spending accounts" for health or "dependent care." Flexible schedules are also on the rise, as is the number of companies offering emergency and "sick-child" centers, *Money* found. And a number of firms are now offering cash or benefit credits for employees who quit smoking or lose weight.

A NEW WAY TO TAKE A VACATION

If you're not getting enough, some companies let you "buy" extra days off

Everyone knows Americans work too hard and here's proof: In a 22-nation comparison of the minimum days off that employers give workers each year, workers in only three countries—Myanmar, Mexico, and the Philippines—got less time off the job than Americans. The average worker in the U.S. gets about 30 days off for vacations and holidays every year—compared with 46 in Germany, for instance, and 33 in Canada.

So, using old-fashioned Yankee ingenuity, American companies have come up with a remedy. An increasing number of companies—including Du Pont, Quaker Oats, Coca-Cola, and American Express—have begun including extra vacation time in their flexible benefits programs. Hewitt Associates, an employee benefit consulting company, estimated that some 15 percent of American companies let employees "buy" or "sell" time, though typically no more than five days a year. "This is becoming a highly valued benefit," Ken McDonnell, a research analyst at the Employee Benefit Research Institute in Washington, D.C., told *The New York Times*.

Quaker Oats, which implemented its program in 1993, estimates that 6,500 of its 10,000 employees take advantage of the system. The company also reported that 35 percent of workers in the program buy vacation days, whereas only 9 percent sell.

No one really knows if working fewer days adversely affects productivity. Indeed, as philosopher Bertrand Russell pointed out in his 1935 essay *In Praise of Idleness*, "there is far too much work done in the world [and] immense harm is caused by the belief that work is virtuous." He urged that the working day be reduced to no more than four hours. "Leisure is essential to civilization," he wrote. "The road to happiness lies in an organized diminuation of work." Now, who's going to argue with that?

EXPERT Q & A

IS YOUR COMPANY FAMILY-FRIENDLY?

Some progressive employers can help you juggle kids and work

Many employers tout themselves as being family-friendly, but what does that really mean? Here Barbara Reisman, executive director of the New York–based Child Care Action Committee, which has been fighting for family rights within the workplace for more than a decade, answers questions about finding and securing family-friendly benefits.

■ What are the most important benefits you should look for in an employer?

The following benefits are becoming common in the more family-friendly companies, and are not unreasonable requests.

- Flexible work time or work space (allowing parents to work at home).
- Part-time work options with benefits.
- Paid parental leave.
- Child-care support, whether it be on- or near-site child care, financial support for employees' child-care needs, emergency or backup child care, before- and after-school care, or contributions to local child-care facilities.
- Information and resources to help employees find dependent care.
- Paid sick-child days (not vacation or employees' own sick days).
- Phase-back work option for new moms (allowing employees to return to work part-time or work from home).

■ Legally, what does a company have to provide?

Under the Family and Medical Leave Act (FMLA), companies that employ 50 or more have to provide unpaid leave, with a job guarantee and continued benefits for 12 weeks in the case of a birth, adoption, or extended illness of child, or if your spouse or other dependent is chronically ill.

■ What if I work for a small company?

While not required by law, many small companies offer family-friendly benefits with little difficulty. One of the most important and cost-effective things a small company can do is look for ways to improve child-care programs already in operation. Small companies can make contributions to local child-care providers, and then arrange for their employees to receive special rates, etc. It's good for employers because it gives them a good public image and their employees won't be worrying about child care.

Pretax set-asides for dependent care is another easy thing for small companies to do because it doesn't cost them any money. Each month, employees can set aside a certain amount of their pretax paycheck to be used for dependent care. They are then reimbursed at a later date.

■ What can you do to make your company more family-friendly if you really need the job and quitting and looking for another employer isn't an option?

Talk to other employees and find out if they're facing the same issues. Find out what your employer's competition offers. As a group, make a list of concerns and suggestions. Present your requests directly to your employer or human resources person.

It's always best to present your concerns in a nonconfrontational manner. Illustrate how these benefits will help the employer and employees alike. Get the company to recognize that it's in both of your interests to address these needs.

■ How do I do that?

A number of recent studies have established that employees who worry about family obligations or child care are not productive workers. Employees who must take sick days or leave work early because they don't have reliable child care cost employers time and money.

At Du Pont, for example, employees can participate in corporate-sponsored work-life programs that ease some of their family and child-care burdens. Du Pont's programs include a toll-free family resource service that provides consultation and referrals, a program that links employees to emergency child care, and reimbursement of dependent care expenses if an employee has an overnight business trip. A recent study shows that the work-life programs are paying off for employee and employer alike: More than 60 percent of employees surveyed said the work-life programs strengthened their relationship with their employer, 75 percent said the service helps their companies retain valuable employees, 45 percent are more likely to agree to "go the extra mile" for Du Pont, and employees who use the work-life programs are the most committed employees in the company.

(For information about the Du Pont or other family-friendly studies, call Work Family Directions ☎ 617–278–4000, or the Family and Work Institute ☎ 212–465–2044.)

■ If a fellow employee is allowed flexible hours, does the company have an obligation to make me a similar offer?

No, but companies tend to be concerned about equity issues. Consult with the employee who has flexible hours and find out more about his or her situation. Then explain to your employer that since flexible time has made the other employee more productive, it's bound to have the same effect on you. Do your research beforehand and have your case well thought out before you present anything to your boss.

■ Do fathers have to be extended the same benefits as mothers?

The Family and Medical Leave Act applies to both fathers and mothers, and has to be adhered to in a nondiscriminatory manner. Beyond that, companies have no obligation to provide fathers with flex-time or phase-back time after a new baby. Fathers can get those benefits, but they must speak up first. Patagonia, Inc., for example, heeded the concerns of men and now offers new dads eight weeks' paid paternity leave. It's important for men to talk about the fact that they are affected by these issues as well.

■ How do I find out more about child care and other important family-friendly initiatives in my area?

Call Child Care Aware at ☎800–424–2246 to find out about resources and referral agencies in your area. You can also request helpful publications, including *Not Too Small to Care: Small Business and Child Care, Investing in the Future: Child Care Financing Options for the Public and Private Sectors,* and *An Employer's Guide to Child Care Consultants.*

FACT FILE:

HERE'S LOOKING AT YOU

■ *The 1996 edition of* The Practical Guide *reported on a recent study that evaluated people on the basis of physical appearance. The study found, among other things, that those deemed unattractive earn, on average, 13 percent less than those deemed beautiful.*

■ *Now, a review of 2,500 lawyers (women and men) and their photos finds that attractive attorneys earned as much as 14 percent more than their less-handsome peers. The study, published by the National Bureau of Economic Research in Cambridge, Mass., also notes that being attractive helped in winning early partnership.*

■ *One other finding: private-sector lawyers generally were better-looking than their government counterparts.*

SOURCE: *The Wall Street Journal.*

FAMILY LEAVE

HOW TO GET YOUR JOB BACK

What to do if you need to take time off to care for a loved one

All politicians say they are pro-family and now they have a law to prove it. The 1993 Family and Medical Leave Act (FMLA) stipulates that all government agencies and all private employers with more than 50 employees must provide up to 12 weeks of unpaid, job-protected leave for an employee for any of the following reasons: the birth or adoption of a child; the care of an immediate relative with a serious health condition; or medical leave for the employee if he or she is unable to work because of a serious health condition. Here, from the Labor Department's *Compliance Guide to the Family and Medical Leave Act*, are answers to some of the most commonly asked questions about the new law.

■ Does the law guarantee paid time off?

FMLA leave is generally unpaid. However, in certain circumstances the use of accrued paid leave—such as vacation or sick leave—may be substituted for the unpaid leave required by the law. FMLA is intended to encourage generous family and medical leave policies. For this reason, the law does not diminish more generous existing leave policies or laws.

■ Does FMLA leave have to be taken in whole days or weeks, or in one continuous block?

The FMLA permits leave for birth or placement for adoption or foster care to be taken intermittently, in blocks of time or by reducing the normal weekly or daily work schedule—subject to employer approval. Leave for a serious health condition may be taken intermittently when "medically necessary."

■ Are there employees not covered by the law?

Yes. About 60 percent of U.S. workers (and about 95 percent of U.S. employers) are not covered. To be eligible for FMLA benefits, an employee must: (1) work for a covered employer; (2) have worked for the employer for at least a year; (3) have worked at least 1,250 hours over the prior 12 months; and (4) work at a location where at least 50 employees are employed by the employer within 75 miles.

■ What do I have to do to request FMLA leave from my employer?

You may be required to provide your employer with 30 days' advance notice when the need for leave is "foreseeable." When the need for the leave cannot be foreseen, you must give your employer notice as soon as "practicable." You may need to submit documentation from the health-care provider treating you or your immediate family member.

■ Will I be allowed to return to the same job?

Ordinarily you will be restored to the same position you held prior to the leave, with the same pay and benefits, if the position remains available. You may be restored to an "equivalent" position rather than to the position you held before taking the leave, if the previous position is not available. An equivalent position must have pay, benefits, and terms and conditions of employment equivalent to the original job.

■ Do I lose all benefits when I take unpaid FMLA leave?

Your employer is required to maintain health insurance coverage on the same terms it was provided before the leave began. In addition, the use of FMLA leave cannot result in the loss of any employment benefit that accrued prior to the start of your leave.

■ What if I believe my employer is violating the law?

You can file, or have someone file on your behalf, a complaint with the Employment Standards Administration, Wage and Hour Division, or you can file a private lawsuit.

EXPERT PICKS

THE 10 BEST COMPANIES FOR WORKING MOMS

Employers who welcome each new kid in the family as if their own

Working Mother magazine annually compiles a list of the 100 best companies for working mothers. The magazine selects companies based on a number of criteria, including pay, opportunities for women to advance, child care, and other family-friendly benefits such as job sharing and flexible hours.

Benefits that were once considered revolutionary, such as job sharing and sick-child days, have become commonplace in many work settings—as the stiff competition for the *Working Mother* list illustrates. The top 10 employers (presented in alphabetical order here) welcome each new kid into the family as if it were their own:

Barnett Bank, *Jacksonville, Fla.*
Fel-Pro Incorporated, *Skokie, Ill.*
Glaxo Wellcome Inc., *Triangle Park, N.C.*
IBM Corporation, *Armonk, N.Y.*
Johnson & Johnson, *New Brunswick, N.J.*
MBNA America Bank, N.A., *Newark, Del.*
Merck & Co., Inc., *Whitehouse Sta., N.J.*
Nationsbank Corporation, *Charlotte, N.C.*
Patagonia, Inc., *Ventura, Calif.*
Xerox Corporation, *Stamford, Conn.*

No single industry or company size dominates *Working Mother*'s top 10 list. In fact, the top 10 list is home to companies as large as IBM, which has 106,323 employees, and Patagonia, Inc., which has only 550 employees.

■ **PAY:** To even be considered for the *Working Mother* list, companies must pay well. No matter how friendly a company may be, parents still have to pay bills. Average entry-level pay in the top 10 companies ranged from $6.50/hour at **Patagonia** to $24,800/year at **Johnson & Johnson.**

■ **EQUAL OPPORTUNITY:** Before you are a working mother, you are a working woman. Companies in the top 10 all provided excellent opportunities for advancement for all women on staff. More than 40 percent of vice presidents at **Barnett Bank** are women.

■ **CHILD CARE:** The companies who made the list either provide on-site or near-site child care. **Johnson & Johnson** provides 550 children with on-site care and provides 50 percent of the centers' operating costs. But 9-to-5 child care is just the beginning. Many of the top companies also offer holiday, after-school, sick-child, and summer programs, as well as pretax set-asides to pay for child care and a dependent-care fund. **Fel-Pro Incorporated** offers a summer camp (children are picked up and dropped off right at the plant) and subsidizes tutoring for children who are struggling in school.

■ **FAMILY BENEFITS:** Many companies offer new moms the option of taking more unpaid leave than the Family and Medical Leave Act (FMLA) mandates. At **Merck & Co.**, for example, new mothers can take FMLA and an additional 66 weeks, with some full pay. **Nationsbank** fathers can take up to 6 weeks paid paternity leave. Phase-back and flextime for mothers who want to ease back into full-time work is a given in the top 10 companies. New to the list, but growing in popularity, are adoption-aid funds. At **Fel-Pro,** adopting parents can receive up to $5,000.

Each **Fel-Pro** baby is welcomed into the family with a $1,000 savings bond and, if the baby goes on to attend college, a $3,500 scholarship. **Merck** provides $400,000 in scholarships to 24 kids each year.

SMART MOVES

MANAGEMENT: Leadership secrets from literary classics, PAGE 365 **EXPERT TIPS:** A top headhunter on how to get noticed, PAGE 367 **THE ZODIAC:** Success may be in your stars, PAGE 368 **BOSSES:** Dealing with office bullies, PAGE 370 **STRESS:** Ways to beat burnout PAGE 372 **SMALL BUSINESSES:** How to be your own boss, PAGE 374 **HOME BUSINESSES:** The hottest home-based businesses, PAGE 377 **ERGONOMICS:** The importance of a good chair, PAGE 379

GETTING AHEAD

A PEP TALK FROM THE WIZARD

A legendary coach's secrets for success on and off the court

Hey, everyone, "Listen up." You know where to find the gurus who know the keys to career success these days? Some of the hottest management messiahs today are not in the boardrooms or the business schools—they're on the playing fields. When he's not huddled with his team on the basketball court, Pat Riley, the former New York Knicks and L.A. Lakers coach who's now coaching the Miami Heat, is in big demand on the corporate lecture circuit. Ten current and former National Football League coaches recently hit the bookstores with *Game Plan for Success* (Little Brown, 1995). In the book, they opine about motivation and coping with prima donnas, among other subjects. *Business Week* magazine recently rounded up three longtime coaches—Tommy Lasorda (Los Angeles Dodgers manager since 1976); Sparky Anderson (Detroit Tigers manager since 1979); and Don Shula (Miami Dolphins head coach from 1970 until his 1996 retirement)—to impart their particular coaching tips to upwardly mobile corporate types.

At 85, John Wooden is the granddaddy of motivational coaches and he's been preaching his "how to succeed in business and life" gospel to striving managers for years. Wooden is the only man inducted into the National Basketball Hall of Fame as both a player and coach, an honor he earned as a three-time All-American guard at Purdue University and as coach of a record 10 NCAA championship clubs at UCLA—including seven straight from 1966 to 1973. (His nearest rival, Adolph Rupp, won four while coaching the University of Kentucky from 1931 to 1972.) The "Wizard of Westwood" credits his accomplishments in part to a philosophy of life he began developing while a high school English teacher in 1934—the Pyramid for Success (see illustration on facing page). The author of an autobiography, with Jack Tobin, called *They Call Me Coach* (Contemporary Books, 1988), Wooden has lectured on the virtues of the pyramid to bankers, mayors, and at over 70 IBM corporate seminars, and he still swears by its basic logic: Industriousness, enthusiasm, and hard work are the best routes to achieving your dreams. Here Coach Wooden discusses his philosophy on and off the court:

■ **What were you trying to show with your management pyramid?**

I wanted to come up with something that I hoped would give kids something to aspire to other than a higher mark in school or more

■ THE WAY TO THE TOP

John Wooden began developing his Pyramid for Success while coaching high school basketball in South Bend, Indiana, in 1934. The pyramid should be interpreted just as it appears, with each block seen as a single step toward the apex of success.

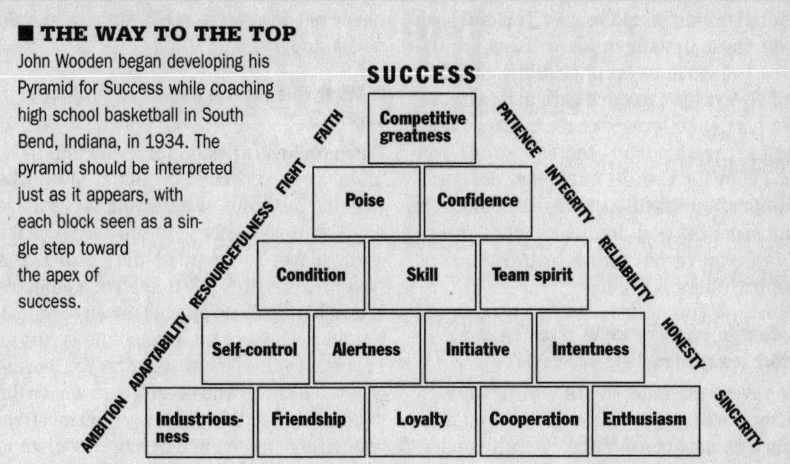

The lower bricks provide the "foundation" for the process, and should thus be given the most early attention; of these, "industriousness" and "enthusiasm" are the cornerstones. The later tiers and blocks build off of the lower levels. The tenets running diagonally up the sides provide the "mortar," more general attributes needed to conquer each tier.

points on the court. First I came up with my definition for success: Success is a peace of mind, which can be attained only from self-satisfaction in knowing you made the effort to become the best of which you're capable. I gave this to my students, but I didn't get the results for which I had hoped. I think something you see makes a better impression, so I got the idea of this pyramid. It took 14 years to finish, but it was the best teaching aid I ever had.

■ What is the significance of your pyramid's order?

I started with the cornerstones of industriousness and enthusiasm. Those were the first two blocks I chose. Between them I selected three blocks—friendship, loyalty, and cooperation—and those five formed the foundation. Above them I had four blocks—self-control, alertness, initiative, and intentness. On the third tier I got down to three blocks—the very heart of the structure. Condition—mental, moral, physical. Skill—the ability to execute properly and quickly. Team spirit—consideration for others and putting the group ahead of self. Just above that I put two blocks—poise and confidence. Poise is just being yourself. Not acting, not pretending, not trying to be something you're not. If you do this, you're going to function near your own particular personal best. But you must have confidence in yourself.

All these things will bring you up to the last block—they'll make you competitive. But you need what's below building up to it. On the corners of the last block, leading up to the apex where success sits, are faith and patience. Good things take time—as they should—and you have to have faith that if you do what you should, things will work out as they should. Maybe not just the way you would like them to, but the way they should.

Everything else along the sides of the pyramid should be thought of as mortar holding up the bricks.

■ Can such simple virtues still work in today's complex world?

Last year in Seattle I spoke before approximately 50 CEOs from some of the biggest companies throughout the nation, and I was kind of surprised myself at how well I was received. The basics have not changed. Long before I taught and long after you and I are gone, those fundamentals will remain the same: industriousness and enthusiasm. You will always have to work hard to reach your own particular level or goals. If you're looking for the shortcut—the easy way—you can get by for a while, but you're not going to improve yourself. As far as enthusiasm is concerned, if you don't like what you're doing, you're not going to influence or inspire others.

■ How do we know we've given enough effort toward reaching our goals?

Who ever overachieved in anything through history? No one! Nobody ever did more than they were capable of doing. We're all underachievers—but to different degrees.

Sometimes I hear an announcer call a guy an overachiever or a real hustler because he dives on the ball, slides out of bounds with it, and winds up giving the other team the ball. He was a real hustler—but he was also stupid at the same time for losing the ball. We never get it exactly right, but we should never stop trying.

■ What role can we play in each other's success?

When you're in a position of leadership, those under your supervision should always be working *with* you, not *for* you. Never have anybody working for you. You need to make every player feel wanted and needed. You have to explain his role to everyone. One role is developing those playing ahead of you. A nut on a wheel of an automobile is just as important as the powerful engine. You lose the nut, you lose the wheel—and then what's the engine going to do? So every person must feel wanted and needed, and he must understand the role he's asked to play. If he can't accept that role, he should be into something else.

It's all about making an effort. Your reputation is what others perceive you to be, but your character is what you are. In the end, you're the only person who really knows if you made every effort to be the best.

EXPERT TIPS

OTHER COACHES HAVE THEIR SAY

Words of wisdom from some of sports' winningest coaches and managers

"It's what you learn after you know it all that counts."

—Earl Weaver, Manager, Baltimore Orioles (1968–82). He won four pennants and one World Series title.

"The secret to managing is to keep the guys who hate you away from the guys who are undecided."

—Casey Stengel, Manager, New York Yankees (1949–60). Under Stengel, the Yankees won 10 American League pennants and seven World Series titles, including five in a row from 1949 to 1953.

"You've got to have integrity to be an effective leader. That's what it all stems from."

—Don Shula, Head Coach, Miami Dolphins (1970–96). Shula's teams played in six Super Bowls, winning twice.

"Managing is like holding a dove...Squeeze too tight, you kill it. Open your hand too much, you let it go."

—Tommy Lasorda, Manager, Los Angeles Dodgers (1976–96). He has won four pennants and two World Series titles.

"I present ideas, not mandates."

—George Seifert, Head Coach, San Francisco 49ers (1989–present). Under Seifert's leadership, the 49ers have won two Super Bowl games.

"Those that worry about getting fired know in their heart that they can't do the job. I never worried."

—Sparky Anderson, Manager, Detroit Tigers (1979–95). Anderson is the only manager to win World Series titles in both the American League and the National League.

LEADERSHIP

MANAGEMENT BY THE BOOK

Literary classics for a good read as well as a few leadership pointers

If you thought reading Shakespeare was only for English literature students, you're in for a surprise. John K. Clemens, a professor of management at Hartwick College in Oneonta, N.Y., has been using literature, including Shakespeare, to teach managerial skills to business students. The literary case studies are now being used by about 70 business school professors across the country. Clemens, who is executive director of the Hartwick Humanities in Management Institute, recommends the following literary classics for managers in search of a good read as well as a few leadership pointers.

■ **HERMAN MELVILLE'S *BILLY BUDD, SAILOR.*** In this Melville novel, a leader must choose between adhering to a rigid organizational policy and doing what he believes is morally right. The case presents an opportunity to explore the problems that arise when company decisions are based on rules rather than circumstance, and understanding the difference between doing the right thing and doing things right. Also, nearly everyone can relate to the book's primary conflict: the effects of one co-worker's dislike for another.

■ **JOHN MASEFIELD'S *THE BIRD OF DAWNING.*** Observe the birth of a leader, as protagonist Cyril Trewsbury is unexpectedly thrust into a position of power and must learn through trial and error which leadership techniques work best. The most important lessons here concern recognizing the ways in which one might transform one's vision into reality, and the critical but often unappreciated importance of challenging employees or co-workers to do more than even they thought possible.

■ **MARTIN LUTHER KING'S *LETTER FROM A BIRMINGHAM JAIL.*** This is a classic lesson in how language is a leader's most effective tool. King's masterful oratory skills come across just as strongly on paper. He also reveals in great clarity his four steps for organizational change. This "recipe" can be used in any social setting including modern corporations.

■ **CHIEF JOSEPH.** In his writings, Native American leader Chief Joseph offers an in-depth look at three styles of leadership, the types of organizations they are associated with (bureaucratic, entrepreneurial, and integrative), and the problems and benefits unique to each of them. This reading offers one of the big lessons for survival in a changing business environment: A corporation ought to look more like a collection of tribes than a monolithic organization. With "tribalism" comes agility, common beliefs, "local" knowledge, and perhaps most important, respect for the individual.

■ **SHAKESPEARE'S *HENRY IV* AND *HENRY V.*** Shakespeare's exploration into the lives of these two kings (and their differing leadership styles) offers lessons on the emergence of a leader, important personal and political traits of leaders, and what works and what doesn't. To lead you must first be a follower. Prince Hal was a great follower, and, subsequently, as king he was a great leader.

■ **HOMER'S *ILIAD.*** This epic poem tells the story of the anger of the great warrior Achilles and the terrible consequences that his community (the Greek army) endured because of it. Clearly, the major figures in Homer's epic are driven by compelling needs and forces not immediately apparent. Once discovered, however, they help to reveal the inner workings of leadership in any setting.

■ **DAVID MAMET'S *GLENGARRY GLEN ROSS.*** This dark play presents a leader whom most readers will not admire. Yet he is in a difficult position, forced to pursue goals that may be unattainable, using an organization that is often untrustworthy and ineffectual. Analyzing him and the other characters in the play

EXPERT PICKS

MOVIES FOR MANAGERS

All it may take to learn how to be a leader is to plunk yourself down, pop in a video, and take in the show. Or so says John Clemens, who is studying 50 films for their potential to teach inspirational—or cautionary—tales about leadership under a grant from the W.K. Kellogg Foundation in Battle Creek, Michigan. Here, he gives a quick overview of the top five films with management lessons:

12 O'CLOCK HIGH
directed by Henry King, starring Gregory Peck and Hugh Marlowe. 1950.

■ This film dramatizes the impact of appropriate leadership style. Watch as two leaders use distinctly different approaches to try to rebuild a bomber group suffering from low morale and heavy losses. Note how one leader succeeds and the other fails.

LORD OF THE FLIES
directed by Peter Brook, starring James Aubrey and Tom Chapin. 1963.

■ Here, a fledgling leader grasps for group cohesion. His failure to coalesce his team resonates for anyone who has witnessed mediocre management. The compelling portrayal of this young leader's challenger shows how quickly a breakaway group can "kill" the organization.

12 ANGRY MEN
directed by Sidney Lumet, starring Jack Klugman, Henry Fonda, and Ed Begley, Sr. 1957.

■ One of the most important aspects of leadership ability is the capacity to sense others' actions. In this film, which shows a jury agonizing over the fate of an alleged murderer, students are asked to predict the order in which the 12 jurors change their votes from guilty to innocent. To do so, they must be astute observers of human behavior.

THE CAINE MUTINY
directed by Edward Dmytryk, starring Humphrey Bogart. 1954.

■ This film about the crew of a minesweeper, the USS *Caine*, provides key lessons in team building and group structure. See how difficult it is for leaders to gain compliance with their desires, let alone their orders. Watch the infamous Captain Queeg as he factionalizes his crew and turns their dislike to hate. This is the ultimate cautionary tale of leadership.

DEAD POETS SOCIETY
directed by Peter Weir, starring Robin Williams and Ethan Hawke. 1989.

■ No managerial task is more difficult than creating change. Here, a young English teacher at a straitlaced boys boarding school makes an ill-starred effort to move it from dictatorship to democracy, providing an unforgettable example of the challenge of change.

surprisingly reveals human qualities that students can identify with. Readers can evaluate the management strategies used in this organization and decide what, if anything, they have to do with the organization's fate.

■ **WILLIAM GOLDING'S *LORD OF THE FLIES.*** This story portrays leadership development and conflict among a group of boys marooned on a desert island. It also explores the alternative ways a subordinate leader can wrest control of the group from an elected leader. The story clearly demonstrates the importance of collaboration and compromise, rather than competition, in achieving organizational objectives.

EXPERT Q & A

HOW TO GET YOUR HEAD HUNTED

A top headhunter on what it takes to get on a "most wanted" list

Headhunters prowl the corporate jungle, trying to lure managers and executives from one job to another. They are constantly on the lookout for the best and brightest in order to snag the top talent for whatever client company has been clever enough to retain them. So why hasn't your phone rung with a juicy job offer? One of the nation's leading headhunters, Gerard Roche, has spent his entire 32-year career at the New York City executive search firm of Heidrick & Struggles, Inc. His clients have included IBM, Kodak, and Westinghouse.

■ How do you get a headhunter's notice?

First off, do an extraordinary job at the job you're in, and get a track record where you get recognition. Don't be distracted by a lot of external situations and superficial activities that take your eye off your main responsibilities. The thing that will get our attention is your reputation at what you're doing in front of you—so keep your focus. Nothing else is even nearly as important. If you succeed to a high extent, we'll sniff you out.

■ Say you're ready to move on. Is it wise to approach a headhunter yourself?

This is a networking game. Now, I get thousands of résumés a week, so just sending a résumé—while it can help—isn't the best move. We do filter them out, try to find the best nuggets and respond. But at our firm we don't count on the write-ins that we get to solve our problems. We count on being aware of who's doing good work out there, and generally speaking, those who are doing a good job aren't writing in to us—we've got to go and get them. If you want to approach a top headhunter, get somebody who you think knows him to call recommending that he pay special attention to you. If you want to use a book to look up names, Jim Kennedy's *Getting Behind the Résumé—Interviewing Today's Candidates* (Prentice Hall, 1987) is as good as any.

One way to get noticed is to be active in your industry—attend association meetings, give a speech, write an article, or get a top newsmagazine to quote you. Do whatever you can to be unique and let people know you're a leader. A strong reputation and résumé are mostly gained through individual effort, not public relations departments.

■ If a headhunter calls, how forthcoming should you be? Should you volunteer your salary, for example?

It's strictly a matter of whether you're the one pursuing a job, or the one being pursued. If you're secure in a position with an established reputation and not looking for a job—which frankly is the type of people we normally go after—then by no means should you open up and tell all. You should do a healthy amount of listening, see what the person has to offer, then respond as you see fit and feel comfortable doing.

If you're looking for a job, one thing to keep in mind is to never take a headhunter's call raw. Ask if you can call back; this gives you a chance to authenticate who the caller is. Find out exactly who it is who's calling, then call back when it's convenient for you.

How forthcoming you are depends on how badly you're interested in a new job. If you're a pursuee of a headhunter, you can be standoffish; if you're looking, you should still have a certain amount of detached interest.

■ Sure, headhunters are hired to search for CEOs. What can you do if you're a smaller fish in the corporate pond?

It sounds simple, and it is—just do your job. If you excel, we'll pick you up on our screen. If you spend most of your time trying to get our attention, you're probably not going to get it. It's the same whether you're looking for a $200,000 job or a $30,000 job.

THE ZODIAC

SUCCESS MAY BE IN YOUR STARS

Can your astrological sign tell you what career path to follow?

Ever wonder why some people just seem to succeed in business while others never seem to get ahead? It may have something to do with their astrological sign—at least, that's the contention of a growing number of astrologers who cater to a business clientele.

Astrologers Grace Morris, president of Astro Economics, Inc., an Oak Brook, Ill., company that advises companies on business and financial moves, and Lynne Palmer, a Las Vegas–based author of several books on financial astrology, including *Prosperity Signs* (Dell, 1981), cater to the many businesspeople who are turning to astrology for guidance in personal career moves and major financial decisions. Whether you're thinking about buying stocks, starting your own business, or signing some important papers, the planetary cycles can influence the outcome, they say.

Typically, astro financial experts use birth charts (literally a picture of the solar system at the time of an individual's birth that shows the alignment and pattern of the planets) to predict the best times to do business, sign important papers, etc. But each Zodiac sign also has its own unique business characteristics. Here, Morris and Palmer summarize the major qualities of each sign:

AQUARIUS Jan. 21–Feb. 19

Aquarius is restless and gets involved in whatever is new and exciting. Thomas Edison was an Aquarius. This is the sign of the computer, so look for Aquarians on the Internet and with anything that involves electronics. It is also a humanitarian sign, so many Aquarians are found in psychology or leading workshops and conferences. Aquarians can be stubborn, and they like to be their own boss. Because of that, many enjoy freelance work.

PISCES Feb. 20–March 20

Those born under this sign have guts—and they use them. Pisceans tend to live in a dream world, but when they put action behind their dreams, they can be very successful. They are idea people with creative imaginations. Many Pisceans are found in the entertainment industry because they are great promoters and are good at wheeling and dealing. They also think big and make big deals.

ARIES March 21–April 20

No long-term savings bonds here. Aries like quick action, taking risks, and accepting challenges. Many Aries do go broke because of their impulsive nature. They like to be in control and have a natural executive ability. Look for Aries in cutting-edge, emerging businesses. They are also attracted to jobs that require physical stamina.

TAURUS April 21–May 22

Unlike the more hyper Aries types, Taureans are most at home in a long-term relationship with their investments. It's not unusual for Taureans to work for the same company their entire career. Taureans are efficient and patient, and can take someone else's invention and perfect it. Money is important to Taureans, and you will find many in the traditional fields of insurance and banking. J.P. Morgan was a Taurus. A Taurus is often chosen as the treasurer of a board or organization.

GEMINI May 23–June 21

A Gemini is the jack-of-all-trades and master of none. Gemini tends to be restless and needs a job that provides mobility. Geminis are most at home in jobs that rely on their minds or their voices. Many are writers, agents, or in the communication fields. They can also sell anything and are very persuasive.

CANCER June 22–July 22

Like Taurus, Cancer likes having roots and long-term commitments. Cancers tends to be the "moms" of their companies. They prefer large companies because they feel protected within that family environment. There are more Cancers in *Who's Who in Business* than any other sign. Look for Cancers in politics or successful family businesses, or the food and restaurant industry, as they enjoy food.

LEO July 23–Aug. 22

Leo is the sign of the entrepreneur and Leo is a natural leader. Many executives, politicians, and movie directors are Leos. Leos may be frustrated if they are not in charge, and many lose their jobs because of their distaste for taking orders, but they are very hard workers. Look for Leos in "executive" positions—everything from executive secretary to executive director. As long as they are at the top of the heap, they're content.

VIRGO Aug. 23–Sept. 22

Virgo is the sign of the workaholic. A Virgo often is a perfectionist with an eye for detail and a penchant for looking after others. Many Virgos are doctors, nurses, and teachers. Look for Virgo in any of the service industries. Virgo is also very analytical and tends toward computer programming and training jobs.

LIBRA Sept. 23–Oct. 22

Libra is the beauty sign and is attracted to jobs that require artistic ability. Look for Libras in the fashion, crystals, linens, and makeup industries. Libras (whose symbol is the scales) also seek balance and make excellent mediators. Rev. Jesse Jackson is a Libra.

SCORPIO Oct. 23–Nov. 21

Scorpios crave control and power, which may explain why so many U.S. presidents are Scorpios. They enjoy the manipulation of power, and are often found around mergers and corporate takeovers. Because they make good executives, look for Scorpios to be the president or CEO of a company.

SAGITTARIUS Nov. 22–Dec. 22

Sagittarius loves travel and communication, and subsequently loves international trade and banking. They make excellent salespeople, but only if they believe in what they're selling. Many are happy-go-lucky, at home in the sports industry or comedy. A Sagittarian is more likely to take chances than most signs and can move quickly when the opportunity presents itself.

CAPRICORN Dec. 23–Jan. 20

Capricorn is the most ambitious sign. Capricorns like structure and control and truly are the captains of industry. They excel at management, are conservative and cautious, but will work tirelessly until they get to the top. They are great negotiators because they have the patience to wait forever, until they get what they want.

FACT FILE:

PISCES POWER

■ *Want to be among the super-rich? It may help to be born between February 20 and March 20. Here's the breakdown of the 256 Forbes Four Hundred with self-made fortunes in their lifetimes:*

PISCEANS	11.3%	AQUARIANS	9.4%
ARIES	9%	CANCERS	9%
CAPRICORNS	8.6%	SCORPIOS	8.2%
TAUREANS	7.8%	LEOS	7.8%
VIRGOS	7.4%	SAGITTARIANS	7.4%
LIBRANS	7%	GEMINIS	7%

■ *Pisceans on the Forbes list: Michael Eisner, CEO, Walt Disney Co.; David Geffen, entertainment mogul; Rupert Murdoch, media mogul; and Laurence Tisch, investor extraordinaire.*

SOURCE: *Forbes* magazine.

EXPERT Q & A

BULLY BOSSES FROM HELL

They tyrannize the workplace. Here's how to escape their clutches

The American workplace can be a brutal place. On any given day, according to Columbia University psychologist Harvey Hornstein, one in five people gets abused by a boss. Using questionnaires filled out by nearly 1,000 men and women over an eight-year period, Hornstein estimates that over 90 percent of U.S. workers experience some form of abusive behavior during their working life.

In his study of managerial abuse, *Brutal Bosses and Their Prey* (Riverhead Books, 1996), Hornstein discusses what separates "bully bosses" from those who are merely "tough, but fair" managers. Here he describes brutal bosses and how to deal with them.

■ Are there any places where bully bosses tend to exist more than others?

No, and that's the scary part. By the end of our research, almost all industries were equally represented. Gender was equally represented. Blue-collar workers and white-collar executives were all represented. In some cases, the abuse may have taken different forms—usually verbal or physical—but I don't know that the pain was any less in each case. Abuse occurs in the boardroom as well as on the shop floor. There really are no differences. Some abuse literally occurred in manholes where utility workers were working, as well as on the 68th floor.

■ Which kind of bully bosses are people likely to encounter?

Our evidence suggests conquerors, performers, and manipulators (see box for descriptions) are the most common. Power organizations focus you on power. That's the name of the game, that's what the trade is about. Turf and power are the issues. It's what's traded. And the subordinates are the ones made to suffer.

However, I have found dehumanizers, blamers, and rationalizers most frequently arise in organizations facing issues such as downsizing or other measures that are taken in the face of difficult times. Whenever companies are making a transition, these three seem to pop up.

■ What is the most effective way to deal with a bully boss?

From an individual perspective, what works well is to try and find protection within the organization.This can usually be found through an ombudsperson, a grievance committee, or even by pursuing legal options. Options do exist, but not always.

One of the reasons I wrote the book was to enable workers to "learn the patterns of the predator." What triggers them? What kinds of issues are their major concerns? And how do workers try to avoid them? In many cases it was quite literally physically avoiding bosses at times when they are at their most volatile. That's how a lot of folks survive working for these kinds of people.

■ What if you can't avoid them?

When you are attacked, it's important to make a good faith response. Focus on the content of what's being said, not on the curses. Focus on the meaning of the message, not the malevolence. Otherwise you just inflame them.

■ What about confronting bully bosses when they are being abusive?

That may be the noble thing to do, but it is often the costly thing to do—very costly. Most of the time you pay the price. If you don't lose your job, you certainly get labeled as someone who is a troublemaker. You get pushed into positions that are undesirable. That's the potential downside of taking legal action or invoking other forms of protection. And that's why people are afraid to do it.

A SPOTTER'S GUIDE TO BRUTAL BOSSES

In his book, Harvey Hornstein identifies six different types of "brutal bosses." Here's his description of each.

■ **CONQUERORS.** Concerned with power and making sure it's not undermined in any way, they use words to bludgeon you. They want to make you feel small. They are the classic schoolyard bullies.

■ **PERFORMERS.** These types are threatened by anyone who challenges their competence, or who they perceive as outperforming themselves. Rather than take a subordinate's performance as a plus for their camp, they see it as a minus for themselves personally. Their favorite weapon is to belittle. They are known to put comments in your personnel file without telling you, and criticize your work without giving you a chance to explain or respond. They are also the types to ask for positive comments to affirm their own self-worth You end up not giving honest feedback, but rather absolute approval.

■ **MANIPULATORS.** Concerned with how they are being valued, whether people like them and care about them is what's important. They will attack you personally. Their weapon is to smear your reputation. They take credit for your successes, but will attribute their failures to you or anyone else who is around. You can't win with these folks.

■ **DEHUMANIZERS.** They turn people into numbers. They look at you as simply cogs. They have a machinelike view of human beings and the social world. That permits them to abuse. It's much easier to abuse someone when the target of your abuse is seen as a "thing" rather than a person.

■ **BLAMERS.** They write off their harm by saying that you and the others "deserved it." This is the blame-the-victim attitude. They will say, "I didn't do a bad thing. They deserved what happened to them."

■ **RATIONALIZERS.** These brutal bosses don't blame the victim of abuse, but use abuse to justify a greater cause. Rationalizing brutal bosses say things such as, "Just helping out the organization," or "Well, someone had to do it." They use these self-justifying terms to cover up their own feelings about the abuse they have inflicted.

I just heard of a case the other day, where a woman took legal action and it's taken two years to go to court. Two years! And her attorney told her that this was a cut-and-dry case. And there is still no remedy. Of course now no one in the company wants this woman working for them. Although up until the time this event occurred, she was a choice employee. It's not easy.

The shortcoming of these solutions is that they really don't solve the problem from an organizational perspective. The brutal characters are still there. Any even if you get out of their way, and mitigate the harm that's coming your way, they are still free to roam the corridors and beat up on someone else. So the organization hasn't solved the problem.

■ **Does senior management need to step in and address the bully boss problem?**

Yes, exactly. Ways to do that include introducing progressive management tools such as 360-degree feedback, which gives employees a greater voice and makes them more equal. It gives them access to senior level management and puts bosses at all levels on notice that their misbehavior will be part of the record and will not go unnoticed.

STRESS

HOW TO BEAT BURNOUT

Smart ways to deal with that "take this career and shove it" feeling

Basketball star Michael Jordan did it. So did Harvard University president Neil Rudenstein and "Far Side" cartoonist Gary Larsen. All three—to name just a few—recently took breathers in their careers to combat battle fatigue. Millions of Americans report that they are burned out, job-weary, bored, frustrated, overworked, or just plain stressed

FACT FILE:

STRESSED OUT

■ *Percentage of senior and middle managers agreeing with each of the following*

	1994	1982
Burnout is a serious problem	68%	40%
Managers are working too many hours	65%	39%
More and more, managers are physically exhausted by the end of the workday	64%	38%
Managers often take too much work home with them	60%	47%
Emotional exhaustion is common among managers	58%	—
Depression is more common among managers than it used to be	45%	—

Source: Opinion Research Corp.

out. A 1992 study of job and personal life stress on 28,000 workers, for example, found that more than half of them reported some degree of career burnout.

Relax, help is just ahead. Cynthia Scott is a clinical psychologist and the author of 10 books on achieving optimal happiness and performance in the workplace. Founding principal of the San Francisco–based firm Changeworks Solutions, she has served as a consultant to executive and management teams from such companies as National Semiconductor and the IRS. Her advice:

■ **KNOW THE BURNOUT SIGNS.** The best indication of burnout is your day-to-day relationship with your immediate supervisor. Supervisors who communicate, share information, collaborate, and allow some control over how work is done produce less burnout in their co-workers. Research suggests burnout is less related to how much pressure people feel than to how meaningful they find their work. People who work hard but love what they do don't get burned out—unless they're working around abusive people or doing a job without a clear goal related to it.

■ **DO AT HOME WHAT YOU CAN'T DO AT WORK.** If you don't have a lot of control in the workplace, you may need to take on more control at home. Vacuum the rug, clean the house, plant a garden, take up a sport—anything that moves your body, lets the tension out, and gives you control. If your work involves long assignments, go home and do things with a quick finishing point. If you're working on real choppy, quick stuff, do something at home that has some longevity, like building a ship in a bottle. If you're isolated all day, go home and talk all night. If you talk to people all day, spend a quiet night reading. Whatever you do, don't get into numbing yourself; that can lead to alcohol and drug abuse, and isn't a real release.

■ **KNOW WHEN TO TAKE A STEP BACK.** If things at work are really getting to you, take a day off and get some distance. Ask yourself: Is the problem short-term stress that you know will be over soon? If I'm overloaded with a short-term stressor, I might just go off for an hour and do something nice for myself. If it's a long-term pressure that doesn't stop—like a long commute you have every day—taking an hour off won't do anything. For a chronic pressure like this, you need to ask yourself, "Is it going to get better?" Then see what options might work.

■ GET INPUT FROM FAMILY AND FRIENDS. I call it bringing together your "board of directors" —the people who know you from different stages of your life. Have a pizza party, bring everyone together, and get their opinions just like you would in a business meeting. It's important to get the perspective of other people, because they each have a different view of you and a different time frame. They can often help you deal with some things you didn't think you could do anything about.

■ SEEK THE TRUTH ABOUT YOUR JOB STABILITY. It's better to actually get laid off than to worry about it. People have their worst anxieties when they don't have information. If you know that you're losing your job in three months or three weeks, you can learn coping strategies. If you hear a bunch of "wells" and "maybes," you stay in a perpetual state of anxiety. You need clarity and the truth. Approach your boss and ask what's going on; this releases you to take other action. If your boss won't be specific, ask him, "Can you at least take this to the next level of understanding?" The more you know, the better.

■ LEARN WHAT WOMEN KNOW ABOUT STRESS. Women inherently have had more opportunities to develop and practice dealing with multiple onslaughts of stress —and establish coping capabilities. Women have had to juggle roles of home and work much more, and the same skills work in each venue. The more traditional male role has been full of onslaughts, but in a narrower vector. In the past, because women didn't have traditional power and authority, they had to get it by sharing their experiences with others in a "friendship network." That's why in many ways women have more success with these new workplaces that are team-based. They also often have a higher emotional literacy, so they can express their concerns—and don't mind doing so to another person. Only now are men getting some permission to have feelings.

■ BRING WORK CONCERNS OUT IN THE OPEN. I'm always a fan of not "choking on it"—of trying to communicate how you feel. Try saying to your boss, "That last comment you made really made me feel devalued, and I'm not sure what role I have in this project now. Could we try and work it out?" If a problem is really stressful, and you don't want to deal with it, do something to get yourself centered again. Try breathing or taking a walk—just get out of the stressful situation.

■ USE MENTAL IMAGERY AND CALMING TECHNIQUES. If you're doing some awful task,

■ THE MOST STRESSFUL JOBS

The *National Business Employment Weekly Jobs Rated Almanac* (John Wiley, 1995) evaluated 250 jobs for stress. Among the criteria used in the ranking: overtime, quotas, deadlines, competitiveness, physical demands, and initiative required. Here's how some common occupations ranked:

RANK	JOB	STRESS SCORE
1.	U.S. president	176.6
2.	Firefighter	110.9
3.	Senior executive	108.6
6.	Surgeon	99.5
22.	Pilot	68.7
25.	Architect	66.9
31.	Lawyer	64.3
47.	Auto salesperson	56.3
144.	Bank officer	35.4
216.	Financial planner	26.3
241.	Bookkeeper	21.5

you need a place where you can go mentally via imagery to get through it. What can you think of that gives you a sense of ease? People choose lots of different things, like lying on the couch, going to the seashore, or sitting in their bathtubs. What I encourage people to do is to always have one image ready. If you practice this kind of self-care strategy ahead of time, you can meditate and go to your safe place mentally whenever you want.

Say you're being screamed at by your boss. You either want to punch him in the nose or run like hell, but this "fight or flight" mentality is not so acceptable in polite society. You can remove yourself from the stress using the meditative technique in 30 seconds. This doesn't mean you have to sit on your desk cross-legged. You can have your eyes open and be attempting to listen, but the rest of you is thinking your way into your place of ease. Sometimes time to unwind is needed to alleviate stress. If you've just left an awful meeting with your boss, don't take the elevator—take the stairs. Ease the butterflies in your stomach by breathing in as you take each step. Let out the tension, and begin to get some oxygen back in your brain.

■ **LEARN HOW TO JUDGE THE STRESS LEVEL OF YOUR JOB.** Jobs that are high demand but have low control are the most stressful. It's more about position than occupation. For instance, a nurse working in a clinic has high demand and low control, with no way of knowing how many patients will be coming in each shift. Firemen have high demand, but it comes in spurts—fires are often followed by long periods of downtime—so it's actually not as stressful. People who fight forest fires have a more stressful time, because these fires seem to go on forever. Air traffic controllers have it really tough, because they are not allowed to leave their controls. Bus drivers not only have to manage the street, but they have to manage all the interpersonal relationships that get on their bus. They have no control over who they pick up, and they can't leave their post either.

SMALL BUSINESS

ON BEING YOUR OWN BOSS

What should you do before taking the plunge to minimize the risk?

At one time or another, almost everyone has considered being his or her own boss. And why not? But being on your own isn't easy. In a 1989 study, Bruce Phillips, director of economic research for the Office of Advocacy of the Small Business Administration, and Bruce Kirchhoff of the New Jersey Institute of Technology found that nearly 40 percent of the new companies they studied survived six years, more than twice the number many had predicted. After eight years, the survival rate was close to 30 percent. Survival rates varied by industry. Manufacturing companies typically had a higher survival rate than retailers. Size was a factor, too. The tiniest companies and those that never added even one employee were more likely to fail than others. On closer examination, Kirchhoff found that only 18 percent of new businesses end in real failure. The rest survive or are closed voluntarily.

Still, being in business for yourself is at least as difficult and challenging as working for others. Bruce Phillips of the Small Business Administration offers some tips on how to minimize the risks.

STAY CLEAR OF ENTERPRISES THAT ARE PRONE TO CYCLICAL DOWNSWINGS.

"Businessess that are tied to discretionary income are always risky in the sense that movements in the economy cause higher interests rates, and businesses that are cyclically sensitive are more likely to be affected," Phillips says. During the 1990–91 recession, for instance, one in six construction workers was out of a job, and construction remains a risky, boom-or-bust business to be in. Auto dealerships are similarly impacted; when interest rates shoot up, car sales tend to go down. And it will hardly come as a surprise to most people that leisure and luxury businesses—recreation, expensive boats, and vacation homes—are also a risk. One less obvious gamble is the apparel industry, which has posted a higher failure rate as of late, in part because of the growth of chain stores.

BEWARE OF SECTORS THAT ARE HEAVILY SATURATED WITH SUPERSTORES.

Home Depot, Borders Books, and other chains known as "category killer stores" have an automatic edge because they have better economies of scale and can overcome the high entry barriers to which they themselves contribute. Any business wanting to go up against these types of stores needs to have a special niche, or four to five stores themselves, in order to spread cost, according to Phillips. It is also increasingly expensive to buy advertising these days unless it is for more than one store.

Over the past two years, Phillips says, the best kind of businesses have been the stable service industries. Leading this growth are business and health services, such as independent consulting firms and those that lease medical equipment such as MRI scanners. Small specialized concerns such as cable repair can also do well. In addition, the whole contracting area has been very successful for small firms, as big firms have continued to downsize. Many larger companies are now contracting out a number of functions, such as bookkeeping, legal services, accounting, advertising, and management consulting. And the failure rates for service industries in general are much less than they are for manufacturing and the wholesale trade.

Phillips recommends talking to people already in the same business. In addition, since many firms fail—either because they don't have enough money when they start out or because they lack management experience—it is important to write a business plan. The Small Business Administration has a mentoring agency that aspiring entrepreneurs can use; call your local SBA office for more information.

■ BEST AND WORST STATES FOR ENTREPRENEURS

Finding the most fertile ground for entrepreneurial activity can sometimes seem like a hitor miss process. Mississippi has become one of the fastest-growing states because of riverboat gambling, and the Rust Belt states of Ohio, Michigan, and Minnesota have experienced a partial rebirth due to increased exports. Cognetics, Inc., a Cambridge, Mass., consulting firm, evaluated the entrepreneurial climate by state, region, and metropolitan area.

BEST TEN STATES	WORST TEN STATES
1. Utah	**1.** Wyoming
2. Nevada	**2.** North Dakota
3. Arizona	**3.** Montana
4. Virginia	**4.** Maine
5. Georgia	**5.** Iowa
6. Tennessee	**6.** Rhode Island
7. Colorado	**7.** Alaska
8. North Carolina	**8.** New York
9. Florida	**9.** West Virginia
10. Maryland	**10.** Oklahoma

SOURCE: Cognetics, Inc., 100 Cambridge Park Drive, Cambridge, MA 02140. 1995 study.

■ THE RISKIEST AND SAFEST BUSINESSES

Bruce Phillips of the Small Business Administration studied "small-business dominated industries" for 1990. Here are the businesses that the study showed to be the five riskiest and five safest:

■ THE RISKIEST	Failure rate per 10,000 (1990)
Amusement and recreation services	578
Oil and gas extraction	166
Lumber and wood manufacturing	106
General building contractors	101
Furniture and home-furnishing stores	99
■ THE SAFEST	
Educational services (private education)	13
Health services	21
Legal services	25
Insurance agents and brokers	28
Personal services	39

FRANCHISES

SEARCHING FOR THE NEXT BIG MAC

A new study finds you're better off starting your own business

Conventional wisdom holds that franchising is a low-risk way to start a business. For an initial investment—up to $600,000 or more for a McDonald's, for example—you get all the training and marketing support you need. Then you manage your business and collect the revenues.

But that's not exactly the way it unfolds, according to Timothy Bates, an economics professor at Wayne State University. Bates tracked the performance of some 21,000 new franchises for four years in the late '80s. His findings are startling: 35 percent of the franchises failed by 1991, compared with 28 percent of conventional start-ups. Franchisees whose companies survived earned just $14,900 a year, compared with $26,600 for other start-ups.

Bates draws several conclusions. For one, franchisees may be picking already saturated or overly competitive markets. For another, perhaps franchisees aren't really getting the management advice and support they need. Finally, says Bates, franchisees may be inherently less likely to take risks than self-starters.

Although nearly two-thirds of franchises do survive, you should look before you leap into a franchise. For starters, contact the Federal Trade Commission, ☎ 202-326-2161, which offers a free packet of information that includes the pros and cons of franchising. Another good source: the International Franchise Association, ☎ 202-628-8000.

EXPERT LIST

THE HOTTEST FRANCHISES

Wondering which franchises are sure bets? Entrepreneur *magazine publishes its Franchise 500 annually, with breakdowns for fastest-growing, lowest-investment, and newest franchises. Franchises are rated on factors such as the length of time they have been in business, the number of franchises and company-owned units, start-up costs, financial stability, growth rates, percentage of terminations, and whether the company provides financing.*

ENTREPRENEUR'S TOP TEN FASTEST-GROWING FRANCHISES

NAME	SERVICE	START-UP COSTS	☎ TELEPHONE
Subway	Submarine sandwiches	$55.72K–$140.7K	800-888-4848
7-Eleven	Convenience stores	$12.5K +	800-255-0711
Burger King	Hamburgers	$247K–$1.32M	800-394-0940 or 305-378-7011
McDonald's	Hamburgers	$363K–$591K	708-575-6196
Dunkin' Donuts	Donuts	$181.6K–$255.1K	800-777-9983 or 617-961-4020
Yogen Fruz/Bresler's	Ice cream	$55K–$129K	905-479-8762
Baskin-Robbin USA	Ice cream	$42.2K–$370K	800-331-0031 or 818-956-0031
Jani-King	Commercial cleaning services	$1.76K+	800-552-5264
Coverall Cleaning Concepts	Commercial office cleaning	$350–$3.5K	800-537-3371 or 619-584-1911
CleanNet USA Inc.,	Commercial cleaning service	$425–$1.3K	800-735-8838 or 410-720-6444

WORKING AT HOME

HOMESPUN SUCCESS STORIES

Make a handsome living without leaving your front door. Here's how

You can't beat this commute: Roll out of bed, go down the hall, switch on your computer, and you're at the office. More than 13 million Americans, according to *Money* magazine, are now running businesses from home. Another 6 million or so work for corporations from home an average of a day and a half a week. Roughly half of the home-based businesses are service firms, says an AT&T survey, ranging from consulting to graphic design. The rest are primarily in sales, technical and administrative support, and repair services.

Judging by the money they make, home entrepreneurs aren't just home visiting the fridge: One study by IDC/Link, a New York City market research firm, found that full-time home-business owners earn an average of $58,000 annually. A 1996 *Money* poll discovered that 20 percent reported that their businesses grossed between $100,000 and $500,000 last year, while 14 percent paid themselves annual salaries of $50,000 to $250,000.

Sound appealing? Paul and Sarah Edwards are the authors of *The Best Home Businesses for the 90s* (Tarcher/Putnam, 1994) and cohosts of weekly cable television and radio shows on the subject. They can be reached via CompuServe's Working From Home Forum and on their Web page *(http://www.homeworks.com)*. Here are their picks of some of today's hottest home-based careers:

SPECIALTY CONSULTING

Large companies are eliminating departments or staff positions, but they still want the service the department or person provided. At the same time, small businesses are growing, but they can't afford to hire people to do training, public relations, or graphic design. So they contract out for those services.

Some of the best specialty consulting fields are technical—software engineers and people who can provide technical and scientific expertise. People in human resources, health administration, education, law, and business can also find lots of work.

An up-and-coming niche position is the "business coach," who works with individuals, often the president of a small business. Coaches ask—and answer—questions that the client would get from a staff and VPs if he or she were the CEO of a large company. You don't need an MBA, just good skills at recognizing problems.

- **TYPICAL ANNUAL GROSS REVENUE:** $30,000–$120,000 per year (billing 15–30 hours a week, 40 weeks a year, at $50–$100 an hour).
- **POTENTIAL DOWNSIDE:** Selling yourself as simply a "marketing consultant" can get you nowhere fast; pick a specialty and stick to it.

BUSINESS PLAN WRITER

The market here is smaller businesses that are growing. When they're seeking venture capital or money from a lender, most companies need a business plan that goes beyond what they might get in a software program.

Independent plan writers should consider teaching a course at a local college. Frequently people who take how-to courses in computer programming or writing business plans will realize the professor knows more than they ever will—and make a job offer.

- **TYPICAL ANNUAL GROSS REVENUE:** $20,000–$100,000. (Median of $55,000 based upon writing 10 plans per year at $5,000 each and editing 10 plans at $500 each.)
- **POTENTIAL DOWNSIDE:** Vulnerable to economic cycles. Because you're dealing with companies in a state of flux, legal or collection problems may arise.

DESKTOP VIDEO PUBLISHER

As the number of cable channels expands, more advertising is needed to support them. Someone working from home is in a great position if he or she can do a decent, quick job producing commercials for local businesses. Related work includes making business pro-

EXPERT Q & A

COURT TIME: THE INS AND OUTS OF JURY DUTY

To meet your civic responsibilitity when you get a summons for jury duty, work and family schedules often need to be revised. As O.J. Simpson's jury consultant, Jo-Ellan Dimitrius of Forensic Technologies, Inc., advised Simpson's lawyers which potential jury members were most likely to give their client a fair hearing. Here, she sheds some light on what to expect when you receive a jury summons.

■ **What should people know when they show up for jury duty?**

Jurors have the right to ask questions: what days will we have off, will I be sequestered, will I remain anonymous? Also, if you anticipate legitimate conflicts, like a long-planned family vacation, the court may be able to work around them.

■ **Who makes the best jurors for criminal and civil cases?**

For a defendant in a criminal trial, or a plaintiff in a civil trial, you look for jurors who are liberal. Someone who is a member of PETA (People for the Ethical Treatment of Animals), for example, or church members and minorities. For defendants in civil cases, or prosecutors in criminal cases, you look for the more conservative, older jurors, perhaps someone who had been the victim of a crime.

In all cases, you want to have one or two firm, authoritarian types who will lead in your direction during the deliberation process. And for the rest you want followers who will listen.

■ **What is the surest way to get excused from jury duty?**

It raises red flags anytime a juror walks in with sunglasses on, anytime anyone's hiding their eyes. I avoid jurors who give very brief answers. It makes me wonder what they are trying to hide. I look at body language—there have been times when jurors are giving me a positive response, but shaking their heads no. Also, the way they talk about the defendant; during the OJ trial, a juror was referring to Simpson as "the incarcerated"—not a good sign. I'll avoid a person who clearly doesn't want to be there.

posals and how-to videos, as well as designing Web pages and producing CD-ROMs.

■ **TYPICAL ANNUAL GROSS REVENUE:** $35,000–$150,000.

■ **POTENTIAL DOWNSIDE:** Huge start-up costs of $10,000–$30,000 for equipment, which must be kept updated. Huge learning curve for those with no prior video or hardware experience.

INFORMATION BROKERING

This position is an investigative reporter, marketing researcher, and librarian rolled into one. The highest incomes go to those who do competitive intelligence—the gathering of information (what a company's competitors are doing, what's happening to the industry, etc.) before marketing decisions are made.

■ **TYPICAL ANNUAL GROSS REVENUE:** $17,500–$75,000.

■ **POTENTIAL DOWNSIDE:** You have to be good at drumming up business, or you can starve.

TEMPORARY HELP SERVICES

Specialize. Develop your database and contacts, then target a very identifiable number of businesses (attorneys, chiropractors, etc.).

■ **TYPICAL ANNUAL GROSS REVENUE:** $70,000 (minus payroll; assumes you have 10 employees working 15 hours a week, $21 an hour).

■ **POTENTIAL DOWNSIDE:** Start-up costs are high ($9,000–$31,000), because your workers get paid before you do. Working capital alone of $5,000–$20,000 is needed to keep folks paid between monthly billing cycles.

ERGONOMICS

A CHAIR FIT FOR A CHAIRMAN

How you sit can make a difference in where you stand

The perfect chair is something to behold. It should meet the contour and size of your body, allowing the torso to rest on the proper muscles to support your weight. An imperfect chair, on the other hand, can be hazardous to your health, inflicting, for example, long-term damage to your spinal disks.

Chances are you haven't given a lot of thought to what you sit on at the office. But Richard Holbrook has. An ergonomics expert with his own industrial design firm in Pasadena, Calif., Holbrook creates chairs, lighting fixtures, and other office furniture for optimal worker comfort and productivity. His "Ambi Chair"—which won a 1996 American Product Excellence Award—is the result of a decade spent studying the health hazards and drops in efficiency that arise from improper seating. "The dictionary defines ergonomics as the 'study of efficiency of persons in their working environment,'" explains Holbrook, "but I look at it as fitting the environment to the person rather than forcing the person to fit the environment." Here are his thoughts on finding this perfect combination:

■ **FIT COMES FIRST.** Find a chair that fits your body. Seat height should be the first concern. A seat that's too low makes it difficult to get to your keyboard and interferes with a comfortable relationship with your desk or computer, so the table and/or chair must be easily adjustable. If you're at the keyboard and feel your arms are in a comfortable, proper position, then the chair height should be adjusted so your thighs are parallel to the ground. If your feet don't touch the ground in this position, you'll need a footrest.

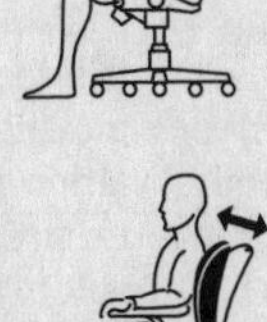

■ **BEWARE CUSHY SEATS.** You don't want too much weight concentrated on your seat bones, the two bony spurs in your pelvis that when you sit cause a stress concentration directly below your hip joint. If a chair seat is too hard, you're going to feel the concentration of stress in the seat bones; if it's too soft you may initially feel good, but eventually you will feel stress on the outside of your hips.

■ **AVOID LONG CUSHIONS.** If you can't get against the backrest, you can't get into a comfortable, healthy posture. You want about 1 to 1½ inches of space between the front of a seat cushion and the back of your calf—a highly sensitive area where a lot of veins and arteries are very close to the surface. Many people sit in office chairs that are too big for them. This can lead to circulation problems in the lower legs like varicose veins, swelling, and pain in the feet and ankles. The front of the seat cushion should have a nice curve; you don't want the sharp front edge of the cushion coming up and cutting off the circulation in the bottom of your thighs.

■ **BACKRESTS AND ARMRESTS.** When you're moving around and bending over, the disks in your back are being compressed, and if the spine is maintained in an unhealthy posture for a long period of time it can permanently damage the disks. A chair with good back support gets the spine back into the natural "S curve" equilibrium it has when we're standing. The backrest should be high enough to also provide some upper-back support—and enable you to lean back, relax, and give your upper arms and shoulders a rest.

Armrests provide a necessary support so you can lean to one side and get relief from your shoulders, and should ideally be height- (up to 4 inches) and width- (2 inches) adjustable. They should provide support from your elbow until a little past the middle of your forearm (about 8 to 10 inches),

EXPERT Q & A

WHAT'S NAUGHTY, WHAT'S NICE

Stick to fruit baskets, golf balls, and other things of nominal value

With workplaces increasingly sensitive to ethical questions, gift giving at the office can be a virtual minefield. W. Michael Hoffman, executive director of the Center for Business Ethics at Bentley College in Waltham, Mass., discusses the whys and wherefores of office giving.

■ How should employees treat gifts from clients or contractors?

Some corporations set a dollar amount, but it's better to say that gifts can only have a "nominal value." It's very hard to police a dollar amount. If someone gives you a ballpoint pen, you have a good idea of the cost. The pen is a way of saying "don't forget us," but it's not going to convince you to do business with a company. If, on the other hand, someone gives you a Mont Blanc pen, that kind of crosses the line.

The real purpose of corporate ethics policies is to try to get employees to think about what they are accepting and, if needed, to check the company's ethics policy. If it is a gift that could be perceived by someone to influence, or in fact actually change, your decision about whether you would do business with that supplier over other suppliers, it should be returned.

■ Should an employee give a gift to his or her supervisor?

Gifts from a subordinate to a supervisor are particularly sensitive; if the gift is too expensive, co-workers could say that the gift giver is trying to gain an edge. That could create resentment and be perceived as being improper if not unethical. It puts both the giver and the recipient in an awkward position, perhaps even influencing improperly a judgment. For instance, if the supervisor wants to promote an employee and then gets a set of golf clubs from that employee, the supervisor could feel uneasy about giving the promotion.

■ Should a supervisor give a gift to a subordinate?

Recognition for employees is fine, but this does not necessarily mean an expensive gift. The supervisor is better off recognizing an employee's performance in some sort of salary fashion. As a rule, though, nominal gifts hold true for the boss-employee relationship as well as the other way around. This is a matter more of common sense than ethics. In internal office giving, the main rule of thumb is to try to avoid giving gifts that could be perceived as trying to win favor or influence.

---

and soft armrests are best. The tissues on the bottom of the arms are sensitive, and cutting off the circulation in those tissues on a harder armrest can cause nerve problems.

■ KEEP MOVING. The best way to stay pain-free is to avoid spending hours on end at your desk. Take a five-minute break every hour to walk around. If you can't do that, make frequent changes of posture as you're sitting. Move around enough to keep your circulation healthy and not get overly fatigued. We've measured fatigue in various sitting positions, and found that when you sit in an uncomfortable position you fatigue more completely.

Taking a break to lean back in your chair is also very important. When your spine is moving, you're maintaining healthy circulation in the spinal column, muscles, and tissues in your back and seat. You should be able to lean forward without feeling uncomfortable, or lean back effortlessly and find a balanced position anywhere from an upright spot to about 20 degrees reclined.

CHAPTER SIX

HOUSE & GARDEN

EXPERT QUOTES

"Warm colors are generally more pleasing and fulfill the basic human need for light."
—Donald Kaufman, architectural color consultant
Page 388

"The mistake most people make on their lawn is watering too frequently."
—Dean Norton, horticulturist at Mt. Vernon
Page 428

"Any time you deal with an exotic animal, there's a tremendous unknown."
—Richard Farinato, Humane Society of the U.S.
Page 431

■ **THE YEAR AHEAD: SAY GOODBYE** to homes with formal dining rooms and other spaces dedicated to a single purpose... **TRY** the new fluorescent lighting fixtures and quartz lamps... **CUT** your home insurance costs by getting a security system... **LOOK FOR** container gardens to attract more urban green thumbs... **PLAN** your garden for year-round color... **SMILE** at the amazing new cat hybrid, the Munchkin... **RETHINK** what you may be feeding the family dog... **BUY** yourself a really comfortable new bed...

AROUND THE HOUSE 382
HOME SAFETY 402
GARDENING 411
PETS 431

AROUND THE HOUSE

RENOVATIONS: What most popular alterations cost, PAGE 384 **EXPERT TIPS:** Finding a contractor you won't regret, PAGE 387 **PAINT:** A color specialist on how to make your home beautiful, PAGE 388 **BEDS:** Tips on buying the right mattress, PAGE 391 **LIGHTING:** Illumination for every room in the house, PAGE 392 **HOME REPAIR:** From stuck windows to trickling toilets, PAGE 395 **POLLUTANTS:** What to do about indoor environmental hazards, PAGE 398

EXPERT Q & A

THE MEANING OF HOME

Houses in the 1990s must fit new lifestyles and psychological needs

Remember the bright orange or avocado-colored Formica kitchen countertops of the 70s? Such fashion and fancy in the home have little or no permanence. The garish colors of yesterday are replaced by the polished granite or stainless steel of today. While such fashions are fleeting, floor plans and the overall organization of homes take longer to evolve. They respond more to lifestyle changes in the family than to designer whim. Here, Linda O'Keeffe, senior editor at *Metropolitan Home* magazine, discusses the modern American home and shares her insights into how people are making the best use of their living spaces today.

■ **Where have you seen the most changes in the home?**

For some time now, floor plans have been evolving to become more open. The kitchen has opened up and is designed to include the family. It's no longer a room occupied by just one person. Figuratively it used to be the center of the house; now, it literally is, too.

The kitchen is also more of a functioning workroom. Everything is no longer sealed away and behind closed doors—there's see-through cabinetry. We are also seeing more center islands.

■ **Have any rooms fallen out of favor in current home designs?**

I think the dining room is disappearing. A separate dining room connotes a formality that really isn't there that much anymore. The living room and family room are also combining more. Rooms for one specific purpose are changing. People have their gyms in their bedrooms, home offices in their dining rooms, and their televisions in their bedrooms. Bathrooms have televisions and telephones; they are also being looked upon as lounging areas. Rooms now have multi purposes, so we are redefining the character of each room.

■ **Do you see more home offices today?**

Absolutely. But we are not seeing a specific room designated as the office. Technologically, you don't need one. You can have a laptop on a plane or a fax in your car, so there is no real need to have an office defined in the traditional sense.

■ **What's behind these renovation trends?**

We have an impression of intimacy because the world is at our fingertips. But there's a backlash to the isolation that comes from interaction that is done through a wire. As our lives become more depersonalized, we want more intimacy and comfort in the home.

■ How do you create intimacy and comfort in a home?

The colors and shapes you have in a space are crucial. A room with 20-foot ceilings dictates the furnishings you choose. The shapes of the furnishings have to be pleasing, as do the negative space they create. We see this with the movement toward *feng shui*—the ancient Asian principles of design and placement of objects. It sounds like nit-picking, but it's all very important as a holistic approach to the space you live in.

■ What should a person do who has trouble imagining how to design a living space to meet his needs?

Today, there's every kind of shelter magazine on the market, so people are more sophisticated than ever in understanding their lifestyles and imagining spaces. The gap between architects and interior designers and the public is lessening. When people hire professionals these days, it's a collaborative effort.

■ Which is more common—adding on to a house or trying to make the most of the space you have?

I think people are re-creating the space they have. They don't think in terms of forever now. Today's homeowners are very aware that they might not be in a home in the foreseeable future. They are much more concerned with what's going to serve their immediate purposes and also increase the property value.

■ What is the biggest mistake that people make when renovating their homes?

I would say ignoring needs. Rather than taking a prescribed floor plan for a room, ask yourself, "What do I use spaces for? What do I want to do with the space? Do I need a dining room, or will a long country table in the kitchen suffice? Do I really need a separate room assigned to be my office?" Needs should dictate and define space more than a set formal plan.

THE DREAM HOUSE AT A DREAMER'S PRICE

A new study shows that Americans still want it all

An English cottage with a kitchen garden? A Federal-style townhouse with lots of shutters? A tepee on the plains, a glass cube with views for miles? Everybody has their vision of the dream house. But what do serious househunters really expect in a newly constructed home? The National Association of Home Builders and Fulton Research, Inc., in association with Home Guides of America, went looking for answers recently, and what they found is that today's new home buyer wants a house that includes:

- **Median size:** 2,196 sq. ft.
- **Front exterior material:** Brick
- **Outdoor features:** Trees, exterior lights
- **Bedrooms:** 4, including one for use as a guest room or home office
- **Bathrooms:** 2 1/2, with master bath to include white tub and sink, separate shower enclosure, private toilet compartment, linen closet, exhaust fan
- **Parking:** 2-car garage
- **Security system:** Internal
- **Kitchen:** Large counter space, table and chairs, double sink, walk-in pantry, island work area, Corian countertop
- **Kitchen–Family room:** Visually open, with a half-wall between
- **Ceilings:** 9 ft. on first floor, with cathedral ceiling in living room
- **Fireplace:** In family room
- **Specialty areas:** Laundry near kitchen or bedroom. Also, a dining room, home office, den/library, soundproofing
- **Master bedroom closet:** Walk-in his & hers, or a single large walk-in
- **Skylights:** In bathroom/kitchen
- **Built-in shelving**

AND THE EXPECTED MEDIAN PRICE FOR ALL THIS: $163,000

RENOVATIONS

THE PRICE OF GETTING IT RIGHT

What most popular alterations cost from coast to coast

You bought the place, but it needs work, and you're not sure where to start. Every house is different, of course, but some remodeling projects offer a better payback than others. Each year *Remodeling* magazine puts some of the most popular home improvement projects to the test, asking real estate agents in 60 cities how much the project would add in the first year to a mid-priced house in an established neighborhood. The results are instructive: Buyers will pay for state-of-the-art kitchens, luxurious master bed and bath suites, family rooms, and extra bedrooms.

Here's a region-by-region breakdown of the projects. The estimates for construction costs come from three well-known publishers of estimating manuals and software: Craftsman Books Company of Carlsbad, Calif., HomeTech Information Systems of Bethesda, Md., and R. S. Means Company of Kingston, Mass. Keep in mind that the prices are averages; actual prices can vary widely depending on materials, labor costs, and design.

FACT FILE:

JOBS TO HIRE OUT

- *Electrical, plumbing, and foundation work that must pass building codes—a licensed professional will know local requirements.*
- *Projects with expensive building materials, such as hand-painted tile or high-end carpeting.*
- *Dangerous jobs, such as installing a new roof.*

MINOR KITCHEN ADDITION

■ **Project description:** In a functional but outdated 200-square-foot kitchen with 30 lineal feet of cabinetry and countertops, refinish cabinets, install new energy-efficient wall oven and cooktop, new laminate countertop, mid-priced sink and faucet, wall covering and resilient flooring, and fresh paint. Job includes new raised-panel wood doors on cabinets.

REGION	JOB COST	RESALE VALUE	COST RECOUPED
East	$8,619	$8,147	95%
South	$7,035	$7,174	102%
Midwest	$7,898	$7,424	94%
West	$8,506	$8,751	103%
National	$8,014	$7,874	98%

MAJOR KITCHEN REMODEL

■ **Project description:** Update outmoded, 200-square-foot kitchen with design and installation of new cabinets, laminate countertops, mid-priced sink and faucet, energy-efficient wall oven, cooktop and ventilation system, built-in microwave, dishwasher, garbage disposal, custom lighting, new resilient flooring, and painted woodwork and ceiling. Features 30 lineal feet of semi-custom-grade wood cabinets and counter space, including 3-by-5-foot center island.

REGION	JOB COST	RESALE VALUE	COST RECOUPED
East	$24,787	$20,185	81%
South	$20,692	$19,463	94%
Midwest	$22,958	$18,078	79%
West	$24,534	$21,463	87%
National	$23,243	$19,797	85%

BATHROOM ADDITION

■ **Project description:** Add a second full bath to a house with one-and-a-half baths. The 6-by-8-foot bath should be within the existing floor plan in an inconspicuous spot convenient to bedrooms. Include cultured marble vanity top, molded sink, standard bathtub with shower, low-profile toilet, lighting, mirrored medicine cabinet, linen storage, vinyl wallpaper, and ceramic tile floor and walls in tub area.

REGION	JOB COST	RESALE VALUE	COST RECOUPED
East	$12,702	$10,471	82%
South	$9,973	$10,214	102%
Midwest	$11,436	$9,118	80%
West	$12,445	$11,709	94%
National	$11,639	$10,378	89%

BATHROOM REMODEL

■ **Project description:** Update an existing 5-by-9-foot bathroom that is at least 25 years old with new standard-size tub, toilet, and solid surface vanity counter with integral double sink. Install new lighting, faucets, mirrored medicine cabinet, and ceramic tile floor and wall in tub/shower area. Vinyl wallpaper elsewhere.

REGION	JOB COST	RESALE VALUE	COST RECOUPED
East	$9,116	$7,154	78%
South	$7,210	$6,571	91%
Midwest	$8,234	$5,873	71%
West	$8,901	$7,390	83%
National	$8,365	$6,747	81%

FAMILY ROOM ADDITION

■ **Project description:** In a style and location appropriate to the existing house, add a 16-by-25 foot, light-filled room on a new crawl space foundation with wood joist floor framing, matching wood siding on exterior walls and matching existing fiberglass roof. Include drywall interior with batt insulation, hardwood tongue-and-groove floor, and 180 square feet of glass, including atrium-style exterior (doors, windows, and two operable skylights). Tie into existing heating and cooling.

REGION	JOB COST	RESALE VALUE	COST RECOUPED
East	$34,583	$27,396	79%
South	$27,681	$23,933	86%
Midwest	$31,700	$24,432	77%
West	$34,131	$30,041	88%
National	$32,024	$26,451	83%

MASTER SUITE

■ **Project description:** On a house with two or three bedrooms, add over a crawl space a 24-by-16-foot master bedroom with walk-in closets. Master bath includes dressing area, whirlpool tub, separate ceramic tile shower, and a double-bowl vanity. Bedroom is carpeted; floor in bath is ceramic tile.

REGION	JOB COST	RESALE VALUE	COST RECOUPED
East	$38,644	$29,730	77%
South	$30,673	$27,190	89%
Midwest	$35,075	$26,708	76%
West	$37,850	$33,379	88%
National	$35,560	$29,252	82%

HOME OFFICE ADDITION

■ **Project description:** Convert an existing 12-by-12-foot room into a home office. Install custom cabinets configured for desk, computer workstation, and overhead storage, and 20 feet of plastic laminate desktop. Rewire room for computer, fax machine, and other electronic equipment as well as cable and telephone lines. Include drywall interior and commercial-grade, level-loop carpeting.

REGION	JOB COST	RESALE VALUE	COST RECOUPED
East	$8,282	$4,583	55%
South	$6,838	$4,407	64%
Midwest	$7,583	$3,823	50%
West	$8,132	$5,190	64%
National	$7,709	$4,501	58%

ATTIC BEDROOM

■ **Project description:** In a house with two or three bedrooms, convert unfinished attic with rafters to 15-by-15-foot bedroom and 5-by-7-foot shower/bath. Add four new windows and a 15-foot shed dormer. Insulate and finish ceiling and walls. Carpet unfinished floor. Extend existing heating and central air conditioning to new space. Retain existing stairs.

REGION	JOB COST	RESALE VALUE	COST RECOUPED
East	$23,646	$18,095	77%
South	$18,848	$16,391	87%
Midwest	$21,425	$16,620	78%
West	$23,262	$20,624	89%
National	$21,795	$17,932	82%

REPLACE SIDING

■ **Project description:** Replace 1,250 square feet

of existing siding with new vinyl or aluminum siding, including trim.

REGION	JOB COST	RESALE VALUE	COST RECOUPED
East	$5,555	$4,154	75%
South	$4,513	$3,077	68%
Midwest	$5,133	$3,489	68%
West	$5,643	$3,517	62%
National	$5,211	$3,559	68%

REPLACE WINDOWS

■ **Project description:** Replace 10 existing 3-by-5-foot windows with aluminum-clad windows, including new trim. Replace sashes, frames, and casings.

REGION	JOB COST	RESALE VALUE	COST RECOUPED
East	$5,840	$4,325	74%
South	$4,855	$3,358	69%
Midwest	$5,453	$3,192	59%
West	$5,805	$4,207	72%
National	$5,488	$3,771	69%

DECK ADDITION

■ **Project description:** Add a 16-by-20-foot deck of pressure-treated pine supported by 4 x 4 posts set in concrete footings. Include built-in bench, railings, and planter, also of pressure-treated pine.

REGION	JOB COST	RESALE VALUE	COST RECOUPED
East	$7,107	$4,910	69%
South	$5,601	$4,221	75%
Midwest	$6,444	$3,958	61%
West	$6,960	$5,334	77%
National	$6,528	$4,606	71%

TWO-STORY ADDITION

■ **Project description:** Over a crawl space, add a 24-by-16-foot two-story wing with a first floor family room and a second floor bedroom with full bath. Features a prefab fireplace in family room, 11 windows and atrium-style exterior door, carpeted floors, and painted drywall. Five-by-8-foot bath has fiberglass bath/shower, standard-grade toilet, wood vanity with ceramic sink top, ceramic tile flooring, mirrored medicine cabinet with light strip above, and wallpapered walls. Add new heating and cooling system to handle addition.

REGION	JOB COST	RESALE VALUE	COST RECOUPED
East	$54,374	$45,860	84%
South	$44,121	$39,729	90%
Midwest	$49,514	$38,623	78%
West	$53,649	$47,805	89%
National	$50,415	$43,004	85%

For a complete copy of the 1995–1996 *Cost vs. Value Report*, send a check for $5.50 to Hanley-Wood, Inc., One Thomas Circle, NW, #600, Washington, D.C., 20005, Attn. Remodeling Reprints.

SOURCE: *Remodeling* magazine, October 1995.

■ HOW REMODELING PROJECTS DEPRECIATE

A new garage is your best bet for increasing the long-term value of your house.

PROJECT	PERCENTAGE OF ORIGINAL RENOVATION COSTS ADDED TO THE VALUE OF HOUSE AFTER		
	1 YEAR	3 YEARS	5 YEARS
Kitchen renovation	77%	62%	47%
Bathroom renovation	77%	62%	44%
Roof replacement	69%	52%	39%
Fireplace addition	76%	68%	61%
Swimming pool addition	53%	42%	31%
One-car garage	84%	78%	71%
Wood deck addition	79%	66%	55%
Solar room addition	72%	61%	53%
Living/dining/family room update	79%	59%	37%

SOURCE: Marshall & Swift National Cost-Reporting Service.

EXPERT TIPS

A CONTRACTOR YOU WON'T REGRET

Your sanity and bank balance are at stake. How to avoid mistakes

Sometimes even the most intrepid do-it-yourselfer is cowed by a home repair or renovation project. That's when it's time to call in a professional. But being certain that you're hiring a dependable contractor is tricky. Most contractors are reliable and hardworking, insists Thomas Kraeutler, a veteran home inspector and president of HomeChek of New Jersey, Inc. But to guard against the few who aren't, here he suggests ways to avoid a home improvement disaster.

BID APPLES TO APPLES

Know exactly what you want before you pick up the phone and call any contractor. Pick out specific products (by brand name, model, and style) to include in the renovation. Tell the contractors which brand and style you've chosen. Don't leave the choice of materials to the contractor—you're likely to get the cheapest stuff available.

CONTRACT WITH YOUR CONTRACTOR

For jobs costing more than a couple of hundred dollars, have a written agreement. Make sure the contract states what is to be done, in as much detail as possible, and when it is to be completed. A common complaint is that the job takes longer to complete than a contractor estimated. To avoid this, include a "time of essence" clause, which charges the contractor penalties if the work takes too long. The contractor should also set forth a payment schedule. As a general rule, put up a small down payment and space out the remainder. Reserve at least 25 percent of the total amount for a final payment and release it only when you're completely satisfied with the work.

If a contractor doesn't give you a contract, you can draw up one of your own. Or you can write the contractor a letter that outlines everything discussed. For a minor repair, the letter could simply read: "This confirms that you have agreed to fix my leaky toilet for $50. Per our agreement, I'll look forward to seeing you next Tuesday at 3 p.m. Thank you for your assistance."

CHECK INSURANCE

A contractor must have full insurance—this includes worker's compensation as well as general comprehensive liability insurance. Some contractors skimp on insurance, leaving you exposed in the case of an accident. When checking insurance, make sure the contractor provides a "certificate of insurance," which names you as an "additional insured." This guarantees that the contractor's insurance company will attempt to notify you if the policy is canceled for any reason. Also, be sure to check the policy limit of the general comprehensive coverage. A basic policy offers a limit of $50,000. This isn't very much coverage in today's litigious world. For peace of mind, insist on a least $300,000 coverage.

KEEP A WRITTEN RECORD

Good documentation of the job is crucial if something goes wrong later or if disputes arise. Keep written notes of starting and stopping times, how many people are working, and what's getting (or not getting) done. This is especially important if you are paying for the job by the hour. Also, for bigger jobs, keep notes of conversations you've had with contractors about problems, changes, etc.

GET AN OUTSIDE REVIEW

If any question arises about the quality of the job, have the work inspected by an independent professional, such as a home inspector. With all contracts, be sure to have them reviewed by your attorney before signing. The expense of such a review can be well worth it in the event of future problems.

EXPERT TIPS

THE SECRET LIFE OF PAINT

A color specialist on how to make your home beautiful with pigment

Each season, paint manufacturers debut scores of new paint colors with such imaginative names as Treasure, Lucia Blue, and WinterMoss. While these names may be pleasing to the ear, they are of little help when it actually comes to choosing a color for the walls of your living room or kitchen. Here, architectural color consultant Donald Kaufman has some genuinely practical tips for choosing paint for the home. Kaufman, co-author with Taffy Dahl of *Color: Natural Palettes for Painted Rooms* (Clarkson Potter, 1992), has worked with renowned architects I. M. Pei and Philip Johnson, and has his own line of paint colors, The Donald Kaufman Color Collection (☎201-568-2226).

■ **Start by noticing which colors are already in and around your home.** An old rug, a painting, a stone terrace outside the house, or even a favorite pair of pants may provide the perfect inspiration. Computers can help turn these colors into paint, but they have limited formulas. Getting a painter to mix the paint often results in more complex colors.

■ **Understand the psychological effects of color.** People have different reactions to cool and warm colors. Cool colors—especially blues and violets—tend to create a sense of darkness and depression. They are the most difficult to use successfully because of these unsettling effects. Warm colors—reds, oranges, and yellows—are generally more pleasing and fulfill the basic human need for light. For this reason, they account for nearly 90 percent of the paints on store shelves. Warm colors are a safe choice for the dining room and kitchen because they improve the look of food. They also flatter the skin color of guests surrounding the table. If a cool color is a must, use green or a blue that has some yellow in it.

■ **Take the time to test samples.** A major complaint about final paint jobs is that they are too bright. Colors on a paint swatch appear twice as bright and twice as light when applied to a wall. Therefore, an adequate mock-up is essential. Paint a five-foot-wide sample swath from floor to ceiling. Block out existing colors with your hand and see how the new colors interact with the room and especially with the color of the floor. Look at the test area at different times of the day to see how it reacts to fluctuations in natural light and to artificial light at night. People who want to paint a brightly colored room a neutral color should prime the entire room before trying samples. Reflected light from strong colors will alter the perceived color of the mock-up.

■ **Brighten rooms.** The common solution to a dark room is throwing white paint on the walls to reflect more light. But the lack of light generally makes the white room look washed-out and gray. A better solution is to use a warmer and deeper color, which often can provide the luminosity that is missing from the room. Yellows are particularly effective, because the color value can be kept light enough while still adding warmth.

■ **Enlarge living spaces.** If you have light-colored floors, choose a deeper wall color and a light ceiling color to reflect the floor. Walls will appear to recede above the floor. If you have dark floors, keep walls and ceiling light and the same color. Eyes are attracted to contrast, and high contrast between walls and ceiling closes spaces. Some people think they can lift a ceiling by painting it white.

That is often the case, because a white ceiling reflects more light. But if there's already plenty of light, similarly colored walls and ceiling can make a room appear more open and atmospheric.

■ **Use the same trim color throughout a number of rooms.** The wall color in each room will make the trim appear different. Keep the trim lighter than the walls. Using darker trim colors can be beautiful, but it is much more difficult to pull off.

■ **Think about how the colors of adjoining rooms interact.** Colors in abutting rooms tend to reinforce each other—which can have dramatic or unpleasant results. A subtle beige room can appear much stronger if viewed from a subtle blue room, and vice versa. Also, thinking about rooms as a series of colors can make cramped quarters seem roomier. For a three-room apartment, if the kitchen and living room have light, warm colors, a bedroom with stronger and deeper colors can provide a perfect escape.

■ **Address the architecture.** Architectural details can be divided into two categories—structural and decorative. Neutral colors work better with structural details such as columns or door frames. Something that looks like it provides support is not the place for a pale peach color. Decorative colors would be more appropriate with friezes and other ornate moldings.

■ **Use top-of-the-line paint from any of the major manufacturers.** It lasts the longest and provides the best coverage. Don't overlook regional paint companies. Their top paints are just as good and sometimes better. But preparation is all-important. Clean, smooth surfaces lead to the best results.

■ **And remember, there are no bad colors.** Colors change and create different perceptions depending on where and how they are used. A very bright, garish green might seem a bad color for a dining room, but it could be absolutely beautiful as a thin stripe underneath crown molding in a beige living room.

NOT ALL PAINTS ARE CREATED EQUAL

Before you paint yourself into a corner, know your oil from your latex

When it comes to paint, there are two basic options: oil or latex. Convention has it that oil paint is more durable, has more sheen, hides brush stokes better, and is easier to clean when dry.

Today's latex paint equals the performance of oil on many of these scores. And because it's easy to use, latex now is the most popular type of paint on store shelves. With latex paint, there's less odor, drying times are shorter, brushes clean up with water, and errant paint splatters can be wiped away with a damp sponge. It also costs less and is better for the environment—latex paint contains fewer volatile organic compounds.

Oil paint is less forgiving. Odors are stronger, drying time can take a day, and clean-up requires turpentine or paint thinner. But in damp areas such as the kitchen and bathroom, it is better at repelling water.

For this reason, many professionals insist that oil makes a superior exterior paint. Latex paint, though, has a porous quality, which allows it to breathe. In homes where a lot of interior water vapor exits through exterior walls, use of latex paint can limit peeling. Keep in mind that both types of exterior paint cost more because of additional resins, pigments, and mildewcides.

Sheen is also an important factor to consider. Glossier finishes are harder and more durable. Use them in high wear or high humidity areas, such as on woodwork or in kitchens and bathrooms. Low luster finishes generally have greater hiding power. Use them on walls and ceilings.

PUT A LITTLE SPRING IN YOUR SOFA

If you're in the market for a new sofa, you're probably wondering what makes a $2,000 sofa any different from one that costs a mere $600. The difference lies in the frame, padding, cushions, springs, fabric, and finish:

■ **PADDING:** Sofas often wear at the arms because the maker has scrimped on padding. The better sofas have a layer of cotton or polyfiber over a layer of foam. Cheaper sofas have fabric right on top of the foam.

■ **FABRIC:** The grade of a fabric determines the price, but is not a measure of the fabric's durability. Grades are based largely on fiber content and on how much waste results from matching the pattern. For durability, consider spending the extra $50 or so for treating the sofa with fabric protection.

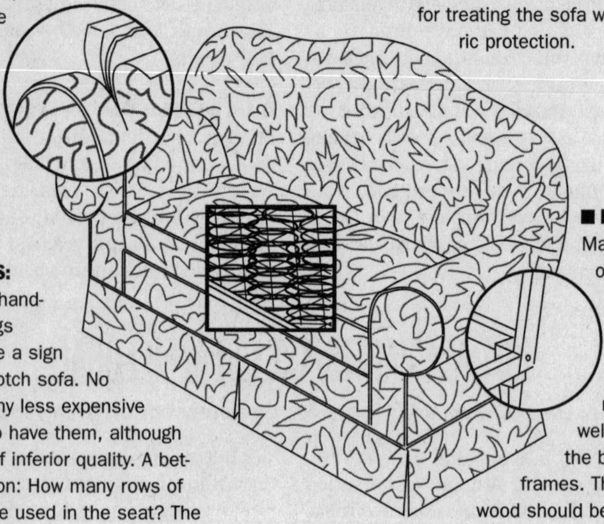

■ **FRAME:** Maple and other hardwoods that grip nails well make the best frames. The wood should be kiln-dried to prevent shrinkage and warping. The best frames are $1^1/_2$ inches thick. (Experts refer to it as a $^6/_4$ frame.) To keep a sofa from sagging, joints and legs must be firmly attached to the frame. The best joints are double- or triple-doweled at the top corners and firmly attached with reinforcing blocks where the arms meet the seat.

■ **SPRINGS:** Eight-way hand-tied springs used to be a sign of a top-notch sofa. No more. Many less expensive sofas also have them, although they are of inferior quality. A better question: How many rows of springs are used in the seat? The best use four rows.

■ **CUSHIONS:** Top-quality foam cushions are made from virgin foam with a density of 2.2 pounds per cubic foot. Accept no less than 1.8. Lower-density foam deteriorates more quickly. If you're looking for a soft down cushion, be sure the cushion has at least 30 percent down feathers in it. Otherwise, you'll be paying for down and getting far less.

■ **FINISH:** Attention to detail makes a difference. In a high-quality sofa, seams are straight, pleats lie flat, corners fill out, and cushions have metal zippers.

EXPERT TIPS

BEDS YOU WON'T LOSE SLEEP ON

Almost a third of life is spent sleeping, so take your mattress seriously

Your mattress sags, creaks, wobbles, and sways. It's probably time to toss this relic and invest in a new one. Is there any purchase that's more personal? Dr. Howard Levy of the Emory Spine Center in Atlanta, Ga., believes that a mattress should be firm and support the natural curves of the spine. Many of his colleagues agree. In a recent survey by Levy of orthopedic surgeons, he found that of the 134 respondents, 67.7 percent recommended a firm mattress, 8.9 percent hard, 1.6 percent a waterbed, and just under 1 percent a soft mattress. The next time you go mattress shopping, keep these tips in mind from the Better Sleep Council:

■ **SUPPORT:** Wear comfortable clothes to your local mattress retailer, so you can lie down on a number of mattresses. The best ones support your body at all points. Pay attention to your shoulders, hips, and lower back. Too little support can result in back pain; too much can lead to uncomfortable pressure.

■ **SPACE:** Sleepers toss and turn 40 to 60 times a night. If you are constantly fighting your partner for space, it may be time to upgrade to a queen- or king-size bed. Both are several inches longer and wider than the standard double bed.

■ **COIL COUNT:** The common innerspring mattress gets its support from tempered steel coils. A full-size version should have more than 300 coils, a queen-size more than 375, and a king-size more than 450.

■ **WIRE GAUGE:** The lower the number, the thicker, stronger, and more durable the wire. Stronger coils generally provide better support. Many manufacturers are introducing wire-engineered innersprings that employ lighter wire. They claim these systems make less noise and offer more support. Lie down and shift positions—it's the best way to test these claims and to see which mattress lends your body's curves the most support.

■ **COVER:** Look for superior stitching, quality seams, and an extra-soft surface. Don't buy a bed based solely on a pretty treatment.

■ **PADDING:** Layers of upholstery insulate and cushion the body from the innersprings. Once you've purchased a mattress that meets your comfort needs, remember to flip it regularly from head to toe. This extends mattress life and helps prevent creating an uncomfortable impression in the padding.

■ **FOUNDATION:** Don't blame a bad night's sleep on the mattress alone. The foundation, or box spring, may also be showing some signs of wear and tear. A mattress and its companion foundation are designed to work as a system. Putting a new mattress on an old foundation can reduce the life and comfort of a mattress.

■ **WARRANTIES:** Top brands generally come with 15 years' protection against product defects, but don't let the salesperson sell you a mattress based solely on the warranty. Let comfort and support guide your decision.

■ **FOAM MATTRESSES:** Made of a solid core or different types of foam laminated together, these mattresses should come with a minimum density of 2.0 pounds per cubic foot. High-resilience polyurethane and the more traditional latex, or synthetic rubber, mattresses provide the best performance.

■ **WATERBEDS:** Whether full motion or waveless, make sure the mattress vinyl is a minimum of 20 mil. in thickness, and pay close attention to seam durability. Even if you live outside of California, look to see if the system meets California Waterbed Standards.

LIGHTING

FIXING THE LIGHT FANTASTIC

The right lighting will flatter, accent, and fill a home with warmth

For years lighting design has been nearly an afterthought for many residential architects and general contractors. The attitude was, what more could there be than a ceiling-mounted fixture in the center of the room or a homeowner's table lamps? But such light fixtures often tend to call attention to themselves and cast shadows in unflattering ways. Here, lighting designer Randall Whitehead, the owner of Light Source, a lighting store in San Francisco, and author of *Residential Lighting: Creating Dramatic Living Spaces* (Rockport Publishers,1993) and *Lighten Up* (Light Source Publishing, 1996), tours the home and offers some advice on lighting.

■ **THE ENTRY.** The entrance sets the mood and tone for the rest of the house. In the entryway, lighting can be used to open up the space and provide a welcoming environment for guests. Make sure lights create a warm glow. Avoid harsh shadows by using uplighting instead of recessed downlights.

■ **THE LIVING ROOM.** The goal here is to create a soft island of illumination that invites people in to relax and converse. Layering the light creates an environment that is humanizing and dramatic. Wall sconces and torchères can generally provide ambient illumination, which softens shadows on people's faces and fills the room with a soft glow. Recessed adjustable fixtures or track lighting can be utilized to provide the necessary accent light for artwork, plants, or table-

LIGHT BULBS ARE NO JOKE

The right light takes the right bulb, as the following guide shows

■ **FLUORESCENT.** California, the bellwether of eco-friendly laws, now mandates that ambient lighting in new or remodeled kitchens and baths be fluorescent. Once derided for its cold, unfriendly illumination, advancements in fluorescent technology have increased its usefulness: There are over 200 color variations, and dimming possibilities are much greater than before. Now people can use energy-efficient fixtures without totally sacrificing the warm glow of more traditional light sources.

■ **INCANDESCENT.** This was the first light source created, and it still has a strong hold over the general public with its warm, amber illumination. But its color tonality shifts colors within a given space—reds turn orange, whites go yellow, and blues shift to green. Be aware of this when you choose paints and fabrics.

■ **QUARTZ AND TUNGSTEN HALOGEN.** These light sources are a recent improvement in incandescent lighting. They provide a whiter source of illumination, so colors are truer. Quartz lamps also produce twice as much illumination as standard lamps so you have a more energy-efficient source by using less wattage for the same amount of light.

■ **H.I.D.** (High Intensity Discharge). These lamps are used mostly in commercial and landscape lighting. Most street lights use these lamps, but the mercury vapor and metal halide varieties are seeing more use in residential landscape designs.

tops. But be sure not to let accent lighting overpower you or your company.

■ **THE DINING ROOM.** This is where dramatic lighting can come into play. Wall sconces are a good source of ambient lighting in this room. A chandelier should only give the illusion of providing the lighting in the room, as otherwise it will be too bright or distracting. Using recessed, adjustable fixtures on either side of the chandelier will produce the necessary focal point lighting for the table, without eclipsing the decorative fixture.

■ **THE KITCHEN.** With today's open floor plan designs, the kitchen should be as inviting as the rest of the house. Mount fluorescent lights above cabinets, so light is bounced off the walls and ceilings, providing ambient lighting. Lights under cabinets provide good, unobstructed task light for the counters. Pendant-hung fixtures can be used for task light where cabinets are not present. Skylights can provide a cheery feeling during the day, and, through the use of fluorescent fixtures mounted in them, will avoid becoming "black holes" at night. A pot rack over a center island may appear to be a perfect idea, but how do you light work surfaces without creating shadows by trying to light through pots and pans? If you have sloped ceilings, special care must be taken to select fixtures that don't glare into people's eyes. Also, remember that an all-white kitchen is going to require dramatically less light than a kitchen with dark wood cabinets.

■ **BATHROOMS.** Lighting at the mirror is most important. Vertically mounted strip fixtures generally provide the best task light. Wall sconces or fluorescent strip fixtures mounted above cabinets, ledges, or beams provide the necessary ambient illumination.

■ **BEDROOMS.** It is important that there is good color-corrected light, especially in closets, to aid in the selection of properly color-matched clothes. Aside from the usual ambient light concerns, easily adjustable reading lamps at the bed are a must. A "panic switch" for outside lighting is often a desirable feature.

EXPERT TIPS

FRAME THE WORLD AROUND YOU

A picture's display can be the difference between wow! and ho-hum

For millennia, people have understood the importance of using a frame to separate a work of art from its surroundings. Ancient Pompeians framed wall paintings with lines of painted color, while artists in the Middle Ages used wood carved in an ornate Gothic style. Here, Greg O'Halloran (GOH), conservation framer at A.P.F., Inc., in New York, Lou Stovall (LS), archival framer and master printer at Workshop, Inc., in Washington, D.C., and Andrew LaBonte (AL), manager of Boston framers Haley & Steele, discuss how to frame art and display it in the home.

THE FRAME

✔ "A good framer will allow the art to make the choice. If you look at the art, it really can talk to you in terms of what is supposed to surround it. If it is done correctly, you can make a second-rate work of art look like a museum piece. For example, you can't take a scoop molding and put it on a 1850s Bierstadt. A period piece should have a style of frame from the same period. It really has to be a marriage of frame and art." (GOH)

✔ "Aside from aesthetics, the frame has to be sturdy enough to hold the artwork in the glass. A large work requires large moldings. Using a thin frame for a more streamlined look requires extra supports on the back. When it comes to frame styles, the options include gold leaf, burnished frames, ones with antiquing, ornamented styles, and plainer models. Generally, people match the frame to the style or period of the art. However, a lot of modern art really works extremely well with antique frames, even very heavily ornamented, gold-leaf frames. It even works well with modern decor." (AL)

✔ "You frame for the art. In rare cases, it's okay to frame the art to complement the living environment where the art will be located. Generally speaking, you want the molding to have some sensitivity to the furniture in the room. If you have traditional furniture, you would probably want a traditional frame, such as carved wood. If you have modern or contemporary furniture, you would go for a simple wood, or, most likely, a metal frame. If you have a dining room with brass wall sconces, you might want a brass frame. If you are hanging over wonderful, natural wood paneling, you would probably want a nice maple or cherry frame." (LS)

THE MAT

✔ "You always want acid-free, 100 percent cotton mats. You can have single, double, or triple mats. Mats set the work back from the glass for protection and give a nice surrounding. I tend to frame with white mats. I don't think much of colored mats, because the art should speak for itself. If the artist required more color around the border, he would have indicated it. But if you are hanging in a dark room painted deep red or forest green, you might consider a colored mat. It softens the blow between the darkness of the room and the art. Mat widths range from 2 1/2 to 5 or 6 inches. If something is larger than 36 by 40 inches, chances are you would want a 5 1/2- or 6-inch band around it. Anything under 20 inches square, you would want something 2 1/2 or 3 inches." (LS)

✔ "The bottom border is usually a small increment larger than the top and sides, for visual balance. If you make the margins all the same, the bottom will actually end up looking narrower—it's an ancient principle of proportion. For this reason, columns in Greek architecture are wider at the bottom, and, usually on a chest of drawers, the bottom drawers are wider than the top drawers. A common border size is 3 inches on the top and sides and 3 1/4 on the bottom. Instead of using color mats, I paint lines or panels on the mat in the traditional English and French style. Usually, you see this style of mats used on decorative pieces, botanicals, landscapes, things like that. I also wrap mats in pure silks or pure linens. For instance, on Beacon Hill, if someone has watered silk wallpaper, I will do silk mats for their pictures. Silk mats also go well on master drawings." (AL)

HANGING THE PICTURE

✔ "With anything large, you want to use Plexiglas because it is light and won't break if the work falls from the wall. With something of value, you want to use UV reflective glass or Plexiglas to diminish the damaging effects of light. Also, you want to place the art on walls washed by light rather than on those with direct light. If you are going to install art lights, you want to place them on the ceiling 30 inches from the wall and at an angle so that light shows brightest on either edge of the frame. You don't want to have the lights on all the time, though. All light takes a toll." (LS)

✔ "One of the largest causes of damage to art and frames is that they fall off the wall. The wire breaks or mounting screws pull out—so make sure the hardware is top-quality. To hang the art on masonry walls, use a masonry screw or drill a hole and insert a lead slug and a lag screw. If you have Sheetrock, traditional hangers will support up to 100 pounds. Anything heavier than that, or if the walls are plaster, I use molly bolts. You should also avoid putting adhesives like glue or tape on the artwork. There are a lot of mechanical mounts that hold the art and work very well." (AL)

HOME REPAIR

PROTECT YOUR CASTLE FROM TIME

From stuck windows to trickling toilets, here's how to fix it yourself

The roof leaks, the basement is damp, and the toilet won't stop running. For many homeowners, such a scenario represents their worst nightmare. But who can afford to call a plumber at the first sign of a leak? Here, Thomas Kraeutler and George Pettie, president and vice president, respectively, of the home inspection firm HomeChek of New Jersey, provide a repair and maintenance guide that will help you protect your number one investment.

LEAKY ROOF

Watch out for unscrupulous contractors who try to sell you a new roof that you don't need. Most roof leaks can be remedied with minor flashing repair. Look for loose or deteriorated flashing around chimneys and vent pipes. Fill any gaps with a good asphalt roof cement. A neatly applied bead of sealant from a caulking gun is better than a thick, troweled-on application.

Loose flashing should be tightened up with masonry nails before resealing. Expect to seal flashing every two years. If sealing doesn't fix the problem, the roof shingles may be in fact worn out. To check your roof for signs of wear and tear, look for cracked, curled, or broken shingles. If the worn area is small, it can be repaired by replacing the old shingles or patching with asphalt roof cement. If all of the roof looks this way, entire replacement is best. Shingles that are allowed to deteriorate can cause major leaks leading to expensive repairs.

WET BASEMENT

Kraeutler and Pettie recount how one homeowner recently attempted to fix a leaky basement by calling a waterproofing contractor. Quotes ranged from $7,500 to $20,000. Yet the homeowner was eventually able to correct his outside drainage and easily fix the problem for under $500.

In fact, good gutters and properly sloping soil on a home's exterior can fix 99 percent of wet basement problems. Start by cleaning out gutters, downspouts, and underground drain pipes. A water hose is very useful for flushing out debris. When the accumulated mess in downspouts and drain pipes proves stubborn, rent a power auger to clear a passageway. If the gutter system doesn't empty into underground pipes, be sure to install downspout extensions that carry water 4 to 6 feet from the foundation. Also, inspect gutters for leaks and sags. Aluminum gutters can be sealed with polyurethane or butyl caulk. Ideally, copper and steel gutters should be resoldered, but they

■ WHAT TO LOOK FOR ON A LEAKY ROOF

The source of a leak may not be where you see the leak, so inspect entire roof. **Flashing** is material—usually rustproof metal or plastic—used at joints (see right) to keep water from getting into the house. Check for looseness, gaps, and holes. Check **shingles** for rips, curled edges, missing sections.

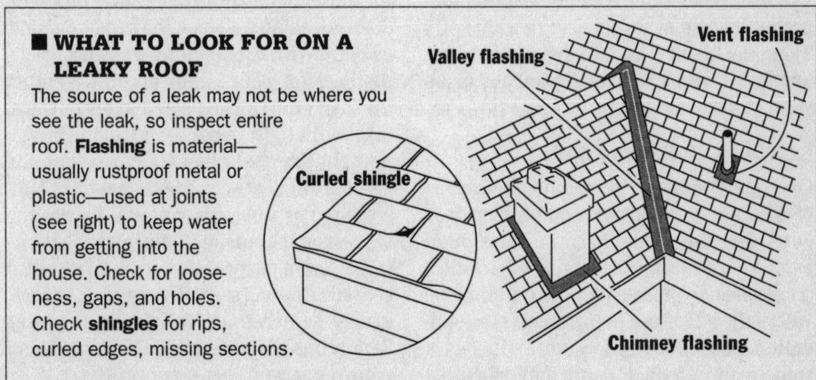

WHEN TO FIX IT, WHEN TO JUNK IT

To help you decide whether to repair or replace an appliance, consult the chart devised by Thomas Kraeutler below. In one typical scenario, you're stuck with an air conditioner that dies because the compressor is seven years old. An entirely new system would cost $2,500, but the compressor repair alone would be $850. According to the chart, a seven-year-old central air conditioner has a low risk of repetitive failure, so it's okay to spend up to 50 percent of the replacement cost on repair. Since the $850 repair cost is 50 percent of the replacement value, go ahead and call for service.

APPLIANCE:	ESTIMATED REPLACEMENT COST[1]	AGE RANGE RISK OF FAILURE[2]: % REPAIR COST LIMIT		
		Low Risk	Medium Risk	High Risk
FURNACE	$1,500–$2,500	up to 12 years: 30%	12–24 years: 20%	25 years & up: 10%
WATER HEATER	$350–$700	up to 7 years : 30%	7–14 years: 20%	15 years & up: 10%
CENTRAL A/C	$1,500–$3,000	up to 8 years: 50%	8–15 years: 30%	16 years & up: 10%
REFRIGERATOR	$700–$1,500	up to 8 years: 40%	8–15 years: 30%	16 years & up: 20%
KITCHEN RANGE	$700–$1,400	up to 15 years: 30%	15–25 years: 20%	26 years & up: 10%
DISHWASHER	$350–$750	up to 10 years: 40%	10–15 years: 30%	16 years & up: 20%
WASHER	$350–$700	up to 10 years: 40%	10–15 years: 30%	16 years & up: 20%
DRYER	$350–$700	up to 10 years: 50%	10–20 years: 40%	21 years & up: 10%
BUILT-IN MICROWAVE	$400–$800	up to 4 years: 20%	4–10 years: 15%	11 years & up: 10%
GARBAGE DISPOSAL	$150–$350	up to 1 year[3]	1 year & up: Always replace	—

NOTES:
1. Assumes replacement with like kind and quality as original appliance.
2. Risk of failure or breakdown increases with age. Percentage indicates minimum cost of repair limit. If cost of repair is greater than percentage of replacement cost shown, then replacement is recommended. If cost of repair is less than percentage of replacement cost show, then repair is likely to be cost-effective.
3. Repair disposals only if under manufacturer's warranty. Otherwise, always replace.

can be resealed with a similar caulk. Repair sags by removing the spikes that hold the gutter in place, raising the gutter so that it slopes evenly to downspouts, and nailing the gutter back in place.

To keep rainfall from collecting near foundation walls, soil should slope downward 6 inches over the first 4 feet from the foundation wall. Thereafter, it can be graded more gradually. Use clean fill dirt (not topsoil). Tamp the fill dirt down to the correct slope and finish with a layer of topsoil and grass seed, mulch, or stone.

EXTERIOR JOINTS AND GAPS

Open joints and gaps in the outside envelope of a house waste energy and provide easy entry for insects and vermin. Gaps often exist where siding meets trim, where electric cables or pipes enter the building, or where the sill of the house meets the foundation. For cracks up to 1/4 to 5/16 inches, a smooth, even bead of caulk applied with a caulking gun is best. For wider openings, use an aerosol spray foam insulation. Let the foam expand to fill cracks and slice away the excess after a day's drying time.

STUCK WINDOWS

Stuck windows are an inconvenience as well as a potential hazard, because they can impede escaping from fire. Most stuck windows are painted shut on the inside, outside, or both. With double-hung windows, place the heels of your hands on either end of the sash's top rail and rap sharply upward. Start with light impacts and don't get violent. If the sash doesn't move, cut the painted joint between the sash and the window stop or weatherstripping. Repeat the process on the outside. If cutting sash joints fails, work a putty knife deep into the joint between stop and sash. If it still won't budge, it may be necessary to remove the stop. Removing the stop will chip paint and requires careful carpentry skills.

BATHROOM CAULKING AND GROUTING

Neglecting to replace old grout and tired caulking in the bathroom is one of the most common home maintenance failures. It may not seem to be a big problem, but over time, the ceramic tiles loosen, allowing moisture to damage underlying wall materials. To prevent headaches later on, old grout, especially at horizontal tile joints where water penetration is greatest, should be scraped out. Before replacing grout, thoroughly wash tiles and joints with a tub and tile cleaner and then rinse.

Faucet, control, and spout joints in the shower or tub also should be well sealed. If they are not, remove the faucet escutcheon plates. Many of these plates have small set screws that must be loosened first. Some plates can be unscrewed after you've removed the faucet handles. Using a putty knife or blade scraper, remove all old caulking, dirt, mildew, and soap residue. Finish cleaning with a tub and tile cleaner and then rinse thoroughly. Next, seal all faucet penetrations with a good adhesive caulk. Before reinstalling the escutcheon plates, run a bead of caulk around the plates' mating edges. Tighten the plates against the wall and run another bead of caulk around the outside, where the plates meet the wall.

Don't neglect replacing the worn-out caulk between the tub and the wall tile. Dig out the old caulk to full depth with an old screwdriver or sharp utility knife. Squirt tub and tile cleaner in the joint. Remove all residual caulk, grout, dirt, and mildew by working a rag or paper towel with a putty knife into the gap. Keep working until the towel comes out clean and dry. To seal the gap, run a bead of caulk into the joint. Placing a strip of masking tape along the tile just above the tub results in a neat, crisp edge. The caulk should fill the joint 1/4- to 3/8-inch deep. Smooth in the caulk with your finger, wipe away excess from the tub and tile, and then let dry for several hours.

TRICKLING TOILETS

Toilets are one of the most used, yet least understood home appliances. They have two basic moving parts: the flush valve, which lets water out of the tank and down the drain; and the fill valve, which lets the toilet fill up after the flush cycle is complete. Small leaks in either of these valves can waste thousands of gallons of water in the course of a year. Here's how to tell if your valves are leaking:

To test the flush valve, open the top of the tank and pour a small amount of food coloring into the water. After an hour, if there is any colored water in the bowl, the flush valve is leaking and should be replaced.

To test the fill valve, open the top of the tank and find the hollow plastic pipe that sticks up from the bottom of the tank. The water level should be about an inch below the top of the pipe. If the water level is even with the top, the fill valve may be leaking or improperly adjusted and should be repaired or replaced. Next, flush the toilet and watch the top of the valve. If any water squirts up, you may have a leaky seal, which also means you need a new fill valve.

Both of these parts are easy to replace and cost less than $10. Fluidmaster makes good replacement valves with clear instructions that teach you how to do the job. You can find them at any home center.

■ HELP FOR A LEAKING TOILET

Most leakages in a toilet can be traced to problems in one of two places. Here's where they are inside the tank:

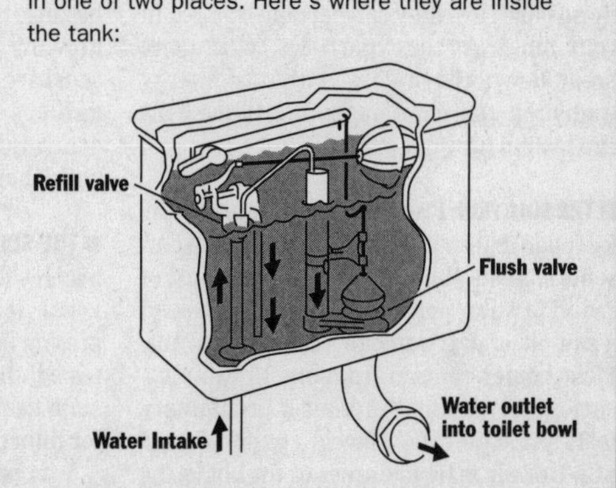

POLLUTANTS

IF A HOUSE IS A HOT ZONE

What to do if your home is plagued by environmental hazards

Environmental pollution can make a mockery of the sanctuary of one's home. To advise potential homeowners of the environmental hazards that may be present in your home's walls, plumbing, and foundations, a group of government agencies and private organizations, including the Environmental Protection Agency (EPA), the Department of Housing and Urban Development, and the National Association of Realtors have joined forces to develop a primer for consumers. Highlights follow:

RADON

Radon is an odorless, tasteless gas that occurs as a byproduct of the natural decay of uranium present in the earth. Over time it breaks down into radioactive particles that remain in the air. Out of doors, this is not a problem, because the gas diffuses in the atmosphere.

■ **THE PROBLEM:** When radon gas and its decay products enter your home, they remain in circulation in the enclosed air. As you breathe these particles, they can become trapped in your lungs. As these particles continue to break down, they release bursts of energy (radiation) that can damage lung tissue. This can lead to lung cancer.

■ **THE SOLUTION:** Preliminary screen-test kits for radon in the air are available for do-it-yourselfers. Tests that measure the amount of radon in water normally require you to send a sample of tap water to a lab for analysis. Most homes contain from one to two picocuries (pCi) per liter (L) of air. If preliminary tests indicate radon levels greater than 4 pCi/L of air in livable areas of the home, the EPA recommends that a follow-up test be conducted. The EPA estimates that the risk of an annual radon level of 4 pCi is equivalent to the risk from smoking 10 cigarettes a day or having 200 chest X rays a year.

In some cases homeowners may be able to treat the problem themselves. However, radon source diagnosis and mitigation normally require skills and tools not available to the average homeowner.

Installing radon reduction equipment can cost from several hundred to several thousand dollars. If the treatment involves fans, pumps, or other appliances, operating costs for these devices also may increase monthly utility bills. When seeking a contractor to deal with a radon problem, ask local, county, or state government agencies for a recommendation.

LEAD

Lead is a metallic element found worldwide in rocks and soils. Its toxic effects have been known since ancient times. The substance can be present in drinking water, in interior or exterior paint, in the dust within a house, or in the soil outside.

■ **THE PROBLEM:** When ingested, lead accumulates in the blood, bones, and soft tissue of the body. High concentrations can cause death or permanent damage to the central nervous system, the brain, the kidneys, and red blood cells. Even low levels of lead may increase high blood pressure in adults.

Infants, children, pregnant women, and fetuses are most vulnerable to exposure because the lead is more easily absorbed into growing bodies and their tissues are more sensitive to its damaging effects. Because of a child's smaller body weight, an equal concentration of lead is more damaging to a child than it would be to an adult.

■ **THE SOLUTION:** The only way to determine lead levels in water is to test a sample of the water. If homeowners suspect that lead is present in water, or if they wish to have water tested, they should contact local, county, or state health or environmental departments for information about qualified testing labs.

It is best to leave lead-based paint undisturbed if it is in good condition and there is little chance that it will be eaten by children. Other procedures include covering the paint with wallpaper or some other building material, or completely replacing the painted surface. Pregnant women and women who plan to become pregnant should not do this work.

Professional paint removal is costly, and everyone not involved in the procedure is required to leave the premises during removal and cleanup.

ASBESTOS

Asbestos is a fibrous mineral found in rocks and soil throughout the world. It has been used in construction because it is strong, durable, fire-retardant, and a good insulator.

■ **THE PROBLEM:** When ingested, asbestos fibers lodge in the lungs, where they remain in tissues and concentrate as repeated exposures occur. Prolonged work-related exposure can cause cancer of the lung and stomach. The health effects of lower exposures in the home are less certain; however, experts are unable to provide assurance that any level of exposure is completely safe.

■ **THE SOLUTION:** Asbestos is sometimes found around pipes and furnaces in older homes; in some vinyl flooring materials; in ceiling tiles; in exterior roofing shingles and siding; in some wallboards; mixed with other materials around pipes, ducts, and beams; in patching compounds or textured paints; and in door gaskets on furnaces and ovens.

Generally, if the material is in good condition and is where it is not likely to be disturbed, you can leave it in place. Great care should be used in handling, cleaning, or working with material suspected of containing asbestos. If it is likely to be banged, handled, or taken apart (especially during remodeling), hire asbestos-removal workers; they are protected under federal regulations that specify special training, protective clothing, and special respirators as needed.

FORMALDEHYDE

Formaldehyde is a colorless, gaseous chemical compound generally present at low, variable concentrations both indoors and outdoors. In homes, the most significant sources are in the adhesives used to bond pressed wood building materials and in the plywood used in construction.

■ **THE PROBLEM:** Formaldehyde has been shown to cause cancer in animals, although there is no hard evidence linking it to cancer in humans. Higher-than-normal levels of formaldehyde in the home can trigger asthma attacks in those who suffer this condition. Other symptoms may include skin rashes; watery eyes; a burning sensation in the eyes, throat, and nasal passages; and breathing difficulties.

Materials containing formaldehyde were used extensively in certain prefabricated and manufactured homes. Although the federal government has curtailed the use of materials containing formaldehyde since 1985, formaldehyde compounds are still widespread in the manufacture of furniture, cabinets, and other building materials.

■ **THE SOLUTION:** In the case of a new home, consult with the builder before you purchase. Most builders will be able to tell you if construction materials contain urea-formaldehyde, or they can direct you to manufacturers who can provide specific product information.

In older homes, materials containing formaldehyde may not be apparent, and the current owners may not have specific product information. Consider hiring a qualified building inspector to examine the home. Home monitoring kits are also available.

In older homes with a formaldehyde problem, increasing ventilation through the home may help the situation. If new furniture, drapery, or other sources are the culprits, removing these items (or limiting their number) may be all that's needed.

If subflooring, walls, or foam insulation is the problem's source, and increased ventilation is inadequate, removal of the materials may be necessary, at considerable expense of time and money.

SOURCE: Adapted from *A Home Buyer's Guide to Environmental Hazards*.

ENVIRONMENTALIST'S GUIDE

FIRST YOU USE 'EM, THEN YOU LOSE 'EM

Many household products contain hazardous chemicals that, if not discarded properly, can do lasting harm to the environment. Here's how to dispose of them and some homemade alternatives that you can use the next time around.

HOUSEHOLD CHEMICALS

ABRASIVE CLEANING POWDER

Corrosive, irritant, contains trisodiumphosphate, ammonia, and ethanol.

■ **DISPOSAL:** Rinse container thoroughly, then it may be sent to landfill; also check with water treatment plants—certain bacteria may detoxify the material.

■ **ALTERNATIVES:** Use baking soda or borax, or rub area with half a lemon dipped in borax (toxic to children and pets).

AMMONIA-BASED CLEANER

Corrosive, irritant, contains ammonia and ethanol.

■ **DISPOSAL:** Same as abrasive cleaner.

■ **ALTERNATIVES:** Use undiluted white vinegar.

BLEACH CLEANER

Corrosive, contains sodium or potassium hydroxide, hydrogen peroxide, sodium or calcium hypochlorite.

■ **DISPOSAL:** Fully use products, then dispose of waste, can be at landfill.

■ **ALTERNATIVES:** For laundry, use 1/2 cup white vinegar, baking soda, or borax per load.

DISINFECTANT

Corrosive, contains diethylene or methylene glycol, sodium hypochlorite, and phenols.

■ **DISPOSAL:** If products are fully used and rinsed, and no waste remains in container, it may go to landfill, if necessary.

■ **ALTERNATIVES:** Mix 1/2 cup borax with 1 gal. boiling water. Not a disinfectant, however.

DRAIN CLEANER

Corrosive, contains sodium or potassium hydroxide, sodium hypochlorite, hydrochloric acid, and petroleum distillates.

■ **DISPOSAL:** Store safely until community organizes hazardous waste program.

■ **ALTERNATIVES:** Pour in 1/2 cup baking soda followed by 1/2 cup vinegar; let set for 15 minutes, follow with boiling water; snake or plunger.

FURNITURE POLISH

Flammable, contains diethylene, glycol, petroleum distillates, and nitrobenzene.

■ **DISPOSAL:** Same as drain cleaners.

■ **ALTERNATIVES:** Mix 3 parts olive oil to 1 part vinegar. For water stains, use toothpaste on damp cloth.

HOUSEHOLD BATTERY

Contains mercury, zinc, silver, lithium, and cadmium.

■ **DISPOSAL:** Recycle your waste, bring to a gas station or reclamation center.

■ **ALTERNATIVES:** Solar power, wind-up watches, rechargeables (may contain toxic heavy metals).

MOTHBALLS

Contain naphthalenes and paradichlorobenzene.

■ **DISPOSAL:** Same as abrasive cleaner.

■ **ALTERNATIVES:** Cedar chips or blocks; clean clothes well, put in airtight storage bag.

OVEN CLEANER

Corrosive, contains potassium or sodium hydroxide and ammonia.

■ **DISPOSAL:** If products are fully used and rinsed, and no waste remains in container, it may go to landfill.

■ **ALTERNATIVES:** Let mixture of 2 tbs. castile soap, 2 tsp. borax, and 2 cups water set in oven for 20 minutes; scrub with baking soda and salt.

PHOTOGRAPHIC CHEMICALS

Corrosive, irritant, contain silver, acetic acid, hydroquinone, sodium sulfite.

■ **DISPOSAL:** Store safely until community organizes a hazardous waste program.

■ ENVIRONMENTALIST'S GUIDE

■ **ALTERNATIVES:** Unknown.

POOL CHEMICALS

Corrosive, contain muriatic acid, sodium hypochlorite, and algicide.

■ **DISPOSAL:** Rinse container thoroughly and it may be sent to landfill; check with water treatment plants, as certain bacteria may detoxify the material.

■ **ALTERNATIVES:** Disinfectants: ozone or UV-light system. pH: consult baking soda box for amount to add for proper pH.

RUG AND UPHOLSTERY CLEANER

Corrosive, contains naphthalene, perchloroethylene, oxalic acid, diethylene, and glycol.

■ **DISPOSAL:** Store safely until community organizes a hazardous waste program.

■ **ALTERNATIVES:** Clean with soda water or baking soda paste, then vacuum.

TOILET BOWL CLEANER

Corrosive, irritant, contains muriatic (hydrochloric) or oxalic acid, paradichlorobenzene, and calcium hypochlorite.

■ **DISPOSAL:** Same as oven cleaner.

■ **ALTERNATIVES:** Coat bowl with paste of lemon juice and borax (toxic to children), let set, then scrub.

PAINTS

ENAMEL OR OIL-BASED PAINT

Flammable, toxic. Contains aliphatic and aromatic hydrocarbons, some pigments.

■ **ALTERNATIVES:** Latex or water-based paint.

■ **DISPOSAL:** Recycle wastes by bringing to service station or reclamation center.

LATEX OR WATER-BASED PAINT

May be toxic. Contains ethylene glycol, glycol ethers, phenyl mercuric acetate, some pigments, resins.

■ **DISPOSAL:** Check with water treatment plants; waste can be disposed of at some treatment plants where certain bacteria can detoxify the chemical; also may be recycled.

■ **ALTERNATIVES:** Latex without the above ingredients or limestone-based (whitewash) paint.

RUST-PROOFING COATING

Flammable, toxic. Contains methylene chloride, petroleum distillates, toluene, xylene, some pigments.

■ **DISPOSAL:** Should be safely stored until community organizes a hazardous waste program.

■ **ALTERNATIVES:** Unknown.

PAINT THINNERS, TURPENTINE

Toxic, flammable. Contain alcohol, acetone, esters, ketones, turpentine, petroleum distillates.

■ **DISPOSAL:** Check for disposal at local water treatment plants.

■ **ALTERNATIVES:** Use water in water-based paints.

PAINT AND VARNISH REMOVER

Flammable, toxic. Contains acetone, ketones, alcohol, xylene, toluene, methylene chloride.

■ **DISPOSAL:** Wastes should be safely stored until community organizes hazardous waste program.

■ **ALTERNATIVES:** For lead-free paint, use sandpaper or scraper and heat gun.

WOOD PRESERVATIVE

Flammable, toxic. Contains copper or zinc naphthenate, creosote, magnesium fluorosilicate, petroleum distillates, chlorinated phenols (PCP).

■ **DISPOSAL:** Wastes should be safely stored until community organizes hazardous waste program.

■ **ALTERNATIVES:** Use water-based wood preservatives. (Note that these products may still contain some of the ingredients mentioned above.)

STAIN AND VARNISH

Flammable, toxic. Contains mineral spirits, glycol ethers, ketones, toluene, xylene.

■ **DISPOSAL:** Wastes should be safely stored until community organizes a hazardous waste program.

■ **ALTERNATIVES:** Use latex or water-based finishes.

SOURCE: Environmental Hazards Management Institute, Durham, N.H.

HOME SAFETY

CAR THEFT: Stopping auto rustlers, PAGE 404 **SECURITY SYSTEMS:** Prices are often negotiable and you don't need all the bells and whistles, PAGE 405 **SELF-DEFENSE:** Improve your odds of fending off an attacker by having a plan, PAGE 406 **DEFENSIVE MOVES:** Three basic self-defense maneuvers, PAGE 407 **GUNS:** Owning a gun is a matter of state and federal laws, PAGE 408 **GUN GUIDE:** State-by-state requirements for owning a gun, PAGE 409

CRIME FOILS

A COP'S GUIDE TO HOME SECURITY

Know what crooks look for so you don't become a crime statistic

Washington, D.C., has the dubious distinction of being known not only as the nation's capital, but the country's crime capital as well. Not that the federal city has any monopoly on crime, of course; there is a burglary every 10 seconds in the United States. With the right knowledge, however, you can make your house far more crime-proof.

D.C. police officer Steven Jackson is the ultimate insider: His job is to teach people in Washington how to stay safe. He's analyzed the burglar's mind and warns, "The thief is riding around looking for people who are careless." Jackson's do's and don'ts of crime-fighting may seem simple, but they are often disregarded with disastrous consequences.

DO'S:

■ **Do** keep doors and windows locked, even when you're at home. Most burglars enter a home through the front door, either by breaking a lock or just opening an unlocked door.

■ **Do** identify visitors through a peephole or window before letting someone in—whether you live in a house or an apartment. Don't allow a stranger in to use your phone, no matter what the person says the emergency is. Instead, offer to call the police or tow truck.

Women who live alone should only list their last names and first initials on mailboxes, telephone directories, and doors.

■ **Do** make your house look occupied when you are away. Timed lights that go on before it gets dark, usually about 5:30 p.m., are a good idea. Jackson advises placing a timer in the living room, kitchen, and main bedroom. When you go on vacation, have someone pick up your mail and newspapers. Parking a car in the driveway may suggest to criminals that you are home, but it also leaves the car outside and unwatched. Jackson suggests putting your car in the garage, if you have one.

■ **Do** vary your schedule from day to day. It's a bad idea to jog, open the door to pick up the paper, or do yard work every day at the same time. Criminals like to prey on victims who are easy to predict.

■ **Do** participate in a neighborhood watch program. Programs in which neighbors keep an eye on each other's houses can be extremely effective. To join one, call your district police department. Being a nosy neighbor can be good, but only if you are aware and informed. Jackson tells of a neigh-

A HOME IS WHERE YOU FEEL SAFE

Here are some simple steps you can take to make your home a castle:

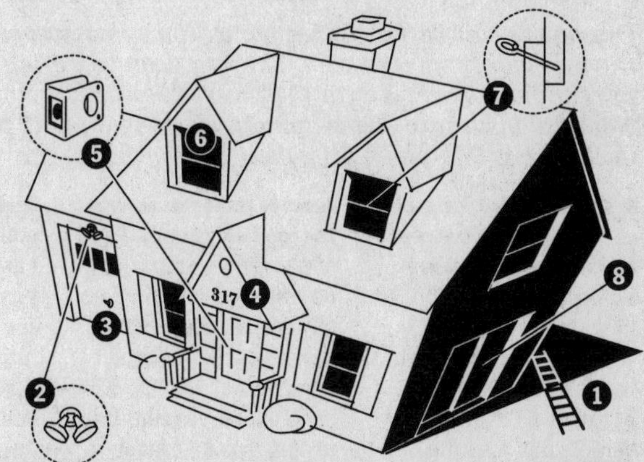

1. Don't leave ladders or other tools outside where they can be used to reach or pry open windows.

2. Lighting can be an effective deterrent. Install economical, high-pressure sodium lights. Motion detector spotlights also are good.

3. Keep your garage door locked at all times. If you have a door that opens mechanically, remove the disconnect rope from the bar when you're on vacation. If you have an electric door opener, turn the system off and put a padlock on the inside.

4. Put large, reflective numbers on your home or mailbox so police and other emergency vehicles can locate your home.

5. The weakest part of a door is where the locks are installed. Invest in a door reinforcer such as the MAG Install-A-Lock. Install an anti-pry plate on the outside of the door. If there is glass within 40 inches of the lock, replace it with unbreakable glazing. Don't depend on door chains. Also install a wide-angle door viewer so you can see who is there.

6. Prepare your master bedroom for use as an emergency refuge if an intruder comes into your home. Install a solid wood door with a good lock. Equip it with a phone, a fire extinguisher, first aid kit, and noisemaker.

7. Windows should be kept closed and locked. To make a lock for a double-sashed window, drill a hole at a slight downward angle where the sashes overlap and insert a sturdy eyebolt. To secure a single-sashed window, install a lock similar to a Blasi lock, two per window.

8. Sliding glass doors should be secured by a special steel or wood bar that you can buy at the hardware store to prevent jimmying or prying. Install a series of roundhead screws and angle irons to secure the stationary panel.

SOURCE: Adapted from "The 10-Minute Crime Safety Audit," Aetna Insurance Company and the National Crime Prevention Institute.

bor who saw a moving van across the street and was so kind to the burglars that she made them iced tea.

DON'TS:

■ **Don't** plant big bushes around your front door. A criminal can hide in the bushes until someone comes home. Don't ever put a house key under an outside doormat, either. Instead, give a copy of your keys to one or two trusted neighbors.

■ **Don't** confuse your address when calling 911. The biggest problem with the emergency number is that people often don't know where they are when they call or don't give directions, Jackson says.

■ **Don't** forget your lines—or your exit strategy—if you are at home when a person with a weapon breaks in. If you feel the person is going to harm you, pretending to comply will give you some time to figure out a plan to gain control. Since you know your house, plot your escape route or figure out what you can grab as a weapon.

EXPERT TIPS

STOPPING AUTO RUSTLERS

Our homes may be our castles, but we sometimes seem to spend more time in—and money on—our cars. The American love of automobiles is shared by criminals: There is a car theft every 20 seconds, according to the National Insurance Crime Bureau. Washington, D.C. police officer Steve Jackson has this advice from the streets on foiling car rustlers.

■ **Don't advertise yourself as an easy mark with unlocked doors and open windows.** Whether you are stopped in your car at a downtown intersection in the middle of the night, or have left your vehicle in a parking space for just a minute while you run into the dry cleaner's, keeping your doors unlocked and windows down is tempting fate.

Leaving purses and bags on the seat next to you is like hanging out a sign that you want to be robbed, says Jackson. People are especially vulnerable while stopped in traffic. Here's the scam: The thief stands on a corner until a driver with a purse on the passenger seat stops at a light or stop sign. If luck is on the crook's side, the criminal quickly opens an unlocked door and grabs the goods. "You can't leave your car because you're in the middle of traffic, so kiss the pocketbook goodbye," says Jackson.

■ **Plan your route, and make sure you have enough gas and money to get to your destination and back.** Running out of gas is dangerous because you could end up stranded in the middle of nowhere, a prime target for criminal activity. And don't expect gas stations to donate you an emergency gallon. If your car breaks down, lift the hood or tie a white cloth to the car. When somebody stops, ask him to phone for help, but stay in your car and keep it locked.

If you have a cellular phone, which Jackson strongly recommends, call the police before calling a motor club like AAA.

■ **Deny car thieves the time and privacy they need to do their thing.** The Club is a great deterrent to car theft, says Jackson, because it takes so long to saw through. Car alarms are also good deterrents because they draw attention. But buy one that stops after one minute, so it won't run itself out. Otherwise, he warns, "Your neighbors will get so sick of it they might smash the car windows themselves."

■ **Mace your assailant.** Jackson suggests that drivers carry Mace or pepper gas, preferably attaching it to a key chain. If you are attacked, "Look for an opportunity to spray him right in the face," Jackson says.

■ **Beware of fashions.** Different cars go in and out of fashion for car thieves. In the nation's capital today, Toyota Camrys are the hot wheels among thieves. Nationwide, Honda Accords top the hot list.

■ HOT WHEELS

This list of the 10 most often stolen cars in 1995 shows that thieves prefer parts over luxury.

1. **Honda Accord**
2. **Oldsmobile Cutlass Supreme**
3. **Chevrolet 1/2 Ton Pickup**
4. **Toyota Camry**
5. **Chevrolet Blazer**
6. **Honda Civic**
7. **Ford Mustang**
8. **Toyota Corolla**
9. **Chevrolet Caprice**
10. **Oldsmobile Delta 88 Royale**

SOURCE: National Insurance Crime Bureau.

SECURITY SYSTEMS

BUYING SAFETY ON A BUDGET

Prices are often negotiable and you don't need every bell and whistle

Home security systems can be far beyond most people's means. But depending on the elements you choose, you can increase the security of your home without bankrupting yourself. Many insurance companies will give discounts on homeowners' policies to those who install a security system. That's because burglars are three times more likely to enter a home without an electronic security system as a protected house, according to the Security Industry Association.

Top-of-the-line systems can include everything from high-tech detectors that can sense the presence of a human in a room, to closed-circuit TV systems that will let you monitor and record what's going on inside or outside your home, to sprinkler systems that spray dye on intruders. "You could spend anything," says Tricia Parks, president of Parks Associates, Dallas, Texas, a market research firm specializing in home technologies. "It's a cash-flow issue."

A good security system should cover the entire perimeter of the house, alert home dwellers to a problem, and let the intruder know he's been detected. Installing good locks and automatic lighting that makes it appear people are home is a start, says Parks. With more complicated systems, you must decide whether to buy a self-installation system or lease one from a company, and whether it should be one that automatically calls the police when the alarm goes off.

A low-end, off-the-shelf system that a consumer can install can cost as little as $500 for a 2,000-square-foot home. But a custom system rented from a security system company starts at about $1,200 to $2,500, says Parks. Getting one with a procedure that will automatically call the police is likely to carry a monthly fee of at least $20. But keep in mind that prices vary widely and are often negotiable.

LEAVING A CHILD HOME ALONE

Teaching kids how to deal with an emergency is the best way to avoid one

■ To decide if a child is ready to be left home alone, ask yourself, can the child:

- Be trusted to go straight home after school.
- Easily use the telephone, locks, and kitchen appliances.
- Stay alone without being afraid or lonely.

■ Before leaving a child home alone, make sure he or she knows:

- How to call your area's emergency number.
- How to give directions to your home.
- How to use the door, window locks and alarm system if you have one.
- How to escape in case of fire.
- To check in with you or a neighbor after arriving home.
- To never accept gifts or rides from strangers.
- To never let anyone into the home without your permission.
- To never let a caller at the door or on the phone know they are alone (say, "Mom can't come to the phone now.").
- To not go into an empty house if things don't look right, such as a broken window, ripped screen, or open door.
- To let you know about anything that frightens them or makes them feel uncomfortable.

SOURCE: The National Crime Prevention Council, Washington, D.C.

SELF-DEFENSE

WHEN A WOLF IS AT YOUR THROAT

You up the odds of fending off an attacker when you have a plan

Remember the movie *Paper Chase*, in which the haughty Harvard law professor played by John Houseman told his first-year students on the first day of class to look to their left and then to their right because one or the other of their neighbors would not be graduating? Well, Houseman's character might better have told his class to consider that one out of three women in America will be attacked in her lifetime, according to the Justice Department.

It's no wonder that women—and men, too—are anxious about walking to their cars in parking lots, going somewhere by themselves at night, or even opening their front door at the end of the day. But no one wants to go through life being paranoid, and learning self-defense is a viable way to reach a balanced awareness.

The first step in self-defense, says Rosalind Wiseman, author of *Defending Ourselves* (Noonday Press, 1995), is to figure out a plan, whether it is running to safety or delivering a crippling blow. "Just as you have a fire escape plan in your house, you should have a plan for physical safety," she advises. Wiseman, who has a second-degree black belt in karate, is the founder of a self-defense school in Washington, D.C., called Woman's Way, where she trains everyone from Girl Scout troops to civil servants. "The techniques are easy — teaching your brain that you can do them is the hard part," says Wiseman. Her tips:

■ Women should be conscious of their body language when they are walking in public places. A confident stride, with eyes up and shoulders down, is preferable. Avoid carrying numerous bags or otherwise showing that you could not immediately fight back.

■ If a person stops you to ask for directions while you are walking, make sure you can see his feet in your peripheral vision. That means he's a safe distance away. If he asks you for help, volunteer to call the police rather than going anywhere with him.

■ Carrying Mace or pepper spray can be an effective defense tool, but only if you are both prepared to use it and have practiced. A can of Mace in your purse with a safety latch you've never tried isn't going to do you much good in an emergency.

■ If someone with a weapon demands your wallet, you should comply—whatever you have in there is not worth your life. Wiseman suggests throwing the wallet away from you at a 45-degree angle. When the attacker goes after it, run to safety. Go where other people are—to a neighbor, a store, a gas station, but be sure to think about your destination instead of running blindly. Without a plan, a woman robbed in a parking garage, for example, might run into a stairwell, setting herself up for a second attack.

■ If you are being followed, use verbal self-defense. State loudly and clearly what you want the person to do, such as: "Go away! Leave me alone!" Fighting back should only be used as a last resort, but it can be a very powerful tool because it greatly reduces your chances of being raped or otherwise harmed. Says Wiseman: "Most assailants aren't looking for someone who will be a tough fight."

■ If you are a woman fighting back, remember that your lower body is five times stronger than your upper body. When using self-defense techniques, aim for the attacker's eyes, nose, throat, groin, knees, or feet. If it seems you can't defend yourself—if the attacker has a knife to your throat, for example — try to lull the assailant into thinking he has control. Convince him he's got you but needs to put down the knife. When he does, strike.

SOME BASIC MOVES IN YOUR OWN DEFENSE

There are two times when experts say you should fight back physically right away. One is if the attacker has rope or duct tape or another means of tying your hands and feet, which will probably make it impossible for you to escape. The other is if someone wants to take you somewhere else; chances of surviving are lower if you are moved to a second location.

■ **A FRONTAL ATTACK.** The palm strike has the power of a punch but reduces injury to your hand and fingers. The primary target is the nose, but you can hit the mouth, chin, throat, ear, or Adam's apple.

■ The proper hand position is shown at far left.

■ Strike quickly and return quickly to prevent the attacker from swatting or grabbing your hand. Don't telegraph your intentions (i.e., don't let him see you *preparing* to strike). The element of surprise is critically important in self-defense.

■ **CLOSE QUARTERS.** You can use your knee if you are at a close distance to the attacker. The two main targets with the knee are the attacker's groin and his head.

■ As you knee the groin, pull the attacker toward you. At the same time, pull your body to his side to minimize his ability to strike you.

■ A knee to the head is for when his body is partially bent—for example, after he's been kneed in the groin. To do this, hold the attacker's head with both hands as you would a basketball.

■ **ATTACKS FROM BEHIND.** If you are attacked from behind or the side, you need to break the attacker's hold and create space between you. When you are touched, immediately yell and round your shoulders to protect your lungs and sternum.

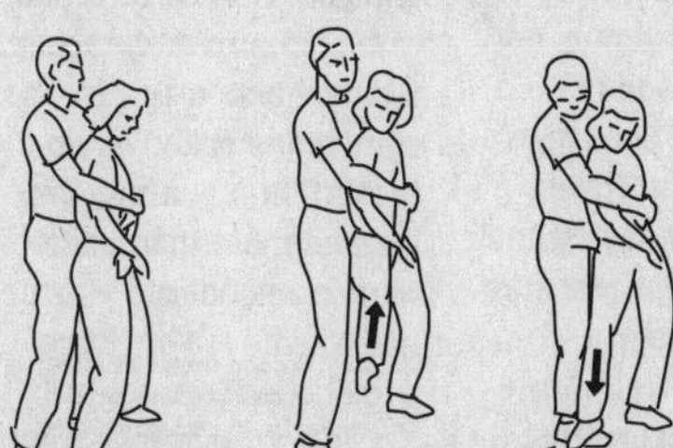

■ Crossing your wrists in front of you will help you round your shoulders, minimizing injury to your upper body from the force of someone grabbing you from behind.

■ Then look for his closest foot and stomp on it. For best results, stomp across (not parallel to) his foot. If you stomp hard enough, you might break a bone, making it difficult for him to chase you.

SOURCE: *Defending Ourselves*, Rosalind Wiseman (Noonday Press, 1995), reprinted by permission.

GUN LAWS

THE RIGHT TO BEAR ARMS

Owning a handgun is a matter of both federal and state regulation

Most of the gun laws in this country are state laws. Carrying permits, in fact, are issued not by a federal agency but by state or local governments. But anyone thinking about buying, transporting, or selling a gun should also be familiar with the federal Gun Control Act and its amendments, which are administered by the Treasury Department's Bureau of Alcohol, Tobacco and Firearms.

For example, handguns and ammunition for handguns may only be sold to persons 21 and older. Long guns, such as rifles, and accompanying ammunition may be sold to those 18 and over. It is against the law for certain other people, including illegal aliens, former Armed Forces personnel with dishonorable discharges, those under certain restraining orders, and criminals convicted for a crime that is punishable by more than one year, to possess or send firearms.

One of the most significant changes in federal gun law took effect on September 14, 1994, as part of omnibus anticrime legislation. Subsequent to that date, it became illegal to import, manufacture, possess, or transfer semiautomatic assault weapons. The ban includes 19 specific rifles, pistols, and shotguns, as well as copies of those makes that have at least two of the features identified with assault weapons. The ban also includes large-capacity ammunition clips. Exempted are owners of any such weapons at the time of the law's passage, as well as law enforcement and military personnel.

Another landmark change to federal legislation was the 1993 Brady law, which requires a background check on the buyer and a five-day waiting period before licensees can walk away with a handgun. Some states have waiting period requirements that differ from federal laws. Where the state provision exceeds five days, the state law overrides the federal one.

WEAPONS GLOSSARY

ASSAULT RIFLE: A military or police rifle usually capable of full automatic fire. Also used to describe military-style civilian rifles capable only of semiautomatic fire.

AUTOMATIC WEAPON: A firearm that continues to fire as long as the trigger is held down or until the ammunition magazine is emptied. The manufacture of machine guns, which are fully automatic, was halted in 1986.

BACKGROUND CHECK: A police department records check to make sure an applicant for a gun license would not violate any federal or state laws by possessing a gun.

CARTRIDGE: A self-contained firearm load consisting of a case, primer, propellant powder charge, and projectile.

CLIP: A metal strip used to hold cartridges; it may be more quickly loaded into a gun's magazine than loading individual cartridges.

HAIR TRIGGER: A trigger that requires only light pressure.

HANDGUN: A firearm designed to be fired with one hand. Handguns that have a revolving cylinder with several individual firing chambers are called revolvers. Handguns fed by a box magazine that has self-loading action are classified as pistols, or auto pistols.

MAGAZINE: A container for the ammunition supply of a repeating rifle, handgun, or shotgun. Can be attached to the firearm or detached; a detachable magazine is sometimes called a clip.

REPEATER: A gun that can be fired more than once without reloading.

SOURCES: Handgun Control Inc., Washington, D.C.; National Rifle Association of America, Fairfax, Va.; Bureau of Alcohol, Tobacco and Firearms, Department of the Treasury.

CITIZEN'S GUIDE

THE LAW OF THE LAND FOR GUN OWNERS

The following chart provides highlights of state firearms laws as of January 1, 1996.[1] Gun owners are also subject to federal gun laws (see opposite page), and in some cases city and other local ordinances.

	SELECTIVE GUNS BANNED[12]	INSTANT BACKGROUND CHECK	SALE REPORTED TO GOVT.	WAITING PERIOD: 5-DAY FEDERAL APPLIES[9]	WAITING PERIOD: STATE (Number of days) –HANDGUNS	WAITING PERIOD: STATE (Number of days) –LONG GUNS	LICENSE OR PERMIT TO PURCHASE REQUIRED (HANDGUNS/LONG GUNS)	SEPARATE REGISTRATION REQUIRED (HANDGUNS/LONG GUNS)	CARRYING OPENLY PROHIBITED	CONCEALED WEAPONS LAW
ALABAMA			✔	YES	–[10]	–	NO	NO	✔	Permitted with specific need
ALASKA				YES	–	–	NO	NO		Concealed carry permit
ARIZONA		✔		YES	–	–	NO	NO		Concealed carry permit
ARKANSAS				YES	–	–	NO	NO	✔[5]	Concealed carry permit
CALIFORNIA	✔		✔	NO	15	15	NO	NO	✔	Permitted with specific need
COLORADO		✔		YES	–	–	NO	NO		Permitted w/law enf. permis.
CONNECTICUT	✔		✔	NO	14	14	NO	NO	✔	Concealed carry permit
DELAWARE		✔		YES	–	–	NO	NO		Permitted with specific need
D.C.	✔		✔	YES	–	–	BOTH[3]	BOTH	✔	Prohibited
FLORIDA		✔		YES	–[10]	–	NO	NO	✔	Concealed carry permit
GEORGIA		✔		YES	–	–	NO	NO	✔	Concealed carry permit
HAWAII	✔		✔	YES	–	–	BOTH[11]	BOTH	✔	Permitted with specific need
IDAHO		✔		YES	–	–	NO	NO		Concealed carry permit
ILLINOIS		✔	✔	YES	–[10]	–[10]	BOTH[8, 11]	NO[4]	✔	Prohibited
INDIANA			✔	NO	7	–	NO	NO	✔	Permitted with specific need
IOWA			✔	YES	–	–	HANDGUNS[11]	NO	✔	Permitted with specific need
KANSAS				YES	–	–	NO[2]	NO[2]		Prohibited
KENTUCKY				YES	–	–	NO	NO		Prohibited
LOUISIANA				YES	–	–	NO	NO		Permitted with specific need
MAINE				YES	–	–	NO	NO		Concealed carry permit
MARYLAND	✔		✔	NO	7	7	NO	NO	✔	Permitted with specific need
MASSACHUSETTS			✔	YES	–	–	BOTH[11]	NO	✔	Permitted with specific need
MICHIGAN			✔	YES	–	–	HANDGUNS	HANDGUNS	✔	Permitted with specific need
MINNESOTA			✔	NO	7	–	BOTH	NO	✔	Permitted with specific need
MISSISSIPPI				YES	–	–	NO	NO		Concealed carry permit
MISSOURI			✔	NO	7	–	HANDGUNS[11]	NO		Prohibited
MONTANA				YES	–	–	NO	NO		Concealed carry permit
NEBRASKA		✔		YES	–	–	NO	NO		Prohibited
NEVADA		✔		YES	–	–	HANDGUNS	NO[2]		Permitted with specific need
NEW HAMPSHIRE		✔	✔	YES	–	–	NO	NO		Concealed carry permit
NEW JERSEY	✔		✔	NO	7	–	BOTH[11]	LONG GUNS	✔	Permitted with specific need
NEW MEXICO				YES	–	–	NO	NO		Prohibited
NEW YORK	–		✔	YES	–	–	HANDGUNS[11]	HANDGUNS	✔	Permitted with specific need
NORTH CAROLINA			✔	YES	–	–	HANDGUNS[11]	NO		Concealed carry permit
NORTH DAKOTA			✔	YES	14	14	NO	NO	✔	Concealed carry permit

■ EXPERT LIST

	SELECTIVE GUNS BANNED[25]	INSTANT BACKGROUND CHECK	SALE REPORTED TO GOVT.	WAITING PERIOD: 5-DAY FEDERAL APPLIES	WAITING PERIOD: STATE (Number of days) –HANDGUNS	WAITING PERIOD: STATE (Number of days) –LONG GUNS	LICENCE OR PERMIT TO PURCHASE REQUIRED (HANDGUNS/LONG GUNS)	SEPARATE REGISTRATION REQUIRED (HANDGUNS/LONG GUNS)	CARRYING OPENLY PROHIBITED	CONCEALED WEAPONS LAW
OHIO				YES	–[2]	–	NO	NO		Prohibited
OKLAHOMA				YES	–	–	NO	NO	✔	Concealed carry permit
OREGON		✔	✔	YES	–	–	NO	NO		Concealed carry permit
PENNSYLVANIA		✔[7]	✔	YES	–	–	NO	NO	✔	Concealed carry permit
RHODE ISLAND			✔	NO	7	7	NO	NO	✔	Permitted with specific need
SOUTH CAROLINA		✔	✔	YES	–	–	NO	NO	✔	Permitted with specific need
SOUTH DAKOTA			✔	YES	–[10]	–	NO	NO		Concealed carry permit
TENNESSEE			✔	NO	15	–	NO	NO[5]	✔	Concealed carry permit
TEXAS				YES	–	–	NO	NO	✔	Concealed carry permit
UTAH		✔		YES	–	–	NO	NO	✔	Concealed carry permit
VERMONT				YES	–	–	NO	NO[5]	✔	No restrictions
VIRGINIA	✔	✔		YES	–[2,6]	–	NO[6]	NO		Concealed carry permit
WASHINGTON			✔	YES	5	–	NO	NO	✔	Concealed carry permit
WEST VIRGINIA				YES	–	–	NO	NO		Concealed carry permit
WISCONSIN		✔	✔	YES	–[10]	–	NO	NO		Prohibited
WYOMING				YES	–	–	NO	NO		Concealed carry permit

SOURCE: National Rifle Association.

■ NOTES AND EXPLANATIONS

1. Since state and local laws frequently change, this chart is not to be considered legal advice or a restatement of the law.

2. Certain cities or counties have legal requirements of their own as well.

3. Applies only to handguns registered prior to D.C.'s 1977 handgun ban and to all long guns. No additional handguns may be acquired by D.C. residents.

4. Except in Chicago, where separate registration is required.

5. Arkansas prohibits carrying a firearm "with a purpose to employ it as a weapon against a person." Tennessee prohibits carrying "with the intent to go armed." Vermont prohibits carrying a firearm "with the intent or purpose of injuring another."

6. Handgun purchases limited to one per 30-day period, with certain exceptions.

7. Pennsylvania passed instant check legislation in 1995; however, the federal and state waiting periods still apply until the new system becomes operational.

8. Firearm owner's I.D. card required for both handguns and long guns; except where handguns are prohibited, which includes Evanston, Oak Park, Morton Grove, Winnetka, Wilmette, and Highland Park.

9. As interpreted by the federal Bureau of Alcohol, Tobacco and Firearms.

10. Alabama, South Dakota, and Wisconsin have a 2-day waiting period for handguns; Florida and Illinois have a 3-day waiting period for handguns, and in Illinois a 1-day waiting period for long guns. But in all these cases the state provisions are overridden by the federal 5-day waiting period.

11. The permit-to-purchase system constitutes a waiting period for first-time buyers in the following states: Illinois, Massachusetts, Missouri, New Jersey, New York and North Carolina. In Iowa, permits-to-purchase are good only after 3 days from date of issue. Hawaii's permit-to-purchase system constitutes a 14- to 20-day waiting period for first-time gun buyers as the law requires law enforcement to hold the permit-to-purchase for 14 days and no longer than 20 days. Subsequent permits may be granted in less time.

12. California, Connecticut, New Jersey, New York City and other towns in New York, and several Ohio cities have banned "assault weapons." Some Ohio cities also forbid the possession and sale of handguns with a certain magazine capacity. In Illinois, Chicago and certain other cities have banned handguns and "assault weapons." Maryland has banned several small, low-caliber, inexpensive handguns and "assault pistols." Hawaii forbids "assault pistols." Virginia bans Street Sweeper shotguns. D.C. bans handguns, semiautomatic firearms with the ability to use a magazine holding more than 12 rounds (except as noted in footnote 3).

GARDENING

SOIL: An expert's advice on preparing the foundation for a great garden, PAGE 416 **COLOR:** How to achieve year-round splendor, PAGE 420 **EXPERT TIPS:** Picking the best plants at the garden center, PAGE 421 **ROSES:** No-fuss varieties for no-mess gardeners, PAGE 423 **PESTS:** Organic remedies for problem insects and diseases, PAGE 424 **TREES:** When and how to prune, PAGE 426 **LAWNS:** The best grasses for your region, PAGE 427

EXPERT Q & A

PARADISE IN A TIGHT SPACE

If your gardening area isn't spacious, try container planting

Time was when having a garden meant having a big yard, but these days having your garden in containers is the "in" thing. Being short on space need not limit your gardening ambitions. Container gardens allow you to grow plants of every type and provide color and seasonal interest to areas where an in-ground garden is impractical. Even if you have a conventional garden, plants in containers can provide changing accents and focal points: Flowers, vegetables, herbs, shrubs, trees—and even aquatics—can be grown in a variety of containers to add new dimensions to your landscape. Portability is also a big plus if you like growing plants that need to be brought indoors when the weather turns cold, but you don't like digging them up in the fall. Holly Shimizu, a host of the PBS gardening program, *Victory Garden,* and assistant director of the U.S. Botanic Gardens in Washington, D.C., offers us her thoughts on this adaptable gardening style:

■ What are your favorite trends in container gardening?

One trend is to put containers into beds and borders. Raise them up on a log or a rock, and use plants with seasonal interest—an azalea when it is blooming, pansies in the cool season, basil or other heat lovers in the summer. It's a fun way to do creative things in a bed or border. Planting a water garden in a container is another trend. You can buy water garden containers or make your own by taking a pot and lining it with pool liner; then you can grow aquatic plants. Another trend is gardening with kids. By giving them a container you can give them their own garden. I use big wooden containers that are perfectly attractive and very low-maintenance.

■ Which containers work best for growing plants?

People are looking for alternatives to terra-cotta, because although terra-cotta is beautiful, it's also high-maintenance. They are easy to blow over in the wind, break down in the elements, and crack in the winter. And because they "breathe" so much, plants in them tend to need much more watering. Plastic containers break down because of the reaction of plastic to sunlight—they become brittle. There are some pots I like that are cement but look like stone and are so elegant. They are heavy and very durable, so they can freeze and thaw without being affected. Be sure any container has a hole in the bottom; if it doesn't, you might as well forget it.

MIX AND MATCH WHAT'S IN THE BOX

When planning container gardens, color, fragrance, and texture are great themes

Petunias and geraniums are staples of most window boxes, hanging baskets, and patio planters, but if you're planning to decorate your surroundings with container plants, you needn't limit yourself to old standbys. Experimenting with more unusual combinations of plants often leads to stunning results. Plant combinations are limitless—consider the color, texture, height, fragrance, and seasonality of plants rather than their traditional uses.

Holly Shimizu of the U.S. Botanic Gardens in Washington, D.C., suggests beginning with a theme. It could be a kitchen garden, with all your favorite herbs from parsley and tarragon to rosemary and oregano. Try dressing up the container with edible flowers like violets and nasturtiums. For height, add a bay tree topiary.

Color offers many creative opportunities—plants with blossoms in shades of blue, for example, or a combination of yellow and purple flowers. Fragrance themes also work. A "lemon" garden, for example, could include plants with a lemony fragrance such as lemon thyme, lemon basil, lemon balm, or lemon-scented geraniums, set off, perhaps, by yellow marigolds.

Plants with attractive foliage often show flowers to their best advantage. The soft gray-green leaves of garden sage, the intense green of tansy, or the silvery white of dusty miller or artemisia provide a splendid foil for bright blooms. Combining plants with purple, bronze, or variegated leaves enhances foliar interest. In fact, a dramatic container display need not include any flowers whatsoever: Simply combine plants with contrasting foliage colors, textures, and heights.

If you thought vegetables were just for eating, think again. Red-ribbed rhubarb, chard and red romaine are especially attractive combined with blue and yellow flowers. Ruffled leaf lettuce in red and green varieties makes a great edging to flower borders or window boxes and can also be harvested for the salad bowl.

■ Do gardening containers need more drainage than the drainage hole provides?

Yes. I usually put a little screen over the hole so it won't get blocked with a rock or something else. Then I often put in a layer of gravel, rock, or even broken crockery. Some people say you don't need it, but I feel it's insurance.

■ How should plants for containers be selected?

Consider the heat that reaches the root system of plants in containers. You don't want to grow plants that originally came from regions where roots remain cool and moist; the ones that thrive tend to come from hot regions. For example, oleander does well in a pot because its roots don't care if they get hot. I grew them at the National Herb Garden at the National Aboretum around the pool where there was not only direct light, but reflected light and heat from the hard surfaces surrounding them. It never fazed them as long as they were watered properly.

■ Do container plants have to be watered differently from plants in the ground?

Watering plants in a container isn't that hard. You get a feeling for how much water the plants need. If it's not raining, you can probably water them almost every day. But be aware of seasonal changes. In spring you water much less, and toward summer's end, if the plants have become potbound, their watering needs are tremendous.

■ Are there special soil and fertilizing requirements?

You need a little more fertilizer in a container

■ WHERE THE GROWING ZONES FALL

Most plant catalogs specify the regions in which perennial plants thrive. The standard zones are defined by the minimum temperatures each region reaches in an average year; the 11 zones are shown.

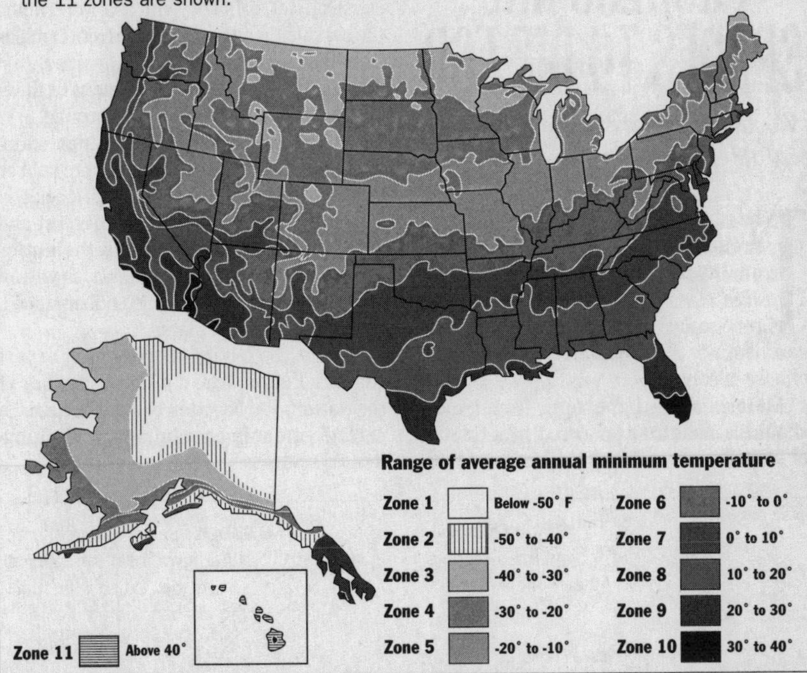

because you don't have much to draw from. I've had very good luck with commercial mixes like Miracle-Gro or Peter's. I also use a combination of seaweed together with fish emulsion. It's so good, I can see immediate results. I sometimes use slow-release fertilizers like Osmocote. The soil that I like is a combination of one part good, loamy topsoil—that's actually challenging, because it's sometimes hard to get—with one part of good soilless mix such as Promix or Metromix with micronutrients in it. We use that at the Botanic Gardens, then amend accordingly. If we were growing Mediterranean plants, we would mix in chicken grit to improve drainage. If we were growing moisture-loving plants, we would add more organic matter.

■ Does planting in a container differ from in-ground planting?

I like to put plants closer together when I'm using a container. I like to make sure I have beautiful things falling over the edge, plants with contrasting textures behind them that are a little taller, and behind that, plants that are even taller, to create layers. You need to whack them back if they become too big. Just as in an in-ground garden, the stronger growers take over. Deadhead, or cut off dead flowers, on a regular basis and you can keep your plants blooming.

■ Does planting different plants in a single container cause growing problems?

Most middle-of-the-road plants are fine. You wouldn't combine an alpine with an aquatic, of course, but otherwise, I don't think much about it. One of the nice things about gardening in containers is that some plants will die, or die back, or die out, and it doesn't matter. That's normal. Just replace them with something else.

TOOLS

PRUNERS AND SPADES TO DIE FOR

Wooden handles cause few blisters, anvil pruners cut most sharply

The gardening rage in recent years has brought forth an abundance of top-quality tools, many of them fashioned after classic English tools. But at current prices, equipping yourself fully can be quite an investment, so you must choose wisely.

Materials are important. Metal tools should be made from tempered, heat-treated, or forged metal. Stainless steel tools are most expensive, but they are also the strongest and should last you a lifetime. Choose wooden-handled tools over metal ones whenever possible because they are less likely to cause blisters. Hickory and ash wood make the best handles. Handles made from Douglas fir will be weak and should be avoided. And make sure that there are no cracks or flaws of any kind in the wood before buying.

Look for pitchforks with springy stainless steel tines, and hoses made from rubber or Flexogen last longer than plastic ones.

Bamboo lawn rakes are the lightest and easiest to handle. They're usually the best for raking leaves. But for raking leaves within flower beds, use a rake that is rubber-tipped. It won't damage the plants.

Here is the advice of gardening expert Alastair Bolton, who did his spadework at the National Arboretum before becoming a private gardening consultant in Washington, D.C.:

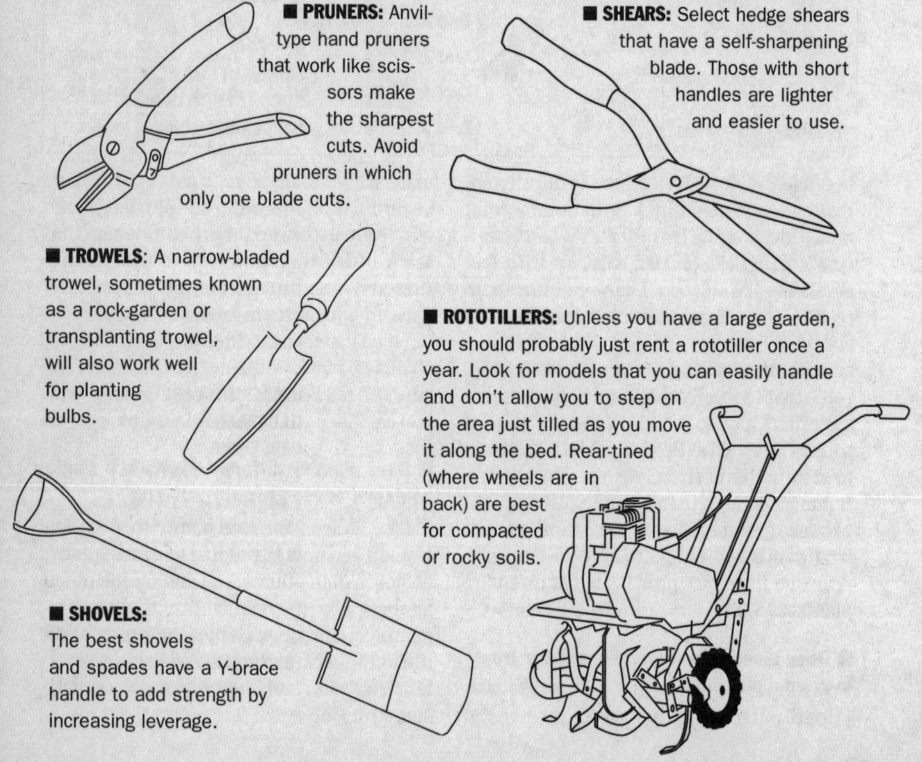

■ **PRUNERS:** Anvil-type hand pruners that work like scissors make the sharpest cuts. Avoid pruners in which only one blade cuts.

■ **SHEARS:** Select hedge shears that have a self-sharpening blade. Those with short handles are lighter and easier to use.

■ **TROWELS**: A narrow-bladed trowel, sometimes known as a rock-garden or transplanting trowel, will also work well for planting bulbs.

■ **ROTOTILLERS:** Unless you have a large garden, you should probably just rent a rototiller once a year. Look for models that you can easily handle and don't allow you to step on the area just tilled as you move it along the bed. Rear-tined (where wheels are in back) are best for compacted or rocky soils.

■ **SHOVELS:** The best shovels and spades have a Y-brace handle to add strength by increasing leverage.

EXPERT SOURCES

TOOLS AND EQUIPMENT TO DO THE JOB

Where to get a great rake or the best English trowel, the best new seeds and plants, and some essential information for a beautiful garden

TOOLS

AMES
P.O. Box 1774
Parkersburg, WV 26102
■ Good selection of child-sized tools.
☎ **800–624–2654**

E. C. GEIGER
P.O. Box 285
Harleysville, PA 19438
■ Tools, equipment, soil testers, fertilizers, etc.
☎ **800–443–4437**

LANGENBACK
P.O. Box 1420
Lawndale, CA 90260
■ Top-of-the line English and other imported tools.
☎ **800–362–1991**

SMITH & HAWKEN
25 Corte Madera
Mill Valley, CA 94941
■ Tools, gifts, clothing.
☎ **800–776–3336**

SEEDS AND PLANTS

W. ATLEE BURPEE
P.O. Box 5114
Warminster, PA
18974–4818
■ Flower and vegetable seeds, bulbs, shrubs, and gardening supplies.
☎ **800–888–1447**

HARRIS SEEDS
P.O. Box 22960
Rochester, NY 14692
■ Flower and vegetable seeds and plants.
☎ **716–442–0410**

J. W. JUNG SEED CO.
335 S. High St.
Randolph, WI 53957
■ Flower and vegetable seeds; fruit trees.
☎ **414–326–3121**

GEO. W. PARK SEED CO.
Cokesbury Rd.
Greenwood, SC
29647–0001
■ Seeds, plants, and gardening supplies.
☎ **800–845–3369**

JACKSON & PERKINS
2518 S. Pacific Hwy.
Medford, OR 97501
■ Wide selection of roses and perennials, also garden accessories.
☎ **800–854–6200**

SHEPHERD'S GARDEN SEEDS
30 Irene St.
Torrington, CT 06790
■ Specialty vegetable, herb, and flower seeds.
☎ **806–482–3638**

THOMPSON & MORGAN
P.O. Box 1308
Jackson, NJ 08527
■ English catalog with over 2,500 varieties of flower and vegetable seeds.
☎ **800–274–7333**

WAYSIDE GARDENS
1 Garden Lane
Hodges, SC 29695–0001
■ Large selection of perennials, trees, and shrubs.
☎ **800–845–1124**

WHITE FLOWER FARM
Litchfield, CT 06759–0050
■ Perennials, bulbs, trees, and shrubs. Excellent catalog with detailed plant and growing instructions.
☎ **800–503–9624**

BOOKS

AMERICAN HORTICULTURAL SOCIETY ENCYCLOPEDIA OF GARDEN PLANTS
Christopher Brickell, ed., Macmillan, 1989, $59.95
■ A comprehensive volume of information on most of the trees, shrubs, flowers, and foliage plants grown in American gardens.

READER'S DIGEST ILLUSTRATED GUIDE TO GARDENING
Carroll C. Calkins, ed., Reader's Digest Association, 1989, $30
■ If you had no other source, you could develop terrific skills with this book alone. Easy-to-understand and has excellent illustrations.

EXPERT TIPS

DIG AND YOU SHALL REAP

Start with a soil test and a little nutrition for dirt that's lacking

Soil is the foundation for any garden. The effort given to its preparation will, to a large degree, determine the success of your garden. While soil quality varies widely depending on location, and your local agricultural extension service is likely to be the best information source about the soil in your region, some steps to soil preparation apply to any yard. Chris Curless, a horticulturist at White Flower Farm, the famous Litchfield, Ct., grower and supplier of ornamental plants to home gardens in the United States and Canada, explains how to get your garden ready for planting:

■ Test your soil to find out how well it will support plant growth and what you might have to do to improve it.

A soil test will show your soil pH and how to adjust it if needed, as well as the levels of specific nutrients to determine fertilizer needs. Extension services can perform these lab tests on your soil and give you a detailed profile of what you've got in your yard. Most plants prefer a slightly acidic-to-neutral soil. Your soil test will indicate how much lime or sulfur needs adding if adjustment is required. It will also recommend what other nutrients may be needed as supplements.

■ Mark the area for your garden before you dig.

If it's a simple shape like a rectangle or square, stakes and string are an easy way to do this. For a curved bed, a garden hose will allow you to make smooth bends. Mark the edge of the bed with white spray paint or powdered lime so you know exactly where you want to dig. It's easy to think you know and still get lost in the middle of your digging.

■ Remove existing grass to get to the soil.

If you are going to put a border into a lawn, you want to get rid of the turf. If it's a large, relatively flat area, consider renting a sod cutter—a heavy, gas-powered machine. It's not great at corners and awful on a hillside because it weighs about 300 pounds, but for flat areas it is very fast. Smaller mechanical gadgets are also available to cut turf. But the tried-and-true method is to use a sharpened spade to undercut the turf. Since you're removing the top inch or so of soil and a lot of green material, put it in the compost pile so you can use it again in the future.

■ Add a hefty layer of organic matter.

Next, spread three to six inches of organic matter on top of the entire area with a rake. Organic matter benefits all kinds of soil, whether it's light and sandy or heavy. In a sandy soil, organic matter improves moisture retention; in a heavy, clayey soil it improves the drainage. Remember: if you're planting woody stock or perennials, you only have one chance to work the soil like this, so take advantage of the opportunity. Some good types of organic matter include aged manure, peat moss, or leaf mold. In some areas of the South, ground-up pine bark is recommended because it lasts longer in warm, moist soil. If you need to add soil amendments, spread them evenly on top of the organic matter.

■ Thoroughly mix the organic matter and other additions into the soil.

The next step is digging. I think turning the soil to a depth of a shovel is enough. Many books recommend double-digging—which means digging twice as deep—but for most people, that's just way too much work.

Start at one corner and work your way backward, so you don't compact the area you have turned. Break up big clods as you go. Digging and incorporating the organic matter and fertilizer creates air spaces in the soil, making it easier for the roots of your plants to get around. The goal of all this is to make it easier for plants to grow.

PLANTER'S GUIDE

CHOOSING VEGETABLES FOR EVERY TABLE

Planting should begin well before the last frost of the season. The following table provides a timetable for when vegetable seeds should be started.

Vegetable	Optimum temp. (°F)	Germination time (days)	WEEKS RELATIVE TO LAST FROST TO: Sow inside	Transplant outside	Sow outside	SPACE BETWEEN: Rows	Plants	Planting per person
ASPARAGUS	60-85	21	7-8 BEF.	5-6 AFT.	†	3 FT.	15 in.	9-15 ROOTS
BEANS, BUSH	75-80	7	*	—	1 AFT.	24 in.	4 in.	10-15 FT.
BEANS, LIMA	85	7-10	*	—	2 AFT.	18 in.	6-8 in.	10-15 FT.
BEANS, POLE	75-80	7	*	—	1 AFT.	4 FT.	36 in.	3-5 HILLS
BEETS	75	7-14	8 BEF.	4 BEF.	1-2 BEF.	15 in.	3 in.	5-10 FT.
BROCCOLI	60-75	5-10	5-7 BEF.	3-4 BEF. to 3 AFT.	3-4 BEF.	30 in.	24 in.	5-10 PLANTS
BRUSSELS SPROUTS	68-75	5-10	10-12 BEF.	5-6 BEF.	5-6 BEF.	24 in.	18 in.	5-10 PLANTS
CABBAGE, CHINESE	50-75	10	10 BEF.	—	AFT.	18 in.	12 in.	5-10 PLANTS
CABBAGE, HEAD	68-75	5-10	7-9 BEF.	2-3 BEF.	1-4 AFT.	24 in.	18 in.	3-5 PLANTS
CARROTS	75	12-14	*	—	4-6 BEF.	14 in.	3 in.	5-10 ft.
CAULIFLOWER	68-86	5-10	6-8 BEF.	2-4 BEF.	†	24 in.	18 in.	3-5 PLANTS
CELERY	68-76	21-28	3-5 BEF.	3 AFT.	†	24 in.	6 in.	2-3 PLANTS
CORN, SWEET	70-86	7-10	*	—	1 AFT.	3 ft.	10 in.	15-25 ft.
CUCUMBERS	70-86	7-10	*	—	2 AFT.	6 ft.	48 in.	2-3 HILLS
EGGPLANT	70-86	10	4-6 BEF.	4-6 AFT.	†	3 ft.	24 in.	2-3 PLANTS
KALE	68-75	5-10	5-7 BEF.	0-2 BEF.	2-4 BEF.	18-24 in.	12-15 in.	5-10 ft.
LETTUCE, HEAD	68-70	7-1	1-6 BEF.	2 BEF. to 3 AFT.	4 BEF. to 4 AFT.	14 in.	10 in.	5-10 ft.
LETTUCE, OTHER	68-70	7-10	1-6 BEF.	2 BEF. to 3 AFT.	4 BEF. to 4 AFT.	14 in.	6 in.	5-10 ft.
MUSKMELONS	80-86	4-10	2-4 BEF.	0-3 AFT.	1 AFT.	6 ft.	36 in.	3-5 HILLS

HOW DEEP IS YOUR CABBAGE?

As a general rule, you should plant at a depth four times the seed's diameter.

SOURCE: *Family Circle*, Spring 1994.

■ PLANTER'S GUIDE

Vegetable	Optimum temp. (°F)	Germination time (days)	Weeks relative to last frost to: Sow inside	Transplant outside	Sow outside	Space between: Rows	Plants	Planting per person
OKRA	80-86	7-14	3-4 BEF.	3-4 AFT.	1-2 AFT.	2-4 ft.	10 in.	2 PLANTS
ONIONS	68-70	10-14	2-10 BEF.	5 BEF.to 3 AFT.	3-5 BEF.	15 in.	2 in.	10-15 ft.
PARSNIPS	68-70	14-21	2-9 BEF.	4 BEF.to 3-4 AFT.	6-8 BEF.	18 in.	3 in.	10-15 ft.
PEANUTS	75-80	7-14	4-6 BEF.	AFT.	†	30 in.	12 in.	9-25 PLANTS
PEAS	65-70	7-14	*	—	2-4 BEF.	24 in.	8 in.	10-15 ft.
PEPPERS	75-85	10	2-4 BEF.	4-6 AFT.	†	24 in.	24 in.	2-3 PLANTS
POTATOES	65-70	10-14	*	—	1-3 BEF.	3 ft.	12 in.	50-100 ft.
PUMPKIN	68-75	7-10	1-2 BEF.	3-4 AFT.	2 AFT.	12 ft.	60 in.	3-5 HILLS
RADISH	65-70	5-7	*	—	2-4 BEF.	14 in.	2 in.	5-10 ft.
SALSIFY	65-70	7-20	4-12 BEF.	6 BEF. to 2 AFT.	†	14 in.	3 in.	10-15 ft.
SPINACH	68-70	7-14	*	—	3-5 BEF.	14 in.	3 in.	5-10 ft.
SQUASH, SUMMER	70-85	7-14	0-1 BEF.	4-5 AFT.	2 AFT.	3 ft.	48 in.	2-3 HILLS
SQUASH, WINTER	70-85	7-14	1-2 BEF.	3-4 AFT.	2 AFT.	6 ft.	60 in.	3-5 HILLS
SWEET POTATOES	75-85	18	6-8 BEF.	2-3 AFT.	†	3 ft.	12 in.	9-20 PLANTS
SWISS CHARD	68-75	7-14	*	—	1-2 BEF.	18 in.	9 in.	5-10 ft.
TOMATOES	75-80	7-14	5-7 BEF.	0-4 AFT.	†	3 ft.	36 in.	3-5 PLANTS
TURNIPS	65-70	7-14	*	—	2-4 BEF.	15 in.	3 in.	10-15 ft.
WATERMELONS	75-85	7-14	1-2 BEF.	1-4 AFT.	†	8 ft.	96 in.	3-5 HILLS

* Direct sowing in garden preferred †Transplant preferred

SOURCE: *Foolproof Planting*, 1990, Rodale Press editors and Anne Halpin; American Horticultural Society.

■ WHEN TO FERTILIZE YOUR VEGETABLE PLANTS

"Side-dressing" is simply a mid-season fertilizer boost. Here are the vegetables that require it, and the best times to apply it:

ASPARAGUS	Before growth starts in spring, and after harvesting to promote fern growth.
BEANS*	No need to side-dress.
BEETS*	No need to side-dress.
BROCCOLI	Three weeks after transplanting.
CABBAGE	Three weeks after transplanting.
CARROTS*	No need to side-dress.
CAULIFLOWER	Three weeks after transplanting.
CUCUMBERS	At "stand-up" stage, just before they start to run.
EGGPLANT	When plants start to blossom.
KALE	Four weeks after planting.
LETTUCE*	No need to side-dress.
MUSKMELON	At "stand-up" stage, just before they start to run.
ONIONS	Four weeks and six weeks after planting.
PEAS*	No need to side-dress.
PEPPERS	When plants start to blossom.
POTATOES	At last hilling, before plants start to blossom.
SPINACH*	No need to side-dress.
SQUASH	At "stand-up" stage, just before they start to run.
TOMATOES	When plants start to blossom.
TURNIPS*	No need to side-dress.
WATERMELON	At "stand-up" stage, just before they start to run.

* Assumes that the fertilizer has been added to the rows before planting.

SOURCE: *Down-to-Earth Gardening Know-How for the 90's*, Dick Raymond, Garden Way, 1991.

THE ORGANIC ALTERNATIVES

Organic fertilizers are substances derived from plants, animals, or minerals. They contain essential elements for plant growth. In contrast to synthetic fertilizers, they occur naturally, which means they may be physically processed but are never chemically altered or mixed with synthetic materials. To ensure effective use, consult these application guidelines from the American Horticultural Society, adjusting them when necessary to take into account soil conditions and the type of plants being raised.

Fertilizer	Application rate per 1,000 sq. ft.	Uses
ALFALFA MEAL	40–50 lbs. (4 appl./yr.)	A "green manure." Breaks down easily to provide nitrogen.
BLOOD MEAL	10–30 lbs. (1 appl./yr.)	Readily available nitrogen; speeds decomposition of compost.
BONE MEAL	10–20 lbs. (1 appl./yr.)	Excellent source of phosphorus; raises pH. Good for fruits, bulbs, flowers.
CATTLE MANURE	30 lbs.	Valuable soil additive. If fresh, will burn.
COMPOST	2-inch depth (1 appl./yr.)	Valuable source of trace elements such as calcium, iron, magnesium, manganese, sulfur, and zinc.
COTTONSEED MEAL	20–30 lbs. (1 appl./yr.)	Acidifies soil; lasts 4–6 months.
FISH EMULSION	2 oz. per gal. water (2–3 spray appl./yr.)	A good "foliar spray," or liquid fertilizer, for early spring.
FISH MEAL	20 lbs. (1–2 appl./yr.)	Readily available nitrogen; speeds decomposition of compost.
SEAWEED	1 oz. per gal. water	Contains natural growth hormones.
SUL-PO-MAG	20 lbs. (1 appl./yr.)	High in potash. Recommended for plants suffering iron chlorosis.

SOURCE: American Horticultural Society.

■ CONVERTING FERTILIZER RATES

Fertilizers often are labeled with big-time planters in mind, but if you are planting only a small corner of your backyard, it's easy to convert the application rates. Gardening expert Dick Raymond says it's better to measure by volume than by weight when you are dealing with small quantities of fertilizer. The table at right shows how to convert rates assuming that two cups of fertilizer weigh about a pound—the standard weight of most commercially available fertilizers.

Area in square feet	Pounds of fertilizer to apply, where amount to be applied per acre is:		
	100 lbs.	400 lbs.	800 lbs.
100	0.25	1	2
500	1.25	5	10
1,000	2.50	10	20
1,500	3.75	15	30
2,000	5.00	20	40

SOURCE: *Down-to-Earth Gardening Know-How for the 90's*, Dick Raymond, Garden Way, 1991.

EXPERT Q & A

THE COLOR OF BEAUTY

Gardening creatively all year round is a many-hued splendor

It's easy to have garden color in the summer, but what about the rest of the year? At famed Callaway Gardens in Pine Mountain, Ga., the demonstration gardens offer visitors plenty of ideas for keeping the garden colorful and interesting in spring and beyond. It's important to think about more than just flowers: Careful selection of plants, wise use of color, and an eye toward arrangement will go a long way to providing interest in your home landscape in every season, as Callaway's garden display manager, Parker Andes, explains here:

■ How should a gardener plan for year-round color?

We all see how great English flower borders look. But here in the South we have such a long summer that we end up with bare spots in such gardens. And in winter, a herbaceous border dies down to the ground. You're better off taking that same ground and mixing it with trees and flowering shrubs to create little vignettes around the yard. Mix something like 'Winter King' hawthorn, which produces a great berry crop, with some rhododendrons. Then add a few annuals and perennials, and your little corner can have a lot of color throughout the year. The most important thing is to grow what's right for your area. Go to your local nursery to find out what does well. Pay attention to the native flora.

■ How would you plan for a succession of blooms?

Plan a border that includes herbaceous plants, woody shrubs, and trees. Maybe you even will want to add vines for more interest. Take a shrub like a spring-blooming viburnum and plant a summer- or fall-blooming clematis nearby and allow it to grow through the shrub. It has to be a good, sturdy shrub to support the vine, but you can find a number of shrubs that will work. That's a good trick to using the same space for flowers in two seasons. Another idea is planting daffodils, daylilies, and Oriental lilies together. The daffodils bloom early, and the daylilies grow to hide the fading daffodil foliage. Then the daylilies bloom, followed by the Oriental lilies, so you are getting a lot of blooms from the same square footage.

■ How do you suggest grouping plants for color?

The traditional way of stepping plants down with the tallest in the back, medium in the middle, and the shortest plants along the edge works well in borders. Placing brighter colors in the back of the border is supposed to draw your eye. I'm not sure that's always true, but brighter colors do stand out from a distance. The darker the color, the less it stands out—it tends to get muddy-looking from a distance and doesn't come through. The same holds for flesh tones. Some of the new chrysanthemums with pale pink or flesh-colored flowers tend to bleed together. They don't stand out like a bright white, yellow, or orange.

■ Which backdrops are particularly useful for setting off colors?

Some of the variegated grasses work very well to set off flowering plants. And purple leaf plants like the purple *Cotinus* (smoke tree) give that burgundy color, which blends with everything so well. Chartreuse is another blender and it helps picks up other colors. If you have a deep red flower with a yellow center, like a mum, chartreuse in that planting really picks up the yellow and brightens it up.

■ Can you get visual interest without a lot of color?

A garden done in shades of green is a contemplative gar-

EXPERT TIPS

BEDDING PLANTS THAT MAKE THE GRADE

Buds are fine, blooms are not, when picking plants. You know how much sun or shade your garden gets in the growing season so you can select plants to suit those conditions. But what to look for when you get to the local nursery? Nona Wolfram-Kivula of the National Garden Bureau offers these tips:

■ Select plants that are not in full bloom. Plants without flowers are usually younger and tolerate transplanting stress better than those with lots of flowers, but buds showing are fine.

■ If you want immediate color, pick plants in larger pots. Larger plants also generally transplant more successfully, because they have larger root systems.

■ Look for dark green leaves. If lower leaves are yellow, the plants are probably older.

■ Buy your plants in small quantities so you can plant them promptly. It's best to plant them the same day you buy them.

■ Always look for a label that gives the variety name—not just "red impatiens"—because that could be any of 20 varieties, and some are superior to others. Save the labels; if the plant grows well and you like it, you can remember to get the same variety next year.

■ Also buy some fertilizer along with your plants. Annuals, especially, require a lot of nutrients because their entire life cycle lasts only about six months.

den. Color can be used as an accent, but not necessarily a bright red. White works very well as an accent for this kind of garden. Textures are also important to consider—for example, leaves with various sizes and shapes. You can use green grasses, broadleaf ground covers, needle-leaf shrubs, and other bold textured plants. We use fatsia down here at Callaway for that bold look, but any large-leaf plant works to provide that variation in texture.

■ Do you use containers to extend color in the garden?

Yes. We put them right in the flower bed, not just to add seasonal color, but to add height. Say we have a coleus that may have a maximum height of two to three feet, and we want that color in a bed of big caladiums. We will set a pot of the coleus among the caladiums, and it brings the color right up to the level we want it.

■ Winter is typically the toughest time to provide interest in the garden. How do you plan for winter color?

Most people don't spend too much time in the yard in winter, so plantings should be in line with what you can see out of the windows and wherever you generally walk outside. Consider plants with ornamental bark and berries. Trees with exfoliating bark and ornamental grasses are particularly outstanding viewed with the winter sun setting behind them. This turns a nice planting into a fantastic one.

■ How can you bring out color in the winter garden?

Evergreen backdrops are really important for things that bloom or fruit in the winter. If you have a deciduous holly in front of a mountain laurel, for example, you get that double effect—the evergreen background and red berries.

PLANTER'S GUIDE

A BULB LOVER'S FAVORITE CHOICES

They can come back to brighten the same spot for decades, or you can dig them up and move them to a new home.

	Height (in.)	Planting depth (in.)	Planting time	Blooming time
SPRING-FLOWERING BULBS				
CROCUS *Crocus* species	3–5	3–4	EARLY FALL	EARLY SPRING
CROWN IMPERIAL *Fritillaria imperialis*	30–48	5	EARLY FALL	MIDSPRING
DAFFODIL *Narcissus* species	12	6	EARLY FALL	MIDSPRING
DUTCH IRIS *Iris xiphium*	24	4	EARLY FALL	LATE SPRING
FLOWERING ONION *Allium giganteum*	48	10	EARLY FALL	LATE SPRING
GRAPE HYACINTH *Muscari botryoides*	6–10	3	EARLY FALL	EARLY SPRING
HYACINTH *Hyacinthus orientalis*	12	6	EARLY FALL	EARLY SPRING
SNOWDROP *Galanthus nivalis*	4-6	4	EARLY FALL	EARLY SPRING
TULIP (early) *Tulipa* species	10–13	6	EARLY FALL	EARLY SPRING
TULIP (Darwin hybrid) *Tulipa* species	28	6	EARLY FALL	MIDSPRING
TULIP (late) *Tulipa* species	36	6	EARLY FALL	LATE SPRING
WILDFLOWER *Anemone blanda*	5	2	EARLY FALL	EARLY SPRING
SUMMER-FLOWERING BULBS				
ANEMONES *Anemone* species	18	2	**NORTH:** EARLY SPRING **SOUTH:** LATE FALL	LATE SUMMER
BUTTERCUP *Ranunculus*	12	2	SOUTH: LATE FALL	MIDSUMMER
CROCOSMIA *Crocosmia* species	24	4	APRIL-MAY	MID- TO LATE SUMMER
DAHLIA (dwarf varieties) *Dahlia* species	12	4	AFTER LATE FROST	LATE SUMMER
DAHLIA (large varieties) *Dahlia* species	48	4	AFTER LATE FROST	LATE SUMMER
GALTONIA *Galtonia candicans*	40	5	APRIL-MAY	MID- TO LATE SUMMER
GLADIOLUS (large flower) *Gladiolus* species	60	3–4	APRIL-JUNE	MIDSUMMER
GLADIOLUS (small flower) *Gladiolus* species	30	3–4	APRIL-JUNE	MIDSUMMER
LILY *Lilium* species	36–84	8	FALL OR EARLY SPRING	ALL SUMMER
TIGER FLOWER *Tigridia paronia*	16	3	EARLY SPRING	MID- TO LATE SUMMER

SOURCE: *Landscaping with Bulbs*, Ann Reilly, Storey Com Inc., 1988.

■ HEIGHT AND DEPTH

A bulb that is planted deep will not necessarily grow tall.

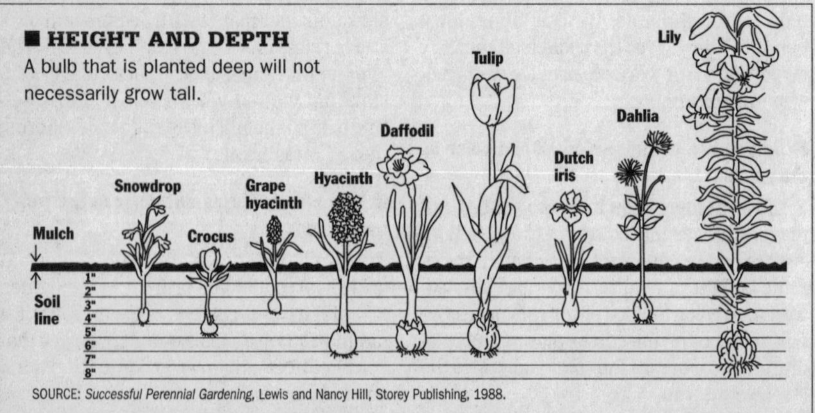

SOURCE: *Successful Perennial Gardening*, Lewis and Nancy Hill, Storey Publishing, 1988.

EXPERT TIPS

WE PROMISE YOU A ROSE GARDEN

Raising roses may not need a ton of chemicals and constant worry

The rose's reputation as an aristocrat is well deserved—it is a regal flower that requires the attention usually reserved for royalty. But rose lovers need not quit their jobs and sell their silver to grow beautiful roses in their gardens. For 15 years, rose breeders Ping Lim and Martin Nemko have been combing the world for the most disease-resistant and beautiful rose varieties, and they have been cross-breeding them to create super-roses. Nemko, who serves as a consultant to the Minnesota-based firm Bailey's Nurseries, a leading breeder of easy-care roses, offers these tips for the busy gardener:

■ **Choose disease-resistant varieties.** Most varieties of roses become so diseased that they look like they were dunked in weed killer unless bombarded each week with enough chemicals to make Saddam Hussein proud. But a few widely available rose varieties, such as Cliffs of Dover, Sun Flare, and Flower Carpet have disease-resistant genes. By choosing healthy varieties, you can pretty much chuck the sprayer. If you look closely, you might notice an insect or two or a nibbled leaf or bloom, but you don't need to get compulsive about your rose bushes. In most areas of the country, the stalwart varieties listed below (see box) should look just fine without a weekly shower of Orthene and Daconil 2787.

■ **Use an automated watering system.** During the growing season, roses love to drink, but you can quench their thirst while saving water, too. Just use a timer that's hooked up to plastic irrigation spritzers. Many home or garden centers sell kits—the two-gallon per hour size works best. Set the timer to water every other day for 30 minutes.

■ **Feed your bushes just once a year.** When the ground starts to warm in the spring, place a time-release fertilizer such as Osmocote+Iron directly underneath the spritzers. The fertilizer you select should be a once-a-growing-season formulation.

NO-FUSS ROSES FOR NO-MESS GARDENERS

Rose breeder Martin Nemko recommends these roses, arranged by color, if you don't have time for hassles. Unless otherwise noted, Nemko's picks are 2 to 3 feet tall and wide and can be found at most well-stocked nurseries.

WHITE

■ **GOURMET POPCORN:** Dark green foliage covered in a cloud of white.

■ **CLIFFS OF DOVER:** 18 in. tall and perhaps the healthiest of all.

YELLOW

■ **SUN FLARE:** The glossiest forest-green foliage you'll ever see on a rose.

PINK

■ **FLOWER CARPET:** A great way to cover a 4- to 5-foot-wide space.

■ **CAREFREE DELIGHT:** Hundreds of old-fashioned roses on a newly bred plant.

■ **CAREFREE WONDER:** A well-mannered 3-foot-tall by 2-foot-wide plant.

■ **HAPPY TRAILS:** The perfect plant for a hanging basket or cascading in a rock garden.

■ **ALEXANDER MCKENZIE:** Winter-hardy and especially bred for the North.

RED

■ **CHAMPLAIN:** Another rose that flourishes in northern climes.

HOMEMADE CURES FOR PESTS AND DISEASES

Organic gardening specialists recommend these do-it-yourself recipes for ridding your garden of unwanted visitors.

COOKING OIL SOLUTION

Effective against eggs and immature insects.

1 cup cooking oil
1 tbsp. liquid dish soap

■ Mix oil and soap. Use 2 1/2 tsps. per 1 cup of water. Pour into a spray bottle and spray surface and undersides of leaves. Apply once every 2 to 3 weeks until pest is gone.

BAKING SODA SOLUTION

Usually effective in preventing foliage fungus, especially on roses.

1 tbsp. baking soda
1 gal. water
1/2 tsp. insecticidal soap

■ Dissolve baking soda in the water. Mix in the soap and pour into a spray bottle. Test this solution on just a few leaves before spraying an entire plant. Some plants may be sensitive and the solution may need to be diluted to prevent foliage discoloration. Spray to cover the top and underside of foliage about twice a week from spring through early fall.

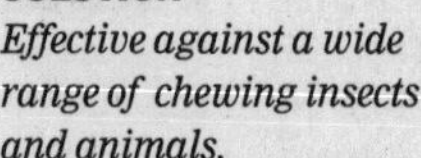

GARLIC-PEPPER SOLUTION

Effective against a wide range of chewing insects and animals.

2 cloves garlic
1 tsp. liquid detergent
2 tsps. cooking oil
1 tbsp. cayenne pepper
2 cups water

■ Put all the ingredients in a blender and mix until the cloves are thoroughly pureed. Spray solution on affected plants. Reapply as needed.

BORDEAUX MIXTURE

Effective against common fungal disease. Often used on small fruits.

2 heaping tbsps. fresh hydrated spray lime
2 level tsps. copper sulfate crystals
3 gals. water

■ Dissolve lime in 2 gallons of water. In a separate container, dissolve the copper sulfate in 1 gallon of water. Add the copper sulfate solution to the lime solution.Strain the solution through a cheesecloth directly into a sprayer. Spray to cover foliage. When dry, it forms an insoluble copper precipitate that prevents fungal spores from entering and infecting plants. Begin applications in spring, repeat once every 7 to 14 days through early fall. Don't apply during cool and wet weather.

INSECTS THAT WILL SET YOU FREE

You can use natural predators to fight insect pests. Here are some friendly enforcers and what they can help control, as well as some places to get them:

■ **ASSASSIN BUG:** Aphids, caterpillars, leafhoppers, and a variety of beetles.

■ **LADYBUGS:** Aphids, chinch bugs, rootworms, scale, spider mites, weevils, whiteflies.

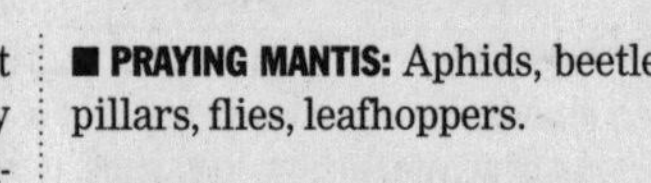

■ **PRAYING MANTIS:** Aphids, beetles, caterpillars, flies, leafhoppers.

■ **ROBBER, SYRPHID, AND TACHINID FLIES:** Aphids, Japanese beetles, leafhoppers, mealybugs, scale, caterpillars.

SOURCES

Bozeman Bio-Tech	☎**800-289-6656**
Gempler's	☎**800-272-7672**
Peaceful Valley	☎**916-272-4769**

EXPERT Q & A

FROM ROOT TO BRANCH

Tree-planting is usually a fall pursuit. Here's how to do it

The selection of trees is one of the largest investments and most important decisions that a homeowner may face in landscaping a property. A well-chosen tree on the right site can transform even the plainest house into a home with visual appeal. Frank Santamour, research geneticist and tree expert at the National Arboretum in Washington, D.C., has been providing practical advice on growing trees for many years. Here he shares his experience and knowledge on tree selection and planting techniques.

■ What factors go into selecting a tree for a landscape?

First of all you look at ultimate size. You don't want to plant a tree that's going to get too big during the time you are paying off your house. Consider then what type of tree you want—evergreen or deciduous, flowering, or something that may have other attractions, like colored leaves in the autumn, or colored leaves all season. Finding trees that have practically no disease or insect problem is also important.

■ What should you look for at the nursery when buying a tree?

Most of the trees at nurseries are sold in containers nowadays. Look for a tree that has a large enough container so that a pretty decent portion of the root system will be intact. It's very difficult to make any judgments when you are viewing a plant at a nursery, because even a plant with a really tacky root system can look good if it's kept watered. You can't pop it out of the container to see the roots. So you've got to go on the general reputation of the nursery.

■ How about mail order trees?

I would stay away from them, quite frankly. There are some firms with a pretty decent reputation, but there are many horror stories—poor quality, small plants. Specialty items can be an exception, but go to your local nursery first and ask if they can get it for you. They should know where to get the best quality material.

■ When is the best time for planting?

That depends on where you live. I come from New England, and we plant in the spring because fall comes a little fast. Ideally, spring planting is done before growth begins, though with container-grown plants, you can plant a little later. In most of the United States, fall planting is also good. When you plant in the fall, wait until after the buds have set on the tree and growth has ceased, and do not fertilize afterward, which could promote new growth on the tree that sets it up for a killing frost.

■ How should a new tree be planted?

One of the myths people have is that they must fill a planting hole with manure and peat moss to make a nice home for the tree. If the tree is going to survive, the roots have to get out of that hole. In most areas, your home soil is worthless. My recommendation is to dig a hole twice the size of the container. When you take the tree out of the container, cut down the roots to promote their growth outward. Make enough room in the hole so the roots can escape that bound mess. Otherwise, they will continue to circle. When you backfill the hole, use what you have taken out of the hole—beat it up and put it back. If you have to amend the soil, use some loam or sandy loam. Do not plant the tree too low.

■ How deep should the hole be?

If the plant comes in a container, look where the soil level is and plant it just a tad high in the ground. It's going to settle in.

■ Should the burlap be removed if the roots are covered with it?

If there are any ties, burlap, plastic wrap, or anything, remove it. In the days when burlap was burlap, it might have rotted, but now, with the synthetic things being used, it's just a tragedy to leave them. The roots just can't get out. More trees die because of a lack of planting care than any other factor, although they don't die immediately. At least unwrap the burlap to let those roots get out.

■ What should you do once a tree has been planted?

Mulch. It keeps the soil relatively warm; if you are planting in the fall, it might allow more root growth before the cold weather sets in. It also keeps the lawnmower and weeding equipment away from the tree. I recommend about a 2-inch layer of mulch.

■ How about watering?

Absolutely the first thing you have to do is water, and make sure the plant is well-seated. Keep the tree watered in times of stress without overwatering.

■ Should new trees be staked?

The average homeowner is dealing with a tree that has a trunk with a 2- to 2½-inch maximum caliper. If it's well planted, well watered in originally, and well sited, it's not going to blow over. Just tamp it down.

■ Should you fertilize your tree?

Most trees do not need fertilization, but if your tree is in your lawn, and you fertilize your lawn, don't worry about it. If you do fertilize, use a slow-release fertilizer. A common mistake is when people use lawn fertilizers with weedkillers. This material leaches into the ground and is taken up by the roots. Eventually it's going to get your tree.

■ Should a newly planted tree be pruned?

Tree growth promotes root growth. The only pruning that should be done on a newly planted tree is if there is a broken branch.

■ PRUNING TREES

Once a tree is established, it will need periodic pruning. The best time to prune deciduous trees is in winter, when trees are dormant—it's also easier to see the problem branches and the general shape of the tree without the leaves. If you're pruning an evergreen tree, wait until spring. Remember to prune with a light hand; overpruning can destroy your tree's look—and your investment.

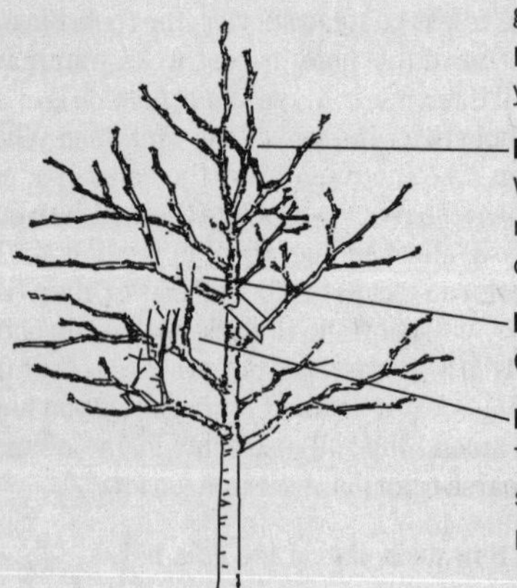

■ Crossing branches

When branches rub against each other, they may damage the bark and make the tree susceptible to disease and insects.

■ Dead, diseased, or broken branches

Cut back to a healthy branch.

■ Crowded branches

Thinning weak branches improves the tree's shape and allows better air circulation and light penetration.

■ HOW TO PRUNE

When pruning a tree, be sure that you cut just above a branch's slightly swollen base at the point where that branch meets another branch. This base consists of plant tissues that help the cut to heal. Leaving too much of a stub creates a conduit for diseases to attack the tree.

If you want to shorten a branch that's grown too long, make a cut on the branch just above a bud at a 45-degree angle. Pick a bud facing the direction that you want a new branch to grow.

LAWNGROWER'S GUIDE

THE GRASS IS ALWAYS GREENER

To pick the best grass seed for your lawn, take into account the growing region (defined by humidity level and mean temperature), microclimate (how much sun the lawn gets throughout the day), maintenance time, and expected foot traffic.

BAHIAGRASS *Paspalum* **Gulf Coast**

■ This wide, coarse-bladed grass is not particularly attractive, but its ruggedness and deep root system make it good for erosion control.

MICROCLIMATE	FOOT TRAFFIC	MAINTENANCE
Sunny to partly shady	High	Low

BENTGRASS *Agrostis* **Northern**

■ Often used on putting greens, this high-maintenance grass should be used only on low-traffic areas or where soft-soled shoes are worn.

MICROCLIMATE	FOOT TRAFFIC	MAINTENANCE
Sunny to partly shady	Low	High

BERMUDAGRASS *Cynodon* **Southern**

■ Fast-growing, this wide-bladed grass requires frequent edge-trimming, but will tolerate high traffic. Popular in the South for its vigor and density.

MICROCLIMATE	FOOT TRAFFIC	MAINTENANCE
Sunny	High	Medium to high

BUFFALOGRASS *Buchloe* **West Central**

■ Like wheatgrass, a native turf that is thick and rugged, requires low maintenance and will not grow over 4 or 5 inches if left unmowed. It is very tolerant of drought.

MICROCLIMATE	FOOT TRAFFIC	MAINTENANCE
Sunny	Medium	Low

CARPETGRASS *Axonopus* **Southern**

■ Coarse but sensitive to wear, this grass is used primarily on hard-to-mow places because of its low maintenance and slow growth rate.

MICROCLIMATE	FOOT TRAFFIC	MAINTENANCE
Sunny	Low	Low

CENTIPEDEGRASS *Eremochloa* **Southern**

■ A good "middle-of-the-road" grass—easy to care for, will tolerate some shade, and is vigorous and attractive. It requires two seasons to grow.

MICROCLIMATE	FOOT TRAFFIC	MAINTENANCE
Sunny to partly shady	Low	Low

KENTUCKY BLUEGRASS *Poa* **Northern**

■ The most popular of cool-season grasses for its beauty and ruggedness and flexibility. It will excel with minimum maintenance almost anywhere.

MICROCLIMATE	FOOT TRAFFIC	MAINTENANCE
Sunny to partly shady	Medium to heavy	Low to high

PERENNIAL RYEGRASS *Festuca* **Northern**

■ This quick-growing and reasonably hardy grass is used in seed mixes to provide cover and erosion control while the other seeds take root.

MICROCLIMATE	FOOT TRAFFIC	MAINTENANCE
Sunny to partly shady	Medium	Medium to high

ST. AUGUSTINE GRASS *Stenotaphrum* **South Atlantic**

■ Dense and spongy, this low-growing, coarse-textured grass is prized for its high shade tolerance. Not available in seed form, but usually sold as fairly inexpensive sod.

MICROCLIMATE	FOOT TRAFFIC	MAINTENANCE
Sunny to shady	Medium	Medium to high

TALL FESCUES *Festuca* **Northern**

■ Though it is a cool-season grass, this tough wide-bladed turf has good heat tolerance and grows well in areas with a steep range of weather. Often used on play-

■ LAWN GROWER'S GUIDE

grounds because of its ruggedness.

MICROCLIMATE	FOOT TRAFFIC	MAINTENANCE
Sunny to partly shady	Heavy	Medium

WHEATGRASS *Agropyron* **High plains**

■ Thick and tough, this grass is native to the high plains of the Northwest. It withstands weather extremes and heavy traffic and needs mowing about once a month.

MICROCLIMATE	FOOT TRAFFIC	MAINTENANCE
Sunny	High	Low

ZOYSIA *Zoysia* **Southern**

■ Takes root very quickly and crowds out other grasses and weeds. It turns a not entirely unattractive straw yellow in cold weather and requires little maintenance in general. Heat- and drought-tolerant.

MICROCLIMATE	FOOT TRAFFIC	MAINTENANCE
Sunny to partly shady	High	Low to medium

SOURCE: Dr. H. A. Turgeon, Pennsylvania State University.

EXPERT TIPS

THE GRASS IS GREENER FOR A REASON

Dean Norton, horticulturist at Mt. Vernon, the Virginia estate of our nation's first president, has these tips on growing turf hardy enough to resist many of the problems backyard lawns may encounter.

■ **Spend a little more and buy certified grass seed.** It is important to get certified seed, because there is less weed seed in it.

■ **Water deeply.** The mistake most people make is watering too frequently and not enough at one time—this encourages the grass to grow shallow roots. The key is to water deeply, the equivalent of an inch of rainfall each time. (An inch of water should penetrate 6 to 8 inches in average soil.) The frequency will change with the season, the temperature, and the humidity. You'll want to keep it uniformly moist without overwatering.

■ **Water in the morning to prevent disease problems.** If you water in the evening, you open yourself up to a lot of disease problems. Lawn pathogens generally need at least 6 hours of moisture to start cooking. If you water at night, they've got it.

■ **Aerate the soil to improve the ground's capacity for absorbing water.** Grass has a harder time growing in a compacted soil than in a loose soil, and there's less penetration of water. If there's any kind of slope at all, you'll be wasting your time when you water because it just runs off. You can rent gas-powered aerating machines—they put small holes throughout your lawn, opening up the soil.

■ **Fertilize cool-season grasses in the fall.** Fertilize in the fall, and split up your applications—one early and one late—so it's more of a constant feed. If you fertilize in the spring, you will work the turf to death as you try to keep up with the mowing.

■ **Mow at the correct height.** Though the cutting height may change with the season, you should not cut grass too hard at any one time, to prevent stressing it. A good rule of thumb: Never remove more than one-third of the leaf blade.

INDOOR GARDENER'S GUIDE

HOUSEPLANTS FOR EVERY WINDOW

How to match up a plant's light, temperature, and humidity needs to the location in your home or office that will best provide them.

■ **NORTH WINDOWS:** Receive no direct sun—but, if unobstructed, they do receive good light. Plants grown in a shaded north window during the winter months would appreciate extra light. When choosing plants for a dark window, remember that plants with variegated leaves require more light than ones with strictly green leaves. Consult the key below.

PLANT	WATER	TEMPERATURE	HUMIDITY	FERTILIZER
CAST-IRON PLANT *Aspidistra elatior*	WD	I	MEDIUM	INTERMEDIATE
FERN, BIRD'S NEST *Asplenium nidus*	EM	I	HIGH	LOW
FIG *Ficus pumila*	EM	I	HIGH	LOW
PHILODENDRON, VELVET LEAF *Philodendron scandens var. micans*	W	I	HIGH	LOW
PRAYER PLANT *Maranta leuconeura*	EM	W	MEDIUM	INTERMEDIATE
SAGO PALM *Cycas revoluta*	W	I	MEDIUM	LOW
SPATHE FLOWER *Spathiphyllum*	EM	W	MEDIUM	INTERMEDIATE
WANDERING JEW *Zebrina pendula*	EM	I-W	MEDIUM	INTERMEDIATE

■ **EAST AND WEST WINDOWS:** Both are excellent for growing houseplants. East windows tend to be cooler than west. If you can't grow the following plants in east or west windows, they should do fine in a south window—but add some shading during the day in the summer, especially for ferns.

PLANT	WATER	TEMPERATURE	HUMIDITY	FERTILIZER
BROMELIAD	W	I	MEDIUM	LOW
CAPE PRIMROSE *Streptocarpus*	W	I	HIGH	HIGH
FERN, BOSTON *Nephrolepsis exaltata*	W	I	HIGH	LOW
IVY, GRAPE *Cissus rhombifolia*	EM	I	MEDIUM	INTERMEDIATE
LILY, AMAZON *Eucharis grandiflora*	EM	I-W	MEDIUM	HIGH
LILY, KARRIR *Clivia minnata*	W	I	MEDIUM	INTERMEDIATE
LADY PALM *Rhapsis excelsa`*	W-EM	I	HIGH	INTERMEDIATE
NORFOLK ISLAND PINE *Araucaria heterophylla*	EM	C	MEDIUM	LOW
BEGONIA REX *Rex begonia*	EM	I	HIGH	HIGH
ROSARY VINE *Ceropegia woodii*	WD	I	LOW	INTERMEDIATE
RUBBER PLANT *Ficus elastica*	W	W	MEDIUM	LOW
SHAMROCK PLANT *Oxalis*	EM	I	MEDIUM	LOW
FIG, WEEPING *Ficus benjamina*	W	W	MEDIUM	LOW
VIOLET, AFRICAN *Saintpaulia*	W	I-W	MEDIUM	HIGH

Key:

WATER:

WD: Water thoroughly, let dry fully before rewatering.
W: Water thoroughly but don't let it totally dry out before rewatering.
EM: Keep soil evenly moist, but don't let it stand in water. Top inch of soil should always feel moist.

TEMPERATURE:

C: Cool: 45° nights, 55° to 60° days.
I: Intermediate: 50° to 55° nights, 65° to 70° days.
W: Warm: 60° nights, 75° to 80° days.

HUMIDITY:

LOW: 20 to 40 percent.
MEDIUM: 40 to 50 percent.
HIGH: 50 to 80 percent.

FERTILIZER:

HEAVY: Use balanced fertilizer recommended for frequent feeding, feed each watering.
INTERMEDIATE: Feed every other week with a balanced fertilizer.
LOW: Feed about once per month with a balanced fertilizer.

■ **INDOOR GARDENER'S GUIDE**

■ **SOUTH WINDOWS:** South windows receive the most light. During the summer months they even can be too bright for many kinds of houseplants—you may need to shade them a bit. All of these plants, while preferring south windows, can also be grown in east or west exposures.

PLANT	WATER	TEMPERATURE	HUMIDITY	FERTILIZER
ALOE	WD	I	LOW	LOW
BEGONIA, TRAILING *Cissus discolor*	EM	I	MEDIUM	INTERMEDIATE
CACTUS	WD	I-W	LOW	LOW
GERANIUM *Pelargonium*	W	I	MEDIUM	LOW
GERANIUM, STRAWBERRY *Saxifraga stolonifera*	W	I	MEDIUM	LOW
IVY *Hedera helix*	EM	I	MEDIUM	INTERMEDIATE
IVY, GERMAN OR PARLOR *Senecio mikanioides*	WD	I	LOW	INTERMEDIATE
JADE PLANT *Crassula argentea*	W	I	LOW	LOW
PASSION FLOWER *Passiflora*	EM	I	MEDIUM	INTERMEDIATE
POMEGRANATE, DWARF *Punica granatum 'Nana'*	EM	I	MEDIUM	INTERMEDIATE
SHEFFLERA, HAWAI'IAN *Erassaia arboricola*	W	I	LOW	INTERMEDIATE

SOURCE: *Landscaping That Saves Energy Dollars,* Ruth Foster, Globe Pequot, 1994.

SHEDDING LIGHT ON HOUSEPLANTS

Fluorescent bulbs are best because they don't throw off a lot of heat

Unless you have a sunroom or greenhouse, the biggest dilemma of having plants indoors is providing them with enough light. Even if you have windows, they may be less than ideal if they're facing in a direction that gets little sun, or if they're shaded by a tree or porch overhang. Plants suffering from light deprivation are often lanky, with pale or yellowed leaves. Luckily, you can lend a helping hand with artificial lighting.

The best type of artificial light is fluorescent. Incandescent light doesn't provide the right kind of light for optimal growth, and it also produces lots of heat, which can burn your plants. Fluorescent light comes in several varieties: the standard ones, which you can find at any hardware store or home improvement center, are fine for growing small plants such as African violets, but for larger plants, go for higher-output fluorescents, which emit much more light and can be found at most well-equipped garden centers or through mail-order gardening supply catalogs. Bear in mind, too:

■ When growing plants under artificial light, choose those that prefer low to medium sunlight.

■ Keep your plants very close to the light source—no more than 6 to 12 inches away. The intensity of light diminishes drastically the farther away you move from it. To increase intensity, add more fluorescent tubes, grouped together.

■ Rearrange your plants regularly around their light source to ensure that they all receive equal exposure. The greatest amount of light is emitted from the center of a fluorescent tube.

■ Leave the lights on 14 to 16 hours each day. A couple of hours daily won't suffice. But don't leave the lights on all the time; plants need periods of darkness for rest.

PETS

DOG BREEDS: A dog's breed is no guarantee that it will make a good companion, PAGE 433 **INBREEDING:** Purebreds can be genetic disasters, PAGE 435 **CANINE HEALTH:** Holistic medicine is for the dogs, PAGE 436 **CAT BREEDS:** A guide to picking a pet, PAGE 437 **ODDITIES:** Meet the Munchkin, a new breed of cat, PAGE 439 **SHOTS:** Vaccinations to keep your pet healthy, PAGE 440 **VET BILLS:** Health insurance for Fido? PAGE 442

EXOTIC ANIMALS

PETS THAT GO BUMP AT NIGHT

Creatures that get the neighbors talking are the "in" thing

Pop star Michael Jackson has an entire menagerie of exotic animals at his Los Angeles retreat, Neverland Ranch. But it's not necessary to be an international celebrity or a member of royalty to own an exotic pet today. Animals as unusual as miniature donkeys, mute swans, African bush babies, and reindeer can even be ordered from a popular catalog called the "Animal Finders Guide."

One indication of the current boom in exotic animals comes from the U.S. Fish and Wildlife Service, which reports that between 1980 and 1992 "legal animal shipments," which require official government notification, grew from 45,000 to 70,000. Many exotic animals are also brought into the country illegally each year, according to animal experts.

But taking animals out of their natural environments and selling them to people who are often uncertain how to care for them can endanger both the animals and their owners. "Any time you deal with an exotic animal, you are dealing with a tremendous amount of the unknown," says Richard Farinato, director of the captive wildlife protection program at the Humane Society of the United States.

Like hairstyles and skirt lengths, exotic animal fashions shift frequently. For example, the movie *Jurassic Park* caused a boom for pet reptiles. But when the animals are no longer wanted, says Farinato, they are often abandoned. In the Washington, D.C. area, for instance, so many pot-bellied pigs are now being cast off by fickle owners that an animal sanctuary had to be established as a refuge for these animals. That sanctuary now has a waiting list.

Many exotic pets aren't so lucky. Half of all birds and reptiles shipped to the U.S. die before they arrive. Some states have laws against owning exotic pets. California and Georgia, for example, ban most exotic animals. All of the exotic pets that Farinato describes below are perfectly legal in the United States. Even so, he advises, don't buy a pet just because it's unusual and cute; make sure you know exactly what's needed to take care of it. "There's no such thing as an easy-care pet," he warns.

■ **HEDGEHOGS.** A favorite character in children's books, hedgehogs are the most popular exotic pet today. They are usually an African species, which means they are accustomed to a tropical environment. Because they are small and cute, says Farinato, "They were tailor-made for a boom." Most people keep pet hedgehogs in an aquarium, which is a very unnatural place for animals that are burrowers. Hedgehogs eat live insects and are nocturnal. That means they are usually asleep when the owner is awake— not the ideal arrangement if you want a companion. **Cost: $50 to $300**

■ **IGUANAS.** A popular Christmas gift item, iguanas are being brought in by the thousands from South and Central America. Young iguanas are usually about six to eight inches long, but they can grow to six feet. If they get that large, they can be dangerous because of their large tails and long nails, especially to small children. Even worse, iguanas naturally harbor salmonella, a bacteria commonly associated with food poisoning, in their digestive tracts. This can be deadly to children or anyone with a weak immune system, such as people with AIDS. The Centers for Disease Control and Prevention has reported an increased incidence of salmonella illness in 12 states, all linked to exposure to iguanas and other reptiles. Natives of the tropics, iguanas need an enclosure where the temperature is kept at 78 to 95 degrees Fahrenheit. Without that heat, the lizard will refuse to eat and become lethargic. Iguanas eat plants and insects, although their diet in the wild consists mainly of flower petals. **Cost: $25 to $100**

■ **SUGAR GLIDERS.** Native to Australia, and similar to a flying squirrel in appearance, these animals are now bred mostly in captivity. They are a nocturnal species with extremely sharp teeth, which can make balancing one on your shoulder a risky endeavor. Most owners keep them in small cages. At chow time, sugar gliders require a diet of fresh fruits. Unless you have the time to buy and cut up fruit for them every day, which few people do, this is not the pet for you. **Cost: $100**

■ **BALL PYTHONS.** As pythons go, they're not the biggest around, but ball pythons do grow to about three to five feet. They are also extremely finicky eaters, preferring live rodents. Few will eat dead animals, and some are so particular that they will only eat a certain color live rodent. These snakes can be dangerous; even a three-foot python is a constrictor. A small child with a snake around his neck could be in big trouble. As with most exotic pets, Farinato advises: "Don't keep these animals near small kids." **Cost: $40 to $100**

■ **BENGAL CATS.** A hybrid of a wild and domestic cat, Bengals are finding their way into more people's homes. They range in size from a large housecat to a large bobcat when fully grown. While they are manageable as infants, they get wilder and more unpredictable, not to mention bigger, as they grow up. Bengals eat what other cats eat, including commercial cat food. **Cost: $300 to $500**

■ **AFRICAN GRAY PARROTS.** One of the longest-living animals around, African Grays can last 50 to 80 years. In fact, they can often outlive their owners. As pets they are very demanding. If not part of a flock, the bird needs to develop a close one-on-one relationship with the owner. Without that relationship, the parrot will become neurotic and pull out its feathers. To forge this bond, the owner must talk to the bird often and feed it by hand. In return, a happy African Gray is one of the most talkative birds around. **Cost: $700 to $1500**

■ **OSTRICHES, EMUS, AND RHEAS.** Sold mainly for their meat until recently, these birds are beginning to find favor as pets. Acquiring an ostrich is something that most people will want to leave to Michael Jackson, but emus and rheas are more affordable. **Cost: Ostriches: $10,000 to $20,000; Emus: $1,000; Rheas: $100 to $1,000**

CANINES

PICKING A DOG TO PLAY ROVER

A dog's breed is no guarantee that it will act according to the book

Every dog has its own personality. But some breeds are better suited to being jostled by children than others, while the circumstances of other pet lovers may require quite different choices. Here, veterinarian Sheldon L. Gerstenfeld suggests which dogs make good pets for families with children, owners with active lifestyles, and people who are older and looking for easy pet companionship. Gerstenfeld is the author of seven books about pet care, including *The Dog Care Book* (Addison-Wesley, 1989). He also writes a pet column for *Parents* magazine.

DOGS FOR CHILDREN

■ **GOLDEN RETRIEVER:** Easygoing, active, and alert, golden retrievers have the best temperaments. They love to interact with kids and to play ball, which provides a young child a playmate. It also gives a child a sense of controlling a situation—when the child throws the ball, the dog brings it back. The adult female weighs 50 to 60 pounds, and the adult male 70 to 90 pounds. They need to be groomed and fed, and that teaches kids about being responsible. The golden retriever is the seventh most popular breed of the American Kennel Club (AKC).

■ **LABRADOR RETRIEVER:** Black, yellow, and chocolate Labs are generally known for being even-tempered and friendly. They are always ready to play, and kids can just lie on them. Adult dogs weigh 60 to 70 pounds. They need grooming, so they also teach kids to be responsible.

Avoid the Chesapeake Bay retriever, which has a curlier coat. It isn't good with kids because it can be a little nasty and unpredictable and will bite more readily than the others. Labrador retrievers are the fifth most popular AKC breed.

■ **COLLIE:** These are sweet dogs. They're gentle and predictable and won't bite around your kids. They're easy to train and really want to please. Adult collies weigh about 50 pounds and their long hair requires grooming. The rough-coated collie, which is what Lassie is, is the 9th most popular AKC breed; the smooth-coated collie is the 13th most popular.

■ **STANDARD POODLE:** A gentle dog that is very intelligent. A standard poodle will let a kid lie on it. You need to groom them, but a fancy hair cut is not necessary. Poodles, including miniature and standard, are the most popular breed in the United States. Because they are so popular, prospective owners have to watch out for puppy-mill degradation. Before choosing one, make sure the dog is well-bred. The larger they are, the less active they are

FACT FILE:

BRINGING UP BABY

■ *Dogs make wonderful companions, but they don't come free, as these cost estimates from the Humane Society of the United States indicate.*

Adopting a dog from a shelter	**$55**
First-year vaccinations	**$200**
Each year thereafter	**$65**
Initial training	**$50–$100**
Each year thereafter	**$50–$200**
Other annual veterinary care [1]	**$135**
Annual feeding	**$115–$400**
Annual toys, grooming supplies	**$160**
Grooming, per visit [2]	**$50**
Annual flea and tick care	**$80**
Daily boarding	**$21–$30**

1. 1991 figures. 2. Varies with size and breed.

and the more exercise they need. Adult standard poodles weigh 50 to 55 pounds.

DOGS FOR THE ACTIVE PERSON

■ **GREYHOUND:** They are a little aloof, but also very gentle. Most are adopted from the racetrack. Greyhounds have a regal personality and don't slobber with affection like a retriever. They're also very athletic, so they're good for active people. Adult greyhounds weigh 70 to 80 pounds. High-strung and easily upset by sudden movements at times, greyhounds are the 105th most popular AKC breed.

■ **BOXER:** Animated, with outgoing personalities, boxers respond readily to playfulness. They are the 24th most popular AKC breed. Prospective owners looking for a dignified dog, however, should be wary of the boxer: They tend to drool and snore.

■ **TERRIER:** Terriers start out their morning as if they had eight cups of coffee, so they are good for an active person. I'd recommend the bull terrier, which was bred for pit fighting. They are always ready to frolic and so need firm training, but they are also known for their sweet personalities. The adult bull terrier weighs in at about 50 pounds. It is the 65th most popular AKC breed.

■ **ENGLISH COCKER SPANIEL:** These are sweet dogs, and they haven't been inbred. They're playful and alert at all times and great for children and active people. The English cocker spaniel is a medium-size dog with long hair. An adult usually weighs 23 to 25 pounds, 3 to 11 pounds more than its cousin, the American cocker spaniel. The English cocker is the 64th most popular AKC breed.

EXPERT QUOTE

It doesn't help to send pets off somewhere unless you are part of the training. Dogs that are sent away come back again and fall into the same old habits and routines again. It's best to do it yourself.

—Steve Berens, Hollywood stunt dog trainer

DOGS FOR OLDER PEOPLE

■ **CHIHUAHUA:** If they are from a good breeder, they will have a good personality. Chihuahuas have short hair, so they don't need a lot of grooming and so are a good choice for an older person living alone. The Chihuahua is the smallest of all the breeds. The barkless variety was once used by the Aztecs as a sacrificial animal to eradicate the sins of the dead. Chihuahuas can be yappy and clannish at times. An adult Chihuahua weighs about 3 pounds and is the 21st most popular AKC breed.

■ **MINIATURE POODLE:** These poodles are intelligent. And they're good for older people because they're small and don't shed a lot. They love attention. Again, the poodle is the most popular AKC breed, so owners have to make sure the dog is not inbred. All poodles are considered fast learners compared with other breeds, but generally the smaller they are the faster they learn. The adult miniature poodle weighs in at about 15 pounds.

■ **TOY POODLE:** These are good dogs for older people. Toy poodles love to be cuddled and are intelligent. They do have to be groomed, but they don't shed, so there's not much hair to clean up. The adult toy poodle weighs less than 10 pounds. It is the brightest of all the toys and will demand its owner's continuous attention. Because of the toy poodle's popularity, inbreeding can be a problem.

■ **YORKSHIRE TERRIER:** These dogs are small, easy to care for, and can be picked up. They weigh about 7 pounds and are about 7 inches tall, with long silky hair that drapes like a sheet over the body. Their coats require grooming, however, which may not be good for an elderly person who doesn't have the energy, or who has arthritis. The Yorkshire terrier is the 14th most popular AKC breed.

INBREEDING

A FANCY FAMILY CAN BE A DOWNER

Purebred pets may be genetic disasters because of overbreeding

Too much of a good thing can be very bad news when animal breeding is concerned. As a breed becomes popular, says Janet Hornreisch, an animal care specialist at the Humane Society of the United States, there is often inbreeding or overbreeding of animals related to each other in order to achieve a certain coat color, spot pattern, or tail length. Some animals are even inbred with the idea of heightening a certain quality, such as loyalty in German shepherds, which can't be done.

Worse yet, inbreeding often produces genetically flawed offspring with problems that range from skin disease to meanness. Great Danes today suffer from heart defects, collies are prone to deafness, toy poodles often experience epilepsy, and Labrador retrievers tend to have cataracts. More than 300 genetic abnormalities have been found in dogs.

All too often, these abnormalities manifest themselves in behavioral problems. In the 1970s, for example, cocker spaniels were considered great family dogs. But as their popularity grew and they were inbred, many cockers lost their agreeable dispositions and became ill-tempered instead. Today that pattern is repeating itself with rottweilers, who are fast developing a reputation for biting.

In fact, about 25 percent of the animals in shelters today are purebred, according to the Humane Society, and many of those animals were abandoned because of physical and behavioral problems caused by inbreeding, and the related practices known as line breeding and overbreeding. Line breeding is when grandparents of a species mate with their grandchildren, or cousins with each other. Overbreeding involves a single desirable male, or even a set of desirable parents, producing many litters. If it is later determined that the male, or the parents, have a genetic disease, it will have already been widely dispersed in the offspring.

Cats are losers, too, as a result of these practices. Persian cats, for example, tend to have malformed tear ducts. That problem stems from inbreeding to achieve a "cute" scrunched up face. "The fact that something is cute doesn't mean it's healthy to the animal," says Hornreisch. Below is her list of the most commonly inbred dogs, and the problems that they most often suffer because of inbreeding.

■ COMMON CONGENITAL DEFECTS IN DOGS

Before selecting a best friend, check this watchlist for problems.

- **COCKER SPANIEL:** Cataracts, kidney disease, hemophilia, spinal deformities, behavior abnormalities
- **COLLIE:** Deafness, epilepsy, hemophilia, hernia
- **DACHSHUND:** Bladder stones, diabetes, cleft lips and palate, jaw too long or short, spinal deformities, limbs too short
- **GERMAN SHEPHERD:** Cataracts, epilepsy, kidney disease, bladder stones, hemophilia, cleft lips and palate, behavior abnormalities
- **LABRADOR RETRIEVER:** Cataracts, bladder stones, hemophilia
- **TOY POODLE:** Epilepsy, nervous system defects, collapsed trachea, diabetes, spinal deformities, limbs too short, skin allergies, behavior abnormalities.

EXPERT Q & A

A WELLNESS GUIDE FOR CANINES

A holistic approach to health can help your pooch, too

What's good for the goose is good for the gander, goes the familar saying. The same is often true of dog owners and their pets. But while health-conscious dog owners may be eating fresh veggies and fruits and jogging regularly, the family dog is often stuck inside with a bowl of food that has the nutritional equivalent of a candy bar. Wendy Volhard, author with veterinarian Kerry Brown of *The Holistic Guide for a Healthy Dog* (Macmillan/Howell Book House, 1995), has this advice on taking care of your canine companion.

■ What is holistic pet care?

It's looking at the whole animal rather than individual parts. Holistic pet care includes training, housing, feeding, and medical care.

■ Why is a new form of animal care necessary?

What was traditionally used is no longer working. For one thing, standards in commercial dog food were changed in 1985. Most of the protein in commercial dog food now comes from cereal grains, which has the effect of turning a carnivore into a semi-vegetarian. Dog food is also subjected to great heat in processing, which destroys nutrients. Although dog food is fine as supplement, it lacks animal protein, vitamins, and amino acids, and therefore shouldn't be a dog's sole source of nutrition.

Vaccines are also a problem. They actually break down a dog's immune system. Some dogs get 47 vaccines before they are six months old, though some are combined into one shot so it doesn't seem like that many. In contrast, a puppy in the 1970s was more likely to get only two vaccines in the first six months of life. All vaccines, no matter what the sequence, should be given in minimum intervals of three weeks.

Owners are often totally unaware of these health issues until there is a sickness or behavioral problem with their dog. The majority of dogs are put to sleep because of behavior problems.

■ What should dog owners feed their pets?

Start with dog food, but realize it doesn't meet all your dog's nutritional needs. In addition to the regular serving of wet or dry dog food, you should give your dog fresh raw beef for protein every day. It needs to be raw because a dog's system is set up to digest raw, not cooked meat. For calcium, feed the dog either cottage cheese, yogurt, or a five-minute cooked egg with the shell—a pure form of calcium. Then give him a serving of fresh raw vegetables. Any vegetable is fine. Then give the dog a vitamin/mineral mix, much like a human supplement, but designed for dogs. Extra vitamin C and B-complex should finish off the meal. But don't mix the dog food with the other food—give it to the dog separately.

■ How much exercise does a dog need?

Running in the backyard is not enough. Dogs really need one hour in the morning and one hour in the afternoon of exercise. For little dogs, some of that can be running around and playing in an apartment or house. But big dogs need to get outside. Get up earlier and go to the park. People are busy, but that's something they need to have considered before they decided to take care of a dog. For people who are too busy, a new cottage industry has sprouted up— day care for dogs.

■ What kind of dog training should be done?

Training should be positive, with a reward rather than punishment. All dogs need to be trained. It makes them easier to live with. It's worth an eight-week course—you'll be able to take them everywhere with you and they'll have a lot of freedom.

CAT BREEDS

MEOWS FOR ALL SEASONS

From pharaoh's favorites to loving tabbies, choose your companion

Celebrated for their highly independent nature, cats have been everything from lap companion to religious idol in the pages of human history. Today, over 200 million cats reside in American homes, making them nearly as popular as dogs for household pets. Here's the book on the best, brightest, most elegant, and most cuddly cats from which to choose.

■ **ABYSSINIAN:** One of the oldest known breeds, their slender, elegant, muscular bodies were often featured in paintings and sculptures in ancient Egyptian art. Abyssinians have arched necks, large ears, almond-shaped eyes, and long, tapered tails. The Abyssinian's soft and silky medium-length coat is one of its most unusual features. Each hair has two or three distinct bands of black or dark brown, giving the breed a subtle overall coat color and lustrous sheen. Abyssinians also can have a rich copper red coat. They are particularly loyal and make good companions.

■ **AMERICAN CURL:** The name comes from the breed's unique curled ears, which curl away from the head to make it look as if this cat is always alert. The American curl is moderately large, with walnut-shaped eyes. Its ears are straight at birth, and curl within 2 to 10 days. A relatively rare breed, the American curl usually weighs 5 to 10 pounds. Curls are short-haired, and their coats come in all colors possible. Even-tempered and intelligent with a playful disposition, American curls adore their owners and display affection in a quiet way. They adapt to almost any home, live well with other animals, and are very healthy.

■ **AMERICAN SHORTHAIR:** The descendents of house cats and farm cats, American shorthairs are easy to care for and resistant to disease. They have big bones and are docile and even-tempered. The breed is strongly built, with an agile, medium to large body. They have a short, thick coat that ranges in colors from black to white to red to tabby.

■ **AMERICAN WIREHAIR:** Uniquely American, the breed began as a spontaneous mutation in a litter on a farm in New York in 1966. Its dense coarse coat is hard to touch and sets these cats apart from any other breed. Some also have curly whiskers. The breed is active and agile and has a keen interest in its surroundings. Although it is quiet and reserved, owners find the breed easy to care for.

■ **BALINESE:** Related to the Siamese, it has a long silky coat, but unlike most long-haired cats, its coat doesn't mat. Endowed with a long, muscular body, the Balinese can come in several colors, including seal point, blue point, and chocolate point. Intelligent, curious, and alert, the Balinese is as affectionate and demonstrative as the Siamese, but it isn't as talkative and has a softer voice.

FACT FILE:

TALLYING A TABBY'S TAB

■ *From the Humane Society of the United States, estimates of what it costs to be a cat owner on average:*

Adopting a cat from a shelter	**$25**
First-year vaccinations	**$200**
Each year thereafter	**$27**
Other annual veterinary care[1]	**$80**
Annual feeding[1]	**$145**
Annual kitty litter	**$78**
Annual toys, grooming supplies	**$160**
Daily boarding	**$10**

1. 1991 figures.

■ **BRITISH SHORTHAIR:** Perhaps the oldest natural English breed, the British shorthair is enjoying new popularity. These cats tend to be reserved, devoted, and good companions. Because of their dense coats, they also are easy to groom.

■ **BURMESE:** Known as the clown of the cat kingdom, the Burmese thrives on attention and is very gregarious. It has a compact body and a glossy coat that comes in several colors, including sable and champagne. Burmese live well with children and dogs. They are smart, loyal, and devoted. Despite their hefty appetites, they seldom are fat. They are very expensive, though, costing as much as $1,500.

■ **CORNISH REX:** Considered "ultra-refined," the Cornish Rex has the body of a greyhound, huge ears set high on its head, and large eyes. It is surprisingly heavy and warm to the touch, with a very soft coat and muscular body. Not only do these cats fastidiously groom themselves, but they want to groom their human companions as well. If that's not to your liking, you may want another cat, because the problem may be impossible to eliminate. The Cornish Rex are highly intelligent and will adapt to almost any environment. They are skillful hunters, love children and dogs, and make superb pets. They generally like to be handled and are excellent choices for people who love cats but dislike cat hair, because they have an undercoat but no outer coat.

■ **DEVON REX:** Devons are considered a mutant breed. The mature female averages 6 pounds; the male averages 7.5 pounds. Devons have a full, wavy coat, large eyes, a short muzzle, prominent cheekbones, and huge low-set ears, which make them look a bit elfin. They are concerned for their owner's safety and are very curious. They refuse to be left out of anything, always knowing where they are going and what they will do there. People with allergies to cat hair can happily live with a Devon Rex because they do not shed.

■ **EXOTIC SHORTHAIR:** Sometimes called the "Teddy Bear" cat, exotic shorthairs require little maintenance because their medium-to-long coat does not mat. They are Persian-like in temperament and type but have an easy-to-care-for plush coat. They will jump in your lap to take a nap, but generally prefer cooler places to sleep. They are very quiet, but they will retrieve a toy until you get tired of throwing it.

■ **JAPANESE BOBTAIL:** The Japanese consider bobtails a symbol of good luck. They are medium-sized and muscular with a short tail which resembles a rabbit's tail. They have high cheekbones, a long nose, and large ears. Born much larger than other cats, the sturdy breed learns to walk earlier than others and starts getting into mischief earlier as well. Active, intelligent, and talkative, their soft voices have a whole scale of tones; some people say they sing. They almost always speak when spoken to and enjoy a good game of fetch and riding around on their human companion's shoulders. Japan-

FACT FILE:

HOUSEHOLD FAVORITES

Cats don't have to be purebred to earn affection.

■ **CALICO:** *Japanese sailors used to like to have a calico cat on their ships because they thought the cats warded off evil spirits. Calicos have characteristic three-colored patches—white, black, and red—on their coats. But the cat's personality is a little snitty.*

■ **RED TABBY:** *Two of the most popular red tabbies are Morris and the cartoon cat Garfield. The red tabby is a ginger or marmalade color with markings in darker red. These cats are gentle and loving with people, but they're not good with other cats.*

A TALE OF ONE CAT'S KITTENS

The Munchkin is one weird-looking new breed of pussycat

Sometimes inbreeding reaches such a level that it does the unthinkable: it creates an entirely new breed. The Munchkin, a cat with short stubby legs that are half the length of a normal cat's, is such a creature. It looks somewhat like a feline version of a dachshund, or like a rabbit when it sits back on its haunches.

The new breed, which traces its history to 1983, was the result of one Louisiana woman breeding the offspring of Blackberry, a single cat she rescued from a pit bull. While it's impossible to say how many Munchkins are around today, Blackberry's progeny are thought to number in the hundreds.

The Munchkin has reportedly caused havoc in cat show circles; Munchkin owners say the breed is adorable, others say it is a freak. Those that think of the stubby legs as an attribute rather than a deformity are willing to pay up to $1,500 for Blackberry's offspring.

ese bobtails are good travelers and good with dogs and children.

■ **MAINE COON CAT:** The Maine coon cat was chosen as best cat at the first cat show ever held in America. It is a native American long-hair. Originally a working cat, it is a very good mouser. The Maine coon cat is solid and rugged and can endure a harsh climate, like Maine's. It has a smooth, shaggy coat and is known for its loving nature and great intelligence. The breed is especially good with children and dogs and has always been a popular and sought-after companion.

■ **ORIENTAL SHORTHAIR:** The extremely long Oriental shorthair is described by the Cat Fanciers' Association as "demonstrative and silly, as well as sinuous and sensuous. Its emerald eyes can gleam with wit, flash and arrogance." These cats are medium-sized and are choosy eaters at times. They are easy to care for and make a practical pet. The Cat Fanciers' Association says,"Their innate sensibility verges on psychic. Once communication is established, you'll never need an alarm clock, or wonder where the cat is when you arrive home from work."

■ **PERSIAN:** The most popular cat breed, Persians are known for their long, flowing coats, which require an indoor, protected environment. They must be combed every day and need an occasional bath to prevent their fur from matting. Persians have a massive head and a very round face. Their necks are short and thick and they have short, heavy legs and broad, short bodies. Persians don't like to jump , but they are very responsive to affection. They have gentle personalities that fare best in secure, serene households. But given a little time, even they can adjust to a boisterous household with lots of children.

■ **RUSSIAN BLUE:** Fine-boned, with short hair and a regal appearance, Russian blues are clean, quiet cats that don't shed a lot. They are very intelligent and are well-attuned to the moods of their owners. They will tolerate being left alone all day while their human companions are at work, and generally do well in a house full of kids and dogs.

■ **SIAMESE:** Siamese cats are like dogs. They will fetch and do other tricks, talk a lot, and follow their owners around the house. They will also sit on your lap. They have blue eyes, and a dark, raccoonlike "mask" around them. They have long svelte bodies and long tapered lines with coats that are short, finely textured, and close to the body. Siamese cats have persistent, distinctive voices and are intelligent, dependent, and affectionate. But be advised: because they have been highly inbred, Siamese cats can be extremely timid, unpredictable, or aggressive.

PREVENTIVE CARE

SHOTS YOUR PET WILL APPRECIATE

Vaccinations will keep your dog or cat free of many common diseases

Since the discovery in the 18th century that it was possible to build up immunities against certain diseases in both people and animals by injecting them with tiny amounts of living virus, hundreds of vaccines have been created. By immunizing pets in their early months and bolstering the protection with annual "booster" vaccinations, pet owners can shield their animals from diseases that often are highly contagious to other animals and, in cases such as rabies, pose a serious threat to humans as well. Here, from the American Veterinary Medical Association, is a rundown of the diseases against which your dog or cat should be immunized.

BOTH CATS AND DOGS

■ **RABIES:** A viral disease that can attack the central nervous system of all warm-blooded animals, including humans. It is fatal if not treated. Most states require dog and cat owners to vaccinate their pets against rabies. The disease is transmitted by saliva, which is usually transferred by a bite from an infected animal and is frequently found in wild animals, such as skunks, raccoons, and bats.

There are two types of rabies—"dumb" and "furious." Both cause a departure from normal behavior. Animals with furious rabies will have a period immediately prior to death in which they appear to be "mad," frothing at the mouth and biting anything that gets in their way. Dumb rabies differs in that there is no "mad" period. Instead, paralysis, usually of the lower jaw, is the first sign. The paralysis spreads to limbs and vital organs and death quickly follows. Wild animals that are unusually friendly and appear to have no fear of man or domestic animals should be avoided and reported immediately to the police or animal control authorities.

Rabies is almost totally preventable by vaccination. Dogs and cats should receive an initial rabies vaccination by the age of three to four months. Protection lasts from one to three years. Regular boosters are required.

DOGS ONLY

■ **CANINE BORDETELLOSIS:** Caused by bacteria in the respiratory tracts of many animals, it is the primary cause of kennel cough. Besides the cough, some dogs suffer from a purulent nasal discharge. Transmission usually occurs through contact with other dogs' nasal secretions. Vaccination is generally administered by nasal spray.

■ **CANINE DISTEMPER:** A highly contagious viral disease, canine distemper is transmitted by direct or indirect contact with the discharges from an infected dog's eyes and nose. Direct contact is unnecessary because the virus can be carried by air currents and inanimate objects. Early signs are similar to those of a severe cold and often go unrecognized by the pet owner. The respiratory problems may be accompanied by vomiting and diarrhea. A nervous system disorder may also develop. The death rate from canine distemper is greater than 50 percent in adult dogs and even higher in puppies. Even if the dog survives, distemper can cause permanent damage to a dog's nervous system, sense of smell, hearing, and sight. Partial or total paralysis is not uncommon.

■ **CANINE LEPTOSPIROSIS:** A bacterial disease that harms the kidneys and can result in kidney failure. Vomiting, impaired vision, and convulsions are all tipoffs. Transmission results from contact with the urine of infected animals, or contact with something tainted by the urine of an infected animal.

■ **CANINE PARAINFLUENZA:** A viral infection of the respiratory tract, it is frequently accompanied by other respiratory viruses and is usually spread through contact with the nasal secretions of other dogs.

■ CANINE PARVOVIRUS (CPV): A serious problem because the virus withstands extreme temperature changes and even exposure to most disinfectants. The source of infection is usually dog feces, which can contaminate cages and shoes and can be carried on the feet and hair of infected animals.

CPV attacks the intestinal tract, white blood cells, and heart. Symptoms include vomiting, severe diarrhea, a loss of appetite, depression, and high fever. Most deaths occur within 48 to 72 hours after the onset of clinical signs. Infected pups may act depressed or collapse, gasping for breath. Death may follow immediately. Pups that survive are likely to have permanently damaged hearts.

■ INFECTIOUS CANINE HEPATITIS: Caused by a virus that can infect many tissues, the disease usually attacks the liver, causing hepatitis. In some instances a whiteness or cloudiness of the eye may accompany the disease. Another strain of the same virus can cause respiratory tract infections. These viruses are transmitted by contact with objects that have been contaminated with the urine from infected dogs. Infectious canine hepatitis is different from human hepatitis.

CATS ONLY

■ FELINE PANLEUKOPENIA: Also known as feline distemper, the disease comes from a virus so resistant that it may remain infectious for over a year at room temperature on inanimate objects. Spread through blood, urine, feces, nasal secretions, and fleas from infected cats, the virus causes high fever, dehydration, vomiting, and lethargy and destroys a cat's white blood cells. It is 50 to 70 percent fatal, but immunity can be developed through vaccination of kittens and annual boosters.

■ FELINE LEUKEMIA VIRUS: A disease of the immune system that is usually fatal, its symptoms include weight loss, lethargy, recurring or chronic sickness, diarrhea, unusual breathing, and yellow coloration around the mouth and the whites of the eyes. Confirmation of the virus requires a blood test. Fortunately, there is a new vaccine that provides protection.

■ FELINE VIRAL RHINOTRACHEITIS, FELINE CALICIVIRUS, AND FELINE PNEUMONITIS: All three are highly infectious viruses of the respiratory tract, for which vaccinations are available.

■ CALLING THE SHOTS ON YOUR PET'S HEALTH

The American Veterinary Medical Association recommends the following vaccination schedule:

	AGE AT VACCINATION (IN WEEKS)			Revaccination
Disease	First	Second	Third	intervals (months)
■ DOGS				
Distemper	6–10	10–12	14–16	12
Infectious canine hepatitis (CAV-1 or CAV–2)	6–8	10–12	14–16	12
Parvovirus infection	6–8	10–12	14–16	12
Bordetellosis	6–8	10–12	14–16	12
Parainfluenza	6–8	10–12	14–16	12
Leptospirosis	10–12	14–16		12
Rabies	12	64		12 or 36*
Coronavirus	6–8	10–12	12–24	12
■ CATS				
Panleukopenia	8–10	12–16		12
Viral rhinotracheitis	8–10	12–16		12
Caliciviral disease	8–10	12–16		12
Rabies	12	64		12 or 36
Feline Leukemia	10	12 & 24 or 13–14*		12

* Check with your veterinarian for type of vaccine.

SOURCE: American Veterinary Medical Association.

VET BILLS

INSURANCE FOR THE ONE YOU LOVE

It may not make money sense, but to some owners there's no alternative

Should you buy pet insurance for your animals? Most insurance companies don't even offer it, or advise you to drop it when you are looking for ways to trim your bill. But then few people ever imagined that animal lovers would one day consider pacemakers, kidney transplants, or chemotherapy for an ailing animal. "Pet owners are accepting more sophisticated care for pets," said Dr. Jack Stephens, a veterinarian with the best-known pet insurance company, Veterinary Pet Insurance, of Anaheim, Calif. "People consider pets to be like children."

Before you sign up, however, consider these cost factors: According to the American Kennel Club, the average veterinary visit for a dog costs $290. Over the lifespan of a dog that lives 11 years, that's $3,340. Pet insurance does not usually cover routine care, such as vaccinations, but would cover a dog being hit by a car or an illness.

Most pet insurance companies, like people insurance companies, base their rates on age and previous illness. The fees are likely to rise as the animal gets older. At Veterinary Pet Insurance (☎800–USA–PETS), for instance, premiums begin at $59 annually for puppies and kittens. Rates rise to $159 annually as the animal ages. Deductibles start at $20. VPI insurance covers surgery, hospitalization, prescriptions, X rays, office calls, and laboratory fees. Some services won't even insure animals once they're past a certain age, which is usually when the pet owner would need it most.

A VIRTUAL WALK WITH YOUR VIRTUAL DOG

For those who only like the "idea" of a pet, check out these cyber versions

Does walking, feeding, and training a dog sound like too much work? There is a solution for the apartment dweller, the fair-weather owner, or the person who has enough trouble taking care of himself: the virtual pet.

Bruce Blumberg, a Ph.D. student at the Massachusetts Institute of Technology's Media Lab, has created Silas, a computerized pet that is ready to play when you want but never needs to be walked too early in the morning. Silas is one of a growing number of digital "friends." Silas acts like a real dog; he runs up to you wagging his tail and will bring you a ball. However, this is not a simple computer game. To get the "you" in the picture, you stand in front of a video camera and look at a screen showing you, and through the computer program, Silas. The dog responds to your gestures, but, like a real dog, will ignore your "sit" command and help himself to a drink of water if he is thirsty. "This is making people appreciate how incredible animals really are," says Blumberg. More information about Silas can be found through the Media Lab's home page at *http://www.media.mit.edu.*

Fictitious dogs have also shown up directly on the World Wide Web. The site "Dogz: Your Computer Pet" can be found at *http://www.fido.dogz.com.dogz/*. The home page invites you to adopt a computer puppy. You can download the software for free, although the purveyors of the site hope you will pay $19.95 for a full-fledged adoption. The site lets you play catch, teach the dog tricks, reward it with treats, groom it, and throw it a bone. Just like the real thing. Only no paper-training.

CHAPTER SEVEN

TRAVEL

EXPERT QUOTES

"If you encounter a rhino, make sure that you give it plenty of distance."

—Jim Fowler, adventurer and author of *Jim Fowler's Wildest Places.*

Page 510

"Rafting down the Colorado is the type of experience that makes people go home and quit their jobs."

—Jeff Renakee, author of *River Days: A Collection of Essays*

Page 536

"Those who like shuffleboard, mints on their pillow at night, and driving golf balls off the after deck... freighter travel is not for you."

—Christopher Buckley, author of *Steaming to Bamboola*

Page 555

THE YEAR AHEAD: CHECK OUT Hawaii's Lanikai Beach, which garnered the top-ranking in Dr. Beach's annual survey... **EXPLORE** La Ruta Maya to see North America's most magnificent ruins... **INVADE** Vietnam, which is now welcoming tourists... **PROMENADE** around Paris' new monuments... **DISCOVER** one of America's little-known national parks... **REQUEST** a wingside seat if you worry about air safety... **CRUISE** on a new mega-ship... **PULL OVER** at a weird roadside attraction...

HOT SPOTS 444

NATURAL TREASURES 480

ADVENTURE 510

GETTING THERE 538

HOT SPOTS

HAWAII: Catch the hula, PAGE 448 **BEACHES:** Best places to avoid the crowds, PAGE 451 **RUINS:** Exploring Mayan culture, PAGE 452 **CARIBBEAN:** An island-by-island guide, PAGE 455 **ENGLAND:** Touring country homes, PAGE 466 **PARIS:** New sights in the city of light, PAGE 468 **INNS:** An expert picks Europe's finest, PAGE 469 **SHOPPING:** Hot sales events around the world, PAGE 474 **RETREATS:** Get thee to a monastery, PAGE 479

ISLANDS

HAWAII'S HIDDEN TREASURES

A guide to finding your perfect piece of paradise in the Pacific

It's a long way from anywhere, so you want to choose carefully. There are eight Hawaiian islands, but it's only possible to visit six of them. Kahoolawe is uninhabited and dangerous because of unexploded ammunition left over from World War II. Niihau is privately owned; visiting the island is prohibited. The remaining six are a visitor's paradise. Oahu is the most popular. Kauai is, perhaps, the wildest and the most scenically beautiful. All of them have fabulous beaches and first-class resorts. Here's an island-by-island guide.

HAWAII

4,038 sq. mi.; pop.; 122,300

Known as the Big Island, Hawaii is dominated by twin volcanoes: the ominously smoking Mauna Loa and the extinct Mauna Kea. The island is so incredibly varied geographically and climatically—temperatures range from frigid in the mountains to tropical by the beach. There are relatively few beaches—some with white sand, others black or green from volcanic residue. Developers have created oases of self-contained luxury resorts along the arid western Kona coast.

★**MAIN ATTRACTIONS: Hawaii Volcanoes National Park** covers more vegetation zones than any national park; you can climb to the top and peek into the caldera. The **Parker Ranch,** the largest cattle ranch in the U.S. (355 sq. mi.), is well worth visiting. The island has two world-class golf courses—one at the Mauna Kea Beach Resort and the other, **Francis H. I'i Brown Course** at Mauna Lani Resort. There is also some of the world's

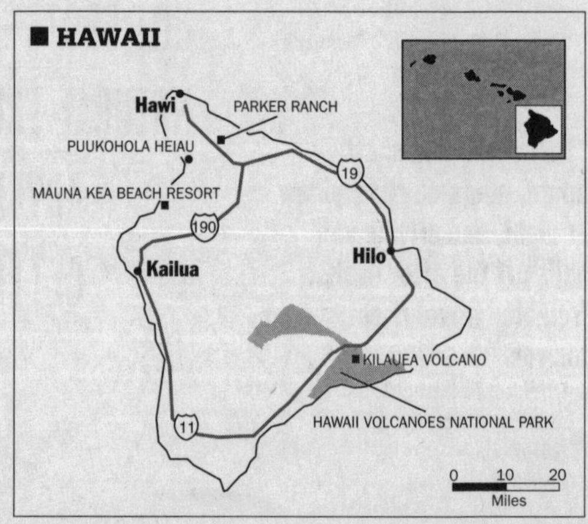

best skin and scuba diving along the island's coral reefs and underwater caves. On the Kona coast lies the town of **Kailua-Kona,** famous for its deep-sea fishing. It is small and tourist-filled but still retains vestiges of old fishing village charm. Hawaiian royalty used to hang out here. A famous heiau (place of worship) is **Puukohola Heiau,** overlooking Kawaihae Bay, now a national historic site. A lesser-known, but legendary, heiau, Mookini Heiau, is off Route 270, about seven miles beyond Lapahaki Park.

☛ **OFF THE BEATEN TRACK:** Although it is the island's largest town, rain-sodden **Hilo** doesn't attract the sunbathing crowd. It is lush with greenery and beautiful flowers, and parts of it have an old-fashioned town ambience. To visit a relatively unspoiled Tahiti-like spot on the **East Rift Zone** of the Kilauea Volcano of Cape Kumukahi, proceed along Route 132, and after the juncture with Route 137, turn right and continue to the sea. There you will find a paradise of rain forest, coconut groves, and mango trees. **Wai Opae Coral Pools** on the Puna Coast South is a showcase for extraordinary coral and is superb for snorkeling and diving.

WHERE TO STAY:

$$$: Most of the posh resorts are on the Kohala Coast. *Condé Nast Traveler* magazine calls **The Ritz-Carlton Mauna Lani,** (☎ 800–885–2000) "signature Ritz: old-world elegance . . . on 32 stunning acres of Pauoa Bay coastline." The **Mauna Lani Bay Hotel & Bungalows** (☎ 800–367–2323), with its lovely open-air architecture and secluded beach, is a haven for many Hollywood honchos.

$: Volcano House (☎ 808–967–7321) is located at the edge of Kilauea Caldera. In Hilo, **Dolphin Bay** (☎ 808–935–1466) is located in an old residential area. All rooms have kitchenettes. On Hamakua Coast, **Tom Araki's Waipio Hotel** (☎ 808–775–0368) is in the isolated Waipio Valley of the Kings. It's cheap and primitive (there's no electricity), but charming.

❢ **INSIDE SCOOP:** There are some gems of little beaches down hidden roads. Lodging prices in Hilo are among the lowest in the Hawaiian Islands.

☎ Local tourist office: (Hilo) 808–961–5797; (Kailua–Kona) 808–329–7787.

MAUI

***729 sq. mi.; pop.:100,000.** The climate in Maui varies from subtropic to subarctic with just about every variety of landscape imaginable: lofty cliffs, waterfalls, tropical rain forests, volcano, and white sand beaches. However, this is a flawed island paradise. The west coast—or Gold Coast—has been subject to intense '90s development and you'll find the usual accoutrements of tourists, traffic, swinging bars, and boutiques. Nevertheless, much of the resort development has been worked into the natural environment, resulting in low-level, beautifully landscaped, spacious, all-inclusive, super-luxury, and super-expensive resorts.*

★**MAIN ATTRACTIONS: Haleakala National Park** includes the crater of the dormant Haleakala volcano. You can drive up to it on the steepest paved road in the world (8,000 feet high and 20 miles long), and then hike over to the crater. The old whaling port of **Lahaina** on the west coast is touristy and lively—with scrimshaw shops, restaurants, and discos. The historic south end resembles an old New England sea town with charming

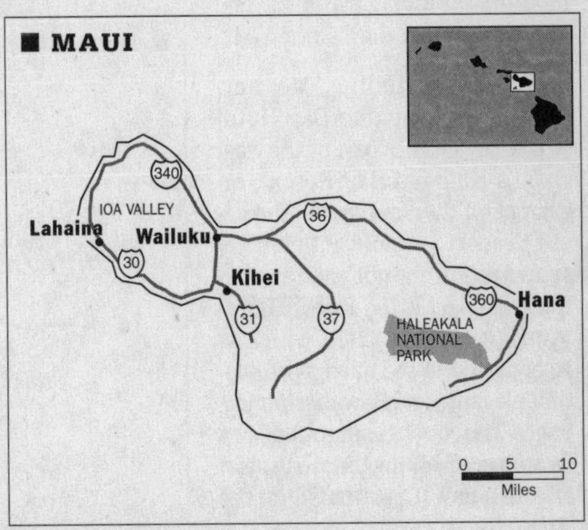

little wooden structures. Carthaginian II, the only authentic replica of a 19th-century square rigger in the world, is moored in the harbor. The Lahainaluna School (founded in 1831) was the first secondary school west of the Rockies, and now is devoted to preservation of the native culture and its important spiritual dimension—you acquire an understanding of Old Hawaii that you might not get elsewhere. **Hana Highway** is a narrow 52-mile highway with 600 curves and lots of traffic. A speed of no more than 15 miles per hour is advisable. Although the destination is Hana, the best part is what lies on the way. Practically every turn-in is a waterfall and every turn-out, a beach. A tribute to Hawaii's diverse cultural roots can be found at the **Kepaniwai Park and Heritage Gardens** in the Iao Valley, a junglelike place, with mist-filled valleys and sweet-smelling flowers.

☛ **OFF THE BEATEN TRACK:** By bike, a 58-mile trip from Hana to Kula and Kahului via Karpo and Ulupalakua Ranch on Route 31 is beautiful, with few cars or people and lovely upcountry scenery. Another good pedal is from Keanae to Hana, with a side trip to **Blue Pool.** The pool is hard to find, but worth the effort—a fine spot for snorkeling and diving. Honolua Bay is a windsurfer's mecca, isolated and beautiful, with some of the best waves on the islands—though it's for experts only. Kanaha Beach Park is good for beginners and experts. The north shore has the best dive sites. Molokini Island and "The Cathedrals" provide excellent surfing.

WHERE TO STAY:

$$$: Award-winning, Mediterranean-style **Kapalua Bay Hotel** (☎ 808–669–5656) is part of the west coast's Kapalua Bay Resort, an example of the new type of "spread-out" resort. Arnold Palmer designed one of the golf courses. On the east coast is the **Hotel Hana-Maui** (☎ 808–248–8211), which is very posh and secluded, with old-time elegance and Hawaiian atmosphere. The cottages surrounded by flowers overlooking the ocean start at $360 a day. It is situated on the Hana Ranch, and very horsey.

$: Plantation Inn (☎ 800–433–6815) has the ambience of an old Victorian house. It's located in a residential area of Lahaina. Also in Lahaina, facing the harbor, is the **Pioneer Inn** (☎ 800–457–5457), a relic of the old whaling era, with noisy saloon and all.

INSIDE SCOOP: A great variety of places for water activities exists on this island—some suitable for beginners, others for only the very experienced. Time of year and weather conditions are important factors. Be sure to check weather reports in advance. That goes for hiking too. Many trails are arduous and run along steep precipices. You might want to sidetrack Kihei, which is over-built and over-visited.

☎ Local tourist office: 808–872–3893, or 808–244–3530.

MOLOKAI

***263 sq. mi; pop.: 6,900.** This island is a far cry from the sumptuous resorts, mod water sports, and lively nightlife of the Big Island or Maui. Here, you step back to a simpler time, when there were few cars and no traffic lights—just quiet little villages. Much of the island is hard to access. The coast in the north is forbidding—and awe-inspiring—with the world's highest sea cliffs. Kamakou (4,970 feet), the highest mountain, lies in the east, surrounded by jungles, deep, secluded valleys, and pools.*

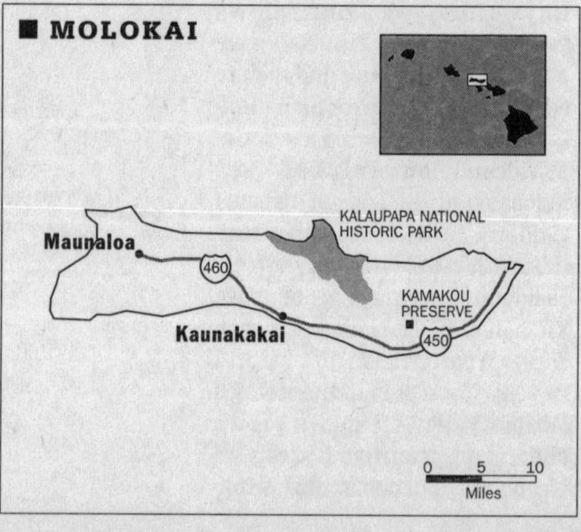

The west is dry, with marvelous beaches and the island's one resort complex. The south is flat, with offshore coral reefs, but the waters are often murky. The interior is remote; a large part of it is privately owned. Many of the numerous beaches are unswimmable. But if you are a Sierra Club–type traveler, you will love this island.

★ **MAIN ATTRACTIONS:** Kamakou Preserve is a 2,774-acre refuge for endangered and indigenous wildlife, wet obia forests, waterfalls, and lush vegetation. Contact the Nature Conservancy (☎ 808–553–5236) to visit. The Molokai Ranch Wildlife Park, is a little taste of Africa, with animals mostly from Tanzania and Kenya. The Illiliopae Heiau (permit needed), which is listed on the National Register of Historic Places, is an ancient religious site. Kalaupapa Lookout, on a high cliff above the peninsula of the same name, is an extraordinary experience. The cliff overlooks the site of the infamous leper colony, established in 1866. About 100 patients still live there voluntarily.

Kawakiu Beach is one of the best swimming beaches and is also a protected nature preserve. (It is part of the Kaluakoi Resort.) **Papohaku Beach** is one of the island's prettiest for walking, but be careful of swimming (it is subject to rip currents). Other water sports are not big here—you can find better spots on the other islands. This is, however, a great place for hiking and biking: There is a particularly nice ride along an unpaved coastal road beginning west of Kaunakakai along 9 miles of isolated beach.

☛ **OFF THE BEATEN TRACK:** Visit **Kalokoeli Fish Pond,** an ancient type of fish pond unique to Hawaii. A strenuous, but rewarding hike is into the beautiful **Halawa Valley.** You pass through lush vegetation, groves of fruit trees, and **Moaula Waterfall,** a 250-foot cascade.

WHERE TO STAY:

$$$: There aren't many on the island. The closest to one is the Kaluakoi Resort complex, which contains the best hotel; **Kaluakoi Hotel and Golf Club** (☎ 808–552–2721) is somewhat in need of renovation, but offers many amenities.The golf course is excellent, and it is right on beautiful Kepuhi Beach, which unfortunately is unsuitable for swimming because of its high waves and strong currents. **Paniolo Hale** (☎ 808–552–2731) are condominium units sited on a high ledge with spectacular ocean and garden views.

$: Honomuni House (☎ 808–558–8383) is a rental cottage in a tropical garden setting with a stream and waterfall. **Kamalo Plantation Bed & Breakfast** (☎ 808–558–8236), on five acres of tropical gardens, is surrounded by fruit trees.

? INSIDE SCOOP: Because of the paucity of restaurants, you might want to consider renting a condo and doing your own cooking. There is virtually no cultural or night life, unless you enjoy square dancing and church suppers. There is, however, local music at the **Pau Hana Inn** (☎ 800–432–MOLO or 808–553–5342).

☎ Local tourist office: 808–553–3876.

LANAI

140 sq. mi.; pop.: 2,200. Formerly owned largely by the Dole Pineapple Co., Lanai is now being eyed by business interests intent on developing tourism. At the moment, however, this small island retains much of

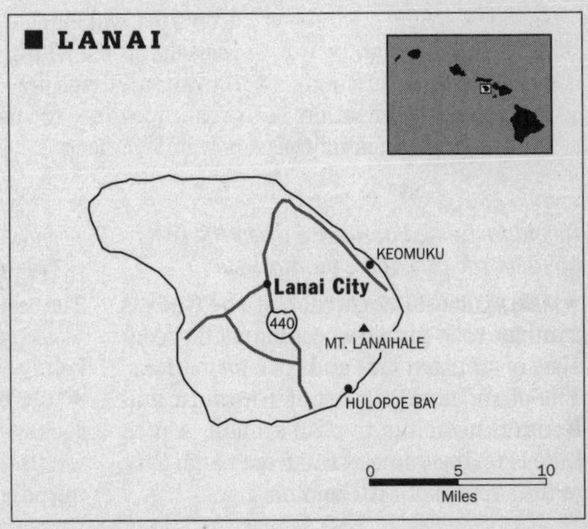

EXPERT PICKS

NO HOOPS, BUT PLENTY OF HULA

Real hula dances are stories in motion—spicy tales of love, war, and beauty. Early 19th-century missionaries suppressed the unapologetically sexual dances, deeming them licentious and barbaric. For nearly 150 years, public performances were a rarity. Instead, the hula kahiko (Hawaiian for "ancient") was passed secretly from one generation to another until the 1960s, when a few traditionalists began dancing and chanting at island festivals. Now, the hula is staging a strong comeback. There are dozens of schools, called hula halau, and the dance has become the focal point of a revival of the Hawaiian culture that existed before Captain Cook arrived in the islands in 1779. Ray Fonseca runs a hula school and teaches over 300 students ages 3 to 60 the historic dance. Here are his picks for the best places to watch hula.

HULA KODAK SHOW
Waikiki

■ The performances, which have been going on for over 30 years, are a bit touristy, but still a lot of fun and a great introduction to the hula. There are daily shows at the Shell, a concert pavilion.

U.S.S. CONSTITUTION
Big Island

■ Once a week, there are great hula performances on the big ship.

HAWAII NANI LOA
Hilo, Big Island

■ The hotel's nightly torch-lighting ceremony is a popular destination for hula lovers, featuring performances by Fonseca's students.

MERRIE MONARCH FESTIVAL
Hilo, Big Island

■ Thousands of hula dancers compete in a three-day festival, which includes arts and crafts and the crowning of Miss Aloha Hula. Held annually around Eastertime.

HULA ONI E
Honolulu

■ The October keiki (the Hawaiian word for "children") festival for 5- to 12-year-olds at the Hilton Hawaiian Village is a great time to see the best new hula dancers.

QUEEN LILIUOKALANI KEIKI COMPETITION
Oahu

■ A very traditional and prestigious competition held in August where all of the hula halaus come together to compete.

POLYNESIAN CULTURAL CENTER
Laie, Oahu

■ Models of Polynesian villages pepper the cultural center grounds run by the Mormon Church. Each village performs its own unique hula dances throughout the day, followed by an evening extravaganza where all the villages perform.

its old-fashioned ambience when life centered on the pineapple plantations.

★ **MAIN ATTRACTIONS: Garden of the Gods** is a unique rock garden whose foundation consists of unusual lava and rock formations. The abandoned villages of **Kaunolu** and **Keomuku** are fun to poke around. A nice hike is up the Munro Trail from Lanai City to the summit of Mt. Lanaihale.

There are splendid golf courses at each of the twin resorts, both with marvelous views. The best beach is **Hulopoe.** It has a partly protected swimming area and tidal pools. Snorkeling and scuba diving are excellent.

☛ **OFF THE BEATEN TRACK:** The black **Luahiwa** rocks with their ancient petroglyphs are worth seeing. A remote beach great for walking only is **Lopa,** near Keomuku Village.

WHERE TO STAY:

$$$: The Lodge at Koele (☎ 800–321–4666) is situated in the highlands among the cool Norfolk pine trees for which the island is famous. The **Manele Bay Hotel** (☎ 800–321–4666) is a luxurious resort with a Hawaiian flavor; it's situated on the beach and offers views of Hulopoe Bay.

$: Hotel Lanai (☎ 800–321–4666) is an old-fashioned inn with a wide front porch and wicker chairs, flower gardens, and three meals a day, if you wish.

INSIDE SCOOP: Do not swim at **Polihua Beach.** If you go hiking or biking, be sure to carry your own water, as there is practically no surface water on the island.

☎ Local tourist office: 808–565–7600.

OAHU

608 sq. mi. ; pop.: 840,000. Oahu has Waikiki, Honolulu, and 80 percent of the entire population of the Hawaiian islands—and that's not counting the tourists. There are more megahotels than you can count and gridlock traffic, too. It may come, then, as a surprise to learn that three-quarters of this island consists of rain forests, mountains, isolated valleys, and empty beaches.

★ **MAIN ATTRACTIONS: The Bernice Pauahi Bishop Museum and Planetarium,** 1525 Bernice St., Honolulu (☎ 808–848–4129), is one of four of the most important folklore museums in the U.S. The **Nuuanu Pali Outlook** at the head of Nuuanu Valley is certainly worth seeing—Mark Twain called it the most beautiful in the world. Also noteworthy is The **Puu-O-Mahuka Heiau,** a religious shrine, which has spectacular views and is on the National Register of Historic Places.

For swimming, **Waikiki,** of course, is the place. If you prefer something less crowded, try **Malaekahana** (safer than many others), or Waialee, near the University of Hawaii Research Farm. The best places for water sports are on the dry leeward coast, which is less developed. The best snorkel and dive spots are the crowded **Hanauma Bay** (ideal for kids), and **Three Tables** on the north shore, which has lots of coral and crevices. All the top surfing spots on the island are crowded. **Makaha** is one of the best. On the windward side, those with experience can try the less crowded surfing off the 7th Hole of Kahuku Municipal Golf Course. **Kailua Bay** is a good family windsurfing spot. If you like hiking, a nice, short two-mile hike to **Sacred Falls Wild Park** will take you up to the 80-foot-high waterfall, which has a delicious pool for a swim. For other good hikes, of which there are many, call the Sierra Club (☎ 415–922–5522).

☛ **OFF THE BEATEN TRACK:** From Malaekahana Beach, you can wade out to **Mokuauia,** a flat nearby island which is a seabird sanctuary with small beaches of its own. A remote, windswept place that is great for exploring is **Kaena Point Natural Area Reserve.**

WHERE TO STAY:

$$$: The Kahala Mandarin Oriental (☎ 800–367–2525) is more isolated than the other megahotels. It is bordered by the Waialae golf course and the ocean and is a favorite of the glitterati. **Halekulani Hotel:** (☎ 800–367–2343) many say this is the best in modern ultra everything. It also has two of the best restaurants in Honolulu.

$: Manoa Valley Inn (☎ 808–947–6019), just two miles from Waikiki, is a country-style inn with antique four-poster beds. **Pat's** at

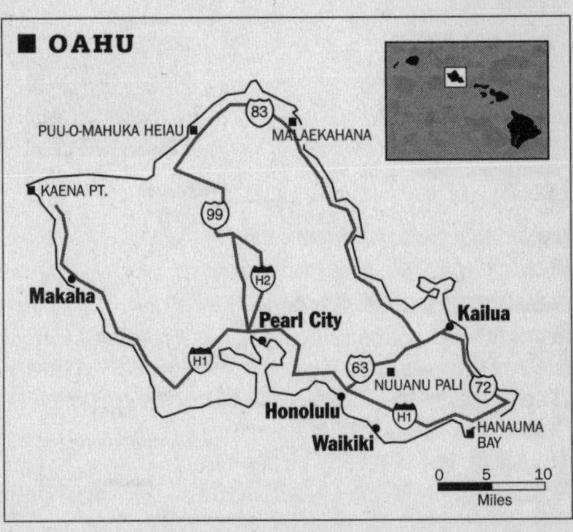

Punaluu (☎ 808–293–8111) offers privately owned condos on Punaluu Beach. A good choice if you like water sports.

INSIDE SCOOP: On the west side, where there are fewer tourists, be careful to respect the privacy of those who live there—tourists are often unwelcome. Be careful of "homestead landsites," which are often located near beautiful areas. These could be dangerous. Also don't camp alone in the campgrounds.
☎ Local tourist office: 808–923–1811.

KAUAI

553 sq. mi.; pop.: 51,000. Of all the islands, Kauai has the most beautiful natural scenery. It receives heavy rainfall, particularly in the northwestern part. The top of Mt. Waialeale (5,238 feet) is the rainiest place on earth. The vegetation is incredibly lush. The interior is virtually inpenetrable.

★ **MAIN ATTRACTIONS:** The **Grove Farm Homestead** presents a picture of life on a 19th-century plantation,which was originally designed to be a self-contained community. The **Wailua Falls** and the coconut grove at Lydgate State Park are also interesting. The state forest climb to the top of Waialeale provides a unique (and wet) experience. **Kilauea National Wildlife Refuge** is home to many exotic birds, monk seals, green turtles, and, sometimes, whales and dolphins.

For all water sports, there is nothing like **Mahaulepu Beach,** with its reef-protected shoreline and pocket beaches. Remains of extinct birds and petroglyphs have been found here. It also has 100-foot sand dunes. **Nukolii Beach Park** has all the above, including good swimming. This is a good island for horseback riding, particularly in Waimea Canyon. There's outstanding golfing at the **Princeville Makai golf course,** designed by Robert Trent Jones. The Kiele course was created by Jack Nicklaus.

☛ **OFF THE BEATEN TRACK:** There are many gems of beaches, some very isolated, all around the island down little dirt roads. They are too numerous to mention, but are there all the same, and you just have to find them. The small village of **Hanalei,** the setting for the movie *South Pacific*, is well worth a visit.

WHERE TO STAY:
$$$: Princeville Resort is the retreat of choice of the very wealthy. Magnificent views from just about everywhere. Superb golf facilities. The premier hotel in this complex is the **Princeville Hotel** (☎ 800–782–9488). The **Outrigger Kauai Beach Hotel** (☎ 800–688–7444) comprises a low-rise building complex in the shape of a horseshoe, surrounding a pool, waterfalls, and exotic flowers.
$: Waimea Plantation Cottages (☎ 800–992–4632) on the northwest side is one of the most secluded settings on the island. It is a group of plantation-era cottages with period pieces in a coconut grove. **The Rosewood B&B** (☎ 808–822–5216) offers rooms in an 80-year-old plantation house, with two charming cottages on the same property. **Keapana Center** (☎ 800–822–7968) is a hilltop B&B, a real retreat, with nearby hiking and beach opportunities.

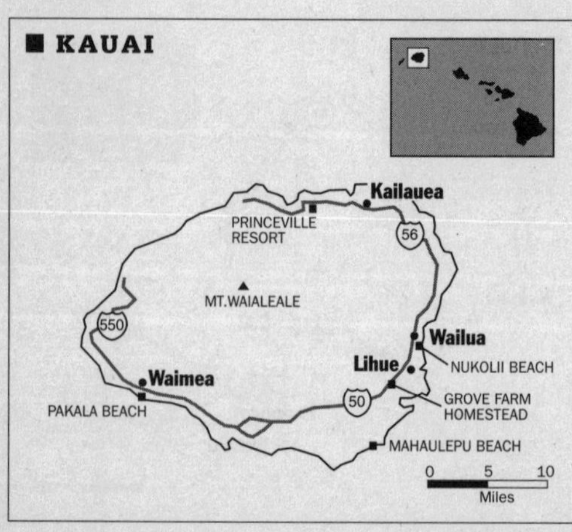

INSIDE SCOOP: Pakala Beach is a wonderful untouristy beach surrounded by lush greenery in back and 12-foot waves in front. It's perfect for all water sports, except swimming. **Smith's Tropical Paradise** is a tourist trap in the form of a tropical theme park.
☎ Local tourist office: 808–245–3971.

EXPERT LIST

THE NEXT BEST THING TO A DESERT ISLAND

The beach might be the best place to beat the heat but most of the time it is not the best place to beat the crowds. Fortunately, there are still a few beaches as yet ungirded by tarmac, summer homes, or boardwalks. Often requiring a hike or a ferry ride, these wilderness beaches reward the extra effort with a guaranteed secluded spot at the shore. Stephen Leatherman (also known as Dr. Beach) is a leading coastal ecologist who has been exploring beaches all over the country for the last 20 years studying the effects of coastal erosion. His annual best beach survey (see below) always makes headlines. Here is his never-yet-been-published list of the best wilderness beaches in the country.

JASPER BEACH
Near Machiasport, Maine
■ Named for the smooth pebbles of jasper, a reddish volcanic rock from the glacial cliffs found in this area. It's a 10- to 20-minute trek from the parking lot to see the eagles.

HIGHLAND LIGHT BEACH
Near Truro, Massachusetts
■ The heather-covered cliffs of Outer Cape Cod are reminiscent of the Scottish highlands. A short trek from Cape Cod Light, which is accessible by paved road.

HAMMOCKS BEACH
On Bear Island, just south of Borgue Banks and Morehead City, North Carolina
■ Access to this four-mile-long island is only by pedestrian ferry. No buildings but for a park concession. No vehicles allowed.

PADRE ISLAND
About 20 miles south of Corpus Christi, Texas
■ The longest barrier island in the world—over 110 miles in length. There is some development at the two ends. Travel is best by off-road vehicle.

LITTLE RIVER
Near Mendocino, California
■ Due to the deep water just offshore and the coastal upswelling of ice-cold water, not a good swimming beach, but great for hiking.

SHI SHI BEACH
Part of Olympic National Park, Washington
■ This area is only reached by a 13-mile hike on which you will see a variety of wildlife. Shi Shi is next to a large Indian reservation, where permission is required to venture.

KALALAU BEACH STATE PARK
On the Napali coast on the island of Kauai, Hawaii
■ The number-one eco-tourism resort destination in Hawaii. There is an 11-mile hiking trail.

■ AND THE WINNERS ARE...

In his annual best beach survey, Stephen Leatherman evaluates over 50 criteria, including beach cleanliness, number of sunny days, sand softness, and number of lifeguards. He takes first-place beaches out of the running in subsequent years.

1996 BEST BEACHES

1. Lanikai Beach, Hawaii
2. Kailua, Hawaii
3. Caladesi Island, Florida
4. Kaunaoa, Hawaii
5. Wailea, Hawaii
6. Hulopoe, Hawaii
7. Cape Florida, Florida
8. Fort Desoto Park, Florida
9. Hanalei Beach, Hawaii
10. Delnor-Wiggins Pass, Florida
11. St. Joseph Peninsula, Florida
12. St. George Island, Florida
13. Ocracoke Island, N. Carolina
14. Perdido Key, Florida
15. Sand Key Park, Florida
16. East Hampton Beach, N.Y.
17. Westhampton Beach, N Y.
18. Bald Head Island, N. Carolina
19. Coast Guard Beach, Mass.
20. Clam Pass, Florida

PREVIOUS WINNERS

1991 Kapalua, Hawaii
1992 Bahia Honda, Florida
1993 Hapuna, Hawaii
1994 Grayton Beach, Florida
1995 St. Andrews, Florida

CENTRAL AMERICA

THE PYRAMIDS NEXT DOOR

Mayan ruins are as magnificent as those in Egypt—and a lot closer

Scattered throughout Central America are more ancient cities and ruins than are found in all of Egypt. They are from the Mayan civilization, the most advanced and longest lived in ancient America. Starting in 300 B.C., the Mayans began organizing city-states, cleared vast tracts of rain forest for agriculture (now grown back), and established a stratified society that included kings, merchants, artisans, and peasant farmers. The metropolises they built rivaled those of Rome and Greece. Mayan architecture was monumental: large pyramids, ornate palaces, and temples. The sculpture, carved without metal tools, is among the most intricate and sophisticated in all of the ancient world.

The Mayans created a complex, highly developed civilization. They discovered the concept of zero before their contemporaries in Western Europe. They developed a calendar more accurate than the Spanish, who conquered them, and built libraries (later burned by the Spanish) to house their bark paper books called codices. Their understanding of astronomy and astrology was so thorough that they were able to predict lunar and solar eclipses. But in A.D. 900, due to war and possibly diminishing natural resources, Mayan civilization began to decline, and it was only a flutter of its previous glory when the Spanish arrived in the 1520s.

La Ruta Maya, also known as Mundo Maya, is a 1,500-mile route that runs through the lands of the Maya—western Honduras, northern Belize, Guatemala, El Salvador, and the Mexican states of Yucatán, Quintana Roo, Tabasco, Campeche, and Chiapas. Mostly paved, except for a section in Guatemala, the route is a modern creation, dedicated to the preservation of Mayan heritage as well as important wildlife habitats. It passes through a wide variety of terrain, including modern resort towns and remote jungles, extending in a figure-eight past ancient cities and temples. Although most travelers probably do not have time to travel the whole route, below is a list of some of the most significant Mayan cities, compiled with the help of Gordon Willey, professor of archeology at Harvard, and Joyce Kelley, author of *An Archeological Guide to Mexico's Yucatán Peninsula* (University of Oklahoma Press, 1993).

CALAKMUL, Campeche, Mexico

Calakmul was one of the largest Mayan cities. It is estimated that over 60,000 people have lived here at one time. It is also one of the oldest Mayan sites, having been established around 1500 B.C. So far, 6,500 structures have been mapped at Calakmul, including a 175-foot-high, 500-square-foot pyramid that archeologists believe is the largest Mayan structure ever built. From the top of it one can see the Danta Pyramid at El Mirador, another preclassic Mayan city over 20 miles away.

Only recently, Calakmul, located in a large jungle reserve that protects five of Mexico's six cat species, including the jaguar and puma, was practically inaccessible, reachable only by an overgrown jeep path. However, now a road has been built into the site, and travel time from the main road is only several hours.

■ **NEARBY:** In this relatively undeveloped part of the Yucatán, the principal attractions are the Calakmul Reserve, a number of under-visited but significant Mayan sites, and the lively ambience of small Mexican farm towns such as Escarcega. An excellent place from which to make day excursions, Escarcega offers a variety of budget accommodations ranging from rustic pensiones to comfortable hotels.

CHICHÉN ITZÁ, Yucatán, Mexico

Chichén Itzá, which over 3 million people visit every year, is the most well known and most extensively excavated Mayan city. It is

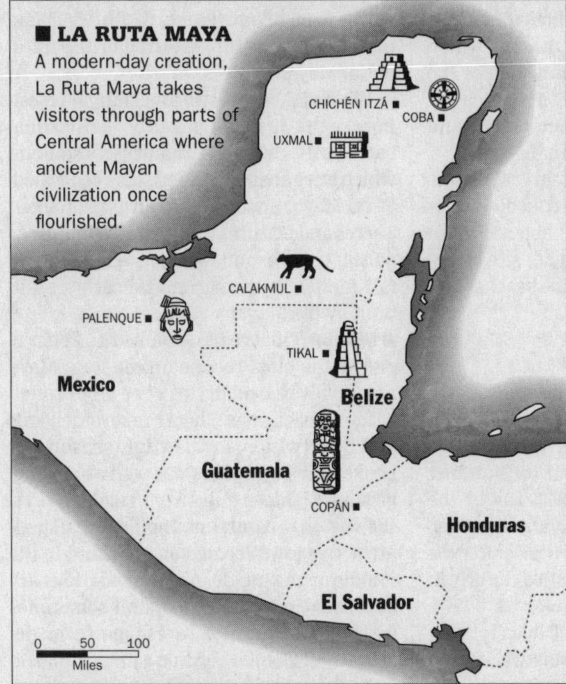

■ **LA RUTA MAYA**
A modern-day creation, La Ruta Maya takes visitors through parts of Central America where ancient Mayan civilization once flourished.

a two-hour drive from either Cancún or Mérida. Built around A.D. 500, Chichén Itzá was the most important city in the late classic period. Between the 11th and 13th centuries, this was where some of the last great Mayan buildings were constructed. Of all the Mayan cities, Chichén Itzá has the most varied architecture and sculpture, due in part to the influence of the Toltec Indian civilization of central Mexico. The murals and sculpture, with their vivid portrayals of war and human sacrifice, are the most gruesome in the Mayan world.

■ **NEARBY:** The well-developed tourist facilities near Chichén Itzá are mostly overpriced. The resorts of Cancún and the coast immediately south of it have some of the flashiest and most famous resorts in the world.

UXMAL, Yucatán, Mexico

Uxmal has some of the finest of the restored ruins and is considered by many to be the most beautiful of the Mayan cities. Many important satellite sites such as Kabah, Sayil, and Labnó are nearby.

Uxmal is where Mayan civilization reached its apogee in the years between A.D. 800 and 1000. The style of architecture that predominates here is characterized by complex geometric designs, stone veneering, moldings, and ornate mosaics. Noticeably absent from the Puuc style are the bloody sacrificial and militaristic themes emphasized at other Mayan sites.

The city boasts one of the most famous examples of astrological symbolism in the Mayan world, the Governor's Palace. The central doorway of this intricately sculpted, 24-room building is aligned with the path of the planet Venus. At the bright planet's southern solstice, the doorway is suffused with light illuminating the throne in the courtyard, as well as a temple on a hilltop 10 kilometers away.

■ **NEARBY:** There are a number of modern hotels and restaurants along the Ruta Puuc Highway. Several hours' drive away is Mérida, with just under a million inhabitants, the largest city in the Yucatán. Built by the Spanish in the 16th century on top of a Mayan city, Mérida has notable examples of Spanish colonial architecture, excellent cuisine, a vibrant nightlife, and is a good departure point for many day trips to the Gulf Coast.

COBA, Quintana Roo, Mexico

One of the lesser-visited of the large sites, Coba is located in dense low-lying jungle, surrounded by five lakes. The ruins of Coba cover an area of about 20 square miles. From the 140-foot-high Nohoch Mul pyramid, the tallest pre-Colombian building in the northeastern Yucatán, the views across the jungle and of the other ruins are magnificent. In contrast to the other ruins, Coba is essentially a set of sites, most of which have not been excavated, connected by the largest network of remaining Mayan causeways made of a limestone cement and raised 1 to 8 feet off the ground.

■ **NEARBY:** At Coba there are several restaurants and lodgings. Villa Arqueológica is owned by Club Med. Coba lies about 25 miles from Tulum, the famous Mayan site by the sea, south of which are pristine beaches bordered by verdant jungles.

PALENQUE, Chiapas, Mexico

Palenque is known for having some of the most unusual sculpture and calligraphy in the Mayan world. The architecture is pagoda-like and has been compared to Buddhist temples in Cambodia. In 1952, one of the most important Mayan excavations uncovered the intact tomb of Lord Pacal, one of the greatest Mayan kings, who ruled the city in the 7th century.

The tomb, in the Temple of Inscriptions, is designed so that at winter solstice, the sun enters a doorway, hits the back wall, and appears to descend the stairway into a tomb. Scholars interpret this as a metaphor equating the dying of the sun with the dying of Pacal. In addition, there is a 1,300-year-old palace, one of the most striking and best-preserved buildings in the Mayan world.

■ **NEARBY:** Five miles from the ruins is the town of Santo Domingo de Palenque, an easy place to reach by bus, where there is a wide variety of accommodations available. Directly adjacent to the ruins is a campground that has become popular with bohemian tourists who eat the same pyschedelic mushrooms that the Maya did. Within 30 miles of Palenque and accessible by bus are two famous waterfall sites, Agua Azul and Misol-Ha.

TIKAL, Tikal National Park, Guatemala

Tikal, situated in the Maya Biosphere Reserve, is the most important of Guatemala's 3,000 sites and, after Calakamul, probably the largest of the Mayan cities. Tikal was a great commercial and political power from about 100 B.C. to A.D. 900, making it one of the longest-lived of the influential Mayan centers.

What makes this site especially interesting are the different layers of civilization, each built alongside the other—some of which were abandoned and some renovated. Plaza Mayor encompasses an area of about 2 acres and features well-restored buildings dating from around 200 B.C. The 212-foot-tall temple is the second-tallest pyramid built by the Mayans.

■ **NEARBY:** The area known as the Petén is one of the most remote on the Ruta Maya and involves long drives over often rough roads to reach sites. There are several hotels at Tikal (which in the high season are booked far in advance), as well as a campground. Eighteen miles from Tikal is Flores, the regional capital of the Petén, a small attractive town located on an island in the middle of the jungle. Accommodations are expensive, often crowded, and sometimes wanting in quality. To escape from the crowds, El Gringo Perdido campground on Lake Petén Itzá is a pleasant and inexpensive place to stay.

COPÁN, Honduras

The southernmost Mayan city, Copán lies in one of the most remote parts of Honduras and receives significantly fewer tourists than the other major Mayan sites, with the exception of Calakmul. For more than 1,000 years, Copán flourished as a center of culture and learning. The Hieroglyphic Stairway is composed of 2,500 blocks of stone and records the history of 17 rulers of a single royal dynasty. Some of the finest pottery, jewelry, and jade carvings are on display at the Museo Regional de Arqueológica near the site.

■ **NEARBY:** Located near the Guatemalan border, the charming little town of Copán Ruinas, one of a number of interesting Spanish colonial villages in the area, is situated a couple of miles from the ruins. There are a number of small hotels that offer simple but comfortable lodgings. About 10 miles from Copán is Agua Caliente, where one can swim in hot springs.

ISLAND-HOPPER'S GUIDE

CHILLIN' IN THE CARIBBEAN

Confused about the Caribbean? Can't decide whether to zero in on Montserrat or Anguilla to soak up the rays? Or should it be the Caymans or Guadeloupe? No wonder. The Caribbean islands describe a 2,500-mile-long arc stretching from south of Florida to the coast of Venezuela. All told, there are more than 2,700 islands. A large number of isles are uninhabited, but many others beckon. Here's a guide to help you narrow the choices. Each entry includes some basic information: the number for the island tourist office and a listing of the airlines that fly there (see the key below to sort out all the abbreviations). But also provided is some more subjective information to help you assess whether the island's personality and yours are a good match.

GREATER ANTILLES

The islands in the northern Caribbean closest to the U.S. include the Cayman Islands, Jamaica, Puerto Rico, Hispaniola, and Cuba, which is omitted here because of travel restrictions.

CAYMAN ISLANDS

100 sq. mi.; pop.: 30,000

■ A scuba-diving paradise: great underwater scenery, including the Cayman Wall (coral-covered underwater mountains), tropical fish, coral reefs, and green turtles, as well as 325 submerged shipwrecks. Believe it or not, the Caymans is the 5th largest financial center in the world. High standard of living—expensive, very little crime.

■ **GRAND CAYMAN.** Among the top diving sites is Stingray City, where snorklers pat the rays. Seven-Mile Beach is world famous, but crowded with hotels and tourists. Worth seeing: the award-winning Queen Elizabeth Botanic Park and the Turtle Farm.

❢ Queen Elizabeth II stayed at the Clarion Grand Pavilion Hotel (☎ 800-CLARION). It's been recently renovated in West Indian style. Nature lovers will appreciate unspoiled Rum Point.

■ **CAYMAN BRAC.** Jagged cliffs provide a dramatic landscape. There is beautiful coral, and more than 100 caves. The diving and snorkeling on the western side of the island can't be beat. Noteworthy is a drop-off called "The Hobbit," because of its fairyland-like appearance. There is also an impressive 180-acre parrot reserve.

■ **LITTLE CAYMAN.** Bloody Bay Marine Park has coral gardens, huge sponges, trees of black coral, sea fans, and eagle rays; and for fish: yellowtails, sergeant majors, angelfish, octopi, and jewel fish. There is also a dive spot at Bloody Bay Wall with a drop-off that begins at 18 feet of water and plunges to 1,200 feet. Sport fishing is big here, especially for tarpon and bonefish.

❢ It's far from the action on Grand Cayman—98 percent undeveloped, very secluded.

☎ 809–949–0623;
US: 212–682–5582

✈ Cayman Airways, American Airlines, United Airlines, Northwest. Inter-island: Air Jamaica, Cayman Airways, Island Air.

KEY:
❢ **INSIDE SCOOP**
☎ **LOCAL TOURIST OFFICE**
✈ **WHO FLIES THERE**

JAMAICA

4,411 sq. mi.; pop.: 2,572,000

■ Pulsing reggae music, Rastafarians, polo, and English-style pubs are all part of the island's vibrant culture. You can also enjoy hiking or canoeing in the lush and mountainous interior—or staying in one of the hedonistic resorts in Negril.

❢ Island specialty is the all-inclusive resort such as: Ciboney Ocho Rios (☎ 809–974–1027) where, according to *Condé Nast Traveler*,

■ ISLAND-HOPPER'S GUIDE

"guests are treated like royalty." The elegant and peaceful Half Moon Golf and Tennis Bay Club (☎809–953–2211) is a favorite haunt of royalty and celebrities.
☎ 809–929–9200;
US: 212–856–9727
✈ Air Jamaica, American Airlines, Caribbean Airlines, Northwest. Inter-island: Trans-Jamaica, Air Jamaica, Caribbean Airlines

HAITI
10,714 sq. mi.; pop.: 7,328,000
■ The Caribbean's most mountainous country, Haiti comprises about one-third of Hispaniola, which it shares with the Dominican Republic. Also, Haiti is voodoo's birthplace, which, in some areas, still flourishes. Unique and increasingly popular "naive" art (no perspective, bright, vibrant colors) is in evidence everywhere, even on the "taptaps," the flamboyant buses that go careening about. Fine Creole cuisine.
❢ Stay away: the U.S. State Department has issued a travel advisory because of political instability. The poorest country in the Western Hemisphere.
☎ 509–686–150; US: Haitian Consulate, NYC: 212–697–9767
✈ American Airlines, Haiti Trans Air, United Airlines

DOMINICAN REPUBLIC
18,816 sq. mi; pop.: 8,050,000
■ Occupies about two-thirds of the eastern part of Hispaniola. Beautiful scenery, including majestic Pico Duarte, the Caribbean's highest peak, and the dazzling 22-mile-long white beach of La Costa del Coco. Also, splendid examples of Spanish Renaissance architecture in the old colonial part of Santo Domingo. The island vibrates with merengue, the joyful national rhythm.
❢ Lively, Latin, and lovely—but the economy is in shambles. Due to the poor tourist infrastructure, it's wise to consider an all-inclusive package vacation (generally cheaper here than elsewhere in the Caribbean) at one of the self-sufficient resorts. Punta Cana, a group of resorts on the east coast with good beaches and long a favorite with Europeans in the know, is just beginning to be discovered by Americans.
☎ 809–689–3655/3657;
US: 212–944–9937
✈ American Airlines, Dominicana; Inter-island: Antillean Air, American Eagle

PUERTO RICO
3,515 sq. mi.; pop.: 3,522,000
■ This island contains the best example of the Caribbean's Spanish colonial architecture in beautifully restored old San Juan and adjoining El Morro, a six-level fortress. The "new" San Juan abounds in sizzling nightlife: glitzy discos, casinos, and shows. The luxurious Sands Hotel and Casino attracts big-name performers. For contrast, visit the 28,000-acre El Yunque Rain Forest, with its 100-foot-high trees, hiking trails, and huge caves.
❢ The art musuem in the restored colonial city of Ponce contains a superb collection of Pre-Raphaelite paintings. This island is one of the best deals for an economy family vacation. Because of the growing crime problem, avoid beaches at night and consider taking "publicos" rather than cars because of carjackings. Also, some of the beaches can be crowded; avoid Condado and choose Fajardo, with its world-class resorts, or the rural beaches of Luquillo or Humacao instead. As yet relatively undiscovered by tourists are the nearby islands of Vieques, which has magnificent beaches, and Culebra, which has a teeming wildlife refuge and sheltered deep water bay.
☎ 809–791–1014;
US: 800–223–6530
✈ American Airlines, American Eagle, USAir, Eastern, Delta; Inter-island: Air Jamaica, BWIA, Dominicana

LESSER ANTILLES
A chain of smaller islands and islets that includes the U.S. Virgin Islands, the British Virgin Islands, followed by the Leeward

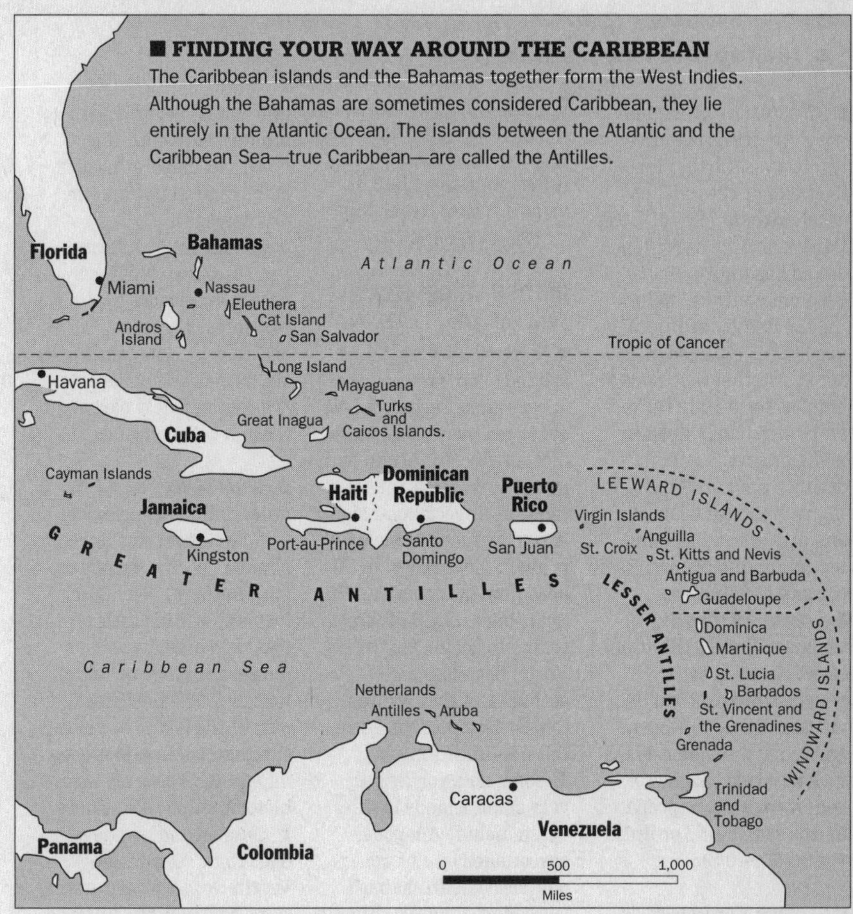

■ FINDING YOUR WAY AROUND THE CARIBBEAN

The Caribbean islands and the Bahamas together form the West Indies. Although the Bahamas are sometimes considered Caribbean, they lie entirely in the Atlantic Ocean. The islands between the Atlantic and the Caribbean Sea—true Caribbean—are called the Antilles.

Islands to the north and the Windward Islands to the south, and ending with the islands off Venezuela: Trinidad and Tobago, and the "ABC" Islands of Aruba, Bonaire, and Curaçao.

US VIRGIN ISLANDS

132 sq. mi.; pop.: 102,000

■ Beautiful beaches, clean, clear water, stunning scenery, world-famous shopping. Well over a million and a half people visit these islands. St. Thomas and St. Croix are American tourist playgrounds with crowds and traffic. St. John, much of which is a national park, is a nature lover's paradise.

☎ 212–332–2222

✈ American Airlines, Delta, USAir, Continental; Inter-island: Air BVI, American Eagle, LIAT, Virgin Air

■ **ST THOMAS:** Charlotte Amalie is a world-famous shopping center and the biggest duty-free port in the Caribbean. The largest charter yacht fleet in the Caribbean is found here. The Coral World underwater observatory at Coki Point has a three-story observatory where visitors can descend to the ocean floor to view its wonders. A panoramic view of 100 islands can be seen from Drakes Seat.

! Cruise ships crowd the harbor, and cruise passengers clog the streets and crowd the beaches. Beware of a growing crime problem, especially around Charlotte Amalie.

☎ 809–774–8784

■ **ISLAND-HOPPER'S GUIDE**

■ **ST. CROIX:** Dry, flat, and not as pretty as the other two islands. Christiansted, the historic capital, has excellent examples of early Danish architecture. The island has unparalleled accommodations, including the luxurious Buccaneer Hotel, situated on 240 acres. Another distinctive hotel is Sprat Hall, the oldest continuously lived-in mansion on the island, dating from the 1650s. There are great beaches and dive sites all around, including Buck Island Reef National Monument.
❢ Lower-key than St. Thomas. Whim Plantation Great House may be crowded, but well worth visiting. Beware of crime and racial problems; do not visit deserted beaches on your own. Also, be prepared for the cruise ship crowds.
☎ 809–773–0495

■ **ST. JOHN:** Virgin Islands National Park comprises two-thirds of the 19 sq. miles of this sparsely populated island (pop: 3,504). Spectacular mountains with an extensive network of trails. Trunk Bay, with its underwater trail, and Cinnamon Bay are outstanding beaches. Sea-kayaking is the coming sport here.
❢ No glitz. This is a haven for the quietly rich and for nature lovers (although Cruz Bay can be quite lively). There are relatively few accommodations, ranging from simple camping facilities to rental villas to luxurious Caneel Bay. No airport. Water travel only.
☎ 809–776–6450

BRITISH VIRGIN ISLANDS
59 sq. mi.; pop.: 13,000
■ Some of the best sailing grounds in the world, with superb anchorages, the BVI consist of over 100 islands, most of volcanic origin with mountains soaring out of the sea—a spectacular sight if you approach by water. At present, they are less developed than the American Virgin Islands. The BVIs are harder to get to than the US Virgin Islands, which accounts for their slower tourist development. Also, there is little crime.
❢ Some noteworthy but very small islands in this chain include Anegada, surrounded by a treacherous coral shelf that has sunk more than 300 ships. It is a wildlife reserve with magnificent beaches. Also worth a visit: Norman Island, Salt Island, and Sandy Cat.
☎ 809–494–3134; US: 800–835–8530
✈ American Airlines, Delta, with connecting flights through San Juan with LIAT, Virgin Air

■ **TORTOLA.** A sailor's paradise, particularly on the south coast with its myriad little coves, protected bays, and coral reefs. This 21-sq.-mile island is very mountainous, with stunning views: Mt. Sage, at 1,780 ft., is the highest point in the archipelago.
❢ Cuisine is not outstanding. Also, Tortola is beginning to experience the pressures of tourist-oriented development. Fuchsia, lavender, and magenta are unfortunately part of the new color schemes.

■ **VIRGIN GORDA:** This 7-sq.-mile island is a geological wonder: It contains huge boulders of mysterious origin. One area, "The Baths," forms charming little grottoes with pristine water (beware, though, of lots of tourists). The northeast part of the island has many spits and islets, and is good for sailing. These are also historic shipwreck waters.
❢ Quieter and less developed than Tortola and Virgin Gorda. There are some surprisingly luxurious low-key places to stay. Try Biras Creek (☎ 888–494–3555) with its elegant English ambience. Or, you can hire all of Necker Island (☎ 800–225–4255), which can accommodate up to 20 people. Princess Diana vacations here.

LEEWARD ISLANDS

Part of the Lesser Antilles, the Leeward Islands are so called because they are sheltered from the trade winds. The islands include Anguilla, Netherlands

■ ISLAND-HOPPER'S GUIDE

Antilles I, St.-Barthélemy, St. Kitts and Nevis, Antigua and Barbuda, Monserrat, and Guadeloupe.

ANGUILLA

35 sq. mi.; pop.:500

■ This rather barren island has 33 magnificent white sand beaches, considered among the best in the Caribbean. Surrounding coral reefs provide excellent diving and snorkeling opportunities.

❢ Traditionally, the island has catered to the very rich who prefer a quiet lifestyle. Slow-growing tourism is creating facilities for the less affluent. One of the safest Caribbean islands.

☎ 809–497–2759; US: 800–553–4939

✈ American Eagle, Air Anguilla, Air BVI, LIAT and WINAIR, and Tyden

NETHERLANDS ANTILLES I

308 sq. mi.; pop.: 185,000

■ This chain is part of the kingdom of the Netherlands, but each island is autonomous.

■ **SABA.** There are no beaches on this tiny island, but it boasts the highest mountain in this chain, Mt. Scenery (2,855 ft.), which harbors a tropical rain forest par excellence. From the airport (situated at Flatpoint) you ascend the one very steep road, called "The Road," with 19 serpentine curves, through Hell's Gate to "The Bottom," one of two main villages (the other is Windwardside). A 1,000-step stone stair, known as "The Ladder," takes you to the crest of the mountain. A small-town atmosphere; extremely clean, unspoiled, tiny picturesque cottages, and tropical gardens provide a unique appeal.

❢ The lack of beaches, most water sports, and yachting facilities keeps the masses away. Scuba diving is just about the only water sport. Saba is one of the great unspoiled dive sites in the Caribbean.

☎ 599–46–2231
US: 305–741–2681

✈ WINAIR

■ **SINT MAARTEN.** If you are a sailor, you will find this island one of the best in this part of the Caribbean. There are good anchorages in the bay. Philipsburg is cruise ship heaven.

❢ A good island to stay away from, unless your idea of a good getaway is a preponderance of casinos, malls, boutiques, bargain

■ **AIRLINES THAT FLY TO THE CARIBBEAN FROM THE U.S.**

✈	☎
AIR JAMAICA	800–523–5585
AMERICAN AIRLINES	800–433–7300
BWIA INTERNATIONAL	800–538–2942
CAYMAN AIRWAYS	800–422–9626
CONTINENTAL AIRLINES	800–231–0856
DELTA AIR LINES	800–221–1212
NORTHWEST AIRLINES	800–447–4747
TRANS WORLD AIRLINES	800–221–2000
UNITED AIRLINES	800–538–2929
USAIR	800–622–1015

■ **INTER-ISLAND AIRLINES**

✈	☎
AIR ANGUILLA	809–497–2643
AIR GUADELOUPE	800–522–3394
AIR MARTINIQUE	011–596–511111
ALM (ANTILLEAN AIR)	800–327–7230
AMERICAN EAGLE	800–433–7300
LIAT	800–253–5011
MUSTIQUE AIRWAYS	800–526–4789
TYDEN AIR	800–842–0261
WINAIR	011–599–552664
AIR JAMAICA	800–523–5585
BWIA	800–327–7401
CAYMAN AIRWAYS	800–422–9626
ISLAND AIR	800–922–9626
VIRGIN AIR	800–522–3084
AIR BVI	800–468–2485
AIR ST KITS–NEVIS	465–8571
AIR ARUBA	800–433–7300
AIR ST. BARTHELEMY	53150–877346
AIR ST MARTIN	829663
HELENAIR	444–2266
SVG AIR	456–5610
AIR CARAIBES	449–1416
ANTILLES AERO SERVICE	516688

■ ISLAND-HOPPER'S GUIDE

shopping—and, oh yes, fast-food joints. For those who are interested, there are two nude beaches.
☎ 599–52–23–37;
US: 212–953–2084
✈ American Airlines and Continental; Inter-island: Air Aruba, Air Guadeloupe, Air Martinique, Air St.-Barthélemy, Air St.-Martin, Antillean Air, LIAT, WINAIR

■ **SINT EUSTATIUS (STATIA).** A good place to avoid tourists. Sint Eustatius is the least developed island in the Northeastern Caribbean, and perhaps the poorest.
❢ The Atlantic side of the island has a strong undertow and is unsafe for swimming. There is a paucity of beaches, which probably accounts for the lack of commercial development.
☎ 599–38–2433
US: 516–261–9600
✈ WINAIR

ST.-BARTHÉLEMY

8 sq. mi.; pop.: 5,043

■ This very French island has marvelous beaches surrounded by a myriad of coves and protected by the mountainous headland. Anse du Grand Colombier is a very secluded beach, and Lorient, off the beaten track, is great for children.
❢ Playground of exclusive millionaire jet-setters. Lots of French-style chic. Many very expensive, first-rate hotels. A good hangout is the restaurant and hotel Carl Gustaf.
☎ 590–27–87–27;
US: 900–990–0040
✈ Air Guadeloupe, Air St.-Barthélemy, Virgin Air, WINAIR

ST. KITTS AND NEVIS

101 sq. mi. and 36 sq. mi.; pop.: 44,000

■ An eco-tourist's dream with lush rain forests and a monkey population higher than the human one. The Caribbean's finest examples of the old 18th-century plantation houses (now mostly hotels) are found on both islands. A prime example is the Rawlins Plantation, situated on the slopes of Mt. Liamulga. Calm waters make for excellent waterskiing and small boating here—many little coves and coral reefs. Nevis, the sister island, still retains remnants of the old West Indies culture and is noted for its great beaches and "small-island life." and a relatively new Four Seasons hotel (☎ 809–469–1111).
❢ Although this is fine sailing territory, sailors should be aware that there are limited services.
☎ 809–465–4040;
US: 212–535–1234
✈ American Eagle connecting from American Airlines hub in San Juan; also, Air St. Kitts-Nevis, LIAT

ANTIGUA AND BARBUDA

171 sq. mi. and 625 sq. mi.; pop.: 69,000

■ Another sailor's paradise with many little coves and coral reefs. Full support services for sailors as well as 365 beaches and a beautifully preserved 18th-century port called English Harbour, one of the most picturesque in the Caribbean. The annual Classic Yacht Regatta, which follows Race Week (a major Caribbean sailing event), is a scene from the past with ships, many with beautiful configurations, no longer seen outside of a museum. Antigua, the sister island of Barbuda, has none of the commercial trappings of many of the other islands, (not even paved roads!) but some of the most beautiful beaches in the Caribbean. It is less-known and quieter, with a feeling of timelessness, and a few vastly expensive hotels.
❢ Very British and conservative; traditionally a retreat for rich expatriates. Recently, the island has become popular due to the development of the all-inclusive resort package. Since sailing is difficult here, sailors should be very experienced. On the south coast is Coco Point Lodge (☎ 212–986–1416), with its own palm-lined beaches, private cottages, and spectacular views.
☎ 809–462–0480; US: 212–541–4117
✈ BWIA, American Airlines, Continental

MONTSERRAT

39 sq. mi.; pop.: 13,000

■ Some of the best sailing

■ **ISLAND-HOPPER'S GUIDE**

in the area is around the offshore islands of Montserrat. The island is still largely undeveloped. There are few beaches, sailing facilities, or hotels. In addition to one of the world's best dive spots with very unusual coral reefs, lush tropical greenery, and bird sanctuary, the main draw here is a quiet, unpretentious lifestyle that has attracted a large population of retirees.

! There is virtually no crime, but beware of sitting under a manchineel tree: the poisonous apples will blister you. Don't come to Montserrat if you're in search of nightlife.

☎ 809–491–2230; US: 212–818–0100

✈ Montserrat Airways and LIAT connecting from Antigua

GUADELOUPE

658 sq. mi.; pop.: 345,000

■ One of the best islands in the Caribbean for abundance of flora: There are 75,000 acres of scenic national park with rain forest, gardens, and ponds. The beaches are only average, however. The northeast reef of North Pigeon Island is one of the world's best dive sites. Lively nightlife. The cuisine is outstanding, and the blend of French, East and West Indian, and African cultures creates a unique mix.

☎ 590–82–09–30; US: 900–990–0040

✈ Air France; American Eagle; Air Guadeloupe, Air St.-Barthélemy, LIAT

WINDWARD ISLANDS

The southern part of the Lesser Antilles arc, it includes Dominica, Martinique, St. Lucia, St. Vincent and the Grenadines, and Grenada.

DOMINICA

290 sq. mi.; pop.: 71,000

■ The least developed of the Windwards, this is one of the "greenest" islands in the Caribbean.There is freshwater swimming, bird-watching, and hiking through a country of riotous vegetation, and of rivers with magnificent cascades and waterfalls. A very special place to stay, with an Eden-like environment, is the Papillote Wilderness Retreat, near Trafalgar Falls. There is a syndicate-protected reserve in the northwest—a haven for botanists and bird-watchers. Plans are being developed to establish a scientific research center here.

! One of the poorest islands in the Caribbean. Although there is a modest amount of tourism, there are few restaurants and little in the way of water sports except for scuba diving. The beaches are a volcanic gray or black, and swimming on the Atlantic side can be dangerous. Swimming in the rivers and charming waterfall pools is a more than satisfactory alternative. There is a beautiful unspoiled beach at Woodford Hill.

☎ 809–44 8–2351; US: 212–682–0435

✈ Air Caraibes, Air Guadeloupe, LIAT, WINAIR

MARTINIQUE

425 sq. mi.; pop.: 360,000

■ Nicknamed the "Island of Flowers," Martinique has both rain forest and open fields of sugarcane and bananas. There are lots of lovely coral beaches. A hotel that's unsurpassed in elegance and French Caribbean chic is Habitation La Grange. If you're interested in good food, the island also has just about the best Creole cuisine in the Caribbean.

! Stay away from underbrush, home of the fer de lance, a very poisonous snake.

☎ 596 63–79-60; US: 900–990–0040

✈ Air France, American Airlines; Air Martinique, Antilles Aero Service, LIAT

ST. LUCIA

238 sq. mi.; pop.: 144,000

■ Although St. Lucia is the most developed of the Windward Islands, there is still great natural beauty, including a rain forest, and the people are exceptionally friendly. There is a lively nightlife in the capital, Castries—irresistible limbo dancers, calypso

■ ISLAND-HOPPER'S GUIDE

singers, and steel bands. A rich Indian culture flourishes—Nobel Prize–winning poet and author Derek Walcott comes from this island.

❢ Jalousie Plantation, a new 110-acre resort, is a grand house–style hotel, which attracts jet-setters and aristocrats.The Green Parrot restaurant in Castries is well worth checking out. However, don't look for the best beaches or nightlife here.

☎ 809 452–4094;
US: 212–867–2952

✈ American

ST. VINCENT AND THE GRENADINES

133 sq. mi. and 17 sq. mi.; pop.: 113,000

■ With 32 islands to explore, ranging from the undeveloped to those with lap-of-luxury development, this is one of the world's premier sailing haunts. St. Vincent will appeal to those with botanical interests; it is incredibly lush and fertile and home to the oldest botanical garden in the Americas—20 acres of exotic tropical plants.

❢ St. Vincent has black volcanic sand beaches and is not yet fully developed. Consequently, equipment for water activities is rather limited. Landlubbers will enjoy the varied terrain, valleys, hills, farmlands, rustic fishing villages, and wide-porched hilltop hotels.

■ **BEQUIA:** A former whaling station. Excellent beaches and many good small hotels.

❢ Popular with the international jet set and a favorite playground for the yachting crowd.

■ **MUSTIQUE:** Scotland's Lord Glenconner has turned what was a rather barren island into a verdant paradise.

❢ Chic playground of the rich and famous, tony rock stars, and British royalty. Those who don't rent or own one of the 50 houses on the island, hang out at the Cotton House Hotel (☎ 809–456–4777).

☎ 809 457–1502;
US: 800–729–1726

✈ Air Martinique, LIAT, Mustique, SVG

GRENADA

13 sq. mi.; pop.: 91,800

■ This island is pristine, with mountains, rain forests, coves, white sandy beaches, and beautiful views all around. The capital, St. Georges, which sits in an ancient volcanic pit surrounded by green slopes dotted with red-tiled roofs, is the most charming harbor in the Caribbean. Much of the interior is wild, remote, and uninhabited. However, commercial development is starting to pick up.

☎ 809–443–7948; US: 800–927–9554

✈ American, BWIA; Antillean Air , HelenAir, LIAT

VENEZUELAN ISLANDS

The islands of Barbados, Trinidad, and Tobago belong to this group, which is a geographical designation only, as they do not belong to Venezuela.

BARBADOS

166 sq. mi.; pop.: 264,000

■ Best climate in the Caribbean, this beautiful coral island also has many of the best beaches, which provide a fine setting for all water sports. There are handsome old plantation houses with beautiful gardens.

❢ One of the most populated islands in the area, Barbados is a favorite winter retreat of the wealthy. Quite cliquey and snobbish. Horse racing and cricket are the "in" sports—have been for a long time. Special places to stay are the small hotels on the wilder west coast. Look elsewhere for the best shopping, nightlife, and beaches.

☎ 809–427–2623;
US: 212–986–6516

✈ American, BWIA, Aeropostal, Air Martinique, LIAT

TRINIDAD AND TOBAGO

1,846 sq. mi. and 116 sq. mi.; pop.: 1,273,000

■ Trinidad is a rich mix of ethnic groups, resulting in a unique cuisine, music, and culture—steel-band orchestras, calypso, Hindu temples, gingerbread houses, and Asian bazaars. There is a rain forest with

■ **ISLAND-HOPPER'S GUIDE**

200-foot-tall trees and spectacular wildlife. Tobago is a quiet getaway—remote, undisturbed, with lovely beaches, rain forest, waterfalls, and tropical birds.

! Trinidad is highly industrialized. There is oil there and growing tourism.

☎ 809–623–1932;
US: 800–232–0082

✈ American, BWIA, LIAT

NETHERLANDS ANTILLES II

Also called the ABC Islands, because they consist of Aruba, Bonaire, and Curaçao. The three islands were formerly all part of the Netherlands; Aruba became independent in 1986.

ARUBA

70.9 sq. mi.; pop.: 82,000

■ You might as well be on a cruise ship—theme parties, casinos galore, all packed onto a very small island. The Caribbean's largest sunken wreck lies just off the northwest coast of this island.

! There is another Aruba. Wander into the countryside and you will find deserts, secluded old Indian caves, and geologically interesting beaches, although they are unsuitable for swimming because of huge waves.

☎ 297–8–23777;
US: 201–330–8757

✈ American, Air Aruba, Antillean Air, Aeropostal

BONAIRE

112 sq. mi.; pop.: 11,500

■ Eco-tourists will find what they're looking for on this arid island, including a treasure trove of exotic and varied wildlife. The Bonaire Marine Park, which covers the entire coastline, is a protected underwater paradise with one of the most unspoiled reef areas in the world and 80 dive sites.

! Good restaurants but not much else to attract the cruise crowd. But development pressures are rising, even though, at this writing, there are still no traffic lights on the island!

☎ 599–7–8322;
US: 212–832–0779

✈ Antillean Air; Air Aruba, American

CURAÇAO

180 sq. mi.; pop.: 150,000

■ Willemstad, which is a mini-Amsterdam,with its Dutch-inspired architectural details on the gaily painted houses and inland waterways, offsets the—in some places—rather dreary countryside. Water sports, reef diving, great shopping, and relatively low-key tourism flourish.

! For a culinary treat, try the rijsttafel, a many-course Indonesian dinner, ending with curaçao liqueur, produced at the 17th-century Chobolobo estate with an orange that only grows here.

☎ 599–9–6160–00;
US: 212–751–8266

✈ Air Aruba, Antillean Air, BWIA

■ SETTING SAIL IN AN AZURE SEA

If you're going to the Caribbean to take in the ocean, why not skip the land altogether? Charters generally last a week to 10 days. Weekly rates run from $1,900 to $6,000 during the high season and as little as half that in the off-season. The only requirement is that you have at least one proficient sailor in your group (though it's probably better to have more. If your skills aren't up to snuff, you can hire a skipper at $80 to $120 a day). Here, one of *Yachting* magazine's executive editors, Kenny Wooton, picks the top outfitters.

	☎
CARIBBEAN YACHT	800–225–2520
CATAMARAN CHARTERS	305–462–6506
THE MOORINGS	800–535–7289
NAUTOR'S SWAN	800–356–7926
STARDUST MARINE	800–634–8822
SUNSAIL	800–327–2276
SUN YACHT CHARTERS	800–772–3500

VIETNAM

BACK TO THE RICE PADDIES

An old Asia hand's tour of the beautiful, war-ravaged land

It's probably the last place a Vietnam vet expected he would ever visit again. At the height of the Vietnam War there were over half a million American soldiers stationed in this faraway land. The last Americans left in 1975 as Saigon fell, evacuated from the roof of the American embassy by helicopter. It wasn't America's finest hour.

These days, former Vietcong guerrillas are laying out the welcome mat for once-reviled capitalists. Whether there are bitter memories of the war, of course, remains to be seen. Bombing targets are now tourist traps. But the countryside, dotted with rice paddies and pagodas, is still as beautiful as it always was, and the cities are teeming with energy. Saigon, once known as the Paris of the Orient, may one day soon reclaim the moniker. Stanley Karnow covered the VietnamWar as a journalist and later wrote *Vietnam: A History* (Viking/Penguin, 1984), which was also a PBS television series. Here are his sightseeing recommendations:

■ **(HO CHI MINH CITY) SAIGON.** Saigon still has the look of a 19th-century French provincial capital. The architecture from that time predominates, with a legacy that includes a replica of the Paris Opera and a Cathedral of Notre Dame. The most interesting and beautiful building is the old French City Hall, called the Hôtel de Ville—now the headquarters of the Ho Chi Minh's People's Party. Visitors are not allowed inside, but the elegant facade is worth going to see, especially at night when it is covered with little lizards called geckos.

The Continental Hotel, which was built in 1880 and was the setting of Graham Greene's novel *The Quiet American*, has the most distinctive accommodations in town. Around the famous terrace bar (now an enclosed air-conditioned pizzeria), once referred to as the "Continental Shelf," secret agents, journalists, underworld figures, and prostitutes congregated during the Vietnam War. For traditional Vietnamese fare, the Lemon Grass restaurant at 63 Dong Khoi St. is one of the tastiest and most atmospheric.

■ **CAODAI GREAT TEMPLE.** Outside the town of Tay Ninh, west of Saigon, is where the see of Caodaism is located. This unique sect, founded in the 1920s, incorporates both western and eastern icons: among the venerated spirits are Victor Hugo, Gandhi, and Lenin. At the compound are the Great Temple, administrative offices, and a herbal medicine hospital to which people travel from all over Vietnam. The large temple is built on nine levels, which represent the steps to heaven.

■ **MEKONG DELTA.** Some of the most savage fighting during the Vietnam War took place in the picturesque countryside of the Mekong delta. Cantho, a small city in Tien Giang province, is an excellent place from which to take a boat trip through the mangrove forest swamps and tall grasses, where the Vietcong sought refuge from American bombs. Another interesting place to visit is Mytho, the capital of Tien Giang province, where the boat trips are much more expensive because they are controlled by the government.

■ **DALAT.** A six-hour drive from Saigon, this beautiful, largely French-built hill town is one of the most scenic cities in Vietnam. Long a resort area as well as an escape from the stultifying heat of the Mekong delta, wealthy Vietnamese and French expatriates built some outstanding villas here. Among the great houses is the old emperor's palace, now the Palace Hotel, owned and operated by an American. Because both sides used the area as a getaway from the war there was not the destruction here that occurred in the rest of the country.

ANGKOR WAT'S MAGNIFICENT TEMPLES

During the reign of terror in Cambodia that followed the end of the Vietnam War, the Khmer Rouge killed thousands of their countrymen. However, except for a few bullet holes, the brutal regime left largely intact the ruins of what was once the most magnificent city in Indochina, Angkor. Now, most of the land mines around the site have been removed and Angkor's numerous and elaborate temples are once again beguiling visitors.

The earliest of the ruins collectively known as Angkor date from the 9th century when King Jayavarman established a capital at Rouluous, southeast of the modern town of Siem Reap. At its height, the Khmer empire extended from the coasts of Vietnam to the borders of Burma. Angkor Wat, the most famous of the ruins, as well as one of the better preserved, was built in the 12th century. The walls of Angkor Thom, one of the successive capitals in the area, enclose a space larger than that of any medieval European city.

The Khmer cities were allegorical representations of the heavens, built around temples constructed atop natural or man-made hills. Most of the architecture combines Hindu and Buddhist symbolism. Angkor Wat boasts the longest bas-relief in existence, extending over 12,000 feet.

If you go: Allow at least two or three days to adequately take in the most significant sites near Angkor. There are daily flights from Phnom Penh to Siem Riep, and occasional direct flights from Ho Chi Minh City in Vietnam. A small town oriented toward tourism, Siem Riep has a variety of accommodations, from budget to luxury. Most travelers arrive as part of tour groups. However, Angkor is accessible to the independent traveler. For more information, contact Phnom Penh tourism (FAX) 855–23–26043.

■ **HANOI.** One of the oldest cities in Asia, Hanoi is more subdued than Saigon, but recently it has started to emulate Saigon's frenetic moneymaking pace. Architecturally, Hanoi is more interesting and unique. A style called Norman Pagoda, a hodgepodge of French and Asian architecture, predominates here. The 36 area streets (each named for a separate craft: weavers, dyers, goldsmiths, etc.) have a lively marketplace where you'll find some of the most talented artisans and craftspeople in Indochina. Ten miles outside Hanoi is the village of Bat Trang, whose 3,000 inhabitants pursue a tradition of ceramic making that goes back over six centuries.

■ **HA LONG BAY.** Occupying a central place in Vietnamese mythology, art, and history, the strangely shaped islands of Ha Long Bay are truly among the most magnificent sights in Vietnam. Situated about a 12-hour drive north of Hanoi, the over 1,600 limestone islands look magical with their grottoes, caves, dense foliage, and secret beaches. Here is where a strange Loch Ness–type monster supposedly prowls. Ho Chi Minh's old summer villa is located here. You can rent a boat for around $50 a day and go exploring throughout the islands and caves.

■ **SE PA.** This area is just beginning to be discovered by Western tourists. Se Pa is a French hill station that was built in the remote mountains of northwest Vietnam and abandoned during the colonial war in the 1950s. Today, it bears little trace of this or any other Western influence. About a 12-hour train trip from Hanoi, Se Pa is an excellent base from which to visit the Hmong, Zao, and Tay tribes who still practice their traditional cultures. From the town, arrangements can be made to climb Fan Si Pan, which, at 10,300 feet is. the highest mountain in Vietnam.

ENGLAND

HOUSES IN THE COUNTRY

Visiting the grandest of the Britain's grand old homes

Hollywood's homage to the English country house is in full swing—the backdrop for Emma Thompson's Oscar-winning adaptation of Jane Austen's *Sense and Sensibility* (as well as *Persuasion* and *Emma*) and *The Remains of the Day*, made several years earlier. And no wonder. These houses represent the finely tooled tradition of 400 years of pomp and circumstance and epitomize a level of decorative arts and architecture that is impossible to re-create today.

Neither castle nor palace, the rise of the English country house is directly linked to the early subjugation of the feudal aristocracy and ecclesiastical influence in England by Henry VIII (he didn't like the idea of his nobles living in castles, where they could defend themselves). Because English country houses essentially descended from squires' houses, their exteriors are markedly absent of the extreme architectural distinctions that characterized aristocratic palaces in other European countries.

Today, due to the immense cost of upkeep, over 400 of these houses are open to the public for at least part of the year. Around 200 are operated by the National Trust, while others are run under a variety of arrangements. You're unlikely to visit them all. Here are some of the most significant, chosen by Fred Maroon, author of *The English Country House: A Tapestry of Ages* (Pavilion Books, 1988).

HADDON HALL

Bakewell, Derbyshire. 14th–early 17th centuries

■ Haddon Hall was originally a medieval manor house and a defensive wall dates from the 12th century. From medieval times onward, Haddon Hall was updated, but there were no major alterations after the early 17th century. As a result, the house contains some of the most authentically historic rooms in England, such as the cavernous kitchen, which still has medieval cupboards, and the 16th-century parlor.

LONGLEAT

Warminster. Late 16th century; altered late 19th century

■ Begun in 1547, Longleat House is considered the first Great House of English Renaissance style. Built on the ruins of an ancient priory, it marks a departure from the fortified look of the medieval house. The early Elizabethan architecture emphasizes a tall, compact building, with many windows, and the Renaissance ideals of balance and symmetry. Longleat is situated in a park designed by Capability Brown. The interior was redone around 1860 in the Italian style, but retains the traditional great hall. The library contains Henry VIII's Great Bible of 1541 and several original editions of Chaucer.

CHATSWORTH

Bakewell, Derbyshire. Late 17th, early 18th and 19th centuries

■ One of the most majestic houses in England, it was begun in the mid-1500s by Sir William Cavendish and his Lady, the famous Bess of Hardwick, who kept Mary Queen of Scots a prisoner here. The exterior of the house is massive and austere. The painting collection includes works by Rembrandt, Veronese, Frans Hals, Poussin, Van Dyck, Reynolds, Sargent, and Lucien Freud. There are magnificent gardens and even a canal.

HARDWICK HALL

Chesterfield, Derbyshire. Late 16th century

■ Hardwick Hall, built by Bess of Hardwick between 1590 and 1597 near the family seat at Chatsworth, is situated on a hilltop with an expansive vista, surrounded by walled courtyards and gardens. It is perhaps the most impressive and least altered of the grand Elizabethan Renaissance houses. The 166-foot long gallery contains huge glass windows, which were unusual for that time. The house is full of tapestry and fine embroidery, much of it done by Bess herself.

KNOLE

Sevenoaks, Kent. Mid- to late 15th century, enlarged 16th and 17th centuries

■ Knole was the childhood home of Vita Sackville-West, the lover of writer Virginia Woolf, who memorialized the house in her book *Orlando*. The house is an excellent example of the early Jacobean period (1600–1650) with its trademark shaped gables, grand hall, and the seven courtyards. The great staircase is a fine example of the new fashion of treating a staircase as a highly decorative entity.

HATFIELD HOUSE

Hatfield, Hertfordshire. Early 17th century

■ Hatfield House is more like a palace than a private house, fitting for its owners the Cecils, who have provided many of England's greatest statesmen. Built in 1608 by Robert Cecil, the first Earl of Salisbury, and Minister to Elizabeth I and James I, it is one of the finest examples of Jacobean architecture, with its classical symmetrical exterior, impressive wide staircase (the intricate Mannerist carving on it is world famous), and great state rooms.

CASTLE HOWARD

Malton, Yorkshire. Early to mid-18th century

■ The setting for the TV series *Brideshead Revisited*, Castle Howard was designed by Sir John Howard. Horace Walpole said of it: "I have seen gigantic palaces before, but never a sublime one." The finest example of the rare English classical Baroque style, which emphasized grandeur and flamboyance, construction of this building took the greater part of the 18th century. Rubens's famous painting *Salome* hangs here.

BLENHEIM PALACE

Woodstock, Oxfordshire. Early 18th century

■ Queen Anne and a grateful Parliament provided funds for Blenheim as a gift to John Churchill, the first Duke of Marlborough, for his famous victories over France. Winston Churchill was born in the cloakroom during a ball that his mother was attending at the time. The house is in the English Baroque style, but with a great deal of rustication. Capability Brown designed the park, replete with lakes and formal gardens.

SYON HOUSE

Brentford, Greater London. Rebuilt mid-16th century, altered late 18th century

■ Still owned by the family who built it, Syon House is set amid 80 acres of picturesque parkland along the Thames, not far from London. Although most of the rather banal exteriors date from the 15th and 16th centuries, the interior of the property was extensively remodeled by renowned neoclassicist Robert Adam in the 1700s. The grand entrance hall is is one of the most magnificent in Britain.

FACT FILE:

POUND FOR POUND

■ Holiday Which?, *a counterpart to* Consumer Reports *in England, rated the following British sights.*

BEST VALUE: *Brighton Pavilion*

GOOD VALUE: *Roman Baths (Bath), Dover Castle, Edinburgh Castle, Fountains Abbey, Hampton Court*

MODERATE VALUE: *Bodiam Castle, Osborne House, Polesden Lacey*

POOR VALUE: *Tower of London, Stonehenge, St. Paul's, Windsor Castle*

WORST VALUE: *Buckingham Palace*

SOURCE: *Consumer Reports Travel Letter* (November 1995).

PARIS

NEW LIGHT ON THE CITY OF LIGHT

There's lots more to explore than the Eiffel Tower

Francophiles hardly need an excuse to visit Paris. But, in case you do, here's one: inspired largely by the late French president François Mitterrand, the City of Light has been undergoing a facelift over the past few years. The overall result is a more modern and functional appearance, with glass and concrete architecture complementing the classical structures of old. And many of the newest additions have yet to make it into the standard guidebooks. Here native Parisian Annie Cohen-Solal, biographer of Jean-Paul Sartre and a politics professor at New York University, offers a guided tour of some of the newer sights.

THE LOUVRE

Quai du Louvre, 1er Arr. ☛***Metro:*** *Palais-Royal/Musée du Louvre, or Tuileries*

■ When it opened in 1989, the $1.3 billion glass pyramid rising out of the Louvre's courtyard was a subject of great controversy. The structure, designed by I. M. Pei, creates an imposing entryway to a central subterranean court containing ticket services, shops, and food stands. Among the highlights: French sculpture from the Middle Ages to the 19th century, the apartments of Napoleon III, and 200 French paintings from the 15th to early 17th centuries.

INSTITUT DU MONDE ARABE

1 rue des Fossés Saint-Bernard, 12e Arr. ☛***Metro:*** *Jussieu, Cardinal-Lemoine, Sully-Morland*

■ Facing Notre Dame, the institute houses exhibits of Arab-Islamic civilization from the 7th to the 19th centuries. Designed by architect Jean Nouvel, the building resembles a ship. Windows modeled after camera shutters open and close with the sun. The restaurant on the 9th floor offers the best view of Paris.

CITÉ DES SCIENCES ET DE L'INDUSTRIE

Parc de la Villette, 19e Arr. ☛***Metro:*** *Porte de la Villette*

■ This very hands-on science and technology museum has exhibits on communications, environment, health, and astronomy. Children will enjoy the planetarium, hemispherical cinema, and the *Argonaute*, a retired submarine.

BIBLIOTHÈQUE NATIONALE

Quai François Mauriac, 12e Arr. ☛***Metro:*** *Quai de la Gare*

■ France's new national library has four glass towers, each in the L-shape of an open book; it stands on the Left Bank of the Seine, about a mile from Notre Dame. Each tower is separated by a small pine forest; a staircase made from Amazonian hardwood leads down to the river, a quarter of a mile away.

GRANDE ARCHE DE LA DÉFENSE

1 parvis de la Défense. ☛***Metro:*** *RER A: Grande Arche de la Défense*

■ The Arch, also known as "the cube," provides a beautiful view down the newly restored Champs Elysée. It's part of the huge La Défense complex at the city's western edge and the crowning jewel of Mitterrand's legacy.

LA CITÉ DE LA MUSIQUE

221, av. Jean Jaurès, 19e Arr. ☛***Metro:*** *Porte de Pantin*

■ This cultural hall, which opened in 1995, features concerts by some of the city's younger musicians.

OPÉRA NATIONAL DE PARIS BASTILLE

Place de la Bastille, 12e Arr. ☛***Metro:*** *Bastille*

■ Inaugurated in 1989, the building, with its glass facade, provides Paris a famous venue for performances that alternate between dance and opera—all of it lyrical.

EXPERT PICKS

EUROPE'S CHOICEST COUNTRY INNS

Small European hotels with charm and character can be difficult to find through tourist agencies and guides. But Karen Brown has made that her specialty. She has been traveling through Europe for the past 20 years, evaluating small inns, hotels, and bed and breakfasts and publishing 18 discerning guidebooks of her discoveries—all part of Karen Brown's Country Inn *series (Travel Press, ☎ 800–395–0440). Here are some of her choices of the best ones in or near some of the continent's most popular destinations. While not necessarily the most luxurious or the best bargains, the hotels are chosen for their charm and most of them offer excellent value. Prices are approximate and from 1996.*

FRANCE

HÔTEL DES QUARTRE DAUPHINS, *Aix-en-Provence*

■ This small cheerful hotel is located in the old quarter of Aix. The rooms are simply but tastefully decorated with prints and dried flowers. The top rooms with exposed beams have the most character.

$ Double: 326–386 francs
☎ 42.38.16.39
FAX 42.38.60.19

HÔTEL LE HAMEAU, *St. Paul de Vence*

■ A true country inn yet only a five-minute drive from the glitter of Nice and the Riviera. It is a converted farm, nestled amid fruit trees and flower gardens in one of the classic hill-perched villages of the Riviera. According to Brown, it's one of the best values in southeast France.

$ Double: 390–600 francs; Suite: to 750 francs
☎ 93.32.80.24
FAX 93.32.55.75

HÔTEL LIDO, *Paris*

■ This family-run inn is very safe, comfortable, and quiet. Situated right around the block from the elegant Place de la Madeleine, its location cannot be beat. The decor is lovely, with numerous antiques, Oriental rugs, tapesties, and carved-wood paneling.

$ Open all year. Singles from 1,155 francs; Suites: to 1,465 francs
☎ (1) 42.66.27.37
FAX (1) 42.66.61.23

SWITZERLAND

ROTE ROSE, *Reggensberg*

■ This country hotel is located in a medieval walled town 15 miles from Zurich. To stay in comparable quarters in Zurich, according to Brown, would cost three times as much. The Rote Rose is beautifully restored. There is also a fantastic rose garden.

$ Single: 250–300 Sw. francs
☎ (01) 85.31.013,
FAX (01) 85.31.559

HÔTEL LES ARMURES, *Geneva*

■ President Clinton paid a visit here when he was last in town. The Hôtel Les Armures, originally a private residence that dates back to the 17th century, is located in the old quarter of the city. It's a quiet, elegant place with real old-world charm and a very good, reasonably priced restaurant.

$ Double: 380–460 Sw. francs
☎ (022) 310.91.72
FAX (022) 310.98.46

GERMANY

HOTEL MONDIAL, *Berlin*

■ This newly built hotel is a little antiseptic but everything is done very tastefully. The hotel has a darkened glass exterior and an outside shaded sitting area from which you can watch the action along the Kurfürstendamm, Berlin's main shopping street.

$ Double: DM 230–480; Suite: from DM 690
☎ (030) 884110
FAX (030) 88411150)

DOM HOTEL, *Cologne*

■ In the pedestrian square near Cologne's magnificent cathedral, this old-world hotel is characterized by formal public rooms, mar-

■ **EXPERT PICKS**

ble stairways, luxurious bedrooms, and antique furniture. In the spring and summer an outside café offers informal dining right in front of the cathedral.
$ Double: DM 430–730; Suite: DM 1,300
☎ (0221) 20240
FAX (0221) 2024444

SPLENDID HOTEL, *Munich*
■ This hotel is located on the Maximilianstrasse, Munich's most chic street. There is a comfortable salon with antiques and Oriental carpets. The guest rooms have traditional painted armoires and wooden beds.
$ Double: DM 265–325; Suite: DM 450–680
☎ (089) 296606
FAX (089) 2913176

HOTEL ABTEI, *Hamburg*
■ One of the top 25 hotels in Germany, this converted private residence is personally run by an owner who insists on the finest of everything, including fresh flowers throughout, excellent service, and handsome bedroom furnishings. Although not inexpensive, it is one of the best values in Hamburg.
$ Double: DM 350–450; Suite: DM 450–490
☎ (040) 442905
FAX (040) 449820

HOTEL BULOW RESIDENZ, *Dresden*
■ In a baroque building that dates from 1730, this small, elegant hotel is just a short walk from the major museums and historic sites of Dresden. It has a beautiful vine-covered courtyard for breakfast, elegant formal restaurant for dinner, and a cozy small piano bar for aperitifs.
$ Double: DM 440–490; Suite: DM 490–600
☎ 0351–80030
FAX 0351–8003100

AUSTRIA

HOTEL ELEFANT, *Salzburg*
■ A charming, small family-owned inn that has been in the same family for generations. The building is over 700 years old and has served as an inn for 400 years. It is much less expensive than the others in the area.
$ Double: AS 1,390–1,790
☎ 0662–84.3397
FAX 0662–84.01.09.28

ROMISCHER KAISER, *Vienna*
■ Located just off the Kärntnerstrasse, the major commercial street, and only blocks from the opera, this hotel has a rather formal atmosphere, and the service is impeccable. It is expensive but has a great deal of charm.
$ Double: AS 2,150–2,950
☎ (1) 51.27.751
FAX (1) 51.27.75.113

ITALY

HOTEL D'INGHILTERRA, *Rome*
■ Costing less than most other deluxe hotels, this is one of the best small ones in Rome. It is in a very old building, with a superb restaurant and a charming wood-paneled bar. Be sure to ask for one of the rooms with small breakfast terraces, which have wonderful views.
$ Double: Lire 420,000–495,000
☎ (06) 69.981
FAX (06) 69.92.22.43

VILLA BRUNELLA, *Capri*
■ The beach is just down the hillside and the center of town a 10-minute walk away. The views of the island and the ocean from the terraced guest rooms are outstanding.
$ Double: Lire 345,000; Suite: Lire 410,000
☎ (081) 83.70.122.
FAX (081) 83.70.430

HOTEL PIERRE, *Milan*
■ This charming small hotel is located in the historic Sant' Ambrogio district. It is expensive but offers an elegant atmosphere with excellent service. Each room has its own individual decor.
$ Double: Lire 370,000–500,000
☎ (02) 72.00.05.81
FAX (02) 80.52.157

HOTEL LOGGIATO DEI SERVITI, *Florence*
■ A fabulous value in a city where hotels are either outrageously priced or inexpensive and dreary. The hotel is situated on an

■ **EXPERT PICKS**

arcaded square and occupies a building that dates to the 16th century. Although not deluxe, it provides excellent accommodations and service. It is run by an attentive owner who has filled the hotel with lovely antiques. Everything is white, bright, and cheerful.
$ Double: from Lire 240,000
☎ (055) 21.91.65
FAX (055) 28.95.95

SPAIN

HOTEL COLON, *Barcelona*

■ This hotel is fairly large and replete with an old-world atmosphere. It is located in the Barrio Gothico, the section of the city that dates from medieval times. The rooms have high ceilings; some are terraced and face the city's most famous cathedral.
$ Double: Ptas 25,885–41,045
☎ (3) 30.11.404
FAX (3) 31.72.915

TABERNA DEL ALABARDERO, *Seville*

■ This small seven-room hotel is one of the best buys in Spain. Only a short walk from Seville's cathedral, the hotel is operated by one of the most famous restaurants in town, which takes up most of this historic three-floor converted house. The hotel rooms are located on the top two floors around an iron-railed gallery beneath a skylight.
$ Double: Ptas 15,000
☎ (5) 45.60.637
FAX (5) 45.63.666

HOTEL DESTINY VILLA REAL, *Madrid*

■ This well-run antique-filled hotel is one of the best-value luxury hotels in Madrid. The hotel has an old-world ambience and an attentive staff. The rooms are plush, large, and most have balconies facing onto a small plaza in the middle of Madrid's famous triangle near the Prado Museum.
$ Double: from Ptas 34,400
☎ (1) 42.03.767
FAX (1) 42.02.547

IRELAND

HIBERNIAN HOTEL, *Dublin*

■ A large brick building that was once a nurses' residence is now one of Dublin's most outstanding hotels. It is very comfortable, with a well-appointed library and drawing room. The bedrooms are well equipped with everything, including fax modem connections. A 10-minute walk from St. Stephens Green.
$ Double: £135–160
☎ (01) 6687666
FAX (01) 6602655

OAKHILL HOUSE, *Belfast*

■ This large Victorian house with its landscaped gardens is an elegant, comfortable home whose owner rents out rooms. Guests have the run of the house and the owner makes hearty dinners for those guests who prefer to eat in.
$ Double: from £70
☎ (01232) 610658
FAX (01232) 621566

ENGLAND

THE STAFFORD, *London*

■ The Stafford is conveniently situated just a few blocks from Picadilly Circus.The atmosphere is that of an old-fashioned gentlemen's club with comfortable sitting areas, a small bar, and an excellent dining room. The best deluxe bedrooms are in the carriage house, a converted 350-year-old stable.
$ Double: from £240; Suite: from £416
☎ (071) 4930111
FAX (0122) 50446065

OLD PARSONAGE HOTEL, *Oxford*

■ A wisteria-covered building that dates from 1660. The rooms are small and the floors uneven, but the place really feels like Merry Olde England, albeit with TVs and phones. The largest bedrooms are in the original house.
$ Double: from £140; Suite: from £180
☎ (01865) 310210
FAX (01865) 311262

THE QUEENSBERRY HOTEL, *Bath*

■ This simple but very attractive hotel is a bargain. It is a converted mansion, and many of the rooms have high ceilings and ornate moldings. There is also an excellent restaurant on the premises.
$ Double: from £102
☎ (01225) 447928
FAX (01335) 44065

VILLA RENTER'S GUIDE

PALACES THAT COULD BE YOURS

The best way to save money on a vacation rental home is to bypass the middleman. You can save 20 to 30 percent by renting directly through the owner. Options include writing the local tourist board or looking through the classified sections of college alumni magazines. Rental agencies, on the other hand, offer the convenience of an experienced pro minding the details. Some resources:

RENTAL AGENCIES

If you use a rental agency, it's wise to choose one with a local agent based near the town in which you intend to rent. That way, you'll have someone to contact in case anything goes wrong.

AT HOME ABROAD
New York, New York
■ Caters to an upscale market. Rates from $3,500 to $50,000 per month, although many of their Caribbean and Mexican villas also are available by the week. Requires a $20 registration fee.
☎ 212-421-9165

BARCLAY INTERNATIONAL
New York, New York
■ Specializes in apartment and villa rentals in most of the major cities around the world. Properties include flats in some luxury hotels. Catalogs are available.
☎ 800-845-6636
(New York State residents: 212-832-3777)

BRITISH TRAVEL INTERNATIONAL
Elkton, Virginia
■ Properties in France, England, Spain, Portugal, and Italy. A color catalog is available for a small fee.
☎ 800-327-6097

CREATIVE LEISURE INTERNATIONAL
Petaluma, California
■ Properties primarily in Hawaii, the Caribbean, and Mexico. Will arrange everything from airfare to baby-sitting.
☎ 800-426-6367

EUROPA LET
Ashland, Oregon
■ Listings in Europe, Mexico, Hawaii, the Caribbean, and the Pacific Islands. A good choice for sailors seeking seaside homes. There is a $25 booking fee.
☎ 800-462-4486

HOMES AWAY
Toronto, Canada
■ A relatively new branch of Butterfield and Robinson, which is well known for organizing hiking and biking trips; offers houses not usually for rent—an old silk farm, for example.
☎ 800-374-6637

INTERHOME
Fairfield, New Jersey
■ In its 31st year and with over 20,000 listings, Interhome is one of the oldest and largest home rental agencies in the world. Rentals in Europe only.
☎ 201-882-6864

RENT A HOME INTERNATIONAL
Seattle, Washington
■ Listings in Europe, Australia, the Caribbean, Mexico, the U.S., and Canada. Prices from $600 to $25,000 per week. Information on its properties is not very detailed. Several catalogs are available for $15.
☎ 206-789-9377

VILLAS INTERNATIONAL LTD
San Francisco, California
■ Listings include a villa on Phuket Island in Thailand that costs from $1,200 to $1,600 per week, but they specialize in properties in Europe and the Caribbean.
☎ 800-221-2260

RENTER'S LIST HOME EXCHANGE

An economical way to take a vacation. Usually there is a listing fee, but other arrangements are left to the homeowners.

INTERVAC
■ International and domestic listings.
☎ 800-756-4663

VACATION EXCHANGE CLUB
Key West, Florida
■ The club offers a free information package. A

■ VILLA RENTER'S GUIDE

directory of rental listings is available for $78.
☎ 800-638-3841

RENTING BY COUNTRY

Renting through an institution abroad can be challenging. But it also can save you money.

DENMARK

■ **SCANDINAVIA DANCENTER:** Offers Danish rentals only. Material is written in German and Danish.
✏ Sotorvet 5, DK 1371. Copenhagen, Denmark
☎ 45-3333-0102

■ **SCANAM WORLD TOURS:** Rents throughout Scandinavia.
✏ 933 Highway 23, Pompton Plains, NJ 07444.
☎ 800-545-2204

ENGLAND

■ **LANDMARK TRUST:** A charitable trust that preserves everything from medieval halls to concrete bunkers by restoring them and renting them to vacationers. Prices during high season range from $320 per week for simple two-person accommodations to $2, 200 for a manor hall with accommodations for 15. A catalog of all 160 properties costs $19.95.
✏ RR1, Box 510, Brattleboro, VT 05301
☎ 802-254-6868

■ **NATIONAL TRUST HOLIDAY BOOKING OFFICE:** Determined travelers can find real bargains at this branch of the

National Trust. From July through August, prices range from $300 to $1,200 per week, mostly for old cottages. At other times of the year renters can save as much as two-thirds off these prices. Write to the address below or call the Royal Oak Foundation, a sister organization in New York (☎ 212-966-6565) for the $5 brochure of properties.
✏ PO Box 536, Melksham, Wiltshire, England SN128SX

FRANCE

■ **FEDERATION NATIONALE DES GITES RURAUX DE FRANCE:** A nonprofit institution that preserves old country houses and promotes tourism in rural areas. The network consists of over 50,000 houses and modest apartments, or gites.
✏ 35 Godot de Mauroy, 75009 Paris, France
☎ (011-33-1) 49-70-75-75

■ **THE FRENCH EXPERIENCE:** Rents more upscale French gites. In the high season, July and August, prices range from $400 to $750 per week. It also handles about 50 small hotels, as well as short-term rentals.
✏ 370 Lexington Ave., New York, NY 10017
☎ 212-986-1115

GERMANY

■ **RING DEUTSCHER MAKLER:** A private association of German rental agencies. All of the reputable rental agencies are registered with it.
✏ Mönckebergstrasse 27, D-2 0095, Hamburg, Germany
☎ 011-49-40-331210

ITALY

■ **GRAND LUXE INTERNATIONAL:** Full-service rental agency that lists villas, castles, farmhouses, and apartments all over Italy. A catalog costs $18.50.
✏ 165 Chestnut St., Allendale, NJ 07401
☎ 201-327-2333

SCOTLAND

■ **NATIONAL TRUST SCOTLAND:** This is the Scottish equivalent of the National Trust in England.
✏ 5 Charlotte Square, Edinburgh, Scotland EH2 4DU,
☎ 011-44-31-243-9331

SWEDEN

■ **VARMLAND TOURIST BOARD:** Specializes in rentals around several of the lakes in Sweden's Lake District.
✏ Sodra Kyrkogatan 10, S-651 08 Karlstad, Sweden
☎ 46-54-102160

■ **SWEDISH TRAVEL & TOURISM COUNCIL:** A resource for rentals all over Sweden.
✏ PO Box 4649, Grand Central Station, New York, NY 10163
☎ 212-949-2333

BARGAINS

SPOTS TO SHOP 'TIL YOU DROP

A traveler's guide to great bargains round the world

Inveterate shoppers have a knack for finding the best buys, no matter where they are. But true shopaholics might want to plan their next travel itinerary around the global retail calendar. The following are some of the best seasonal sales worldwide, from *Travel & Leisure* magazine.

■ **PARIS:** Lines start forming early in the morning at the twice yearly sale at Hermès (24 Rue du Faubourg-St. Honoré; ☎ 33–1/40–17–48–10; held in June and January), where shoppers can buy the designer's famously expensive silk and leather accessories at up to 50 percent off. Some of the offerings are discontinued styles, others have minor flaws.

■ **LONDON:** Several hundred thousand patrons appear for the first day of Harrods' semiannual sale (Knightsbridge; ☎ 44–171–730–1234; held mid-July and in January). Among the deals: half-price reductions on women's fashions, furnishings, and Oriental carpets, and 30 percent discounts on accessories.

■ **HONG KONG:** The semiannual sale at Joyce (202 The Landmark; ☎ 852/2525–3655; and the Galleria, 9 Queen's Road, Central; ☎ 852/2810–1120; in July and January) offers bargains on leading fashion designers, including Karl Lagerfeld, Issey Miyake, Dolce & Gabbana, and Calvin Klein—at up to 30 percent off.

■ **ROME:** Fendi (36-40 Via Borgognona, ☎ 39–6/679–7641; and 76 Via Piave; Rome, ☎ 39–6/486–868; July and January) offers an array of the store's famous leather goods, furs, and men's and women's apparel discounted up to 50 percent.

■ **CHICAGO:** In early December, the School of the Art Institute of Chicago (112 S. Michigan Ave.; Student Union Office; ☎ 312–345–3589) offers for sale original paintings, sculpture, ceramics, photographs, and textiles—most items costing under $50. Admission is free.

■ **NEW DELHI:** Asia's largest handicrafts bazaar, the Indian Handicrafts & Gifts Fair (Pragati Maidan; ☎ 91–11/600–871 or 91–11/687–5377, FAX 91–11/606–144; end of January) is geared primarily to wholesalers and retailers, but the enterprising individual shopper can also revel in the 215,000-square-foot fair that includes woodcrafts, textiles, fashion jewelry, carved stone, papier-mâché, musical instruments, and more. Prices are slightly higher than open markets, but the selection makes this sale well worth the trip.

■ **BANGKOK:** If you love baubles, go to the annual Bangkok Gems & Jewelry Fair (Queen Sirikit National Convention Center, 60 New Rajadapisek Rd., Klong Toey; call the Thai Trade Center in New York, ☎ 212–466–1777; held in March). As the world's leading producer of rubies and sapphires, and the second-largest manufacturer of jewelry, Thailand offers low to moderate prices even for top-of-the-line goods. Loose stones are a special value.

■ **NEW YORK CITY:** Bibliophiles can rejoice at the New York Book Fair (Seventh Regiment Armory, 643 Park Avenue; contact Sanford L. Smith & Associates, ☎ 212–777–5218; held in April), where first-edition, out-of-print, and rare books are still reasonable, and the people-watching opportunities are first-rate.

■ **LOIRE VALLEY:** Antique-lovers will rejoice in the two-day auction held at the 17th-century Château de Cheverny (contact Flore de Brantes, Château du Fresne, Authon, France; ☎ 33–54/80–33–04, FAX 33–54/80–34–41; held in May). Organized by the daughter of an American marquise, this auction of local families' superfluous heirlooms also offers the chance to mingle with celebrities such as Mick Jagger and Jerry Hall, who own a nearby château.

SOURCE: Jennifer Farley, *Travel & Leisure*, June 1995.

DINER'S GUIDE

TEN TOP TONGUES' TASTES OF CHOICE

It's a big country with food that's getting better all the time, so coming up with the best restaurants in America could be a daunting task. We tackled it by asking the food critics in 10 cities their favorites. Prices listed are for dinner.

RESTAURANT ▸ Address ☎ **Phone** ✦ Cuisine $ **Prices** ✍ *Critic's comment*

■ **ATLANTA:** *Christiane Lauterbach, the dining critic for* Atlanta *magazine, suggests some of the finer places to dine.*

BRASSERIE LE COZE ▸ 3393 Peachtree Rd., Lenox Square Mall ☎ **404-266-1440** ✦ French Bistro $ **Entrees $10 to $20**
✍ *Best French restaurant in town; authentic, unpretentious food.*

BUCKHEAD DINER ▸ 3073 Piedmont Rd. ☎ **404-266-1440** ✦ American $ **Entrees $7.50 to $17.50**
✍ *The glamour spot of the Big Peach, creative American cuisine coupled with visiting celebrities such as Elton John.*

THE DINING ROOM ▸ 3434 Peachtree Rd. NE ☎ **404-237-2700** ✦ Creative continental $ **Prix Fixe, $56, $80 w/ wine.**
✍ *The best restaurant in Atlanta; renowned chef Gunter Seeger creates daring and fresh seasonal cuisine.*

CANOE ▸ 4199 Paces Ferry Road, NW ☎ **770-43CANOE** ✦ American $ **Entrees $13 to $18**
✍ *Creative American cuisine in a glamorous location on the Chattahoochee River.*

THE HORSERADISH GRILL ▸ 4320 Powers Ferry Rd. ☎ **404-255-7277** ✦ Southern $ **Entrees $8.95 to $18.95**
✍ *Traditional southern cooking translated for the modern world.*

■ **BOSTON:** *Mat Schaffer, the restaurant critic for* Boston *magazine, makes his picks.*

GRILL 23 & BAR ▸ 161 Berkeley St. ☎ **617-542-2255** ✦ American $ **Entrees $18 to $28**
✍ *Classic steakhouse fare elevated by Chef Robert Fathman's signature specials, like roast pork with apple, apricot, and sun-dried cranberry stuffing, or seared tuna with sesame-ginger glaze.*

CARL'S PAGODA ▸ 23 Tyler St. ☎ **617-357-9837** ✦ Chinese $ **Entrees $4.75 to $17.95**
✍ *Don't ask for a menu. Bring your own wine and order the tomato soup, steamed sea bass, Hong Kong–style steak, and Carl's special rice.*

GALLERIA ITALIANA ▸ 177 Tremont St. ☎ **617-423-2092** ✦ Regional Italian $ **Entrees $14 to $19.50**
✍ *Chef Barbara Lynch makes exceptional northern Italian food with an Abruzzian influence. Ask the sommelier to pour you a glass of vino in Miss Kitty's salon, a cozy wine/antipasti bar at the front of the restaurant.*

HAMERSLEY'S BISTRO ▸ 553 Tremont St. ☎ **617-423-2700** ✦ French Provençal $ **Entrees $19 to $28**
✍ *Simple but sophisticated Provençal cuisine. Look for Chef Gordon Hamersley in the Red Sox baseball cap.*

ROWES WHARF RESTAURANT ▸ 70 Rowes Wharf ☎ **617-439-3995** ✦ New England $ **Entrees $18 to $35**
✍ *Exceptional cuisine well worth the price. Chef Daniel Bruce hooks, forages, hunts and grows many of his ingredients. Don't miss the wild mushrooms on stone-ground polenta, or the Maine lobster fricassee with corn pudding.*

■ **CHICAGO:** *Phil Vitell, restaurant critic for the* Chicago Tribune, *picked the first three; Bill Rice, the* Tribune*'s food and wine columnist, picked the second two.*

ARUNS ▸ 4156 N. Kedzie Ave. ☎ **312-539-1909** ✦ Thai $ **Entrees $13.95 to $23.95**
✍ *A beautiful dining room with museum-quality art is combined with culinary excellence.*

EVEREST ▸ 440 South La Salle St. ☎ **312-663-8920** ✦ French $ **Entrees $28 to $32**
✍ *Located on the 40th floor of a building. Try the pork cheeks with lentils.*

TOPOLOBAMPO FRONTERA GRILL ▸ 445 N. Clark St. ☎ **312-661-1434** ✦ Mexican $ **Entrees $14 to $21, Grill, $8 to $17**
✍ *Two restaurants in one space, Topolobampo is a smaller, more upscale dining room, while Frontera is more crowded and casual. Both offer unsurpassed regional Mexican food.*

CHARLIE TROTTER'S ▸ 816 W. Armitage ☎ **312-248-6228** ✦ New American $ **Entrees $68 and up**
✍ *A temple of gastronomy. Many culinary influences. Elegant and very expensive.*

SPIAGGIA ▸ 980 N. Michigan Ave. ☎ **312-280-2750** ✦ Italian $ **Entrees $25 to $30**
✍ *Elegant dining room with view of Lake Michigan. Chef Paul Bartolota prepares high-level, pure Italian dishes with top-quality ingredients, some of which are flown in from Italy.*

■ **DINER'S GUIDE**

■ **DALLAS:** Dallas Morning News *lifestyles editor Dotty Griffith's favorites are less upscale than the renowned Mansion at Turtle Creek, and a little more off the beaten path.*

CITY CAFE ▸ 5757 W. Lovers Lane ☎ **214-351-2233** ✦ Regional American $ **Entrees $13 to $19**
✍ *Seasonally based, creative food with a menu that changes every two weeks.*

MATT'S RANCHO MARTINEZ ▸ Lakewood Plaza, 6312 La Vista Dr. ☎ **214-823-5517** ✦ Tex-Mex $ **Entrees $7.25 to $15.75**
✍ *Stupendous chiles rellenos.*

THE PALM RESTAURANT ▸ 701 Ross Ave. at Market ☎ **214-698-0470** ✦ American $ **Entrees $14 to $25**
✍ *Steaks, lobsters, and the beautiful people crowd.*

STAR CANYON ▸ 3102 Oaklawn Ave., Suite 144 ☎ **214-520-7827** ✦ New Texas $ **Entrees $14 to $23**
✍ *Sophisticated food with Texas roots. Favorite dish: chilled shrimp and jicama soup with fresh buttermilk and basil.*

MIPIACI ▸ 14854 Montfort Dr. ☎ **214-934-8424** ✦ Northern Italian $ **Entrees $20 and up**
✍ *Lots of fresh pasta and fresh herbs (they grow their own on the roof).*

■ **LOS ANGELES:** *Irene Virbila, the restaurant editor for the* Los Angeles Times, *made picks that varied as much in style as they did in price—from under $10 all the way up to $300.*

THE BAR BISTRO AT CITRUS ▸ 6703 Melrose Ave. ☎ **213-857-0034** ✦ French $ **Entrees $9.50 to $17.50**
✍ *French comfort food from the same kitchen as Michel Richard's French-California flagship, Citrus.*

CAMPANILE ▸ 624 S. La Brea Blvd. ☎ **213-938-1447** ✦ California-Mediterranean $ **Entrees $15 to $26**
✍ *Great breakfasts and lunches. At dinner try the flattened grilled chicken with parsley salad or bistecca fiorentina.*

CHINOIS ON MAIN ▸ 2709 Main St., Santa Monica ☎ **310-329-9025** ✦ East-West fusion $ **Entrees $19 to $29**
✍ *Wolfgang Puck's—the creator of L.A. restaurant/institution, Spago—best restaurant yet.*

GINZA SUSHI-KO ▸ 218 N. Rodeo Dr., Beverly Hills ☎ **310-247-8939** ✦ Japanese $ Entrees **$200 to $300**
✍ *The most expensive restaurant in Los Angeles, this exquisite little sushi bar has the fish flown in daily from Japan.*

VALENTINO ▸ 3115 Pico Boulevard, Santa Monica ☎ **310-829-4313** ✦ Italian $ **Entrees $18 to $25**
✍ *Possibly the best Northern Italian restaurant in North America. Instead of ordering from the menu, ask chef Piero Selvaggio to prepare a series of small courses.*

■ **MIAMI:** *Not just for retirees anymore, Miami these days is hot, filled with celebrities and great restaurants. Geoffrey Tomb, a restaurant critic at* The Miami Herald, *surveys the scene.*

CHEF ALLEN'S RESTAURANT ▸ 19088 N.E. 29th Ave., Miami Beach ☎ **305-935-2900** ✦ Fusion-American $ **Entrees $22.95 to $29.95**
✍ *Don't miss the 16-ounce veal chop with double mustard sauce, wild-mushroom risotto, and ginger-flavored calabaza.*

EAST COAST FISHERIES ▸ 300 West Flagler St., Miami ☎ **305-577-3000** ✦ American $ **Entrees $9 to $49**
✍ *Very fresh fish served in indigenous old riverside fish house off the beaten track.*

LE SANDWICHERIE ▸ 229 14th St., Miami Beach ☎ **305-532-8934** ✦ Casual fare $ **Entrees $5 to $10**
✍ *Open till 5 a.m. on weekends, this sidewalk joint is as likely to serve people in tuxedos as cabdrivers.*

OSTERIA DEL TEATRO ▸ 1443 Washington Ave., Miami Beach ☎ **305-538-7850** ✦ Italian $ **$14 to $24**
✍ *Excellent Italian food and maybe the best restaurant in town. Emphasis is on seafood.*

THE RALEIGH RESTAURANT ▸ 1775 Collins Ave., Miami Beach ☎ **305-534-1775** ✦ Creative American $ **Entrees $9 to $19**
✍ *A 1940s gem; the ghost of Esther Williams lives here. Sit outside and order the warm goat cheese–potato cakes.*

■ **NEW YORK:** *Five restaurants, impossible! That was Florence Fabricant, a food and restaurant columnist for* The New York Times. *We let her cheat a little.*

C.T. ▸ 111 East 22nd Street ☎ **212-995-8500** ✦ Fusion French $ **Entrees $19.50 to $26.50**
✍ *The food here reflects chef Claude Proistros's great French heritage intertwined with the vibrancy of his 10 years in Brazil—all in a fun, relaxed atmosphere.*

GOTHAM BAR AND GRILL ▸ 12 E. 12th St. ☎ **212-620-4020** ✦ American $ **Entrees $10 to $32**
✍ *The finesse of Alfred Portale's food arranged in breathtaking pinnacles matches the celebratory, high-ceilinged space in which it is so deftly served.*

■ **DINER'S GUIDE**

LE BERNARDIN ▸ 155 W. 51st St. ☎ **212-489-1515** ✦ French $ **Entrees $68**

The ultimate in seafood in the hands of chef Eric Ripert is as sublime as ever, witness truffled sea scallops and foie gras in cabbage.

LE CIRQUE ▸ 58 E. 65th St. ☎ **212-794-9292** ✦ French $ **Entrees $22 to $32**

A wondrous restaurant, tiny copper casseroles with exotic mushrooms, a simple bouquet of vegetables bathed in olive oil, and heady lobster risotto.

NOBU ▸ 105 Hudson St. ☎ **212-219-0500** ✦ Fusion $ **Dinner $45 to $50**

The most inventively delicious food in town: Deep-fried kelp adorns roasted lobster nuggets or caviar on seared tuna.

REMI ▸ 145 W. 53rd St. ☎ **212-581-4242** ✦ Italian $ **Entrees $15 to $28**

Francesco Antonucci unerringly commands pasta, risotto, foie gras, anchovies, duck, salmon, and zabaglione.

■ **SAN FRANCISCO:** *The challenge to good eating is the transient nature of restaurants in San Francisco, says Michael Bauer, the* San Francisco Chronicle*'s restaurant critic. His picks:*

THE FRENCH LAUNDRY ▸ 6040 Washington St., Yountville ☎ **707-944-2380** ✦ French $ **Prix Fixe $49**

The $49 menu includes five courses, all reminiscent of a three-star country restaurant in France.

FRINGALE ▸ 570 Fourth St. at Bryant ☎ **415-543-0573** ✦ French $ **Entrees $10 to $15**

The best casual French restaurant in San Francisco; don't miss the mussels flecked with parsley and fried garlic.

MASAS ▸ 648 Bush St. ☎ **415-989-7154** ✦ French $ **Prix Fixe $68 to $75**

A great special-occasion restaurant with a four- to six-course classic French menu.

YANK SING ▸ 427 Battery St. ☎ **415-781-1111** ✦ Chinese $ **Entrees $10 to $15**

Unparalleled dim sum, minced squab in crunchy lettuce cups, and Peking duck with sweet, doughy buns.

ZUNI CAFE ▸ 1658 Market ☎ **415-552-2522** ✦ American $ **Entrees $10 to $28**

Great people-watching and casual food. Signature dishes: chicken with bread salad and hamburger on focaccia.

■ **SEATTLE.** *Tom Sietsema, the food and restaurant critic for the* Seattle Post-Intelligencer, *defines his favorite restaurants by the ones he returns to over and over again. His regulars:*

CAFE CAMPAGNE ▸ 1600 Post Alley ☎ **206-728-2233** ✦ French $ **Entrees $6.95 to $14.95**

A fantastic, gourmet meal-to-go place with a tiny bar serving samplings of upscale wine and appetizers.

LAMPREIA ▸ 2400 First Ave. ☎ **206-443-3301** ✦ American $ **Entrees $19 to $22**

A luxurious and seasonal menu; opt for the cheese course after dinner, which includes handcrafted local samples.

MACRINA BAKERY ▸ 2408 First Ave. ☎ **206-448-4032** ✦ American $ **Entrees $8 to $20**

The bakery is well known for its rustic loaves and European coffee cakes, but the witty little café adjoining the bakery also turns out excellent lunches and dinners.

PIROSMANI ▸ 2220 Queen Ann Ave. ☎ **206-285-3360** ✦ Georgian $ **Entrees $16 to $22**

Inspired food from the Republic of Georgia, which also embraces the sunny flavors of the Mediterranean.

THE HERB FARM ▸ 32804 Southeast Issaquah–Fall City Rd., Fall City ☎ **206-784-2222** ✦ Regional $ **Prix Fixe $115**

An extraordinary restaurant 30 minutes east of Seattle. The prix fixe price includes nine herb-infused courses.

■ **WASHINGTON:** *Phyllis Richmond, the food critic for* The Washington Post, *recommends:*

GALILEO ▸ 1110 21st St., NW ☎ **202-293-7191** ✦ Italian $ **Entrees $18 to $28**

Chef Roberto Donna's pappardelle and risotto with first-of-the-season alba truffles are famous.

GERARD'S PLACE ▸ 915 15th St., NW ☎ **202-737-4445** ✦ French $ **Five-course special $55**

Chef Gerard Pangaud cooks simple dishes of great sophistication. Try his lobster with a ginger-lime sauce.

INN AT LITTLE WASHINGTON ▸ Middle & Main St., Washington, Va. ☎ **703-675-3800** ✦ New American $ **Full course $78 to $98**

Self-taught American chef Patrick O'Connell coaxes wonders out of local ingredients such as Virginia ham, Chesapeake Bay crabs, berries, and herbs. A bit of a drive from the District.

GKINKEAD'S ▸ 2000 Pennsylvannia Ave., NW ☎ **202-296-7700** ✦ American $ **Entrees $14.50 to $24**

Regional seafood shines here in an informal and energetic atmosphere.

OBELISK ▸ 2029 P St., NW ☎ **202-872-1180** ✦ Italian $ **Prix Fixe $38**

A tiny restaurant that personifies Italian simplicity—excellent wine and grappa.

HONEYMOONER'S GUIDE

WHERE ROMEOS CAN TAKE JULIETS

Marriage is a great adventure. Here are some places to start the journey. The editors of Honeymoon Magazine *offer their top picks for the most unusual honeymoon spots from their upcoming honeymoon encyclopedia.*

AMAZON RAIN FOREST
Ecuador

❤ Visit Vilcabamba, Ecuador, otherwise known as the "Valley of the Elders," with its astonishing number of centenarians. Take a cruise to the Galápagos Islands to view the interesting wildlife there. Best place to stay: Hacienda Cusin, in Otavalo.

BANFF SPRINGS
Canadian Rockies

❤ The Banff Springs Hotel in Alberta has been a vacation mecca since it opened in 1888. There are majestic mountains, glacial lakes, and other breathtaking scenery. The hotel has a new addition, the Solace, a 35,000-square-foot spa and fitness center.

CHICHÉN ITZÁ
Yucatan Peninsula, Mexico

❤ Just a couple of hours drive from Cancún, all that remains of this former Mayan ceremonial city are centuries-old ruins, including a pool where virgins were once sacrificed. (For more about Mayan ruins, see page 452.) Visitors can climb to the top of one of the towering temples. Bordering the ruins, the Mayaland Hotel (☎ 800–235–4079) is a lush tropical hideaway with a local mariachi band.

GREAT BARRIER REEF
Australia

❤ This is the longest barrier reef on earth, teeming with tropical fish, colorful coral, giant clams, and large marine animals. For day trips or deluxe live-aboard boats, call Taka Dive ☎ 800–241–7690.

VOLCANOES NATIONAL PARK
Hawaii

❤ By day, hike together through the mists surrounding the volcanoes. At night, watch fountains of lava shooting up from the earth. A helicopter tour gives great views. The most unusual hotel in Hawaii is Kona Village (☎ 800–325–5555), in Kailua-Kona, featuring thatch-roofed cottages. (For more about Hawaii, see page 444.)

THE LION'S CITY
Singapore

❤ You can stay at the beautifully renovated Raffles Hotel and visit Sentosa, a theme-park island with a beach, an aquarium, and a model Asian village.

REVENTAZON RIVER
Costa Rica

❤ There's good rafting on the Reventazon River. You can hike around the Poas Volcano or visit a butterfly farm. The Casa Turire (☎ 503–531–1111), a Spanish-style hacienda located in the middle of a coffee and macadamia nut plantation, is a nice place to stay.

"STINGRAY CITY"
Grand Cayman Island

❤ This is a "must dive," according to *Skin Diver* magazine. The water is quite shallow, so the stingrays can be fed by snorkelers. (For more information about the Cayman Islands, see page 455.)

YUCATÁN PENINSULA
Belize

❤ The world's second-largest barrier reef lies just off the Peninsula. It's worth taking in the famous blue hole, a 480-foot-deep limestone sinkhole, with giant stalactites in an ancient cavern. Call Lighthouse Reef ☎ 800–423–3114.

CRYSTAL CAVES
Bermuda

❤ Wonderful diving and snorkeling, beautiful pink-sand beaches and fantastic limestone caves. For romantic luxury, stay at Grotto Bay Beach Hotel & Tennis Club (☎ 800–582–3190).

CONTEMPLATOR'S GUIDE

GET THEE TO A MONASTERY

St. Benedict (the founder of Western monasticism) made it a tenet that guests should be received "as Christ himself." Ronald Regalbuto, author of A Guide to Monastic Guest Houses *(Morehouse, 1992), has been visiting monasteries since he was in prep school. The rooms are usually spare; but the surroundings are often quite splendid. (Costs for a day of room and board run $20 to $40 per person at many of the monasteries.) A guest must be ready to abide by certain customs. Usually monasteries impose periods of quiet and often some of the ceremonies and parts of the compounds are off-limits to visitors. Here's Regalbuto's favorites:*

THE RETREAT HOUSE
Camaldolese monks (Roman Catholic)

† Located on 500 acres in the St. Lucia mountains with great views of the Pacific. The monks here practice the hermetical life.
Big Sur, CA 93292
☎ 408–667–2456

INCARNATION PRIORY
Order of the Holy Cross (Episcopal) and Camaldolese Benedictine monks (Roman Catholic)

† The only joint Anglican and Roman Catholic venture in the world. The monastery is mostly empty during the day.
Berkeley, CA 94709
☎ 510–548–3406 Episcopal
☎ 510–548–0965 Catholic

HOLY CROSS ABBEY
Benedictine monks (Roman Catholic)

† The Gothic revival buildings of this monastery have been placed on the National Register of Historic Places.
Canon City, CO 81212
☎ 719–275–8631

ST. AUGUSTINE'S HOUSE

† Located outside Detroit, with beautiful views, this is the only Lutheran monastery in the United States.
Oxford, MI 48371
☎ 810–628–5155

SAINT LEO ABBEY
Benedictine monks (Roman Catholic)

† Distinguished by a 2100-pound marble crucifix at the center of the sanctuary, the monastery is situated on a lakefront in the Florida countryside.
Saint Leo, FL 33574
☎ 352–588–2881

SKETE OF SAINT SERAPHIM
Synod of Bishops of the Russian Orthodox Church in Exile

† This monastery was once an ordinary suburban home. The traditional service combined with the incense and vestments make this one of the most impressive Russian Orthodox liturgies outside of Russia.
Minneapolis, MN 55432
☎ 612–574–1001

THE COMMON
Discalced Carmelite Friars (Roman Catholic)

† A beautiful old summer residence built in a traditional Gothic style. Nearby is Mount Modnadnock, the second most-climbed mountain in the United States.
Peterborough, NH 03458
☎ 603–924–6060

SAINT HILDA'S HOUSE
Community of the Holy Spirit (Episcopal)

† This convent is located in Manhattan. Some of the sisters are craftswomen who merchandise their work.
New York, NY 10025
☎ 212–666–8249

WESTON PRIORY
Benedictine monks (Roman Catholic)

† Located in a beautiful village, Weston Priory is well known for its crafts and music.
Weston, VT 05161
☎ 802–824–5409

SABBATHDAY LAKE SHAKER COMMUNITY
United Society of Shakers

† The only Shaker community left in the world. The meetinghouse, built in 1794, is largely untouched.
Poland Spring, ME 04274
☎ 207–926–4597

NATURAL TREASURES

NATIONAL PARKS: The 10 most popular, PAGE 484 **EXPERT SOURCES:** The best guides—in print and online—to the parks, PAGE 495 **CONSERVATION:** Imperiled wild places, PAGE 496 **LODGING:** Where to find a cozy cabin in the woods, PAGE 498 **WILDLIFE:** Best spots to see a manatee and other creatures, PAGE 500 **TRAILS:** Following historic pathways across the nation, PAGE 502 **DRIVES:** A fall foliage guide for leaf-peepers, PAGE 508

NATIONAL PARKS

WHERE THE CROWDS AREN'T

Places you've never heard of are just as beautiful as Yellowstone

Getting away from it all is getting more difficult all the time in America's national parks. Increasingly, people are running into the same urban ills that they are trying to escape: traffic jams, pollution, and even crime. While most people go for the blockbusters such as Yellowstone and Grand Canyon, there are parks just as magnificent and just as resource-rich with significantly fewer visitors. These lesser-known parks in many cases lie farther from population centers or just don't yet have local T-shirt and calendar industries.

There's a strong argument to be made that the undervisited reserves are the way national parks are meant to be. Without the car horns and camera-toting tourists, they better preserve that sense of yesteryear—and besides, you can grab a campsite at the last minute, instead of having to reserve a year in advance.

Noted National Park expert Yale history professor and environmental chair Robin Winks once sleuthed some important national secrets in a book called *Cloak and Gown*, about the CIA's involvement on college campuses. Here, Winks puts his formidable abilities to decidedly more pleasurable national secrets—the lesser-known national parks (see his choice list below). No armchair intellectual, Winks did his homework for two new books by visiting all 369 units in the National Park System. The first, *The Rise of the National Park Ethic* (Yale University Press, 1996), is a history of the National Park system. The second book will be a hard-nosed guide that describes all 369 units in the National Park system and rates them according to the quality of visitor experience.

CUMBERLAND ISLAND NATIONAL SEASHORE

40,743 visitors per year ☛ *33,900 acres*
Nearest big town: Accessible via the National Park Service ferry, from St. Mary's, Ga., 95 miles from Savannah

■ Cumberland Island, the largest of Georgia's Atlantic barrier islands, is also the most unspoiled. The southernmost of Georgia's Golden Isles, it has magnificent beaches, dunes, maritime forests, salt marshes, and a number of old estates, as well as raccoon, deer, and loggerhead turtles. The island can be reached only by ferry. Accommodations are available in five campsites on the island.

✉ PO Box 806, St. Mary's, GA 31558–0806
☎ 912–882–4336

THE BIGGEST PARK IN THE LOWER 48

Adirondack State Park is the size of Yosemite and Yellowstone combined

While the Northeast can lay claim to only one national park and one of the smallest at that—Acadia in Maine—outdoor enthusiasts really have nothing to complain about. Sprawling over the northeastern part of New York State is Adirondack State Park. Roughly the size of Yellowstone and Yosemite combined, and larger than either the states of Massachusetts or New Jersey, it is the largest protected landmass in the lower 48 states. The park is a unique blend of public and private land—43 percent is state-owned, while development on the remaining privately owned 3.7 million acres (much of which is accessible to the public) is strictly regulated.

The statistics are impressive: 46 mountain peaks over 4,000 feet, more than 2,000 miles of trails, and 1,200 miles of rivers. The only mountains in the east that are not part of the Appalachians, the Adirondacks are among the oldest mountains in the world. In addition, the park is the watershed for most of the major basins in the Northeast, offering some of the best canoeing and fishing in the region. At the center of the park is Lake Placid, the resort town that hosted the 1932 and the 1980 winter Olympics. Today it is one of the major winter sports training centers in the country.

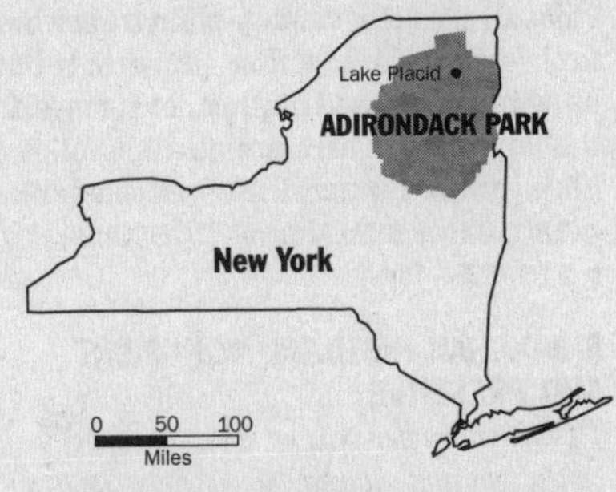

The most stunning scenery is found in the high peaks region in the northeastern part of the park, where there is rare alpine fauna. This is also where the crowds are between the months of June and October—although a crowd in the Adirondacks is much smaller than the summertime crunch in the better-known national parks. To escape the summer crowds, try exploring the northwest lake region of the park, where there is a lot more land to cover and also the opportunity to canoe to deserted islands (state-owned canoes can be used free). Another good bet is the southeastern and southern sections of the park, where numerous networks of dirt roads make it easy to find secluded spots at which to set up camp.

VOYAGEURS NATIONAL PARK

224,181 visitors per year ☛ 218,034 acres
Nearest big town: Duluth 280 miles

■ Much of the park is accessible only by boat (free canoes are available from the Park Service). There is, in fact, only one road. This wilderness is composed of 70,000 acres of dense forest, 30 lakes, and 900 islands teeming with wildlife, including a pack of timber wolves. The area is relatively unchanged from the days of trappers and explorers. ✉3131 Highway 53, International Falls, MN 56649-8904, ☎218-283-9821

GRANT–KOHRS RANCH NATIONAL HISTORIC SITE

363,441 visitors in 1994 ☛ 3,973 acres
Nearest big town: Butte 45 miles

■ This was one of the largest and best-known ranches in the country at the end of the 19th century. Today, the ranch is almost unchanged: cowboys still gallop by, herds of cattle bellow, and the smells of a working ranch waft through the place. In addition, the site preserves the original log buildings, the main Victorian-style ranch house, and an impressive collection of saddles,

wagons, buggies and other artifacts.
✏PO Box 790, Deer Lodge, MT 59722–0790
☎406–846–2070

GREAT BASIN NATIONAL PARK

88,024 visitors per year ☛ 77,180 acres
Nearest big town: Salt Lake City 230 miles

■ Situated in one of the most rugged and remote parts of the country, this park is reminiscent of the wide open Old West. It has vast stretches of desertlike open country, dramatic tall mountains, including the 13,063-foot Wheeler Peak, which descends to the Great Basin, one of the lowest points in the state. Among the park's attractions are ancient bristlecone pines, which, at 4,000 years old, are among the oldest living things in the world. Lehman Cave, one of the largest limestone caves in the country; and remnants of Pleistocene lakes.
✏Baker, NV 89311–9700, ☎702–234–7331

NORTH CASCADES NATIONAL PARK

19,323 visitors per year ☛ 504,781 acres
Nearest big town: Seattle 115 miles

■ This is one of those hike-all-day-and-not-see-anyone-else parks, largely because Washington's other better-known park, Olympic, is more accessible. Northern Cascades is sometimes called the American Alps because of its numerous immense jagged glaciers— 318 in all. This enormous wilderness boasts 248 lakes, 1,700 species of plants, 207 species of birds, and 85 species of mammals, including grizzly bears and cougars.
✏2105 Highway 20, Sedro Woolley, WA 98284, ☎360–856–5700

EXPERT SOURCE

The U.S. Government Printing Office publishes an excellent guide to the less well-known but in many cases no less spectacular parks called *National Parks: Lesser-Known Areas* ($1.75). Available from:

Consumer Information Center,
PO Box 100,
Pueblo, CO 81002.

CHANNEL ISLANDS NATIONAL PARK

175,226 visitors per year ☛ 249,354 acres
Nearest big town: Ventura on the coast is about 14 miles away by boat or plane

■ Because of the abundant wildlife, which includes the world's largest creature, the blue whale, biologists refer to these five tiny islands as North America's Galapagos. There are also sea lions, sea otters, pelicans, and cormorants. Remains of Spanish farms offer examples of how some of the earliest settlers in California lived.
✏1901 Spinnaker Drive, Ventura, CA 93001–4354, ☎805–658–5730

LASSEN VOLCANIC NATIONAL PARK

385,489 visitors per year ☛ 106,372 acres
Nearest big town: Chester 35 miles

■ Before Mount St. Helens erupted in 1980, Lassen Peak was considered the most active volcano in the lower 48 states. The park provides an excellent vantage point from which to observe volcanic action—fumeroles, bubbling mud pots, and hissing hot springs dot the landscape. There are also 150 miles of hiking trails through densely forested areas.
✏38050 Hwy 36E, Mineral, CA 96063
☎916–595–4444

ANIAKCHAK NATIONAL MONUMENT AND PRESERVE

1,193 visitors per year ☛ 137,176 acres in the Monument and 465,603 acres in the Preserve
Nearest big town: Anchorage 400 miles

■ This wilderness is the most remote and difficult to visit in the National Park System. The quickest way to get to the focal point of Aniakchak, which is a giant crater, one of the largest in the world, is to fly into the crater. For every 10 attempts, only one is successful; winds are constantly closing the only gap a plane can enter. Inside the crater, Surprise Lake's waters course through the wall of the crater to form the Aniakchak River.
✏PO Box 7, King Salmon, AK 99613–0007
☎907–246–3305

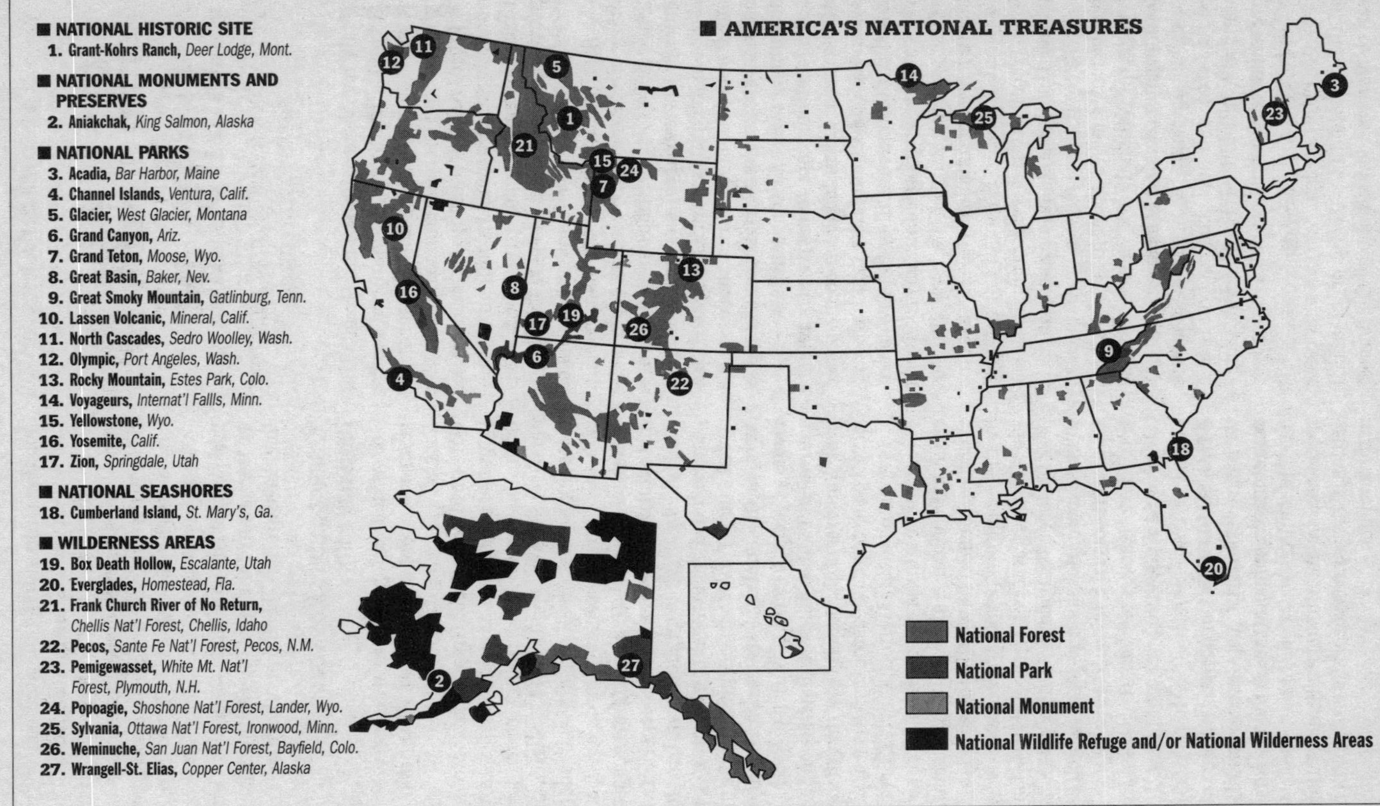
AMERICA'S NATIONAL TREASURES
NATIONAL HISTORIC SITE
1. Grant-Kohrs Ranch, Deer Lodge, Mont.
NATIONAL MONUMENTS AND PRESERVES
2. Aniakchak, King Salmon, Alaska
NATIONAL PARKS
3. Acadia, Bar Harbor, Maine
4. Channel Islands, Ventura, Calif.
5. Glacier, West Glacier, Montana
6. Grand Canyon, Ariz.
7. Grand Teton, Moose, Wyo.
8. Great Basin, Baker, Nev.
9. Great Smoky Mountain, Gatlinburg, Tenn.
10. Lassen Volcanic, Mineral, Calif.
11. North Cascades, Sedro Woolley, Wash.
12. Olympic, Port Angeles, Wash.
13. Rocky Mountain, Estes Park, Colo.
14. Voyageurs, Internat'l Fallls, Minn.
15. Yellowstone, Wyo.
16. Yosemite, Calif.
17. Zion, Springdale, Utah
NATIONAL SEASHORES
18. Cumberland Island, St. Mary's, Ga.
WILDERNESS AREAS
19. Box Death Hollow, Escalante, Utah
20. Everglades, Homestead, Fla.
21. Frank Church River of No Return, Chellis Nat'l Forest, Chellis, Idaho
22. Pecos, Sante Fe Nat'l Forest, Pecos, N.M.
23. Pemigewasset, White Mt. Nat'l Forest, Plymouth, N.H.
24. Popoagie, Shoshone Nat'l Forest, Lander, Wyo.
25. Sylvania, Ottawa Nat'l Forest, Ironwood, Minn.
26. Weminuche, San Juan Nat'l Forest, Bayfield, Colo.
27. Wrangell-St. Elias, Copper Center, Alaska
National Forest
National Park
National Monument
National Wildlife Refuge and/or National Wilderness Areas

NATIONAL PARKS

...AND WHERE THE CROWDS ARE

Folks flock to the 10 most popular parks for a reason

Italy has Venice. China, the Great Wall. The United States, its national parks, which collectively encompass some of the largest protected wildernesses in the world. All together, the national parks annually attract around 270 million visitors. Unfortunately, the popularity of the parks is proving ruinous to their health. Unless visits drop off, which seems unlikely, or major changes are made in crowd management, many of our natural treasures could be in jeopardy. Pollution, traffic jams, and honky-tonk resorts are part of many people's experience in the national parks, especially the most popular ones. While there are 54 national parks, the 10 most popular parks account for over half the visitors.

The environmental threat posed by rapidly increasing tourism has been compounded by severe budget cutbacks that have curtailed park rangers' ability to provide services and keep parks clean. Many roads and sewer systems built in the 1930s and '40s have not been maintained. Recently, a failing sewer at Yosemite National Park, which wasn't repaired due to a lack of funds, almost polluted the water supply of San Francisco.

To stave off the ecological threat tourism has become, and to adapt to its shrinking budget, the National Park Service is getting back to nature. Roads are closing and in many cases just not being repaired; gift shops are being razed; and new construction is at a standstill. In addition, backcountry camping is now increasingly regulated by a new permit system.

With a little foresight, you can steer clear of the crowds and parking problems. If you're planning to visit one of the 10 most popular parks during the summer, try to make reservations far in advance. While some campsites are on a first-come, first-served basis, a large number can be reserved through the National Park Service's Destinet system, ☎ 800-365-2267.

Following are the 10 most popular national parks ranked by popularity (as of 1995) and a description of the most interesting tracks they have to offer—beaten or otherwise.

1. GREAT SMOKY MOUNTAINS NATIONAL PARK

8.62 million visitors per year ☛ *800 square miles* ☛ *Largest national park east of the Rockies*

■ A world unto itself, Great Smoky Mountains National Park has over 1,500 species of flowering plants, 10 percent of which are considered rare, and over 125 species of trees—more than in all of Europe. In addition, there are 200 species of birds, about 50 species of fish, and 60 species of mammals, including wild hogs and black bears.

A hike or drive from mountain base to peak is equivalent to the entire length of the Appalachian Trail from Georgia to Maine in terms of the number of species of trees and plants—every 250 feet of elevation is roughly equivalent to 1,000 miles of distance on the trail. A quarter of the park is virgin forest, the largest concentration east of the Mississippi.

In addition to its natural attributes, Great Smoky Mountains is one of the most interesting national parks historically, with farms, churches, cabins, and working gristmills left by the mountain people who moved away when the park was established in 1934. The park has been designated a United Nations International Biosphere Reserve as well as a World Historical Site.

✉ 107 Park Headquarters Rd., Gatlinburg, TN 37738, ☎ 615-436-1200

■ **PEAK SEASON TIPS:** During the summer, in the lower elevations, expect haze, humidity, and afternoon temperatures in the 90s—and terrible traffic jams. Cades Cove, the less spectacular but more historically interesting section of the park, is generally less crowded in the summer.

■ **CAMPING:** Reservations are required May 15 through October 31 for Elkmont, Smokemont, and Cades Cove campgrounds. Contact the National Park Service's Destinet system. Sites at other campgrounds are on a first-come, first-served basis. Stays of up to 7 days are allowed from mid-May through October, and up to 14 days the rest of the year. Rarely filled are the Look Rock and Cosby campgrounds, which are in more remote parts of the park.

Also of note is the LeConte Lodge, located on the park's third-highest peak, Mt. LeConte (elevation, 6,593 feet), a six-hour hike from the main road. Accommodations are in cabins with no electricity or running water, but do include beds and hot meals. The lodge is open from mid-March through mid-November, ☎615–429–5704.

■ **BEST ONE-DAY TRIP:** Entering the park from Gatlinburg, continue on U.S. 441, and stop at the Newfoundland Gap, where there are spectacular views of the mountains. From there, turn onto Clingmans Dome Road (closed in the winter), which ends at a parking lot where there is a strenuous half-mile hike to a lookout tower atop 6,643-foot Clingmans Dome—the highest peak in the park. Back on U.S. 441, continue to the Smokemont Campground, where the easy, two-mile Chasten Creek Falls Trail meanders along a stream through a hardwood forest ending at one of the park's many waterfalls.

■ **BEST EXPERIENCE:** The Great Smokies is one of the premier places in the East to enjoy magnificent fall foliage. The season lasts from September through October. Peak time: October 15 to October 31.

2. GRAND CANYON NATIONAL PARK

4.36 million visitors per year ☛ 1,904 square miles ☛ The 277-mile canyon is nearly a mile deep in places

■ A Grand Canyon sunset is glorious, but even during the day, the canyon walls' many layers of stone refract hues of red, yellow, and green light. On a good day, you can see 200 miles across vast mesas, forests, and the Colorado River.

The park consists of three different areas: the North Rim, the South Rim, and the Inner Canyon, which is accessible only by foot, boat, or mule. The North Rim and the South Rim are only 9 miles apart as the eagle flies, but 214 miles by road.

The different rims are located in entirely different temperate climate zones. The North Rim on average is 1,000 feet higher and is heavily forested with blue spruce and alpine vegetation. It is open only from May to late October. The more popular South Rim is closer to population centers and has the juniper bushes and Gambel oak typical of the arid Southwest. The Inner Canyon is desertlike; temperatures there often exceed 110 degrees in the summer.

✉PO Box 129, Grand Canyon, AZ 86023
☎520–638–7888

■ **PEAK SEASON TIPS:** The South Rim is crowded all year. To escape the masses, take one of the many trails off East Rim Drive to a private spot overlooking the canyon, or try

■ THE BIGGEST PARKS

The largest parks cover more ground than some of our smallest states

NATIONAL PARK OR STATE	ACRES
1. Wrangell–St. Elias, Alaska	8,331,604
2. Gates of the Arctic, Alaska	7,523,888
3. Denali, Alaska	5,000,000
4. Katmai, Alaska	3,716,000
5. Death Valley, Calif.	3,367,628
6. Glacier Bay, Alaska	3,225,284
CONNECTICUT	**3,118,080**
7. Lake Clark, Alaska	2,636,839
8. Yellowstone, Wyo.	2,219,790
9. Kobuk Valley, Alaska	1,750,421
10. Everglades, Fla.	1,506,499
11. Grand Canyon, Ariz.	1,217,158
12. Glacier, Mont.	1,013,572
13. Olympic, Wash.	922,163
14. Big Bend, Tex.	801,163
15. Joshua Tree, Calif.	793,954
RHODE ISLAND	**675,200**

SOURCE: *Backpacker* magazine, December 1994.

the North Rim, which gets only 10 percent of the park's visitors.

■CAMPING: For lodging reservations in the South Rim, including Phantom Ranch, ☎ 602–638–2401. North Rim lodging reservations: ☎ 801–568–7686. Recorded general park info: ☎ 602–638–7888.

■ BEST ONE-DAY TRIP: The West Rim Drive offers wonderful views of the main canyon. In the summer, it is open only to buses, which can be taken from the visitor center. A paved trail runs along the South Rim offering an easy hike. All hikes into the canyon are strenuous. Of them, only the Bright Angel and the South Kaibab trails are regularly maintained.

■ BEST EXPERIENCE: A raft ride down the Colorado River is a great way to enjoy the splendor of the canyon. Motorboat trips take 7 to 10 days, raft trips take 10 to 12 days, and trips on wooden dories usually last 18 days, though 3- to 8-day partial trips can be arranged. Write the park superintendent for a complete list of outfitters licensed by the National Park Service.

3. YOSEMITE NATIONAL PARK

3.96 million visitors per year ☛ *1,170 square miles* ☛ *Home of the giant sequoia*

■ Yosemite's majestic granite peaks, groves of ancient giant sequoia trees, and waterfalls (including Yosemite Falls, which at a height of 2,425 feet is the nation's highest) inspired some of the earliest attempts at conservation in the United States. In 1864, Congress enacted laws protecting the valley. Journalist Horace Greeley noted that he knew of "no single wonder of Nature on earth which can claim a superiority over the Yosemite." And naturalist John Muir, whose efforts led to the park's formation, said of the valley, "No temple made with hands can compare with Yosemite."

The enormous park occupies an area comparable to Rhode Island, with elevations of up to 13,114 feet.

✉PO Box 577, Yosemite National Park, CA 95389, ☎209–372–0200

EXPERT TIP

The dramatic domes and soaring pinnacles in Yosemite make it one of the best places in the world for rock climbing. The Yosemite Mountaineering School and Guide Service offers beginning through advanced classes in the summer; for information, call:

☎ 209–372–1244.

■ PEAK SEASON TIPS: During the busy summer months, forgo the sights and splendors of the seven-mile Yosemite Valley, which attracts the hordes.

■ CAMPING: Of the 18 campgrounds in Yosemite, the 5 main ones in the valley offer "refugee-style camping"—over 800 campsites crammed into a singularly unspectacular half-mile. For more space and better views, head for the hills and try one of the eight Tioga Road campgrounds. There also are five tent camps about a day's hike from one another on the High Sierra Loop Trail. Campers can obtain meals, showers, and cots there. Reservations via Yosemite Reservations are advised, ☎ 209–252–4848.

Reservations also are required year-round in Yosemite Valley's auto campground and for Hodgdon Meadow, Crane Flat, and Tuolumne Meadows campgrounds. Other campgrounds are operated on a first-come, first-served basis. Camping reservations may be made up to, but no earlier than, eight weeks in advance through Destinet. Reservable campsites fill up quickly from mid-May to mid-September. Your best bet for snagging a spot is to start calling the Destinet reservation number at 7 a.m. Pacific Standard Time eight weeks in advance of the date you want to camp.

■ BEST ONE-DAY TRIP: Avoid the congested route to Yosemite Valley, grab a tour bus and get off at either shuttle stop 7, for an easy half-mile, 20-minute hike to Lower Yosemite Falls, or

SURE WAYS TO BEAT THE CROWDS

Travel in the off-season has its own rewards—and its own perils

Traffic on the main roads slows to a crawl, people are everywhere. Morning drive time in New York City? No, it's the summer rush to the nation's most popular national parks. Traffic has gotten so bad at some parks that tourists can spot wildlife simply by looking where other cars have pulled over to the side of the road to gawk.

The surest way to beat the crowds is to visit in the off-season. From June through October, Great Smoky National Park typically gets over a million visitors a month, but roughly half that number visit in the months between November and April, when temperatures in the lower elevations average about 50 degrees and occasionally reach into the 70s—perfect hiking weather, in other words.

There are other off-season rewards, too. At Rocky Mountain National Park, the bighorn sheep come down from higher elevations in May to feed on the mud deposits, and wildflowers there are spectacular in the spring. Yosemite National Park's waterfalls rush from the melting winter snows. In the fall, the foliage in many parks is absolutely superb. September is the sunniest month at Rocky Mountain National Park. And Grand Teton National Park is open all winter, allowing access to excellent cross-country skiing.

Of course, seasonal difficulties abound. There are, for instance, sudden snowstorms at Yellowstone National Park as early as September. And spring weather at Zion National Park is unpredictable; flash floods are not uncommon. Mammoth Cave can be especially dank in the dead of winter.

If such perils are too daunting for you, it is possible to avoid the masses in the summer simply by venturing into the backcountry. Most visitors don't wander very far from their cars.

shuttle bus stop 8, for a strenuous one- to three-hour round-trip hike to Upper Yosemite Falls. Other sites include the Native American Yosemite Village and El Capitan, a 3,000-foot face crawling with black specks which, on closer inspection, turn out to be rock climbers.

4. OLYMPIC NATIONAL PARK

3.38 million visitors per year ☛ 1,441 square miles ☛ The best example of virgin temperate rain forest in the country

■ On a relatively isolated peninsula with no roads traversing it, Olympic is one of the most pristine of the nation's parks. It has been referred to as the "last frontier." It divides into three distinct environments: rugged coastline, virgin temperate rain forest, and mountains, at the foot of which is the largest intact strand of coniferous forest in the lower 48 states. The park also has 60 active glaciers. ✉600 East Park Ave., Port Angeles, WA 98362, ☎360–452–4501

■ **PEAK SEASON TIPS:** Though three-quarters of the precipitation falls from October 1 to March 31, Olympic still receives more rain than any other area in the United States. Always bring rain gear.

■ **CAMPING:** Nestled in thickets of spruce, the main coastal campgrounds of Kalaloch and Mora provide privacy and a sense of wilderness. For an even greater sense of solitude, try one of the two smaller campgrounds, Ozette Lake or Ericson's Bay. (The latter is accessible only by canoe.) All of the coastal campgrounds are available on a first-come, first-served basis.

The Hoh campground is the largest in the rain forest. The four smaller campgrounds, especially the 29-site July Creek campground on Quinault Lake, have more privacy and better wildlife-watching.

On the mountain, the Deer Park campground (elevation 5,400 feet), feels remote but is accessible by car and provides an excellent base from which to explore the mountains.

Most of the 17 developed mountain campgrounds are available on a first-come, first-served basis, but group reservations at Kalaloch and Mora can be made through the Kalaloch park ranger, ☎360–962–2283, or the Mora park ranger, ☎360–374–5460.

■ **BEST ONE-DAY TRIP:** On a drive up Route 101, you can take in the park's harbor seals, gigantic driftwood, and tide pools teeming with activity along the coast. On the right, you'll pass a sign for the world's largest cedar tree. Get off onto the spur road to the Hoh Rain Forest visitor center. There is a 3/4-mile round-trip hike that winds through the dense rain forest at the end of the road. Back in your car, turn onto the road to the Mora campground, where there are several short scenic trails along the beach.

5. YELLOWSTONE NATIONAL PARK

3.04 million visitors per year ☛ 3,400 square miles ☛ The largest concentration of geysers and hot springs in the world

■ The center of what is now Yellowstone Park erupted 600,000 years ago. The explosion left behind a 28-by-47-mile crater that contained the world's greatest concentration of geothermal phenomena, including hot springs, fumaroles, steam vents, mud pots, and over 300 geysers. Among the geysers is Steam Boat, which shoots columns of water a record 350 feet high.

Yellowstone is the second-largest park in the lower 48 states, encompassing an area larger than the states of Delaware and Rhode Island combined. It is also the oldest park in the country, established in 1872. It has the largest mountain lake (Yellowstone Lake, with 110 miles of shoreline); the biggest elk population in America (90,000 strong); and is the last place in the country where there is a free-ranging herd of bison (3,500 of the woolly beasts).

✉PO Box 168, Yellowstone National Park, WY 82190, ☎307–344–2002

■ **PEAK SEASON TIPS:** This is one of the coldest parks in the continental United States. Be prepared for winter weather at any time of the year. The park receives half its visitors in July and August, overcrowding the roads and limited visitor facilities. The solution: head for the backcountry. Most visitors never venture far from their cars.

■ **CAMPING:** The 13 campgrounds at Yellowstone are available on a first-come, first-served basis except for Bridge Bay, where reservations can be made through Destinet. They often fill early in late summer. Winter camping is available only at Mammoth campground.

■ **BEST ONE-DAY TRIP:** From the west entrance, drive along Grand Loop Road to the mile-long Upper Geyser Basin, where boardwalks and trails run among the most outstanding geothermal phenomena in the world. Continue on to Yellowstone Lake.

6. ROCKY MOUNTAIN NATIONAL PARK

2.96 million visitors per year ☛ 414 square miles ☛ One of the highest regions in the country: 114 mountains above 10,000 feet

■ On both sides of Rocky Mountain National Park's 44-mile Trail Ridge Road, the highest paved road in America, are craggy snow-capped mountain peaks shrouded in clouds, alpine fields ablaze with wildflowers, and crystal-clear mountain lakes. Elk, deer, moose, coyotes, marmots, ptarmigan, and bighorn sheep—the symbol of the park—can often be seen.

✉Superintendent, Estes Park, CO 80517
☎303–586–1399

EXPERT TIP

Yellowstone is one of the few national parks where snowmobiles are permitted. In addition, snow coaches—winter buses on skis—provide a unique way to travel. Call TW Recreational Services Inc. for information on snow coaches and snowmobile rentals: ☎ 307-344-7311.

■ **PEAK SEASON TIPS:** The road to Bear Lake is one long traffic jam in the summer. Consider spending most of your time on the west side of the park; it's less spectacular but also less crowded, and there are better opportunities to see wildlife.

■ **CAMPING:** There are five campgrounds in the park, each with a seven-day camping limit. For reservations to Moraine Park and Glacier Basin campgrounds, call Destinet. The other three are available on a first-come, first-served basis. In the summer, Timber Creek, on the west side of the park, is recommended—it doesn't fill up until about 1:30 p.m. Aspenglen and Longs Peak, where one begins the ascent to the summit, are often full by 8 a.m. Privately owned campgrounds also are available.

■ **BEST ONE-DAY TRIP:** For a sampling of the varied topography, take Fall River Road to the Alpine visitors center at Fall River Pass, 11,796 feet above sea level. Drive back along Trail Ridge Road. If time permits, turn off Trail Ridge Road onto Bear Lake Road, which winds past lakes and streams to Bear Lake, where there is an easy 2/3-mile nature walk around the lake and a 1.1-mile hike to Dream Lake. A less-crowded trail nearby is the Glacier Gorge Junction Trail to Alberta Falls. Those who are in peak physical condition may want to attempt Longs Peak Trail, a strenuous 8-mile hike. A third of the 15,000 people who try it every year don't make it—at 14,000 feet, there is 40 percent less oxygen in the air.

■ **BEST EXPERIENCE:** Eighty percent of the park's trails can be ridden on horseback, and there are two historic ranches at the center of the park. Horses can be rented in Glacier Basin and Moraine Park. For a list of nearby ranches, many of which offer accommodations, write:

✏Colorado Dude and Guest Ranch Association, PO Box 6440, Cherry Creek Station Rd., Denver, CO 80206.

7. ACADIA NATIONAL PARK

2.71 million visitors per year ☛ 54 square miles ☛ The highest coastal mountains on the East Coast

■ The park is made of two islands and a peninsula: Mount Desert Island (which is accessible by a land bridge), Isle au Haut, and Schoodic Peninsula.

Artists and writers flocked to Mount Desert Island in the 1850s, attracted by its dramatic natural beauty and the rustic life it offered. In the 1890s, wealthy vacationers, inspired by the paintings, came and built "cottages" of a level of opulence that the country had not seen before. Many of the cottages were burned to the ground in the great fire of 1947, but the magnificent landscape that the painters celebrated remains—jagged granite cliffs with forests of birch and pine that grow right up to the coastline.

The park's proximity to the ocean gives it a milder climate than that of the mainland, which helps it to sustain more than 500 varieties of wildflowers and makes it one of the best places on the eastern seaboard to take in fall foliage. The park also is known as the Warbler Capital of the United States. Over 275 species of birds, including 26 varieties of warblers as well as the endangered peregrine falcon, inhabit the park.

✏PO Box 177, Bar Harbor, ME 04609
☎207-288-3338

■ **PEAK SEASON TIPS:** Expect nothing but bumper-to-bumper traffic on the Park Loop Road on the east side of Mount Desert Island in the summer. To avoid crowds, try the island's much less crowded western side. Also consider taking a ferry trip either to Baker Island or to Isle au Haut. June is the best month to see birds in the forests. August is the best month for sea birds.

■ **CAMPING:** The landscaped Blackwoods campground on the east side of Mount Desert Island has 310 campsites interspersed among groves of trees. It is open all year. Reservations via Destinet are advised.

On the less-crowded west side is the 200-site Seawell campground, which is open only during the summer. You have to hike in from a parking lot to reach it, but it's worth the effort. Sites are available on a first-come, first-served basis only.

Particularly remote are Isle au Haut's five small lean-to shelters. Here you can escape the cars and crowds without sacrificing convenience. The ferry there lands at a nearby hamlet where you can get provisions.

■ **BEST ONE-DAY TRIP:** From the visitor center, take Park Loop Road to the 3.5-mile road that leads to Cadillac Mountain, where a short, paved trail winds around the 1,530-foot mountain, the highest coastal mountain in the United States. Back on Park Loop Road, turn around and continue down the East Coast. Stop at Sand Beach for a dip and the 1.4-mile Great Head Trail for a hike around a rocky, forested peninsula. Continue on Park Loop Road to Route 3 and turn onto Route 198. Look for Hadlock Pond Carriage Road Trail where there is a 4-mile loop across three granite bridges. This trail goes past the highest waterfall in the park and is one of the best places to enjoy the color of flowering plants in the spring.

■ **BEST EXPERIENCE:** Take the charming carriage ride through the park that is offered by the Wild Wood Stables near Jordan Pond, ☎ 207-276-3622.

If carriages are too old-fashioned for you, this also is one of the few national parks where snowmobiles are allowed. The network of carriage roads provides excellent terrain.

EXPERT TIP

Maine's windjammers breeze past parts of the rugged coastline that are best left unhiked. The handcrafted schooners can carry anywhere from 12 to 25 passengers.

On summer trips, they leave Monday morning and return Saturday, visiting places such as the scenic Isle au Haut. For more information, write:

Maine Windjammer Assoc.
PO Box 317B
Rockport, ME 04856.

8. GRAND TETON NATIONAL PARK

2.54 million visitors per year ☛ 485 square miles ☛ Best part of the beautiful Teton range

■ There are not many places in the world where you can literally stand next to a mountain. (Foothills usually intervene.) Imagine then Grand Teton, where the mountains rise sharply out of the relatively flat Jackson Hole Valley like stark granite skyscrapers.

Another geological oddity formed during the ice age, Jackson Hole Valley looks as if some gargantuan infant sculpted it out of Play-Doh. When the valley formed, little driblets from the glaciers formed rocky deposits, called moraines, around the six sparkling mountain lakes that were incongruously punctured into the landscape.

Winding gently through this strange valley is the Snake River, along the banks of which grow willows, cottonwoods, and the blue spruces in which bald eagles prefer to nest. Beavers have built dams up and down the river, forming wetlands that have an incredibly dense concentration of wildlife, including bears, elk, moose, trumpeter swans, sandhill cranes, and Canada geese.

✏PO Drawer 170, Moose, WY 83012
☎307-739-3300

■ **PEAK SEASON TIPS:** From June through August, the crowds are near Jenny Lake, which has sand beaches and sometimes is warm enough for a quick swim.

■ **CAMPING:** Campgrounds are generally open from late May to October. In summer, Jenny Lake campground fills the fastest and has a seven-day camping limit—the other five parks have two-week limits. Camping at all six campgrounds is available on a first-come, first-served basis except at Colter Bay Trailer Village, where reservations are required, ☎ 307-543-2855.

■ **BEST ONE-DAY TRIP:** Beginning at the south entrance on Route 191, stop at Mentor's Ferry and the Chapel of the Transfiguration for a look at the dwellings of some of the area's first pioneers. Then drive north along Teton Park Road to Lupine Meadow and take the spur road to the trailhead, where

SPECTACULAR SPOTS STILL WORTH SAVING

There's a debate over what lands should be preserved by granting them national park status. Our expert picks several

Death Valley has been around for quite a while, but only in 1994, when Congress passed the California Desert Protection Act, was it officially designated a national park (☎619–786–2331). What is and isn't worth protecting and preserving are, of course, hotly debated issues these days.

Also included in the 1994 act, Mojave National Preserve (☎619–928–2572) was originally proposed as a national park but was then downgraded to a national preserve to allow hunting, grazing, and existing mining claims. Even so, it has not been able to operate fully because hostile congressmen voted only $1 in funding.

Congress is still mulling over whether to designate as a national park the Tall Grass Prairie National Preserve (in Kansas), one of the last remaining expanses of tall grass prairie in the U.S. But other magnificent wilderness areas lack the political midwifery to gain designation as a "national park." Many are only partially protected as, for example, "national forests" or "national recreation areas," where logging, off-road vehicles, and some development is allowed. Here are three spots worth visiting that Paul Pritchard, president of the National Parks and Conservation Association, one of the nation's most respected conservation groups, thinks need further protection:

Hell's Canyon (Wallowa-Whitman National Forest, Snake River Office, ☎509–758–0616) lies in an area that borders Idaho, Oregon, and Washington. It is the deepest erosion-carved canyon on earth and a place of rich biological, cultural, and geologic significance. Legislation has repeatedly but unsuccessfully been introduced in Congress since the early '70s to upgrade the canyon to national park status.

The proposed Cascades International Park and Stewardship Area, in Washington State and in British Columbia, would link together wildernesses in both countries, including North Cascades National Park (☎360–856–5700). Currently, many of these wildernesses are partially protected, but because they are not physically linked together and because of differing bureaucratic imperatives, many animals and natural resources are threatened.

The North Georgia Wilderness on the border of Tennessee and Georgia includes the 37,000-acre Cohutta Wilderness Area (☎706–695–6763), a place of exquisite natural beauty, only about an hour's drive from Chattanooga, Tenn. Currently there are no National Park Service proposals for the Cohutta and adjacent areas.

there is a difficult hike to Amphitheater Lake near the timberline. (Attempt this only if you are in good physical shape.) Head back up Teton Road for a stop at South Jenny Lake, located at the bottom of the tallest Teton peak. An easy six-mile hike there circles the lake and affords spectacular views of the mountain. Finally, stop at Colter Bay for a one-mile hike that loops around the wetlands.

■**BEST EXPERIENCE:** In winter, horse-drawn sleighs take visitors to see the herd of 11,000 elk that live in the valley.

9. ZION NATIONAL PARK

2.27 million visitors per year ☛ 229 square miles ☛ The 319-foot Kolub Arch is the world's largest sandstone formation

■ Nineteenth-century Mormons named the main canyon in this park Zion after the Heavenly City and gave religious names to many of the rock formations. With its brilliantly shaded sandstone cliffs, wide variety of flowers, and strange geological formations, the park does indeed look otherworldly. Some of the park's outstanding features include massive stone arches, hanging flower gardens, forested canyons, and isolated mesas.

The varied topography and plant life of the canyon have been caused by differences in the amount of water that reaches the various parts of the park. The microenvironments shelter a wide variety of animals, from black bears to lizards.

✉Springdale, UT 84767, ☎801–772–3256

■ **PEAK SEASON TIPS:** Expect exceedingly unpleasant traffic jams on summer weekends, when temperatures climb to over 100 degrees and over 5,000 cars visit the park. The west side generally is less crowded.

■ **CAMPING:** Watchman campground is open all year, but reservations are necessary, ☎ 801–772–3256.

The south campground is open only in the summer on a first-come, first-served basis and has restrooms and a disposal station. Lava Point primitive campground is usually open from May to October and offers camping by reservation for groups of nine people.

■ **BEST ONE-DAY TRIP:** A spectacular stretch of Utah Route 9 descends 2,000 feet in 11 miles into the park. As you enter the half-mile-wide canyon, the road turns into Zion Canyon Scenic Drive and runs north to the Temple of Sinawava. Riverside Walk, an easy 2-mile round-trip and the most popular trail in the park, begins here.

10. GLACIER NATIONAL PARK

2.15 million visitors per year ☛ 1,583 square miles ☛ One of the most varied displays of trees, wildlfowers, and plants in the West.

■ Glacier National Park in Montana lies alongside several borders, both political and geographic. It is part of the first international park, Wharton Glacier, created in 1910; Wharton lies in Canada and is administered separately.

Geographically the park sits astride the Continental Divide. Indeed, the trees one finds on the eastern side are eastern trees—Engelman spruce, subalpine fir, and lodgepole pine—while on the western slopes, due to more precipitation, grow ponderosa pine, Douglas fir, larch, and western red cedar. Two endangered species, the grizzly bear and the recently reintroduced gray wolf, call Glacier National Park home. The park is also one of the best places in the country to view wildflowers.

Glacier is one of the few parks that you can get to by train. Amtrak's Empire Builder stops daily at both West Glacier and at East Glacier from late April through late October.

✉West Glacier, MT 59936, ☎406–888–5441

■ **PEAK SEASON TIPS:** The traffic on Go-to-the-Sun-Highway piles up in July and August. To avoid the crowds, try Wharton Lakes on the Canadian side of the border.

■ **CAMPING:** All campgrounds are available on a first-come, first-served basis. During July and August there is a 7-day limit on stays; the rest of the year it is 14 days. Backcountry camping is free but by permit only, and permits are issued on a first-come, first-served basis a maximum of 24 hours in advance. At Avalanche campgrounds the park service allows camping only in vehicles or in "bear cages"—barbed wire enclosures that keep the bears out.

■ **BEST ONE-DAY TRIP**: Entering the park at the Apgar visitor center, turn onto Go-to-the-Sun Road (open from early June until mid-October), which runs 56 miles over the divide and is one of the most scenic roads in the country. The road passes by Lake McDonald, a 10-mile-long, 462-foot-deep lake. At Avalanche Creek there is a 4-mile-round-trip trail up to Avalanche Lake, one of the many distinctive, milky blue, glacier-fed lakes in the park. Back on the road, continue the steep drive up to Logan Pass, where near the visitor center, the Hanging Garden Walk offers an excellent chance to see the wildflowers for which the park is famous. The road continues on past glaciers and descends into the eastern part of the park, ending at Divide Creek on the border of the Blackfoot reservation.

■ **BEST EXPERIENCE:** Cross-country skiing is immensely popular here. A ski trails guide is available at visitors centers. There are also numerous lodges throughout the park that stay open during the winter. For information on lodges: From mid-May through September, call ☎ 406–226–5551; from October to mid-May, call ☎ 602–207–6000.

VISITOR'S GUIDE

ALL OF AMERICA'S CROWN JEWELS

America has designated over 80 million square miles as 54 National Parks for the enjoyment of its citizenry and the generations to come. The parks, how to get in touch with them, and their claims to fame

NATIONAL PARK ☎ Telephone number for information ✔ **Claim to fame** ☞ *Special activities*

ALASKA

DENALI ☎ 907-683-2294 ✔ **Mt. McKinley, N. America's highest mountain** ☞ *Dog sledding, cross-country skiing, hiking*

GATES OF THE ARCTIC ☎ 907-456-0281 ✔ **Greatest wilderness in N. America** ☞ *River running, fishing, mountaineering*

GLACIER BAY ☎ 907-697-2232 ✔ **Tidewater glaciers, wild terrain from ice to rain forest** ☞ *Sea kayaking, fishing*

KATMAI ☎ 907-246-3305 ✔ **Alaskan brown bears, the world's largest carnivores** ☞ *Sport fishing, kayaking*

KENAI FJORDS ☎ 907-224-3175 ✔ **300-sq.-mile Harding Ice Field, varied rain forest** ☞ *Sea kayaking, charter boats*

KOBUK VALLEY ☎ 907-442-3890 ✔ **Entirely north of the Arctic Circle** ☞ *Canoeing, exploring archeological sites*

LAKE CLARK ☎ 907-271-3751 ✔ **Headquarters for red salmon spawning** ☞ *Charter river trips, fishing*

WRANGELL-ST. ELIAS ☎ 907-822-5234 ✔ **Chugach, Wrangell, & St. Elias mtns. meet here** ☞ *Rafting, x-country skiing*

AMERICAN SAMOA

PARK OF AMERICAN SAMOA ☎ 011-684-633-7082 ✔ **Paleotropical rain forests, coral reefs** ☞ *Bird watching, sunbathing*

ARIZONA

GRAND CANYON ☎ 602-638-7701 ✔ **The mile-deep canyon itself** ☞ *River rafting, hiking, mule rides*

PETRIFIED FOREST ☎ 602-524-6228 ✔ **Petrified trees, Indian ruins** ☞ *Self-guided auto tours, photography*

SAGUARO ☎ 602-670-6680 ✔ **Greatest variety of desert life in N. America** ☞ *Photography, bird-watching, hiking*

ARKANSAS

HOT SPRINGS ☎ 501-624-3383 ✔ **Some 950,000 gals. of water a day flow through 47 thermal springs** ☞ *Hot baths*

CALIFORNIA

CHANNEL ISLANDS ☎ 805-658-5700 ✔ **Seabirds, sea lions, and unique plants** ☞ *Scuba diving, bird-watching*

DEATH VALLEY ☎ 619-786-2331 ✔ **Lowest point in Western Hemisphere** ☞ *Photography, jeep riding, horseback riding*

JOSHUA TREE ☎ 619-367-7511 ✔ **20- to 40-foot Joshua trees, stunning dunes** ☞ *Wildlife-watching, nature walks*

KINGS CANYON ☎ 209-565-3341 ✔ **The enormous canyons of the Kings River** ☞ *Hiking, photography*

LASSEN VOLCANIC ☎ 916-595-4444 ✔ **Huge lava-flow mountains, steaming sulfur vents** ☞ *X-country, downhill skiing*

REDWOOD ☎ 707-464-6101 ✔ **Redwood forests and 40 miles of scenic coastline** ☞ *Whale-watching, guided kayaking*

SEQUOIA ☎ 209-565-3341 ✔ **Giant sequoias include General Sherman, the largest living tree** ☞ *Hiking, fishing*

YOSEMITE ☎ 209-372-0200 ✔ **Granite peaks and domes, and the nation's highest waterfall** ☞ *Skiing, rock climbing*

COLORADO

MESA VERDE ☎ 303-529-4465 ✔ **Pre-Columbian cliff dwellings and other artifacts** ☞ *Guided lectures, exhibits*

ROCKY MOUNTAIN ☎ 303-586-1399 ✔ **Trail Ridge Rd., highest in the lower 48** ☞ *Mountain climbing, horseback riding*

FLORIDA

BISCAYNE ☎ 305-247-2044 ✔ **Pristine wilderness, living coral reefs** ☞ *Glass-bottom boat tours, snorkeling, scuba*

DRY TORTUGAS ☎ 305-242-7710 ✔ **Largest all-masonry fort in the west** ☞ *Fishing, snorkeling, scuba diving*

EVERGLADES ☎ 305-242-7710 ✔ **Largest remaining subtropical wilderness in U.S.** ☞ *Backcountry canoeing, fishing*

HAWAII

HALEAKALA ☎ 808-572-9306 ✔ **Inactive volcano, chain of pools linked by a waterfall** ☞ *Sunrise- and sunset-watching*

HAWAII VOLCANOES ☎ 808-967-7311 ✔ **Devastation from recent eruptions** ☞ *Backpacking, bird-watching*

VISITOR'S GUIDE

KENTUCKY

MAMMOTH CAVE ☎ 502-758-2251 ✔ **Longest recorded cave system in the world** ☞ *Cave tours, cave boating*

MAINE

ACADIA ☎ 207-288-3338 ✔ **Cadillac Mountain, highest on East Coast north of Brazil** ☞ *Boat tours, skiing*

MICHIGAN

ISLE ROYALE ☎ 906-482-0986 ✔ **The largest island in Lake Superior** ☞ *Lake kayaking, hiking*

MINNESOTA

VOYAGEURS ☎ 218-283-9821 ✔ **Thirty lakes and over 900 islands** ☞ *Canoeing, x-country skiing, ice-skating*

MONTANA

GLACIER ☎ 406-888-5441 ✔ **Nearly 50 glaciers, glacier-fed streams, lakes** ☞ *Excursion-boat cruises, snowshoeing*

NEVADA

GREAT BASIN ☎ 702-234-7331 ✔ **Ice field on 13,063-ft. Wheeler Peak, Lehman Caves** ☞ *Fishing, climbing, spelunking*

NEW MEXICO

CARLSBAD CAVERNS ☎ 505-785-2251 ✔ **U.S.'s deepest cave (1,593 ft.) and largest chambers** ☞ *Guided cave tours*

NORTH DAKOTA

THEODORE ROOSEVELT ☎ 701-623-4466 ✔ **The arid badlands, Roosevelt's Elkhorn Ranch** ☞ *Fishing, photography*

OREGON

CRATER LAKE ☎ 503-594-2211 ✔ **Deepest lake in the U.S. (1,932 feet)** ☞ *Boat tours, snowmobiling, x-country skiing*

SOUTH DAKOTA

BADLANDS ☎ 605-433-5361 ✔ **The scenic western badlands** ☞ *Hiking, wildlife-watching*

WIND CAVE ☎ 605-745-4600 ✔ **Beautiful limestone cave and the scenic Black Hills** ☞ *Spelunking, cave tours, hiking*

TENNESSEE

GREAT SMOKY MOUNTAINS ☎ 615-436-1200 ✔ **Loftiest range in the East, diverse plant life** ☞ *Hiking, photography*

TEXAS

BIG BEND ☎ 915-477-2251 ✔ **Rio Grande passes through canyon walls for 118 miles** ☞ *Horseback riding, fishing*

GUADALUPE MOUNTAINS ☎ 915-828-3251 ✔ **Portions of world's most extensive fossil reef** ☞ *Hiking, historic sites*

UTAH

ARCHES ☎ 801-259-8161 ✔ **Giant arches, pinnacles change color as the sun shifts** ☞ *Interpretive walks, auto tours*

BRYCE CANYON ☎ 801-834-5322 ✔ **Colorful, unusually shaped geologic forms** ☞ *X-country skiing, snowshoeing*

CANYONLANDS ☎ 801-259-3911 ✔ **Canyons of Green, Colorado rivers** ☞ *Mountain biking, backcountry drives, rafting*

CAPITOL REEF ☎ 801-425-3791 ✔ **Waterpocket Fold, a 100-mile-long wrinkle in earth's crust** ☞ *Hiking, photography*

ZION ☎ 801-772-3256 ✔ **Unusual geologic formations–Kolub Arch, world's largest at 310 feet** ☞ *Hiking, photography*

VIRGINIA

SHENANDOAH ☎ 703-999-3200 ✔ **The scenic Blue Ridge Mountains** ☞ *Skyline Drive, horseback riding, nature walks*

VIRGIN ISLANDS

VIRGIN ISLANDS ☎ 809-775-6238 ✔ **Secluded coves, white beaches fringed by lush hills** ☞ *Snorkeling, swimming*

WASHINGTON

MOUNT RAINIER ☎ 360-569-2211 ✔ **Greatest single-peak glacial system in U.S.** ☞ *Skiing, snowshoeing, climbing*

NORTH CASCADES ☎ 360-856-5700 ✔ **Half the glaciers in the U.S., 318 are active** ☞ *Backpacking, hiking*

OLYMPIC ☎ 360-452-4501 ✔ **One of the biggest temperate rain forests in the world** ☞ *Mountain climbing, fishing*

WYOMING

GRAND TETON ☎ 307-739-3300 ✔ **The flat Jackson Hole Valley and the Teton mountains** ☞ *Hiking, climbing, skiing*

YELLOWSTONE ☎ 307-344-7381 ✔ **World's largest concentration of geothermal phenomena** ☞ *Skiing, snowmobiling*

SOURCE: National Park Service; individual parks.

EXPERT SOURCES

THE BEST NATIONAL PARK GUIDES

The National Park Service publishes an excellent series of guides with color photos and maps; for more information call ☎ 304–535–6018. Michelle Morris, senior editor of Backpacker *magazine, also recommends:*

IN PRINT

CAMPER'S GUIDE TO U.S. NATIONAL PARKS: Where to Go and How to Get There (Volumes 1 & 2)
Mickey Little and B. Morva, Gulf Publ., Houston, Texas, 1994, $18.95 per volume
■ More recreation and less backpacking, this book is especially good for families and beginning campers. It has maps of all the parks, plus tips about hiking.

THE COMPLETE GUIDE TO AMERICA'S NATIONAL PARKS
Jane Bangley McQueen, ed., National Park Foundation, biannual 1995–96 $15.95
■ A handy reference guide to all the national parks. Practical information on permits, fees, and useful climate tables.

THE ESSENTIAL GUIDE TO WILDERNESS CAMPING AND BACKPACKING
Charles Cook, Michael Kesenel Publ. Ltd., 1994, $24.95
■ Provides comprehensive information on all the national parks with good tips on hiking and backpacking. Includes a good thumbnail guide to camping in national forests and a listing of notable trails.

THE MOUNTAINEER SERIES
Mountaineer Guide Books, Seattle, Wash., guides range $12.95 to $14.95
■ The best trail guides and the largest selection of destinations, these focus mostly on wilderness areas in the West.

NATIONAL GEOGRAPHIC GUIDE TO THE NATIONAL PARKS OF THE UNITED STATES
Elizabeth L. Newhouse, ed., National Geographic Society, 1992, $24
■ Perfect for the windshield tourist, this book is packed with itineraries, quick hikes, and beautiful pictures.

ONLINE

NATIONAL PARK SERVICE HOME PAGE
http://www.nps.gov/
■ Currently provides brief but useful information on the parks and links to the home pages of major parks.

NATIONAL PARKS AND CONSERVATION ASSOCIATION
http://www.npca.org/
■ A nonprofit citizen group that is dedicated to preserving and protecting the Appalachian Trail and the national parks. It provides information on various activities, including volunteer opportunities. The site also provides a link to the latest issue of *National Parks* magazine.

GORP (GREAT OUTDOORS RECREATION PAGES)
http://www.gorp.com/
■ This commercial Web site has a vast array of offerings: ATTRACTIONS provides detailed reports on national parks, forests, wildlife refuges, etc; ACTIVITIES offers information on hiking, biking, fishing, skiing, caving, etc., as well as tours of wilderness areas.

PRINCETON UNIVERSITY OUTDOOR ACTION HOME PAGE
http://www.princeton.edu
■ Designed for both Princeton and the Internet community, this is an excellent resource with in-depth information that can be downloaded, including guides to outdoor careers, animal tracking, winter shelters, etc. It also has links to other outdoor resources on the Internet.

WILDERNESS CONSERVATION

IMPERILED WILD WONDERS

They're here today, but they could be gone tomorrow

The battle is raging for control of America's remaining unprotected and underprotected wildernesses between the extractive industries and the environmental groups. "A war is being waged on the national parks, with no concern for the natural and cultural heritage that will be lost," says Paul Pritchard, president of the National Parks Conservation Association.

We asked Ben Beach of the Wilderness Society, one of the country's foremost environmental groups, to put together the following list of the most-imperiled natural treasures in the United States.

STERLING FOREST

■ Among the largest tracts of privately owned wilderness in the Northeast, Sterling Forest is 40 miles north of New York City. The owners have plans for development; Congress has taken some tentative steps to provide funds to help buy key tracts in Sterling Forest but has yet to complete work on this project.

✏NY–NJ Trail Conference, 232 Madison Ave., #401, New York, NY 10016, ☎212–685–9699

YELLOWSTONE NATIONAL PARK

■ One of the most intact ecosystems in the lower 48 states, this park is now being threatened by Crown Butte's New World Mine, to be located on land adjacent to the park. Mining would destroy wildlife habitats in the park and create 5.5 million tons of toxic waste. (See also page 488 for more on Yellowstone.)

✏PO Box 168, Yellowstone, WY 82190 ☎ 307–344–7381

EVERGLADES NATIONAL PARK

■ Because of its proximity to urban centers, the Everglades is probably the most endangered national park today. Efforts to eliminate the sugar subsidy program, which would have removed a main source of river pollution, were thwarted once again in 1996.

✏National Park Service, Homestead, FL 33034, ☎305–242–7700

TONGASS NATIONAL FOREST

■ Home to bald eagles, brown bears, and Sitka black-tailed deer, the ancient forest also contains economically important fisheries. Legislation initiated by Republican Senator Ted Stevens and supported by the rest of the Alaskan state delegation would increase timber-cutting by 75 percent.

✏Juneau, AK 99835, ☎907–586–8751

UTAH WILDERNESS

■ The Utah Public Lands Mangagement Act of 1995, introduced by Utah Senators Orrin Hatch and Robert Bennett, would open the Redrock Wilderness in southern Utah to development. An alternative bill supported by conservation groups would designate 5.7 million acres as protected wilderness.

✏Moab Interagency Visitor Center, Moab, UT 84532, ☎801–259–8825

KLAMATH NATIONAL FOREST

■ This remote wilderness contains ancient mixed conifers and rare Port Orford cedars. The U.S. Forest Service currently allows logging in the Dillon Creek watershed area. Pending legislation, supported by Senator Slade Gorton (R-WA) and Congressman Wally Herger, (R-CA) would allow heavier logging.

✏Yreka, CA 96097, ☎916–842-6131

ARCTIC NATIONAL WILDLIFE REFUGE

■ Legislation before Congress would open 1.5 million acres of untouched tundra land for oil and gas drilling. Oil accounts for 80 percent of Alaska's income, and the legislation has the backing of Alaska's Congressmen, Senators Frank Murkowski and Ted Stevens and Rep. Don Young. President Clinton can protect this refuge by declaring it a National Monument.

✏U.S. Fish and Wildlife Service, Fairbanks, AK 99701, ☎907–456–0250

EXPERT PICKS

INTO THE WILDERNESS

Wilderness areas—some 96 million acres—are the most strictly protected lands in the country. "Carry out what you carry in" policies are enforced so that, in the words of the 1964 Wilderness Act, "the imprint of man's works" remains "substantially unnoticeable." Buck Tilton, a freelance columnist for outdoor magazines, has just written America's Wilderness Areas *(Foghorn Press, 1996), a comprehensive guide. Here are his top picks.*

PEMIGEWASSET

■ One of the most extensive roadless areas in the East, this is New Hampshire's largest wilderness. Almost the entire forest was removed for timber between 1890 and 1940, but 55 years of regeneration have brought it back.

White Mountain National Forest, Pemigewasset Ranger District, Plymouth, NH
☎603–536–1310

EVERGLADES

■ Florida's "river of grass," 6 inches deep and 50 miles wide, forms the heart of this 1,296,500-acre wilderness area.

Homestead, FL
☎305–242–7700

SYLVANIA

■ This area contains 35 deep lakes (many edged with white sand), 84 established campsites, and a well-maintained trail system.

Ottawa National Forest, Ironwood, MI
☎906–932–1330

FRANK CHURCH RIVER OF NO RETURN

■ Besides Alaska, no area provides a wilderness experience to match its magnitude (it lies in six national forests). The canyon carved by the Main Salmon River lies deeper than the Grand Canyon.

Chellis National Forest, Middle Fork Ranger District, Chellis, ID
☎208–879–5204

POPO AGIE

■ This rugged area encompasses about 25 miles of the southern Wind River Mountain Range. A perennial snowfield lies along the Continental Divide.

Shoshone National Forest, Washakie Ranger District, Lander, WY
☎307–332–5460

WEMINUCHE

■ Colorado's largest and most popular wilderness has 63 ice-blue high country lakes and 500 miles of trails, including the Continental Divide Trail and the Colorado Trail.

San Juan National Forest, Columbine Ranger District, Bayfield, CO
☎970–844–2570

PECOS

■ Much of Pecos lies in the high country of New Mexico and features the 13,103-foot South Truchas Peak, the second highest in the state.

Sante Fe National Forest, Pecos–Las Vegas Ranger District, Pecos, NM
☎505–757–6121

BOX–DEATH HOLLOW

■ Vertical gray and orange walls of Navajo sandstone stand above two canyon tributaries of Utah's Escalante River.

Dixie National Forest, Escalante Ranger District, Escalante, UT
☎801–826–5400

WRANGELL–ST. ELIAS

■ The largest unit of the National Park System, this Alaskan wilderness holds 9 of North America's 16 highest peaks, the 90-mile-long and 4,000-foot-thick Bagely Icefield, and the Malaspina Glacier, which is 50 percent larger than the state of Delaware.

National Park Service, Copper Center, AK
☎907–822–5234

LODGING

COZY CABINS IN THE WOODS

Almost all the comforts of home in the middle of the wilderness

America's national parks contain some of the best-preserved rustic hotels in the United States. These capacious lodges were built with stones and trees hewn directly from the stunning landscapes they occupy in an attempt to re-create the great outdoors indoors. But suppose you yearn for a less refined experience, yet sleeping on a bed of pine needles doesn't appeal. Rustic cabins offer a happy middle ground and, unbeknownst to many, the national parks have a variety of offerings. Most of the cabins were built during the Great Depression by the Civilian Conservation Corps; the Park Service is not allowing any new construction. Rates are reasonable, from $12 to $130 a night per person depending on the location, type of cabin, and whether meals are provided.

PHANTOM RANCH

Grand Canyon National Park, Arizona

■ Accessible only by mule, foot, or raft, Phantom Ranch is a series of 14 cabins and other buildings about 10 miles from Grand Canyon Village on the South Rim. All but one of the cabins are for mule travelers; each can sleep up to 10 people. The remaining one is for hikers and sleeps 4. Mule riders pay about $265 per person per day, including mule rental and meals; hikers and rafters pay about a quarter of that amount. All cabins have baths, electricity, and heat. Open year-round. Book 11 months in advance. The reservation desk opens on November 30.

☎520-638-2631

HIGH SIERRA TENT CAMPS

Yosemite National Park, California

■ High up in the alpine meadows are a series of tent camps spaced 8–10 miles apart. The most remote tent camp is Merced Lake, which sleeps up to 60. There is a separate bath building with showers and a main dining room, also in a tent. Applications are on a lottery basis and are due November 30 for the following summer. Open mid-June–mid-September. Mule rentals are available.

☎209-454-2002

LA CONTE LODGE

Great Smoky Mountain National Park, Tennessee

■ It takes a good part of a day to hike to these cabins located on the third-highest peak in the Smokies. There are 7 one-room and 3 group cabins; bathroom facilities are in a separate structure, no showers. Open March 29–November 24, but start booking in October for the following summer.

☎423-429-5704

GRANITE PARK CHALET

Glacier National Park, Montana

■ Dating from 1914, the 11-room Granite Park Chalet and Sperry Chalet, a sister lodge, lie deep in the wilderness. Hike in or rent a horse. No reservations are needed—just show up at the Apgar visitor center about 24 hours in advance. It is a steep 5-mile hike up to the hut. This is bear country—bring pepper spray in case of an encounter with a grizzly.

☎406-387-5654

NORTH CASCADES STEHEKIN LODGE

North Cascades National Park, Washington

■ Situated on the banks of Lake Chelan, North Cascades' Stehekin Lodge is a complex of fully equipped cabins that sleep 2 to 8 people, but it's accessible only by boat or a day-long hike. There is a restaurant, cross-country ski trails, and fishing boats.

☎509-682-4494

ROSS LAKE RESORT

Ross Lake National Recreation Area, Washington

■ Probably the only floating resort in the National Park System, the resort consists of 10 rustic cabins and 3 bunkhouses on floating log rafts along the steep shoreline of

Ross Lake in the Ross Lake National Recreation Area. The cabins all have stoves and fireplaces. The modern cabins have baths; the little cabins have outside facilities. You can hike 2 miles in or go by boat. Open mid-June to the end of October. Book at least a year in advance.

☎206–386–4437

POTOMAC APPALACHIAN TRAIL CLUB CABINS

Shenandoah National Park, Virginia

■ Some of the cabins for rent in the Shenandoah were original settlers' homes. The 26 operated by the Potomac Appalachian Trail Club sleep 8 to 12 people and are reached by hiking from 1/5 to 4 miles along backcountry trails. All have fireplaces or woodstoves, outhouses, and even dishes. Corbin, a 2-story cabin at the end of Corbin Cabin Cutoff Trail, is on the National Register of Historic Buildings. It sleeps up to 12 people.

☎703–242–0315

CEDAR PASS LODGE

Badlands National Park, South Dakota

■ Bison and pronghorn and bighorn sheep can be seen from these cabins. There are also fossil beds formed 37 million years ago during the Oligocene epoch. The 24 pine cabins are heated and air-conditioned, have showers and baths, and sleep 4 to 6. Meals with such dishes as buffalo steak are served nightly. The cabins are available from May to October. Closed November 1 to April 15.

☎605–433–5460

MAHO BAY CAMP

Virgin Islands National Park

■ Half the island of St. John and much of its shoreline is national park. Its pristine coral reefs are a perfect place for snorkeling and there are miles of mountain trails. Maho Bay Camp is built on wooden platforms with walkways to preserve the vegetation beneath. The canvas- and screen-covered tent cottages sleep 5 to 6 people. Beds, linens, cooking facilities, and fans are provided. Book at least a year in advance. There is a restaurant on the premises.

☎800–392–9004

KETTLE FALLS HOTEL

Voyageurs National Park, Minnesota

■ Voyageurs is a paddler's dream with more than 30 lakes. Accessible by ferry, about a half mile from the historic Kettle Falls Hotel, are 12 separate units in 4 cabins that sleep 4 to 6 people. All rooms have baths, and some, fully equipped kitchens. Bedding, towels, and cleaning service are included and meals can be had at the nearby Kettle Hotel. Closed mid-October to mid-May.

☎ 800–322–0886

HALEAKALA NATIONAL PARK CABINS

Haleakala National Park, Hawaii

■ Cabins are a 4- to 10-mile hike into a volcanic wilderness of striking lava scenery, unusual plants, and exotic birds. Three cabins sleep up to 12 people and have wood-burning stoves, bunks, pit toilets, and firewood. The cabins are very popular and available through a monthly lottery. Write at least 2 1/2 months in advance and address requests to Haleakala National Park, attn: Cabins, PO Box 369, Makawao, HI 96768.

CAPE LOOKOUT CABINS

Harker's Island, North Carolina

■ The only undeveloped part of the Outer Banks, these islands can be reached by boat or ferry. Each island has 20 to 30 cabins that sleep 2 to 12 people. There is no electricity, and you must bring your own supplies. However, there are bathrooms and hot and cold water. The busy time is during the fall fishing season. Open year-round.

☎919–225–4261

APPALACHIAN MOUNTAIN CLUB CABINS

White Mountains National Forest, New Hampshire

■ These 8 "backcountry huts," each a day's hike apart, sleep 36 to 90, and include meals and bunks. The most spectacular is Lakes of the Clouds Hut on Mt. Washington, 5,050 feet above sea level. Open late spring until early October. One of two self-service huts is Carter Notch Hut. You get a bunk, pillow, and blanket, and use of a kitchen. There is running water and toilets but no shower or electricity.

☎603–466–2727

WILDLIFE

WHERE TO SPOT A MANATEE

A wildlife expert on the best places to see some magnificent animals

It seems to be an inexorable law that as the human population expands, wild animal species decline. Viewing large numbers of wild animals in a relatively pristine habitat is increasingly a rare experience. But it's still possible—even in America. We asked Mark Damian Duda, a noted wildlife expert who has worked as a consultant to over 30 state fish and wildlife agencies, for the best places to see wildlife in their natural habitat in the United States. His choices are drawn from his new book, *Watching Wildlife* (Falcon Press, 1995). The book also provides information on seasonal migrations, tips on how to watch wildlife, and helpful photography pointers. A series of state guides to wildlife are also available from Falcon Press ($5.95–$8.95).

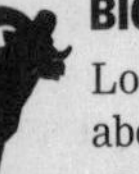

BIGHORN SHEEP

Located along Interstate 70, about halfway between Denver and Vail, the Georgetown Viewing Site is probably the most accessible place for viewing Rocky Mountain bighorn sheep. Between 175 and 200 bighorns occupy the rocky cliffs along the north side of Clear Creek Canyon. Fall and winter are the best times to look for them. (There's a lookout tower shaped like a ram's horns.) An exhibit includes interpretative displays and mounted viewing scopes.

■ **WHERE:** Georgetown Viewing Site, Georgetown, Colorado, ☎303–297–1192.

MANATEES

The gentle, slow-moving, endangered Florida manatee is a large aquatic mammal, typically 10 feet long and weighing 1,000 pounds. Manatees live in shallow, slow rivers, river mouths, estuaries, saltwater bays, and shallow coastal areas. In recent years, more than 200 manatees have used the Kings Bay area as wintering grounds.

■ **WHERE:** Crystal River National Wildlife Refuge, Florida, ☎904–563–2088.

ROCKY MOUNTAIN ELK

During September and October, bull elk bugle as a physical release and to challenge other males during the fall rut. Bugling usually begins an hour before sunset and starts off as a low, hollow sound, rising to a high-pitched shriek, culminating in a series of grunts.

■ **WHERE:** Horseshoe Park, Rocky Mountain National Park, Colorado, ☎306–586–1206.

■ **WINTERING ELK**

When snow comes to high country in the Grand Tetons, elk migrate from their high-elevation summer range to winter range in the valley. Almost 7,500 elk inhabit the area. Elk arrive in early November and return to the high country in early May. In the winter, visitors can view elk from a horse-drawn sleigh. Sleighs run from late December to March, 10 a.m. to 4 p.m. daily. Tours operate from the Natural Wildlife Art Museum, three miles north of Jackson on U.S. Highway 26/191.

■ **WHERE:** National Elk Refuge, Jackson Hole, Wyoming, ☎307–733–9212.

SANDHILL CRANES

For about five weeks in early spring (usually starting in March), more than three-quarters of the world's population of sandhill cranes gathers along the Platte River in central Nebraska. More than 500,000 of these stately birds rest and fatten up here on their way back to breeding grounds in the Arctic.

The local chamber of commerce sponsors a three-day program known as "Wings over the Platte," which includes bus tours, seminars, and wildlife art exhibits.

■ **WHERE:** Platte River, Nebraska. For more information contact: Field Supervisor, U.S.

Fish and Wildlife Service, ☎308–382–6468 or Grand Island/Hall County Convention and Visitors Bureau, Nebraska, ☎800–658–3178.

CALIFORNIA AND STELLER'S SEA LIONS

After descending more than 200 feet in an elevator to Sea Lion Caves on the coast of Oregon, you will find dim light, the hollow sound of waves crashing against cliffs, and the echoed barks of hundreds of Steller's sea lions (present year-round) and California sea lions (present from September to April). Sea lions swim and loaf below a cliff-top observation deck.

■ **WHERE:** Sea Lion Caves, Oregon ☎503–547–3111.

GRAY WHALES

The annual wintertime migration of the endangered gray whale brings these giant cetaceans directly off the coast of Southern California. Watching a gray whale thrust its 50-foot-long body out of the water, rotate in midair, and crash back to the ocean is an unforgettable experience. Some of the best whale-watching takes place aboard commercial boats that offer trips. But there are also good viewing opportunities from shore at the many inlets.

■ **WHERE:** Channel Islands National Marine Sanctuary, California, ☎805–966–7107.

MEXICAN FREE-TAILED BATS

On warm summer evenings in the Chihuahuan Desert, thousands of Mexican free-tailed bats exit in a whirling, smokelike column from the natural mouth of Carlsbad Caverns. An estimated 300,000 bats inhabit the caverns. They emerge at dusk to feed on moths; other flights occur in late August and September, when young bats born in June join the evening ritual.

Flight Amphitheater, which is located at the mouth of the cavern, seats up to 1,000 people. Park rangers offer programs about the bats from Memorial Day to Labor Day prior to the evening flights. But don't expect to see bats if you visit during the winter—they will have migrated to Mexico.

■ **WHERE:** Carlsbad Caverns National Park, New Mexico, ☎505–785–2232.

BALD EAGLES

One of the largest concentrations of wintering bald eagles in the lower 48 states occurs at the Skagit River Bald Eagle Natural Area in northern Washington State. More than 300 bald eagles gather along the river's gravel bars between 7 a.m. and 11 a.m. to feed on spawned-out salmon. The eagles feast here between November and early March, with peak numbers occurring in mid-January.

■ **WHERE:** Skagit River, Mount Baker–Snoqualmie National Forest, Washington. For more information contact: The Nature Conservancy, Washington Field Office, ☎206–343–4344; Mount Baker Ranger District, Sedro Woolley, Washington, ☎360–856–5700; or Washington Department of Wildlife, ☎206–775–1311.

FACT FILE:

DANCES WITH WOLVES

■ *Early in this century, a government-sponsored predator-eradication program almost caused the extinction of the gray wolf* (Canis lupus) *in the lower 48 states. In Yellowstone, the last gray wolf was killed in the late 1950s. Today, the wolf is protected by the Endangered Species Act, and gray wolves from Canada are being reintroduced into Yellowstone and Glacier National parks and the Frank Church River of No Return Wilderness. About 25 gray wolves have been resettled in Yellowstone; the park service hopes to have about 100 around the year 2000.*

NATIONAL TRAILS

PATHS ACROSS THE NATION

Some are no wider than a fat guy, all are of scenic or historic value

While they may not have hiked it top to bottom, most Americans have heard of the Appalachian Trail. Many are unaware, though, that the Appalachian belongs to a much larger system of trails. In 1968, Congress passed the National Trails Assistance Act to establish a national trail system. The trails fall into two categories: national scenic trails, which are protected scenic corridors for outdoor recreation, and national historic trails, which recognize prominent past routes of exploration, migration, and military action and may consist of no more than a series of roadside markers. The entire system includes 19 trails and covers most of the country.

NATIONAL SCENIC TRAILS

Benton MacKaye, the man who created the Appalachian Trail, thought it should be no wider than the space required by the average fat man. The majority of the trails are open to hikers only, although some allow mountain bikes and horses. Many are works in progress and have large sections closed to the public. Call ahead to inquire about available sections, allowable modes of transportation, and camping permits.

APPALACHIAN NATIONAL SCENIC TRAIL

Length: 2,159 miles ☛ The first interstate recreational trail, the Appalachian was conceived in 1921 by Benton MacKaye as a national preserve parallel to the East Coast. Beginning in Georgia and ending in Maine, the trail hugs the crest of the Appalachian Mountains and is open only to hikers. There are shelters every 6 to 12 miles, making it possible to hike the entire span without leaving the trail. Approximately 175 people hike the entire length of the trail every year, while millions of other hikers find inspiration and adventure on shorter segments.

✎ Appalachian Trail Conference, PO Box 807, Harpers Ferry, WV 25425, ☎ 304–535–6278

CONTINENTAL DIVIDE NATIONAL SCENIC TRAIL

Length: 3,100 miles ☛ The Continental Divide Trail provides spectacular backcountry travel through the Rocky Mountains from Mexico to Canada. It is the most rugged of the long-distance trails. About 75 percent of the entire 3,100 miles is finished in some form, and the Forest Service hopes to complete the rest by the year 2000. (It is possible for the more adventurous to hike from border to border now, though.) The longest continuous finished stretch reaches 795 miles from Canada through Montana and Idaho to Yellowstone National Park, and there is another solid 400-mile stretch through Colorado. The trail is open to hikers, pack and saddle animals, and, in some places, off-road motorized vehicles.

✎ Continental Divide Society, 3704 N. Charles St., Baltimore, MD 21218, ☎ 410–235–9610

FLORIDA NATIONAL SCENIC TRAIL

Length: 1,300 miles ☛ The Florida Trail extends from Big Cypress National Preserve in South Florida to just west of Pensacola in the northern part of the Florida Panhandle. Formed in 1964, the trail will eventually extend through Florida's three national forests to Gulf Islands National Seashore in the western panhandle. The trail passes through America's only subtropical landscape, making it especially popular with winter hikers and campers. Side-loop trails connect to nearby historic sites and other points of interest. At present, Forest Service officials estimate that about 600 miles of the trails are in place and open to public use.

✎ Florida Trail Association, PO Box 13708, Gainesville, FL 32064
☎ 904–378–8823

ICE AGE NATIONAL SCENIC TRAIL

Length: 1,000 miles ☛ At the end of the Ice Age, some 10,000 years ago, glaciers

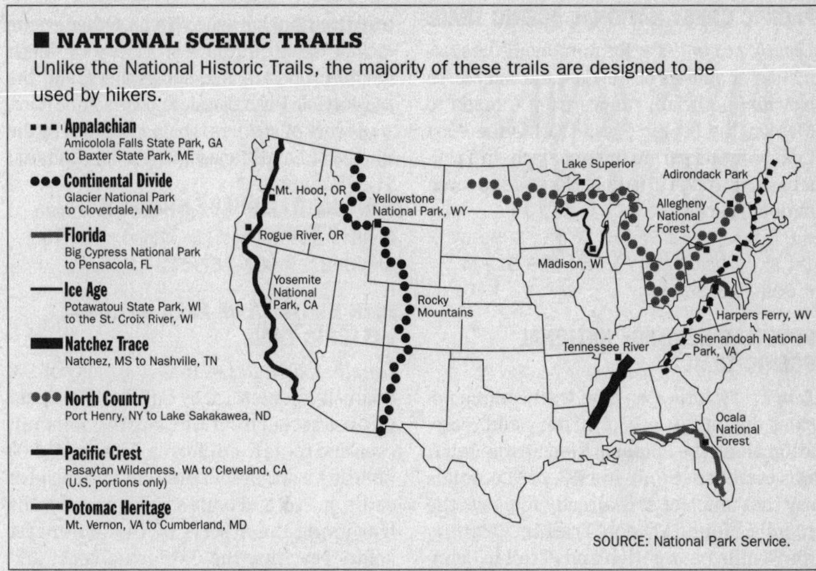

retreated from North America and left at their southern edge a chain of moraine hills made of rocks and gravel that the glaciers had accumulated along their journey. In Wisconsin, this band of hills zigzags across the state for 1,000 miles from Lake Michigan to the St. Croix River. Almost half the trail is open to the public, and certain sections are sometimes even used for marathons, ski races, and super-long-distance running.

✉National Park Service, 700 Rayovac Dr., Suite 100, Madison, WI 53711
☎ 608–264–5610

NATCHEZ TRACE NATIONAL SCENIC TRAIL

Length: 110 miles ☛ The trail lies within the boundaries of the as yet uncompleted Natchez Trace Parkway, which extends 450 miles from Natchez, Miss., to Nashville, Tenn. The parkway will commemorate the historic Natchez Trace, an ancient path that began as a series of animal tracks and trails used by Native Americans. It was later used by early explorers, "Kaintuck" boatmen, post riders, and military men, including Andrew Jackson after his victory at the Battle of New Orleans. Segments near Nashville (26 miles), Jackson (20 miles), and Rocky Springs (15 miles), which is near Natchez, are close to completion. There also are about 20 shorter "leg-stretcher" trails throughout. The Park Service hopes to connect the entire 445 miles within the next 10 to 20 years.

✉Natchez Trace Parkway, RR 1, NT 143, Tupelo, MS 38801
☎ 800–305–7417 or 601–680–4004

NORTH COUNTRY NATIONAL SCENIC TRAIL

Length: 3,200 miles ☛ Conceived in the mid-1960s, the North Country National Scenic Trail links the Adirondack Mountains with the Missouri River in North Dakota. The trail journeys through the grandeur of the Adirondacks, Pennsylvania's hardwood forests, the canals and rolling farmland of Ohio, the Great Lakes shorelines of Michigan, the glacier-carved lakes and streams of northern Wisconsin and Minnesota, and the vast plains of North Dakota—not to mention nine national forests and two national parks. About half of the trail is now completed for hiking.

✉National Park Service, 700 Rayovac Dr., Suite 100, Madison, WI 53711
☎ 608–264–5610

PACIFIC CREST NATIONAL SCENIC TRAIL

Length: 2,638 miles ☛ Running along the spectacular shoulders of the Cascade and Sierra Nevada mountain ranges from Canada to Mexico, the Pacific Crest Trail is the West Coast counterpart to the Appalachian Trail. It passes through 25 national forests and seven national parks.

✉U.S.D.A. Forest Service, PNRO, 333 S.W. 1st St., 1 Oak Plaza, Portland, OR 97204 ☎ 503–326–3644

POTOMAC HERITAGE NATIONAL SCENIC TRAIL

Length: 700 miles ☛ The trail commemorates the unique mix of history and recreation along the Potomac River. Although it was established only in 1983, park officials say that much of it is already in place: the 18-mile Mount Vernon Trail in Virginia, the 70-mile Laurel Highlands Trail in Pennsylvania, and the 184-mile towpath of the Chesapeake and Ohio Canal. The last 20 or so miles of the trail along the Chesapeake and Ohio provide a wonderful bicycle ride that ends in the heart of Washington, D.C.

✉National Park Service National Capital FDO, 1100 Ohio Dr., S.W., Washington, D.C. 20242 ☎ 202–619–7027

NATIONAL HISTORIC TRAILS

National historic trails are somewhat more conceptual than national scenic trails. Their objective is to preserve any historic remnants of the trail rather than provide a continuous footpath across its entire length. The "trails" often are no more than a series of roadside signs that direct travelers to historic sites or markers, though foot trails do appear from time to time at the roadside stops. The main exception to this description is the Iditarod in Alaska.

IDITAROD NATIONAL HISTORIC TRAIL

Length: 2,450 miles ☛ The trail was made famous by prospectors and their dog teams during the Alaska gold rush at the turn of the century. Most of the trail is usable only during Alaska's six-month winter, when rivers and tundra are frozen. Each year, the 1,150-mile Iditarod sled dog race is run along the trail from Anchorage to Nome. Other events include the 210-mile Ididasport race for skiers, mountain bikers, and snowshoers, and the Alaska Gold Rush Classic Snowmachine Race. A network of shelters is being installed by the Bureau of Land Management and the Iditarod Trail Committee.

✉Bureau of Land Management–Anchorage District, 6881 Abbott Loop Road, Anchorage, AK 99687, ☎ 907–267–1207

JUAN BAUTISTA DE ANZA NATIONAL HISTORIC TRAIL

Length: 1,200 miles ☛ In 1775, a party of 200 Spanish colonists led by Col. Juan Bautista de Anza set out from Mexico to establish an overland route to California. The band of 30 families, a dozen soldiers, and 1,000 head of cattle, horse, and mule spent three months traversing the deserts of the Southwest before reaching the California coast and another three months traveling up the coast to what is now San Francisco. There they established a presidio, or military headquarters, that is still in use today.

✉National Park Service, Western Region Division of Planning, 600 Harrison St., Suite 600, San Francisco, CA 94107 ☎ 415–744–3968

LEWIS AND CLARK NATIONAL HISTORIC TRAIL

Length: 3,700 miles ☛ President Thomas Jefferson in 1803 doubled the area of the United States by purchasing from France 885,000 square miles of land west of the Mississippi. The following year he commissioned Meri-

EXPERT SOURCE

The first comprehensive guide to America's trails, *Trails Across America* by Arthur and Marjorie Miller (Fulcrum, 1996, $19.95), describes all the National and Historic Trails and includes maps of each one.

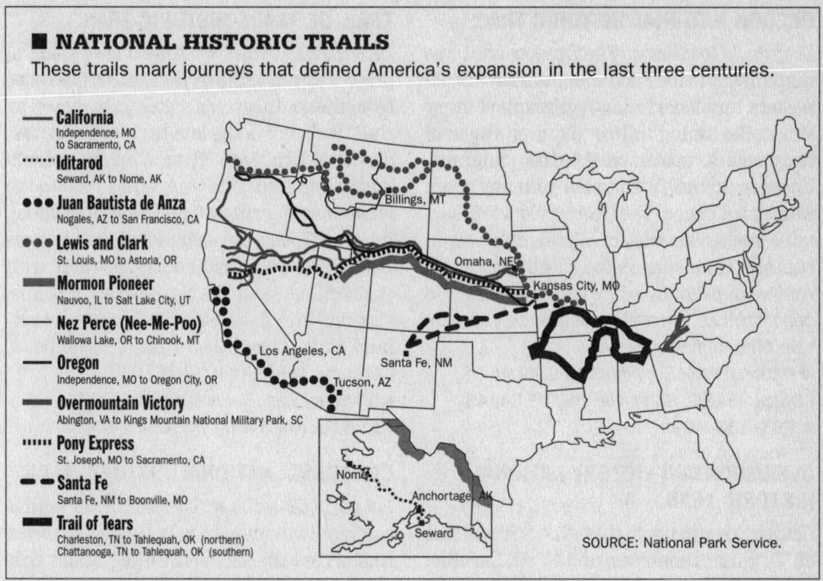

wether Lewis and William Clark to explore and map his $125 million "Louisiana Purchase." They took the Missouri River upstream from what is today Wood River, Ill., and eventually reached the Pacific Ocean at the mouth of the Columbia River in 1805. State, local, and private interests have established motor routes, roadside markers, and museum exhibits telling the Lewis and Clark story along the route.

✏National Park Service, 700 Rayovac Dr., Suite 100, Madison, WI 53711
☎ 608–264–5610

MORMON PIONEER NATIONAL HISTORIC TRAIL

Length: 1,300 miles ☛ Mormon emigration was one of the principal forces of settlement of the West. Seeking refuge from religious persecution, thousands of Mormons in 1846 left their settlement in Nauvoo, Ill., where church-founder Joseph Smith had lived. They spent the next winter in the Council Bluffs, Iowa, and Omaha, Neb., areas. Early in 1847, Brigham Young led an advance party west along the Platte River to Fort Bridger, Wyo., where they turned southwest and eventually came to the Great Salt Lake. The 1,624-mile route through five states generally is marked with a logo and closely follows the trail's historic route.

✏National Park Service, PO Box 45155, Salt Lake City, UT 84145, ☎ 801–539–4093

NEZ PERCE (NEE-ME-POO) NATIONAL HISTORIC TRAIL

Length: 1,170 miles ☛ The Nez Perce in 1877 were forced to leave their ancestral homelands in the Wallowa Valley of the Oregon Territory and move to the Lapwai Reservation in Idaho. Hostilities broke out between white settlers and some of the Nez Perce during the journey. Three of the settlers were killed. The U.S. Army was called in, and five bands of the Nez Perce, one of them led by Chief Joseph, headed north across the Rocky Mountains hoping to find refuge in Canada. They eluded capture for months, but just short of reaching the Canadian border in Montana, they were captured by the army and forced to settle in Oklahoma. Within two years, they were returned to Idaho and Washington. Joseph became an eloquent spokesman for peace until his death in 1904.

✏U.S. Forest Service, Nez Perce National Historic Trail Coordinator, PO Box 7669, Missoula, MT 59807, ☎ 406–329–3511

OREGON NATIONAL HISTORIC TRAIL

Length: 2,170 miles ☛ The Oregon Trail was the pathway to the Pacific for fur traders, gold seekers, missionaries, and emigrants of every stripe. Beginning in 1841 and over a span of two decades, an estimated 300,000 emigrants undertook the five-month journey from Kansas to Oregon. The trail corridor still contains some 300 miles of discernible wagon ruts and 125 historic sites. The approximate route can be followed by car; there are also opportunities to travel by foot, horse, or mountain bike in many places.

✏National Park Service, 324 S. State St., PO Box 45155, Salt Lake City, UT 84145
☎ 801–539–4094

OVERMOUNTAIN VICTORY NATIONAL HISTORIC TRAIL

Length: 300 miles ☛ In the fall of 1780, citizens of Virginia, Tennessee, and North Carolina formed a militia to drive the British from the southern colonies. This trail marks their 14-day trek across the Appalachians to the Piedmont region of the Carolinas. There they defeated British troops at the Battle of Kings Mountain, setting in motion events that led to the British surrender at Yorktown and the end of the Revolutionary War. Much of the trail is now roadway; only a 20-mile portion remains as a foot trail across the mountains.

✏National Park Service, 75 Spring St., S.W., Atlanta, GA 30303, ☎ 404–331–5465

SANTA FE NATIONAL HISTORIC TRAIL

Length: 1,203 miles ☛ After Mexican independence in 1821, U.S. and Mexican traders developed this trail using American Indian travel and trade routes. It quickly became a commercial and cultural link between the two countries. It also became a road of conquest during the Mexican and Civil wars. With the building of the railroad to Santa Fe in 1880, the trail was largely abandoned. Of the 1,203 miles of the trail route between Old Franklin, Mo., and Santa Fe, N.M., more than 200 miles of wagon ruts remain visible; 30 miles of them are protected on federal lands.

✏National Park Service, PO Box 728, Santa Fe, NM 87504, ☎ 505–988–6888

TRAIL OF TEARS HISTORIC TRAIL

Length: 2,200 miles ☛ After many years of pressure from white settlers, 16,000 Cherokee from the southeastern states were moved by the U.S. Army in the late 1830s to lands west of the Mississippi River. Various detachments followed different routes west to the Oklahoma Territory. Thousands died along the way. Today the designated trail follows two of the principal routes: a water trail (1,226 miles) along the Tennessee, Ohio, Mississippi, and Arkansas rivers; and an overland route (826 miles) from Chattanooga, Tenn., to Tahlequah, Okla.

✏National Park Service, PO Box 728, Santa Fe, NM 87504, ☎ 505–988–6888

CALIFORNIA NATIONAL HISTORIC TRAIL

Length: 5,665 miles ☛ The California Trail is commonly thought of as a single and direct line across the western United States that was trampled by fortune seekers during the gold rush of 1849. In fact, it was a collection of routes developed in the decade prior to the gold rush by land-seeking immigrants. Officially opened in 1992, the system includes an estimated 320 historical sites and the natural landmarks that guided immigrants.

✏Oregon-California Trails Association, 524 S. Osage St., Independence, MO 64050
☎ 816–252–2276

THE PONY EXPRESS TRAIL

Length:1,666 miles ☛ During its 18 months of operation, riders for the privately owned Pony Express carried mail between St. Joseph, Mo., and San Francisco in an unprecedented 10 days. The horse-and-rider relay system became the most direct and practical means of east-west communications before the telegraph. The trail proved the feasibility of a central overland transportation route that could be used year-round, paving the way for a cross-country railroad. About one-third of the 150 relay stations, where the riders were allowed exactly two minutes to exchange mail with the stationmaster, show identifiable remains and are historical sites along the trail.

✏National Park Service, 324 S. State St., PO Box 45155, Salt Lake City, UT 84145
☎ 801–539–4093

HISTORY BUFF'S GUIDE

OUR NEWEST DEPOSITS

Here are some of the newest sites and parks to receive a legislative blessing

CANE RIVER CREOLE NATIONAL HISTORICAL PARK
Opening: Late 1996
■ Established in 1714, Cane River is the oldest permanent settlement in the Louisiana Purchase territory. The site includes the Oakland and Magnolia Plantations and the historic district in the town of Natchitoches.
✏Jean Lafitte National Historical Park and Preserve, 365 Canal Street, Ste. 3080, New Orleans, LA 70130
☎318–357–4237

NEW ORLEANS JAZZ NATIONAL HISTORICAL PARK
Opening: Late 1996
■ This educational park preserves and interprets jazz as it has evolved in New Orleans. In late 1996, park officials hope to open a small visitor center. Later plans are for a full-scale center with jazz educational programs, including live music.
✏Jean Lafitte National Historical Park and Preserve
☎504–589–3882, ext. 111

STEAMTOWN NATIONAL HISTORIC SITE
■ Steamtown was once the main headquarters for the Delaware, Lackawanna & Western Railroad. There is a train tour through the railroad yard past the former locomotive erecting shop. The site has 29 steam locomotives, including one of the biggest steam locomotives ever built: a 133-foot-long monster that could run at more than 80 miles an hour.
✏150 South Washington Ave., Scranton, PA 18503
☎717–340–5200

PRESIDIO NATIONAL HISTORIC LANDMARK
■ Who says an army base can't be beautiful? Spain, Mexico, and the United States have used the Presidio as a fort for 219 years. Eleven miles of hiking trails and 14 miles of biking paths will wind through this 1,480-acre area. There are over 500 historic buildings on the base, some spectacular shoreline, and a military airfield.
✏Fort Mason, Building 201, San Francisco, CA
☎415–561–4000

KOREAN WAR VETERANS MEMORIAL
■ Dedicated to the memory of American soldiers who served in the Korean War, the first part of the memorial consists of a triangular-shaped area over which 19 soldiers advance toward the flag. A polished granite wall with the etched-in faces of over 2,500 soldiers, taken from archive photographs, reflects the scene. The second part of the memorial is composed of a grove of linden trees surrounding the circular Pool of Remembrance.
✏National Capital Park Central, 900 Ohio Drive, S.W., Washington, D.C. 20242

QUINEBAUG & SHETUCKET RIVERS VALLEY NATIONAL HERITAGE CORRIDOR
■ This historic area comprises a large area in the northeastern part of Connecticut. In 1995, it was designated an "affiliated area," a new classification that provides stewardship by the National Park Service, although the land continues to be owned by state or local authorities. The valleys include important archeological sites and architecturally significant mill structures. Currently there are markers identifying historic trails, factory buildings, and houses.
✏Northeast Visitors District 162 Main St. Putnam, CT 06260
☎860–928–1228

BEST DRIVES

WHEN THE LEAVES CHANGE COLORS

Our expert steers you to 10 perfect spots to watch the fall folliage

Nature does not go to bed quietly. Instead, each fall for a few choice weeks the forest erupts in a symphony of colors that has delighted countless generations—from the reds and oranges of the maples to the varied yellows of beeches and birches. Some of the best places for a fall foliage drive are in the country's national forests, along roads pretty enough that Congress has passsed legislation designating them as "scenic byways."

National forests are usually more accessible and less crowded than national parks. Yet, they encompass more than twice the landmass of the national parks and have only slightly more visitors. The scenic byway program was established by Congress in 1988. Now, 100 byways cover more than 3,000 miles, through or adjacent to national forests and provide easy access to many trailheads and recreation facilities, as well as offering some of the most scenic and traffic-free driving in America's wildernesses. We asked Beverly Magley, author of *Scenic Byways* (Vols. I and II), to pick the 10 best fall foliage drives.

■ FALL FOLIAGE HOTLINES

The Hotline is a collaborative effort among the Forest Service, Bureau of Land Management, Fish and Wildlife Service, and the National Park Service. In the spring, between April and July, the number turns into the Wildflower Hotline. To find out the fall foliage or spring wildflower conditions on over 630 million acres of public lands, call:

☎ 1-800-354-4595

For fall foliage conditions in the northeastern states, these state tourism numbers provide information:

Connecticut:	**☎ 800-282-6863**
Massachusetts:	**☎ 800-632-8038**
New Hamphsire:	**☎ 800-258-3608**
New York:	**☎ 212-827-6255** or **☎ 800-225-5697**
Vermont:	**☎ 800-828-3239**

KANCAMAGUS HIGHWAY

(State Highway 112) White Mountain National Forest, New Hampshire

32 miles ☛ Starting from Lincoln, at an elevation of 811 feet, the road, one of the most spectacular fall foliage drives in the country, climbs to 2,855 feet in its first 10 miles.

■ **PEAK WEEK:** First week in Oct.

■ **BEST STOP:** The C.L. Graham Overlook (at the top of the mountain).

■ **NEAREST TOWN:** Conway.

LONGHOUSE SCENIC BYWAY

Allegheny National Forest, Pennsylvania

29 miles ☛ The road runs along a plateau with views of flat-topped mountains covered with a lush growth of black cherry, maple, northern red oak, beech, aspen, and white oak. Rivers and streams have cut steep channels into the mountains and exposed interestingly shaped rock outcrops.

■ **PEAK WEEK:** Second week in Oct.

■ **BEST STOP:** Jakes Rocks Overlook,on a spur off the drive.

■ **NEAREST TOWN:** Warren.

COVERED BRIDGE SCENIC BYWAY

Wayne National Forest, Ohio

44 miles ☛ The road winds through a region of farms and rolling hills and offers splendid views of American beech, sugar maple, shagbark, and pignut hickory, and black, white, and swamp oaks.

■ **PEAK WEEK:** Second and third week in Oct.

■ **BEST STOP:** Hune Covered Bridge, which spans the Little Muskingum River.

■ **NEAREST TOWN:** Marietta.

NORTHWOODS SCENIC BYWAY

Chippewa National Forest, Minnesota

22 miles ☛ The road travels along the edge

of two designated nonmotorized recreational areas bordering hardwood forests and freshwater lakes. Pick up a copy of *The Fall Color Tour* at the ranger station, which details a 36-mile trip via side roads in the forest.

■ **PEAK WEEK:** Last week of Sept.
■ **BEST STOP:** Surprise Lake.
■ **NEAREST TOWN:** Grand Rapids.

GLADE TOP TRAIL

Mark Twain National Forest, Missouri

23 miles ☛ This is a two-lane gravel road meandering over the rolling hills of the Ozark Plateau. Make sure to stop at the Smoke Tree Scene, an interpretative site at the beginning of the trail. Smoke trees are locally known as yellowwood because of the tree's color when the bark is removed. The trees dot the entire hollow and turn magnificent hues of red and orange in the autumn.

■ **PEAK WEEK:** Mid-Oct.
■ **BEST STOP:** Caney picnic ground (at midpoint).
■ **NEAREST TOWN:** Branson.

MOUNT MAGAZINE SCENIC BYWAY

Ozark National Forest, Arkansas

25.9 miles ☛ The road climbs from the Arkansas River Valley up to flat-topped Mount Magazine, the highest mountain in Arkansas (2,753 ft.). Views on a clear day can extend 50 miles. Fall colors include the yellows and oranges of the sweet gum, the deep red of the black gum, and yellows and reds of oaks. Wildlife include white-tailed deer, black bears, bobcats, eagles, owls, and a variety of songbirds.

■ **PEAK WEEK:** Mid- to late Oct.
■ **BEST STOP:** Cameron Bluff, about halfway to the top of the mountain, just off the byway.
■ **NEAREST TOWN:** Paris.

SPEARFISH CANYON HIGHWAY

Black Hills National Forest, South Dakota

20 miles ☛ Spearfish Canyon Highway winds alongside Spearfish Creek through a high-walled limestone canyon. The buff-colored rocks soar as high as 1,200 feet overhead, while oaks, birches, cottonwoods, willows, ashes, and aspens provide a brilliant canopy to shade the canyon floor.

■ **PEAK WEEK:** First or second week of September.
■ **BEST STOP:** Midway, at the Savoy, an old railroad stop.
■ **NEAREST TOWN:** Spearfish, at the north end of the highway.

SAN JUAN SKYWAY

San Juan and Uncompahgre National Forests, Colorado

232 miles ☛ The skyway crosses four high mountain passes and weaves alongside sparkling streams, drops down into the high desert country of prehistoric and modern Indians, and passes near Mesa Verde National Park. The fall foliage is especially spectacular near the Dolores River.

■ **PEAK WEEK:** Last week in Sept. and first week in Oct.
■ **BEST STOP:** Molas Pass (35 miles north of Durango).
■ **NEAREST TOWN:** Durango. Drive passes through this town.

BOULDER MOUNTAIN HIGHWAY

Dixie National Forest, Utah

30 miles ☛ The road climbs rapidly out of desert slickrock country and ascends 2,500 feet along the side of Boulder Mountain before winding back down. At Round Up Flat there are wildflowers and groves of aspen trees, which turn vivid gold.

■ **PEAK WEEK:** Mid-Sept.
■ **BEST STOP:** Larb Hollow (halfway across the mountain).
■ **NEAREST TOWN:** Torrey.

ROBERT AUFDERHEIDE MEMORIAL DRIVE

Willamette National Forest, Oregon

70 miles ☛ The road runs along the wild and scenic Willamette River, through a lush forest of mixed conifers and hardwoods with a thick underbrush of ferns and shrubs. The forest is so thick in some places that the drive is like passing through a tunnel of leaves.

■ **PEAK WEEK:** Mid-Sept.
■ **BEST STOP:** The Gorge, at the lower end of the drive. Also, the Old Growth Constitution Grove.
■ **NEAREST TOWN:** Eugene (40 miles).

ADVENTURE

EXPERT Q & A: Travel tips from the world's most-traveled man, PAGE 514 **SAFARI$:** Where the wild things are, PAGE 515 **RAIN FORESTS:** Ecological gems not be missed, PAGE 519 **HIKING:** Trips for global trekkers, PAGE 523 **THE ALPS:** Walking excursions in Switzerland, PAGE 526 **BARGES:** The slow way to see Europe, PAGE 530 **WHALES:** The best places to watch these gentle giants, PAGE 532 **RAFTING:** Family fun on the rapids, PAGE 534

EXPLORING

THE LAST GREAT PLACES ON EARTH

Progress exacts its price, but these 10 spots are still pristine and wild

The great wildernesses have long been a challenge to the more adventurous travelers. Whatever their reasons—self-renewal, getting back to nature, or just to see what's there—adventurers have risked life and limb to get to these, until recently, blank spots on the map. Yet these wildernesses are the last best places for adventure travel, not only because they have wild rivers, unclaimed mountains, and unpenetrated rain forest, but because just to travel through them is an adventure—a reminder of where we came from.

Now, with the advent of adventure tour operators as well as the inevitable roads and airstrips, you don't have to be a Richard Burton, the famous 19th-century explorer who spent years tramping through African jungles in search of the source of the Nile, to visit these remote areas. And although tourism does have an impact on wilderness, many conservationists now view eco-tourism and adventure travel as a major factor in the protection of these places. A properly conducted eco-tour offers the twin satisfactions of not only seeing a completely different world, but also of providing governments and local peoples with a dollar incentive to protect their natural resources.

Jim Fowler, co-host of Mutual of Omaha's *Wild Kingdom*, author of *Jim Fowler's Wildest Places* (Time-Life Books, 1993), conservationist, and worldwide explorer, has been to wild places on every continent. He has lived with Bushmen in the Okavango Delta, rafted down wild rivers on the island of Sumatra in Indonesia, rappelled down cliffs in Patagonia, and wrestled crocodiles and boa constrictors in Africa and South America. He knows the wildernesses of the world in a way that very few do. Here is his list of the wildest places in the world that should tempt any modern-day adventurer.

TORRES DEL PAINE, *Chile*

■ Designated a world biosphere reserve by the United Nations, this park comprises 935 square miles of pristine Patagonian wilderness. Despite being one of the world's most wind-battered wildernesses, it contains some of the most varied habitats, greatest extremes of climate, and least-explored regions. The stunning peaks that pierce through the perpetual storm clouds are so steep that they were not successfully climbed until the 1950s. Runoff from immense ice fields feeds dense forests replete with lakes, streams, and prowling 150-pound pumas and dwarf deer. In

EXPERT TIPS

LIONS AND TIGERS AND BEARS, OH MY

You never know when you might confront a bear in the woods or a lion in the bush. Some beast-by-beast advice from adventurer Jim Fowler

■ **BROWN BEAR OR SLOTH BEAR:** Be aggressive and make a lot of noise. If you act submissive, you risk being attacked.

■ **GRIZZLY BEAR:** Act submissively, but if the bear is about to attack you, challenge it.

■ **TIGER:** Tigers will usually not attack unless they are able to sneak up on you or you have your back turned. In Nepal, for instance, natives wear a mask with eyes in the back to scare them off. If you do encounter a tiger, act aggressively. Hopefully, this is enough to make the largest predator in the world flee.

■ **LION:** Lions will usually not attack people unless they do not have anything else to eat. Nevertheless, make sure that you are not alone in an area inhabited by lions.

■ **RHINO:** Rhinos have bad eyesight and only attack if panicked. If you encounter a rhino, make sure that you give it plenty of distance.

■ **GORILLA:** When a gorilla attacks you, kneel down and don't look it in the eye.

mountain meadows there are herds of guanacos (relative to the llama). Farther down in the pampas, Darwin's rhea (a 3-foot-high flightless bird) grazes.

■ **JUMPING-OFF POINT.** Punta Arenas, the southernmost city in the world. Hotel Explora, bordering the park, provides comfortable accommodations for those who are averse to roughing it (☎ 56–2–228–8081; FAX 56–2–228–4655. In the U.S., you can also fax 800–858–0855).

■ **ESSENTIAL EQUIPMENT.** The best wind and wet weather clothing that you can afford.

SKELETON COAST, *Namibia*

■ When people refer to Namibia's Skeleton Coast as a place of haunting beauty, they aren't just using a figure of speech. The bones of lost adventurers, shipwrecked sailors, and dead animals lie here in perpetuity—the salt, air, and lack of rain preserve their skeletons. Yet there is extraordinary beauty: Garnet crystals shimmer in the sun, shifting sands settle in sensually curved dunes called *barchans*, and underground streams nourish long corridors lined with trees and bushes such as acacia and mopane. Wildlife—including elephants, black rhinos, ostriches, and over 200 species of birds—flourish along this protected 300-mile strip of the Atlantic coast.

■ **JUMPING-OFF POINT.** Walvis Bay, a large town where there are inland camping areas with thatched roof huts that are just now being developed for tourists.

■ **ESSENTIAL EQUIPMENT.** Wind and sun protection, especially bandannas and scarves for the face. Boots that lace up to keep sand out.

■ **TRAVEL ADVISORY.** Don't sleep on the beach. There are giant carnivorous land crabs, a foot tall and several feet wide. Much of the water is polluted; filter and boil it before using.

GUNUNG LEUSER NATIONAL PARK, *Indonesia*

■ The 3,120-square-mile park preserves what is left of one of the world's most unusual and fastest-disappearing wildernesses. (Indonesia is the world's leading exporter of tropical hardwood.) This particular tropical forest is haven to one of the richest varieties of plant and animal species found anywhere. Fowler reports that this is where he saw the largest concentrations of butterflies he has ever seen, massed in migration, sipping moisture on small sand beaches. The best way to visit this wilderness is along the Alas River, which descends through10,000-foot-high Mount Alas.

■ **JUMPING-OFF POINT.** Madian, a city located several hours' drive from the Alas river. Mountain Travel–Sobek (☎ 800–227–2384) is one of the few operators that run rafting trips here.

■ **ESSENTIAL EQUIPMENT.** Extra insect repellent for brown jumping leeches, which are so tenacious that they will jump through the eyelets of your boots. Also, avoid using tents that are like plastic wrap because of the tropical humidity; instead, sleep on a hammock underneath a tarpaulin.

ROYAL CHITWAN, *Nepal*

■ When malaria was eradicated in the 1950s, poachers and settlers streamed into the region, and endangered species such as the rhino were nearly decimated within a decade. With little time to lose, the king of Nepal established a rhino sanctuary. Today, the enlarged sanctuary is the 360-square-mile Chitwan National Park, which contains the best-preserved section of a jungle that used to run the entire length of southern Nepal. Within this region are some of the biggest and most dangerous animals found in eastern Asia—including a recovering Asian rhino population of 400 (a quarter of the world's total), tiger, king cobra, crocodile, and the unfriendliest creature of all—the sloth bear, which attacks unprovoked.

Despite the dangerous animals, this is one of the easier wild places to explore—if precautions are taken—and savvy travelers can make a go at it on their own. Knowledgeable native guides from the villages such as Saurha can be hired. For less intrepid and more affluent explorers, elephant safaris are conducted from the Tiger Top Lodge (see below).

■ **JUMPING-OFF POINT.** Tiger Top Lodge inside the park has an airstrip where planes from Katmandu land. Contact Durbar Marg, PO Box 242, Katmandu, Nepal (TELEX: 2216 Tiger Top NP). Reserve 6 to 12 months in advance.

■ **ESSENTIAL EQUIPMENT.** Elephantback is the recommended mode of travel for viewing tigers and rhinoceroses.

WOLONG NATURE RESERVE, *China*

■ The western half of Sichuan province is one of the most densely populated places in the world; the rugged eastern half is one of the greatest remaining wildernesses. If you take the tortuous two-week bus trip from Chengdu east to Lhasa in Tibet—aside from Litang (the highest settlement in the world) and a few domesticated yaks—you would just see pure wilderness.

The Wolong reserve preserves a large slice of this vast wilderness encompassing ecosystems ranging from 11,000-foot mountains to tropical rain forest. Also found here are some of the world's most famous endangered animals, including snow leopards and the largest remaining population of giant panda.

■ **JUMPING-OFF POINT.** From Chengdu, capital of Sichuan province, it is an 11-hour bone-jarring bus drive to the dormitories for ecotourists in Wolong Reserve.

■ **ESSENTIAL EQUIPMENT.** Although dormitories have mattresses, you won't regret bringing your own sleeping bag. Also, exchanging of gifts is customary in this region, so bring plenty of trinkets (preferably baseball hats).

■ **TRAVEL ADVISORY.** Watch out for the alcohol that is served at the dormitory; it is similar to moonshine.

LAKE BAIKAL, *Russia*

■ Lake Baikal is the oldest, the largest, the deepest, and one of the cleanest lakes in the world. It contains 20 percent of the world's freshwater (more than all five Great Lakes combined). Surrounding the lake is the world's largest contiguous forest, which extends more than 3,000 miles from the Ural mountains in the west to the Sea of Japan. The lake lies in a deep rift valley surrounded by tall mountains, which accounts for its high endemism; of the more than 2,500 species of plants and animals that live here 1,500 are unique to the lake. Some of the species include the Baikal seal (the only freshwater seal in the world), the sable, and the giant fish-eating flatworm.

■ **JUMPING-OFF POINT.** From Irkutsk on the southern tip of Lake Baikal take a launch or helicopter to Barguzin camp on the northern wild part of the lake.

■ **ESSENTIAL EQUIPMENT.** A cot—to avoid the rodents that live in many areas around the park. Also, fishing equipment: Lake Baikal is one of the best places in the world to fish.

ANTARCTIC PENINSULA

■ The continent is so vast and incomprehensible in its natural beauty as to be almost part of another planet. There are floating icebergs 50 miles wide, millions of penguins, and reflections of mountain peaks that are so clear as to cause one to wonder sometimes which way is up. Once you cross the stormy seas of the Drake Passage, you enter a tranquil land of black still water, rock, and ice. However, the coast, skies, and seas abound with wildlife, including the 700-pound leopard seal and the giant albatross (the world's largest bird).

Terrestrial adventure is limited to the very hardiest of travelers. These intrepid souls have sleeping bags rated to -30 degrees, special chemical packs that can be mixed for warmth, and consume three times their normal daily calorie intake—including whole sticks of butter. For all others, specialized cruise ships equipped with zodiac landing craft suffice. Fowler recommends including the Falkland Island, South Georgia Island, and the Ross Ice Shelf on your itinerary.

■ **JUMPING-OFF POINT.** Falkland Islands

■ **ESSENTIAL EQUIPMENT.** Russian ice breakers with two engines, in case the krill, the ubiquitous crustaceans that surround Antarctica, clog one of your ship's engines.

RORAIMA (THE LOST WORLD), *Venezuela, Guyana, Brazil*

■ This is an equatorial ecosystem: vast, diverse, hot, wet, and primeval. Throughout the tropical forest are unique flat-topped mountains called "tepuis." It was these tepuis that served as the inspiration for Conan Doyle's *The Lost World*. The tallest of the tepuis, Mount Roraima, has become a famous site for professional mountain climbers. In addition, Angel Falls, the largest waterfall in the world (20 times the height of Niagara Falls), is located here. Diamond snakes, giant anaconda snakes up to 20 feet long, and vampire bats are common.

■ **JUMPING-OFF POINT.** From Caracas, Venezuela, fly into Canaima, a small town at the outskirts of Canaima National Park. For the remotest parts there are landing fields in Guyana that can be reached from Georgetown, its capital.

■ **ESSENTIAL EQUIPMENT.** Machetes, light hammocks (the local ones are superior to ones from the States), and tarpaulins (instead of A-tents). Make sure that you have mosquito nets to fit the hammock to avoid getting buzzed by vampire bats.

MOUNTAINS OF THE MOON, *Zaire, Rwanda, Uganda*

■ Located in a region with live volcanoes, the Mountains of the Moon comprise some of the most varied wildernesses in Africa. High, wet, and cold, these equatorial mountains support strange vegetation such as forests of gigantic lobelias (a plant that grows only a few feet high in North America) and rare animals such as the mountain gorilla. Mount Margherita soars to 16,000 feet.

■ **JUMPING-OFF POINT.** Kahuzi Biega in Zaire

■ **ESSENTIAL EQUIPMENT.** A good quality ski jacket and lots of layered clothing. Be prepared for changes in the climate.

■ **TRAVEL ADVISORY.** Locate your campsite away from a game trail and your hammock high enough so that if a lion chasing its prey goes through your camp, it will go under you.

EXPERT Q & A

HE'D GO ANYWHERE —AND HE HAS

Travel pointers from the world's most-traveled man

Ever spin the globe, wondering what some far-off place is like? Well, John Clouse doesn't—because he's been there. In fact, there are only six places in the world that he hasn't been. And these are small dots such as Kingman Reef 1,000 miles south of Honolulu, the type of place you wouldn't want to visit unless, of course, you wanted to maintain your status in the *Guinness Book of World Records* as the world's most-traveled man. Below, Clouse, a 71-year-old lawyer who has been known to spend four months a year on his global journeys, offers some travel tips.

■ Do you take many things when you travel?

No, people take too much stuff. And dry-cleaning is hazardous in other parts of the world—a size 50 suit can often change into size 36! I take things that I can wash. Sometimes, I save old socks and underwear and things that I can throw away. I always dress down, but I usually bring a suit and tie just for those places that won't let you in if you are not wearing them.

■ What kind of shoes do you wear?

I like something flexible and low-cut, like sneakers. I don't like boots because I like to feel where I am going. Hell, I went up Longs Peak in Colorado in sneakers!

■ Do you have tips on visiting dangerous places?

If you are visiting a dangerous area, don't tell the driver until you get in the car—otherwise he won't take you. In 1988, I went to Gaza and the driver didn't want to take me there. But afterward he said that he learned more about the Palestinians than he had ever known before. Also, if you are visiting a dangerous area, always go in the morning; the revolutionaries and terrorists usually stay up late!

■ What are some spectacular places overlooked by tourists that are worth visiting?

Lake Naivasha in Kenya is one of the most gorgeous places on earth—like the Garden of Eden. It's located about 100 miles south of Nairobi. Namibia, formerly Southwest Africa, has spectacular horizons. There's a beautiful feeling of openness in the place. On Irian Jaya, the Indonesian side of New Guinea, Djajapura is one of the most beautiful harbors in the world. Its dense foliage, natural hills and inlets put it on par with the great harbors of the world, such as San Francisco and Hong Kong. Only this harbor is perfectly preserved and looks like something out of another age.

■ What are some of the most romantic places in the world?

Paris is the most romantic place on earth, but everyone knows that. In French Polynesia, the island of Tahiti has been overrun, but the islands near it, such as Moorrea and Raiatea have that romance that people associate with the South Pacific. The landscape has a softness and femininity to it with palm trees swaying and beautiful intoxicating sultry breezes.

■ What places haven't you visited yet?

In the South China Seas, I have yet to visit the Spratley Islands and the Paracel Islands. In the Pacific, there's Kingman Reef, 1,000 miles south of Honolulu, and also the Baker, Howland, and Jarvis Islands, a group of islands in the South Pacific. Then there is Mainland Norwegian Antarctica (also known as Queen Maud Land) and Bouvet Island in sub-Antarctica, which is also claimed by Norway.

■ Any other tips for the traveler?

Bring a beautiful person of your sexual orientation. Sex always enhances a trip and it's also nice to share a trip with someone else.

SAFARIS

JOURNEYS INTO AFRICA

There are more destinations for today's adventurer into the bush

For years, if you were heading out on a safari, you headed for the game parks of Kenya and Tanzania in East Africa—most notably Serengeti National Park, the Ngorongoro Conservation Area, and Masai Mara Natural Reserve—where huge herds of animals still wander across the plains. Nowhere else in Africa can you see such a vast collection of wildlife in its natural habitat. And there are safari options for every type of traveler from the pampered who treasure their creature comforts to the rugged outdoors person who doesn't mind being without a hot shower.

These days, however, others parts of Africa also beckon. The civil war that ravaged Uganda is over and outsiders are once again starting to visit the region, where gorilla and other primates can be seen. More notably, southern Africa (Namibia, Zimbabwe, and Botswana) is becoming a favored spot now that the political strife and guerrilla skirmishes that terrorized the region have seemingly ended.

Instead of the endless wide open savannahs of eastern Africa, immense swamps and forests predominate in southern Africa. In general, safaris to the southern part of the continent offer more options for the active tourist—from walking safaris to expeditions on elephant and horseback. Also, night drives are much more common, an activity prohibited in national parks in eastern Africa. Such forays afford a different perspective on the wild kingdom, since some animals, like leopards, are nocturnal.

Below, with the help of Gaby Whitehouse, former director of planning for Harvard's Comparative Museum of Zoology, John Hemingway, chairman of the African Wildlife Foundation, and Peter Alden, co-author of the *The National Audubon Society Field Guide to African Wildlife* (Random House, 1995), is an assessment of the best game-viewing spots, and camps and lodges not to be missed in Africa. Note: for a successful safari, timing is all. At certain times of the year the animals you wish to see may be away on migration or dispersed amid thick vegetation during the rainy season, so plan ahead.

EAST AFRICA

KENYA

■ Kenya has the highest concentrations of animals and tourists. Its biggest draw is the greatest game migration on the planet, which moves from the Serengeti in Tanzania up to the Masai Mara every year. Over a million wildebeests and hundreds of thousands of zebra can be found here from mid-July to mid-September. The best places to see game are in central Kenya at the national parks—Tsavo, Samburu, Amboseli, and Masai Mara (which boasts the largest lion population in Africa). Visitors to the national parks must be able to countenance the crowds as well as the constraints of watching the game from within an open safari vehicle. Kenya is also one of the best places in the world to see birds; over 1,000 species of birds live here in a variety of different habitats. In addition, Kenya has some of the most varied and distinctive tribal cultures in Africa, including the Masai, who still maintain their traditional nomadic life.

EXPERT PICK ☛ Little Governors Camp. One of the smaller fixed-tented camps located near the epicenter of wildlife viewing, this camp is a welcome escape from the more mass-market tourist camps in the Masai Mara preserve. ✉ PO Box 48217, Nairobi; ☎ 254-2-33104.

TANZANIA

■ Tanzania has Kenya's game without the

crowds, albeit this is in good part due to its less-developed tourist facilities and much bumpier roads. The Serengeti and the Ngorongoro Crater (the largest caldera in the world and the best place to see black rhino in Africa) abound with large herds of zebra and wildebeest. Like Kenya, tourists are restricted to safari vehicles in the national parks. For more adventurous walking or canoe safaris, head south to the Selous Game Reserve, the largest wildlife preserve in Africa, uninhabited except for a half dozen small tourist camps.

EXPERT PICK ☛ Tarangire Safari Lodge. Like the permanent tented camps of the old days—simple, secluded, and with a setting that cannot be beat. It is perched on a cliff overlooking a mini rift valley filled with zebras and wildebeests.

✉ Factory area, plot 2/3, Box 1182, Arusha
☎ 255-57-6886/6896

UGANDA

■ This landlocked country is mostly forested and mountainous, with a terrain reminiscent of Asia—very green, with terraced farming. Having recently emerged from a time of terror and political instability, Uganda is one of the most exciting places to visit in Africa right now. It is the best place in Africa to see primates and also the only safe place (safe from warring humans that is) where one can comfortably see gorillas. Visitors to the primate forests—the most notable of which is called the Bwini or Impenetrable Forest—must be ready for hard hikes and prepared for occasional deluges of rain.

EXPERT PICK ☛ Buhoma Gorilla Camp. One of the few outfitters with an established presence in Uganda, this is a very comfortable fixed-tented camp from which hikes are arranged into the primate-inhabited forests. Run by Abercrombie & Kent (see outfitters box on page 518 for how to contact).

SOUTHERN AFRICA

BOTSWANA

■ One of the most popular safari countries in southern Africa, Botswana has incredible wildlife, comfortable isolated safari lodges, and good transportation. The government has been successful so far in keeping out the large mass-market tent camps and lodges, which makes Botswana a more expensive place to visit than other African countries. While much of the country is arid and desert-like, the Okavango delta, in the northern part of the country, is like a primordial oasis. The only inland delta in the world, the Okavango is a lush swamp whose numerous rivulets and waterways empty directly into the Kalahari desert; the best way to explore it is by canoe. It's also one of the few bodies of fresh water in Africa where westerners can swim without worrying about parasites. In addition, this wilderness contains more plant species than all the rain forests of West and Central Africa combined. Adjoining the Okavango, the Moremi Reserve and Chobe National Park have one of the most varied and greatest concentrations of wildlife (including some of the largest elephant herds) in Africa. Botswana is also, together with Namibia, home to the majority of the 60,000 Bushmen in Africa.

EXPERT PICK ☛ Xaxaba Tented Camp. A small tented camp in the western and most remote part of the Okavango delta, Xaxaba is a particularly good location to see wildlife, since it is the camp that is located farthest away from the hunting preserves.

✉ PO Box 147, Maun, Botswana
☎ 267-660-351

ZIMBABWE

■ This is one of the all-around best countries to go on a safari. Zimbabwe has a good tourist infrastructure, excellent conservation, and perhaps the widest variety of safari options, including walking, kayaking, houseboat safaris, and some of the best white-water rafting in the world. In additon, camps and lodges here are usually small scale, have good food, and offer personalized service. Seven percent of the country is protected, and the national parks—especially Mana Pools, on the Zambezi river gorge—offer opportunities to see one of the great-

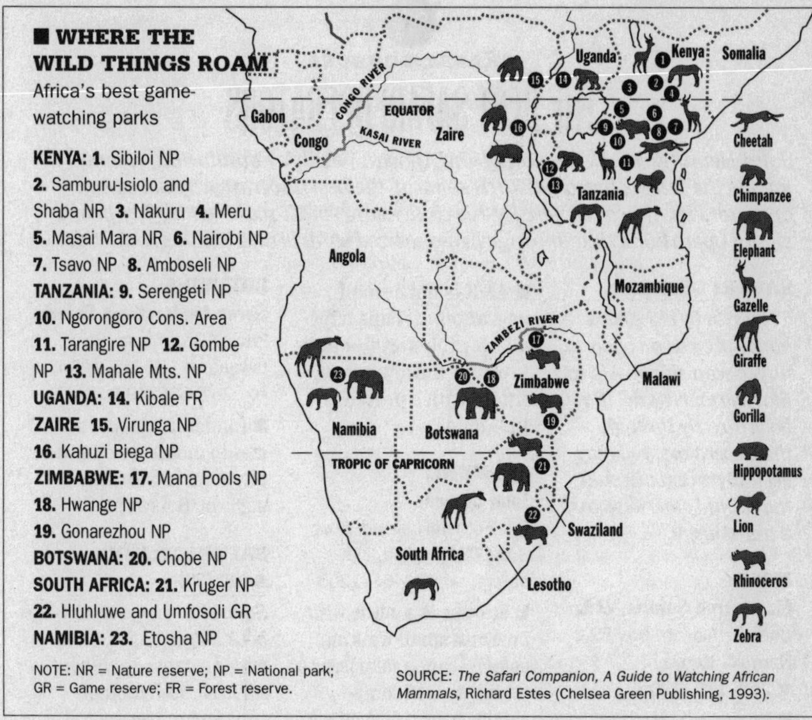

NOTE: NR = Nature reserve; NP = National park; GR = Game reserve; FR = Forest reserve.

SOURCE: *The Safari Companion, A Guide to Watching African Mammals*, Richard Estes (Chelsea Green Publishing, 1993).

est concentrations of wildlife during the dry season.

EXPERT PICK ☛ Victoria Falls Hotel. Located by the falls, the highest in Africa, this is one of the continent's grand old hotels. The terrace is perfect for high tea as well as the sunsets.
✉ PO Box 10, Victoria Falls, Zimbabwe
☎ 800–521–7242 (For reservations in U.S.)

ZAMBIA

■ More of a challenge to get to and travel through than other African countries, Zambia rewards the intrepid traveler. The Luangwa Valley is one of the most beautiful places in Africa. Crisscrossed by numerous rivers, the valley is home to many birds, African buffalo, hippos, crocodiles, zebras, and elephants. Walking and night safaris are readily available.

EXPERT PICK ☛ Chibembe Lodge. A 40-bed lodge and base for walking safaris. The lodge has a pool and landscaped grounds.
✉ Eagle Travel, Permanent House, Cairo Road, Box 35254, Lusaka;
☎ 260–1–229060/226857

MALAWI

■ There is not much tourism in Malawi, although there are numerous game-watching opportunities. Lake Malawi, which takes up a fifth of the country, contains over 300 varieties of fish, the greatest diversity of tropical freshwater fish of any lake in the world; it's also an excellent snorkeling spot. Zomba plateau, an enormous 8,000-foot plateau that topographically looks like Switzerland—except for the plethora of brilliantly colored orchids, and the leopards and antelope roaming about—can be explored on horseback.

EXPERT PICK ☛ Club Makokola. This hotel's comfortable rooms located right on the beach offer beautiful views of Lake Malawi.
✉ PO Box 59, Mangochi, Malawi
☎ 265–584–244 FAX 265–584–417.

EXPERT SOURCES

THE BEST SAFARI OPERATORS

John Hemingway, chairman of the African Wildlife Foundation, recommends the guides listed below as some of the best adventure travel safari operators in Africa. Generally, his choices are small-scale but highly professional operations that arrange personalized safaris and small group tours.

SAFARI GUIDES

Trips run by old Africa hands provide an opportunity to see a side of Africa that few tourists do. If you book directly through these operators, you may get a 15 percent discount that would otherwise go to a travel agent.

KENYA:
Flame Tree Safaris, Ltd.
Chrissie Aldrich, Box 82, Nanyuki, Kenya
☎ 254–176–22053

■ Chrissie Aldrich arranges mobile tented camp and walking tours on private preserves.

TANZANIA:
Richard Bonham Safaris
PO Box 24133, Nairobi, Kenya, ☎ 254–2–882521
TELEX 25547 BONHAM

■ Outfitted author and photographer Peter Matthiessen for the safari chronicled in *Sand Rivers* (out of print). Conducts walking tours and other expeditions in Tanzania and in Kenya.

UGANDA:
Abercrombie & Kent
1420 Kensington Road, Oak Brook, IL 60521
☎ 800–323–7308

■ A&K is not a small operation—it runs trips all over the world—but it is one of the few outfitters with a presence in Uganda.

ZIMBABWE:
John Stevens
C/o Fothergill Island, Post Bag 2081, Kariba, Zimbabwe; FAX 263–61–2253

■ Stevens is a guide who operates small walking safaris, canoe safaris, and mobile tented camp safaris from a seven-bed tented camp located near the Zambezi river.

ZAMBIA:
Robin Pope Safaris Ltd.
PO Box 320154, Lusaka, Zambia

■ From Tena Tena camp, a small base camp set on the Luangwa River, Robin Pope conducts walking safaris and movable tent safaris.

MALAWI:
Heart of Africa Safaris
PO Box 8, Lilongwe, Malawi, ☎ 265–740848

■ Run by David Foote, a well-known operator who arranges horseback safaris in the high country as well as walking safaris.

BOTSWANA:
Soren Linderstrom Safaris
Private Bag, Maun, Botswana; ☎ 267–660–994;
FAX: 267–660–493

■ Linderstrom specializes in mobile photography safaris to remote parts of Botswana.

SAFARI TRAVEL AGENTS

Safari travel agents can book lodges, safaris, and tented camps throughout Africa as well as make travel arrangements.

■ **BUSHBUCK SAFARIS**
48 High St., Hungerford, Berkshire, Eng., RG17 One
☎ 011–44–1–488–684702
FAX 011–44–684868

■ **EAST AFRICA SAFARI CO**
250 West 57th St.
New York, NY 10017
☎ 800–772–3214

■ **OVERSEAS ADVENTURE TRAVEL**
349 Broadway
Cambridge, MA 02139
☎ 800–221–0814

■ **GAMETRACKERS INTERNATIONAL, INC**
1000 East Broadway
Glendale, CA 91205
☎ 800–421–8907

RAIN FORESTS

GLORIES OF THE WET AND WILD

More life thrives in these tropical habitats than anywhere else

Tropical rain forests occupy only 7 percent of the earth's land surface, yet they contain over half its living organisms. What makes all that life possible is warm weather—averaging 80 degrees—and, of course, rain—lots of it. Tropical rain forests average 100 to 400 inches of rainfall a year, whereas New York City receives 43 inches a year and San Francisco only about 20 inches a year.

In contrast to other places on earth, most of the plant life in rain forests is in the treetops. Rain forests have several layers. Beginning at the top is an overarching canopy of profusely flowered and fruited treetops that can range from 100 to 130 feet high, with intermittently spaced emergent trees towering 160 feet or higher. Interlaced among the treetops are thick vines, as well as numerous plants called epiphytes, which grow on other plants. Below this primary canopy is a secondary one where shrubs and bushes and smaller trees grow 50 to 80 feet high.Underneath this is often an understory level of scrublike growth. Plant life on the forest floor is limited because of the lack of light.

Where should one go to witness the glories of the rain forests up close? Thomas Lovejoy, special adviser to the Smithsonian Institution, and Russell Mittermeier, president of Conservation International suggested these South American spots; James Castner, a tropical scientist and author of *Rain Forests: A Guide to Research and Tourist Facilities* (now out of print), who has visited these forests, recommended the best lodges in which to stay.

■ AND DON'T FORGET YOUR RAIN GEAR

The following groups organize eco-sensitve expeditions to many of the rain forests discussed here.

INTERNATIONAL EXPEDITIONS
Birmingham, Ala. ☎ 800–633–4734

MOUNTAIN TRAVEL/SOBEK EXPEDITIONS
El Cerrito, Calif. ☎ 800–227–2384

VICTOR EMANUEL NATURE TOURS
Austin, Texas ☎ 800–328–8368

FIELD GUIDES
Austin, Texas ☎ 512–327–4953

RAIN FOREST VENTURES
Gainesville, Fla. ☎ 352–371–6439

COSTA RICA

Costa Rican rain forests do not have the staggering variety of species or sheer density of plant and animal life of the most significant rain forests in the world, such as those along the eastern Andes. However, they are among the most important in the Northern Hemisphere, containing about 5 percent of the thousands of species of plants and animals that exist in the world.
RATE OF DEPLETION: *Costa Rica has the highest annual rate of deforestation in Central America.*

PARQUE NACIONAL CORCOVADO

On the Peninsula de Osa, about 115 miles southeast of San José.

■ The largest primary lowland rain forest in Costa Rica. The jungle canopy here contains over 400 species of birds, including numerous scarlet macaws, the most beautiful parrots in the world and supposedly as intelligent as dogs. The park is also home to pumas, ocelots, tapirs, and jaguars, as well as numerous rare butterflies and the almost extinct Harpy eagle.

MONTEVERDE CLOUD FOREST RESERVE

A four-hour drive north of San José.

Situated on a mountain 4,600 feet above sea level, the reserve contains six different ecozones. It is called a tropical cloud forest because of the constant low clouds that hover in the treetops, creating a highly humid environment. The park is home to over 2,000 species of wildlife, including three-wattled bellbirds, buffy tufted cheeks, prong-billed barbets, golden toads, and mantled howler monkeys. Also, one of the last remaining nesting sites of the quetzal, supposedly the most beautiful bird in the world.

EXPERT PICK ☛ Costa Rica Expeditions operates small deluxe eco-sensitive lodges in both Corcovado, at the edge of the forest on the beach, and in Monteverde National Park—with Jacuzzis, fireplaces, and excellent food.
✏ Mikail Kaye, Costa Rica Expeditions,
☎ 506-257-0766 FAX 506–257–1665
WEB SITE: *Crexped@sol.Rasca.Co.Cr*

EASTERN SLOPES OF THE ANDES

This area extends from the southern part of the Colombian Amazon through Ecuador and Peru. Norman Myers, one of the world's leading experts on biodiversity, says these rain forests constitute the richest biotic zone on earth.

RATE OF DEPLETION: *According to Myers, 90 percent of the original forest will have been converted to agriculture or have been severely damaged by extractive industries by the year 2000, and 50 percent of the species will have disappeared or be on the point of elimination.*

YASUNI NATIONAL PARK

The Oriente region of Ecuador.

■ The lakes in Yasuni National Park are home to piranhas and caimans (relatives of the crocodile). Other animal inhabitants include howler monkeys, bat falcons, mocking thrushes, sun grebes, and claw-winged hoatzins. A number of Indian tribes also live here, including the Waorani, who until recently have avoided contact with outsiders.

EXPERT PICK ☛ La Selva Lodge, located on Garzacocha Lake, accommodates 35, is easily accessible, and has won various eco-tourism awards. It runs a field studies program in conjunction with Harvard University.
✏ Eric Schwartz, La Selva Lodge, 6 de Diciembre 2816, PO Box 1712–635
Quito, Ecuador
☎ 593–2–550–995/554–686 FAX 567–297

TAMBOPATA-CAUDANO RESERVE AREA AND NATIONAL PARK

About 40 miles south of Puerto Maldonado in the Madre de Dios region of Peru.

■ This park is contiguous with the Madidi National Park in Peru, and together the two form the largest uninterrupted rain forest on earth. Tambopata-Caudano is also the best place in the world to see butterflies—over 1,100 butterfly species live here. In addition, this park has the largest known macaw lick in South America.

EXPERT PICK ☛ The Explorers Inn is located only 100 meters from the Tambopata River. It has accommodations for 75 in seven bungalow-style buildings. There is a bar, library, and a bathroom in each room, but no electricity.
✏ Dr. Max Gunther, Peruvian Safaris S.A.
Garcilazo de la Vegas 1334,
PO Box 10088, Lima, Peru
☎ 51–1–431–304–7 FAX: 51–1–432–88–66

MANU NATIONAL PARK

About 75 miles northeast of Cuzco in Peru.

■ This rain forest is the largest biosphere reserve zone in South America. It has the highest documented diversity of life in the world, containing an estimated 8,000 plant species, which is almost half of the number found in all the United States. There are 200 animal species—more than the number in the United States and Canada combined—and over 900 species of birds, which is 200 more bird species than in all of North America.

EXPERT PICK ☛ The Manu Lodge is a small, remote but comfortable rustic building built from mahogany logs taken from the Manu River. It accommodates 25 guests. A small electric generator powers appliances, and latrines are a short walk away. The food is simple, but good.
✏ Boris Gomez, Manu Nature Tours,
Avenida Pardo 1046, Cuzco, Peru
☎ 51–84–252721 FAX 51–84–234793
E-MAIL: *MNT@Amauta.RCP.NET.PA*

ATLANTIC FOREST REGION RAINFOREST, BRAZIL

This belt of rain forest once extended along the coast of South America; today, only a

GIVING "WORKING VACATIONS" A NEW MEANING

Why pay for a vacation on which you work? Actually, some people find research vacations quite rewarding: You learn something while helping to fund valuable scientific research. Participants of various ages and backgrounds roll up their sleeves and work together—sometimes under the lead of world-renowned scientists. We asked Stephanie Ocko, author of Environmental Vacations *(John Muir, 1991), to evaluate some of the options:*

EARTHWATCH

Two-week programs, about $1,500

■ The biggest volunteer research organization with offices worldwide, Earthwatch draws volunteers and scientists from all over to participate in over 100 different research programs—from excavating medieval sites in Moscow to monitoring climate change through the study of glaciers in Patagonia. Expeditions vary in quality. Also, because of remote locations, accommodations are sometimes spartan and travel can be complicated.

Watertown, MA 02272
☎ 617–926–8200

UNIVERSITY RESEARCH EXPEDITIONS PROGRAM

Two-week programs, $900–$1,500

■ Drawing on University of California at Berkeley faculty exclusively, this is one of the best-run research organizations. Its work covers the whole research spectrum—archeology, sociology, and ecology. Some of its expeditions planned for 1996–97: tracking a species of manatee in Costa Rica; excavating a 17th-century palace in West Africa; and studying prehistoric rock art images in Baja.

University of California
Berkeley, CA 94720
☎ 510–642–6586

OCEANIC SOCIETY

Seven- to 10-day programs: $230–$3,000; lodging on land or aboard

■ This water-oriented research organization usually conducts research programs aboard ships. Facilities are upscale and comfortable. The water-oriented programs are generally a little less demanding than land-based ones. The Society's programs include studying whales, dolphins, sea turtles, and howler monkeys (among others) near, in, and under the waters off North, Central, and South America.

San Francisco, CA 94123
☎ 800–326–7491

small bit of it remains. Up to half of the plant species found here are not found anywhere else. The forest contains the largest variety of primates in South America—over 24 different species.

RATE OF DEPLETION: *Most of the remaining rain forest is partially protected, but it still faces threats from expanding agriculture, logging, and industrial development.*

ITATIAIA NATIONAL PARK

Located halfway between Rio de Janeiro and São Paulo near the town of Itatiaia, Brazil.

■ This park, with its numerous hiking trails, is very accessible, unlike the Amazon. Over 100 plants found here are endemic to the Atlantic rain forest. Itatiaia National Park is also home to many distinctive animals, including the pale-throated three-toed sloth and the red-breasted toucan.

EXPERT PICK ☛ Rustic accommodations are available in the park and should be booked 30 days in advance during the busy season. There are also several hotels around the park's perimeter.

✉ Administração do Parque Nacional de Itatiaia, Caixa Postal 83657, Itatiaia 27580–000 RJ, Brazil
☎ 0243–52–1652

EXPERT PICKS

GOING FOR THE GREEN

When it comes to defining "eco-tour," lexicographers must be scratching their heads. Like "natural," "eco-tour" is a label used to sell such a wide variety of offerings that it has almost lost its meaning. To help clear things up, we went to Lisa Tabb, editor and publisher of EcoTraveler *magazine. Tabb defines a successful eco-tour as "a trip that provides a financial incentive for communities to preserve intact cultures and ecosystems." Here, she recommends trips that epitomize eco-tourism at its best.*

SAIL IN THE GALAPAGOS

■ Small sailboats glide noiselessly among these starkly beautiful islands, enabling you to get up close to multitudes of rare reptiles and birds.

✏Mountain Travel–Sobek
☎510–527–8100
☎800–227–2384

POLAR BEAR WATCHING IN MANITOBA

■ This outfit operates three-day trips out in Manitoba in southern Canada. Tundra buggies keep you propped up high enough to safely get within 10 feet of a polar bear.

✏Tundra Buggy Tours
☎204–675–2121

CAMEL TREK IN ISRAEL

■ Live like a Bedouin for seven days as you plod across Israel's Negev desert by camelback.

✏Society for Protection of Nature of Israel, 3 Hasfela St., Tel Aviv, Israel
☎011971–369–0644

THE MAYAS IN BELIZE

■ In southern Belize, outside of Punta Gorda, you can hike from Mayan village to Mayan village staying along the way in Mayan guest houses and eating with Mayan families.

✏Mayan Guesthouse Program, Nature's Way, 65 Front St., Punta Gorda, Belize
☎ 501–7–22119

TRACKING GAME IN SOUTH AFRICA

■ Conservation Corporation owns some of the highest-end lodges in South Africa. At Phinda lodge you stay in a glass-walled cabin, propped high enough above the bush to allow lions to meander underneath. There are expeditions for tracking rhinos, giraffes, and elephants with reformed poachers-turned-guides.

✏For U.S. bookings: Baobob Safari Tours
☎415–391–5788;
Park East Tours
☎800–223–6078; or
Abercrombie & Kent
☎800–323–7308

ABORIGINES IN AUSTRALIA

■ Spend eight days on a reserve where non-Aborigines are allowed only with special permission. There you will sleep under the stars and meet Pitjantjatjara elders who speak only their native tongue.

Adventure Center
☎510–654–1879 (ask about Desert Track Tours)

YURT-TO-YURT CROSS-COUNTRY SKIING IN IDAHO

■ Cross-country ski all day long in the Sawtooth Mountains and then return to a backcountry yurt where a gourmet meal, hot mulled wine, and a wood-burning sauna await.

✏Bob Jonas, Sun Valley Trekking ☎208–788–9585

CAMP ON A VIRGIN ISLAND

■ This is your basic beautiful Caribbean beach resort, but the lodging at Maho Bay camp on St. John in the U.S. Virgin Islands is made from recycled plastic, the bread is baked in a solar oven, and the food is organic.

✏Maho Bay Booking, 17 E. 73rd. St., NY, NY 10021
☎800–392–9004

TOURISME VERT IN FRANCE

■ For as little as $50 a night you can stay at a farmhouse inn and eat gourmet food with a working farmer.

✏Maison de Gites, 35 rue Godot-de-Mauroy, 75439 Paris Cedex 09

HIKING

JUST FOR THE TREK OF IT

A world-wise veteran chooses 10 classics not to be missed

The current vogue for trekking can be traced, in part, to the post-1960s crowd who traveled the world, exploring non-Western cultures and becoming inadvertent wanderers along the way. Today, trekking has gone mainstream. Tony trekking companies with glossy brochures offer deluxe trips to every imaginable corner of the globe. You can take your pick from a classic trek in Nepal to a pure wilderness experience in New Zealand. And you pay Ritz-Carlton prices to sleep in tents under the stars.

The immense popularity of trekking is sparking some environmental concerns. Once-pristine environments have become less so as trekkers have passed through. Cultures once isolated from outside influences now experience them with fair regularity.

We asked veteran trekker Robert Strauss, who has trekked on six continents and written numerous books on the subject including *Adventure Trekking: A Handbook for Independent Travelers* (Mountaineers, 1996), to pick what he considers to be the world's 10 classic treks. Strauss also provided the names of the outfitters listed.

KENYA

■ A five-day trek to Point Lenana (16,350 feet) in Mt. Kenya National Park (camping or staying in mountain huts en route) can be done with or without porters and guides. Rain forest on the lower slopes gives way to bamboo groves that thin into moorland—and, at higher altitude, the extraordinary giant species of groundsel and lobelia. Wildlife in the area includes elephants, buffaloes, monkeys, and rock hyrax. Appropriate high-altitude experience and sufficient warm and waterproof gear are essential. Daily fees for park entry and camping are payable in advance.

■ **OUTFITTERS:**

Tusker Trail & Safari Co. ☎ 800–747–2728

Africatours ☎ 212–563–3686 or 800–23–KENYA

PERU

■ The Inca Trail, a once-secret passage between Cuzco and Machu Picchu, the legendary lost city of the Incas, was rediscovered in 1911. The three-day trek features high passes, forests, and ancient ruins. It is strenuous in parts and often crowded, since it is easily the most well-known trekking destination in South America. For improved security, travel in a group and keep an eye on your tent and possessions.

■ **OUTFITTERS:**

Exploration Inc. ☎ 800–446–9660

International Expeditions ☎ 800–633–4734

VENEZUELA

■ In the southeast of the country is La Gran Sabana, a region renowned for its many tepui, or tablelike mountains of sandstone. The Roraima tepui rises 9,216 feet and is accessible via the village of San Francisco de Yuruaní. The trek to the top takes about five days. The trail starts in flat savannah, rises through rain forest, passing waterfalls and streams before the final steep ascent to the stepped plateau. It is strenuous in parts; take warm gear for the cold nights, rainproofs, and insect repellent. Hiring local guides is advisable. Overnighting en route consists of sleeping under rock overhangs or in caves.

■ **OUTFITTERS:**

Condor Adventures ☎ 800–729–1262

Southwind Adventures ☎ 800–377–WIND

TASMANIA

■ The delightful island state of Tasmania is a bushwalking magnet. Weather can change with amazing speed, so be prepared with cold-weather and wet-weather gear. In the center of the island, the popular, 50-mile-long Overland Track in the Cradle Mountain–Lake St. Clair National Park can be covered in a week or less. The trailheads at Cynthia Bay and Waldheim, at the southern and northern ends of the park respectively, are served by a shuttle bus during the prime summer season. Permits are issued by park offices at both points.

■ **OUTFITTERS:**

Adventure Center ☎ 800–227–8747

Mountain Travel–Sobek ☎ 800–227–2384

NEW ZEALAND

■ Tramping (the New Zealand term for hiking/trekking) has become a passion for the locals. At the southern end of the South Island lies Mt. Aspiring National Park and Fiordland National Park, which are straddled by the Routeburn Track. This very popular three-day tramp has great alpine scenery and passes through valleys covered by rain forest. A booking system for huts and campsites on the Routeburn has recently been introduced. (Less crowded tracks in the same area are The Greenstone and The Caples.) Information is available from the Department of Conservation (DOC) in Queenstown, which provides a transport base to access the northern end of the trail; Te Anau is convenient for the southern end.

■ **OUTFITTERS:**

Down Under Answers ☎ 800–788–6685

Swiss Hike, Olympia, WA ☎ 360–754–0978

CORSICA

■ GR20 (GR for Grande Route) passes through the national park (Parc Naturel Régional de la Corse) in the interior and extends 86 miles from Calenza in the north to Conca in the south—almost the full length of this Mediterranean island. There are beech and pine forests, aromatic scrub (maquis), high pasturelands, exposed mountaintops, and wild pigs with an aggressive craving for hikers' victuals! The walk can be split into two by starting in the middle at Col de Vizzavona. (The prime season for the northern section is early summer; autumn is best for the southern section.) You'll need at least two weeks to complete the full route, which requires fitness and experience in dealing with exposed terrain and major elevation changes. Unattended mountain huts (rifugios) provide shelter, but you need to carry your own food. Camping is prohibited within the park.

■ **OUTFITTERS:**

Himalayan Travel ☎ 800–225–2380

Adventure Center ☎ 800–227–8747

GREENLAND

■ A demanding terrain, lack of trails (for navigation at these latitudes you'll need to adjust your compass), and fickle weather make this destination a challenge even for experienced trekkers. The five- to six-day trek between Qaqortoq, the major town in southern Greenland, and Igaliku offers the scenic variety of icebergs, bays, waterfalls, and boulder fields. There are also Norse church ruins dating back to medieval times.

■ **OUTFITTERS:**

Greenland Travel, Denmark ☎ +45 (33-13-10-11)

Black Feather, Canada ☎ 800–5RIVER5

ALASKA

■ Three-quarters of Alaska is protected wilderness. Backcountry trekking through Denali National Park is regulated through zoning and permit quotas. Free permits are issued a day in advance by the Visitor Access Center (VAC). Once you have your permit, a shuttle bus will drop you off at your assigned zone. The park has no marked trails; hikers find their way with topographical maps. Denali, which is dominated by Mount McKinley, America's highest mountain at 20,320 feet, is accessible from Anchorage by car, bus, and rail.

■ **OUTFITTERS:**

Sunlight North Expeditions, Anchorage, AK ☎ 907–346–2027

Hugh Glass Backpacking Co., Anchorage, AK ☎ 907–344-1340

NEPAL

■ The main gateway for the Annapurna region is the town of Pokhara. The Annapurna Conservation Area Project (ACAP), based in Pokhara, provides regional support for minimizing impact on the environment. The Annapurna Circuit is a trekking tour de force: it passes through alpine forests to arid semidesert characteristic of Tibet; crosses over the Thorong La pass with dazzling views at 17,650 feet; and drops into the Kali Gandaki gorge, the world's deepest. The full circuit

EQUIPMENT THAT'S MORE RELIABLE THAN BREAD CRUMBS

A whole array of new gadgets ensure that civilization is never far away. The new gadgets, of course, have their limitations—they can break and do not always work properly in deep valleys or under thick tree cover. Think of them as helpful accessories, not substitutes for real wilderness skills.

GPS UNIT (Global Positioning System)

$ Approximately $300 and up

■ The same technology that guides missiles can also help you find your way home. Using a compass requires calculation, but with a GPS, a Star Wars spinoff, you just plug in the data and the unit tells you where you are. At the start of your trip, enter your coordinates and then periodically update the unit. The system can also calculate your estimated time of arrival.

AVALANCHE BEACONS

$ Start around $300

■ These beacons have been around but boast some new features. One is the Ski Mouse, which you can hitch onto your skis so that you can find them if they become detached, something that's useful in very deep powdery snow. Powder cords—brightly colored materials that you attach to your bindings—go for under $15.

WATCH ALTIMETERS

$ Sophisticated devices cost $300 and up; more limited ones start around $130.

■ Altimeters are now available as watches. In addition to indicating barometric trends, altitude, and temperature readings, some come with graphics. You have to know enough about how they work in order to make needed adjustments and interpretations.

CELLULAR PHONES

$ Around $200 without service. Deeply discounted when purchased with a service plan.

■ Cell phones are increasingly being used in the wilderness by hikers who get lost or injured; however, they will work only in the vicinity of a cellular transmission tower. They do not work well in mountainous areas.

SATELLITE PHONE

$ Start at $3,300, with additional charge for telephone service.

■ Satellite phones enable one to make phone calls from anywhere. They are available now in portable briefcase size. The lid of the briefcase functions as a satellite dish with a compass and map for positioning. They come with fax and computer capabilities.

takes around 18 days for seasoned trekkers putting in some 7 hours of hiking each day. Be prepared for the effects of high altitude and a possible wait to cross the pass if it's snowbound. The trail has plenty of teahouses and lodges en route.

■ **OUTFITTERS:**

Himalayan High Treks ☎ 800-455-8735
Trek Direct ☎ 800-873-5347

PAKISTAN

■ The northernmost region of Pakistan, where four ranges (Himalaya, Hindu Kush, Pamirs, and Karakorum) meet, boasts the largest number of high peaks in the world. The Concordia trek, passing through this area, is rated as one of the world's best. Because of the travel restrictions, most trips are organized through a tour operator. From the trailhead in Askole, the trek takes two weeks or longer, crossing awesome wilderness and glaciers into a natural amphitheater where colossal mountains (K2, Gasherbrum, Chogolisa, Broad Peak, and others) soar above you.

■ **OUTFITTERS:**

Snow Lion Expeditions ☎ 800-525-TREK
Wilderness Travel ☎ 800-368-2794

HIKING

SIX WONDERFUL SWISS WALKS

The scenery is unsurpassed and backpacks are unnecessary

No one thought of climbing around in the Alps for fun until the great influx of British travelers arrived in Switzerland in the 19th century. Of course the Swiss had been hiking around the mountains for a millennium, but in their case it was work. Today, people hike for recreation from Katmandu to Kandersteg. Many Europeans, especially, spend their summer holidays in the mountains hoofing it and an increasing number of Americans are quite literally following in their footsteps.

True to their stereotype of hyper-efficiency, the Swiss have transformed the art of walking into a science. Not only are there a plethora of signposts at every fork in the footpath, but the distance to various points is indicated down to the minute. People of all ages and abilities are able to knock about the mountains with the reassurance that they can stop practically whenever they want to for refreshment or a rest. Throughout the mountains, tramways, trains, and cable cars run so that one can cross high passes or access otherwise hard-to-reach hillside villages. There's no need to carry a heavy backpack, either. Your bags can be shipped for a modest fee from one destination to the next, and local inns and hotels will gladly fetch your gear for you after you've checked in. There's no camping in the Alps, but you can stay at Swiss Alpine Club huts at the top of many mountain passes or hotels or pensions in most villages. Even the remotest spot isn't terribly far from a train that can speed you to Zurich or Geneva or anywhere else in Switzerland in a matter of hours. The hiking season, however, is short: from June to late August, when the first snows usually arrive.

We asked Eve Preminger, a judge in New York City's Surrogate Court who spends most of her summers walking in the Alps, for her favorites hikes. The hikes chosen are moderate to slightly challenging, meaning that anyone in reasonably good physical shape should be able to handle them comfortably. (Walking poles, available at most outdoor equipment stores, are advisable; they make descents, especially, less wearing on your knees.) Most of the chosen hikes can be accomplished in a day. But the most satisfying way to experience the Alps is to plan a walking trip of, at least, 3 to 4 days. Preminger and her husband usually plan a route that takes a week or two, using a favorite hotel as a base for a couple of days and then moving on.

The walks are chosen from three of Switzerland's most scenic cantons: Valais, noted for its vineyards and for being one of the most inaccessible regions of Switzerland; Graubünden with its rural villages, and magnificent vistas of lakes, meadows, and mountains; and the Bernese Oberland, the southern part of the canton of Bern, with its famous Jungfrau.

VALAIS WALKS

Valais, in the southern part of the country along the Italian border, is the most mountainous region in Switzerland, containing the country's 10 highest mountains.

Zermatt to Hornlihutte

Round trip: 10 miles ➤ Altitude: 6,300 ft. ➤ 6–7 hours

■ Start and, perhaps, stay in Zermatt, one of the great mountain villages of the world, dominated by the legendary Matterhorn. The town allows no cars, which contributes to its pristine air and quality of timelessness, and which is also enhanced by the horse-drawn carriages lining the single main thoroughfare, the Bahnhofstrasse. On either side are grand chalets, antique buildings, and fashionable boutiques and not-so-fashionable T-shirt shops. Of special note is the alpine museum, which has exhibits on mountain ascents.

Although the village can be very crowded in the summer, five minutes by foot takes you to an extensive network of pleasant

THE TRULY AWESOME ALPS

The highest mountain in the Alps (Mont Blanc) is in France, but Switzerland claims the greatest number of peaks 13,000 feet or higher. The Valaisian Alps, a magnificent chain of high peaks and glaciers, stretches across the southwest of Switzerland. On the other side of the Rhone Valley are the Bernese Alps, with peaks nearly as high. Cable cars, cog railways, and a fine public transportation system make even high alpine valleys easily accessible.

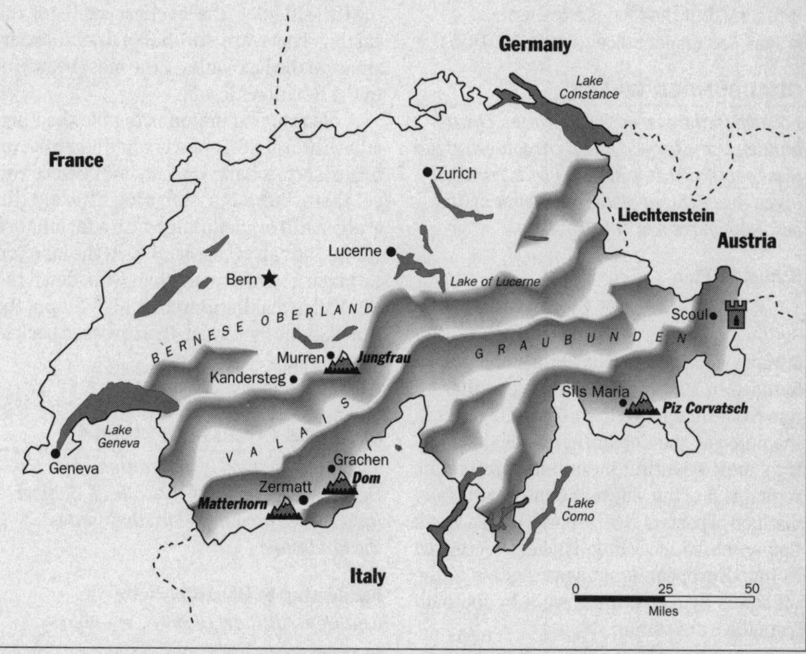

walks. First take the cable car, skipping the trail that passes underneath the car, to the Hotel Schwarzee, which provides views of the Matterhorn and the Gorner Glacier. From the hotel it is about a three-hour hike to Hornlihutte, a little mountain inn that serves as the base camp for hardy souls preparing to climb the Matterhorn. This lonely, pyramid-shaped mountain can only be attempted by experienced climbers with technical climbing skills, but for hikers, there are some lovely walks. You can spend the night at the Hornlihutte, which is operated by the Swiss Alpine Club, then get up at 4 a.m. and breakfast with the mountaineers attempting to climb the summit, or you can walk back to Zermatt the same day and dine more elegantly.

☎Zermatt tourist office: (4128) 66 11 81

Grächen to Saas Fee

9 miles ➤ Altitude: 6,200 ft. ➤ 6–7 hours

■ Saas Fee is, separated from Zermatt by the Dom (14,941 ft.), the highest peak of the Mischabel range. Although lesser known than Zermatt, Saas Fee rivals it as one of the most spectacular mountain villages in the Valais. Like Zermatt, no cars are allowed. The environs allow for relatively easy walks as well as challenging hikes into the heights overlooking the Saas valley. There are 170 miles of clearly marked trails.

For this hike take the bus to Grächen and hike back to Saas Fee above the Saas valley. It is a demanding hour's hike along ridge trails with a few steep sections and occasional drop-offs. About half an hour from Saas Fee, on the forested trail (inaccessible by car) is the Fletchorn Inn, perched on a cliff with a terrace that has a spectacular view. A famous chef, Irma Douce, presides. It is very informal, but the food is excellent.

☎ Saas Fee tourist office: (4128) 57 14 57

GRAUBÜNDEN WALKS

Located in the east of Switzerland, Graubünden is the largest Swiss canton—and the least populated. It is known for its rural villages, magnificent vistas, and some of the best-known resorts in Europe.

Schuol to Ftan

7 miles ➤ Altitude: over 6,200 ft. ➤ 1 1/2 hours

■ Make your base in Guarda, a small village founded in 1197 and not that much different now from what it was then. The village lies in the midst of the Engadine, one of the country's most beautiful mountain ranges. The region is one the oldest and most culturally distinctive parts of Switzerland; people speak Romansch, which is linguistically not related to Indo-European languages. Access to the village is by a 20-minute walk by footpath from the train station.

The walk starts in Schuol, 20 minutes by foot from Guarda. Before you embark on your hike, cross over the Inn river to the Tarasp castle, a beautifully preserved medieval structure perched on its own demi-mountain. Then from Schuol, take the lift up the mountain and head for the ridge trail going west. There's a panoramic vista looking south to the snow-capped mountains that divide Switzerland from Italy. The trail descends through the woods into Ftan, a charming old town. In Ftan, perched on its own precipice with magnificent views, is the Hotel Paradiso, which is expensive but very good. From Ftan, you can take a 45-minute walk or bus back to Schuol.

☎ Guarda Tourist office: (4181) 862 23 42

Sils-Maria to Sgrisches Lake and back

6 miles ➤ Altitude: 6,200 ft. ➤ 3–4 hours

■ Sils-Maria is a small (pop. under 500) and quiet resort in the upper Engadine. The village lies at the beginning of the Engadine valley on a slope beneath the peak of Piz Corvatsch and between the lakes of Silvaplana and Sils. The German philosopher Friedrich Nietzsche, not known for his uplifting prose, lived here from 1881 to 1888—one can visit the room where he stayed. He called the little hamlet "the loveliest corner of the earth." There are still horse-drawn excursions up the Fex Valley—the most beautiful in the Bernina Massif.

A pleasant excursion is to take the Furtcillas lift from Sils-Maria and then hike up to Sgrishches Lake. Half an hour before you get there, there is a charming little alp (literally a hill or mountain) with a farmhouse where you can get fresh milk. At the lake you can take a chilly swim, then walk down the Fex Valley, making a circular hike. Stop at the Hotel Sonne for dinner, then proceed back to Sils-Maria.

☎ Sils-Maria tourist office: (4182) 4 52 37

BERNESE OBERLAND WALKS

The southern part of the canton of Bern, where the Jungfrau, one of Switzerland's most famous peaks, dominates the landscape.

Kandersteg to Blumslialphutte

6 miles ➤ Altitude: 10,900 ft. ➤ 4 hours

■ At the north end of the 9-mile-long Lotschberg Tunnel (which links Bern and the Rhone Valley), Kandersteg lies in a lush valley with cattle-grazed alpine meadows. The town, known as a hiker's paradise, has a variety of trails, ranging from easy to difficult. Skip the trail and take the lift up to the Hotel Oeschinensee—the veranda of the hotel overlooking the Lake Oeschinensee is one of the most scenic spots in Switzerland to have lunch. Tall, imposing pine trees grow on the edge of the lake and there's a waterfall at one end. At the end of the lake, a path leads onward and upward to Blumslialphutte, a hut atop Hohturli—a demanding hike. Stay overnight at the Swiss Alpine Club–operated

EXPERT TIPS

FAR FROM THE MADDENING CROWDS

Some are remote, supplied only by mules or, in this modern age, helicopters. Many are converted farmhouses, typically with scrubbed pine walls and floors and book-lined parlors. Most do not have TVs, private bathrooms, or electric blankets. However, the Swiss berghaus do offer comfortable beds, hearty meals, and a homey atmosphere. Here are some recommendations from Marcia and Philip Lieberman, authors of numerous books on Switzerland, including The Berghaus *(to be published), a guide to Swiss mountain inns.(All prices are double occupancy and include dinner.) You should phone, at least a day or two ahead, for reservations.*

UPPER KIENTAL VALLEY
Both these inns in the Bernese Oberland region can be reached pretty easily by road.

■ **PENSION GOLDERLI.** Located in the tiny hamlet of Griesalp. The new owners used to run a hotel outside St. Moritz.
$110 per night
☎41-33762192

■ **WALDRAND.** Like the Golderli, a good base for going over the passes to Mürren or Kandersteg.
$100 per night
☎41-33761010

LAUTREBRUNNENTAL VALLEY
To reach the following two inns, take a bus to Stecshelberg hamlet. Walk on a trail for 2 1/2 hours to reach Tschingelhorn. After another half an hour walk, you'll reach Obersteinberg.

■ **TSCHINGELHORN.** You reach the end after a rather steady and steep climb through the woods.
$80 per night
☎41-36551343

■ **OBERSTEINBERG.** The inn sits across from a spectacular waterfall. Retire early, there's no electricity in the rooms.
$90 per night
☎41-36552033

ABOVE ZERMATT
You can take a cable car to Zunnegga or to Blowherd, then it's a short walk to the hotel.

■ **HOTEL FLUHALP.** One of the older berghaus, it has a great view of the mountains, especially the Matterhorn. Often frequented by climbers.
$110 per night
☎41-2661181

hut, which sits on the edge of a glacier, or return to Kandersteg.
☎Kandersteg tourist office: 41-75-2233

Griesalp to Murren
10 miles ➤ Altitude: 6,100 ft ➤ 7 hours

■ Start from the tiny hamlet of Griesalp nestled high up in the alpine meadows. You can stay at the Pension Golderli, a charming, but simple mountain inn with a spectacular valley views (see box). The first hour and a half of the walk winds through mountain meadows. After another hour and a half you reach Ober Durrenberg, at 6,000 feet, the highest occupied farm in Europe. Here you can have refreshments and, if you feel like spending the night, there is a hayloft above the cows and the goats where you can sleep. A two-hour difficult hike from Ober Durrenberg takes you to the top of Sefinenfurkepasse, a pass where you begin a spectacular walk down into Mürren. Halfway down, stop at a little hut called Rotstockhutt for a rosti, a Swiss dish made from potatoes. As you descend, you'll see the Eiger, Monch, and Jungfrau, three of the most famous mountains in Switzerland. Mürren (pop. 350) is located on a rocky shelf overlooking the Lauterbrunnen Valley in the shadow of the Jungfrau massif.
☎Griesalp tourist office: (4135) 55 16 16

BARGES

SLOW BOATS THRU EUROPE

With your craft moving at a snail's pace, you won't miss a thing

Before roads, canals and rivers were the major thoroughfares of Europe, criss-crossing the fields and wending their way through towns. Almost all the major cities of Europe were built on the banks of a river. Canals are hardly the avenues of commerce they once were, but they haven't fallen into total disuse. Pleasure boats and refitted barges laden with tourists now ply the waterways. At 8 to 12 mph, the scenery hardly goes whizzing by—and that's the beauty and charm of this antiquated mode of travel. The canals pass through some of the oldest and most picturesque parts of many European towns. It's possible for passengers to disembark for a walk or bicycle ride. The quarters on board have been modernized. Depending on the barge, the food can be of gourmet standard.

FACT FILE:

ALONG EUROPE'S WATERWAYS

■ *Approximate lengths of (mainly) interconnected navigable rivers and canals*

England and Wales	3,500 miles
Scotland	167 miles
Ireland	500 miles
France	5,000 miles
Germany	4,430 miles
Belgium	969 miles
Netherlands	4,600 miles

There are several barge options: Hotel barges are the most leisurely way to go; you don't have to maneuver boats into locks, and meals, cocktails, and excursions are included. However, the price can run to $300–$500 per person per day. Less pricey are self-driven barges, which accommodate 4 to 10 people. Many of these are converted commercial vessels and can be steered by a beginner, after a minimal amount of instruction. In France the average price of a four-person self-drive barge is about $1,000 a week.

We asked Hugh McKnight, one of the pioneers in the self-drive barge vacation who has taken barge trips throughout Europe for the past 30 years and is the author of many books on barges, including *Cruising French Waterways* and *Slow Boat Through Germany* (available through Shepperton Swan Ltd. in England ☎ 44–181–01932), to recommend the continent's best barge trips.

ENGLAND

■ **LEEDS AND LIVERPOOL CANAL.** This early 19th-century waterway in the north of England connects the east and west coasts via the rugged moorland scenery of Yorkshire and Lancashire. The canal features stone-built locks, many manually operated swing bridges, and appealing small mill towns.

■ **RIVER THAMES.** A historic and beautiful river with locks and weirs, crossing southern England from London to Gloucestershire and the Cotswolds. Famous towns and cities include Windsor (an 11th-century royal castle), Henley (Europe's premier rowing regatta), and the university center of Oxford.

SCOTLAND

■ **CALEDONIAN CANAL.** This early 19th-century engineering feat provides a coast-to-coast navigation through the Scottish Highlands from Fort William to Inverness. Spectacular "staircase" (multiple-chambered) locks and lengths of artificial canal link a series of natural lakes, including Loch Ness, renowned for its elusive monster.

IRELAND

■ **RIVER SHANNON.** The longest waterway in

EXPERT SOURCES

WHERE TO RENT-A-BARGE

Author, barge veteran, and trip guide Hugh McKnight offers these suggestions. He can be reached in England at ☎ 44–181–01932.

HOTEL BARGES & SHIPS

U. K. W. H. LTD.
■ British waterways.
✉1, Port Hill, Hertford, SG14 1PJ ☎ FAX (441992) 587392

HIGHLAND MINI-CRUISES
■ Luxury barge cruises in Scotland's Caledonian Canal.
✉Muirtown Top Lock, Caledonian Canal, Inverness, Scotland, IV3 6NF
☎ (441463) 711913

RENT A CANAL CRUISER

CROWN BLUE LINE LTD.
■ Britain, France, Netherlands, also Erie Canal, USA.
✉8 Ber St., Norwich, Norfolk, NR1 3EJ. Great Britain
☎ (441603) 630513

HOSEASONS HOLIDAYS
■ Britain and France.
✉Sunway House, Lowestoft, Suffolk, NR32 3LT, Great Britain
☎ (441502) 501010

FRENCH COUNTRY CRUISES

■ Trips in France, Netherlands, and Mecklenburg/Germany.
✉Andrew Brock Travel Ltd, 54 High St East, Uppingham, Rutland, LE15 9PZ, Great Britain
☎ (441572) 821330

EMERALD STAR LINE
■ Irish waterways.
✉Star Line, 47 Dawson St., Dublin, Ireland
☎ 353–1–6798166

the British Isles, navigable from the south coast and via lakes large and small to the border of Northern Ireland. A 19th-century canal has been restored to provide a link with the huge and island-studded Lough Erne. This route is very thinly populated.

FRANCE

■ **CANAL DU MIDI ROUTE.** Together with the Canal lateral à la Garonne, the largely 17th-century Canal du Midi provides a navigable link through southern France from the Mediterranean to the Atlantic. Locks, buildings, and aqueducts are all over 300 years old.

■ **RIVER MEUSE.** From its upper reaches near the city of Nancy, this canalized river is one of the most beautiful in all Europe, especially as it passes through the Ardennes forests near the border with Belgium.

■ **WATERWAYS OF ALSACE.** The Canal de la Marne au Rhin and associated waterways in the northeastern part of the country have a Germanic character. Radar-operated locks are totally automatic as the route passes through pine forests in the valley of the Zorn River.

GERMANY

■ **RIVER RHINE.** The Rhine runs for 640 miles through Europe. The uppermost reaches (Strasbourg to Switzerland) are canalized with giant ship locks. Elsewhere, it flows unimpeded, especially through the castle-filled Rhine Gorge (Bingen to Koblenz). The river is most conveniently visited aboard one of the many large cruise ships, which take four to five days exploring the major part of the river.

■ **RIVER LAHN.** The Lahn is a Rhine tributary, branching off near Koblenz and terminating in the cathedral city of Limburg. Although the river is only 40 miles long, a return journey can easily fill a week, for every one of the towns and villages en route is well worth exploring.

■ **MECKLENBURG LAKES.** This is a complicated network of interconnected lakes north of Berlin in former East Germany. Because the area has been practically untouched by development since the 1930s, one of its attractions is the large number of traditional pre–World War II privately owned pleasure craft.

SIGHT-SEEING

A WHALE OF A GOOD TIME

The largest, oldest living mammals are a source of endless fascination

While whale hunting dates from time immemorial, whale-watching as a commercial activity began as recently as 1955 in North America. Today, whale-watching takes place in the waters of over 40 countries. Unfortunately, the hunters got a good jump on the watchers and of the 32 species of whales, 8 are endangered. Today, whale hunting for profit has been banned, although a number of countries continue to kill whales under the subterfuge of conducting scientific research. And now there's a new danger, as well. Evidence has shown that the accumulation of toxic wastes in the ocean, most notably PCBs, has caused a life-threatening condition in many whales.

In his book *Among Whales*, renowned whale scientist Roger Payne claims that whales have brains at least as complex as humans. Part of the fascination of watching these gargantuan creatures comes from the many behaviors that we share with them—singing to each other for pleasure, romping, and communicating vocally.

More impressive is the whale's endurance—they have existed about 63 million years longer than humans. The gray whale is the largest thing (including the dinosaur) that ever lived, but the whale genus also includes species ranging from the killer whale to the dolphin. Here's a guide to the more common species and how you can spot them:

BLUE

Blue whale calves can gain 200 pounds a day, feeding on an 8-ton daily diet of small crustaceans known as krill. Long and streamlined, with a mottled blue-gray color and a small dorsal fin, blue whales have tall, dense spouts with flat snouts that appear U-shaped from above.

HUMPBACK

Humpbacks are noted for their leaps from the water and their singing voices. They reach a maximum length of 53 feet, and have a white right lower lip and a white edge on the upper jaw.

GRAY

Now extinct in the North Atlantic, gray whales continue to populate the North Pacific. The California group is well known for its annual migration along the west coast of North America from November through May. Instead of dorsal fins, they have a series of bumps on the back behind a larger bump. They reach a top length of 49 feet and are often covered with barnacles and "whale lice."

RIGHT (BOWHEAD)

The first whale to be hunted commercially, bowhead whales are still hunted by Alaskan natives—a big source of controversy since they're considered the most critically endangered whales. They reach a top length of 60 feet and have large broad flippers. All black except for a white blotch, their most distinctive feature is patches of grayish, rough skin on their heads—known as callosities.

SPERM

The toothed whale made famous by Herman Melville's *Moby-Dick*, the sperm whale is the most numerous of large whales. They can remain submerged for hours, and sonars have tracked sperm whales to depths of 9,200 feet. They can grow 65 feet long and their distinct, rectangular heads make them easy to spot.

ORCA (KILLER)

These distinctively colored black-and-white whales are the only predators of their fellow whales (besides man). They reach a length of 31 feet and live at the high latitudes of the northern and southern hemispheres.

EXPERT LIST

WHERE TO WATCH THE WHALES

Thar she blows, or so says the World Wildlife Fund. Here are the spots where whales are most likely to spout off.

SOUTHERN OCEAN WHALE SANCTUARY
Antarctica. Boat access only.

■ **SIGHTS.** Humpback, southern right, and minke whales. On occasion, these whales can be seen creating a "net" of bubbles around a school of fish that they will feed upon, or "spy-hopping," holding themselves up vertically to inspect the boats of people watching them.
■ **PEAK SEASON:** Summer.

SAMANA BAY
Dominican Republic. Boat and shoreline access.

■ **SIGHTS.** Humpback, pilot, and Bryde's whales. Behaviors include breeching, singing, courtship, social gathering, and feeding.
■ **PEAK SEASON:** January–March.

CAMPBELL RIVER
British Columbia. Shoreline, motorboat, or sailboat access.

■ **SIGHTS.** Minke and orcas (killer whales). Behaviors include feeding and belly-rubbing, where orcas rub their ventral surfaces on shallow rocks, presumably to get rid of parasites.
■ **PEAK SEASON:** June–September.

CAPE COD
Massachusetts. Boat access only.

■ **SIGHTS.** Humpback, fin, northern right, minke, and pilot whales. Watchers can see bubble-net feeding, spy-hopping, breeching, social gathering. Notable for diversity of species, but watching limited to good weather.
■ **PEAK SEASON:** April–October.

BAJA CALIFORNIA
Mexico. Shoreline and boat access.

■ **SIGHTS.** Gray, blue, and humpbacks. Behaviors include breeching, logging (sleeping), spy-hopping, feeding, calving, and social gathering. Grays breeding and calving on the Pacific shores, humpbacks and blues in the Sea of Cortez.
■ **PEAK SEASON:** Almost year-round.

LOFOTEN ISLANDS
Norway. Boat access only.

■ **SIGHTS.** Sperm, minkes, and orcas. Hearty watchers can see feeding, pairing, and breeching.
■ **PEAK TIME:** Summer.

KAIKKOURA
New Zealand. Boat and shoreline access.

■ **SIGHTS.** Sperm whale (one of the few places to see these deep-water whales so close to shore) and orcas, also Hector's and dusky dolphins. Behavior includes feeding and diving.
■ **PEAK SEASON:** Year-round.

WHALE ROUTE
South Africa. Shoreline access.

■ **SIGHTS.** From Cape Town to Cape Aguihas, species include southern right whale, humpback, Bryde's whale, and orca. Feeding, breeching, and breeding behaviors can be seen.
■ **PEAK SEASON:** August–November.

PATAGONIA
Argentina. Boat and shoreline access.

■ **SIGHTS.** Southern right whale and orcas. Breeching, singing, social gathering can be seen. Watchers with fortitude can observe as orcas swim up onto the beach and nab baby sea lions for food.
■ **PEAK SEASON:** June–December.

SHIKOKU
Japan. Boat access only.

■ **SIGHTS.** Bryde's whales can be observed. Social gathering, breeching behavior can be seen. Fishermen conduct well-organized trips.
■ **PEAK SEASON:** Year-round.

RAFTING

WHITE WATER RUNS THROUGH IT

Ten rafting journeys the whole family can enjoy

White-water rafting isn't for the faint of heart, but it isn't just for daredevils, either. Outfitters all across the country now offer trips for families. Children generally need to be 11 and up, as well as reasonably good swimmers. But those are the only requirements, plus perhaps an ample supply of adrenaline. We asked Jeff Bennett, a contributing editor at *Canoe and Kayak* magazine and author of *The Complete White-water Rafter* (MacGraw Hill/Ragged Press, 1996), for his picks of the 10 best white-water rafting trips for families, along with the best guides.

South Fork of the American River

California ➤ 21 miles ➤ Class III

■ This stretch of river has long been California's most popular commercial trip. Dozens of Class II and III rapids, rich gold-era history, and easy access to big cities combine with sunshine and scenic rolling hills to create the perfect family trip. The big thrills happen at the river's two Class III rapids, Troublemaker and Satan's Cesspool.

■ OUTFITTERS:

Beyond Limits Adventures ☎ 800-234-7238
Tributary Whitewater Tours ☎ 916-346-6812
Whitewater Voyages ☎ 800-488-7238

Deschutes River

Oregon ➤ 13 to 98 miles ➤ Class III

■ Running through the heart of Oregon's high-desert country, the Deschutes River provides a suprisingly sunny getaway for Pacific Northwesterners accustomed to damp, drizzly weather. Rafters can enjoy a bouncy one-day jaunt down the crowded Maupin section, or opt for a two- to five-day canoeing trip down the Deschutes's more remote corridors. Stair-stepped basalt cliffs, grassy meadows, and world-class fishing holes add to the experience.

■ OUTFITTERS:

Ewing's Whitewater ☎ 800-538-7238
Hunter Expeditions ☎ 503-389-8370
Rapid River Rafters ☎ 800-962-3327

Salmon River, Upper Main

Idaho ➤ up to 35 miles ➤ Classes II to III +

■ Just 90 minutes north of Sun Valley, the headwaters of the Salmon River cut a path through the Sawtooth National Recreation Area. At normal summer flows, the Salmon's emerald currents slip past smooth granite boulders and towering pines, occasionally erupting into series of big roller-coaster-style waves.

■ OUTFITTERS:

The River Company ☎ 800-398-0346
Triangle C Ranch Whitewater ☎ 208-774-2266
White Otter Outdoor Adventures ☎ 208-726-4331

Snake River (Grand Teton)

Wyoming ➤ 30 miles ➤ Classes I to II

■ One of the best ways to soak in the breathtaking beauty of Great Teton National Park is to float the Snake River downstream from Jackson Lake. You can comfortably gawk at the Teton's distant spires or search the banks for moose, bears, otters, and a variety of waterfowl.

■ OUTFITTERS:

Barker-Ewing Float Trips ☎ 800-365-1800
Fort Jackson Float Trips ☎ 800-735-8430
OARS ☎ 800-346-6277

Colorado River, Glenwood Canyon

Colorado ➤ 10 to 15 miles ➤ Classes II to III

■ Just three hours from downtown Denver, the Glenwood Canyon section of the Upper Colorado River carves a narrow, cliff-lined gorge alongside Interstate 70. Layers of sandstone, limestone, and granite rise from the riverbed, while cavalcades of big waves accent the toughest rapids.

■ OUTFITTERS:

Blazing Paddles Raft Adventures ☎ 800-282-7238
Blue Sky Adventures ☎ 303-945-6605
Timberline Tours ☎ 800-831-1414

Rio Grande, State Park and Racecourse sections

New Mexico ➤ 6.5–10.8 miles ➤ Classes II to III+

■ The Rio Grande rises along the eastern flanks of the southern Colorado Rockies, then flows 1,887 miles south to the Gulf of Mexico. Near Taos, N.M., it enters a spectacular and challenging gorge known as the Taos Box. To catch a taste of the Box, without the hazards of big rapids, families can paddle the Rio Grande's State Park and Racecourse sections near the quaint town of Pilar.

■ **OUTFITTERS:**

Far Flung Adventures ☎ 800-359-4138
New Wave Rafting Company ☎ 505-984-1444
Rio Grande Rapid Transit ☎ 800-222-7238

Kennebec River

Maine ➤ 6 to12 miles ➤ Classes III to IV+

■ Controlled releases from the Central Maine Power Company's Harris Station Dam guarantee reliable summertime flows, while memorable rapids like Magic Falls ensure tons of excitement. For a more sedentary experience through the Kennebec wilderness, run the Carry Brook section.

■ **OUTFITTERS:**

Eastern River Expeditions ☎ 800-634-7238
New England Whitewater Center ☎ 800-766-7238
North Country Rivers ☎ 800-348-8871

Youghiogheny River

Pennsylvania ➤ 7.5 miles ➤ Classes II to IV

■ The lower Youghiogheny was the first river east of the Mississippi to be commercially rafted. Tracing a serpentine path through the Laurel Mountains near Ohiopyle State Park, the Lower Youghiogheny alternates between challenging rapids and calm pools. Although scheduled launch times help keep the river traffic in check, plan your trip ahead of time, as over 100,000 people run it every year!

■ **OUTFITTERS:**

Mountain Streams & Trails ☎ 800-245-4090
White Water Adventures ☎ 800-992-7238
Wilderness Voyageurs ☎ 800-272-4141

Ocoee River

Tennessee ➤ 4.5 miles ➤ Class III to IV

■ Recently made famous by hosting the 1996

■ A QUICK GUIDE TO WHITE-WATER RAPIDS

River conditions can vary widely and unpredictably. The following ratings were developed to give those unfamiliar with a river a feel for what they are getting into—before they get into it.

■ **CLASS I:** Flat water, some current.

■ **CLASS II:** Small waves.

■ **CLASS III:** Big waves, requires maneuvering through "hydraulic holes" in which the water breaks back on itself over a rock.

■ **CLASS IV:** Big waves, many rocks, and very fast, powerful water. Requires precise maneuverability. Not fun to swim in if you make a mistake.

■ **CLASS V:** Pushing the limits of navigability, should be done only by experts. Extremely steep gradient of river: 30- to 40-foot drops. Mistakes or capsizing will result in injury or possibly death.

■ **CLASS VI:** Pushing the absurd. Paddlers on the West Coast define it as not runnable. Those on the East recommend it only for experts, lunatics, or both. Injury or death is a distinct possibility.

EXPERT PICKS

THE ULTIMATE RIVER RAFTING TRIP

Going down the Colorado through the Grand Canyon

"The type of experience that makes people go home and quit their jobs," is how Jeff Renakee, veteran river rat and author of *River Days: A Collection of Essays* (Fulcrum Press, 1988), refers to a rafting trip through the Grand Canyon. In Renakee's years as a guide on the river, he never saw anyone glad to go home. The trip, along 226 or 270 (depending where you get off) unspoiled miles of the Colorado River is the longest and wildest river trip in the lower 48 states.

Nothing matches the magnitude of the Grand Canyon and the stupendous force that created it. Along the edge of the canyon is writ the geologic history of the last two billion years—from the relatively recent Jurassic period, 1.2 million years old, to the bottom layer of Vishnu rock, at approximately 2.0 billion years, some of the oldest rock in the world.

Three-quarters of the trips down the river are via motorized boats, which whisk though the canyon in about 6 days. Kim Crumbo, author of *A River Runner's Guide to the History of the Grand Canyon* (Johnson Press, 1981), and a former guide who has been down the canyon over a hundred times, recommends non-motorized boats, because they don't interfere with the majestic quiet of the canyon. It takes 12 to 18 days to make the trip in a nonmotorized boat; from Memorial Day to December they are the only craft allowed on the river.

The most common type of nonmotorized craft are oar boats, where one or two river guides control the oars while passengers sit back and take in the scenery. For more adventurous types who want an active participatory experience, a few companies run paddle boats where everyone paddles.

Rafting down the canyon may be the experience of a lifetime, but many people have to wait part of a lifetime to do it. The number of people allowed each year has been frozen at the 1972 limit of 20,000—roughly 800 trips down the river. For a commercial trip that averages about 25 passengers, you have to plan at least a year in advance. If you are an experienced rafter, you can apply for a permit, but these days, the average wait for private trips is 12 years. The best times to go are in the spring and the fall, when it's less crowded, and more temperate. Average summer highs are 106 degrees.

■ **FOR A LIST OF OUTFITTERS CONTACT:**
River Subdistrict Office, Grand Canyon National Park, PO Box 129, Grand Canyon, AZ 86023

Olympic white-water competitions, the Ocoee has long been a favorite among southeastern rafters. A healthy gradient and an endless assortment of boulders combine to form nearly continuous rapids on the section between the Ocoee Diversion Dam and its powerhouse downstream.

■ **OUTFITTERS:**
Nantahala Outdoor Center ☎ 800–232–7238
Ocoee Outdoors ☎ 800–533–7767
Southeastern Expeditions ☎ 800–868–7238

Nantahala River

North Carolina ➤ 8 miles ➤ Classes II to III

■ The Nantahala, just east of Great Smoky Mountains National Park, runs along a valley thick with rhododendron, mountain laurel, and princess trees. Nantahala Falls (a sharp Class III+) highlights the trip.

■ **OUTFITTERS:**
Nantahala Outdoor Center ☎ 800–232–7238
USA Raft ☎ 800–872–7238
Wildwater Ltd. ☎ 800–451–9972

WILDERNESS SCHOOLS

CLASSES AS BIG AS ALL OUTDOORS

Where you can learn how to start a fire and other survival skills

Unlike many things that you can learn on your own, the consequences of failure while teaching yourself outdoor adventure skills can be disastrous—freezing to near-death in the wilderness, falling off a cliff face, or losing your kayak in the rapids, to name some of the grimmer possibilities. Fortunately, there are ways to avoid that fate. One is to go on guided expeditions with skilled chaperons. Or, you can sign up for a wilderness course. Here are some options for the dedicated outdoorsperson.

OUTWARD BOUND

Tanzania, Nepal, Russia, Mexico, and all over the United States.

■ The original outdoor school, Outward Bound is the biggest and has the most varied offerings. An Outward Bound program usually includes a one- to three-day solo, when a student goes off by him- or herself into the woods with little or no food.

■ **TUITION:** $600 for a five-day course to $7,300 for an 81-day semester course.

■ **AGE RANGE:** 14 and up, but there are courses for all ages as well as special groups (e.g., women-only, troubled youngsters, etc.).

☎914–424–4000 or 800–243–8520

NATIONAL OUTDOOR LEADERSHIP SCHOOL

British Columbia, Mexico, Chile, Kenya, and all over the United States.

■ NOLS focuses on developing technical wilderness skills; programs are developed for those who are in shape and already somewhat comfortable in a wilderness setting. NOLS does have programs for younger kids, but most programs are more suited to older adolescents and adults.

■ **TUITION:** $2,600 for a 30-day basic wilderness skills course; $6,300 to $7,900 for a 70- to 90-day semester course.

■ **AGE RANGE:** 14+ (average age: 20); there are also courses for 25+ as well as 50+.

☎307–332–6973

NANTAHALA OUTDOOR CENTER

Primarily the South, but there are also special expeditions that take beginners to Honduras, Fiji, Costa Rica, and Corsica.

■ The leading white-water school in the country, Nantahala Outdoor Center is the place to learn kayaking and white-water rafting. Recently, the school added mountain biking and rock climbing courses to its repertoire.

■ **TUITION:** $330 for a two-day basic course to $1,025 for a seven-day course. Courses offered March through November.

■ **AGE RANGE:** Minimum, 16.

☎704–488–6737

APPALACHIAN MOUNTAIN CLUB

Courses are run primarily in New Hampshire's White Mountains, but there are also courses throughout the Northeast.

■ This club is involved in conservation, outdoor trips, and maintaining the Appalachian Trail. It also sponsors low-cost outdoor workshops that focus on handling yourself in the wilderness.

■ **TUITION:** Ranges from $80 for a two-day backpacking workshop to $675 for a two-week medical first response course.

■ **AGE RANGE:** No minimum age.

☎603–466–2721

AMERICAN ALPINE INSTITUTE

Alaska, Argentina, Bolivia, Canada, Mexico, Chile, Ecuador, Nepal, and Switzerland.

■ The AAI is the largest, and widely regarded as the best, all-around mountaineering school in North America. A skills school, the AAI focuses on getting up and down mountains safely, not on group dynamics or wilderness ethics.

■ **TUITION:** Six-day program, $760; 36-day alpine mountaineering program, $4,880.

■ **AGE RANGE:** Based on the level of student experience.

☎360–671–1505

GETTING THERE

FLYING: The best airlines in the sky, PAGE 541 **BOOKINGS:** What to do if you are bumped from a flight, PAGE 543 **FREQUENT FLYERS:** Where you'll get the best deals, PAGE 543 **AIRFARES:** Four ways to fly for less, PAGE 547 **RAILWAYS:** Trains to travel the world, PAGE 549 **CRUISES:** A guide to the best ships, PAGE 552 **HOTELS:** Top-ranked places to crash for the night, PAGE 557 **SIGHT-SEEING:** Ten of America's weirdest attractions, PAGE 558

AIR TRAVEL

HOW SAFE IS YOUR PLANE?

A checklist for worrywarts who fear that they might not beat the odds

If you're a white-knuckle flyer, there's almost no amount of reassurance that can allow you to sit back, relax, and enjoy the flight. Not the fact that over the five-year period ending in 1994, your chance of being killed while flying was approximately one in 2.7 million. Nor the fact that your chance of being killed while flying on a major U.S. airline is even more remote—there's only one death per every 7.5 million passengers. Nor the fact that even if your plane did crash, these days one-third of the passengers typically survive, up from one-quarter not very long ago. "The United States has fifty percent of the world's traffic," reports FAA administrator David Hinson, "and only eight percent of the fatalities."

But doesn't your fate depend on what airline you're flying? Of course it does and here the statistics can be elucidating and misleading, sometimes at the same time. For example, consider the cases of Southwest Airlines and USAir. Southwest has the best safety record of the world's 85 major airlines since its first flight in 1971, according to *Condé Nast Traveler*, which compiled data from a variety of official air transportation sources. Southwest has carried 300 million passengers without a fatality—at least, that was the case as this book was going to press in mid-1996. USAir, by contrast, comes in 47th place when ranking airlines from least to most fatal accidents. Does that mean that USAir's planes are inherently more unsafe than Southwest's? Probably not. Southwest is fortunate that most of its routes are in an area of the country that has generally good weather, while many of USAir's routes crisscross the Northwest, where frequent inclement weather conditions make flying more dangerous. Also, USAir has been in the business a lot longer than Southwest, consequently logging about two-and-a-half times as many flights.

However, the worriers will find plenty to keep worrying. As the number of air passengers increases, the number of fatalities will also surely rise. By one calculation, there could be a 77 percent increase in fatal accidents by the year 2003, if safety procedures are not improved. The U.S. government is trying to do its part. The Federal Aviation Administration and the Department of Transportation have announced a "zero accidents" goal and are spending billions on programs in different areas, including upgrading obsolete aircraft control equipment.

EXPERT TIPS

THE SAFEST SEATS ON BOARD

Since in most accidents, an aircraft travels with its nose down as well as bumping along the ground for a bit after impact, it stands to reason that sitting in one of the front rows won't increase your chances of survival. But, are some seats on a plane really safer than others? Experts usually duck the question since there are so many possible crash scenarios, but there are some precautions you can take when reserving a seat:

■ **BOYCOTT BULKHEAD ROWS.** Although seats that face the bulkheads and interior dividers provide more legroom, they can also be more hazardous. Serious head injuries resulting when passengers hit their heads on the walls during air turbulence and landings top the list of non-crash injury concerns. The FAA, airlines, and safety researchers are investigating ways to lessen the danger, such as shoulder belts and airbags. Currently, only the Boeing 777, which has cushioned walls, passes the new federal standards. Until an appropriate solution is designed for other aircraft, Hamid Lankarani, an airline crash injury specialist at the National Institute for Aviation Research, advises passengers who are above average in height to sit elsewhere: the taller the person, the greater the chance of hitting the bulkhead.

■ **REQUEST A WINGSIDE SEAT:** Seats close to the aircraft wings are structurally more sound and have better support.

■ **LOOK FOR AN EXIT ROW:** Sitting by an emergency exit not only provides more legroom but also allows easier escape from fire and smoke dangers. But wherever you sit, be sure to count the number of rows you are from an exit; that way, if the lights go out, you can still find your way to safety.

■ **SETTLE FOR A GOOD BOOK:** Video screens or phone sets in the seat back, increasingly common now, may make your trip more enjoyable, but they also add danger. Like the bulkhead, these stiff objects may cause head injuries. You're better off staring at a plain seat back.

Most of the burden, however, falls on airline manufacturers and the carriers themselves. So far, newer planes are proving themselves safer than older models. Yet, passengers are not entirely at the mercy of the airlines. Here are some factors you may want to consider:

■ Avoid airlines that show systemic problems. Between 1989 and 1994, for example, three carriers, according to an analysis by *Condé Nast Traveler* magazine, continued to have accident rates similar to those recorded during the previous 20 years. Aeroflot, which since the breakup of the Soviet Union has been fragmented into many carriers, had 103 fatal accidents during that five-year period. Indian Airlines (but not Air India, which hasn't had a fatal accident since 1989) and Philippines Airlines have each had more than 10 fatal accidents in the last 25 years.

■ Keep abreast of updates from an FAA task force investigating the use of unapproved airplane parts. (The *Federal Register* and aviation publications are sources of information, as are newspapers and TV reports.) If you have a concern about the misuse of parts, call the FAA Safety Hotline ☎ 800-255-1111.

■ You can choose to postpone your flight

because of inclement weather, even if the airline does not. However, you may be subject to penalties, depending on the airline.

■ The rates for accidents and fatalities on commuter airlines and on-demand air taxis are many times higher than those of the nine major U.S. carriers—and so are the risks.

■ Of the world's 50 biggest airports, New York's JFK has had the most crashes—22 since 1955. With 14 accidents, Chicago's O'Hare is second worst. Los Angeles International and London's Heathrow tie for third, with 12 accidents each. (Crash statistics also exist for individual aircraft types, see table at right.)

■ If you're traveling abroad, contact the FAA to determine if your destination has been cited for failing to meet international safety standards. Call ☎ 800–FAA–SURE.

■ Because safety is directly related to the amount of material and space that's available under your seat to absorb the energy of an impact, you have a better chance of surviving a crash if you're flying on a big plane. The key column in the following table is the percentage of survivors. The Boeing 727 has had 0.7 fatal crashes per million flights; the 737, 0.65 per million; and the 747, 1.46 per million. The next generation of Boeing planes—the 757 and 767—have an even better safety record. Each type has flown about 4.5 million times with only one fatal accident. Data wasn't available for the number of flights for the Airbus and McDonnell Douglas planes.

■ THE BIGGER, THE BETTER

Service	Entry date	Fatal accidents	% of survivors
AIRBUS INDUSTRIE			
A300	1974	4	25.3
A310	1983	3	0.0
A320	1988	3	41.6
BOEING			
727	1964	41	20.3
737	1968	36	38.8
747	1970	14	49.7
LOCKHEED L-1011			
TriStar	1972	5	47.5
MCDONNELL DOUGLAS			
DC-9	1965	34	22.4
DC-10	1971	8	45.6
MD-80	1980	4	47.1

SOURCE: "How Safe Is Flying," *Condé Nast Traveler*, December 1995.

CABIN FEVER: SOMETHING IN THE AIR

Do you get a headache, a cold, allergies, or nausea every time you fly? Any of these maladies might be caused or exacerbated by the cabin air you've been breathing. Two decades ago, ventilation systems on DC-9s or 727s circulated 100 percent fresh air throughout the cabin during a flight. But planes designed since the early 1980s recycle up to 50 percent of cabin air to burn less jet fuel and save money.

Some planes are known to have better air than others. Boeing 757s have high carbon dioxide levels in the cabin, according to *Travel & Leisure* magazine. Recycled air on narrow-body planes, like the 757 and 737, often becomes stale because there is so little space per passenger. A *Consumer Reports* study of air quality on 158 flights, however, found that "passenger cabin air in almost one in four commercial airline flights flunks a ventilation industry guideline for freshness."

Complaining during flights about stuffy air can sometimes help. Unfortunately, many newer planes have no ventilation adjustment dials; all the pilot can do is turn on or off a ventilation pack that has been preset either by the airline or by the manufacturer. If your plane has a stop en route, get off and take in the fresher air in the terminal. Ventilation is usually worse when a plane is parked than during flight.

AIR TRAVEL

THE BEST AIRLINES IN THE SKY

Results of the surveys are in. Here are the facts to help you pick

May we have the envelope, please. Southwest Airlines won top carrier honors in the 1996 Airline Quality Rating Report of America's nine largest airlines, moving up from second place a year earlier. American Airlines, which had won top honors three of the last five years, slipped to second place.

The AQR Report, conducted by the National Institute of Aviation Research at Wichita State University and the Univeristy of Nebraska at Omaha, is different from other surveys: it relies on objective data, not the opinions of passengers. The scores are based on 19 weighted factors including such things as mishandled baggage, average cost per seat-mile, and on-time performance. The numbers are crunched according to a complicated formula and an "airline quality rating" is produced. Southwest earned top marks in a number of the categories the AQR Report uses for its ratings. It had the youngest fleet and the best on-time record, for example (see table on page 542).

Other surveys, based on passenger opinions, produced quite different, and not entirely comparable, results. When *Frequent Flyer* magazine, for example, polled its readers about the nine largest U.S. carriers, Delta came out on top for overall service, placing first in 9 of 21 categories, such as baggage delivery speed, both short-haul and long-haul service, in-flight amenities, airport check-in, gate location, seating comfort, service with a smile, and on-time arrival. American Airlines came in a not-so-close second, earning first places in four categories: food service, food quality, availability of seat preference, and keeping flyers informed of schedule delays. United placed third.

Condé Nast Traveler's annual airline survey includes large and small airlines—not just the Big Nine included in the AQR and *Frequent Flyer* reports. Midwest Express came in number one, with 60.5 percent of the respondents grading it as "excellent" or "very good." It also came in first for cabin comfort/service and food. Alaska Airlines won the highest marks for scheduling, punctuality, and baggage handling. The lowest scores went to Northwest for punctuality, Kiwi for scheduling, and Reno Air for baggage handling.

Unlike the other surveys, *Condé Nast Traveler* also asks its readers' opinions of international carriers. The clear favorite: Singapore Airlines, which earned the top spots in four categories—scheduling, cabin comfort/service, food, and baggage han-

FACT FILE:

MOVE OVER, JULIA CHILD

■ *For those who just can't get enough of airline food, American Airlines is offering recipes so passengers can re-create the "subtle flavors and tantalizing aromas" in their own kitchens. The 18-page cookbook—*A Taste of Something Special*—contains a few recipes that verge on the complicated, such as "peanut crusted chicken with roasted banana honey sauce," but others, such as "ice cream sundae," that require little culinary skill: "Scoop ice cream into a clear, footed glass bowl or sundae glass; layer toppings and finish with whipped cream and nuts to create your very own premium class dessert."*

SOURCE: Associated Press.

dling. Singapore only stumbled in one category, punctuality, where Swissair, not surprisingly, placed first. Only two U.S. companies made the top 20, with Midwest Express coming in 15th and Alaska Airlines 17th. Interestingly, the *Condé Nast* results mirror a 1995 Zagat survey, the most comprehensive of the consumer preference studies with over 9,000 respondents. Midwest Express was the only American carrier in Zagat's top ten of international and domestic airlines. The top three overall: Singapore Airlines, Swissair, and Cathay Pacific. Among domestic carriers, the Zagat survey rated Midwest tops, followed by Alaska Airlines, Kiwi International, and American.

Of course, like a lot of other things in life, which airline is best for you ultimately depends on your individual likes and needs. For instance, TWA was touted in *Frequent Flyer*'s survey as having the most comfortable seats, and Northwest for the best frequent flyer program. Got a lot of bags to bring on board with you? America West had the best overhead storage. Absolutely have to get somewhere on time? Delta came in first for on-time arrival, but Southwest had the best ratings for overall on-time performance—it scored first for on-time departure and second for on-time arrival.

It's sometimes hard to square the results among the different surveys. By the AQR Report's objective criteria Southwest was tops, but it placed sixth overall in both the *Frequent Flyer* and *Condé Nast Traveler* reader surveys. Indeed, Southwest came in dead last when *Condé Nast* asked passengers about cabin comfort, service, and food—criteria that the AQR Report doesn't consider as a matter of course, unless there have been consumer complaints. The report does, however, consider cost per seat-mile in its rankings, where a budget carrier like Southwest excels.

Still, on occasion, there is conspicuous agreement between the results of the objective and subjective surveys. In both the AQR Report and *Frequent Flyer* survey, Continental came in last.

EXPERT PICKS

STACKING UP AMERICA'S BIG AIRLINES

The National Institute for Aviation Research at Wichita State University and the Aviation Institute at the University of Nebraska at Omaha combined forces to produce the 1996 Airline Quality Rating Report, which analyzes 19 objective criteria and assigns each of America's big nine carriers an "air quality rating." Below are the 1996 results and some of the factors that went into that rating.

Airline	Mean airline quality rating	Average on time (percentage)	Bags mishandled per 10,000 pass.	Denied boardings per 10,000 pass.	Average age of fleet (years)	Phone
1. SOUTHWEST	0.221	.823	42.6	3.430	7.5	800–435–9792
2. AMERICAN	0.164	.775	50.8	0.450	8.9	800–433–7300
3. UNITED	0.058	.777	52.3	0.410	10.7	800–241–6522
4. DELTA	–0.024	.762	52.8	0.800	10.6	800–221–1212
5. AMERICA WEST	–0.145	.776	48.2	2.280	9.4	800–235–9292
6. NORTHWEST	–0.222	.807	63.3	0.340	18.3	800–225–2525
7. USAIR	–0.262	.798	49.0	1.350	11.5	800–428–4322
8. TRANS WORLD	–0.303	.743	63.7	0.820	19.0	800–221–2000
9. CONTINENTAL	–0.340	.795	46.9	0.670	13.4	800–525–0280

SOURCE: National Institute for Aviation Research, Wichita, Kan., and Aviation Institute, Omaha, Neb.

TICKETS

IF YOU'RE BUMPED FROM A FLIGHT

How to turn bad news to good news when your plane is overbooked

The departure lounge is overflowing. The gate attendant announces the flight is overbooked. Should you accept the airline's offer for another flight? David S. Stempler, president of Air Trav Advisors, offers some counsel.

■ What is overbooking?

For any given flight, a certain percentage of people will not show up for whatever reason. Airline companies track the average no-show rate for specific routes and overbook accordingly. If the no-show rate is usually about 10 percent, the airline then books the flight at 110 percent capacity.

■ How do I avoid being bumped from an overbooked flight?

You should get to the airport early, check in early, and get to the gate early. But watch out: sometimes just checking in at the gate doesn't necessarily count—your options change from airline to airline. Your best bet to avoid being bumped is to actually be on the plane as soon as possible. Possession is nine-tenths of the law.

■ If I volunteer to be bumped, what should I expect in the way of compensation?

Usually, the airlines start with the minimum that they can get away with, which is about $200. You're at the mercy of the lowest offer from other bidders though, so if the airline offers a free ticket, you should grab it. Be warned: the savvy traveler will ask when the next guaranteed trip to his

EXPERT PICKS

A REPORT CARD ON FREQUENT FLYER PROGRAMS

Earning miles may be easier, but on many airlines you need more miles to get a reward. In 1995, many airlines increased the number of miles needed to get a free ticket in the U.S. from 20,000 to 25,000, although America West and TWA stayed at 20,000. All the ways to earn miles can be found in a new book, The Miles Guide, *available at ☎ 800–333–5937. Here's how Randy Peterson, editor of* InsideFlyer *magazine (☎ 719–597–8889), rates the airlines' frequent flyer programs. Peterson has analyzed frequent flyer programs since their inception in 1981.*

PROGRAM	Grade	EASE OF EARNING		BLACKOUT		SEAT AVAILABILITY		Customer	Hotel	Tie-Ins
		Dom.	Int	Dom.	Int.	Dom.	Int.	Service	Partners	
Northwest WorldPerks	B+	B+	A	B	A	A	C	**A+**	B	B
American Aadvantage	B+	**A+**	B–	A	C	A	C	C	A	A
United Mileage Plus	B+	B+	B	B	C	A	C	A	A	A–
USAir Frequent Traveler	B	B	B	A	C	A	C	B	A	B+
Amer. West Flight Fund	B	B	B–	A	B	A	C	**A+**	B–	B–
Alaska Mileage Plan	B	B	B	B+	C	A–	C	B+	B	A–
Continental OnePass	B–	B+	B–	C–	D+	B	C	A–	B	B+
Delta SkyMiles	B–	B	B	C	D	A	C	A–	A	B–
Southwest Company Club	B–	C	NA	**A+**	NA	**A+**	NA	A–	F	D
TWA Freq. Flight Bonus	C+	B–	C	C	D	B	C	B	C–	C+

EXPERT SOURCES

GETTING IN TOUCH WITH AIRLINE WATCHDOGS

To find out more about different airlines, lodge a complaint, or educate yourself about passenger rights, consider these organizations:

U.S. DEPARTMENT OF TRANSPORTATION

■ **Consumer and Community Affairs Office:** Specializes in problems with baggage handling, overbooking, and delayed flights. Also releases monthly statistics based on consumer complaints and airline reports.
☎ 202–366–2220

FEDERAL AVIATION ADMINISTRATION

■ **Consumer Hotline:** An FAA watchdog, the hotline is for complaints about problems with airport security, carry-on baggage, or the FAA itself.
☎ 800–322–7873

■ **Safety Hotline:** To report violations of federal airport and airplane regulations or unsafe situations. Often the first stop for insider whistle-blowers.
☎ 800–255–1111

AVIATION CONSUMER ACTION PROJECT

■ Founded in 1971 by Ralph Nader, ACAP researches consumer issues and publishes the brochure *Facts and Advice for Airline Passengers*. Will advise you about passenger rights and safety issues over the phone.
☎ 202–638–4000

INTERNATIONAL AIRLINE PASSENGERS ASSOCIATION

■ Like members of the American Automobile Association, IAPA's 150,000 members can buy travel accident insurance or participate in the lost luggage retrieval assistance program. Their bimonthly travel-safety alert is a good resource for travelers worried about airline safety and other travel problems.
☎ 214–404–9980

AMERICAN SOCIETY OF TRAVEL AGENTS

■ A travel trade organization, ASTA represents some 23,000 airlines, hotels, travel agents, car rentals, and other travel businesses around the world. Its consumer office can provide info about packing or preparing to travel abroad and also can informally mediate consumer disputes with ASTA members.
☎ 703–739–2782

destination is available or risk being stranded on standby. Also, ask yourself what out-of-pocket expenses you will incur in waiting for the next plane, and if the airline will cover them.

■ What are my rights if I end up being bumped against my will?

When you buy a ticket, you've made a contract with the airline. Before you do anything, you have to make sure you've held up your end. Did you check in on time, for instance? Also, if the airline can get you to your destination within an hour of your originally scheduled time, it is free of any liability. Between one and two hours, though, it has to pay the amount of a one-way ticket to your destination (maximum $200). After that, the compensation doubles.

In all cases you get to keep the original ticket to use on another flight or can turn it in for a refund. Also, the Supreme Court has said that you can sue for compensatory damages to recoup whatever loss the delay might have cost you. If, for instance, being bumped forced you to miss a cruise that was paid for in advance, you can sue for the amount of that cruise, though the airline will probably try to get you to the cruise late rather than have to pay for the whole thing.

AIRFARES

DO'S AND DON'TS OF CHEAP FLYING

Coupons, regional airlines, and "split fares" can save you money

As the editor and publisher of *Best Fares* magazine, Tom Parsons has been studying the ins and outs of airline pricing and helping travelers fly cheaply since 1983. Here Parsons gives some money-saving tips.

DO

■ **Search for and use discount coupons.** Parsons says that airlines offer 350 to 400 unadvertised and unpublished travel deals every year. Most can be had by redeeming discount coupons that are distributed by retail outlets and with specific products. An example: people who bought three rolls of Kodak film at a Walgreen Drug Store recently could request a mail-in certificate redeemable for four $60-off coupons good on American Airlines. This sort of coupon can usually be used during fare wars to further reduce already low prices.

■ **Look into niche and regional airlines.** Several small upstart airlines, such as Kiwi, now offer service between select areas at very low prices. These airlines concentrate on specific pockets, usually limiting their flights to only a handful of cities, and deep-discount their ticket prices to make up for their lack of name recognition and to encourage passengers to fly the short haul rather than drive.

■ **Take advantage of "split fares."** Surprisingly, splitting fares may enable a traveler to combine two cheap tickets for much less than the cost of the original single ticket, especially with the aforementioned rise of niche markets. Rather than buying a single ticket from Dallas to Kansas City, for example, Parsons suggests that a consumer look into the option of flying from Dallas to Tulsa, Oklahoma, and then from Tulsa to Kansas City.

ALL'S FAIR IN THE FARE WARS

If this week's fare is half of what you paid last week, here's what to do:

You've already bought your ticket when you see the ad in the newspaper: a lower fare on the same route. Getting your ticket rewritten for the lower fare—and pocketing the savings—is not always possible. First you must meet all the qualifications listed in the ad in the small print: there must be the right number of days in advance of your trip; you must have been booked to travel when the fare applies; and there must still be seats available in the cheaper fare category. Even then, you might be charged $50 or so to have your ticket rewritten.

Don't give up if the first airline person who answers tells you your ticket is nonrefundable and nonchangeable, though. Insist on speaking with a supervisor. Also, move fast. The number of seats available at the lower fare is probably limited. Even if you meet all the restrictions, you will not be able to claim one of the cheap seats unless they are still unsold when you call.

A travel agent can give you further assistance. Some agents now guarantee you the lowest fare through use of a computer that monitors reservations systems overnight. Your agent may call you when a lower fare pops up. (You certainly won't hear about it from the airline.) If the agent is still holding your tickets, he or she could rewrite your ticket at the new price even before you open your morning paper.

THE GUY SITTING NEXT TO YOU PAID LESS

The price of an airline seat isn't locked till the plane leaves the ground. Below is a snapshot of what people paid on a recent American Airlines flight from Miami to New York on takeoff—the average fare: $196.89.

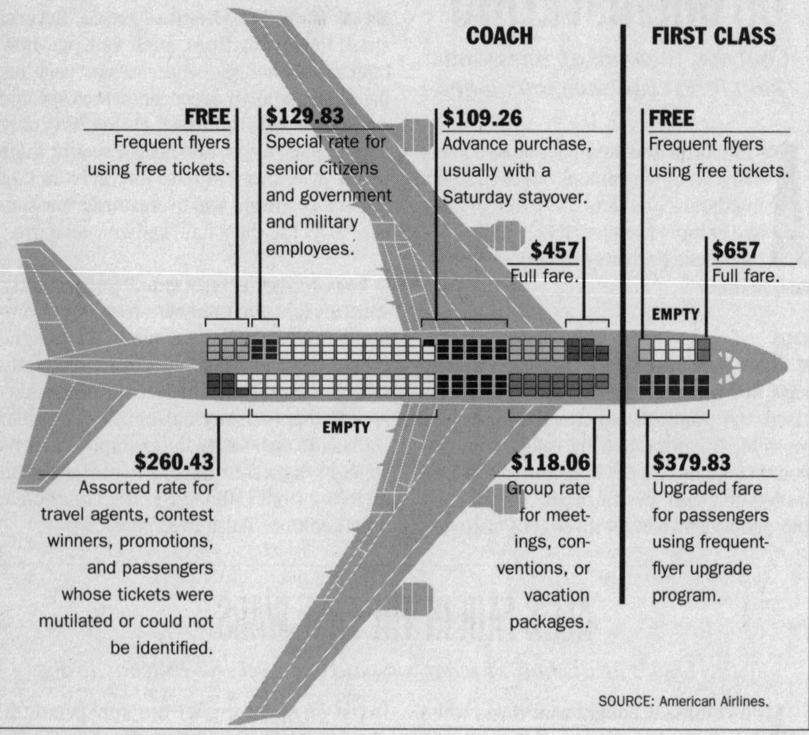
COACH
FIRST CLASS
FREE
Frequent flyers using free tickets.
$129.83
Special rate for senior citizens and government and military employees.
$109.26
Advance purchase, usually with a Saturday stayover.
FREE
Frequent flyers using free tickets.
$457
Full fare.
$657
Full fare.
EMPTY
EMPTY
$260.43
Assorted rate for travel agents, contest winners, promotions, and passengers whose tickets were mutilated or could not be identified.
$118.06
Group rate for meetings, conventions, or vacation packages.
$379.83
Upgraded fare for passengers using frequent-flyer upgrade program.

SOURCE: American Airlines.

■ **Consider flying to and from alternative cities.** Some air routes are significantly cheaper than others. If you are willing to make the journey to and from an out-of-the-way airport before and after a long trip, you may be able to save big. A one- or two-hour drive, according to Parsons, can take as much as 70 percent off of a single ticket price. Washington, D.C. flyers, for example, should consider making the trek to the airport in nearby Baltimore, and Chicago flyers should look into flying by way of Milwaukee.

DON'T

■ **Buy tickets immediately.** Most discount fares need only be purchased 14 days in advance. Buying sooner may simply mean a loss of future savings, because people who buy early can't get any money back when prices drop. Buy tickets immediately only if you wish to travel during busy holidays like Christmas or New Year's Day.

■ **Always pick a flight time.** Tell travel and flight reservation agents that a cheap ticket is more important than, say, arriving at nine in the morning. The relationship between time and cost is not always obvious, so you should inquire about the least expensive times to fly a chosen route—some cost more than others, and some special fares only apply at specific times.

AIRFARES

FOUR WAYS TO FLY FOR PEANUTS

Couriers, consolidators, charters, and rebaters are cheap—but tricky

In 1959, when *How to Travel without Being Rich* was a hot seller, a 10-day trip from New York to Paris including airfare, lodging, and sight-seeing cost $553. Today, that price would elude even the most serious of cost-cutters. But bargains still abound for travelers willing to do some research.

AIR COURIERS

The absolute cheapest way to fly is as a courier. Although most large courier companies such as Federal Express and UPS use their own couriers, smaller companies use "freelance couriers." A typical courier fare can be as low as one-fourth of the regular airline economy class fare. Last-minute tickets are especially cheap—one courier company recently listed a fare from Los Angeles to Tokyo of $100. A full-fare ticket would cost around $1,800.

In exchange for a drastically reduced fare, couriers have minimal duties. After booking a flight with a company, the courier meets a representative of the company at the airport a few hours before departure. The agent hands baggage checks for the cargo and other paperwork over to the courier. The courier then boards the plane and, on arrival at his international destination, accompanies the cargo through customs. Once through customs, the courier hands over the paperwork to the company agent. After that he is free to go.

■ **DRAWBACKS:** Because air courier companies use a courier's allotted baggage space for cargo, couriers generally are limited to carry-on baggage only. More important, courier travel can be unreliable. On rare occasions, for instance, courier companies will cancel or postpone their shipments because of last-minute cargo changes. In this instance, if a courier does not have flexible travel plans and cannot wait for the next courier flight, he or she may have to buy a full-fare economy ticket from a regular airline.

■ **WHERE TO GO:** Most courier flights leave from New York, Los Angeles, San Francisco, or Miami. The best way to find them is to join the International Association of Air Travel Couriers, ☎407–582–8320. A one-year membership costs $45; you get a bimonthly bulletin and access to twice-daily updates of available courier flights online or via fax.

CONSOLIDATORS

Consolidators are the Price Club of airline travel—large brokerage houses that buy blocks of tickets from airlines at wholesale prices and then pass the savings on to individual flyers. Airlines sell to consolidators at reduced prices because they fear that the tickets would otherwise go unsold. Consolidators buy seats mostly on established carriers for flights that are headed to overseas destinations. Travelers booking flights with consolidators can save anywhere from 20 to 50 percent off the price of a regular ticket.

■ **DRAWBACKS:** Most consolidators are reliable, but to protect against illegitimate businesses, travelers should use a credit card whenever possible. Consolidator tickets are nonrefundable, so a traveler who cannot use his or her ticket will most likely end up eating the fare. Consolidator tickets typically are not honored by other airlines, so ticket holders who miss their flights or whose flights are canceled will have to wait for another flight on the issuing airline. Also, flights generally are not direct and sometimes have as many as three stops.

■ **WHERE TO GO:** Travel agents rarely volunteer information about consolidator tickets. Should a travel agent plead ignorance, it may help to suggest that he look up the fare in *Jax Fax*, ☎ 800–952–9329, a monthly newsletter that lists consolidator fares and is widely distributed to travel agents. Consolidator fares are also listed in small ads in the travel sections of major newspapers like *The New York Times* and *USA Today*. For flights from Europe, the Air Travel Advisory Bureau in London, ☎ 44–1–636–5000, has a complete listing of consolidators (or, as they are called in Britain, "bucket shops").

CHARTER FLIGHTS

Charter flights offer savings that are competitive with consolidator tickets, but generally they are only for nonstop routes. Charter companies are able to profit by running less often than regularly scheduled airline flights and by booking to complete capacity. On transatlantic flights especially, travelers can save between $200 and $400.

Charters also are a good alternative for those who like to fly first class but don't want to pay for it. *Consumer Reports Travel Letter* editor Ed Perkins says, "One of the best values around is the premium class service on some of the transatlantic charters. First class on charter planes is a third of the price of regular airlines with many of the same amenities."

■ **DRAWBACKS:** Infrequency of flights and overcrowding of planes are common complaints. If a charter flight is canceled close to departure, there usually are no other planes available, nor will a charter ticket be honored on another airline. Travelers can often have a lengthy wait for another flight, or worse, will have to pay full fare on a regular airline. Also, despite the aforementioned first-class options, charter flights are not known for luxury service. The meals often come in a brown bag, and you're packed in like the proverbial sardine.

■ **WHERE TO GO:** Travel agencies are an excellent source for charter listings. Charter companies also advertise heavily in the travel sections of major newspapers. Martinair Holland, ☎ 800–366–4655, Tower, ☎ 800–221–2500, and Balair Ltd., ☎ 800–322–5247, get high marks from Perkins for first-class service.

REBATERS

Rebaters are "no-frills" travel agents who pay the ticket buyer all or part of the commission they are paid by airlines for selling the ticket. Rebaters profit by charging a flat fee for making a reservation and issuing a ticket to the buyer. A traveler headed from New York to Stockholm might be quoted a round-trip fare of $800. By using a rebater, the fare would drop to $750. The reason: Rebaters refund their commission, in this case, $80 or 10 percent of the fare. They then tack on a $20 fee to issue the ticket and sometimes an extra $10 to make the reservation. Still, the total price of the ticket is $50 less than it would have been with a regular travel agent.

■ **DRAWBACKS:** For the money saved by using a rebater, a traveler gives up a lot in service. A rebater will make a reservation and issue a ticket, but all other travel details, such as seat assignments, hotel reservations, and ground transportation, will need to be made by the traveler. "The amenities a consumer loses using a rebater instead of a full-service travel agent are not worth the savings unless you are buying expensive tickets," Perkins says.

■ **WHERE TO GO:** One of the most prominent rebaters is Travel Avenue in Chicago, ☎ 800–333–3335. In addition, *Consumer Reports Travel Letter*, ☎ 800–234–1970, lists major rebaters throughout the country once a year.

FACT FILE:

ROOM AT THE TOP

■ *Wide-body aircraft—L-1011s, 767s, A310s, MD-11s, 747s, and the new 777s—have larger overhead compartments. Many also have closets though often these are reserved for first class. The exception: most DC-10s have relatively small bins.*

SOURCE: *Travel & Leisure.*

TRAIN TRAVELER'S GUIDE

ROMANCING THE RAILS AROUND THE WORLD

"Railway terminals are our gates to the glorious and the unknown. Through them we pass out into adventures and sunshine, to them, alas! we return," wrote E. M. Forster. No doubt, the novelist would have jumped at the chance to purchase a railway pass that guarantees unlimited travel for a set price during a set period had they been available in his day. Usually it takes only one or two trips for you to come out ahead, as compared with a regular round-trip ticket. Below are just some of the options available for your train treks across the world.

AUSTRALIA

Air travel across this continent is more practical, but riding the rails gives a better view of the outback. RailAustralia offers two different passes, Austrailpass and Austrail Flexi-Pass, both of which present several different options. Because many of the major rail services are heavily patronized, advance reservations are often necessary.

■ **PRICE RANGE:** The Austrailpass gives unlimited First-class and economy travel. Costs range from $359 for a 14-day economy pass to $1,521 for a 90-day first-class; options also include 21, 30, and 60 days. The Flexi-Pass gives you six months to use up 8, 15, 22, or 29 days of travel. Costs range from $281 for 8 days of economy travel to $1,201 for 29 days of first-class. Note: the 8-Day Flexi-Pass cannot be used on the Ghan and Indian Pacific route.

■ **TRAIN TIP:** Train lovers should not miss riding the Queenslander, which runs only from April to January. Its 1,000-mile journey from Cairns to Brisbane takes you through a rain forest, past lakes where scores of black swans swim, and by hundreds of kangaroos and kookaburras. Inside, there are orchids in every room, a lively piano bar, and, according to one traveler, "a dining car like a jewel." Everyone here goes first class, so economy riders must temporarily upgrade their tickets, and all railpass holders must pay a supplement of $234.

☎ **ATS Tours:** 800–423–2880

CANADA

VIARail links Montreal's old-world milieu, Vancouver's mountain views, and the arctic tundra. The Canrail Pass allows unlimited coast-to-coast economy-class travel for 12 days within a 30-day period.

■ **PRICE RANGE:** Cost of the Canrail Pass depends on the time of year. For traveling during the peak season (May 15 to Oct. 15), it's $419; for off-peak, it's $286. A nonpeak pass is cheaper than a one-way ticket from Toronto to Vancouver, and a peak pass is only $39 more; however, passes are not honored Dec. 15 to Jan. 5.

■ **TRAIN TIP:** In 1992, VIARail launched a restored, stainless steel fleet built in the '50s. The passenger cars retain their art deco sleekness but are updated with showers and advanced suspension systems. On the run between Jasper and Vancouver, there are exhilarating views of the Canadian Rockies. You may want to consider upgrading your pass to upper-berth accommodations just this route; in addition to other amenities, you will receive access to the Park Car, whose dome roof lets you relax under the stars.

☎ **VIARail:** 800–561–3949

EUROPE

The Continent's railways, which serve more than 30,000 cities, have united to offer plenty of different pass options to meet individual needs: you can focus on just one country, a couple, or all. To help you compare prices and set your itinerary, Rail Pass Express offers a complete online database that shows the prices for passes as well as for point-to-point tickets. It's available on the Internet at *http://www.eurail.com.*

■ **TRAIN TRAVELER'S GUIDE**

Also, American Youth Hostels offers free assistance to nonmembers and nonyouths alike in making European rail plans.

■ **PRICE RANGE:** The well-known Europass encompasses Germany, France, Italy, Spain, and Switzerland; its costs depend on the number of countries and number of days chosen. Consumers are given 11 options for adult fares, ranging from a three-country, 5-day pass ($316); to a five-country, 15-day pass ($736). All adult fares are first-class; all youth fares (for ages 12 to 25) are second-class. Thus, adults traveling with youths must either upgrade the youth pass to the more expensive first-class or choose to sit in the second-class areas, without receiving a price break, or sit separately. To ease this dilemma, Europass has instituted a 50 percent discount for the second person in a party of two for all first-class fares; however, the pair must travel together at all times. Travelers can add countries—that is, Austria, Belgium/Luxembourg/Netherlands, Greece, and Portugal—Greece and Portugal for nominal fees ranging from $29 to $90; the cost for Greece includes ferry service. A Eurail Pass makes sense only if you plan to do a lot of city hopping across the continent. It allows for unlimited travel in 17 countries during a specified time, ranging from 15 days for $522 to 3 months for $1,468. Additionally, there are flexipasses that range from 10 days of travel in two months for $616 to 15 days in two months for $812.

■ **TRAIN TIP:** Gena Holle, editor of *International Railway Traveler*, highly recommends the line from Nice, France, to Livorno, Italy: This scenic route along the banks of the Mediterranean offers a chance to stop off at Cinqueterre, a unique spot made up of five beautiful seaside towns all connected by walkways.

☎ **Rail Europe:**
800–438–7245

☎ **American Youth Hostels:**
202–783–4943

INDIA

Indian Railways boasts the world's largest railroad system, daily running more than 7,000 passenger trains. They offer a better alternative to driving, given the crowds in the cities and potentially rugged roads elsewhere. Indrail passes come in three classes: air-conditioned; first-class (which varies from line to line, but often specifies an air-conditioned chair car); and second-class, usually crowded non–air-conditioned cars.

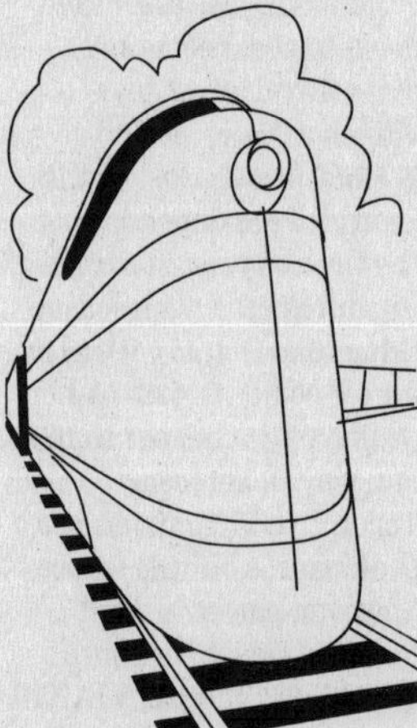

■ **PRICE RANGE:** For unlimited travel within a specified period, costs run from $10 for a half-day, second-class pass to $1,060 for a 90-day, air-conditioned-class pass. In all, 10 different pass lengths are available. Regular tickets may be cheaper if you're planning only one or two trips, but the passes make it easier to get reservations.

■ **TRAIN TIP:** Delays and strandings at stations used to be common because of telex failures, but faxes now offer a more reliable backup system for rail reservations. *India by Rail* by Royston Ellis (Globe Pequot Press, 1994) offers descriptions of some scenic routes. Trains tend to be slow (52 mph), so you have more time to soak in the views.

☎ **Hari World Travels, Inc.:**
212–997–3300

JAPAN

The extensive Japan Railway (JR) system rivals that of continental Europe for speed and convenience,

■ TRAIN TRAVELER'S GUIDE

and it reaches nearly every tourist spot. Rail passes offer a great investment: an economy-priced 7-day pass with unlimited travel can cost less than one round-trip ticket between some cities.

■ **PRICE RANGE:** JR passes come in two classes: superior, also called "green," and ordinary. Both include travel on most Shinkansen (bullet trains) and all ferries. Fares run from $280 for a 7-day ordinary pass to $768 for a 21-day superior.

■ **TRAIN TIP:** The bullet train from Tokyo to Osaka, the nation's second-fastest train, bolts by Mount Fuji at 167 mph. Despite the speed, you can get great views in clear weather.

☎ **TBI Tours:** 800–223–0266

UNITED KINGDOM

BritRail no longer offers combination packages with Continental Europe's lines, having recently discontinued its BritFrance and BritGermany passes. Also, it no longer offers the limited England/Wales package. Instead, BritRail pass holders can travel anywhere in England, Wales, or Scotland. Also, one can opt to add Ireland, including Northern Ireland as well as the Republic.

■ **PRICE RANGE:** For unlimited consecutive days of travel, costs run from $235 for a second-class 8-day pass to $765 for a first-class 1-month pass. BritRail flexipasses range from four days of second-class travel for $199 to 15 days of first-class travel for $615. All passes must be used within one month. The Plus Ireland Pass comes in two versions, 5 days in one month ($405, first-class; $299, second-class) and 10 days in one month ($599; $429). Irish Sea ferry service is included, but reservations are required.

■ **TRAIN TIP:** Stephen Forsyth, the only U.S. distributor of the Thomas Cook Overseas Timetable (a must-have for rail travelers), recommends the short trip from Southhampton to Bournemouth; it travels through the New Forest, created in the 1200s, and past thatched-roofed cottages. At the forest's southeast corner is Buckler's Hard, a town where sailing ships used to be built.

☎ **Forsyth Travel Library:** 800–Forsyth

☎ **Rail Pass Express:** 800–551–1977

U.S.A.

Several accidents, including an act of sabotage that killed a crew member, have hurt Amtrak's reputation. However, a report released by the Federal Railroad Administration shows that despite an average of 4 accidents per million miles, Amtrak (including its commuter services in 6 cities) had no passenger fatalities in 1995. Indeed, Amtrak's fatality rate per million riders has been lower than that of the U.S. airlines for 12 of the last 16 years. Amtrak offers two passes: All Aboard America, good for 45 days, and Explore America, for 30 days. For these fares, it divides the country into three regions, basically drawing two lines from north to south: Chicago to New Orleans and Denver to Albuquerque. One can opt to buy unlimited travel in one region, two, or three. The eastern region includes Montreal.

■ **PRICE RANGE:** Peak fares for All Aboard passes run from June 14 to August 18, then again from Dec. 13 to Jan. 5: $228 for one region, $318 for two, and $378 for three. Nonpeak fares are $198, $258, and $318, respectively. The Explore America Fare offers similar deals, but at lower rates and with some restrictions.

■ **TRAIN TIP:** The Coast Starlight from Los Angeles to Seattle is Amtrak's most popular trip. The scenic ride along the Pacific shore to the snow-crested Cascades takes about 35 hours, but first-class passengers are kept busy with wine tastings, live entertainment, and fine dining.

☎ **Amtrak** 800–872–7245

*All prices are subject to change, and certain restrictions can apply; for instance, with the exception of Amtrak and Canrail passes, all must be purchased outside the relevant country, sometimes only in the U.S. Be sure to ask about rates for children, students/youths, and senior citizens.

SAILOR'S GUIDE

WHERE EVERYTHING IS SHIPSHAPE

The way cruise ships are being outfitted these days, the passengers hardly realize that they're at sea. The newest boats contain practically everything anyone could possibly want—except, perhaps, sandy beaches. Here's a highly selective guide to cruise ships, new and old, plying the high seas.

THE NEW MEGAS

The biggest ships just keep getting bigger. Carnival Cruise Line's 100,000-ton Destiny, due out August 1996, will be topped in 1997 by the Princess Line's Grand Princess, with a tonnage of 105,000. All told, the cruise lines are rushing out approximately 26 new ships in the next two years, many with tonnages of 70,000 or over. These boats are faster, have high-atrium lobbies, multilevel dining rooms with lighter menus, larger cabins, and revolving stage theaters, among many other things.

DESTINY (1996)

Carnival Cruise Line

■ **WHERE:** Year-round, 7-day cruises to eastern and western Caribbean. Home port: Miami.
■ **WHO:** Mass market.
■ **ON BOARD:** There's a 15,000-foot, two-level Nautica spa, which is 25 percent larger than those on other Carnival ships. Sixty percent of the cabins will have ocean views, and 60 percent of those in turn have private balconies.
☎ 800–327–9501

GALAXY

Celebrity Cruises

■ **WHERE:** Western Caribbean from Ft. Lauderdale. Vancouver inside passage.
■ **WHO:** Adults ages 35 to 60, with a median income of $50,000 and over.
■ **ON BOARD:** One of the most technically advanced ships in 1996 in terms of interactive systems and computer programs.
☎ 800–437–3111

GRANDEUR OF THE SEAS (1996)

Royal Caribbean Cruise Line

■ **WHERE:** The eastern Caribbean, year-round. Home port: Miami.
■ **WHO:** Mass market. 1,950 passengers, with average age of 43 and a median household income of $50,000 or more.
■ **ON BOARD:** More square feet of glass than on any other ship afloat. With a cruising speed of 22 knots per hour, it will be one of the speediest ships.
☎ 800–327–6700

GRAND PRINCESS (1997)

Princess Cruises

■ **WHERE:** The Caribbean only, on a year-round basis
■ **WHO:** This will be a family-oriented ship accommodating 2,600; and appealing primarily to 35- to 45-year-olds.
■ **ON BOARD:** At 105,000 tons, it will be the largest ship built—probably for some time to come; 750 of the cabins will have verandas.
☎ 800–LOV–BOAT

LUXURY ON A SMALL SCALE

These ships accommodate 250 passengers or less. The appeal is attentive service. The cuisine is apt to be first-class. Life on board is generally unstructured and low-key. Entertainment is often cabaret style. Many of the ships also provide lectures on a variety of subjects. For exercise, the emphasis is on water sports.

SEA GODDESS I & II

Cunard

■ **WHERE:** Sea Goddess I operates 7-day cruises to the Caribbean, spring and fall, Amazon in winter, Mediterranean in summer. Sea Goddess II goes to Asia in winter, east Mediterranean in summer.
■ **WHO:** 116 passengers—generally executive and professional types; predominantly couples, half from North America and half from Europe.
■ **ON BOARD:** A "country club" atmosphere, with lots of water sports, a spa, danc-

DECK BY DECK

Your cabin's location can have a profound effect on your enjoyment of a cruise. The higher you go, for example, the more likely you are to suffer the ill effects of the ship's pitching and rolling. On the other hand, if you are too close to the nightlife, you might not get much sleep. No two ships are alike, but here is what you generally can expect on various decks.

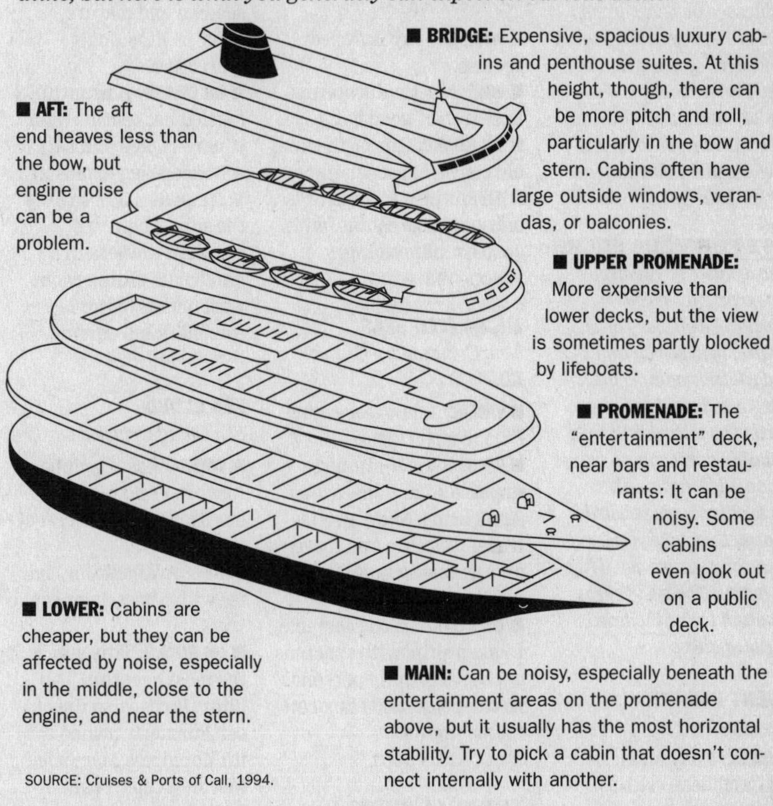

■ **BRIDGE:** Expensive, spacious luxury cabins and penthouse suites. At this height, though, there can be more pitch and roll, particularly in the bow and stern. Cabins often have large outside windows, verandas, or balconies.
■ **AFT:** The aft end heaves less than the bow, but engine noise can be a problem.
■ **UPPER PROMENADE:** More expensive than lower decks, but the view is sometimes partly blocked by lifeboats.
■ **PROMENADE:** The "entertainment" deck, near bars and restaurants: It can be noisy. Some cabins even look out on a public deck.
■ **LOWER:** Cabins are cheaper, but they can be affected by noise, especially in the middle, close to the engine, and near the stern.
■ **MAIN:** Can be noisy, especially beneath the entertainment areas on the promenade above, but it usually has the most horizontal stability. Try to pick a cabin that doesn't connect internally with another.

SOURCE: Cruises & Ports of Call, 1994.

ing, and just relaxing. All drinks are included.
☎ 800–221–4770

SEABOURN'S PRIDE & SPIRIT
Seabourn Cruise Line
■ **WHERE:** Europe, Asia, Alaska, Mediterranean, and Caribbean.
■ **WHO:** 204 passengers. Median age is 45 to 50—apt to include financiers, professionals, members of the English upper class, and the "glitterati"; 70 percent are repeat passengers.
■ **ON BOARD:** These ships are larger than the Goddesses, with more facilities and entertainment, and larger cabins. The fares are higher too.
☎ 800–929–4747

SONG OF THE FLOWER
Radisson Seven Seas Cruises
■ **WHERE:** Summers in Europe, winters in Asia.
■ **WHO:** 214 passengers; likely to be well educated, include active executive

■ SAILOR'S GUIDE

types, 45+, as well as many retirees.

■ **ON BOARD:** Cheaper than Goddesses, but cabins not as beautifully decorated as Goddesses or Seabourns. This is a spotless ship, with wonderful space, great service. The atmosphere is low-key and unpretentious. This ship can enter ports inaccessible to larger ones.

☎ 800-333-3333

BEST FOR YOUR BUCKS

Ever wonder if you are overpaying for a cruise vacation? Well, very often you are. Maybe you don't need all that pampering, glitz, or supreme cuisine. But on the other hand, you probably don't care to travel "troopship" style, either. These ships were selected because they give you good value for your money. They are not all "budget" ships, although we've included a couple of those.

REGENT RAINBOW

Regency Cruises

■ **WHERE:** 4-day Mexican and Caribbean cruises.

■ **WHO:** 960 passengers, mostly Americans in the 40 to 60 age range who like to live modestly. Recently, the ship has been attracting a number of foreigners because of its reputation for excellent value.

■ **ON BOARD:** A midsize ship with no glitz, but modern and comfortable. Wide range of entertainment from classical music to cabaret and western. There is also afternoon tea.

☎ 800-388-5500

AMERIKANIS

Fantasy Cruises

■ **WHERE:** 7-day European cruises.

■ **WHO:** Mostly Europeans in search of good value

■ **ON BOARD:** One of the fine old converted ocean liners with lots of wood and brass, and good-size cabins (with good soundproofing).

☎ 800-433-2100

ENCHANTED SEAS

New Commodore Cruise Line

■ **WHERE:** 7-day, year-round Caribbean cruises.

■ **WHO:** Budget-minded upper- and middle-income Americans. Many groups travel this ship and there is an increasing number of younger people.

■ **ON BOARD:** A comfortable, relaxed ship, with spacious deck space, quite personalized service, and elaborate theme nights.

☎ 800-237-5361

THE TALL SHIPS

"Tall Ships" are replicas of old sailing schooners that sail under canvas—with ropes and salt spray, and moonlit nights at ocean level. The modern versions of these ships come in two styles: authentic replicas that depend on the sails to get places, and the so-called sail-cruise ships that are largely powered.

LILI MARLEEN

Peter Deilmann Reederei

■ **WHERE:** Caribbean and Baltic.

■ **WHO:** Experienced seamen and mature, older professionals and retirees.

■ **ON BOARD:** A beautiful 3-masted barkentine (one square-rigged and two schooner-rigged masts). You can assist in sailing the ship. There are candlelit dinners in a handsome dining room with menus featuring international cuisine.

☎ 800-348-8287

SEA CLOUD

Sea Cloud Cruises

■ **WHERE:** East Caribbean in winter and many different itineraries the rest of the year.

■ **WHO:** Available for charter with a passenger capacity of 69.

■ **ON BOARD:** This may be the most beautiful Tall Ship afloat—also the oldest. Formerly owned by millionairess Marjorie Merriweather Post. There's handcrafted carved oak paneling, antique furniture, and fine original oil paintings. (Note: Sea Cloud Cruises is based in Hamburg, Germany.)

☎ 011-49-40-369-0272

THE POLYNESIA

Windjammer Barefoot Cruises, Ltd.

■ **WHERE:** 6-day cruises

EXPERT TIPS

IF SHUFFLEBOARD ISN'T YOUR THING

And you like staring at salt water, a trip on a freighter may be just the ticket

Before turning to poking fun at Washington pooh-bahs (*Thank You for Smoking* and *The White House Mess*), Christopher Buckley penned *Steaming to Bamboola*, a first-person account of his trip from South Carolina to the North Sea on a tramp freighter. Freighter travel is still available to the general public today. *Ford's Freighter Travel Guide and Waterways of the World* (Ford's Travel Guides, 19448 Londelius St., Northridge, CA 91324) publishes semiannual listings of itineraries for more than a hundred different vessels. But freighter travel isn't for everybody. Buckley's counsel:

Those who like shuffleboard, mints on their pillow at night, and driving golf balls off the after deck, read no further. Freighter travel is not for you. It's also not for people with medical conditions, because there's no doctor on board. That's why only 12 people are allowed on board at once. But for those who enjoy reading or rereading the classics and long, long hours of boring, endless blue salt water, this is your trip. It's a reader's vacation—or a writer's vacation. Nelson Algren reread all of Hemingway's works while on a freighter from San Francisco to Yokohama, then wrote about the experience in *Diary of a Sea Voyage—or Hemingway All the Way*.

A generation ago, you could go down to the dock, talk to a freighter captain, and get a job and berth on board. I arranged to work with the crew to pay my way on a freighter; you can't do that today. But a freighter is still less expensive than traveling on a cruise ship—and you're not going to have Kathie Lee Gifford twirling around telling you to eat more shrimp.

My first freighter trip came when I was 17 and about to start college; I saw a bit of the world at a young age, and developed a real relationship with the men on board. I only made $20 a week, but felt rich because I could buy cigarettes for $1 a carton and beer for $3 a case at the ship store.

It's like apples and oranges between the way I traveled and a freighter trip today. I doubt someone traveling now would be able to really get to know the crew, or to sample the local whorehouse with them. I guess going by freighter is still kind of a romantic idea, but if you're looking for romance, this ain't it.

around the Caribbean (the itinerary depends on the wind).

■ **WHO:** Singles, retirees, families, and young marrieds. A high record of repeat passengers.

■ **ON BOARD:** This is a legendary old fishing schooner. Some cabins are made over into bachelor quarters. Singles and other theme cruises are featured.

☎ 800-327-2602

SIR FRANCIS DRAKE

Tall Ship Adventures

■ **WHERE:** Year-round, 3- to 7-day cruises, usually around the British Virgin Islands.

■ **WHO:** Young and middle-aged couples and singles. Median age of passengers is mid-40s.

■ **ON BOARD:** An authentic 3-masted ship that is not as luxurious as the Sea Cloud, and not as simple as the Polynesia. All cabins have private baths (unlike Polynesia). Very casual.

☎ 800-662-0090

MOTELS

NOT EXACTLY THE RITZ

Our intrepid expert's advice: pack a 100-watt bulb and a bed board

For most of the postwar period, motels have occupied a unique place in American life. For some, they bring to mind long-forgotten family vacations; for others, they are more closely connected with Hitchcock's most famous film character, Norman Bates. John Margolies, a photographer, lecturer, and prolific traveler, has been studying motels as cultural icons for more than 20 years. Here are some pointers from his recent book, *Home Away from Home: Motels in America* (Bullfinch Press, 1994).

■ Are motels really "homes away from home" anymore?

There's no substitute for home, and really no sleep replenishment, no true regaining of energy and empathy or feeling to be had in any motel or hotel, regardless of the price. They are anonymous, functional places that are used for people to crash in, and some of them are nicer than others.

■ What should travelers be looking for in a motel?

There's something to be said for the Holiday Inn slogan of the 1970s that the best surprise is no surprise. The full range of alternatives for the genre is still there today, from campgrounds to mom-and-pop motels to franchises to hotels. The first step for travelers should be looking at guidebooks like those put out by Mobil or AAA.

What I look for in a motel is a hard bed and peace and quiet, the latter being harder to achieve than the former. I don't usually stay in the types of motels I take photos of, because they don't have hard beds. But you can always pull the mattress onto the floor. I used to carry a collapsible bed board.

■ What should you be looking for once you choose the motel?

You want to be away from soda and ice machines, out of the circulation patterns. I generally circle a motel in my car before I get to the office, trying to figure out where the quietest rooms might be. You don't want to be near entrance and exit doors. You want the room that is halfway between the registration desk and the door at the end. Unfortunately, at many hotels, even though there are only three people staying there, they put them in rooms next to one another. As a rule, it is better to stay on the second floor. Paul Simon of Simon & Garfunkel said it very well: One man's ceiling is another man's floor. But then again, if you are carrying a lot of luggage, you want a first-floor room in the back end of the motel.

And if you are deep in the heart of nowhere, you want to ask where the train is. The train sound is going to be there for a long time before the train actually reaches you.

■ Do you have any favorite motel chains, or areas of the country?

I used to stay in Holiday Inns, but can't afford them anymore. If you are over 50 and you reserve on the 800 number, you get 30 percent off at Quality, Comfort, and Choice motels. I like Quality and Comfort Inns, although there are variations within the chain. There are some really good mom-and-pops, and sometimes when you are way out there, away from the interstate, you are not going to find a lot of chains. If you are way out in Roosevelt, Utah, you'd be lucky to stay in the Frontier Motel. They have hard beds, first-floor rooms you can pull right up to, the restaurant was delicious, and it was relatively quiet.

■ Do you have any other tips for motel travelers?

A clothespin or safety pin, or a couple of them, are a good idea for keeping drapes shut entirely. Finally, a high-wattage lightbulb will come in handy because motels tend to be the land of 30-watt lightbulbs.

EXPERT'S PICKS

THE BEST PLACES TO BED DOWN IN AMERICA

Here are the top-ranked hotels from four of the most respected travel authorities. The American Automobile Association (AAA) and the Mobil Travel Guide *both release a yearly list of the nation's best hotels. Also in the hotel rating game are two well-known travel publications: the* Hideaway Report, *a newsletter, and* Condé Nast Traveler *magazine. AAA and Mobil utilize roving teams of inspectors, whereas* Hideaway *and* Condé Nast *rely on reader polls. To appear on our list, a hotel had to get top marks from at least two of the four authorities we consulted. Fourteen hotels—marked by hollow checks—made it on to all four lists.*

HOTEL	☎	HIDEAWAY	CONDE NAST	AAA	MOBIL
AUBERGE DU SOLEIL, Rutherford, CA	800-348-5406	✓	✓	✓	✓
THE BOULDERS, Scottsdale, AZ	800-553-1717	✓	✓	✓	✓
THE BROADMOOR, Colorado Springs, CO	800-634-7711	✓	✓	✓	✓
THE CARLYLE, New York, NY	800-227-5737	✔	✔		✔
THE CLOISTER, Sea Island, GA	800-732-4752	✓	✓	✓	✓
C LAZY U RANCH, Granby, CO	303-887-3344			✔	✔
FOUR SEASONS, Boston, MA	800-332-3442	✔	✔	✔	
FOUR SEASONS, Chicago, IL	800-332-3442	✔	✔	✔	
FOUR SEASONS–RITZ-CARLTON, Chicago, IL	800-332-3442	✔	✔	✔	
FOUR SEASONS, Washington, DC	800-332-3442	✔	✔	✔	
FOUR SEASONS RESORT, Maui, HI	808-874-8000	✔	✔	✔	
FOUR SEASONS HOTEL, Newport Beach, CA	800-332-3442		✔	✔	
FOUR SEASONS, New York, NY	800-332-3442	✔	✔		✔
FOUR SEASONS, Philadelphia, PA	800-332-3442		✔	✔	
FOUR SEASONS–OLYMPIC, Seattle, WA	800-332-3442		✔	✔	✔
GRAND HERITAGE–CLIFT, San Francisco, CA	415-775-4700	✔	✔		
GRAND WAILEA BEACH RESORT, Maui, HI	808-875-1234		✔	✔	
THE GREENBRIER, White Sulphur Springs, WV	800-624-6070	✓	✓	✓	✓
HALEKULANI, Oahu, HI	800-367-2343	✔	✔	✔	
HOTEL BEL-AIR, Los Angeles, CA	800-648-4097	✔	✔		
INN AT LITTLE WASHINGTON, Washington, VA	703-675-3800	✓	✓	✓	✓
THE LITTLE NELL, Aspen, CO	800-525-6200	✓	✓	✓	✓
LODGE AT KOELE, Lanai, HI	800-321-4666	✔	✔		
LODGE AT PEBBLE BEACH, Pebble Beach, CA	800-654-9300	✔	✔		
MANSION ON TURTLE CREEK, Dallas, TX	800-527-5432	✓	✓	✓	✓
MARRIOTT'S CAMELBACK INN, Scottsdale, AZ	800-242-2635		✔	✔	✔
MAUNA LANI BAY, Big Island, HI	800-367-2323	✔	✔	✔	
MEADOWOOD, St Helena, CA	800-458-8080	✔	✔		
THE PENINSULA, Beverly Hills, CA	800-462-7899	✓	✓	✓	✓
THE PHOENICIAN, Scottsdale, AZ	800-888-8234	✔	✔		✔
RITZ-CARLTON BUCKHEAD, Atlanta, GA	800-241-3333	✔	✔	✔	
RITZ-CARLTON, Boston, MA	800-241-3333	✔	✔		
RITZ-CARLTON, Laguna Niguel, CA	800-241-3333	✓	✓	✓	✓
RITZ-CARLTON, Naples, FL	800-241-3333	✓	✓	✓	✓
RITZ-CARLTON, San Francisco, CA	800-241-3333	✓	✓	✓	✓
STOUFFER RENAISSANCE WAILEA BEACH RESORT, HI	800-992-4532		✔		✔
ST. REGIS, New York, NY	800-759-7550	✓	✓	✓	✓
SCOTTSDALE PRINCESS, Scottsdale, AZ	800-344-4258		✔	✔	
VENTANA INN, Big Sur, CA	800-628-6500	✔	✔		
WILLIAMSBURG INN, Williamsburg, VA	800-447-8679		✔		✔
WINDSOR COURT, New Orleans, LA	800-262-2662	✓	✓	✓	✓

SIGHTSEEING

WEIRD ROADSIDE ATTRACTIONS

Take a dancing lesson from the gods at 10 of America's strangest sites

For over 10 years now Doug Kirby, Ken Smith, and Mike Wilkins have been exploring America's highways and byways and recording what they found in books, articles, and online projects that are known collectively as the Roadside America Project. They and their book—*New Roadside America* (Fireside, 1992)—are the country's recognized authorities on unusual domestic tourist attractions that aren't listed in run-of-the-mill travel guides—like alligator farms, mermaid shows, and giant concrete statues of farm animals. Of the more than 5,000 odd entries in their ever-growing database, here are 10 of their favorites.

THE SIT-IN GAS CHAMBER

Rawlins, Wyoming

■ At the Rawlins Territorial Prison, tours are staffed by enthusiastic youngsters who happily allow visitors to sit inside the gas chamber where five lawbreakers were executed. They'll strap you in—and even shut the door, if you so desire. And there's a bonus: Just across the street at The Carbon County Museum are The Shoes Made From The Skin of Executed Killer, Big Nose George. When Big Nose George, a notorious outlaw, was lynched, the attending physicians took skin from the outlaw's chest and made a pair of saddle shoes. They also sawed off the top of his skull to make a pipe holder which is displayed at the Union Pacific Museum in Omaha.

BABYLAND GENERAL HOSPITAL

Cleveland, Georgia

■ The nationwide Cabbage Patch Kid craze is no longer, but true believers still pilgrimage to the site where the stuffed and certified dolls are "born." The surrounding parking lots of this old doctors' clinic are packed during the summer as hordes of couples gather around the "Magic Crystal Tree" inside. At the base of the tree, a Cabbage Patch fetus head pokes through cloth cabbages and suddenly, over the intercom: "Code Green, Cabbage Dilation!" A woman dressed as a nurse emerges from a door in the Crystal Tree and, poking one of the doll heads with a dental tool, she readies for delivery. With a flourish, she yanks the doll from the cabbage and into the world, ready for adoption—at $195.

COW CHIP THROWING CAPITAL OF THE WORLD

Beaver, Oklahoma

■ Beaver gets high marks for not only hosting the annual chip throwing contest and for sending gift-boxed cow chips to loved ones anywhere in the world, but also for erecting, on Main Street, a 10-foot-tall fiberglass beaver holding a four-foot-wide fiberglass cow chip. King Cow Chip, an anthropomorphized dried bovine fecal wad wearing a rakishly-tilted crown, is the town's registered trademark.

PREHISTORIC FOREST

Marblehead, Ohio

■ This gets our nod as the country's best dinosaur park because in addition to seeing huge statues of the prehistoric creatures, tourists are also placed in a tram, each given a toy M-16, and commanded to "Kill the monsters!" whenever the tram passes one. The forest then echoes with the chatter of toy gunfire in all directions.

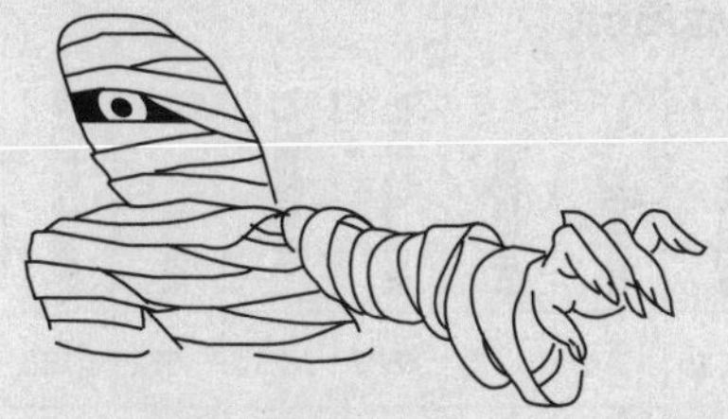

MUMMIES OF THE INSANE

Philippi, West Virginia

■ Back in the 1880s, an enterprising farmer named Graham Hamrick experimented with embalming fluid in an attempt to re-create the secrets of the pharaohs. Using cadavers from the local insane asylum, he finally succeeded, and the well-dried fruits of his labor are still here. Two mummies are displayed in glass-topped wooden coffins in the bathroom of the Barbour County Historical Museum. You can see them for a dollar a peek. Airwick disks in their coffins help stave off the stench of time.

PRECIOUS MOMENTS CHAPEL

Carthage, Missouri

■ Precious Moments figurines are America's number-one selling porcelain bisque representations of teardrop-eyed kids who wear angel wings. Inside Precious Moments Chapel, these dead-child figurines are painted Sistine Chapel–style on the walls and ceiling in poses drawn from the Bible. The centerpiece mural shows an original scene, though: a recently departed cartoon child being welcomed to the gates of heaven by those cartoon child-angels who came before. Precious Moments aficionados stand awed in the midst of this experience. You will too.

SOUTH OF THE BORDER

Dillon, South Carolina

■ Billboards like "Keep Yelling, Kids, They'll Stop," and "20 Honeymoon Suites: Heir Conditioned" beckon for 150 miles in either direction of this 135-acre Mexican-themed mega-attraction located just south of the North Carolina border. The centerpiece is the 200-foot-high Sombrero Tower. Take an elevator ride up to the lookout deck on its brim. Wander the 14 different gift stores and buy the gift-boxed "Pyromaniac" assortment of fireworks or one of 22 different styles of SOB coffee mugs. Eat at The Casateria, then luxuriate overnight in pedro's Pleasure Dome. Pose with sombrero-wearing dinosaurs or even with a neon-pink serape-wearing statue of pedro himself, who, like e.e. cummings, insists that his name not be capitalized.

THE TITAN II MISSILE MUSEUM

Green Valley, Arizona

■ It's actually a decommissioned Titan II missile silo, and a 100-foot-tall Titan II resides there still—though a hole has been cut in its nose cone so that Russian satellites can tell that it's been deactivated. The tour takes you deep into the silo's heart, and once down there, the highlight is a simulated end of the world scramble. As Armageddon approaches, the guide gets the launch codes, inserts two keys . . . and there's no turning back. Sorry: high-heeled shoes cannot be worn in the silo.

THE OXEN STATUES THAT PEE

Three Forks, Montana

■ Two large oxen statues appear to be pulling a restaurant that is shaped like a covered wagon. Under the cash register inside is a valve. When the cashier sees people admiring the statues, she turns on the valve and . . . well, folks around The Prairie Schooner restaurant call them "New Faithful."

BEHN'S GAME FARM

Aniwa, Wisconsin

■ Seventy-five-year-old self-taught lion tamer Wilbert Behn gets in a homemade cage with the big cats daily. The tranquillity of the surrounding dairy farms gives no warning of the snarling jungle kings, which Behn makes jump through hoops as "The Theme From S.W.A.T." plays on a portable cassette player.

FROM HERE TO THERE ACROSS AMERICA

Mileages between major U.S. cities	ATLANTA	BOSTON	CHICAGO	CLEVELAND	DALLAS	DENVER	DETROIT	HOUSTON	KANSAS CITY	LOS ANGELES	MIAMI	MINN.-ST. PAUL
ATLANTA, Ga.		1,084	715	727	826	1,519	741	875	882	2,252	662	1,136
BOSTON, Mass.	1,084		976	643	1,868	2,008	706	1,961	1,442	3,130	1,547	1,399
CHICAGO, Ill.	715	976		349	936	1,017	297	1,073	505	2,189	1,386	416
CLEVELAND, Ohio	727	643	349		1,225	1,373	173	1,356	799	2,487	1,365	769
DALLAS, Texas	826	1,868	936	1,225		797	1,194	241	505	1,431	1,394	940
DENVER, Colo.	1,519	2,008	1,017	1,373	797		1,302	1,038	604	1,189	2,126	871
DETROIT, Mich.	741	706	297	173	1,194	1,302		1,326	752	2,448	1,395	693
HOUSTON, Texas	875	1,961	1,073	1,356	241	1,038	1,326		746	1,564	1,306	1,181
KANSAS CITY, Mo.	882	1,442	505	799	505	604	752	746		1,631	1,485	435
LOS ANGELES, Calif.	2,252	3,130	2,189	2,487	1,431	1,189	2,448	1,564	1,631		2,885	2,033
MIAMI, Fla.	662	1,547	1,386	1,365	1,394	2,126	1,395	1,306	1,485	2,885		1,786
MINNEAPOLIS-ST. PAUL, Minn.	1,136	1,399	416	769	940	871	693	1,181	435	2,033	1,786	
NEW ORLEANS, La.	518	1,625	938	1,132	495	1,292	1,143	349	809	1,947	881	1,228
NEW YORK, N.Y.	863	217	818	502	1,649	1,852	632	1,742	1,223	2,911	1,325	1,261
OMAHA, Neb.	1,027	1,451	477	816	681	540	745	931	185	1,668	1,686	371
PHILADELPHIA, Pa.	776	308	767	425	1,561	1,770	588	1,648	1,141	2,829	1,231	1,179
PORTLAND, Ore.	2,873	3,229	2,250	2,599	2,145	1,347	2,523	2,368	1,953	1,016	3,438	1,830
RENO, Nev.	2,611	2,953	1,980	2,310	1,849	1,038	2,239	1,975	1,654	475	3,217	1,782
ST. LOUIS, Mo.	582	1,188	293	545	643	858	514	780	254	1,942	1,231	553
SALT LAKE CITY, Utah	1,959	2,431	1,411	1,796	1,240	501	1,725	1,502	1,105	704	2,621	1,309
SAN DIEGO, Calif.	2,230	3,119	2,210	2,476	1,421	1,243	2,445	1,578	1,706	125	2,817	2,138
SAN FRANCISCO, Calif.	2,554	3,198	2,233	2,563	1,791	1,267	2,492	1,984	1,903	383	3,238	2,077
SEATTLE, Wash.	2,954	3,163	2,184	2,533	2,222	1,426	2,457	2,445	1,984	1,193	3,469	1,691
WASHINGTON, D.C.	641	443	696	358	1,414	1,707	525	1,501	1,066	2,754	1,096	1,116

NEW ORLEANS	NEW YORK	OMAHA	PHILADELPHIA	PORTLAND, ORE.	RENO	ST. LOUIS	SALT LAKE CITY	SAN DIEGO	SAN FRANCISCO	SEATTLE	WASHINGTON, D.C.	
518	863	1,027	776	2,873	2,611	582	1,959	2,230	2,554	2,954	641	**ATLANTA,** Ga.
1,625	217	1,451	308	3,229	2,953	1,188	2,431	3,119	3,198	3,163	443	**BOSTON,** Mass.
938	818	477	767	2,250	1,980	293	1,411	2,210	2,233	2,184	696	**CHICAGO,** Ill.
1,132	502	816	425	2,599	2,310	545	1,796	2,476	2,563	2,533	358	**CLEVELAND,** Ohio
495	1,649	681	1,561	2,145	1,849	643	1,240	1,421	1,791	2,222	1,414	**DALLAS,** Texas
1,292	1,852	540	1,770	1,347	1,038	858	501	1,243	1,267	1,426	1,707	**DENVER,** Colo.
1,143	632	745	588	2,523	2,239	514	1,725	2,445	2,492	2,457	525	**DETROIT,** Mich.
349	1,742	931	1,648	2,368	1,975	780	1,502	1,578	1,984	2,445	1,501	**HOUSTON,** Texas
809	1,223	185	1,141	1,953	1,654	254	1,105	1,706	1,903	1,984	1,066	**KANSAS CITY,** Mo.
1,947	2,911	1,668	2,829	1,016	475	1,942	704	125	383	1,193	2,754	**LOS ANGELES** Calif.
881	1,325	1,686	1,231	3,438	3,217	1,231	2,621	2,817	3,238	3,469	1,096	**MIAMI,** Fla.
1,228	1,261	371	1,179	1,830	1,782	553	1,309	2,138	2,077	1,691	1,116	**MINNEAPOLIS-ST. PAUL,** Minn.
	1,406	994	1,312	2,654	2,350	690	1,735	1,879	2,300	2,731	1,165	**NEW ORLEANS,** La.
1,406		1,295	89	3,088	2,789	969	2,275	2,900	3,082	3,025	232	**NEW YORK,** N.Y.
994	1,295		1,213	1,749	1,499	439	938	1,788	1,726	1,824	1,150	**OMAHA,** Neb.
1,312	89	1,213		3,006	2,707	887	2,193	2,818	2,960	2,943	141	**PHILADELPHIA,** Pa.
2,654	3,088	1,749	3,006		666	2,207	768	1,137	611	175	2,943	**PORTLAND,** Ore.
2,350	2,789	1,499	2,707	666		1,908	516	576	222	856	2,644	**RENO,** Nev.
690	969	439	887	2,207	1,908		1,359	1,931	2,157	2,238	812	**ST. LOUIS,** Mo.
1,735	2,275	938	2,193	768	516	1,359		812	730	924	2,130	**SALT LAKE CITY,** Utah
1,879	2,900	1,788	2,818	1,137	576	1,931	812		525	1,314	2,743	**SAN DIEGO,** Calif.
2,300	3,082	1,726	2,960	611	222	2,157	2,157	525		786	2,897	**SAN FRANCISCO,** Calif.
2,731	3,025	1,824	2,943	175	856	2,238	2,238	1,314	786		2,880	**SEATTLE,** Wash.
1,165	232	1,150	141	2,943	2,644	812	812	2,743	2,897	2,880		**WASHINGTON,** D.C.

EXPERT PICKS

A GUIDE TO THE TRAVEL GUIDES

With gazillions of titles, here's how to pick your trusty companion

During 10 years as co-owner of the Traveler's Bookstore in Rockefeller Center, Martin Rapp saw hundreds of travel guides come and go. Now a travel agent at Altour International in New York City and a contributing editor at *Travel & Leisure* magazine, he has become an expert at picking the best of the bunch. Here are his views on the current crop.

■ **AAA.** If you're on the road in some obscure place, don't care about charm, and just want to find a place to stay, these guides are complete and very useful. The maps and "Tripticks" (succinct notebook-style maps designed for easy flipping while driving) are excellent.

■ **ACCESS.** Great city guides (e.g., *New York City*, 250 pages, $12) for first-time visitors tell you everything found within a geographic neighborhood using color-coordinated entries. Access guides pioneered the technique of interviewing leading citizens of all types for lists of "bests." However, the entries are not very detailed, and the books are weak on general travel advice. Stylized but good maps.

■ **BIRNBAUM.** Their strength is special sections like "For the Body," "For the Mind," and "Unexpected Pleasures and Treasures." They don't do pricing, just say "expensive" or "cheap," which doesn't really help me. They do provide driving itineraries, which are not extensive, but a great starting-off point. Their Mexico guide (640 pages, $19) is excellent.

■ **CADOGAN.** A British import, so what you get are very extensive descriptions of sites and historical info. I like them because they give you some out-of-the-way hotels and restaurants. They're not extensive listings, but they're more personal. These guides are good for the intellectual traveler. Their Sicily book (375 pages, $14.95) is excellent.

■ **FODOR'S AND FROMMER'S.** Great for people who want to see the sights but are not adventurous. For a wider choice of hotels and restaurants in the medium- and lower-price range, I've always liked Frommer's. Frommer's guides are a little more user-friendly, with more personal flavor. Fodor's guides are dependable, middle-of-the-road books with which you can't really go wrong. Both are great for people who want to know a little about a lot.

■ **LONELY PLANET.** When the Wheelers, Lonely Planet's editors, started their books, they were young backpackers traveling with no money through Southeast Asia. As they have grown older, they've learned to list some of the more expensive places, but the books are still firmly rooted in the budget end. Their India handbook (1,150 pages, $24.95) is probably the best travel guide ever for that country.

■ **MICHELIN "RED GUIDES."** The most detailed restaurant and hotel guides there are for Europe, with the most accurate range of prices. Almost everything has a symbol—whether or not there is an elevator, whether dogs are allowed, whether there is a swimming pool, etc. The city maps are superb, including one-way streets, parking areas, hotels, and restaurants listed in the guide, and many other features. The green Michelin guides are just for sight-seeing.

■ **MOON.** These guides are great for Southeast Asia and that part of the world. What I like about them in comparison to Lonely Planet is they are a little more upscale.

■ **ROUGH GUIDES.** The English version of the Lonely Planet guides, although the Lonely Planet guides are more complete. A trendsetter in offering advice for female, gay, and disabled travelers. Weak on maps.

CHAPTER EIGHT

AUTOS

EXPERT QUOTES

When car bargaining, "knock 10 percent off the sticker price automatically."
—Mark Eskeldson, author of *What Car Dealers Don't Want You to Know*
Page 571

"Excessive charges for early termination and wear and tear are the two biggest leasing abuses."
—Randall McCathren, car leasing expert
Page 574

"Maintaining a three-second distance between cars allows adequate time."
—Lyn St. James, professional race car driver
Page 584

■ **THE YEAR AHEAD: TAKE ADVANTAGE** of the revolution in used car selling... **DO** your car bargaining by fax machine... **KEEP** the financing period on your next car as short as possible... **LEARN** about HMOs for the family auto... **MAKE SURE** that the motorcycle you buy is big enough... **INTRODUCE** teenage drivers to the road in stages through the graduated licensing approach...

BUYING & LEASING 564

DRIVING & MAINTENANCE 584

BUYING & LEASING

ROAD TESTS: The best cars for 1996, PAGE 567 **DEALERSHIPS:** Doing your homework is the best way to get a good deal, PAGE 571 **BUYING SERVICES:** Let someone else buy your car for you, PAGE 573 **LEASING:** Some common errors to avoid, PAGE 574 **CRASH TESTS:** How various models compared in safety, PAGE 576 **INSURANCE:** Some cars cost more to insure than others, PAGE 578 **REPAIRS:** HMOs and PPOs for your car? PAGE 581

TRENDS

NEW WAYS TO BUY USED CARS

A host of marketing heavyweights want your business

Turned off by new car prices that have increased 10 percent over the last two years, you decide to brave the Damoclean sword and shop the used-car market. You're familiar with the process: driving from lot to lot in search of a suitable vehicle, all the while haggling with slick salesmen. The day's first stop is at the new used-car dealership outside of town. The lot's landscaped lawn almost makes you forget you're car shopping. Inside, you're overwhelmed by the acres of selection. You drop your child off at the store's day-care facility and browse the dealer's stock via computer. After compiling a list of suitable cars, you move to the coffee bar to ponder your selection. You've narrowed your choice to two cars, but you need some more information, so, with trepidation, you ask the salesman for help. Curiously, he steers you away from the higher-priced choice, indicating the lower-priced car meets your needs just as well as the higher-priced vehicle. To your surprise you find that all the prices are set and non-negotiable, so you go directly to the dealer's financing department, work out a deal, and drive away in your newly purchased automobile.

Have you reach car lot nirvana? Actually, you just shopped at a used-car superstore. In the last few years, a number of entrepreneurs have set out to revolutionize the used-car industry the way WalMart revolutionized retailing. Circuit City, which grew to a national powerhouse selling TVs and computers, is applying its formula to high quality used cars. H. Wayne Huizenga, the former chairman of Blockbuster Entertainment Corp., plans to do for cars what he did for videos with a competing chain, AutoNation. Financial heavyweights, including New York financier Marshall S. Cogan, Leon D. Black of Apollo Advisors, and J.P. Morgan Capital, are major investors in United Auto Group, the nation's fourth largest new car chain.

The new players bring a new kind of retailing savvy to car sales. They see cars as essentially the same as shoes or TV sets, products that sell best with the right blend of selection, convenience, service, and price.

So far, these new superstores have focused on used cars, where they don't have to wrestle with state franchise laws that prevent dealers from issuing a new franchise within 15 miles of another dealer. All the cars are relatively new, two- to five-year-old vehicles. Best of all, you can choose from as many as 700 automobiles of nearly every make and model.

■ WHAT YOUR CAR WILL BRING FIVE YEARS LATER

The percentage to the right of each vehicle represents how much of its original value the vehicle will retain at the end of five years. Resale value is based on the car's rate of depreciation. Vehicles with better resale values have slower rates of depreciation.

HIGHEST RESALE VALUE

■ SUBCOMPACT	
Honda Civic CX 2 Door	66%
Saturn SC1	63
Toyota Tercel DX 2 Door	61
■ COMPACT	
Saturn SL	66
Toyota Corolla DX 4 Door	61
Volkswagen Jetta GL	60
Honda Accord DX 4 Door	60
■ MIDSIZE	
Mazda 626 DX	57
Toyota Camry DX 4 Door	56
Nissan Maxima SE	55
■ LARGE	
Buick LeSabre Custom	52
Pontiac Bonneville SE	51
Ford Crown Victoria	50
■ SMALL LUXURY	
Lexus ES 300	63
Mercedes-Benz C220	60
BMW 328 iS 2 Door	59
■ LARGE LUXURY	
Lexus GS 300	63
Lexus SC 400	63
Lexus SC 300	63
Mercedes-Benz E320/C280	61
■ SMALL SPORT	
Ford Mustang GT	57
Chevrolet Camaro Z28	54
Acura Integra GS-R 2	54
Mazda MX-5 Miata	54
■ LARGE SPORT	
Mitsubishi 3000GT VR-4 4wd	59
Porsche 911 Carrera Cabriolet	59
Chevrolet Corvette	58
■ SUBCOM./COMPACT WAGON	
Saturn SW	66
Toyota Corolla DX	62
Honda Accord LX	57
■ MIDSIZE/LARGE WAGON	
Toyota Camry LE	55
Subaru Legacy L AWD	55
Eagle Summit AWD	53
■ SM SPORTS UTILITY VEHICLES	
GMC Jimmy	70
Chevrolet Blazer	69
Jeep Cherokee Sport 4WD	68
■ LGE SPORTS UTILITY VEHICLES	
GMC Suburban K2500 4WD	76
GMC Suburban K1500 4WD	74
GMC Yukon	73

LOWEST RESALE VALUES

■ SUBCOMPACT	
Eagle Summit ESi 4 Door	46
Subaru Impreza Brighton AWD	46
Ford Probe	48
■ COMPACT	
Oldsmobile Achieva SC III Series 2 Door	41
Mercury Tracer LTS 4 Door	43
Buick Skylark Limited 2 Door	44
■ MIDSIZE	
Buick Century Special	43
Olds Cutlass Supreme SL Series IV 2 Door	44
Ford Taurus LX	45
Mercury Sable LS	45
Olds Cutlass Ciera SL Series II	45
■ LARGE	
Eagle Vision TSi	42
Buick Roadmaster	45
Chevrolet Caprice Classic Special Value SB	45
■ SMALL LUXURY	
Chrysler LHS	43
Chrysler New Yorker	44
Olds Ninety-Eight Regency Elite Series I	45
■ LARGE LUXURY	
Lincoln Town Car Cartier Designer	43
Cadillac Fleetwood	44
Lincoln Mark VIII	44
■ SMALL SPORT	
Eagle Talon TSi Turbo	45
Pontiac Firebird Formula	49
Ford Mustang Cobra	49
■ LARGE SPORT	
Nissan 300ZX 2+2	45
Subaru SVX L AWD	47
Toyota Supra Turbo	49
■ SUBCOM./COMPACT WAGON	
Subaru Impreza Outback AWD	46
Ford Escort LX	50
Mercury Tracer	50
■ MIDSIZE/LARGE WAGON	
Buick Century Special	43
Chevrolet Caprice Classic Special Value SD	45
Oldsmobile Cutlass Ciera SL Cruiser	45
■ SM SPORTS UTILITY VEHICLES	
Geo Tracker Soft Top	53
Oldsmobile Bravada 4WD	57
Ford Explorer XLT 4WD	59
Suzuki Sidekick JS	59
■ LGE SPORTS UTILITY VEHICLES	
Land Rover Range Rover 4.0 SE 4WD	60
Ford Bronco Eddie Bauer 4WD	64
Chevrolet Tahoe 4WD	68
GMC Yukon 4WD	68

Source: *The Complete Car Cost Guide* (Intellichoice, 1996).

Although the huge selection may catch a shopper's eye, it's the low-stress, customer-friendly shopping environment the superstores consider the key to winning customer patronage. The salesmen work on salary and not commission; touch-screen computers allow you to browse the entire inventory without walking the enormous lot; and fixed sticker prices have replaced the stressful haggling process. Most of the extended services available from new-car dealerships are also provided through the superstores, including warranties ranging from the existing manufacturer's warranty to the store's own three-month warranty to options on extended warranties. Also available are fully equipped service centers, roadside assistance, and finance departments. Some shops may even offer coffee shops and day-care centers. Consumers have evidently taken to the new trend: In one month alone, four CarMax stores did an estimated $288 million in sales.

Does this mean the end of franchise dealerships? Art Spinella, a noted industry analyst at Oregon-based CNW market research, doubts it. Dealers now realize, he says, that to compete they must place greater emphasis on marketing their used-car departments and becoming more customer-friendly. Already, franchises have begun stressing their "traditional" advantages—namely, price and manufacturer agreements. A customer willing to haggle can still get the same car from a dealer for hundreds of dollars less than at a superstore. Maintenance is another selling point. Regardless of where you buy a car, if it has an existing manufacturer's warranty, it must be brought back to the dealerships for any needed repairs.

Dealers also realize that the day has come to shed their plaid-suit image. "Dealerships are no longer mom-and-pop operations; they are $2 million investments. To successfully maintain a dealership requires business understanding and acumen," says Ted Orme, executive director of communication of the National Automotive Dealers Association (NADA). Indoor showrooms have replaced banner-laden outdoor used lots. The dealerships have also tried to emulate many of the popular selling practices of the superstores, such as low-pressure sales, a short-term dealership warranty, and money-back guarantees. In a recent customer satisfaction poll taken by CNW, the franchise dealers fared very well against the superstores. Atlanta's CarMax dealership received a very impressive 8.1 (out of 10) Customer Satisfaction Rating (CSR); however, the typical new-car dealer trailed close behind, registering a 7.8 CSR.

Other dealer reactions have been even more assertive. Nine of the country's leading franchise dealers have formed their own auto superstore. Drivers Mart, of Grand Rapids, Mich., had 10 stores opened by early 1996 and planned to open 100 more within three years. The owners are not your stereotypical car salesmen. Karl Selvel is a well-known customer service guru, and Bert Bockman runs a successful Saturn dealership. Like the other superstore chains, Drivers Mart offers huge selection, technological shopping aids, low-pressure sales, and a variety of customer-friendly amenities. Many other dealers have shown great interest in opening superstores.

Not that superstores will run away with all the business. "The supply of two- to four-year-old cars just isn't available," says analyst Spinella, "and these are the automobiles the public craves and that provide the dealers with the most profit." Superstores, he predicts, "will be left with cars five years or older. These automobiles are less reliable and difficult to recondition. More important, the people who buy five-year-old cars are driven by one thing: price. They may be just as willing to haggle with a dealer, or shop the independent market, than buy at Drivers Mart or Circuit City."

So where does this leave the consumer? It is highly doubtful that we will once again be at the franchise dealers' mercy. The market is in the midst of enormous change and will unlikely fall back on outmoded habits. Since Drivers Mart is made of franchise dealers, it is not likely to have problems obtaining prime used cars. Furthermore, Chrysler stunned its dealers and competitors when it gave CarMax a new car franchise in Duluth, Ga., giving the store access to Chrysler-Plymouth-Jeep-Eagle closed auctions. If successful, manufacturers may cut similar deals with other superstores. Even Saturn, the highly respected subsidiary of GM, has now announced it too will enter the used-car market.

In the topsy-turvy world of car sales, the only player who may claim victory is the consumer. With unprecedented buying options now available, and dealers getting religious about the importance of service, the consumer is finally in the driver's seat.

EXPERT PICKS

THE BEST CARS OF 1996

Everyone wants a car that starts when it's supposed to and gets you to where you need to go. But many drivers expect an automobile to be more than just a reliable appliance. For drivers who love the road, the magazines Car and Driver *and* Automobile Magazine *are among the first places they turn for car evaluations. Here are the cars their editors picked as the very best of model year 1996:*

$12,000–$18,000

CHRYSLER CIRRUS/DODGE STRATUS

Front-drive, 4-door, 5-passenger sedan, 20 mpg.* Base: $17,560.

■ Efficient packages often resemble boxes, but these two sedans have a smart and distinctive look that stands out in the humdrum sedan segment. They also have an electronically controlled automatic transmission and an independent suspension with control arms in front and multilink setup in the rear—the only such arrangement on a domestic front-drive sedan and one that yields a good ride and good handling.

CAR AND DRIVER

FORD CONTOUR/MERCURY MYSTIQUE

Front-drive, 4-door, 5- or 6-passenger sedan, 18–20 mpg. Base: $16,170.

■ Okay, so it costs a little more than a Ford Tempo. It should; the Ford Contour is a four or five times better car than the best Tempo ever made. The all-alloy Contour V-6 gives us four valves per cylinder, service-free running for 100,000 miles (well, you do have to change the oil and filter), and all the sounds and feel of the finest sports car engines, suitably subdued for family appreciation.

CAR AND DRIVER

HONDA CIVIC

Front-drive, 3- or 4-door, 5-passenger sedan; 28–33 mpg. Base: $12,300.

■ Honda's Civics have always been technological leaders in the economy-sedan segment, and the redesigned 1996 models are no exception. The lean-burn VTEC-E engine with its staged intake valves produces an outstanding blend of power and fuel economy, and the high-revving VTEC powerplant puts out 127 hp. Another innovation is the continuously variable transmission that combines the convenience of an automatic with the performance and efficiency of a manual. Despite these virtues, these Civics are very reasonably priced.

CAR AND DRIVER

$18,000–$25,000

ACURA INTEGRA COUPE

Front-drive, 3-door, 4-passenger coupe, 24–25 mpg. Base: $21,300.

■ The Integra coupe is a blast to drive, and that's why the GS-R model won a spot on our 1996 Ten Best Cars list. There are four models of the two-door Integra: the budget RS, the mid-level LS, the speedy GS-R, and a new Special Edition trim package that falls between LS and GS-R. Everything is done right on these cars. Though the Integra is not inexpensive, driving it will make you feel as if you spent your money wisely.

CAR AND DRIVER

FORD MUSTANG COBRA

Rear-drive, 2-door, 4-passenger coupe, 18 mpg. Base: $24,810.

■ It will come as a shock to techno-twits and nomenclature sniffers that a car with a 32-year-old name, a modified 17-year-old platform, and a solid rear axle is mentioned in the same breath with the term All-Star. But the new Mustang Cobra is not only a contender for the honor, it wins hands down. The credit goes to the 305-bhp, 32 valve, DOHC aluminum V-8, a paragon of high performance.

AUTOMOBILE MAGAZINE

FORD TAURUS/MERCURY SABLE

Front-drive, 4-door, 5-passenger

■ EXPERT PICKS

sedan, 20 mpg. Base: $21,295.

■ While we're divided on the appearance of the new Taurus and Sable, we're unanimous on our assessment of their performance and drivability. Two areas stand out: the basic structure and the optional Duratec all-aluminum, four-cam V-6 engine. The three-liter Duratec engine is a paragon of internal-combustion virtue and will probably put more Americans into cars with four-cam engines than any previous automotive development has ever done.

AUTOMOBILE MAGAZINE

MAZDA MX-5 MIATA

Rear-drive, 2-door, 2-passenger convertible, 23 mpg. Base: $18,450.

■ After 30 minutes behind the Miata's fat little wheel, we're convinced it's still a modern classic—nippy, fun to drive, and remarkably responsive. In keeping with the car's subtle evolution, changes were carefully chosen to preserve the Miata's exquisite balance. For 1996, there's 133 bhp (up from 128 bhp) and 114 pound-feet of torque (up from 110). There are three pricey option packages, but we prefer the base car without power assists and fancy trim.

AUTOMOBILE MAGAZINE

NISSAN MAXIMA SE

Front-drive, 4-door, 5-passenger sedan, 22 mpg. Base: $22,677.

■ The Maxima seems ordinary at first glance but grows in our estimation with every mile we spend behind the wheel. The latest Maxima offers excellent accommodations front and back, along with handsome leather furnishings in our preferred SE trim level. Its seemingly standard-for-the-class, 24-valve, 3.0-liter, all-aluminum V-6 engine makes Maxima the quickest car in its class.

CAR AND DRIVER

$25,000–$35,000

AUDI A4

4-wheel-drive, 4-door, 5-passenger sedan, 19 mpg. Base: $26,500.

The A4 became a favorite during All-Star testing because it did so many things well. For the generation weaned on a Volkswagen GTI who are now looking for something with four doors and a little more room for their partner or—gasp—baby, the A4 presents an appealing alternative to the BMW 328I, while saving a couple thousand dollars.

CAR AND DRIVER

HONDA PRELUDE VTEC

Front-drive, 2-door, 2+2-passenger coupe, 22 mpg. Base: $26,000.

■ We're mesmerized by the Prelude's driver delights. The 2.2-liter all-aluminum VTEC engine is instantly responsive, revs to 7500 rpm effortlessly, and develops 190 hp in the process. Then there's the delightful gearbox, coupled to a smooth, light clutch. The Prelude's steering disproves the notion that a front-driver can't steer with the accuracy and feel of a rear-driver. Finally, the suspension provides uncanny balance, letting a sensitive drive position both ends of the car with predictable precision.

CAR AND DRIVER

$35,000 AND ABOVE

BMW 328is/M3

Rear-drive, 2- or 4-door, 5-passenger sedan, 19–20 mpg. Base: $33,410–$39,972.

■ Year in and year out, these tidy six-cylinder BMWs rank among our favorite cars. From the 328i sedan to the glorious M3, the 3-series cars drive with distinction. The classic BMW in-line six defines these cars with its smooth-sounding, eager-revving, energtic performance. In the 1996 models an increase in engine displacement from 2.5 to 2.8 liters makes for improved performance and more relaxed cruising. They feel more like refined sports cars than compact luxury sedans. As all-around sporting sedans, the BMW 3s remain the ones to beat.

CAR AND DRIVER

LEXUS SC300

Rear-drive, 2-door, 4-passenger coupe, 18 mpg. Base: $43,400.

■ The Lexus SC300 exudes elegance. The SC300 repre-

■ **EXPERT PICKS**

sents old-money sensibilities with its blend of opulence and minimalism. Under the charm, grace, and elegance lies a mischievous heart, though. There are sportier cars and cars with far more power, but the combination of this raspy 225-bhp, 3.0-liter DOHC in-line six and the short-throw five-speed manual transmission will bring out the feisty side of any driver.

AUTOMOBILE MAGAZINE

NISSAN 300ZX TURBO

Rear-drive, 3-door, 2- or 4-passenger coupe, 18–19 mpg. Base: $44,679.

■ This is the last year the current 300ZX Turbo will appear on our Ten Best list, because Nissan will stop importing the car after the 1996 model year. That's a shame. The current model is not only the fastest and most powerful in a long line of Z-cars, but it's also as user-friendly as 150 mph two-seaters get.

CAR AND DRIVER

PORSCHE 911 CARRERA

Rear-drive, 2-door, 2+2 coupe, 17 mpg. Base: $105,000.

■ It has earned plaudits for the purity of its design but has been criticized for faults that include Stone Age ergonomics and dodgy on-the-limit behavior. Most of the deeply ingrained niggles about such factors as offset pedals are forgiven, if not forgotten, when you tune in to the 911 Carrera's exhilarating air-cooled, 3.6-liter engine that now develops 282 bhp at 6300 rpm.

AUTOMOBILE MAGAZINE

SPORTS UTILITY

CHEVROLET TAHOE/GMC YUKON

4-wheel drive, 4-door, 5-passenger utility vehicle, 13 mpg. Base: $28,585.

■ Somewhere between the massive Chevrolet Suburban and the compact Blazer lies perfection. It is the Tahoe. It is absolutely dandy in the dirt, with higher ground clearance than any of its chief competitors and a new push-button electronic transfer case for one touch shifting between two- and four-wheel-drive.

AUTOMOBILE MAGAZINE

MINIVAN

CHRYSLER TOWN AND COUNTRY

Front- or 4-wheel drive, 4- or 5-door, 7-passenger van, 17–20 mpg. Base: $30,500.

■ The new Chrysler Town and Country runs and feels like a luxury car on the highway. Plus, it's got the high-up view of a minivan, and the interior room of, well, a big room on wheels. The Town and Country for the first time comes in a short-wheelbase model, which is built in Ontario, as well as the long-wheelbase, from St. Louis.

CAR AND DRIVER

* All mpg results were rated according to EPA city driving estimates.
SOURCES: *Automobile Magazine*, February 1996; *Car and Driver, '96 Buyers Guide.*

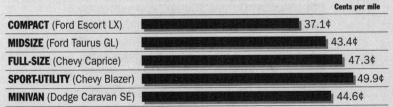

■ **CRUISIN' GETS COSTLIER**

Costlier depreciation, insurance, and financing raised the average cost of owning and operating a 1996 car, $204 to $6,384 per year, or 42.6 cents per mile. By vehicle type:

NOTE: Depreciation, insurance, financing, fuel, oil, repairs, licenses, and taxes for 4-year, 60,000-mile ownership period.
SOURCE: Runzhaimer for the American Automobile Association.

THE QUALITY LEADERS

The research firm J.D. Power and Associates in 1996 asked more than 44,000 owners of new cars, light trucks, and sports-utility vehicles to evaluate their autos 90 days after they had purchased them. The average number of new-car problems per 100 vehicles was 100 in 1996, a record year for the auto industry, in which consumers reported fewer problems overall than ever before, compared with 110 in 1994. J.D. Power and Associates expects further quality improvements to reduce vehicle problems by another 30 percent in the next five years. Here are the top three least problematic autos in each car category:

COMPACT CAR

Subaru Impreza	57
Mazda Protege	64
Toyota Tercel	68

ENTRY MIDSIZE CAR *(less than $20,000)*

Nissan Altima	73
Honda Accord	77
Chevrolet Lumina	78

PREMIUM MIDSIZE CAR *(over $20,000)*

Oldsmobile 88	70
Toyota Camry	82
Nissan Maxima	83

SPORTY CAR

Toyota Paseo	68
Acura Integra	85
Mazda Miata	88

ENTRY LUXURY CAR *(under $35,000)*

Lexus ES300	54
Mazda Millenia	61
Infiniti J30	62

PREMIUM LUXURY CAR *(over $35,000)*

Lexus SC300/400	45
Lexus LS400	52
Infiniti Q35	58

COMPACT PICKUP TRUCK

Toyota Tacoma	76
Ford Ranger	78
Mazda B-pickup	115

FULL-SIZE PICKUP

Chevrolet C/K	94
Toyota T100	102
GMC Sierra	113

COMPACT VAN

Toyota Previa	76
Mercury Villager	105
Chevrolet Lumina APV	114

COMPACT SPORTS UTILITY VEHICLE

Ford Explorer	104
Geo Tracker	108
Jeep Grand Cherokee	127

FULL-SIZE SPORTS UTILITY VEHICLE

Toyota Landcruiser	70
Chevrolet Suburban	118
GMC Yukon	120

SOURCE: J.D. Power and Associates, 1996.

TRYING HARDER PAYS OFF

When J.D. Power and Associates asked U.S. customers to rate the performance of the major car rental agencies at airport locations, Avis scored slightly higher than Hertz or National. Taking 100 as an average score, Dollar and Alamo placed lowest.

SOURCE: J.D. Power and Associates, 1996. Domestic Car Rental Satisfaction Study.

EXPERT TIPS

WHAT DEALERS DON'T TELL YOU

With the right data, the salesman will be at your mercy

Most people approach buying a new car with the same apprehension as sitting in rush hour traffic with a car full of quarreling children. But there's no need to feel at the mercy of a car salesman, says Mark Eskeldson, author of *What Car Dealers Don't Want You to Know* (Technews, 1995), and host of Shop Talk: America's Radio Car Clinic. Here, Eskeldson offers these tips on how to gain control of your car buying experience and save a great deal of money in the process:

■ Knock 10 percent off the sticker price automatically.

First and foremost, determine how much you can afford to spend. For a rough estimation, take a vehicle's sticker price and deduct 10 percent. For example, if you're interested in purchasing a vehicle listed at $20,000, estimate the monthly payments based on a purchase price of $18,000. After you've settled on an affordable price range, start shopping. Make a list of the cars that fit your style and budget. You don't necessarily need to visit dealerships to do this, you can make your list from television commercials or magazines. If you do visit a dealership, stay away from salesmen. If one approaches you, tell him or her, "I'm just looking and I am not buying a car."

To research the cars on your list, use consumer guides, reviewing cars for reliability, safety, performance, and the like. This is the area where people typically make their biggest mistakes. People who fail to research a car's reliability can lose a great deal of money to depreciation and the repair shop. If the car you like isn't among the top-rated, try compromising style for reliability. Choose a car you find attractive, but that rates well in the car assessments.

■ Don't begrudge a dealer a modest profit.

Books and magazines provide very, very basic car cost numbers. For a number of reasons, the actual amount that a dealer pays for a vehicle can change from day to day. For accurate and daily up-to-date information on true dealer cost, you should consider phoning a service called Fighting Chance (☎ 800–288–1134). The charge of $19.95 per call will provide you with the amount the dealer is paying for any new vehicle—including secret factory incentives and other market shifts that will affect the automobile's true price.

Once you have figured out a car's true cost, add in a reasonable amount for dealer profit. For cars costing $10,000–$13,000, allow $400–$500 for the dealer's profit. For cars in the $20,000 range, add on approximately $500. For luxury cars, a dealer typically won't accept an offer for less than $1,000 profit.

■ Solicit bids by fax if possible.

Before you tangle directly with the dealers, I encourage customers to first try the "fax strategy." Fax a form letter to a number of dealerships. Inform the dealer you've already done your research and you are shopping for the best offer. Describe in detail the automobile you intend to purchase and the names of the dealer's competitors. For example, "I'm looking for a blue '96 Taurus four-door sedan, with option package X, Y, Z. I am soliciting offers from Bob's Cars and Joe's Autos and will accept the lowest offer." Don't mention an amount, but let the dealer know you've done your homework. In closing, notify the dealer that if it is interested in selling a car, it should fax or call you with a price. In about three days you should hear from all interested parties.

Choose the offer you are most comfortable with and visit the dealer. You may only have to visit one dealer before closing a deal. I recently had great success using this method to purchase my own car. I sent out seven faxes, received three responses, and

EXPERT SOURCES

WHERE TO GET A FIX ON PRICES

Invoice prices can be found in two annuals, The Complete Car Cost Guide *(IntelliChoice, Inc.) or* Edmund's New Car Price Guide *(Edmund Publications). The services below will mail or fax you that and more for $11 to $23.*

CAR PRICE NETWORK
■ Everything from dealer invoices and factory rebates to market overviews and negotiating tips.
☎ 800-227-3295

CENTER FOR THE STUDY OF SERVICES
■ Its biweekly newsletter, *Car Deals*, provides info on factory incentives for $4.50 a copy.
☎ 202-347-7283

FIGHTING CHANCE
■ Like Car Price Network, it offers dealer invoices, factory rebates, market overviews, and negotiating tips.
☎ 800-288-1134

CAR/PUTER
■ Information about dealer invoices and factory rebates.
☎ 800-992-7404

CONSUMER REPORTS NEW CAR PRICING
■ Dealer invoice, factory rebates, negotiating tips.
☎ 800-933-5555

INTELLICHOICE
■ Dealer invoice, factory rebates, resale values, and ownership costs.
☎ 800-227-2665

closed the deal without ever leaving my home. If this method fails, resort to plan B—visiting the dealer.

■ Be wary of "deals" at the end of the model year.

Most salespersons have quotas to meet at the end of each month. Whether he needs one more sale to keep his job or win a trip to Hawaii, the dealer may be willing to sell the car at little or no profit simply for the sale.

Beware of model year-end sales, however. Buying a model before the new versions arrive may appear to offer great savings, but it rarely makes up for the depreciation difference. Because the greatest depreciation occurs in an automobile's first two years, a year-end model has already lost 20 to 25 percent of its value.

■ Use walking out as a negotiating strategy.

You're never going to get the best price unless you're willing and ready to walk out. Don't waste your time fighting with dealers—you will always lose. Once you begin haggling, the dealer has gained the advantage. This is his specialty. The dealer makes his living haggling a deal; he does so nearly every single day.

When you visit the dealer, keep the process very impersonal. Submit an offer, and make it clear that if they turn you down, you are willing to offer their competitors the same deal. Usually the dealer will call your bluff and let you walk out. I'd be shocked if they didn't run out to catch you in the parking lot. At this point you have gained the advantage. Tell the salesman you will not go back inside unless they accept your price. The key ingredient to the strategy is competition. Most dealers accept the fact that a low-profit sale is better than no sale. Remember, it is a buyer's market. Use this to your advantage.

■ Keep the financing period as short as possible.

Never walk in and ask the salesperson for financial advice. A car dealer will always steer you toward the most expensive car and long-term financing. Don't be fooled by the low monthly payments. Financing a car is a "no pain, no gain" proposition—if it doesn't hurt, you haven't done it correctly. The intelligent way to finance a car is with a large

EXPERT SOURCES

LEAVE THE BARGAINING TO THE PROS

The easiest way to spare yourself showroom face-offs with car salespersons you don't trust is to engage an auto-buying service that will do the negotiating for you. The best services are ones whose fees are paid by customers, not car dealers rewarding buying services for sending clients their way. Among the best-known national services are:

AUTO ADVISOR

■ This Seattle-based company's basic service costs $359, and the sales price it negotiates for a car is guaranteed. Its enhanced service ranges from $419 for four- to eight-week delivery to $679 for one-week delivery. The service permits customers to price more than one car at a time and includes an hour of consultation in the base fee. Extra advice costs $120 an hour.
☎ 800–326–1976

AUTOMOBILE CONSUMER SERVICES

■ Work begins with a $75-per-vehicle service fee. The final bill is based on a percentage of the savings between the sticker price and purchase price. Total costs average about $295.
☎ 800–223–4882

CAR BARGAINS

■ Operated by the Center for the Study of Services in Washington, D.C., on a nonprofit basis. For a fee of only $135, Car Bargains solicits bids from five dealers in your area. You get the actual dealer quote sheets as well as information on financing, service contracts, and the value of your used car.
☎ 800–475–7283

CONSUMERS AUTOMOTIVE

■ Fees are $195 for a car with a sticker price up to $15,000, $295 for a car between $15,000 and $30,000, and $395 for more expensive cars. Prices are guaranteed.
☎ 703–631–5161

down payment and as high monthly payments as possible.

Under no circumstance should you agree to a six-year car loan. A six-year loan is financial suicide. The interest will kill you. For example, if you purchased a $20,000 car, financed at 9 percent over three years, your total payment in interest will be $2,896. Paying the same price and rate, but agreeing to a six-year loan, your interest payment is now $5,963. If you can't afford at least a five-year loan, you are better off buying your car used or settling for a lower-priced model. A five-year loan is your compromise. Even there you'll save $1,000 in interest, while paying only $54 more a month than for a four-year loan.

■ Avoid extended warranties in almost all situations.

Extended warranties are where people make the biggest financial mistakes. If people do their homework and find a reliable car in the first place, an extended warranty becomes unnecessary. Statistically, you're better off banking or investing your money than purchasing a three-year warranty. But if you did buy a poorly rated car, then you should purchase an extended warranty for a reasonable price—$2,000 is not a reasonable price.

Most major insurance companies will sell you an extended warranty for well under $1,000. You can typically purchase an extended warranty for around $400. A credit union is your best bet. Of course these rates are contingent upon the reliability of your car. If your vehicle rates poorly, you will pay more. If you pay $1,800 at a credit union for your warranty, there is a very good chance your car is going to wind up in the repair shop.

THE INS AND OUTS OF SMART LEASING

Auto leasing is a cheap way to drive an expensive vehicle

Leasing a car can be a smooth ride if you map out your route in advance. But it can be one of the great auto scams of the 1990s if you don't understand how the lease you agree to really works. Here, Randall McCathren, executive vice president of Bank Lease Consultants, Inc., a consulting company that deals with auto lease financing, and the author of *Automobile Lending and Leasing Manual* (Warren, Gorham & Lamont, 1989), steers you toward your destination.

■ What is the difference between buying and leasing a car?

When you lease a car, you have no obligation for the car when you reach the end of the lease term on the closed-end lease (if you have observed the mileage and wear-and-tear restrictions). You have a guaranteed trade-in value equal to the end-of-term lease balance, and if you want to keep the car, you exercise your purchase option. When you buy a car, there is no guaranteed trade-in value any time you want to terminate the loan and trade in the car.

■ What are the advantages to leasing?

Leasing has become attractive to people who understand the benefits of cash conservation and guaranteed trade-in value. Leasing traditionally requires no down payment, though some special manufacturer lease programs require 5 to 10 percent down to get the financial terms being offered. Leasing has much lower payments than financing because the consumer only pays for depreciation, or the portion of the vehicle expected to be used up, rather than for the total price of the vehicle. The higher the down payment on the lease, the lower the monthly payment. The guaranteed value means the customer can walk away from the vehicle when the lease is up without obligation even if the vehicle is worth less than projected.

Another benefit of leasing is deferring the purchase decision until after you've driven the vehicle for a while. Even consumers who think they want to keep the vehicle for 10 years are better off leasing it for 3 to 5 years first, then deciding whether or not they want to keep it for the full 10 years.

■ Why are people hesitant to lease a car?

Leasing can be very confusing. Unfamiliar words, lengthy technical contracts, and manipulative sales techniques can make shopping for a lease more difficult than shopping for a car. With no capitalized cost disclosure (which is analogous to the selling price in a purchase) and no annual percentage rate (APR) disclosure, it's difficult to be comfortable that you've gotten a good deal. Now, however, most of the largest lessors, such as Ford Credit, GMAC, Toyota Motor Credit, and General Electric Credit, require dealers to disclose the capitalized cost. Eleven states have also mandated capitalized cost disclosure. By mid-1997, a federal mandate for capitalized cost disclosure should be in effect for all consumer leases.

■ What pitfalls should consumers avoid when leasing?

If consumers put down $1,000 less and pay $50 to $75 a month less on a five-year lease than a five-year loan, they can't expect to have the same lease balance after three years as they would have had on the loan.

Some lessees plan to terminate early when the structure of the lease is intended to avoid building equity. If lessees pay for 15,000 miles per year and drive 25,000, they can't expect to drop the car off with no obligation; if they had purchased the car, its trade-in value would be lower because of the extra mileage. The same is true in cases of excess wear and tear.

Finally, as in any business there are some unscrupulous lessors who try to take advan-

READING THE FINE PRINT ON A LEASE

Monthly payments are just the beginning. Randall McCathren, executive vice president of Bank Lease Consultants, Inc., a consulting firm that tracks trends in auto lease financing, advises that, in addition to monthly payment, which is the main shopping comparison consumers use, potential lessees shoud consider these variables:

■ **CAPITALIZED COST:** Don't lease a car without getting it in writing. Leasing has $300 to $500 of costs not found in loans (such as contingent liability insurance and credit insurance), so expect to pay at least that much more than for a purchase. The other benefits of leasing may also be worth a higher purchase price, particularly a highly subsidized rate, but the capitalized cost can be negotiated just like the selling price of the vehicle.

■ **RESIDUAL VALUE:** This is the predicted value of the car at the end of the lease term, and it's guaranteed. The higher it is, the more likely it is that the lessor will lose money at the end.

■ **PERMITTED MILEAGE:** Most deals are now only 10,000 or 12,000 miles a year, but don't choose the lower mileage if you're likely to end up paying excess mileage charges at lease end.

■ **EARLY TERMINATION RIGHT AND CHARGE:** Look for a lease that permits early termination and has a constant yield (where interest is earned at the same rate every month and is precalculated), at least after the first 12 months.

■ **PURCHASE OPTION:** Look for a residual value fixed-price purchase option or, if you can find it, the lesser of the published wholesale value and the residual value.

■ **EXCESS MILEAGE CHARGE:** Make sure it is reasonable if you drive extra miles. For a car worth up to $15,000, you shouldn't pay more than 10¢ per extra mile. For a car worth $15,000 to $30,000, excess mileage shouldn't cost more than 15¢ a mile, and for cars above $30,000, no more than about 18¢ a mile.

■ **TERM:** Don't sign a lease for longer than you plan to drive the car. The guaranteed value only benefits you at the end of the term. Never plan to terminate early. If you can't afford the payments on the shorter term, choose a less expensive car.

■ **LIABILITY AFTER CASUALTY LOSS:** Ask if the lease includes "gap insurance." If not, don't pay more than $200 for coverage and consider self-insuring the risk.

tage of customers. Excessive charges for early termination and wear and tear are the two biggest areas of abuse. One or two bad apples can create a lot of negative publicity.

■ How can I make sure I'm getting a good lease price?

Negotiate the purchase price first. Get it in writing. Then negotiate the lease and get a statement of the capitalized cost in writing. If the dealer or independent leasing company says they don't know what the capitalized cost is or that there isn't one, take your business elsewhere. Shop around and talk to a number of lessors. Compare rates and terms before making a decision. When you're ready to lease, don't agree to a longer term than you reasonably expect to keep the vehicle. Don't choose a car so expensive that you won't be able to pay for early termination if you need to.

And make sure you're comfortable with the vehicle. A great lease on a car you don't really want is not a good deal.

CRASH TEST DUMMY'S GUIDE

HOW YOUR CAR DOES IN A CRUNCH

Each year the National Highway Traffic Safety Administration conducts crash tests of new cars under conditions that are the equivalent of having a head-on collision with an identical vehicle at 35 mph. The tables below include results for cars tested for the first time in 1996 as well as results for previously tested vehicles that were essentially the same cars being sold in model year 1996. Vehicles should be compared only to other vehicles in the same weight class—if a light vehicle collides head-on with a heavier vehicle at 35 mph, for example, the occupants in the lighter vehicle would experience a greater chance of injury than indicated. Vehicles are classified by the estimated chance of injury for the driver or passenger, and receive a one- to five-star rating, with five stars indicating the best protection.

VEHICLE	Driver / Passenger:	AIRBAG	CRASH RATING
MINI PASSENGER CARS			
GEO METRO		§	★★★★
4-dr. sedan, 1,986 lbs.		§	★★★★
LIGHT PASSENGER CARS			
FORD ASPIRE		§	★★★★
4-dr. HB, 2,086 lbs.		§	★★★★
HONDA CIVIC		§	★★★★
4-dr. sedan, 2,337 lbs.		§	★★★★★
HYUNDAI ACCENT		§	★★★
4-dr. sedan, 2,261 lbs.		§	★★★★
MAZDA MX-5		§	★★★★
2-dr. convertible, 2,312 lbs.		§	★★★
MAZDA PROTEGE		§	★★★
4-dr. sedan, 2,429 lbs.		§	NO DATA
NISSAN SENTRA		§	★★★★
4-dr. sedan, 2,454 lbs.		§	★★★★
SATURN SL		§	★★★★
4-dr. sedan, 23,32 lbs.		§	★★★★
TOYOTA TERCEL		§	★★★
4-dr. sedan, 2,176 lbs.		§	★★★★
COMPACT PASSENGER CARS			
ACURA INTEGRA		§	★★★★
4-dr. sedan, 2,709 lbs.		§	★★★
CHEVROLET CAVALIER		§	★★★
4-dr. sedan, 2,731 lbs.		§	★★★
CHEVROLET CORSICA		§	★★★
4-dr. sedan, 2,741 lbs.		NO	★★
DODGE AVENGER		§	★★★★★
2-dr., 2,952 lbs.		§	★★★★★
DODGE NEON		§	★★★★
4-dr. sedan, 2,547 lbs.		§	★★★★
FORD ESCORT		§	★★★★
4-dr. sedan, 2,509 lbs.		§	★★★★
FORD PROBE		§	★★★★★
2-dr., 2,773 lbs.		§	★★★★
HONDA ACCORD		§	★★★★
4-dr. sedan, 2,901 lbs.		§	★★★
HYUNDAI SONATA		§	★★★
4-dr. sedan, 2,761 lbs.		§	★★★★
MAZDA 626 DX		§	★★★★
4-dr. sedan, 2,762 lbs.		§	★★★★★
MITSUBISHI ECLIPSE		§	★★★★
2-dr., 2,853 lbs.		§	★★★★
MITSUBISHI GALANT		§	NO DATA
4-dr. sedan, 2,832 lbs.		§	★★★★
NISSAN 240 SX		§	★★★
2-dr., 2,795 lbs.		§	★★★★
NISSAN ALTIMA		§	★★★★
4-dr. sedan, 2,941 lbs.		§	★★★★
NISSAN MAXIMA		§	★★★★
4-dr. sedan, 2,970 lbs.		§	★★★
PONTIAC GRAND AM		§	★★★★
4-dr. sedan, 2,987 lbs.		§	★★★★
SUBARU LEGACY		§	★★★★
4-dr. sedan, 2,654 lbs.		§	★★★★
TOYOTA CAMRY		§	★★★★
2-dr., 2,992 lbs.		§	★★★★★
TOYOTA COROLLA		§	★★★
4-dr. sedan, 2,553 lbs.		§	★★★
MEDIUM PASSENGER CARS			
AUDI A4		§	★★★★
4-dr. sedan, 3,096 lbs.		§	★★★★★
AUDI A6		§	★★★★★
4-dr. sedan, 3,373 lbs.		§	★★★★★
BMW		§	★★★★
4-dr. sedan, 3,234 lbs.		§	★★★★
BUICK CENTURY		§	★★★★
4-dr. sedan, 3,049 lbs.		NO	★★★★

■ **CRASH TEST DUMMY'S GUIDE**

VEHICLE Driver / Passenger:	AIRBAG	CRASH RATING
CHEVROLET CAMARO	§	★★★★★
2-dr. HB, 3,408 lbs.	§	★★★★★
CHEVROLET LUMINA	§	★★★★★
4-dr. sedan, 3,344 lbs.	§	★★★★
CHEVROLET MONTE CARLO	§	★★★★
2-dr., 3,284 lbs.	§	★★★★
DODGE INTREPID	§	★★★★
4-dr. sedan, 3,254 lbs.	§	★★★★
DODGE STRATUS	§	★★★
4-dr. sedan, 3,144 lbs.	§	NO DATA
FORD CONTOUR	§	★★★★★
4-dr. sedan, 3,020 lbs.	§	★★★★
FORD MUSTANG	§	★★★★
2-dr., 3,119 lbs.	§	★★★★
FORD MUSTANG	§	★★★★★
2-dr. convertible, 3,317 lbs.	§	★★★★★
FORD TAURUS	§	★★★★
4-dr. sedan, 3,368 lbs.	§	★★★★
FORD THUNDERBIRD	§	★★★★★
2-dr., 3,460 lbs.	§	★★★★★
HONDA ODYSSEY	§	★★★★
4-dr. wagon, 3,459 lbs.	§	★★★★
MAZDA MILLENIA	§	★★★★
4-dr. sedan, 3,150 lbs.	§	★★★★★
MERCEDES-BENZ C220	§	★★★★
4-dr. sedan, 3,190 lbs.	§	★★★★
PONTIAC GRAND PRIX	§	★★★★
2-dr., 3,210 lbs.	§	★★★
SAAB 900	§	★★★★
4-dr. HB, 3,064 lbs.	§	★★★★
TOYOTA AVALON	§	★★★★
4-dr. sedan, 3,290 lbs.	§	★★★★★
TOYOTA CAMRY	§	★★★★
4-dr. sedan, 3,128 lbs.	§	★★★
VOLKSWAGEN PASSAT	§	★★★★
4-dr. sedan, 3,124 lbs.	§	★★★★
VOLVO 850	§	★★★★★
4-dr. sedan, 3,241 lbs.	§	★★★★
HEAVY PASSENGER CARS		
CHEVROLET CAPRICE	§	★★★★
4-dr. sedan, 4,177 lbs.	§	★★
CHRYSLER NEW YORKER	§	★★★★
4-dr. sedan, 3,589 lbs.	§	★★★★
FORD CROWN VICTORIA	§	★★★★★
4-dr. sedan, 3,849 lbs.	§	★★★★★
INFINITI J30	§	★★★★
4-dr. sedan, 3,840 lbs.	§	★★★★
LEXUS GS300	§	★★★
4-dr. sedan, 3,765 lbs.	§	★★★
OLDSMOBILE AURORA	§	★★★
4-dr. sedan, 3,883 lbs.	§	★★★
PONTIAC BONNEVILLE	§	★★★★★
4-dr. sedan, 3,558 lbs.	§	★★★

VEHICLE Driver / Passenger:	AIRBAG	CRASH RATING
SPORTS UTILITY VEHICLES		
CHEVROLET S-10 BLAZER	§	★★★
4-dr. 4X4, 4,156 lbs.	NO	★
CHEVROLET TAHOE	§	★★★★
4-dr. 4X4, 5,276 lbs.	NO	★★★
FORD BRONCO	§	★★★★★
2-dr. 4X4, 4,763 lbs.	NO	★★★★★
FORD EXPLORER	§	★★★★
4-dr. 4X4, 4,242 lbs.	§	★★★★
ISUZU RODEO	§	★★★★
4-dr. 4X4, 4,105 lbs.	§	★★★
JEEP CHEROKEE	§	★★★★
4-dr., 2,983 lbs.	NO	★★★★
JEEP WRANGLER VJ	NO	★★
4-dr., 2,896 lbs.	NO	★★★★
LAND ROVER DISCOVERY	§	★★★
4-dr. 4X4, 4,486 lbs.	§	★★★
LIGHT TRUCKS		
CHEVROLET S-10 PU	§	★★★
2-dr., 3,091 lbs.	NO	★
DODGE DAKOTA PU	§	★★★★★
2-dr., 3,924 lbs.	NO	★★★★
DODGE RAM 1500 PU	§	★★★★★
2-dr., 4,469 lbs.	NO	NO DATA
FORD F150 PU	§	★★★★★
2-dr., 4,444 lbs.	NO	★★★★★
FORD RANGER PU	§	★★★★
2-dr., 3,245 lbs.	NO	★★★★
MITSUBISHI PU	NO	★★★
2-dr., 2,731 lbs.	NO	★★★
TOYOTA T100 PU	§	★★★★
2-dr., 3,382 lbs.	NO	★★★★★
TOYOTA TACOMA PU	§	★★
2-dr., 2,560 lbs.	NO	★★★
VANS		
DODGE GRAND CARAVAN VAN	§	★★★
4,000 lbs.	§	★★★★
DODGE RAM B250 VAN	§	★★★
4,056 lbs.	NO	★★★★
FORD AEROSTAR VAN	§	★★★★
3,670 lbs.	NO	★★★
FORD ECONOLINE VAN	§	★★★★
5,166 lbs.	NO	★★★
FORD WINDSTAR VAN	§	★★★★★
3,801 lbs.	§	★★★★★
MERCURY VILLAGER VAN	§	★★★★
3,862 lbs.	§	★★★
PONTIAC TRANS SPORT VAN	§	★★★★★
3,708 lbs.	NO	★★★
TOYOTA PREVIA VAN	§	★★★★
3,644 lbs.	§	★★★

AUTO SHOPPER'S GUIDE

THE OTHER CAR PAYMENT TO REMEMBER

When you shop for a new car, considering the insurance cost of the make and model you select can give you a substantial savings over time

The cars listed to the right are grouped alphabetically by make. Next to each model is Allstate's rating of that car's insurance cost when compared with other models in the same price range. The five rating groups range in price from "much better than average" to "much worse than average." The guide compares similarly priced cars because consumers tend to shop for cars in a certain price range.

Generally, the more expensive a car is, the more it costs to insure. That's because higher-priced cars cost more to repair and are more likely to be targeted by thieves. Thus, a Toyota Celica rated "average" will cost more to insure than a Chevrolet Beretta rated "average." But there are exceptions. For example, a Honda Civic may cost about the same to insure as an Audi 90, even though the Civic's suggested retail price is about $11,000 less.

The examples below illustrate this relationship in three price ranges. For the sake of comparison, insurance costs were calculated using identical rating factors.

STICKER PRICE: $12,501–$15,000

BETTER THAN AVERAGE	Chevrolet Corsica	$741
AVERAGE	Saturn SC2	$867
WORSE THAN AVERAGE	Honda Civic	$939

STICKER PRICE: $15,001–$20,000

BETTER THAN AVERAGE	Chrysler Concorde	$795
AVERAGE	Buick Century	$865
WORSE THAN AVERAGE	Acura Integra	$957

STICKER PRICE: $20,001–$30,000

BETTER THAN AVERAGE	Buick Park Avenue	$863
AVERAGE	Infiniti G20	$957
WORSE THAN AVERAGE	Mitsubishi Eclipse	$1,205

1996 MAKE & MODEL		INSURANCE VALUE
■ ACURA		
Integra		§ WORSE THAN AVERAGE
Legend	◊	§ WORSE THAN AVERAGE
NSX	◊	§ AVERAGE
TL Series	◊	§ AVERAGE
SLX	◊	§ AVERAGE
■ AUDI		
A4 Series	◊	§ AVERAGE
A6 Series	◊	§ AVERAGE
Cabriolet	◊	§ AVERAGE
■ BMW		
318 Series	◊	§ MUCH WORSE THAN AVERAGE
325, 328 Series	◊	§ MUCH WORSE THAN AVERAGE
525 Series	◊	§ AVERAGE
530 Series	◊	§ WORSE THAN AVERAGE
540 Series	◊	§ AVERAGE
740 Series	◊	§ BETTER THAN AVERAGE
750 Series	◊	§ AVERAGE
840 Series	◊	§ AVERAGE
850 Series	◊	§ AVERAGE
M3 Series	◊	§ AVERAGE
Z3 Series	◊	§ AVERAGE
■ BUICK		
Century	◊	§ AVERAGE
Le Sabre	◊	§ BETTER THAN AVERAGE
Park Avenue	◊	§ BETTER THAN AVERAGE
Regal	◊	§ BETTER THAN AVERAGE
Riviera	◊	§ AVERAGE
Roadmaster	◊	§ BETTER THAN AVERAGE
Skylark	◊	§ BETTER THAN AVERAGE
■ CADILLAC		
Concours	◊	§ BETTER THAN AVERAGE
DeVille	◊	§ BETTER THAN AVERAGE
Eldorado	◊	§ AVERAGE
Fleetwood	◊	§ BETTER THAN AVERAGE
Seville	◊	§ BETTER THAN AVERAGE

■ AUTO SHOPPER'S GUIDE

1996 MAKE & MODEL			INSURANCE VALUE
■ CHEVROLET			
Astro Vans	◊	§	BETTER THAN AVERAGE
Beretta	◊	§	AVERAGE
Blazer	◊	§	AVERAGE
C & K Series Pickups	◊	§	AVERAGE
Camaro	◊	§	MUCH WORSE THAN AVERAGE
Caprice	◊	§	BETTER THAN AVERAGE
Cavalier	◊	§	AVERAGE
Corsica	◊	§	BETTER THAN AVERAGE
Express, Chevy Vans	◊	§	AVERAGE
Impala	◊	§	AVERAGE
Lumina APV	◊	§	BETTER THAN AVERAGE
Lumina	◊	§	BETTER THAN AVERAGE
Monte Carlo	◊	§	AVERAGE
S-10 2WD Pickups	◊	§	WORSE THAN AVERAGE
S-10 4WD Pickups	◊	§	AVERAGE
Suburban	◊	§	BETTER THAN AVERAGE
Tahoe	◊	§	BETTER THAN AVERAGE
■ CHRYSLER			
Cirrus	◊	§	AVERAGE
Concorde	◊	§	BETTER THAN AVERAGE
LHS	◊	§	AVERAGE
New Yorker	◊	§	BETTER THAN AVERAGE
Sebring	◊	§	AVERAGE
Town & Country Van	◊	§	MUCH BETTER THAN AVERAGE
■ DODGE			
Avenger		§	AVERAGE
Caravan		§	BETTER THAN AVERAGE
Dakota Pickups		§	AVERAGE
Intrepid		§	BETTER THAN AVERAGE
Neon		§	AVERAGE
Ram Pickups		§	AVERAGE
Ram Vans & Wagons		§	BETTER THAN AVERAGE
Stealth		§	MUCH WORSE THAN AVERAGE
Stratus	◊	§	AVERAGE
Viper			AVERAGE

KEY:
◊ antilock brakes standard § airbags
† significantly worse than other models in the much worse category

1996 MAKE & MODEL			INSURANCE VALUE
■ EAGLE			
Summit		§	WORSE THAN AVERAGE
Talon		§	AVERAGE
Vision		§	BETTER THAN AVERAGE
■ FORD			
Aerostar		§	BETTER THAN AVERAGE
Aspire		§	MUCH WORSE THAN AVERAGE
Bronco	◊	§	BETTER THAN AVERAGE
Club Wagons	◊	§	BETTER THAN AVERAGE
Contour		§	AVERAGE
Crown Victoria		§	BETTER THAN AVERAGE
Econoline Vans	◊	§	BETTER THAN AVERAGE
Escort LX		§	AVERAGE
Escort GT		§	MUCH WORSE THAN AVERAGE
Escort Standard		§	MUCH WORSE THAN AVERAGE
Explorer	◊	§	BETTER THAN AVERAGE
F Series 2WD Pickups		§	AVERAGE
F Series 4WD Pickups		§	AVERAGE
Mustang		§	MUCH WORSE THAN AVERAGE
Probe		§	WORSE THAN AVERAGE
Ranger Pickups		§	AVERAGE
Taurus (Excluding SHO)	◊	§	BETTER THAN AVERAGE
Thunderbird		§	AVERAGE
Windstar	◊	§	AVERAGE
■ GEO			
Metro		§	MUCH WORSE THAN AVERAGE
Prizm		§	WORSE THAN AVERAGE
Tracker		§	AVERAGE
■ GMC			
Jimmy	◊	§	AVERAGE
Safari Vans	◊	§	MUCH BETTER THAN AVERAGE
Savana Vans	◊	§	AVERAGE
Sierra Pickups	◊	§	AVERAGE
Sonoma 2WD Pickups	◊	§	WORSE THAN AVERAGE
Sonoma 4WD Pickups	◊	§	AVERAGE
Suburban	◊	§	MUCH BETTER THAN AVERAGE
Yukon	◊	§	MUCH BETTER THAN AVERAGE
■ HONDA			
Accord		§	AVERAGE
Civic		§	WORSE THAN AVERAGE

■ AUTO SHOPPER'S GUIDE

1996 MAKE & MODEL			INSURANCE VALUE
Del Sol		§	WORSE THAN AVERAGE
Odyssey	◊	§	AVERAGE
Passport		§	WORSE THAN AVERAGE
Prelude		§	MUCH WORSE THAN AVERAGE
■ HYUNDAI			
Accent		§	AVERAGE
Elantra		§	MUCH WORSE THAN AVERAGE
Sonata		§	WORSE THAN AVERAGE
■ INFINITI			
G20	◊	§	AVERAGE
I30	◊	§	AVERAGE
J30	◊	§	WORSE THAN AVERAGE
Q45	◊	§	AVERAGE
■ ISUZU			
Hombre		§	AVERAGE
Oasis	◊	§	AVERAGE
Pickups		§	WORSE THAN AVERAGE
■ MITSUBISHI			
3000GT		§	WORSE THAN AVERAGE
Diamante		§	AVERAGE
Eclipse		§	WORSE THAN AVERAGE
Galant		§	AVERAGE
Mirage		§	MUCH WORSE THAN AVERAGE
Montero		§	MUCH WORSE THAN AVERAGE†
Pickups			WORSE THAN AVERAGE
■ NISSAN			
200SX		§	WORSE THAN AVERAGE
240SX		§	MUCH WORSE THAN AVERAGE†
300ZX	◊	§	MUCH WORSE THAN AVERAGE†
Altima		§	AVERAGE
Maxima		§	AVERAGE
Pathfinder	◊	§	WORSE THAN AVERAGE
2WD Pickups			WORSE THAN AVERAGE
4WD Pickups			AVERAGE
Quest		§	BETTER THAN AVERAGE
Senta 4 Door		§	AVERAGE
■ OLDSMOBILE			
88,LSS	◊	§	BETTER THAN AVERAGE
98	◊	§	BETTER THAN AVERAGE
Achieva	◊	§	AVERAGE

1996 MAKE & MODEL			INSURANCE VALUE
Aurora	◊	§	AVERAGE
Bravada	◊	§	AVERAGE
Ciera	◊	§	AVERAGE
Cutlass Supreme	◊	§	BETTER THAN AVERAGE
Silhouette	◊	§	BETTER THAN AVERAGE
■ PLYMOUTH			
Breeze		§	AVERAGE
Neon		§	AVERAGE
Voyager		§	BETTER THAN AVERAGE
■ PONTIAC			
Bonneville	◊	§	BETTER THAN AVERAGE
Firebird	◊	§	WORSE THAN AVERAGE
Grand Am	◊	§	AVERAGE
Grand Prix		§	BETTER THAN AVERAGE
Sunfire	◊	§	AVERAGE
Trans Sport	◊	§	BETTER THAN AVERAGE
■ PORSCHE			
All Models	◊	§	AVERAGE
■ SAAB			
900 Series	◊	§	AVERAGE
9000 Series	◊	§	AVERAGE
■ SATURN			
Coupes		§	AVERAGE
Sedans & Wagons		§	AVERAGE
■ SUBARU			
Impreza		§	AVERAGE
Legacy		§	AVERAGE
SVX	◊	§	AVERAGE
■ SUZUKI			
Esteem	◊	§	AVERAGE
X-90	◊	§	AVERAGE
Sidekick		§	AVERAGE
Swift		§	WORSE THAN AVERAGE
■ TOYOTA			
4Runner		§	WORSE THAN AVERAGE
Avalon		§	AVERAGE
Camry		§	AVERAGE
Celica		§	WORSE THAN AVERAGE
Corolla		§	WORSE THAN AVERAGE

■ **AUTO SHOPPER'S GUIDE**

1996 MAKE & MODEL			INSURANCE VALUE
Land Cruiser		§	MUCH WORSE THAN AVERAGE†
Paseo		§	AVERAGE
Previa		§	BETTER THAN AVERAGE
RAV4		§	AVERAGE
Supra	◊	§	WORSE THAN AVERAGE
Tacoma Pickups		§	AVERAGE
Tercel		§	MUCH WORSE THAN AVERAGE
T100 2WD Pickups		§	WORSE THAN AVERAGE
T100 4WD Pickups		§	AVERAGE

1996 MAKE & MODEL			INSURANCE VALUE
■ VOLKSWAGEN			
Cabrio	◊	§	AVERAGE
Golf	§	§	AVERAGE
GTI	◊	§	AVERAGE
Jetta		§	WORSE THAN AVERAGE
Passat		§	AVERAGE
■ VOLVO			
850 Series	◊	§	BETTER THAN AVERAGE
960 Series	◊	§	AVERAGE

NOW IT'S CARS THAT HAVE HMOS

Car management organizations are used by insurers to cut repair costs

Smile if you like managed health care, because the idea is about to spread. Auto insurers, eager to duplicate the way managed care has contained health-care costs, have applied similar ideas to fixing automobiles. By using car management organizations, or CMOs as they're being called, insurers can negotiate group discounts with body shops, allowing them to offer lower premiums and more efficient service to customers.

Managed car-care insurance isn't a new concept. Allstate and most major insurance companies have offered such direct repair programs (DRPs) for nearly 20 years. But rising costs have prompted insurers and motorists to take a new look at this little-known service. DRPs allow the insured to choose between repair shops prescreened by their insurer or their own mechanic. They also eliminate the bothersome process of estimate shopping. Since the DRP shop is already authorized by the insurer to start repairs, the insured motorist can rest easy, knowing the insurance company will cover all costs except the deductible. Without delays caused by price disputes or waiting for a claims adjuster, your car is typically ready several days sooner, and repair work often comes with an insurer-enforced guarantee. As of 1996, over one-fourth of drivers with access to DRPs have signed up.

A newer, more restrictive version of DRPs is called the preferred provider option (PPO). Under a PPO, insurance companies limit the motorist's choice to a few network repair shops in exchange for premiums or deductibles that are much lower on average. Going out of network and receiving partial reimbursement may not be an option. Companies in a few states—Florida, Colorado, and California—have been testing the concept, and depending upon the survey, anywhere from 20 to 50 percent of those offered the plan have accepted.

CMOs do have their flaws, of course. Not all customers have seen a significant drop in their insurance rates, and rural customers sometimes have problems finding participating garages nearby. Collision repair shops not included in the networks worry about losing customers and have lobbied hard to restrict the spread of CMOs. It almost sounds like the battles that some doctors have waged against HMOs for years!

EXPERT Q & A

A BIKER'S GUIDE TO CYCLE SHOPPING

Learn to ride before you buy; you may spare yourself a big mistake

When Ed Youngblood describes motorcycling as "a spiritual activity, essential for maintaining a healthy mental perspective," he reflects a viewpoint shared by many motorcycle lovers. Youngblood's romance with the motorcycle began nearly 40 years ago, when he was just 14 and took the $60 he saved from doing odd jobs to purchase his first bike, a 1953 Harley-Davidson 165F. Youngblood has since gone on to become one of the great ambassadors of cycling. The president of the American Motorcycle Association (AMA), Youngblood is a regular contributor to *American Motorcyclist*. For anyone interested in joining America's 6 million motorcycle enthusiasts, Youngblood has this advice:

■ How do you know if a motorcycle is right for you?

I don't believe motorcycles are right for everyone. So before you go out and buy yourself a $10,000 motorbike, register in a motorcycle training course—preferably the Motorcycle Safety Foundation's (MSF). The course will take you through all aspects of motorcycle operation and maintenance. You'll also receive an excellent introduction to motorcycle makes and sizes, so if you do decide to buy a bike, you'll have an idea of the type of bike that fits your personality and needs.

■ What kinds of bikes are there for the motorcycle buyer to choose from?

First, you must decide whether you prefer an on-road or off-road motorcycle. In other words do you plan on riding over dirt trails or on the open highway? If you're in the market for an off-road, you can choose between a total dirt bike and a trail bike made street-legal. The latter comes with turning signals and other requirements of a highway vehicle. If you favor the highway, there are essentially three bike types. The sport bike is styled like a high-performance machine; it is light and quick, best suited for short rides. Cruisers are designed for comfort and local riding. These bikes provide an ideal fit for a commuter or the "weekend" rider. Touring bikes are made for the long-distance traveler. They're larger and often have built-in saddlebags for luggage.

Size is also important. Typically, trail bikes have much smaller engines than road bikes. Trail bike sizes usually top out at 600cc (cubic centimeters), while a touring bike can have an engine as large as 1500cc—comparable to a small automobile engine.

■ Which motorcycle best fits the first-time buyer?

Unlike automobiles, which are typically purchased with practicality in mind, motorcycle selection is determined by personal taste and style. You must remember: The motorbike is a recreational vehicle. Most AMA members own more than two cycles, and many own more than four.

As far as the leading brands or makes available in the U.S., you have Harley-Davidson, Honda, Kawasaki, Suzuki, Yamaha, BMW, and a variety of smaller manufacturers. Typically, all these manufacturers put out high quality products. The choice among them usually comes down to brand loyalty. I know people who have driven Harleys for over 20 years and would never try anything else. The same is true for BMWs and most other brands. You can't explain a person's personal taste for motorbikes any more than you can a person's clothing selection. It's all up to the individual.

■ What is your favorite bike?

Hard to say. There aren't many I don't like. I guess it would depend upon the type of riding I'm doing. At this moment I own a Harley-Davidson F14H6 touring bike and a Kawasaki 1500cc Vulcan Classic cruiser.

■ What should you ask the dealer when shopping for a bike?

As I said earlier, motorcycle selection is very personal, and today's selection is enormous. That's why it's so important to have an informative motorcycle introduction, such as the MSF's safety course, before you begin shopping for a bike. The dealer will actually depend upon you for information. In my early days, the choices were much simpler. The $60 I bought a Harley-Davidson 165 with when I was 14 would not buy me anything today, but at least I'd have more to look at.

■ What is the first-time buyer's most common mistake?

First-time buyers often purchase bikes that are too small. Going into the showroom, most first-timers lack confidence, so they choose the smaller bikes, which are easier to handle. After their first month, they're ready for a larger model. I'm not suggesting every first-time buyer needs a larger bike, but I would recommend some riding experience before going to the dealer.

■ Which, if any, accessories really matter?

This depends upon your cycling plans. If you intend on having a passenger, install a backrest for his or her comfort. A rider taking long trips should consider installing saddlebags. Personally, I prefer a windscreen, simply for the comfort. If you like camping, there's even specially made motorcycle trailers, which many people use to haul their outdoor gear.

■ Any other critical advice for first-time cyclists?

Again, I can't stress how important it is to enlist in motorcycle driving courses *before* you take to the road. For my first 20 years of riding, no instruction was available and I believed I didn't need any. After participating in my first course, I was horrified to learn of my poor technique and riding habits. I was so taken by the course, I became an instructor and lifelong advocate. If you don't intend to go through a training course, don't ride.

BIKERS AND THEIR BIKES

Think of motorcyclists and images of nomadic rebels moving from town to town like modern-day desperadoes come to mind. In actuality, members of the American Motorcycle Association (North America's largest motorcycle organization) represent an established (only 3 percent unemployed), well-educated (79 percent with post–high school educational experience) and financially successful ($57,300 average household income) segment of their community. More important, they know motorcycles. Last year, AMA members rode over a billion miles and purchased over 93,000 motorcycles—spending over $450 million in the process. For prospective first-time buyers, a glimpse at the AMA membership's motorcycle preferences:

■ BRANDS OF ROAD MOTORCYCLES OWNED:

Honda	37%
Harley-Davidson	28%
Yamaha	21%
Kawasaki	20%
BMW	10%
Suzuki	10%
Ducati	3%
Moto Guzzi	2%
Other	9%

Amount spent by AMA members for their most recent Road Motorcycle: $6,190 (avg.)

■ BRANDS OF OFF-ROAD MOTORCYCLES OWNED

Honda	51%
Yamaha	19%
Kawasaki	11%
Suzuki	11%
Husqvarna	9%
KTM	5%
Beta	2%
Other	12%

Amount spent by AMA members for their most recent Off-Road Motorcycle: $2,940 (avg.)

SOURCE: American Motorcycle Assocation.

DRIVING & MAINTENANCE

BRAKING: What it takes to stop on time, PAGE 586 **SAFETY:** Expert advice from AAA on the proper use of your car's safety devices, PAGE 588 **TEENAGERS:** Training young drivers for the road, PAGE 589 **LICENSING:** How to find a good driving school, PAGE 590 **ALCOHOL:** Drinking and driving is a bad mix, PAGE 591 **REPAIRS:** An auto grandma on preventive car care, PAGE 592 **MAINTENANCE:** A checklist for potential problems, PAGE 593

EXPERT Q & A

LYN ST. JAMES HITS THE ROAD

One of the world's great drivers shares her tips on the curves ahead

Since capturing the IMSA Norelco "Driver of the Year Award" in 1985, Lyn St. James has proved beyond a doubt that women have a place in professional auto racing. Named Indy 500 "Rookie of the Year" in 1992, she is also a two-time team winner of the 24-hour endurance race at Daytona, and is the holder of 31 national and international speed records. St. James also heads the Lyn St. James Foundation, an educational organization that promotes automotive safety and driver development programs worldwide. Here, she offers her tips on becoming a better driver.

■ **Who first taught you to drive and what do you remember of that experience?**

My mother was a great lover of cars and introduced me to automobiles at an early age. In fact, when I was 16 and went to take my driver's exam, the police officer administering the driving portion of the test commented that I drove as if I had been doing it for a long time. Being a diagnostic person, my mother taught me more than just how to stay on the road. I learned to identify the sights and smells of a car; I could recognize the smell of burning oil or the color of antifreeze. These are things every driver should know but typically drivers never receive adequate instruction about. You should learn more than simply the driver's relationship with the steering wheel and brakes.

■ **Is there anything a driver should do before turning on the ignition?**

In many cases, drivers do not take the time to adjust seats and mirrors. As long as they can reach the steering wheel and pedals, people will drive away. Before beginning your drive, properly position your seat and all mirrors—especially the side mirrors, which people often neglect. After you've made the proper adjustments, then put on your safety belt.

■ **What is the best way to turn?**

Look ahead and think ahead. Well before you reach the turn, position your car in the proper lane and find a comfortable speed. People tend to make abrupt lane changes or slam on the brake just before a turn. Both of these practices can place you and other drivers in danger. If you have anticipated the turn properly, many times a smooth turn can be achieved by simply removing your foot from the accelerator.

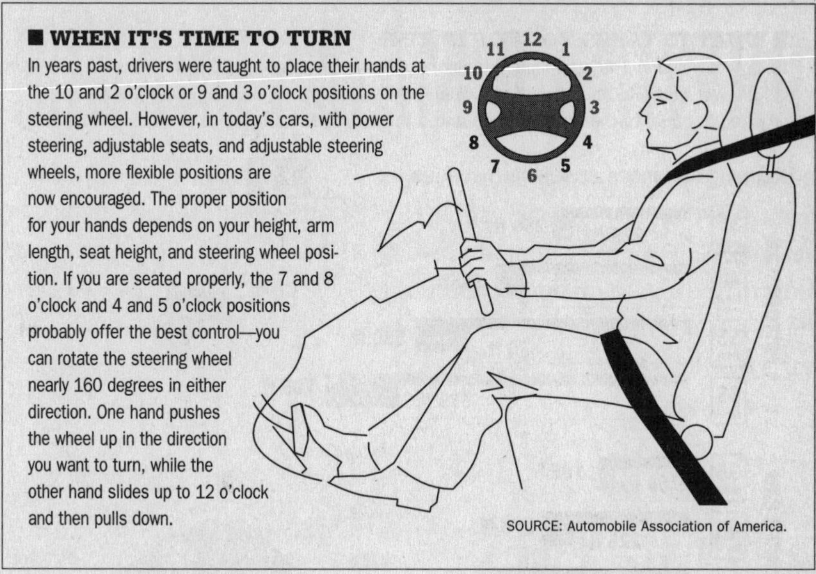

■ WHEN IT'S TIME TO TURN

In years past, drivers were taught to place their hands at the 10 and 2 o'clock or 9 and 3 o'clock positions on the steering wheel. However, in today's cars, with power steering, adjustable seats, and adjustable steering wheels, more flexible positions are now encouraged. The proper position for your hands depends on your height, arm length, seat height, and steering wheel position. If you are seated properly, the 7 and 8 o'clock and 4 and 5 o'clock positions probably offer the best control—you can rotate the steering wheel nearly 160 degrees in either direction. One hand pushes the wheel up in the direction you want to turn, while the other hand slides up to 12 o'clock and then pulls down.

SOURCE: Automobile Association of America.

■ How far back should you be when trailing another vehicle?

Employing the three-second rule is an easy way to measure proper following distance. Using a roadside landmark such as a bridge or road sign as a reference point, time the distance between your car and the vehicle in front of you. Maintaining a three-second distance between cars allows adequate time to brake smoothly and avoid abrupt stops. Abrupt braking is especially common in instances of heavy traffic. A tailgater's constant starts and stops causes a chain reaction that disrupts the flow of traffic. If you are aware of traffic flow, removing your foot from the accelerator will often suffice for deceleration.

■ What is the best technique for passing and changing lanes?

The first mistake most drivers make prior to making a pass or lane change is failure to check their rear and side mirrors. Before the blinker even goes on, determine how much time and space you have to make your move, or whether you should make the move at all. If you've decided you have ample space, check the mirrors one last time for any sudden developments just prior to making the move. When making a pass, do it smoothly, not abruptly; if taken correctly, you can complete your move without excessive acceleration or wheel movement.

Once you've moved into the passing lane, make sure you complete your pass. Often, a driver will pull out from behind another vehicle and ride parallel to the car. When returning to your lane, check the mirrors again. Once you have completed the pass, check your mirrors one last time to evaluate your new position. If you lost count, that's four mirror checks per pass.

■ Is front-wheel drive superior to rear-wheel drive?

Each has its pluses and minuses. With front-wheel-drive vehicles, everything is focused on one spot. The steering, power, and engine all rest in the front, which translates to better handling and traction—especially in adverse weather conditions. The downside is more maintenance. Your alignment, balance, and tires may require greater attention. Since everything is focused in one spot, the added weight on the car's front can make steering more laborious and place greater strain on alignment and tire wear.

The even distribution of weight in rear-

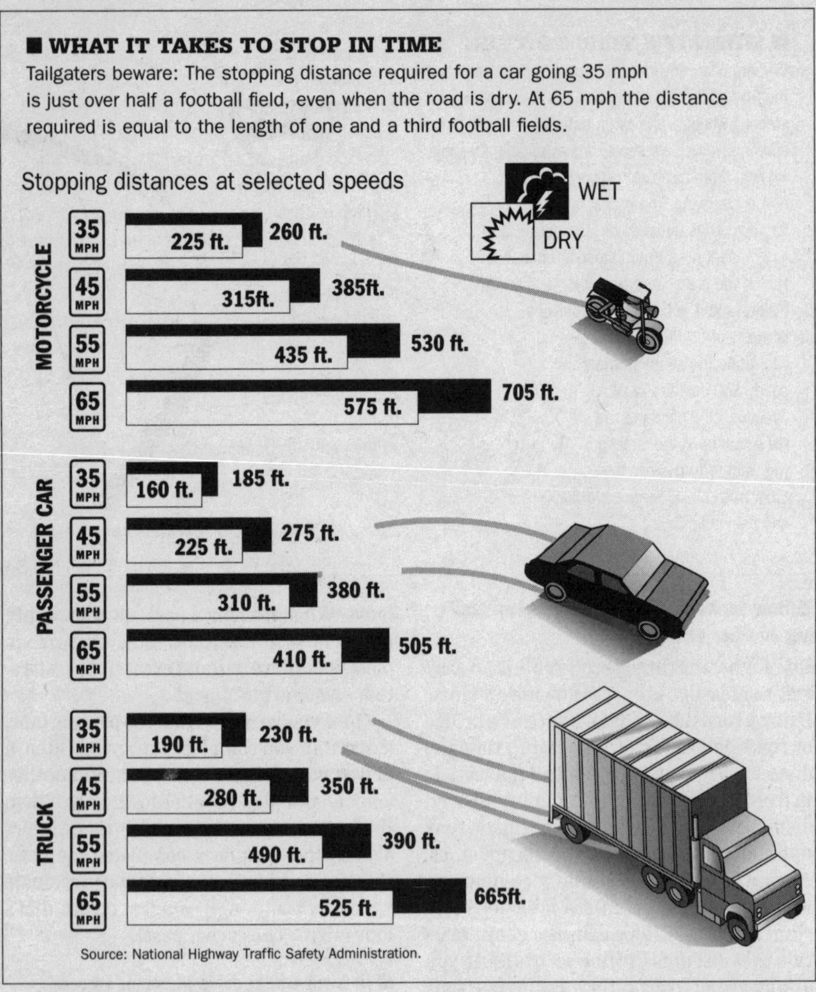

wheel cars allows for a smoother ride and less wear on these parts. The choice between the two may come down to where you live. If you live in an area without a lot of snow or ice, you may find the handling and ride of rear-wheel vehicles more to your liking.

■ What about stick shift versus automatic transmission?

Again, it is a matter of preference. A stick allows the driver more control. You determine when to shift gears instead of the engine doing it for you. I feel I'm more in control over the vehicle in stick shift. The disadvantage is convenience. In rush hour traffic the continual shifting can become a little annoying.

■ Should a motorist alter his habits for nighttime driving?

Most drivers have a tendency to look far ahead when driving. At night this can actually become an impediment. Reflections and oncoming headlights can blind a driver whose gaze remains far out in front. To avoid this, shorten your range of vision by lowering your line of sight and looking for road lines or reflectors. This will shield you from bright lights and also give you a more innate sense of the road's shape. When possible, do not neglect to take full advantage of your highbeams. In many cases a driver will neglect his or her high beams simply to avoid turning them on and off in intermittent traffic. The more you see, the safer you are, so don't let laziness interfere with your safety. Just remember to turn them off when approaching another car.

■ How should a motorist navigate in bad weather?

Driving in poor weather conditions often requires an extra antenna. You have to look more acutely and modify your driving accordingly. If you're driving in a downpour, slow down, put the wipers on full blast, and use lane markers for guidance. If you lose sight of the markers or feel uncomfortable, move off the road. A frightened driver has a tendency to make mistakes.

In snow and ice, keep your car's weight evenly distributed over all four tires. When you brake abruptly, all the weight shifts to one section of the car, causing a loss in control. If you live in a part of the country where you will encounter adverse conditions, go to an empty parking lot and do donuts until you know how to react to skids. Remember, in poor weather conditions, slowing down helps, but this does not mean excessive braking. What causes accidents most often under bad traveling conditions is a person driving at extremely slow speeds. If you're only traveling at 10 mph, and a driver who may be comfortable driving in this weather approaches at 30 mph, a major problem can occur.

■ Should a motorist brake or try to drive through a dangerous situation?

Deciding on the safest approach to a dangerous situation often comes down to a person's personal driving instincts, and being aware of your environment. I am a very visual driver—I know distance and what can be accomplished in an allotted space. For example, when approaching a dangerous situation, I may recognize I have 20 feet before I reach a road hazard, and I also know what I can accomplish within 20 feet.

Other motorists are audible drivers and may rely on sound to determine distance and reaction time. But just because you have confidence that you can avert a dangerous situation does not make it the safest decision. Often, we hear of a motorist who swerves to avoid a dog, only to go off the road and into a ditch. Other drivers swerve to get around a potential pileup, only to veer into oncoming traffic. When avoiding trouble you need a safe outlet, not just an opening. Rule of thumb: If you have little distance, but a lot of space, try and avoid it. If you have plenty of distance, but little room, try and slow your vehicle the best you can.

■ Who drives better—men or women?

There are only two types of drivers: good drivers and bad drivers. Gender and age make no difference. A good driver is alert, with good vision, knows his or her vehicle and how it handles. A bad driver doesn't pay attention, isn't courteous, and doesn't anticipate what could happen.

Having said this, I have been told by many professional driving instructors, and noticed through my own personal experience, that women make better driving students than men. Women tend to listen more attentively and are more desirous to learn. In many cases women never had an adequate introduction to cars, therefore they appreciate the opportunity to learn about the cars they drive. After completing a driving class, the women students will often leave better drivers than the men.

■ Which professional drivers do you most admire?

That's a tough question. I'm always so busy trying to beat them that I've never taken the time to admire them. There are certain drivers I do respect: Al Unser, Jr., always maintains excellent control over his car, especially at Indy. Bill Elliot is very smooth, never putting his car at risk. He understands his car and knows exactly what he can get out of it. This is something all drivers should appreciate and emulate. Knowing your car definitely makes you a better and safer driver.

EXPERT TIPS

BEING SAFE AND NOT SORRY

There's a right way to operate antilock brake systems and airbags

Americans are driving more and dying less often. In 1950, an average of 7.6 Americans died behind the wheel for every 100 million miles driven. Today, the fatality rate has dropped to only 1.7 over the same distance. Much of the credit goes to motorists who demanded safer automobiles. But confusion about the proper use of airbags, antilock brakes, and other recent safety innovations still leads to unnecessary accidents. Here, safety specialist Norman Grimm of the American Automobile Association discusses how to make today's safety features work for you.

■ Antilock brakes work, but only if they are held down, not pumped.

It is true that in the short time we have had ABS there has not been any noticeable difference in the number of accidents. But the problem is not the system—it's the way it is used. There is a prevailing myth that in an emergency you should pump your brakes, but for antilock brakes to work effectively, the driver must press down hard and hold down. The grinding noise and pulsations indicate that ABS is functioning correctly.

■ Airbags need to be used in tandem with seat belts to be effective.

There have been times when airbags have deployed unnecessarily, and other instances when the bag is deployed with such force that it causes injury. Technology is now being developed that will correct these problems, but improvements will only help if the system is used properly. Without the assistance of seat belts, airbags lose their effectiveness.

When buckling your seat belt, use the lap and shoulder harness simultaneously. The lap belt should be worn as low on the abdomen as possible. The shoulder harness should come across the chest and not up by the neck.

■ The safest place to position a child is in the car's middle rear.

This is especially important for infants weighing less than 17 pounds. If the child is in the front seat, with a passenger side airbag, the deployed airbag can dislodge the child. Always keep older children in seat belts and toddlers and infants in child seats, and always read a child seat's manufacturer instructions.

■ Head restraints are a safety device, not a head rest.

Most Americans drive cars with an adjustable head restraint. If used properly it can help prevent neck injuries such as whiplash: the head restraint should support the back of the head, not the neck or shoulders.

■ If you suddenly lose your power steering, don't panic.

You still have steering capabilities, only now you'll have to use more muscle. Any play in your power steering wheel when the car is off indicates a problem that should be checked.

■ BELTS OR BAGS? BOTH IS BEST

Using air bags and lap and shoulder belts together offers drivers the most protection, as shown below:

PERCENTAGE OF DRIVERS SUSTAINING HEAD INJURIES IN FRONTAL CRASHES

	Air bag only	Air bag and belt	Belt only
Brain injuries	25.0%	0.6%	4.0%
Fractures	2.3%	0.0%	0.0%
Facial injuries	48.6%	9.7%	25.5%
FATALITY REDUCTION IN FRONTAL CRASHES			
	25%	75%	50%

SOURCE: *The New York Times* (December 10, 1995).

EXPERT TIPS

PUT TEEN DRIVERS ON A SAFE TRACK

"Graduated licensing" is the way to keep teenagers secure

For teenagers, getting a driver's license can be as inviting a rite of passage as learning to cavort with the opposite sex. For parents of new teen drivers, seeing their offspring slide behind the steering wheel can be a source of high anxiety. That's because teenagers are seven times more likely to be involved in a fatal crash then adult drivers and 44 percent of teenage drivers are involved in a collision before their 17th birthday. Most disturbing, car crashes have become the number one killer of teenagers between the ages of 16 and 19, and the problem is getting worse. For the first time in years, teenage fatalities and accidents are on the upswing. John Undeland, until recently a traffic safety expert for the Automobile Association of America, has this advice for parents facing the teen-driving dilemma:

■ Alcohol and drugs are not the main culprits in teen accidents.

Among 16-year-old drivers involved in fatal crashes nationwide, only 5 percent had a blood alcohol content above the legal standard for drunken driving. Contrary to popular opinion, most accidents result from a combination of overconfidence, carelessness, and lack of experience. Unlike years past, young drivers lack adequate training opportunities. Dual family incomes and longer working hours limit the time parents have to spend with their children, and budget cuts have weakened already spotty school-sponsored driver's education courses. Consequently, young drivers see very little road time prior to receiving their license.

■ Graduated licensing can be an effective way of developing teenage drivers.

Highway deaths are likely to rise in the future, simply because more 16-year-olds will be driving. In five years, the number of 16-year-old drivers will increase 5 percent; by the year 2010 the number will climb to 25 percent. In an attempt to fight the demographic trend, many states have considered enacting a form of "graduated licensing." The program's object is to counteract the major causes of most teen crashes and reward conscientious drivers in three ways: by limiting a young driver to a provisional or restricted license until he or she demonstrates good driving skills over an extended period of time—usually one year; by requiring suspension of driving privileges for traffic or underage drinking or drug violations or failure to use safety belts; and by prohibiting 16- and 17-year-olds who have not yet earned an unrestricted license from driving between midnight and 5 a.m. unless accompanied by a licensed adult.

■ Even where graduated licensing is not the law, parents can use the concept to set ground rules for teenage drivers.

Impose your own limits, suggests Underland. Draw up a contract that gradually increases your teen's driving privileges in accordance with his developing skills and good judgment. Consider limiting his nighttime driving and limiting the number of passengers. Above all else, ban all use of alcohol when the car is involved. "The idea is to insist upon conscientious driving every time a teenager gets behind the wheel and to make this message personal," explains Undeland. "During the one-year provisional period, teenagers gain driving experience and maturity while staying off the road at the times they're most likely to be involved in an accident."

■ Driver's education courses are valuable, but they shouldn't take parents off the hook.

In years past, many could rely upon school-sponsored driver's education programs to provide free driving lessons for their teens. Today, budget cuts have reduced the number of districts still offering the program, and some evidence suggests driver's education contributes little or nothing to a teenager's driving preparedness. Experts also question the effectiveness of "driving schools." "In many cases the instructors teach the drivers how to pass a driver's test and not how to drive," says Undeland. "You won't learn to merge onto a busy highway, but you will become an outstanding parallel parker."

"Regardless of governmental regulation or instructional classes, if the parents are not involved, nothing will work," insists Undeland. "Driver's education classes help, but 6 to 20 hours of road time just doesn't cut it. Parents must pick up the slack in driving instruction." Unlike driver's education, a parent can introduce teenagers to all situations, moving from residential driving to rush-hour traffic on freeways and finally emergency driving. Vacant parking lots offer an excellent initial training ground. Practice smooth starts, stops, and turns, and the use of signals and rear and side mirrors.

After the basic skills are learned, move on to more difficult situations, advises Undeland. Practice proper following distances in residential areas, merging onto major highways, and night driving. Near the end of their training, return to the parking lot and enact emergency situations, like skidding in rain or snow. The idea is to gradually expose young drivers to all aspects of driving, while building road senses and driving experience.

CHOOSING A DRIVING SCHOOL

What to look for in an instruction program that you'd trust your child in

Up at 6 a.m. and out the door by 7, you return home 10 hours later, only to have to drive the kids to soccer practice and prepare dinner. Where is the time for your teenager's driving instruction? Professional driving schools may offer a solution. Here's a quick guide to choosing one that best fits your child's needs:

■ **FINDING SCHOOLS:** High schools often provide a list of driving schools. Many local chapters of the Automobile Association of America also operate driving schools.

■ **CHECKING REFERENCES:** Confirm a school's accreditation by requesting the phone number for the school's accreditation organization and information on its standards. (Regulations vary state to state, and a license does not guarantee a good school.) Reputable schools will offer names of past customers as references.

■ **PERSONAL REVIEW:** Finalize your selection only after visiting each school on your shortlist. Check the following points:

■ **Instructional vehicles** should be late-model cars in good condition. Some states bar the use of driving-school vehicles more than 4 years old.

■ **Textbooks** should be current and in good condition. Each student should also receive a copy of the state's driver's handbook.

■ **Instructional staff** members should have successfully completed professional developmental courses. The Driving School Association of America Inc., the American Driver and Traffic Safety Education Association, and the Association for the Disabled are among the most prominent national instructional driving organizations.

■ **Classroom lessons** should work in-tandem with car sessions. A total of 30 classroom hours is average. Beginners learn best with two 45-minute in-car lessons each week, totaling 6 hours of behind-the-wheel training under varying circumstances and driving environments.

HOLDING YOUR LIQUOR

Percentage of alcohol in the blood one hour after drinking

Examples of alcoholic drinks	Amount of alcohol (oz.)	Body weight (lbs.) 100	120	140	160	180	200
Three Dubonnet cocktails	**3.0**	**.252**	**.208**	**.176**	**.152**	**.134**	**.119**
Four Bloody Marys, Daiquiris, or Whiskey Sours	**2.8**	**.234**	**.193**	**.163**	**.141**	**.124**	**.110**
Two glasses Fish House Punch	**2.6**	**.217**	**.178**	**.151**	**.130**	**.114**	**.101**
Three Martinis or Manhattans or glasses malt liquor	**2.4**	**.199**	**.163**	**.138**	**.119**	**.104**	**.092**
Two Mai Tais or Mint Juleps	**2.2**	**.181**	**.149**	**.125**	**.108**	**.094**	**.083**
Four Champagne Cocktails	**2.0**	**.163**	**.134**	**.113**	**.097**	**.084**	.075
Two Margaritas	**1.8**	**.146**	**.119**	**.100**	**.086**	.057	.066
Two Martinis or Manhattans	**1.6**	**.128**	**.104**	**.087**	.075	.065	.057
Two highballs, Bloody Marys	**1.4**	**.110**	**.089**	.075	.063	.055	.048
Two 3 oz. glasses fortified wine (port, vermouth, etc.)	**1.2**	**.092**	.075	.062	.052	.045	.039
Two glasses beer	**1.0**	.075	.060	.049	.041	.035	.030
One Black Russian	0.8	.057	.045	.037	.030	.025	.021
One Sloe Gin Fizz	0.6	.039	.030	.024	.019	.015	.012
One 1 oz. cordial or liqueur	0.4	.021	.015	.011	.008	.006	.004

THE MEANING OF TIPSY

The figures in red represent the blood alcohol content past which you shouldn't drive:

BLOOD ALCOHOL CONTENT	EFFECTS ON FEELING AND BEHAVIOR	EFFECTS ON DRIVING ABILITY
.40 **.20** **.19** **.18**	At this point, most people have passed out.	Hopefully, driver passed out before trying to get into vehicle.
.17 **.16** **.15** **.14** **.13**	Major impairment of all physical and mental functions. Irresponsible behavior. Euphoria. Some difficulty standing, walking, and talking.	Distortion of all perception and judgment. Driving erratic. Driver in a daze.
.12 **.11** **.10**	Difficulty performing gross motor skills. Uncoordinated behavior. Definite impairment of mental abilities, judgment, and memory.	Judgment seriously affected. Physical difficulty in driving a vehicle.
.09 **.08** **.07**	Feeling of relaxation. Mild sedation. Exaggeration of emotions and behavior. Slight impairment of motor skills. Increase in reaction time.	Drivers take too long to decide and act. Motor skills (such as braking) are impaired. Reaction time is increased.
.06 .05 .02	Absence of observable effects. Mild alteration of feelings, slight intensification of existing moods.	Mild changes. Most drivers seem a bit moody. Bad driving habits slightly pronounced.

SOURCES: National Clearinghouse for Alcohol and Drug Information; National Safety Council.

EXPERT TIPS

CAR REPAIRS MADE EASY

Spare yourself grief; listen to "The Auto Repair Grandmother"

"Grandma" probably isn't the name that comes to mind when you need automotive repair advice, but then your grandmother isn't Lucille Treganowan. The 65-year-old auto-repair grandmother owns two Transmission by Lucille shops in Pittsburgh and hosts a weekly television show that can be seen throughout the country on HGTV. Lucille first learned about fixing automobiles back in the '60s, while working as a bookkeeper for a local Pittsburgh garage. She began reading repair manuals and soon after began directing the shops' most difficult repairs. Now she's a legend in the automotive repair industry and has recently completed her first book, *Lucille's Car Care* (Hyperion, 1996). Here, the "grandmother of auto repair" sets you straight on the essentials of car maintenance:

■ Whatever you do, change your oil.

Today, with convenient and inexpensive drive-in oil-change outlets, you don't even need to bother with this procedure yourself. But don't rely completely on your 60-day visit for oil maintenance. Regularly check oil level yourself. It is one of the simplest things to do yet is often overlooked. Just remember, for an accurate reading you need to turn the car off and park it on level ground before checking the dipstick.

The frequency of your oil change depends upon the type of driving you do. If you're driving a family vehicle, where the majority of driving time is spent on short trips, then you should change the oil about every 60 days. People who spend more time driving highways and interstates, like salesmen, can go longer between changes.

■ Check coolant colors as well as levels: They should be clear or green.

The National Car Care Council reports overheating as the number-one motorist complaint. This usually occurs due to low coolant level. Always make certain you allow the engine to cool for at least 20 minutes before removing the radiator cap. If the fluid level checks, the problem may be a faulty thermostat or even a bad radiator cap.

I like to change my radiator fluid every two years. But depending upon your driving habits, you can go much longer between changes. Get in the habit of checking all your fluids. If the coolant still looks clear and green, you can keep it.

■ When you change one hose, change them all.

With hoses you need to look at the condition of the rubber. Usually, when one goes, others will follow. If you find the hoses have lost their flexibility and feel brittle or stiff, there's the possibility they may split or crack in the near future. Residue around the clamps, caused by leaking, is also a sign a hose may need to be changed.

Unlike hoses, belt wear is much more difficult to see. To play it safe, change your belts every four years.

■ Don't sacrifice qualify for price when buying a battery.

Batteries are like shoes—you can buy good ones or bad ones. The length of time they're good for varies, although typically they'll last three to four years. The complex electrical systems have made batteries much more important than simply a device to start the engine. In some newer cars, a bad battery can send your car into the limp mode—meaning it will limp and sputter its way into the repair shop. Even transmissions and steering have become dependent on the battery.

■ Use your ears when it comes to brakes.

To check your brakes you need to pull the wheels off. Most people aren't going to go

A CHECKLIST FOR AVOIDING GRIEF

You don't have to get yourself covered with grease to tell quickly whether a car has been well maintained. The following tips for reading a car's history will save you lots of headaches later:

STEERING WHEEL: There should be no play for power steering when the engine is off, and no more than two inches for manual steering.
BODY CONDITION: Rust, especially in the rocker panels under the doors, in the trunk, or around the wheels is bad news. Sooner rather than later, your car will fall apart.
INTERIOR: Resale value as well as comfort will be affected by seats and carpets that look shabby or smell musty.
TIRES: Original tires should be good for 25,000 miles. Uneven tire tread can mean an alignment problem, which is easily remedied.
BRAKES: Look for wear on the pads or scars on the rotor disk.

■ **FLUID LEAKS:** Checking a car's fluid levels and condition is like taking a person's blood pressure and doing a blood test. They can indicate both present and future problems. Oil spots around the engine or beneath the vehicle are obvious signs that something's leaking. Other signs are less obvious: transmission fluids should be pink, not dirty.

■ **SUSPENSION:** Does the car look lopsided from the side or rear? Bad springs are probably the culprit. Does the car bounce more than a couple times when you push down hard on a corner? The shocks or struts could need replacing. If a front tire can be noticeably lifted by pulling on the top of the tire with both hands, you may have bad bearings or suspension joints.

through that. Luckily, your ears can pick out most brake problems. When brake pads need to be replaced, listen for a singing/whistling noise. A scratching/metal grinding noise indicates your pads or footings have worn away to the point where metal is rubbing against metal. In such cases, bring your car into a garage immediately. The time it takes for this to occur will depend upon your personal driving habits. I have a tendency to use my brakes a bit much, so I need to change my brake pads about once a year.

■ **Ignore smells at your own peril.** A smoky smell is a good indication of oil leaking onto something hot. A nasty acid odor, like the smell of something caught in your vacuum cleaner, points to wires burning. In the case of the burning wires, you should first pull over, turn the car off, and if the smell persists, disconnect the battery, which will interrupt the flow of electrical currents through the battery.

■ Apply the penny test to check your tire tread.

If you place a Lincoln-head penny in a tire's lowest tread spot, and you can see the president's head, it's time for new tires. The variation in tread height is usually due to a tire's air pressure. If you overinflate your tires, the inside tread will tend to wear first. If your tire is low, the outside tread will wear first. By purchasing a $4 air gauge, you can check your tires for correct inflation.

FACT FILE:

THE FIX-IT FACTOR

■ **ENGINE OVERHAUL:** *If the engine is worn out, making a lot of noise, blowing smoke, or has no power, it might need an overhaul. That's when an engine gets rebuilt to the manufacturer's specification. For a 4-cylinder engine, it might cost $2,000 to $3,000. For an 8-cylinder it can get up to $4,000. That's when you have to evaluate if it's worth putting that much money into the vehicle.*

■ **AUTOMATIC TRANSMISSION:** *The automatic transmission should be serviced every 25,000 miles. Symptoms of automatic transmission failure are that the vehicle feels as if it lacks power, is going nowhere, or is making grinding noises. The majority just won't drive. If you have a transmission failure, it could cost $1,200 to $3,000 to fix.*

■ Don't jump to jump-start a car that won't start.

If you turn the key, and the car slowly turns, or you hear only a series of clicks, you probably have a low battery. In this case, a jump start can remedy the situation, but before you try one, check your owner's manual to make sure it's safe. In many newer cars' sophisticated electrical systems jump starts can cause a number of problems.

When using jumper cables, connect the positive terminal of the fresh battery to the positive terminal of the dead battery, and the negative terminal of the fresh battery to a metal ground. Have the car with the fresh battery running before attempting to start the second.

■ Think of auto mechanics the way you think of doctors.

If you visit a doctor with a stomachache, and before any tests are taken, the doctor recommends immediate removal of your appendix, most people would think the doctor a quack and seek a second opinion. But, if the same person sees a mechanic with a battery problem, and before performing any tests the mechanic recommends replacing your alternator, most people would take the mechanic's advice.

Just like the stomachache, a low battery may have a number of causes. Something as simple as a loose fan belt could be the culprit. Simply taking your car to a second mechanic could end up saving you hundreds of dollars in repair bills—and the hassle of returning to the mechanic because the real problem was never fixed.

Approach with caution any mechanic who won't discuss price. After looking over your car, a competent and honest mechanic should have little problem offering a rough estimate on the cost of parts and labor. Repair scams occur when you allow the mechanic to begin work before discussing price; once they have your car torn apart, they'll tell you you already owe so much in labor that you might as well go ahead with the rest of the repairs.

CHAPTER NINE

ENTERTAINMENT

EXPERT QUOTES

"Too many people shoot pictures with the sun behind them, creating short shadows."

—Sisse Brimberg, *National Geographic* photographer

Page 632

"Ray Bradbury's book *Something Wicked This Way Comes* is the scariest book I ever read."

—R.L. Stine, creator of the Goosebumps children's books

Page 635

"Cedar Point has the most rides of any park in the world—it's everything you'd ever want."

—Mark Wyatt, author of *White Knuckle Ride*

Page 648

■ **THE YEAR AHEAD:** **SCOUT** the indie labels for the next big band... **LOOK FOR** opera diva Cecilia Bartoli to lead a Vivaldi revival... **CHECK OUT** the World Wide Web for the latest movie reviews... **CONSIDER** a home theater system with THX sound... **EXPECT** R.L. Stine's scary stories to stay at the top of best-seller lists... **ENJOY** the many new roller coasters opening across America...

MUSIC 596

MOVIES 608

GEAR & GADGETS 626

JUST FOR KIDS 633

MUSIC

INDIE LABELS: Where to find the next Pearl Jam, PAGE 600 **MUSIC BY MAIL:** Gold mines for r&b and jazz lovers, PAGE 601 **ROCK FESTS:** A guide to the best-known rock festivals around the country, PAGE 602 **GENERATIONAL JUKEBOX:** Music you ought to hear today, PAGE 603 **CLASSICS:** Building blocks for a classical CD collection, from Bach to Gershwin, PAGE 604 **OPERA:** Cecilia Bartoli lists her favorites, PAGE 606

SHRINES

WHERE IT ALL REALLY HAPPENED

Bob Dylan and Nirvana didn't just sleep there. They made history.

Want rock memorabilia, go to the Rock and Roll Hall of Fame Museum or your nearest Hard Rock Café. But if you want to see where music history was really made, check out Aretha Franklin's church in Detroit, Miss Taylor's Restaurant in Memphis, and Antone's nightclub in Austin. For these and other little-known rock-and-roll landmarks around the country, read on. But to find Woodstock or Altamont, get a road map.

THE NORTH

1. HIBBING HIGH SCHOOL

■ Here, 17-year-old **Bob Dylan** formed his first band, the Golden Chords, beginning one of the most dramatic careers in music today. His senior yearbook is in the school's library.

✉ 800 East 21st Street, Hibbing, MN 55746
☎ 218–263–3675

2. NEW BETHEL BAPTIST CHURCH

■ **Aretha Franklin** began singing and recording in this church, where her father, the Reverend C. L. Franklin, was the pastor. True fans of "Lady Soul" may want to check out the candid photographs of a young Aretha in the pastor's office.

✉ 8430 C. L. Franklin Avenue, Detroit, MI 48206, ☎ 313–894–5788

3. BUDDY GUY'S LEGENDS

■ This club, owned and operated by blues guitar master **Buddy Guy,** might as well be called "guitar heaven" because Guy has godlike status in the guitar world. Though still largely unknown to the general public, Guy is considered one of the masters of the electric guitar by artists as renowned as Eric Clapton, Jeff Beck, and Robert Cray.

Located in downtown Chicago, Legends is often the site of all-star jam sessions between the club's owner and his famous friends, particularly during Chicago's annual Blues Festival in early June. The club's kitchen serves up red-hot, spicy, Louisiana-style cuisine. Among the guests in the past: David Bowie, Aerosmith's Joe Perry, and Ron Wood and Bill Wyman of the Rolling Stones.

✉ 754 South Wabash Avenue, Chicago, IL 60605–2111, ☎ 312–427–0333

EAST COAST

4. THE CHELSEA HOTEL

■ The temporary home once to many rock luminaries such as **Bob Marley, Bob Dylan** (whose wife gave birth there), **Janis Joplin, Jimi Hendrix** (who was mistaken for a bell-

■ ROCK MONUMENTS FOR ALL AGES

Before there were stadium tours or Ticketmaster or rock superstars with French villas or their memorabilia was used to decorate chain restaurants, rock flourished in some surprising places. Here's a partial road map:

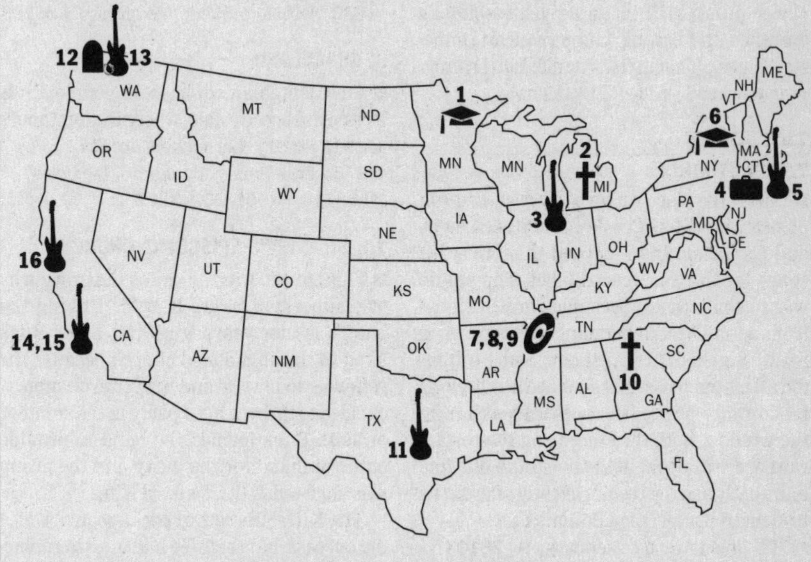

boy by another hotel guest), **Leonard Cohen,** and, of course, punk rocker **Sid Vicious** of the Sex Pistols, who reportedly murdered his girlfriend Nancy Spungen in their room at the Chelsea before overdosing himself a couple of months later. The Vicious episode was dramatized in the Alex Cox film *Sid and Nancy*, and hotel management reports that Sid and Nancy's room, #100, is frequently requested by hotel guests.

✏ 222 West 23rd Street, New York, NY 10011, ☎ 212-243-3700

5. C.B.G.B.'S

■ This club was the birthplace of bands like the **Ramones,** the **Talking Heads,** and **Living Colour.** The club, founded in 1973, was initially supposed to be a country and bluegrass establishment, but it soon became the center for the new wave and punk movements of the late 1970s and early 1980s.

Owner Hilly Krystal books over 75 bands a week today and has opened another venue next door called The Gallery, which spotlights singer-songwriter acts. Among the celebrities who frequent the club: **Brad Pitt** and **Madonna,** who played there early in her career (not as a singer but as the drummer in a band called the Breakfast Club). Its walls are plastered with graffiti and handbills left by customers and performers. A note of caution: Nobody actually uses the club's infamously grungy bathrooms! Seasoned club-goers go next door to the CB's Pizza Boutique, which besides providing a sanitary alternative to the club's restrooms, also offers great food!

✏ 315 Bowery at Bleecker St., New York, NY 10003, ☎ 212-982-4052

6. BARD COLLEGE

■ At Bard, two students, Walter Becker and Donald Fagen, met and formed a group that they named the **Bad Rock Band**. After leaving Bard, Becker and Fagen went on to form the wildly successful **Steely Dan,** while the drummer from the Bad Rock Band, actor and comedian **Chevy Chase,** went on to achieve

fame on Saturday Night Live and the silver screen. Bard rejected an applicant from Duluth, Minn., in 1959, who nevertheless included the line "the pump don't work cause the vandals took the handle," describing the water pump still located at the school's entrance, in his song "Subterranean Homesick Blues." That artist's name: Bob Dylan.
✏Annandale-on-Hudson, NY 12504

THE SOUTH

7. SUN STUDIOS

■ This is the place where early rock-and-roll pioneers like **Elvis Presley, Jerry Lee Lewis,** and **Carl Perkins** recorded their first hit songs for the Sun record label. The studio was so small that it precluded any business from actually being conducted there. As a result, Sun Record's president, Sam Phillips, did all his business next door at Miss Taylor's restaurant—always in the third booth from the window. Both the studio and the restaurant are still open, with the studio offering tours daily and the restaurant still offering its trademark Dixie Fried Banana Pies.
✏706 Union Avenue, Memphis, TN 38103
☎901–521–0664

8. STAX VOLT STUDIOS

■ Once a movie theater, the Stax recording studio was where **Otis Redding, Booker T. and the MG's,** and other soul greats made all of their landmark recordings. The building also housed the Satellite record shop, where consumers could buy Stax recordings, sometimes hot off the presses.
✏926 McLemore Street, Memphis, TN 38103

9. GRACELAND

■ And Memphis also boasts, of course, **Elvis Presley**'s rococo estate, where the tour hours are 9 to 5 every day. Tickets are $17.
✏3765 Elvis Presley Boulevard, Memphis, TN 38116, ☎ 901–332–3322

10. ST. MARY'S EPISCOPAL CHURCH

■ This church was the site of the first gig by '90s superstar group **R.E.M.** During the band's leaner years, guitarist Peter Buck lived in the abandoned church because the rent was so low. He and his "church-mates" decided to throw a huge party in the summer of 1980. Buck formed the band to provide entertainment for the party and the group was christened the Twisted Kites.

The Kites' inaugural performance was a big success, but their fee had to go to replacing the beer taps, which were stolen during the party. Mike Hobbes, booking agent for the Athens club Tyrone's, witnessed the performance and offered the Twisted Kites a gig. The band happily accepted, smartly changed their name to R.E.M. and the rest is rock-and-roll history.
✏980 S. Lumpkin Street, Athens, GA 30605
☎706–353–2330

11. ANTONE'S

■ Antone's, Austin's self-proclaimed "home of the blues," is a nightclub with some major history. Founded in the early '70s by blues enthusiast Clifford Antone, the club was an early home to musicians like **Stevie Ray Vaughan and the Fabulous Thunderbirds.** Legend has it that Vaughan actually used to sleep underneath the tables at the club early in his career!

Today, Antone's is one of the hubs of Austin's vibrant music scene. Presenting live blues music seven days a week, the club brings in blues legends from all over the country as well as booking local tal-

FACT FILE:

THE HOUSE THAT ROCK BUILT

■ *The Rock and Roll Hall of Fame Museum is located on the shore of Lake Erie in downtown Cleveland's north coast harbor. Tickets are $10.90 for adults and $7.65 for seniors and children. For ticket and parking information, call:*
☎ **800–493–ROLL** or
☎ **800–BUCKEYE**

ent. Antone's also has a fascinating collection of photographs on display of the performers it has featured over the years (artists from B.B. King to Howling Wolf). Antone's Record Store, which is located directly across the street, sells releases by artists that play at the club. If you get the chance, check out the Antone's House Band, which over the years has featured top-notch musicians from the bands of John Mellancamp and Stevie Ray Vaughan.

✏2915 Guadalupe Street, Austin, TX 78705
☎512-474-5314

PACIFIC NORTHWEST

12. GREENWOOD MEMORIAL CEMETERY

■ The grave of **Jimi Hendrix,** located just minutes outside of Seattle, is visited daily by fans and admirers of the late rock guitarist. Die-hard fans make the pilgrimage on both Hendrix's birthday (November 27) and on the anniversary of his death (September 18), when Hendrix's father and other family members often come to talk with fans. Many of the most serious fans also make charcoal and pencil rubbings of the guitar engraved in the headstone.

✏350 Monroe Ave., Renton, WA 98056
☎206-255-1511

13. THE OFF RAMP

■ A venue with one of the richest rock histories in the country, during its early years it featured a house band led by **Quincy Jones,** one of today's most successful producers and arrangers. Over the years The Off Ramp has hosted performances by rock legends like **Jimi Hendrix** (a Seattle native), **Janis Joplin, Ray Charles,** and **Guns 'N Roses.** Recently, it has become famous as a launching pad for bands from the Seattle area that have gone on to achieve worldwide success. It played host to early gigs by **Pearl Jam, Soundgarden,** and **Nirvana** and was featured in the motion picture *Singles*. While there, be sure to grab a bite to eat at the club's in-house restaurant, which features such menu items as the Janis [Joplin] Pie and the highly recommended Pearl Jam Pizza.

✏109 East Lake, Seattle, WA 98109
☎206-628-0232

THE COAST

14. THE WHISKY-A-GO-GO

■ The seminal home to L.A. rock and roll, this club, located on famous Sunset Strip, has been home to many of the most controversial bands of all time. **The Doors** worked as the house band for four months in 1966 and singer Jim Morrison kept frequenting the club until his death five years later. Since the Doors era, the club has brought acts like the **New York Dolls, Iggy Pop, Aerosmith,** and most recently **Guns N' Roses** and **Jane's Addiction** to West Coast prominence. Head to the Whisky on Monday nights for a free showcase of the most exciting new bands.

✏8901 Sunset Blvd., West Hollywood, CA 90069, ☎310-652-4202

15. THE RAINBOW BAR AND GRILLE

Owned by the same people as the Whisky, the Rainbow has been a popular hangout for L.A. musicians for years. The restaurant/bar began to display photographs and rock memorabilia years before the Hard Rock Café. Among the items worth checking out: guitars and gold records belonging to **Eddie Van Halen** and **Guns 'N Roses,** and photographs of bands like the **Who** and **Led Zeppelin** performing at the Whisky during their heyday.

✏9015 Sunset Blvd., West Hollywood, CA 90069, ☎310-278-4232.

16. JUSTIN HERMAN PLAZA

■ The place the Irish band **U2** gave a free performance in which lead singer Bono spray-painted the words "Rock and Roll stops the traffic" on a sculpture by artist Bernard Villancourt. The act was immortalized in the band's film, *Rattle and Hum*. City officials demanded an apology and Bono, in typical rock-and-roll fashion, refused, citing freedom of expression to justify his graffito. U2 then contacted Villancourt, who it turned out was a huge fan of the band. Villancourt rushed to San Francisco to defend Bono's "modifications" of his work. The statue still stands in Justin Herman Plaza.

✏San Francisco, CA 94103

INDIE LABELS

TO FIND THE NEXT PEARL JAM...

To catch the next wave, the place to look is the independent labels

Heard of the new Tortoise record, or the latest release by Palace Music? If these bands are wholly unfamiliar to you, don't condemn yourself to the category of completely unhip just yet! You might never have heard of these bands because they release their recordings on small, independently owned record labels.

Largely unknown to the average music consumer, independent record labels are privately owned and smaller than well-known major labels like Sony or Geffen Records. But "indie" labels are home to some of the most exciting and innovative music being created. If you're looking for tomorrow's great bands, there are thousands of indie labels releasing music of every genre. Groups as diverse as the Smashing Pumpkins, Otis Redding, and Nirvana got their start on indie labels.

For many of these labels, making money from the music is only a secondary consideration. Says Chris Taquino, the head of UP Records, a successful Seattle-based independent: "We just want to put out great music without paying too much attention to whether it's commercially viable." Indies almost always give their artists total creative control, so what you hear on an indie release may well be truer to its artist's vision. Major label releases are more likely to reflect not only a band's tastes, but that of record company executives as well.

Indie labels can be difficult to find in retail outlets, but their albums are usually available through mail-order catalogs at a discount. Here, indie executive Taquino and Drew Hauser, director of college radio promotions at Advanced Alternative Media, provide their takes on a few of their favorite labels:

SUB POP RECORDS

■ Perhaps the most prominent indie label today, Sub Pop has been home to bands like Nirvana and Soundgarden. Current Sub Pop bands include the aggressive pop group Six Finger Satellite (which has a fall '96 release date for their newest record) and the L.A.-based dense, heavy rock trio, Plexi. Specializing in the most cutting-edge rock music being played today, the Seattle-based Sub Pop recently sold 49 percent of its shares to Time Warner, and the result has been a huge increase in the promotion and availability of Sub Pop releases. The Sub Pop catalog comes with a coupon worth $1.00 off your first order and can be obtained by sending $1.00 to:

✏ Sub Pop Catalog, 1932 First Ave., Suite 1103, Seattle, WA 98101

EPITAPH RECORDS

■ Owned and run by Brett Gurewitz of the rock group Bad Religion, Epitaph has had great success recently with its distinctive brand of punk-tinged rock. Fans of Epitaph's superstar rock bands, like the Offspring, L7, and Rancid, may want to check out its less well known groups like Pennywise, Wayne Kramer (of the 1960s rock legends the MC5), the Cramps, and the Red Aunts. Epitaph's free catalog, which includes the releases from 12 other indie labels, can be ordered by writing:

✏ 2140 Hyperion Ave., Los Angeles, CA 90027, ☎ 213–664–7070

RYKODISK

■ This indie's motto, "Big enough to matter, small enough to care," is reflected in the quality of the wide variety of records it releases. In addition to reissuing rock classics by artists like Jimi Hendrix, Frank Zappa, and David Bowie, Rykodisk is also home to some of today's most innovative new rock bands like Sugar and Morphine. Rykodisk is far more than merely a rock record label, however; it also releases funk, jazz, folk, reggae, blues, hip-hop, and world music albums by artists from all over the world. Rykodisk's free catalog can be obtained by sending your name and address to:

✏ Rykodisk USA, Pickering Wharf, Bldg. C, Salem, MA 01970

EXPERT SOURCES

FOR R&B AND JAZZ LOVERS

Been through everything in the racks at your local music retailer's? Try these mail-order music gold mines.

CADENCE, THE REVIEW OF JAZZ & BLUES
Cadence Bldg.
Redwood, NY 13679
☎ 315-287-2852

■ *Cadence* is both a catalog and a magazine. Every month it dedicates about 100 pages to jazz. There are features, extensive artist interviews, and dozens of record reviews. But it's the 40 pages of rare albums for sale that really make *Cadence* special. Each title is listed in a no-nonsense, phone-book style; over 9,000 titles indexed and alphabetized by record label. Write or call to order a monthly subscription ($3 per issue, $30 per year).

DOUBLE TIME JAZZ RECORDS
1211 Aebersold Dr.
New Albany, IN 47150

■ Another well-organized jazz outlet, it offers nearly 5,000 titles. All eras of jazz are represented, but Double Time is especially good at locating out-of-print items. Write to receive a catalog.

RHINO CATALOG
10635 Santa Monica Blvd.
Los Angeles, CA 90025
☎ 800-357-4466

■ The label bills itself as the top archival record label in the country—and the extensive catalog bears out that claim. It covers music from the '50s to the '90s, with a great selection of funk anthologies and rock compilation albums. Catalogs may feature thick sections devoted to Cajun music, zydeco, New Orleans r&b, folk, world music, country and western, blues, jazz, vocals, and a lot more. The catalog is free for the asking, and requests are handled at the 800 number.

Rykodisk also offers a CD-ROM featuring an interactive tour through the label's full catalog as well as samples of Rykodisk artists' recordings and videos. The CD-ROM also enables travelers of the information superhighway to order Rykodisk products directly from the company via the Internet. Consumers can receive the CD-ROM, Surf This Disc, by sending $3.00 to:

✏ Rykodisk, Dept. S1, 530 N. 3rd St.
Minneapolis, MN 55401
e-mail: info@rykodisc.com

ALLIGATOR RECORDS

■ *The New York Times* calls Alligator "the leading record label for blues," adding that Alligator has "succeeded where the giants have failed." Founded by Bruce Iglauer in Chicago in 1971, Alligator has released albums from blues legends like Buddy Guy and Johnny Winter and continues to put out some of the finest blues being recorded. The folks at Alligator recently released a special silver anniversary collection. Their free catalog can be obtained by writing:

✏ Alligator Records, P.O. Box 60234,
Chicago, IL 60660
☎ 800-344-5609

DISCHORD RECORDS

■ The ultimate indie label, Dischord shuns all corporate trappings and sells its punk rock releases as cheaply as possible. Founded by Ian Mackaye, the label, based in the nation's capital, is home to some of the biggest and best punk and hard-core rock bands like Fugazi and Slant 6. You can get Dischord's free catalog by sending a self-addressed stamped envelope to:

✏ Dischord Records, Dept. S,
3819 Beecher Street, Washington, D.C.
20007-1802

ROCK FESTS

TAKING THE SHOW ON THE ROAD

Hello, Austin. Hello, Washington. Hello, anywhere there's a bandstand

When the Woodstock music festival was held at Max Yasgur's farm in 1969, over 400,000 people flocked to hear many of their favorite rock bands in a single event. These days it's difficult to choose which of the many rock festivals to attend. From annual music fests to modern-day, traveling road-shows, here is a guide to many of the best-known rock festivals on the calendar:

SOUTH BY SOUTHWEST FESTIVAL

Austin, Texas ☛ *Mid-March* ☛ ***Ticket prices:*** *$35–$50*

■ The SXSW Festival is a music industry event that takes over the already vibrant music scene of Austin, Texas, for a week in March. Bands and labels alike use the Festival to showcase their talents. Established musicians like Johnny Cash also play the festival. Concertgoers can purchase bracelets that give them admission to all the shows, or they can brave the lines at various venues. All types of music are featured, but the focus is on rock and roll. Past performers featured: Willie Nelson, the Supersuckers, Stevie Ray Vaughan, and The Presidents of the United States of America.

HFSESTIVAL

Washington, D.C. ☛ *Early June* ☛ ***Ticket prices:*** *Under $20*

■ This annual, all-day rock festival, sponsored by the radio station WHFS, brings the hottest alternative bands to the nation's capital. Held in the enormous R.F.K. Stadium, the festival attracts thousands of modern rock fans to enjoy the sun and sounds, making it the largest single-day rock festival in the country. Past performers include: Better than Ezra, Counting Crows, and Cracker.

KROQ WEENIE ROAST

Los Angeles, California ☛ *June* ☛ ***Ticket prices:*** *$25*

■ Sponsored by L.A.'s perennial FM radio powerhouse, KROQ, this annual concert brings the best alternative bands to Los Angeles for one big night of live music. Best of all, the proceeds of the Weenie Roast go to charity. Past performers include: Elastica, the Ramones, and Stone Temple Pilots.

LOLLAPALOOZA

Sites nationwide ☛ *June through August* ☛ ***Ticket prices:*** *Vary from city to city; contact Ticketmaster*

■ The ultimate in "alternative" music festivals, Lollapalooza was organized by singer Perry Farrell of Jane's Addiction and Porno for Pyros. It will celebrate its eighth season in 1997. Lollapalooza is staged in large outdoor venues from coast to coast, and features five of the hottest alternative acts on its main stage each show. Local and less prominent bands play on a second stage, and there are exhibits and vendors offering everything from virtual reality to body-piercing. Purchase plenty of water early in the day to avoid the long lines. Water and shade are essential to avoid dehydration and sunstroke. Past performers include: Red Hot Chili Peppers, Hole, and Arrested Development.

THE HORDE FESTIVAL

Sites nationwide ☛ *June through August* ☛ ***Ticket prices:*** *Vary from city to city; contact Ticketmaster*

■ With the passing of Jerry Garcia and the subsequent demise of the Grateful Dead, it's a good bet that many dead-heads can now be found at the "Horizons of Rock Developing Everywhere" Festivals across the country. The HORDE Festival showcases new, improvisation-oriented bands like Phish, Blues Traveler, and Joan Osborne that appeal to dead-heads. The festival also has political and artistic booths. Past performers include: the Spin Doctors, Ziggy Marley and the Melody Makers, and the Allman Brothers Band.

GENERATIONAL JUKEBOX

Even Baby Boomers are getting tired of Classic Rock radio stations that play the same 300 songs over and over again. Thankfully, even those who had their music sensibilities forged in the Sixties can find plenty to like in today's music. From Oasis to Wilco and Son Volt, here's a musical travel guide for the '90s:

IF YOU LIKE:	THEN YOU OUGHT TO HEAR:
MARVIN GAYE	D'Angelo; Tony, Toné, Toni
THE ROLLING STONES	The Black Crowes, Oasis
JANIS JOPLIN	Melissa Etheridge, Joan Osborne
BLACK SABBATH	Alice in Chains, Soundgarden
THE SEX PISTOLS, THE CLASH	Green Day, The Offspring, Rancid
PATSY CLINE, TAMMY WYNETTE	Shania Twain, Mary Chapin Carpenter
THE BEATLES	The Presidents of the United States of America, Gin Blossoms
STEVE MILLER	Hootie and the Blowfish, God Street Wine
THE GRATEFUL DEAD	Widespread Panic, The Dave Matthews Band, Phish
SLY AND THE FAMILY STONE	Fishbone, the Roots
AL GREEN, THE FOUR TOPS	The Tony Rich Project, Boyz II Men, R. Kelly
ARETHA FRANKLIN	Faith, Mary J. Blige, Brandy
RICKIE LEE JONES	Natalie Merchant, Lisa Loeb and Nine Stories
NEIL YOUNG	Wilco, Son Volt, Dinosaur Jr.

SOURCE: Jamie Krents.

BUDWEISER SUPERFEST

Sites nationwide ☛ *June through August* ☛ ***Ticket prices:*** *Vary from city to city; contact Ticketmaster*

■ The Budweiser Superfest hip-hops from city to city, delivering the hottest and biggest acts in modern r&b and rap. The event showcases the talents of both up-and-coming artists as well as established stars. Among past performers: Boyz II Men, TLC, and Mary J. Blige.

THE CMJ MUSIC MARATHON

New York, New York ☛ *Early September* ☛ ***Cost:*** *\$105–\$170 for students; \$235–\$325 for others (depending upon how far in advance tickets are purchased). Concertgoers may also pay the cover charges at each individual venue.*

■ Sponsored by the college radio publication the *New Music Report*, the Music Marathon takes place in Lincoln Center and New York's clubs for four nights in early September. Festival-goers attend panel discussions on everything from marketing your own band to the advent of the Internet in the music business. Past speakers have included David Bowie and Jesse Jackson. The festival's focus is on bringing the hottest college radio acts to the New York crowds—more than 500 bands bring their music to over 35 different venues. Past performers include: Red Hot Chili Peppers, R.E.M., U2, and Green Day.

NORTH BY NORTHWEST FESTIVAL

Portland, Oregon ☛ *October* ☛ *Tickets for concerts only, \$20–\$25*

■ Organized by the same folks who produce the South by Southwest Festival in Austin, Texas, this two-year-old festival is held annually in Portland, Oregon. Occurring over three October nights, the festival brings many of the most promising new bands to the clubs of Portland. The days are filled with panel discussions and information sessions. This festival is smaller than its Texas counterpart, but it's just as good a place to look for tomorrow's superstars. Past performers include: Joan Jett, Pete Krebbs, and Walter Solis Humara.

CLASSICS

LIVING WITH THE MUSIC MASTERS

Building blocks for a classical CD collection, from Bach to Gershwin

"Music is about emotions," says Ted Libbey, host of the weekly National Public Radio show *Performance Today*, "it helps us grow." And, Libbey says, classical music "has a particular richness because it goes back centuries." Libbey is the author of the recently published book *The NPR Guide to Building a Classical CD Collection* (Workman Publishing Co., 1994). Following are the composers that Libbey would make the building blocks of any classical music collection and why he thinks so.

JOHANN SEBASTIAN BACH (1685–1750)

Bach has had a huge influence on music history, much greater than any of his contemporaries would have guessed. He was known mainly as an astounding keyboard virtuoso and a very prolific composer. What has emerged in the two-and-a-half centuries since his death, however, is the absolutely amazing spiritual power of his compositions. There is a beauty of construction and a kind of clarity of conception and detail that goes far beyond what any other composer of the Baroque period achieved.

WOLFGANG AMADEUS MOZART (1756–1791)

Mozart is his favorite, Libbey says, because of the sense of humanity that comes out in the music. People say he was a divine genius, and it's true. But he was also very human. With all the formality of the 18th century, he could evoke tragedy in music and make it burn with emotion. He was a virtuoso keyboardist, the greatest of his age. At the same time he played the violin well enough that he could have had a career as Europe's leading violinist. In his operas he conveys to the listener an understanding of an emotional or dramatic state probably more acutely than any other composer of all time.

FRANZ JOSEPH HAYDN (1732–1809)

Haydn was the most powerful innovator of the later 18th century. In the field of symphonies, he was the leader. He grew the form from a lightweight suite to a very thoroughly worked-out and highly contrasted musical expression for a large orchestra. For Haydn, music was something of a game, and so there are wonderful jokes in his music. He didn't probe the tragic dimension as much as Mozart did, but he was a pioneer in creating the classical style.

LUDWIG VAN BEETHOVEN (1770–1827)

Beethoven was a classical composer who can also be called the first Romantic. He made things more subjective. His music not only conveyed emotions or imagery, but very precise emotions from his own soul as well. Working on the basis of what Mozart and Haydn had done, Beethoven reinvented the string quartet and symphony and expanded their meaning dramatically. His instrumentals set the standards for the entire 19th and 20th centuries. Like an undertow in the ocean, they pull you in.

FRANZ SCHUBERT (1797–1828)

Schubert was the great songwriter in music history; his melodies pin down a state of emotion so effectively. His music is more concerned with contemplation than drama. It puts a very high value on the beauty of sound. Indeed, what you hear in Schubert's music is the beginning of a Romantic concept of sound as color. His music inhabits regions. It's not in a hurry to go from one place to another in a straight line. It's like seeing a strange landscape.

FREDERIC CHOPIN (1810–1849)

There has never been a closer connection between a composer and an instrument than with Chopin and the piano. There is an Italian quality to some of his works: he treated the piano as a human voice. There is an undertone of darkness in much of what he wrote, but also a surreal beauty and lightness to it all—an imaginative release from life.

PIOTR ILYICH TCHAIKOVSKY (1840–1893)

Tchaikovsky has been diminished by the musicologists as a little bit too hysterical and trite in his music. But when you listen to his music, you're not surprised that it's among the most popular. It is music of immediate emotional impact. His ballets—*Sleeping Beauty*, *Swan Lake*, *The Nutcracker*—are among the greatest ever written. His symphonic music has a richness and translucency to it. Many of his musical ideas are almost commonplace, like a simple scale, but he clothed them so gloriously that they come out as very powerful expressions.

CLAUDE DEBUSSY (1862–1918)

Debussy was one of the most profound thinkers in the history of music. He did so much to create modernity. He had an ear for sonority that was completely original. He was influenced by the orchestra of cymbals and gongs from Indonesia that he heard at the World's Fair in Paris. It revolutionized his thinking about sound and resulted in some of the most extraordinary writing for the piano ever. The essential Debussy is in the quiet floating pieces like "Prelude to the Afternoon of the Faun." People tend to compare Debussy to the impressionist painters, but it's more accurate to compare him to the symbolist poets. Most of his work takes a literary point of departure.

GEORGE GERSHWIN (1898–1937)

Gershwin was a lot like Schubert. He was a wonderful melodist. His tunes are all over our musical consciousness. He wrote "Rhapsody in Blue" when he was 25. As he got older, he got more of a sense of organization and structure without losing that freshness he always possessed. His opera, *Porgy and Bess*, is probably the great American opera. It's a tragedy his life ended so early. He still conveys something of the American spirit, especially of the roaring '20s, that no one else has captured in quite the same way.

EXPERT PICKS

The rockers and the pop stars get all the attention at the Grammy Awards, but classical music performances are also honored. Among the winners for 1996:

BEST CLASSICAL ALBUM: Debussy: *La Mer; Nocturnes; Jeux, etc.*, Pierre Boulez, conductor (the Cleveland Orchestra, the Cleveland Orchestra Choir; Franklin Cohen, clarinet) Deutsche Grammophon

BEST ORCHESTRAL PERFORMANCE: Also awarded to Boulez and the Cleveland Orchestra for its performance of Debussy's *La Mer*.

BEST INSTRUMENTAL SOLOIST PERFORMANCE: Franz Schubert: "Piano Sonatas" (B Flat Major & A Major) Radu Lupu, piano, London Records

EXPERT PICKS

CECILIA BARTOLI'S GUIDE TO OPERA

The Italian diva wants to share her favorite operas with all of you

Cecilia Bartoli is one of the most celebrated classical singers performing today. Highly acclaimed for her concert, opera, and recital appearances, she is known to an even wider audience through her immensely popular recordings (see box, next page), which have won numerous awards around the world. Here, the Italian mezzo-soprano known for the warmth and expressiveness of her singing recommends a list of 10 operas for opera-novices and opera lovers alike. She explains:

In trying to compile a list of 10 operas which are my recommendations for seducing people to become opera lovers, I would like to choose only one opera from each of 10 different composers, although each of them has written many other wonderful stage works. They are mentioned here not necessarily in the recommended order for listening.

■ MOZART'S *Le Nozze di Figaro*

Le Nozze di Figaro is a wonderful marriage of perfect music and a perfect story. Some people will chide me for not choosing *Don Giovanni* or *The Magic Flute* as his most perfect opera. I say, start with *Nozze* and then listen to ALL of Mozart's operas.

■ ROSSINI'S *La Cenerentola*

La Cenerentola is Rossini's scintillating setting of the Cinderella fairy tale. It also happens to be one of my favorite roles. And if you like the sparkle of *La Cenerentola*, you will find champagne in such other works as his *Barbiere di Siviglia* or *L'Italiana in Algieri*. Eventually you will find your way also to his serious operas.

■ PUCCINI'S *La Bohème*

Puccini's *La Bohème* is probably the most directly appealing opera. It's about youth, love, and tragedy in the most realistic terms, set to glorious music. And from *La Bohème* one goes so easily to all the other works of this great composer.

■ BIZET'S *Carmen*

Many consider the adventures of the Spanish gypsy to be the perfect opera. This is a timeless story set to timeless music. One could say that it is the first really realistic opera—a path to what later became *verismo* in opera.

■ MASCAGNI'S *Cavalleria Rusticana*

This opera is considered the most important step into the *verismo* era in music. In *verismo*, best translated as "stark reality," there are no gods, no mythical beings, no royalty, no *deus ex machina*—just everyday people in some very realistic, and often violent, circumstances. If it were not for its emotionally charged music, it might be a play or a movie.

■ VERDI'S *Otello*

This is a perfect example of an opera being more powerful than its source. Shakespeare's play is weak in that the jealousy motive built on the missing handkerchief is rather unbelievable. Through Verdi's absolutely glorious music the story becomes not only completely believable but in the end truly heart-wrenching.

■ RICHARD STRAUSS'S *Elektra*

Elektra is probably the prime shocker in music and there will be raised eyebrows as to why I have included it in a 10-most-accessible-operas list. This searing score is built on the Sophocles tragedy and it is unsparing in its assault on our senses. But our senses have become accustomed to so much violence in entertainment that *Elektra* may be the very subject matter that has an immediate audience appeal.

I've purposely left three of the earliest operas for the end of my list. They are from the early Baroque era, the beginning of the

18th century. Strange as it may seem, to some listeners this early music is the most accessible of all, because of its "logic" in composition. To others it is an acquired taste. My advice is that every listener should do his own experimenting.

■ HANDEL'S *Rinaldo*

Written in 1711, *Rinaldo* is based on the text of Torquato Tasso's *Liberation of Jerusalem*. Although it demands female and male singers capable of extraordinary bravura singing, its music has an almost "healing" quality. If one opens one's heart and ears to this music, it can work like a tonic against the burdens of daily life. Let us not forget that because of "Messiah," Handel is no stranger to most of us.

■ PERGOLESI'S *La Serva Padrona*

La Serva Padrona was written in 1733 and its success, in so many countries in addition to its native Italy, established it as groundbreaking in the area of comic opera—or *opera buffa*. The music is inventive, charming, and often "witty." It is extremely easy on the ears, which is a quality to be cherished.

■ VIVALDI'S *Orlando Furioso*

Orlando Furioso, which premiered in 1727, is based on Ariosto's epic poem, which was also the inspiration for the three Handel operas: *Orlando*, *Ariodante*, and *Alcina*. Like Handel's *Rinaldo*, this is an *opera seria*—but listen to the differences in composing styles. To my ears, it takes more liberties within the musical boundaries of that era, just like Vivaldi's "The Four Seasons" is looser in concept than Handel's "Water Music" and "Fireworks Music."

I hope that we will have a real revival of Vivaldi in opera soon—and that I will be part of it.

THE ART AND SOUL OF A SONGBIRD

If you haven't enjoyed Cecilia Bartoli's singing on CDs, you're in for a treat. Here are some highlights and sources for those who can't get enough:

■ **CDs**	**Cecilia Bartoli: A Portrait**	London Records	1995
	If You Love Me	London Records	1993
	The Impatient Lover	London Records	1993
	Mozart Arias	London Records	1991
	Mozart: La Clemenza di Tito	London Records	1995
	Mozart: Le Nozze di Figaro	Deutsche Grammophon	1996
	Mozart Portraits	London Records	1994
	Pergolesi: Stabat Mater	London Records	1990
	Rossini Arias	London Records	1989
	Rossini Heroines	London Records	1992
	Rossini: Il Barbiere di Siviglia	London Records	1989
	Rossini: Il Barbiere di Siviglia (excerpt)	London Records	1993
	Rossini: La Cenerentola	London Records	1993
	Rossini Recital	London Records	1991
	Rossini: Stabat Mater	Philips	1990
■ **VIDEOS**	**Cecilia Bartoli: A Portrait**	London Records	1992
	Rossini: Il Barbiere di Siviglia	RCA	1993
	Rossini: La Cenerentola	London Records	1996
■ **WWW**	**Cecilia Bartoli FanWeb**	*http://www.nwu.edu/music/bartoli*	

MOVIES

ARMCHAIR CRITICS: The Vatican's picks are quieter than what some conservatives like, PAGE 610 **CLASSICS:** Not-to-be-missed flicks that have made it to the National Film Registry, PAGE 611 **OSCARS:** Movie families who have more than one award winner, PAGE 620 **FANS:** Where to get in touch with your favorite star, PAGE 624 **MAIL ORDER:** Sources for hard-to-find videos, PAGE 625

MOVIE REVIEWS

FINDING EYES THAT SEE LIKE YOU

Next time you need a film pick, check out the World Wide Web

It's Friday night, thank God, you say. But when you check your local paper to see which movies are in town, you realize that nearly all the marquees have changed while you were buried by your work. With ticket prices at least $6.50 today in most places, you're not eager to attend another movie as bad as Demi Moore's version of *The Scarlet Letter*. But judging a movie by its blurbs is like taking the claims in "personal ads" at face value. Your salvation may well lie in pulling a few quick yet reliable movie reviews off the Internet.

There's no shortage of opinions from which to choose. The Yahoo index—one of a number of software programs that catalog and steer users of the Internet to the information they need—recently showed over 120 sources of movie reviews on the World Wide Web, with new sites being added almost weekly. Everything from two- to three-sentence reviews with letter grades for the latest pictures, to scholarly discourses on the French antecedents of Sharon Stone's newest thriller, are within a click of your computer mouse. Here are a few of your scouting options and their World Wide Web addresses:

MOVIE REVIEW QUERY ENGINE

http:byron.sp.cs.cmu.edu:9086/movie

■ Just enter the movie title that you're considering and the Movie Review Query Engine will spew out a list of most, if not all of the reviews available of the film online. Click your mouse again and you can access any of the reviews listed. Some of the critiques come from the newsgroup portion of the Internet known as rec.arts.movies, and are posted by anyone who's moved to offer his or her two cents. Other reviews are on the World Wide Web and feature everything from the latest picks from *People* magazine to iconoclastic blasts from a character calling himself "Teen Movie Critic" *(http://www.skypoint.com/members/magic/roger/teencritic.html)*. The Movie Review Query Engine is operated by the Pittsburgh Cinema Project.

THE INTERNET MOVIE DATABASE

http://www.msstate.edu/movies

■ Related to the newsgroup rec.arts.music, the Internet Movie Database is a vast compendium of movie-related information contributed by movie buffs through the newsgroup and then repackaged for easy electronic retrieval by fellow enthusiasts. Users are invited to update the database, known by some as the Cardiff Movie Database, and to post their own reviews.

You can also engage in a kind of running plebiscite by having your ratings of any of the several thousand films on the site factored into the scores posted for each title. If you're trying to decide whether to see the new version of *Diabolique*, for instance, you can check whether users of the Internet Movie Database collectively rated it a 3 or a 9. (Hint: The answer works better with a square root than a squared number.)

MR. SHOWBIZ

http://web3.starwave.com/showbiz

■ Mr. Showbiz is a spirited entertainment magazine in cyberspace. You'll find movie, television, and music reviews, and lots of celebrity features, showbiz news, and dishy gossip. One nice feature of the movie reviews: If you're in a hurry to make a show, there's a quick one-or-two-sentence assessment, followed by a numerical ranking, for each film so you don't have to read the full review.

CINEMANIA ONLINE

http://www.msn.com/cinemania/

■ From the folks at Microsoft, a wide-ranging movie entertainment site with everything from current reviews by byline superstars Leonard Maltin and Roger Ebert as well as Cinemania's own in-house reviewers to film star biographies, highbrow essays, and movie award-winners. The site is still young, but it's fast on its way to becoming a movie lover's destination on the Web.

PATHFINDER

http://www.pathfinder.com

■ All the movie reviews that appear in the Time Warner magazine family, including *Time*, *People*, and *Entertainment Weekly*. Need more be said?

MR. CRANKY

http://internet-plaza.net/zone/mrcranky

■ You might never go to a movie again if you listen to Mr. Cranky, but he's sure to put you in a better mood anyway. The ratings system employed in these reviews is unique: "Almost Tolerable" (1 cherry bomb); "Consistently Annoying" (2 cherry bombs); "Will Require Therapy After Viewing" (3 cherry bombs); "As Good As A Poke In The Eye With A Sharp Stick" (4 cherry bombs); "So Godawful That It Ruptured The Very Fabric Of Space And Time With The Sheer Overpowering Force Of Its Mediocrity" (1 bundle of dynamite).

FILM.COM

http://www.film.com:80/film/

■ This site is meant for people in the movie business—or those who think they should be. It pulls together current reviews, the latest gate receipts, essays, and provides details about things like the finer points of sound tracks. Not to be confused with Film Comment *(http://www.interactive.line.com/film/cover.html)*, the site for the journals published by the Film Society of Lincoln Center, which is most definitely not Hollywood.

EXPERT SOURCES

■ **If you're mired in a movie trivia contest, trying to identify the movie where someone said, "Rugman! It's been a few milennia. Slap me some tassel!" try MOVIE QUOTES: *http://www.cis.ohio-state.edu:/hypertext/faq/usenet/movies/quotes/part2/faq.html***

■ **If it's the answer to the question of whom David Carradine beat out for the lead role in the movie *Kung Fu* (1972), try MOVIE TRIVIA: *http://www.cis.ohio-state.edu:/text/faq/usenet/movies/trivia-faq/faq.html***

ANSWERS: The Genie in *Aladdin*; Bruce Lee

ARMCHAIR CRITICS

THE HOLY AND BULLY PULPIT

The Vatican's film picks are quieter than what some conservatives like

In the Oscar-winning film *Network* in 1976, a liberal network newscaster crazed by ratings pressure rants, "I'm fed up and I'm not going to take it anymore." Lately, it's political conservatives from Bob Dole to William Bennett who have taken up the cry against offensive movies and television programming.

On the theory that you can't beat something with nothing, some prominent conservatives have even begun to recommend movies that do meet their value standards. When readers of William F. Buckley, Jr.'s long time journal, *National Review*, were asked to name their favorite movies recently, their picks as the best modern films about individual conscience and courage included: *Walking Tall* (1973), the story of a Tennessee sheriff who used a baseball bat to rout out local corruption; *Rob Roy* (1995), the heroic tale of a Scotsman fighting for his way of life, based on the novel by Walter Scott; and *Braveheart* (1995), another tale of Scottish patriotism. Odd that all three films have been criticized for showing either needlessly explicit sex or extreme violence.

Other inspirational tales appreciated by *National Review*'s readers included one of Ronald Reagan's favorite flicks, *The Sound of Music* (1965), and *Prisoner of War* (1954), which starred Ronald Reagan as a spy investigating the fate of U.S. POWs in North Korea.

Another conservative group that's gotten into the movie selection business is the Vatican. To help celebrate the 100th anniversary of cinema last year, a group convened by the Pontifical Council on Social Communications issued a list of feature films whose values it applauded. Among them: *Gandhi*, directed by Richard Attenborough (1982); *Chariots of Fire*, directed by Hugh Hudson (1981); *It's a Wonderful Life*, directed by Frank Capra (1939); and *Schindler's List*, directed by Steven Spielberg (1993). The only film on both the Vatican's and *National Review*'s list: *Ben Hur* (1959).

IF FAMILY VALUES ARE NOT YOUR THING

Then check out Quentin Tarantino's must-see films. The director of Pulp Fiction *and* Reservoir Dogs *got his start in the movie business by working as a video store clerk. The movies that most shaped his cinematic attitude:*

- **BAND OF OUTSIDERS,** directed by Jean-Luc Goddard, 1964
- **BLOW OUT,** directed by Brian De Palma, 1981
- **BREATHLESS,** directed by Jim McBride, 1983
- **COFFY,** directed by Jack Hill, 1973
- **FOR A FEW DOLLARS MORE,** directed by Sergio Leone, 1965
- **HIS GIRL FRIDAY**, directed by Howard Hawks, 1940
- **LE DOULOS,** directed by Jean-Pierre Melville, 1962
- **THE LONG GOODBYE,** directed by Robert Altman, 1973
- **ONE-EYED JACKS,** directed by Marlon Brando, 1961
- **RIO BRAVO,** directed by Howard Hawks, 1959
- **ROLLING THUNDER,** directed by John Flynn, 1977
- **THEY LIVE BY NIGHT,** directed by Nicholas Ray, 1949

EXPERT LIST

MOVIES THAT MAKE IT TO THE HALL OF FAME

On your next trip to the video store, bring back something that's really great. Listed below are the feature films in the National Film Registry, organized by category, along with a brief description of the entries and any Oscars they may have won. Most of these films are available on videocassette, as indicated by the icon. Films marked with an asterisk were made before the 1927 inception of the Academy Awards.

COMEDY

ADAM'S RIB
George Cukor, B&W, 1949, 101m

■ Spencer Tracy and Katharine Hepburn are at their best as a husband-and-wife legal team on opposite sides of a case.

ANNIE HALL
Woody Allen, color, 1977, 94m

■ One of the best romantic comedies ever made. Woody Allen stars and directs himself, Diane Keaton, and Tony Roberts through the minefield of relationships in New York and Los Angeles.

■ **OSCARS:** Best Actress, Director, Screenplay, Picture.

THE APARTMENT
Billy Wilder, B&W, 1960, 125m

■ Jack Lemmon stars in this fantastic satire as an insurance clerk who lends his apartment to his superiors for their extra-marital affairs. All's well until he falls for one of the women. Shirley MacLaine and Fred MacMurray co-star.

■ **OSCARS:** Best Art Direction/Set Decoration, Director, Editing, Screenplay.

THE BANK DICK
Eddie Cline, B&W, 1940, 73m

■ W. C. Fields's classic comedy about a reluctant drunk-turned-hero.

BIG BUSINESS
James Horne, B&W, 1929, 30m

■ A Laurel and Hardy short in which they try to sell Christmas trees in July.

BRINGING UP BABY
Howard Hawks, B&W, 1938, 102m

■ Katharine Hepburn and Cary Grant star in the kind of great slapstick comedy that just doesn't get made anymore.

DAVID HOLZMAN'S DIARY
Jim McBride, B&W, 1967, 71m

■ Clever satire on the pretensions of cinema verité. A filmmaker explores the truth in his life by making a film about himself.

FACT FILE:

OSCAR'S LATEST FAVORITES

■ *Hollywood has always loved historical extravaganzas that require lots of extras, from* **Gone With the Wind** *to* **Braveheart.** *In 1996 Mel Gibson's epic about a 13th-century Scottish rebellion took home Best Picture, Best Directing, and three additional Oscars. Other big winners for 1996 included:*

Nicolas Cage, Best Actor, **Leaving Las Vegas**
Susan Sarandon, Best Actress, **Dead Man Walking**
Kevin Spacey, Best Supporting Actor, **The Usual Suspects**
Mira Sorvino, Best Supporting Actress, **Mighty Aphrodite**

■ **EXPERT LIST**

DR. STRANGELOVE (OR, HOW I LEARNED TO STOP WORRYING AND LOVE THE BOMB)
Stanley Kubrick, B&W, *1964, 93m*

■ Peter Sellers plays three roles in this brilliant black comedy about nuclear bombs. George C. Scott, Slim Pickens, and James Earl Jones contribute great comic performances, too. Nominated for Best Picture.

DUCK SOUP
Leo McCarey, B&W, *1933, 70m*

■ The best of the Marx Brothers films. Strangely, it was a box-office disaster when first released.

THE FRESHMAN*
Sam Taylor and Fred Newmeyer, B&W, *1925, 70m*

■ Harold Lloyd stars as a college nerd who'll do anything to be popular. Little does he know that people aren't laughing with him, but at him.

THE GENERAL
Buster Keaton, B&W, *1927, 74m*

■ Keaton stars as an engineer trying to retake his stolen locomotive during the Civil War. His silent magnetism dominates the whole film.

THE GOLD RUSH*
Charlie Chaplin, B&W, *1925, 100m*

■ Chaplin stars as well as directs this historical comedy. Includes the brilliantly inventive "dance of the dinner rolls."

HIS GIRL FRIDAY
Howard Hawks, B&W, *1940, 92m*

■ Based on the oft-filmed Ben Hecht and Charles MacArthur play, *The Front Page*. Cary Grant and Rosalind Russell have combustible chemistry as a battling reporter and her editor.

THE HOSPITAL
Arthur Hiller, color, 1971, 102m

■ Very black hit-and-miss comedy, scripted by Paddy Chayefsky, with a magisterial performance from George C. Scott as a depressed hospital boss faced with a raft of professional crises.
■ **OSCAR:** Best Screenplay.

IT HAPPENED ONE NIGHT
Frank Capra, B&W, *1934, 105m*

■ Clark Gable and Claudette Colbert fall in love one night. Frank Capra directs in the patent "feel-good" style he invented.
■ **OSCARS:** Best Screenplay, Actor, Actress, Director, Picture.

MODERN TIMES
Charlie Chaplin, B&W, *1936, 87m*

■ Chaplin's classic industrial satire features the Little Tramp stuck in an automated nightmare. It probably means more to today's technology-flooded viewers than it did to the moviegoers of 1936.

A NIGHT AT THE OPERA
Sam Wood, B&W, *1935, 92m*

■ A Marx Brothers musical comedy with a love story tacked on for good measure. Fortunately, the romance doesn't spoil the Brothers' weird brand of antic fun.

NINOTCHKA
Ernst Lubitsch, B&W, *1939, 110m*

■ A comedy starring Greta Garbo? The lady with the scowl plays a Soviet commissar checking up on some comrades in Paris. It's still good lightweight entertainment.

THE PHILADELPHIA STORY
George Cukor, B&W, *1940, 112m*

■ Donald Ogden Stewart's adaptation of Philip Barry's hit Broadway comedy, about a socialite wedding threatened by scandal, fires on every cylinder. Katharine Hepburn, Cary Grant, and notably James Stewart are in peak, sophisticated form.
■ **OSCARS:** Best Screenplay, Actor.

SAFETY LAST*
Fred Newmeyer and Sam Taylor, B&W, *1923, 78m*

■ A Harold Lloyd picture about an up-and-comer in the big city. His famous building-climbing scene

■ EXPERT LIST

(Lloyd did his own stunts) stunned early audiences and still keeps viewers on the edge of their seats.

SOME LIKE IT HOT
Billy Wilder, B&W, 1959, 120m

■ A classic. Jack Lemmon and Tony Curtis witness a mob hit and flee to the safe haven of an all-girl band—as girls. Marilyn Monroe is the lead singer of the band in her best performance.
■ **OSCAR:** Best Costume Design.

SULLIVAN'S TRAVELS
Preston Sturges, B&W, 1941, 90m

■ Sturges sends a jaded Hollywood director out into the real world with nothing but a dime in his pocket. Clever satire featuring Veronica Lake.

TROUBLE IN PARADISE
Ernst Lubitsch, B&W, 1932, 83m

■ The story of two jewel thieves who fall in and out of love.

DRAMA

THE ADVENTURES OF ROBIN HOOD
Michael Curtiz and William Keighley, color, 1938, 105m

■ The old yarn is retold with flamboyant gusto on great sets. Errol Flynn and Basil Rathbone duel with unsurpassed panache.
■ **OSCARS:** Best Music, Art Direction, Editing.

THE AFRICAN QUEEN
John Huston, color, 1951, 105m

■ Bogart and Hepburn travel downriver through Africa. Scripted by James Agee. A near-perfect film.
■ **OSCAR:** Best Actor.

ALL ABOUT EVE
Joseph L. Mankiewicz, B&W, 1950, 138m

■ This look at the New York theater scene features a great leading performance from Bette Davis. Also stars Anne Baxter and George Sanders.
■ **OSCARS:** Best Director, Picture, Sound, Supporting Actor.

ALL THAT HEAVEN ALLOWS
Douglas Sirk, color 1955, 89m

■ Glossy weepie that runs a stiletto into the heart of the American Dream. Jane Wyman is the wealthy widow who has an ill-fated affair with young Rock Hudson, her bohemian gardener. Lurid and harrowing.

AMERICAN GRAFFITI
George Lucas, color, 1973, 110m

■ Breakthrough, and very taking, nostalgia picture about California teenage life on a small-town strip in 1962. With Ron Howard, Richard Dreyfuss, and Harrison Ford in top form at the start of their careers. You'll remember the songs.

THE BIRTH OF A NATION*
D. W. Griffith, B&W, 1915, 175m

■ Director John Singleton nominated it for preservation in hopes that the disturbing glorification of

FACT FILE:

MOVIE ROYALTY

■ *Katharine Hepburn has been named Best Actress four times:*

Morning Glory *1933*
Guess Who's Coming to Dinner *1967*
The Lion in Winter *1968*
On Golden Pond *1981*

■ *John Ford won four Oscars for directing:*

The Informer *1935*
The Grapes of Wrath *1940*
How Green Was My Valley *1941*
The Quiet Man *1952*

■ EXPERT LIST

the KKK would serve as a lesson for younger Americans and a reminder for older ones.

THE BLACK PIRATE*
Albert Parker, B&W, 1926, 122m
■ Silent buccaneer film written by and starring Douglas Fairbanks, Sr. It's silly, mindless fun.

THE BLOOD OF JESUS
Spencer Williams, Jr., color, 1941, 50m
■ Williams wrote, directed, and starred in this story of a husband who accidentally shoots his wife.

BONNIE AND CLYDE
Arthur Penn, color, 1967, 111m
■ Warren Beatty and Faye Dunaway reinvented the gangster picture as the infamous crime duo. The final shoot-out in slow motion is one of the most memorable scenes in American film. Also stars Gene Hackman and Estelle Parsons.
■ **OSCARS:** Best Cinematography, Supporting Actress.

CASABLANCA
Michael Curtiz, B&W, 1942, 102m
■ The standard by which every movie romance will forever be judged. Bogart and Bergman are magic at every turn.
■ **OSCARS:** Best Director, Picture, Screenplay.

THE CHEAT*
Cecil B. DeMille, B&W, 1915, 60m
■ A silent melodrama about a high-society woman who loses her shirt and her honor to a Japanese lender.

CITIZEN KANE
Orson Welles, B&W, 1941, 119m
■ The single most influential American film. The story of newspaper tycoon Charles Foster Kane still tops many lists of the greatest films of all time, and it established Orson Welles as the premier talent of his generation.
■ **OSCAR:** Best Original Screenplay.

CITY LIGHTS
Charlie Chaplin, B&W, 1931, 81m
■ Considered Chaplin's masterpiece, the actor's little tramp befriends a blind woman and does all he can to help her. The finale will bring tears to your eyes.

THE COOL WORLD
Shirley Clarke, B&W, 1963, 125m
■ A disturbing, early look at ghetto life. Clarke follows a gang leader on his symbolic pursuit of a gun through the mean streets of Harlem. Every urban film since owes something to this one.

A CORNER IN WHEAT*
D. W. Griffith, B&W, 1909, 1 reel
■ Griffith contrasts the lives of the rich and poor by examining a wheat farmer and a Wall Street broker. The startling ending culminates in the death of the farmer. Based on the writings of Frank Norris.

THE CROWD
King Vidor, b&w, 1928, 90m
■ An examination of a working-class family in a wealthy world. Vidor's best work.

FACT FILE:

NIGHTS TO REMEMBER

■ *The distinction of being the all-time biggest Oscar winners is shared by:*

Ben Hur *1959 and*
West Side Story *1961*

Each was honored in 11 categories, including Best Picture and Directing. So striking was the dancing in West Side Story *that a special Oscar was awarded for choreography.*

■ **EXPERT LIST**

DODSWORTH
William Wyler, B&W, 1936, 101m

■ From the Sinclair Lewis novel of the same name. The finely crafted story follows Walter Huston as Dodsworth, a self-made millionaire and automobile mogul.
■ **OSCAR:** Best Interior Decoration.

EL NORTE
Gregory Nava, color, 1983, 140m

■ A brother and sister flee political persecution in Guatemala for sweated labor in California. Obvious and on the long side, but not unaffecting.

THE FOUR HORSEMEN OF THE APOCALYPSE*
Rex Ingram, B&W, 1921, 114m

■ This grim antiwar movie from a novel by Vicente Blasco Ibáñez made Rudolph Valentino a star. An Argentinean with French blood signs up to the Allied cause in WWI; his brother fights for Germany. An arresting silent spectacular.

FURY
Fritz Lang, B&W, 1936, 94m

■ Atmospheric thriller somewhat softened by MGM in which Spencer Tracy, wrongly accused of kidnapping, escapes a lynch mob and a burning jail, and turns the tables on his "killers." The first and most famous U.S. film by the German master of psychological suspense.

THE GODFATHER
Francis Ford Coppola, color, 1972, 175m

■ The unforgettable first chapter in the Corleone family saga. Marlon Brando stars as the title character, with Al Pacino, James Caan, Talia Shire, Diane Keaton, and Robert Duvall. A great film.
■ **OSCARS:** Best Actor, Adapted Screenplay, Picture.

THE GODFATHER, PART II
Francis Ford Coppola, color, 1974, 200m

■ Robert De Niro joins the star-studded cast as the young Don Corleone, but it's Al Pacino as Michael who eclipses everyone with a skillful, complicated performance. The sequel is just as good as the original.
■ **OSCARS:** Best Adapted Screenplay, Art Direction/Set Decoration, Director, Picture, Supporting Actor, Screenplay.

GONE WITH THE WIND
Victor Fleming, color, 1939, 222m

■ Clark Gable and Vivien Leigh star in the epic telling of the last days of the Civil War. Politically incorrect? Sure. But it remains a beautiful, compelling, and thoroughly entertaining film.
■ **OSCARS:** Best Color Cinematography, Interior Decoration, Screenplay, Editing, Supporting Actress, Actress, Director, Picture.

THE GRAPES OF WRATH
John Ford, B&W, 1940, 129m

■ Henry Fonda is brilliant and Ford is at his best. Adapted from the Steinbeck classic about Okies fleeing the Dust Bowl.
■ **OSCARS:** Best Supporting Actress, Director.

GREED*
Erich Von Stroheim, B&W, 1924, 133m

■ Von Stroheim's tale of corruption must have been a wonder in its original nine-hour length. Even in the VCR-friendly two-hour version, it's a magnificent remnant from the silent era.

HOW GREEN WAS MY VALLEY
John Ford, color, 1941, 118m

■ The story of a Welsh mining family told by 13-year-old Roddy McDowall.
■ **OSCARS:** Best Interior Decoration, Black and White Cinematography, Supporting Actor, Director, Picture.

I AM A FUGITIVE FROM A CHAIN GANG
Mervyn Leroy, B&W, 1932, 90m

■ An honest man convicted of a crime he didn't commit. One of the first films to explore this subject, Paul

■ EXPERT LIST

Muni's performance pulls it all together.

INTOLERANCE*
D. W. Griffith, B&W, 1916, 175m

■ An ironic title, considering the controversy surrounding Griffith's work. This story is an amalgam of four tales of intolerance: two historical, two modern.

IT'S A WONDERFUL LIFE
Frank Capra, B&W, 1946, 129m

■ Jimmy Stewart finds out what the world would be like if he had never been born. A Christmas classic with an ending as sweet as Santa himself.

THE ITALIAN*
Reginald Barker, B&W, 1915, 78m

■ The tragic turn-of-the-century tale of an immigrant Italian family in New York.

KILLER OF SHEEP
Charles Burnett, B&W, 1977, 83m

■ Set in south central L.A., Burnett follows Stan, an aging man struggling to keep his values while the world falls around him. It's a complex tale, beautifully told.

THE LADY EVE
Preston Sturges, B&W, 1941, 94m

■ Barbara Stanwyck stars as a con making the moves on the wealthy but nerdy Henry Fonda. Subtle humor and first-rate lead performances.

LASSIE COME HOME
Fred Wilcox, color 1943, 90m

■ Elizabeth Taylor and Roddy McDowall star, but Lassie steals the show. Perfect family viewing, even 50 years later.

FACT FILE:

NIGHTS TO FORGET

■ *Two pictures,* **The Turning Point** *and* **The Color Purple,** *were nominated for 11 Oscars and came up empty-handed.* **Judgment at Nuremberg** *did slightly better. It had 13 nominations but managed to win two, for Best Actor (Maximilian Schell) and Writing (based on material from another medium). It would have done better had it not been up against* **West Side Story,** *which virtually swept the field that year.*

THE LAST OF THE MOHICANS*
Maurice Tourneur, B&W, 1920, 75m

■ Silent version of James Fenimore Cooper's romance of the wartorn Colonial 1750s, notable for Wallace Beery's performance as the vile Magua.

LAWRENCE OF ARABIA
David Lean, color, 1962, 221m

■ Peter O'Toole gives one of the greatest debut performances in film history as T. E. Lawrence, and David Lean tells the lengthy story with remarkable ease. See it on a large screen if possible.

■ **OSCARS:** Best Art Direction, Set Decoration, Color Cinematography, Sound, Score, Editing, Director, Picture.

THE LEARNING TREE
Gordon Parks, color, 1969, 107m

■ Gordon Parks became the first black director of a major studio film with this autobiographical project. The former *Life* photographer directed, produced, wrote the script, and scored the film himself.

LETTER FROM AN UNKNOWN WOMAN
Max Ophüls, B&W, 1948, 90m

■ Romance starring Joan Fontaine and Louis Jourdan. Director Ophüls gives the film a European

■ EXPERT LIST

feel and stylized look.

THE MAGNIFICENT AMBERSONS

Orson Welles, B&W, 1942, 88m

■ Orson Welles's dark portrait of a midwestern family in decline, from the Booth Tarkington novel. Was nominated for Best Picture; don't miss it.

MARTY

Delbert Mann, B&W, 1955, 91m

■ The tiny but touching story of a Bronx butcher (Ernest Borgnine) who finds love unexpectedly. Borgnine gives (by far) his best performance.

■ **OSCARS:** Best Screenplay, Actor, Director, Picture.

MIDNIGHT COWBOY

John Schlesinger, color, 1969, 113m

■ The only X-rated film to win Best Picture, *Cowboy* is hardly as shocking today as it was then. Dustin Hoffman and Jon Voight star as small-time hustlers. New York never looked seamier than through director Schlesinger's lens.

■ **OSCARS:** Best Adapted Screenplay, Director, Picture.

MOROCCO

Josef von Sternberg, B&W, 1930, 92m

■ Marlene Dietrich's first Hollywood film casts her as a cabaret singer stuck in Morocco. Gary Cooper goes along for the ride.

MR. SMITH GOES TO WASHINGTON

Frank Capra, B&W, 1939, 129m

■ Capra and Jimmy Stewart (as Jefferson Smith) team up to tell the story of a scoutmaster turned senator who brings old-fashioned values back to Capitol Hill. It's every politician's dream role.

■ **OSCAR:** Best Screenplay.

NASHVILLE

Robert Altman, color, 1975, 159m

■ Altman at his best. With a large ensemble cast at his disposal, the director examines American life and the way it was lived in the '70s with acute wit and style.

■ **OSCAR:** Best Song.

NOTHING BUT A MAN

Michael Roemer, B&W, 1964, 95m

■ A quiet look at racial prejudice in the South. Melodrama is kept to a minimum, as director Roemer examines the complexities of black life.

ON THE WATERFRONT

Elia Kazan, B&W, 1954, 108m

■ Marlon Brando stars as Terry Malloy, a boxer-turned-longshoreman. Disgusted by the mob corruption that his older brother (Rod Steiger) has introduced him to, Brando sums himself up with one of the most desperate lines in the movies: "I coulda' been a contender."

■ **OSCARS:** Best Art Direction/Set Decoration, Black and White Cinematography, Editing, Screenplay, Supporting Actress, Actor, Director, Picture.

ONE FLEW OVER THE CUCKOO'S NEST

Milos Forman, color, 1975, 129m

■ *Cuckoo's Nest* and *It Happened One Night* are the only two films to have swept the five major Oscar categories. Jack Nicholson is an inmate at a mental institution who brings the other patients back to life. Based on Ken Kesey's novel. Look for a great early-career performance from Danny DeVito.

■ **OSCARS:** Best Screenplay, Actor, Actress, Director, Picture.

PATHS OF GLORY

Stanley Kubrick, B&W, 1957, 86m

■ Kubrick's specialty, an antiwar movie. Kirk Douglas stars as a World War I sergeant forced to defend three of his troops against charges of cowardice.

A PLACE IN THE SUN

George Stevens, B&W, 1951, 120m

■ Elizabeth Taylor, Montgomery Clift, and Shelley Winters star as the three points of a love triangle.

■ **EXPERT LIST**

■ **OSCARS:** Best Black and White Cinematography, Costume Design, Score, Editing, Screenplay, Director.

THE POOR LITTLE RICH GIRL*
Maurice Tourneur, B&W, 1917, 64m
■ Mary Pickford gives an extraordinary performance as a girl with everything but her family's love.

THE PRISONER OF ZENDA
John Cromwell, B&W, 1937, 101m
■ From the Anthony Hope novel about a power struggle in a small European kingdom. Ronald Colman stars, and Mary Astor, Douglas Fairbanks, Jr., and David Niven also put in appearances.

RAGING BULL
Martin Scorsese, B&W, 1980, 128m
■ Many critics hailed this drama about boxer Jake LaMotta as the best film of the '80s. Robert De Niro gives a fantastic performance as LaMotta, portraying the character from his 20s as a fighting machine to his dissolute later years.
■ **OSCARS:** Best Editing, Actor.

REBEL WITHOUT A CAUSE
Nicholas Ray, color, 1955, 111m
■ The classic tale of teen angst and alienation. James Dean stars in the role that made him an American legend.

SALT OF THE EARTH
Herbert Biberman, B&W, 1954, 94m
■ Deals with a miners' strike in New Mexico from a staunchly pro-union perspective. During the McCarthy era, it was attacked as Communist propaganda.

SCARFACE
Howard Hawks, B&W, 1932, 93m
■ Like the remake, it was censored at first because of its violent content. Hawks's film was the best gangster film until *The Godfather*. Paul Muni plays a Capone-like mob man with deep affection for his sister.

SEVENTH HEAVEN
Frank Borzage, B&W, 1927, 119m
■ Swooning over-the-top melodrama about Parisian waif, Janet Gaynor, rescued and married by a sewerman, Charles Farrell, who is later blinded in the First World War.
■ **OSCARS:** Best Actress, Director, Screenplay.

SHADOWS
John Cassavetes, B&W, 1959, 87m
■ Cassavetes's first directorial effort. The film follows a light-skinned black girl through life in New York City. Lelia Goldoni turns in a strong lead performance.

SHERLOCK, JR.*
Buster Keaton, B&W, 1924, 45m
■ Keaton plays a projectionist with Walter Mitty–like dreams of being a great detective. He walks from the booth onto the screen and enters a fantasy drama. Besides being Keaton's greatest display of skill as a director, the "fourth-wall" fusion of reality and fantasy has been copied by everyone from Woody Allen to Schwarzenegger.

STAGECOACH
John Ford, B&W, 1939, 96m
■ A stagecoach of assorted characters jolts across Monument Valley under threat of Indian attack. John Wayne collaborated with John Ford for the first time in this classic and still matchless Western.
■ **OSCARS:** Best Music, Supporting Actor.

SUNSET BOULEVARD
Billy Wilder, B&W, 1950, 100m
■ A cavalcade of Hollywood's greats appear in this black comedy about Norma Desmond, played by Gloria Swanson in her defining role, a silent film star who's got nothing left. As a Broadway musical starring Glenn Close, it was a hit in 1994.
■ **OSCARS:** Best Art Direction/Set Decoration, Screenplay, Score.

■ EXPERT LIST

SWEET SMELL OF SUCCESS
Alexander Mackendrick, B&W, 1957, 96m

■ Burt Lancaster and Tony Curtis star in a story about a newspaper gossip columnist (Lancaster) and the press agent who'll do anything for him (Curtis). An excellent musical score by Elmer Bernstein of *Magnificent Seven* fame.

TABU
F. W. Murnau and Robert Flaherty, B&W, 1931, 81m

■ The story follows a young diver and his unrequited love for a woman declared "taboo" by the gods.
■ **OSCAR:** Best Cinematography.

TAXI DRIVER
Martin Scorsese, color, 1976, 112m

■ Robert De Niro plays Travis Bickle, a disturbed taxi driver who can't stand New York and goes berserk. Scorsese's portrait of vigilantism was cited by John Hinckley as an influence for his assassination attempt on Ronald Reagan. Costars Jodie Foster, Cybill Shepherd, and Harvey Keitel.

TEVYE
Maurice Schwartz, B&W, 1939, 96m

■ Later known as *Fiddler on the Roof*, this is the story of a Jewish dairyman whose lifestyle is changed by his daughter's wishes to marry outside the faith. From the Sholom Aleichem story.

TO KILL A MOCKINGBIRD
Robert Mulligan, B&W, 1962, 129m

■ Horton Foote's righteous adaptation of Harper Lee's novel about a Southern lawyer, Gregory Peck, who defends a black man wrongly accused of rape.
■ **OSCARS:** Best Actor, Screenplay.

WHERE ARE MY CHILDREN?*
Lois Webber and Phillips Stanley, B&W, 1916, 72m

■ A silent "social" film from woman director Lois Webber, starring Tyrone Power, Sr. Daring, in that it takes a pro–birth control, anti-abortion stand in the early 20th century.

THE WIND
Bud Greenspan, B&W, 1928, 74m

■ Lillian Gish as a girl who marries a farmer to escape her family. One of the last great silent films.

WITHIN OUR GATES*
Oscar Micheaux, B&W, 1920, 79m

■ The earliest surviving film by an African American director. A mixed cast explores racial issues that didn't bubble to the cultural surface for decades.

A WOMAN UNDER THE INFLUENCE
John Cassavetes, color, 1974, 147m

■ Gena Rowlands and Peter Falk star in the story of a woman who is cracking up.

HORROR

CAT PEOPLE
Jacques Tourneur, B&W, 1942, 73m

■ Simone Simon is a dressmaker who believes she's infected with a panther curse in this creepy, well-directed thriller.

FRANKENSTEIN
James Whale, B&W, 1931, 71m

■ Boris Karloff's performance as Mary Shelley's monster is

FACT FILE:

IT HAPPENED TWICE

■ *Only two films have ever won Oscar's quintuple crown by being honored in all five top categories: Best Picture, Directing, Screenplay, Actor, and Actress. They were:*

It Happened One Night *(1934)*
One Flew Over the Cuckoo's Nest *(1975)*

■ EXPERT LIST

still the best, Robert De Niro's friendly monster in the Kenneth Branagh version included.

FREAKS
Tod Browning, B&W, 1932, 64m

■ Director Browning explores relationships between sideshow freaks in this strange horror film. The real story is the humanity of the freak characters, many of whom are real-life sideshow performers.

KING KONG
Merian Cooper and Ernest Shoedsack, B&W, 1933, 105m

■ Big ape rampages through New York until he reaches the Empire State Building. A camp classic.

PSYCHO
Alfred Hitchcock, B&W, 1960, 109m

■ Anthony Perkins stars as Norman Bates, motel proprietor and neighborhood psychotic. Thirty years and several hundred slasher imitators later, *Psycho* still provides some terrifyingly good screams.

MUSICALS

AN AMERICAN IN PARIS
Vincente Minnelli, color, 1951, 113m

■ Gene Kelly stars in this entertaining musical as a GI-turned-painter. Features a stunning, 17-minute ballet sequence with classic Kelly dancing.

■ **OSCARS:** Best Art Direction/Set Decoration, Color Cinematography, Score, Screenplay, Picture.

THE BAND WAGON
Vincente Minnelli, color, 1953, 112m

■ Witty backstage Broadway drama with Cyd Charisse and comeback star Fred Astaire dancing up a storm, and Jack Buchanan as their temperamental producer. "By Myself," "A Shine on Your Shoes," "Dancing in the Dark," and many more. A champagne pick-me-up.

CABARET
Bob Fosse, color, 1972, 128m

■ Glittering if sometimes crude adaptation of John Kander's musical of Christopher Isherwood's prewar Berlin stories, notable for Fosse's stylish chore-

FACT FILE:

FAMILY TIES

Some movie families who have had more than one Oscar winner:

■ *John Huston, Best Directing and Screenplay for* **The Treasure of the Sierra Madre** *(1948); his father Walter Huston, Best Supporting Actor for the same movie; and John Huston's daughter Anjelica Huston, Best Supporting Actress for* **Prizzi's Honor** *(1985).*

■ *Joanne Woodward, Best Actress for* **The Three Faces of Eve** *(1957), and her husband, Paul Newman, Best Actor for* **The Color of Money** *(1986).*

■ *Vincente Minnelli, Best Directing for* **Gigi** *(1958), and his and his one-time wife Judy Garland's daughter, Liza Minnelli, Best Actress, for* **Cabaret** *(1972).*

■ *Jane Fonda, Best Actress for* **Klute** *(1971) and* **Coming Home** *(1978), and her father, Henry Fonda, Best Actor for* **On Golden Pond** *(1981).*

■ *Warren Beatty, Best Directing for* **Reds** *(1981), and sister Shirley MacLaine, Best Actress for* **Terms of Endearment** *(1983).*

■ EXPERT LIST

ography and Joel Grey's silky performance as the Kit Kat Klub's cynical MC.
■ **OSCARS:** Eight in all, including Best Director, Photography, Score Adaptation, and Actress.

CARMEN JONES
Otto Preminger, color, 1954, 105m
■ Oscar Hammerstein II adapted the film from Bizet's opera. Harry Belafonte and Dorothy Dandridge turn in good performances.

FOOTLIGHT PARADE
Lloyd Bacon, B&W, 1933, 100m
■ James Cagney plays a struggling stage director trying to outdo himself (and sound movies) with every musical number.

GIGI
Vincente Minnelli, color, 1958, 116m
■ Leslie Caron is Gigi, a harlot-in-training with Louis Jourdan on her mind. One of the last great movie musicals.
■ **OSCARS:** Best Art Direction, Color Cinematography, Costume Design, Score, Song, Screenplay, Director, Picture.

LOVE ME TONIGHT
Rouben Mamoulian, B&W, 1932, 104m
■ The Rodgers & Hart musical that introduced "Isn't It Romantic" (sung by Maurice Chevalier) to the film world.

MEET ME IN ST. LOUIS
Vincente Minnelli, color, 1944, 133m
■ Set at the 1903 World's Fair in St. Louis. Director Minnelli's musical tracks a family through their expectant, turn-of-the-century lives. Judy Garland carries the picture, although child-star Margaret O'Brien was given a special Oscar for her performance.

SINGIN' IN THE RAIN
Gene Kelly and Stanley Donen, color, 1952, 103m
■ This is the greatest movie musical ever. Kelly's performance of the title song is deservedly one of the most famous scenes in film. Donald O'Connor, Debbie Reynolds, Cyd Charisse, and Jean Hagen also give great performances.

TOP HAT
Mark Sandrich, B&W, 1935, 97m
■ Ginger Rogers and Fred Astaire in their best form. "Cheek to Cheek" and "Top Hat, White Tie, and Tails" are just two of the great songs performed. Look for Lucille Ball in a small early role.

THE WIZARD OF OZ
Victor Fleming, color/B&W, 1939, 101m
■ An American cinema classic based on L. Frank Baum's children's novel of the same name. Judy Garland stars as Dorothy in the role of a lifetime. The music is instantly hummable, the performances are unforgettable. A perfect film.
■ **OSCARS:** Best Song, Score.

YANKEE DOODLE DANDY
Michael Curtiz, B&W, 1942, 126m
■ James Cagney stars in the story of popular song composer George M. Cohan. Cagney proved that he could play something other than a gangster in this sweet musical.
■ **OSCARS:** Best Score, Sound, Actor.

MYSTERY & SUSPENSE

BADLANDS
Terrence Malick, color, 1974, 94m
■ Before there was Oliver Stone's *Natural Born Killers*, there was *Badlands*. Director Malick's creepy thriller stars Martin Sheen and Sissy Spacek as a murderer and his companion. Loosely inspired by a Nebraska killing spree in 1958.

CHAN IS MISSING
Wayne Wang, B&W, 1981, 80m
■ Very off-the-wall Chinese-American San Francisco mystery, by turns funny, suspenseful, and melancholy. There's no payoff, but it's fresh and full of surprises.

■ **EXPERT LIST**

CHINATOWN
Roman Polanski, color, 1974, 131m
■ Jack Nicholson and Faye Dunaway in one of Hollywood's greatest executions of film noir. John Huston, Diane Ladd, and Burt Young co-star.
■ **OSCAR:** Best Original Screenplay.

THE CONVERSATION
Francis Coppola, color, 1974, 113m
■ A master surveillance man cannot find the bug planted on him. Gene Hackman is wholly compelling as the anonymous hero of this riveting psychological thriller.

DETOUR
Edgar Ulmer, B&W, 1946, 69m
■ Ulmer was one of the first low-budget, independent filmmakers. His craft is at its sharpest in this film noir about a drifter, played superbly by Tom Neal.

DOUBLE INDEMNITY
Billy Wilder, B&W, 1944, 106m
■ Fred MacMurray stars as an insurance salesman who joins Barbara Stanwyck in a plot to kill her husband for his insurance. Suspense films don't get any better than this.

FORCE OF EVIL
Abraham Polonsky, B&W, 1948, 100m
■ Noir classic starring John Garfield as a mob lawyer caught between crime and brotherly love. A tremendous performance by Garfield, a too-often underrated actor.

THE MALTESE FALCON
John Huston, B&W, 1941, 101m
■ Bogart is Sam Spade, a P.I. investigating the web of deceit and murder spun around a priceless statue. With a supporting cast featuring Peter Lorre, Mary Astor, and Sydney Greenstreet, this is the best of P.I. flicks.

THE MANCHURIAN CANDIDATE
John Frankenheimer, B&W, 1962, 126m
■ Frank Sinatra gives his best film performance as an Army man who knows more than he thinks he does in Frankenheimer's thrilling adaptation of the Richard Condon novel. The plot revolves around conspiracy and brainwashing at the highest levels of American government.

THE NIGHT OF THE HUNTER
Charles Laughton, B&W, 1955, 93m
■ Robert Mitchum plays a terrifying preacher trying to kill his step-kids. This is one scary flick, and Mitchum turns in a creepy, career-defining performance.

NORTH BY NORTHWEST
Alfred Hitchcock, color, 1959, 136m
■ Cary Grant is the nonchalant advertising executive who escapes abduction and goes on the run across America. An extraordinary mix of comedy and paranoia, and a faultless Hitchcock classic, climaxing on the slippery stone face of a U.S. president.

OUT OF THE PAST
Jacques Tourneur, B&W, 1947, 97m
■ A small film noir starring Robert Mitchum and Kirk Douglas. Mitchum plays a P.I. who gets involved with a gangster's girl. Douglas plays the formidable gangster.

SHADOW OF A DOUBT
Alfred Hitchcock, B&W, 1943, 108m
■ Joseph Cotten stars as Uncle Charlie, a loving relative who may have a murderous secret to hide. This is Hitchcock's personal favorite.

SUNRISE
F. W. Murnau, B&W, 1927, 110m
■ The story of a farmer who plots to murder his wife. The silent film featured innovative camerawork for the times.
■ **OSCAR:** Best Actress.

TOUCH OF EVIL
Orson Welles, B&W, 1958, 108m

■ **EXPERT LIST**

■ In this film, director Welles also stars as the corrupt sheriff of a seedy Mexican border town. Charlton Heston, Janet Leigh, and a host of other stars also appear.

THE TREASURE OF THE SIERRA MADRE
John Huston, B&W, 1948, 126m

■ Humphrey Bogart, Walter Huston, and Tim Holt go prospecting for gold and discover the worst in human nature.
■ **OSCARS:** Best Screenplay, Supporting Actor, Director.

VERTIGO
Alfred Hitchcock, color, 1958, 126m

■ Jimmy Stewart is an ex-cop hired to shadow Kim Novak. He has vertigo. To reveal anything more would be criminal.

WESTERNS

HELL'S HINGES*
William S. Hart and Charles Swickard, B&W, 1916, 65m

■ Director Hart was the first master of the Western, and this fine film had more to do with shaping the formula of the genre than any other.

HIGH NOON
Fred Zinneman, B&W, 1952, 85m

■ The clock ticks down on sheriff Gary Cooper as an old nemesis turns his wedding day into a nightmare. Great suspense and good acting; Cooper won his second Oscar for the role.
■ **OSCARS:** Best Editing, Song, Score, Actor.

MY DARLING CLEMENTINE
John Ford, B&W, 1946, 97m

■ Henry Fonda plays Wyatt Earp in the best version of the oft-filmed shoot-out at the O.K. Corral.

RED RIVER
Howard Hawks, B&W, 1948, 133m

■ One of the most frequently underrated Westerns. John Wayne plays a leathery rancher with surprising skill. Montgomery Clift co-stars in his first film role.

RIDE THE HIGH COUNTRY
Sam Peckinpah, color, 1962, 93m

■ Two gunmen are hired to guard a stash of gold. One has honorable intentions, one doesn't. Starring Randolph Scott and Joel McCrea in their final screen roles.

THE SEARCHERS
John Ford, color, 1956, 119m

■ John Wayne plays a racist old Confederate in search of his niece (Natalie Wood) who was abducted by Indians. Both Wayne and director Ford are in peak form.

SHANE
George Stevens, color, 1953, 117m

■ A great drama from the Jack Schaeffer novel of

FACT FILE:

WAR STORIES:

■ *Cowboy movies haven't fared that well in Oscar history. Only* **Cimarron** *(1930),* **Dances with Wolves** *(1990), and* **Unforgiven** *(1992) have won Best Picture awards. But war movies have been decorated often. Among the best of the Best Picture winners:*

All Quiet on the Western Front *(1929–1930)*
Gone With the Wind *(1939)*
Casablanca *(1943)*
From Here to Eternity *(1953)*
The Bridge on the River Kwai *(1957)*
Patton *(1970)*
Schindler's List *(1993)*

■ EXPERT LIST

the same name. Alan Ladd as the lonesome gunfighter is fantastic.

■ **OSCAR:** Best Color Cinematography.

SCIENCE FICTION

BLADE RUNNER

Ridley Scott, color, 1982, 122m

■ An art-house favorite starring Harrison Ford as an everyday cop in a nightmarish future that resembles L.A. Cast features Daryl Hannah, Sean Young, Edward James Olmos, and Rutger Hauer. The production design is superb.

THE DAY THE EARTH STOOD STILL

Robert Wise, B&W, 1951, 92m

■ The story: Alien robot lands in Washington, D.C. with a dire warning of what will happen if mankind fails to mend its warlike ways. A sci-fi classic, strange and menacing.

E.T. THE EXTRA TERRESTRIAL

Steven Spielberg, color, 1982, 115m

■ This touching adventure of a boy and his alien could only come from the imagination of Steven Spielberg. Henry Thomas as Eliot gives one of the best child-performances ever in a film, and the superior cast (including Debra Winger as the voice of E.T.) makes this the classic of '80s pop-cinema.

■ **OSCARS:** Best Sound, Visual Effects, Score.

INVASION OF THE BODY SNATCHERS

Don Siegel, B&W, 1956, 80m

■ One of the most influential sci-fi horror movies. Aliens replace people with duplicates hatched from pods. Don't watch it alone.

STAR WARS

George Lucas, color, 1977, 121m

■ "A long time ago, in a galaxy far, far away," sci-fi fantasies were drive-in jokes. Then director George Lucas came along and made outer space into a world populated by heroes and monsters drawn from Greek mythology. The special effects set a new standard for film technology.

■ **OSCARS:** Best Art Direction, Set Decoration, Costume Design, Editing, Sound, Visual Effects, Score.

2001: A SPACE ODYSSEY

Stanley Kubrick, color, 1968, 139m

■ The groundbreaking film that took viewers into a future where machine and man are equals. Besides being a visual feast, the philosophical and theological issues raised within make it one of the touchstone films of a generation.

■ **OSCAR:** Best Visual Effects.

EXPERT SOURCE

Where are they now? To get in touch with your favorite actor, whether it's George Lindsey, who played Goober on *The Gomer Pyle Show*, or Susan Sarandon, who was Thelma to Geena Davis's Louise, you can probably make contact through the Screen Actors Guild in Los Angeles. SAG keeps an address file for its 84,000 members, and can usually tell you how to reach a member's agent in most cases. The Guild prefers that you call, not write.

Agency Department, Screen Actors Guild
5757 Wilshire Boulevard
Los Angeles, CA 90036
☎ 213-549-6737

EXPERT SOURCES

VIDEOS THAT ARE HARD TO FIND

The variety of unusual videos that can be ordered through the mail is staggering. While Blockbuster Video might have 140 copies of True Lies, *very often the major video rental chains don't carry a single copy of harder-to-find films. For those videophiles looking for the obscure, whether for rental or purchase, mail-order houses are often the best bet. Some outlets rent and sell only through membership deals, while others are happy to deal with onetime customers.*

ALTERNATIVE VIDEOS
P.O. Box 270797
Dallas, TX 75227
☎ 214–823–6030

■ Specializes in films for those of African descent. The catalog is free, but there's a $25 basic membership charge before you can rent or purchase.

THE BRAUER BETA CATALOG
26 Emery Lane
Woodcliff Lake, NJ 07675
☎ 800–962–7722

■ For those who still insist on clinging to the ol' Beta machine. There's a free catalog, and they sell packs of blank tapes.

COLUMBIA HOUSE
1400 N. Fruitridge Avenue
Terre Haute, IN 47811
☎ 800–262–2001

■ Good deals at first, but read the agreement and respond to your mail—monthly selections are sent unless you say in advance that you don't want them. Free catalog.

CRITICS' CHOICE VIDEO
P.O. Box 749
Itasca, IL 60143
☎ 800–367–7765

■ The free catalog of 2,500 titles is the tip of the iceberg; some 42,000 unlisted titles are available via another special 900 number. Call for information.

DAVE'S VIDEO, THE LASER PLACE
12114 Ventura Blvd.
Studio City, CA 91604
☎ 800–736–1659

■ Ten percent discount on all discs. Dave's insists it can and will find any title currently available on the laser disc format. Catalog available on request.

FESTIVAL FILMS
2841 Irving Ave. S.
Minneapolis, MN 55408
☎ 612–870–4744

■ Specializes in foreign titles at lower-than-average prices. The price of the $2 catalog is applied to your first purchase.

FILMIC ARCHIVES
The Cinema Center
Botsford, CT 06404
☎ 800–366–1920

■ One of the few mail-order houses that only sells to teachers. Three free catalogs: one each for teachers of English, history, and kindergarten through 8th grade.

KEN CRANE'S LASER DISC SUPERSTORE
1521 Beach Blvd.
Westminster, CA 92683
☎ 800–624–3078

■ The superstore claims to have over 100,000 titles available—with an updated list every week. Every purchase is automatically discounted by 10 percent.

MONDO MOVIES
255 W. 26th St.
New York, NY 10001
☎ 212–929–2560

■ The avant-garde specialists, from raunchy B-movies to hard-to-find, experimental art-shorts. Free catalog.

SCIENCE FICTION CONTINUUM
P.O. Box 154
Colonia, NJ 07067
☎ 800–232–6002

■ The name says it all. The catalog costs $1.

WHOLE TOON CATALOG
P.O. Box 369
Dept LM
Issaquah, WA 98027
☎ 206–391–8747

■ Sheer heaven for lovers of animated film, the $2 catalog specializes in hard-to-find imports.

GEAR & GADGETS

VCRS: VCR PLUS+ can help the VCR-impaired record their favorite programs, PAGE 628 **HOME THEATERS:** What you need to set up a mini theater in your TV room, PAGE 629 **AUDIO:** The latest on sound equipment, from CD players to speakers, PAGE 630 **SPEAKERS:** Seting up speakers in the home for optimum performance, PAGE 631 **CAMCORDERS:** Digital equipment joins 8mm and VHS-C on the home video front, PAGE 632

PICTURE THIS, TV SHOPPERS

Some new sets do everything but cook your dinner

For most people, buying home entertainment equipment is a nerve-racking ordeal. "Will I end up with an obsolete system?" "Am I being taken for a ride?" What looks good and sounds great in the showroom can turn out to be a piece of junk when you get it home.

The key to avoiding disappointment is being prepared. Magazines like *Video Magazine*, *Videomaker*, *Stereo Review*, and, of course, *Consumer Reports* are great resources. The following guide should also help get you started.

TELEVISION

The past decade has seen an incredible reduction in the cost of wide screen televisions, and the near elimination of black-and-white models. Today, one of the most important factors in choosing a set is its compatibility with the rest of your system. Will your TV remote work with cable stations? Will you be able to input speakers and a receiver for "surround sound"?

Picture and sound quality are still major considerations, but the next trend is to merge audio and video into one large home theater. You'll want to make sure the investment you make in equipment now will position you for the future.

Most people decide what size TV to buy by how much money they have to spend. But too often, people discover that bigger is not always better. Within a few inches, screen size is not going to vastly improve the viewing experience, and you could end up just paying for special features that you may not want. Regardless of what size TV you buy, there are several features every set should have, and some you can do without. Here's a rundown:

■ **INTERNAL SPEAKERS.** Built-in stereo loudspeakers provide a higher quality sound than traditional mono, but external speakers do the best job. Most high-end sets are going to come with built-in stereo sound, but if you're planning on speakers anyway, don't worry about them.

■ **SLEEP-TIMER.** A built-in timer that turns TV off after a preset amount of time. Good for people who like to fall asleep to the TV.

■ **CLOSE-CAPTIONING.** Required by law on all sets 13 inches or larger. The subtitles are a plus for the hearing-impaired, or people just learning English.

■ **PREVIOUS CHANNEL.** Just press this button, and the TV automatically returns to the last channel viewed. Great for people who flip during commercials.

■ **PRESET AUDIO/VISUAL.** You'll be glad you have this feature after you've mucked around with the treble or brightness. It automatically returns the color and sound to their original settings.

■ **CABLE READY.** Common in better sets, this option allows your TV to accept cable TV directly, without the need for a costly cable converter box. There are certain premium services, however, like Pay-Per-View, that cannot be ordered without the box.

■ **PICTURE-IN-PICTURE.** Allows your TV to display two images simultaneously from different feeds (e.g., TV and VCR). A nice feature, but a baseball game in the corner of a movie love scene can be distracting. Two-tuner sets are also available, and can display two broadcast channels at a time—a boon for news junkies.

■ **REMOTE CONTROL LOCATOR.** Remote emits sound when TV set is turned on. Perfect for people who are always misplacing the clicker.

■ **VOLUME ADAPTER.** Automatically adjusts the sound to a reasonable level, even when the broadcast suddenly changes volume. A good feature for people who are irritated by loud commercials.

EXPERT QUOTE

For the serious consumer who wants as large a screen as possible, rear projection TVs are becoming more and more affordable—they currently go for around $2,500 to $3,000. But except for sports fans and movie buffs, many might find such colossal sets intimidating and space-wasting.

—*Peter Barry,* Video Magazine

■ **CHANNEL BLOCK-OUT.** Allows you to skip over certain channels while channel-surfing. A good option for parents with young children, or people who hate CNN.

SOME BRANDS WORTH CONSIDERING:

20-INCH COLOR TV (with stereo sound):
$200–$250 .... Sharp, Goldstar
$250–$300 .... RCA, Toshiba, Zenith
$300–$350 .... Hitachi, JVC, Sony
REAR PROJECTION TV (with stereo sound):
$2,000–$2,500 .... Pioneer
$3,000–$3,200 .... Sony, Hitachi
$3,200–$3,500 .... Toshiba

SATELLITE TV

Satellite services are becoming both smaller and more affordable. The trend will no doubt continue. RCA has already introduced an 18-inch satellite dish and receiver system called DSS that retails for just under $500. Toshiba and other companies are due to follow suit in 1996. The large backyard dishes that cost upward of $1,000 will soon be dinosaur carcasses.

Although satellite services like Primestar, Alphastar, and Echostar (call ☎ 800–538–2718 for customer assistance or inquiries for all three services), offer various programming packages, beginning as low as $10 to $15 a month, you must still pay for premium channels like HBO, Cinemax, and Showtime. The benefits of satellite dishes over regular cable include better picture quality, dozens more channels, and rates that are more economical in the long run. But satellite services are only a wise choice if you think you'll roam the programming firmament freely. If your tastes run mostly to network television, you'd be throwing your money away.

VIDEOCASSETTE RECORDERS

With digital video players coming on the market now, you might be reluctant to buy a traditional VCR. But just as the advent of the compact disc didn't mean the end of audiocassettes, videotape will be around long

HELP FOR THE VCR-IMPAIRED

With VCR PLUS+, even neophytes should be able to record TV shows

For the legions of Americans who still find setting a VCR's clock daunting, programming the machine to tape a show while you're away may seem truly impossible. But don't give up hope just yet: manufacturers have begun to attack the VCR conundrum with simple, on-screen programming and easy-to-follow manuals.

One of the best weapons in the war against VCR illiteracy is a system called VCR PLUS+, offered as both a built-in feature on some better VCRs and as a standalone gizmo available in electronics stores.

Here's how VCR PLUS+ works: Start by looking at the daily listings in *TV Guide* or other participating publications. You will notice there a long series of numbers following each individual show. These are the PlusCode numbers that must be entered with a special remote to let VCR PLUS+ know what you want to tape. Your machine will ask if you wish to record your program once, daily, or weekly. If any problems arise, you can call ☎ 800–432–1VCR or ☎ 900–454–PLUS for the PlusCode number to any show ($.95 a minute). A word of warning, though: Although VCR PLUS+ makes taping easier in the long run, there is a monotonous, onetime process of calibrating the system to your local listings. In addition, some machines with VCR PLUS+ cannot adapt to cable boxes, making recording a nuisance for some cable subscribers.

A number of other, similar services to VCR PLUS+ are now on the market. One of the most user-friendly is VideoGuide. A remote control tuned into the VideoGuide box allows you to record programming with a touch of a button. VideoGuide also allows you to scan TV listings up to a week in advance, as well as get up-to-the-minute sports and news information. Its cost: under $100.

enough for you to get your money's worth from any VCR you buy in the next few years. Nor are VCR manufacturers sitting on their laurels waiting to become obsolete. Video technology is constantly being improved and options are being added to recorders to meet consumer demand.

Already available are machines with automatic clocks that keep time even if the power is shut off (no more blinking 12:00!) and others that can tape and replay images from digital satellite sources. One word of warning: If you are interested in stereo sound, be sure to get a stereo VCR. Even if your TV has speakers, anything recorded on a mono VCR will sound muffled.

Any decent VCR should come equipped with a range of features to make recording and viewing easier, including preset recording options, remote control, and fast forward at double speed. There are also a number of optional features that true video aficionados might be interested in. They include:

■ **AUTO-TRACKING:** Automatically adjusts tracking to provide optimal image. Perfect for people who hate having to jump up every few minutes to fix the picture.

■ **AUTOMATIC TURN-ON:** Instantly turns on VCR and begins playing when a tape is inserted. A nice, but nonessential labor-saving option.

■ **GO-TO:** Allows you to go to a predetermined point on the tape. Cuts down on time wasted checking fast-forwarding.

■ **POWER-BACKUP:** Preserves preset records and VCR clock in case of power outage.

SOME BRANDS WORTH CONSIDERING:

Price	Brands
$300–$350	Magnavox, GE, Samsung
$350–$400	Panasonic, Quasar, RCA
$400–$450	Mitsubishi, Toshiba

BUILDING YOURSELF A HOME THEATER

For true audio/video connoisseurs, the home theater is even better than a trip to the multiplex.

The combination TV/VCR/Stereo comes close to approximating the feel of a movie theater without the expensive candy and sticky floors. The only limit is your imagination...and your pocketbook.

■ For a simple and inexpensive home theater, all you need is a VCR, a stereo TV with audio inputs, and maybe a pair of external speakers.

■ For something more advanced, consider investing in a special A/V receiver with more power and speaker outlets than your basic television. These receivers start as cheaply as $300–$400, and are a good choice if you plan to upgrade your home theater in the future. The Dolby sound of most movie sound tracks and television shows is wasted on most basic stereo receivers. Receivers with Pro Logic circuitry, available on most receivers over $350, can create acoustics once found only in movie theaters and Pavarotti's shower.

■ If the very best is what you want, get a system with THX sound. Developed by Lucasfilm, THX is replacing Dolby sound in movie theaters. THX is not a piece of machinery, but rather a set of criteria for realistically reproducing film sound tracks. Originally begun as a certification program for theaters, THX broke into the personal stereo market when manufacturers of high-end audio equipment began sending components to LucasArts for certification. Among other things, true THX sound diffuses the output of surround sound, so that the source cannot be located by ear.

■ JUST LIKE BEING THERE

Here's the basic setup for turning your entertainment room into a home theater.

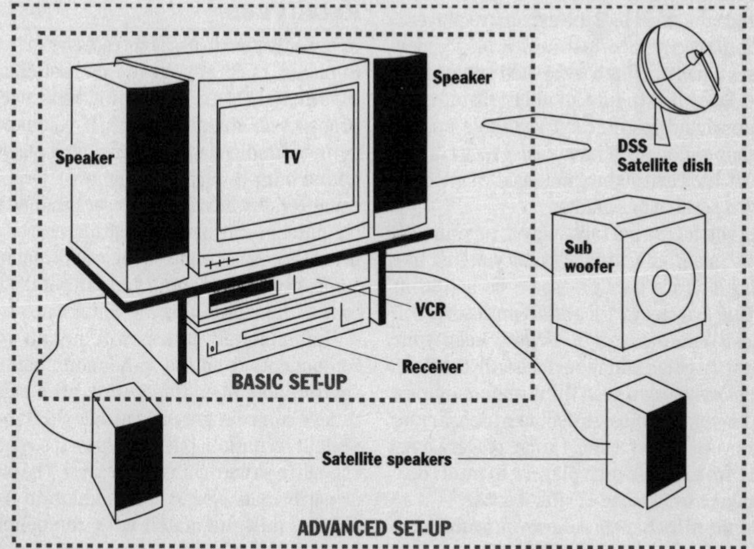

AUDIO

SOUND TIPS ON SOUND SYSTEMS

Speakers matter, but so do the other components of a music center

Boom boxes and rack stereos have their time and place in every music lover's life, but when you get serious about sound quality, you'll want to consider a stereo system with separate components. Consider these tips when shopping for great sound:

CD PLAYERS

Some CD players are better at reducing background noise; others can locate and play a track quickly. Those killer speakers won't do you any good if all they amplify is some hissing and skipping. When you visit a store, try listening to a high-end CD player through a top-of-the-line receiver and speakers. Then test CD players in your price range through the same system, looking for the one that sounds the most like the expensive player.

You should also test how a player performs when playing a scratched or damaged disc. Does it skip like an old hi-fi stereo, or jump ahead to the next readable space? Higher-end models have disc error correction, which can deduce material when faced with a scratch or smudge.

If you have a portable player, or your system's in a high traffic area, or you just like to have dance parties—you'd be better off getting a system with antiskipping capabilitites. Whether you do or not, keep your player on a flat, stable surface OFF the floor.

Before you can even think about buying a CD player, you have to decide which format suits you. In just a short time, players have gone from single-disc players to multi-disc changers to 100-disc CD jukeboxes.

Multi-disc changers allow you to queue up several (usually five or six) CDs at once and choose among them, without having to reload the machine. The two basic formats are carousel changers—with a lazy Susan–style drawer that slides halfway out for loading, and magazine changers—with a loadable cartridge that actually pops out of the machine. Which is better for you is a matter of personal preference, although carousel changers tend to jam less, and give you the luxury of listening to one CD while changing others.

CD jukeboxes are only practical if you have a gargantuan CD collection or are a professional party-thrower. Other features worth considering in a CD player are:

- **FADE OUT/FADE IN:** Adjusts pauses between tracks, making them less noticeable.
- **SAMPLING:** Lets you listen to a few seconds of each track on a disc.
- **FAVORITE TRACKS:** Remembers selected tracks on a disc.

SOME BRANDS WORTH CONSIDERING:

CAROUSEL-CHANGERS:

$150–$200	Teac, JVC
$200–$300	Sony, Onkyo, Denon
$300–$400	Marantz, Kenwood

MAGAZINE LOADING:

$180–$230	Sony, JVC
$240–$300	Pioneer, Optimus

RECEIVERS

If you only plan to use your receiver to listen to music, most any on the market should have digital FM and AM tuning, with at least 20 spaces for channel presets. If you like listening to audiocassettes, consider a receiver with a built-in tape deck (or two). Graphic equalizers are nice, but the basic bass and treble buttons are usually enough for most beginners. Also, some receivers come with loudness compensation, meaning you can get the full bass without cranking the volume up.

Unfortunately, unless you buy all your components from the same manufacturer, you're liable to end up with a grab bag of remote controls. For most people this is only a small irritation, but for others it's reason enough to go with compatible parts. The price or performance edge you might gain from playing mix-and-match with components won't do you any good if you're driven to distraction over remote control incompatibility

SOME BRANDS WORTH CONSIDERING:

$250–$200 .... Sony, Sherwood
$200–$300 .... Technics, JVC
$300–$400 .... Yamaha, Onkyo

SPEAKERS

Important features to examine when comparing speakers include clarity, bass, bandwidth, and distortion. Bring a favorite CD to the store showroom, preferably something with a variety of styles, and a heavy bass. Classical music and acid jazz are good possibilities. Any reputable dealer will allow you to gauge the speakers' performance before making a decision. But make sure the speakers are connected to a stereo comparable to your own. There's no point in buying speakers that sound great with a $1,000 system, when all you have at home is a Sony Discman.

Another important speaker feature is size. Most other stereo components are more or less the same size, but speakers can vary from ones that fit on your desk to ones as big as filing cabinets. For music lovers working with a budget and size constraints, there are two basic categories. Bookshelf speakers (surprise!) are small enough to fit on a shelf—under 3 feet tall—and run under $100. But you do sacrifice bass quality and general sound richness with smaller speakers. At around 3 to 4 feet in height, mini-tower speakers are more expensive (from $100 to $1,000) and generally occupy a square foot of floor space. The sound quality is better, but any imperfections in the music will be amplified.

There are also speakers that specialize in producing exceptional bass, speakers for outside listening, even wireless speakers for that uncluttered look. But you're likely to pay upward of $300 for some of these options. Don't be afraid to do a lot of research before buying—this is a big investment. And keep in mind how much available space you have—or you could end up sleeping on a subwoofer.

SOME BRANDS WORTH CONSIDERING:

$200–$250 .... Pioneer, Sony
$300–$400 .... Boston Acoustics, Allison
$400–$600 ..... Celestion, Infinity, Phase Tech.

■ THAT CARNEGIE HALL SOUND IN YOUR OWN HOME

The ins and outs of arranging speakers for perfect performances

■ Always try to form a triangle with your sound sources if you want great sound.

■ Speaker placements depend on how many speakers you have, their size, and the kind of sound you like.

■ To get the most out of smaller speakers, try putting them on speaker stands. It will diminish the bass slightly, but provide a more uniform sound.

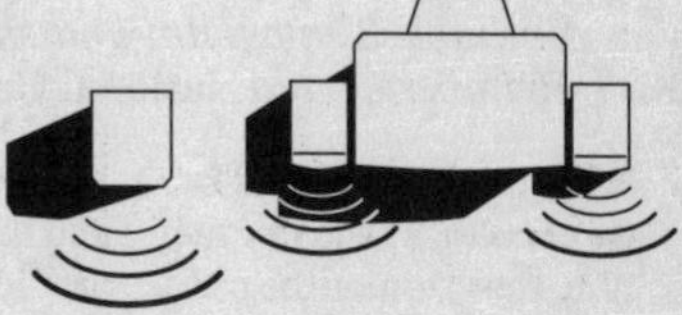

■ Keep speakers clear of walls and corners, and try to maintain a uniform distance from the stereo unit itself.

■ If you like to lie in bed while listening to music, position the speakers about 10 feet away from the bed and separated from each other as well. Additional speakers should line the perpendicular walls, not the opposite wall.

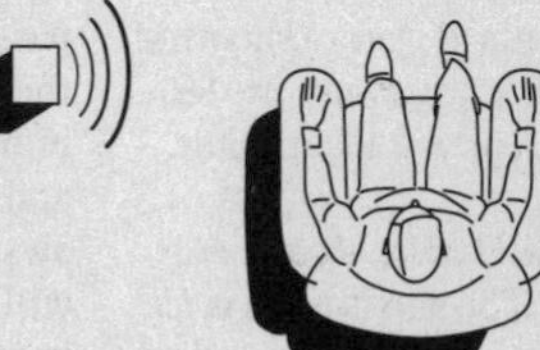

■ Do what works best for you. Every space has unique acoustics, so play around with speaker placement to find the best sound for your room.

CAMCORDERS

CAMERA... READY... ACTION!!!

8mm and VHS-C camcorders that will preserve your every moment

With camcorders there are two basic choices for the typical amateur, 8mm and VHS-C video cameras. While 8mm film allows for more filming time (about two hours, compared to half an hour at regular speed for VHS-C), VHS-C is easier to play back. Both formats weigh around two pounds and cost about the same ($650–$1,000).

For more demanding consumers with fatter wallets, higher-end versions of both models, HI8 and Super-VHS-C, offer better picture quality. Regardless, both 8mm and VHS-C should come with standard features such as auto-focus, built-in microphone, and self-timer. Some other useful options available:

- **IMAGE STABILIZER:** Takes some of the jerkiness out of handheld shots. Useful, but a tripod is always a good alternative.
- **TITLES:** Allows you to spruce up footage with a pregenerated title sequence.
- **FADE:** Lets you stop a sequence without a quick cutoff.
- **ADVANCED EDITING:** Some cameras offer "random-assemble editing," where you can select scenes from the original tape to be recorded and rearranged on the edited copy. A good feature for people who like a more professional look to their footage.

SOME BRANDS WORTH CONSIDERING:

$600–$800............RCA, Sony (8m and VHS-C)
$800–$1,000......Magnav. (VHS-C), Hitachi (8m)
$1,000–$1,500.......Canon (HI8) JVC (S-VHS-C)

DIGITAL CAMCORDERS

Sony, Panasonic, JVC, and Sharp have all released digital camcorders, with Canon expected to follow soon. Models run from $700 to $1,500 for a fully loaded version. Two useful features are image stabilization, which improves picture clarity, and a color viewfinder, which allows you to see while filming the picture as it will look on playback.

EXPERT TIPS

TAKING PHOTOS THAT WILL BE WORTH SAVING

A reliable 35mm point-and-shoot camera can produce great shots Sisse Brimberg, a top National Geographic *photographer, offers these tips:*

- **Use the right film speed for the occasion.** The faster the film, the grainier the picture. Generally, 100 ASA film is fine for outdoors and 400 ASA for indoor events. If you're shooting a sporting event, use 800 ASA or you'll get a blur.

- **Avoid taking shots at midday.** The sun is at its peak then and pictures tend to be faded. Early morning and late afternoon shoots provide the best light.

- **Keep the light source in front of you.** Too many people shoot pictures with the sun behind them, half-blinding their subjects and creating short shadows. Most subject matter will look better with lighting from behind.

- **Get in close to your subject matter.** Unless you're shooting a parade, focus in on one specific image. The more empty space you eliminate, the stronger your picture will be. Frame the picture in your head before shooting. Make sure you're not cropping anyone's head or getting a stray elbow into the picture.

JUST FOR KIDS

EXPERT LIST: R.L. Stine picks his favorite kids' books, PAGE 638 **TOYS:** For toddlers through school-age, what a toy tester says will delight and teach, PAGE 639 **GAMES:** Diversions for kids from around the world, PAGE 643 **AMUSEMENT PARKS:** The best parks for the carousel rider and thrill-seeker, PAGE 645 **ROLLER COASTERS:** The 10 baddest, according to die-hard fans, PAGE 646 **COOKING:** Tips for kids in the kitchen, PAGE 648

MEDIA LITERACY

EARNING AN "A" IN TV WATCHING

Helping children to think critically when they turn on the tube

For parents upset with TV violence , the V-chip that will be built into all new TV sets by the end of 1996 is one kind of quick fix. The blocking device will enable them to screen out programming that they consider inappropriate for their children. Bob McCannon, director of the New Mexico Media Literacy Project in Albuquerque, has a different approach. He is among the educators nationwide teaching children how to watch programs and commercials more critically so that they realize when they are being manipulated. Here is what McCannon advises parents:

■ **Don't tell people what to watch, teach them how to watch.** Media Literacy teaches people to deconstruct media. We teach kids by making our own videos and thinking about what's in them, by looking at mid afternoon talk shows, and analyzing television ads. We have a multimedia database that has hundreds of video, film, and advertising clips that we use to teach. Part of that database can be accessed on the World Wide Web at *http://www.aa.edu/*.

■ **Help children to understand the violence they see on TV.** The "Power Rangers" show is 30 percent pure violence. Every problem that is introduced on the program is eventually found to have one solution, and that solution involves violence. If you teach him to recognize that's not always the case in the real world, he won't be as affected by the program.

Cartoon violence is probably the worst—worse than real-people violence. Cartoon violence never shows any harm coming to the characters and it's all done in the spirit of fun, like the battles between the Road Runner and the Coyote.

■ **Discuss the subliminal messages you see on TV.** We use an ad about a bunch of people at a party for a cable movie company. A girl hits on a guy because she thinks he's a big-shot director. Although he's not, he pretends he is. The whole thing demonstrates a disrespect for the truth. The message is: If you lie, you get ahead.

MTV has such raw power it actually affects a child's central nervous system. The way women are portrayed on MTV is not healthy or appropriate for children.

■ **Make television watching a shared experience.** Plan to watch TV the way you plan other family activities. Watch together and ask your child questions about what he sees. If you see something objectionable, talk about it.

EXPERT PICKS

THE MOVIE MOM'S LATEST FLICKS

Whether it's history, sports, or comedy, your kids will love these

Watching a movie with your child is not just a way to pass time together, says children's film critic Nell Minow, it's also a way to teach children about the past, to expose them to ideas and points of view that will help them grow, and to share with them some of the stories, characters, and music that meant the most to you as a child. As the "Movie Mom," Minow has been organizing film festivals for her children for many years. To help parents find suitable movie fare for their children, the Movie Mom now offers a movie and video review service on the World Wide Web (http://pages.prodigy.com/VA/rcpj55a/moviemom.html). She will also be publishing *The Movie Mom's Guide to Family Movies* (Avon, 1997). Here, she recommends some of her favorite children's movies in a variety of categories, from American history to screwball comedy. All the titles mentioned should be available in video and are arranged by age appropriateness.

AMERICAN HISTORY

BEN AND ME (1954)

For 2- to 6-year-olds

■ Based on the book by Robert Lawson, this is the story of Benjamin Franklin as seen through the eyes of Amos the mouse, who claims credit for many of Franklin's achievements. The charming story is a delightful introduction to the era, to one of America's most colorful characters, and to the importance of creative thinking to solve problems.

JOHNNY TREMAIN (1957)

For 6- to 12-year-olds

■ From the book by Esther Forbes, this is about a boy who gets caught up in the early days of the Revolutionary War. He meets Paul Revere, and participates in the Boston Tea Party and the skirmish at Lexington. While not strictly accurate, the movie does a good job of exploring the reasons for the rebellion, and, unlike many movies, makes it clear that no matter how just the cause, war is always a tragedy.

1776 (1972)

For 6- to 12-year-olds

■ At least once a year, every American should watch this musical about the signing of the Declaration of Independence, preferably on July 4. The characters and the issues are vividly and frankly portrayed, and the founding fathers' faults are there as well as their virtues.

YOUNG MR. LINCOLN (1939) and ABE LINCOLN IN ILLINOIS (1940)

For 10 and up

■ Henry Fonda in the first and Raymond Massey in the second both portray beautifully this icon of American history. The first movie shows his early law practice and his tragic romance with Ann Rutledge. The second covers 30 years of his career, from shopkeeper to lawyer, through the debates with Stephen Douglas, and ending with his election to the presidency.

GLORY (1989)

For 10 and up

■ This is the true story of the all-black 54th Massachusetts Regiment during the Civil War, of their white commanding officers, and how both learned about the brutalities of war and of racism. The courage and discipline of the 54th culminated in a turning point in the war. Denzel Washington won an Oscar for his performance as a runaway slave who insists on better treatment. (R-rated for graphic battle scenes.)

ALL THE KING'S MEN (1949)

For 10 and up

■ Based on the career of Louisiana's Huey Long, this Oscar-winning story of the rise and fall of a populist politician shows how someone with ideals is corrupted by the political process. (Mature themes.) Other good movies about political campaigns include *Alias Nick Beal*, *The Candidate*, and *The Great McGinty*.

SPORTS

IT HAPPENS EVERY SPRING (1949)

For all ages

■ This is a delightful fantasy about a mild-mannered professor who loves baseball. When he invents a chemical that repels wood, he becomes a pitcher who throws balls that can't be hit by a bat. (Those were the days when bats were all made of wood.)

HOOP DREAMS (1994)

For teenagers

■ This documentary about the high school careers of two inner-city basketball players begins when they are both recruited by a mostly white prep school, the alma mater of former NBA star Isiah Thomas. One stays in the school, but the other is let go when he fails to grow and his performance on the team is not what the coach had expected. This is one of the best movies ever made about sports, about families, and about American cultural divides. (Rated PG-13 for strong language and mature themes.)

EIGHT MEN OUT (1988)

For teenagers

■ In 1919, members of the Chicago White Sox agreed to throw the World Series. This is the story of how it happened, told with a sense of the period and of the people, a love for the early days of baseball, and a feel for the loss of its innocence. Other good movies about baseball's history are *Field of Dreams*, also inspired by the Chicago Black Sox debacle; *The Bingo Long Traveling All-Stars and Motor Kings*, about the all-black league; and *A League of Their Own*, about the World War II–era women's teams.

BODY AND SOUL (1947)

For teenagers

■ John Garfield stars as a once-idealistic boxer who gets caught up in corruption and dissolution, and is ultimately redeemed by the love of his girlfriend (Lili Palmer) and his mother (Ann Revere), and by the values that still matter to him. Along with *Golden Boy* and *Champion*, this is one of a great trilogy about the fight business. It also has a rare early portrayal of a strong and capable (though tragic) black man, played by Canada Lee.

RUDY (1993)

For teenagers

■ A young man from a blue-collar family wants to play football for Notre Dame, despite the fact that he has neither the athletic nor the academic skills. His determination and commitment endear him to the team, and he is finally permitted to play for seven seconds of his last game, assuring him a place among the Fighting Irish in the record books. (Some profanity.)

FAMILIES

FIDDLER ON THE ROOF (1971)

For all ages

■ The long-running Broadway musical about the lives of Jewish families in 19th-century rural Russia is lovingly adapted, with all of the wit and poignance of the Sholom Aleichem stories that inspired it, and the songs that have become standards. Each of Tevye's daughters presents him with a new challenge as he struggles to reconcile his commitment to tradition with the changing environment around them.

CHEAPER BY THE DOZEN (1950)

For all ages

■ Based on the children's classic about the real-life pioneers of "motion study" (efficiency and ergonomics) and their 12 children, this movie shows how Frank Gilbreth (Clifton Webb) and his wife Lillian Moller Gilbreth (Myrna Loy) apply the principles of motion study they develop for factories and offices to their home and family. Through a variety of inventive games and projects, they teach the children everything from multiplication of large numbers to how to take a bath in the time it takes to hear one side of the language records Frank insists that the children hear. A sequel, *Belles on Their Toes*, covering the years after Frank's death, is almost as good.

MEET ME IN ST. LOUIS (1944)

For all ages

■ This story of the Smith family in the St. Louis of 1903 is based on the memoirs of author Sally Benson. Its pleasures are in the period detail, the glorious songs (including "The Trolley Song" and "Have Yourself a Merry Little Christmas" sung by Judy Garland) and the loving and nostalgic look at a time of innocence and optimism, where a long-distance call was almost as thrilling as having the World's Fair come to your very own city.

MR. BLANDINGS BUILDS HIS DREAM HOUSE (1948)

For all ages

■ Anyone who has ever tried to preside over renovations will appreciate the experience of the Blandings family (led by Cary Grant and Myrna Loy) after they find their "dream house" (which must then be torn down and rebuilt). Very funny—and if you add a couple of zeroes to the quoted figures, still very accurate. (Warning: There's an affectionate but stereotypical portrayal of the black housekeeper, as usual for that era.)

CLASSIC BOOKS

CHARLOTTE'S WEB (1973)

For all ages

■ E.B. White's farmyard story of the pig befriended by a spider named Charlotte is brought to life in this animated version, with the voices of Henry Gibson, Debbie Reynolds, and Paul Lynde.

HEIDI

For all ages

■ There are several good versions of the story of the girl who goes to live with her hermitlike grandfather in the Alps, and is then taken away from him to live with a wealthy crippled girl. The best are the one with Shirley Temple (1937) and one made in 1969 with Maximilian Schell and Jean Simmons.

NATIONAL VELVET (1944)

For all ages

■ Elizabeth Taylor plays Velvet Brown, a young girl who dreams of winning the Grand National with her horse, the Pi. Anne Revere won an Oscar as one of the kindest and wisest mothers in the history of the movies. Mickey Rooney plays Mi Taylor, who helps Velvet train and race her horse. This film is about faith, and dreams, and what happens after the dream comes true.

THE SWISS FAMILY ROBINSON (1960)

For all ages

■ When the Robinsons (Dorothy McGuire and John Mills) and their three boys are shipwrecked, they use what remains from the ship to build a treehouse with everything they need. But the island turns out to be a hideout for pirates. The Robinsons rescue a young girl and together they fight off the pirates with a series of booby traps. When the girl's grandfather arrives with his ship, the girl and the oldest brother stay to help establish the island as a new colony.

THE SECRET GARDEN

For all ages

■ Frances Hodgson Burnett's story of the sour young girl and the hysterical invalid boy redeemed when they find a locked up garden on the moors of Yorkshire has been beautifully filmed three times, in 1949, 1987 (for television), and 1993. In the 1949 version, featuring Margaret O'Brian and Dean Stockwell, only the garden scenes are filmed in color.

OLIVER TWIST (1948) AND OLIVER! (1968)

For all ages

■ There are at least eight versions of the Charles Dickens story of the orphan boy who becomes a pickpocket, and these are the two best. The 1948 version, directed by David Lean, was once considered too controversial to be shown in America because of Alec Guiness's portrayal of the Jewish Fagin, who teaches the boys to steal, and was not shown uncut in the U.S. until 1970. The 1968 version is a gorgeously filmed production of the long-running Broadway musical, which won an Oscar as Best Picture. Younger children will enjoy Disney's *Oliver & Company* (1988), an animated version featuring dogs as most of the main characters.

JANE EYRE (1944)
For ages 12 and up

■ Joan Fontaine plays the shy, young governess who falls in love with her charge's mysterious guardian (Orson Welles as Mr. Rochester) in this adaptation of the Charlotte Brontë classic. Watch for a very young Elizabeth Taylor as Jane's only friend at school in the early scenes.

PRIDE AND PREJUDICE (1940)
For ages 12 and up

■ Adapted from Jane Austen's novel of the second of five sisters (Greer Garson as Elizabeth Bennet) and her suitor (Laurence Olivier as Mr. Darcy), the movie, like the book, is filled with deliciously foolish characters, including the pompous Mr. Collins and his overbearing patroness, Lady Catherine. Both Elizabeth and Mr. Darcy are able to overcome pride and prejudice to find happiness together.

JUST PLAIN FUN

THE GREAT RACE (1965)
For all ages

■ This movie both spoofs and embodies all of the conventions of the classic old silent movies (it is dedicated to "Mr. Laurel and Mr. Hardy"), as Our Hero (Tony Curtis, as "The Great Leslie," always in white, with eyes and teeth that literally sparkle) competes with The Villain (Jack Lemmon as the evil Professor Fate) in a car race from New York to Paris. Natalie Wood covers the race for a newspaper. Romance, adventure, wonderful antique cars, and the biggest pie fight in movie history make this a sheer delight.

IT'S A MAD, MAD, MAD, MAD WORLD (1963)
For all ages

■ Every comedian in Hollywood—plus Spencer Tracy—appear in this story of a mad dash to buried treasure by an assortment of people becoming increasingly mad with greed. Deliriously chaotic and wildly funny.

BRINGING UP BABY (1938)
For all ages

■ Madcap heiress Katharine Hepburn falls for shy paleontologist Cary Grant and does everything she can to keep him from marrying his straitlaced fiancée. This includes insisting that he help her to deliver a pet leopard named Baby to the wilds of Connecticut. In the meantime, her dog George buries the rare dinosaur bone Grant had just received. This classic of the "screwball comedy" genre has been often imitated, but never surpassed.

DUCK SOUP (1933)
For all ages

■ The Marx Brothers bring their sublime anarchy to politics. Groucho is Prime Minister of Freedonia, and declares war on neighboring Sylvania. But it is just an excuse for a lot of wisecracks and sight gags, including the famous mirror scene, which Harpo later reenacted with Lucille Ball on her TV show.

THE ABSENT-MINDED PROFESSOR (1961)
For all ages

■ Professor Ned Brainerd (Fred McMurray) invents "flubber" (for flying rubber). He puts it on the sneakers of the school basketball team and they jump yards above the court. And he puts it on the wheels of his Model T and it flies all the way to Washington, where it is first reported as an Unidentified Flying Object, but he is finally received as a hero, and he gets the girl, too.

THE SHAGGY DOG (1959)
For all ages

■ A teenager finds a ring that turns him into a shaggy dog, with all kinds of complications from his allergic father who sneezes whenever the dog is in the house to a neighbor who turns out to be a spy. The dog saves the day (even driving a car), captures the spy, saves the girl, and turns back into the boy, just in time for the dog to get all the credit.

EXPERT LIST

BOOKS THAT GIVE R.L. STINE GOOSEBUMPS

"I'm basically a 10-year-old," says writer R.L. Stine, which would put the author of the Goosebumps *series and America's most popular children's author squarely in the middle of his intended audience of children 8 to 12 years old. For readers 10 to 13, Stine has the* Fear Street *series. Between the two series, Stine has written nearly 100 scary books for children at last count.*

Quite a phenomenon for someone whose first writing job was for a soft-drink industry magazine and who now sells over a million books a month. Here, Stine tells which children's books he loves most, and why:

PINOCCHIO
by Carlo Collodi

■ My first book. Pinocchio smashes the advice-giving cricket with a mallet, then falls asleep near the stove and burns his feet off! Obviously, a big influence on me.

WHERE THE WILD THINGS ARE
by Maurice Sendak

■ Very wild—and very dangerous. That's why it's so wonderful.

HUCKLEBERRY FINN
by Mark Twain

■ I loved it as a kid; even more as an adult. Not really a children's book, but it has to go on any list because it's the best American novel.

SOMETHING WICKED THIS WAY COMES
by Ray Bradbury

■ About a midwestern boy who sneaks off to a weird, menacing circus. Scariest book I ever read.

TREASURE ISLAND
by Robert Louis Stevenson

■ A great, gripping adventure written from a boy's point of view. As a kid, I found it absolutely thrilling.

INTERSTELLAR PIG
by William Sleator

■ Inventive, chilling sci-fi thriller by one of my favorite young-adult writers.

WHERE THE SIDEWALK ENDS
by Shel Silverstein

■ Uncle Shelby is hilarious for all ages.

SKINNYBONES
by Barbara Park

■ Wise and very funny. The only author my son ever wrote a fan letter to!

MINE'S THE BEST
by Crosby Bonsall

■ Hilarious picture book that captures the way kids argue better than any book I ever read.

TIGER EYES
by Judy Blume

■ A book that's really about something. Simply the best young-adult novel ever.

EXPERT QUOTE

"I always loved stories in which a ventriloquist dummy comes to life. So in *Night of the Living Dummy* (*Goosebumps #7*) I tried to double the suspense in this book by having TWO dummies come to life and battle it out.

I was pleased with this book because it has the mix of fear and humor I try for, along with a lot of big surprises."

EXPERT PICKS

THE TOYS KIDS WON'T PUT DOWN

Before shopping, learn what a top toy tester says will delight

Don't be daunted by holiday shopping or by that child's birthday around the corner that you need a present for. Every year Herb Weisbaum, the Seattle-based consumer correspondent for CBS' *This Morning*, conducts a huge toy test to find out which new toys kids really like. In his most recent test, which he reported on in a full week of broadcasts on CBS' *This Morning*, Weisbaum arranged for 200 different toys to be tested by 2,600 children at 30 child-care centers in the Seattle area for a full month. Six copies of each toy were made available, so that lots of kids could play with them while their teachers watched and rated the toys. "To make it through this grueling four-week challenge, a toy's got to be pretty darn good," says CBS's toy tester-in-chief Weisbaum. His recommendations and comments:

FOR TODDLERS

1. Pop-Up Pals Piano

Tiger Electronics. About $20.

"The top-rated toy for toddlers is three toys in one. Kids can use the keyboard to make music or animal sounds. But the really fun part is using the built-in microphone to sing along with the prerecorded melodies. The teachers reported that the kids made it a little karaoke thing and sang to the whole class."

2. Little People Farm

Fisher-Price. About $30.

"It takes a toddler's imagination to bring the Little People Farm to life. The open-and-close barn makes it real easy for kids to get at all the fun things inside like the feeding bins and swinging gates. When it's time to clean up, everything fits inside for easy storage."

3. Bumble Ball Bolters

Ertl Toy Company. About $20.

"Turn on these zany-looking characters with the seven legs and seven feet and you never know where they'll go. Just try not to smile, watching them wiggle and waggle about."

4. Little Helper's Workbench

Step2. About $25.

"This comes with all the tools kids need for those make-believe projects. Little boys and girls liked turning the bolts and screws and pounding the pegs all the way through the work surface. The teachers said the toy let the kids be really aggressive if they wanted to and just hammer their little hearts out."

5. Electronic Discovery Desk

Fisher-Price. About $55.

"Baby's first desk is fully equipped for both fun and learning. It's loaded with electronic surprises. The play piano rings, the mirror talks, and so does the mail slot."

FOR PRESCHOOLERS

1. Great Adventures Pirate Ship

Fisher-Price. About $40.

"Shoot the cannon at enemy attackers, put your captives in jail, and when land's found, jump into the removable dinghy and fire the grappling hook of the top-rated toy for preschoolers. The ship, with a captain and crew of four, holds up really well under heavy use."

2. Pickup Truck

Little Tikes. About $80.

"With its off-road wheels and detailed front grille, the Little Tikes pickup looks like the real thing. Kids love to pretend they're filling it up with gas. The drop-down tailgate makes it easy to haul around all sorts of things. Just getting in and out kept the kids busy."

3. Playskool Playstore

Playskool. Battery-powered. About $40.

"Kids are immediately attracted to the Playskool Playstore. It's big, bright, and colorful but, more important, it makes a lot of noise. There's the ringing cash register, the credit card machine, and electronic scanner sounds. It's perfect for role-playing."

4. Big Rig
Step2. About $140.
"This sturdy semi puts your little trucker in the driver's seat. The Big Rig is pedal-powered and has everything a kid needs for those long hauls—front-wheel steering, an enclosed cab seat, even a pretend CB radio. Teachers said it was easy to put together."

5. Le Calin-Malin Charmeur
Corolle. About $80.
"Most dolls are stiff and hard to move; this one has bean-bag stuffing, and the arms are made of cloth, so they're movable, making it easy to get those baby clothes on and off. And it smells like baby powder, even after hundreds of kids used it. The doll's name means 'the sweet charmer' in French and you'll pay for the fact that it's a French import. But it's the most popular doll we've seen in a long time."

FOR SCHOOL-AGE CHILDREN

1. 6.0V Jet Turbo Rebound 4x4
Tyco. About $70, including $20 battery pack and charger.
"The top-rated toy in this category is a remote-controlled vehicle with two distinct body styles—a tough off-road pickup on one side and a sleek sports car on the other. It turns from one to the other when it flips over. Whichever way you land, it keeps on going."

2. Tirestorm
Hasbro. About $100, with required $30 battery pack and charger.
"Tirestorm is a dragster with an attitude. Just lock in the kickstand and watch the tires on this radio-controlled racer grow over 80 percent in diameter. This toy does all sorts of stunts."

3. Animal Shelter
(Set #3634). Playmobil. About $99.
"Kids just love putting all the pieces together and playing vet and zookeeper with the animals in the Playmobil Animal Shelter. It's made with snap-together walls, which makes setting up the building easy."

4. Junior Erector Tool Center
Erector. About $30.
"The new Junior Erector Tool Center comes with everything you'll need to build six models. You can follow the directions or try something on your own. The set is made for little hands. The pieces are study and durable."

5. Crystal Explorer Sub
(Set #6175). LEGO Systems. About $30.
"Teachers gave high marks to this toy, which is fully equipped for deep-sea exploring with its two mechanical arms—one magnetic and the other a pincer. Your mission is to take a rare crystal away from the mighty octopus, but you can make up your own plans, too. The set contains 160 pieces but school-age kids have no problem putting it together."

EDUCATIONAL TOYS

(For preschool and school-age children.)

1. Follow-the-Lights Keyboard
Mattel. About $30.
"An electronic toy that combines the fun of music with the magic of lights. Press any note and the keys brighten as a familiar song is played. Switch to the free-play mode and your kids can make up their own tunes."

2. Build 'N' Play Table
Today's Kids. About $100.
"This big bright activity table for preschoolers has an all-purpose play surface for crafts and coloring, and a building grid for LEGO and Duplo blocks. With the stand-up art easel, two children can color or paint at the same time."

3. Lucky Ducks
Milton Bradley. About $18.
"Kids take turns picking one of the 12 noisy little ducks swimming round and round in a pond, hoping that the color spot underneath matches the color on their nest. Teachers say this toy teaches kids their colors and number concepts. And it keeps on going, so it also teaches them to take turns."

4. The Light-up Picture Maker
Playskool. About $23.
"Kids put their paper on top of the lighted

screen and then they can draw or trace whatever's underneath because the light shines up from below. The pictures being projected onto the paper are on special design discs, and kids can choose from 30 different images."

5. Robotix
Learning Curve Toys. Battery-powered. About $100.

"An all-new, motorized, modular building system for school-age children. The set comes with four motors, so you can make your creations move. It also allows children to create and pretend. The teachers told us they liked the toy as much as the kids did."

VIDEO GAMES

To find the top performers in this category, toy tester Weisbaum set up a one-of-a-kind game arcade at the Pacific Science Center in Seattle for three weeks, where children visiting from across the country put 89 of the newest video games through the gauntlet. Over 11,000 ratings were collected in all. The winners:

1. Battle Arena Toshinden
Sony. Pricing varies.

"The top-rated game in this year's CBS' *This Morning* test, Battle Arena Toshinden is recommended for ages 13 and up and operates on the new Sony PlayStation. Fighters can attack from the side or circle around to get away. That's because this is the first fight game to take place in a true three-dimensional world."

2. Tekken
Namco. Pricing varies.

"Recommended for ages 13 and up, Tekken also operates on the Sony PlayStation. It's a fight game with all sorts of unpredictable moves and is pretty intense."

3. Mortal Kombat 3
Nintendo. Pricing varies.

"Based on one of the most popular games of all time, this one picks up where the last one left off. Recommended for ages 13 and up, Mortal Kombat 3 for the Super Nintendo player has improved graphics, bigger fighters, and new 'Kombat Kodes' to unlock secret moves."

TOYS THAT LAUNCHED A LIFELONG QUEST

The next time you are headed for Toys "R" Us, think of the toys that made a difference for these scientists. None of the things mentioned need batteries!

■ *"As a young child, I remember enjoying playing with a big set of large wooden blocks. Using them, a seemingly infinite number of wooden cities could be built, with wonderful arches, tunnels, and perilously unstable towers."*

Bruce Alberts, cell biologist
President, National Academy of Sciences

■ *"I remember liking gyroscopes and Slinkys as a child, but for me, gadgets and toys had less appeal than specimens—specimens of the real things that scientists study. I was fascinated by a polished piece of turquoise and a glittering crystal of iron pyrite that my Aunt Marguerite gave me."*

Anne K. Behrensmeyer, paleontologist
Acting Associate Director for Science, National Museum of Natural History

■ *"When I was a youngster, age 8 or 9, I received an extraordinary gift—a plastic, raised-relief map of the United States. A map gives free rein to one's imagination, wondering about the history of towns, people who live there, waterways, characteristics of the land, rock formations and topography."*

Gordon P. Eaton, geologist
Director, U.S. Geological Survey

Source: *The Washington Post,* December 13, 1995.

HERB'S TOY HALL OF FAME

After six years of toy testing for CBS, consumer reporter Herb Weisbaum has enshrined a few in his personal Hall of Fame. All are still on the market and virtually guaranteed to delight the child you're fixing to please.

■ **Switch 'n Sound Railroad.** *Mattel. About $50.*

"For the littlest ones on your toy buying list, the Switch 'n Sound Railroad is fun to watch and fun to listen to."

■ **Angel Fish Rocker.** *Step2. About $30.*

"How's this for simple? A big yellow angel fish that's a big hit with the little ones. Something about this friendly fish just invites youngsters to climb in and start rocking. And it's well-balanced so they don't tip over."

■ **Radio Control Raceway.** *Fisher-Price. About $36.*

"Preschoolers couldn't get enough of the radio-controlled raceway. Teachers told us they'd play it over and over again. They like it because they go fast. The set is designed to grow with your child. On slow speed, beginners always stay on the track; switch to expert and the pace picks up."

■ **Elefun.** *Parker Brothers. About $25.*

"Another preschool toy that had the kids squealing with delight. Elefun is a baby elephant that's packed with fun. Just load him up with the colorful plastic and fabric butterflies, turn on the switch and watch them fly. Everytime you put the butterflies back in, you have a whole new game on."

■ **K'NEX.** *K'NEX Industries. About $40.*

"For school-age children, consider K'NEX. It's a better kind of building system, complete with rods, pulleys, tires, connectors, and rubber bands. It's the connectors that make this building set so special. Using them, kids can create all sorts of three-dimensional shapes."

■ **2XL.** *Tiger Electronics. About $30.*

"2XL is the smartest (and smart-alecky) toy robot in the world. The kids just love him. Just put in a cassette tape and 2XL quizzes you on everything from sports to history."

4. Killer Instinct

Nintendo. Pricing varies.

"Recommended for children 13 years and up, Killer Instinct is a 16-bit game, but the sophisticated 3-D graphics for the Super Nintendo player are something to see."

5. (TIED) Donkey Kong Country 2

Nintendo. Pricing varies.

"For ages 6 and up, this is a sequel to the fastest-selling video game in history, with more than 100 new levels to explore. The kids told us that it's even better than the original."

5. (TIED) Virtua Cop

Sega. Pricing varies.

"Recommended for ages 13 and up, Virtua Cop is the hit arcade game, redone for the new Sega Saturn system. It's a 3-D, first-person, in-your-face shoot-em-up game, and may be a little intense for some."

5. (TIED) Wipe Out

Sony. Pricing varies.

"Recommended for ages 6 and up, this futuristic racing and combat game runs on the Sony PlayStation. You control teams of anti-gravity racers as they scream around a series of complex tracks. Fast, fun, and challenging."

5. (TIED) GEX

3DO. Pricing varies.

"For kids 6 and up, Gex is a hyperactive gecko who shimmies up and down buildings, tail-whipping the bad guys and tossing out one-liners. It runs on a 3DO game player."

SOURCE: CBS' *This Morning* Toy Test.

GAMES

GLOBAL DIVERSION FOR YOUR CHILD

From Elizabethan ticktacktoe to French hopscotch, ideas worth a go

In today's plugged-in, high-tech world, kids have more entertainment options than the rich kid in the movie *Richie Rich*. Compared to Nintendo games and CD-ROMs, simple games of coordination and strategy may seem practically quaint. But if you're looking for games to play at your child's next play date or party, here are some world-class ideas: kids' games played in countries around the globe.

NINE MEN'S MORRIS

A strategy game like ticktacktoe, with roots in Elizabethan England. Ages: 8 and up

■ MATERIALS: A drawing utensil and two sets of 9 different colored or shaped objects (such as nickels and pennies or colored chips).

Draw three concentric squares. If using coins, the largest square should have 7-inch sides. Connect the mid-points of the squares, and draw a circle or dot at each point where two lines meet to make a total of 24 spaces (see illustration).

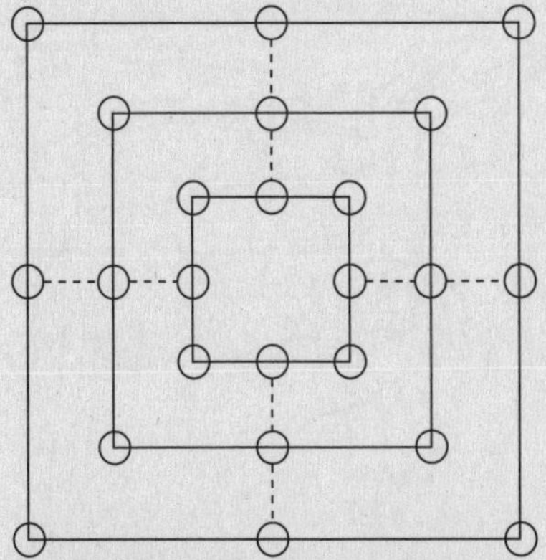

To set up for nine men's morris, draw three concentric squares. Connect the mid-points of the squares, and draw a circle or dot at each point where two lines meet.

■ HOW TO PLAY: The goal of the game is to capture the opponent's pieces and limit his ability to move on the board. When a player lines up three pieces in a row (called a "mill"), he can remove from the board an opponent's piece that itself is not part of a mill—pieces of a mill can be removed only as a last resort.

Players begin by alternately placing their nine pieces on open spaces. (Spaces in the middle of squares—from which you can move in three directions—are most desirable.) After all pieces are on the board, players take turns moving their pieces to an adjacent space, along a line, to try to form a mill. If a player forms a mill and removes an opponent's piece, he may move a piece out of that mill on one turn and move it back into the mill on the next. If your opponent forms a mill, try to block him from reforming it on successive moves.

The game ends when one player has just two pieces left, or when neither player can move. In that case, the player with the most pieces wins.

KULIT K'RANG

A Southeast Asian game of dexterity. Ages: 5 and up

■ MATERIALS: A supply of shells, pebbles, stones, or other small objects.

■ HOW TO PLAY: Players sit in a circle with a bowl in the middle. Each player has a dozen or more stones or shells. The first player places a shell on the back of her hand and flips it in the air. She then grabs a second shell from her lap and tries to catch the shell from the air. If the player keeps both shells in her hand, she keeps them in her pile. If not, she puts one shell in the bowl in the middle of the circle. Play proceeds around the circle.

Players drop out as they lose all their shells, and the last player left wins.

ESCARGOT

A French version of hopscotch. Ages: 5 and up

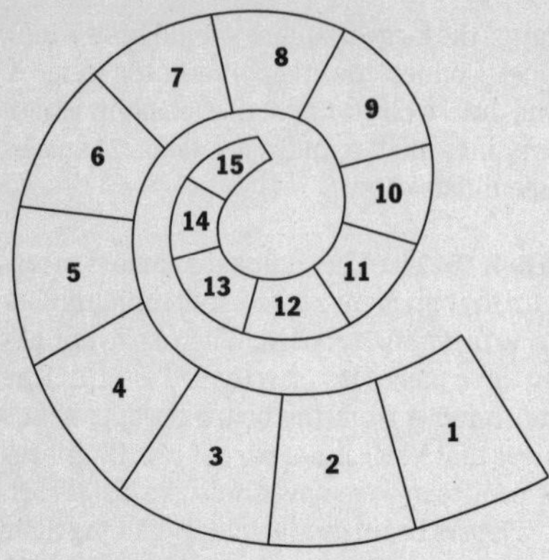

To play escargot, use chalk to draw a large snail shape on the sidewalk, about six feet in diameter. Then divide it into 15 to 20 numbered boxes.

■ **MATERIALS:** Chalk. Draw a large snail shape on the sidewalk, about six feet in diameter. ("Escargot" is French for snail.) Divide it into 15–20 numbered boxes.

■ **HOW TO PLAY:** The first player must hop to the center of the snail and back again (with a rest in the middle, if need be) without stepping on a line or letting the other foot touch down. If she succeeds, she gets to initial one box as "hers." All the other players must jump over that box; she may use it as a resting spot on future turns.

Each player who makes a successful turn gets to initial a box. The game ends when all spaces have been claimed or it is impossible for anyone to hop to the center. At game's end, the person with the most initialed boxes is the winner.

NUGLUTANG

An Eskimo target game that can be played outdoors or indoors, by anywhere from 3 to 10 players. Ages: 6 and up

■ **MATERIALS:** A 3-foot-long narrow piece of wood to use as the target, a string to hang it up, and about a dozen pencils or 1/4-inch dowels.

Eskimos traditionally use a caribou antler as the target, but caribou antlers are hard to come by in most places, so you can use a piece of wood about 3/4-inch in diameter and about 3 feet long. Drill between 10 and 15 holes along the wood, using a 1/4-inch drill bit. The holes don't need to be equal distances apart.

Attach a hook to the exact center of the board. Using a piece of string, hang the wood either from a tree branch or, if inside, from a beam or the ceiling. Hang it at a height reachable by the smallest player with his or her arm outstretched; all players should have to reach up to touch it.

■ **HOW TO PLAY:** Give each player a pencil or 1/4-inch dowel that is sanded to a dull point on both ends and will fit through the drilled holes. Players try to insert their dowels into a hole so that it stays in. That's tricky because players are not allowed to grab onto the wood target, which swings and spins wildly about the players' heads. The first player to get his stick into a hole is the winner and the game continues until the last player has succeeded.

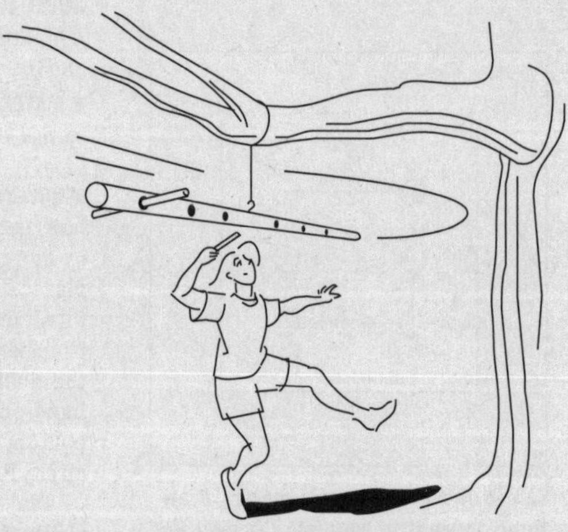

The wood target for nuglutang should be hung at a height reachable by the the smallest player.

EXPERT LIST

THRILLS, CHILLS, AND SOME SPECIAL TRILLS

Roller coasters, cotton candy, Ferris wheels, and bumper cars. Parks these days are a mix of trendy themes and old-fashioned rides, appealing to both the coaster thrill-seeker and the carousel fan. For the past nine years, Mark Wyatt has made a full-time job of checking out amusement parks. "I've loved this since I was a little kid," Wyatt says. He is the editor of Inside Track, *a newsletter that rates amusement parks and their attractions. His book,* White Knuckle Ride, *was published by Random House in 1996.*

AMUSEMENT PARKS

Following are the results of Inside Track*'s ninth annual readers' poll of the best amusement parks in America—in order of preference—and Wyatt's commentary on the winners:*

1. CEDAR POINT
Sandusky, OH
***Season:** May 11 to Labor Day. **Admission:** $25–$30*

■ Cedar Point, a 364-acre park on Lake Erie, has the most rides of any amusement park in the world. Among the 50 rides are 12, count 'em 12, roller coasters. One of the hottest rides is the Mantis, which opened in May 1996, and is the tallest standing roller coaster in the world. The Magnum XL-200, which is more than 200 feet high, was ranked the second-best roller coaster in America by *Inside Track* readers. "It's everything you'd ever want in a park," says Wyatt. The park has no heavy-handed theme—a relief to many.

2. KNOEBELS AMUSEMENT RESORT
Elysburg, PA
***Season:** May 1 to third week in September. **Admission:** Free for the park; individual rides are extra.*

■ One of the very few free-admission parks left in the world. Knoebels charges by the ride, so park-goers can also picnic or walk around for free. Old-fashioned rides such as bumper cars are mixed with attractions such as a haunted house. There's a huge swimming pool and campground, and the whole park is shaded by large trees.

3. KENNYWOOD
West Mifflin, PA
***Season:** April 22 to Labor Day. **Admission:** $14–$16*

■ Although Dollywood, the Tennessee theme park, is actually named after Dolly Parton, Kennywood has no affiliation with her sometimes singing partner Kenny Rogers. At age 100, Kennywood is one of the oldest amusement parks in the country. It has four excellent roller coasters, and is always voted the best park for

EXPERT PICKS

***Inside Track* readers rated these waterparks the best they've tried:**

1. **Schlitterbahn, New Braunfels, TX**
2. **Typhoon Lagoon, Lake Buena Vista, FL**
3. **Wildwater Kingdom, Allentown, PA**
4. **Blizzard Beach, Lake Buena Vista, FL**
5. **The Beach, Mason, OH**
6. **Wet 'n Wild, Orlando, FL**
7. **Six Flags Wet 'n Wild, Arlington, TX**
8. **Splashin' Safari, Santa Claus, IN**
9. **Myrtle Waves, North Myrtle Beach, SC**
10. **Action Park, Vernon Valley, NJ**

Source: Inside Track *(September 1995).*

■ EXPERT LIST

french fries on Wyatt's list.

4. DISNEYLAND
Anaheim, CA
Season: *Every day, except Christmas.* ***Admission:*** *$30–$35*

■ The theme park that came before all other theme parks. All regional theme parks descended from Disneyland, and in the *Inside Track* poll Walt Disney's first love finishes well ahead of the much larger Disney World. Walt Disney was the first person to build a theme park around the idea that adults should also have fun. The world's most famous animated characters stroll through the park as if they own it.

5. HOLIDAY WORLD
Santa Claus, IN
Season: *May 6 to the second week in September*
Admission: *$16–$18*

■ Fifty years old in 1996, Holiday World was originally a park based on the Santa Claus theme that the town's name suggests. Now the park has three sections: permanent versions of Christmas, Fourth of July, and Halloween. The park is located in the middle of nowhere, admits Wyatt, but its number-three-ranked roller coaster, the Raven, and its waterpark, Splashin' Safari, will put it on the map, he guarantees.

6. SIX FLAGS MAGIC MOUNTAIN
Valencia, CA
Season: *Every day*
Admission: *$25–$30*

■ Six Flags is best known for its thrill rides, including 10 roller coasters. Its latest is a 415-foot-high ride called Superman: The Escape. Like all of the Six Flags parks, this one is owned by Time Warner and therefore many Warner Bros. characters amble around the park.

7. BUSCH GARDENS
Williamsburg, VA
Season: *March 25 to October.* ***Admission:*** *$25–$30*

■ One of the most beautifully landscaped parks in the world, Busch Gardens has a European theme, which means that you can explore the food and culture of countries such as Germany, France, and England. Beer fans can take a tour of the Anheuser-Busch brewery, complete with tastings. The Busch Clydesdale horses are a mascot of the park. It also boasts three world-class roller coasters.

8. WALT DISNEY WORLD MAGIC KINGDOM
Lake Buena Vista, FL
Season: *Every day.* ***Admission:*** *$35–$40*

■ The biggest theme park in the world. Disney World has so much more space than Disneyland that what people who have gone to both remember is how big everything is at Disney World, according to Wyatt. The Magic Kingdom has 34 attractions, all kinds of shows, and great rides, including the roller coaster

EXPERT PICKS

The baddest roller coasters in the entire nation, according to *Inside Track's* coaster riders:

1. **Texas Giant, Six Flags Over Texas, Arlington, TX**
2. **Magnum XL-200, Cedar Point, Sandusky, OH**
3. **Raven, Holiday World, Santa Claus, IN**
4. **Raptor, Cedar Point, Sandusky, OH**
5. **Comet, The Great Escape, Lake George, NY**
6. **The Beast, Paramount's Kings Island, OH**
7. **Timber Wolf, Worlds of Fun, Kansas City, MO**
8. **Phoenix, Knoebels Resort, Elysburg, PA**
9. **Kumba, Busch Gardens, Tampa, FL**
10. **Steel Phantom, Kennywood, West Mifflin, PA**

Source: Inside Track *(September 1995).*

■ EXPERT LIST

Space Mountain. Fireworks are shown many nights and Disney characters are ubiquitous.

9. SIX FLAGS OVER MID-AMERICA
Eureka, MO
***Season:** March 25 to Labor Day. **Admission:** $25–$30*

■ Another TimeWarner theme park, with rides based on Warner characters, including Batman. The park features different periods of U.S. history, such as the 1904 World's Fair and the Wild West.

10. SIX FLAGS OVER TEXAS
Arlington, TX
***Season:** March 4 to Christmas. **Admission:** $25–$30*

■ The original Six Flags park, its name comes from the six different flags—those of Mexico, Spain, France, Texas, the Confederacy, and the U.S.—that have flown over Texas. You'll find the top-rated roller coaster on Wyatt's list below. Its name befits it: The Texas Giant.

RIDES

From the man who's probably ridden more roller coasters than anyone alive, here are Mark Wyatt's personal favorites when it comes to rides:

1. RAPTOR
Cedar Point, Sandusky, OH

■ I like rides that are out of control, that are on the edge. The reason to ride a thrill ride is to get thrilled.

2. THE PHOENIX
Knoebels Amusement Resort, Elysburg, PA

■ This is a wooden coaster, as opposed to steel, which has an entirely different feel. There are only about 100 wood coasters left in North America.

3. THE TEXAS GIANT
Six Flags Over Texas Arlington, TX

■ It's really fast, has long, fast drops, and good curves. It always runs well.

4. THE BIG SHOT
Stratosphere Tower Las Vegas, NV

■ This ride starts you off at 930 feet off the ground, then propels you straight up another 200 feet.

5. WHITE WATER CANYON
Paramount's Kings Dominion, Doswell, VA

■ This is one of the wettest water rides. You really get soaked!

EXPERT PICKS

The top amusement park attractions in America, according to *Inside Track* readers:

1. **Haunted House, Knoebels Amusement Resort, Elysburg, PA**
2. **Indiana Jones Adventure, Disneyland, Anaheim, CA**
3. **Back to the Future, Universal Studios, Orlando, FL, and Hollywood, CA**
4. **Skycoaster, Kennywood, West Mifflin, PA**
5. **Escape From Pompeii, Busch Gardens, Williamsburg, VA**
6. **Haunted Mansion, Magic Kingdom, Lake Buena Vista, FL**
7. **Twilight Zone Tower of Terror, Disney-MGM Studios, Orlando, FL**
8. **Noah's Ark, Kennywood, West Mifflin, PA**
9. **Mountain Slidewinder, Dollywood, Pigeon Forge, TN**
10. **Pirates of the Caribbean, Disneyland, Anaheim, CA**

Source: Inside Track *(September 1995).*

EXPERT TIPS

JOYS OF COOKING (WITH YOUR KIDS)

Cooking isn't just fun, it can teach science and develop self-esteem

"We live in a world where children aren't involved in many adult processes," says cookbook writer Mollie Katzen, author of *Moosewood Cookbook* (Ten Speed Press, 1977; rev. 1992), and co-author, with Ann Henderson, of *Pretend Soup & Other Real Recipes: A Cookbook for Preschoolers and Up* (Tricycle Press, 1994). Katzen, who writes a kids' cooking column for *Family Fun Magazine* and is the host of *Mollie Katzen's Cooking Show* on public television, shares her tips:

■ **Contrary to popular belief, children don't always like to make messes.**

They love breaking eggs, for example, but hate having sticky fingers. They also worry that the adult will get angry if they're messy. A child-size table eliminates the fear of dropping things from a counter. Most kids have no idea what goes on in cooking because it's all done above their head. Most of our testers thought pizza comes from the telephone.

■ **Cooking can teach science.**

Kids love to see dry turn into wet, or butter melt. They love to guess whether the muffins will get bigger or smaller. Whether they know it or not, chemistry fascinates them.

■ **Waiting for something to cool off or bake can give a child a sense of time.**

For kids, the most difficult part of cooking is waiting. Patience is an adult skill, a struggle. Cooking can also help a child learn the concept of sequential events—that you can't put the batter in the pan before you've mixed the ingredients.

■ **Never leave a child alone in a kitchen.**

Let him push the button on a blender, but not put the ingredients in. Use only plastic or serrated dinner knives, and unplug all food processors when not in use. Never let a child take anything out of an oven, and remind him every few minutes if something is hot.

■ **When the recipe is finished, share it.**

Children have a strong nurturing drive, and sharing something they have made gives them a good sense of self-esteem.

■ **GREEN SPAGHETTI**

When Mollie Katzen tested recipes with children, their favorite was "Green Spaghetti." Yield: 3 or 4 small servings.

Tools: Pot for boiling spaghetti; colander; can of soup for smashing garlic; cutting board; 1-cup measure; 1/4-cup measure; salt and pepper shakers; food processor or blender; rubber spatula; large bowl for the spaghetti; forks for mixing and eating; plates for eating.

Ingredients: About 1/2 pound uncooked spaghetti; 1/4 cup olive oil; 3 packed cups basil leaves (about 5 sprigs); 6 shakes salt; 3 shakes pepper; 1 medium-small clove garlic; 1/4 cup Parmesan cheese; a little extra olive oil and cheese.

Directions:

1. A grown-up begins cooking the spaghetti.
2. Take all the basil leaves off the stems; put the leaves into the food processor.
3. On a cutting board, smash the garlic with the soup can and peel it. Add it to the basil, and blend.
4. Add cheese, oil, salt and pepper, and blend again until it forms a thick paste.
5. Transfer the paste to a bowlful of hot spaghetti, and mix well with a fork.
6. Optional: drizzle on a little extra olive oil, and sprinkle on extra cheese.
7. Put on individual plates, and eat!

SOURCE: Reprinted with permission from *Pretend Soup & Other Real Recipes: A Cookbook for Preschoolers and Up* (Tricycle Press, ©1994) by Mollie Katzen and Ann Henderson.

CHAPTER TEN

COMPUTERS

EXPERT QUOTES

"No studies have proven that health problems arise directly from using monitors frequently."
—John R. Quain, multimedia maven,
Page 656

"Even if you're not a Jurassic junkie, you'll be hooked on this intelligent, multimedia look at dinosaurs."
—Ron White, senior editor *PC Computing* magazine,
Page 664

"If you want your kids to get the most from your home computer, don't limit your involvement to simply choosing software."
—Cathy Miranker and Alison Elliott, authors of *The Computer Museum Guide to the Best Software for Kids,*
Page 670

■ **THE YEAR AHEAD: EXPECT** computer prices to dip in January, as they usually do... **CHECK** regularly for computer viruses...**WORRY** about the future of Apple's Macintosh... **LOOK AHEAD** to the introduction of the $500 Net PC... **CHEER** as the price of color printers continue to drop... **SIGN UP** for Wow!, CompuServe's new online service for kids... **INVEST** in the fastest modem available... **SURF** the Web for everything under the sun...

HARDWARE 650

SOFTWARE 664

ONLINE 681

HARDWARE

BASICS: The anatomy of a computer, PAGE 652 **EXPERT LIST:** Computer companies you can trust, PAGE 654 **PLATFORMS:** Should you get a PC or a Mac? PAGE 655 **PERIPHERALS:** The essentials on monitors, printers, and modems, PAGE 656 **UPGRADES:** Getting an old computer up to speed, PAGE 659 **PORTABLES:** What to look for in a small computer, PAGE 660 **HACKER'S GUIDE:** How to prevent backaches and eyestrain, PAGE 662

STRATEGIES

THE SMART WAY TO BUY A PC

Buy the latest model, a name brand, and remember prices dip in January

Personal computers don't last forever. It's not that computers die—though some parts will fail eventually—but they become long in the tooth. The technology changes so rapidly that after a few years, a PC can't run the new crop of software. Three to five years is about how long you can expect to be satisfied with your PC. Mary Kathleen Flynn, cyberspace correspondent for MSNBC, the new cable channel, offers some buying tips:

■ **STRETCH YOUR BUDGET.** It may sound extravagant, but in fact the most prudent approach to buying a new PC is to spend as much as you possibly can to get the most leading-edge machine you can afford. Prices are dropping all the time, but generally that's to make way for the next set of PCs with new features. The planned obsolescence cycle in the computer industry is about every six months. Be wary of last year's, or last season's, models.

PCs aren't like televisions or other appliances, where the new features are often just bells and whistles (though there's some of that as you'll see below). The brain and guts of PCs are improving all the time, with new product lines introduced each spring and fall. To get a modern complete system (PC, monitor, and printer), you'll have to pay about $3,000.

It's tempting to keep delaying purchasing a PC. After all, the longer you wait, the more power your $3,000 will buy. But don't make the mistake some people have made with camcorders; they waited so long to buy one that they miss documenting their kids' toddler years. Post-holiday price drops make January an especially good time to buy.

■ **WHAT TO LOOK FOR.** Pass up the bargain-priced entry-level models and move up to the middle of the product line. Currently, the configuration you should choose is a 133 megahertz Pentium or PowerPC, 8 (or better yet, 16) megabytes of memory, a 1.2 gigabyte hard disk, a quadruple-speed (or faster) CD-ROM drive and a 28.8 kilobit-per-second modem.

PC makers are adding more and more fancy features to their machines. Some may be very useful—such as a built-in scanner for photos or documents—while others may seem redundant for home users, like an answering machine. Don't cut corners on the key components listed above to buy an extra frill unless you've really got your heart set on it.

■ **SPECS TO INSIST ON**

Basic computing requires no more than a keyboard, a mouse, a monitor, and a central processing unit (CPU). You don't need to know the exact meaning of all the terms, but you do need to know enough to make sure a potential purchase has the right features in the right amounts and speeds. Keep this in mind when you go shopping for a new system.

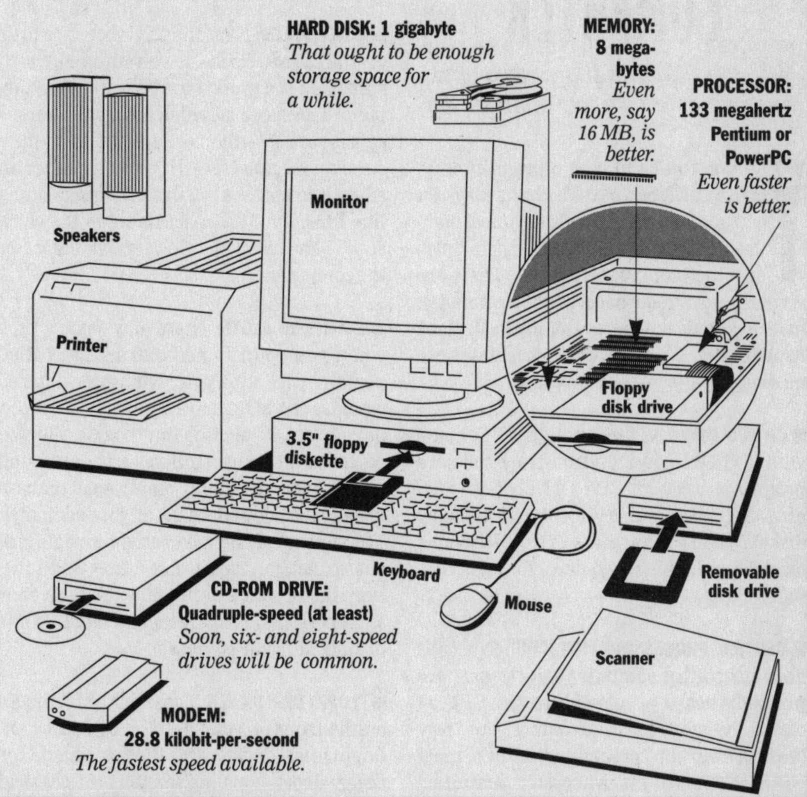

■ **CHOOSE A NAME BRAND.** Although sophisticated computer owners may ask a favorite local company to build them a PC—or they may even "grow their own"—less technically savvy buyers should always choose a name brand. You don't need to stick with the top 10, but make sure the manufacturer you're considering is distributed nationally. Check the reviews in *PC Magazine* and other computer magazines to find reputable companies.

Even with a big name there's no guarantee of smooth sailing. PCs are complicated, and things do go wrong from time to time. But at least with a bigger company, chances are better that it will still be in business a few years later and that it will have a technical staff to help you solve problems.

■ **CONSIDER MAIL ORDER.** Many PC buyers may find the idea of walking into a store more comfortable than buying over the phone. And today, computer warehouses, such as CompUSA and Computer City, offer deals comparable to mail-order houses. But the big advantage to working with a company like Gateway 2000, which doesn't sell through stores at all, is that you can pick and choose exactly which features you want.

THE BASICS

THE ANATOMY OF A COMPUTER

You, too, can talk like a nerd once you've mastered a few basic terms

You don't have to take a programming course or lock yourself up for days on end attempting to decode technical manuals to understand the basic principles on which computers operate. There are virtually no moving parts inside a computer, just electronic messages zipping from place to place. Here's a quick course on how those messages get from place to place.

■ **CD-ROM DRIVE:** Virtually all new PCs come with CD-ROM drives, and most new software programs come on CD-ROM disks (which hold 450 times as much information as floppy disks). When buying a new drive, insist on at least a quadruple-speed drive for smoother video clips.

■ **CENTRAL PROCESSING UNIT (CPU):** The CPU does most of the computer's work; you have probably heard people calling the CPU by one of its more familiar names, the "processing chip" or "processor." In PCs, most CPUs are based on processors manufactured by Intel Corp.'s 80X86 series ("X" stands for a number from 2 to 4). But since folks in the computer industry like to shorten nomenclature, you'll often hear a PC referred to as a "286," "386," or "486." The higher the number, the faster the PC. To make things a bit more complicated, however, the fastest and newest Intel processor doesn't have a number at all; it's called the Pentium processor. The processors inside Macs are made especially for them by Apple, and people don't generally refer to Macs by the speed of the processor—they just identify Macs by model ("Macintosh SE," "Mac II," and so on).

■ **CHASSIS:** This is the metal or plastic case that covers all the stuff inside your computer. Once you become a computer-tinkerer, you can unscrew the chassis and remove it to add more memory, peripheral cards, and other stuff.

■ **CLOCK SPEED:** Near the CPU there is a little crystal called a clock—it whirs around, which speeds up the processing power of the computer. The speed at which the clock whirs is called—ta dah!—the clock speed, and it's measured in megahertz (MHz). When you see an advertisement for a PC, and it reads something like P133, the "133" part refers to the clock speed—the faster the clock speed, the faster the computer.

■ **EXPANSION SLOTS:** There may come a time when you want to add extra stuff, called peripherals, onto your computer—stereo sound, a CD-ROM drive, a scanner, an internal modem. When this time comes, you will be glad that your computer has expansion slots, which are simply empty slots that are usually located at the back of your computer. The slots are designed to accommodate special expansion cards that either add functionality to your computer by themselves or allow peripherals like modems and CD-ROMs to "talk" to your computer.

■ **FLOPPY DISK DRIVES:** Those one or two doors on the front of your desktop computer are floppy disk drives, and they are made for floppy disks—smaller versions (in physical size and storage space) of your hard disk. Floppy disks are handy because they let you carry your data around from computer to computer, unlike hard disks, which stay inside the computer all the time. Floppy disks come in two sizes: 3 1/2 inch and 5 1/4 inch. Some computers have two disk drives for both sizes. It's more common now, however, for computers to have just one 3 1/2-inch drive, because that's the most popular size. Floppy disks get their name from the flexible Mylar disks that are inside their plastic casings.

■ **HARD DISK:** You'll probably never see your hard disk (it's nestled inside your computer),

HOW TO KEEP YOUR PC HUMMING

Like a car, a PC will perform better if you take proper care of it. Here are some tips and tools to help keep it whizzing along nicely.

■ **CHECK FOR VIRUSES.** Every time you use a floppy disk to install a new program or copy files or download a file from an online service or the Internet, you're vulnerable to a computer virus. The damage a virus can cause ranges from silly pranks to complete demolition of all your data. For $50 and up, programs from Symantec (which carry the well-known "Norton" moniker), IBM, McAfee Associates, and others will scan the PC and remove any viruses found. A word to the wise: Buy a program that includes monthly updates.

■ **BACK UP YOUR WORK.** It's a fact of life: Hard disks can fail. To protect yourself from losing information if your hard disk crashes, make frequent copies, known as "backups" of the hard disk. You can use the simple utilities that are included in modern operating systems. If they don't let you do something fancy—such as setting up an automatic backup every Friday night—you can buy more sophisticated backup programs from Symantec and others for less than $100. Got a lot of files, say 200 photos you've scanned in for an electronic family album? Forget about floppy-disk–based backup and buy a tape backup drive, which costs about $150, or one of the new rewritable CD-ROM drives, which range from $350 to $1,000.

■ **CLEAN UP YOUR HARD DISK.** The classic choice for hard-disk maintenance is Norton Utilities from Symantec, available for around $100 for DOS, Macintosh, and Windows users. This program has lots of diagnostic and repair tools. It analyzes the hard disk to find and fix problems like "lost clusters," tiny portions of the disk that seem to be in use but aren't accounted for anywhere. It also "defrags" the hard disk, pulling together scattered fragments of files that can slow down disk access. Every six months or so, give the hard disk a tune-up with a program like Gibson Research's SpinRite (about $90). It looks deep into the surface of the hard disk to spot damaged areas and then blocks them off so data can't be stored in those risky spaces.

but you'll use it all the time. The hard disk is your computer's filing cabinet; it stores all the letters, reports, spreadsheets, and other documents that you work on, as well as all your applications (the software that makes it possible for you to create those documents). When you store something on your hard disk, it's like making an audio recording on a cassette tape—the information is scratched on the disk's magnetic surface, and when you want to look at that information, the disk plays it back to you like a song on a tape. The amount of storage space a hard disk has is measured in megabytes (MB), and most computers aren't sold with less than a 540 MB hard drive today. If you're buying a new PC, get a hard disk no smaller than 1 gigabyte.

■ **KEYBOARD:** A computer keyboard is different from that of a typewriter. Many have "function" keys labeled F1 through F12 that you can program to carry out various—you guessed it—functions. Most have "arrow" keys that let you move the cursor (that blinking bar or square) around the monitor's screen, a "delete" key, and other specialized keys that give the computer information.

■ **MODEM:** Due to the popularity of the Internet, a modem is considered basic equipment these days and comes on virtually all new PCs. It lets you exchange data over the telephone lines. When shopping for a new one, look for a speed of 28.8 kilobits per second (for more buying tips, see page 658).

■ MONITOR: Also called displays, monitors come in different sizes and resolutions, and in color or monochrome (for more info, see page 656). A computer monitor may look like a single component, but it's actually two: the monitor itself and a display adapter. The display adapter is a card that fits into one of your computer's expansion slots, and it produces the video information for the monitor. When you buy a computer, it will come with both of these components—but if, someday, you want to buy a bigger, better monitor, you'll probably have to buy a new display adapter, too.

■ MOTHERBOARD: This circuit board is where the CPU, RAM, and the other "brains" of the computer live. It's called the motherboard because it has to do the most work.

■ MOUSE: Some older PCs didn't come with these, but today most do—and Macs have always come with them. A small plastic gizmo with one or several buttons on top, the mouse attaches to your computer with a cord. Using a mouse is just an easier way of moving the cursor around the screen. Moving the mouse around with your hand, you'll see an arrow or some other symbol (sometimes something called an I-bar) on your screen corresponding with your movements; when you click on the left-hand mouse button at a certain spot, the arrow or symbol will put the cursor there. Some computers come with a "trackball" instead of a mouse; it's a different design, but it does the same thing. Mice and trackballs can carry out more complex commands, too.

EXPERT PICKS

Robert W. Kane supervises the testing of 1,000-plus PCs a year as director of ZD Labs, the world's largest independent computer testing facility. Here are the companies Kane says deliver the highest quality PCs.

■ LEADERS OF THE PACK:
Apple Computer, Compaq Computer Corp., Hewlett-Packard Co., IBM

■ WORTHY FOLLOWERS:
Acer America Corp., Dell Computer Corp., Gateway 2000, Packard Bell Electronics

■ NICHE PLAYERS:
Portables: NEC and Toshiba.
Business: AST Research and Digital Equipment Corp.
Apple clones: Power Computing Corp.

■ RANDOM ACCESS MEMORY (RAM): You know that feeling you get when you're juggling several projects at the same time—that I-only-have-enough-brainpower-to-do-three-things-at-once feeling? That's what a computer's RAM, or just plain "memory," is like: the kind of brainpower a computer needs to let you work on several programs at once. RAM is measured in megabytes (MB), and the more memory you have, the more programs you'll be able to use—faster, at once. To be safe, don't get a computer with less than 4 MB of RAM (otherwise, your programs will run sluggishly). If you need more (you may, especially if you use a lot of graphics applications), you can always buy more (it costs around $40 per megabyte, and prices are dropping). RAM often comes in physical units called SIMMs (Single Inline Memory Modules), which look like little plastic rectangles with computer chips on them. One SIMM can hold 1 MB, 4 MB or, 16 MB of memory. Before you buy your computer, ask the salesperson how much RAM you can add to the system; the ideal answer is "64 MB."

■ SPEAKERS: Today's multimedia PCs come with a sound card and a pair of speakers. (If you've got an old computer and are shopping for new speakers, make sure they are "self-powered.") Typically, speakers are separate units that sit on your desk, but in some new PCs, the speakers are attached to the monitor.

PLATFORMS

SHOULD YOU GET A PC OR A MAC?

It's the toughest decision you'll have to make in buying a computer

If you've ever wandered into a computer store, you've probably left with your head spinning. With so many different kinds of computers—Apple, Compaq, IBM, Gateway 2000, Packard Bell, and countless others—how will you ever know which one to buy? The first thing you should know about computers is that there is basically only one choice for the home user: PCs or Macintosh.

PC stands for "personal computer," the name of the first computer built especially for one person to use. PCs originally were made by IBM, but today many different computer manufacturers make PCs. This is why you sometimes hear people calling PCs "IBM-compatibles," "IBM clones," or "PC-compatibles." Don't worry, they all basically use the same type of software and hardware. PCs make up about 90 percent of the home computers in the world today.

The Macintosh accounts for the remaining 10 percent. Apple Computer released the first Macintosh in 1984 and has held the proprietary rights to its design since then, but announced in 1995, however, that it would begin licensing the design to other manufacturers. Since then, several companies have begun to produce clones of comparable quality.

Macintoshes (also known as "Macs") use completely different software and hardware from PCs, which until recently made it impossible to exchange information between the two systems without special software. A new chip, called the PowerPC, first introduced in 1994, now makes it possible for computers to "read" the different software.

The historical stereotype has been that Macs are more "user-friendly"—that their interface (what you see on the screen when you turn on the computer) is more intuitive (computer-speak for easy to learn, even if you don't read the manual)—while PCs are for so-called "power users," folks who care more about speed and data-crunching capabilities than pretty pictures.

The truth is, with modern technology, there is very little difference between PCs and Macs. The Macintosh continues to enjoy a very loyal following, but the tough times Apple has experienced over the last year may deter all but die-hard fans from buying a new Mac. The Mac's future has never been shakier.

LOOKING AHEAD: A COMPUTER FOR $500

The PC as we know it may soon be out of vogue, if companies like Sun Microsystems and Oracle Corp. get their way. These firms, which are betting heavily on the Internet, are touting a new concept in computers: the Net PC.

Essentially a monitor, keyboard, and network connection, a Net PC could cost as little as $500 and would do nothing but access the Internet. New programming languages, like Java, developed by Sun, mean that mini programs, called applets, can live on the Internet. With a Net PC, you could use these applets on an as-needed basis—and not have to pay today's prices for full-fledged programs that hog space on a hard disk. You could even store files and programs on the Internet, or, more likely, on an "intranet" owned by your employer.

Whether or not this concept takes off—or can, in fact, be executed at the $500 price point—remains to be seen. Some niche products have already come out in 1996, but maintream devices with mass appeal are yet to appear.

PERIPHERALS

WHAT YOU'LL ALSO NEED

A computer isn't complete without a monitor, printer, and modem

Buying a home computing system often doesn't end with the purchase of a spanking new PC. There are some extras you may desire—especially if you bought the machine a few years ago. A faster modem and a bigger monitor are common reasons to return to the computer store. Many families find that a color printer, which sometimes comes bundled with a new PC for a low price, is a must. Here are the buying strategies from well-known experts on how to pick the three devices.

MONITORING MONITORS

Multimedia maven John R. Quain has been staring at monitors for 12 years in the course of testing and evaluating all kinds of computer products for a variety of magazines, including Entertainment Weekly, Fast Company, *and* PC Magazine. *Here are his views on monitors.*

■ What's the most important thing to look for?

The best monitor is the one that looks good to you. Carefully examine a potential purchase in the store. Make sure the onscreen image is not bowed or blurry.

■ What are the key specs?

For sharp, detailed images, get a resolution of at least 800 by 600 pixels and a dot pitch (the distance between pixels of the same color) of .28 or smaller. Also look for a "refresh rate"—how often the monitor can redraw the screen—of 72 Hertz or higher, which causes less eyestrain than lower ones. These days most monitors are "noninterlaced," which is what you want.

■ What size monitor should you buy?

The biggest one you can afford. A 15-inch unit (between $300 and $500) is adequate for most people but not for those who want to view several open windows onscreen at the same time. A better choice, budget permitting, is 17 inches (around $800).

■ Should you be concerned about radiation?

The type of radiation in question is called extremely low frequency (ELF), which is emitted in low doses from computer monitors. No studies have proved that health problems arise directly from using monitors frequently, but ELF from other sources (such as electrical transmission and distribution lines) has been linked with increased incidence of cancer. Current monitors emit low radiation and are considered reasonably safe.

■ Do you recommend anti-glare filters?

No. Most monitors have some form of anti-glare treatment, so extra filters, which cost $50 to $150, are not necessary—unless you work in an especially bright room.

■ Do you need to know anything special to hook up a laptop to a monitor?

Make sure the laptop can accept an external

EXPERT TIP

Monitor dirty? Here's what the editors of *PC Commuting* suggest: Clean it with Windex, ammonia, or even vinegar—but don't use alcohol. And spray your cleanser on a rag first, then clean the monitor. Otherwise you'll remove the coating on your screen.

monitor and that it is able to display the image on both screens at the same time.

■ What's the state of the art?

Professional artists and serious game players will appreciate a 21-inch monitor with 1600 by 1200 resolution and a refresh rate of 85 Hz. Two popular brands are Nanao and Nokia for the high end. These monitors start at $2,000.

7. PICKING A PRINTER

As the director and principal analyst of electronic printer services at Dataquest, a market research firm in San Jose, Calif., Bob Fennell's middle name is hard copy. This is how he shops for the perfect printer.

■ How do you choose between a laser printer and an inkjet?

If you're only interested in printing text, then a laser printer is the best option. But for those planning to print color and graphics, you're better off with an inkjet. Try to get a salesperson to print out a test document you designed yourself. A family newsletter or greeting card will do nicely.

■ How much will you have to spend?

A good laser printer will cost around $300 and up for faster machines. For a decent inkjet, expect to spend between $250 and $550, possibly more for color.

■ What's the best speed?

A decent laser printer should print between four and eight pages per minute. An inkjet printer prints between two and six pages per minute in monochrome. You should get the fastest printer you can afford. To test color printing speed, print out one color page. Bear in mind that it takes longer to print a document that has highly detailed graphics. A regular color printout should take between one and two minutes.

■ What about the resolution?

Resolution in printers is measured in dots per inch (dpi). Resolutions start at 300 dpi, but for crisp, professional-looking output, look for 600 or 720 dpi.

■ Do you recommend multipurpose devices that combine printer, copier, and fax machine?

Make sure that you're not buying anything you don't need; your PC may already have fax capability, for example. One advantage of a multipurpose machine is that it is less expensive than buying all the features separately. A disadvantage is that when one feature malfunctions, the others may also fail.

■ What are the best brands?

For laser: Apple, Brother, Hewlett-Packard, Lexmark, NEC, Okidata, Panasonic, Texas Instruments, and Xerox. For inkjets: Hewlett-Packard, Canon, Apple, Epson, and Lexmark.

■ Should anyone even consider a dot matrix printer these days?

The cost of paper and ink or toner is lower for a dot matrix than for inkjet and laser printers, but the print quality is also lower. Dot matrix printers are most appropriate for those who need to print continuous-form paper and multiple-part forms.

EXPERT TIP

Worried about adding plastic waste to landfills? Then don't throw out spent laser toner cartridges. If you buy a Hewlett-Packard cartridge, you'll find a prepaid United Parcel Service shipping label to HP in the box. When the cartridge is used up, just slip it in the original box and mail it back, where the materials are recycled. Other companies that make toner cartridges may have similar recycling programs.

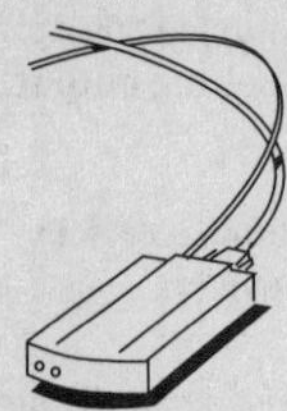

LINKING UP WITH A MODEM

As the technical editor at Communications Week, *Oliver Rist knows modems inside and out. Here's his communications strategy for the rest of us.*

■ Why buy a modem?

With all the new online services popping up, a modem has become as necessary a device as the telephone. A modem allows you to exchange electronic mail with friends and relatives, surf the Internet, receive updated software, and shop without leaving the comfort of home.

■ What should you look for in a modem?

Get the fastest standard modem available. It transfers data at 28.8 kilobits per second.

■ WHAT YOUR MODEM IS TELLING YOU

A guide to those blinking lights, be they vertical or horizontal.

- **HS HIGH SPEED**—Your modem is set to communicate at its highest speed.
- **AA AUTO ANSWER**—Your modem is set to answer incoming calls.
- **CD CARRIER DETECT**—Your modem is connected to another modem.
- **OH OFF HOOK**—Your modem is in use, either answering an incoming call or placing an outgoing one.
- **RT** or **RX RECEIVE DATA**—Your modem is receiving data from another modem.
- **ST** or **SX SEND DATA**—Your modem is sending data to another modem.
- **MR MODEM READY**—Your modem is on.
- **TR TERMINAL READY**— A hardware connection exists between your computer and your modem.

■ Should you replace a slow modem?

Yes, if you think it's likely you'll spend much time on the Internet. Viewing sites on the World Wide Web (see page 681) is painfully slow at speeds lower than 28.8 kbps.

■ How easy is it to hook up a modem to a PC?

To install an internal modem (they start at about $150), you need to open up the computer and replace the old one with it—which could be a hassle for those unfamiliar with the inside of a PC. An external modem ($200 and up) would be a better choice for beginners. Windows 95, which comes installed on most systems sold since the fall of 1995, makes adding an external modem especially simple: just plug the device into the back of the PC and reboot.

■ What are the most popular brands?

Hayes and U.S. Robotics.

■ What about fancy new features being built into modems, like speaker phones or voice mail?

Most new PCs come with these capabilities, so they're superfluous in the modem.

■ What are cable modems and when will they be available?

Instead of the phone lines, cable modems use cable TV wires, which at 128 kbps are much faster than regular modems. Manufacturers are still test-marketing cable modems. Trial runs involve buying the device for about $100 and paying a monthly rental fee of $40. Don't expect to see cable modems widely available before the end of 1996.

■ What about Integrated Services Digital Network (ISDN) lines?

ISDN lines also transmit data at a speed of 128 kbps and can carry voice and data simultaneously. For instance, you can talk on the phone and receive a fax at the same time. To get this service, however, the phone company has to install special lines (for a typical fee of $100 to $250), and the monthly fees of $30 to $85 are prohibitively expensive for casual users.

UPGRADES

PUTTING MUSCLE IN YOUR MACHINE

You don't necessarily need to buy a new computer to be up to speed

If your computer is out-of-date, you can't run the newest software programs. For people who only use the computer to balance their budgets or to write letters, that's fine. But if you're frustrated because you don't have access to the nifty programs your friends are talking about, or you aren't able to log onto the Internet or send electronic mail, it's time to upgrade your PC. You may even need to replace it altogether.

■ **MULTIMEDIA.** Today, all new PCs have built-in multimedia—a sound card and speakers and a CD-ROM drive. And virtually all new programs come on CD-ROM disks.

To take advantage of the latest products and services, you need multimedia. The best course would be to donate your text-only PC to a local school, library, or community center and buy a whizzy new PC. But if you can't afford the investment, you can buy a multimedia upgrade kit for a few hundred dollars.Get at least a quadruple-speed CD-ROM drive and a 16-bit sound card, and, after the dealer has installed it, be prepared for incompatibilities and imperfect performance.

People who bought early multimedia systems may want to update the components. If you've got an 8-bit sound card, consider swapping it out for a 16-bit one. If the CD-ROM drive is "double-speed," you may want a faster one—though many of the current programs work adequately on a double-speed drive. Quadruple-speed, or 4X, is standard; 6X is often optional; and 8X will soon become common, too.

■ **PROCESSOR.** PC makers used to believe that home computer owners didn't need all the power their counterparts in corporations had. The PC-buying public proved them wrong. In fact, home PC owners bought Intel's Pentium processors sooner than companies did. Those buying a new system shouldn't look at anything slower than a Pentium or PowerPC chip on the Mac side, but if you've got a PC or Mac that you purchased three to four years ago, you can still run most software just fine. If you do need to upgrade, consider getting a new machine. Although it's often possible to upgrade a processor, it's not easy to do, and the old components may slow the new processor down, canceling out the reason you upgraded in the first place.

■ **OPERATING SYSTEM.** To be sure you can run the latest software programs, you need the latest operating systems. For IBM-type PC owners, that means Windows 95 (about $100) and for Macintosh owners, System 7.5 (also around $100). Upgrading an operating system can require several hours and a fair amount of tinkering to get everything up and running again, so choose your time carefully.

■ **MEMORY.** To upgrade to a modern operating system like Windows 95 or Macintosh System 7.5—and the programs that require them—you'll need at least 8 MB of memory (16 MB is even better). Check with your PC manufacturer, or a tech-savvy friend, to see if your computer's memory can be expanded and to see what kind of memory it takes (SIMMs are standard, but some machines require proprietary memory made by the system manufacturer). You can buy memory from a computer store; a megabyte will probably cost less than $40.

■ **MODEM SPEED.** To exchange electronic mail with friends and family and to log onto the Internet or commercial online services, you need a modem ($200 and up). The faster, the better. If you don't have a modem or you have a slow 9,600 bit per second or 14.4 kilobit per second, you would do well to replace it with one with a speed of 28.8 kilobits per second. An external modem is easier to install than an internal one, though may cost $10 or $20 more.

EXPERT Q & A

SIZING UP THE SMALL COMPUTERS

Portable computers are hot. Here's what you need to know

Seems like everybody's going mobile. With more and more people working away from the office—at home, on the road, in planes and trains, and other far-flung locations—portable computers are compact, convenient, and are getting so powerful that many people are using them as their primary computers. But other than the size difference, what's to know about portable computers? Here's the lowdown on sized-down machines from some of the editors of *PC Magazine*.

■ What's the difference between portable and desktop computers?

Portables are smaller. It sounds like a ridiculously obvious point, but if you're talking components, that's about the only real difference between desktops and portables. You will, however, have to pay more for those components in miniature. While prices of portables are falling steadily, you'll still pay about a third more for a portable (specifically, a notebook) than you would for a desktop. Why? It's the price of design ingenuity; it takes some pretty fancy engineering to cram all those goodies into a compact package. The other difference is power. By and large, turbo-powered computing always hits the desktop market before it shrinks to portable sizes. In other words, don't expect the same kinds of bells and whistles that you see on desktops now (internal CD-ROM drives or 1 GB hard drives, for example) to be standard fare on a portable until 1997.

Tempted to buy a notebook instead of a desktop—even though you don't plan to take it on the road much? Reconsider. The undersize keyboard and display will cause you discomfort if a notebook is your only home PC.

■ What's the difference between a PowerBook, laptop, notebook, and subnotebook?

Portable computers come in varying sizes and weights. Laptops are the heaviest (seven pounds or more) and, while they were popular in the late '80s, they're outdated now; if you're looking for a laptop, your best bet is the classified section for secondhand sales.

Notebooks are the most popular, practical class of portable. They're slim, weigh less than seven pounds, and many have processing capabilities on a par with powerful desktop PCs. Subnotebooks are smaller versions of notebooks, about four pounds—great for assiduous notetakers and e-mail communicators, but because subnotebooks have such cramped keyboards and tiny screens, they're not appropriate for people who write all the time. And subs are definitely not right for budget-buyers, who will find better bargains in laptop and notebook computers.

PowerBooks are Apple's Macintosh notebooks. The latest and most powerful powerbooks use the PowerPC chip, roughly comparable to the Pentium chip used in PCs.

■ What should you look for in a notebook?

The typical configuration in an average

FACT FILE:

TOP FIVE PORTABLES

■ *The leading brands in the U.S.:*

1. TOSHIBA AMERICA INFORMATION SYSTEMS
2. COMPAQ COMPUTER CORPORATION
3. IBM
4. APPLE COMPUTER
5. TEXAS INSTRUMENTS

SOURCE: Dataquest.

EXPERT TIPS

BATTERIES THAT KEEP ON GOING...AND GOING

Learning about how batteries work can save you trouble on the road, or wherever you're tethered to your computer. Here's what the experts advise:

■ **PUT IT TO SLEEP.** If you're not going to be working on a file for several minutes, don't turn off the laptop (the energy required to boot it up again drains battery juice). Most portable computers have energy-saving utilities that will lull the machine into "sleep mode" after several minutes of non-use, but if you don't have this feature, simply close the cover or use the Suspend/Resume switch.

■ **KEEP THE LIGHT LOW.** A bright monitor setting drains 20 to 65 percent of your computer's energy; keep your screen as dim as is comfortable.

■ **AVOID USING PERIPHERALS.** Switching among your CD-ROM drive, modem—even floppy drive—wastes energy. Try to work only from your hard disk, and save files as infrequently as possible; constant saving can eat up to 80 percent of a battery's power.

■ **TREAD LIGHTLY ON YOUR HARD DRIVE.** The type of software you use and the amount of RAM in your computer affect how often the disk drive is used and therefore the running time of the battery. If you increase the amount of RAM on your computer, say, from 4 MB to 8 MB, the battery will last longer. Also, some programs rely more heavily on the hard drive than others.

■ **PREVENTIVE CARE.** When you buy a new, uncharged battery, charge and discharge it two to four times before taking it on a trip. To discharge a battery, unplug your AC-adapter and leave your laptop on (idle) for a few hours. Discharge it fully before recharging. Also, don't let batteries go dormant too long; unplug your AC-adapter every so often while you're working on your laptop at home, and always disconnect it when you're not using the machine. Discharging and recharging your battery periodically will lengthen its life.

■ **WATCH FOR NEW DEVELOPMENTS.** New technologies are producing lighter batteries that run longer on a single charge. Within the past year, manufacturers introduced lithium ion batteries, which last longer, can be recharged more often, and retain more of their charge during storage than nickel-metal hydride batteries. They are, however, more expensive.

notebook now includes the following: a 75-MHz Pentium processor, 650 MB hard disk, a 9.5-inch dual-scan passive color screen, a PC slot (credit card–sized drives for modems), a 3½-inch floppy drive, built-in trackball—or touch-sensitive pad. The average time for battery life on notebooks and PowerBooks is about three hours. Remember, though, that heavy-duty batteries can saddle you down—they weigh up to half a pound. Make sure that the weight you're quoted for the portable machine includes the weight of the battery and its adapter.

■ What if I wait until next year to get a notebook?

Waiting will get you more computing power for less money. A typical notebook configuration will probably include: a 200-MHz Pentium, a 1.2 gigabyte hard disk, and a 9½-inch active-matrix color screen. But if you know what you want and have the cash, why wait?

HACKER'S GUIDE

WARNING: COMPUTING CAN BE HAZARDOUS TO YOUR HEALTH

If you type 50 words a minute for an hour, you'll have pecked out some 18,000 keystrokes. Keep that up all day, five days a week, and you're giving your digits and wrists a hard-core workout. Typing's repetitive movements can lead to muscle strain, pain, and weakness in the hands, arms, and wrists—all of which are signs of carpal tunnel syndrome and other repetitive stress injuries (RSI). And that's not all. A bad chair or posture can cause back and neck strain, and staring at your monitor (especially if it's a flickery one) is a great way to give yourself a pounding headache, not to mention ruin your eyes.

PREVENTING REPETITIVE STRESS INJURIES

Behavior modification:

■ Make sure that your keyboard is lower than your elbows; your wrists should be slightly higher than your fingers.

■ Don't over-curl your fingers, drop, or twist your wrists—you'll put too much stress on your hands' muscles and tendons. When you're at the keyboard, keep your fingers just slightly curled and sit up straight.

■ Avoid tendonitis in the elbow (a condition also known as tennis elbow) by making sure that your arms rest comfortably on the armrests of your chair and that your elbows do not jut out at an awkward angle. Ideally, your elbows should bend at 90 degrees. The best chairs let you adjust the armrests to fit your body size.

■ Do you peck at the keyboard, using only a few fingers to do all the work? This can cause muscle strain. If you learn to touch-type, you'll reduce the pain—and double your typing speed at the same time.

■ Take plenty of breaks (five minutes every hour if possible).

Products to try:

■ Investing in a wrist-rest—a device that elevates your hands so that your wrists remain straight while typing—is a great way to help prevent repetitive stress injuries in your hands and wrists. They range from the simple (a foam pad, which costs about $10) to the sophisticated (plastic shackles, going for $25 and above). You can find wrist-rests at many computer stores. Don't want to spend the dough? Try a rolled up towel instead.

■ Dozens of keyboards claim to be ergonomic, and some of them actually deliver on that promise. The most comfortable keyboards are Kinesis Ergonomic Keyboard (☎ 206-455-9220) and Microsoft's keyboard.

■ KEYBOARDING

Three common incorrect practices and their symptoms:

TWISTING: Long muscles forced to stretch around elbow, stressing muscles in hands and arms.
SYMPTOMS: Elbow inflammation, throbbing forearm, loss of dexterity in ring and little fingers.

OVER-CURLED FINGERS: Continously flexed muscles that contract cause nerve compression in the wrist.
SYMPTOMS: Pain in the wrist and forearm, tingling or numbness in the fingers.

DROPPED WRISTS: Tendons press against the nerves in the wrist, weakening the thumb, index, and ring fingers.
SYMPTOMS: Numbness, tingling in the fingers at night, swelling of wrist and/or thumb.

■ HACKER'S GUIDE

PREVENTING EYESTRAIN

Behavior modification:

■ Keep at least 20 inches between your eyes and monitor, and adjust the monitor's angle so that you don't have to crane your neck to look at the screen. If you wear bifocals, adjust your monitor so that you're looking down.

■ The light that you work by should be diffuse and come from overhead. A light source that comes from the side, or worse, from behind, will make you squint; over time, you'll develop headaches from eyestrain.

■ It sounds kind of obvious, but have you adjusted the brightness and contrast on your screen? This often overlooked solution can save you from squinting at a screen that is either too dim or too bright.

■ Contact lenses may cause eyestrain in people who stare at a computer screen for hours on end. Try using your glasses instead. Photo-sensitive lenses soften the glare from the screen.

Products to try:

■ Nothing is harder to look at than a bright monitor; it can cause headaches as well as eyestrain. Look for add-on screen filters to correct that problem, such as the ones that are available from Less Gauss.

■ Is your monitor's screen flickering? If it is, it's causing strain on your eyes. A monitor that flickers usually has a low vertical refresh rate or a high dot pitch (see page 656); in either case, it's probably time to get a new monitor.

PREVENTING BACK AND NECK STRAIN

Behavior modification:

■ Bad posture is the most common reason for neck and upper back pain. So learn to sit straight, don't slouch, and keep your shoulders relaxed (but not dropped forward).

Products to try:

■ If you're looking for a computer desk (anything that costs more than $100 is probably called a workstation), keep a few important points in mind: Get one that you can raise and lower from 27 to 29 inches. Make sure it has an adjustable and sliding keyboard holder—one that is a couple of inches below the table level. Finally, spend the extra bucks and get something solid—there's nothing more likely to give you a headache than a wobbly PC.

■ If you tend to slouch in the chair at your desk, try the $49.95 Nada Chair, a contraption that forces you to sit straight. Call ☎ 800-722-2587 for more information.

■ Looking for a new chair? Make sure the backrest is adjustable and tilts backward. Also look for lumbar support, armrests, adjustable height, and easy-rolling wheels.

■ POSTURE

Computer workstations can be equipped to ensure good posture and proper alignment.

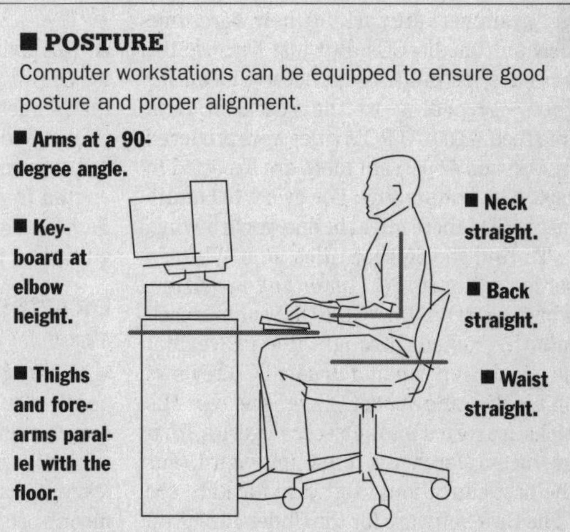
■ Arms at a 90-degree angle.
■ Keyboard at elbow height.
■ Thighs and forearms parallel with the floor.
■ Neck straight.
■ Back straight.
■ Waist straight.

SOFTWARE

KIDS: Helping children make the most of computers, PAGE 670 **PARENT'S GUIDE:** The best software for kids under 10, PAGE 672 **DATABASES:** Do you really need a special program? PAGE 675 **MONEY:** Software that can help your financial life, PAGE 677 **DESKTOP PUBLISHING:** What you need to know for choosing the right package for the job, PAGE 679 **WORD PROCESSING:** The top programs for PCs and Macintoshes, PAGE 680

EXPERT PICKS

THE 50 GREATEST CD-ROMS

With thousands to choose from, here is the cream of the crop in 11 areas

Like miners to the gold rush, book publishers, game developers, Hollywood types, and even business application programmers are packing their wares into multimedia CDs. But just because the box says it's multimedia doesn't mean it's good. According to the research firm InfoTech, 4,000 CD-ROM titles were produced in 1995 and 42 percent more are expected in 1996. The bottom line: For every 100 multimedia CDs, there might be one worth buying.

To find the 50 best titles, Ron White, a senior editor at *PC Computing* magazine, where he writes the "CD-RON" column each month, sorted through the proverbial haystack. You can find updated CD reviews on his Web site at http://www.cdron.com. His picks are sorted into subject categories, from business reference to the simply weird. (For the best educational software for kids, see "The Best Software for the Under-10 Set" on page 672.) The choices are listed alphabetically by title. Except when otherwise indicated, the list price is specified.

REFERENCE

ARGUS CENSUS MAP USA
Argus Technologies, $99.95

■ Here's a complete demographic breakdown of the U.S. into 115 census categories. The data go down to the block level, the smallest demographic unit in the U.S. census. The graphs and maps are great for presentations. A real bargain.

1996 COMPTON'S INTERACTIVE ENCYCLOPEDIA
Compton's NewMedia, estimated street price, $70 to $90

■ With updates issued weekly through America Online, this encyclopedia is never more than a week old. Students can piece together photos, videos, audio, and narration in the "editing room" and use a powerful search engine to scour the disk's 35,000 articles. *Star Trek*'s Patrick Stewart beams in for a guided tour. Outstanding!

ENCARTA 96 ENCYCLOPEDIA
Microsoft Corp., estimated street price, $55

■ Microsoft's updated Encarta is a calmer, gentler encyclopedia with an improved search engine to make it easier to find what you're looking for. "InterActivities" let you learn by experimentation, like altering the moon's orbital speed and distance from earth to demonstrate how those two factors determine the moon's orbit. The well-integrated online connection lets you easily download new articles.

INFOPEDIA

Future Vision Multimedia, estimated street price, $50

■ This newcomer to all-purpose reference CDs makes a strong impression. Seven of its eight titles are comparable to those in Microsoft Bookshelf, but Infopedia contains all 29 volumes of *Funk & Wagnalls Encyclopedia*—the same encyclopedia that Microsoft Encarta is based on—and far more extensive than the one-volume encyclopedia found in Bookshelf.

MICROSOFT BOOKSHELF

Microsoft Corp., estimated street price, $70

■ Bookshelf is the killer CD-ROM application. It includes *Columbia Dictionary of Quotations* (with sound recordings), *The American Heritage Dictionary* (with more than 350,000 entries and sound bites of 80,000 words), *Roget's Thesaurus, People's Chronology, Concise Columbia Encyclopedia, Hammond World Atlas, World Almanac, 1994 Book of Facts,* a zip code finder, and a year in review.

RANDOM HOUSE UNABRIDGED ELECTRONIC DICTIONARY

Random House Reference and Electronic Publishing, estimated street price, $70

■ Word freaks will go ape over the latest version, with 115,000 spoken pronunciations. This is the only newly updated, unabridged dictionary in years. Its 2,200 illustrations make this a must-have reference tool. Toss in $21 more, and you also get the *Random House Dictionary* in hardcover.

3D ATLAS

Creative Wonders, estimated street price, $65

■ 3D Atlas has the usual stuff—political boundaries and flags of the nations—but it also shows ecosystems and geological formations based on satellite photos. There are slide shows for selected countries and cities as well as tables of statistics.

BUSINESS REFERENCE

ALLEGRO REFERENCE SERIES BUSINESS LIBRARY, VOL. 1

Allegro New Media, $59.95

■ What Microsoft Bookshelf is to the writer, this collection of 12 books is to the entrepreneur. Want to know the principles of a successful telemarketing campaign or the tax benefits of real estate trusts? You'll find the answers in the included books on marketing, finance, real estate, international business, selling, and careers.

MULTIMEDIA BUSINESS 500

Allegro New Media, $49.95

■ With this collection of detailed information on the country's 500 biggest businesses from *Hoover's Handbook of American Business* and Standard & Poor's statistics, you can explore companies' finances, stock history, products, and executives' salaries. With a subscription to Prodigy, you can link to current stock quotes.

SCIENCE FICTION:THE MULTIMEDIA ENCYCLOPEDIA OF SCIENCE FICTION

Grolier Interactive, $39.95

■ Forgive the redundant title of one of the best combinations of content and presentation on CD-ROM. Explore by concept, author, or title. Based on an award-winning book, the text explores important authors and concepts in depth. Have fun with film clips, movie posters, and sci-fi factoids.

MULTIMEDIA MBA SMALL BUSINESS EDITION

SoftKey International, $79

■ This collection of tutorials and software is as close as you can get to earning an MBA without having to make an 8 a.m. lecture. Detailed text, supporting illustrations and charts, serious math and accounting tools—they're all here. Worksheets are linked to your own electronic spreadsheet, and legal, advertising, and human resource forms are linked to your word processor.

MOVIES

CINEMANIA 96

Microsoft Corp., estimated street price, $35

■ Cinemania does not have the most film listings nor the most film clips, but it solves the problem most other movie guides face: They're dated a week after they come out. Cinemania lets you connect from your modem directly to the Microsoft Network for monthly updates. Reviews by Roger Ebert, Pauline Kael, and Leonard Maltin are accompanied by complete lists of credits and awards. The snappy search engine lets you find all the films Bette Davis played in or the name of that movie directed by Fellini whose title you can never remember. Or select a category, and it will suggest the type of movie you're in the mood to watch.

COREL ALL MOVIE GUIDE

Corel Corp., estimated street price, $11–$20

■ This is a winner for the sheer number of movies and TV shows listed on a CD-ROM. With detailed information on 90,000 movies and videos, this guide will find just about any movie fact you could ever want—from plot to cast to awards to audience ratings to gross revenues.

HISTORY AND CURRENT EVENTS

EYEWITNESS HISTORY OF THE WORLD

DK Multimedia, $55

■ Though designed for children, this reference is so packed with interesting information and stunning graphics that there's no reason the kids should have all the fun. Explore history from a desktop covered with items that change every time you visit a different era. In each time period you can look at everyday life, culture, writing, innovations, and a who's who of history.

OUR TIMES MULTIMEDIA ENCYCLOPEDIA OF THE 20TH CENTURY

Vicarious, estimated street price, $70

■ Our Times has a photo-studded timeline that highlights important social, scientific, artistic, cultural, political, and international events of the century. A video for each decade brings the highlights to life. The intelligently written text is hyperlinked to the *Columbia Encyclopedia*.

VIETNAM

Medio, estimated street price, $35

■ This compelling study of the war and surrounding issues covers all points of view and includes the complete text of the Pentagon Papers and George Herring's *America's Longest War*.

SCIENCE, ART, MUSIC

A BRIEF HISTORY OF TIME

Creative Labs Inc., $59.95

■ Have you ever sat around with some friends wondering what time really is, how the universe got started, and where it ends? This multimedia version of the best-selling book is beautifully illustrated and explored; author Stephen W. Hawking narrates.

DISTANT SUNS FIRST LIGHT

Virtual Reality Laboratories, $64.95

■ The ultimate astronomy CD-ROM, First Light lets you look at the stars and planets—comets, asteroids, and spacecraft too—from anywhere in the solar system.

EYEWITNESS ENCYCLOPEDIA OF NATURE

DK Multimedia, estimated street price, $55

■ Explanations of everything from how viruses reproduce to how whales feed are supported by videos and animations and presented with a clarity that kids will understand and adults won't find patronizing. A must for any lover of nature or science.

EYEWITNESS ENCYCLOPEDIA OF SCIENCE

DK Multimedia, estimated street price, $55

■ This makes science crackle with excitement, through illustrated explanations of math, and physical and natural sciences. Perfect for a budding Einstein.

MICROSOFT DANGEROUS CREATURES

Microsoft Corp., estimated street price, $60

■ Dangerous Creatures zeroes in on that most enticing aspect of animal behavior—the killer instinct—through guided explorations of the Amazon, Africa, coral reefs, and other parts of the animal kingdom. You'll explore it for days without retracing your steps.

MICROSOFT DINOSAURS

Microsoft Corp., estimated street price, $60

■ Even if you're not a Jurassic junkie, you'll be hooked on this intelligent multimedia look at dinosaurs and paleontology. You can track down the dinos based on the locations or time periods in which they lived or by their biological classifications. A great educational tool—and fun.

MICROSOFT OCEANS

Microsoft Corp., estimated street price, $35

■ This beautiful combination of photos, videos, and sounds takes you from the depths of the oceans to the storms they generate to the pirates who sailed the seas to the treasures and cities hidden beneath them.

RED SHIFT

Maxis Software, $54.95

■ Explore the stars and planets—from vast panoramas to low, sweeping flybys over alien terrain—follow the life cycle of a star, and the birth of a universe. The color photography from NASA is beautiful. Totally absorbing.

THE WAY THINGS WORK

DK Multimedia, estimated street price, $50

■ Based on David Macauley's terrific 1988 best-selling book, this is an instant classic. It explains everything from simple levers to microprocessors through animation, drawing, narration, and video.

A PASSION FOR ART

Corbis Publishing, estimated street price, $45

■ This expertly guided tour from the company that Microsoft chief Bill Gates launched to manage his art collection includes guided tours of Impressionist, post-Impressionist, and early modern painting.

THE ULTIMATE FRANK LLOYD WRIGHT AMERICA'S ARCHITECT

Microsoft Corp., estimated street price, $35

■ This exploration of the architect's ideas and designs takes you on walking tours through 3-D renderings of Wright's buildings. Movable blocks let you experiment with his modular concepts and then create a 3-D vision of your design.

MICROSOFT MUSICAL INSTRUMENTS

Microsoft Corp., $34.95

■ A wonderful combination of fun and education that plays sounds as you see the instruments displayed. Includes endless ways to explore the instruments—by the country they come from to the musical families they belong to.

MULTIMEDIA
BEETHOVEN The Ninth Symphony;
MOZART The Dissonant Quartet;
SCHUBERT The Trout Quintet;
STRAUSS Three Tone Poems;
STRAVINSKY The Rite of Spring

Microsoft Corp., estimated street price, $35 each

MULTIMEDIA COMPOSER COLLECTION (BEETHOVEN, MOZART, SCHUBERT)

Microsoft Corp., estimated street price, $55

■ All of these multimedia disks will engage your mind as you read about the music and listen along. Each disk includes biographies and musical glossaries.

HEALTH

A.D.A.M. THE INSIDE STORY

A.D.A.M. Software, Inc., estimated street price, $50

■ This "animated dissection of anatomy for medicine" takes you on a thorough tour of the human body. From views of the cardiovascular system, skeleton, nervous system, and assorted glands, you can delicately peel away layer after layer of skin, muscle, and other organs for a complete human dissection.

ANNE HOOPER'S ULTIMATE SEX GUIDE

DK Multimedia, estimated street price, $40

■ Filled with tastefully presented information, this guide starts by asking you questions designed to search out your areas of sexual ignorance. It spends a lot of time on the emotional side of sex, hygiene, sexual diseases, and sex techniques. Personal passwords prevent your kids from using the disk, although it is a good way to teach older children about sex.

THE ULTIMATE HUMAN BODY

DK Multimedia, estimated street price, $55

■ Among the many CDs that take you inside the human body, this is a standout. More than an anatomy lesson that identifies organs, it explores the functions of individual organs, the nervous system, skeletal system, and six other body systems. More than 1,000 illustrations and 90 animations are effective teaching tools and stunning works of art.

SPORTS

FLY FISHING: GREAT RIVERS OF THE WEST

IVI Publishing, estimated street price, $35

■ Beautiful art, photos, and maps offer advice on tackle, techniques, flies, and rivers.

MICROSOFT COMPLETE BASEBALL

Microsoft Corp., estimated street price, $50

■ If you believe baseball should last year round, you'll love this one. It's packed with those statistics that fans seem to love so much, along with the history of the game as far back as 1839, photos galore, and even a few key videos. You can subscribe to Microsoft Baseball Daily, a newspaper delivered by modem for $1.25 an issue, to keep those statistics and scores up-to-date.

TRAVEL

BERLITZ LIVE! JAPANESE
BERLITZ LIVE! SPANISH

Sierra On-Line, $44.95 each

■ These language instruction programs are helpful when it comes to doing international business. Their quick-and-dirty approach emphasizes the business phrases you're most likely to need. And because communication is more than words, you also learn key body language, such as Japan's ritual bowing during the exchange of meishi or business cards. These are first rate, all around.

TAXI

News Electronic Data, estimated street price, $160

■ Packed with maps of 20 cities from Boston to San Diego, Taxi maps are linked to the authoritative Zagat travel guides. It offers details on all the places that match your food, service, and pricing criteria and shows you the best route to reach them. Five-city versions are available in different combinations for $60.

HOME

3D LANDSCAPE

Books That Work, $49

■ Design your own garden with trees, shrubs, flowers, ponds, boulders, and lawn chairs; see how it will look after years of growth; learn how to grow the greenery; and figure out how much your fantasy will cost.

HOME REPAIR ENCYCLOPEDIA

Books That Work, $29

■ This is the answer to a do-it-yourself homeowner's prayers. An authoritative and comprehensive collection of videos, animations, and text that teaches you to be handy around the house.

POPULAR MECHANICS NEW CAR BUYERS GUIDE 1996

Books That Work, estimated street price, $30

■ Let the editors of *Popular Mechanics* do all the research for you. You pick the type of car, the price, mileage, safety features, and options, and the software provides details on all vehicles that match your specs. The 1996 edition adds used cars—which you won't find in any competing CD—and tools to figure out what type of a car you can really afford.

GAMES

DESCENT

Interplay and Parallax Software, estimated street price, $35

■ A faster, more frantic game for those who find Doom too slow, Descent gives you not only a 360-degree range of horizontal movement, but also a 360-degree vertical range. Descent's movement takes place only in corridors, but you still have to guard up and down as well as front, back, and sides.

FURY 3

Microsoft Corp., estimated street price, $50

■ Fury is Microsoft's adaptation of Terminal Velocity, one of the first of a stunning new type of game. Like Flight Simulator, you control a flying vehicle, but don't even think about trying to land. Beneath you are 3-D textured landscapes of mountains, valleys, plains, and seas studded with cities and war machines marching to destroy civilization.

THE JOURNEYMAN PROJECT TURBO

Sanctuary Woods, estimated street price, $40

■ World peace is threatened by the building of a time machine that can undo history. This game will have you lying awake at night wondering if you could sneak back downstairs to the computer for a while more and show up late to the office tomorrow.

THE JOURNEYMAN PROJECT 2: BURIED IN TIME

Sanctuary Woods, estimated street price, $65

■ In this clever first-person riddle-solving adventure in the future—and the past—your role as a time cop is to stop others from changing destiny. This is a thinking game. Leave your trigger finger behind.

MYST

Broderbund, estimated street price, $55

■ Myst is the first New Age game. Or maybe it's a nongame. Or an art show. Or maybe a digital sedative. You don't shoot anyone in Myst and you don't die. Instead, you explore a small island searching for.... Well, you don't really know, and it doesn't matter.

THE 7TH GUEST

Virgin Interactive Entertainment, $54.99

■ The 7th Guest is an old computer adventure game raised to an eerie new level of 3-D virtual reality combined with riddles and puzzles. You explore a haunted house with only a skeleton's hand to guide you. Keep the room lights on when you play.

THE ULTIMATE DOOM

id Software and GT Interactive, estimated street price, $37

■ The original game plus a new one, "Thy Flesh Consumed." The title says it all. It's still a DOS game, but it plays just dandy under Windows 95. It also includes five hours' access to Dwango, the dial-up game network where you can play death matches with other Doom fanatics.

DOOM II

id Software and GT Interactive, estimated street price, $50

■ This new version picks up the battle between you and assorted demon meanies. It's got more levels, bad guys, and weapons.

HERETIC AND HEXEN

id Software, Raven Software and GT Interactive, estimated street prices, $40

■ The best of the Doom imitators are rich, imaginative games in their own right. The setting is medieval instead of futuristic, and the monsters are creatures of magic.

PRIMAL RAGE

Time Warner Interactive, estimated street price, $50

■ If Mortal Kombat is sold out, this is the first fallback. The contestants are dinosaurs and giant apes There is blood, lots of it, and cool artwork and creatures.

SIMPLY WEIRD

MONTY PYTHON'S COMPLETE WASTE OF TIME

7th Level, estimated street price, $50

■ Bringing total anarchy to computing, this disk is a compilation of the Pythons' animation and best BBC skits—the cheese shop, the dead parrot, the argument room, among others. Totally Pythonize your computer with the collection of sounds, wallpaper, icons, and screen savers.

EXPERT Q & A

AN ELECTRONIC BABY-SITTER?

Don't just plop the kids in front of the computer. Lend a helping hand

The odds are better than even that your kids are more at home with a computer than you are. But in case they're not, Cathy Miranker and Alison Elliott, authors of *The Computer Museum Guide to the Best Software for Kids* (HarperCollins, 1995), offer some advice about how to make your home computer as comfy as a teddy bear.

■ How involved should parents be when kids play on the computer?

Very. If you want your kids to get the most from your home computer, don't limit your involvement to simply choosing software. Hold toddlers on your lap and be the audience for older kids' artwork and stories. Explore a topic of interest together. Challenge them to a game. Because in the end, the computer is not their teacher. You are.

■ What are some good ways to extend the longevity of a computer game?

Put the game away after two months or so. When you reintroduce it, your kids will be slightly different people. Chances are, they'll use the same software in a new and different way. Check the Web sites of your favorite children's software publishers, too. Their free online activities often let kids get more mileage out of a software title.

■ What kinds of programs are good for sharing?

Most kids' software is even better when played with a friend, sibling, or parent. For older kids, brainteasers, math challenges, thinking games, history simulations, and geography quests make great "together" activities. Children who are too young to play love watching siblings at the keyboard and helping them decide what to do next.

■ How can software reinforce classroom work?

Talk to your child's teacher to learn what the students are doing with computers in school. They may also recommend homework helpers like a writing program, spelling software, or electronic encyclopedia. Also consider programs that complement the subjects your child is studying. Software that presents classroom topics in unclassroom-like ways often sparks the most enthusiasm and discovery.

■ How should parents go about buying software?

Beware of programs that simply repackage movies, TV shows, and books. Too often, they ask kids to do little more than click and watch. Instead, look for software that encourages kids to create, experiment, make decisions, and solve problems. Beyond that, it helps to read reviews, talk to teachers and friends, and surf the Web. If possible, try before you buy—at a store, a children's museum, or an after-school computer center. Then buy from a source that will let you return the software

■ BEYOND THE COOL AND WHIZZY

These packages don't teach programming per se, but include intriguing activities that let kids master challenges that are central to programming. Here are some picks from Cathy Miranker and Alison Elliott:

MY MAKE BELIEVE CASTLE	Ages 4–7
Logo Computer Syst.	☎800–321–5646
ZURK'S ALASKAN TREK	Ages 6–10
Soleil	☎415–494–0114
THINKIN' THINGS COLLECTION	Ages 7–13
Edmark	☎800–320–8378
LOST MIND OF DR. BRAIN	Ages 9+
Sierra On-Line	☎800–757–7707
KLIK & PLAY	Ages 10 and up
Maxis	☎800–526–2947

HOW TO CHILDPROOF YOUR COMPUTER

It's easier than you think to keep kids away from things they shouldn't see

Sharing the home computer with your brood seems like a good idea, both financially and familially—until your seven-year-old deletes an important business report from your hard disk. And you probably don't want the kids wandering around the Internet's red-light district. Here are some inexpensive solutions.

■ **HARDWARE SOLUTIONS:** A solid hardware solution to kid intervention is hard disk partitioning. If you're a computer whiz, you've probably done this already; otherwise, take your computer to a good service store. Disk partitioning allows you to divide a single hard disk into several drives, assigning one to kids, the other to adults. When kids turn the computer on, they're automatically routed into the drive assigned to them; password protection prevents them from accessing the adults' space.

If you decide on this option, just make sure that you have a hard drive that is large enough to divide so adults have enough hard disk space to run their applications and the kids have enough space to run their games. For true division, you can buy two external hard drives; one for parents and one for kids.

■ **SOFTWARE SOLUTIONS:** Give your kids their own desktop software. Kid Desk, from Edmark, ☎ 800–320–8378, makes the computer screen look like a child's desk. Like the Microsoft Windows or Macintosh desktop, Kid Desk displays icons for applications that your kids use, and identifies parents' territory with a single icon, which is password protected. The family edition lets kids leave messages and voice mail on the desktop for other family members.

Launch Pad, from Berkeley Systems, ☎ 510–540–5535, works in the same way, but kids are given the option of selecting one of several desktop wallpaper designs: a spaceship, dinosaurs, a castle, a unicorn, or a creepy old haunted house.

■ **INTERNET SOLUTIONS:** Several software programs are designed specifically to prevent kids from viewing adult material on the Internet. One of the best is SurfWatch, ☎ 800–458–6600, which blocks out thousands of Web sites that contain sexually explicit material and stuff you probably don't want your kids to see. With an annual subscription, you'll get monthly updates. Other Internet filtering utilities include Cyber Patrol, ☎ 800–828–2608, and Net-Nanny, ☎ 800–340–7177.

if it doesn't meet your expectations.

■ **What's the best way to avoid incompatibility surprises?**

Keep the vital statistics about your system on hand when you shop: type of processor, amount of RAM, CD-ROM drive speed, type of monitor, operating system version number, and types of sound card and speakers.

■ **Do most packages have enough facets to keep kids busy?**

Great kids' software has a long life span because smart publishers update successful titles to take advantage of new technology. So start with the software classics; they have a solid track record for keeping kids involved.

■ **What rules should parents enforce?**

Guide your child in striking a balance among homework, sports, after-school lessons, free play, chores, computer use, and TV watching. When you first introduce the Internet, you should always supervise children's online activities. Later, require older children to check with you before using the Internet and be specific about what they're planning to do and how long they'll be online.

PARENT'S GUIDE

THE BEST SOFTWARE FOR THE UNDER-10 SET

Buying good software for your kids is like finding suitable television shows for them: You've got to weed out the junk, then make a parent-child compromise. To help you choose the best family-tested educational software in math, reading, writing, and science, the editors of Family PC *magazine—along with more than 1,500 parents, teachers, and kids—pick the best ones.*

JAMES DISCOVERS MATH

Broderbund, $40, ages 3–6

■ This CD-ROM contains 10 skill-building activities, all accessible by clicking on objects in James's kitchen. At the Fruit Shop, kids can help Mr. Echo fill orders by taking fruit from the stand and placing it in a box. Another game lets kids place features on a blank face, an activity that teaches spatial visualization and recognition of scale. Most games contain verbal instructions and feedback.

ADI'S COMPREHENSIVE LEARNING SYSTEM 2ND AND 3RD MATHEMATICS

Sierra On-Line, $40, ages 7–9

■ In this elementary math curriculum, Adi—an extraterrestrial tutor from the planet Zitron—teaches kids about numbers, calculation, measurement, patterns, and geometry. Each category contains several levels of instruction, making it good for families with more than one child. Correct answers yield a brief animation and points that kids can use to access games within the program. Parents can keep track of progress by viewing graphical reports.

MONEY TOWN

Simon & Schuster/Davidson & Associates, $35, ages 5–9

■ In this learning adventure, inspired by the best-selling books *Money Doesn't Grow on Trees* and *The Common Sense* series by Neale Godfrey, kids help Greenstreet's characters earn money to reopen the town park. Five interactive games teach basic money math, coin recognition, how to make change, and how to save and spend money wisely. With every correct answer, kids earn money needed to purchase items to open the park.

SNOOTZ MATH TREK

Theatrix Interactive, $35, ages 6–10

■ In this intergalactic math adventure, two Snootians crash their spaceship into Earth. Kids can help them fix their ship—and find all the items on their Big List—by solving math and logic problems.

COLOR, SHAPES & SIZE WITH POLDY THE SCARECROW

Starpress, $30, ages 3–6

■ Along with Poldy, Wagtail, Seagull, and Crow, kids explore three narrated and gorgeously illustrated stories that take them to Brazil, China, and Africa. Six activities teach kids about colors, shapes, sizes.

JUMPSTART: PRESCHOOL

Knowledge Adventure, $32, ages 2–5

■ This colorful, fun preschool curriculum offers the youngest kids an early understanding of letters, numbers, shapes, and colors. Kids learn about phonics, letters, numbers, quantities, shapes, and colors through 11 learning areas in an inviting schoolroom. Clicking on the house brings kids to a memory game in which Pierre (complete with French accent) encourages kids to match objects behind the windows of a house. This is the highest-scoring educational program tested by *Family PC;* JumpStart Kindergarten and

JumpStart First Grade also received *Family PC* kudos.

FRANKLIN'S READING WORLD

Sanctuary Woods, $24.95 (disk), $39.95 (CD-ROM), ages 4–7

■ Franklin the turtle and his friends Bear and Beaver invite prereaders to visit the woods, the pond, and the soccer field to learn about phonics, word recognition, reading, and spelling. Kids can move the mouse over different objects and watch the cursor change to one or more letters. Clicking this letter-cursor calls up a word-builder activity.

GET READY FOR SCHOOL, CHARLIE BROWN

Virgin Sound and Vision, $35, ages 4–8

■ Kids help the Peanuts star cope with a hectic school day. They get training in vocabulary, spelling, and reading through seven fun activities and a 1,000-word interactive dictionary that lets kids hear and see the definition of a word and how it's used in a sentence. Activities include Charlie Brown's A Great American Novel, Peppermint Patty's Sentence Scramble, Rhyme Time with Lucy, and Good Grief, It's a Spelling Bee.

ADI'S COMPREHENSIVE LEARNING SYSTEM: ENGLISH 2ND & 3RD

Sierra On-Line, $40, ages 7–9

■ This double CD-ROM provides kids with an entertaining supplement to

LEARNING ISN'T JUST FOR KIDS

Want to learn a new language? Master typing? Prep for a test?

Whatever your hobby, from gardening to opera to remodeling the kitchen, there is, no doubt, a software package to help you be the best you can be.

■ **LEARNING A FOREIGN LANGUAGE.** Power Japanese and Power Spanish from Bay-Ware (☎ 800–538–8867) are among the most popular language tutors you can buy. They are based on a learning philosophy that de-emphasizes rote memorization and helps you formulate your own sentences—warts and all—quickly. You can even record and compare your voice to native speakers. With Berlitz Live! Spanish from Sierra On-Line (☎ 800–757–7707) you can learn survival-level Spanish by listening and conversing in a series of well-organized lessons. Berlitz Live! Japanese is also available. (See review on page 668.)

■ **TEST-PREP.** Need to prepare for a standardized test but don't want to spend the money on a costly prep course? Test-prep software has really taken off recently, thanks in part to a great series from The Princeton Review (☎ 800–221–8180). Inside the SAT includes video of real instructors providing guidance tailored to individual student's answers, witty animation, classroom-tested hints for improving SAT scores, and practice tests. The Princeton Review also makes test-prep software for the GMAT, GRE, and LSAT.

■ **TYPING SKILLS.** Here's one fact about owning a computer that you may as well face up front: You need to have a pretty good handle on your typing skills. The longtime favorite tutor is Mavis Beacon Teaches Typing (☎ 800–542–4222). And to start them out young, there's Mavis Beacon Teaches Typing for Kids. Mavis comes with a 30-day money-back guarantee if you don't see results. Multimedia Typing Instructor, Individual Software (☎ 800–822–3522) makes learning to type about as exciting as it gets.

■ PARENT'S GUIDE

school English studies. Each lesson contains exercises on sentences, grammar, and editing. Correct answers are rewarded with access to a series of games.

CYBERCRAFTS: HANDS-ON-LEARNING FUN WITH ELECTRONICS

Philips Media Home and Family Entertainment, $44.99, ages 8 and up

■ This mini-workbench with 100 electrical components and a CD-ROM teaches kids how to build 25 electronic projects, including a burglar alarm, a siren, and a traffic light. A narrated slide show explains what electricity is and how it works. Then kids can get down to making cool stuff like a transistor radio and a metal detector using the workbench. An animated representation of the circuit board appears on screen and provides step-by-step instructions on how each project is assembled. Setting up the workbench takes time, patience, and, often, parental assistance.

THE MULTIMEDIA BUG BOOK

Compton's NewMedia, $40, ages 5–10

■ Here, kids can observe more than 50 insects up close and learn tips on capturing and identifying their own creepy-crawly neighbors. The fun begins with Dr. Anson Pantz's dilemma: His entire bug collection has escaped. Kids then set out to capture the bugs and conduct buggy experiments like testing the way temperature affects how often a firefly flashes its light.

THE ZOO/OCEAN EXPLORERS BUNDLE

Compton's NewMedia, $40, ages 3–9

■ This two-CD set takes kids on explorations among creatures of land and sea. In a series of video chats, zookeepers describe their work and show off some of their charges, and Miss Hippo invites kids to play a memory game with animals as the key ingredient. There are no tests or curriculum, but there's a lot to learn here just by having a good time.

ADI'S COMPREHENSIVE LEARNING SYSTEM: SCIENCE 4TH & 5TH

Sierra On-Line, $40, ages 9–11

■ This installment of Adi's Comprehensive Learning System provides kids with a fun supplement to their school science studies. The set of two CD-ROMs covers earth, life, and physical sciences, including the planets, gravity, seasons, and conservation, life cycles, habitats, and ecosystems, matter, electricity, magnetism, and energy through multiple-choice, true-or-false, and fill-in-the-blank questions. Correct answers are rewarded with access to a series of games. Parents can keep track of progress by viewing graphical reports of lessons.

WHAT'S THE SECRET? VOL. 2

3M Learning Software, $59.95, ages 7–13

■ Based on the PBS science show *Newton's Apple*, this volume of What's the Secret answers the questions: "How does a plane get off the ground?" "What keeps a kite in flight?" "How can you keep from freezing in the Arctic?" and "How does my brain think?" From these questions, kids can follow many paths—like viewing a cool MRI of the brain—to make discoveries about the subject under study. Kids who read well will get the most out of this one.

BUMPTZ SCIENCE CARNIVAL

Theatrix Interactive, $35, ages 8 and up

■ Kids join zillions of Bumptz on an intergalactic field trip to the Great Galaxies Amusement Park and experiment with light, gravity, buoyancy, and magnetism. A science carnival contains over 200 animated puzzles to instruct and test the scientist in every kid. When kids master an area, they can construct their own science puzzles.

EXPERT TIPS

SOFTWARE FOR LIST LOVERS

Chances are the database program you need already exists

Many people need to keep lists, but they don't need a typical database program, says Alfred Poor, *PC Magazine* contributing editor and author of *The Underground Guide to PC Hardware* (Addison Wesley, 1996). While these programs can make short work of tasks that would take hours by hand, it's important to make sure that you're using the right tool for the job. Poor's advice:

■ **YOU PROBABLY HAVE A DATABASE ALREADY:** If you have Microsoft Windows 3.1, you already have a simple "flat file" database program. Cardfile is like a set of 3x5 file cards that you can use to keep simple lists of information. This program can't create complex reports, but it's a good place to start and to find out whether you need a more powerful program. Another easy way to create a quick and dirty list is to use a spreadsheet program such as Microsoft Excel or Lotus 1-2-3.

■ **LET SOMEONE ELSE DO THE WORK:** Chances are excellent that someone else has already created a program to handle the specific task you have in mind. Rather than reinvent the wheel, consider taking advantage of their efforts. Want to track contacts and addresses? Think about trying a sales management program such as Act! or Sales Ally or a personal information manager like Day Runner Planner. Need to handle your finances? Quicken, QuickBooks, and Managing Your Money are specialized database programs that can do the job with ease. Want to make order out of your hobby, such as antiques or genealogy? There are specialized programs for dozens of different activities, from baseball-card collections to pilots' flight logs. Many are shareware programs that you can download from online services such as CompuServe.

■ **FLAT FILE VS. RELATIONAL:** One big mistake people make is picking a program that is either too simple or too complex for the task. Simple "flat file" programs can keep track of information that you might keep on 3x5 file cards—one card for each piece of information. This isn't sufficient in some cases where the information is more complex. For example, consider a list of family addresses and birthdays. With a file-card system, you'd have to make a separate card for every person, even if they live at the same address as someone else. A relational database like Lotus Approach can handle more complicated data structures like linking information from different files.

■ **YOU DON'T NEED A PROGRAMMING DEGREE:** If you can't find a specialized program that

■ **LEADING PERSONAL INFORMATION MANAGERS**

These programs can help you organize your contacts and schedules.

ACT!	*Symantec Corp.*	☎ 800–441–7234
DAY RUNNER PLANNER	*Day Runner Inc.*	☎ 800–232–9786
DESKTOP SET	*Okna Corp.*	☎ 201–909–8600
ECCO PRO	*NetManage*	☎ 206–885–4272
GOLDMINE	*GoldMine Software Corp.*	☎ 800–564–3526
LOTUS ORGANIZER	*Lotus Development Corp.*	☎ 800–343–5414
MAXIMIZER	*Modatech Systems Int'l*	☎ 800–804–6299
PACKRAT	*Polaris Software*	☎ 800–722–5728
SHARKWARE PRO	*CogniTech Corp.*	☎ 770–454–9260
SIDEKICK	*Starfish Software*	☎ 800–765–7839

EXPERT TIPS

THE BOTTOM LINE ON SPREADSHEETS

It's hard to find a bad spreadsheet program, says PC Magazine *contributing editor Craig Stinson, because all of the major players are capable of heavy lifting. Here's Stinson's list of things to check before you buy*

■ **ANALYSIS AND MODEL BUILDING:** A good spreadsheet application can analyze numbers and interpret them in a way that allows you to build models based on the data. Clues that tell you whether or not a spreadsheet can do this are number of data entry tools, function library, ability to annotate, special features that organize and consolidate data, as well as features that let you access databases.

■ **CHARTING:** This feature transforms your data into different types of charts for presentation purposes. Look at the number and quality of chart formats that the spreadsheet offers, its ability to automate simple charting tasks, and options such as customizable titles, notes, multiple typefaces, objects, colors, shading.

■ **WORKSHEET PRESENTATION:** Make sure that the application produces boardroom quality documents, on screen and on paper. Generally, if the program offers a print previewer, a number of preconfigured document styles, as well as a broad range of fonts, shading, ruling, and color options, it's up to snuff.

■ **WORKGROUP COMPUTING:** A good spreadsheet program should support e-mail so you can quickly route files to others, multiple versions, and conversion of tables to HTML format so you can post on the Web. The ability for multiple users to work on the same file simultaneously is also a plus.

■ **CUSTOM DESIGN:** Once you have become a spreadsheet whiz, you may want to have the option of making macros, or programming keys on your keyboard to carry out certain functions automatically. Each spreadsheet application has its own "macro language" that allows you to do this. Before you buy the software, examine the macro language.

■ **APPLICATION DEVELOPMENT:** Ideally, a program's development language should work across other applications, allowing the spreadsheet to work with database programs, word processors, and presentation programs.

does what you need, then it's time to consider creating your own with a database program. There are a number of them on the market that make it relatively easy to create, modify, and maintain a database of information. Some of the easiest relational programs include Approach from Lotus, Alpha Five from Alpha Software, and File Maker Pro from Claris. Be sure to plan your database on paper carefully before you start to work on the computer, and then test it to make sure that it does what you want before you commit to entering all your information. Good programs will let you make changes to the database structure after you've entered data, but it's always better to get it right from the start rather than have to fix it later.

MONEY MANAGER'S GUIDE

PROGRAMS THAT DO EVERYTHING–EXCEPT MAKE MONEY

Stumped by a money matter? A software program can help you organize your financial affairs by computer. Some simply handle record keeping, banking, and check writing; others help you plan your budget, choose a portfolio of stocks, bonds, and mutual funds, and then buy and sell them for you. For tax season, there are tax programs with scores of income tax forms and money-saving tips. How do you choose? Here's a comparison of some of the top-selling software. The prices indicated are suggested retail prices, but you can generally get the software for 20 to 30 percent less at discount stores

RECORD KEEPING AND BANKING

For basic financial chores like bill paying, keeping records, and budgeting, these programs fit the bill. All can print checks and envelopes and track a stock or mutual fund portfolio. Beyond that, here's how they compare:

QUICKEN

Intuit, $29.95

■ The top-selling personal finance software. Excels at budgeting and graphing what happens to your money. Makes it easy to pay bills, track expenses, graph the results, budget your income, and get current balances. The online banking feature gets current account balances, transfers funds between accounts, and pays bills online.
☎ 800–624–9096

QUICKEN DELUXE

Intuit, $49.95

■ The upgraded deluxe version has the Investor Insight online service that provides updates on mutual-fund performance

and tells you the returns on your investments. A home inventory management feature is useful for valuing your valuables for insurance purposes.
☎ 800–624–9096

MICROSOFT MONEY

Microsoft Money, $24.95

■ Good for beginners who want to create a budget by using their spending patterns as a guide. Its online banking ability also makes it appealing to more sophisticated investors. Online services are available for a monthly fee. The online bill payment feature works in conjunction with your checking account. The online banking service is available from participating banks only.
☎ 800–426–9400

MONEYCOUNTS

Parsons Technology, $89

■ One of the few packages that include a general ledger and a trial balance. Allows you to keep large mailing lists and to address envelopes and labels.
☎ 800–223–6925

FINANCIAL PLANNING

These programs offer tools for choosing investments. They allow you to pick a goal, such as paying for college tuition, then figure out how much you need to save to meet it. You can put together a portfolio of stocks or funds and track its performance. You can also handle specific tasks, like analyzing life insurance.

WEALTHBUILDER

Reality Online, $49.95

■ Everything you need to put together a thorough financial plan. Designed with *Money* magazine, the program scopes out your financial philosophy—from very conservative to very aggressive—by asking questions about your holdings. It has financial data on thousands of stocks,

■ MONEY MANAGER'S GUIDE

bonds, and mutual funds.
☎ 800–346–2024

MANAGING YOUR MONEY
Meca, $19.95
■ Advice from financial planning guru Andrew Tobias. Strong on how to manage your portfolio and investments.
☎ 800–288–6322

KIPLINGER SIMPLY MONEY
Computer Associates, $34.95
■ Helpful tips from the folks who publish *Kiplinger's Personal Finance* magazine on how to manage your money. Good graphics. Easy to learn, with clear, lively commentary.

QUICKEN FINANCIAL PLANNER
Intuit, $39.95
■ A step-by-step guide to creating a custom financial plan for retirement, along with guidance on how much you should save, how to invest, and how to track your progress.

PERSONAL INVESTING

The following programs are for experienced investors. They let you screen stocks, bonds, or mutual funds and then manage your portfolio. All except Pulse also let you trade securities by modem through discount brokerage houses.

REUTERS MONEY NETWORK
Reality Online, $24.95 (Free with WealthBuilder)
■ Good choice for mutual fund watchers. This combination software and online service lets you sort through a database of stocks, bonds, and certificates of deposit. The program suggests CDs, mutual funds, and money market funds that fit your investment goals. It also updates and analyzes Quicken and Microsoft Money portfolios.
☎ 800–346–2024

CAPTOOL
Techserve, $149
■ For the serious investor who is primarily interested in individual stocks. Does sophisticated calculations, such as your stock, bond, or mutual fund portfolio's internal rate of return.
☎ 800–826–8082

STREET SMART
Charles Schwab, $39
ON-LINE XPRESS
Fidelity Investment $49.95
■ For those who have accounts with Schwab or Fidelity, these programs let you place trades before the market opens and download account information. Both offer 10 percent off the firms' standard discount brokerage commissions for customers who trade with the software.
Schwab: ☎ 800–334–4455
Fidelity: ☎ 800–544–9375

WINDOWS ON WALL STREET
MarketArts, $49.99
■ For technically minded investors who need to chart and analyze performance. A deluxe version for $179 comes with seven years of historical data.
☎ 800–998–8439

TAX PREPARATION

Returning consumer information cards to manufacturers is especially important to buyers of tax software, which is updated yearly. Manufacturers can then send information about new editions. The price of all tax software, of course, is tax deductible. The following three programs allow you to take charge of your taxes.

TURBOTAX DELUXE
Intuit, $39.95
■ The top seller. Visual displays are easy on the eye. Good at finding deductions.
☎ 800–964–1040

KIPLINGER TAXCUT
Block Financial Corp., $29.95
■ Tips on just about everything, even tricky questions. Also included: Kiplinger Tax Estimator program for tax planning and a tax guide, Sure Ways to Cut Your Taxes.
☎ 800–457–9525

PERSONAL TAX EDGE
Parsons Technology, $19
■ Includes 80 of the most popular federal forms, schedules, and worksheets (for individual tax prep only) and a good help system. A bargain if you're on a tight budget.
☎ 800–223–6925

TOOLS

FOR BUDDING PUBLISHERS

This software lets you design pages—from book to Web

Desktop publishing (DTP) software allows you to arrange words and pictures on a page in complex layouts. You can format text, resize and crop pictures, and move elements freely around a page. Luisa Simone, contributing editor of *PC Magazine* and author of *Microsoft Publisher by Design* (Microsoft Press, 1996) and *The Windows 95 Scanning Book* (John Wiley, 1996), helps beginning desktop publishers make some important decisions.

■ **WORD PROCESSING VS. DESKTOP PUBLISHING** Word processing programs are geared toward a linear flow of text, while DTP programs allow for much more flexible placement of text and pictures. If you are producing a document where stories flow in sequence from page to page, a word processor is sufficient. If you want to produce a highly formatted document that includes three or more columns, lots of pictures, or stories that jump to noncontiguous pages, you should seriously consider a DTP program so you can control typographic elements like interword spacing (called tracking) and intercharacter spacing (called kerning), align text across columns, control the way text wraps around pictures, and prepare files for high-resolution output at a service bureau or for commercial printing.

■ **MAC OR PC?** The Mac has long been the preferred platform for DTP, but Windows users no longer have to feel like second-class citizens. In fact, the two most popular desktop publishing programs—QuarkXpress and Adobe PageMaker—are available for both the Mac and PC, as is FrameMaker. If you are planning to send your projects to a service bureau or commercial printer, look for a program that has a Mac counterpart and produces what's called binary-compatible files. This means that the files you create on your PC can be opened directly on the Mac—without any special conversion routines.

■ **COMPARISON SHOPPING:** If you want to produce standard business publications for a small business, turn to products that offer both ease of use and low cost, like Microsoft Publisher or Serif PagePlus. To produce design-intensive documents that require a high degree of typographic control, full-color separations, and robust prepress functions, Adobe PageMaker and QuarkXpress are the programs of choice. For generating long documents like reference books or technical manuals, Adobe FrameMaker and Corel Ventura let you create and maintain complex cross-references, contents lists, and indexes.

■ **PRICING:** Prices will vary depending upon where you buy your software. In general, you can buy Microsoft Publisher and Serif PagePlus for under $100 and Ventura for slightly more than $400. High-end programs, like Adobe PageMaker, QuarkXpress, and Adobe FrameMaker hover between $600 and $700.

■ **HARDWARE:** Most DTP software runs fine on a 486 processor. However, if you are using a DTP program for business, you'll probably

■ LEADING DESKTOP PUBLISHING PACKAGES

COREL VENTURA
Corel Corp. ☎ 800-772-6735

FRAMEMAKER
Adobe Systems ☎ 800-628-2320

MICROSOFT PUBLISHER
Microsoft Corp. ☎ 800-426-9400

PAGEMAKER
Adobe Systems ☎ 800-628-2320

SERIF PAGEPLUS PUBLISHING SUITE
Serif ☎ 800-489-6719

QUARKXPRESS
Quark Inc. ☎ 800-676-4575

EXPERT LIST

THE WRITE STUFF FOR WRITERS

Edward Mendelson, Columbia University English professor and contributing editor of PC Magazine *picks the best of the batch. These packages are expensive: expect to pay between $100 and $400. The good news is you can't really make a mistake: all the programs listed are good. Because word processing software is updated frequently, we haven't listed specific versions. The features referred to were available as this book went to press in mid-1996.*

FOR PCS

LOTUS WORD PRO
Lotus Development Corp.
■ This Windows-based word processor excels at group editing and consolidating multiple versions of documents. Also an excellent desktop publishing application. Built-in Internet features let you import and export Web pages.

MICROSOFT WORD FOR WINDOWS, *Microsoft Corp.*
■ Automation features, like correcting misspelled words as you type, make text-entry, formatting, and graphics features easy to use. With a free add-on available at Microsoft's Web site, you can prepare documents for the Web.

WORDPERFECT FOR WINDOWS, *Corel Corp.*
■ A great package for people who love program shortcuts to customize their word processors. Great at handling complex, multipart documents that require precise formatting. Includes a full-feature spreadsheet and advanced graphics tools.

WORDPERFECT FOR DOS
Corel Corp.
■ This package proves you don't need an advanced operating system to enjoy one of the most advanced word processors. Offers nearly all the features of WordPerfect for Windows.

FOR MACINTOSHES

MACWRITE PRO, *Claris*
■ Not as feature-rich as other Mac word processors but a bargain at under $100. With a communications link, you can send e-mail directly from the word processor. Also has great search-and-replace and graphics capabilities.

WORD FOR THE MAC
Microsoft Corp.
■ Probably the best of the Mac word processors. Has every feature that its Windows counterpart does.

WORDPERFECT FOR MAC
WordPerfect Corp.
■ For point-and-click addicts, WordPerfect for the Macintosh has a toolbar for everything—mail merges, formatting, fonts, tables, and more.

SOURCE: Reprinted from *PC Magazine*, November 21, 1995.

need to increase both your storage capacity and memory (RAM). You'll probably have to upgrade your hard disk (think in gigabytes, not megabytes), and you may also consider buying a high-capacity removable storage device, such as a Syquest drive or a Zip drive, in order to transport files to a service bureau.

■ **WEB PUBLISHING:** To publish documents on the Web, you must produce a standard format called HTML (HyperText Markup Language). Authoring programs, such as SoftQuad's HoT-MetaL allow you to easily insert HTML codes into plain text documents. Programs like In Context Spider and Attachmate Emissary let you preview HTML documents, and utility programs such as Microsoft's Internet Assistant add HTML capability to Word for Windows. You can expect to see HTML functions in most DTP programs by 1997.

ONLINE

ONLINE SERVICES: A guide to your options, PAGE 683 **E-MAIL:** Electronic correspondence is fast, PAGE 685 **TECH TALK:** The lingo of cyber-communication, PAGE 686 **TOOLS:** Some software and search engines to help you navigate online, PAGE 688 **WEB SITES:** The top places for a plethora of interests, PAGE 689 **HOME PAGES:** You can create your own, PAGE 694 **TIPS:** How to avoid trouble on the Internet, PAGE 696

CYBERSPACE

THE ABC'S OF THE INTERNET

Things you need to know about the online world but were afraid to ask

These days, the Internet is everywhere. World Wide Web addresses are plastered on the sides of buses, displayed on television, and printed throughout books like this one. Businesses, colleges, and charities of every variety are busy designing home pages. Managers and executives are getting their e-mail addresses printed on their business cards. Wall Street is in a virtual frenzy when fledgling companies whose business has anything to do with the Internet offer stock to the public. It doesn't seem to matter that almost no one has found a way to make money on the Internet yet. Only dyed-in-the-wool skeptics doubt that the Internet is the communications medium of the future and that the future is now.

But, what exactly is the Internet? And what is all this fuss about going online? More to the point, how can you sign up, set up, and find out for yourself what all the hype and hoopla is all about? What follows is an Internet primer for the uninitiated.

INTERNET BASICS

The Internet is a globally linked network of computers that began life as a means of communication for academia and the military. Since then, the Net has evolved into a resource that anyone can use for just about anything—academic, professional, or leisure pursuits or whatever else brings you online. The Net is not run by any single entity; instead, it is maintained by those who've contributed content to it. You learn the rules of the Internet by being online and by participating.

What seems like a seamless web to users, isn't. The Internet is actually divided into several distinct parts:

THE WORLD WIDE WEB— The Web is the graphical component of the Internet—meaning that information is presented with words, pictures, photos, tables, charts—and, increasingly, advertisements.

INTERNET E-MAIL— This is exactly what you would expect. It is used for exchanging e-mail messages and file attachments with anyone who has access to the global network.

USENET NEWSGROUPS— A collection of thousands of topic-specific bulletin boards that cover every subject under the sun.

INTERNET RELAY CHAT (IRC)— This part of the Net is used for "talking" online with others.

FILE TRANSFER PROTOCOL (FTP)— The part of

cyberspace used for downloading files from Internet sites.

A lot of information is available on the Net, but finding what you're looking for is another matter. And chances are, you will not be entirely satisfied with the process or the result. Because of the Internet's decentralized nature, information is haphazardly organized, at best. To search the Internet's vast resources—the World Wide Web, FTP, and Usenet newsgroups—you'll need to consult an Internet directory, also known as a search engine. (See "Online Tools You Can Use," page 688.) Think of a search engine as a spontaneously generated yellow pages. You tell the search engine what you're looking for, using either a keyword or phrase, and the search engine consults its continually updated index of Internet resources and returns a listing of items—often with literally thousands of entries—that match your request. Some matches may be more accurate than others. Furthermore, the different search engines have different methods of indexing the Internet and conducting searches, thereby often yielding different results. Like the yellow pages, you may or may not find what you're looking for.

FACT FILE:

HOW BIG IS THE INTERNET?

There's no question that the Internet is immense—and growing at warp speed. Just how big is a hot topic for debate. Here are some recent estimates:

- **20 to 30 million people** *throughout the world use the Internet.*
- *As of mid-1996, there were more than* **22 million pages of content** *on the World Wide Web.*
- *Over* **1 million new pages** *are added each month.*

SOURCE: Dataquest.

GETTING ONLINE

The first thing you'll need is a modem and a phone line. Ideally, you'll use a 28.8-Kbps modem for a fast connection and a phone line with call-waiting disabled so your online session will not be interrupted.

Then you have a few choices. Most commonly, you'll get online by dialing up a commercial online service or a dedicated Internet service provider (ISP). When you go online with an ISP, you're establishing what is called a dial-in connection. Dial-in connections make use of either SLIP (Serial Line Internet Protocol) or PPP (Point-to-Point Protocol), and are the next best thing to having a permanent connection like the one you may find at your office or university. Your modem dials up an Internet server directly. With an online service, your modem dials up the computer of a service provider that has a permanent connection. It's kind of a twice-removed connection to the Internet. The commercial online services and most national Internet service providers (see chart, facing page) provide you with a package that includes all the software and files needed to get you online quickly and easily, as well as provide a technical support line in case you run into problems. Local ISPs are sometimes less expensive than national ISPs, but they often don't provide one-step software installation or an accessible technical support line.

ONLINE SERVICES VS. INTERNET SERVICE PROVIDERS

Online services—such as America Online and CompuServe—are akin to boutique department stores, providing specialty items as well as merchandise generally available elsewhere. Each offers its own content, which is only accessible to members of the service, as well as an on-ramp to most of the Internet.

The biggest difference between the Internet access you'd get from an online service and that which you'd get from a dedicated Internet service provider lies in the speed of your connection. The online service is slower—searches aren't as speedy and it takes longer for graphics and text to appear on your screen. Also, there's often greater congestion than you'd likely experience with an ISP.

On the other hand, each online service has its unique content to offer, sometimes making a trip to the Internet unnecessary. If you're choosing between the online services, consider the content of the service; the pricing; and whether the service is geared toward families, businesses, or both (see chart below). CompuServe gets high marks for the depth of its offerings. America Online is generally considered more user-friendly—meaning that it's easier to move around the site and find things. Wow!, a new service from CompuServe, is aimed at kids and families.

If you're going online primarily for Internet access, you face a different set of questions. First and foremost, how much time do you plan on spending on the Internet? As of mid-1996, the online services were generally charging $9.95 per month with your first five hours free, and additional hours billed at $2.95. Internet service providers tend to charge around $19.95 to $24.95 per month for unlimited access. In another words, if you are going to spend nine hours or more surfing the Net, you might pay less with an Internet service provider.

Those savings could evaporate quickly, however, if the service you choose does not have a local access number for your area. Toll charges can add up. All the big online services offer local access numbers across the U.S., but in some rural areas, you might be better off with an ISP. Another consideration: how many members of your household will want to be online. Some online services, such as America Online and Wow!, allow multiple user names under one account. This means that everyone in your family can have his own e-mail address and personalized settings. ISPs, generally, do not allow multiple users.

SUBSCRIBER'S GUIDE

COMPARING THE ONLINE SERVICES

Ready to go online? Use this comparison chart to help you decide which online service or Internet service provider is right for you. Keep in mind that most of these services offer a one-month free trial so you can try the service out. Also, The Microsoft Network and Wow! from CompuServe are only for Windows 95; all of the other services are available for the Macintosh, Windows 3.1, and Windows 95.

AMERICA ONLINE

■ Excellent content, including *The New York Times*, *Entertainment Weekly*, *Consumer Reports*, and *Business Week*. A solid selection of business resources, second only to CompuServe. Strong integration with the Internet (including Microsoft Internet Explorer Browser), a streamlined interface, and Internet child-proofing makes this a great service for the entire family.

■ **FEE:** $9.95 for 5 hours; $19.95 for 20 hours.
☎ 800–827–6364

AT&T WORLDNET

■ AT&T has adapted Netscape Communications Corp.'s Netscape Navigator Personal Edition to make setting up an Internet account as painless as it gets. Plus, AT&T has added its own Customer Care tools, which make trouble-shooting a snap. A downside is that AT&T's Navigator is at least one step behind the latest available version.

■ **FEE:** $4.95 for 5 hours; $24.95 for unlimited hours. Prices are less for AT&T long-distance phone customers.
☎ 800–967–5363

COMPUSERVE

■ In spite of its unwieldy interface, nothing matches CompuServe's depth of research resources or Internet access tools. The

■ EXPERT LIST

premium databases include Dun & Bradstreet Online, and the invaluable Database Plus series (offering full-text article retrievals of business, computers, health, and general interest magazines).

■ **FEE:** $9.95 for 5 hours; $24.95 for 20 hours.
☎ 800–848–8199

THE MICROSOFT NETWORK

■ A great interface is coupled with such strengths as integration with the Web and selective but strong content. A solid choice for home and business users. Included are online versions of Microsoft's Bookshelf reference and Encarta encyclopedia, NBC News online, Deloitte & Touche Online, and Schwab Online.

■ **FEE:** $4.95 for 3 hours; $19.95 for 20 hours.
☎ 800–386–5500

NETCOM

■ Offering easy access to the Internet, Netcom includes a copy of Netscape Navigator 2.0 with your sign-on software.

■ **FEE:** $19.95, unlimited use.
☎ 800–353–5600

PRODIGY

■ The interface and speed of Prodigy needs improvement. Still, Prodigy offers safeguards to protect kids on the Net, as well as some excellent children's areas. Homework Helper is a wonderful research resource, as is Dow Jones News/Retrieval Service.

■ **FEE:** $9.95 for 5 hours.
☎ 800–776–3449

PSINET PIPELINE USA

■ The software is easy to set up, but if you want to use a browser other than the one provided by Pipeline, you'll need to download it first. Features localized, city-specific, online communities for: Atlanta, Boston, Dallas, Las Vegas, London, Los Angeles, New York, and Washington, D.C.

■ **FEE:** $19.95, unlimited use.
☎ 703–904–4100

WOW! FROM COMPUSERVE

■ Great for families, this is the newest kid on the online services block. Offering the Internet on training wheels, Wow! caters specifically to novices. Kids have their own interface and content, while parents have the peace of mind about their kids' safety online. Wow! has the easiest-to-navigate interface, which can best be described as colorful and unintimidating. The content is still revving up and has a ways to go before matching the likes of America Online.

■ **FEE:** $17.95, unlimited use.
☎ 800–943–8969

Sources: Individual companies.

■ **BASIC FEATURES:**

	America Online	AT&T Worldnet	CompuServe	Microsoft Network	Netcom	Prodigy	PSINet Pipeline	Wow! from CompuServe
Supports any Web browser	✔	✔	✔	✔	✔	NO	✔	NO
24-hour technical support	✔	✔	NO	✔	✔	✔	✔	✔
Multiple screen names per account	✔	NO	NO	NO	NO	✔	NO	✔
Direct Internet access services division	✔	NO	✔	NO	NO	✔	NO	NO
Free personal home pages	✔	NO	✔	NO	✔	✔	✔	NO

E-MAIL

THE CYBER-POSTMAN

Snail mail may soon be as antiquated as Pony Express

E-mail is cheaper, faster, and can be more convenient than snail mail, as the cyberhip refer to correspondence that arrives in envelopes with canceled stamps in the corner. So what's the rub? Well, you can't enclose a check—at least, not yet, so it is not a great way to pay your bills. You have to have access to a computer. It takes a lot of 32¢ stamps to buy one of those. Getting an invitation electronically—whether it's for a fancy dress ball or a kid's birthday party—just isn't the same. But, otherwise, e-mail probably has the post office beat. If only more people would rely on it—as they undoubtedly will.

Actually, there's another e-mail hassle to overcome. Using e-mail at home requires that you pay monthly fees to an online service or Internet service provider. That used to be a somewhat expensive proposition. Now, however, you can find low-maintenance plans, offered by AT&T Worldnet, The Microsoft Network, and others, for as little as $4.95 per month for five hours online. If you prefer a commercial online service, America Online and CompuServe have the best e-mail systems, but they are more expensive.

If you can type, composing e-mail is a breeze. First, you'll use an e-mail editor—such as Qualcomm's Eudora Light or the editors built in to online services—to create your message. Once you're online and send your message, it travels across the Internet's global maze of interconnected computers until it arrives at its destination. Delivery time ranges from a few minutes to a few hours. If, say, you're on America Online and you're sending a message to someone else who is also a member of AOL, delivery can be virtually instantaneous.

E-mail addresses may seem more complicated than zip codes, but they're actually rather simple to deconstruct. Addresses consist of two parts: your user name (whatever name or number you would enter to sign on online) and your domain's name (which specifies where your service provider is located on the Internet). The two segments are separated by an @ sign. So veryimportantperson@aol.com would be read as: "very important person at aol dot com," where "veryimportantperson" is the user name, "aol" indicates that the address is on America Online, and "com" indicates that the site is a commercial site (as opposed to, say, ".edu," which indicates an academic institution, or ".gov," which indicates a government organization).

A bonus to using e-mail is that you can easily attach documents, spreadsheets, and graphics to your messages. If you send an attachment via the Internet, you'll be using what's called Multipurpose Internet Mail Extensions (MIME), a standard e-mail protocol that automatically encodes attachments. The attachment must be "decoded" with special software before it may be properly viewed. If you send an attachment from one of the commercial online services to someone on the same service, decoding isn't a problem.

EXPERT SOURCES

Looking for the e-mail address of an old friend? Try checking either of these growing online e-mail directories.

Bigfoot Directory
http://bigfoot.com

Four11 Directory Services
http://www.four11.com

TECH TALK

LEARNING THE LANGUAGE ONLINE

A handy glossary of terms and symbols that'll get you fluent online

Talking in cyberspace is not impersonal; you just have to know how to speak the language. People express emotions online with "emoticons," symbols that denote happiness, sadness, anger, and other garden-variety, as well as complex, feelings. Abbreviations are shortcuts for commonly used online idioms: slang, in other words. Online etiquette requires knowing the language; you would be well advised to learn the following emoticons and abbreviations before you go online, just as you would study a bit of useful French before you travel to France.

■ FREQUENTLY USED ABBREVIATIONS

<bg> Big grin.
<g> or <G> Grin.
AFKB Away from keyboard.
BTW By the way.
f2f Face to face, used when referring to meeting an online friend in person, or when you'd like to.
FAQ Frequently Asked Questions (see next column).
IMHO In my humble opinion.
IMNSHO In my not so humble opinion.
IOW In other words.
IRL In real life.
ITRW In the real world.
LOL Laughing out loud.
MorF? Male or female? Used when your online name is gender-neutral.
OTF On the floor (laughing).
RTFM Read the f***ing manual, usually in response to a question you could have figured out on your own.
WRT With regard to.
YMMV Your mileage may vary.

■ FREQUENTLY USED TERMS

Browser—Software, such as Internet Explorer or Netscape, for PC Windows- or Mac-users that allows one to point and click one's way around the World Wide Web.

BBS—Bulletin board service. Cheaper than major online services, BBSes are generally run by a small number of people as a hobby bringing together people who share a common interest. Most are regional. Generally, you join a BBS by paying an annual fee (between $30 and $50 a year) as well as an hourly online fee (35¢ to $2.50 an hour). To find lists of BBSes (there are thousands of them), consult magazines such as *Boardwatch Magazine* (☎ 303-973-6038) or *Computer Shopper* (☎ 212-503-3800).

FAQ (Frequently Asked Questions)—Electronic handbooks filed at most Usenet newsgroups that answer most questions you'll have about that site; read them before you participate to avoid getting flamed (see below).

Flame—An inflammatory statement that is often rude, and occasionally crude. Flames are common on online services and the Internet. Newcomers sometimes are flamed for ignoring "netiquette."

Gopher—A search tool that helps you find files, services, and sites on the Internet by listing them in menu form. People at the University of Minnesota developed the software, so they got to name it (after their mascot).

Home page—The reception area for World Wide Web sites (see below). A home page welcomes you, lists the site's features and areas, and gives you a menu of choices about which to access.

Hypertext—Highlighted text in a file (a hyperlink) that is linked electronically to another file. Point and click on a word, and a new file pops up. Hypertext is the primary means of navigating the World Wide Web (see below).

Internet Relay Chat (IRC)—Instead of exchanging messages via e-mail, this tool lets you talk

■ COMMONLY EXPRESSED EMOTICONS

Here are some codes for getting your point across in cyber-conversations.

- :-) Smile; happy; "I'm joking."
- :-(Frown; sadness; "Bummer."
- :-| Can't decide how to feel; no feelings either way.
- :-D Big, delighted grin.
- :-P Sticking out your tongue.
- :-O Yelling, or completely shocked.
- :-() Can't (or won't) stop talking.
- :-& Tongue-tied.
- :-X Lips are sealed.
- :-)~ Drooling.
- ;-) Wink; denotes pun or sly joke.
- |-O Yawning or snoring.
- %-) Confused but happy; drunk or under influence of controlled substances.
- %-(Confused, unhappy.
- :'-(Crying.
- :'-) Crying happy tears.
- :-} or :-] Sarcastic smile.
- :-\ Mixed feelings, mostly happy.
- :-/ Mixed, but mostly sad.
- {} or [] Hug.
- * Kiss.
- {{{* *}}} Hugs and kisses.
- (:-) User is a skinhead.
- B-) User wears horn-rimmed glasses.
- :-# User wears braces.
- -:-) User has a mohawk.
- C=:-) User is a chef.
- +-:-) User is the Pope or holds some Christian office.
- (8-o User is Saturday Night Live–alumnus Mr. Bill.

in "real time" with people: It's a typed, instead of spoken, conversation.

HTML (HyperText Markup Language)—The traditional computer programming language for developing documents on the World Wide Web, HTML identifies (or marks up) the various components, such as the title, and allows for hyperlinks to other pages.

Java—A newer computer programming language for embedding a mini program (or "applet"), such as an animation, into a document on the World Wide Web.

Lurk—To read posts in a Usenet newsgroup (see below) for a time without posting, virtually listening in on conversations without participating in them; one who lurks is a "lurker." Lurking is encouraged when you first join a newsgroup to get a sense of the atmosphere and conversations, but if you lurk for too long, you may inspire suspicion and get flamed.

URL (Uniform Resource Locater)—A World Wide Web site's address, the URL typically looks something like this: http://www.somethingorother.

Usenet newsgroups—The group of over 7,000 Internet discussion groups, whose diverse topics range from Elvis to toxic waste to computer programming.

VRML (Virtual Reality Modeling Language)—A programming language for making 3-D images on the World Wide Web.

World Wide Web—The "cool" multimedia portion of the Internet, the Web is where all the action is these days.

EXPERT SOURCES

ONLINE TOOLS YOU CAN USE

NAVIGATION SOFTWARE

To surf the World Wide Web, you'll need a Web browser; if one of these two popular browsers is not included with your online access software, you can download a copy.

NETSCAPE NAVIGATOR

Netscape Communications Corp., free

■ Arguably the Web browser of choice, Netscape Navigator is the innovator, always at the cutting edge. Download the latest version from: http://www.netscape.com

MICROSOFT INTERNET EXPLORER

Microsoft Corp., free

■ Microsoft's Internet Explorer is your best alternative to Netscape. Download a copy of the latest version from: http://www.microsoft.com

OFFLINE NAVIGATION UTILITIES

To download Web pages or Usenet newsgroups for reading at your leisure, check out these utilities.

WEBWHACKER

The Forefront Group, $49.95

■ This handy program lets you download individual Web pages, groups of pages, or entire Web sites, retaining the pages' original format and storing them on your hard disk. Download a trial copy at: http://www.ffg.com.

NETBUDDY

Internet Solutions, free

■ NetBuddy will monitor your favorite sites for changes and alert you. You can download the latest version from: http://www.netree.com/netbuddy.html.

SMART BOOKMARKS

First Floor Software, $24.95

■ Smart Bookmarks helps you organize your browser's bookmarks. You can also monitor your favorite pages for changes, and download them for reading offline.

OUI

Dvorak Development, $39

■ OUI lets you subscribe to your favorite Usenet newsgroups, and then locate, retrieve, download, and post information to and from those newsgroups. Download a trial copy at: http://www.dvorak.com.

CYBERSEARCH

Frontier Technologies Corp., $29.95

■ This useful CD-ROM provides offline searching of the first half-million records in the Lycos database.

ONLINE DIRECTORIES

There are plenty of Internet directories, or "search engines," for locating what you want quickly and easily. Because each search engine combs the Net differently, you may get different results from each. To use any of the ones listed below, simply enter their Web address when you are online and follow the instructions on each home page.

■ **YAHOO!**
http://www.yahoo.com.

■ **LYCOS**
http://www.lycos.com.

■ **A2Z**
http://a2z.lycos.com.

■ **INFOSEEK GUIDE**
http://www.infoseek.com

■ **EXCITE**
http://www.excite.com.

■ **POINT**
http://www.pointcom.com

■ **ALTA VISTA**
http://www.altavista.digital.com.

■ **HOTBOT**
http://www.hotbot.com.

CYBERNAUT'S GUIDE

THE ULTIMATE HOT LIST

On the World Wide Web, finding the gems among the junk can be tough. That's why the editors at Wolff New Media, which publishes the best-selling NetBooks *series, launched a Web site that describes and recommends places to visit in cyberspace* (http://www.ypn.com). *Your Personal Net, or YPN, contains reviews of thousands of sites, which you find by keying in a subject that interests you. Here are YPN's favorites.*

GETTING STARTED

■ Best Place to Get Direction: Yahoo is the cleanest, fastest, and simplest online directory around. Just plug in a keyword describing what you want to investigate and Yahoo will offer you hundreds of sites to visit.
http://www.yahoo.com

■ Best General Computer Site: c|net offers general-interest reporting on the computer industry, as well as recommendations about equipment, all within a clean, easy-to-navigate site.
http://www.cnet.com

SOUND ADVICE

■ Best Place for Rockers: Atlantic's beautiful Web site allows the rock faithful to check in on Atlantic artists such as Brandy, Edwin McCain, Frances Dunnery (who contributes an online road diary to the site), and Jill Sobule; chew the fat with other fans in Atlantic's chat room; or download sound and movie clips. The Atlantic Web site also serves as a promotional site for Spew+, a high-tech, high-energy, enhanced CD-ROM magazine.
http://www.atlantic-records.com

■ Best Place for Alterna-kids: High-end graphics, cutting-edge sound compression, and a firm sense of purpose are the hallmarks of the Internet Underground Music Archive (IUMA), a huge site with information on every aspect of the independent music industry.
http://www.iuma.com

■ Best Place for New York's Underground: After more than a year as one of the leading independent rock bulletin boards, SonicNet has moved onto the Web, and it's a wonderful site that concentrates on alternative music in the New York City area.
http://www.sonicnet.com

■ Best Personal Music Agent: Tell your personal online agent your musical tastes and firefly retrieves from cyberspace communities, movies and musical gems that may interest you. After the agent makes a recommendation, you can search firefly's extensive database of album listings to listen to sound clips, purchase albums, or discuss with other netizens what interests you.
http://www.ffly.com

ENTERTAINMENT

■ Best Place to Go for TV Listings: TVNet tells you what's on TV right now, no matter where you are. Tune in, turn on, and then turn on the TV.
http://www.tvnet.com

■ Best Place to Track an Entertainment Behemoth: Sony is one of the biggest entertainment companies in the world, and its Web site delivers on that stature, with areas devoted to film, music, video, and more.
http://www.sony.com

■ Best Place to Go for a Laugh: Comedy Central has long been earning its reputation as the smart aleck of cable channels, and the network's Web site not only reports on on-air programs but develops Internet-only content that's guaranteed to leave you in stitches.
http://www.comcentral.com

■ Best Tinseltown Surrogate: Hollywood Online delivers press releases, promotional

stills, plot summaries, and the latest gossip on today's hottest new movies.
http://www.hollywood.com

■ **Best Place for Fans of the Silver Screen:** For film trivia buffs, there's no place better than the Internet Movie Database, which includes detailed hyperlinked cast lists and credits for every movie imaginable.
http://www.msstate.edu/movies/

■ **Best Place for Quality Film:** Miramax has produced some of the best films of the '90s, and now the studio has produced one of the most interesting Web sites of the first phase of Internet development. With contests, articles, and an online chat area called the Miramax Cafe, this is the place to go if you want to cement your celluloid aficionado credentials.
http://www.miramax.com

■ **Best Online Magazine (Sort Of):** It's hard to single out only one magazine in a medium stuffed with publications of every shape and size. But Salon has succeeded where other publications have failed, in part because it has tried to understand how the technology of the Web can be maximized for design and editorial ends, and in part because it isn't afraid to deliver substantial articles on topics ranging from national politics to cutting-edge literature.
http://www.salon1999.com

THE SPORTING LIFE

■ **Best Place to Dunk:** Didn't get a large enough dose of hoops on TV? The NBA's site offers basketball fans up-to-date scores, schedule information, player profiles, and Dennis Rodman's spectacular hair.
http://www.nba.com

■ **Best Place for Everything Sports:** ESPN's inexhaustible coverage loses no steam online. Included are top sports stories of the week, scores for the games you missed, trivia, athlete bios, a program schedule, and live chat rooms for various sports. There are even audio clips of your favorite sports show's theme music.
http://espnet.sportszone.com

■ **Best Place for the Fan:** Fan chat rooms, contests, and polling stations breed visitor participation. The real attraction, however, is Sportsline's comprehensive listing of statistics.
http://www.sportsline.com

OFF AND ON THE BEATEN TRAIL

■ **Best Traditional Guidebook:** Fodor's has been guiding travelers for 60 years, and if you're smart, you'll let the venerable travel publisher continue to guide you. The Fodor's Web site contains thousands of entries for restaurants, hotels, and recommended activities the world over. Useful information abounds for all travelers from seniors to currency-lacking college globe-trotters. Information can be searched by keyword.
http://www.fodors.com

■ **Best Nontraditional Guidebook:** The publishers of the ecologically and politically correct Lonely Planet travel guides have gone online. Use the interactive map to gain excellent, illustrated descriptions of the climate, history, economy, and culture of countries worldwide.
http://www.lonelyplanet.com

■ **Best Place to Learn Foreign Tongues:** A remarkably useful site for travelers to research key phrases in preparation for a voyage to a foreign-speaking country. Users select their native language followed by the language they want to learn and instantly are thrown into a linguistic crash course. Have a craving for the obscure? Esperanto offered.
http://www.travlang.com/languages/

IN SICKNESS, IN HEALTH

■ **Best Place for General Medical Info:** Medaccess promotes family health by providing downloadable health work-

■ CYBERNAUT'S GUIDE

books to keep track of children's immunizations and illnesses (user-friendly for the organizationally challenged), a health and safety alert section direct from the Federal Food and Drug Administration for the latest toxin reports on common household goods, and a section called You Are What You Eat, which investigates just what's in that chicken and rice casserole.
http://www.medaccess.com/home.htm

■ **Best Place to Get Quick Answers to Medical Questions:** Got a health-related question? Well, why not Ask Alice, a service of the Health Education and Wellness program of Columbia University. In the past, the service has answered queries about air-popped popcorn, the health value of avocados, and problems with body odor. The site archives the answers and allows users to search them. It's certainly one of the most user-friendly and valuable health resources on the Net.
http://www.columbia.edu/cu/healthwise/

■ **Best Use of Web Technology to Save Lives:** Want to find out who's donating bone marrow and in what quantity anywhere in the world? Go to the Bone Marrow Donor's Web. Broken down by region, this service not only furnishes interesting bone-marrow donation trivia—for instance, there are more donors in New York than in the whole of Poland—but also includes an online match program to tell needy patients where they might find a matching donor.
http://BMDW.LeidenUniv.NL

■ **Best Place for a Healthy Family:** The University of Iowa Family Practice Handbook provides in-depth definitions, lists of symptoms, and types of treatments for most common maladies. The handbook has few graphics and is therefore pretty speedy, which means that even if you long for the friendliness of your local doc, you won't wait in periodical purgatory for upwards of an hour listening to the hum of fish tank filters.

FINANCIAL FINDS

■ **Best Place for Money Information:** Don't like the idea of mongers wrapping fish in your business journal tomorrow morning? Not only does this site offer the latest business news, but articles for the personal investor on money and business management.
http://www.cnnfn.com

■ **Best Place to Make Mutual Friends:** NetWorth not only gives you all the information you'll ever need about mutual funds—ratings, prospectuses, and investment tips from Morningstar—but also includes a fund manager that helps you pick the mutual fund that's best for you.
http://networth.galt.com

■ **Best Place for Corporate Info:** Company information—size, history, corporate philosophy—is a precious commodity in today's world, and Hoover's Online is the Net's biggest gold mine for this sort of data.
http://www.hoovers.com

ALL THE NEWS THAT'S FIT TO DOWNLOAD

■ **Best Place for News, Now:** Six weeks' worth of daily news—including today's—from the CNN folks who brought you Tiananmen Square and the Gulf War. Download a video clip of the latest news item, and read submissions from CNN's contributors.
http://www.cnn.com

■ **Best Place for the Times:** Though *The New York Times*'s online presence is anchored by cultural coverage, the paper also reprints the day's top economic and financial news stories. Beware: Don't cancel your subscription, this is only a selection—and, anyway, you'd miss the crossword puzzle.
http://www.nytimes.com

■ **Best Place for In-Depth News Coverage:** In addition to

news coverage, the National Public Radio Web site offers transcripts of online and radio pieces, interviews with cultural leaders, and a special election area. Everything that you would expect from NPR—even pre-recorded radio shows.
http://www.npr.org

■ **Best Place for Domestic Interests:** News, weather, sports, features, and more. Updated constantly and subscription-based. The *USA Today* Web site is as colorful as its print counterpart.
http://www.usatoday.com

■ **Best Utility News Center:** For a survey of all news, *U.S.News & World Report* offers breaking international and domestic news including a section recapping the day's news for those short on time. Opinion pieces and photo essays give the site a comfortable magazine feel. And, as always, the college and graduate school issues are a real draw.
http://www.usnews.com

■ **Best Magazine Stand:** Visitors can leaf through such popular magazines as *Time*, *People*, *Money*, *Vibe*, and *Entertainment Weekly*. Time-Warner also provides a daily news service.
http://pathfinder.com

MODEMOCRACY

■ **Home Sweet White House:** Our President's home is now online, with recorded greetings from the President and the Vice President, as well as pictures of the First Family, a tour of the grounds, a history of the building, and even a link for Socks the White House cat that finds the First Feline meowing a greeting. (The content could change after the November election.)
http://www.whitehouse.gov

■ **Best Political Joint Venture:** Allpolitics, incorporating the resources of CNN and *Time* correspondents, offers numerous articles on America's political leaders both inside and outside of the Beltway. Feeling alienated from your representatives? Find solace in political discussion groups or vent your frustrations in discussions with key policy makers.
http://allpolitics.com

■ **Best Place to Practice Informed Voting:** Project Vote Smart goes a long way toward keeping the public apprised of what the "hired help" is up to. Simply plug in any Congressperson's name or state and a complete profile pops up, with bios, special interest funding sources, contact information, voting records, and performance evaluations by special interest groups. Vote Smart also follows state governments and the courts, providing analysis of decisions by everyone from Sandra Day O'Connor to the Court of Appeals judge for Skagit County.
http://www.vote-smart.org

ART AND LITERATURE

■ **The Best Electronic Book Clearinghouses:** Alex is one of the largest clearinghouses of electronic-text links, with thousands of books ranging from classical Greek plays to 19th-century fiction to contemporary political philosophy.
http://www.lib.ncsu.edu/stacks/alex-index.html

■ **The Best Shelf Variety:** Amazon.com books offers over one million titles for sale, ranging from the masterpiece to the mediocre. This site doesn't have discriminating tastes and confesses frankly that its only goal is to carry every book in print. Large discounts are available every day.
http://www.amazon.com

■ **Best Web Museum:** The site offers beautiful online art exhibits ranging from a study of Japanese woodblock prints of the Edo era to a thorough examination of Cézanne and his influence on 20th-century artists and art movements. Cancel the trip to the Louvre; it's all here.
http://www.emf.net/louvre/

■ **Best Place for the Booksellers:** Sponsored by the

■ CYBERNAUT'S GUIDE

American Booksellers Association, BookWeb guides the visitor to thousands of bookstores across the country while supplying the latest news about books and publishing. Geared toward members of the publishing world, feature articles tend to be industry-specific, ranging from first amendment issues to marketing ideas.
http://ambook.org/bookweb

■ **Best Book Archive:** The Library of Congress isn't just a huge collection of books; it's also a legislative agency, entrusted with maintaining the documents that bear the nation's laws. Find out all about the library—its holdings, its exhibits, and even its electronic catalog.
http://www.loc.gov

LOOKING IT UP

■ **Best Place for Wordsmiths:** If you're trying to remember the meaning of "punctilious" but can't quite put your finger on it, visit the Hypertext Websters, where looking up words is as easy as sliding your mouse and pressing down.
http://c.gp.cs.cmu.edu:5103/prog/webster

■ **Best Legal Lounge:** The Web site for Nolo Press is as friendly as a legal self-help center can get. Read articles on recent legal developments, leaf through a large archive of briefs and view a catalog that lists related books, videotapes, and software. Message boards are available for curious citizens to post legal queries to experts.
http://gnn.com/gnn/bus/nolo

COMPUTERS

■ **Best Computer Magazines:** A useful site for computer articles, updated daily, from such magazines as *MacUser*, *MacWeek*, *PC Week*, and *PC Magazine*. Also, the site offers a small software archive and an index to Ziff Davis's advertisers' sites.
http://www.zdnet.com

■ **Best Industry News:** CMP Publications is responsible for many of the best-selling computer magazines on the market, and CMP's site delivers the content of those publications, along with computer news and a buyer's guide for the latest high-tech products.
http://techweb.cmp.com/

■ **Best Place to Complain:** Having trouble with your printer? Got a monitor that won't show colors? Go to the Moan and Groan List, which collects tech complaints from hardware and software users around the world.
http://www2.tsixroads.com/Moan

THE NET LOOKS AT ITSELF

■ **Best Place for Giant-Killing:** If you want to see industry leaders and media leviathans lampooned and skewered, come to Suck, the daily column with insight, wit, and a surplus of attitude.
http://www.suck.com

■ **Best Place for Internet Insiders:** The Netly News covers the Internet beat with an eye toward entertainment, supplementing its regular Web-industry features with irreverent news articles, guest rants from luminaries like Penn and Teller, and regular site spotlights.
http://pathfinder.com/netly

■ **Best Place to Get a Handle on the Online World:** Become a regular reader of Flux, and terms like "Luddite revival," "online circulation audit," and "Web demography" will soon be popping up in your everyday speech. And if industry gossip isn't your cup of poisoned tea, pay a visit to the rest of HotWired (http://www.hotwired.com), the online version of the world's premier online magazine.
http://www.hotwired.com/flux

■ **Best Place to Follow Online Media:** Media Central covers everything from cable modems to magazines to subscription services, and does it all with a style that's quick and direct.
http://www.mediacentral.com

THE WEB

A PAGE TO CALL YOUR OWN

It's easy to create a home page. But if you build it, will anyone come?

The early American pioneers who headed west were lured by the promise of 40 acres and a mule. The closest 20th-century equivalent may be a home page on the World Wide Web. Putting down your stake requires little effort and not much expertise. Making it easier still, the building tools you'll need are readily available from the various online services and other sources at little or no cost.

A home page is a page or document on the World Wide Web. Like the home you live in, it has an address—called a URL, the abbreviation for Uniform Resource Locator. Like houses in an old neighborhood, each home page has a different look. Once you have wandered inside, the differences can be even more dramatic, depending upon what you choose to put in it. Your home page can be linked to other Web pages that you've created or others have created.

Before starting construction, you should, of course, give some thought to what you want to appear on your Web page and what you want it to look like. If you need some inspiration, visit the personal home pages created by members of:

America Online: *http://home.aol.com*
CompuServe: *http://ourworld.compuserve.com*
Prodigy: *http://pages.prodigy.com*

Creating a Web page can be as simple as filling in the blanks. America Online, CompuServe, and Prodigy all offer software that will walk you step-by-step through the process. In addition, all three services will, at no extra charge beyond your monthly fee, "host" your page on the Web, which amounts to giving you some space on their computers to store your material. CompuServe's home page software is the easiest to use and the most flexible, but AOL and Prodigy also do a reasonable job.

If you're determined to build your Web page from scratch, you'll need to learn a few more skills, namely the basics of Hypertext Markup Language, or HTML, which is the standard computer programming language of the Internet. The codes that make up HTML are used to apply different styles and attributes to a Web page, which in turn tell your Web browser how to display the page. HTML is continually being updated, which is the reason why many Web pages carry a caveat stating that the page is best viewed when using a particular version of a Web browser. The latest browser versions will support the latest innovations, and viewing a Web page with an older version of a browser or a different browser than the one specified will often affect how the page is displayed on your screen.

More advanced types can create their Web pages using a specialized word proces-

EXPERT SOURCES

Time to learn HTML? Check out these Web sites for HTML reference guides, Web design aids, and links to other resources:

Microsoft's Internet Resources
http://www.microsoft.com/intdev/author

HTML Style Guide & Test Suite
http://www.charm.net/~lejeune/styles.html

Netscape's Creating Net Sites
http://home.netscape.com/assist/net_sites/index.html

A WEB DESIGNER'S DECORATING MAXIMS

Ready to do your own home page? Darrell Sano, a user-interface designer at Netscape Communications Corp. and author of Designing Large-Scale Web Sites: A Visual Design Methodology *(John Wiley & Sons, 1996), offers beginners these five tips:*

■ **Plan your message and objectives.**

Ask yourself, "Why am I creating this Web page? What do people want to know, or what information would people find useful?" This is especially important if you are planning to sell products or services. Your message should be focused toward your users. Building a Web site requires planning and forethought. Even an individual's personal home page should be carefully planned out; after all, your home page is a reflection of you.

■ **Start rough and slowly refine.**

You don't have to be an artist to complete rough sketches of your page. Sketching out Web pages is a quick, easy way to visualize alternative site layouts.

■ **Don't let your users get lost.**

Your visitors should always know where they are within a Web site. They should also know where they can go—and where they came from. Identification information should be placed on all pages and displayed in a consistent manner so users won't have to scan the page, looking for clues as to where they are. Consistency contributes to a welcome predictability and familiarity, enhancing usability.

■ **Use images wisely.**

Graphics should add value to the user's experience. The opportunities for creative expression are great, but keep in mind how the page will appear from the user's point of view. It's always a good practice to provide a text equivalent for any graphic link, especially large image maps, since many Web users temporarily defer image loading in exchange for increased speed when loading a Web page. Also, make sure backgrounds do not interfere with the legibility of your text. Finally, it's always a good idea to test your page with various browsers. You'd be surprised how different your page may appear!

■ **Keep it simple.**

Remember that simple designs are easier to understand than complex ones. A Web page packed with text and meaningless graphics can repel users. Keep in mind that reading on a computer screen is more difficult than on paper, so brevity is important. A simple Web page will stand out from all the visual "noise" currently found on many Web sites.

sor called an HTML editor, and then post their pages online through an Internet service provider, rather than relying on one of the online services. Some popular HTML editors include Netscape Communications Corp.'s Netscape Navigator Gold; Microsoft's Internet Assistant, which enables you to edit HTML files from within your familiar Microsoft Word environment; Sausage Software's Hot Dog Standard Web Editor; and SoftQuad's HotMetal Pro. Another option is utilizing programs such as DeltaPoint's QuickSite and Corel Corp.'s CorelWEB.Designer, which provide a graphical way to design Web sites without any prior knowledge of HTML.

EXPERT TIPS

AVOIDING TROUBLE ON THE NET

Caution kids, don't give out credit-card numbers, and hold your tongue

By now everyone has heard horror stories about life on the Net. And indeed the dangers are real. There are sites unsuitable for children. Credit-card transactions are not 100 percent safe. You could pick up a computer virus from a downloaded file or get slapped with a lawsuit for saying something stupid. But don't let the naysayers spoil your fun. Follow these tips, and you'll face a minimum of hassles.

PROTECTING THE KIDS

■ There's a movement under way—and legislation pending—to rid the Internet of obscene material. But it's not clear yet whether it will succeed. In the meantime, the best defense against online creeps is to teach children that cyberspace is a public space, like the park or a grocery store. The same rules apply about strangers. Personal information, like home or school address, should not be given out to strangers online. Younger children should be supervised by adults.

■ To prevent older children from accessing sites with adult content, there are parental control programs such as SurfWatch Software's SurfWatch or Microsystems Software's Cyber Patrol. These programs deny access to sites known for showing nude photos and the like, as well as sites with telltale words (sex and "XXX," for example) in their titles. Typically, they cost about $50, and you can often buy monthly updates that screen recent sites for less than $20. But they're no substitute for good parenting; they won't catch every bit of naughtiness on the Web, and they may block some perfectly respectable sites.

■ Another way to restrict children to areas designed for them is to choose an online service made especially for kids, such as CompuServe's Wow! Like a children's book, there's no adult content here.

BUYER BEWARE

■ The Internet is not yet a secure environment for conducting financial transactions, although lots of work is being done to solve this problem. The safest course is to refrain from giving out your credit-card information until the latest efforts to make the Internet secure are well established. You can always phone the proprietor whose goods or services you're interested in purchasing and give your credit-card information that way—assuming you think the telephone is safe.

AVOIDING VIRUSES

■ The effects of computer viruses range widely from essentially pranks that advocate the legalization of marijuana or protest nuclear testing to disasters that wipe out the entire contents of your hard disk. Smart computer users scan their hard disks and floppy disks for viruses frequently with programs from Symantec, McAfee Associates, and others ($50 and up).

WATCH WHAT YOU SAY

■ Legally speaking, communication on the Net is up for grabs. So until the legal eagles get all the thorny issues sorted out, it's best to keep your head low. Strategies for staying out of trouble: Assume that people who want to can find out who you are even if you use an alias. Don't say anything you wouldn't say in any other public forum—or that you wouldn't want your parent, spouse, or boss to read in the paper the next day. If there's any doubt in your mind about a message you've keyed in, sleep on it; you'll be more rational, and cautious, in the morning.

CHAPTER ELEVEN

SPORTS & GAMES

EXPERT QUOTES

"Be a good teacher to your kids, and they'll learn to love the game from you."
—Cal Ripken, Jr., Baltimore Orioles shortstop
Page 703

"It's a big immortal cycle, and you're the mortal angler."
—James Prosek, author of *Trout: An Illustrated History*
Page 727

"Buy everything you can, until you get around to the three most expensive set of properties."
—Roger Craig, reigning U.S. Monopoly champ
Page 747

■ **THE YEAR AHEAD: EXPECT** Cal Ripkin, Jr., to play shortstop forever... **WATCH** as more and more cities build state-of-the-art stadiums... **BET** that sports gambling will continue to flourish... **DRIVE** to the new Golf Hall of Fame in Ponte Vedra Beach, Florida... **CLICK ON** to ESPNET, the best sports site on the Web... **SKI** Montana, where the crowds aren't... **TRY** snowboarding, which is no longer just for the grunge set... **BUCKLE UP** your inline skates and try America's fastest-growing outdoor sport... **LEARN** how to be an "efficient" swimmer...

A FAN'S GUIDE 698

THE GREAT OUTDOORS 713

WINTER FUN 733

PARLOR GAMES 747

A FAN'S GUIDE

EXPERT TIPS: How to win the office pool, PAGE 701 **BASEBALL:** Take me out to the old ball game, PAGE 702 **CAL RIPKEN:** Advice on how to turn a Little Leaguer into an All-Star, PAGE 703 **PRO FOOTBALL:** Get ready for the kick-off, PAGE 706 **PEEWEE FOOTBALL:** Is the game safe? PAGE 707 **BASKETBALL:** A who's who of hoopsters, PAGE 708 **HOCKEY:** The fastest game on ice, PAGE 710 **HALLS OF FAME:** Shrines for the great and not-so-great, PAGE 711

BEING THERE

JUST THE TICKET FOR YOU

Watch the game, not the box. Here's how to get a seat for big events

Most couch potatoes' idea of a good seat for the Super Bowl is in front of a wide-screen television. But for real sports fans, nothing beats being there—whether it's the Super Bowl, the World Series, the Masters, or whatever. Getting tickets to some of the nation's sporting events—like the Masters, for example—is next to impossible. But you can get in the door to some of the others if you do some advance planning and are prepared for a little hustle. Here's the lowdown on how and where to get tickets to some of the hottest sporting events.

THE SUPER BOWL

January 26, 1997; Superdome, La.

■ Football's biggest game is the world's most-watched television event each year, but the Super Bowl itself is not all that hard to see in person, if you're willing to pay the hefty ticket price ($350 on average last year). Season-ticket holders of the participating teams have the best shot; the AFC and NFC champs split 35 percent of the Super Bowl ducats, most of which are made available to their faithful fans. The host team gets another 10 percent of the tickets, and every other NFL team gets hundreds of tickets, which they generally sell to their own ticket-holders. The league also distributes several thousand tickets each year through a lottery it conducts, which you can enter by sending a self-addressed stamped envelope to the league's office between February and June. The NFL's address is 410 Park Ave., New York, NY 10022.

WORLD SERIES

October 1997; Place to be determined

■ The participating teams control virtually all the tickets to baseball's Fall Classic, so your best bet is to hold season tickets for your favorite team—and hope they make it all the way.

NCAA FINAL FOUR

March 29–31, 1997; Hoosier Dome, Ind.

■ You practically have to jump through hoops to watch the best college-basketball teams fight for the national championship each year. Last year, for instance, just 1,000 of the 18,500 seats at the Final Four went to the general public; some went to the competing colleges and the host, and the rest to coaches, corporate sponsors, and college sports officials. The NCAA received more than 91,000 applications for those 1,000 tick-

THE BEST VALUES IN SPORTS

You' ll get the most for your money in Cleveland

The Cleveland Indians fell short in their 1995 quest to win a World Series for the first time in 47 years. But they are second to none when it comes to being the best fan value in American sports.

That' s according to a 1995 *Money* magazine survey, which ranked teams using a wide range of criteria. It asked fans what mattered most to them, and then rated individual franchises on how well they met the fans' desires. Their top demands were no surprise: parking under $8 and ticket prices under $25. But they also yearned for clean and comfortable facilities, a home team with a winning record, and a local star who's among the top 10 in his sport.

The average cost of attending a game in Cleveland's sparkling new Jacobs Field for the 1995 season was $35.62 for two, including parking, tickets, and two hot dogs and sodas. By comparison, a day for two at Texas Stadium to see Emmitt Smith and the rest of the Dallas Cowboys would cost $92.34. Baseball teams dominated the list of the top values. While every major league team has average ticket prices under $25, just three National Basketball Association teams and no National Football League teams have ticket prices that low.

■ TOP 10 SPORTS VALUES:

Picks from *Money* magazine's survey:

Team	Cost
1. Cleveland Indians	$35.62
2. Chicago Cubs	$45.84
3. Indianapolis Colts	$67.36
4. Kansas City Royals	$31.10
5. San Francisco Giants	$37.14
6. San Diego Padres	$27.24
7. Atlanta Braves	$40.00
8. Green Bay Packers	$62.26
9. Dallas Cowboys	$92.34
10. Miami Dolphins	$84.12

ets, which means you had about as good a chance of winning the lottery as you did of sitting courtside at the New Jersey Meadowlands for the Final Four. The NCAA's decision to hold most future championship games in arenas that hold 30,000 seats or more will alleviate the problem somewhat, but Final Four tickets will still be tough to get. The NCAA begins taking applications just after the previous year's tournament. Write to NCAA, 6201 College Blvd., Overland Park, KS 66211.

THE MASTERS

April 7–13, 1997; Augusta, Ga.

■ It's almost as hard to watch golf's big event in person as it is to play a round at Augusta National, the famous Georgia course on which it is played each year. Only the lucky few on Augusta National's "patron's list" are allowed to buy tickets each year. The list is made up primarily of people who had been attending the tournament before 1968, and those people who've been added to it off the very long waiting list—which itself was closed to new members in 1978. Your best chance of seeing top golfers play at Augusta National is to go a few days early for the practice rounds. Fans interested in those tickets should write the club just after the end of the previous year's tournament: Augusta National, PO Box 2086, Augusta, GA 30903.

If you care more about great golf than the majesty of the Masters, you might check out the U.S. Open. The 1997 Open, which will be held June 12–15 at Congressional Country Club in Bethesda, Md., will make 25,000 of its 35,000 tickets available to the general public. Tickets are first-come, first-served, and go on sale, by mail, the day after the 1996 Open ends. Write the U.S. Golf Association at P.O. Box 1500, Far Hills, NJ 07931, or call at ☎ 800-336-4446.

INDIANAPOLIS 500

May 25, 1997; Indianapolis Motor Speedway

■ Hundreds of thousands of people turn out every year for auto racing's big day, which is also one of the world's biggest parties. But despite the huge number of seats, it's still a tough ticket. About 95 percent of the 300,000 seats are filled through renewals—people who attend the race one year and, within a week, request renewals or upgrades for the next year's 500. Only after all renewals and upgrades are accommodated do new requests get considered. To request tickets for the first time, you must send a check or money order (no credit cards) to the Indianapolis Motor Speedway, 4790 W. 16th St., Indianapolis, IN 46222, immediately after the end of the prior year's race. Your timing must be good: Requests received before the race will be returned. New requests are considered in the order of the date received. The only seats that are ever available to new requesters are the least-expensive seats ($30 in 1997); all other seats, which range in price up to $140 and average about $65, are filled by repeaters.

While many new requests get turned down, there is hope: If you're turned away one year, your request will get considered before other new requesters if you apply for tickets again the following year. And if you really want to see the race, the speedway sells general-admission, standing-room-only tickets the day of the race. But these are a last resort: Peggy Swalls, director of ticket operations, describes them as "partial view."

KENTUCKY DERBY

May 3, 1997; Churchilll Downs, Ky.

■ The infield is the place to be for the Run for the Roses; more than 80,000 people mill around inside the track oval drinking juleps each year, while about 48,000 sit in the cushier boxes. The box seats (sold in sets of six) and the infield tickets are available by writing to the Kentucky Derby ticket office at 700 Central Ave., Louisville, KY 40208, at the conclusion of the previous year's race.

SNAGGING A SEAT, WHEN THERE AREN'T ANY

Just because the game is sold out doesn't mean that you can't get a ticket. Here's a scalper's guide

Selling tickets at more than face value is illegal in many places. But it is the scalpers who face arrest, not the ticket buyers. And if a game is completely sold out—or so the newspaper says—buying a scalped tickets can be your best and only way to see the game in person.

Scalping, of course, is somewhat of a covert activity. Reselling tickets at any price on stadium grounds is illegal in some places, so much of the commerce takes place in surrounding areas. You may get a good deal here, but you're probably better off waiting.

The more scalpers you see, the more patient you should be; as game time approaches, the prices will drop. If the game is not sold out, or if demand is not high, try to wait until right before the game starts, and you' ll discover a buyer's market. Desperate to unload tickets, scalpers will sell them for as little as a third of the price they paid.

If it's a very big game, the seekers will far outnumber the sellers, and prices may be steep. Scalped tickets at events like the Super Bowl and Final Four can run as high as $1,000. Try to bargain for the best price you can get. Most scalpers are trying to do brisk business, so they may take your reasonable offer.

Before you decide to buy, make sure to get a good look at the tickets; fake ones are often sold, and while you may not be able to recognize them, it's worth a try. Whatever you do, don't buy a press pass; it's probably fake, and even if it's not, you're almost sure to get discovered and thrown out.

EXPERT TIPS

HOW TO WIN THE OFFICE POOL

The odds are you'll lose even if you follow our oddsmaker's advice

Americans bet billions of dollars in office pools every year, part of an estimated $100 billion that they wager on sporting events overall. Most people would be better off giving the money to charity—at least they'd get a tax writeoff that way.

Sports gambling is a losing proposition for all but the savviest—and luckiest—bettors. The odds are better than for casino games like roulette and blackjack, where the house's statistical edge ensures that you will lose over time. But if you bet (legally) through a casino sports book, or (illegally) with your local bookie, you still give up a share of your bet in payment, so you have to win more than half the time just to break even.

Knowing full well that bettors won't be deterred, we asked Russ Culver, who runs the sports book at Palace Station Casino in Las Vegas, and helps set the Associated Press odds that appear in hundreds of newspapers each day, for his tips on successful sports gambling in general, and on winning the office pool in particular.

■ **Avoid "analysis by paralysis."** That's what Culver calls the overdependence on statistics and sports trivia. "Knowing that a guy is successful stealing bases 87 percent of the time isn't going to help you figure out if his team will win," says Culver.

■ **Look for trends.** The currency of the smart sports bettor isn't stats but psychology—looking for shifts in a team's fortunes and abilities as they happen, or even before. If you spot such a trend, and it makes intuitive sense, go with it—but realize that it may be nothing more than a coincidence. Differentiating between relevant trends and those that aren't takes time, but it's worth the effort. "Knowing that a team goes 8–1 on Thursdays probably isn't important, but knowing that the Bears haven't won a road game straight up since 1987 may well be," Culver says.

■ **Ignore the polls.** The Associated Press polls of the nation's best college basketball and football teams are "nothing more than beauty contests," Culver says. The rankings are heavily skewed toward the best-known programs with the most popular players and famous coaches. Frequently, he notes, oddsmakers will give the lower-ranked teams an edge in the betting line. So when looking at the NCAA tournament bracket in the office pool, bet against the glamour teams when they're playing a strong team that's not as popular.

■ **Momentum matters more than records.** When analyzing a baseball matchup, Culver focuses primarily on a pitcher's last five starts. In college basketball, he recommends looking at how a team played down the stretch in the period just before the NCAA tournament. A team that finished third in its league in the regular season, but came on strong to win the conference tournament, deserves a good look.

■ **The seedings mean little in the NCAA tournament.** Around tournament time, pundits will spout statistics about how many times 13th-seeded teams have upset 4th-seeded teams. Ignore that, says Culver: "The NCAA will never admit it, but those seedings are gerrymandered to give them the best matchups for television. The No. 1 and No. 2 ranked teams are accurate, but once you get from No. 4 to about 12, they screw around with those for TV."

■ **Parity makes NFL betting a nightmare.** The National Football League has few truly dominant teams right now, and while that equity makes for exciting competition, it makes betting that much harder. Culver notes that of teams favored by 10 points or more, only about 1 in 3 covers the spread these days. It's also very hard to read momentum in the NFL, he says.

BASEBALL FAN'S GUIDE

TAKE ME OUT TO THE BALL GAME

You can still get peanuts and Cracker Jacks, of course. But the fare is getting fancier at a lot of America's ballparks. In Baltimore, you might try the crab cakes; in L.A., the sushi; in Miami, the empanadas and Cuban sandwiches. But the game is the same. Here's the batting order for the 1997 season. As always, the World Series is scheduled for October.

Team	LAST TITLE World Series	LAST TITLE League	Stadium	Capacity	Ticket information
AMERICAN LEAGUE EAST					
BALTIMORE ORIOLES	1983	1983	Oriole Park at Camden Yards	48,079	410–685–9500
BOSTON RED SOX	1918	1986	Fenway Park	33,871	617–267–8661
DETROIT TIGERS	1984	1984	Tiger Stadium	52,416	313–962–4000
NEW YORK YANKEES	1978	1981	Yankee Stadium	57,545	718–293–6000
TORONTO BLUE JAYS	1993	1993	Skydome	50,516	416–341–1111
AMERICAN LEAGUE CENTRAL					
CHICAGO WHITE SOX	1917	1959	Comiskey Park	44,321	312–924–1000
CLEVELAND INDIANS	1948	1995	Jacobs Field	42,400	216–241–5555
KANSAS CITY ROYALS	1985	1985	Kauffman Stadium	40,625	816–921–8000
MILWAUKEE BREWERS	—	1982	County Stadium	53,192	414–933–1818
MINNESOTA TWINS	1991	1991	Hubert H. Humphrey Metrodome	56,783	612–375–7444
AMERICAN LEAGUE WEST					
CALIFORNIA ANGELS	—	—	Anaheim Stadium	64,593	714–634–2000
OAKLAND ATHLETICS	1989	1990	Oakland–Alameda County Stadium	47,313	510–638–0500
SEATTLE MARINERS	—	—	Kingdome	59,702	206–628–3555
TEXAS RANGERS	—	—	The Ballpark in Arlington	48,100	817–273–5222
NATIONAL LEAGUE EAST					
ATLANTA BRAVES	1995	1995	Centennial Olympic Stadium*	49,831	404–683–6100
FLORIDA MARLINS	—	—	Joe Robbie Stadium	46,238	305–626–7400
MONTREAL EXPOS	—	—	Olympic Stadium	46,500	800–463–9767
NEW YORK METS	1986	1986	Shea Stadium	55,601	718–507–8499
PHILADELPHIA PHILLIES	1980	1993	Veterans Stadium	62,238	215–463–1000
NATIONAL LEAGUE CENTRAL					
CHICAGO CUBS	1908	1945	Wrigley Field	38,765	312–404–2827
CINCINNATI REDS	1990	1990	Riverfront Stadium	52,952	513–421–7337
HOUSTON ASTROS	—	—	Astrodome	53,821	713–799–9555
PITTSBURGH PIRATES	1979	1979	Three Rivers Stadium	47,972	412–321–2827
ST. LOUIS CARDINALS	1982	1987	Busch Stadium	57,078	314–421–4060
NATIONAL LEAGUE WEST					
COLORADO ROCKIES	—	—	Coors Field	50,400	303–762–5437
LOS ANGELES DODGERS	1988	1988	Dodger Stadium	56,000	213–224–1400
SAN DIEGO PADRES	—	1984	San Diego Jack Murphy Stadium	46,510	619–283–4494
SAN FRANCISCO GIANTS	1954	1989	Candlestick Park	63,000	415–467–8000

* Beginning with 1997 season.

EXPERT Q & A

HOW TO BE LIKE CAL

Advice from a legend on turning a Little Leaguer into an All-Star

With major-league baseball stars signing multimillion-dollar contracts and basking in the spotlight, it's tempting for parents to look at their little athletes and say: "Hmmm. If I just push him a little harder..."

Don't do it, says Cal Ripken, Jr. The baseball star, who plays for the Baltimore Orioles and wowed the world with his gritty, gracious pursuit of Lou Gehrig's consecutive-game streak, understands the temptation that parents feel (he's got two kids of his own, after all). But he counsels parents to let kids develop an appreciation for baseball and other sports at their own pace. Pushing them won't help, he says. "In order to instill passion for the game, it has to be inside of you. And it's only going to develop if a kid comes to it on his or her own, and if it's fun."

Although Ripken grew up in a baseball family (his dad, Cal Sr., was a longtime coach for the Orioles), he was not pushed into playing the game. Still, his desire to play in the big leagues burned inside him, and from an early age: The night before his first Little League game, he surreptitiously slept in his uniform, his glove by his side. He just wanted to be ready, he said.

Here are Ripken's tips for the nearly 3 million kids who play on Little League teams, and for their parents:

■ What's the best way to get kids interested in baseball?

The most important thing is to keep it on a fun level. You've got to gear it to whatever makes kids enjoy playing. The worst thing you can see is to go to a little-league game and have parents yelling at the kids. I understand the competitiveness, but too much emphasis on winning saps a lot of the fun out of it. Kids should be encouraged to play any position they want, and to experiment.

■ How do you make it fun?

Just let them see how much you enjoy it. I take my young son to the batting cage, and he watches me having a good time. Be a good teacher to your kids, and they'll learn to love the game from you.

■ What's the right age to start?

My first competition was as an 8-year-old, which was the age

FACT FILE:

UNBREAKABLE RECORDS?

■ *Nobody thought Lou Gehrig's record of 2,130 consecutive games played would ever be broken, but Cal Ripken did it. Here are some other "unbreakable records." But don't ever think they won't be broken. Says Ripken: "If you'd asked me 15 years ago if I thought I or anybody else could play that many straight games, I'd have said 'No chance.' But now I think every record can conceivably be broken, because I don't consider myself to be an iron man, or think there's anything super special about me."*

HOME RUNS IN A SEASON:
Roger Maris 61

MOST HOME RUNS IN A CAREER:
Hank Aaron 714

HITS IN CONSECUTIVE GAMES:
Joe DiMaggio 56

CAREER STRIKEOUTS
Nolan Ryan 5,714

IF YOU CAN'T WAIT UNTIL OPENING DAY

For spring training, fans have two choices: the Grapefruit League in Florida or the Cactus League in Arizona. Here are the places to catch a game before the regular season starts.

	TEAM	STADIUM	CAPACITY	TICKET INFO
AMERICAN LEAGUE				
EAST	Baltimore Orioles	Fort Lauderdale Stadium, Fort Lauderdale, Fla.	8,340	954-776-1921
	Boston Red Sox	City of Palms Park, Fort Myers, Fla.	6,850	813-334-4700
	Detroit Tigers	Joker Marchant Stadium, Lakeland, Fla.	7,027	813-499-8229
	New York Yankees	Legends Field, Tampa, Fla.	10,000	813-879-2244
	Toronto Blue Jays	Grant Field, Dunedin, Fla.	6,218	813-733-9302
CENTRAL	Chicago White Sox	Ed Smith Stadium, Sarasota, Fla.	7,500	813-287-8844
	Cleveland Indians	Chain O'Lakes Stadium, Winter Haven, Fla.	7,042	813-291-5803
	Kansas City Royals	Baseball City Stadium, Davenport, Fla.	7,000	407-839-3900
	Milwaukee Brewers	Compadre Stadium, Chandler, Ariz.	10,000	602-895-1200
	Minnesota Twins	Lee County Stadium, Fort Myers, Fla.	7,500	800-338-9467
WEST	California Angels	Diablo Stadium, Tempe, Ariz.	9,785	602-678-2222
	Oakland Athletics	Municipal Stadium, Phoenix, Ariz.	8,500	602-392-0217
	Seattle Mariners	Peoria Stadium, Peoria, Ariz.	10,000	602-784-4444
	Texas Rangers	Charlotte Co. Stadium, Port Charlotte, Fla.	6,026	813-625-9500
NATIONAL LEAGUE				
EAST	Atlanta Braves	Municipal Stadium, West Palm Beach, Fla.	7,200	407-683-6100
	Florida Marlins	Space Coast Stadium, Melbourne, Fla.	7,200	407-633-9200
	Montreal Expos	Municipal Stadium, West Palm Beach, Fla.	7,200	407-966-3309
	New York Mets	St. Lucie Co. Stadium, Port St. Lucie, Fla.	7,400	407-871-2115
	Philadelphia Phillies	Jack Russell Stadium, Clearwater, Fla.	7,195	813-442-8496
CENTRAL	Chicago Cubs	HoHoKam Park, Mesa, Ariz.	8,963	800-638-4253
	Cincinnati Reds	Reds Spring Training Complex, Plant City, Fla.	6,700	813-752-7337
	Houston Astros	Osceola Co. Stadium, Kissimmee, Fla.	5,100	407-839-3900
	Pittsburgh Pirates	McKechnie Field, Bradenton, Fla.	6,562	813-748-4610
	St. Louis Cardinals	Al Lang Stadium, St. Petersburg, Fla.	7,600	813-822-3384
WEST	Colorado Rockies	Hi Corbett Field, Tucson, Ariz.	7,726	800-638-7625
	Los Angeles Dodgers	Holman Stadium, Vero Beach, Fla.	6,500	407-569-6858
	San Diego Padres	Peoria Stadium, Peoria, Ariz.	10,000	602-878-4337
	San Francisco Giants	Scottsdale Stadium, Scottsdale, Ariz.	10,000	602-784-4444

when kids could really play the whole game—hitting, throwing, and running. I think it's great you're now shown parts of the game through T-ball and other games like that. Kids can learn how to slide and run a lot earlier than I did.

■ A lot of kids love to play but hate to practice. How do you make practice fun?

To learn baseball, like other things, you have to teach fundamentals, and then give kids ample time to practice them. Repetition is key. But it's got a downside: It's boring. The answer is to try to figure out creative ways to make it fun—to find games within the games. Take a game like pepper, and come up with a system where you get points for catches and good throws and make it a competition. All of a sudden the kids won't even realize they've fielded 100 ground balls.

STRIKING OUT SOUTH OF THE BORDER

Who says the season's over in October? Try the Caribbean League

The winter months are dark days for baseball fans. The World Series is a distant memory, and the promise of spring training is still months away. But there's no need to fret: The answer is just a plane ride away. Visit the Caribbean winter leagues.

Each winter, from November through January, some of baseball's best players head south to play for teams in the Dominican Republic, Mexico, Puerto Rico, and Venezuela. Many of the players are Latinos who return to the home countries that helped get them to the big leagues. Others are younger players sent by their major-league teams for intensive off-season training. Still others are older free agents trying to impress potential suitors.

Roberto Alomar of the Baltimore Orioles, Edgar Martinez of the Seattle Mariners, and Carlos Perez of the Montreal Expos were among the big-league stars who ventured south to keep their skills sharp in the winter leagues last season. The most established players are found in the Puerto Rican league; Mexico features the fewest.

The baseball comes cheap (most tickets are $5 or less) and the sideshows are distinctly Caribbean—scantily dressed cheerleaders dancing on the dugouts, salsa music between innings, and piña coladas hawked by vendors in the aisles.

For a real treat, take in the Caribbean Series, in which the winning team, from each of the four winter leagues—joined by all-stars from the league's remaining teams—go head to head for the regional championship each February. And if the baseball bug makes you want to venture even farther afield, winter leagues are emerging in Hawaii and Australia, too.

■ FOR MORE INFORMATION:
Call or write these leagues for details.

DOMINICAN LEAGUE
Estadio Quisqueya, Santo Domingo, Dominican Republic
☎809–567–8371

MEXICAN PACIFIC LEAGUE
Pesqueria No. 301–R. Navojoa, Sonora, Mexico
☎52–642–2–3100

VENEZUELAN LEAGUE
Avenida Sorbona, Edif. Marta–2do. Piso, #25, Colinas, De Bello Monte, Caracas, Venezuela
☎582–751–2079

PUERTO RICAN LEAGUE
PO Box 1852, Hato Rey, P.R. 00919
☎809–765–6285

■ Is burnout for young pitchers a real threat?

In order to develop your arm you need to develop arm strength, and the way you do that is by throwing straight. Throwing curves doesn't help build up kids' arms. I don't think that you want to not allow them to throw it, but you should make sure that they throw 70 to 80 percent fastballs. You can always teach a kid who has a good arm to throw breaking balls, but if you don't have arm strength, you can't learn to throw a fastball.

■ Major leaguers aren't always the best role models; some big stars catch with one hand and violate other basic fundamentals. What do you tell a kid who notices that?

I'll be at a clinic telling kids how important it is to throw overhand, to develop arm strength and accuracy, and a kid'll say, "But I saw you on TV and you threw the ball sidearm on a double play." I'll say, "When you get older, you can do some of these things to speed up your throws. But when I was your age, I threw overhand." That's the truth, and it's about all you can say.

FOOTBALL FAN'S GUIDE

GET READY FOR THE KICK-OFF

Not since the Romans put a gladiator in a ring with a lion has a sport been so brutal and so popular. Men and boys—and increasingly women and girls—huddle in front of the TV set to watch hulking grown men throw themselves at each other. But that experience doesn't compare to being at the stadium in person.

Team	LAST TITLE		Stadium	Capacity	Ticket information
	Super Bowl	Conference			
AMERICAN FOOTBALL CONFERENCE EAST					
BUFFALO BILLS	—	1994	Rich Stadium	80,091	716-649-0015
INDIANAPOLIS COLTS	1971	1971	RCA Dome	60,272	317-297-7000
MIAMI DOLPHINS	1974	1985	Joe Robbie Stadium	73,000	305-620-5000
NEW ENGLAND PATRIOTS	—	1986	Foxboro Stadium	60,794	508-543-1776
NEW YORK JETS	1969	1969	Giants Stadium	76,891	516-538-7200
AMERICAN FOOTBALL CONFERENCE CENTRAL					
BALTIMORE RAVENS	—	—	Memorial Stadium	60,020	410-547-5696
CINCINNATI BENGALS	—	1989	Riverfront Stadium	60,389	513-621-3550
HOUSTON OILERS	—	—	Astrodome	62,439	713-797-1000
JACKSONVILLE JAGUARS	—	—	Jacksonville Stadium	73,000	904-633-6000
PITTSBURGH STEELERS	1980	1996	Three Rivers Stadium	59,600	412-323-1200
AMERICAN FOOTBALL CONFERENCE WEST					
DENVER BRONCOS	—	1990	Mile High Stadium	76,273	303-433-7466
KANSAS CITY CHIEFS	1970	1970	Arrowhead Stadium	77,872	816-924-9400
OAKLAND RAIDERS	1984	1984	Oakland–Alameda County Stadium	65,000	310-322-5901
SAN DIEGO CHARGERS	—	1995	San Diego Jack Murphy Stadium	60,836	619-280-2121
SEATTLE SEAHAWKS	—	—	Kingdome	66,400	206-827-9766
NATIONAL FOOTBALL CONFERENCE EAST					
ARIZONA CARDINALS	—	—	Sun Devil Stadium	73,521	602-379-0102
DALLAS COWBOYS	1996	1996	Texas Stadium	65,024	214-579-5000
NEW YORK GIANTS	1991	1991	Giants Stadium	77,311	201-935-8222
PHILADELPHIA EAGLES	—	1981	Veterans Stadium	65,187	215-463-5500
WASHINGTON REDSKINS	1992	1992	Robert F. Kennedy Memorial Stadium	56,454	202-546-2222
NATIONAL FOOTBALL CONFERENCE CENTRAL					
CHICAGO BEARS	1986	1986	Soldier Field	66,950	312-663-5100
DETROIT LIONS	—	—	Pontiac Silverdome	80,500	313-335-4151
GREEN BAY PACKERS	1968	1968	Lambeau Field	59,543	414-496-5719
MINNESOTA VIKINGS	—	1977	Metrodome	63,000	612-333-8828
TAMPA BAY BUCCANEERS	—	—	Tampa Stadium	74,296	813-870-2700
NATIONAL FOOTBALL CONFERENCE WEST					
ATLANTA FALCONS	—	—	Georgia Dome	70,500	404-223-8000
CAROLINA PANTHERS	—	—	Carolinas Stadium	72,300	704-358-7000
NEW ORLEANS SAINTS	—	—	Louisiana Superdome	69,065	504-522-2600
SAN FRANCISCO 49ERS	1995	1995	Candlestick Park	66,513	415-468-2249
ST. LOUIS RAMS	—	1980	Trans World Dome	67,000	314-982-4267

PEEWEE FOOTBALL

SHOULD KIDS PLAY FOOTBALL?

Is soccer a safer alternative? Our experts tackle the questions

Your eight-year-old comes home one day and proudly announces his intention to try out for the local peewee football team. You've just finished watching another NFL quarterback get carried off the field on a stretcher. It's hard not to picture your son in the same position some day. Do you let him play?

Dr. Jeffrey L. Brown, a clinical associate professor in pediatrics and psychiatry at New York Hospital–Cornell Medical Center, compares such a decision to the many other major choices parents must make each day about their children, from what kind of school they should attend to whether and when they should drive a car. "You take into account the child's wishes, and the risk or benefit for them. But ultimately, the decision should always be the parents'," says Brown, who writes a monthly column for *Child* magazine.

Okay, so you know your child's wishes: He wants to play. What are the risks and benefits?

How you weigh the two varies to some extent from child to child, especially as they grow older. Participating in a sport like football may be more important for children who "need it for self-esteem," Brown says, because it makes them "stand out" in high school or is their "ticket to college." Those factors must be considered against the chances of "putting the body at risk."

How great is that risk? That, too, varies depending on the level of play. In general, football has become much safer in the last 25 years as equipment has improved and rules have been tightened to prevent certain kinds of hitting, says Frederick O. Mueller, who heads the National Center for Catastrophic Sports Injury Research at the University of North Carolina at Chapel Hill. The number of deaths and paralyzing injuries caused by football has dropped dramatically since the late 1960s. In 1968, 36 people died from football-related injuries; in 1994, the latest year for which statistics are available, just one person died. Similar declines in the number of permanently disabling head and neck injuries have brought the annual number down to fewer than 10 a year, says Mueller. "Those numbers are low," he says, though that won't be any consolation "if it's your son or daughter."

While catastrophic injuries are relatively rare these days, knee injuries and concussions appear to be on the rise. Knee injuries especially trouble doctors. "If you screw up your knees playing football," says Brown, "they're hurt for the rest of your life." Brown and Mueller both warn parents to be cautious, but neither aggressively discourages kids from playing football, especially at younger ages, when the level of play is less intense and knee injuries are generally less severe. Mueller advises parents to look carefully at the coach and the kind of program he runs—finding out what kind of emergency equipment is on the sidelines at games, for instance, and what kind of preparation is taken to prevent players from getting heat stroke, which has killed several football players in recent years.

Many other sports are just as dangerous as football, if not more so. Per capita, the rates of serious injury are higher in ice hockey, gymnastics, and pole vaulting. Indeed, soccer, often the alternative of choice for those who eschew football, has some drawbacks of its own. Recent studies suggest that soccer players may have abnormal brain-wave readings and lower IQs than other people, probably attributable to hitting the ball repeatedly with their heads. Repeated heading puts soccer players at the same kind of risk as boxers, the studies suggest. "I've been sending kids off to play soccer," Brown admits, "but the better choice may be lacrosse."

BASKETBALL FAN'S GUIDE

A WHO'S WHO OF HOOPSTERS

When the Basketball Association of America and National Basketball League merged just after the 1948–49 season, the National Basketball Association was born. But it wasn't until the early '80s that the NBA exploded in popularity. In 1995, the NBA added expansion teams in Vancouver and Toronto. Starting in the 1997 season, the Washington Bullets will be known as the Wizards. Here's the line-up for the 1996–97 season.

Team	LAST TITLE		Stadium	Capacity	Ticket information
	League	Conference			
EASTERN CONFERENCE ATLANTIC DIVISION					
BOSTON CELTICS	1986	1987	FleetCenter	18,400	617–523–3030
MIAMI HEAT	—	—	Miami Arena	15,200	305–577–4328
NEW JERSEY NETS	—	—	Byrne Meadowlands Arena	20,029	201–935–8888
NEW YORK KNICKERBOCKERS	1973	1994	Madison Square Garden	19,763	212–465–6000
ORLANDO MAGIC	—	1995	Orlando Arena	16,010	407–649–2255
PHILADELPHIA 76ERS	1983	1983	CoreStates Center	21,000	215–339–7676
WASHINGTON BULLETS	1978	1978	USAir Arena	18,756	301–622–3865
EASTERN CONFERENCE CENTRAL DIVISION					
ATLANTA HAWKS	1958	1961	The Omni	16,368	404–827–3865
CHARLOTTE HORNETS	—	—	Charlotte Coliseum	23,698	704–357–0489
CHICAGO BULLS	1996	1996	United Center	21,500	312–455–4000
CLEVELAND CAVALIERS	—	—	Gund Arena	21,500	216–420–2000
DETROIT PISTONS	1990	1990	The Palace of Auburn Hills	21,454	313–337–0100
INDIANA PACERS	—	—	Market Square Arena	16,530	317–263–2100
MILWAUKEE BUCKS	1971	1974	Bradley Center	18,633	414–227–0500
TORONTO RAPTORS	—	—	SkyDome	22,500	416–366–3865
WESTERN CONFERENCE MIDWEST DIVISION					
DALLAS MAVERICKS	—	—	Reunion Arena	17,502	214–939–2800
DENVER NUGGETS	—	—	McNichols Sports Arena	17,171	303–893–3865
HOUSTON ROCKETS	1995	1995	The Summit	16,611	713–627–0600
MINNESOTA TIMBERWOLVES	—	—	Target Center	19,006	612–673–1313
SAN ANTONIO SPURS	—	—	Alamodome	20,640	210–554–7787
UTAH JAZZ	—	—	Delta Center	19,911	801–355–3865
WESTERN CONFERENCE PACIFIC DIVISION					
GOLDEN STATE WARRIORS	1975	1975	Oakland Coliseum Arena	15,025	510–638–6300
LOS ANGELES CLIPPERS	—	—	Los Angeles Memorial Sports Arena	16,005	213–748–0500
LOS ANGELES LAKERS	1988	1991	The Great Western Forum	17,505	213–480–3232
PHOENIX SUNS	—	1993	America West Arena	19,023	602–379–7867
PORTLAND TRAIL BLAZERS	1977	1992	Rose Garden	21,401	503–231–8000
SACRAMENTO KINGS	1951	1996	Arco Arena	17,317	916–928–6900
SEATTLE SUPERSONICS	1979	1979	Key Arena	17,102	206–283–3865
VANCOUVER GRIZZLIES	—	—	GM Place	20,004	604–688–5867

HOT SHOTS

THE HOME COURT ADVANTAGE

What you need to know to build the hoop of your dreams

Dr. James Naismith created the first home basketball hoop by nailing a peach basket to a pole more than a century ago. Designing your home court today is not so easy or inexpensive. But your options are many, ranging widely in quality, durability, and price.

Mobility is crucial to playing basketball, and it's also a key factor in setting up a home court. The traditional 10-foot mounted backboards and pole-secured backboards are still available for those gym rats who want to practice on a regulation hoop. But players trying to dunk like Michael Jordan or shoot three-pointers like Larry Bird can get awfully frustrated if Dad pulls the car into the driveway under the hoop.

Portable baskets and baskets with adjustable heights are no longer as flimsy as they once were. Players who compete in leagues or gyms should be especially careful in selecting a rim. A springed rim (which gives a little when the ball hits it) will give the shooter a better bounce, but it can cause frustration when the player returns to a real court where tighter steel rims are the rule. To get the ultimate home-court advantage, here are your options:

MOUNTED BACKBOARD

Price: around $80

■ The most common of home-court hoops can be attached to the house or garage with a few nuts and bolts.

■ **PROS:** Very sturdy because it has to be attached to a wall or the side of a building.

■ **CONS:** The backboard cannot be moved. The height can't be adjusted either.

PORTABLE BACKBOARD

Price: $200–$300.

■ Wheels on the base of the basket allow you to move it easily by simply tilting the basket forward. The base should be filled with sand or a combination of water and antifreeze to keep the basket from moving. The height can be adjusted from 7 to the regulation 10 feet. Less expensive portable backboards are made of graphite. The more expensive ones have acrylic backboards that shake less and hold up better in inclement weather.

■ **PROS:** The basket can be easily moved to other locations, and the height can be easily adjusted for players of all ages.

■ **CONS:** Even with the acrylic backboard, the basket will still shake on hard shots. Because the base is portable, it can at times be wobbly.

IN-GROUND HOOP

Price: around $300

■ The acrylic backboard is attached to a steel pole and inserted in the ground. The height can be adjusted from 7 to 10 feet.

■ **PROS:** With an acrylic backboard and base in the ground, this is the sturdiest option.

■ **CONS:** It's the most expensive option, and the game cannot be moved.

FACT FILE:

WINNERS AND LOSERS

■ **MOST NBA TITLES**

Boston **Celtics**	16
Minneapolis/Los Angeles **Lakers**	11
Chicago **Bulls**	4
Philadelphia/S. F./Golden State **Warriors**	3
Syracuse Nationals/Philadelphia **76ers**	3

■ **MOST LOSSES IN THE NBA FINALS**

Minneapolis/Los Angeles **Lakers**	13
New York **Knicks**	5
Syracuse Nationals/Philadelphia **76ers**	5
Boston **Celtics**	3
Philadelphia/S. F./Golden State **Warriors**	3
Washington **Bullets**	3
F. Wayne/Detroit **Pistons**	3
St. Louis/Atlanta **Hawks**	3

HOCKEY FAN'S GUIDE

THE FASTEST GAME ON ICE

The top eight teams in each conference qualify for the Stanley Cup playoffs, the outcome of which determines the League's champion. At least one team from each division makes the playoffs. These division leaders are seeded first and second. One plays eight, two plays seven, and so on. The divisions:

TEAM	First season in NHL	Stanley Cups* (most recent win)	Stadium	Capacity	Ticket information
EASTERN CONFERENCE ATLANTIC DIVISION					
FLORIDA PANTHERS	1993–94	0	Miami Arena	14,500	305-358-5885
NEW JERSEY DEVILS	1974–75	1 (1995)	Meadowlands Arena	19,040	201-935-3900
NEW YORK ISLANDERS	1972–73	4 (1983)	Nassau Coliseum	16,927	516-888-9000
NEW YORK RANGERS	1926–27	4 (1994)	Madison Square Garden	18,200	212-465-6741
PHILADELPHIA FLYERS	1967–68	2 (1975)	The CoreStates Center	17,380	215-336-2000
TAMPA BAY LIGHTNING	1992–93	0	ThunderDome	26,000	813-229-8800
WASHINGTON CAPITALS	1974–75	0	USAir Arena	18,130	301-386-7000
EASTERN CONFERENCE NORTHEAST DIVISION					
BOSTON BRUINS	1924–25	5 (1990)	The FleetCenter	17,200	617-227-3200
BUFFALO SABRES	1970–71	0	Crossroads Arena	19,500	716-856-8100
COLORADO AVALANCHE	1979–80	1 (1996)	McNichols Arena	16,058	303-893-6700
HARTFORD WHALERS	1978–79	0	Hartford Civic Center	15,635	800-469-4253
MONTREAL CANADIENS	1917–18	23 (1993)	Montreal Forum	21,400	514-932-2582
OTTAWA SENATORS	1993–94	0	Ottawa Paladium	18,500	613-721-4300
PITTSBURGH PENGUINS	1967–68	2 (1992)	Civic Arena	17,537	412-323-1919
WESTERN CONFERENCE CENTRAL DIVISION					
CHICAGO BLACKHAWKS	1926–27	3 (1961)	United Center	17,742	312-559-1212
DALLAS STARS	1967–68	0	Reunion Arena	16,914	214-467-8277
DETROIT RED WINGS	1926–27	7 (1955)	Joe Louis Arena	19,275	313-396-7544
ST. LOUIS BLUES	1967–68	0	Kiel Center	18,500	314-291-7600
TORONTO MAPLE LEAFS	1917–18	13 (1967)	Maple Leaf Gardens	15,642	416-977-1641
WINNIPEG JETS	1979–80	0	Winnipeg Arena	15,405	204-982-5304
WESTERN CONFERENCE PACIFIC DIVISION					
MIGHTY DUCKS OF ANAHEIM	1993–94	0	Arrowhead Pond of Anaheim	17,250	714-704-2500
CALGARY FLAMES	1972–73	1 (1989)	Olympic Saddledome	20,230	403-777-4646
EDMONTON OILERS	1979–80	5 (1988)	Northlands Coliseum	17,503	403-471-2191
LOS ANGELES KINGS	1967–68	0	Great Western Forum	16,005	310-419-3870
SAN JOSE SHARKS	1991–92	0	San Jose Arena	17,190	408-287-9200
VANCOUVER CANUCKS	1970–71	0	GM Place	19,056	604-280-4400

*As of the end of the 1995–96 season.

EXPERT Q & A

THE HALL OF FAME OF HALLS OF FAME

Over 1,000 shrines honor the great and—well—not-so-great

Pick a sport or pastime and, chances are, there's a hall of fame that honors its legends. Baseball, football, and basketball have their well-known and popular halls, of course, but so do bodybuilding, show jumping, and drag racing. Heck, there's even a dog musher's hall of fame in Knik, Alaska, and a jousting hall in Virginia.

Halls of fame are a peculiarly American phenomenon. (North American, actually; Canada probably has more halls of fame per capita than the U.S.) Such pantheons are rare elsewhere in the world, but well over 1,000 are spread across America. The vast majority are sports-themed, but scores of others feature leading lights in other fields. There's a Barbie Doll Hall of Fame in Palo Alto, Calif., for instance, and an Aviation Hall of Fame in New Jersey. The National Fresh Water Fishing Hall of Fame is housed in a five-story building shaped like a muskie.

Choosing which halls of fame to visit and which to skip can be a daunting task. We asked Paul Dickson, a co-author of the *Volvo Guide to Halls of Fame* (Living Planet Press, 1995), for some recommendations.

■ Of the four major sports—baseball, basketball, football, and hockey—which has the best hall of fame?

It's really hard to beat the baseball hall in Cooperstown, N.Y. It's got everything, and it keeps reinventing itself to stay vital. But all four of them are good, because they realize they're in show business. The day when a hall of fame was a room full of dusty trophies and exhibits is long gone.

■ What are some of your favorites?

The bowling hall is a real sleeper. I'm biased because I discovered a picture of my great-grandfather on a wall there. It's a great place to bowl and have some laughs, and there's a wonderful collection of bowling ceramics, and a collection of 60 antique beer steins all depicting bowling. The Indiana Basketball Hall of Fame and Museum gives you a chance to replicate the buzzer-beater from the movie *Hoosiers*.

■ What are some up-and-coming halls?

Boxing was the last major sport to get its own hall, but they're making up for it now—they're building a whole area for sparring. The soccer hall is now a storefront in Oneonta, N.Y., but it's going to be a big deal—part of a national soccer campus. And look for the new Golf Hall of Fame. It's supposed to open next spring in Ponte Vedra Beach, Fla.

■ If you were planning a trip to see halls of fame, where would you go?

There are three places that come to mind

■ HOW TO GET TO THE HALLS OF FAME

Practice, practice, practice. But if you need directions, call first.

International Ph[illegible]raphy Hall of Fame and Museum, Oklah[illegible] City, OK	☎800-532-7652
Inventure Place—[illegible]ne of the National Inventors Hall of Fame, Akron, OH	☎216-768-4463
Naismith Memorial Basketball Hall of Fame, Springfield, MA	☎413-781-6500
National Baseball Hall of Fame and Museum, Cooperstown, NY	☎607-547-7200
National Bowling Hall of Fame and Museum, St. Louis, MO	☎314-231-6340
National Cowboy Hall of Fame, Oklahoma City, OK	☎405-478-2250
National Fresh Water Fishing Hall of Fame, Hayward, WI	☎800-826-3474
National Jousting Hall of Fame, Mount Solon, VA	☎703-350-2510
National Soccer Hall of Fame, Oneonta, NY	☎607-432-3351
National Softball Hall of Fame, Oklahoma City, OK	☎405-424-5266

EXPERT SOURCES

GOING BY THE BOOKS

Some sports fans aren't satisfied just watching the games and reading about them in the newspaper. So where should you look for the best sports-reference information? We turned to Howie Schwab, a long-time manager of research for ESPN broadcasts, now coordinating producer of the cable network's new online news service. Here are his suggestions for the best sports reference books now available:

BASEBALL

TOTAL BASEBALL: The Official Encyclopedia of Major League Baseball, 4th ed.
Edited by John Thorn and Pete Palmer, with Michael Gershman, Viking, 1995, $59.95
■ The baseball fan's bible. Indispensable.

FOOTBALL

1995 PRO FOOTBALL HANDBOOK
STATS Publishing, 1995, $17.95
■ A relative newcomer to the field, Stats Inc. is ESPN's official provider of sports statistics.

BASKETBALL

OFFICIAL NBA GUIDE, OFFICIAL NBA REGISTER
Sporting News Publishing Co., 1995, $13.95
■ The guide offers team-by-team analysis and statistics; the register provides information on every coach and player in the NBA. *The Sporting News* publishes similar books for all the major sports, and they're all very good.

TENNIS

ATP TOUR OFFICIAL PLAYER GUIDE
Triumph Books, 1995, $12.95
■ Among the best reference books put out by a sports league or governing body itself.

COLLEGE SPORTS

NCAA FOOTBALL AND NCAA BASKETBALL,
National Collegiate Athletic Association, 1996, each $10
■ The official record books of NCAA football and NCAA college hoops, men's and women's. Well done.

GENERAL GUIDES

SPORTS ILLUSTRATED 1996 SPORTS ALMANAC
Little, Brown and Co., 1996, $11.95.
■ Stats and more on everything from football to figure skating.

BEST ONLINE SITES

ESPNET:
http://www.sportszone.com
■ Like the network that spawned it, the current leader in the field.

USA TODAY INFORMATION NETWORK
http://www.usatoday.com
■ Not just sports, but well organized and fun to read, just like the newspaper.

where you can see several great halls of fame. Oklahoma City has three really diverse ones: the National Cowboy Hall of Fame, which is spectacular and one of the biggest; the American Softball Association Hall of Fame, which is a real treat; and the International Photography Hall of Fame. Another prime spot is in upstate New York: You have the baseball hall of fame and the Corvette Americana museum in Cooperstown, boxing in Canastota, and soccer in Oneonta. And one of the great hall-of-fame trifectas is the Canton-Akron-Cleveland area: Canton has the football hall, Cleveland has the new rock and roll hall, and Akron has Inventure Place, which is one of my favorites. It pays tribute to our greatest inventors, like the guy who invented MRI and the inventor of the Kevlar vest, which has saved something like 1,100 cops.

THE GREAT OUTDOORS

ROCK CLIMBING: Best places to get a view in the U.S., PAGE 715 **EXPERT LIST:** The world's toughest endurance competitions, PAGE 717 **CYCLING:** A pro's advice on picking the right bike, PAGE 718 **GOLF:** Ten top public courses, PAGE 721 **TENNIS:** Zina Garrison-Jackson's tips for winning, PAGE 723 **FLY-FISHING:** Where to go in search of trout, PAGE 727 **SWIMMING:** Three ways to start swimming more efficiently, PAGE 731

IN-LINE SKATING

WHEN YOU'RE REALLY ON A ROLL

A glider's guide to the fastest-growing outdoor sport in America

A decade ago, in-line skating was a specialized training device for hockey players during the off-season, as little-known as those little skis with wheels used by the Olympic cross-country ski team during the summer months. These days, in-line skating—still known to some as "rollerblading," after the popular skate manufacturer—is the fastest-growing outdoor sport in the country. At last count, there were more than 20 million participants. Kids ages 6 through 11 account for almost half of all skaters. But the activity is catching on among the parent set, too—people over 35 now account for about 20 percent of skaters.

There are four varieties of in-line skating. Most skaters simply do it for recreation. They're the ones you see coasting down sidewalks or through the local park. Aggressive skating, which resembles skateboarding and is the most difficult and dangerous in-line activity, involves leaping, twisting moves on ramps and stairways. Roller speed skating, now usually practiced with in-line skates, is similar to the same event on ice. But the fastest growing in-line activity is roller hockey, which is similar to the game played on ice. Roller hockey has the backing of the National Hockey League and is now more popular than baseball among California youths. Some colleges are starting up in-line hockey teams.

In-line skating is good exercise. A study published in the American College of Sports Medicine's journal found that in-line skating is as good as running for burning calories and aerobic conditioning. The average person skates at 10 to 12 mph, according to John Porcari, executive director of the LaCrosse Exercise and Health Program at the University of Wisconsin, who conducted the study. A person running at an 8 to 8½ mph pace would feel the effort involved to be about the same.

Here are some pointers before you hit the pavement.

SAFETY AND GEAR

There's a reason in-line skaters suit up with helmets, and pads for knees, elbows, and wrists. According to the International In-Line Skating Association, 73,000 trips to the emergency room in 1995 were caused by in-line injuries. A 1995 study by the Consumer Product Safety Commission revealed 25 deaths from the sport in the last three years. "On a bicycle, it's a matter of *if* you fall. On skates, it's *when* you fall," says Gordon Sanders, an in-line skating instructor.

■ PICKING YOUR PAIR

There are hundreds of in-line skates available. Here are some recommendations for different kinds of skating from *In-line Skater* magazine. Prices are approximate, as of mid-1996.

■ RECREATIONAL SKATING

Roces MEX 4 **$429**
Top of the line speedy skate.

Rollerblade Maxxum **$279**
For the intermediate skater

CCM Tomcat **$155**
Quality for the advanced beginner.

Roller Derby's "The Rail" **$75**
A basic beginner skate.

■ ROLLER HOCKEY

CCM 755 **$539**
For serious competitive play.

Motive M6 **$225**
For an intermediate-level player.

CCM RH 105 **$99**
A beginner's budget skate.

■ AGGRESSIVE SKATING

Roces '62 Impala **$399**
Extra ankle padding and an anti-shock footpad.

Rollerblade Tarmac CE **$249**
Rollerblade's only aggressive skate has a stiff, nylon frame.

Roces Lil' Street **$145**
Aggressive skate for smaller feet.

■ SPEED SKATING

Roces BER **$1,099**
A five-wheel leather skate, with gel padding in the ankle.

K2 2Extreme **$230**
Racing frame sold separately.

■ THE DEVIL IS IN THE DETAILS

■ **PLASTIC BOOT.** Supportive, durable, and designed to flex.

■ **WHEELS.** Bigger isn't always better. Big wheels are faster, but less stable.

■ **RATCHET BUCKLES.** Faster to put on and off, and they tighten better.

■ **NYLON FRAME.** The material of choice—rigid and responsive, yet absorbs shock.

■ **HEEL BRAKE.** Works like a charm.

With an outer layer of plastic, knee pads and wrist guards are made to slide across the ground to transfer the impact of a fall, rather than absorbing it. The helmet and wrist guards are the most important gear. Head injuries are the most serious; wrist injuries, the most common. Elbow pads can prevent nasty scrapes.

The International In-Line Skating Association (☎ 404–728–9707) has instructors all over the country who charge about $25 per hour lesson. Most YMCA chapters provide lessons for about $10. Stores that sell in-line equipment have information on where to take lessons, as well.

THE SKATES

Expect to spend at least $150 to ensure quality wheels, ball bearings, and frames. A decent pair of children's skates costs $50 to $90. Buying used skates is a money-saving option. Paula Caballero, a former editor of *In-Line Skater* magazine, recommends aluminum-framed skates for heavier skaters, because they will support weight better. Women, she says, should ask for skates that are made specifically for women—not just smaller skates that happen to be pink.

The more expensive skates may be too fast for inexperienced recreational skaters. Hockey players should stick with what they know. (Bauer and CCM make in-line skates that are nearly identical to their ice-hockey cousins.) Aggressive skaters should buy cheaper skates, because the sport's wear and tear will break skate frames no matter how well they are made. Novice speed skaters should look into brands that can be converted from four wheels to five. With any skates, the wheels should be rotated to avoid wearing down the edges, and bearings should always be cleaned, particularly after skating in wet areas.

ROCK CLIMBING

CLINGING TO THE CRAGS

For some, it's a sheer delight, for others sheer madness

Some hope to savor what the poet Alfred, Lord Tennyson called the "joy in steepness overcome ... [the] joy in breathing nearer heaven." For others, it is a way to overcome faint-heartedness. Rather than being daredevils, most climbers, in fact, work to reduce the dangers. "Climbers like to have control over their risks," explains George Bracksieck, editor of *Rock and Ice*, a climbing magazine.

High-tech innovations developed over the past 30 years, like spring-loaded gadgets that lock into cracks and stop falls, help minimize the inherent risks of the sport. Besides, climbers can limit their risk according to what style of climbing they take on. Using "top roping," which employs a block and tackle system, a climber can only slip a few inches before the rope stops the fall. Mountaineering, which combines traditional climbing—in which each climber sets his or her own anchors—and ice climbing on high peaks, can be much more dangerous, mainly because of uncontrollable risks, such as avalanches and blizzards.

Climbers must always work in pairs, with one "belaying," protecting the other by controlling the rope. And because the belayer literally holds the climber's life in just one hand, it's crucial that climbers have proper training. Rock gyms and many college outdoor clubs offer instruction. The American Mountain Guides Association (☎ 303–271–0984) and the American Alpine Club (☎ 303–384–0110), willingly give out advice and guidance.

Across the country, there are plenty of cliffs to climb. Brent Bishop has climbed all over the U.S. and the world, including an ascent of Mt. Everest, which his late father also conquered. Currently, Bishop is the director of the Sagarmatha Environmental Foundation, which is dedicated to cleaning tons of expedition gear off Everest. Here are his favorite climbing spots in the U.S.

YOSEMITE NATIONAL PARK, *California*

■ A spectacular area with no rival in the U.S. Many climbs demand not only expertise, but also spending nights hanging in a bivouac sack, tied to the rock.

■ **CLASSIC ROUTE:** Astroman, possibly the best vertical crack climb in the world for its high degree of difficulty. It's well over 1,500 feet long.

■ **OUTFITTER:** Yosemite Mountaineering School
☎ 209–372–8344

FACT FILE:

HIGH ALTITUDES CAN POSE MANY DANGERS

■ **EXTREME COLD:** *Can cause hypothermia, which slows the heart and can lead to death.*
Wear insulated layers of clothing to minimize exposure.

■ **OXYGEN DEPRIVATION.** *Summit air can contain just one third of the oxygen at sea level.*
Some climbers carry extra oxygen.

■ **IMPAIRED JUDGMENT:** *High altitudes can affect the brain, creating confusion and bad judgment.*
Climb in teams, so members can help each other in crisis.

■ **DRY AIR:** *The water content in a climber's blood can drop drastically, increasing the chance of frostbite.*
Drink plenty of water. Bring stoves to melt snow.

SOURCE: *Newsweek*.

CITY OF ROCKS, *Idaho*

■ Scores of granite blocks, many 100 to 120 feet high, cater to every ability level and offer both awesome traditional crack climbs and hard-core sport routes, most of them safe and user-friendly.

■ **CLASSIC ROUTE:** Bloody Fingers, a 115-foot-long crack that just fits your fingers.

■ **OUTFITTER:** Exum Mountain Guides ☎ 307–733–2297

DEVIL'S TOWER, *Wyoming*

■ Every route up this 365-foot-high core of an ancient volcano requires a sustained crack climb. There's a voluntary hiatus on climbing in June, out of respect for Native Americans who consider this a sacred site.

■ **CLASSIC ROUTE:** Durrance. Though the climb is rated as moderate in difficulty, it's still an amazing route every foot of the way up.

■ **OUTFITTER:** Jackson Hole Mountain Guides ☎ 307–733–4979

SENECA ROCKS, *West Virginia*

■ There are more than 200 routes here, most of them challenging, up this bizarre slab of quartzite, which looks like two gigantic fins cutting through the forest. The summit is only a dozen feet wide. The cliffs have some good sport climbs and also several easy routes for beginners.

■ **CLASSIC ROUTE:** Castor and Pollux, two side-by-side cracks, which are steep and scary.

■ **OUTFITTER:** Seneca Rocks Climbing School ☎ 304–567–2600

SHAWANGUNK MOUNTAINS, *New York*

■ "The Gunks," as they are better known, are actually four major cliff areas spread over seven miles and offering more than 1,300 different ways up, each topping out anywhere between 30 and 200 feet high. One unique feature here is that beginners' routes are often right next to ones that can defy the proficient, giving everyone a great chance to mingle.

■ **CLASSIC ROUTE:** Foops, one of the best climbs in the country. It's a tough roof problem—meaning that you climb as if you're hanging on a ceiling.

■ **OUTFITTER:** High Angle Adventures. ☎ 800–777–2546

EXPERT SOURCES

READINGS ON THE ROCKS

Duane Raleigh, equipment editor for Climbing Magazine, *co-authored with Michael Benge* Rock, Tools, and Technique *(Climbing Magazine, 1995, $11.95), a comprehensive, up-to-date climbing manual. He recommends the following how-to guides for safety-conscious climbers.*

KNOTS FOR CLIMBERS
Craig Luebben, Chockstone Press, 1993, $5.95.
■ Numerous, well-done illustrations and descriptions clarify how to tie the knots used in rock climbing and mountaineering.

SPORT AND FACE CLIMBING
John Long, Chockstone Press, 1994, $11.95.
■ Covers the nuances of face climbing and strategies for sport and indoor competition climbing.

MOUNTAINEERING, FREEDOM OF THE HILLS
Don Graydon, ed., Mountaineers, 1992, $22.95.
■ Textbook format covers everything you need to know for mountaineering, as well as for rock and snow climbing.

ROCK 'N ROAD: Rock Climbing Areas of North America
Tim Toula, Chockstone Press, 1995.
■ A comprehensive guide describing more than 2,000 places to climb.

■ For a listing of other books and guides, contact: **The Adventurous Traveler Bookstore** ☎ 800–282–3963.

EXPERT LIST

FOR MACHO MEN AND WOMEN ONLY

O.K, tough guy. Let's see how tough you really are. Sure, lots of Americans have run a marathon, a 26-mile race. But that's a cakewalk compared to the really tough endurance races out there. Outside *magazine compiled a listing a few years ago of the toughest endurance races — rating the seven events on such factors as the toughness of the course, the rigor of the action, and the percentage of competitors who reach the finish line (it's often small). The events are presented here from easiest (relatively, of course) to most hell-bent.*

IRONMAN WORLD TRIATHLON COMPETITION

A 2.4-mile ocean swim, followed by 112 miles of cycling and a 26.2-mile marathon.

■ **WHERE:** Kailua-Kona, Hawaii
■ **WHEN:** October 1997
■ **HOW TOUGH:** The oldest and probably best-known of the endurance events. Eight to nine hours of grueling competition for some of the world's fittest men—and women.

BADWATER

A 139-mile run and walk from Badwater, Calif., the lowest point in the contiguous U.S., to near the top of Mount Whitney, the highest.

■ **WHERE:** Death Valley, Calif.
■ **WHEN:** September 1997
■ **HOW TOUGH:** Temperatures range from 130 degrees in the desert to 30 on the mountaintop. Runners can face everything from sandstorms to ice storms and take anywhere from 26 to 60 hours to finish the course.

LA TRAVERSEE INTERNATIONALE DU LAC SAINT-JEAN

A 25-mile swim across a lake in Northern Quebec

■ **WHERE:** About 500 miles north of Montreal
■ **WHEN:** July 1997
■ **HOW TOUGH:** Three-to-four-foot swells make for a rough ride, and no wetsuits are permitted during the nine-plus-hour swim, even though the water temperatures often fall to the low 60s.

RAID GAULOISE

A "wilderness endurance competition" in which five-person teams must navigate a 300-mile course and finish together.

■ **WHERE:** The site varies from year to year, and is kept secret until hours before the race.
■ **WHEN:** December 1997
■ **HOW TOUGH:** Recent races have been held over brutal terrain in Patagonia, Argentina, Costa Rica, Oman, and Madagascar. In this week-long event participants may engage in mountain climbing, kayaking, white-water canoeing, horseback riding, and skiing—among other things.

IDITAROD SLED DOG RACE

A 1,100-mile race through Alaskan wilderness that takes the mushers and their dogs 10 to 20 days to finish.

■ **WHERE:** Anchorage to Nome, Alaska.
■ **WHEN:** March 1997
■ **HOW TOUGH:** Like the Ironman, this race has become an icon. The wintry conditions can be brutal, but the race is even tougher on the dogs when it's overly warm.

VÉNDEE GLOBE

A four-month solo sailing race around the world.

■ **WHERE:** From France's Bay of Biscay, past Western Africa, Antarctica, and Cape Horn.
■ **WHEN:** Every four years, including November 1996.
■ **HOW TOUGH:** Participants can't go ashore or get assistance, so they're totally on their own for four months.

RACE ACROSS AMERICA

A 2,900-mile bicycle race in 8 to 10 days.

■ **WHERE:** California to Savannah, Georgia.
■ **WHEN:** July 1997
■ **HOW TOUGH:** The winners cycle 350 miles in a day and sleep little more than an hour. About a third of the entrants finish.

EXPERT Q & A

A PEDALER'S GUIDE TO BIKES

A cycling pro's advice on the best deals on wheels

A stroll into today's bike shop is not for the faint of heart. The days of banana seats and coaster brakes are long gone, replaced by the likes of titanium steel frames and shock-absorbing suspension forks. But don't be intimidated—or fooled. Inside that shop, there is a bike that is exactly what you need—and lots more that you don't need. Here to guide you through the maze of bike styles and sizes and help you pick one that best suits your needs (and pocketbook) is the editor of *Bicycling* magazine, Geoff Drake.

■ How do I know what type of bike I need?

There are three types of bikes: road, mountain, and hybrid. Each is built for a certain type of riding. A breakdown:

ROAD BIKES: The lightest and fastest of the three bicycle types, these bikes are primarily for people who will be doing distance riding on smooth pavement. The skinny, smooth tires and low handlebars give riders speed and low wind resistance but also make some cyclists feel vulnerable in traffic. Most road bikes weigh between 20 and 30 pounds, but new high-end models can weigh as little as 18 pounds. The majority of people riding road bikes today are athletes who use them for training purposes.

MOUNTAIN BIKES: Mountain bikes, created by outdoors enthusiasts in Northern California, are now the most popular bike in the United States. The upright seating, fat, knobby tires, and easy gearing make these bikes ideal for off-road riding. But even if you live in the heart of the city and only occasionally hit a trail, mountain bikes offer comfort and stability. If you use your bike only for riding with the kids or short trips around town, a mountain bike is probably better suited to your needs than a road bike.

HYBRID BIKES: Hybrids, relative newcomers to the bike market, are rapidly gaining in popularity. Hybrids combine the upright seating and shifting of mountain bikes, but offer the thin, smooth tires of road bikes for speed. Many people like the versatility a hybrid offers; you can ride on some less-challenging trails, and also make better time than you would on a mountain bike. But don't buy a hybrid if you are a serious cyclist: the limitations on both roads and trails will frustrate you. If you want to ride on tough trails, the hybrid's frame and thin tires can't handle the challenge. And if you want to take it on the open road, you'll be battling wind resistance the whole ride.

■ How much should I spend on a bike?

Bikes aren't cheap. You can spend anywhere from several hundred to several thousand dollars for a high-end model. It's hard to purchase a bad bike today, though—you can find a decent bike for $300 to $400. So don't worry if your budget is tight, but remember you get what you pay for. Don't expect a less-expensive bike to perform as well or last as long as a high-end model. Your extra money is buying lighter, sturdier frames, and components (like gears and brakes) that can take a beating and last a long time.

■ How do I know if my bike fits me?

One of the most common errors is buying a bike that is too large. The best advice is buy the smallest bike that you can comfortably ride. Tests to determine if the size is right for you include: straddling the bike frame and lifting the front tire up by the handlebars. There should be several inches of clearance between your crotch and the bike frame, 1 to 2 inches for a road bike, and at least 3 to 4 inches for a mountain bike.

When riding, you should be able to straighten—but not strain—your leg. Adjust-

■ THE NUTS AND BOLTS OF MOUNTAIN BIKES

Bike shops are dangerous places for those with an itchy wallet finger. There are hundreds of bike accessories you could purchase, but a much smaller number that you actually need. Here are a few of the basics, and some exotic innovations:

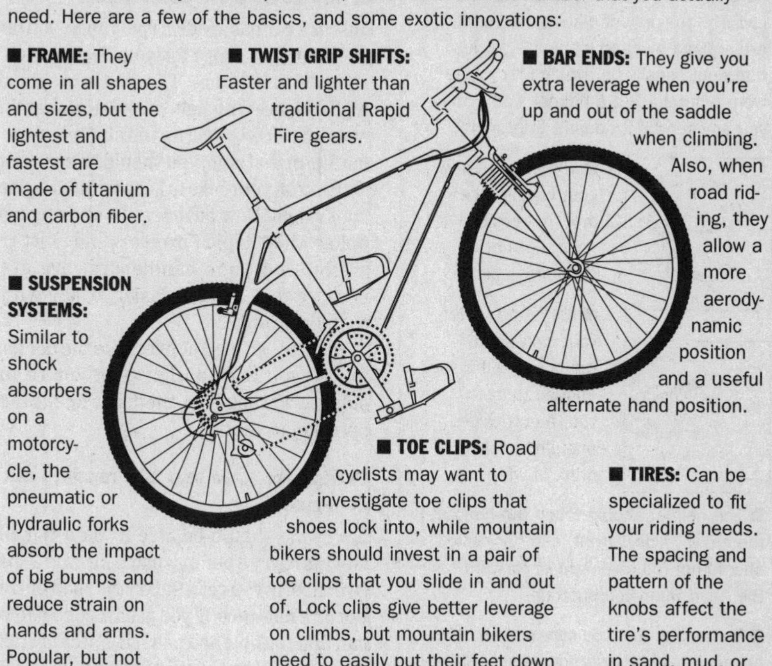

■ FRAME: They come in all shapes and sizes, but the lightest and fastest are made of titanium and carbon fiber.

■ TWIST GRIP SHIFTS: Faster and lighter than traditional Rapid Fire gears.

■ BAR ENDS: They give you extra leverage when you're up and out of the saddle when climbing. Also, when road riding, they allow a more aerodynamic position and a useful alternate hand position.

■ SUSPENSION SYSTEMS: Similar to shock absorbers on a motorcycle, the pneumatic or hydraulic forks absorb the impact of big bumps and reduce strain on hands and arms. Popular, but not necessary.

■ TOE CLIPS: Road cyclists may want to investigate toe clips that shoes lock into, while mountain bikers should invest in a pair of toe clips that you slide in and out of. Lock clips give better leverage on climbs, but mountain bikers need to easily put their feet down when navigating tricky trail turns.

■ TIRES: Can be specialized to fit your riding needs. The spacing and pattern of the knobs affect the tire's performance in sand, mud, or hard-packed trails.

ing the seat height can help this. Also, especially on road bikes, be sure that you can comfortably reach the handlebars and that your knees are just barely brushing your elbows as you pedal.

■ There are so many frames to choose from. What's best for me?

Frames vary in price and expense, with the heaviest and least expensive being a steel frame. More expensive and lighter are aluminum, carbon fiber, and titanium steel frames, in that order. One-piece, molded composite frames are the lightest of all and are a hot new item, but they also carry a hefty price tag. Some composite-frame bikes cost as much as $3,250.

If you are planning on racing with your bike, a light frame is a necessity. But for weekend riders, it is merely a luxury that will make your ride somewhat more enjoyable.

■ Which bikes do you recommend?

Bike models come and go, and what's hot this year may be outdated by next year. The surest way to purchase a quality bike is to avoid the hot gimmicks and new names, and stick with companies that produce high-quality bikes year-in and year-out.

For mountain and hybrid bikes, try Trek and Cannondale, two of the biggest American companies. Bikes made by GT, Specialized, and Schwinn are also good.

For road bikes: Specialized and Trek are always reliable. For sure-fire winners , look to the Italian-made bikes. Some bike shops carry Pinarello and De Rosa, which are top-of-the line. They often cost as much as $5,000.

■ BUYING A HELMET

Wearing a bike helmet is no longer nerdy. In fact, in many cities it's the law. The majority of bike-related deaths are caused by head injuries—injuries that could easily be avoided if cyclists wore helmets. But a helmet won't do you any good if it doesn't fit properly.

■ The experts suggest buying a helmet that feels snug, but not uncomfortable.

■ The strap under your chin should feel snug, but loose enough to open your mouth wide enough to take a drink of water.

■ The helmet should touch the head at the crown, sides, front, and back and should not roll backward or forward on the head when you push up.

■ Remember that you can make a tight helmet looser by inserting smaller sizing pads or sanding down existing pads.

■ I'd like a better bike, but don't have the money for a new one. Can I upgrade my bike?

Absolutely. If you have a mountain bike, the first thing to add would be a suspension fork if you don't already have one—it absorbs the impact of big bumps and gives you a smoother ride. Also, clipless pedals make riding a lot nicer. If you're looking at replacing an entire component group (gears, brakes, etc.), you may want to look into a new bike. There are significant cost savings on individual components when you buy them as part of a bike, as opposed to individually.

If you have a road bike, look into clipless pedals. Also, a cycle computer that goes on your handlebars can tell you your speed, distance, time, and sometimes your heart rate. Computers run $20 to $100. For greater speed on your road bike, you could also buy new, lighter wheels.

■ How do all those gears work?

Just as a car has an ideal rpm range, you have an ideal rpm range for your legs, which is about 80 to 100 rpms. The idea is to spin at a high cadence with light pressure, rather than pedaling slowly. Just as you shift your car to maintain that rpm, you should be constantly shifting on your bike to keep within the ideal rpm range. New advances in shifting technology (like Rapid Fire gears and twist grip shifters on your handlebars) are great because they make it easier to stay within that ideal range.

Remember, a higher gear is a harder gear, and if you're in a high gear, you're in a smaller sprocket in the back or a bigger sprocket in the front.

■ What are some easy bike repairs I can do myself?

Everyone should be able to fix a flat tire. Always carry a pump, a patch kit, and a spare tire tube. If you get a flat on the road or trail, put on a new tube. If you get a second flat, you can find the hole and patch it. Patching takes practice and you should try it at home a few times before you go on a trail—you don't want to be stuck out in the woods with a flat and no way to fix it. You should always carry what is called a mini tool—the Swiss Army knife of the bike world. It's an all-in-one tool, including an Allen wrench and spoke wrench, and it can be bought at any bike shop.

People often forget to keep their bike chains clean and lubricated. If you have a really grimy chain, first spray the chain and derailleurs with degreaser, then wet an old sponge with warm, soapy water and hold it around the chain as you spin the wheels. Continue this until the chain is clean, then dry with rags. Instead of using a sponge, you could buy a chain cleaning kit that snaps around your chain and then cleans and degreases it. Remember to regularly lubricate your chain—lubricants made specifically for bike chains are available at all bike shops. If you ride in the rain, be sure to lubricate your chain every time.

GOLFER'S GUIDE

THE TEN BEST PUBLIC COURSES

Many of the best American golf courses are available to you for the price of a greens fee. Golf *magazine recently published a list of the "Top 100 You Can Play," featuring public courses, courses at resorts, and semiprivate clubs that are open, at least partially, to nonmembers. The survey was based on the views of about 200 golf fanatics from around the country. Twenty-eight states placed courses on the list; California led the way with 13, followed by Florida with 10, Arizona and Michigan with 7 each, and North Carolina and Hawaii with 4 apiece. More than a third of the courses have opened since 1990, indicating a boom in public courses, and good ones at that. But the quality doesn't come cheap: 35 of the courses have a greens fee of more than $100, and another 24 run $75 to $100. Here is* Golf*'s top 10:*

1. PEBBLE BEACH
Pebble Beach, Calif.

■ The experts in *Golf*'s survey picked Pebble Beach as the most scenic public course as well as tops over all. But you pay for what you get at this stunning resort course overlooking Carmel Bay: It's the most expensive course in the survey.
■ $325
☎ 408–624–3811

2. PINEHURST (No. 2)
Pinehurst, N.C.

■ This resort is one of numerous multicourse facilities that placed more than one course on *Golf*'s top 100 list (the No. 7 course at Pinehurst placed 36th on the list). *Golf* cites Pinehurst's clubhouse as the nicest in the survey, and its practice area, Maniac Hill, as one of the best.
■ $101 and over
☎ 910–295–8141

3. BLACKWOLF RUN (River Course)
Kohler, Wisc.

■ This resort course is

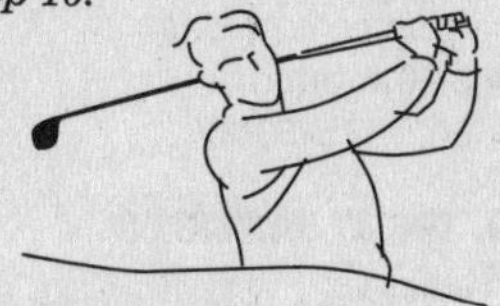

one of six in *Golf*'s top 18 designed by Pete Dye, an architect known for driving golfers mad with his challenging layouts. Its sister course, Meadow Valleys, which is part of the same facility, is No. 46 on *Golf*'s list.
■ $76 to $100
☎ 414–457–4448

4. SPYGLASS HILL
Pebble Beach, Calif.

■ Pebble Beach's neighbor on California's Monterey coastline, this resort course was rated one of the best-groomed and toughest courses in the country. It's also one of the prettiest.
■ $101 and over
☎ 408–624–3811

5. PUMPKIN RIDGE (Ghost Creek)
Cornelius, Ore.

■ *Golf* singled out this daily-fee course, built on rolling

FACT FILE:

HOW MANY DIMPLES ON YOUR BALL?

■ *Traditional golf balls have anywhere from 384 to 500 dimples, but there are balls on the market with as few as 252 and as many as 812. Makers of the balls with more dimples promise golfers increased distance and control on their shots. But if a ball has too many dimples, the impressions are smaller, and the effect is largely lost. "Anything beyond 500 and there are too many," says Frank Thomas, technical director for the U.S. Golf Association.*

■ **GOLFER'S GUIDE**

farmland 20 miles outside Portland, as among the best-groomed in the country.
■ $51 to $75
☎ 503–647–4747

6. BETHPAGE
Farmingdale, N.Y.
■ *Golf*'s choice as the best value in the survey, this daily-fee course is part of a state park on Long Island, an hour's drive from Manhattan.
■ $25 and under
☎ 516–249–0700

7. COG HILL (No. 4)
Lemont, Ill.
■ In its list of brutal courses, *Golf* describes this daily-fee course outside Chicago as one of a handful of "classic round-wreckers, time-honored toughies."
■ $76 to $100
☎ 708–257–5872

8. TROON NORTH (Monument)
Scottsdale, Ariz.
■ Voters picked this daily-fee course as perhaps the best-kept course in the survey, with impeccably groomed fairways and velvety smooth greens.
■ $150 a round
☎ 602–585–5300

9. TPC AT SAWGRASS (Stadium)
Ponte Vedra Beach, Fla.
■ This resort course, not far from Jacksonville, was picked as one of *Golf*'s most challenging courses. You wouldn't know it from playing it, but this Pete Dye course actually has been softened over the years.
■ $76 to $100
☎ 904–285–7888

10. WORLD WOODS (Pine Barrens)
Brooksville, Fla.
■ Rounding out *Golf*'s top 10, this course features an unmatched practice facility that includes a four-sided, 700-yard driving range and several stunning practice holes. The only downside: its out-of-the-way location, 90 minutes from Tampa and Orlando.
■ $51 to $75
☎ 352–796–5500

■ THE REST OF THE BEST COURSES

The following courses placed 11th through 25th on the *Golf* magazine ranking of the Top 100. The full list is available from *Golf* magazine, Times-Mirror Magazines, 2 Park Ave., New York, NY 10016–5675 (☎ 212–779–5000), or online at *http://www.golfonline.com*

NAME	LOCATION	COST	TYPE	TELEPHONE
11. PASATIEMPO	Santa Cruz, Calif.	$76–$100	Daily-fee	408–459–9155
12. HARBOUR TOWN	Hilton Head Island, S.C.	$76–$100	Resort	803–842–8484
13. THE HOMESTEAD (Cascades)	Hot Springs, Va.	$51–$75	Resort	540–839–1766
14. KIAWAH ISLAND (Ocean)	Kiawah Island, S.C.	$76–$100	Resort	803–768–2121
15. BAY HILL	Orlando, Fla.	$101 and up	Ltd.	407–876–2429
16. MAUNA KEA	Kohala Coast, Hawaii	$76–$100	Resort	808–885–4288
17. LA QUINTA (Mountain)	La Quinta, Calif.	$101 and up	Resort	619–564–7111
18. PGA WEST (Stadium)	La Quinta, Calif.	$101 and up	Resort	619–564–7111
19. THE DUNES	Myrtle Beach, S.C.	$101 and up	Ltd.	803–449–5236
20. DORAL (Blue)	Miami, Fla.	$101 and up	Resort	305–592–2000
21. HORSESHOE BAY (Ram Rock)	Horseshoe Bay, Texas	$51–$75	Resort	210–598–2511
22. TREETOPS SYLVAN (Smith)	Gaylord, Mich.	$51–$75	Resort	517–732–6711
23. WILD DUNES (Links)	Isle of Palms, S.C.	$101 and up	Resort	803–886–6000
24. TREETOPS SYLVAN (Fazio)	Gaylord, Mich.	$76–$100	Resort	517–732–6711
25. SUGARLOAF	Carrabassett Valley, Me.	$51–$75	Resort	207–237–2000

A PRIVATE LESSON WITH ZINA

A Wimbledon finalist's five-step program to playing a better game

Zina Garrison-Jackson knows a thing or two about playing top-flight tennis. She's been one of the best and most-popular players on the women's tennis tour for more than a decade, winning more than a dozen tournaments and well over $4 million during that time, including a second-place finish to Martina Navratilova at Wimbledon in 1990. Here is her advice for preparing to play smart tennis, mentally and physically.

Step 1: ASSESS YOUR OPPONENT

If you get the chance, watch your opponent play or practice before your next match, Garrison-Jackson says. "You want to see their movements and their strokes, to figure out where their weaknesses are," she says. Once you've identified those failings, shape your game to determine "how you'll be able to maneuver him or her to take advantage of the weaknesses."

That advice is somewhat self-evident: If the player has a much weaker backhand than forehand, hit to the weaker side. But don't go too far, Garrison-Jackson says, that you change your own game. "If you're primarily a baseline player, and you're playing a hard-core baseliner, don't suddenly become a serve-and-volleyer that match. Instead, hit a lot of balls around the court, a lot in the corners and a lot of deep balls, so you'll force mistakes and be in a position to move in occasionally and attack."

Step 2: VISUALIZE

Yogi Berra once said that half of baseball is 90 percent mental. Well, you know what he meant, and tennis is, too. Like many top athletes, Garrison-Jackson is a strong believer in visualization, in which she prepares for a match by playing it out, point by point, in her mind. She closes her eyes and pictures herself "hitting the strokes exactly the way I want to." She takes this process to its logical end, "to the point where I'm smiling after the match rather than frowning."

Step 3: HAVE A GAME PLAN

Say you've developed a good game plan based on your strengths and your opponent's failings. But once the match begins, you fall behind five games to one. Do you dump your plan and try something else? "You should believe enough in your game plan to stick with it win, lose, or draw," Garrison-Jackson says. That doesn't mean that you don't adapt if you find a bigger hole in your challenger's game than the ones you spotted in practice. But if you were thorough and thoughtful going in, you probably picked the right game plan for you, and dumping it probably won't produce a better one, says Garrison-Jackson.

Step 4: HITTING WINNERS

A lot of tennis players actively try to hit winners: They rear back and try to rip a hole in the opponent's racquet, or try desperately to drop a ball daintily over the

FACT FILE:

TENNIS ELBOW, ANYONE

■ *Fewer than 5 percent of those who get tennis elbow play tennis, according to* Tennis *magazine. Golfers, violinists, and surgeons also suffer from it. If you get tennis elbow (an inflammation or tiny tear of the muscle in the forearm), wait 20 minutes to let your body heat return to normal, then use ice to reduce the pain. Severe pain may need a prescription of cortisone.*

EXPERT TIPS

PICKING A TENNIS RACQUET

You naturally look for an exact fit in shoes, clothes, and everything else you buy. Do the same with racquets, which are individualized instruments that must be chosen carefully. Any racquet can be made more or less powerful by adjusting the three systems—handle size and shape, overall weight and balance, and string type and tension. You should plan to adjust the systems of any racquet you buy depending on what you want the racquet to do. Warren Bosworth is a racquet consultant to stars like Pete Sampras, Ivan Lendl, and Martina Navratilova, and chairman of Bosworth International, a racquet-testing company. His suggestions:

■ **BODY:** Today's wide-body racquets provide power, but at the sacrifice of control. Conventional wisdom suggests that the wider the body, the more power; the more conventional the racquet, the more control.

Weight is also a critical factor. Too heavy a racquet will strain your wrist, arm, elbow, or shoulder, but the new ultralights have also been a principal cause of injury because they are just too light to overcome the impact of the ball.

■ **STRING:** Strings are the most important part of the racquet in regard to storing energy and influencing the spin of the ball. Essentially, you have two choices: gut and synthetics. Synthetics, which are much cheaper, are thought to last longer, but you really have to take into account climate and humidity (dry weather is better for strings), surface (clay is harder on strings), the type of racquet (some have grommets, or stringholds, that are harder on strings than others) and the type of player you are (spin players are harder on their strings).

Gauge, or string thickness, is as critical as string type. Thicker gauges—that is, fatter strings—last longer. The thinner ones provide more feel. Recreational players should expect to get several months out of a set of strings before it loses its flexibility.

Tension is another factor. The looser the strings, the more power. Tighter strings may give you more spin control, but also may add shock.

■ **COST.** Expect to spend $150 to $250 for a standard retail purchase. Look for the previous year's model, which is often just as good as the new ones.

net. Bad idea, Garrison-Jackson says. "Your best bet is to learn the basics of tennis first, and concentrate on making your opponent miss. Do that until you get to the point where you place that ball so well that you get your opponent totally out of position. That's how you hit winners. You basically do it without trying to."

Step 5: THE RIGHT MENTAL ATTITUDE

Garrison-Jackson says she sees a lot of players who are either over- or underconfident. The overconfident types, she says, believe they're better than they really are and try shots they have no business trying, usually unsuccessfully. "The other type of player says, 'Oh, I'm a hacker,'" Garrison-Jackson says. The hacker assumes he'll lose, while the overconfident player assumes he'll win. Both mind-sets are equally damaging to good, smart tennis, Garrison-Jackson says. "The key is not to think about the level of the person you're playing, but just to go out and compete as hard as you can, one point at a time."

SOFTBALL

BE A HITTER, EVERY TIME

Two slow-pitch sluggers reveal how the bat should meet the ball

Every time he steps to the plate, Carl Rose tries to smack the ball out of the park. Rose, a professional softball player, has cleared the fences of seven major-league ballparks and once hit 240 home runs in a 90-game season. If you're counting, that's nearly three a game. "I always wanted to hit the ball further than I did before," he says. "That's what everyone talks about: how far you hit the ball."

Dirk Androff takes another approach to hitting a softball. "The game is about not making outs," Androff says. He doesn't make many: He hit .779 for the Louisville Slugger team in 1995, and has been named player of the year by major softball publications in two of the last three years.

Both players have aggressive strategies for hitting well. Each begins with hours of off-season weightlifting and batting practice, but their differing goals at the plate mean they pursue different approaches. Here's what they do before they get to the on-deck circle and once they're in the batter's box.

TRAINING

Both Rose and Androff have learned how to transfer training with weights into hitting with more power. Though he concentrates on his batting average, Androff still hit 153 home runs last year.

Both players say that developing strong leg muscles is important to good hitting, because that's where the spring in your swing comes from. Androff also says that having a strong lower back is critical to reducing the wear and tear from constant swinging. He works on his stomach muscles to keep up with the lower back. For that final burst of power and building bat speed, Rose and Androff concur: Work on strengthening your wrists, forearms, and biceps.

HITTING THE LONG BALL

The key to hitting home runs for Rose, a former minor-leaguer in the Pittsburgh Pirates organization, is knowing how to hit bad pitches hard. "It's really easy to hit pitches in the heart of the plate, but I seldom see strikes during a game," says Rose.

Rose tailors his swing to the location of the pitch. If it comes in low, he swings with a slight uppercut; for high pitches, he swings straight through the ball. The key to hitting any pitch out of the park, he says, is rolling the shoulders: turning the hips and transferring weight from the back foot to the front one at the time of contact. Because the pitch floats in in slow-pitch softball, the hitter must provide all the momentum.

To get even more power on his swing, Rose also uses a nontraditional grip. A 34-inch bat is the longest permitted by the American Softball Association, so Rose holds the bat with left ring finger on the knob, and then overlaps his right hand over the left. The extra length gives him more bat whip and thus more power, he says.

GETTING A HIT EVERY TIME

The hitter should decide where to hit the ball *before* he sees the pitch, Androff says. Once he decides where he wants to hit the ball, Androff times his swing accordingly. If he wants to pull the ball, he extends the barrel, the widest part of the bat, in front of his hands at the point of contact. In other words, at the time the bat strikes the ball, the bat barrel is closer to the pitcher than Androff's hands. If he wants to hit the ball up the middle, he keeps the barrel even with his hands, and to hit to the opposite field, he points his shoulder in that direction when the bat meets the ball.

Androff also tries to use a level swing no matter where the ball is pitched. Any uppercut, he says, can lead to pop outs. The three key factors in hitting, he says, are timing the swing, keeping an eye on the ball, and transferring your weight at the right moment.

ANGLER'S GUIDE

MAYBE THIS WILL BE YOUR LUCKY DAY

If you consult the chart below before you schedule your next fishing trip, you might not have to come back and talk about the ones that got away.

Key: MORNING: B BEST, G GOOD, F FAIR, P POOR
EVENING: **B** BEST, **G** GOOD, **F** FAIR, **P** POOR

DAY	JAN	FEB	MAR	APR	MAY	JUN	JUL	AUG	SEP	OCT	NOV	DEC
1	P	B	**G**	F	G	P	P	G	**P**	**P**	**F**	**P**
2	P	P	P	G	B	F	P	P	**P**	**P**	**P**	**P**
3	P	P	P	G	B	P	P	**P**	**P**	**F**	**P**	**F**
4	G	F	F	B	P	P	**G**	**P**	**P**	**G**	**P**	**G**
5	G	P	F	G	P	**P**	**G**	**P**	**P**	**G**	**F**	**G**
6	P	F	F	P	**P**	**G**	**P**	**F**	**G**	**P**	**F**	**B**
7	P	**F**	**F**	P	**P**	**G**	**P**	**P**	**G**	**P**	G	B
8	**P**	**G**	**G**	**P**	**P**	**B**	**P**	**P**	**G**	**F**	G	P
9	**P**	**G**	**G**	**P**	**P**	**P**	**F**	**P**	P	F	B	P
10	**F**	**P**	**P**	**P**	**B**	**P**	**F**	**G**	P	F	B	G
11	**G**	**P**	**P**	**P**	**B**	**F**	**P**	G	F	G	F	G
12	**B**	**F**	**F**	**P**	**P**	F	P	P	F	B	F	G
13	**B**	**F**	**F**	**B**	**P**	F	P	P	B	B	G	**F**
14	**P**	F	**P**	B	P	P	G	P	B	B	**G**	**F**
15	P	P	P	P	F	P	G	G	B	**F**	**F**	**B**
16	F	P	B	P	F	G	F	G	**B**	**F**	**F**	**B**
17	F	B	B	P	F	B	F	B	**F**	**G**	**B**	**P**
18	P	B	B	F	P	B	G	**B**	**F**	**G**	**B**	**P**
19	P	B	P	G	F	F	**G**	**B**	**G**	**P**	**B**	**F**
20	F	F	F	F	B	**F**	**B**	**B**	**F**	**P**	**P**	**F**
21	B	F	G	F	B	**G**	**B**	**F**	**P**	**B**	P	F
22	B	**G**	G	**F**	**F**	**G**	**B**	**P**	**P**	B	F	P
23	**F**	**G**	**G**	**B**	**F**	**B**	**B**	P	P	P	F	P
24	**F**	**G**	**F**	**B**	**G**	**G**	**P**	F	B	P	F	G
25	**F**	**F**	**F**	**F**	**G**	**B**	**P**	P	B	P	P	G
26	**G**	**P**	**B**	**P**	**F**	**B**	F	P	P	F	P	G
27	**F**	**G**	**G**	**F**	**G**	P	F	B	P	F	F	P
28	**P**	**G**	**G**	**F**	**G**	P	F	B	F	P	F	P
29	**P**		**P**	G	B	F	P	B	P	P	**P**	**P**
30	**P**		**P**	G	B	F	P	P	P	P	**P**	**P**
31	G		F		P		G	P		**F**		**F**

SOURCE: 1997 Wright's Fishing Calendar, Hart-Wright Co.

FLY-FISHING

A YOUNG ANGLER'S FAVORITE STREAMS

A talented author and illustrator picks his special trout spots

James Prosek makes you want to fly-fish, even if you've never had the slightest inclination to do so. He doesn't do it purposefully: He's not a salesman or a shill for the sport. But his appreciation for fly-fishing, and for everything that surrounds it, is infectious.

He lovingly describes the trout as "elegant, streamlined, and beautiful." He details the remarkable, brief life of the mayfly, which arises from the water as a nymph, hatches in the air, mates, and dies in the course of a single day. And he places himself as a fisherman in the context of the awesome natural cycle of the fishing stream. "It's a big immortal cycle, and you're the mortal angler," he says. "You step into that water and see your reflection, and you've become part of that cycle. It's powerful."

Prosek, a 21-year-old senior at Yale University, shares his love for fly-fishing in *Trout: An Illustrated History* (Alfred A. Knopf, 1996), a book of watercolor paintings and text describing about 70 types of trout. Here he volunteers some of his favorite fishing streams.

HOUSATONIC RIVER, *Cornwall Bridge, Conn.*

■ This is Prosek's "home" stream, located not far from where he lives. The trout season here is short because the water warms up by late June, making it inhospitable for trout. But from late April through June, the green rolling hills make it a perfect place to catch some big rainbows and brown trout, as well as take in some terrific scenery. Phil Demetri at the Housatonic Meadows Fly Shop (☎ 203–672–6064) will set you up with all you need.

CONNECTICUT RIVER, *Pittsburgh, N.H.*

■ This fishing hole near the river's headwaters in northern New Hampshire offers a delightful surprise. Wild rainbow and brown trout are the dominant catch, but the river also contains a nice population of landlocked salmon. When you catch one, they leap around wildly.

ANDROSCOGGIN RIVER, *Lewiston, Me.*

■ The alder fly hatches in early to mid-June, and trout just gobble up the fat fly with the zebra-colored wings.

LITTLE KENNEBAGO RIVER, *Rangeley, Me.*

■ Prosek's recommended spot is where the river flows into Mooselookmeguntic Lake, one of the Rangeley Lakes. Each September, landlocked salmon go there to spawn, though Prosek admits that he has never been present at quite the right moment himself.

FALLING SPRINGS CREEK, *Chambersburg, Pa.*

■ This is Prosek's favorite among the unusual spring-fed creeks in central Pennsylvania. The creeks are fed by cold, slightly chalky water that pours forth from limestone outcroppings. The limestone raises the pH of the streams, which increases plant life and, in turn, fattens up the trout. Don't fish these streams with traditional mayflies or other flies, Prosek warns; use imitations of insects such as ants, beetles, or cicadas.

MADISON RIVER, *Ennis, Mont.*

■ This very famous river lives up to its reputation. Prosek suggests taking a guided float trip the first time you fish it; after that you can pull off the road and fish your favorite spots yourself. There's a big hatch of stoneflies at the end of June; flies based on this huge two-inch-long insect attract large brown trout.

ROCK CREEK, *Missoula, Mont.*

■ Buffalo and elk frequently stroll along the banks of this stream in west central Montana. Look for the striking-looking West Slope cutthroat trout; cutthroats get their name from the two red slashes below their neck.

SEARCHING FOR BIGGER, MEANER FISH

Landing a tarpon or a bonefish with a fly rod poses quite a challenge

Fly-fishing has stood the test of time. It's always been popular with serious anglers and, of course, still is. But these days, stream fishing is having to share the limelight with its coastal cousin: saltwater fly-fishing. While fly-fishing on the high seas may lack the bucolic beauty and some of the fly-making artistry of fly-rodding in the streams of Montana, what it offers instead is simple: "Bigger, meaner fish," says Art Scheck, an editor of *Saltwater Fly-Fishing* magazine.

Tarpon, bonefish, striped bass, and sailfish are the hard-running—and often mammoth—quarry of saltwater fly-rodding. Big trout, a primary target of stream fishers, run to 20 pounds; tarpon and sailfish can easily tip the scales at 100 pounds or more. But saltwater fly-fishing isn't just about size; striped bass and bonefish can take your line and tear away from you at dazzling speeds, and the fight to reel them in can give you a workout that'll make a day in the gym look like a walk in the park.

Ocean fly-fishing isn't as accessible as stream fishing, which you can dabble in in most states in the country. And to do some of the best saltwater fly-rodding, you have to travel to exotic locales like the Florida Keys. But you can find good ocean fishing up and down the East Coast, and a few other places besides. (Unfortunately, if you live on the West Coast, most experts say the Pacific Ocean fly-fishing just doesn't measure up.)

It's nice to have an expensive boat that can take you to more far-flung, and less-fished, spots. But shallow water is in many ways the best place to fly-fish, and you can do so successfully off beaches and cliffs, and in and around estuaries. This is not a sport of kings.

Some of the equipment you'll need can cost a princely sum, though. The specialized gear is much heavier and stronger than for stream fishing, reflecting the bigness and meanness of your foe. The high-end equipment can be outrageously expensive, but you don't have to spend a fortune for quality gear.

For most of the fishing that you'll probably do, you'll need a saltwater-grade graphite rod in the 8/9 or 9/10 weight class, which typically runs anywhere from about $100 to $400. Big-game rods, for going after tarpon or sailfish, say, will run a little more. The rest of the equipment that you'll need—line, leader, flies, etc.—will probably run you at least a few hundred dollars more.

GREEN RIVER, *Pinedale, Wyo.*

■ Prosek raves about the fishing and hiking in the mountains of the Wind River Range in central Wyoming. The lakes that feed off the headwaters of the Green River get stocked regularly by airplane drops; the fish get deposited as fingerlings and are left to develop in the wild. Any tackle store in Pinedale will be able to outfit you for a several-day pack trip.

FRYING PAN RIVER, *Western Colo.*

■ Freshwater springs are so plentiful in the Colorado mountains that you can pull off Highway 70 and fish in ditches and do well. A better bet, however, is this beautiful river that runs through brick-red hills. It features some enormous brown and rainbow trout, but the native fish here is the Colorado River cutthroat.

PROVO RIVER, *Heber City, Utah*

■ Utah may be best-known for its salt lakes, but this stream in the central part of the state, not far from Brigham Young University, has some of the prettiest wild trout ever seen.

SNORKELING

WHERE TO DON A MASK AND FINS

Ten spots where the underwater views are nothing if not spectacular

Jacques Cousteau is best known for his scuba diving adventures. The television films he produced made the ocean come alive, revealing the teeming life and incredible vibrancy of the world's waters. His own eyes, however, were opened not by scuba diving—which he invented—but by snorkeling. In 1936, he first donned a pair of goggles and floated on the surface of the sea. "Sometimes we are lucky enough to know that our lives have been changed, to discard the old, embrace the new and run headlong down an immutable course. It happened to me on that summer's day, when my eyes were opened to the sea," he later wrote.

Today, the sport of scuba diving has largely supplanted snorkeling in the public imagination. But free diving, as snorkeling was originally known, still has the power to captivate, and more people actually snorkel each year than scuba. Partisans say snorkeling offers more freedom than scuba diving, which requires clunky gear and sometimes keeps you tethered to a boat. For snorkeling, all you need are fins, a mask, and a snorkel. It's significantly cheaper, and you don't need to undertake the rigorous certification that scuba diving requires (see box, page 730).

David Taylor, executive editor of *Scuba Diving* magazine, has some tips for getting started with snorkeling. Take great care in picking a mouthpiece and mask that fit comfortably. To test whether a mask fits, hold it to your face, sniff slightly to hold it in place, and let go. If the mask stays on and there are no leaks, the fit is sufficient. Try on as many as five masks with different shapes to see which fits best. Buy fins that cover your entire feet, instead of the open-heeled fins. And buy your equipment in a dive store, not in some discount department store, Taylor says: "You are buying serious sports equipment, not tennis shoes." Ready to plunge in? Taylor suggests these top destinations:

LOOE KEY, FLORIDA

Best time to go: Year-round, though winds can limit visibility during the winter.

■ There are dozens of incredible snorkeling spots in the Florida Keys, the most popular diving location in the world. Looe Key features a national marine sanctuary, and stands out for its remarkable fish life and the numerous sunken ships that the schoolmasters, snappers, and barracuda dart through.

■ **CONTACT:** Outcast Charters and Florida Keys House, ☎ 305–872–4680.

BAHAMAS, OUT ISLANDS

Best time to go: February–September.

■ In some diving spots, snorkelers take a backseat to scuba divers. Not here. More than 30 hotels on Abaco, Bimini, Eleuthera, and the other smaller islands in the Bahamas offer a snorkeling package that is top-notch. The Out Islands don't have the posh hotels and casinos of Freeport and the other main tourist islands, but the snorkeling sights are sure luxurious.

■ **CONTACT:** Out Island Tourism ☎ 305–359–8097.

BONAIRE MARINE PARK, NETHERLANDS ANTILLES

Best time to go: Year-round.

■ This boot-shaped island off Venezuela's coast is less famous than neighboring Aruba and Curaçao. But its snorkeling—from its coral gardens to its tube sponges, which are as long as a person—is unmatched. The island's license plate says all you need to know: "Diver's Paradise."

■ **CONTACT:** Sand Dollar Dive and Photo ☎ 800–288–4773.

WHERE TO LEARN TO BLOW BUBBLES

Four ways to get yourself properly trained

Most countries require that you be certified before you strap on your tanks and dive in, and for good reason—mishandled equipment or an error in judgment in the lower depths can lead to a life-threatening case of the bends. Here are three ways to get certified, and a fourth way to dip your toe into diving without making a three-week commitment.

■ **CERTIFICATION CLASSES:** They are usually offered at the local dive shop or YMCA. The three- to six-week programs combine classroom instruction, pool-time, and open-water dives in an ocean or other body of water with currents and waves. Look for programs certified by one of the two largest American diving associations, the National Association of Underwater Instructors (NAUI), or the Professional Association of Diving Instructors (PADI). Both set clear standards for everything from equipment to instructor credentials. Also, try to meet your instructor before committing to the class. Diving is a high-risk activity; a novice needs to feel comfortable with the instructor. Tuition, equipment, and textbook should run about $250.

■ **RESORTS:** Most resorts that offer diving also offer on-premise certification classes. They usually last three to four days and cost $350 to $450. You should make sure that the program is certified by NAUI or PADI before signing on.

■ **AT-HOME INSTRUCTION WITH ON-SITE DIVE:** A combination program for those who live in cold-weather climates. You do all your instruction at home in an indoor pool, and then do your open-water test at a resort with a referral program. Costs vary widely.

■ **PASSPORT PROGRAM:** For people who want to try diving but don't want to commit the time or money to getting certified, these half- or one-day programs review the basics and conclude with an open-water or shore-dive accompanied by the instructor. The cost is usually about $50.

HERON ISLAND, AUSTRALIA

Best time to go: April–July.

■ One of about 900 islands that make up the 1,200-mile Great Barrier Reef, Heron sits amid a protected marine sanctuary, so the diversity of fish life is virtually unmatched in the world. Park rangers are accessible and knowledgeable, so you learn as you dive.
■ **CONTACT:** P & O Resorts, Ltd.
☎ 800–225–9849.

STINGRAY CITY, GRAND CAYMAN

Best time to go: September–June.

■ Ever yearned to get up close and personal with a stingray? It may not sound inviting, but snorkelers rave about the experience in this British colony 450 miles south of Miami. Groups of 15 to 20 tame stingrays—drawn to the surface by the squid and other treats that divers bring—swarm around you, above you, even through your legs.
■ **CONTACT:** Red Sail Sports, ☎ 809–947–5965.

SANTA BARBARA ISLAND, CALIF.

Best time to go: Year-round, although weather conditions are variable.

■ This tiny island, one of the so-called Channel Islands off the Pacific coastline near Los Angeles, offers an extremely unusual bonus: a huge sea lion rookery on its north side.
■ **CONTACT:** Atlantis Charters
☎ 310–592–1154.

PROVIDENTIALES, TURKS AND CAICOS

Best time to go: June–August.

■ These British colonies, which are composed of eight small islands, are largely undeveloped, which makes for terrific diving in an unspoiled setting. The reefs surrounding Provo, as Providentiales is commonly known, sit on a shallow shelf surrounded by deep water, so snorkelers can see sharks, turtles, and other marine life that usually swim in far deeper water.

■ **CONTACT:** Turks and Caicos Tourist Board ☎ 809–94–64970.

GULF OF AQABA, RED SEA

Best time to go: June–October.

■ Deep walls of coral reef begin in just 18 inches of water near the gulf's mouth, so snorkelers can glimpse up close sights typically seen only by scuba divers. Those who make the trip to what *Scuba Diving* magazine calls the "most-unexplored of the world's divable seas" can also see unusual regional fishlife, like the bump-head wrasse. Hard to get to, but worth it.

■ **CONTACT:** Sinai Divers, ☎ 011–2062–600158.

MADANG, PAPUA NEW GUINEA

Best time to go: Year-round, though monsoons can hit from November–April, and are worst in January.

■ Madang is bounded by a tropical rain forest and the Bismarck Sea. The turquoise waters here contain some of the world's last primitive reefs, largely untouched and unspoiled by human encroachment. The corals and sea life are astounding, matched by the remarkable ancient land creatures found in the rain forest.

■ **CONTACT:** Trans Nuigini Tours ☎ 800–521–7242.

DELOS, GREECE

Best time to go: April–September, except mid-August, when the the seas can be rough.

■ Scuba diving is now banned here, because scavengers have taken off with many of the cultural artifacts that lie just below the surface, remnants of Greece's Golden Age more than 2,000 years ago. Snorkelers, however, can view what remains, including pieces of mosaic and sunken temple columns.

■ **CONTACT:** Hard to get to, so see your local travel agent.

SWIMMING

HOW TO SWIM LIKE A FISH

Sure, you can stay afloat, but are you an "efficient" swimmer?

Remember those mind-numbing and exhausting laps you had to do when you were learning to swim? Unfortunately, many of the swimming techniques you've been taught probably won't help you swim better or faster. Terry Laughlin, who runs Total Immersion Adult Swim Camp in Goshen, N.Y. (☎ 914–294–3510), is a world-class swimming coach who's dedicated his career to teaching advanced swim techniques to people who hit the pool for fun and fitness, not gold medals. Students who attend his weekend seminars know how to swim, but he teaches them to be more efficient swimmers.

Laughlin believes you improve your "stroke efficiency" not with endless laps but by making your body more "slippery," so that it glides through the water by offering less resistance. The formula for swimming speed is this: Velocity = Stroke length (how far you travel with each stroke) x stroke rate (how fast you take them). Swim-

EXPERT TIP

If you're trying to improve your kicking when you swim, using a kickboard isn't the answer, says Terry Laughlin, because it keeps your hips locked—and you need to move them to propel yourself. Instead, try swim fins, which get you to stretch your feet and help make your legs stronger.

■ **HOW TO BOB LIKE A BOAT**

Swim long, swim tall, and swim on edge

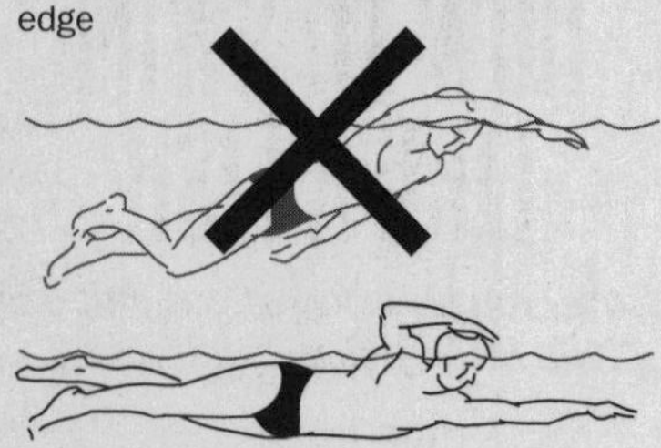

1. Learn to sink evenly, instead of like a ship with all its cargo shifted to the stern.

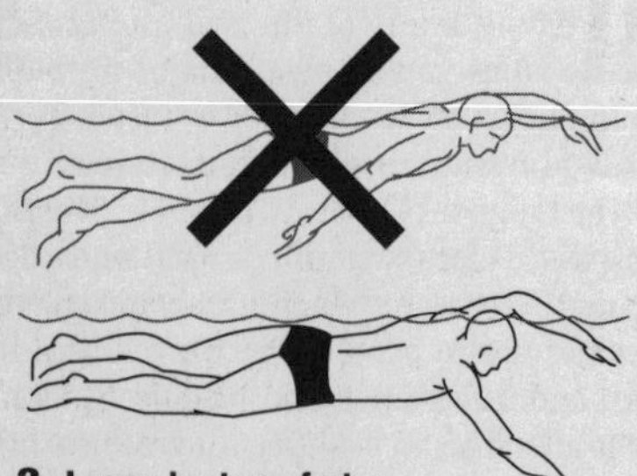

2. Longer boats go faster. Longer bodies do, too. The best swimmers make themselves "taller" by keeping their arms extended in front as much as possible.

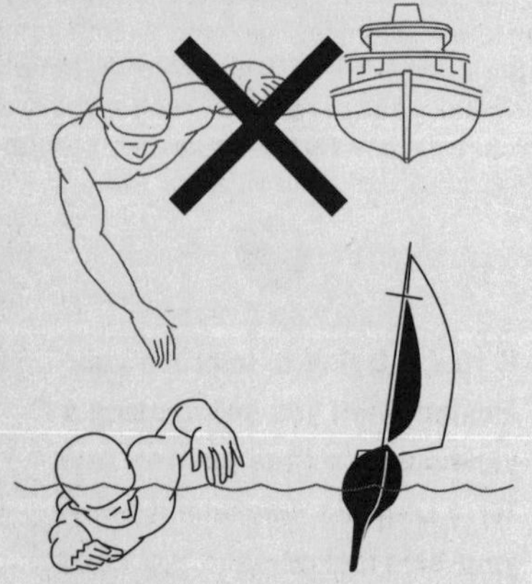

3. The world's fastest swimmers roll until they're nearly perpendicular to the water and glide there for as long as possible, in each stroke cycle.

mers are naturally inclined to stroke faster, but the potential for improvement there is limited, and the work it takes burns more energy than it's worth. According to Laughlin, most of the best swimmers in the world actually stroke fewer times than other swimmers; their speed, he argues, comes from increasing the length they travel on each stroke. Your body's tendency will be to do that by stroking and kicking harder, but churning your hands and legs won't help much. A much better bet, Laughlin says, is to improve your body position in three ways:

1. BALANCE YOUR BODY. Many swimmers find that the lower half of their body—the longer, heavier end—lags beneath the surface when they swim, like a lot of excess baggage in a boat. They kick harder—but it won't help. The solution is what Laughlin calls "pressing your buoy": pushing your chest down into the water as you swim, which has the effect of lifting your hips and hence your legs. It takes some practice to master this, but it works.

2. "SWIMMING TALLER." By this, Laughlin means stretching out your body, which helps you glide through the water. As each hand enters the water, reach forward—not down—before starting your pull. This will be difficult: Your inclination will be to automatically reach for the bottom as your hand hits the water. To fight that tendency, Laughlin says to begin each stroke as if you're reaching for the wall at the end of a lap. Leave your hand extended for as long as you can before beginning to stroke. It may seem odd to spend more time than you're accustomed to with both arms stretched in front of you, but it will help you glide.

3. SWIM ON YOUR SIDE. Yachts move more easily through the water than barges do. Yet most of us swim more like barges—which lie flat in the water—than like yachts, which are frequently leaning to the side, leaving only a narrow sliver in the water. So when you swim, roll from side to side as you stroke. It's not natural, and your body will fight it because you'll feel unbalanced. But master it and you'll swim more fluidly with less effort.

WINTER FUN

SKIING: A look at the best resorts for ski bums and ski bunnies, PAGE 735 **UP AND COMING:** Seven resorts for great skiing—but without the crowds, PAGE 738 **EQUIPMENT:** Hourglass skis are the new thing on the slopes, PAGE 739 **ESCAPADES:** From curling to ice climbing, other sports for winter fun, PAGE 741 **HUNTING:** A beginner's guide to bagging a duck or bringing home the venison, PAGE 744

SNOWBOARDING

A HEAD-TO-TOE GUIDE TO AIR

Boarding is no longer just for the grunge set

Sixteen-year-old grunge boarders are still the norm, but now some of their parents are buying snowboards and joining them. Some skiers, attracted by the prospect of fewer knee blowouts and familiar with the slalom movements of snowboarding, are making the switch. Other adults, simply eager to spend time outdoors and get a good workout, are seeking advice from their teenagers.

Meet Paul Graves, 41, who began snowboarding in 1964 on one huge wooden ski with a leather belt binding. Graves and partner Gordon Robbins run the Over-the-Hill-Gang snowboard camps, which cater primarily to middle-aged beginners. Here, Graves offers a head-to-toe guide to snowboard gear, including snowboard lingo, that will get you up and skying fat in no time!

■ **THE BOARD:** The first thing you'll need is, of course, a board. Unfortunately, the popularity of the sport has only fueled its high costs. You can plan on spending close to $500 for a board with bindings. There are two styles of boards: freestyle and alpine. Freestyle, with its roots in the skateboard culture, is more common in the U.S. There is no true front or back of a freestyle board, as boarders can ride "fakie"—spin and reverse the direction of the board. Alpine, which is popular in Europe, is done on a thinner board designed to carve the snow and work the board's edges more.

■ **BINDINGS AND BOOTS:** Freestyle boards use boots that are similar to regular snow boots. Alpine boards use a rubber-soled hard boot that resembles a ski boot. The binding of the back foot is quickly released, as boarders must skate themselves through the lift line. Boarders either ride regular (left foot forward, right foot skates) or goofy (right foot forward, left foot skates).

■ **LEGS AND BUTT:** Loose-fitting clothing is not only a fashion statement, it's a necessity on a snowboard. Snowboard pants come with reinforced knees because you'll spend a lot of time on your knees, either after a fall or simply resting. Some snowboard companies sell extra padding for your butt. But no matter how much you pad, beginners will spend a majority of their time falling on their butt and knees and will feel it afterward. Also, your lead quad and upper thigh will begin to burn before too long.

■ **TORSO AND ARMS:** Most jackets come with a

BASIC MOVES

All you do is work just one edge at a time, heel or toe side. Traversing 1, the board will hold a line like a ski when tilted on edge;

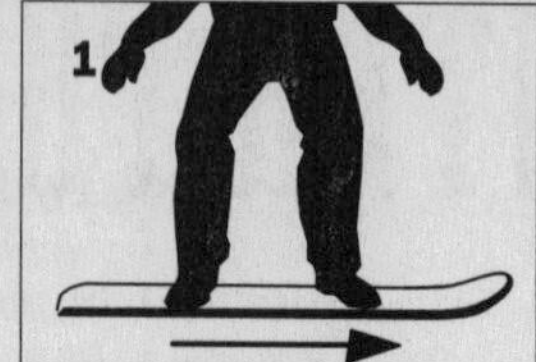

Release the edge 2, and the board will sideslip down the fall line.

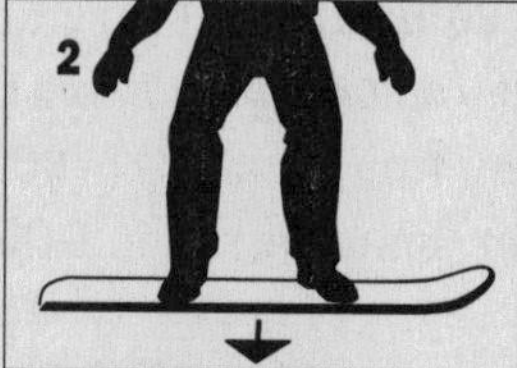

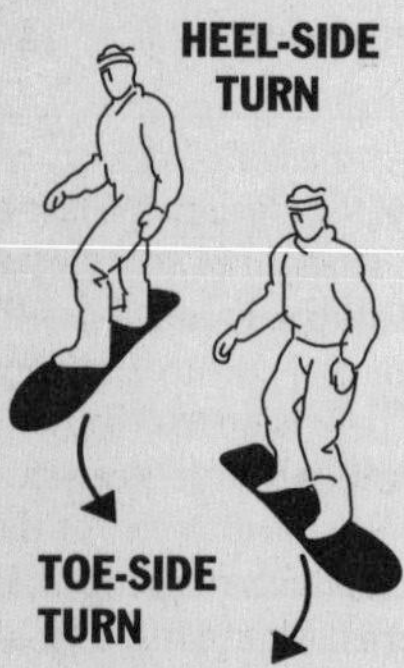

To make the basic turn, from heel edge to toe edge, say, release the heel edge 3,

pivot the back foot in the direction of the turn 4,

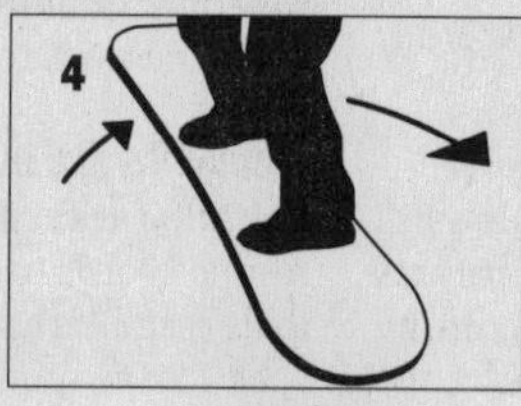

engaging and weighting the toe edge 5. The board's sidecut draws a curve in the snow.

SOURCE: *Men's Journal*, Dec. 1994/Jan. 1995.

SNOWBOARD LINGO

- **Bomb hole.** *If you land so hard after a jump that you leave a dent/hole in the snow.*
- **Butt rocker.** *Being on your butt a lot.*
- **Catching air.** *As in, "You caught some awesome air that time!" Catching air is the time spent in the air after a jump.*
- **Doing hits.** *Any kind of move.*
- **Fresh powder hits.** *A powder hit happens when you attack a jump that's all powder snow. When you hit, the jump "explodes" into a blur of white powder.*
- **Headin' to the half-pipe?** *Many mountains have half-pipes built in where snowboarders can show off their moves.*
- **Laying down an arc.** *Being so far over on your board's edges that you're almost lying flat on the snow and your body is almost parallel to the ground. Done at high speeds.*
- **Poser.** *One who walks the walk and talks the talk, but can't catch air.*
- **Sky fatter.** *If someone is skying fatter than you, they are going higher and catching more air.*
- **$%&#*!!!.** *Foul language is common and welcome in the snowboard world.*

butt flap that makes sitting on a chilly chairlift more comfortable. The baggy plaid, pseudo-Seattle look that has dominated snowboarding the last few years is still popular, but it is slowly giving way as some ski apparel companies enter the snowboard market in force. Thick gloves with gaiters that come up to the elbows are important, as you will spend much time with your hands on the snow in front of you.

HEAD: Many snowboarders wear elaborate headgear, including long jester hats that flow down nearly to their boards. Also popular is the plain wool skull cap, a nice touch if you're going with the gangsta-look theme. Snowboarders wear sunglasses and goggles under the same conditions that skiers do, but many boarders opt for sunglasses all the time to add to the total look. Pierced nose or tongue optional.

SKIING

IT'S DOWNHILL FROM HERE

Our annual look at the best resorts for ski bums and ski bunnies

Like beauty, a ski resort's charms are often in the eye of the beholder. One skier's Heavenly is another's Purgatory. And so it goes for Killington, Vail, Whistler/Blackcomb, and many other resorts. According to *Skiing* magazine, experts rank Squaw Valley, Alta, and Whistler/Blackcomb as their top three choices, while *Ski* magazine gives Jackson Hole, Whistler/Blackcomb, and Mammoth Mountain gold medals for terrain. The only resort in the East that earned an A+ in any category in *Snow Country*'s 1995 rankings was Quebec's Mont-Ste. Anne, which received the grade for its network of cross-country trails. The only A+ in the West was awarded to Lake Louise in the Canadian Rockies for scenery.

The rankings on these pages show the top 10 resorts for each of the three major ski magazines (and, where applicable, how those resorts ranked in the two other surveys). Below are some of the pros and cons of the ski areas that made *Ski* magazine's top 10 list. We've noted readers' top preferences at the different resorts.

1. WHISTLER/BLACKCOMB, B.C.

TOP RATINGS: Terrain, lifts and lines, value, challenge, food, lodging, après-ski.

■ Say hello to the new #1 ski resort. Whistler/Blackcomb (connected mountains that can be skied with the same lift pass) knocked perennial #1 Vail from the top by offering North America's largest ski resort, an awesome vertical drop, some of the most breathtaking scenery around and a base village with a European feel. Whistler/Blackcomb's proximity to the Pacific, however, can lead to rain, fog, and wet snow. The sheer size and variety on the mountain, however, more than makes up for a few days of bad weather.

2. SUN VALLEY, IDAHO

TOP RATINGS: Terrain, lifts and lines, challenge, food, lodging, après-ski.

■ No, Bruce Willis does not own Sun Valley, just a nearby small town. Hollywood movie stars have been retreating to Sun Valley for decades. New high-speed lifts and lodges, part of a multimillion-dollar makeover, bumped this western favorite from #22 last year all the way up to #2 in *Ski*'s 1995 survey. The 3,400 feet of vertical can challenge any skier, but there's also some wide-open cruisers for beginners. Sun Valley can be a little difficult to get to, but that also means smaller crowds and shorter lines once you get there.

3. MAMMOTH MOUNTAIN, CALIF.

TOP RATINGS: Snow conditions, terrain, value, challenge.

■ Blessed with 335 inches of annual snowfall and 3,400 skiable acres, Mammoth is just that. Add to

FACT FILE:

HOW MUCH IS A GOLD MEDAL WORTH?

■ *There can be big money in doing bumps. According to* Snow Country *magazine, Tommy Moe earned close to $1 million in the season after he captured two Olympic medals in 1994, ten times his earnings the previous season. By the early '80s, after an Olympic gold medal and three World Cup titles, Phil Mahre pulled in an average of $500,000 annually. Skiing's biggest current moneymaker: Alberto Tomba, the popular Italian technician who has won five Olympic medals and over 40 World Cup races. His estimated 1995 earnings: $10 million.*

that its relative proximity to Los Angeles (a 5-hour drive) and San Francisco (a 7-hour drive), and it's no wonder that Mammoth has upwards of a million skier visits a year. But with 31 lifts and 150 runs (not to mention the many off-trail opportunities), you'll be more overwhelmed with the size of the mountain than the size of the crowd. The only area Mammoth receives poor ratings in is its base village.

4. STEAMBOAT, COLO.

TOP RATINGS: Snow conditions, terrain, lifts and lines, challenge, fair weather, lodging.

■ A popular Steamboat tourism poster features a group of ranchers riding on horseback through downtown Steamboat in dusters and cowboy hats. The poster is more real than staged, which adds to the laid-back, friendly feel of this western resort.

■ HOW THEY RANKED

Each year, the editors of *Ski, Snow Country,* and *Skiing* magazines ask their readers to rank the nation's top resorts. Here are the '95–'96 results. We've included each magazine's top 10 and, if applicable, the corresponding rank on the other surveys.

AREA	SKI	SNOW COUNTRY	SKIING
Whistler/Blackcomb, B.C.	1	1	2
Sun Valley, Idaho	2	16	6
Mammoth Mountain, Calif.	3	3	N/A
Steamboat, Colo.	4	5	N/A
Snowbird, Utah	5	N/A	9
Vail, Colo.	6	2	1
Snowmass, Colo.	7	13	N/A
Telluride, Colo.	8	26	4
Jackson Hole, Wyo.	9	19	N/A
Aspen Mountain, Colo.	10	4	5
Squaw Valley, Calif.	22	6	10
Alta, Utah	11	28	3
Beaver Creek, Colo.	14	7	N/A
Big Sky, Mont.	18	9	N/A
Park City, Utah	19	8	N/A
Keystone, Colo.	29	10	N/A
Taos, N.M.	21	22	7
Val d'Isere, France	N/A	N/A	8

Steamboat can be difficult to get to, though—it's a nail-biting drive from Denver, but more and more airlines are offering direct flights. The combination of Steamboat's dry snow, steep vertical, breathtaking scenery, and the friendly staff and locals makes Steamboat a nice place to call home—for at least a week. Families with young kids give the place particularly high marks.

5. SNOWBIRD, UTAH

TOP RATINGS: Snow conditions, terrain, challenge, fair weather, accessibility.

■ Snowbird ranked high in all categories having to do with its mountain (challenge, snow conditions, and terrain). Like all Utah resorts, Snowbird receives its share of dry powder, but unlike other Utah resorts, it offers a 3,240 vertical rise. The base village has all the charm of a well-stocked nuclear fallout shelter. One of Snowbird's major attractions is its accessibility. It's a short drive (29 miles) from the Salt Lake City airport, a major hub.

6. VAIL, COLO.

TOP RATINGS: Snow conditions, terrain, challenge, food, après-ski.

■ It was no fluke that Vail topped *Ski* readers' list for so long. The front side of the mountain offers run after run of groomed forested trails, and the back side offers seven bowls to keep experts busy. If you don't ski or need a day off from skiing, Vail is the place to be. The base village is famous for its shopping, food, and high prices. Last year the resort instituted its Mountain Plus ticket, which can be used for skiing, snowmobiling, lessons, or rentals. Despite the many advantages, you can't avoid Vail's primary disadvantage: the crowds. Long lift lines are a commonplace.

7. SNOWMASS, COLO.

TOP RATINGS: Snow conditions, terrain, challenge, fair weather.

■ Big Burn (a long, intermediate cruising run) is one of the most famous runs in Colorado and is Snowmass's most identifiable feature. But don't write off Snowmass as a one-run mountain. While Snowmass is a great family resort with lots of beginner and

■ SNOW STATS FOR SKIERS

Here are the key stats on the top-rated resorts. The list includes all the resorts mentioned in the rankings by the top three ski magazines. For lift ticket prices and other travel and lodging information, call the individual resorts

Resort	Vert. rise (ft.)	Skiable acres	% of runs that are... Exp.	Int.	Beg.	Lifts/ gondolas	Snowfall (in./yr.)
WHISTLER/BLACKCOMB, B.C. ☎ 604-932-3141	5,280	3,340	30	55	15	13/1	400
SUN VALLEY, Idaho ☎ 800-786-8259	3,400	2,067	17	45	38	17/0	220
MAMMOTH MOUNTAIN, Calif. ☎ 800-832-7320	3,100	3,500	30	40	30	27/2	335
STEAMBOAT, Colo. ☎ 800-879-6111	3,668	2,500	31	54	15	19/1	300
SNOWBIRD, Utah ☎ 800-453-3000	3,240	2,000	45	10	25	8/1	500
VAIL, Colo. ☎ 800-525-8930	3,330	4,112	32	36	32	25/1	335
SNOWMASS, Colo. ☎ 800-923-8920	4,087	2,560	38	52	10	18/0	300
TELLURIDE, Colo. ☎ 800-525-2717	3,522	1,050	32	47	21	11/0	300
JACKSON HOLE, Wyo. ☎ 800-443-6931	4,139	2,500	50	40	10	9/1	400
ASPEN MOUNTAIN, Colo. ☎ 800-923-8920	3,267	6,310	65	35	0	7/1	300
SQUAW VALLEY, Calif. ☎ 800-545-4350	2,850	4,000	30	45	25	30/2	450
ALTA, Utah ☎ 801-942-0404	2,100	2,200	35	40	25	8/0	500
BEAVER CREEK, Colo. ☎ 800-525-8930	3,340	1,191	43	39	18	11/0	330
BIG SKY, Mont. ☎ 800-548-4486	3,030	2,100	40	44	16	11/2	400
PARK CITY, Utah ☎ 800-545-7669	3,100	2,000	17	44	39	13/1	350
KEYSTONE, Colo. ☎ 800-222-0188	2,340	1,739	51	36	13	18/2	230
TAOS, N.M. ☎ 505-776-2291	2,612	1,094	51	25	24	11/0	312
VAL D'ISERE, France ☎ 0113-79-06-60	4,290	10,000 h.	9	76	15	97/5	390

intermediate runs, there are also plenty of bumps and extreme runs for the more adventurous. Located right up the road from Aspen, it has more than its share of excellent dining and lodging, without the "Aspen scene."

8. TELLURIDE, COLO.

TOP RATINGS: Snow conditions, terrain, lifts and lines, challenge.

■ If it weren't so difficult to get to, Telluride might be the world's perfect ski resort. Then again, the fact that it is difficult to get to adds to the resort's funky charm. While Telluride is known for its difficult and steep terrain, intermediates will enjoy their own novice mountain with a 1,600-foot vertical rise. The base village has excellent dining, and hasn't been spoiled yet by overdevelopment.

9. JACKSON HOLE, WYO.

TOP RATINGS: Snow conditions, terrain, challenge.

■ For years, families and intermediate skiers have shied away from Jackson Hole, intimidated by its many expert runs. But a booming town, spectacular views of the Tetons, and half a mountain of beginner and intermediate runs is changing all that. If, however, you still want to tackle the expert black diamonds, help yourself to 1,250 acres and 4,139 vertical feet of terrain, including the famous Corbet's Couloir. Jets are a common sight at Jackson's airport today, but flights fill up fast and securing a seat can be difficult.

10. ASPEN, COLO.

TOP RATINGS: Terrain, challenge, food, après-ski.

■ You could spend your entire vacation in Aspen and never ski—the town is nearly as famous as the mountain. Finer dining is hard to find, and there are as many stars wandering the streets as there are in the night skies. But beyond the town is the mountain, which offers not a lot (600+ acres) but challenging terrain. Nearby Aspen Highlands and Snowmass give some more options for off-days.

SKIING

BEYOND VAIL AND ASPEN

Chances are you'll be hearing a lot more about these seven resorts

Love skiing, but hate standing in lift lines? Beyond the Vails and Aspens is a wide variety of smaller—and cheaper—resorts that offer great skiing and less crowded runs. *Ski* magazine's executive editor Lisa Gosselin recommends these up-and-coming ski resorts as the spots of the future:

BIG SKY, *Montana*

■ Big Sky could now officially change its name to Closest to the Sky: A newly added tram gives Big Sky the greatest vertical rise in the United States. A new conference center will allow visitors to mix more business with pleasure. Drawbacks include a 45-minute to 1-hour drive from the closest airport, and chilly temperatures. But you'll work up such a sweat skiing the crowd-free slopes you may not notice the temps.

PURGATORY RESORT, *Durango, Colorado*

■ This quiet little resort in southwestern Colorado is quickly making a big name for itself. Purgatory, recently under new management, offers a variety of creative packages, including a "total ticket" that allows visitors to buy one ticket for skiing, train rides, sleigh rides, and other resort attractions. An increased number of daily flights from Dallas is making it easier to get in and out of Durango.

MONT TREMBLANT, *Quebec, Canada*

■ More than $430 million in renovations has turned Mont Tremblant into one of the best vacation spots in North America. The new base village offers some of the tastiest food around—a vast improvement from the typical lodge chili and overpriced french fries. East Coast skiers will appreciate a shorter flight and a premier resort in their own backyard.

SUGARBUSH, *Vermont*

■ A perennial New England favorite, Sugarbush is now in league with the best of the West. More than $25 million in renovations added more lifts and spruced up the mountain and base area.

NORTHSTAR-AT-TAHOE, SIERRA-AT-TAHOE, BEAR MOUNTAIN, *California*

■ California skiers can thank the Fibreboard Corp. for making their lives easier. The company has recently assumed ownership of all three resorts and instituted a number of creative packages, including a lift-ticket good at all three resorts. Bear Mountain, a 2½-hour drive from Los Angeles, offers lodging at the mountain base and in the nearby town of Big Bear Lake. Sierra and Northstar are about a 3½-hour drive from San Francisco. There is no lodging at Sierra-at-Tahoe, but nearby South Lake Tahoe has plenty, and Northstar-at-Tahoe offers lodging at its base.

■ SNOW STATS

Resort		Vert. rise (ft.)	Skiable acres	% of runs that are... Exp.	Int.	Beg.	Lifts/ gondolas	Snowfall (in./yr.)
Big Sky	☎800–548–4486	3,030	2,100	40	44	16	8/2	400
Purgatory	☎970–247–9000	2,029	2,722	26	51	23	9/0	250
Mont Tremblant	☎800–461–8711	2,131	493	35	45	20	9/1	144
Sugarbush	☎802–583–2381	2,650	412	29	48	23	18/0	270
Northstar-at-Tahoe	☎916–562–1010	2,200	2,280	25	50	25	8/1	300
Sierra-at-Tahoe	☎916–659–7453	2,212	2,000	25	50	25	10	450
Bear Mountain	☎909–585–2518	1,665	195	25	50	25	11	120

EQUIPMENT

THE GREATEST THING SINCE GORP

"Hourglass" skis can make an expert out of an intermediate

There's a revolution under way in the world of skiing. For years, ski manufacturers have fiddled with ski technology, producing faster, lighter, safer equipment, but the fundamental shape of the ski has remain unchanged. Now, parabolic or hourglass skis are challenging the traditional ski design. "Hourglass skis will do for skiing what the Prince oversized rackets did for tennis and the Big Bertha oversized driver did for golf," says Steve Still, director of the Vail Ski School. Still is such a proponent of hourglass skis that the Vail Ski School has converted to them. We asked Still about some of the whys and wherefores.

■ What are hourglass skis?

Hourglass skis are a new style of ski that is narrow in the middle and wider at the tip and tail. They're also sometimes called "super-sidecut" or "parabolic" skis.

■ How do they work?

All skis have sidecut (a tapering in the middle). When a ski is turned on edge, the sidecut helps to make the turn. Without sidecut, skis would not turn at all. On traditional skis, the sidecut is not extreme and skiers must shift their weight and lift their legs and feet in order to turn their skis. On hourglass skis, however, the sidecut is so extreme that skiers just shift their weight from ski to ski.

■ What type of skiers would benefit most?

All skiers. Because less energy is needed to turn hourglass skis, all skiers will feel less

SKIING IN CYBERSPACE

Snow reports, trail maps, and just about everything else is a few keystrokes away. If you have a connection to the Internet and a Web browser, it's easy to do a search, using either "ski" or your favorite resort as a keyword. But here are some of the better skiing Web sites:

■ SKINET: *Ski* and *Skiing* magazines have gone online. This site offers vital stats on resorts, equipment reviews, snow conditions, same-day race results, chat forums, travel information, links to other ski pages, and a resort finder, which will help you choose the resort that suits your interests and skiing ability. *http://www.skinet.com*

■ SKI WEB HOME PAGE: Offers links to most major ski resorts and information on discount tickets. *http://diamond.sierra.net:80/skiweb/*

■ SKI MAP SERVER: Includes maps of nearly every ski resort. *http://www.cs.umd.edu/~.regli/ski.html*

■ THE SOUTHLAND SKI SERVER: Creator Mark Bixby has made it his own personal crusade to keep California skiers informed and entertained. Bixby provides a wealth of information on most California resorts and offers links to nearly every ski resource. *Snow Country* magazine recently dubbed his page "the best ski link out there." *http://www.cccd.edu/ski.html*

■ SKI GATE: Features everything from equipment to ski products and resort information. *http://www.aescon.com/skigate/index.htm*

EXPERT TIPS

HOW LONG SHOULD YOUR SKIS BE?

Some skis are too big, some are too small, and some are just right. Greenwood's Ski Haus in Boise, Idaho—consistently rated one of the best ski shops in the country by Snow Country *magazine—offers these sizing tips*

■ The first question you need to ask yourself is: What type of skier are you?

• If you are a beginner to intermediate skier, you should probably buy skis about 4 inches taller than yourself

• If you are a more accomplished, aggressive skier, you could go 4 to 8 inches over your head.

• If you are very, very aggressive, you could venture up to 12 inches over your head.

■ If you are buying hourglass skis, they may be much shorter.

AT A GLANCE:

■ In general, you should buy skis that are on the long side. In the old days, beginners and intermediates were steered toward very short skis. Not anymore.

■ The longer the ski, the faster the ride. Add 5 cm. for fast skiing on groomed slopes. Subtract 5 cm. for skiing mostly bumps, or if you are a slow, conservative skier.

■ Intermediate skiers looking for a basic, all-purpose ski should use the chart below as a general guide.

Height	Ski length (cm.)
5'0"–5'1"	158
5'2"–5'3"	168
5'4"–5'5"	178
5'6"–5'7"	183
5'8"–5'9"	188
5'10"–5'11"	193
6'0"–6'1"	198
6'2"–6'3"	201
6'3"+	201

fatigued and will be able to ski longer and safer. Beginners will see improvement almost immediately; intermediates will soon be skiing effortlessly; experts will be able to get more performance out of their skis while expending less energy; even pros can benefit—many of today's World Cup skiers have switched to hourglass skis.

■ Do they work better in some conditions?

Soft, cruising runs with room were made for hourglass skis. Some complain the sidecut on hourglass skis makes it tough to run them fast and straight on quick runs.

■ What are the disadvantages?

Hourglass skis are funny-looking. If you can handle the muffled giggles in the lift lines, you may have overcome the biggest challenge facing hourglass skis.

■ Are all hourglass skis the same?

The severity of the sidecut varies by ski. Many rental shops now carry hourglass skis, so you can comparison-shop before you buy. Elan and Head are two of the biggest producers of hourglass skis, but expect the hourglass market to expand rapidly.

■ Do they cost the same as regular skis?

Skis aren't cheap. If you're not used to dropping $500 on a pair of skis, you may be turned off by the cost of hourglass. Expect to spend between $450 and $550.

ESCAPADES

GOING OUT INTO THE COLD

Who says you have to stay in and get fat? Try curling, for example

Just because winter is here doesn't mean you should settle for riding a stationary bike or climbing a fake set of steps in a gym. But what if skiing isn't your thing? Here's a guide to other winter activities that team up well with ice, snow, and chilly weather.

CURLING

Curling is a team sport played on ice. Teams of four shove "rocks" down the ice toward a target. Team members slide along the ice with the rock, steering it by sweeping long-handled brooms in front of it. While curling is found mostly in the colder northern tier of the country, there are curling clubs as far west as San Francisco and as far south as Houston. More than 15,000 curling enthusiasts do their stuff all winter long, some of those with dreams of gold: Curling will debut as a full-medal sport in the 1998 Olympics.

■ **GEAR:** Clubs are also good places to start because many lend equipment to beginners. Once you're serious, you'll need your own Teflon slider (about $18); a broom (about $40); and curling shoes (about $80), but flat sneakers will also do.

■ **TRAINING TIP:** Sweeping (the rapid back and forth with the broom in front of the curling rock) is an exhaustive workout for the arms and shoulders. But don't forget about your quads: curling is done primarily in a squat.

■ **KEEP AN EYE ON:** The skip (the "captain" of the four-person team). The skip is the strategist and controls the flow of the shots and movement.

■ **WHO TO CALL:** U.S. Curling Association ☎715–344–1199. Curling is a club-oriented sport. Your first step is to get in touch with one of the 130 area clubs. Most clubs also offer instruction for beginners.

SNOWSHOEING

Snowshoes are no longer relics of the Nordic past. In fact, snowshoe sales have tripled of late and snowshoers are popping up at ski resorts the way snowboarders did in the '80s. New lightweight equipment is making snowshoeing easier and faster for experts and beginners alike. Many serious athletes now do their winter training on snowshoes and there is an annual snowshoe marathon, but you don't need to be an iron man to snowshoe. It is, perhaps, the world's simplest sport: If you can walk, you can snowshoe.

■ **GEAR:** One of snowshoeing's most appealing aspects is its lack of cumbersome gear. The old-fashioned wood and rawhide snowshoes have given way to lightweight aluminum shoes with crampons. But in deeper powder, you need more flotation and the new running snowshoes are not as effective. A set of Nordic ski poles will give you more balance and stability and also add an upper-body workout. Like cross-country skiers, snowshoers should dress in layers that will keep out the cold but allow you to strip down once you really start sweating—which you will. Top-of-the-line snowshoes can cost about $250, but many outdoors stores rent them.

■ **TRAINING TIP:** Snowshoeing is an excellent cardiovascular workout. In steep terrain, a 150-pound snowshoer can burn up to 500 calories per mile. A simple way to get in shape for snowshoeing is walking up and down hills. When you first start, you'll feel a burn in the tops of the legs at the hip and groin area from lifting a snow-filled shoe.

■ **KEEP AN EYE ON:** The scenery. Snowshoeing can take you places you couldn't get to on skis or in boots. But if you're in the mountains, be careful in the backcountry and keep an eye out for avalanches.

■ **WHO TO CALL:** There is no national snowshoe association, but check local newspapers and local outdoors stores for information on any clubs in your area. For further information, you could call self-appointed sport spokesman Dave Felkley ☎303–258–3157, a snowshoe guide in Boulder, Colorado.

HOCKEY

Want to be more than a hockey parent? Want to relive those glory days of Pee Wee hockey? Then strap on your skates and join an amateur hockey league. There are organized hockey leagues all over the country (no checking, or blocking an opponent, is allowed in older leagues) and the amateur popularity of the sport continues to rise.

■ **GEAR:** You'll need a lot. Hockey requires a fair amount of equipment. You can't play league hockey in your college sweatshirt and a pair of skates; you'll need all the proper body padding (including shoulder pads, shin pads and elbow pads), gloves, a stick, and a helmet. Plan on spending anywhere from $200 to $700. You might want to check with used sports stores for good prices on skates and equipment.

■ **TRAINING TIP:** Hockey is a grueling cardiovascular workout, so don't hit the ice without some preconditioning. Also, although most over-35 leagues outlaw checking, expect to take some knocks and spills—and not complain. Before you even think about joining a team, make sure you're confident on your skates—forward, backward, and stopping.

■ **KEEP AN EYE ON:** The obvious—the puck, your teammates, and the opposing team. If you're playing hockey to relieve a little stress and aggression, you may want to throw the occasional hip check. But if you're playing for pure cardiovascular reasons, watch out so you don't end up with your face plastered against the Plexiglas.

■ **WHO TO CALL:** USA Hockey ☎719–599–5500 is the national governing body for hockey in the United States. USA Hockey can provide information on area leagues. For more information on old-timers' leagues in your areas, check the Yellow Pages for ice rinks.

SNOWMOBILING

A nice, noisy snowmobile can take you everywhere a wimpy pair of cross country skis can—and make a lot more noise doing it too. There are about 1.4 million registered snowmobiles in the U.S. Tour operators offer everything from half-day to three- to four-day trips. Women-only trips are a sign of the sports growing popularity.

■ **GEAR:** The average snowmobile costs between $5,000 and $6,000, but used ones can be found for about $2,000. Daily rentals can run from $50 to several hundred dollars, depending on the package. If you don't own them, you'll also need to rent a snowmobile suit, gloves, and a helmet.

■ **TRAINING TIP:** Always wear a helmet and follow general safety guidelines. There are a number of snowmobile deaths every year, caused mostly by drunk and reckless driving. Just like cars, snowmobiles must abide by a set of operating laws. Most operators offer a free lesson on mechanics, handling, and safety. Physically, riding a snowmobile may not seem taxing, but controlling a large machine for several hours at a time wears out anyone. Don't be too ambitious and be sure to head back before you're beat.

■ **KEEP AN EYE ON:** Where you are. Snowmobiling on private land without prior consent could land you in jail. There are over 100,000 miles of groomed, marked snowmobile trails in North America. Always be extra cautious about snowmobiling on frozen lakes. And if you're snowmobiling near a road, don't assume the traffic can see you.

■ **WHO TO CALL:** The American Council of Snowmobile Associations ☎517-351-4362 is the best place to start. The council can help you organize a trip or direct you to one of 27 state organizations for more region-specific information. The council also offers a variety of snowmobiling publications, including safety manuals and a complete North American snowmobile directory.

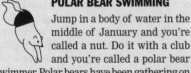

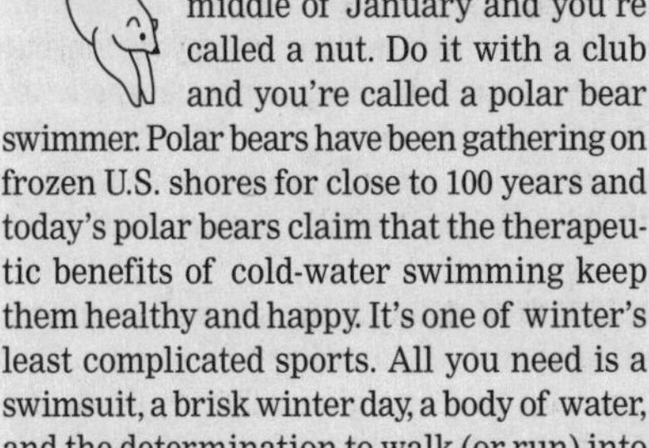

POLAR BEAR SWIMMING

Jump in a body of water in the middle of January and you're called a nut. Do it with a club and you're called a polar bear swimmer. Polar bears have been gathering on frozen U.S. shores for close to 100 years and today's polar bears claim that the therapeutic benefits of cold-water swimming keep them healthy and happy. It's one of winter's least complicated sports. All you need is a swimsuit, a brisk winter day, a body of water, and the determination to walk (or run) into icy cold waves.

■ **GEAR:** A swimsuit, goggles, water-proof booties optional, a big warm towel.

■ **TRAINING TIP:** Those with heart troubles should check with their physicians before jumping in icy water. The sudden drastic change in temperature could cause problems, but many polar bears are octogenarians who claim the cold water is precisely what keeps them going.

■ **KEEP AN EYE ON:** Frolickers. Polar bear swimming is as much about frolicking and splashing in the icy water as it is about exercise. Polar bears swim together because it's fun. If you want a serious, competitive workout, turn down the temperature in the pool and do some laps.

■ **WHO TO CALL:** Although you could jump in any old frozen water, it's more fun to do it with a club. The Coney Island Polar Bears (at 91 years old) is the nation's oldest club, ☎718-748-1674. If you're in or near Boston, there's the L Street Swimming Club and Brownies, ☎617-635-5106. On the West Coast, jump in with San Francisco's Dolphin Swimming and Boating Club ☎415-441-9329.

ICE CLIMBING

Ice climbing was invented by restless rock climbers looking for a way to pass the winter months. It is similar to rock climbing, but climbers scale frozen waterfalls, instead of sheer cliffs. Climbers can be found anywhere the temperature drops. The mecca for ice climbers is the San Juan Range, near Telluride, Colorado, but East Coasters can find excellent ice climbing outside North Conway, N.H., and midwestern diehards have been known to ice silos for a good climb. The sport's popularity has soared in recent years, mostly due to rock climbing's popularity and advances in safety equipment.

■ **GEAR:** To be properly outfitted, you'll need: ice climbing boots, which are plastic versions of stiff hiking boots and run \$200–\$250; crampons, the stiff iron spikes you strap to your boots that cost \$125–\$150; two hand tools, basically handles with fancy picks on them that cost about \$200; a helmet. Most climbers stick to low climbs, but anything higher requires ropes and harnesses.

■ **TRAINING TIP:** Climbing is done with all parts of your body, not just the arms, as many people assume. Women often make excellent climbers because they lack upper body strength, and are forced to use ingenuity instead of brawn.

■ **KEEP AN EYE ON:** Melting ice, so you can avoid it. A sunny, warm day may tempt you outside, but resign yourself to the fact that ice climbing is best—and safest—on chilly, cloudy days.

■ **WHO TO CALL:** There are no organized ice climbing organizations, but your local outdoors clubs and retail outlets are good sources. In the San Juans, call Ryder–Walker Alpine Adventures in Telluride, Colorado ☎970-728-6481. In New England call International Mountain Equipment in North Conway, New Hampshire ☎603-356-6316.

HUNTING

HAVE GUN, WILL TRAVEL

Choose your prey, dress warmly, and head for the woods

Mention hunting and most people picture a middle-aged man in an orange vest wielding a rifle and, perhaps, a beer can. But the sport of hunting has become so popular that hunters—many of them women—are too diverse to be easily stereotyped. The United States Fish and Wildlife Service estimates that some 40 million Americans hunt or fish. The average hunter spends about $1,000 a year, making the sport a $40.9 billion annual industry. (For more information about fishing, see The Great Outdoors, page 726.)

Hunting is a sport of precision, skill, challenge, and being outdoors. You have four sports to choose from. You can hunt waterfowl (ducks and geese), upland birds (quail, dove, grouse, and pheasant), deer, or elk. Each sport has its own seasons, locations, and pros and cons. Dave Petzal, editor-in-chief of *Field and Stream,* has compiled a beginner's guide to the basics of hunting.

WATERFOWL

Waterfowl are, of course, found near water. Duck hunters spend their time crouched in fields and blinds (structures that hunters erect to conceal them from the ducks) alongside lakes, ponds, and marshes.

The North American geese population is larger than the duck population. One reason: Many geese have adapted to their surroundings and may stay in one spot all year long, rather than migrating.Hunting geese is similar to hunting ducks. The only differences are the seasons and limits. Check with your local fish and wildlife department or a good sporting goods store for local information.

■ **WHERE TO HUNT:** There are four principal North American migration routes. So no matter where you live, you're not more than a state or two away from a duck thoroughfare. Much of the best duck hunting land is private. You will need to stick to public land or pay a user's fee for the private land.

■ **WHEN TO HUNT:** Early in the morning. You can't shoot until the first daylight, but plan on starting your day about 3 a.m., so you can get set up and ready by sunrise. The best shooting is generally at sunrise and sunset.

Duck hunting seasons vary by region, but you can plan on hunting somewhere between November and January, depending on how far south you live. Seasons are set each August by the local fish and wildlife department.

■ **ESSENTIAL GEAR:** A license and (in many states) proof of a hunting safety course. The limits on ducks are generally very small and some species are limited or restricted. It's essential you have a license and are within local limits. For information on licenses, check with your local sporting goods store.

- **12-gauge shotgun**—the accepted gun of choice for all duck hunters. Shotguns actually fire hundreds of tiny pellets, which make them ideal for moving targets, but they don't shoot far, so don't fire at ducks beyond your 40-yard range.
- **Camouflage raingear and hip boots.** Plan on being cold and wet. The best duck hunting is always in the worst weather.
- **A duck call,** very important and worth any investment. A good one costs about $30.
- **Decoys** made of lightweight plastic help lure ducks within range.
- **A good retriever dog** is crucial. Labrador retrievers are best, followed by golden retrievers.

■ **HUNTING TIP:** Don't shoot at anything more than 40 yards away. Wait until the ducks are lured into your decoys, and then pull the trigger as they're descending. Also, the hunting is best on rainy, overcast days.

UPLAND BIRDS

Upland generally refers to the hunting of inland birds. The most popular targets are dove, followed by quail, grouse, and pheasant.

■ **WHERE TO HUNT:** Upland hunters generally stand around in fields and prairies, near where birds eat, and wait for the birds to descend and take off. Upland hunting is common in all parts of the country, but find out where the private and public lands are.

■ **WHEN TO HUNT:** Upland seasons are generally in the fall and early winter months. The bird populations are more dense than waterfowl populations, so seasons are longer and limits are larger. Inland birds feed at all times of day, so you don't necessarily need to be shooting at sunrise or sunset.

■ **ESSENTIAL GEAR:** Proper licenses and safety courses, of course. Unlike waterfowl, no calls or decoys are necessary.
• **Any type of shotgun,** from a 12-gauge to a .410-gauge shotgun, will do.
• **Brush pants** (heavy canvas pants faced with leather or nylon) for trudging through briers and thickets. A jacket of the same material is also essential.
• **A game vest with multiple pockets** provides a handy place to store shells and also a place to stuff the game you shoot.
• **A good dog,** either a pointer (to track down birds), a retriever (to bring back your kill), or a springer (to flush the birds up).

■ **HUNTING TIP:** Because you're using a shotgun, don't shoot at anything beyond 40 yards.

DEER

Two deer species are hunted: the white-tail (the most commonly hunted and found throughout the U.S.) and the mule (only found west of the Mississippi).

■ **WHERE TO HUNT:** You can hunt as far south as South Carolina and as far north as Canada. Access to hunting on private land can easily cost several hundred dollars. In some areas, membership in a hunting club grants you access to private areas.

■ **WHEN TO HUNT:** Deer hunting seasons tend to be short, simply because the deer can't handle constant hunting pressure. Depending on your latitude, deer season is somewhere between August and January.

■ **ESSENTIAL GEAR:** License and proof of hunter-safety course. Safety courses are usually conducted by the local fish and game department at a shooting range.
• **Weapon of choice.** There are three types of weapons to hunt deer, each having its own season. Most common is the modern rifle. But more primitive weapons—bow and arrows and muzzle-loading rifles—are also used. The primitive weapons offer a greater challenge and demand a higher skill level—though animal rights activists argue that bow-hunting in particular can be more cruel to the animals. Proficiency in all three weapons prolongs your hunting season.
• **Camouflage gear** made of soft fabrics. Your clothes must not rustle when you move or bump into trees. The slightest noise can ruin a day of tracking.
• **A bright orange hunting vest** is required in most states.
• **A telescopic scope on your rifle** will help you track your target.
• **A good set of binoculars** is a must. Using your scope exclusively can lead to misfires.
• **Survival kit,** including equipment to start a fire. The woods can be cold, and you may end up spending a full day or night outdoors.
• **Compass.** Don't assume

FACT FILE:

BRINGING HOME THE VENISON

■ *Expenses for a day of deer hunting:*
$50—*license*
$200—*proper clothes*
$500—*rifle*
$300—*scope*
$500–$1,000—*Either a trespassing fee on private land, or lodging near public land*
$300—*binoculars*

$1,850–$2,350—*total*

FALCONRY: A SPORT OF SULTANS

An ancient field sport favored by kings and sultans is making a modest modern-day comeback of sorts. There are 2,000 or so falconers in the U.S. currently, but their numbers are soaring. Falconers spend years training falcons and red-tailed hawks to respond to commands, hunt prey, and then return to their masters. They track down and kill everything from duck and pheasant to rabbits and squirrels. The thrill of the sport, falconers say, is spending time outside and the awesome sight of a falcon diving at 200 m.p.h. to attack its prey.

Wannabe falconers must spend several years in training—earning first the title of apprentice, then general, then master falconer. You can't just purchase a falcon, you must find a master who is willing to be your sponsor. There are strict state and federal regulations (designed to protect the birds) and multiple levels of examinations to pass. In response to the sport's growing popularity, several resort areas now offer day- or week-long falconry schools. The North American Falconers Association (125 S. Woodstock Drive, Cherry Hill, NJ 08034) can put you in touch with your local falconers club.

■ **WHERE TO HUNT:** Falconry is currently outlawed in Delaware, Hawaii, and Connecticut, but you can take your falcon pretty much anywhere else. (Falcons generally hunt game birds; red-tailed hawks generally hunt smaller land animals.)

■ **WHEN TO HUNT:** There is no set falconry season. Indeed, if you own a falcon, you must work with, train, and care for it every day. You also must first pass a written exam and housing inspection before you can begin training your own bird.

■ **ESSENTIAL GEAR:** A falcon or hawk. Apprentice falconers trap wild birds and spend two years training them. Once you are a master or general, you can buy a bred bird.

- **Appropriate housing** for your bird.
- **Classic falconers' bells** alert you to the whereabouts of your bird when it is off hunting.
- **Leather glove** allows the bird to rest on your arm.
- **Game bag** (sack) to bring home your catch.
- **Lure to bring your bird back.** If properly trained, your falcon will identify the lure with a food-reward and promptly return.

■ **HUNTING TIP:** These birds of prey are not pets. They are working animals and will only return to you because they want to.

---

you can find your way back to your car. Trees start to look alike after a while.

■ **HUNTING TIP:** Rifles are more precise than shotguns, but you only get one chance. Unlike shotguns, rifles shoot a single, conical-shaped bullet. A careless shot can ruin an entire day of tracking and scare off all deer within earshot, and deer have great ears.

ELK

Hunting elk is similar to hunting deer, but it's harder, you need to travel farther to do it, and you need more expensive stuff.

■ **ESSENTIAL GEAR:** Elk are found in the western and Alaskan mountains, so factor in a plane ride if you don't live in the Rocky Mountains or the 49th state.

- **A big-game rifle,** which can cost about $2,000, is essential.
- **A guide who knows the area.** It's not worth the money to fly out there and spend three days getting the lay of the land.
- **An out-of-state elk hunting license,** if you don't live in one of the Rocky Mountain states, which runs about $300–$500.
- **An access fee.** It's not uncommon to pay $5,000 for prime elk country.

PARLOR GAMES

SCRABBLE: Advice from a Scrabble master on how to win in the war of words, PAGE 749 **BOARD GAMES:** The rules for checkers, chess, and backgammon, PAGE 750 **CARD GAMES:** A primer on poker, gin rummy, spades, and solitaire, PAGE 753 **BLACKJACK:** When to stick and when to take a hit, PAGE 755 **BRIDGE:** Essential reading for the enthusiast, PAGE 757 **POOL:** Cue tips from a world champion, PAGE 759

STRATEGIES

SECRETS OF A MONOPOLY CHAMP

Don't buy Boardwalk, skimp on hotels, and gobble up the orange

At the Monopoly Game Championship in New York City in the fall of 1995, Roger Craig astonished onlookers when, on his first pass around the board, he opted not to buy Boardwalk, the most expensive property in the game and one highly coveted by lesser players. But about 90 minutes later, Craig, a 34-year-old tire salesman from Harrisburg, Ill., emerged as the U.S. Monopoly champion for the next 4 years. We tracked Craig down and asked him to share some of his secrets of success. Craig's strategy is based on the "traditional" game, in which each player starts with $1,500 and gives all tax and fine money over to the bank. (Nontournament matches often include the "untraditional" $500 bonus pot into which all taxes and fines are placed—a bounty awarded to any player landing directly on Free Parking.)

■ An important tactical question first. Do you prefer a particular token?

I use the iron. It's the smallest piece on the board, and as you're moving it around you can hide it behind hotels and get away without paying rent. It's amazing how much money I've saved over the years using that piece. Once the dice are rolled by two people beyond yourself, you can't be caught for owing money on your last move. In the championship final they announced every move to the crowd, so I couldn't get away with it.

■ What is your basic strategy in acquiring property?

You buy everything you can, until you get around to the three most expensive sets of properties—the yellow ones (Atlantic, Ventnor, Marvin Gardens), green ones (Pacific, North Carolina, Pennsylvania) and blue ones (Park Place, Boardwalk). They cost too much to buy, get a monopoly on, then have to improve with houses and hotels. If I get one of the green ones or the yellow ones, that's all I'm interested in. It blocks the other monopolies, and it gives me something to trade later in the game.

■ Which properties are the best to acquire?

The orange ones—St. James, Tennessee and New York. The two most common numbers rolled on the dice are six and eight—and rolling them just pops you onto the orange ones. You get those three or the red ones—Kentucky, Indiana, and Illinois—and you're going to win 75 percent or more of the time unless you roll very poorly. They don't cost

■ THE MOST LANDED-ON MONOPOLIES

In the 1980s, Parker Brothers, Monopoly's manufacturer, made a list of the most frequently landed-upon monopolies. The list shows the odds a player is going to land on one property of a monopoly in one trip around the board.

■ GO DIRECTLY TO JAIL...

1	**RAILROADS** – B&O, Reading, Short Line, Penn	64%
2	**ORANGES** – N.Y., St. James, Tennessee	50%
3	**REDS** – Illinois, Indiana, Kentucky	49%
4	**YELLOWS** – Marvin Gardens, Atlantic, Ventnor	45%
5	**GREENS** – Pacific, Pennsylvania, N. Carolina	44%
6	**LIGHT PURPLES** – St. Charles, States, Virginia	43%
7	**LIGHT BLUES** – Oriental, Connecticut, Vermont	39%
8	**UTILITIES** – Water Works, Electric Co.	32%
9	**DARK BLUES** – Boardwalk, Park Place	27%
10	**DARK PURPLES** – Mediterranean, Baltic	24%

■ DO NOT PASS GO, DO NOT COLLECT $200...

Using a computer, Irvin Hentzel, a mathematics professor at Iowa State University and a frustrated Monopoly player, calculated the 10 spaces you can count on landing on more than others. (The most landed-upon space was Jail, but Hentzel deleted that from his list, since a player in Jail had to remain there for three turns or roll doubles to get out.) Upon making his findings in 1973, Hentzel promptly quit playing. "It was no fun anymore," he explained. "I had figured it out."

1. **Illinois Avenue**
2. **Go**
3. **B&O Railroad**
4. **Free Parking**
5. **Tennessee Avenue**
6. **New York Avenue**
7. **Reading Railroad**
8. **St. James Place**
9. **Water Works**
10. **Pennsylvania Railroad**

too much to build up, and they bring in the best return for what you spend.

Knowing that, if you have one of the yellows and two of the greens—or vice-versa—you can trade them for oranges or reds to people who don't know what it takes to win. They see the yellows and greens cost more, and they're only thinking about how much they'll get when someone lands there—not how much it will cost to build them up. I figure how much cash a player can generate. I would never make such a trade if a guy was sitting there with $1,000 in cash.

■ How does your strategy change once you have a monopoly?

If you can get a monopoly of your own without having to trade for it, you ought to have the game in hand. Then you can spend the rest of your time blocking everybody else—making a trade that doesn't help any opponent and gets you a piece of property that will block someone else. If you're holding all the single cards to a bunch of monopolies and you've got one monopoly yourself, they can't beat you. The only time I will make a trade that gives someone a monopoly is if I get an outright monopoly itself in exchange.

It usually takes eight or nine times around for everything to be bought up. When all the properties are sold, you start looking around at all the deals you can make. Hardly anybody ever tries to get Boardwalk or Park Place as part of a deal, because they cost so much to improve—and at that stage of the game you don't have any money.

■ How much should you build up your properties with houses and hotels?

Everybody wants to build up as many houses as they can—as fast as they can. A good rule is to only build up to the three-house level—as quick as possible. Your return on your money from one house to two houses is

EXPERT TIPS

A-D-V-I-C-E FROM A SCRABBLE MASTER

Seven things you can do to score big

Joe Edley was already a self-admitted games guru when he began playing Scrabble. After two years of "fanatical study," he won the National Scrabble Championship in 1978. Since then, he has won another national title (1992) and consistently has been one of the 15 top-ranked players in the U.S. Edley is the co-author, with John Williams, of *Everything Scrabble* (Pocket Books, 1985). Both men are officials with the National Scrabble Organization (☎ 516–477–0033). The words Edley suggests mastering can all be found in the *Official Scrabble Players Dictionary* (Merriam-Webster, 1993). The third edition, published in 1996, contains approximately 1,200 more words than the 1991 second edition—but without some 100 "offensive" words that have been removed from the game.

- Learn the 94 2-letter words.
- Learn the 996 3-letter words.
- Learn the 17 "Q without U" words. Seven of them (Faqir, Qintar, Qanat, Tranq, Qoph, Qaid, Qat) can also be made plural with the addition of an "S", and "Qindar" (an Albanian monetary unit) can become "Qindarka."
- Learn the approximately 1,200 four- and five-letter words containing a J, Q, X, or Z.
- Learn to use "vowel dumps"—words containing multiple vowels such as "ourie" (shivering with cold) and "warison" (a battle cry) that get four or more low-scoring vowels out of your rack in one move.
- "S" and "A" are "hook letters" that can often be used to form two words off of one existing word (e.g., "board" can lead to "aboard" and "ape").
- Learn "bingos"—words that by using all seven of your tiles earn a 50-point bonus. Included in the bingo list are about 200 "6 to make 7" words that can all be built off just three six-letter words (saltine, satire, retain) and one blank tile.

almost nothing, but once you make the jump to the third house—that's where your real money is made. The jump from the third to the fourth house and the fourth house to a hotel isn't that big. So save your money for something else.

The biggest mistake I saw people make during the championships was that as soon as they got a monopoly, they would spend everything in front of them to build their land up—without regard to where they or the other players were on the board. You need to leave yourself enough money to cover yourself. If there are several monopolies out, I'll take whatever money I figure I can spend and put it aside, then see where everyone else is on the board. As soon as they get real close to my property, then I'll build on the property and take a chance they'll land there. I also wait until I pass opposing monopolies before spending cash.

■ What else should players keep in mind?

Don't always go for cash. Say an opponent lands on your property, and they owe you $800. You can see by what they have in front of them that they can raise that much cash with what they have on hand and by mortgaging properties. It's not always smart to let them do that, because if you leave them with three or four mortgaged properties, the next person who lands there is going to be able to get those properties. So a lot of times, I'll take whatever property they have instead of cash.

BOARD GAMES

WHERE KINGS AND QUEENS REIGN

The rules that rule the pieces in checkers, chess, and backgammon

The most exciting board games require a unique mix of brains and imaginative brawn. In the best of matches, the rules metamorphose from simple mathematical variations into the physics of a new world in which pawns become warriors and you are the mastermind behind a war in which everything good and decent is at stake. Here are the rules that govern the battlefield.

HOPSCOTCHING THE CHECKER BOARD

Learning to play checkers is child's play, but devising strategies to triumph over a good player takes skill and lots of practice. The winner, of course, is the first player to capture all of an opponent's men or to block them so that they can't move anywhere on the board. To test your mettle, follow these instructions:

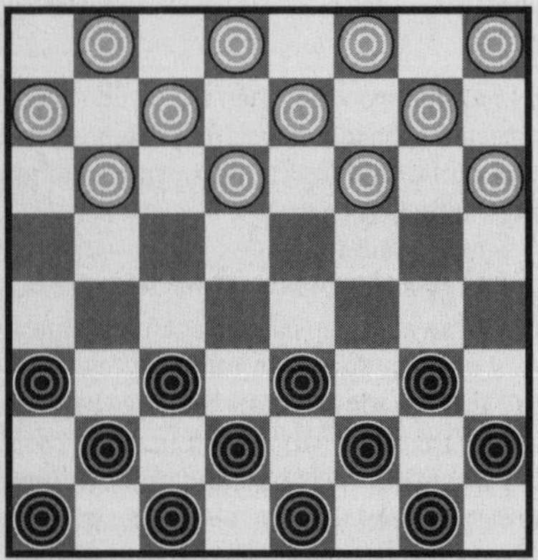

RANK AND FILE: In both checkers and chess, the rows across are known as ranks; the columns as files. In checkers, only the red squares are used.

■ Opponents face each other across the board, which has eight rows of eight squares each, alternately red and black. One player takes the red pieces, or men, and puts them on the black squares in the three horizontal rows nearest him. The opponent places the black checkers on the black squares in the three rows facing him.

■ The opponents take turns—black goes first, then red—moving a man forward diagonally toward the opponent's side. Only the black squares are used. With each turn, a player moves one man to an adjacent empty square. When one player's man comes up against an enemy checker and there is an empty space behind it, the player jumps over the enemy, landing on the unoccupied square. The captured checker is removed from the board.

■ One man can jump two or more enemy pieces consecutively, by moving diagonally left or right after the first jump, as long as there are empty spaces to land on between each jump. A checker that makes it to any square in the opponent's first row becomes a king—at which time it gets crowned by a man of the same color that is not in play. The king can now move, and jump, forward and backward.

THE MIND FIELDS OF CHESS

When it comes to drama, intrigue, and byzantine rules, few games can match chess, which is thought to date back to sixth-century India or China. Odds are you won't become the next Bobby Fischer, who at age 15 was the youngest international grandmaster in history, but here are the rules that will take you to the endgame: capturing the enemy's king.

■ Opponents face each other across the board, which has eight rows of eight squares each, alternately white and black. Each player gets 16 pieces of one color, black or white. From least to most important, the pieces are: 8 pawns, 2 knights, 2 bishops, 2 rooks (or castles), 1 queen, and 1 king.

■ Place the board so that each player has a light square at the nearest right-hand corner.

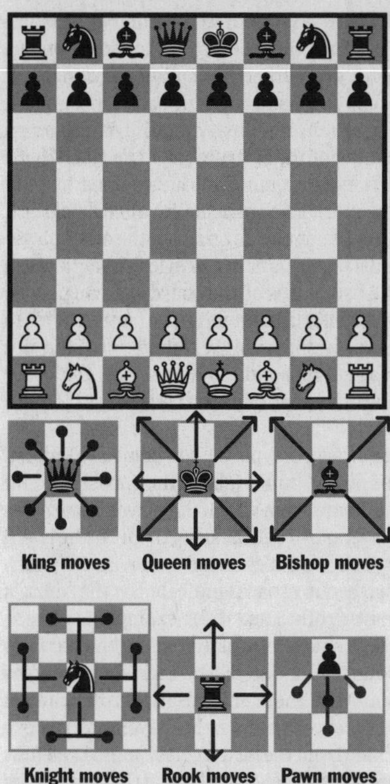

MANEUVERS: As shown here, the six chess pieces can move in a variety of ways. The knight, however, is the only one that can actually move through, or jump over, other pieces. That ability, combined with its unusual L-shaped moving pattern, makes it an endgame linchpin.

In the row closest to you, place in order from left to right: rook, knight, bishop, queen, king, bishop, knight, and rook. Line up the pawns next to each other in the row directly in front these pieces.

■ A piece can move only into a square that's not occupied by another piece owned by the same player. If an enemy piece occupies the square, it is captured. You remove the captured piece from the board and put your piece in its place.

■ A pawn moves forward one square at a time, except for its first move when it can go one or two squares. A knight makes an L-shaped move, going two squares forward, backward, or sideways, then another square at a right angle. It's the only piece that can jump over another piece. A bishop goes diagonally forward or backward, but has to stay on the same color. A rook moves forward, backward, or sideways, for any distance. The queen is a potent force. She moves forward, backward, sideways, and diagonally for any number of squares in one direction. The king's moves are like the queen's except that he moves one square at a time, as long as it's unoccupied or not under attack by an enemy piece.

■ When a king is under attack by an enemy piece, the king is in check. The player whose king is in check has several options: to move the king to safety, to capture the attacker, or to move another piece to a square between the king and the attacker. If a player can't take any of these moves, the king is captured or "checkmated," and the game is over.

■ Pieces capture an opponent's man by moving as they normally do, except for the pawn. It can capture any of its opponent's pieces that are diagonally next to and ahead of it.

■ A pawn can also take an enemy pawn "en passant," or in passing. Say an opponent starts by moving his pawn two squares, instead of one, putting it next to one's pawn. You can take that piece by moving diagonally to the square directly behind it. But do it immediately: you can't wait for your next turn.

■ Once in each game, in a move called castling, a king gets to move two spaces. Castling is done only if the king is not in check, there are no pieces between the king and a rook, and neither piece has yet made a move. The two-part move is done by moving the king two squares toward the rook and then putting the rook on the square passed over by the king. Castling counts as one move.

THE FINER POINTS OF BACKGAMMON

Backgammon is a game played by two players, each with 15 markers or stones—but these days checkers can be used in a pinch. The object is to be the first player to move all one's markers around the board and then off it.

■ To set up, the markers are placed on the board as shown in the diagram below. The board is divided into four "tables" with numbered triangular spaces, or "points." The bar in the middle is also used in the game.

■ Each player rolls a die to determine who goes first. The higher one starts. Players then take turns rolling two dice to determine how many spaces to move the stones, with black moving around the board in one direction and white moving in the opposite direction. The numbers on each die can be combined so that one piece moves the total amount indicated. Alternatively, each die's value can be applied separately to a single marker.

■ Throwing "doubles" (for example, two 4s), allows a player to move twice as many points as shown on the dice—in this case, either four markers can be moved four spaces each, one can be moved four spaces and one 12 spaces, two can be moved 8 spaces each, or one marker can be moved 16 spaces.

■ There is no limit to the number of markers of the same color that may stay on one point, but markers of opposite colors may not occupy the same point. If two or more markers are on a point, the point is closed—a marker of the opposite color can't land there. However, a point that is occupied by only one marker is open and is called a "blot." If an opponent lands on a blot, the other player must move his or her man to the bar between the two halves of the board and can play no other man till the one on the bar reenters. To do so, the player must make a roll of the dice that corresponds to a space on the other player's inner table that is open or blotted.

■ Once all of a player's 15 men have entered his or her "inner table" (the opposite side of the board from which the player began), the player may begin bearing them off the board by rolling the dice and removing any men that occupy spaces indicated by the roll. If a player rolls 5 and 4, for example, he or she may remove one of the men that occupies point 5 and one of the men that occupies point 4. If the number is higher than any of the occupied points, the player may remove a man from the next highest point. Double 6s are an especially good roll at this point. Play continues until one of the players has removed all of his or her men.

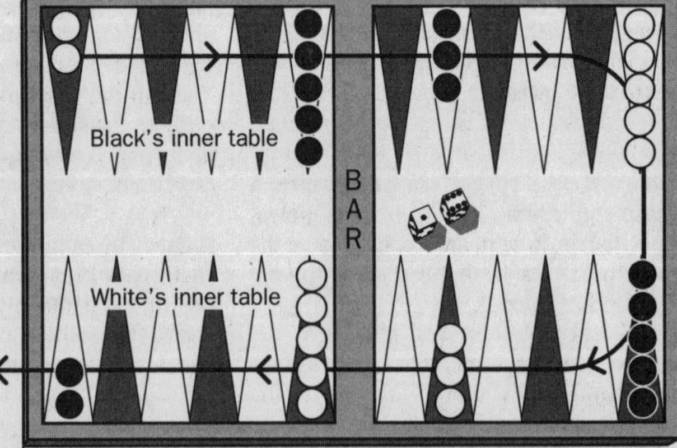

BACKGAMMON: Board is shown in the starting position. The goal is to move your men from your opponent's inner table to your own inner table on the opposite side of the board. White moves in the direction indicated by the arrows, black moves in the opposite direction. When all of your men reach your inner table, you may begin bearing them off by throwing dice that (hopefully) correspond to the number assigned each point.

CARD GAMES

CUT THE DECK, PLEASE

A quick review of how to play poker, gin rummy, spades, and solitaire

If you want to learn how to play bridge, you need to either read a book or take lessons. But here are the rules—and some tricks of the trade—for popular card games that almost anyone can play. That's no guarantee, of course, that you'll draw good cards, but at least you'll be prepared to call the other guy's bet.

■ POKER (FIVE-CARD DRAW)

Poker pits one player against another. Casinos that provide poker tables make their money by taking a percentage of the winnings or charging by the hour for the use of their table and dealer. If you are not an expert, a casino is definitely not the place to test your skill. Better to wager chips or change in the comfort of your own home.

There are hundreds of card games based on slight modifications of standard poker or "five-card draw." Variations include adding wild cards, changing the way in which players bet, and altering the size of each hand. The goal is always the same: get a better hand (selection of cards) than the other players.

To play five-card draw, shuffle a regular 52-card deck and deal 5 cards to each of three to seven players. Typically each player pays a small sum, called an "ante," for the privilege of seeing his or her hand. All bets (and antes) are placed in the pot, a pile of money in the center of the table.

Players bet on their cards in a clockwise fashion, starting at the dealer's left. The first player has several betting options:

- **FOLD:** Throwing in the cards and sitting out the rest of the hand. Any time a player folds at this stage, the ante remains in the pot and goes to winner.
- **BET:** Placing a wager in the pot.
- **PASS:** Choosing not to make a wager and allowing the next player to go.

If the first player doesn't make a bet, then the next player has the same options. Once a player has made a bet, however, other players may no longer pass, and are required to do one of the following:

- **FOLD:** And lose one's bets and ante.
- **CALL:** Match the other player's bets by placing an equal wager into the pot.
- **RAISE:** Place a higher wager than others have bet into the pot. All other players will need to match this raised bet in order to stay in the game.

After a round of betting, all remaining players are then allowed to exchange up to three of their cards with those from the top of the remaining deck in the same order that the cards were dealt. At this time, the players have a second round of betting. After this round, all remaining players show their cards to each other. The player with the highest hand wins the entire pot.

Cards are ranked in the following order, from lowest to highest: 2, 3, 4, 5, 6, 7, 8, 9, 10, Jack, Queen, King, Ace. The box on the next page helps illustrate the ranking. Each level of the table beats ALL hands below it. For example, even the lowest straight (2, 3, 4, 5, 6) will beat the highest three of a kind (Ace, Ace, Ace, King, Queen).

If two players have the same type of hand, the one who has the higher cards wins the hand. For example, a player with a 9, 9, 9, Jack, 2 (three 9s) would beat a player with a 6, 6, 6, Ace, Queen (three 6s). Extra cards, such as the Ace, Queen, Jack, and 2 in this example, only matter when two players have identical winning combinations. For example, a player with a 9, 9, 5, 5, King (two pair, with a King) would beat a player with a 9, 9, 5, 5, Queen (two pair, with a Queen).

■ LOW-HAND POKER

The rules for this game are identical to poker, except for an exciting 180-degree switch. In

WHAT BEATS WHAT

Hand	Number possible	Odds of obtaining
ROYAL FLUSH The highest straight flush—10, J, Q, K, A all of the same suit	4	1:649,739
STRAIGHT FLUSH A straight, and all five cards are of the same suit	40	1:64,973
FOUR OF A KIND Four cards of the same value with one extra	624	1:4,164
FULL HOUSE Three cards of one value and two of another	3,744	1:693
FLUSH Five cards of the same suit, such as five spades	5,108	1:508
STRAIGHT Five cards in a sequence of different suits, such as 5-6-7-8-9	10,200	1:254
THREE OF A KIND Three cards of the same value with two extra	54,912	1:46
TWO PAIR Two pairs of cards with one extra	123,552	1:20
ONE PAIR (Two of a kind) Two cards of the same value with three extra	1,098,240	1:1.37
HIGH CARD In a hand with no winning combination of cards, the highest card	1,302,540	1:1

low-hand poker, it is the player with the lowest (and not the highest) hand who wins. The lowest hand possible is a 2, 3, 4, 5, 7—known as a "seven-high" hand. There is no such thing as a six-high, because a 2, 3, 4, 5, 6 would make a straight. In this game, it is common to see players discarding Aces and pairs of cards to rid themselves of their beastly hand.

HIGH-LOW POKER

Two players split the pot—the one with the highest hand and the one with the lowest hand. If all but one player folds, then the entire pot goes to the winner.

FIVE-CARD STUD

Unlike draw, five-card stud begins by dealing only two cards to each player. One of these cards is placed facedown and one is placed face up, in plain view of all players at the table. Each player is allowed to look at his or her facedown card, after which a round of betting ensues. Betting starts with the player showing the highest card. After this round, another card is placed faceup for each player (so that each player has two cards showing and one hidden card) and there is another round of betting. Again, betting starts with the player showing the highest cards. This pattern continues until each player has five cards. At any time during the game, a player can fold and the person with the highest hand at the end wins.

SEVEN-CARD STUD

This is an extremely lively and often high-stakes game. It is played in a similar fashion to five-card stud, except that the game begins by dealing three cards to each player—two are facedown and one is face up. Rounds of betting are then interspersed with receiving additional faceup cards until each player has two facedown cards and four faceup cards. At this time, a final card is dealt facedown and the final round of betting occurs.

Players can use any of their seven cards to make their best five-card hand. The catch to this game is that the odds are thrown haywire. Having seven cards makes it much easier to achieve good hands. It is common to see full houses, straights, and flushes.

■ BASEBALL

Baseball is a popular variation on seven-card stud, which makes the chances of achieving a high hand ridiculously easy. The game has wild cards, ones that can represent any other card in the deck at the player's discretion. In the game, all 3s and 9s (the number of strikes and innings in baseball) are wild. But they come with a price; players must either purchase 3s and 9s (at a predetermined price) if they are dealt these cards faceup or they must fold the hand. If a player is dealt a 4 faceup (the number of balls in baseball), the player is immediately dealt another card facedown.

Because of the wild cards in baseball, and the possibility of having more than seven cards (if a 4 is dealt), it is common for players to obtain the absurd "five of a kind." For example, a hand of 5, 5, 5, 3, 9 would be five 5s. Five of a kind is the highest hand possible, and beats a royal flush.

■ BLACKJACK

The object of blackjack is to have a hand with a point value that is higher than the dealer's. You must do this without going over 21 points, which is why the game is also known as Twenty-one. A player or dealer with 22 points or more has busted and automatically loses the hand. All numbered cards are worth their face value; picture cards (Jacks, Queens, and Kings) are worth 10 points each; and Aces are worth either 1 or 11—which the player gets to determine. Suits and colors are disregarded in the game.

Before each deal, all players make their bets, if you're playing at a casino. Two cards are then dealt to everybody including the dealer, who is dealt one card facedown. A player whose first two cards add up to 21 (e.g., an Ace and a Queen) has a Blackjack and is immediately paid 3–2, unless the dealer also has a Blackjack. Whenever a dealer and player tie, it is known as a push, and neither one wins the hand.

Once everyone has been dealt, players have several options to choose from. The best move depends both on what you have been dealt and on the one exposed card of the dealer's hand. A player can:

- **HIT:** Take an additional card.
- **STAND:** Take no additional cards.
- **DOUBLE DOWN:** Double the original bet and take only one additional card.
- **SPLIT:** When a player has been dealt two cards of identical value (e.g., two 9s), he can choose to double the original bet and play the two cards as separate hands.

HOW TO WIN AT BLACKJACK

You got to know when to hold 'em, and know when to fold 'em.

■ **Always hit when you have been dealt 8 or less.** You have no chance of busting, and you need to get closer to 21.

■ **Always stand on hard hands of 17 or more, regardless of what the dealer is showing.** A hard hand is a hand that either has no Aces or has an Ace or Aces that must be worth only one point because to be worth more would mean a bust (e.g., a 6, a Jack, and an Ace). If you hit, odds are you will bust.

■ **Always hit if you have 16 or less and the dealer's card is a 7, 8, 9, 10, or Ace.** These are the best cards and it is likely that the dealer will beat you. Although you have a good chance of busting, it is worth the risk of getting closer to 21.

■ **Always stand on hard hands of 12 or more if the dealer's first card is a 2, 3, 4, 5, or 6.** These are the worst cards and it is likely that the dealer will bust. But, you don't win if you bust first!

■ **Always stand on soft 19s and 20s.** A soft hand is one that has an Ace that can still be valued at either 1 or 11. Don't risk losing the good hand.

- **CLAIM INSURANCE:** When a dealer is showing an Ace, players are invited to claim insurance that the next dealer's card will be worth 10 (and thus Blackjack). Insurance involves risking half the amount of the original bet and pays off at two to one, if the dealer has a Blackjack.
- **SURRENDER:** Forfeit the hand and lose half of the original bet. (Not an option in many casinos.)

Once all the players are either satisfied with their hands or have busted, the dealer proceeds. Unlike the players, who get to make choices, the dealer must proceed according to set rules: drawing on any hand that is less than 17 and standing on anything 17 or higher.

GIN RUMMY

Gin Rummy (or simply "Gin") is one of the most popular two-handed card games. It can be played for fun or for money. All 52 cards are used. Suits, however, do not play a role in the game. Face cards are worth 10 points each; numbered cards are worth their face value; and Aces are worth one point each. One common variation, however, is to allow Aces to be either high or low. Usually when this is done, Aces are worth 15 points instead of one. The object is to get rid of the cards in your hand by creating sets of three or more cards that can be "melded." Timing is important, though—the sets are played differently depending on who melds his or her cards first. The sets can be formed in two ways:

- **SERIES:** Three or more cards form a series in sequential order, such as a 4-5-6-7 or a 10-J-Q.
- **MATCHING SETS:** This is when cards are put in groups of the same value, such as an 8-8-8 or an A-A-A-A.

To play, 10 cards are dealt to each of two players and the remainder of the deck is placed in a pile between them. The dealer turns over the top card from this pile and places it faceup to begin a discard pile. The second player then has the option of taking this card and switching it with one of the cards in his hand or passing and giving the dealer the same option. If the dealer also passes, the second player takes the card that is on the top of the pile—so that momentarily there are 11 cards in his hand. One of the 11 cards is then placed faceup on top of the discard pile.

The dealer must then either take the card that has been discarded or the next card from the deck. This continues until a player decides to end the round of play by melding his or her cards to reveal the hand.

Here's where it gets complicated. The first player to meld or "knock" must have fewer than 10 points in hand that are not part of sets. For example, after several rounds of drawing cards, a player might knock with the following hand: 5-5-5 (a set), 8-9-10-J (another set), and A, 2, 2, K (not a set). This player can discard the King and then meld with the set of 5s, the 8 through Jack sequence, and five points (A+2+2).

The second player then must meld his or her cards, too. In doing so, the second player has the added advantage of being able to play cards off the first player's hand.

For example, the second player might have the following hand: 2-3-4, 9-9-9, 4, 5, 8, Q. The 2 through 4 sequence and the 9s would be played in their own right. However, the Q could also be played off the 8 through Jack sequence of the first player, as would the 5 with the three 5s. This would leave the second player with only 12 unused points (4+8). The player who knocked would earn the difference between the two hands, or seven points (12–5).

If a player knocks and then is beat (or underscored), then the second player gets an additional 25 points for the feat. If a player melds an entire hand, with no extra cards, then he is entitled to say "gin" and obtains an extra 25 points. The winner of each round deals the next hand.

The game continues until one player reaches 100 points (or any score that the players have agreed to before the game). To play for money, players typically bet a certain sum per point. For example, a final score of 105 to 80 would result in 25 points to the winner.

SPADES

Spades can be played by three people, but four

EXPERT SOURCES

THE BOOKS ON BRIDGE

We asked Bob Hamman, a championship player who's won the Bermuda Bowl, the Olympiad, and World Open Pairs, to choose the volumes that best teach the game. He has played with and against many authors on this list.

WHY YOU LOSE AT BRIDGE
S. J. Simon (Devyn, reprinted1997, $9.95)
■ A classic with great humor. Not really a book about bridge but about how to be a competitor.

KILLING DEFENSE AT BRIDGE
Hugh Kelsey (Houghton Mifflin, 1966, $9.95)
■ All Kelsey's books are good. He does an excellent job of laying out a problem and putting you in the position of the player, then allowing you to make the decision along with the player.

ADVENTURES IN CARD PLAY
Hugh Kelsey and Geza Ottlik (Trafalgar, 1983, $19.95)
■ The high end of books on card-playing. This is stuff that's tough for everyone, including myself. Ottlik was a mediocre player at the table, but an excellent theorist.

MASTER PLAY IN CONTRACT BRIDGE
Terrence Reese (Dover 1974, $3.95)
■ Reese has worked on over 50 books as an author and collaborator, and this is the best (also published as *The Expert Game*). A classic for the high-level player.

RIGHT THROUGH THE PACK
Robert Darvas and Norman de V. Hart (Devyn, 1947, out of print)
■ Problems cast in a narrative form, with interesting hands that give you other things to think about. Very good for the moderate player.

HOW TO READ YOUR OPPONENTS' CARDS
Mike Lawrence (Devyn, 1991, $9.95)
and **COMPLETE DEFENSIVE BRIDGE PLAY**
Eddie Kantar (Wilshire, 1974, $20)
■ The best of the modern high-tech theorists who are still living and playing. Beginning players can't go wrong reading anything by Lawrence and Kantar, who have both won a couple of world championships.

THE LAWS OF TOTAL TRICKS
Larry Cohen (Cohen, 1992, $12.95)
■ Excellent for a basic understanding of the game. It's about bidding, not card play, and will really help someone who has played just a little bit.

is ideal. The goal is to score as many points as possible by collecting "tricks."

To begin, the entire 52-card deck is dealt evenly to each of the players. If there are four players, each will have 13 cards. The first round is begun by whoever has the 2 of clubs, which is laid in the center of the table. The player to his or her left then must lay down any card of the same suit. The next player does likewise, and the next, till each has laid a card. The highest card wins the trick. (Aces are played high in spades; 2 is the lowest.)

If a player doesn't have a card in the suit that is being played, he or she may trump the trick by playing a spade. However, if any of the following players in that round also has no cards in the original suit, he or she may "trump the trump" with a higher spade. (No one may open with a spade until spades have been "broken"—that is, played as a trump.) The winner of the book plays the next card, and the round continues till all 13 books have been played.

Scoring is what makes spades challenging. Each trick is worth 10 points. After a hand is dealt, players must make a bid on how many tricks they expect to get based on the strength of the cards they were dealt. Because each player in a four-person game has 13 cards, there are 13 possible tricks (130 points). A player who found among his or her 13 cards a couple of Kings, some Queens, and several spades of any value would rightly feel justified in making a high bid because those cards are all likely to make a trick. The catch: If a player has a strong hand and so bids, say, 6 tricks, that player must make at least those 6. If not, he or she will instead lose 60 points (–10 points for each trick bid).

On the other hand, if the player makes over the amount bid, say 7 tricks instead of the 6 bid, he or she receives only a single point for each extra trick—in this case 61 points. Another catch: if a player receives more than 10 of those extra single points, he or she loses 100 points. This is called "sandbagging."

A player who is behind by more than 100 points may bid "blind six," a bid of six made before the cards are even dealt. If the six are made, the player receives 100 points; if not, the player loses 100 points.

Players can play as many hands as they like to a preset score. About 500 points is a good goal for a satisfying evening.

■ SOLITAIRE

Klondike is the most common form of solitaire in the United States—so common, in fact, that it is often known simply as "solitaire." In reality, there are many varieties of solitaire which, as the name implies, refers to any card game played by one person.

To play Klondike, deal one card faceup from a standard deck. Then deal six additional cards facedown, to form a row to the right of the first card. Next a card is dealt faceup on top of the second card in the row, and five more cards are dealt facedown on top of the remaining piles to the right. This pattern continues until 28 cards have been used and there are seven piles or columns of cards, ranging from one card (in the left column) to seven cards (in the right column). The remainder of the deck is placed facedown on the table.

Cards are then shifted from one column to another to form descending sets (from King to 2) that alternate by color (red-black or black-red). In the example below, the red 8 can be placed on top of a black 9. Then, the card beneath the 8 can be flipped over. If a red 10 were to appear, then the 9 and 8 could be placed on top of the 10, allowing the player to flip over more cards.

Aces are immediately removed from the layout when they appear, and are used as starting points to build ascending sets. These sets are based on suit, rather than the black-red pattern already described. In this example, the Ace of diamonds has been set aside for this purpose. If the two of diamonds appears, it will be placed on top of the Ace, and then the 3 of diamonds, and so on. The game is won if all four of these Ace piles are built into Ace-through-King sequences.

If one of the seven columns ever becomes empty because all of its cards have been shifted, a King (and anything stacked beneath it) can be moved to the column to fill the empty space. Once there are no cards that can be moved, cards are taken three at a time from the remainder of the deck, and played off on any of the columns if possible. If you can play the top card, you can play the next one as well. The cards that can't be played are set aside, faceup. When the entire deck has been played through three times, the game is over.

A variation on the game involves flipping the discard pile over and going through the cards a second time, or even a third time before calling it a loss.

■ LAYOUT FOR KLONDIKE

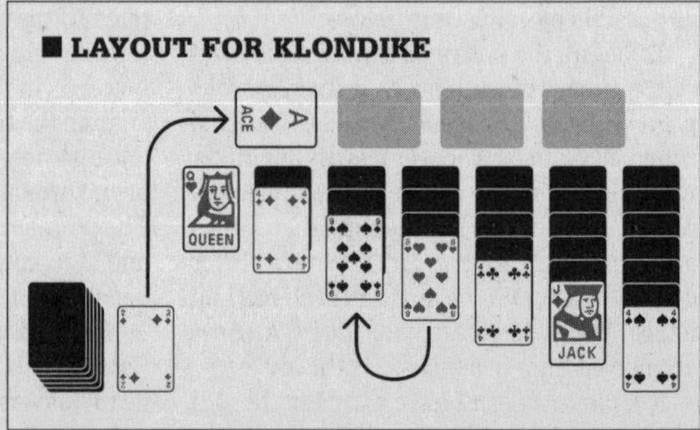

POOL

TAKING CUES FROM A SHARK

Forget that triple bank shot until you've mastered these basics

Loree Jon Jones began her pool career at the age of 4 in her father's billiard room. She won two world championships at 15, and since joining the Women's Professional Billiards Association (WPBA) tour has been one of the sport's top stars. In 1995, she won four of the first five tournaments she entered, earning a record $99,800 for the year. Since 1988, she has been women's editor for *Pool and Billiard Magazine* (☎ 800-247-6172). Here are some of Jones's pointers:

■ FINDING THE RIGHT CUE STICK

The most important thing in choosing a stick is comfort. A big key is the material it's made of—especially the shaft (or top) part. I don't like fiberglass sticks, and the cheaper wooden ones are very grainy. Definitely buy one with a hard-rock maple shaft. People think a heavy stick gives them more control, but it doesn't. Men should use a stick weighing between 19 and 21 ounces, women between 18 and 19½. If you're just pulling a stick off the wall to use, make sure it's not too heavy or warped. Sticks can be specially made small for kids, but I was using a regulation cue when I was 4 years old.

■ START CHALKING

This should be done before every shot. Don't twist and turn the chalk over the top of your stick, just hold the chalk between your thumb, index, and middle fingers and stroke downward while turning the middle of the stick. Make sure the tip is covered. The majority of tips are made of leather, and if you hit a ball straight on without chalking, you'll slide off and miscue. Chalk creates a friction to prevent this.

■ BUILDING BRIDGES

Here are five bridges for a beginner to master.

The "basic" or "regular" bridge is used for average shots where the cue ball rests in the middle of the table. Place thumb against middle finger, put cue stick between them, then wrap index finger around cue stick and touch thumb. Ring finger and pinkie should be spread out for flexibility. Palm and side of hand need to be on table, and the three locking fingers can be moved to make bridge tighter or looser.

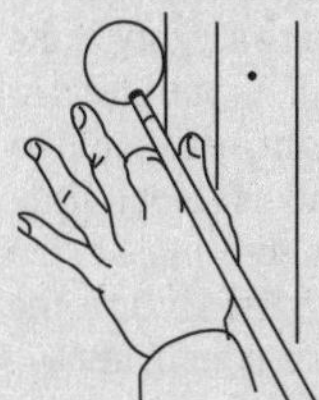

The "rail bridge" is used when the cue ball is frozen against a rail. Place palm on table by rail, hanging it off edge if necessary. Keep cue stick level, curl index finger underneath, then make a "V" with thumb and lay stick against it. The key here is to keep hand flat.

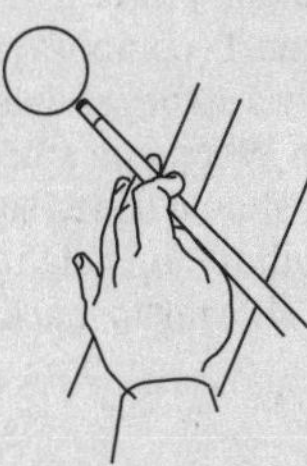

The "near rail" bridge is used if your cue ball is 1½–3 inches off the rail; you need more stability than the rail bridge offers. Put thumb under hand, place cue stick on side of thumb, and rest cue stick on felt of rail. Bring index finger over cue stick so stick sits between index finger and thumb. Stick should remain touching felt throughout shot.

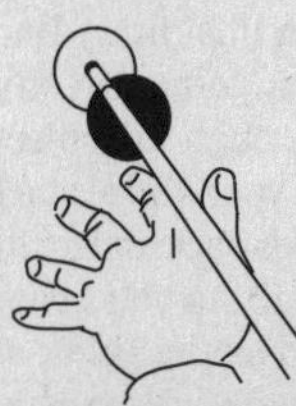

The "over the ball" bridge is used when you have a ball sitting directly behind the cue ball—blocking room for a normal bridge. Get on tips of fingers as best as you can, place them behind the blocking ball, and form a "V" by raising thumb. Not very comfortable, but necessary if you want to avoid using the mechanical bridge.

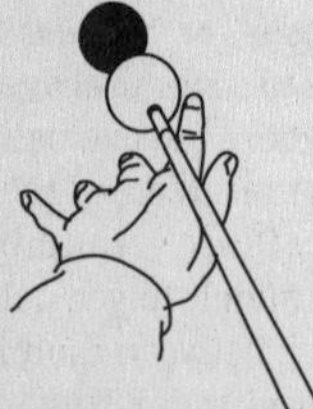

The "open bridge" is used to stretch way over the table for a shot. Put hand flat on table, stretch out fingers, and raise hand up to knuckles. Lay cue stick over index finger and raise thumb for support. If you stroke with right hand, raise right leg in air and stand on left tiptoe for more stretch.

DEVELOPING A STRONG STANCE

When you see a great player ready to shoot, everything is lined up. If you're a righty, make a bridge with your left hand. As you stand at table lining up your shot, right foot should be under back of cue stick and left foot a little more forward and at a 45-degree angle to the right. Both feet should be pointed a little to the right, but make sure you're comfortable—that's the key to every facet of the game.

Before shooting, lean down and get as low as you can to the ball. A few of us touch our chins to the cue stick; you don't have to do that, but get as low as you can. People always wonder how far back or forward they should hold the butt of the stick. When cue stick meets cue ball, back elbow should be at a 90-degree angle. It's OK to adjust for height, moving hand forward if shorter or backward if taller.

STROKING THE BALL

Now you're ready to shoot. Not moving the rest of your body, bring the cue stick back with your stroking arm as you begin eyeing the shot. Making sure your bridge is close enough to cue ball, draw an imaginary line with your eyes or cue stick going directly from middle of cue ball through the object ball and into the pocket. Set your aim at start of that line, moving your eyes back and forth between cue and object ball. As you bring your stroking arm forward again, think of your body as a pendulum—nothing else moving besides your lower arm. As you make contact, your head should remain down. Keep your eyes on the object ball—following it all the way into the pocket.

SHOTS YOU CAN USE

Follow Shot. When you want the cue ball to roll forward after hitting the object ball to set up your next shot, hit the cue ball above its center spot so it spins forward. If you imagine the cue ball as a clock, you would be aiming at 12 o'clock. The bridge should be very high on follow shots; pull your middle finger toward you to make it higher. Don't use too much power; it's not power that makes a better roll, it's how high you hit the cue ball.

Draw Shot. If you want the cue ball to roll backward after hitting the object ball, strike the cue ball below its center spot at 6 o'clock. To make the shot more effective, snap your stroking wrist back as you make contact with the cue ball—but don't force it.

Stop Shot. To make the cue ball stop dead after making contact with the object ball, hit the cue ball just a bit lower at 6 o'clock than on the draw shot. A little wrist action helps.

English Shot. This is used to send the cue and object ball to the right or left rather than straight ahead. Try this shot only after you've mastered everything else. If you want the ball to veer to right, hit it on the right side at 3 o'clock; if you want it to veer left, hit it on the left at 9 o'clock. The higher you hit the ball on either side, the less it cuts down an angle shot. The lower you hit it, the wider the angle.

EXPERT TIP

Straight pool (where players must sink balls 1–15 in order) is the best game for beginners; you can really work on patterns, and with the shots in numbered sequence it's easy to think ahead.

—Loree Jon Jones

INDEX

A

abdominals, exercises for, 140-41, 143, 146
abdominoplasty, 191
Abe Lincoln in Illinois, 634
Abercrombie & Kent (A&K), 518
Abington Memorial Hospital, 180
abortion:
drugs for, 270, 274-75
laws on, 275
Absent-Minded Professor, The, 637
abstinence, periodic, 273
Abyssinian cats, 437
Academy Awards, 466, 611, 634
Acadia National Park, 489-90
Access guides, 562
accountants, 109
fees of, 102
selection of, 105-6
acetaminophen (Tylenol), 232, 244
acquired immune deficiency syndrome (AIDS), 260, 265, 278-80, 432
hospitals specializing in, 217-18
oral sex as transmitter of, 280
tests, 279-80
acrophobia, 234
Actron, 232
acupuncture, 247-49
Acura Integra Coupe, 567
acyclovir, 278
Adam, Robert, 467
Adam's Rib, 611
A.D.A.M. the Inside Story, 667
Adirondack State Park, 481
Adi's Comprehensive Learning Systems, 672-74
adjustable rate mortgages (ARMs), 62, 68, 70
Administration on Aging, 47
administrative occupations, 353
administrative support occupations, 354
Adobe:
FrameMaker, 679
PageMaker, 679
adolescents, 292, 589-91
after-school jobs for, 111
on benefits of music education, 299
contraception and, 269
driver's licenses for, 589-90
female, 300
foreign language education for, 295
movies for, 635, 637
physical development in, 256, 260
winter sports and, 733
adoption, 204-5, 265
Advanced Alternative Media, 600
Advanced Placement exams, 303-4
Adventures in Card Play (Kelsey and Ottlik), 757
Adventures of Robin Hood, The, 613
Adventure Trekking, 523
Advil (ibuprofen), 232, 244
Aeroflot, 539
Aerosmith, 599
aerospace engineering, 320-21
Africa, travel to, 515-18, 522-23
African Gray parrots, 432
African Queen, The, 613
African Wildlife Foundation, 515, 518
age, aging:
and adoption, 204-5
and back problems, 244-45
and breast cancer, 238, 240
and diet, 153
and discounts, 48
and drugs, 233
and education, 283-84
and HRT, 241
and injuries, 146-47
and looking great, 179-82, 187-89
and melatonin, 237
and pregnancies, 194-95, 200-203
and prostate cancer, 242-43
and sexuality, 255, 257-58, 260, 268, 276
and weight, 134
see also retirement
Agency for Health Care Policy and Research (AHCPR), 234, 244-46
aggressive funds, 26-27, 34
agoraphobia, 234
Agriculture Department, U.S. (USDA), 134, 148, 159-60, 175
airbags, 588
air conditioner repairs, 396
air couriers, 547
airline mileage credit cards, 116
Airline Quality Rating (AQR) Report, 541-42
airlines, air travel, 538-48
best carriers for, 541-42
to Caribbean islands, 459
fares for, 545-48
and frequent flyer programs, 543
insurance for, 126
overbooking in, 543-44
safeness of, 538-40
seats in, 539
ventilation in, 540
watchdogs for, 544
Air Travel Advisory Bureau, 548
Alan Guttmacher Institute, 271
Alaska, 346
guided expeditions to, 537
hiking in, 524
national parks in, 493
retirement in, 44
Alaska Airlines, 541-42
Alaska Gold Rush Classic Snowmachine Race, 504
Alberts, Bruce, 641
Alchemy of Love and Lust, The (Crenshaw), 254
alcohol, 160, 248
abuse of, 101, 372
career burnout and, 372
in desserts, 165, 167
drugs and, 232, 235
pregnancies and, 208
teenage drivers and, 589, 591
Alden, Peter, 515
Aldrich, Chrissie, 518
Aleichim, Sholom, 635
Aleve, 232, 244
Algren, Nelson, 555
Alias Nick Beal, 635
Alice Let's Eat (Trillin), 178
All Aboard America, 551
All About Eve, 613
Allegheny National Forest, 508
Allegro Reference Series Business Library, Vol. 1, 665
Allen, Jeanne, 288
allergies, 250-51
Alligator Records, 601
allowances, children's, 110-12
Allstate, 578, 581
All That Heaven Allows, 613
All the King's Men, 635
Alman, Isadora, 261-62
Alomar, Roberto, 705
alpha-fetoprotein (AFP) tests, 200-202
Alpha Five, 676
alpha hydroxy acids (AHAs), 180
alphas, of mutual funds, 34
Alphastar, 627
alprazolam (Xanax), 235
alprostadil, 276
Alsace, waterways of, 531
alternative medicine, 247-49
Alternative Videos, 625
Altour International, 562
alumni, 330-32
benefits for, 330-31
return to college towns by, 331-32
Alzheimer's disease, 221, 237
Amazon.com Books, 692
Amazon Rain Forest, 478
Ambi Chairs, 379
American Academy of Dermatology, 179, 181
American Academy of Family Physicians, 207
American Academy of Orthopaedic Surgeons, 244
American Academy of Pediatricians (AAP), 206-7
American Airlines, 541, 545-46
American Alpine Club, 715
American Alpine Institute (AAI), 537
American Arbitration Association, 20
American Art Dealers Association, 79
American Association of Homes and Services for the Aging, 46-47
American Association of Individual Investors (AAII), 21, 23
American Association of Investors, 40
American Association of Retired Persons (AARP), 47, 59-60
American Association of University Women (AAUW), 300-301
American Automobile Association (AAA), 404, 554-57, 562, 588-90
American Booksellers Association, 693
American Cancer Society, 238-39, 243
American cocker spaniels, 434
American College of Obstetricians and Gynecologists (ACOG), 206, 241
American College of Sports Medicine, 135, 142, 713
American Council of Life Insurance, 129
American Council of Snowmobile Associations, 743
American Council on the Teaching of Foreign Languages, 287
American Demographics, 76
American depository receipts (ADRs), 12
American Dietetic Association, 174
American Driver and Traffic Safety Education Association, 590
American Express, 357
American Football Conference (AFC), 698
American Fried (Trillin), 178
American Graffiti, 613
American Hair Loss Council, 186
American Heart Association, 136, 158, 161
American Heritage Dictionary, The, 665

American history, films on, 634
American Home Products Corp., 13
American Horticultural Society, 419
American Horticultural Society Encyclopedia of Garden Plants (Brickell), 415
American Hospital Association (AHA), 216
American in Paris, An, 620
American Institute for Cancer Research, 174
American Institute of Philanthropy, 122
American Institute of Wine and Food, 165
American Journal of Health Promotion, 142
American Junk (Carter), 89
American Kennel Club (AKC), 433-34, 442
American Medical Association (AMA), 226-27
American Motorcycle Association (AMA), 582-83
American Mountain Guides Association, 715
American Philatelic Society, 94
American Psychiatric Association, 208, 236
American Psychological Association, 263
American Resort Development Association, 76
American River, rafting on, 534
American Samoa, 493
American shorthairs, 437
American Society of Plastic and Reconstructive Surgeons, 187
American Society of Travel Agents (ASTA), 544
American Softball Association, 712, 725
American Stock Exchange, 19
Americans with Disabilities Act (ADA) (1990), 265, 348
American Tea Masters Association, 173
American Urological Association (AUA), 242-43
American Veterinary Medical Association, 440-41
American wirehairs, 437
American Woman's Cookbook, The (Berolzheimer), 178
American Youth Hostels, 550
America Online (AOL), 23, 346-47, 664, 682-85, 694
America's Best Beers (Finch and Griffiths), 175
America's Job Bank, 346
America's Longest War (Herring), 666
America's Top Internships (Oldman and Hamadeh), 340
America's Wilderness Areas (Tilton), 497
America West, 542-43
Amerikanis, 554
Ames, 415
amethysts, 86
amitriptyline (Elavil), 235
amniocentesis, 201-2
amok, 236
Among Whales (Payne), 532
amoxicillin, 252
Amtrak, 551
amusement parks, 645-47
Anafranil (clomipramine), 235
analysis and model building, spreadsheets for, 676
Anchor Brewing Company, 175
ancient coins, collecting of, 93
Anderson, James, 158
Anderson, Sparky, 362, 370
Andes, eastern slopes of, 519-20
Andes, Parker, 420-21
Androff, Dirk, 725
Androscoggin River, 727
anencephaly, 200
angel cake, recipe for, 167-68
Angel Falls, 513
Angel Fish Rocker, 642
angina, diet and, 156-57
angioplasty, 213, 215
Angkor Wat, 465
Anguilla, 459
Aniakchak National Monument and Preserve, 482
"Animal Finders Guide," 431
Animal Shelter, 640
Aniston, Jennifer, 184
ankles:
  injuries to, 147
  swelling of, 232
Annapurna Conservation Area Project (ACAP), 524
Anne, Queen of England, 467
Anne Hooper's Ultimate Sex Guide, 667-68
Annie Hall, 611
Annuities, 60
answering machines, 650
Antarctica, 513, 533
anthropology, 323
Antibiotic Paradox, The (Levy), 228
antibiotics, 228-29, 252
antidepressants, 209, 233-35, 268
Antigua, 460
antihypertensives, 268
anti-inflammatories, 232
anti-lock brakes, 588
antioxidants, 149-50, 153, 160, 237
antiques:
  collecting of, 81-87, 89-90
  examination of, 82-84
  home insurance and, 75
  name-brand, 83
  silver, 85
antiseizure medications, 231
Antone's, 596, 598-99
anxiety, 233-35, 249
Anza, Juan Bautista de, 504
Apartment, The, 611
A.P.F., Inc., 393
Apollo Advisors, 564
Appalachian Mountain Club, 499, 537
Appalachian National Scenic Trail, 502
apparel industry, 375
Apple Computer, 342, 652, 654-55, 657, 660
apples, 169
applets, 655
application development, 676
appraisal fees, 101
apricots, 169
Aquariana, collecting of, 88
Aquarius, 368
Archeological Guide to Mexico's Yucatan Peninsula, An (Kelley), 452
Arctic National Wildlife Refuge, 496
Argentina:
  guided expeditions to, 537
  whale watching in, 533
Argus Census Map USA, 664
Aries, 368
Arizona:
  house purchases in, 62
  national parks in, 493
  pre-season baseball games in, 704
  retirement in, 44
Arkansas, national parks in, 493
arms, exercises for, 140, 142, 147
Army, U.S., 506
art, arts:
  for art's sake, 80-81
  CD-ROMs on, 666-67
  collecting of, 79-81, 86, 89
  education in, 286-87, 298
  framing and displaying of, 393-94
  and home insurance, 75
  Web sites on, 692
Art & Auction, 79, 86
Art Auction Trends (Coleman), 80
art history, 319
arthritis, 232, 248-49, 274
Arthur Andersen Personal Financial Planning Newsletter, 56
Artnet Auctions Prices On-Line, 81
ARTnewsletter, 79
Art of Eating, The (Fisher), 178
Art of Investing, The (Carret), 2
Aruba, 463
asbestos, 399
Asia, investing in, 11-12
Ask Alice, 691
Aspen, Colo., 737
aspirin, 232
assassin bugs, 424
asset allocation funds, 39-40
assets, 4-5, 71, 101
assisted reproductive technologies, 202-3
Associated Press, 701
Association for the Disabled, 590
assumable mortgages, 69
asthma, 232, 248, 399
Astor, Bart, 321
AST Research, 654
Astro Economics, Inc., 368
astrological signs, career selection and, 368-69
astronomy, 322
astrophysics, 322
As You Like It (Shakespeare), 7
AT&T, 120, 342, 377
  Worldnet, 683, 685
ataque de nervios (nervous attack), 236
atherosclerosis, 156, 268
At Home Abroad, 472
Ativan (lorazepam), 235
Atlanta, Ga., dining in, 475
Atlanta Magazine, 475
Atlantic Forest Region Rainforest, 520-21
Atlantic Web, 689
ATP Tour Official Player Guide, 712
Attachmate Emissary, 680
Attenborough, Richard, 610
Attention Deficit Hyperactivity Disorder (ADHD), 208-9, 290
"At Time of Diagnosis," 211
Aubrey, James, 366
Audi A4, 568
Audi 90, 578
audio equipment, 629-31, 652
augmentation mammoplasty, 187
Augusta National, 699
Austen, Jane, 466, 637
Austenfeld, Mark, 242-43
Australia:
  Aborigines in, 522
  honeymoons in, 478
  snorkeling in, 730
  train travel in, 549
Austria, country inns in, 470
autism, 208
Auto Advisor, 573
auto-buying services, 573
Automobile Consumer Services, 573
Automobile Lending and Leasing Manual (McCathren), 574
Automobile Magazine, 567-69
AutoNation, 564
autos, 563-94
  bargains, 573
  best of 1996, 567-70
  body condition of, 593
  buying of, 564-74, 578-81
  CD-ROMs on, 668
  crash tests of, 576-77
  depreciation of, 565, 569, 571-72, 574
  driving of, 584-91
  fatality rates and, 588-89
  financing of, 564-65, 569, 571-74
  front wheel vs. rear wheel drive in, 585-86
  insurance on, 126, 128, 569, 578-81
  interiors of, 593
  leasing of, 570, 574-75
  least problematic, 570
  mechanics for, 595
  men vs. women in, 587
  model year-end sales of, 572
  operating costs of, 569
  prices of, 564-66, 571-72
  repairing of, 581, 592-93
  resale values of, 565
  research on, 571
  safety and, 588-91
  smells of, 593-94
  standard vs. automatic transmissions in, 586
  stopping times of, 586
  teenage drivers of, 589-90
  thefts of, 404
  used, 564-66, 573
  weather conditions and, 587
avalanche beacons, 525
Aviation Consumer Action Project (ACAP), 544

Aviation Hall of Fame, 711
avocados, 169
AZT, 278

B

baby boomers, 241
careers of, 338-39, 342
house purchases and, 61-62, 76
late pregnancies among, 194
memorabilia collected by, 88
music for, 603
retirement of, 44-45, 50
Babyland General Hospital, 558
Bacall, Lauren, 161
Bach, Johann Sebastian, 604
back, back problems, 244-46
and alternative therapies, 248-49
and chiropractors, 246
and computer health hazards, 662-63
exercises for, 141, 146, 244-45
backgammon, 752
Backpacker, 495
bacteria, 252
drugs and, 228-29
food contaminated by, 177
bacterial vaginosis, 277
Badlands, 621
Badlands National Park, 499
Bad Rock Band, 597
Badwater, 717
Bahamas, snorkeling in, 729
Bahia grass, 427
Bailey, Susan McGee, 300
Bailey's Nurseries, 423
Baja California, 533
Bakken, Johan, 252
Bakker, Robert, 95
balanced funds, 39
bald eagles, 501
balding, 185-86, 190-91
Baldwin, Jerry, 172
Balinese, 437
balloon mortgages, 68
Ball pythons, 432
Baltimore Orioles, 364, 703, 705
bananas, 169
Bande a Part, 610
Band Wagon, The, 620
Banff Springs, 478
Bangkok, 474
Bankcard Holders of America (BHA), 114
Bank Dick, The, 611
banking, 677-78
online, 119
Bank Lease Consultants, Inc., 574-75
Barbados, 462
Barbara Walters' Baked Apple Delight, 167
barbecues, 174
Barbie Doll Hall of Fame, 711
Barbie dolls, collecting of, 88
Barbuda, 460
Barclay International, 472
Bard College, 597-98
barge trips, 530-31
Barkley, Russell A., 208-9
Barnard, Melanie, 174
Barnett Bank, 361
Barrett, John, 184
Barron-Tieger, Barbara, 345
Barry, Peter, 627
Bartoli, Cecilia, 606-7
basal cell carcinoma, 211
baseball (card game), 755
baseball (sport):
books on, 712
Caribbean winter league, 705
fan's guide to, 699-700, 702-5, 711-12
pre-season, 704
Baseball Hall of Fame, 711-12
basements, leaks in, 395-96
basil, 412
basketball:
books on, 712
fan's guide to, 698-700, 708-9, 711-12
at home, 709
Basketball Hall of Fame and Museum, 711
Bates, Timothy, 376
bathrooms, 382-85, 387, 392
addition of, 384-85
caulking and grouting of, 397
lighting in, 393
remodeling of, 385
bats, 440
batteries:
auto, 592-94
household, 400
portable computer, 661
Battle Arena Toshinden, 641
Bauer, Michael, 477
Baywatch Production Co., 340
Beach, Ben, 496
beaches, 444, 446-49, 451, 456-62, 470
Beard, James, 178
Beardstown Ladies' Common Sense Investment Guide, The, 16
Bear Mountain, Calif., 738
Beating the Dow (O'Higgins), 7-8
Beck, Nuala, 334-36
Beck, Simone, 178
Becker, Walter, 597-98
bedrooms, 382-85, 389
in attic, 385
lighting in, 393
beds, 82-83, 391
beers, 175
Beethoven, Ludwig van, 604, 667
Beethoven, The Ninth Symphony, 667
Begley, Ed, Sr., 366
behavior, 320
Behn's Game Farm, 559
Behrensmeyer, Anne K., 641
Belize, 478, 522
Bell Atlantic/NYNEX, 120
Belles on Their Toes, 636
belt wear, 592
Belyski, Richard, 88
BEMW Inc., 344
Ben and Me, 634
Benedict, Saint, 479
Bengals, 432
Benge, Michael, 716
Ben Hur, 610
benign prostatic hyperplasia (BPH), 243
Benjamin Graham on Value Investing (Lawe), 24
Benna, Ted, 51-52
Bennett, Jeff, 534
Bennett, Robert, 496
Bennett, William, 610
Benson, Sally, 636
bent grass, 427
Bentley College, 380
benzodiazepines, 235
Bequia, 462
Bergdorf Goodman, 184
Bergfeld, Wilma, 179-81
Berghaus, The (Lieberman and Lieberman), 529
Berkeley Systems, 671
Berlitz Live! Japanese, 668, 673
Berlitz Live! Spanish, 668, 673
Bermuda, honeymoons in, 478
Bermuda grass, 427
Bernese Oberland walks, 528-29
Bernstein, Anne C., 259-60
Bernstein, Jake, 24
Berolzheimer, Ruth, 178
Berry, Bessie, 177
Best Fares, 545
Best Home Businesses for the 90s, The (Edwards and Edwards), 377
beta carotene (vitamin A), 150-51, 161, 180
Beta Carotene and Retinol Efficacy Trial (CARET), 150
betas, of mutual funds, 34
Betaseron, 221
Beth Israel Medical Center North, 146
Bethlehem Steel, 8
Betholle, Louisette, 178
Bethpage, 722
Better Sleep Council, 391
Betty Crocker Cookbook, The (Hustad), 178
Bibliothèque nationale, 326, 468
bicep curls, 142
bicycles and bicycling, 140, 718-20
Big Business, 611
Big Cypress National Preserve, 502
Bigfoot Directory, 685
bighorn sheep, 500
Bigos, Stanley, 244
Big Rig, 640
Big Shot, The, 647
Big Sky, Mont., 738
Bill Nye the Science Guy's Big Blast of Science (Nye), 296
Bill Nye the Science Guy's Consider the Following (Nye), 296
Billy Budd, Sailor (Melville), 365
Bingo Long Traveling All-Stars and Motor Kings, The, 635
biochemistry, 320
biofeedback, 247-48
biological clocks, 195, 202
biology, developmental, 320
biomedical engineering, 321
biostatistics, 323
biotechnology, 334, 338-39
biotin (vitamin B), 153
Bird, Larry, 146, 709
Bird of Dawning, The (Masefield), 365
Birnbaum guides, 562
birth control pills, 270-72
birth defects, 200-202
diet and, 152-53, 160
Birth of a Nation, The, 613-14
Bishop, Brent, 715-16
Bixby, Mark, 739
Bizet, Georges, 606
BJ's Wholesale Club, 118
Black, Leon D., 564
Black Hills National Forest, 509
blackjack, 755-56
Black Pirate, The, 614
black tea, 173
Blackwolf Run, 721
bladder cancer, 153
Blade Runner, 624
Blair, Steven, 135
Blenheim Palace, 467
blepharoplasty, 187, 188-89
Block, John, 90
Blockbuster Entertainment Corp., 564
Blockbuster Video, 625
Block Financial Corp., 678
Blood of Jesus, The, 614
blood thinners, 231-32
Blow Out, 610
Blue Pool, 446
blue whales, 532-33
Blumberg, Bruce, 442
Blume, Judy, 638
Blumslialphutte, walking from Kandersteg to, 528-29
blush, 182-83
BMWs, 568
board games, 750-52
Board of Immigration Appeals, 265
Boardwatch Magazine, 686
Bockman, Bert, 566
Bodleian Library, 326
Bodnar, Janet, 110, 112
Body and Soul, 635
Boeing, 539-40
Bogart, Humphrey, 366
Bohème, La (Puccini), 606
Bolivia, 537
Bolles, Richard, 344
Bolton, Alastair, 414
Bonaire, 463
Bonaire Marine Park, 729
Bon Appetit, 174
bond funds, 15
bonds, 3-6, 11, 13-15, 19, 21-22, 104, 125
art vs., 80
fixed-income, 14
hard assets vs., 4
home ownership and, 66
for retirement, 50, 52-53, 56
software for, 677-78
taxes on premiums of, 101
tips on, 15
yield curve and, 14
bonefish, 728
Bone Marrow Donor's Web, 691
Bonnie and Clyde, 614
Bono, 599
Bonsall, Crosby, 638
Booker T. and the MG's, 598
Book of Old Silver, The (Wyler), 85
Books That Work, 668
BookWeb, 693
boomerabilia, 88

Borders Books, 375
Boston, Mass., dining in, 475
Bosworth, Warren, 724
Botswana, 516, 518
Boulder, Colo., 46
Boulder Mountain Highway, 509
Boulez, Pierre, 605
Bove, Alexander, 59
Bove, Geoffrey, 246
bowhead (right) whales, 532-33
Box-Death Hollow, 497
boxers, 434
Boxing Hall of Fame, 711-12
Boyer, Edward, 80
boys, physical development in, 256
Bracksieck, George, 715
Bradbury, Ray, 638
Brady law, 408
Brainerd, Minn., 77
brain fag, 236
Brauer Beta Catalog, The, 625
Braveheart, 610
Bravo, Ellen, 263
Brazil:
  business investments in, 12
  rain forest in, 520-21
  wilderness areas in, 513
breast cancer, 136, 216
  alternative medicine and, 249
  birth control pills and, 271
  diet and, 148, 151, 153, 240
  HRT and, 241
  risks, precautions, and treatment of, 238-41, 243
breasts:
  enlargement of, 187
  implants and, 187, 193
  lifts and, 187
  self-examination of, 238-39
  during sexual intercourse, 258
Breathless, 610
Brickell, Christopher, 415
Brideshead Revisited, 467
bridge, 757
Brief History of Time, A, 666
Brigham and Women's Hospital, 193
Brimberg, Sisse, 632
Bringing Up Baby, 611, 637
Brinkley, Christie, 161
British Columbia, 533, 537
British Library, 326
British shorthairs, 438
British Travel International, 472
Broderbund, 669, 672
brokers, 12, 15, 19-22
  bypassing of, 22
  discount, 20-22
  full service, 20-22
  real estate, 325
  selection of, 19-20
  settling disputes with, 20
  taxes and, 101
  women as, 339
Brook, Peter, 366
Brooks, Diana, 86
browlifts, 190
Brown, Capability, 467
Brown, Jeffrey L., 707
Brown, Karen, 469-71
Brown, Kerry, 436
Brown, Louise, 202-3
brown bears, 511
browsers, 686
bruises, 147
Brutal Bosses and Their Prey (Hornstein), 370-71
Buck, Peter, 598
Buckingham Palace internships, 340
Buckley, Christopher, 555
Buckley, William F., Jr., 610
Budweiser Superfest, 603
buffalo grass, 427
Buffett, Warren, 2-3, 7, 24
Build 'N' Play Table, 640
bulbs, 422
bulletin board services (BBSes), 686
bull terriers, 434
Bumble Ball Bolters, 639
Bumptz Science Carnival, 674
burglaries, 402-7
  of autos, 404
  of homes, 402-3, 405-7
Burmese, 438
Burnett, Frances Hodgson, 636
burros, purchasing of, 78
Burton, Richard, 510
Busch Gardens, 646
business, businesses:
  CD-ROMs for, 665-66
  coaches for, 377
  education in, 286
  equipment for, 98-99
  and gift-giving, 101, 380
  and Internet, 681, 683
  tax deductions for, 98-99
  woman-owned, 338
  see also employment; managers and management
business plan writers, 377
Business Week, 35, 362, 683
Butler, Robert N., 268
buttocks, exercises for, 143
buy-down mortgages, 70
Buying Stocks Without a Broker (Carlson), 22
Bwini, 516

C

Caballero, Paula, 714
Cabaret, 620-21
cabbage, planting of, 417
Cabbage Patch Kids, 558
Cactus League, 704
Cadence, 601
Cadogan guides, 562
caffeine, 171-72
Caicos, 730-31
Caine Mutiny, The, 366
caladiums, 421
Calakmul, 452
calcium, 154, 161, 436
Caledonian Canal, 530
California:
  exotic pet bans in, 431
  national parks in, 493
  rafting in, 534
  snorkeling in, 730
  vacation homes in, 76
California Desert Protection Act (1994), 491
California National Historic Trail, 506
California sea lions, 501
California Technology Stock Letter, 18
California Waterbed Standards, 391
Calin-Malin Charmeur, 640
Calkins, Carroll C., 415
Callaway Gardens, 420-21
calories, 713
  cholesterol and, 156-57
  diet and, 149, 161, 165, 174
  exercise in burning of, 138-39
Cambodia, travel to, 465
camcorders, 632, 650
camel treks, 522
cameras, 632
Campbell River, 533
Campeche, 452
Camper's Guide to U.S. National Parks, The (Little and Morva), 495
camping, 522
Campus Consultants Inc., 316
Camusi, Paul, 175
Canada:
  guided expeditions to, 537
  honeymoons in, 478
  ski resorts in, 735, 738
  train travel in, 549
Canal de la Marne au Rhin, 531
Canal du Midi route, 531
Cancer (astrological sign), 369
cancer (disease), 135-36, 245, 248, 274
  birth control pills and, 271
  diet and, 148, 150-51, 153, 159-60
  hospitals specializing in, 218
  insurance for, 126-27
  melatonin and, 237
  of reproductive tract, 220
  see also specific types of cancer
Candidate, The, 635
Cane River Creole National Historic Park, 507
Canima National Park, 513
canine bordetellosis, 440
canine distemper, 440
canine hepatitis, infectious, 441
canine leptospirosis, 440
canine parainfluenza, 440
canine parvovirus (CPV), 441
Canoe and Kayak Magazine, 534
cantaloupes, 169
Cao Di Temple, 464
Cape Cod, Mass.:
  vacation homes in, 76
  whale watching in, 533
Cape Lookout Cabins, 499
Cape May, N.J., 77
capital gains and losses, 38, 58, 102, 106
Capra, Frank, 610
Capricorn, 369
Captool, 678
Car and Driver, 567-69
carbohydrates, 150, 153
carcinogens, 174
Car Deals, 572
Cardfile, 675
card games, 753-58
cardiologists and cardiology, 211, 219, 227
career counselors, 334, 344-45
careers, 333-80
  astrological signs in selection of, 368-69
  competition and, 347
  continuing education and, 324-25
  dealing with burnout in, 372-74
  downsizing and, 336
  entrepreneurship and, 374-78
  fastest-growing, 337
  getting started in, 334-48
  and gift-giving at office, 380
  at home, 98, 377-78, 382-83, 385
  hunting in cyberspace for, 343, 346-47
  internships and, 340-41
  interviews and, 343, 348
  knowledge professions as, 334-36
  office chairs and, 379-80
  power lunches and, 345
  psychological profiles in selection of, 344-45
  for slackers, 342-43
  top industries for, 335
  of women, 338-39, 361, 373
  worst industries for, 335
  see also employment; managers and management; perks; salaries
Caribbean islands:
  airlines to, 459
  sailing around, 463
  travel to, 455-63, 478
Caribbean League, 705
Carlsbad Caverns National Park, 501
Carlson, Charles, 22
car management organizations (CMOs), 581
CarMax, 566
Carmen (Bizet), 606
Carmen Jones, 621
Carmony, Kathryn, 347
Carnegie, Andrew, 326
Carnegie Museum, 95
Carnival Cruise Line, 552
carpal tunnel syndrome, 662
carpet grass, 427
Car/Puter, 572
Carret, Philip, 2-3
cars, *see* autos
Carter, Mary Randolph, 89
Cartier, 90
cartoon violence, 633
cartridges, 408
Casablanca, 614
Cascades International Park and Stewardship Area, 491
Case, Karl, 76
Case Shiller Weiss, 76
cash, 4-6
  dollars & sense guide to, 110, 113
  stocks vs., 4-5
cash-value homeowner's insurance, 128
cash-value life insurance, 125, 129
Castle Howard, 467
Castner, James, 519
cataracts, 148, 153, 224
category killer stores, 375
Cathay Pacific, 542
Cat People, 619

cats, 435, 437-42
diseases of, 441
inbred, 435, 439
Cavalleria Rusticana (Mascagni), 606
Cavendish, Sir William, 466
Caverject, 276
Cayman Islands, 455
C.B.G.B.'s, 597
CBS' *This Morning,* 639, 641-42
CD players, 630-31
CD-ROM drives, 650-53, 659-61, 671
CD-ROMs, 643, 688
software on, *see* software
Cedar Point, 645, 647
ceftriaxone, 278
Celebrity Cruises, 552
Celis Brewery, 175
cell biology, 320
cellular phones, 101, 120, 525
Cellular Treatment Foundation/ Satin, 183
Cenerentola, La (Rossini), 606
Center for Applied Linguistics, 295
Center for Civic Education, 287
Center for Education Reform, 288
Center for Mind-Body Medicine, 247
Center for the Study of Services, 572-73
Centers for Disease Control and Prevention (CDC), 135, 206-7, 228, 252, 277-80, 432
centipede grass, 427
Central America:
coffees from, 171
traveling to, 452-54, 478
central processing units (CPUs), 651-52, 654, 659-61
CENTURY 21, 77
certificates of deposit (CDs), 22, 54
certified public accountants (CPAs), 105-6
cervical cancer, 153
cervical caps, 272
Cesarean sections (C-sections), 195, 206, 215
Cezanne, Paul, 692
CFA Insurance Group, 126, 129
chairs:
antique, 83-84
computer health hazards and, 662-63
for office workers, 379-80
Chall, Jean, 293
Challenging Child, The (Greenspan and Salmon), 282
Champion, 635
Champlain roses, 423
Changeworks Solutions, 372
Chan Is Missing, 621
Channel Islands National Marine Sanctuary, 501
Channel Islands National Park, 482
Chany, Kalman, 316
Chapin, Tom, 366
charcoal grilling, 174
chard, 412
Chariots of Fire, 610
charitable remainder trusts, 104
charities, 60
dollars & sense guide to, 113, 121-23
Internet and, 681
largest, 123
retirement and, 57-58
taxes and, 96-98, 101, 104-6, 109, 113, 122
watchdog groups monitoring, 122
Charles, Prince of Wales, 90, 130-31
Charles, Ray, 599
Charles Schwab, 20-23, 36, 678, 684
Charlottesville, Va., 46
Charlotte's Web, 636
Charmed Lives (Korda), 345
charter flights, 548
charter schools, 288-89
charting, spreadsheets for, 676
Chartist, The, 18
chartreuse, 420
Chase, Chevy, 597-98
Chatsworth, 466
Cheaper By the Dozen, 635-36
Cheat, The, 614
checkers, 750
Cheek Color, 183
cheese, 160
cheese reaction, 235
Chellis National Forest, 497
Chelsea Hotel, 596-97
chemical engineering, 321
chemical peels, 187-88
chemicals:
household, 400
photographic, 400-401
pool, 401
chemistry, 322
chemotherapy, 218
Cherokees, 506
cherries, 169
Chesapeake Bay retrievers, 433
chess, 750-51
chest, exercises for, 140-42
chests of drawers, antique, 82-83
Chevrolet Beretta, 578
Chevrolet Tahoe, 569
Chiapas, 454
Chicago, Ill., 474-75
Chicago Black Sox scandal, 635
Chichén Itzá, 452-53, 478
chicken, 174, 177
chicken soup, 176
Chihuahuas, 434
Child, 707
Child, Julia, 178
child care, 358-61
children:
adoption of, 204-5
alternative medicine and, 248
in autos, 588
books for, 638
and careers for women, 338
cholesterol and, 156
computers and, 650, 671
cooking with, 648
developing morality in, 285
diets of, 154
in divorces, 130-31
dollars & sense guide to, 110-13, 126, 130-31
drugs and, 229, 232
education of, 282-301
entertainment for, 633-48
estate planning and, 57-58
foreign language skills of, 286-87, 295
of gay and lesbian couples, 265
gifts to, 104
health of, 207-9
and HGE and Lyme disease, 252
in home emergencies, 405
home environmental hazards and, 398
homework of, 292
hospitals for, 222, 224
hyperactive, 208-9
immunization schedule for, 207
Internet and, 671, 684, 689, 696
loans to, 57
mental disorders among, 236
misbehavior in, 289-90
from newborn to pre-schooler, 206, 283, 639-41
pets and, 431-34, 439
physical fitness for, 145
rafting with, 534
reading and, 293-94
sexual education of, 259-60
software for, 666, 670-74
sports and, 703-4, 706-7, 713
survival skills for, 537
taxes and, 105-6, 109
therapy for, 290
time management for, 290
toys for, *see* toys
traveling with, 460, 468
vision problems of, 207
wills and, 59
see also adolescents; infants; pregnancies
child support, 102
Chile:
guided expeditions to, 537
wilderness in, 510-11
China:
accupuncture in, 248
business investments in, 11-12
sexuality in, 258, 266-67
teas from, 173
wilderness in, 512
Chinatown, 622
Chippendale, Thomas, 83
Chippewa National Forest, 508-9
chiropractors, 246
Chitwan National Park, 512
chlamydia, 277-78
chlortetracycline, 277
Chobe National Park, 516
chocolate sauce, recipe for, 168
Choice motels, 556
cholesterol, 219, 241, 247
diet and, 150-51, 154, 156-58, 160
good vs. bad, 156
lowering of, 156-57
screenings for, 215
sexuality and, 276
short course on, 156-57
soy protein for, 158
Chopin, Frederic, 605
chores, 112-13
chorionic villus sampling (CVS), 201-2
Christie's, 79, 81, 84, 94
Chronicle of Philanthropy, The, 121, 123
Chrysler, 566-67
Chrysler Cirrus, 567
Chrysler Town and Country, 569
Churchill, John, 467
Churchill, Winston, 467
Cinemania 96, 666
Cinemania Online, 609
Cinemax, 627
Circuit City, 564, 566
circumcision, 258
cirrhosis, 232
Cité de la Musique, La, 468
Cité des Sciences et de l'Industrie, 468
Citibank Bank/Direct Access, 119
Citizen Kane, 614
City Lights, 614
City of Rocks, 716
civics, education in, 286-87
civil engineering, 321
Civilian Conservation Corps, 498
Civil War, 506, 634
Claiborne, Craig, 178
Claris, 676, 680
Clark, William, 505
classic books, films for children based on, 636-37
cleaners, household, 400-401
Cleeman, James, 156, 158
cleft lips, 200
cleft palates, 200
clematis, 420
Clements, John K., 365
Cleveland Indians, 699
Cleveland Orchestra, 605
Climbing Magazine, 716
clinical psychologists, 233
Clinique, 183
Clinton, Bill, 97, 206, 264, 286, 496
Cloak and Gown (Winks), 480
Clomid, 202
clomipramine (Anafranil), 235
closed-end leases, 574
Clouse, John, 514
Club, The, auto theft and, 404
CMP Publications, 693
CMU Music Marathon, 603
c/net, 689
CNN, 691-92
CNW, 566
coaches, 362-64, 377
Coast Starlight, 551
Coba, 453-54
Coca-Cola, 357
cocker spaniels, 434
cocoa powder, 165, 168
coffee, 171-72
Coffy, 610
Cogan, Marshall S., 564
Cog Hill, 722
Cognetics, Inc., 375
cognitive behavioral therapy, 234
Cohen, Franklin, 605
Cohen, Larry, 757
Cohen, Leonard, 597
Cohen-Solal, Annie, 468
Cohutta Wilderness Area, 491
coins:
ancient, 93
in circulation, 93
collecting of, 92-95
foreign, 93
Coleman, James, 80
Coles, Judy, 330

coleus, 421
Colgate-Palmolive Co., 349
collagen/fat injections, 187-88
collecting, 79-95
of antiques, 81-87, 89-90
of art, 79-81, 86, 89
of boomerabilia, 88
of coins, 92-95
flea markets and, 85, 89
of fossils, 95
of gems and jewelry, 86-87, 89-91
investing in stocks vs., 4
and law of supply and demand, 87
of possessions of celebrities, 86
of possessions of historic personalities, 86
preparation for, 288
of silver, 84-85, 87, 90, 92-94
of stamps, 94-95
college and graduate school, 302-23, 377, 707
alumni benefits of, 330-31
application deadlines for, 303
applying early to, 302-3
best in U.S., 306-13, 319-23
books on sports in, 712
and careers, 336, 342-47
community, 289
and computers, 304, 317-18
and contraception, 270
finances for, 99, 101, 302-4, 314-16, 321
and Internet, 681
in liberal arts, 307-8, 310-13
and life insurance, 124-25
national, 306-8, 312-13
and part-time work, 321
regional, 308-11, 313
and salaries, 350, 352
and SAT scores, 305
College Entrance Examination Board, 298, 304, 314
College Park, Md., 46
college towns:
alumni and teachers returning to, 331-32
retirement in, 44-46, 332
collies, 433, 435
Collodi, Carlo, 638
colon cancer, 148, 153-54
colonialism, books on, 327-28
Color (Kaufman and Dahl), 388
Colorado:
gay rights in, 265
national parks in, 493
rafting in, 534, 536
retirement in, 44-46
Colorado Brewing Company (Tabernash), 175
Colorado River, 534, 536
Color Shapes & Size with Poldy the Scarecrow, 672
Columbia Dictionary of Quotations, 665
Columbia Encyclopedia, 666
Columbia House, 625
Columbus, Christopher, 94
comedy, Web sites for, 689
comic films, 611-13
for children, 637
Common, The, 479
Common Application, 304
Common Cents New York, 113
common colds, 228
chicken soup for, 176
zinc and, 155
Common Sense, The (Godfrey), 672
communications, careers in, 335
Communications Week, 658
community colleges, 289
Compact Disc Eyeshadow in Brown #7, 183
Compaq Computer Corp., 349, 654-55
comparative literature, 319
Complete Book of Wills & Estates, *The* (Bove), 59
Complete Car Cost Guide, The, 572
Complete Defensive Bridge Play (Kantar), 757
Complete Guide to America's National Parks, The (McQueen), 495
Complete Job Search Handbook (Figler), 344
Complete White-water Rafter, The (Bennett), 534
Compliance Guide to the Family and Medical Leave Act, 360
Compton's NewMedia, 664, 674
CompUSA, 651
CompuServe, 23, 346-47, 377, 682-85, 694, 696
Computer Associates, 678
Computer City, 651
Computer Museum Guide to the Best Software for Kids, The (Miranker and Elliott), 670
computers, 377-78, 649-96
anatomy of, 652-54
in buying used cars, 564-65
careers and, 334-36, 339, 343, 368-69
care of, 653
childproofing of, 671
college and, 304, 317-18
cycle, 720
education and, 288-89, 294, 304, 317-18
for $500, 655
hardware and, 650-63, 671, 679-80
as health hazards, 656, 662-63
home insurance and, 75
as investment tools, 23
Mac vs. PC, 655
mail-order, 651
name brand, 651
for paint mixing, 388
peripherals for, 656-58, 661
pets and, 442
portable, 654, 660-61
purchasing of, 650-51
specs to insist on, 651
tax filing with, 107-8
upgrades for, 659
Web sites on, 693
see also Internet; software
computer sciences, 322
Concise Columbia Encyclopedia, 665
Condé Nast Traveler, 445, 455-56, 538-39, 541-42, 556-57
condoms, male and female, 272
Coney Island Polar Bears, 743
Confide, 279
Congress, U.S.:
college loans and, 314
on education, 286
on fossil collecting, 95
on maternal hospital stays, 206
on national parks, 486, 491, 496, 507
on national scenic trails, 502
on scenic byways, 508
on Social Security, 51
on taxes, 96-100
Web sites on, 692
Congressional Country Club, 699
Connair, 184
Connecticut River, 727
Connoisseur's Guide to the World's Best Beers, A (Finch), 175
Conservation International, 519
consolidators, 547-48
Constitution, U.S.S., 448
construction trades, 355
Consumer Federation of America, 112
consumer price index, 80
Consumer Product Safety Commission, 713
Consumer Reports, 47-48, 540, 683
Guide to Income Tax, 108
New Car Pricing, 572
Travel Letter, 548
Consumers Automotive, 573
Consumer's Directory of Continuing Care Retirement Communities, 47
Consumer's Guide to Long-Term Care Insurance, 60
Consumer's Guide to Medicare and Supplement Insurance, 60
contact lenses, 101, 663
insurance on, 126
container planting, 411-13
Conte Lodge, La, 498
ContextSpider, 680
Continental Divide National Scenic Trail, 502
Continuing Care Retirement Community, 47
continuing education, 324-25
contraception, 101, 260, 269-73
efficacy rates of, 272-73
morning after pills, 269-70
sterilization for, 271, 273
see also specific contraceptives
Conversation, The, 622
convertible bond funds, 26, 29
Conway, Patrick and Daniel, 175
Cook, Captain, 448
Cook, Charles, 495
cookbooks, 178
cookie dough, 165
cooking, children and, 648
cookware, non-stick, 165
Cool World, The, 614
Cooper Institute for Aerobics Research, 135
Coors Brewing Company, 340
Copán, 454
copper, 155
Corbis Publishing, 667
Cordon Bleu Cookbook, The (Lucas), 178
Corel Corp., 680, 695
All Movie Guide, 666
CorelWEB, 695
Ventura, 679
Corner in Wheat, A, 614
Cornish Rex, 438
Corolle, 640
coronary bypasses, 215, 219
corporate bond high-yield funds, 26, 29
corporate bonds and bond funds, 15, 26, 30
Corsica:
guided expeditions to, 537
hiking in, 524
cosmetics, 182-83
Costa Rica:
coffee from, 171
guided expeditions to, 537
honeymoons in, 478
rain forests in, 519
cost of living:
and retirement, 45-46
and salaries, 350
Cost vs. Value Report, 386
Cotinus, 420
Council of Institutional Investors, 9
Council on Chiropractic Education, 246
Country Baskets, 12
country inns, European, 469-71
Cousteau, Jacques, 729
Covered Bridge Scenic Byway, 508
cow chip throwing, 558
Cox, Alex, 597
Cox, Courteney, 184
crabs, 277
Cradle Mountain–Lake St. Clair National Park, 523-24
Craft of Investing, The (Train), 24
Craftsman Books Company, 384
Craig, Roger, 747-49
Creative Leisure International, 472
Creative Wonders, 665
credit cards:
best and most popular, 115-17
dollars & sense guide to, 110-11, 114-17, 126, 128
Internet and, 696
credit unions, 573
Crenshaw, Theresa, 254-55
crêpes, 167
Crested Butte, Colo., 76
criminology, 324
critical dose drugs, 231
Critics' Choice Video, 625
Crowd, The, 614
cruise ships, 552-55
Cruising French Waterways (McKnight), 530
Crumbo, Kim, 536
Crystal, Graef, 350
Crystal Caves, 478
Crystal Explorer Sub, 640
Crystal River National Wildlife Refuge, 500
CSC Credit Service, 114
CSS/Financial Aid Profile, 314
cue sticks, 759
Cuhaj, George, 92

Culver, Russ, 701
Cumberland Island National Seashore, 480-81
Cunard, 552-53
Curaçao, 463
Curless, Chris, 416
curling, 741
current events, CD-ROMs on, 666
Curriculum and Evaluation Standards for School Mathematics, 287
Curtis, Peter, 246
Curtis, Tony, 637
Custom Blend Powder, 183
custom design spreadsheets, 676
Cybercrafts, 674
cyber-investing, 23
Cyber Patrol, 671, 696
Cybersearch, 688
cycle computers, 720

D

dachshunds, 435, 439
Daconil 2787, 423
daffodils, 420
Dahl, Taffy, 388
Dalat, 464
DALBAR, Inc., 43, 71
Dallas, Tex., dining in, 476
Dallas Cowboys, 699
  internships with, 340
Dallek, Geraldine, 213
Dallow, Ted, 78
Dana-Farber Cancer Institute, 216, 280
Danta Pyramid, 452
Darvas, Robert, 757
Database Plus, 684
Dataquest, 657
Dave's Video, 625
David Holzman's Diary, 611
Davis, Bette, 666
daylilies, 420
Day Runner Planner, 675
Day the Earth Stood Still, The, 624
DDI, 278
Dead Poets Society, 366
Dean Witter Intercapital, 32-33
  Capital Growth fund of, 37
death, education and, 290
Death Valley National Park, 491
debts, 71
  see also credit cards; loans
Debussy, Claude, 605
deciduous trees, 425-26
decks, cost of addition of, 386
Declaration of Independence, 634
deductions on tax returns, 96-104, 108-9
  itemized, 96-100, 103, 106
  standard, 96-97, 103
  see also specific tax deductions
deer hunting, 745-46
DEET, 252
Defending Ourselves (Wiseman), 406
defined benefit plans, 55
defined contribution plans, 356
de Gaulle, Charles, 165
deli foods, 177
Dell Computer Corp., 654
Deloitte & Touche Online, 684
Delos, 731
Delta, 541-42
DeltaPoint, 695
DeMark, Thomas R., 24
Denali National Park, 346, 524
Denmark, villa rentals in, 473
dental insurance, 356
dependent care expenses, 359-60
Depo-Provera, 272-73
depression, 249, 255
  drugs for, 209, 233-35, 268
Depression, Great, 2, 5, 498
dermabrasion, 188
dermatology, 211
Descent, 668-69
Deschutes River, 534
Designing Large-Scale Web Sites (Sano), 695
desipramine (Norpramin), 235
desktop publishing (DTP), software for, 679-80
desktop video publishing, 377-78
desserts, low-fat, 165-68
Destiny, 552
detached retinas, 224
Detour, 622
Detroit Tigers, 362, 366
developmental biology, 320
Devil's Tower, 716
Devon Rex, 438
DHEA, 255
diabetes, 134-36, 219, 268, 276
  diet and, 159, 165
  drugs for, 231
diamonds, 86, 90
  collecting of, 4
Diana, Princess of Wales, 90, 130-31
diaphragms, 272
Diary of a Sea Voyage (Algren), 555
diazepam (Valium), 235
Dickens, Charles, 636
Dickson, Paul, 711-12
Dick Tracy, 87
diet, 148-78, 191, 246, 300
  alternative medicine and, 248-49
  Asian pyramid and, 159
  beer in, 175
  breast cancer and, 148, 151, 153, 240
  charcoal grilling and, 174
  cholesterol and, 150-51, 154, 156-58, 160
  coffee in, 171-72
  cookbooks and, 178
  deli foods in, 177
  desserts and, 165-68
  drugs and, 235
  fish in, 162-64
  low-fat, 161, 165-68, 241
  melatonin and, 237
  milk in, 161, 167
  minerals in, 148, 154-55, 160
  for pets, 436
  pregnancies and, 194, 208
  red wine and, 160
  relationship between disease and, 148
  research on, 148-50
  sexuality and, 276
  snack foods in, 161
  soup and, 176
  tea in, 173
  vegetarian, 152, 154, 159-60, 178
  vitamins in, *see* vitamins; *specific vitamins*
  weight and, 134-35, 157
Different Lipstick in Tender Heart, 183
digital rectal exams (DREs), 243
Dimitrius, Jo-Ellan, 378
dining rooms, 382-83
  lighting in, 393
Dinosaur National Monument, 95
Direct Access Diagnostics, 279
Directory of Retirement Facilities, The, 47
direct repair programs (DRPs), 581
disability income, 102
disability insurance, 125-28
  as perk, 356-57
Dischord Records, 601
discounts, 75
Discover card, 114-15
disease:
  homemade cures for, 424
  relationship between diet and, 148
  see also health and health care; *specific diseases*
disinfectants, 400
Disneyland, 646
Distant Suns First Light, 666
Ditre, Cherie, 179-80
diuretics, 232
dividends, 6-9, 13, 16, 22, 100, 104, 106
divorces:
  dollars & sense guide to, 130-31
  education and, 290
Dixie National Forest, 497, 509
DK Multimedia, 666-68
Dmytryk, Edward, 366
Dr. Koop's Self-Care Advisor: The Essential Home Health Guide (Koop), 210
doctors, 210-16, 225-29
  allergies and, 250
  alternative medicine and, 247, 249
  auto mechanics compared to, 595
  back problems and, 245
  chiropractors and, 246
  contraception and, 270-71
  drugs and, 228-29, 233-34
  fees of, 226-27
  and HGE and Lyme disease, 252
  HMOs and, 213-15
  hospitals and, 225
  HRT and, 241
  for mental disorders, 225, 233-36
  and patient's bill of rights, 216
  prostate cancer and, 242
  selection of, 210-12
  women and, 210, 338
  see also specific medical specialties
Dr. Strangelove, 612
Dodge Stratus, 567
Dodsworth, 615
Dog Care Book, The (Gerstenfeld), 433
dogs, 433-36, 440-42
  diseases of, 440-41
  inbred, 435
  selection of, 433-34
  wellness guide for, 436
Dogs of the Dow Jones Industrial Average, 8
Dolby sound, 629
Dole, Bob, 242, 610
dollar-cost averaging, 6
dollars & sense guide, 110-32
  to cellular phones, 120
  to charities, 113, 121-23
  to credit cards, 110-11, 114-17, 126, 128
  to divorces, 130-31
  to insurance, 124-29
  to loans from family members, 131
  to online banking, 119
  to penny saving, 113
  to shopping, 118
  to small claims courts, 132
  to teaching children about money, 110-13
  to tipping, 117
  see also finances
dolls, antique, 87
Dolphin Bay, 445
Dom Hotel, 469-70
Dominica, 461
Dominican Republic:
  travel to, 456
  whale watching in, 533
  winter baseball in, 705
Donkey Kong Country 2, 642
Doom II, 669
doors, locking of, 402-4
Doors, The, 599
Dornbush, Sanford, 111
DOS, 653, 677
Double Indemnity, 622
Double Time Jazz Records, 601
Doulos, Le, 610
Dow dividend approach, 7-9
Do What You Are (Tieger and Barron-Tieger), 345
Dow Jones Industrial average, 2, 5, 7-9
Dow Jones News/Retrieval Service, 684
downsizing, 375
  careers and, 336
  salaries and, 350-51
Down's syndrome, 195, 198, 200
doxepin (Sineqan), 235
doxycycline, 252, 277-78
Doyle, Arthur Conan, 513
Drake, Geoff, 718-20
Drake, Sir Francis, 555
dramatic films, 613-19
Dreyfus Investments, 33, 60
DRIP Investor, 22
driver's education courses, 589-90
Drivers Mart, 566
driving schools, 590
Drolling, Martin, 86
Drucker, Richard, 91
drug and alcohol abuse:
  career burnout and, 372
  treatment for, 101
drugs, 228-35

for abortion, 270, 274-75
for ADHD, 209
alternative medicine and, 247-48
back problems and, 244
brand-name vs. generic, 230-31
for cholesterol, 157
for depression and anxiety, 209, 233-35, 268
HMOs and, 213-14
hospitals and, 225
over-the-counter, 232, 244
and patient's bill of rights, 216
prescription, 228-31
sexuality and, 268, 276
for STDs, 277-78
teenage drivers and, 589
see also specific drugs
duck hunting, 744
Duck Soup, 612, 637
Duda, Mark Damain, 500
Dun & Bradstreet Online, 684
Du Pont, 357, 359
durable power of attorney, 59
Durango, Colo.:
retirement in, 45
skiing in, 738
vacation homes in, 77
Dvorak Development, 688
Dylan, Bob, 596-98
dyslexia, 294
dysthymia, 234

E

Eagle, 566
ear infections, 229
earned-income credit, 100
Earthwatch, 521
East Africa:
coffees from, 171
traveling in, 515-16
East Africa Safari Co., 518
Eastern Europe, investing in, 11
East Rift Zone, 445
eating disorders, 300
Eaton, Gordon P., 641
Ebert, Roger, 609, 666
Echostar, 627
ecology, 320
economics:
books on, 329
graduate schools for, 323
eco-travel, 522
Ecuador:
guided expeditions to, 537
honeymoons in, 478
rain forests in, 520
Edison, Thomas, 368
Edley, Joe, 749
Edmark, 671
Edmund's New Car Price Guide, 572
education, 102, 281-332
careers and, 336
continuing, 324-25
in driving, 589-90
Internet and, 681
in science, 286-87, 296-97, 300-301
on sexuality, 259-60
single-sex, 300
software and, 664, 670, 672-74
on World Wide Web, 330-31
see also college and graduate school
education, primary and secondary, 282-301
and charter schools, 288-89
developing intellectually active children in, 282-85
and dropouts, 285
emotionally involved approach to learning in, 282-83
girls in, 300-301
and homework, 292
and music, 290, 298-99
and parent aid in after-school work, 292
and parent-teacher relations, 291
reading in, 293-94
and student behavior, 289-90
testing national standards in, 286-87
Educational Resources Information Center, 291
educational toys, 640-41
Education Department, U.S., 286
Edwards, Paul and Sarah, 377-78
eggs:
whites of, 165, 167-68
yolks of, 160
Eight Men Out, 635
Elavil (amitriptyline), 235
elbows:
injuries to, 147, 222
winter sports and, 734
Eldercare Locator Service, 60
electrical engineering, 321
electronic bill-paying services, 119
Electronic Discovery Desk, 639
electronics, 674
Elefun, 642
Elektra (Strauss), 606-7
Elizabeth I, Queen of England, 467
elk, 500, 746
Elkind, David, 289-90
Elle, 182
Elliot, Bill, 587
Elliott, Alison, 670-73
Ellis, Royston, 550
Elon College, Henton at, 332
e-mail, 317, 658-60, 681, 685-87
emergency contraceptive pills, 269-70
emerging-market funds, 11
Emory Spine Center, 391
emoticons, 686
empathy, 285
Employee Benefit Research Institute, 357
Employer's Guide to Child Care Consultants, An, 359
employment, 360, 521
after-school, 111
commuting and, 99
gays and, 264-65
mortgages and, 71
part-time, 113, 321, 358
beyond retirement age, 51
see also careers
employment agency fees, 101
emus, 432
enamel paints, 401
Encarta 96 Encyclopedia, 664-65, 684
Enchanted Seas, 554
endocrinology, 219-20
endometrial cancer, 271
endorphins, 248
endurance races, 717
engagement rings, 90
English:
education in, 286-87, 295
graduate schools for, 319
software for children on, 673-74
English cocker spaniels, 434
English Country House, The (Maroon), 466
English shots, 760
English silver, 85
Enlighten Skin-Enhancing Makeup, 183
enrolled agents, 105
entertainment:
books on, 328
for children, 633-48
gear and gadgets for, 626-32
Web sites on, 689-90, 693
see also movies; music and musicians
Entertainment Weekly, 609, 656, 683, 692
entrepreneurs, 374-78
fastest-growing franchises for, 376
in working at home, 377-78
environmental hazards, 398-401
environmental policy and management, 324
Environmental Protection Agency (EPA), 398
Environmental Vacations (Ocko), 521
Epitaph Records, 600
Epstein, Joyce, 292
Equal Employment Opportunity Commission, 348
Equifax, 114
Equity Fund Outlook, 18
equity income funds, 26
erections, 258
Erector, 640
Ernst & Young, 74, 101, 104
Ernst & Young Tax Guide, 108
Ertl Toy Company, 639
erythromycin, 277-78
Escaping the Coming Retirement Crisis (Benna), 51
Escarcega, 452
escargot, 643-44
Escoffier, George Auguste, 178
Eskeldson, Mark, 571-73
esophageal cancer, 153
E-Span Employment Database Search, 346
ESPN, 690, 712
ESPNET, 712
Essential Guide to Psychiatric Drugs, The (Gorman), 234
Essential Guide to Wilderness Camping and Backpacking, The (Cook and Kesenel), 495
estate planning, 57-59
estate taxes, 57-59
Estée Lauder, 183
estimated tax, 100
estrogen, 240-41, 254-55, 268-69, 271
Ethiopia, coffee from, 171
ethyl chloride, 278
E.T. The Extra Terrestrial, 624
Eudora Light, 685
Eurax, 278
Europa Let, 472
Europe:
country inns in, 469-71
sexuality in, 258
train travel in, 549-50
European Continental silver, 85
European stock funds, 26
Evangelical Council for Financial Accountability, 122
Everest, Mount, 715
Everglades National Park, 496-97
evergreens, 421, 425-26
Everything Scrabble (Edley and Williams), 749
evolution, 320
Ewert, Hank, 303
Exact Makeup 2 Makeup+, 183
Excite, 688
executive occupations, 353
executive recruiters, 339, 367
executors, 58-59
exercise, 191, 241
alternative medicine and, 248-49
back and, 141, 146, 244-45
breast cancer and, 240
calories burned in, 138-39
choices of, 137-39
diet and, 157
for fitness, 134-43
for flexibility, 141
heart rates and, 136
injuries and, 146-47
less effective, 140-41
for muscle tone, 142-43
for pets, 436
pregnancies and, 198
shoes for, 144
for strength and endurance, 140
weight and, 134-35, 138
see also sports
exotic pets, 431-32
exotic shorthairs, 438
extremely low frequency (ELF) radiation, 656
eyelid surgery, 187-89
eyeliner, 182
eyeshadow, 182-83
eye strain, 662-63
Eyewitness Encyclopedia of Nature, 666
Eyewitness Encyclopedia of Science, 666
Eyewitness History of the World, 666

F

Fabricant, Florence, 476-77
Fabulous Thunderbirds, 598
facelifts, 187-90
face powder, 182-83
Face Stockholm, 183
facial implants, 190
facial surgery, 222

Facts and Advice for Airline Passengers, 544
Fagen, Donald, 597-98
falconry, 746
fall foliage, 508
Falling Springs Creek, 727
Fallon, Lee, 200
falls, 225
Families USA, 213
Family and Medical Leave Act (FMLA), 358-61
Family Fun Magazine, 648
family histories, 201
FamilyPC, 672
family rooms, 382-85
  addition of, 385
Fannie Farmer Cookbook, The (Merritt), 178
fantasies, sexual, 261-62
Fantasy Cruises, 554
Farinato, Richard, 431-32
Farrell, Eileen, 90
"Far Side" (Larsen), 372
Fast Company, 656
fat, 187-88
  breast cancer and, 240
  cholesterol and, 156-57
  in diet, 148-50, 153, 156-57, 160-61, 163, 165-68, 174, 240
  fake, 161
fatsia, 421
faxes, 657-68
  and auto purchases, 571-72
Federal Aviation Administration (FAA), 538-40, 544
Federal Direct Student Loan Program, 315, 321
Federal Express, 547
Federal Family Education Loan Programs (FFELP), 315
Federal Housing Administration (FHA), 78
Federal National Mortgage Association (Fannie Mae), 69, 71
Federal PLUS loan, 315
Federal Register, The, 539
Federal Reserve Bank of New York, 112
Federal Reserve Board, 4
Federal Trade Commission, 67, 203, 376
Federation Nationale des Cités Ruraux de France, 473
fee-for-service care, 213-14
feline calicivirus, 441
feline leukemia virus, 441
feline panleukopenia, 441
feline pneumonitis, 441
feline viral rhinotracheitis, 441
Felkley, Dave, 742
Fellini, Federico, 666
Fel-Pro Incorporated, 361
feng shui, 383
Fennell, Bob, 657
fertility:
  contraception and, 270
  pregnancies and, 195
  see also infertility
Fertility Institute, 203
fertilizers, 412-13, 416, 418-19, 421, 423, 425-26, 428
Festival Films, 625
fetuses, 199-202
  abortion and, 275
  growth of, 197
  threats to, 199
  in utero checkups for, 200-202
fevers, 232
Fibreboard Corp., 738
Fiddler on the Roof, 635
Fidelity Insight, 18, 41
Fidelity Investments, 21, 33, 60, 116, 678
  Equity Income II fund of, 41
  Growth Company fund of, 41
  Magellan fund of, 7, 13, 37
  On-Line Xpress of, 23
  Value fund of, 41
Field and Stream, 744
field audits, 109
Field of Dreams, 635
fifteen-year mortgages, 62, 67, 74
fighting, close quarters, 407
Fighting Chance, 571-72
Fiji, 537
File Maker Pro, 676
file transfer protocols (FTPs), 681-82
Filmic Archives, 625
Film Society of Lincoln Center, 609
finances:
  software for, 677-78
  Web sites on, 691
  see also dollars & sense guide
Financial Advisers, Inc., 49
financial services, 339
Finch, Christopher, 175
Finkel, Charles, 175
Fiordland National Park, 524
firefly, 689
fireplaces, 383
Fischer, Bob, 35
fish:
  cleaning of, 163
  in diet, 162-64
  grilling of, 174
  guide to, 164
Fish and Wildlife Service, 431, 508, 744
Fisher, M.F.K., 178
Fisher-Price, 639, 642
fishing, 726-28
  fly-, 727-28
  saltwater, 728
fitness, 134-47
  exercise for, 134-43
  in-line skating for, 713
Fitzgerald, F. Scott, 57
five-card draw, 753
five-card stud, 754
fixed rate mortgages, 61-62, 67, 70, 72, 74
flames, 686
Flame Tree Safaris, Ltd., 518
flashing, roof, 395
flat tax, 96, 105
flea markets, 85, 89
flex time, 351, 357-59, 361
Flight of the Stork (Bernstein), 259
floppy disk drives, 651-52, 661
Florida:
  house purchases in, 62
  national parks in, 493
  pre-season baseball games in, 704
  retirement in, 44-45
  snorkeling in, 729
Florida National Scenic Trail, 502
flower boxes, 412, 429-30
flowering trees, 425
fluid leaks, 593
fluorescent light, 392-93, 430
fluoxetine (Prozac), 225, 235
fly-fishing, 727-28
Fly Fishing: Great Rivers of the West, 668
Flynn, Mary Kathleen, 650-51
Flynn, Michael, 42
Fobel, Jim, 178
Fodor's guides, 562, 690
Folger Library, 326
folic acid (vitamin B), 152-53
follow shots, 760
Follow-the-Lights Keyboard, 640
Fonda, Henry, 366, 634
Fong, Roy, 173
Fonseca, Ray, 448
Fontaine, Joan, 637
Foo, Susanna, 178
food, *see* diet
Food and Drug Administration (FDA), 149, 151-52, 154, 161, 180-81, 193, 230, 239, 248, 270-71, 274, 276, 279-80, 691
Foods of the World, 178
football:
  books on, 712
  for children, 707
  fan's guide to, 698-700, 706-7, 711-12
Foote, David, 518
Footlight Parade, 621
foot massage, 266-67
For a Few Dollars More, 610
Forbes, 35, 369
Forbes, Esther, 634
Force of Evil, 622
Ford Contour, 567
Ford Credit, 574
Ford Mustang Cobra, 567
Ford's Freighter Travel Guide and Waterways of the World, 555
Ford Taurus, 567-68
Ford Tempo, 567
Forefront Group, The, 688
forehead lifts, 190
foreign languages:
  education in, 286-87, 295
  software for, 673
  Web sites on, 690
foreign stocks and funds, 11-12, 26
foreign taxes, 101
Forensic Technologies, Inc., 378
Forest Service, 496, 502, 508
formaldehyde, 399
Forrest, Jacqueline Darroch, 271
Forrester Research Inc., 23
Forster, E. M., 549
Forsyth, Stephen, 551
Fortune, 350
Forty Acres and a Mule Filmworks, Inc., 340-41
40+ Guide to Fitness (Stutz), 137
fossil collecting, 95
foundations (cosmetic), 182-83
Four11 Directory Services, 685
Four Horsemen of the Apocalypse, The, 615
401(k) plans, 48-49, 52-53, 104, 350, 356
Fowler, Jim, 510-13
France:
  abortion drugs in, 274
  barge trips in, 530-31
  country inns in, 469
  tourism vert in, 522
  villa rentals in, 473
franchises, 376
  for used-car dealerships, 564-66
  women in, 338
Frank Church River of No Return, 497
Frankenstein, 619-20
Franklin, Aretha, 596
Franklin, Benjamin, 93, 634
Franklin's Reading World, 673
Fratta, Domenico Maria, 79
Freaks, 620
Fredericksen, Burton, 81
Free Application for Federal Student Aid (FAFSA), 314
free radicals, 237
freighter travel, 555
French, Arnold, 86
French Culinary Institute, 165
French Experience, 473
Frequent Flyer, 541-42
frequent flyer programs, 543
Freshman, The, 612
Friends, 161, 184
Fringe Benefits Mascara, 183
Frommer's guides, 562
Frontier Technologies, 688
fruits:
  in desserts, 165
  in diet, 148-55, 157, 159-60, 165-70
  shopper's guide to, 169-70
fruit sorbets, recipes for, 166
Frying Pan River, 728
Ftan, walking from Scuol to, 528
Fulton Research, Inc., 383
Fundline, 18
Funicello, Annette, 181
Funk & Wagnalls Encyclopedia, 665
furniture:
  antique, 83-84, 87
  polish for, 400
Fury, 615
Fury 3, 669
futures, 22
Future Vision Multimedia, 665

G

Galapagos Islands, sailing in, 522
Galaxy, 552
gambling, 101, 701
Game Plan for Success, 362
games:
  on CD-ROMs, 668-69
  for children, 643-44
  parlor, *see* parlor games
  simulation, 318
gamete intrafallopian transfer (GIFT), 203
Gametrackers International, Inc., 518
Gandhi, 610

Gandhi, Mohandas, 464
Ganley, Nika, 304
garages, 383, 383
Garcia, Jerry, 602
Garden of the Gods, 448
gardens and gardening, 411-30
  all-year round, 420-21
  beneficial insects for, 424
  bulbs for, 422
  and container planting, 411-13
  fertilizer in, 412-13, 416, 418-19, 421, 423, 425-26, 428
  grasses in, 420-21, 427-28
  growing zones for, 413
  homemade pest and disease cures for, 424
  indoor, 429-30
  roses for, 423
  tools for, 414-15
  trees in, 420-21, 425-26
  see also plants and planting
Gardner, David and Tom, 7
Garfield, John, 635
Garland, Judy, 636
garlic, 247
  health benefits of, 158
  -pepper solution, 424
Garrison-Jackson, Zina, 723-24
Garson, Greer, 637
gas chamber sit-ins, 558
gastroenterology, gastro-enterologists, 211, 227
Gates, Bill, 667
Gateway 2000, 651, 654-55
Gault, Stanley, 349
geese hunting, 744
Gehrig, Lou, 703
Gemini, 368
gems:
  collecting of, 86-87, 89-91
  value of, 91
General, The, 612
General Electric, 349
General Electric Credit, 574
General Foods, 339
generalized anxiety disorders, 234-35
General Motors (GM), 566
generation-skipping tax, 58
genetics:
  breast cancer and, 240
  graduate schools for, 320
  looking great and, 179
  pregnancies and, 195, 200-202
genital warts, 277
gentility, books on, 329
geography, education in, 286-87
Geography for Life, 287
Geological Survey, 641
George Auguste Escoffier Cookbook Collection (Escoffier), 178
Georgetown Viewing Site, 500
Georgia:
  exotic pet bans in, 431
  retirement in, 44
geosciences, 322
Geo. W. Park Seed Co., 415
geraniums, 412
German shepherds, 435
Germany:
  barge trips in, 531
  collecting coins from, 93
  country inns in, 469-70
  villa rentals in, 473
Gershman, Michael, 712
Gershwin, George, 605
Gerstenfeld, Sheldon L., 433
Gerstner, Louis, 286
Get Ready for School, Charlie Brown, 673
Getting Behind the Résumé (Kennedy), 367
Getty, John Paul, 131
Gex, 642
ghost sickness, 236
Gibson, Henry, 636
Gibson Research, 653
gifts, 101-2, 131
  to children, 104
  at office, 101, 380
  taxes on, 57
gigabytes, 651, 653, 660-61
Gigi, 621
Gin Rummy, 756
girls:
  education of, 300-301
  physical development of, 256
  see also women
Girl Scouts, 301, 406
Glacier National Park, 492
Glade Top Trail, 509
Glass, Philip, 298
glass pieces, collecting of, 87
glaucoma, 224
Glenconner, Lord, 462
Glengarry Glen Ross (Mamet), 365-66
Glenwood Canyon, rafting in, 534
Glory, 634
GMAC, 574
GMC Yukon, 569
Goals 2000, 286
Godfather, Part II, The, 615
Godfather, The (film), 615
Godfather, The (Puzo), 345
Godfrey, Neale, 112, 672
goiters, 155
gold, 86, 90, 92, 94
  investing in, 4
Golden Boy, 635
golden retrievers, 433
Golding, William, 366
Gold Rush, The, 612
golf courses, 721-22
Golf Hall of Fame, 711
Gone with the Wind, 615
gonorrhea, 277-78
Goodman, James, 79
Goodman Gallery, 79
Goodyear Tire & Rubber Co., 349
Goosebumps series (Stine), 638
gophers, 686
Gordon, James, 247
Gorham, 84-85, 87
gorillas, 511, 513, 516
Gorman, Jack, 234
Gorton, Slade, 496
Gosselin, Lisa, 738
government bond general funds, 26, 30
government bond mortgage funds, 26, 30-31
government bond treasury funds, 26, 30
Government Printing Office, 482
Graceland, 598
Grachen, walking to Saas-Fee from, 527-28
graduated payment mortgages, 68-69
Graham, Benjamin, 24
grains, 148, 151-52, 154-55, 157, 159
Grammy Awards, 605
Grand Canyon National Park, 480, 485-86, 498
  rafting in, 536
Grand Cayman Island, 455
  honeymoons in, 478
  snorkeling in, 730
Grande Arche de la Défense, 468
Grandeur of the Seas, 552
Grand Junction, Colo., 45
Grand Luxe International, 473
Grand Princess, 552
Grand Teton National Park, 487, 490-91, 534
Granite Park Chalet, 498
Gran Sabana, La, 523
Grant, Cary, 636-37
Grant-Kohrs Ranch National Historic Site, 481-82
Grapefruit League, 704
grapefruits, 169
grapefruit sorbet, 166
grapes, 169
Grapes of Wrath, The, 615
grasses, 420-21, 427-28
  types of, 427
Grateful Dead, 602
Graubunden walks, 528
Graves, Paul, 733
Graydon, Don, 716
Graystone Partners, 42
gray whales, 501, 532-33
Great Adventures Pirate Ship, 639
Great Barrier Reef, 478
Great Basin National Park, 482
Great Britain:
  barge trips in, 530-31
  country inns in, 471
  train travel in, 551
  travel to, 466-67, 471, 473-74
  villa rentals in, 473
Great Danes, 435
Greater Antilles, 455-56
Great Lakes Brewing Co., 175
Great McGinty, The, 635
Great Outdoors Recreation Pages (GORP), 495
Great Race, The, 637
Great Smoky Mountains National Park, 484-85, 487, 498
Greece:
  collecting coins from, 93
  snorkeling in, 731
Greed, 615
Greeley, Horace, 486
Greene, Bert, 178
Greene, Graham, 464
Greene, Richard, 109
Greenland, hiking in, 524
Green River, 728
green spaghetti, recipe for, 648
Greenspan, Stanley, 282, 285
green teas, 173
Greenwood, Robert, 46
Greenwood Memorial Cemetery, 599
Greenwood's Ski Haus, 740
Greer, Gaylon, 65
Gregorian, Vartan, 326
Greif Brothers, 3
Greisalp, walking to Murren from, 529
Grenada, 462
Grenadines, 462
greyhounds, 434
Griffith, Dotty, 476
Griffiths, Scott, 175
Grimm, Norman, 588
grizzly bears, 511
Grolier Interactive, 665
gross domestic product (GDP), 11-12
Grossman, Ken, 175
ground covers, 421
Grove Farm Homestead, 450
growing equity mortgages, 70
growth and income funds, 26
growth funds, 26-27
Growth of the Mind and Its Endangered Future, The (Greenspan), 285
GT Interactive, 669
Guadeloupe, 461
guaranteed-permanent life insurance, 125
guaranteed replacement cost homeowner's insurance, 128
guardians, 58
Guatemala:
  coffee from, 171
  travel to, 454
guidebooks, 562
  to national parks, 495
  Web sites on, 690
Guide to Free Tax Services, 108
Guide to Monastic Guest Houses, A, 479
Guiness, Alec, 636-37
Guiness Book of World Records, 514
Gulf Islands National Seashore, 502
Gulf of Aqaba, 731
Gun Control Act, 408
guns, 408-10
Guns N' Roses, 599
Gunung Leuser National Park, 512
Gurewitz, Brett, 600
Guy, Buddy, 596, 601
Guyana, wilderness areas in, 513
gymnastics, 707
gynecology, 220-21
gynecomastia, 191

Haddon Hall, 466
Hagstrom, Robert G., Jr., 24
hair, 184-86
  loss of, 185-86, 190-91
  styling of, 184
  transplanting of, 185-86, 190-91
  wigs and, 186
Haiti, 456
Haleakala National Park, 445, 499
Haley & Steele, 393
halogen lamps, 392
Ha Long Bay, 465
ham, 177
Hamadeh, Samer, 340

Hambrecht, Patricia, 79
Hamer, Dean, 264
Hamilton, George, 181
Hamman, Bob, 757
Hammocks Beach, 451
Hammond World Atlas, 665
Hamrick, Graham, 559
Hana Highway, 446
Hanalei, 450
Hanauma Bay, 449
Handel, George Frederic, 607
handguns, 408
H&R Block, 107
hand surgery, 222
hanging baskets, 412
Hanley-Wood, Inc., 386
Hanoi, 465
hard disks, 651-53
Harder, Deb, 204-5
Hard Rock Café, 596
Hardwick, Lady Bess of, 466
Hardwick College, 365
Harley-Davidson, 582-83
Harris Seeds, 415
Harry, Prince, 130-31
Harry Winston, Inc., 90
Hart, Norman de. V., 757
Hasbro, 640
Hatch, Orrin, 496
Hatfield House, 467
Hauser, Drew, 600
Havala, Suzanne, 159
Hawaii:
  coffee from, 171
  honeymoons in, 478
  national parks in, 444, 493
  same-sex marriages in, 264-65
  travel to, 444-50, 478
Hawaii Nani Loa, 448
Hawaii Volcanoes National Park, 444, 493
Hawke, Ethan, 366
Hawking, Stephen W., 666
Haydn, Joseph, 604
hay fever, 248, 250
HBO, 627
headaches, 232, 241, 248
  as computer health hazards, 662-63
head injuries, 225
  restraints for, 588-90
  sports and, 707, 720, 734
health and health care, 133-252, 375
  careers in, 334-38
  CD-ROMs on, 667-68
  of children, 207-9
  in college towns, 332
  computers and, 656, 662-63
  and gays, 264-65
  of newborns, 206
  of pets, 436
  and pregnancies, *see* pregnancies
  proxies, 59, 216
  and sexuality, 268, 276
  see also diet; doctors; drugs; exercise; fitness; hospitals; looking great; *specific diseases*
Health and Human Services (HHS) Department, U.S., 134, 148, 159-60, 246
Health Care Information Analysts, Inc., 47
health insurance:
  abortion and, 275
  AIDS and, 279
  alternative medicine and, 248-49
  chiropractors and, 246
  dollars & sense guide to, 126-29
  as perk, 356-57
  tax deduction for, 99
Health Insurance Association of America, 60, 127, 129
health maintenance organizations (HMOs), 127, 210, 212-16, 356, 581
  accreditation of, 215
  getting most out of, 213-14
  preventive care from, 214
  report cards of, 215
Health Plan Employer Data and Information Set (HEDIS), 215
Healthy People 2000, 215
heart attacks, 134
  drugs and, 232-34
heartburn, 232
heart defects, congenital, 200
heart disease, 135-36, 238, 240-41, 276
  alternative medicine and, 249
  diet and, 148-50, 152, 156-60, 162-63
  HMOs and, 213-14
  hospitals and, 219
Heart of Africa Safaris, 518
Heathrow Airport, 540
Heckman, Leila, 11-12
hedgehogs, 431-32
Heidi, 636
Heidrick & Struggles, Inc., 367
Heisey glass, 87
Hell's Canyon, 491
Hell's Hinges, 623
Hemingway, Ernest, 555
Henderson, Ann, 648
Hendrix, Jimi, 596-97, 599-600
Hennekens, Charles, 193
Henry IV (Shakespeare), 365
Henry V (Shakespeare), 365
Henry VIII, King of England, 466
Henry J. Kaiser Family Foundation, 270-71
Hentzel, Irvin, 748
hepatitis B, 277
Hepburn, Audrey, 179
Hepburn, Katharine, 637
Hepplewhite, George, 83
herbaceous plants, 420
herbs, 248, 412
Heretic and Hexen, 669
Herger, Wally, 496
Heron Island, 730
herpes, 278
Herring, George, 666
Hesse-Darmstadt, 93
Hewitt Associates, 357
Hewlett-Packard (HP) Co., 654, 657
HFSestival, 602
Hibbing High School, 596
Hibernian Hotel, 471
Hideaway Report, 557
high blood pressure, *see* hypertension
High Density Discharge (H.I.D.) lamps, 392
high-density lipoproteins (HDLs), 156-57
High-Flavor, Low-Fat Vegetarian Cooking (Raichlen), 178
Highland Light Beach, 451
high-low poker, 754
High Noon, 623
high-quality corporate bond funds, 26
High Sierra Tent Camps, 498
hiking:
  equipment for, 525
  on Swiss walks, 526-29
  for travelers, 523-29
Hill, Anita, 263
Hilo, 445, 448
Hinson, David, 538
Hirsch, Alan, 258
Hirsch, Yale, 24
His Girl Friday, 610, 612
history:
  CD-ROMs on, 666
  education in, 287
  graduate schools for, 323
  movies for children on, 634
Ho Chi Minh City, 464-65
hockey, 707
  amateur, 742
  fan's guide to, 710-11
  on in-line skates, 713
Hoffman, W. Michael, 380
Holbrook, Richard, 379
Holiday Inns, 556
Holiday World, 646
Holistic Guide for a Healthy Dog, *The* (Volhard and Brown), 436
holistic medicine, 247
  for pets, 436
Holle, Gena, 550
Hollywood Online, 689-90
Holocaust, 329
Holy Cross Abbey, 479
Home Away from Home (Margolies), 556
HomeChek of New Jersey, Inc., 387, 395
Home Depot, 375
Home Guides of America, 383
homeopathy, 247-49
home pages, 686, 694-95
Homer, 365
Home Repair Encyclopedia, 668
Homes Away, 472
HomeTech Information Systems, 384
home theaters, 629
Homework Helper, 684
homosexuality, 260, 262, 264-65, 300
Honda Civic, 567, 578
Honda Prelude VTEC, 568
Hondas, 582
Honduras:
  guided expeditions to, 537
  travel to, 454
honeydews, 169-70
honeymooner's guide, 478
Hong Kong:
  bargain shopping in, 474
  business investments in, 11-12
Honolulu, 448
Hoop Dreams, 635
Hoover's Handbook of American Business, 665
Hoover's Online, 691
HORDE Festival, 602
hormone-producing tumors, 219
hormone replacement therapy (HRT), 241, 255
hormones, sexual, 240-41, 268-69, 271
Hornlihutte, walking from Zermatt to, 526-27
Hornreisch, Janet, 435
Hornstein, Harvey, 370-71
horror films, 619-20
hoses, 414, 592
Hospital, The, 612
hospital indemnity insurance, 127
hospitals, 216-25
  best in U.S., 217-25
  HMOs and, 213-14
  maternal stays in, 206
  patient's bill of rights and, 216
HotBot, 688
Hot Dog Standard Web Editor, 695
Hotel Abtei, 470
Hotel Bulow Residenz, 470
Hotel Colon, 471
Hôtel des Quartre Dauphins, 469
Hotel Destiny Villa Real, 471
Hotel d'Inghilterra, 470
Hotel Elefant, 470
Hotel Fluhalp, 529
Hotel Hana-Maui, 446
Hotel Lanai, 449
Hôtel le Hameau, 469
Hôtel les Armures, 469
Hôtel Lido, 469
Hotel Loggiato dei Serviti, 470-71
Hotel Mondial, 469
Hotel Pierre, 470
HotMetal, 680, 695
Hot Wheels, 88
Hot Wired, 693
Housatonic River, 727
Houseman, John, 406
houseplants, 429-30
houses and homes, 61-78, 381-410
  appreciating value of, 61-62, 77
  basketball hoops at, 709
  CD-ROMs on, 668
  down payments on, 62, 65-68, 71
  "dream," 383
  environmental hazards in, 398-401
  and firearms, 408-10
  first-time buyers of, 62, 67
  in fitting lifestyles and psychological needs, 382-83
  foreclosed, 78
  framing and displaying art in, 393-94
  furnishings of, 383, 390-94
  and gays, 264
  hiring contractors for, 387
  insurance on, 62, 69, 75, 127-29, 387
  and investing, 4, 62, 65-66, 71, 74, 76
  lighting in, 392-93
  mortgages on, *see* mortgages
  painting of, 388-89

preventing burglarization of, 402-3, 405-7
prices of, 63, 383
renovation of, 383-87
rental income from, 102-3
renting vs. buying of, 65-66
repairing of, 395-97
and retirement, 45-49
safety in, 402-10
and salaries, 350
sales of, 102
security systems for, 383, 405
and self-defense, 406-10
and taxes, 62, 65-67, 69-70, 74, 78, 96-97, 101, 105, 109
ten least affordable markets for, 65
ten most affordable markets for, 65
top 134 markets for, 63-64
trade-up, 62
vacation, 76-77
windows of, *see* windows
working at, 98, 377-78, 382-83, 385
Housing and Urban Development Department, U.S., 398
How Green Was My Valley, 615
"How Schools Shortchange Girls" (Bailey), 300
How to Buy Foreclosed Real Estate for a Fraction of Its Value (Dallow), 78
How to Read Your Opponents' Cards (Lawrence), 757
How to Travel without Being Rich, 547
Huckleberry Finn (Twain), 638
Hugo, Victor, 464
Huizenga, H. Wayne, 564
hula dances, 448
Hulbert Financial Digest, 17
Humane Society of the United States, 435, 431
human granulocytic ehrlichiosis (HGE), 252
human immunodeficiency virus (HIV), 265, 278-80
human papilloma virus, 277
humpback whales, 532-33
hunting, 744-46
Huntington Library, 326
Hurried Child, The (Elkind), 289
Hustad, Marjorie Child, 178
hybrid funds, 26, 28
hyperactive children, 208-9
hypertension, 135, 185, 232, 255
alternative medicine and, 249
diet and, 154, 159-60
sexuality and, 276
hypertext, 686
Hyper Text Markup Language (HTML), 687, 694-95
Hypertext Websters, 693
hypnosis, 248
hypochondria, 236

I

I Am a Fugitive from a Chain Gang, 615-16
Ibbotson Associates, 5-6
IBM Corporation, 286, 361-62, 367, 653-55, 659
ibuprofen (Advil), 232, 244
I Can Do Anything, If I Only Knew What It Was (Sher and Smith), 344
Ice Age National Scenic Trail, 502-3
ice climbing, 743
Idaho:
rafting in, 534
rock climbing in, 716
yurt-to-yurt cross country skiing in, 522
IDC/Link, 377
Iditarod National Historic Trail, 504
Iditarod Sled Dog Race, 717
Iglauer, Bruce, 601
iguanas, 432
Iliad (Homer), 365
Illinois, 265
imipramine (Tofranil), 235
immigration, 265
immunizations, *see* vaccinations
impotence, 276
impressionism, 80
incandescent light, 392
Incarnation Priory, 479
Inca Trail, 523
income, *see* salaries
independent appraisers, 129
independent practice associations (IPAs), 214
independent record labels, 600-601
index funds, 38
India:
business investments in, 12
train travel in, 550
India by Rail (Ellis), 550
Indian Airlines, 539
Indianapolis 500, 700
Indianapolis Motor Speedway, 700
Individual Investor's Guide to Computerized Investing, The, 23
individual retirement accounts (IRAs), 48, 53-54, 316
taxes and, 100, 104, 106
Indonesia:
business investments in, 12
coffees from, 171
wilderness areas in, 512
indoor gardening, 429-30
Industrial Revolution, 334
infants:
around the clock care for, 198
in autos, 588
education of, 282-83
home environmental hazards and, 398
infectious canine hepatitis, 441
infertility, 202-4, 219
adoption and, 204
pregnancies and, 202-3
see also fertility
inflation:
house prices and, 61
investing and, 4-6, 14
life insurance and, 124
retirement and, 50
salaries, 349-50
taxes and, 96
Infopedia, 665
information technology, 334
Infoseek Guide, 688
Info Tech, 664
injuries:
to elbows, 147, 222
exercise and, 146-47
football and, 707
to head, *see* head injuries
from in-line skating, 713-14
to knees, 147, 222, 707, 733
to spine, 225
in-line skating, 713-14
In Praise of Idleness (Russell), 357
insects:
beneficial, 424
repellents for, 252, 424
Inside Flyer, 543
Inside Track, 645, 647
Insight Management, Inc., 41
installers, salaries of, 355
Institut du Monde Arabe, 468
Institute of Medicine, 269
insurance, 573
automobile, 126, 128, 569, 578-81
to avoid, 126
dental, 356
disability, *see* disability insurance
dollars & sense guide to, 124-29
health, *see* health insurance
on homes, 62, 69, 75, 127-29, 387
on pets, 442
sources for advice on, 129
Integrated Services Digital Network (ISDN) lines, 658
Intel Corp., 652
Intellasearch, 81
Intellichoice, 572
interest rates:
on auto loans, 573-74
on credit cards, 114-15
dollars & sense guide to, 114-15
entrepreneurship and, 374-75
investing and, 11-12, 14
on loans to family members, 131
of mortgages, 61-63, 66-74, 76
taxes and, 96-97, 100, 102, 105-6
Interhome, 472
Interior Department, U.S., 78
Internal Revenue Service (IRS), 130-31, 372
on loans to family members, 131
retirement and, 52, 56
taxes and, 97-101, 105-9
International Airline Passengers Association (APA), 543-44
International Association of Air Travel Couriers, 547
International Biosphere Reserves, 484
international bond funds, 26, 31
International Franchise Association, 376
international funds, 26, 28
International In-Line Skating Association, 713-14
International Mountain Equipment, 743
International Photography Hall of Fame, 712
International Railway Traveler (Holle), 550
Internet, 681-96
avoiding trouble on, 696
basics of, 681-83
and childproofing computers, 671
computers and, 653, 655, 658-59
e-mail and, 681, 685-87
getting online on, 682
online services of, 683-84
online services vs. ISPs of, 682-83
online tools for, 638
terms and symbols used on, 686-87
see also World Wide Web
Internet Movie Database, 608-9, 690
Internet relay chat (IRC), 681, 686-87
Internet service providers (ISPs), 682-83
Internet Solutions, 688
Internet Underground Music Archive (IUMA), 689
Internship Bible, The (Oldman and Hamadeh), 340
internships, 340-41
Interplay and Parallax Software, 668-69
Interstellar Pig (Sleator), 638
Inter Vac, 472
interviews, 343, 348
Intolerance, 616
intracytoplasmic sperm injection (ICSI), 203
intrauterine devices (IUDs), 269-70, 272-73
Intuit, 677-78
Invasion of the Body Snatchers, 624
inverted stamps, 94
Investech Mutual Fund Advisor, 18
investing, 2-24
in ADRs, 12
in art, 80-81
in bonds, 3-6, 11, 13-15, 19, 21-22
books on, 24
brokers for, 12, 15, 19-22
and bull vs. bear markets, 5-6, 10
clubs for, 16
cyber-, 23
in foreign countries, 11-12
houses and, 4, 62, 65-66, 71, 74, 76
inflation and, 4-6, 14
life insurance and, 125
newsletters on, 17-18
patience in, 3-6
perks and, 356-57
in pure plays, 10
for retirement, 48-56, 58
risk in, 50
salaries and, 350
selling and, 5

software for, 678
taxes and, 6, 100, 104-6, 108-9
tips on, 2-3, 7-9, 17
Web sites on, 23, 691
of women vs. men, 16
see also mutual funds; stocks
Investing in the Future, 359
Investment Biker (Rogers), 24, 50
Investment Company Institute, 42
Investor's Business Daily, 14
in vitro fertilization (IVF), 202-3
iodine, 155
Ireland:
barge trips in, 530-31
country inns in, 471
iron, 154, 160
Ironman World Triathlon Competition, 717
irrevocable life insurance trusts, 58
isocarboxazid (Marplan), 235
isoflavones, 158
Israel, camel treks in, 522
Italian, The, 616
Italy:
country inns in, 470-71
villa rentals in, 473
Itatiaia National Park, 521
It Happened One Night, 612
It Happens Every Spring, 635
It's a Mad, Mad, Mad, Mad World, 637
It's a Wonderful Life, 610, 616

J

Jackson, Andrew, 503
Jackson, Jesse, 369
Jackson, Michael, 89, 431-32
Jackson, Steven, 402-4
Jackson & Perkins, 415
Jackson Hole, Wyo., 735, 737
Jack White, 22-23
Jacobs Field, 699
Jacques Pépin's Simple and Healthy Cooking (Pépin), 166
Jamaica, 455-56
James I, King of England, 467
James Beard Cookbook, The (Beard), 178
James Discovers Math, 672
Jane Eyre, 637
Jane's Addiction, 599
Japan:
business investments in, 11-12
sexuality in, 258
train travel in, 550-51
whale watching in, 533
Japanese bobtails, 438-39
Jasper Beach, 451
jaundice, 206
Java, 655, 687
Jax Fax, 547
Jayapura, 514
Jayavarman, King of Khmer Empire, 465
jazz, 601
J.D. Power and Associates, 570
Jeep, 566
Jefferson, Thomas, 504-5
Jenkins, William, 294
Jensen, Georg, 84, 87
jewelry:
collecting of, 86-87, 89-91
home insurance and, 75
JFK Airport, 540
Jim Fobel's Big Flavors (Fobel), 178
Jim Fowler's Wildest Places (Fowler), 510
Jim Henson Productions, 341
job-protected leaves, 360
job sharing, 361
Jobsmarts for Twentysomethings (Richardson), 342
John Carter Library, 326
John Hancock, 32
Johnny Tremain, 634
Johns, Jasper, 79
Johnson, Philip, 388
Johnson, Virginia, 254
Johnson & Johnson, 3, 279, 361
Johnston, Richard, 152
joint pain, 232
Jones, Loree Jon, 759-60
Jones, Quincy, 599
Jones, Robert Trent, 450
Joplin, Janis, 596-97, 599
Jordan, Michael, 372, 709
Joseph, Chief of Nez Perce, 365, 505
Journeyman Project 2: Buried in Time, The, 669
Journeyman Project Turbo, The, 669
Joyce, Jack, 314
Joy of Cooking, The (Rombauer), 178
J. Paul Getty Museum, 81
J. P. Morgan Capital, 564
Juan Bautista de Anza National Historic Trail, 504
jumper cables, 595
jumping jacks, 140
Jumpstart: Preschool, 672-73
Junior Erector Tool Center, 640
junk insurance, 126
Jurassic Park, 95, 431
jury duty, 378
Justice Department, U.S., 406
Justin Herman Plaza, 599
JVC, 632
J. W. Jung Seed Co., 415

K

Kael, Pauline, 666
Kaena Point Natural Area Reserve, 449
Kalalau Beach State Park, 451
Kander, Lillian, 178
Kandersteg, walking to Blumslialphutte from, 528-29
Kane, Robert W., 654
Kantar, Eddie, 757
Karen Brown's Country Inn series (Brown), 469
Karnow, Stanley, 464-65
Karp, Jonathan, 345
Katz, Lilian, 291
Katzen, Mollie, 648
Kauai, 444, 450
K. Aufhauser, 22
Kaufman, Donald, 388-89
Kawakiu Beach, 447
Kelley, Joyce, 452-54
Kelly, Grace, 179
Kelsey, Hugh, 757
Ken Crane's Laser Disc Superstore, 625
Kennebec River, 535
Kennedy, Jim, 367
Kennedy, Joe, 58
Kennedy, John F., 58, 86, 145, 244
Kennywood, 645
Kentucky, national parks in, 494
Kentucky bluegrass, 427
Kentucky Derby, 700
Kenya:
coffee from, 171
guided expeditions to, 537
hiking in, 523
travel in, 515, 518, 523
Keogh plans, 48, 55, 104
Kepaniwai Park and Heritage Gardens, 446
Kesenel, Michael, 495
Kessler, Alan, 194-95
ketoprofen, 232
Kettle Falls Hotel, 499
keyboards, 651, 653, 655, 660
computer health hazards and, 662-63
Keynes, John Maynard, 7
Keystone, 32
Kid Desk, 671
kiddie tax rates, 104
kidney disease, 232
Kiehl's Creme, 184
Kilauea National Wildlife Refuge, 450
Killer Instinct, 642
Killer of Sheep, 616
killer (orca) whales, 532-33
Killing Defense (Kelsey), 757
Kinesis Ergonomic Keyboard, 662
King, Henry, 366
King, Martin Luther, Jr., 365
King Kong, 620
King's College Library, 326
Kings Dominion, 647
Kings Mountain, Battle of, 506
Kinsey, Alfred C., 258
Kiplinger's, 35
Kiplinger's Personal Finance, 108, 110, 678
Kiplinger Washington Editors, Inc., 112
Simply Money, 678
TaxCut, 108, 678
Kirby, Doug, 558-59
Kirchhoff, Bruce, 374
kitchens, 382-84, 388-89
addition of, 384
herb gardens and, 412
lighting in, 392-93
remodeling of, 384
kiwifruits, 169-70
Kiwi International, 541-42
kiwi sorbet, 166
Klamath National Forest, 496
Klondike, 758
Klugman, Jack, 366
knee bends, 140
knees:
to chest exercise, 141
injuries to, 147, 222, 707, 733
K'NEX, 642
Knoebels Amusement Resort, 645, 647
Knole, 467
Knots for Climbers (Leubben), 716
Knowledge Adventure, 672
knowledge professions, 334-36
Kobren, Eric, 41
Kohl, Kay, 324
Koop, C. Everett, 210
Korda, Michael, 345
Korea, South, 11
Korean War Veterans Memorial, 507
koro, 236
Kovel, Terry, 88
KPMG Peat Marwick, 213
Kraeutler, Thomas, 387, 395-97
Kraft, 339
Krauss, Ronald, 158, 161
KROQ Weenie Roast, 602
Krystal, Hilly, 597
kulit k'rang, 643
Kwell, 277-78

L

LaBonte, Andrew, 393-94
Labor Department, U.S., 360
Labrador retrievers, 433, 435
lacrosse, 707
ladybugs, 424
Lady Eve, The, 616
Lahaina, 445
Lahn River, 531
Laie, 448
Lake Bakail, 512-13
Lake Malawi, 517
Lake Naivasha, 514
Lake Oeschinensee, 528
Lamar, Howard, 330
Lambda Legal Defense and Education Fund, 265
land contract mortgages, 70
Landmark Trust, 473
Langenback, 415
language learning disorders, 294
Lani, 447-49
Lankarani, Hamid, 539
laptop computers, 656-57, 660-61
Larsen, Gary, 372
laser resurfacing, 189
Lasorda, Tommy, 362, 366
Lassen Volcanic National Park, 482
Lasser, J. K., 108
Lassie Come Home, 616
Last of the Mohicans, The, 616
Las Vegas, Nev., 45
Late Show with David Letterman, The, 341
latex paints, 389, 401
Latin America, 12
Laughlin, Terry, 731-32
Launch Pad, 671
laundry services, 101
Lauterbach, Christiane, 475
Lautrebrunnental Valley, 529
law, lawyers:
dollars & sense guide to, 130
salaries of, 359
for sexual harassment, 263

Web sites on, 693
women as, 338-39
Lawrence, Mike, 757
Lawrence of Arabia, 616
Laws of Total Tricks, The (Cohen), 757
Lawson, Robert, 634
lead, 398-99
leadership, *see* managers and management
leaf mold, 416
League of Their Own, A, 635
leaking toilets, 397
Lean, David, 636-37
Learning Curve Toys, 641
learning disabilities, 293-94
Learning to Read, the Great Reading Debate (Chall), 293
Learning Tree, The, 616
Leatherman, Stephen, 451
Lee, Canada, 635
Leeds and Liverpool Canal, 530
Leeward Islands, 458-60
Legg Mason, 35
LEGO Systems, 640
legs:
exercises for, 140, 143, 147
winter sports and, 733
Leitch, A. Marilyn, 238
Lemmon, Jack, 637
lemon gardens, 412
lemons, 170
Lendl, Ivan, 724
Lenin, V. I., 464
Leo, 369
Leonardo da Vinci, 81
Lereah, David, 61
lesbians, 264-65
see also homosexuality
Lesser Antilles, 456-58
Less Gauss, 663
Let's Talk (Alman), 261
Letter from an Unknown Woman, 616-17
Letter from Birmingham Jail (King), 365
Letterman, David, 341
lettuce, 412
Levitt, Arthur, 19
Levy, Howard, 391
Levy, Stuart, 228
Lewis, Jerry Lee, 598
Lewis, Meriwether, 504-5
Lewis, Myrna I., 268
Lewis and Clark National Historic Trail, 504-5
Lexus SC300, 568-69
Leybourn, Michael, 175
Libbey, Ted, 604-5
liberal arts colleges, 307-8, 310-13
Liberation of Jerusalem (Tasso), 607
Liberty Financial Companies, Inc., 112
Libra, 369
libraries, 326, 332
Library of Congress, 326, 693
Lichtenstein, Roy, 79
Lieberman, Marcia and Philip, 529
life-cycle funds, 39
life expectancies, 243
life insurance, 102
dollars & sense guide to, 124-26, 128-29
as perk, 356-57
Life Insurance Advisers Association, 129
life insurance trusts, 58
Life on the Screen (Turkle), 317
lifestyles:
homes and, 382-83
salaries and, 350
weight and, 134
lifting techniques, 245
Lighten Up (Whitehead), 392
Lighter, Quicker, Better (Sax and Simmons), 178
lighting, 392-93
burglaries and, 402-3
for houseplants, 430
Light Source, 392
Light-up Picture Maker, The, 640-41
Lili Marleen, 554
Lim, Ping, 423
limes, 170
linguistics, 319
Linn's Stamp News, 94
Lionel trains, collecting of, 88
lions, 511, 513
Lion's City, The, 478
lipoproteins, 156-57
liposuction, 187-88, 191
Lipper, A. Michael, 40
lipstick, 182-83
literature:
landmarks of, 327
on management, 365-66
Web sites on, 692-93
lithium, 232
lithographs, 80
Little, Micky, 495
Little Cayman, 455
Little Helper's Workbench, 639
Little Kennebago River, 727
Little League, 703
Little People Farm, 639
Little River, 451
Little Tikes, 639
liver disease, 232
Living Colour, 597
living rooms, 382, 388-89
lighting in, 392-93
living trusts, 59
living wills, 59, 216
loans:
on autos, 564-65, 569, 571-74
to children, 57
for college, 99, 101, 302-4, 314-16, 321
from family members, 131
from 401(k)s, 53
online banking and, 119
tax refund, 107
see also mortgages
Lockheed, 540
locura, 236
Lofoten Islands, 533
Loire Valley, 474
Lollapalooza, 602
London, 474
Lonely Planet guides, 562, 690
Long, Huey, 635
Long, John, 716
longevity:
diet and, 148, 160
exercise and, 135
melatonin and, 237
Long Goodbye, The, 610
Longhouse Scenic Byway, 508
Longleaf Partners, 41
Longleat, 466
Looe Key, 729
looking great, 179-93
cosmetics and, 182-83
hair and, 184-86, 190-91
plastic surgery and, 187-93
skin care and, 179-81, 187-90
Lopa, 448
lorazepam (Ativan), 235
Lord of the Flies (film), 366
Lord of the Flies (Golding), 366
Loren, Sophia, 179, 182
Los Angeles, Calif., 476
Los Angeles Dodgers, 362, 366
Los Angeles International Airport, 540
Los Angeles Lakers, 362
Lost World, The (Doyle), 513
Lotus Development Corp., 680
Approach, 675-76
1-2-3, 675
Word Pro, 680
Louisiana Purchase, 505, 507
Louvre, 468, 692
Lovejoy, Thomas, 519
Love Me Tonight, 621
Lover and Sex after 60 (Butler and Lewis), 268
low-density lipoproteins (LDLs), 156-58
lower back, exercises for, 141
lower body, exercises for, 140-41, 143
Low-Fat Grilling (Barnard), 174
low-hand poker, 753-54
Loy, Myrna, 635-36
L Street Swimming Club and Brownies, 743
L-tryptophan, 237
Luangwa River, 518
Luangwa Valley, 517
Lucas, Dione, 178
Lucasfilm, 629
Lucille's Car Care (Treganowan), 592
Lucky Ducks, 640
Luebben, Craig, 716
Lukins, Sheila, 178
Lumet, Sidney, 366
lumpectomies, 240
Lumpen, 347
lung cancer, 238, 242
diet and, 148, 150, 153
home environmental hazards and, 398-99
Lupu, Radu, 605
lurk, 687
Lycos, 688
Lyme disease, 252
Lynch, Peter, 7, 13, 23
Lynde, Paul, 636

M

M.A.C, 183
McAfee Associates, 653, 696
Macauley, David, 667
McCannon, Bob, 633
McCartney, Marion, 198
McCathren, Randall, 574-75
McDonald's, 376
McDonnell, Ken, 357
McDonnell Douglas, 540
McGuire, Dorothy, 636
Macintoshes (Macs), 652-55, 659-60, 671, 677
DTP for, 679
Internet and, 683, 686
PCs vs., 655
word processing software for, 680
Mackay, Benton, 502
Mackaye, Ian, 601
McKinley, Mount, 524
McKnight, Hugh, 530
McLaughlin, Donald R., 87
McLaughlin, Michael, 178
MacMurray, Fred, 637
McNally, Connie, 84-85
McQueen, Jane Bangley, 495
macular degeneration, 148-49
MacUser, 693
Madang, 731
Madidi National Park, 520
Madison River, 727
Madonna, 597
magazines (ammunition containers), 408
MAG Install-A-Lock, 403
Magley, Beverly, 508-9
magnesium, 155
magnetic resonance imaging (MRI) scanners, 375
Magnificent Ambersons, The, 617
Mahaulepu Beach, 450
Maine:
national parks in, 494
rafting in, 535
retirement in, 44-45
vacation homes in, 76
Maine Antique Digest, 82, 85
Maine coon cats, 439
Maine Windjammer Assoc., 490
Main Street Beats Wall Street (Maturi), 16, 24
Malawi, 517-18
mal de ojo (evil eye), 236
male breast reduction, 191
male pattern baldness, 185
Malkiel, Burton, 38
Maltese Falcon, The, 622
Maltin, Leonard, 609, 666
Mamet, David, 365-66
mammograms, 214, 238-39, 243
Mammoth Cave, 487
Mammoth Mountain, Calif., 735-36
managers and management, 362-72
abusive, 370-71
astrological signs of, 368-69
burnout among, 372
family-friendly, 358-59
headhunters for, 367
and Internet, 681
literary classics on, 365-66
movies for, 366
salaries in, 349-50, 352-54
tips for, 362-63
Managing Your Money, 675, 678
Mana Pools National Park, 516-17
manatees, 500
Manchurian Candidate, The, 622
Manifesto for a New Medicine (Gordon), 247
Manu National Park, 520

manure, 416, 425
marbles, collecting of, 87
March of Dimes Birth Defects Foundation, 152
Margolies, John, 556
marigolds, 412
Marriott Corporation, 331
Mark, Reuben, 349
Markese, John, 40
MarketArts, 678
marketing occupations:
salaries in, 354
women in, 339
Market Masters (Bernstein), 24
market timers, 40
Mark Twain National Forest, 509
Marley, Bob, 596-97
Marlowe, Hugh, 366
Maroon, Fred, 466-67
Marplan (isocarboxazid), 235
marriage:
abortion and, 275
gays and, 264-65
taxes and, 103
Marshall, Deirdre, 185-86
Martinez, Edgar, 705
Martinique, 461
Marty, 617
Marx Brothers, 637
Mary, Queen of Scotland, 466
Masai Mara Natural Reserve, 515
Mascagni, Pietro, 606
mascara, 183
Masefield, John, 365
Massachusetts, 265
massage therapy, 247
mass entertainment, 328
Massey, Raymond, 634
mastectomies, 240
MasterCard, 115
Mastering the Art of French Cooking, Volume One (Child, Beck and Bertholle), 178
Mastering the Art of French Cooking, Volume Two (Child and Beck), 178
Master Play (Reese), 757
Masters, William, 254
Masters Golf Tournament, 699
mastopexy, 187
materials science, 322
mathematics:
education in, 286-87, 298, 300-301
graduate schools for, 322
SAT in, 305
software for children on, 672
Mathers Fund, 40
Mathiessen, Peter, 518
Matisse, Henri, 80
Mattel, 88, 640, 642
mattresses, 391
Maturi, Richard J., 16, 24
Maui, 445-46
Mavis Beacon Teaches Typing, 673
Mayan civilization, 452-54, 478, 522
Maytag, Fritz, 175
Mazda MX-5 Miata, 568
MCI, 120
meat, 160, 174
Meca, 678
mechanical engineering, 322
mechanics, 355, 595
Mecklenburg Lakes, 531
Medaccess, 690-91
Media Central, 693
media literacy, 633
Medicaid, 47-48
Medical Economics, 226-27
medical technology, 335-36
medical transportation, 101
Medicare, 47, 99, 210, 246
Medicare supplement health insurance, 127
medications, *see* drugs
Medio, 666
Mediterranean diet, 249
Medtronic Inc., 13
Meet Me in St. Louis, 621, 636
megabytes (MBs), 651, 653-54
megahertz (Mhz), 650, 652
Mekong Delta, 464
melanoma, 211
melatonin, 237
Meller, Steven, 294
Melville, Herman, 365, 532
memory, computer, 650-51, 654, 659, 661, 671, 680
Mendelson, Edward, 680
Mendelson, Irene, 344-45
Mendocino Brewing Company, 175
meningitis, 228-29
menopause, 195, 238, 240-41, 255, 268
menstruation and menstrual cycles, 238, 240, 258, 270
and cramps, 232, 248
mental disorders:
culturally triggered, 236
drugs for, 225, 233-36
Mer, La (Debussy), 605
Mercer Inc., 21
Mercer's 1995 Discount Brokerage Survey, 22
Merck & Co., 361
Mercury Mystique, 567
Mercury Sable, 567-68
Merida, 453
Merrie Monarch Festival, 448
Merrill Lynch Asset Management, 32-33, 36, 50
Merritt, Fannie, 178
Merzenich, Michael, 294
Mesa Verde National Park, 509
Methode, La (Pépin), 178
methotrexate, 274
Metromix, 413
Metronidazole, 277
Metropolitan Home, 382
Metropolitan Life Insurance Company, 134
Meuse River, 531
Mexican free-tailed bats, 501
Mexican War, 506
Mexico:
coffee from, 171
guided expeditions to, 537
honeymoons in, 478
travel to, 452-54, 478
whale watching in, 533
winter baseball in, 705
Miami, Fla., dining in, 476
Miami Dolphins, 362, 366
Miami Heat, 362
Michael, Liz, 182-83
Michelin red guides, 562
Michigan:
entrepreneurs in, 375
national parks in, 494
Microsoft Corp., 662, 664-69, 671, 675, 680, 688
Bookshelf, 665, 684
Complete Baseball, 668
Dangerous Creatures, 666-67
Dinosaurs, 667
Excel, 675
Internet Assistant, 680, 695
Internet Explorer Browser, 683, 686, 688
Internet Resources, 694
Money, 119, 677-78
Musical Instruments, 667
Oceans, 667
Publisher, 679
Word, 695
Word for Windows, 680
Microsoft Network, The, 23, 666, 684-85
Microsoft Publisher by Design (Simone), 679
Microsystems Software, 696
Mid America Paleontology Society, 95
middle class salaries, 350
Midnight Cowboy, 617
Midwest:
house prices in, 63
vacation homes in, 76-77
Midwest Express, 541-42
mifepristone (RU-486), 270, 274-75
migraine headaches, 232
Miles Guide, The, 543
military service, gays and, 264
milk, low-fat, 161, 167
Milken, Michael, 242
Miller, Arthur and Marjorie, 504
Miller's Market Report, 88
Mills, John, 636
Milton Bradley, 640
mind, books on, 328
mind-body medicine, 247
minerals, 148, 154-55, 160
for pets, 436
Mine's the Best (Bonsall), 638
Ming Tian, Xiao, 248
miniature poodles, 434
Minnesota:
entrepreneurs in, 375
national parks in, 494
Minow, Nell, 634-37
minoxodil, 185
Miracle Grow, 413
Miramax, 690
Miranker, Cathy, 670-73
mirrors, antique, 82-84
misoprostol, 274
Miss Galaxy, 142-43
Mississippi:
entrepreneurs in, 375
retirement in, 44
Miss Taylor's Restaurant, 596, 598
Mr. Blandings Builds His Dream House, 636
Mr. Cranky, 609
Mr. Showbiz, 609
Mr. Smith Goes to Washington, 617
Mittermeier, Russell, 519
Mitterrand, François, 468
Moan and Groan List, 693
Mobil Travel Guide, 556-57
modems, 650-53, 656, 658-59, 661, 682
evaluation of, 658
upgrading of, 659
Modern Times, 612
Mojave National Preserve, 491
molecular biology, 320
molecular genetics, 320
Mollie Katzen's Cooking Show, 648
Molokai, 446-47
monastic guest houses, 479
Mondo Movies, 625
money, 1-132
sex vs., 258
wills and, 59
see also collecting; dollars & sense guide; investing; mutual funds; real estate; taxes
Money, 35, 356, 377, 677, 692, 699
Money Doesn't Grow on Trees (Godfrey), 672
money managers, 42, 60
money market funds, 5
money purchase plans, 55
monitors, 650-51, 654-57, 661-63, 671
computer health hazards and, 662-63
evaluation of, 656-57
of portable computers, 661
Monjan, Andrew, 237
monoamine oxidase inhibitors (MAOIS), 235
Monopoly, 747-49
Montana:
national parks in, 494
retirement in, 44
Montana, Joe, 146
Montana Coffee Traders, 172
Monteverde Cloud Forest Reserve, 519
Montreal Expos, 705
Montserrat, 460-61
Mont Tremblant, 738
Monty Python's Complete Waste of Time, 669
Moody's Handbook of Dividend Achievers, 13
Moon guides, 562
Moore, Demi, 608
Moosewood Cookbook (Katzen), 648
morality, 285
Moremi Reserve, 516
Morgan, J. P., 368
Morgan Stanley Asset Management, 12
International Index of European and Asian Stocks of, 38
Morland, George, 81
Mormon Pioneer National Historic Trail, 505
Morningstar Inc., 12, 25-27, 32, 35-37, 39-40, 56, 691
Morocco, 617
Morris, Grace, 368-69
Morris, Michelle, 495
Morristown Memorial Hospital, 194, 198
Mortal Kombat 3, 641
Mortgage Bankers Association, 61
Mortgage Money Guide, The, 67

mortgages, 66-74, 78
evaluating lenders for, 71
income needed for, 68-69, 71
information needed by lenders for, 71
interest rates of, 61-63, 66-74, 76
life insurance and, 124-25
monthly payments on, 62, 67-70, 72-74
payment tables for, 72-73
points on, 97, 101
refinancing of, 62, 68-71, 74
taxes and, 96-97, 101, 105, 109
types of, 67-70
Morva, B., 495
Mosley, Alisa, 351
motels, 556-57
mothballs, 400
motherboards, 654
mothers:
best companies for, 361
working, 361
Motley Fool Investment Guide, The (Gardner and Gardner), 7
motorcycles, 582-83
Motrin, 232
mountain bikes, 718-19
Mountaineering, Freedom of the Hills (Graydon), 716
Mountaineer Series, The, 495
mountain inns, 529
mountain laurels, 421
Mountains of the Moon, 513
Mt. Aspiring National Park, 524
Mount Baker-Snoqualmie National Forest, 501
Mt. Kenya National Park, 523
Mount Magazine Scenic Byway, 509
Mt. Vernon, Va., 428
Mouree, 514
mouses, 651, 654
Movie Mom, 634-37
Movie Quotes, 609
Movie Review Query Engine, 608
movies, 608-25
CD-ROMs on, 666
for children, 634-37
conservatives on, 610
hard to find, 625
for managers, 366
recommended, 610-24
Tarantino on, 610
Vatican on, 610
Web sites on, 608-9, 634, 690
moving expenses, 101
Mozart, The Dissonant Quartet, 667
Mozart, Wolfgang Amadeus, 298, 604, 606, 667
MPT Review, 18
MSNBC, 650
MTV, 633
Mueller, Frederick O., 707
Muir, John, 486
mulch, 426
Multimedia Bug Book, The, 674
Multimedia Business 500, 665
Multimedia Composer Collection (Beethoven, Mozart, Schubert), 667
multimedia computers, 659
Multimedia MBA Small Business Edition, 665-66
Multimedia Typing Instructor, 673
multiple sclerosis (MS), 214, 221
Multipurpose Internet Mail Ex-tensions (MIME), 685
multisector bond funds, 29
Multi-User Domains (MUDs), 317
mummies, 559
mums, 420
Munchkins, 439
municipal bonds and funds, 15, 19, 26, 31, 102
Murkowski, Frank, 496
Murphy, Barry, 16
Murren, walking from Greisalp to, 529
Museum of the Rockies, 95
museums, Web sites of, 692
music and musicians, 596-607
CD-ROMs on, 666-67
classical, 604-7
and education, 290, 298-99
equipment for, 629-31
films with, 620-21
graduate schools for, 319
and independent labels, 600-601
mail-order, 601
for Nineties, 603
and operas, 606-7
Web sites on, 689
see also rock-and-roll
Music Educators National Council, 287
Mustique, 462
Mutual Beacon fund, 41
Mutual Discovery fund, 41
mutual funds, 4, 9-12, 15, 19, 22-23, 25-43, 104
analysis of, 34
asset allocation, 39-40
classification of, 25-26
expense ratios of, 33, 40
families of, 33, 37
index, 38
investment style and mix of, 34, 40
large, 37
leverage of, 34
new, 37
no-load, 22, 33, 36
owning too many, 41
private money managers vs., 42
rankings of, 35
for retirement, 50, 52, 54, 56
returns of, 34, 37-39
risk of, 25-26, 34
selection of, 25-26
services provided by, 43
software for, 677-78
standard deviations of, 34
taxes and, 26, 34-35, 38, 42-43, 106
top 140, 27-31
Web sites on, 691
worst performing, 32
Mutual of Omaha, 510
My Darling Clementine, 623
Myers, Norman, 520
Myers-Briggs Type Indicator (MBTI), 344-45
Myst, 669
mystery films, 621-23

N

Nada Chair, 663
Nader, Ralph, 544
Nadig, Perry, 276
Naismith, James, 709
Nambia, wilderness in, 511-12
Namco, 641
Nanao, 657
nanny tax, 97
Nantahala River, 536
Napoleon III, Emperor of France, 468
naproxen sodium, 232
Nardil (phenelzine), 235
Nashville, 617
Natchez Trace National Scenic Trail, 503
National Abortion Rights Action League, 275
National Academy of Sciences, 269, 641
National Adoption Center, 205
National Adoption Information Clearinghouse, 205
National Aeronautics and Space Administration (NASA), 161, 667
National AIDS Hotline, 279
National Arboretum, 412, 414, 425
National Association of Child-bear-ing Centers, 198
National Association of Enrolled Agents, 105
National Association of Home Builders, 383
National Association of Investors Corporation (NAIC), 16, 112
National Association of Life Underwriters, 60
National Association of Realtors, 67, 398
National Association of Secondary School Principals, 304
National Association of Securities Dealers (NASD), 19-20, 22
National Association of Underwater Instructors (NAUI), 730
National Association of Working Women, 263
National Audubon Society Field Guide to African Wildlife, The (Alden), 515
National Automotive Dealers Association (NADA), 566
National Basketball Association (NBA), 635, 690, 708, 712
National Basketball Hall of Fame, 362
National Board for Certified Counselors, 345
National Bureau of Economic Research (NBR), 103, 359
National Business Employment Weekly Jobs Rated Almanac, 373
National Cancer Institute (NCI), 240, 264
National Car Care Council, 592
National Center for Education in the Economy, 286
National Center for Financial Education, 112
National Center for Health Statistics, 194, 279
National Charities Information Bureau, 122
National Cholesterol Education Program (NCEP), 156, 158
National Collegiate Athletic Association (NCAA), 362, 700-701
Final Four tournament, 698-700
National Commission for Quality Assurance (NCQA), 215
National Council of Individual Investors (NCII), 20
National Council of Mathematics, 287
National Council of Teachers of English, 287
National Cowboy Hall of Fame, 712
National Educational Standards and Improvement Council, 286
National Eldercare Locator Service, 47
National Elk Refuge, 500
National Film Registry, 611
National Fisheries Institute, 164
National Football League (NFL), 362, 698-99, 701, 707
National Fresh Water Fishing Hall of Fame, 711
National Garden Bureau, 421
National Geographic, 632
National Geographic Guide to the National Parks of the United States (Newhouse), 495
National Geographic Society, 287
National Governors Association, 286
National Heart, Lung, and Blood Institute, 156, 158
National Highway Traffic Safety Administration, 576
national historic trails, 503-6
National Hockey League, 713
National Institute for Aviation Research, 539
National Institute of Aviation Research, 541-42
National Institute of Environmental Health Sciences, 203
National Institute of Mental Health, 233, 300
National Institute on Aging, 237
National Institutes of Health (NIH), 60, 156, 158, 247-48, 346
National Insurance Consumer Helpline, 129
National Insurance Consumer Organization, 124
National Insurance Crime Bureau, 404
National Marine Fisheries Service, 164
National Merit Scholarship Qualifying Test (NMSQT), 303
National Museum of Natural History, 641
National Opinion Research Center, 217

National Outdoor Leadership School (NOLS), 537
national parks, 444, 480-99
areas considered for status of, 491
best guide books on, 495
largest, 485
lesser-known, 480-83
lodging in, 498-99
map of, 483
most popular, 484-92
newest, 507
off-season visits to, 487
visitor's guide to, 493-94
National Park Service, 484, 497-98, 503, 508
home page of, 495
National Public Radio (NPR), 604, 692
National Registry of Historic Buildings, 499
National Registry of Historic Places, 447, 449, 479
National Research Council (NRC), 287, 319
National Review, 610
national scenic trails, 502-4
National Science Education Standards, 287
National Scrabble Organization, 749
National Semiconductor, 372
National Standards for Art Education, 287
National Standards for Civics and Government, 287
National Standards for United States History, 287
National Standards in Foreign Language Education, 287
National Trails Assistance Act, 502
National Trust, 466
National Trust Holiday Booking Office, 473
National Trust Scotland, 473
National University of Continuing Education Association (NUCEA), 324-25
National Velvet, 636
"Nation at Risk, A," 286
Nationsbank, 361
Nature, 298
nature, books on, 327
Nature Conservancy, 324, 447
nausea, 232
Navratilova, Martina, 146, 723-24
NBC News online, 684
NCAA Basketball, 712
NCAA Football, 712
NEC, 654, 657
neck, 146
computer health hazards and, 662-63
exercises for, 141, 146
football and, 707
nectarines, 169-70
neighborhood watch programs, 402
Nemko, Martin, 423
Nepal:
guided expeditions to, 537
hiking in, 524-25
wilderness areas in, 512
net asset values (NAVs), 26
NetBooks, 689
NetBuddy, 688
Netcom, 684
Netherlands Antilles, 459-61, 463, 729
Netly News, 693
NetNanny, 671
Net PC, 655
Netscape Communications Corp., 683, 695
Navigator Gold, 695
Navigator Personal Edition, 683
Navigator 2.0, 684, 686, 688
Network, 610
networking, 367
careers and, 342-43
Net Worth, 691
neurology, 221-22
neurosciences, 320
neurosurgeons, 227
Neutrogena, 3
neutrophils, 176
Nevada:
national parks in, 494
retirement in, 44
Neverland Ranch, 431
Nevis, 460
New Age Health Spa, 267
New Belgium, 175
New Bethel Baptist Church, 596
newborns, 206, 283
New Commodore Cruise Line, 554
New Delhi, 474
New England Journal of Medicine, 158, 203, 247
New Hampshire, 537
Newhouse, Elizabeth L., 495
New Issues, 18
New Jersey, 265
New Jersey Meadowlands, 699
New Lifestyles, 47
New Mexico:
national parks in, 494
rafting in, 535
retirement in, 44
New Mexico Media Literacy Project, 633
New Music Report, 603
New Orleans, Battle of, 503
New Orleans Jazz National Historical Park, 507
New Roadside America (Wilkins, Kirby, and Smith), 558
news, Web sites for, 691-92
New Science of Technical Analysis, The (DeMark), 24
News Electronic Data, 668
Newton's Apple, 674
New York:
rock climbing in, 716
same-sex marriages in, 265
New York City:
bargain shopping in, 474
dining in, 476-77
New York Dolls, 599
New York Knicks, 146, 362
New York Public Library (NYPL), 326-27
New York Public Library's Books of the Century, The, 327-29
New York Stock Exchange, 12, 20
New York Times, 110, 248, 357, 476, 548, 601, 683, 691
New York Times Cookbook, The (Claiborne), 178
New York Yankees, 364
New Zealand:
hiking in, 524
whale watching in, 533
Nez Perce (Nee-Me-Poo) National Historic Trail, 505
Ngorongoro Conservation Area, 515
Ngorongoro Crater, 516
niacin (vitamin B3), 151
Niagara Falls, 513
Nicklaus, Jack, 450
Nietzsche, Friedrich, 528
Night at the Opera, A, 612
Night of the Hunter, The, 622
Night of the Living Dummy (Stine), 638
Nike, internships with, 341
nine men's morris, 643
1995 Pro Football Handbook, 712
1994 Book of Facts, 665
1996 Compton's Interactive Encyclopedia, 664
9 to 5 Guide to Combating Sexual Harassment, The (Bravo), 263
Ninotchka, 612
Nintendo, 641-42
Nirvana, 599-600
Nissan Maxima SE, 568
Nissan 300ZS Turbo, 569
Nixon, Richard, 94
Nocturnes (Debussy), 605
Nohoch Mul pyramid, 453
Nokia, 657
No-Load Fund Analyst, 35
Noload Fund Investor, 18
Nolo Press, 693
nonsteroidal anti-inflammatory medications, 146-47, 244
Norplant, 272
Norpramin (desipramine), 235
Norte, El, 615
North:
grasses for, 427-28
rock-and-roll shrines in, 596
North American Falconers Association, 746
North American Menopause Society, 241
North By Northwest, 622
North By Northwest Festival, 603
North Carolina, 45, 536
North Cascades National Park, 482, 491
North Cascades Stehekin Lodge, 498
North Country National Scenic Trail, 503
North Dakota, 494
Northeast:
house prices in, 63
vacation homes in, 76-77
North Georgia Wilderness, 491
Northstar-at-Tahoe, 738
Northwest Airlines, 541-42
Northwestern Coffee Mills, 172
Northwoods Scenic Byway, 508-9
Norton, Dean, 428
Norton Utilities, 653
nortriptyline (Pamelor), 235
Norway, whale watching in, 533
nose surgery, 187-88, 191
Nothing But a Man, 617
Not Too Small to Care, 359
Nouvel, Jean, 468
Nozze di Figaro, Le (Mozart), 606
NPR Guide to Building a Classical CD Collection, *The* (Libbey), 604
nuglutang, 644
Nukolii Beach Park, 450
Numismatic News, 94
Nuprin, 232
Nuremburg Museum, 93
nurses, 225, 237, 241
nursing homes, 46-48
Nye, Bill, 296-97

O

Oahu, 444, 448-50
Oakhill House, 471
Obersteinberg, 529
Oberweis Report, 18
O'Brien, Margaret, 636
obsessive-compulsive disorders, 234-35
obstetrician-gynecologists (OB-GYNs):
fees of, 226
women as, 338
Occupational Outlook Handbook, 353
occupational therapists, 225
Oceanic Society, 521
oceanography, 322-23
Ocko, Stephanie, 521
Ocoee River, 535-36
office audits, 109
Office of Alternative Medicine, 247
Office of Investor Assistance, 20
Official NBA Guide, 712
Official NBA Register, 712
Official Scrabble Players Dictionary, 749
Off Ramp, The, 599
O'Halloran, Greg, 393
O'Hare Airport, 540
O'Higgins, Michael, 7-8
Ohio, 375
Ohio Casualty Corp., 13
Ohiopyle State Park, 535
oil-based paints, 389, 401
Okavango, 516
O'Keeffe, Linda, 382
Okidata, 657
Oldman, Mark, 340
Old Parsonage Hotel, 471
olestra, 161
Oliver!, 636-37
Oliver & Company, 636-37
Oliver Twist, 636-37
Olivier, Laurence, 637
Olney, Richard, 178
Olympic National Park, 487-88
omega-3 fatty acids, 162-63
Onassis, Jacqueline Kennedy, 86
One-Eyed Jacks, 610
One Flew Over the Cuckoo's Nest, 617
100 dollar bills, redesign of, 93
O'Neil, Patti, 331
OneSource, 36
On-Line Xpress, 678
On the Waterfront, 617
oolong tea, 173

Opéra National de Paris Bastille, 468
operas, 606-7
operating systems, 659
ophthalmology, 224
optimism, 329
Oracle Corp., 655
oral mucosal transudate (OMT), 280
oral sex, 280
oranges, 170
OraSure HIV-1 Oral Specimen Collection device, 280
orca (killer) whales, 532-33
Oregon:
national parks in, 494
rafting in, 534
retirement, 44
Oregon National Historic Trail, 506
organic matter, 416, 419
Oriental lilies, 420
oriental rugs, 75
Oriental shorthairs, 439
Origins, 183
Orlando (Woolf), 467
Orlando Furioso (Vivaldi), 607
Orme, Ted, 566
Orphan Annie, 87
Orthene, 423
orthopedics, 222
orthopedic shoes, 101
orthopedic surgeons, 227
Orudis KT, 232
O'Shaughnessy, James P., 24
Osmocote, 413
Osmocote+Iron, 423
osteoporosis, 161, 219, 222, 241
Ostergren, Lucy, 267
ostriches, 432
OTC Insight, 18
Otello (Verdi), 606
Ottawa National Forest, 497
Ottlik, Geza, 757
Oui, 688
Our Times Multimedia Encyclopedia of the 20th Century, 666
outdoor sports, 713-22
Out of the Past, 622
Outside, 717
Outward Bound, 537
ovarian cancer, 271
oven cleaners, 400
Overmountain Victory National Historic Trail, 506
Overseas Adventure Travel, 518
Over-the-Hill-Gang snowboard camps, 733
owned real estate (OREs), 78
oxen statues that pee, 559
Ozark National Forest, 509

P

Pacal, Lord, King of the Mayans, 454
Pacific Brokerage, 20-21
Pacific Crest National Scenic Trail, 504
Pacific Northwest, 599
Pacific Science Center, 641
Pacific stock funds, 26
Packard Bell Electronics, 654-55
Packwood, Robert, 167
Padre Island, 451
Paine Webber, 32
painkillers, 232, 244
paintings:
collecting of, 79-81, 86, 89
framing and displaying of, 393
paints and painting, 388-89, 401
Pakistan, 525
Palace Station Casino, 701
Palenque, 454
Palmer, Arnold, 446
Palmer, Lili, 635
Palmer, Lynne, 368-69
Palmer, Pete, 712
Palmer, Stacy, 121
Pamelor (nortriptyline), 235
Panasonic, 632, 657
panic disorders, 234-35
Paniolo Hale, 447
pantothenic acid (vitamin B5), 151-52
Paper Chase, 406
Papillote Wilderness Retreat, 461
pap smears, 214-15
Papua New Guinea, 731
Parc Naturel Régional de la Corse, 524
parental leave, 358
parents:
ADHD and, 208-9
adoption for, 204-5
after-school work and, 292
education and, 282-85, 288-95, 301
gays and, 264-65
Internet and, 696
loans to children by, 57
reading and, 293-94
relations between teachers and, 291
and software for children, 670-71
sports and, 703-4, 707, 733
of teenage drivers, 589-90
and telling children about sex, 259-60
see also pregnancies
Parents, 433
Paris:
bargain shopping in, 474
travel to, 468-69, 474, 514
Park, Barbara, 638
Parker Brothers, 642, 748
Parker Ranch, 444
Parkinson's disease, 237
Parks, Tricia, 405
Parks Associates, 405
parlor games, 747-60
board, 750-52
card, 753-58
Monopoly, 747-49
pool, 759-60
Scrabble, 749
Parnate (tranylcypromine), 235
paroxetine (Paxil), 235
Parque Nacional Corcovado, 519
parsley, 412
Parsons, Tom, 545-46
part-time jobs, 113, 321, 358
Pasadena Nifty Fifty, 37
Passion for Art, A, 667
pastrami, 177
pastry dough, 165
Patagonia, 533
Patagonia, Inc., 359, 361
paternity leave, 359, 361
Pathfinder, 609
Paths of Glory, 617
Patient Education Media, Inc., 211
Patient Investor, The (Carret), 2
patient's bill of rights, 216
patio planters, 412
Pat's, 449-50
Paxil (paroxetine), 235
Payne, Roger, 532
PBS, 46, 165, 296, 411, 674
PC Computing, 656, 664
PC Financial Network, 23
PC Magazine, 651, 656, 660, 675-76, 679, 680, 693
PC Week, 693
peaches, 169-70
Pearl Jam, 599
pears, 169-70
peat moss, 425
Pebble Beach, 721
Peck, Gregory, 366
Pecos, 497
pediatrics and pediatricians, 224, 226
pediculosis pedis, 277
Peet's Coffee & Tea, 172
peewee football, 707
Peggy Guggenheim Collection, 341
Pei, I. M., 388, 468
Pell Grants, 321
Pemigewasset, 497
penicillin, 228, 278
penis envy, 258
Pennington, Sam, 82
Pennsylvania, rafting in, 535
Penny Saved..., A (Godfrey and Richards), 112
Pension Goderli, 529
pension plans, 48, 55, 316
life insurance and, 124
as perks, 356
see also specific types of pension plans
Pentium processor, 650, 652, 659-61
People, 608-9, 692
People's Chronology, 665
Pépin, Jacques, 165-67, 178
perennial ryegrass, 427
Perez, Carlos, 705
"Performance Today," 604
Pergolesi, Giovanni Battista, 607
Perkins, Carl, 598
Perkins, Ed, 548
Perkins Loan Program, 315
perks, 349-50, 356-61
of family-friendly employers, 358-59
flexible benefits and, 357
of interns, 340-41
job-protected leaves as, 360
more choices and less coverage of, 356-57
stagnation of, 349-50
vacations as, 357, 360
for working mothers, 361
Persian cats, 435, 439
personal communications systems (PCS), 120
Personal Finance, 18
Personal Tax Edge, 678
Persuasion, 466
Peru:
hiking in, 523
rain forests of, 520
Pesando, James, 80
Peter's fertilizer, 413
Peterson, Randy, 543
pets, 431-42
cats, 435, 437-42
dogs, 433-36, 440-42
exotic, 431-32
holistic care for, 436
inbred, 435, 439
insurance for, 442
vaccinations for, 436, 440-42
virtual, 442
Pettie, George, 395-97
petunias, 412
Petzal, Dave, 744-46
Pez candy dispensers, 88
Pez Collectors News, 88
Pfeiffer, Eckhard, 349
Phantom Ranch, 498
Pharmacia & Upjohn, Inc., 185
pharmacology, 320
phase-back work option, 358-59, 361
phenelzine (Nardil), 235
Philadelphia Story, The, 612
Philanthropic Advisory Service (PAS), 122
Philippines Airlines, 539
Philips Media Home and Family Entertainment, 674
Phillips, Bruce, 374-75
Phillips Fine Art Auctioneers, 95
philosophy, 319
phobias, 234-35
Phoenix, The, 647
phosphorus, 154
photographic chemicals, 400-401
physicals, 214
physical therapists, 222, 225
women as, 339
Physician's Health Study, 150
physics, 323
physiology, 320
Piano Sonata K. 448 (Mozart), 298
Piano Sonatas in B Flat Major and A Major (Schubert), 605
pibloktoq, 236
Picasso, Pablo, 80-81
Pickup Truck, 639
Pierpont Morgan Library, 326
Pike Place Brewer, 175
pineapples, 170
pineapple sorbet, 166
pine bark, 416
Pinehurst, 721
Pinocchio (Collodi), 638
Pioneer Fund, 2
Pioneer Inn, 446
Pisces, 368
pitchforks, 414
Pitt, Brad, 597
Pittsburgh Cinema Project, 608
Pittsburgh Pirates, 725
Place in the Sun, A, 617-18
Planning Your Retirement, 60
plants, planting, 415-18, 420
container, 411-13
preparations for, 416
selection of, 421

vegetable, 417-18
plaque, 156
plastic surgery, 187-93
platinum, 90
Playground Politics, The (Greenspan and Salmon), 282
Playmobil, 640
Playskool, 639-40
Playskool Playstore, 639-40
plums, 169-70
Plum Stain, 183
Plymouth, 566
pneumonia, 228-29
podophyllin, 277
Point, 688
point-of-service care, 213-14
Point-to-Point Protocols (PPPs), 682
poker:
  five-card draw, 753
  high-low, 754
  low-hand, 753-54
polar bear swimming, 743
polar bear watching, 522
pole vaulting, 707
polishes, furniture, 400
political memorabilia, 87
political science, 323
politics, Web sites on, 692
Polk, Melanie, 174
Polo Ralph Lauren, 341
Polynesia, The, 554-55
Polynesian Cultural Center, 448
Ponce de Leon, Juan, 237
Pontius Pilate, 93
Pony Express Trail, The, 506
poodles, 433-35
pool, 759-60
pool chemicals, 401
Poor, Alfred, 675-76
Poor Little Rich Girl, The, 618
Pop, Iggy, 599
Pope, Robin, 518
Popo Agie, 497
popular culture, books on, 328
Popular Mechanics New Car Buyers Guide 1996, 668
Population Council, 274
Pop-Up Pals Piano, 639
Porsche 911 Carrera, 569
portfolios, 286-87
posers, 734
post-traumatic stress disorder, 234
posture, 662-63
potassium, 154-55
Potomac Appalachian Trail Club Cabins, 499
Potomac Heritage National Scenic Trail, 504
pottery, collecting of, 87
Povich, Lynn, 338
Power! (Korda), 345
Power Books, 660-61
Power Computing Corp., 654
Power Japanese, 673
power lunches, 345
power of attorney, durable, 59
Power PC chip, 655, 659-60
"Power Rangers," 633
Power Spanish, 673
Prairie, La, 183
praying mantises, 424
Precious Moments Chapel, 559
preferred provider option (PPO), 581
preferred provider organizations (PPOs), 213-14
pregnancies, 194-203, 208
  ADHD and, 208
  birth defects and, 200-202
  fetus growth and, 197
  figuring due dates for, 196-97
  hospital stays and, 206
  infertility and, 202-3
  late, 194-95, 200-203
  timing sexual intercourse for, 203
  what to expect in, 198
  see also abortion; contraception
prehistoric forest, 558
Preliminary SATs (PSATs), 303
premenstrual cramps, 232
Preminger, Eve, 526-29
premiums, collecting of, 87
preschoolers, 283
  toys for, 639-41
Prescriptives, 183
President's Council on Physical Fitness and Sports, 145
Presidio National Historic Landmark, 507
Presley, Elvis, 598
Pretend Soup & Other Real Recipes (Katzen and Henderson), 648
previous channel, 627
Price-Costco/Price Club, 118
price/earnings ratios, 11, 16
Pride and Prejudice, 637
Primal Rage, 669
Primestar, 627
Princess Cruises, 552
Princeton, N.J., 46
Princeton Review, 673
  The Student Access Guide to Paying for College 1995 Edition, 316
printers, 650-51
  color, 656-57
  copies and faxes in combination with, 657
  evaluation of, 657
prints, collecting of, 80
Prisoner of War, 610
Prisoner of Zenda, The, 618
Pritchard, Paul, 491, 496
Procari, John, 713
Procter & Gamble (P&G), 161, 339
Prodigy, 23, 684, 694
  Bill Payer, 119
Produce Marketing Association, 169
production occupations, 355
Professional Association of Diving Instructors (PADI), 730
professional specialty occupations, 353-54
professions, *see* careers
profit-sharing plans, 48, 55
progesterone, 254-55
progestin, 241, 269, 271
progress, books on, 327
Project Vote Smart, 692
Pro Logic circuitry, 629
Promix, 413
property taxes, 66
Prosek, James, 727
Prosperity Signs (Palmer), 368
prostate cancer, 148, 242-43, 255, 273
prostate specific antigen (PSA), 242-43
prostate surgery, 223, 242
protein:
  cholesterol and, 156, 158
  in diet, 153, 158-60
  for pets, 436
protest, books on, 327
Providentiales, 730-31
Provo River, 728
Prozac (fluoxetine), 225, 235
Prudential, 32
Prudent Speculator, The, 18
pruners and pruning, 414, 426
PSINet Pipeline USA, 684
psychiatrists and psychiatry, 233-34, 344
  hospitals specializing in, 225
  and therapy, 233, 290
Psycho, 620
psychoactive drugs, 233-35
psychological profiles, 344-45
psychologists and psychology, 225, 344-45
  graduate schools in, 323
  and homes, 382-83
psychopharmacology, 225
public accountants, 105
Public Health Service, 243, 272
public land purchases, 78
Puccini, Giacomo, 606
puerh tea, 173
Puerto Rico:
  travel to, 456
  winter baseball in, 705
Pulp Fiction, 266, 610
Pumpkin Ridge, 721-22
purchase option, 574-75
Purgatory Resort, 738
Puzo, Mario, 345
Pyramid for Success, 362-63
pyroxidine (vitamin B6), 152

Q

Quain, John R., 656-57
Quaker Oats, 357
Qualcomm, 685
qualified terminable interest property (QTIP) trusts, 57-58
Quality/Comfort Inns, 556
Quantum Fund, 7
QuarkXpress, 679
quartz lamps, 392
Queen Elizabeth II, 455
Queensberry Hotel, 471
Quest for Value Opportunity fund, 40
Quick & Reilly, 21
QuickBooks, 675
Quicken, 119, 675, 677-78
  Deluxe, 677
  Financial Planner, 678
QuickSite, 695
Quiet American, The (Greene), 464
Quin, Bradley J., 305
Quinebaug & Shetucket Rivers Valley National Heritage Corridor, 507
Quintana Roo, 453-54
Quotesmith, 129

rabies, 440
raccoons, 440
Race Across America, 717
radiation, 218, 223, 656
radiator fluid, 592
Radio Control Raceway, 642
radio premiums, 87
Radisson Seven Seas Cruises, 553-54
radon, 398
rafting trips, 534-36
  guide to, 535
  ultimate, 536
Raging Bull, 618
Raichlen, Steven, 178
Raid Gauloise, 717
rail bridges, 759
rail travel, 549-51
Rainbow Bar and Grille, The, 599
rain forests, 519-21
Rainforests (Castner), 519
rain insurance, 126
Raisin, 183
rakes, 414
Raleigh, Duane, 716
Ramones, 597
RAND Corporation, 246
random access memory (RAM), 654, 661, 671, 680
Random House, 345
  Unabridged Electronic Dictionary, 665
Random Walk Down Wall Street, A (Malkiel), 38
Raphael, 81
Rapp, Martin, 562
Raptor, 647
raspberry souffles in raspberry sauce, recipe for, 168
Rattle and Hum, 599
Rauscher, Frances, 298
Rawlins Territorial Prison, tours of, 558
Raymond, Dick, 419
RCA, 627
Reader's Digest Illustrated Guide to Gardening (Calkins), 415
reading, 293-94, 318, 673
Reagan, Ronald, 610
real estate, 61-78
  brokers for, 325
  public land purchases and, 78
  wills and, 59
  see also houses and homes
real estate investment trusts, 38
realism, 80
Reality Online, 677-78
rebate credit cards, 114, 116
rebaters, airlines, 548
Rebel Without a Cause, 618
receivers, audio, 630-31
recessions:
  entrepreneurship and, 374
  house purchases and, 61-62

recipes:
for children, 648
for desserts, 165-68
record keeping and banking, 677-78
records and record labels, 600-601
Redding, Otis, 598, 600
Red River, 623
Red Shift, 667
red wine, 160
Reebok, 343
Reederei, Peter Deilmann, 554
Reese, Terrence, 757
reference:
CD-ROMs for, 664-66
on sports, 712
Web sites for, 693
reflexology, 267
Regalbuto, Ronald, 479
Regency Cruises, 554
Regional Financial Associates, 61
rehabilitation:
hospitals specializing in, 225
women's careers in, 339
Reisman, Barbara, 358
Reiter, Russel, 237
religion, 319-20
REM, 598, 603
Remains of the Day, The 466
Rembrandt van Rijn, 81
Remodeling, 384
Renakee, Jeff, 536
renal disease, 232
Renaud, Serge, 160
renegotiable rate mortgages, 68
Rennard, Stephen, 176
Reno, Janet, 265
Reno Air, 541
Renova, 180-81
Rent A Home International, 472
rental car insurance, 126, 128
repairers, salaries of, 355
repeaters, 408
repetitive stress injuries (RSI), 662
replacement cost homeowner's insurance, 128
reproductive tract cancers, 220
Reservoir Dogs, 610
Residential Lighting (Whitehead), 392
Resnik, Barry, 185
restaurants, 475-77
Reston, James, 248
résumés, 367
careers and, 342-43, 346-47
retardation, 208
Retin A, 180
retinas, detached, 224
retirement, 44-60
assisted-living for, 47
careers and, 342
in Caribbean, 461
in college towns, 44-46, 332
congregate housing for, 46-47
distribution, 100
estate planning for, 57-59
financial and legal mileposts of, 48
401(k) plans and, 48-49, 52-53
independent-living for, 46-47
inflation and, 50
IRAs and, 48, 53-54, 100, 104, 106, 316
life-care communities for, 48
money management in, 60
in nursing homes, 46-48
perks and, 356
places for, 44-46
salaries and, 350
savings for, 48-56
SEP plans and, 55
Social Security and, 48-51, 55, 60
software for planning of, 22, 60
in Sun Belt, 44
taxes and, 44-45, 51-59, 97, 100, 104
vacation homes for, 77
variable annuities for, 56
wills and, 57-59
Retirement Places Rated (Savageau), 44-46
Retreat House, The, 479
Reuters Money Network, 678
Reventazon River, 478
Revere, Ann, 635-36
reverse annuity mortgages (RAMs), 70
Revolutionary War, 506
Reynolds, Debbie, 636
rheas, 432
Rhine River, 531
Rhino catalog, 601
rhinoplasty, 187-88, 191
rhinos, 511-12, 516
Rhodes, Nancy, 295
rhododendrons, 420
rhubarb, 412
rhytidectomy, 187-90
riboflavin (vitamin B2), 151
Rice, Bill, 475
Richard Band's Profitable Investing, 18
Richard Bonham Safaris, 518
Richards, Tad, 112
Richardson, Bradley G., 342-43
Rich Die Richer and You Can Too, The (Zabel), 57
Richie Rich, 643
Richmond, Phyllis, 477
rides, amusement park, 645-47
Ride the High Country, 623
rifles, assault, 408
Right Through the Pack (Darvas and Hart), 757
right (bowhead) whales, 532-33
Riley, Pat, 362
Rinaldo (Handel), 607
Ring Deutscher Makler, 473
rings, 90
Rio Bravo, 610
Rio Grande, rafting on, 535
Ripken, Cal, Jr., 703
Rise of the National Park Ethic, The (Winks), 480
Rist, Oliver, 658
Ritalin, 209
River Days (Renakee), 536
River Runner's Guide to The History of The Grand Canyon, A (Crumbo), 536
Roadside America Project, 558
Roasters Select Coffee of the Month Club, 172
robber flies, 424
Robbins, Gordon, 733
Robert Aufderheide Memorial Drive, 509
robotics, 335
Robotix, 641
Rob Roy, 610
Roche, Gerard, 367
Rock, Tools, and Technique (Raleigh and Benge), 716
Rock and Ice, 715
rock-and-roll, 605
festivals, 602-3
shrines, 596-99, 712
Web sites for, 689
rock climbing, 715-16
Rock Creek, 727
Rockers, Glenn, 95
Rock 'n' Road (Toula), 716
Rocky Mountain elk, 500
Rocky Mountain National Park, 487-89, 500
Roe v. Wade, 275
Rogaine, 185
Rogers, Jim, 24, 50
Roget's Thesaurus, 665
roller coasters, 645-47
roller hockey, 713
Rolling Thunder, 610
romaine lettuce, 412
Roman Empire, coins from, 93
Rombauer, Irma, 178
Rome, bargain shopping in, 474
Romischer Kaiser, 470
roof leaks, 395
Rooney, Mickey, 636
Root, Waverley, 178
Roraima (The Lost World), 513
Rorschach tests, 344
Rose, Carl, 725
rosemary, 412
roses, 423
Rosewood B&B, 450
Rossini, Gioacchino, 606
Ross Lake Resort, 498-99
Rosso, Julee, 178
Rote Rose, 469
rototillers, 414
rotweilers, 435
Rough guides, 562
Royal Caribbean Cruise Line, 552
Royal Chitwan, 512
Royal Tyrrell Museum of Paleontology, 95
R.S. Means Company, 384
Rubens, Peter Paul, 467
Rudenstein, Neil, 372
Rudy, 635
RU-486 (mifepristone), 270, 274-75
rug cleaners, 401
Ruhm, Christopher, 111
running shoes, 144
runny nose, 229
Rupp, Adolph, 362
Russell, Bertrand, 357
Russia:
guided expeditions to, 537
sexuality in, 258
wilderness areas in, 512-13
Russian blues, 439
rust-proofing coatings, 401
Rutledge, Ann, 634
Rwanda, wilderness areas in, 513
Ryato, 514
Ryder-Walker Alpine Adventures, 743
Rykodisk, 600-601

S

Saas Fee, walking from Grachen to, 527-28
Saba, 459
Sabbathday Lake Shaker Community, 479
Sackville-West, Vita, 467
Sacred Falls Wild Park, 449
safaris, 515-18
Safety Last, 612-13
Sagarmatha Environmental Foundation, 715
Sagittarius, 369
Saigon, 464-65
sailfish, 728
sailing:
in Caribbean, 463
in Galapagos, 522
St. Augustine grass, 427
St. Augustine's House, 479
St.-Barthélemy, 460
St. Croix, 458
Saint Hilda's House, 479
St. James, Lyn, 584-87
St. John, 458, 522
St. Kitts, 460
Saint Leo Abbey, 479
St. Lucia, 461-62
St. Mary's Episcopal Church, 598
St. Stan's Brewery, 175
St. Thomas, 457
St. Vincent, 462
salaries, 102, 349-55
average entry-level, 361
of CEOs, 349-50, 352
and current trends in workplace, 352
for interns, 340-41
maintaining middle-class lifestyle and, 350
of men vs. women, 338, 349
mortgages and, 68-69, 71
by occupation, 353-55
physical appearance and, 359
raises and, 349, 351
stagnation of, 349-51
sale of assets, commissions on, 101
Sales Ally, 675
sales contracts, 71
salespersons, 339, 354
Salisbury, Robert Cecil, First Earl of, 467
Salmon, J., 282
Salmon River, 534
Salome (Rubens), 467
Salomon, R. S., Jr., 4
Salon, 690
salt, 150, 155
Salt of the Earth, 618
Saltwater Fly-Fishing, 728
Salvation Army, 113
Samana Bay, 533
Sampras, Pete, 724
Sam's Club, 118
Sanctuary Woods, 669, 673
Sanders, Gordon, 713
sandhill cranes, 500-501

Sandpoint, Idaho, 45
Sand Rivers, 518
San Francisco, Calif., 477
San Francisco 49ers, 364
San Juan National Forest, 497, 509
Sano, Darrell, 695
Santa Barbara Island, 730
Santa Fe National Forest, 497
Santa Fe National Historic Trail, 506
Santamour, Frank, 425
Santangelo, Anthony, 186
sapphires, 90
Sarcev, Ursula, 142-43
Sartre, Jean-Paul, 468
satellite phones, 525
Satin Finish Foundation, 183
Satin Taupe, 183
Saturn, 566
Savageau, David, 44-46
Savage-Marr, Pamela, 174
savings:
  careers and, 342
  houses and, 62, 71
  penalties for early withdrawal of, 101
  of pennies, 113
  for retirement, 48-56
Savings Bonds, U.S., 102
Sawgrass, TPC at, 722
Sax, Richard, 178
scalping tickets, 700
Scanam World Tours, 473
Scandinavia Dancenter, 473
scanners, 650-52
Scarface, 618
Scarlet Letter, The, 608
scenic byways, 508-9
Scenic Byways (Magley), 508
scents, sexually arousing, 258
Schaffer, Mat, 475
Scheck, Art, 728
Scheiber, Anne, 6
Schell, Maximilian, 636
Scheluchin, Andre, 22
Schiller, Donald, 130-31
Schindler's List, 610
scholarships, 102
Scholastic Assessment Tests (SATs), 298, 303-5, 314, 673
  dates for, 303
  recentering scores of, 305
schools, 102
  charter, 288-89
  see also education, primary and secondary
Schubert, Franz, 604-5, 667
Schubert, The Trout Quintet, 667
Schulte Roth & Zabel, 57
Schwab, Howie, 712
Schwarzenegger, Arnold, 86
Schwarzkopf, Norman, 242
Science, 264
science and scientists, 641
  CD-ROMs on, 666-67
  education in, 286-87, 296-97, 300-301
  experiments in, 297
  software for children on, 674
Science Fiction: The Multimedia Encyclopedia of Science Fiction, 665
Science Fiction Continuum, 625
science fiction films, 624
Scientific Learning Principles, 294
Scorpio, 369
Scotland:
  barge trips in, 530
  villa rental in, 473
Scott, Cynthia, 372-74
Scott, Norman, 146
Scott, Walter, 610
Scott Catalog, The, 94
scouting, 406
  education and, 290, 301
Scrabble, 749
Scuba Diving, 729
Scuol, walking to Ftan from, 528
Seabourn's Pride & Spirit, 553
Sea Cloud, 554
seafood, grilling of, 174
Sea Goddess I & II, 552-53
Sea Lion Caves, 501
Searchers, The, 623
sea salvage coins, 94
Seated Liberty half dollars, 92
Seattle, Wash., dining in, 477
Seattle Mariners, 705
Sebastian Thick Ends, 184
second opinions, 212
Secret Garden, The, 636
Section 179 deductions, 98
secured credit cards, 117
Securities and Exchange Commission (SEC), 12, 19-20, 23
Securities Industry Association, 112, 405
security systems, 383, 405
seeds, 415
Sega, 642
Seifert, George, 364
selective serotonin reuptake inhibitors (SSRIs), 235
Selectquote, 129
self-defense, 406-10
self-employed health insurance, 99
self-employment tax, 101-2
seller take-back mortgages, 69
Selous Game Reserve, 516
Selvel, Karl, 566
semiconductors, 334
Sendak, Maurice, 638
Sense and Sensibility, 466
Se Pa, 465
Serengeti National Park, 515-16
Serial Line Internet Protocols (SLIPs), 682-83
Serif PagePlus, 679
serigraphs, 80
sertraline (Zoloft), 235
Serva Padrona, La (Pergolesi), 607
service firms and industries, 375
  careers in, 337
  home-based, 377-78
  salaries in, 355
Settlement Cookbook, The (Kander), 178
seven-card stud, 754-55
1776, 634
7th Guest, The, 669
Seventh Heaven, 618
7th Level, 669
sex, sexuality, 203, 253-80, 514
  and age, 255, 257-58, 260, 268, 276
  and AIDS, 278-80
  CD-ROMs on, 667-68
  and contraception, *see* contraception
  drive for, 254-55
  and embarrassment, 261-62
  and foot massage, 266-67
  and harassment, 263
  and homosexuality, 260, 262, 264-65, 300
  and impotence, 276
  and intimate experiences over lifetime, 257
  of men vs. women, 254-55, 257-58
  money vs., 258
  telling children about, 259-60
  see also abortion; contraception
Sex Information (Alman), 261
sexually transmitted diseases (STDs), 259-60, 277-78
Sgrisches Lake, walking from Sils Maria to, 528
Shadow of a Doubt, 622
Shadows, 618
Shaggy Dog, The, 637
Shah, D. J., 131
Shaindlin, Andy, 330
Shakespeare, William, 7, 326, 365
Shane, 623-24
Shannon River, 530-31
shared appreciation mortgages, 69
Shaw, Gordon, 298
Shawangunk Mountains, 716
shears, 414
Shekelle, Paul, 246
Shelley bone china, 87
Shenandoah National Park, 499
shenkui (shen-k'uei), 236
Shepherd's Garden Seeds, 415
Sher, Barbara, 344
Sheraton, Thomas, 83
Sherlock, Jr., 618
Shifting Gears (Beck), 334
Shikoku, 533
Shimizu, Holly, 411-13
shingles, roof, 395, 399
Shi Shi Beach, 451
shoes, 144
shopping:
  dollars & sense guide to, 118
  for fruits, 169-70
  for records, 601
  for travelers, 474
shopping clubs, 118
Shopping for Health (Havala), 159
Shop Talk, 571
"Shortchanging Girls, Shortchanging America," 300
short-term world income funds, 26
Shoshone National Forest, 497
shoulders:
  exercises for, 140-41, 147
  injuries to, 146-47
shovels, 414, 416
Showtime, 627
Shriver, Maria, 86
Shula, Don, 362, 366
Siamese, 439
sick-child days, 358, 361
sick leave, 360
Sid and Nancy, 597
siding, 399
  replacement of, 385-86
Siegel, Jeremy J., 4, 24
Sierra-at-Tahoe, 738
Sierra Club, 449
Sierra Nevada Brewing Co., 175
Sierra Online, 668, 672-74
Sietsema, Tom, 477
sildenafil (Viagra), 276
silicon gel-filled breast implants, 193
Silk Groom, 184
Sils Maria, walking to Sgrisches Lake from, 528
Silver, 84-85
silver collecting, 84-85, 87, 90, 92-94
Silver Palate Cookbook, The (Rosso, Lukins, and McLaughlin), 178
Silverstein, Shel, 638
silverware, 75
simian immunodeficiency virus (SIV), 280
Simmons, Jean, 636
Simmons, Marie, 178
Simon, Paul, 556
Simon, S. J., 757
Simon & Schuster, 345, 672
Simone, Luisa, 679-80
Simple French Food (Olney), 178
simplified employee pension (SEP) plans, 55
Simpson, O. J., 378
simulation games, 318
Sineqan (doxepin), 235
Singapore, honeymoons in, 478
Singapore Airlines, 541-42
Singin' in the Rain, 621
Single Inline Memory Modules (SIMMs), 654, 659
Sint Eustatius (Statia), 460
Sint Maarten, 459-60
Siscovick, David, 162-63
Six Flags amusement parks, 646-47
6.0V Jet Turbo Rebound 4x4, 640
60 Minutes, 160
Skeleton Coast, 511-12
Skete of Saint Seraphim, 479
Ski Gate, 739
skiing, 522, 733-40
  best resorts for, 735-37
  hourglass skis for, 739-40
  ski lengths for, 740
  smaller and cheaper resorts for, 738
  snow stats for, 737-38
  on World Wide Web, 739
skill-based salaries, 351
skin:
  breast cancer and, 238
  cancer of, 179-81, 211
  care of, 179-81, 187-90
  HRT and, 241
  laser resurfacing of, 189
Skinnybones (Park), 638
Skolnick, Arnold, 88
skunks, 440
skylights, 383, 393
slackers, 342-43
Slater, Robert, 24
Sleator, William, 638
sloth bears, 511

Slow Boat Through Germany (McKnight), 530
Small Business Administration (SBA), 374-75
small claims courts, 132
small company stock and funds, 6-7, 9, 26, 37
Smart Bookmarks, 688
SmartMoney, 22, 32
Smell & Taste Treatment and Research Foundation, 258
Smith, Barbara, 344
Smith, Emmitt, 699
Smith, Joseph, 505
Smith, Ken, 558-59
Smith & Hawken, 415
Smith Barney, 11, 36
Smithsonian Institution, 519
Smith's Tropical Paradise, 450
smoking:
  birth control pills and, 271
  diet and, 149-50, 153
  looking great and, 180-81
  pregnancies and, 194, 208
snack foods, guilt-free, 161
Snake River, 534
Snootz Math Trek, 672
snorkeling, 729-31
Snowbird, Utah, 736
snowboarding, 733-34
Snow Country, 735-36, 739-40
Snowmass, Colo., 736-37
snowmobiling, 742-43
snowshoeing, 741-42
soccer, 707, 711-12
social phobias, 234-35
Social Security:
  life insurance and, 124
  retirement and, 48-51, 55, 60
  taxes on benefits from, 97
Social Security numbers, 106
Social Security tax, 99, 101-2
social workers, 225
Society of Actuaries, 125-26
sociology, 323
Socrates, 332
sofas, purchasing of, 390
softball, 725
SoftKey International, 665-66
SoftQuad, 680, 695
software, 655, 664-80
  on CD-ROMs, 664-69, 673-74
  and childproofing computers, 671
  for children, 666, 670-74
  computer upgrades and, 659
  for DTP, 679-80
  educational, 664, 670, 672-74
  for finances, 677-78
  for list lovers, 675-76
  for retirement planning, 22, 60
  spreadsheets and, 676
  for tax preparation, 108, 677-78
  women's careers in development of, 339
  for writers, 680
soil testing, 416
solitaire, 758
Some Like It Hot, 613
Something Wicked This Way Comes (Bradbury), 638
Song of the Flower, 553-54
SonicNet, 689
Sony, 632, 641-42, 689
sorbets, fruit, 166
Soren Lindstrom Safaris, 518
sore throats, 229
SOROS (Slater), 24
Soros, George, 7
Sotheby's, 81, 84, 86, 88, 90
sound cards, 659, 671
Soundgarden, 599-600
Sound of Music, The, 610
sound systems, 629-31, 652
soups, 176
South:
  grasses for, 427-28
  rock-and-roll shrines in, 598-99
  vacation homes in, 77
South Africa:
  tracking game in, 522
  whale watching in, 533
South American coffees, 171
South By Southwest (SxSW) Festival, 602-3
South Dakota:
  national parks in, 494
  retirement in, 44
Southern Africa, 516-17
Southern Ocean Whale Sanctuary, 533
Southland Ski Server, The, 739
South of the Border attraction, 559
South Pacific, 450
Southwest Airlines, 538, 541-42
soy protein, 158, 160
spades (card game), 756-58
Spain, country inns in, 471
spaniels, 434-35
spatial reasoning, 298
speakers:
  for computers, 671
  for sound systems, 631
  for TVs, 626
Spearfish Canyon Highway, 509
specialists, 210-12, 214, 217, 223-24
special schooling, 102
specialty consulting, 377
specialty funds, 26, 28
speech therapists, 225
sperm, 202-3, 273
  production of, 258
spermicides, 272
sperm whales, 532-33
Spielberg, Steven, 610
spina bifida, 200, 222
spine:
  injuries to, 225
  manipulation of, 246
Spinella, Art, 566
SpinRite, 653
spiritual books, 328
Splendid Hotel, 470
Sport and Face Climbing (Long), 716
sports, 697-746
  best values in, 699
  betting on, 701
  CD-ROMs on, 668
  education and, 290, 301
  fan's guide to, 698-712
  films for children on, 635
  and getting tickets, 698-700
  in great outdoors, 713-32
  halls of fame of, 711-12
  injuries in, 146-47, 222, 225
  Web sites on, 690, 712
  in winter, 705, 733-46
  see also specific sports
spreadsheets, 676
Spyglass Hill, 721
squamous cell carcinoma, 211
Stafford, The, 471
Stafford loan, 315, 321
Stagecoach, 618
stain, 401
stamps:
  collecting of, 94-95
  dollars & sense guide to, 113
Standard & Poor's (S&P), 665
  500 stock index of, 5-6, 9, 13, 34, 37-38, 40-41, 80
Standard Catalogue of World Coins, 92
standard of living, 49
standard poodles, 433-34
Standards for English and Language Arts, 287
Starpress, 672
Star Trek, 664
Star Wars, 624
statistics, 323
Stax Volt Studios, 598
Stay Young the Melatonin Way, 237
Steamboat, Colo., 736
Steaming to Bamboola (Buckley), 555
Steamtown National Historic Site, 507
Steely Dan, 597-98
Steinberg, Laurence, 111
Steinroe's Young Investor Fund, 112
Steller's sea lions, 501
Stempler, David S., 543
Stengel, Casey, 364
Stephens, Jack, 442
Step One diets, 156
Step 2, 639-40, 642
Step Two diets, 157
step-ups, 143
stereo sound, 652
sterilization, 271, 273
Sterling Forest, 496
sterling silverware, 85
Stern Stewart, 10
Stevens, John, 518
Stevens, Ted, 496
Stevenson, Robert Louis, 638
Stewart, Patrick, 664
Still, Steve, 739-40
STI Management, 4
Stine, R. L., 638
Stingray City, 478, 730
Stinson, Craig, 676
Stockmarket Cycles, 18
stocks, 104, 125, 316
  art vs., 80
  capital loss on, 102
  dividends of, 6-9, 13, 16, 22
  Dow dividend approach to, 7-9
  foreign, 11-12
  hard assets vs., 4-5
  homeownership and, 66, 74, 76
  Internet and, 681
  no-load, 22
  on-line banking and, 119
  price/earnings ratios of, 11, 16
  for retirement, 50, 52-54, 56
  of small companies, 6-7, 9
  software for, 677-78
  taxes and, 106
  underachievers among, 9
  wills and, 59
Stocks for the Long Run (Siegel), 4, 24
Stock Trader's Almanac, 24
Stockwell, Dean, 636
Stolper, Michael, 42
stomach cancer, 399
  diet and, 148, 153
Stovall, Lou, 393-94
Stratford Advisory Group, 42
Stratosphere Tower, 647
Strauss, Richard, 606-7, 667
Strauss, Robert, 523
Strauss, Three Tone Poems, 667
Stravinsky, Igor, 667
Stravinsky, The Rite of Spring, 667
strawberries, 170
strawberry sorbet, 166
Street Smart, 678
Streisand, Barbra, 89
strength training, 142-43
strep throat, 229
stress, dealing with, 372-73
Stretch, Bonnie, 79
striped bass, 728
strokes, 225, 248
  drugs and, 232-33
Strom, Brian, 230
Strong Interest Inventory, 344-45
Stutz, David, 137
subnotebook computers, 660-61
Sub Pop Records, 600
Success! (Korda), 345
Suck, 693
suction-assisted lipectomy, 187-88, 191
sugar, 150, 161, 165-68
Sugarbush, Vt., 738
sugar gliders, 432
Sullivan's Travels, 613
sun, 179-81, 187, 191
Sun Belt, retirement in, 44
Sun Microsystems, 655
Sunrise, 622
sunscreens, 181
Sunset Boulevard, 618
Sun Studios, 598
suntan lotion, 181
Sun Valley, Idaho, 735
Super Bowl, 698, 700
support occupations, 354
Supreme Court, U.S., 544
  on abortion, 275
  on gay rights, 265
SurfWatch, 671, 696
surgeons and surgery, 211, 218, 222-23, 242
  cost of, 226-27
  plastic, 187-93
  questions to ask before, 212
survival skills, 537
Susan B. Anthony dollars, 92, 94
Susanna Foo Chinese Cuisine (Foo), 178
suspense films, 621-23
suspensions, 593
Susswein, Ruth, 114
Swalls, Peggy, 700
Sweden, villa rental in, 473
Swedish Travel & Tourism Council, 473

Sweet Smell of Success, 619
swimming, 731-32, 743
Swissair, 542
Swiss Alpine Club, 526-29
Swiss Family Robinson, The, 636
Switch 'n Sound Railroad, 642
Switzerland:
  country inns in, 469
  guided expeditions to, 537
  hiking in, 526-29
  map of, 527
  mountain inns of, 529
Sylvania, 497
Symantec, 653, 696
Syon House, 467
syphilis, 277-78
syrphid flies, 424
Systems & Forecasts, 18
System 7.5, 659

T

Tabb, Lisa, 522
Taberna del Alabardero, 471
tables, antique, 83
Tabu, 619
tachinid flies, 424
Tacrine, 221
tai chi, 247, 249
taijin kyofusho, 236
tailgaters, 585
Taking Charge of ADHD (Barkley), 208
Talking Heads, 597
Tallal, Paula, 294
tall fescues, 427-28
Tall Grass Prairie National Preserve, 491
Tall Ships, 554-55
Tambopata-Caudano Reserve Area and National Park, 520
tamoxifen, 241
tangerines, 170
Tanzania:
  guided expeditions to, 537
  traveling in, 515-16, 518
Taquino, Chris, 600
Tarantino, Quentin, 610
tarragon, 412
Tasmania, hiking in, 523-24
Tasso, Torquato, 607
Tate Museum, 95
Taurus, 368
tax attorneys, 106
taxes, 96-109
  audits on, 109
  charity and, 96-98, 101, 104-6, 109, 113, 122
  deductions on, *see* deductions on taxes
  electronic filing of, 107-8
  errors to avoid in, 106
  on estates, 57-59
  forms for, 97, 106-7
  on gifts, 57
  houses and, 62, 65-67, 69-70, 74, 78, 96-97, 101, 105, 109
  investing and, 6, 100, 104-6, 108-9
  life insurance and, 125
  on loans to family members, 131
  marriage and, 103
  mutual funds and, 26, 34-35, 38, 42-43, 106
  preparation of, 102
  professional preparation of, 105-6
  refunds and, 107
  retirement and, 44-45, 51-59, 97, 100, 104
  revising rules on, 96
  salaries and, 350
  software for, 108, 677-78
  and sources of tax-free income, 102
  state and local, 105-6
  tips on, 104
Taxi, 668
Taxi Driver, 619
tax preparation chains, 105
tax rates, 96, 99
tax refund loans, 107
Taylor, David, 729-31
Taylor, Elizabeth, 636-37
Tchaikovsky, Piotr Ilyich, 605
teachers, 317, 330-32
  education and, 284, 286-93, 299-301
  relations between parents and, 291
  return to college towns by, 331-32
  and software for children, 670
teas, 173
technicians, 354
Technique, Le (Pépin), 178
technology, books on, 329
Techserve, 678
Teen Movie Critic, 608
Tekken, 641
telecommunications, 335, 339
television (TV), 564, 571, 626-29, 650
  CD-ROMs on, 666
  for children, 633
  education and, 290
  rear projection, 627
  and software for children, 670-71
Telluride, Colo., 737
Temple, Shirley, 636
temporary help services, 378
tendonitis, 662
Teniers, David, 81
Tennessee:
  national parks in, 494
  rafting in, 535-36
tennis:
  books on, 712
  racquets for, 724
  tips on, 723-24
Tennyson, Alfred, Lord, 715
term life insurance, 124, 129
terriers, 434
testosterone, 254-55, 258
testosterone replacement therapy (TRT), 255
test-prep software, 673
tetracycline, 277-78
Tevye, 619
Texas:
  national parks in, 494
  retirement in, 44
Texas Giant, The, 647
Texas Instruments, 657
Texas Stadium, 699
Thames River, 530
Thank You for Smoking (Buckley), 555
Theatrix Interactive, 672, 674
They Call Me Coach (Wooden), 362-63
They Live By Night, 610
thiamin (vitamin B1), 151
Third Helpings (Trillin), 178
35mm point-and-shoot cameras, 632
thirty-year mortgages, 61-62, 68, 72, 74
Thomas, Clarence, 263
Thomas, Isiah, 635
Thomas Cook Overseas Timetable, 551
Thompson, Emma, 466
Thompson & Morgan, 415
Thorn, John, 712
Thornton, Yvonne, 194-95, 198
3D Atlas, 665
3D Landscape, 668
3DO, 642
Three Tables, 449
THX sound, 629
thyme, 412
thyroid disorders, 219
ticks, 252
Tieger, Paul, 345
Ties That Stress (Elkind), 289
Tiffany, 84, 87, 90
Tiger Electronics, 639, 642
Tiger Eyes (Blume), 638
tigers, 511-12
Tikal, Tikal National Park, 454
Tilton, Buck, 497
Time, 609, 692
Time-Life, 211
Timer Digest, 18
Time-Warner, 600, 609, 692
  Interactive, 669
tipping, 117
Tirestorm, 640
tire tread, 593-94
Titan II Missile Museum, 559
Tobago, 462-63
Tobias, Andrew, 678
Today's Gourmet, 165
Today's Kids, 640
Tofranil (imipramine), 235
toilet bowl cleaners, 401
toilets, leaking, 397
To Kill a Mockingbird, 619
Tomb, Geoffrey, 476
Tongass National Forest, 496
tools, gardening, 414-15
Top Hat, 621
Torres del Paine, 510-11
Tortola, 458
Toshiba, 627, 654
Total Baseball (Thorn, Palmer, and Gershman), 712
total hip replacements, 222
Total Immersion Adult Swim Camp, 731
totalitarianism, books on, 329
total return funds, 26-27
Touch of Evil, 622-23
Toula, Tim, 716
tourism vert, 522
Toyota Celica, 578
Toyota Motor Credit, 574
toy poodles, 434-35
toys, 639-42
  collecting of, 87
  recommended, 642
  scientists on, 641
Toys 'R' Us, 641
trackballs, 654, 661
tracking game, 522
Tracy, Spencer, 637
Trail of Tears Historic Trail, 506
Trails Across America (Miller and Miller), 504
Train, John, 24
train travel, 549-51
Transmission by Lucille, 592
Transparent Facecolor Allover Tint, 183
Transportation Department, U.S., 538, 544
transsexuals, 264
Trans Union, 114
tranylcypromine (Parnate), 235
travel, travelers, 443-526
  adventure for, 510-36
  in Africa, 515-18, 522-23
  air, *see* airlines, air travel
  bargain shopping for, 474
  on barges, 530-31
  beaches for, 444, 446-49, 451, 456-62, 470
  to Cambodia, 465
  to Caribbean, 455-63, 478
  CD-ROMs on, 668
  to Central America, 452-54, 478
  diner's guide for, 475-77
  eco-, 522
  European country inns for, 469-71
  to Great Britain, 466-67, 471, 473-74
  guides for, 562
  Hawaii for, 444-50, 478
  hiking for, 523-29
  honeymooner's guide for, 478
  hot spots for, 444-79
  mileage chart for, 560-61
  monastic guest houses for, 479
  motels for, 556-57
  to national historic trails, 503-6
  to national parks, 480-99
  to national scenic trails, 502-4
  to Paris, 468-69, 474, 514
  pointers on, 514
  rafting for, 534-36
  to rain forests, 519-21
  scenic byways for, 508-9
  by ship, 552-55
  survival skills for, 537
  by train, 549-51
  unusual attractions for, 558-59
  to Vietnam, 464-65
  villa rentals for, 472-73
  whale watching for, 532-33
  to wilderness areas, 496-99, 510-13, 516
  and wildlife, *see* wildlife
  see also vacations
travel agents, 518
Travel Avenue, 548
Traveler's Bookstore, 562
Traversee Internationale du Lac Saint-Jean, La, 717

Treasure Island (Stevenson), 638
Treasure of the Sierra Madre, The, 623
Treasury securities, 4-6, 14-15, 17, 25-26, 50
trees, 420-21, 425-26
  pruning of, 426
Treganowan, Lucille, 592-93
tricyclics (TCAs), 235
Trillin, Calvin, 178
Trinidad, 462-63
trolls, 88
Troon North, 722
Trouble in Paradise, 613
Trout (Prosek), 727
trowels, 414
T. Rowe Price, 50, 60
Trussell, James, 270
trustees, 58
trusts, 22, 38, 57-58
TRW, 114
Tschingelhorn, 529
tuberculosis, 228-29
tummy tucks, 191
Turbo Tax software, 108, 678
turkey, 176-77
Turkle, Sherry, 317-18
Turks, 730-31
Turnaround Letter, 18
turpentine, 401
TVNet, 689
TWA, 542-43
Twain, Mark, 449, 638
12 Angry Men, 366
12 O'Clock High, 366
Twenty-one, 755-56
2001: A Space Odyssey, 624
2XL, 642
TW Recreational Services Inc., 488
Tylenol (acetaminophen), 232, 244
typing, software for, 673-74

U

Uganda:
  traveling in, 516, 518
  wilderness areas in, 513
ulcers, 231-32, 274
Ultimate Doom, The, 669
Ultimate Frank Lloyd Wright America's Architect, The, 667
Ultimate Human Body, The, 668
ultrasound screening, 200-202
Uncharted Grounds, 172
Uncompahgre National Forest, 509
Undeland, John, 589-90
Underground Guide to PC Hardware, The (Poor), 675
Understanding Social Security, 60
unemployment tax, 97
Uniform Resource Locator (URL), 687, 694
United Auto Group, 564
United Nations, 484
United Parcel Service (UPS), 547, 657
United States:
  best colleges in, 306-13, 319-23
  best grad schools in, 319-23
  best hospitals in, 217-25
  best restaurants in, 475-77
  guided expeditions in, 537
  mileage chart for, 560-61
  sexuality in, 258
  train travel in, 551
unit-investment trusts, 22
universal life insurance, 125
University Research Expeditions Program, 521
Unser, Al, Jr., 587
upland birds, hunting for, 744-45
Upper Kiental Valley, 529
UP Records, 600
urinary tract infections, 229
urology, 223
USA Hockey, 742
USAir, 538
USA Today, 548
  Information Network of, 712
  Web page of, 692
U.S. Botanic Gardens, 411, 413
U.S. Curling Association, 741
Usenet newsgroups, 681-82, 687
U.S. Golf Association, 699
U.S. Open, 699
U.S. News & World Report, 217, 306-13, 692
U.S. Robotics, 658
Utah, national parks in, 494
Utah Public Lands Management Act, 496
Utah Wilderness, 496
uterine cancer, 136, 241
Utian, Wulf, 241
utopia, books on, 329
Uxmal, 453

V

Vacation Exchange Club, 472-73
vacation homes, 76-77
vacations:
  burglaries and, 402-3
  as perk, 357, 360
  working, 521
  see also travel and travelers
vaccinations, 214-15
  for children, 207
  for pets, 436, 440-42
Vail, Colo., 735-36
Vail Ski School, 739
Valais walks, 526-29
Valium (diazepam), 235
Value Line Investment Survey, 18
Van Gogh, Vincent, 79
Vanguard Group, 33, 60
  Index Trust 500 Portfolio of, 10
  Intermediate Corporate Bond fund of, 41
  Retirement Planner of, 60
  Windsor fund of, 37
Vanity Fair, 182
variable annuities, 56
variable life insurance, 125
Varmland Tourist Board, 473
varnish and varnish remover, 401
vasectomies, 273
Vatican:
  Library of, 326
  on movies, 610
Vaughan, Stevie Ray, 598-99, 602
Vaughn Next Century Learning Center, 288
VCR PLUS+, 628
vegetables, 436
  in diet, 148-49, 151-55, 157, 159-60, 174
  grilling of, 174
  planting of, 417-18
vegetarian diets, 152, 154, 159-60, 178
Vegetarian Resource Group, 159
Venezuela:
  hiking in, 523
  wilderness areas in, 513
  winter baseball in, 705
Venezuelan islands, 462-63
Venice Biennale, 341
Verdi, Giuseppe, 606
Vermont:
  retirement in, 44-45
  same-sex marriages in, 265
  vacation homes in, 76
Vertigo, 623
Veterans Administration (VA), 78
Veterinary Pet Insurance, 442
Viagra (sildenafil), 276
VIA Rail, 549
Vibe, 692
viburnum, 420
Vicarious, 666
Vicious, Sid, 597
Victory Garden, 411
video, videos, 634
  and education, 290
  equipment, 626-29, 632
  games, 294, 641
  mail-order, 625
video cassette recorders (VCRs), 627-29
Vietnam:
  CD-ROMs on, 666
  travel to, 464-65
Vietnam (Karnow), 464
Vietnam War, 464-65
Villa Brunella, 470
Villancourt, Bernard, 599
villa rentals, 472-73
viral infections, 228-29
Virbila, Irene, 476
Virgin Gorda, 458
Virginia, national parks in, 494
Virgin Interactive Entertainment, 669
Virgin Islands, British, 458
Virgin Islands, U.S., 522
  national park in, 458, 494, 499
  travel to, 457-58
Virgin Sound and Vision, 673
Virgo, 369
viropause, 255
Virtua Cop, 642
virtual pets, 442
Virtual Reality Laboratories, 666
Virtual Reality Modeling Language (VRML), 687
viruses, computer, 653, 696
vision problems, 207, 662-63
visiting students, 102
visual imagery, 247-48
vitamins, 148-53, 160
  A (beta carotene), 150-51, 161, 180
  B (biotin), 153
  B (folic acid), 152-53
  B-complex, 436
  B1 (thiamin), 151
  B2 (riboflavin), 151
  B3 (niacin), 151
  B5 (pantothenic acid), 151-52
  B6 (pyroxidine), 152
  B12, 152, 160
  C, 436
  D, 153, 161
  E, 149-50, 153, 161
  K, 161
  for pets, 436
Vitell, Phil, 475
Vivaldi, Antonio, 607
voice-mail, 658
Volcanoes National Park, 478
Volcano House, 445
Volhard, Wendy, 436
Volvo Guide to Halls of Fame (Dickson), 711
Voyageurs National Park, 481, 499

Waikiki, 448-49
Walcott, Derek, 462
Waldman, Sandra, 274
Waldrand, 529
Walking Tall, 610
Wallis, Donald R., 173
Wallowa-Whitman National Forest, 491
Wall Street Equities, 20-21
Wall Street Journal, 7, 14, 342, 349
WalMart, 564
Walpole, Horace, 467
Walt Disney World Magic Kingdom, 646-47
war, books on, 329
Warhol, Andy, 80-81, 86
warranties:
  extended, 573
  on used-cars, 565-66
Warren Buffett Way, The (Hagstrom), 24
Washington:
  national parks in, 494
  retirement in, 44
Washington, D.C.:
  crime in, 402
  dining in, 477
  same-sex parenting in, 265
  U.S. Botanic Gardens in, 411, 413
Washington, Denzel, 634
Washington Bullets, 708
Watching Wildlife (Duda), 500
waterbeds, 391
waterfowl hunting, 744
watermelon, 170
watermelon sorbet, 166
waterparks, 645
W. Atlee Burpee, 415
Wayne National Forest, 508
Wayside Gardens, 415
Way Things Work, The, 667
Wealthbuilder, 677-78
weapons, automatic, 408
Weaver, Earl, 364
Webb, Clifton, 635
Webwhacker, 688
wedding bands, 90
weight, 134-36

around belly vs. hips, 136
diet and, 134-35, 157
exercise and, 134-35, 138
guidelines for, 134-35
looking great and, 180
pregnancies and, 194
weight lifting, 142-43
weight training, 146-47
Weinstein, Steven B., 56
Weir, Peter, 366
Weisbaum, Herb, 639-42
Weiss, Paul, 189
Welch, John F., Jr., 349
Welles, Orson, 637
Weminuche, Colo., 497
West:
grasses for, 427
rock-and-roll shrines in, 599
vacation homes in, 77
westerns, 623-24
Westinghouse, 367
Weston Priory, 479
whale watching, 532-33
What Car Dealers Don't Want You to Know (Eskeldson), 571
What Color Is Your Parachute? (Bolles), 344
What's the Secret? Vol. 2, 674
What Works on Wall Street (O'Shaughnessy), 24
wheat ear pennies, 93
wheatgrass, 428
Where Are My Children?, 619
Where the Sidewalk Ends (Silverstein), 638
Where the Wild Things Are (Sendak), 638
Whipple, John, 233-34
Whisky-A-Go-Go, The, 599
Whistler/Blackcomb, B.C., 735
White, E. B., 636
White, Ron, 664-69
White Flower Farm, 415-16
Whitehead, Randall, 392
Whitehouse, Gaby, 515
White House Mess, The (Buckley), 555
White Knuckle Ride (Wyatt), 645
White Mountains, guided expeditions in, 537
White Mountains National Forest, 497, 499, 508
white teas, 173
White Water Canyon, 647
whole life insurance, 125, 129
Wholesale Insurance Network, 129
Whole Toon Catalog, 625
Who's Who in Business, 369
Why You Lose at Bridge (Simon), 757
wigs, 186
wilderness areas, 496-99, 510-13, 516
wild horses, purchasing of, 78
wildlife, 78, 500-501
in Africa, 515-17, 522
in rain forests, 519-20
in wilderness areas, 510-13
Wilkins, Mike, 558-59
Willamette National Forest, 509
Willett, Walter, 134, 148, 150
Willey, Gordon, 452-54
William, Prince, 130-31
William M. Mercer, Inc., 349, 351
Williams, John, 749
Williams, Robin, 366
wills:
living, 59, 216
retirement and, 57-59
Wilshire 5000 Stock Index, 17, 38
Wind, The, 619
Windjammer Barefoot Cruises, Ltd., 554-55
windows (of houses):
flower boxes in, 412, 429-30
locking of, 402-4
replacement of, 386
stuck, 396
Windows (software), 653, 671, 677, 679-80
Internet and, 683, 686
Windows 3.1, 675, 683
Windows 95, 658-59, 683, 686
Windows 95 Scanning Book, The (Simone), 679
Windows on Wall Street, 678
Windsor, Duchess of, 86
Windsor chairs, 84
Windward Islands, 461-62
wine, red, 160
Winks, Robin, 480-83
Winn-Dixie Stores, 13
Wintergreen/Orchard House, 302
Winter King hawthorns, 420
winter sports, 705, 733-46
Wipe Out, 642
Wise Giving Guide, 122
Wiseman, Rosalind, 406
Wishcraft (Scher), 344
Within Our Gates, 619
Wizard of Oz, The, 621
Wolff New Media, 689
Wolfram-Kivula, Nona, 421
Wolmer, Bruce, 86
Wolong Nature Reserve, 512
Woman's Way, 406
Woman Under the Influence, A, 619
women:
abortions and, 270, 274-75
biological clocks of, 195, 202
books on, 328-29
breast cancer in, *see* breast cancer
burglaries and, 402, 406
careers of, 338-39, 361, 373
contraception and, 269-73
depression in, 233
diets of, 149, 152-54, 161
doctors and, 210, 338
egg supplies of, 258
home environmental hazards and, 398
HRT and, 241
in-line skates for, 714
investing of men vs., 16
looking great and, 180-85, 187, 189, 193
men drivers vs., 587
mental disorders in, 236
perks for, 359, 361
salaries of men vs., 338, 349
sexual harassment of, 263
sexuality of, 254-55, 257-58
STDs of, 277
weight and, 134-36
weight training for, 142-43
see also girls; mothers; pregnancies
Women's Professional Billiard's Association (WPBA), 759
Wood, Natalie, 637
Wooden, John, 362-64
wood preservative, 401
Woodstockiana, collecting of, 88
Woodstock music festival, 602
woody shrubs, 420
Woolf, Virginia, 467
Woolworth's, 8
Wooton, Kenny, 463
Word for the Mac, 680
WordPerfect:
for DOS, 680
for Mac, 680
for Windows, 680
word processing software, 679-80
Wordsworth, William, 283
Working Mother, 361
Working Woman, 338
work-life programs, 359
workplace:
chairs for, 379-80
salaries and, 352
sexual situations in, 262-63
worksheet presentations, 676
Workshop, Inc., 393
World Almanac, 665
World Antique Dealers Association, 87
World Bank, 11
World Equity Baskets (WEBs), 12
World Historical Sites, 484
World Series, 698-99, 702, 705
world stock funds, 26
World War II, 635
World Wide Web, 120, 681, 687-95
on CD-ROMs, 664
collecting and, 81
college and, 304, 317
creating home pages on, 694
distance education via, 330
education on, 330-31
investment sites on, 23, 691
job hunting on, 343, 346-47
libraries on, 326
media literacy and, 633
movie reviews on, 608-9, 634
national park guides on, 495
online tools for, 688
publishing documents on, 680
on rail travel, 549
recommended places to visit on, 689-93
record shopping on, 601
ski information on, 739
software for children on, 670-71
sports on, 690, 712
taxes and, 108
video reviews on, 634
virtual pets on, 442
and working at home, 378
World Wildlife Fund, 533
World Woods, 722
Worth, 13, 258
Wow! from CompuServe, 683-84, 696
Wrangell-St. Elias, 497
wraparound mortgages, 70
Wright, Frank Lloyd, 667
Wright Institute, 259
wrinkles, 179-81, 188-89
Wyatt, Mark, 645-47
Wyler, Seymour B., 85
Wyoming:
national parks in, 494
rafting in, 534
retirement in, 44
rock climbing in, 716

Xanax (alprazolam), 235
xylocaine cream, 278

Yachting, 463
Yahoo!, 23, 608, 688-89
Yankee Doodle Dandy, 621
Yasgur, Max, 602
Yasuni National Park, 520
Yellowstone National Park, 480-81, 487-88, 496, 502
yellow teas, 173
Yemen, coffee from, 171
yoga, 247, 249
Yorkshire terriers, 434
Yosemite National Park, 481, 484-87, 498
rock climbing in, 715
Youghiogheny River, 535
Young, Brigham, 505
Young, Don, 496
Youngblood, Ed, 582-83
Young Investor Parents' Guide, The, 112
Young Mr. Lincoln, 634
Your Income Tax (Lasser), 108
Your Personal Net (YPN), 689
Yucatán Peninsula, 452-53, 478
yurt-to-yurt cross country skiing, 522

Z

Zabel, William D., 57
Zaire, wilderness areas in, 513
Zambezi River, 518
Zambia, 517
Zantac, 231
ZD Labs, 654
Zeitz, Joyce, 203
Zermatt, 529
walking to Hornlihutte from, 526-27
zero coupon bonds, 22
Zervoudakis, Ioannis, 198, 206
Ziff Davis, 693
Zimbabwe, 516-18
zinc, 155, 160
Zion National Park, 487, 491-92
Zip City Brewing Co., 175
zodiac, 368-69
Zoloft (sertraline), 235
Zomba plateau, 517
Zoo/Ocean Explorers Bundle, The, 674
zoysia, 428
Zweig Performance Ratings, 18
zygote intrafallopian transfer (ZIFT), 203

ACKNOWLEDGEMENTS

The second time around, things are supposed to get easier. But for the second edition of *The Practical Guide,* we started almost from scratch—with new ideas, new experts and new writers. The result is a new book and we have many new contributors and experts to acknowledge.

First, though, we would like to express our thanks to *The Practical Guide*'s earliest supporters. Our publisher, Harold Evans at Random House, continues to champion this endeavor with great enthusiasm. Our editor, Jonathan Karp, is a terrific source of creative ideas and is always at the other end of the phone when we need him. The same is true of the entire Random House team.

Our most constant partners in this enterprise have been our spouses, Nathalie Gilfoyle and Amy Bernstein, and our children, Olivia, Rohan, Elisabeth, Alexander, and Nicky, who are indispensable sounding boards for all sorts of ideas—good and bad. Not only have they been understanding about our work schedules, but they have helped us hone our headlines and even let us use the phone to send our copy from one place to another.

Our editorial designer, Janice Olson, patiently labored over every page in the book and many others that ended up on the cutting room floor. Her innumerable editorial suggestions never failed to improve our work. We again were fortunate to have as our illustrator, Steve McCracken, as our chartmaker, David Merrill, and as our design consultant, Rob Covey, who designed the cover this year.

Behind every complex operation are a couple of people who with seemingly effortless efficiency make sure everything gets done. Our miracle workers have been Anna Mulrine and Mary Yee. Besides contributing a number of articles to the book, Anna managed our considerable production operation. Mary meticulously edited and fitted the copy, no small task. We also benefited from the superb work of writer Michele Turk, our copy editors Eva Young, Michael Burke, and Evan Stone, and our indexer, Sydney Cohen and his associates. Thanks are also due our attorney Robert Barnett, publicist Donald Lehr, and our friends Ibby Jeppson, Joanne Lawson, Susie Goldman, Di and Lou Stovall, Rich Lodish, and John Pym.

We remain fortunate to have the continuing support and encouragement of our editor-in-chief at *U.S. News & World Report,* Mortimer Zuckerman, and the magazine's co-editors Merrill McLoughlin and Mike Ruby. As always, Cornelia Carter, Mary Jean Hopkins, and Susan LeClair lent help at key times. Thanks, too, to Kathy Bushkin, Bruce Zanca, and Elizabeth Gross, and to the *U.S. News* library staff and the staff of Applied Graphics Technologies.

This book would not exist, of course, without the enormous help, creativity, and knowledge of the hundreds of experts who grace our pages and the dedicated skills of the journalists who sought them out. Some of our experts even wrote their own articles this year—our hats go off to opera sensation Cecilia Bartoli and her publicist, Edgar Vincent; Brown University president Vartan Gregorian; *Goosebumps* author Bob Stine and his partner Jane Stine of Parachute Press; Don Wallis of the American Tea Masters; Bill Nye the Science Guy; Herb Weisbaum of CBS' *This Morning*; and Nell Minow, the Movie Mom. You mustn't hold any of our wonderful contributors responsible for our failings.

Peter Bernstein and Christopher Ma

From the editors

WE'D LIKE TO HEAR FROM YOU,

Please help shape the next edition of *The Practical Guide to Practically Everything*. We need to know what you liked about this book—and what you'd like to see done differently—so that we can make next year's version even more useful to you. Let us know if we've made a mistake or left out an important piece of information. And share with us your ideas for what to include next time so that *The Practical Guide* will become as much your book as ours. We look forward to your suggestions.

1. Would you like more, less or the same amount of coverage of the following subjects:

	MORE	LESS	THE SAME
MONEY	❑	❑	❑
HEALTH	❑	❑	❑
SEXUALITY	❑	❑	❑
EDUCATION	❑	❑	❑
CAREERS	❑	❑	❑
HOUSE & GARDEN	❑	❑	❑
TRAVEL	❑	❑	❑
AUTOS	❑	❑	❑
ENTERTAINMENT	❑	❑	❑
COMPUTERS	❑	❑	❑
SPORTS & GAMES	❑	❑	❑

2. Should more editorial attention be paid to any of the following groups?

- Teenagers ❑
- Young adults ❑
- People at midlife ❑
- Seniors ❑
- Single people ❑
- Couples ❑
- Families in which both spouses work ❑
- Families with young children ❑

READER'S QUESTIONNAIRE

3. Do you have a question that you would like to see answered, or a subject or expert that you wouid like to see included in next year's book? Please be as specific as possible.

....

....

....

....

....

....

....

....

....

....

4. Would you be interested in receiving updated information on the subjects included in the *Practical Guide* more often than once a year? How?

Online ❑ **Newsletter** ❑ **Other periodical** ❑

5. Your name:
....

Address:
....

....

....

Age:
....

Questionnaires should be returned to: **THE PRACTICAL GUIDE,**
c/o Random House
201 East 50th St.,
New York, NY 10022

We look forward to hearing from you and we thank you for your suggestions.